Special Edition Using

Using

MICROSOFT®

Windows 95 with Internet Explorer 4.0

QUE®

Using

MICROSOFT®

Windows 95 with Internet Explorer 4.0

Using Special Edition

Ed Bott, Ron Person, et al.

Special Edition Using Windows 95 with Internet Explorer 4.0

Library of Congress Catalog No.: 97-80803

ISBN: 0-7897-1553-8

00 99 98 6 5 4 3 2 1

Interpretation of the printing code: The rightmost double-digit number is the year of the book's printing; the rightmost single-digit number, the number of the book's printing. For example, a printing code of 98-1 shows that the first printing of the book occurred in 1998.

Screen reproductions in this book were created using Collage Plus from Inner Media, Inc., Hollis, NH.

Contents at a Glance

Table of Contents

II Navigation Skills

VI Customizing Windows 95 and Sharing Data Effectively

Appendix

Credits

SENIOR VICE PRESIDENT/PUBLISHING
Don Fowley

PUBLISHER
David Dwyer

GENERAL MANAGER
Joe Muldoon

DIRECTOR OF EDITORIAL SERVICES
Carla Hall

MANAGING EDITOR
Sarah Kearns

EXECUTIVE EDITOR
Jeff Koch

ACQUISITIONS EDITOR
Cari Skaggs

DEVELOPMENT EDITOR
Mark Cierzniak

PROJECT EDITOR
Tom Lamoureux

COPY EDITOR
Julie MacLean

TECHNICAL EDITORS
Henly Wolin
Alexandria Haddad

SOFTWARE SPECIALIST
Julie Maynard

MANUFACTURING COORDINATOR
Brook Farling

BOOK DESIGNER
Ruth Harvey

COVER DESIGNER
Sandra Schroeder

DIRECTOR OF PRODUCTION
Larry Klein

PRODUCTION MANAGER
Laurie Casey

PRODUCTION ANALYSTS
Dan Harris
Erich J. Richter

PRODUCTION TEAM
Jeanne Clark
Heather Howell
Christy Lemasters
Julie Searls
Sossity Smith

INDEXER
Cheryl Jackson

Composed in *Century Old Style* and *ITC Franklin Gothic* by Que Corporation.

To Judy, my best friend and partner for life

About the Authors

Ed Bott is a best-selling author and award-winning computer journalist with more than 10 years experience in the personal computer industry. As senior contributing editor of *PC Computing,* he is responsible for the magazine's extensive coverage of Windows 95, Windows 98, Windows NT, and Microsoft Office. From 1991 until 1993, he was editor of *PC Computing,* and for three years before that he was managing editor of *PC World* magazine. Ed has written numerous books for Que Publishing, including the "User Friendly" editions of *Using Windows 95* and *Using Microsoft Office 97.*

Ed is a two-time winner of the Computer Press Award, most recently for *PC Computing's* annual Windows SuperGuide, a collection of tips, tricks, and advice for users of Windows 95 and Windows NT. He lives in Redmond, Washington, with his wife, Judy Merrill, and two incredibly smart and affectionate cats, Katy and Bianca.

Ron Person has written more than 18 books for Que Corporation, including *Special Edition Using Excel for Windows 95, Web Publishing with Word for Windows,* and *Special Edition Using Windows 3.11.* He has an M.S. in physics from The Ohio State University and an MBA from Hardin-Simmons University. Ron was one of Microsoft's original twelve Consulting Partners and is a Microsoft Solutions Partner.

Jim Boyce, the lead author for *Windows NT Installation and Configuration Handbook,* is a Contributing Editor and columnist for *WINDOWS Magazine* and a regular contributor to other computer publications. He has been involved with computers since the late seventies, and has worked with computers as a user, programmer, and systems manager in a variety of capacities. He has a wide range of experience in the DOS, Windows, and UNIX environments. Jim has authored and co-authored over two dozen books on computers and software.

Jerry Cox has been involved in computers since 1982. He has worked the last 10 years as a computer sales consultant for MicroAge Computer Center of Fort Wayne. He has received certifications from Apple, IBM, Hewlett Packard and Compaq. He has tech edited *Upgrading and Troubleshooting PC's 2nd, 3rd, and 4th editions; Upgrading and Troubleshooting PC's Workbook; Winn Rosch's Hardware Bible; Peter Norton's Inside the PC Premiere Edition; Easy Troubleshooting and Upgrading PC's; Using the PS/1;* and several other Prentice Hall/Macmillan titles.

Dick Cravens lives and works in Columbia, MO, where he is a product manager designing the Next Big Thing from DATASTORM TECHNOLOGIES, Inc., a publisher of fax, data and TCP/IP communications software for Windows PCs. In previous lives he designed training programs for support technicians, answered a gazillion questions about modems, worked as production manager for an advertising agency, sold television programming to evil cable TV empires, managed a chain of one-hour photo shops, ran a commercial photographic studio, and chased Angus cows, kind of in that order. Since he just bought the classic fixer-upper bungalow and has an addiction to way-cool-wicked-fast computer stuff, he writes the occasional computer book, too. His son Jesse, budding MUD freak, abuses the hand-me-down computers, slops the cats and orders the pizzas.

Michael Desmond is Senior Editor of News at *PC World* magazine, the world's largest computer publication with a circulation rate base of over 1.1 million readers. He is also vice-president of the Computer Press Association, an organization dedicated to promoting the computer press and its writers and editors. In 1996, Michael earned a Jesse H. Neal award from the American Business Press for runner up in the best investigative article category. Previously executive editor at *Multimedia World* magazine, Michael has an M.S. in Journalism from Northwestern University's Medill School of Journalism, and a B.A. in Soviet Studies from Middlebury College in Vermont. Michael has also written for other publications, including *Working Woman* and *Video* magazines, and is a contributing author to *Platinum Edition Using Windows 95* from Que Publishing. A native of Cleveland, Ohio, Michael is an inveterate Cleveland Indians fan, and will never ever forgive Art Modell for moving the Cleveland Browns football team to Baltimore.

Glenn Fincher has worked in the Computer Industry for the last 12 years. Working in the fast moving electronic manufacturing industry, the early years were spent in Test Engineering at SCI Systems, Inc., the world's largest computer contract manufacturer. Spending the bulk of the SCI years in component, board, and unit testing he became intimately familiar with the building blocks of today's computer technology. Joining Intergraph Corporation in 1991 as a Customer Support Analyst, he has applied his wealth of computer knowledge to providing Intergraph's customers with quality, timely and accurate support for the MicroSation CAD product. Leading the software certification efforts for the successful release of MicroSation 5.0, he continues to be involved in the day-to-day world of Intergraph's partner Bentley Systems' MicroStation product. Sharing the knowledge gained in the experience of these years in the industry has always been a priority, so it is no surprise that he is in demand as a speaker, writer, and presenter throughout Intergraph. With his present involvement in Intergraph's WWW effort as Webmaster for Intergraphs Software Solutions, Glenn continues to remain at the leading edge of this industry. Continually seeking to stay on this edge has required both the support and understanding of wife Jan and their three children—Ashely, Will, and Aimee—without whom this and all his other endeavors would have been a lonely journey indeed. Glenn can be reached by electronic mail at **gtfinche@ingr.com**.

William S. Holderby is a computer engineering graduate from the University of Central Florida. He has 20 years of experience in systems design and applications development for the federal government and commercial markets. Mr. Holderby frequently contributes magazine articles covering computer systems technology. He is a network systems developer and integrator and is currently working with the Naval Computer Telecommunications Station based in New Orleans, Louisiana.

Gerald "Jerry" Paul Honeycutt, Jr. provides business-oriented technical leadership to the Internet community and software development industry. He has served companies such as The Travelers, IBM, Nielsen North America, IRM, Howard Systems International, and NCR. Jerry has participated in the industry since before the days of Microsoft Windows 1.0, and is completely hooked on Windows 95 and the Internet.

Jerry is the author of *Using Microsoft Plus!*, *Using the Internet with Windows 95*, *Windows 95 Registry & Customization Handbook*, *Special Edition Using the Windows 95 Registry*, *VBScript by Example*, *Special Edition Using the Internet 3E*, *Using the Internet 2E*, and *Windows NT and Windows 95 Registry and Customization Handbook* published by Que. He is also a contributing author on *Special Edition Using Netscape 2*, *Platinum Edition Using Windows 95*, *Visual Basic for Applications Database Solutions*, *Special Edition Using Netscape 3*, *Windows 95 Exam Guide*, *Netscape Navigator 3 Starter Kit*, *Using Java Workshop*, *Using JScript*, and *Internet Explorer ActiveX and Plugins Companion* published by Que. His articles have been printed in *Computer Language* magazine and he is a regular speaker at the Windows World and Comdex trade shows on topics related to software development, Windows 95, and the Internet.

Jerry graduated from the University of Texas at Dallas in 1992 with a B.S. degree in Computer Science. He currently lives in the Dallas suburb of Frisco, Texas with Becky, two Westies, Corky and Turbo, and a cat called Scratches. Jerry is an avid golfer with a passion for fine photography. Feel free to contact Jerry on the Internet at **jerry@honeycutt.com** or visit his Web site at **http://rampages.onramp.net/~jerry**.

Peter Kent lives in Lakewood, Colorado. He has spent the last 14 years training users, documenting software, and designing user interfaces. Working as an independent consultant for the last nine years, Peter has worked for companies such as MasterCard, Amgen, Data General, and Dvorak Development and Publishing. Much of his consulting work has been in the telecommunications business.

Peter is the author of the best-selling Internet book *The Complete Idiot's Guide to the Internet* (QUE). He has also written another six Internet-related books—including *The Complete Idiot's Guide to the World Wide Web*—and a variety of other works, such as *The Technical Writer's Freelancing Guide* and books on Windows NT and Windows 3.1. His articles have appeared in many periodicals, including *Internet World*, *Windows Magazine*, *Windows User*, *The Dallas Times Herald*, and *Computerworld*. Peter can be reached electronically at **PeterKent@msn.com**, **71601.1266@compuserve.com**, **pkent@lab-press.com**.

Doug Kilarski is a freelance writer and an accomplished computer industry analyst. Doug is a former technical editor for Computer Shopper magazine and former editor-in-chief for *Computer Monthly* and *Reselle World* magazines. He is currently developing global marketing and distribution strategies for the internetworking and telephony industries. Doug can be reached on the Internet at **dkilarski@mcimail.com**.

Bradley Lindaas is a project consultant for Follett Software Company, a library automation solutions provider based outside of Chicago. Brad started his career working in a computer lab while attending the University of Wisconsin, Madison, where he received his B.A. in English Literature. After graduating he took a job with Softmart, an outsourcer of software technical support and Microsoft Windows 95 Launch Partner, working with MS-DOS, Windows 3.1 and then Windows 95.

After Softmart, Brad worked for Wingra Technologies of Madison, Wisconsin supporting their UNIX- and VAX-based email integration product called Missive. Currently he consults K-12 schools on the implementation of district-wide technology plans involving Follett's NetWare-based LANs and WANs. Brad is a Microsoft Certified Professional and can be reached at **lindaas@fsc.follett.com**.

Gordon Meltzer has been teaching himself about computers since they were made with vacuum tubes. Recently, Gordon had designed and built workgroup networks for a music marketing division of Time-Warner and several New York City law firms. He is a consultant on computing issues to NBC Post Production, also in Manhattan.

Gordon has produced a number of jazz records for people like Miles Davis, Michel LeGrand, Al Di Meola, and Wallace Roney, and has a special interest in using computers in the business side of the music business.

Brady P. Merkel is a Senior Software Consultant and Technical Webmaster for Intergraph Corporation in Huntsville, Alabama. He has co-authored popular internet books such as *Web Publishing with Word for Windows* and *Building Integrated Office Applications*. One of his ongoing projects includes the development of Intergraph Online, Intergraph Corporation's World-Wide Web server at **http://www.intergraph.com**. Brady can be reached by email at **bpmerkel@ingr.com**.

Francis Moss has been involved with computers for 12 years, a Microsoft beta tester for five years, and a writer—primarily in television but more recently, books—for fifteen years. With his writing partner, he is co-author of *Internet for Kids* from Price Stern Sloan. He likes computers because he enjoys cursing at unarmed inanimate objects. With his wife and two children, he lives in North Hollywood, California. He can be reached at **fcmoss@directnet.com**.

Michael O'Mara is a freelance author and technical writer. Previously, he was a staff author with The Cobb Group where he wrote innumerable articles about leading computer software programs and served as Editor-in-Chief of several monthly software journals. He has co-authored or contributed to other Que books including *Using DOS*; *Using Windows 3.11*; *Special Edition Using CompuServe*; *Special Edition Using Windows 95*; *Special Edition Using Windows NT Workstation 3.51*; *10 Minute Guide to Freelance Graphics 96 for Windows 95*; and *Using Your PC*. He can be reached at **76376.3441@compuserve.com**.

Sue Plumley has owned and operated her own business for eight years; Humble Opinions provides training, consulting, and network installation, management, and maintenance to banking, education, medical, and industrial facilities. In addition, Sue has authored and co-authored over fifty books for Que Corporation and its sister imprints, including *10 Minute Guide to Lotus Notes 4*, *Special Edition Using Windows NT Workstation*, and *Easy Windows 95*. You can reach Sue via the Internet at **splumley@citynet.net** or on CompuServe at **76470.2526@compuserve.com**.

Kenneth W. Poore is a marketing consultant for the Technical Information Management and Delivery division of Intergraph Corporation in Huntsville, Alabama. He currently develops strategic product plans, but has written technology white papers, conducted customer training, and worked in pre-sales and marketing roles over the past 10 years. Ken lives with his wife Molly in Harvest, Alabama and can be reached at **kwpoore@ingr.com**.

Paul Robichaux, who has been an Internet user since 1986 and a software developer since 1983, is currently a software developer for LJL Enterprises (**http://www.ljl.com**), where he writes data security and cryptography software for Win32 and MacOS platforms. In his spare time, he writes computer books and develops Macintosh applications; he still manages to spend plenty of time with his wife and young son. He can be reached via e-mail at **paulr@hiwaay.net**.

Rob Tidrow has been using computers for the past six years and has used Windows for the past four years. Mr. Tidrow is a technical writer and recently was the Manager of Product Development for New Riders Publishing, a division of Macmillan Computer Publishing. Rob is co-author of the best-selling *Windows for Non-Nerds*, and has co-authored several other books including *Inside the World Wide Web, New Riders' Official CompuServe Yellow Pages, Inside Microsoft Office Professional, Inside WordPerfect 6 for Windows, Riding the Internet Highway, Deluxe Edition*, and the *AutoCAD Student Workbook*. In the past, Mr. Tidrow created technical documentation and instructional programs for use in a variety of industrial settings. He has a degree in English from Indiana University. He resides in Indianapolis with his wife, Tammy, and two boys, Adam and Wesley. You can reach him on the Internet at **rtidrow@iquest.net**.

Robert Voss, Ph.D., deserves special thanks for his help in bringing this book together. Beyond applying his writing and training skills to the original writing, Bob made a significant contribution to this book and many of Que's best-selling books, including *Using Word Version 6 for Windows*, Special Edition. Bob is a senior trainer in Microsoft Excel and Word for Windows for Ron Person & Co.

Craig Zacker has been employed as a network administrator, a technical writer and editor, a Webmaster, a technical support engineer and supervisor, a courseware developer, and a freelance network consultant. He now spends most of his time tinkering with computers and writing about them. His previous credits for Que include *Special Edition Using NetWare 4.1, Platinum Edition Using Windows 95, Windows NT 4.0 Workstation Advanced Technical Reference*, and *Upgrading and Repairing Networks*, among others. He can be reached at **craigz@tiac.net**.

Acknowledgments

A book of this size and scope doesn't just happen overnight. It takes a hard-working team of professionals to put all the pieces together. Literally dozens of people—co-authors, editors, designers, proofreaders, technical reviews, and others—had a hand in the making of this book. It's impossible to thank them all personally, but a few deserve special thanks for special efforts.

It was a pleasure to work with Development Editor Mark Cierzniak, who succeeded at the unenviable job of keeping the entire team focused on a single objective. Thanks, too, to Executive Editor Jeff Koch, who made sure everything happened on time and within budget, and to Associate Publisher Dean Miller, who said yes when it counted.

Technical editors Henly Wolin and Alexandria Haddad checked the manuscript for accuracy and added some helpful suggestions in key chapters. Behind the scenes, Production Editor Tom Lamoreux did a superb job of making sure that all these bits wound up in the right places on the right pages.

And a very special thank you to Claudette Moore and Debbie McKenna of Moore Literary Agency, who dealt with all the boring but essential business details so I could concentrate on Windows 95 and Internet Explorer.

We'd Like to Hear from You!

Que Corporation has a long-standing reputation for high-quality books and products. To ensure your continued satisfaction, we also understand the importance of customer service and support.

Tech Support

If you need assistance with the information in this book or with a CD/disk accompanying the book, please access Macmillan Computer Publishing's online Knowledge Base at **http://www.superlibrary.com/general/support**. If you do not find the answer to your questions on our Web site, you may contact Macmillan Technical Support by phone at **317/581-3833** or via e-mail at **support@mcp.com**.

Also be sure to visit Que's Web resource center for all the latest information, enhancements, errata, downloads, and more. It's located at **http://www.quecorp.com/**.

Orders, Catalogs, and Customer Service

To order other Que or Macmillan Computer Publishing books, catalogs, or products, please contact our Customer Service Department at **800/428-5331** or fax us at **800/882-8583** (International Fax: 317/228-4400). Or visit our online bookstore at **http://www.mcp.com/**.

Comments and Suggestions

We want you to let us know what you like or dislike most about this book or other Que products. Your comments will help us to continue publishing the best books available on computer topics in today's market.

Mark Cierzniak
Development Editor
Que Corporation
201 West 103rd Street, 4B
Indianapolis, Indiana 46290 USA
Fax: 317/581-4663
Email: mcierzniak@mcp.com

Please be sure to include the book's title and author as well as your name and phone or fax number. We will carefully review your comments and share them with the author. Please note that due to the high volume of mail we receive, we may not be able to reply to every message.

Thank you for choosing Que!

Introduction

In this chapter

Windows 95 is more than a piece of computer software—it's a genuine phenomenon. Since its original release on August 24, 1995, Microsoft has sold more than 100 million copies of Windows 95, and it has become the undisputed standard for personal computing. Today, virtually every PC sold includes a copy of Windows 95, and there are thousands of productivity programs, utilities, and games that run on top of Windows 95.

Microsoft released its first web browser within weeks of shipping Windows 95. If you tried to use that crude 1.0 version to explore the World Wide Web today, you'd have trouble viewing even the simplest pages, and you'd appreciate the enormous progress the Internet has made in that time. A little more than two years later, Internet Explorer 4.0 appeared; more than just a great web browser, it's a sweeping upgrade to Windows 95.

The first copies of *Special Edition Using Windows 95* hit bookstore shelves the same day as Windows 95, and through the years that book had become an international bestseller. This updated edition follows the same basic organization as that first release, but more than half of the material in this book is completely new. Just as Microsoft has continually updated Windows 95 and Internet Explorer, we've produced a brand-new volume designed to help you work effortlessly and productively with both products.

It doesn't matter how you use Windows 95 and Internet Explorer 4.0. If your computer sits on the kitchen table and you dial in to a local Internet service provider, you will find plenty of help here. We've also included detailed information that can help you integrate your computer into a business network, whether your business is a simple storefront or a far-flung multinational corporation.

How to Use This Book

This book was designed and written expressly for intermediate and advanced users of Windows 95 who understand the importance of keeping up with advances in technology. *Special Edition Using Windows 95 with Internet Explorer 4.0* contains detailed information about each version of Windows 95 (including OEM service releases) and Internet Explorer. It also includes step-by-step instructions on how to find and install online updates, including Internet Explorer and its components.

Special Edition Using Windows 95 with Internet Explorer 4.0 is a comprehensive reference that makes it easy for you to accomplish any task quickly and effectively. It covers every version of Windows 95 and every component of Internet Explorer 4.0. To help organize this enormous breadth of coverage, we've divided the book into eight parts, beginning with the essentials and progressing to more specialized or advanced subjects.

Part I: Installing & Configuring Windows 95

This chapter covers the absolute essentials of Windows 95 and Internet Explorer 4.0. Pay particular attention to Chapter 1, "What's New in Windows 95 and Internet Explorer 4.0," which includes an overview of the new features that Internet Explorer adds to Windows 95. If you're still using the original retail version of Windows 95, turn to Chapter 2, "Installing and Upgrading Windows 95," for details on how you can add important patches and updates to your system.

Part II: Navigation Skills

You will notice dramatic improvements to Windows 95 when you install the Windows Desktop Update. This optional (but highly recommended) component of Internet Explorer 4.0 completely replaces the old-style Windows Explorer with a single browser that enables you to manage files, folders, and web pages in the same window. If you're puzzled by new features such as Web view and the Active Desktop, you're not alone. Read Chapter 11, "The Overview of the Windows Desktop Update," for step-by-step instructions on how to install and configure the Windows Desktop Update, as well as a clear explanation of what it does and how the new Windows shell can help you become more productive.

Part III: Working with Files and Folders

After you install the Windows Desktop Update, you will have access to a new set of file-management tools. In this completely revised section, you will learn basic and advanced techniques for programs, files, and folders, whether they're stored on a local disk or on a corporate network. You also will find detailed information to help you customize the new Explorer and manage associations between data files and programs. Are you puzzled by disk compression and the FAT32 file system? Chapter 15, "Working with Disks and Disk Drives," demystifies both features.

Part IV: Working with the Internet

When Windows 95 was first released, the Internet was an obscure research tool and playground for techies. Today it's a crucial source of information for tens of millions of people, and increasingly, it's a major force in banking, commerce, and stock trading. This comprehensive section is completely new for this edition. It covers every aspect of Internet connectivity, from configuring TCP/IP options to downloading files from FTP servers. If you have questions about the World Wide Web, email, newsgroups, or Internet security, you can find the answers here.

Part V: Working with Applications

There are literally tens of thousands of applications available for Windows 95. Collectively, they give you the power to organize your thoughts, communicate with other people, run a business of any size, and even create your own custom applications. This section covers the essentials of installing, running, and managing applications—including 32-bit programs written for Windows 95, as well as older 16-bit Windows and MS-DOS programs. You also will find details about applets included with Windows itself.

Part VI: Customizing Windows 95 and Sharing Data Effectively

Windows 95 owes much of its enormous popularity to its incredible flexibility. This section details how you can modify Windows 95 to suit your personal preferences. Customize the Windows desktop, Start menu, and taskbar. Change the colors, fonts, and background images to make Windows more visually appealing. Reset the many system-level options that help define how Windows works—from which keyboard layout and language you prefer to which sounds play in response to system events.

You will also find a chapter covering basic information-sharing tools, as well as how to link data from one document to another. Turn here for help on cutting, copying, and pasting within and between documents in Windows.

Part VII: Networking with Windows 95

Even a two-person office can benefit from Windows 95's capability to communicate and share files over a network. In this section, we cover the full range of network topics: setting up a simple workgroup, sharing resources on a small network, using shared printers, and setting up Windows 95 as a client on larger networks with Novell NetWare and Windows NT servers.

Appendix

Appendix A, "Additional Help and Resources," tells you where to find what wouldn't fit between the covers of this book. This appendix lists the telephone and FAX support numbers for Microsoft and third-party suppliers. You will also learn how to use the Internet, The Microsoft Network, CompuServe, and TechNet CDs to access the same comprehensive databases that Microsoft's telephone support staff and consultants use.

Special Features in This Book

Que has over a decade of experience writing and developing the most successful computer books available. With that experience, we've learned what special features help readers the most. Look for these special features throughout the book to enhance your learning experience.

A sidebar on the first page of each chapter contains a list of topics to be covered in the chapter. This list serves as a road map to the chapter so that you can tell at a glance what is covered. It also provides a useful outline of the key topics you will be reading about.

NOTE Notes present interesting or useful information that isn't essential to the discussion. This secondary track of information enhances your understanding of Windows, but you can safely skip notes and not be in danger of missing crucial information. ■

Tips present quick advice on shortcuts or often-overlooked procedures.

CAUTION

Cautions warn you about potential problems that a procedure may cause, unexpected results, and mistakes to avoid.

TROUBLESHOOTING

What is a troubleshooting section? No matter how carefully you follow the steps in the book, you eventually come across something that just doesn't work the way you think it should. Troubleshooting sections anticipate these common errors or hidden pitfalls and present solutions.

Throughout this book, you will find Internet references that point you to World Wide Web addresses or online addresses where you can find out additional information about topics. Internet references look like this:

ON THE WEB

You can learn about the Registry's organization on the Internet, too. *PC Magazine* has a three-part description of the Registry on the Web that you can read by pointing your web browser at:

www.zdnet.com/~pcmag/issues/1418/pcm00083.htm

www.zdnet.com/~pcmag/issues/1419/pcm00116.htm

www.zdnet.com/~pcmag/issues/1422/pcm00140.htm

Throughout the book, you see references to other sections and pages in the book (like the one that follows this paragraph). These cross references point you to related topics and discussions in other parts of the book.

▶ **See** "Improved Performance and Reliability," **p. xxx**

Conventions

In addition to these special features, several conventions are used in this book to make it easier to read and understand. These conventions include the following.

Shortcut Key Combinations

In this book, shortcut key combinations are joined with plus signs (+). For example, Ctrl+V means hold down the Ctrl key and then press the V key.

Menu Commands

Instructions for choosing menu commands have this form:

> Choose File, New.

This example means open the File menu and select New, which is one way to open a new file.

Instructions involving the new Windows 95 Start menu are an exception. When you are to choose something through the Start menu, the form is as follows:

> Open the Start menu and choose Programs, Accessories, WordPad.

In this case, open the WordPad word processing accessory. Notice that in the Start menu, you simply drag the mouse pointer and point at the option or command you want to choose (even through a whole series of submenus); you don't need to click anything.

This book also uses certain typeface enhancements to indicate special text, as described in the following table:

Typeface	Description
Italic	Italic indicates new terms and variables in commands or addresses.
Boldface	Bold indicates text you type, as well as Internet addresses and other locators in the online world.
MYFILE.DOC	Filenames and directories are set in all caps to distinguish them from regular text, as in MYFILE.DOC.
`Monospace`	Mono indicates screen messages, code listings, and command samples.
Underline	Underline indicates keyboard hotkeys. For example, to choose the Properties button, press Alt and then R.

PART I

Installing and Configuring Windows 95

CHAPTER 1

What's New in Windows 95 and Internet Explorer 4.0

by Ron Person and Ed Bott

In this chapter

Keeping Your Copy of Windows 95 Up to Date

Every new wave of technology brings sweeping changes in its wake. In the last 25 years, we've seen the rise of personal computers, the growth of graphical computing, and the astonishing surge of Internet awareness. Windows 95 is arguably the most popular piece of software ever sold, and you can't turn on a television or pass a billboard without seeing a World Wide Web address. It's only natural that Windows and the web would come together.

In combination, Windows 95 and Internet Explorer 4.0 create a personal computing environment that integrates local and network resources with information on the World Wide Web. This chapter gives you an overview of how Windows 95 and Internet Explorer 4.0 work together.

NOTE If you are an experienced Windows 95 user familiar with web browsing, turn to the chapters that provide details of new features in Internet Explorer 4.0. Chapter 11, "The Overview of the Windows Desktop Update," details changes in the Windows 95 interface. For information about web browsing, turn to Chapter 18, "Web Browsing with Internet Explorer 4.0," Chapter 19, "Finding, Organizing, and Saving Web-Based Information," Chapter 20, "Internet Explorer 4.0 and Security," and Chapter 21, "Working with Web Subscriptions and the Active Desktop."

If you are new to Windows 95 but have experience with Windows 3.1, start with Chapter 10, "Navigating and Controlling Windows," and Chapter 12, "Managing Files with My Computer and Windows Explorer," to see a few of the main user interface changes. ■

Windows 95 first appeared on retail shelves August 24, 1995. At that time, Microsoft announced its intention to deliver frequent updates to Windows 95, both to fix the bugs inevitable in any complex piece of software and to add new features. Since Windows 95's initial release, there have been four significant updates and dozens of patches to update or repair individual components.

The first update, known as Service Pack 1, appeared in the first quarter of 1996. The CD-ROM version of Service Pack 1 contained repairs for several bugs, some add-on software, new hardware drivers, and Internet Explorer 2.0. All of these updates are also available for download from Microsoft's web site.

ON THE WEB

Service Pack 1 is available in a variety of formats, including a 1.2MB self-extracting update file or a collection of 14 files sized to fit on floppy disks. There is also a corresponding collection of utilities designed to help system administrators. To download any of these components, use this URL:

http://www.microsoft.com/windows95/info/service-packs.htm

To order a copy of the Microsoft Windows 95 Service Pack 1 on CD-ROM, call 800-360-7561. There is a shipping and handling charge of $14.95.

The second major Windows 95 update appeared in August 1996, when Microsoft released Windows 95 OEM Service Release 2 (OSR2). At its core, this is still Windows 95, although it includes significant new features. OSR2 includes all the updates from Service Pack 1, as well as additional hardware drivers, improved multimedia components, power-management and networking enhancements, and support for the new FAT32 file system, which improves performance and storage efficiency on large hard disks. There are no significant user-interface changes between OSR2 and the original release of Windows 95. (Some manufacturers include a slightly updated version called OSR2.1; it adds basic support for the Universal Serial Bus but is otherwise identical to OSR2.)

You cannot buy a shrink-wrapped copy of OSR2; instead, this version of Windows 95 was released only to hardware manufacturers who sell it as part of a new system. It is possible to download many of the OSR2 components from the Microsoft web site for free. (Turn to Chapter 2, "Installing and Upgrading Windows 95," for detailed descriptions of each of these components and their download locations.) Throughout this book, OSR2 enhancements are indicated by the icon shown at the left.

The third major update to Windows 95 represents a major change in the direction of personal computing. Microsoft released the final version of Internet Explorer 4.0 (IE4) on September 30, 1997, after a lengthy public preview program. It includes a key component called the Windows Desktop Update, which replaces the Windows 95 shell with a single Explorer that enables you to find and organize information on your own computer, on company networks, and on the World Wide Web. Other applications included as part of the IE4 package include a capable personal web page editor, a useful email reader that also connects with newsgroups, collaborative software that enables you to communicate and share applications over the Internet, and a collection of multimedia players that enable you to tap into streaming audio and video sources. Throughout this book, IE4 enhancements are indicated by the icon shown at left.

Chapter 18 explains how to download a free copy of Internet Explorer 4.0 for use with any version of Windows 95.

In late 1997, the fourth and most recent Windows update appeared. OEM Service Release 2.5 integrates OSR2 and Internet Explorer 4.0 in a single package. Like previous Windows updates, this package is not available for retail purchase; you can buy it only with new hardware.

NOTE To identify which version of Windows 95 is installed on your computer, right-click the My Computer icon on the Windows desktop, choose Properties, and inspect the information under System. The original release of Windows 95 appears as 4.00.950. An A after that string means Service Pack1 has been added; a B identifies OSR2. If Internet Explorer 4.0 is installed, its version number appears below the Windows 95 information. The original release identifies itself as IE 4.0 4.71.1712.6. ■

Installing Windows 95 and Internet Explorer 4.0

These days, it's nearly impossible to purchase a new PC without a copy of Windows 95. Most new computers sold since early 1997 come with OSR2 installed. If your computer is running the original version of Windows 95, it's possible to upgrade to OSR2, although it requires some extra work to find a legal copy and to prepare your system for the upgrade. If you want to convert your FAT16 formatted hard disk to the more efficient FAT32, then you need to back up all your data, repartition and reformat your hard disk, install OSR2, and reinstall your applications and data. It takes a lot of time, but it's not particularly difficult, especially if you follow the instructions in Chapter 2.

Upgrading an existing copy of Windows 95 to include Internet Explorer 4.0 and the Windows Desktop Update is almost completely automatic. Use an existing Internet browser to access the Microsoft web site and download the updates. You can choose the Active Setup option to install IE4 automatically over the web or download the IE4 setup package and install it from your local drive. Chapter 18 describes both installation options in detail.

▶ **See** "Installing the Windows 95 OEM Service Release 2 (OSR2)," **p. 31**

▶ **See** "Installing Internet Explorer 4.0," **p. 28**

Improving Windows with OSR2

OEM Service Release 2 incorporates the changes from Service Pack 1, but it also includes a number of additional enhancements. One of its most significant enhancements is a new 32-bit version of the File Allocation Table file system (FAT32). With FAT32, Windows 95 enables you to format hard drives larger than 2GB (up to a theoretical limit of 2 terabytes in size) without requiring multiple partitions. Because FAT32 uses a more efficient cluster size, it makes much better use of the space on disk partitions over 512MB in size—you can easily store 400MB more data on a disk formatted with FAT32 compared with the same disk using the FAT16 file system.

If you are currently using the original release of Windows 95 with a FAT16 hard drive, the only way you can change to the more efficient FAT32 is to upgrade to OSR2, and even then the process is complex and technically demanding. Third-party software enables you to access large hard disks, but you'll have to wait for Windows 98 before Microsoft will offer a supported utility to convert FAT16 drives to FAT32. Read the section "The FAT32 File System" in Chapter 15, "Working with Disks and Disk Drives," to learn more about the tradeoffs and alternatives.

OSR2 includes a wide range of enhancements. Some of the enhancements are as follows:

Enhancements	Description
DriveSpace 3	Contains code originally released as part of Microsoft Plus! pack to compress volumes up to 2GB; note that DriveSpace 3 will not work on a FAT32-formatted disk.

New storage devices	Support for Zip and 120MB floptical drives, CD changers, removable IDE media, and IDE Bus Mastering.
PC Card/PCMCIA	Support for newer 32-bit PC Card standard, improved modem power management, 3.3 volt PC Cards, network/modem PC Cards, and global positioning systems.
Power management	Support for Advanced Power Management 1.2, support for drive spin-down, new Control Panel Power properties.
Internet	Includes Internet Explorer 3, Internet Connection Wizard, Internet Mail and News, NetMeeting, and Personal Web Server; installing IE4 updates these components.
Improved multimedia	Includes DirectX 2.0, OpenGL, and support for Intel MMX processors.
Networking	New Dial-Up Networking interface, improved infrared communication tools, NDIS 4.0 drivers, and support for multiple DNS configurations when using TCP/IP.
Netware	Full support for NetWare 4.x including NetWare Directory Services.
Automatic ScanDisk	ScanDisk runs automatically when you restart Windows after an abnormal shutdown.
Online Services	Installable client software for America Online, CompuServe, AT&T WorldNet, and The Microsoft Network.

Some OSR2 enhancements are available individually for free from the Internet. For information on downloading and installing components from OSR2, refer to Table 2.1 in Chapter 2.

▶ **See** "Installing the Windows 95 OEM Service Release 2 (OSR2)," **p. 31**

CAUTION

Be aware that there is some risk of hardware and software incompatibilities with OSR2, and disk utilities must be specifically designed to work with the FAT32 file system. You need to obtain updated versions or patches for programs such as the Norton Utilities, for example. OSR2 includes FAT32-compatible updates to system utilities such as ScanDisk and Defrag.

A Web-Oriented Interface

To most personal computer users, the interface they see on the screen is the computer. MS-DOS, which required users to type commands at a C:> prompt, imposed a disheartening learning curve on users trying to handle even simple tasks. The advent of Windows, with its point-and-click interface and pull-down menus, improved computer usability substantially. After a few hours of instruction, even a novice user can learn by simply clicking on Windows icons and pulling down menus.

The explosive growth of the Internet and the rising popularity of web browsers have ushered in a new set of user interface elements: web pages and hyperlinks. With the release of Internet Explorer 4.0, Microsoft has begun merging web browser conventions into the Windows 95 interface. For example, you can choose double-clicking (the Windows 95 standard) or single-clicking (the web browser convention) to activate icons on the Windows desktop and in folders.

When you install the Windows Desktop Update, the old-style Windows Explorer and My Computer windows disappear, replaced by a single Explorer that uses the same program code as Internet Explorer. Click the Address bar, and you can type a web address, a folder name, or even the name of a Windows resource such as My Computer or Control Panel, and then watch the contents of the Explorer window change. The exact appearance of the Explorer window depends on how you opened it in the first place, and as you move from local folders to web locations and back, notice that toolbars and menus change accordingly.

▶ **See** "Single-Click or Double-Click?," **p. 274**

Perhaps the most dramatic and noticeable change to the Windows 95 user interface is the Active Desktop, which enables you to add web-based content to the Windows desktop, where it's updated frequently and always available. By using the Active Desktop (available only when the Windows Desktop Update is installed), you can display a ticker showing current stock quotes, a weather map, or the home page of your favorite computer magazine.

Think of the Active Desktop as a graphical layer that sits above the desktop and underneath the shortcut icons found there (My Computer, Recycle Bin, and so on). You control the look of the Active Desktop: With web view turned off, it looks exactly like the standard Windows 95 desktop. When you enable the option to view the desktop as a web page, you can display objects such as graphics, web pages, ActiveX components, or Java applets, and you can customize any of these objects so that they connect to the Internet and update on a regular schedule. With the Active Desktop enabled, you can even display a local HTML page. For examples of how you can use this feature, see Chapter 21, "Working with Web Subscriptions and the Active Desktop."

As soon as you're comfortable with the concept of Windows as an extension of the web, it's easy to imagine a web view of a folder's contents. Most Windows users are familiar with the four choices that Windows 95 offers when viewing any folder: Large Icon, Small Icon, Detail, and List. Web view works with these familiar views to display a folder's contents within an

HTML page. You can use any HTML editor to modify a folder's HTML page and thus modify how the files or folders appear. For example, you can display help information next to each file, telling the user how to use the files in a given folder. Or you can hide the display of files within a folder and, instead, create hypertext links to those applications or documents. In this organizational scheme, users can click a link to open a file instead of having to browse through a cluttered folder and interpret confusing file names. Internet Explorer 4.0 includes FrontPage Express, a simple HTML editor, so intermediate level users can make personal web pages for their own web views.

In addition to these major changes, the Windows Desktop Update makes dozens of minor user-interface improvements that help make Windows 95 easier to use. For example, you no longer have to open a special folder to reorganize items on the Start menu—instead, you just click the Start button and drag a menu item to another position.

Experienced Windows users appreciate the power of the Windows taskbar and customizable toolbars in applications such as Office 97. When you install the Windows Desktop Update, you receive a collection of new Windows toolbars to use on the desktop. The Address toolbar enables you to quickly enter a pathname or URL and open an Explorer window. The Links toolbar stores buttons that give you one-click access to frequently used locations. The Desktop toolbar enables you to work with shortcut icons on the desktop, even when those icons are covered by one or more open windows. The Quick Launch toolbar gives you instant access to frequently used programs and documents. Of course, you can customize any toolbar and even create your own new toolbars.

Internet Explorer 4.0

Microsoft has included much more than a web browser in Internet Explorer 4.0. In addition to the Windows Desktop Update, IE4 includes a suite of products designed to create an integrated work environment on the web. Internet Explorer 4.0 includes the following free products:

Product	Description
Internet Explorer 4.0	Microsoft's Internet browser, with dozens of usability improvements and support for web subscriptions and offline browsing
Outlook Express	Integrated email and news reader
FrontPage Express	An HTML editor, useful for creating personal web pages
Task Scheduler	A system tool that enables you to use an Explorer-style window to schedule repetitive tasks, such as backing up files or defragmenting disks

NetMeeting	Collaborative software that enables teams to work over the Internet by using shared applications, chat space, whiteboard, audio, and video
NetShow Player	Receive streaming audio and video over the Internet or a corporate intranet for training and entertainment
Microsoft Chat	A simple chat client for carrying on text-based conversations over an Internet connection

Internet Explorer 4.0: Offline Browsing and Web Subscriptions

In interactive mode, with a live Internet connection, Internet Explorer 4.0 is noticeably faster than previous Microsoft web browsers. You can dramatically increase even that level of performance by using subscriptions. When you subscribe to a web site by using IE4, the browser automatically downloads those web pages to your local drive. Select the Work Offline option from IE4's menu, and those pages pop into your browser almost instantly, because they're being loaded from a fast local drive instead of a slow Internet connection.

Internet Explorer 4.0 gives you two alternatives for subscribing to web sites. (There's no cost associated with subscribing to a web site.) If the web site supports Microsoft's Channel Definition Format (CDF), it comes down to your computer as a prepackaged file on a schedule defined by the web designer. For web sites that don't use CDF files, you start with a single web page; subscription options enable you to tell IE4 to gather pages linked to that page and to specify a schedule for updating your local copy. This variety of web subscription works with any web site—it even enters your username and password automatically in protected web sites.

If you've enabled IE4's Active Desktop, you can add any web page or HTML component to your desktop and use a subscription to keep information constantly updated. This method of moving information from web servers to the desktop, sometimes called Webcasting or "push technology," enables content providers to tailor information for you or your corporation and deliver it directly to you, without requiring you to open a browser. IE4 gives you access to a sweeping collection of these Active Channels, for information such as news headlines, stock prices, and corporate bulletins.

▶ **See** "Navigating Internet Explorer," **p. 435**

▶ **See** "Subscribing to Web Sites," **p. 504**

Stay in Touch with Outlook Express

One of the most welcome "extras" in Internet Explorer 4.0 is Outlook Express, a complete email client and news reader. For anyone who uses only standard Internet mail protocols, Outlook Express is a welcome alternative to the Exchange Inbox and Windows Messaging Programs included with Windows 95.

Outlook Express enables you to filter and store messages by category. Messages can consist of plain text or richly formatted HTML, and you can attach one or more files to any message. In fact, you can even send a complete web page to another Outlook Express user by selecting a menu option from within Internet Explorer 4.0.

▶ **See** "Using Outlook Express for Email and News," **p. 517**

FrontPage Express, a Simple Web Page Editor

If you've seen Microsoft's FrontPage 97 and Front Page 98, the award-winning web site development software, then you've seen FrontPage Express. FrontPage Express includes the page-editing portion of FrontPage 97, without its web-management features, and it's free with Internet Explorer 4.0. FrontPage Express enables you to design and edit simple web pages; it also enables you to customize the HTML templates Windows uses to display files in web view.

▶ **See** "Using FrontPage Express," **p. 570**

NetMeeting and the Future of Collaboration

There's much more to the Internet than mail and web pages. Microsoft has invested significant development resources in NetMeeting, an application that turns the Internet and corporate networks into a powerful communication channel. At its simplest, one-to-one level, NetMeeting enables individuals to place long-distance calls over the Internet. In a business setting, it enables two or more Windows users to collaborate over an intranet or the Internet, communicating with voice and video, using an electronic whiteboard and chat window, and even sharing applications and documents in real time.

NetMeeting is entertaining and useful over the Internet, but it's especially zippy over high-speed corporate networks. Many companies expect to use it to reduce training and support costs. Studies have found that it takes about as long to resolve a user's problem via remote training over the Internet as it would if the user called for support over the telephone. But unlike telephone support, NetMeeting makes it much less likely that the user will call back with additional questions, because the support person can see the exact problem on the remote user's screen, and the caller can watch the resolution.

NetMeeting also has potential as a group editing and collaboration tool. It supports international telephone standards and will support group conference standards so that telecommuters can work with other members of their team from home, on the road, in the office, or in a group meeting.

▶ **See** "Using NetMeeting 2.0," **p. 587**

CHAPTER 2

Installing and Upgrading Windows 95

by Dick Cravens, Robert Voss, and Ed Bott

In this chapter

System Requirements for Windows 95

No matter how hard you try, you can't avoid the Windows Setup program. Even on brand-new systems that arrive with Windows 95 already installed, chances are good that a component you need is missing or misconfigured, and you'll have to set it up on your own. Microsoft regularly issues patches and updates to Windows, including the mother of all updates, Internet Explorer 4.0, but to keep Windows running smoothly, you'll need to manage that collection of updates on your own. And if Windows ever stops working, you might need to run Setup from scratch to get back to work. This chapter explains how to install Windows 95 from scratch, how to upgrade an existing system with a newer version of Windows, and how to use patches and updates to keep Windows running smoothly and safely.

Before you install Windows 95, make sure that your system meets the following requirements:

- *A 486 or later processor* A Pentium or compatible processor running at 100 MHz or more is recommended. Although you can install Windows 95 on a system with an 80386 processor, this configuration results in unacceptable performance for most users.
- *A Microsoft- or Logitech-compatible mouse* If you have another type of mouse, you might need to provide drivers for it when you run Windows Setup.
- *A high-density (1.44M) 3.5-inch floppy drive or CD-ROM drive* A CD-ROM drive is highly recommended, because many software packages are available only in CD formats).
- *16MB of RAM* Although you can run Windows 95 with 8MB of RAM, 16MB is the minimum recommended configuration, and you should have 32MB or more if you plan to work with multiple applications or use large graphic, photo-editing, and database applications.
- *VGA graphics video display* Super VGA recommended.
- *A version of Windows or a disk from Microsoft Windows 3.0 or later (including Windows for Workgroups)* If you're installing the upgrade version of Windows 95, you need to provide this during setup. The full version of Windows 95 does not require a previous installation of Windows.
- *417KB free conventional memory*
- *25MB to 40MB of free hard drive storage space partitioned with the FAT file system* This depends on your upgrade path and installation options. If you plan to run Microsoft Office 95 or Office 97, you should have at least a 1GB hard drive.
- *Up to 14MB of additional free storage space for the Windows 95 swap file* This depends on the amount of RAM installed on your system.

Although you can install Windows 95 on a computer with as little as 4MB of RAM, you won't be able to do much with it. To experience the full performance potential of Windows 95, you really need at least 16MB of memory. And when running multiple applications, you will see a noticeable performance increase with 32MB or more of RAM. Processor speed is also important, and with the drop in price for Pentium systems, it is almost always more cost-efficient to replace an older 386 or 486 system than it is to upgrade it.

NOTE Windows 95 is compatible with Microsoft DriveSpace and DoubleSpace disk compression utilities included with older versions of MS-DOS. It is also compatible with older third-party compression programs, including Stacker versions 3.*x* and 4.*x*.

Exercise caution when upgrading a system that uses disk compression, however, as these utilities can affect the estimate of free drive space available for installation. If you're nearly out of room on an older drive, with or without disk compression, consider replacing the drive or adding a second drive to the system; cost of a new multi-gigabyte drive is typically under $200.

Keeping Your Copy of Windows 95 Up to Date

Most PCs sold today include a copy of Windows 95 already installed. For the most part, PC makers use the Typical option to set up a Windows configuration that includes components that meet the needs of most Windows users. Like any one-size-fits-all solution, however, it's virtually certain that the Typical setup will miss some components that you need or add others that you will never use. PC manufacturers are also unlikely to add the most recent security patches and system updates when configuring a Windows 95 system. Most important, unless your system included a copy of OSR 2.5 with Internet Explorer 4.0, you'll need to obtain a copy of IE4 and install the Windows Desktop Update before you can use the shell enhancements described in this book.

Adding and Removing Windows Components

The Add/Remove Programs icon in Control Panel enables you to install and remove Windows components and accessories, as well as applications. Therefore, you can reconfigure your copy of Windows 95 without reinstalling it.

To use the Windows Setup feature to add or remove a Windows components, follow these steps:

1. Open the Start menu and choose Settings, Control Panel.
2. Open the Add/Remove Programs properties sheet by double-clicking the Add/Remove Programs icon.
3. Click the Windows Setup tab to display a list of Windows components, as shown in Figure 2.1.

   In the Components list box, a check mark next to an item indicates that the component is already installed on your system. If the check box is gray, the Windows component includes more than one part, and some (but not all) of those parts are currently installed. For instance, in Figure 2.1, only some of the components in the Accessories option are installed. To see a full listing of the parts included in a component, choose Details.
4. Select a component in the Components list box. When you do, the Description box in the lower portion of the dialog box displays a description of that component.

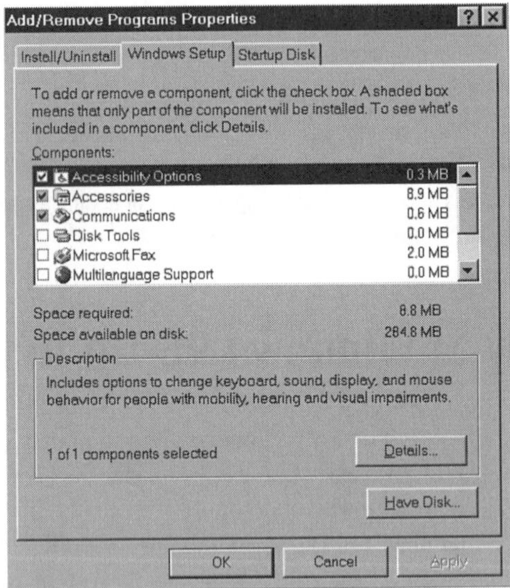

FIG. 2.1
The Windows Setup tab of the Add/Remove Program properties sheet enables you to add and remove parts of Windows.

5. If the component you select consists of more than one part, choose Details to open a dialog box listing the individual parts. (For example, Figure 2.2 shows the Accessories dialog box, which lists all the components of the main Accessories option.) In some cases (the Screen Savers option, for example) you can choose Details again to narrow your selection further.

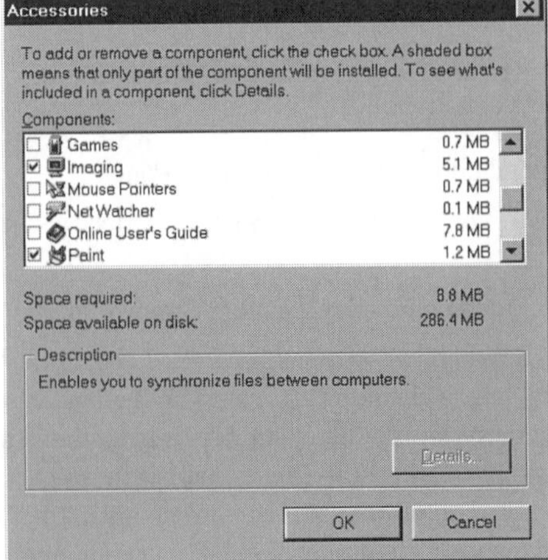

FIG. 2.2
The Accessories dialog box lists a component's parts. By choosing Details, you can narrow your selections.

6. Mark components for installation or removal by clicking the check box beside that item in the Components list. Adding a check mark to a previously blank check box marks that item for installation. Conversely, clearing a previously checked box instructs Windows to uninstall that component.

7. If you're selecting components in a dialog box that you opened by choosing a Details button, click OK to close that dialog box and return to the Add/Remove Programs properties sheet.
8. When the check marks in the Components lists specify the components that you want composing your Windows system, choose Apply in the Add/Remove Programs properties sheet. You might need to supply the Windows Setup disks or CD when prompted.

TROUBLESHOOTING

When I use the Windows Setup feature to add new components, it adds those components, but it also removes other components. Why? When you clear a check box for a component that was checked when you opened the Add/Remove Programs dialog box, Windows removes the component. This behavior can be confusing if you are not experienced with the Windows Setup program. Leave the check mark next to those components that are already installed unless you want to remove them.

Installing Unlisted Components

Eventually, you might want to install a Windows component that doesn't appear on the Components list in the Windows Setup tab of the Add/Remove Program properties sheet. For example, you might want to install the System Policy Editor from the Admin folder of the Windows 95 CD-ROM.

To install a Windows component not listed in the Components list box, open the Add/Remove Program properties sheet, click the Windows Setup tab, and choose the Have Disk button at the bottom of the dialog box. This opens the Install From Disk dialog box. When adding Windows components from a supplemental disk, you must supply the full path to the correct INF file.

In the Copy Manufacturer's Files From field, specify the path to the setup information file (with the extension INF) for the Windows component that you want to install. (The setup information file tells Windows Setup what is available to install and how to do it.) You can either type the path and filename of the folder where the INF file is stored or choose Browse and select the file in the Browse dialog box. After specifying the correct path, click OK. Windows opens the Have Disk dialog box (see Figure 2.3), which lists the components available for installation. Check the ones that you want to add and then choose Install. You might have to supply disks and browse for needed files when prompted.

Windows not only installs the component but also adds the component to the list of installed software on the Install/Uninstall tab of the Add/Remove Programs dialog box. Later, you can remove the component just like any other in the list.

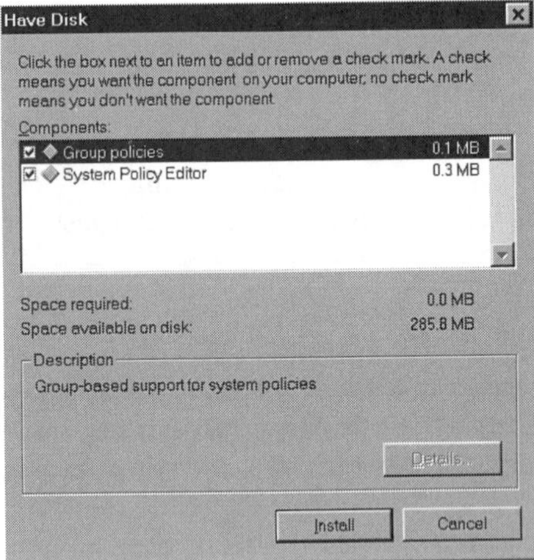

FIG. 2.3
The Have Disk dialog box lists the Windows components available on the supplemental disk, or at least the components described in the INF file that you selected.

Installing Service Packs and Patches

Microsoft regularly issues patches and updates intended to repair bugs or to enable new features in Windows 95. Unlike Windows components, which use the Windows Setup program to add themselves to your configuration, patches and updates are usually self-executing files. The most common way to obtain a patch file is to download it from Microsoft's web site. After downloading the file, double-click its icon to launch the patch program, which typically replaces one or more files and updates Windows Registry entries, as needed.

As of November 1997, there were dozens of updates and patches available for Windows 95. Table 2.1 includes a comprehensive list of these files. Don't just blindly install patches and updates, however. Some fixes, such as the security updates that strengthen password encryption, belong on any Windows 95 system, but others are intended to repair bugs that occur only with specific hardware or network configurations, and installing the patch on another type of system or network can cause more problems than it solves. Whenever possible, read the Knowledge Base article that explains the reason for the update before downloading and installing the file.

ON THE WEB

The most up-to-date list of Windows 95 patches and updates is available from **http://support.microsoft.com/support/downloads/LNP195.asp**. Each entry in the list includes a description of the file, references to any relevant Knowledge Base articles, and a link to the downloadable file.

Table 2.1. Available Updates for Windows 95

Filename	Title	Description
ANSINST.EXE	Microsoft	Windows 95 add-on support tool for users of VoiceView-compatible modems. Included with OSR2.
BACKUPD2.EXE	Updated Backup.exe for Windows 95	Repairs minor bugs; does not contain any new functions.
CDCHNGER.EXE	Updated Drivers for CD-ROM Changers	Updated protected-mode CD-ROM changer drivers that correct problems working with multiple disc CD-ROM changers.
COM32UPD.EXE	Updated Comctl32.dll file for Windows 95	Corrects problems with garbled text on tabs in Windows properties sheets.
COVERPG.EXE	Microsoft Fax Cover Page Update	Corrects a problem with the Microsoft Fax service in Exchange Inbox and Windows Messaging.
DLC32UPD.EXE	DLC Update for the MSDLC32 Protocol	Update for the Microsoft 32-bit Data Link Control (MSDLC32) protocol used to communicate with mainframe systems.
DSKTSUPD.EXE	Disk Type Specific Driver Update for Windows 95	Repairs a serious bug that can cause data loss when using large EIDE drives with multiple partitions on computers that support LBA and extended INT 13 functions.
EXUPDUSA.EXE	Microsoft Exchange Inbox Update for Windows 95	The Microsoft Exchange Inbox Update for Windows 95 provides support for Microsoft Mail Server shared folders and other minor updates.
IMGINST.EXE	Imaging for Windows 95 Version 1.0	New accessory to create, annotate, view, and print TIFF, BMP, and Microsoft Fax (AWD) image documents. Included with OSR2.
IOSUPD.EXE	Microsoft SAME IDE Channel N CDROM & Hard Disks	Fixes problem with CD-ROM performance when CD-ROM is set as slave on same IDE channel as master hard drive.
KRNLUPD.EXE	Updated Kernel32.dll file for Windows 95	Repairs a memory leak that can occur when using Windows Sockets connections.

continues

Table 2.1. Continued

Filename	Title	Description
MSISDN11.EXE	ISDN 1.1 Accelerator Pack	Upgrades Dial-Up Networking components and adds support for multilink connections over ISDN line; despite name, does not require ISDN connection. Included in OSR2.
MSPWLUPD.EXE	Enhanced Encryption for Windows 95 Passwords	Substantially strengthens the encryption used for the Microsoft Windows 95 password cache.
NWREDUP4.EXE	Windows 95 Update to Enhance Password Security	Increases security of locally cached passwords on systems that use Microsoft Client for NetWare Directory Services.
OLEUPD.EXE	OLE Update for Windows 95	Corrects a problem that enables embedded Office files to include deleted text. Included with IE4.
PAINT95.EXE	Updated Microsoft Paint for Windows 95	New version of Microsoft Paint that corrects “Illegal Operation” messages when attempting to open graphics files after installing Microsoft Office 97.
PINGUPD.EXE	New Ping Tool for Windows 95	Prevents other networked resources from hanging when you use Ping.exe.
PLUSUPD1.EXE	New Sage.dll Corrects Floating-Point Errors	Corrects a problem with incorrect results from floating-point calculations when System Agent (from Microsoft Plus!) is running. Included with IE4.
QFECHKUP.EXE	Update Information Tool for Windows 95	Verifies which Service Pack components have been added and that the versions installed match the versions listed in the registry. Installed automatically with Service Pack 1 and OSR2.
RAS2UPD.EXE	Updated Rasapi32.dll for Windows 95 OSR2	OSR2-specific update to correct Dial-Up Networking bug noted in previous item.
RASUPD.EXE	Updated Rasapi32.dll version 4.0.953	Install if, when using Dial-Up Networking to dial into a remote network, you receive the following error message: “No domain controller was available to validate your logon.” For original release of Windows 95 only.

Filename	Title	Description
RPCRTUPD.EXE	Remote Procedure Call DLL Update for Windows 95	Update to the Windows 95 remote Procedure Call runtime. Recommended for developers only.
SECUPD.EXE	Windows 95 Update to Enhance Password Security	Increases security of locally cached passwords. For original release of Windows 95 only.
SECUPD2.EXE	Windows 95 Update to Enhance Password Security	Increases security of locally cached passwords. For Windows 95 OSR 2 and 2.1 only.
THEMES.EXE	Updated Themes.exe version 4.40.311	Prevents "Illegal Operation" error messages after installing a program that modifies the JPEG graphics filter.
VIPUPD.EXE	Updated TCP/IP Protocol Stack for Windows 95	Repairs a TCP/IP bug that can cause system hangs when accessing the Internet or a multicast network.
VRDRUPD.EXE	Windows 95 Update to Prevent Sending Clear-Text Password Over Network	Fixes a potential security bug when connecting with older SMB servers on UNIX networks, including connections over the Internet.
VREDRUPD.EXE	Updated Vredir.vxd File	Corrects a problem that might cause local files to be deleted when attempting to delete files on Samba servers running on UNIX- based computers.
VTCPUPD.EXE	Update to Windows 95 TCP/IP Out-Of-Band issue	Corrects a security flaw that enables out-of-band packets by using the TCP/IP protocol to crash a Windows 95 computer.
VVSETUP.EXE	Microsoft File Transfer Tool	Enables users of VoiceView-capable modems to transfer files while talking over the telephone.
W95IR.EXE	Infrared Data Connectivity for Windows 95	Adds support for Infrared Data Association (IrDA) connectivity. Included with OSR2.
WSOCKUPD.EXE	Windows 95 WinSock Update to Improve Multihoming Support	WinSock update for Windows 95 to improve multihoming support. Do not install on OSR2 systems!

Installing Internet Explorer 4.0

Perhaps the most important Windows upgrade of all is the Windows Desktop Update, included with Internet Explorer 4.0. This book assumes that you've installed IE4 and enabled the changes to the Windows shell, included as part of the Desktop Update. If you purchased a brand-new PC with OSR 2.5, the PC manufacturer has already installed IE4 with Windows; otherwise, installing IE4 is not particularly difficult. Depending on your system configuration, you have three options, decribed in the following sections.

NOTE If you've installed one of several beta versions of IE4 (Microsoft officially refers to them as Platform Preview editions), remove the old code completely before installing the released version. The old edition is on the list of installed applications when you activate the Add/Remove Programs option in Control Panel. ■

Installing from Desktop Icon Some computer manufacturers ship PCs with Internet Explorer 3.0 or Internet Explorer 4.0 available for setup; the compressed files might be on your hard disk or on a separate CD-ROM. If the IE4 option is available on your system, you see an IE4 Setup icon on the desktop. Double-click this icon and the Setup program prompts you to choose the components to install.

Installing from CD-ROM Because Internet Explorer 3.0 was included with OSR2, some computer manufacturers might include the older version of Internet Explorer on the hard disk, with the IE4 program code available on a separate CD-ROM. You can also order a copy of IE4 on CD if you'd prefer not to download the large IE4 setup files, which range in size from 13MB to more than 25MB.

Free downloadable upgrades are usually available from Microsoft on CD-ROM for a nominal fee, typically under $15. In the first few months after the official release of IE4, Microsoft offered CD versions for as little as $4.95 to users in the United States and Canada. Order the CD version online by following the links from **http://www.microsoft.com/ie/ie40/**; you also can call Microsoft at 800-485-2248 to order from a customer service representative. A deluxe version of IE4, called Internet Explorer Plus, is available at retail outlets for around $30; it includes the same code as the free versions and adds a number of third-party utilities.

To install from CD-ROM, insert the CD-ROM in its drive; then click Start, Settings, Control Panel. Double-click Add/Remove Programs, select the Install/Uninstall tab, and click the Install button. Follow the directions when prompted.

Installing from the Microsoft Web Site There is no charge to download Internet Explorer 4.0 from Microsoft's web site. You'll find the necessary links at **http://www.microsoft.com/ie/ie40**.

Installing IE4 is a two-step process. In the first step, you run a small program called the Active Setup Wizard. You can save this wizard to hard disk and run it later, or you can launch the wizard directly from the Internet and begin installation immediately. In the second step, you use the Active Setup Wizard to choose the version of IE4 to install, and you specify whether you want to install directly from the Internet or download the setup files and install them later.

For most users, the option to download and install later is more prudent, because it enables them to control when and how they perform the installation, and it enables them to reinstall components at a later date without having to establish an Internet connection again.

To get started, follow the links to the download page, select a preferred language, and download the small IE4SETUP program (at approximately 400KB, it should take no more than 5 minutes over an analog connection). A dialog box enables you to choose whether to run the program immediately or download it. If you choose the second option, save the file to a location on your hard disk, and when the download is complete, find the icon for IE4SETUP.EXE and launch it.

As Figure 2.4 shows, the Active Setup Wizard enables you to choose one of three versions of IE4 for download. The Standard Installation option, selected by default, includes the web browser, Windows Desktop Update, Outlook Express, and several multimedia components. Avoid the Browser-only option, which does not include the Windows Desktop Update or mail software. The Full Installation adds all IE4 components, including NetMeeting, FrontPage Express, and several streaming-media players. The Standard option requires you to download approximately 13MB of data, which takes more than an hour with a 28.8KB modem running at full speed, and the Full option represents a download of more than 25MB.

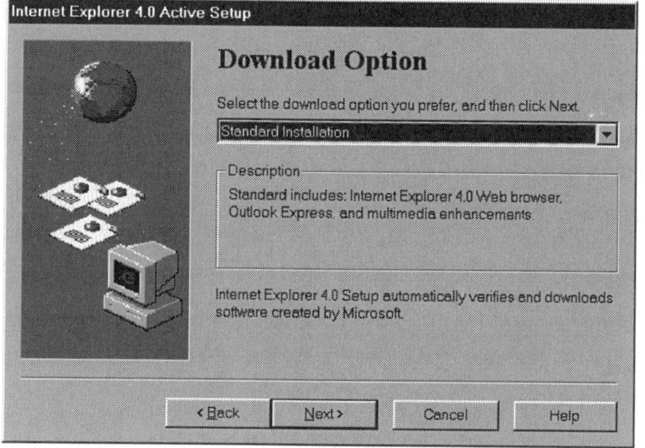

FIG. 2.4 This Active Setup Wizard enables you to choose which components to download when you first install IE4.

If you're concerned about download times, a good strategy is to start with the Standard Installation and then return later for additional components as you need them. To add new components or check for upgraded versions of those you've already installed, open IE4 and choose Help, Product Updates; this takes you to Microsoft's web site, and an ActiveX control on your computer scans your system to see which components are already installed, compares that list to the inventory of available components, and presents a summary screen like the one shown in Figure 2.5. Check the box to the left of each component you want to add or reinstall, and click the Next button to proceed to the rest of the wizard.

NOTE Although IE4 uses its own setup and update routines, you must use the Add/Remove Programs option in Control Panel to remove individual components of IE4. ■

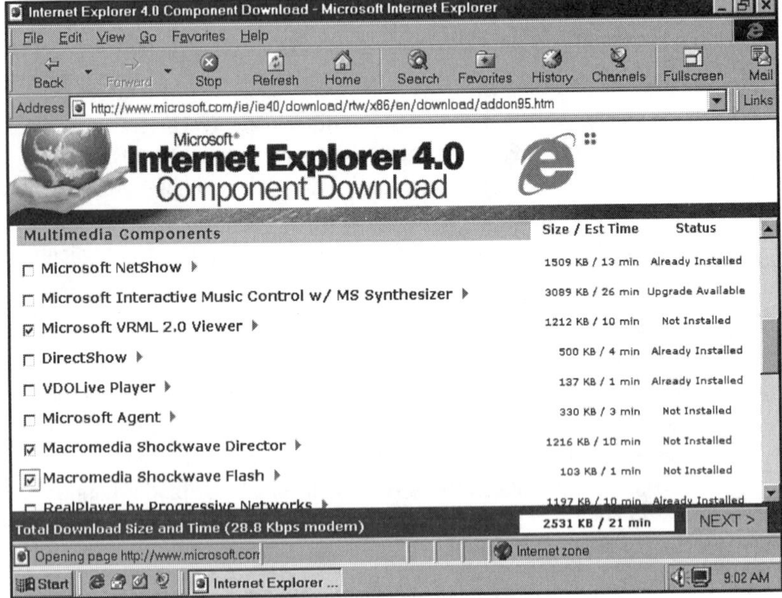

FIG. 2.5
This page on Microsoft's web site enables you to see at a glance the components that are available for you to install for the first time or upgrade.

Determining the Current Version of Windows

How can you tell which version of Windows 95 is installed on a given system? Right-click the My Computer icon on the Windows desktop and choose Properties. Look at the information under the System heading on the General tab—if OSR2 is installed, the version number for Windows 95 appears as 4.00.950 B, as shown in Figure 2.6. If there is no letter after the 950 identifier, the original release of Windows 95 is installed; 950 A indicates that Service Pack 1 has been installed.

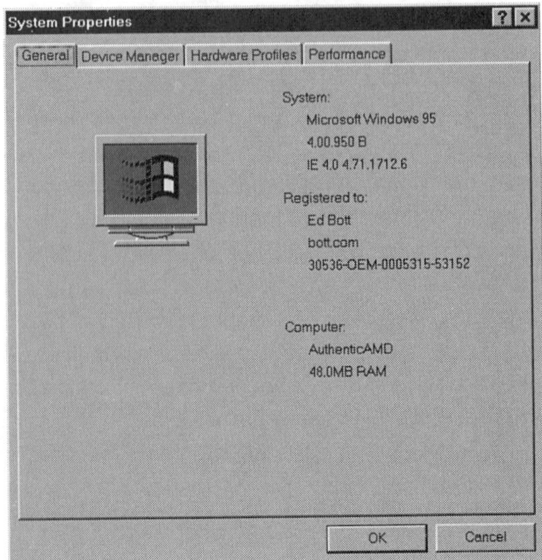

FIG. 2.6
View the System Properties sheet to find out if a system is using the OSR2 release of Windows 95 (designated as 4.00.950 B).

To verify the Windows 95 version from an MS-DOS prompt, type **ver**. If you are running OSR2, the version number is listed as Version 4.00.1111.

To verify that you have installed the FAT32 file system, open the My Computer window, right-click the drive icon you want to check, and choose Properties. If your hard disk is using FAT32, you will see the FAT32 file system designation in the General tab (see Figure 2.7).

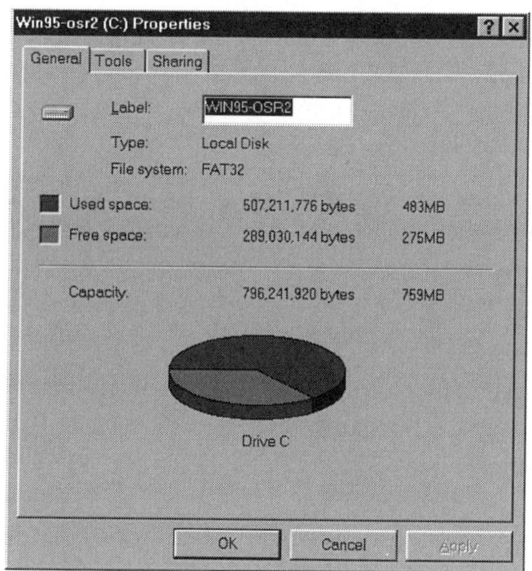

FIG. 2.7 If your hard disk is using FAT32, you will see the FAT32 designation in the Properties sheet for the hard disk.

Installing Windows 95 OEM Service Release 2 (OSR2)

Microsoft Windows 95 OEM Service Release 2 (OSR2) incorporates all of the enhancements included in Service Pack 1, many patches and fixes that were released after Service Pack 1, and a long list of new features. (OEM is an acronym for Original Equipment Manufacturer, a term used in the computer industry to refer to companies that manufacture personal computers and peripherals.) As the name implies, OSR2 is sold only by OEMs when installed on new systems; it is not available for retail sale. You can, however, download some of the new components from Microsoft's web site and install them on your computer without having to obtain the OSR2 update. Other components, including the FAT32 file system update, are available only when you install Windows 95 OSR2.

Chapter 1, "What's New in Windows 95 and Internet Explorer 4.0," summarizes the new features in OSR2. On most new systems sold since the beginning of 1997, OSR2 is already included.

Do You Want to Upgrade to OSR2?

Although it's not easy, it is possible to upgrade an existing system to OSR2. Should you bother? The most compelling reason for upgrading to OSR2 is the new FAT32 file system, which makes it easier to work with large hard disks. (We'll discuss FAT32 options in the following section.) Users of portable computers will also see noticeable benefits from the improved-power management features for portables.

If you are not interested in FAT32 or power management but would like to take advantage of some of the other components in OSR2, check Table 2.1 to see if those components can be downloaded individually. If this is the case, you don't need to upgrade to OSR2 to take advantage of the enhancements that interest you.

What are the main disadvantages of OSR2? First of all, it is not easy to get a copy of the upgrade. Because of Microsoft's OSR2 distribution policy, you either have to purchase a new system or buy a new hard drive or motherboard from a vendor who will sell you a copy of OSR2 with the item you purchase. You can't run down to your local software dealer to buy a copy of OSR2.

Microsoft's official explanation for this policy is that because most of the enhancements apply to new hardware devices, there is no reason to upgrade existing systems. A second reason, which Microsoft doesn't officially acknowledge, is that they are unwilling to provide technical support to end users attempting to upgrade to the new version because of the complications involved.

After you have obtained a copy of the OSR2 upgrade, there are several steps you need to undertake to successfully upgrade your system. We will show you two methods for installing OSR2 on your system. The first approach involves repartitioning and reformatting your hard disk with the new versions of FDISK and FORMAT that Microsoft released with OSR2. You need the updated versions of these utilities to format your hard disk with the new FAT32 file system. As soon as you reformat your hard disk, you install OSR2 from scratch.

The second method for upgrading eliminates the need for repartitioning and reformatting the hard disk when you install OSR2. Using this method does not enable you to use FAT32.

Also be aware that you might encounter hardware and software incompatibilities with OSR2, and any disk utilities you have that are designed to work with the FAT16 file system will not work on a FAT32 disk. You will need to obtain updated versions or patches for your disk utilities. The versions of ScanDisk and Disk Defragmenter that come with OSR2 are compatible with FAT32.

If you currently dual-boot between Windows 95 and either Windows 3.*x*, Windows NT 3.51, or 4.0, you might lose this capability if you install OSR2. Neither Windows 3.*x* nor current versions of NT can access FAT32 partitions.

NOTE For instructions on restoring dual-boot capabilities with Windows NT after installing Windows 95, go to **http://support.microsoft.com** and search for Q136547. This Knowledge Base article describes the problem and the cure. ■

Another serious consideration is that you will almost certainly lose the right to technical support from the manufacturer of your PC if you install a version of OSR2 that they did not sell you. In fact, some computer companies install OSR2 on new computers without enabling FAT32 and state that you will invalidate your technical support and warranty if you install it. If technical support is important to you, read your PC's documentation carefully and contact the manufacturer before you inadvertently invalidate the warranty.

ON THE WEB

http://www.compuclinic.com/osr2faq/ Check out this web site for in-depth coverage of OSR2 and the FAT32 file system.

Understanding Your FAT32 Options

The original version of Windows 95, as well as DOS, uses a file system called FAT16, a 16-bit file system. There are two major drawbacks to the FAT16 file system in this age of larger and larger hard disks. First, FAT16 can support only single disk volumes (partitions) of up to 2GB. With larger hard disks, you are forced to partition your drive into 2GB or smaller volumes. Second, the cluster size increases dramatically as you increase partition size. A 2GB partition, for example, stores each file in clusters 32KB in size; that means even a small text file of only a few bytes will use a full 32KB cluster, and a file that is even one byte larger than 32KB will use two clusters. On a hard disk with thousands of files, the result is extremely inefficient use of disk space. This wasted storage space is called slack.

With the OSR2 release, Microsoft introduced a new 32-bit file system called FAT32. The FAT32 file system supports single disk volumes (partitions) up to 2 terabytes in size and uses much smaller clusters. For partitions up to 8GB, FAT32 uses 4KB clusters, resulting in much more efficient file storage. On a FAT32 volume with 4KB clusters, eight small files occupy the same space that a single small file uses on a FAT16 volume with its 32KB clusters. With thousands of files on a large hard disk, converting to FAT32 typically reclaims hundreds of megabytes of usable storage space.

Unfortunately, OSR2 does not include a utility for converting FAT16 partitions to FAT32. If your new PC came preinstalled with OSR2 but the manufacturer did not enable FAT32, you can use PowerQuest's Partition Magic utility to resize or convert hard disk partitions dynamically, so you don't have to back up and then restore your data and applications (as you do with FDISK).

ON THE WEB

http://www.powerquest.com For more information on Partition Magic, call PowerQuest at 801-226-8977 or visit their web site.

NOTE If you don't want to risk upgrading to OSR2 and the FAT32 file system, don't despair. Windows 98, a major upgrade to Windows 95 due in mid-1998, will incorporate all of the features in OSR2, including FAT32. It will also include the capability to upgrade over any version of Windows 95 and to upgrade disk partitions from FAT16 to FAT32. ■

Setting Up OSR2 from Scratch

If you decide you want to install OSR2 on your system from scratch, there are several steps you must complete. First, create a startup disk by using the OSR2 CD-ROM or disks. The startup disk will include the updated versions of FDISK and FORMAT; you need it to repartition and reformat your hard disk with the FAT32 file system.

To create an OSR2 startup disk, follow these steps:

1. Insert the Windows 95 OSR2 CD-ROM in your CD-ROM drive and a blank, high-density disk in your floppy disk drive.
2. Open the Start menu and choose Settings, Control Panel.
3. Double-click the Add/Remove Programs icon.
4. Click the Startup Disk tab and choose Create Disk. Follow the instructions that appear onscreen.

   Windows copies files from the Windows 95 CD-ROM to create the startup disk. Because you inserted the OSR2 version of Windows 95 in step 1, the newer versions of FDISK.EXE and FORMAT.COM will be copied to the startup disk.

After you create the OSR2 startup disk, copy the files needed to access your CD-ROM drive from the DOS prompt onto the startup disk. This enables you to access the Windows 95 OSR2 CD-ROM from the DOS prompt after you have partitioned and formatted your hard drive, using the OSR2 startup disk. See the tip in "The Typical Windows 95 Setup Process" section (later in this chapter) that shows you what files you need to add to your startup disk to access your CD-ROM.

After you create an OSR2 startup disk, you are ready to repartition your hard disk. To partition your hard disk with the FAT32 file system, complete the steps that follow.

CAUTION

Be sure you back up all critical files on your hard disk before you repartition and reformat. You will lose all the data on your hard disk when you repartition it.

1. Insert the startup disk you just created into the floppy disk drive and reboot your computer.
2. Run FDISK from the A:> prompt.

   If your hard disk is larger than 512MB, a message appears, informing you that your hard disk is larger than 512MB and that you have the option of enabling large disk support. You are warned that if you do so, you will not be able to access the drive by using other operating systems and that some disk utilities not designed for the FAT32 file system will not work.
3. Assuming that you accept these caveats, type **Y** and press Enter.
4. Use FDISK to delete the existing DOS partitions on your hard disk.

   Do not proceed with this step unless you have backed up your files on the hard disk.

5. After you delete all existing DOS partitions, use FDISK to create a new Primary DOS partition. Make this partition the active one.

   At this point, you can use FDISK to partition your drive into smaller, logical drives. Keep in mind, however, that one of the benefits of the FAT32 file system is that you can create a single partition of up to 2 terabytes and that partitions up to 8GB in size will use 4KB clusters.

6. When you finish partitioning your hard disk, exit FDISK and reboot your computer by using the startup disk.
7. Use the Format command on the startup disk to reformat your hard disk.

After you repartition and reformat your hard drive with the OSR2 startup disk, you can install Windows 95 from the OSR2 CD-ROM. Reboot your computer and run Setup from the DOS prompt. If your CD-ROM is designated as the D: drive, for example, type **d:setup**. The procedure from this point onward is identical to the procedure described in "Installing Windows 95 for the First Time," later in this chapter; please refer to this sections for details on the Windows setup.

Upgrading to OSR2 Without Reformatting

The OSR2 release of Windows 95 is not designed to be an upgrade. If you try to set up OSR2 on a system that has the original release of Windows 95 installed, a message box informs you that you cannot upgrade your system. However, there is an alternative to the laborious process described in the previous section for installing OSR2 from scratch. The following workaround enables you to trick the OSR2 setup program into thinking you are installing Windows 95 on a system that does not have the original version of Windows installed. Please note that this procedure is not supported by Microsoft; if you get into trouble, you will have no technical support options.

NOTE If you use the workaround to upgrade to OSR2 without reformatting, you cannot use the OSR2 system to convert existing disk partitions from FAT16 to FAT32. You will need a third-party conversion utility such as Power Quest's Partition Magic to complete this process. ■

To upgrade your system to OSR2, follow these steps:

1. Create a temporary folder on your hard disk and name it FLAT.
2. Copy all of the setup files from the WIN95 folder on the OSR2 CD-ROM to the FLAT folder.
3. Extract the file named SETUPPP.INF from the Precopy2.cab file.

   To extract the file, open an MS-DOS Prompt window and switch to the FLAT directory. Type the following at the DOS prompt:

   extract precopy2.cab setuppp.inf

4. Close the DOS window.

5. Using Notepad, make the following change in the file LAYOUT.INF (which is located in the FLAT folder):

   Change `SETUPPP.INF=2,,4550` to `SETUPPP.INF=0,,4550`

6. Save the changes in LAYOUT.INF.
7. Using Notepad again, make the following change in SETUPPP.INF:

   Change `ProductType=9` to `ProductType=1`

8. Save the changes in SETUPPP.INF.
9. Run SETUP from the FLAT folder by double-clicking SETUP in Windows Explorer. OSR2 will now run as an upgrade.

Before you start the upgrade procedure, create a temporary folder and move all the items in your Windows\Start Menu\Programs\StartUp folder. When you have finished the upgrade, move these items back to the StartUp folder. This step saves you the trouble of having to restore these items to the StartUp folder.

Upgrading from Windows 3.*x*

When Windows 95 was first released, the most common Setup option was upgrading to Windows 95 over an existing copy of Windows 3.1 or Windows for Workgroups 3.11. Today, that option is increasingly less common. Most systems still using Windows 3.*x* consist of older hardware that is unsuited for use with Windows 95; it's more common for system buyers to replace old Windows 3.*x* systems with new hardware on which a copy of Windows 95 is already installed. Still, upgrading over Windows 3.*x* is possible, and, in fact, the Setup program makes the upgrade as simple as possible.

Before upgrading, it's a good idea to confirm that Windows and all attached devices are working properly. Windows 95 uses previous settings to confirm your peripheral configurations. If those settings are incorrect, Windows 95 tries to install the specified hardware anyway—and will certainly fail. Even if your current installation and peripherals are working perfectly, it's a good idea to have device drivers available on floppy disks in case Windows 95 Setup needs to refer to them during installation.

To make a complete backup copy of your existing Windows 3.*x* files in case you need to restore them later, use the following MS-DOS command (substitute the directory names you actually use):

```
XCOPY  /S C:\WIN31\*.* C:\WIN31BAK
```

If you have installed a substitute shell for Program Manager, such as Norton Desktop for Windows, you should remove it. Edit the `SHELL=` line in the [boot] section of SYSTEM.INI to read `SHELL=PROGMAN.EXE`. Defragment your hard drive before running the Setup program, and clean out any existing Program Manager groups and icons that you no longer need. Windows 95 will detect existing Windows 3.*x* configuration details, such as real-mode device drivers, and carry them forward if necessary. Any Program Groups you have created in Windows 3.*x* will appear as items on the Windows 95 Start menu.

To start Windows 95 Setup from within Windows 3.*x*, open Program Manager and choose File, Run from the main Program Manager menu. Windows displays the Run dialog box. Type **a:setup** and click OK to begin the installation process. From that point forward, the procedure is the same as described in the next section.

Installing Windows 95 on a New System or Hard Drive

Before you can install a fresh, clean copy of Windows 95, you must be able to boot to an MS-DOS prompt, and you must have a formatted hard disk. If you need instructions on how to create and format a partition, see "Setting Up OSR2 from Scratch" in the preceding section. Note that a startup disk created by the original release of Windows 95 supports FAT16 partitions only.

Although Windows 95 Setup generally does a good job of configuring most systems, you can save time and trouble by preparing your machine for installation. Before you begin the Setup process, determine if you are installing Windows from an existing MS-DOS prompt or reformatting your hard disk and doing a clean install. The following sections help you prepare for installing Windows 95.

Preparing Your System for Windows 95 Setup

You need to take several steps before running Windows 95 Setup. Before you install Windows 95, make sure you do each of the following:

- Confirm that your system meets the minimum Windows 95 hardware and software requirements, as listed at the beginning of this chapter.
- Confirm the boot drive sequence for your system.
- Confirm that you have a working boot floppy disk for your current operating system configuration.
- Back up critical data and configuration files, if necessary (a complete system backup is preferred).
- Know the location of all required drivers for any peripherals, including network interface cards.
- Know all the usernames and passwords you'll need to log in to your network.
- Disable all memory-resident programs (loaded in AUTOEXEC.BAT and CONFIG.SYS files).
- Disable antivirus programs, screen savers, disk scan utilities, and any similar programs.
- Disable third-party memory managers.

Although this list might seem like a lot to do before you can upgrade to Windows 95, bear in mind that changing the operating system on your computer is no small matter. In fact, you should follow most of these procedures before making any major change in hardware or software. Anything less is simply begging to fall victim to Murphy's Law of Personal Computing: If anything can go wrong, it's most likely to do so when you don't have a recent backup or a boot disk.

Configuring a Startup Disk

A good boot disk is not just a bootable floppy; on that disk, you should have the tools you need to edit startup files, work with disks, and access your CD-ROM. It might take a few minutes to create this "boot backup" now, but the effort could save you hours of scrambling if you run into trouble later.

A great boot disk is worthless if your system can't read it. Most systems are configured to search the drives during startup to find a bootable disk, but some are configured to look only at a specific drive, either as a time-saving startup step or for security reasons. If in doubt about your system, make sure you can boot by using the startup disk. If you create a boot disk and the system won't read it from a cold start, check the system CMOS settings and correct the boot sequence to use the A: drive first.

Performing a Clean Installation

A disadvantage to installing Windows 95 over an earlier copy of Windows 3.*x* or DOS is that you might end up with bits and pieces of the previous operating system on your hard disk, which might affect the performance or stability of your system. The best solution is to do a "clean" install, with no traces of any earlier drivers or operating system, by repartitioning and reformatting your hard disk and then setting up Windows 95 from scratch.

To perform a clean install of Windows 95, follow these steps:

1. Create a boot disk for your system. A startup disk from another Windows 95 system works, or you can copy FDISK.EXE and FORMAT.COM from the \DOS directory of an MS-DOS system. If you plan to install Windows 95 from a CD-ROM, be sure to copy the real-mode drivers for the CD-ROM on the disk, a copy of the MS CD Extensions (MSCDEX.EXE), and AUTOEXEC.BAT and CONFIG.SYS files for loading the drivers at startup.
2. Reboot your computer by using the boot disk.
3. Repartition your hard disk by using FDISK.

CAUTION

Repartitioning your hard drive destroys all the information on it. Make sure you have a reliable backup of all your important data.

4. Reformat the drive by using FORMAT.COM.

5. Reboot your computer by using the startup disk and run Setup from the DOS prompt, as described in "Installing Windows 95 from an MS-DOS Prompt," later in this chapter.
6. Reinstall all of your applications and restore your data files from your backups.

NOTE If you are installing the final version of Windows 95 on a system that had beta versions of Windows 95, Microsoft recommends that you perform a clean install to remove any traces of the earlier versions. ■

CAUTION

If your computer system is completely new and has no operating system installed, or if you are doing a clean install, be sure you have the non-upgrade version of Windows 95 or you have access to Windows 3.*x* Setup disks. Otherwise, you'll get in trouble, because the standard upgrade version requires a previous version of Windows (or at least earlier Windows disks) to operate. If Windows 3.*x* is not installed on your system, the Windows 95 Setup program asks you for the first Windows 3.*x* install disk during the installation.

How Windows 95 Setup Works

Before you begin to install Windows 95, it's a good idea to know what to expect and when to expect it. Windows 95 Setup has four basic phases:

- Detection
- Question and answer
- File copy
- Startup

Phase One: Setup Detection—Software and Then Hardware

Windows 95 Setup starts by detecting what environment it was started from. If you opt to install from within a running Windows 95 or Windows 3.*x* installation, Setup skips a few steps and gets to the business of analyzing your hardware. If you don't have Windows installed or choose to start from the MS-DOS prompt, Setup first copies and executes a bare-bones version of Windows that runs the remainder of the Setup program and then moves on to hardware detection.

Setup checks your system for the following:

- An extended memory manager and cache program. If either HIMEM.SYS or SMARTDRV.EXE is missing, Setup loads its own copies.
- Installed hardware devices.
- Connected peripherals.
- IRQs, I/O, and DMA addresses available.
- IRQs, I/O, and DMA addresses in use.

Don't be surprised if the hardware detection phase takes a few minutes. Windows 95 Setup uses a variety of techniques to perform this hardware query. Most PCs respond well to this procedure, which results in the creation of a hardware tree in the Registry. Older PCs might represent a problem if the devices do not follow modern industry standards for IRQs or I/O addresses; newer machines with Plug and Play technology report their configurations more quickly, fully, and accurately.

When the hardware detection phase finishes, Setup displays a dialog box offering you an opportunity to review the detected equipment and settings for accuracy. If they are correct, you can proceed to the next phase. You can deal with any problem directly or tell Windows to ignore it for the time being.

Phase Two: Providing Additional Information

As soon as Setup has the basic information regarding your hardware, it knows most of what it needs to install Windows on your system. However, you must provide a few details, as well as select which Windows components you want to install. Setup guides you through this process with a few clear dialog boxes. We'll look at these options in more detail in the next section.

Phase Three: Copy Chores

Windows 95 Setup asks most questions up front and then performs most of the actual installation process without interruption. You might have to click a dialog box on one or more occasions to reboot as part of the setup process. When all Windows 95 files are copied, Setup adds the Windows 95 operating system files—most notably, Command.com, Msdos.sys, and Io.sys—to your boot drive. If there is an existing version of MS-DOS on that drive, Setup replaces those startup files with their Windows 95 counterparts.

Phase Four: System Startup

When it has replaced the startup files, Setup restarts your system and finishes the final cleanup chores required for installation. When this is finished, you're ready to roll with Windows 95.

Installing Windows 95 from an MS-DOS Prompt

Now that you have an overview of the basic logic and operation of Windows 95 Setup and some tips for how to prepare your system, you are ready to begin installation.

NOTE If you are using Windows NT or OS/2, you must boot from a floppy disk or use a dual-boot option to start Windows 95 Setup from an MS-DOS prompt. ■

At the MS-DOS prompt, change to the drive that contains the Windows Setup files (D: for many CD-ROMs, A: if installing from floppies). Type **setup** and press Enter.

Basic Setup Steps

The Windows 95 Setup program first runs the Windows 95 version of ScanDisk, which performs a routine check of disk integrity. Follow the prompts to deal with any drive anomalies. When ScanDisk finishes, choose the option to exit and Setup continues. Setup copies a small version of Windows 3.1 to your system so the graphical portions of Setup can run. After that is complete, Setup displays a Welcome screen.

Setup performs a brief check of your hardware, current operating system, and current running programs before proceeding. It then displays the End-User License Agreement. Read it and click Yes to continue. Windows copies files to your hard drive to prepare for the rest of the installation.

Setup begins the first major phase requiring user interaction by collecting information about your system and how you'll use it. By default, Setup installs Windows 95 in a new Windows directory on the C: drive. You can choose a different directory name if you want, although we strongly recommend accepting the default directory name.

Compact, Typical, or Custom?

Setup then checks your system for available installed components and disk space. After Setup determines that you have sufficient available drive space, it asks you to select one of four installation types, as shown in Figure 2.8.

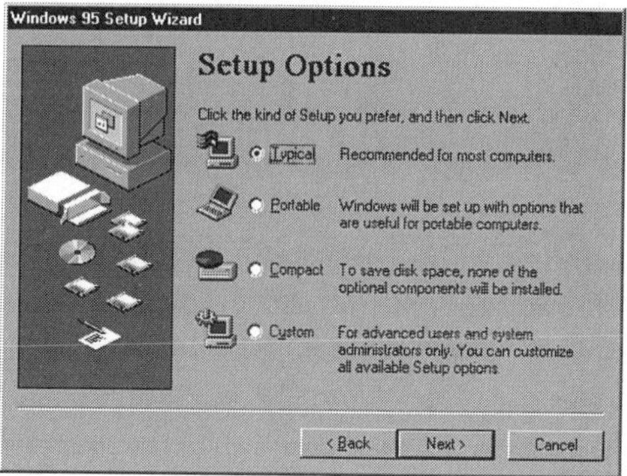

FIG. 2.8
You can choose from Typical, Portable, Compact, or Custom installation profiles.

Your choice depends upon how you use your computer and Windows. With the Typical installation option, you need to provide only some user and computer information and tell Setup whether or not you want an emergency startup disk (highly recommended).

NOTE The "Typical" selection won't install all the Windows accessories or games that you might expect. To select these components on initial setup, use the Custom option.

The Portable setup option is best for laptop or mobile computer users. Setup installs the Windows Briefcase tools for file synchronization and transfer.

The Compact setup option is for systems where you must absolutely minimize the Windows "footprint." This option is for those with truly limited free disk space; it's also appropriate for quickly installing a version of Windows from which you will restore backup tape. In a Compact setup, Windows is completely installed, but most optional components are not—disk compression and maintenance tools are the only accessories added in this configuration.

The Custom option enables you to select exactly which components will or will not be installed. If you want to install Microsoft Exchange (known as Windows Messaging in OSR2), Microsoft Fax, the Microsoft Network, the Network Administration Tools, or the Online User's Guide, you must use the Custom installation.

Selecting a Typical Setup

To continue with a Typical installation, confirm the default selection (Typical) by clicking Next or pressing Enter. Windows displays the User Information dialog box (see Figure 2.9).

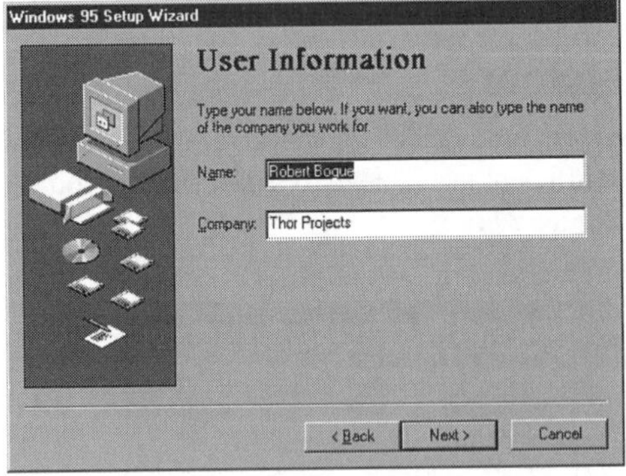

FIG. 2.9
Providing your name helps Windows properly identify you in later application installations and helps Windows identify your system when you connect to a network.

Fill in the appropriate information for your installation, and click Next or press Enter. The next several stages enable you to specify peripherals and to select individual Windows components. If you're setting Windows up on a single-user, non-networked machine, the default settings will usually be fine. Be sure to create a startup disk when prompted.

If you installed Windows 95 from a CD-ROM, you should add some additional files to your Startup disk when you finish installing Windows 95, enabling you to access the CD-ROM should you ever have to reinstall Windows. You need to copy HIMEM.SYS, MSCDEX.EXE (needed to access your CD-ROM drive), and the real-mode driver file(s) for your CD-ROM to the floppy disk.

Create a CONFIG.SYS file that loads HIMEM.SYS and the driver(s) for your CD-ROM and save it on your boot floppy. Next, create or edit AUTOEXEC.BAT on the boot floppy to run MSCDEX.EXE automatically. If you require other DOS device drivers to run in MS-DOS mode (to access a Zip drive, for example), copy the appropriate driver files to the boot floppy and add the appropriate entries to the CONFIG.SYS or AUTOEXEC.BAT files there.

The entry in AUTOEXEC.BAT should contain a line that resembles the following:

```
MSCDEX.EXE  /D:OEMCD001 /L:D
```

The CONFIG.SYS file on the startup disk should contain entries similar to this:

```
DEVICE=HIMEM.SYS
DEVICE=SAMPLE.SYS /D:OEMCD001
```

Replace SAMPLE.SYS with the actual name of the real-mode driver file used by your CD-ROM. The OEMCD001 statement must match in the AUTOEXEC.BAT and CONFIG.SYS. The documentation for your CD-ROM drive specifies any additional command-line switches that can be required.

Setup can now begin moving the Windows 95 files to your hard drive. The Windows 95 Setup background includes a progress gauge that indicates how much of the copying remains to be done. After Setup copies all Windows 95 files to your hard drive, the Finishing Setup dialog box appears. When you choose Finish and your system reboots, you'll actually boot Windows 95 for the first time.

TROUBLESHOOTING

My system froze up while the Startup disk was being made. Run Setup again and bypass making a Startup disk during setup. After Windows 95 is installed, create a startup disk by using the Startup Disk tab in the Add/Remove Programs Properties dialog box.

Restarting Setup, Starting Windows 95

When Setup resumes, it continues the Windows 95 installation by updating remaining configuration files and asking you a few more questions regarding your system peripherals. Most of these tasks are done by a system component called the Run-Once Module, which launches the appropriate system wizards to help you complete your installation.

The process begins with a quick scan of the system hardware. After this quick scan, Setup runs several short routines that can only be performed from within Windows 95 (setting up Control Panels for all appropriate devices, setting up program icons in the Start menu, initializing Windows Help, and confirming the local time zone), as shown in Figure 2.10.

The Time Zone dialog box enables you to click the map near your part of the planet and adjust the system clock accordingly, even down to daylight savings time. If you've already adjusted your system clock, you might want to uncheck the DST option.

There's a bug in the original version of Windows 95 that strikes every fall and causes Windows 95 to skip back two hours instead of one when returning to Standard time. This bug is fixed in OSR2.

When the Run-Once tasks finish, Setup is complete, and Windows 95 is fully installed.

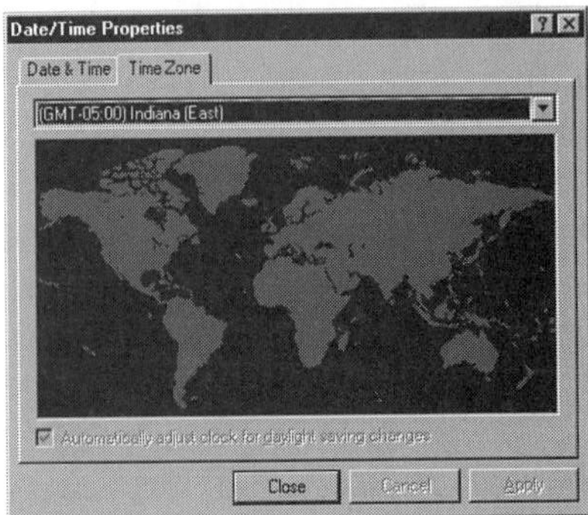

FIG. 2.10
As soon as Windows 95 is running, it can complete Windows 95-specific setup tasks.

TROUBLESHOOTING

When I run Setup, it hangs during the system check. First, check your hard disk for the presence of a virus; that's one common cause for system hangs during the routine check performed by ScanDisk. After you check for viruses, run ScanDisk from the DOS prompt and then run Setup again. If you get hung up at the same point, run Setup again with the /IS switch to bypass the routine ScanDisk check.

Advanced Installation Techniques

Although most Windows 95 installations are relatively simple, some situations demand special consideration. If you want complete control over all aspects of Setup, specify a Custom setup; if you run into difficulties during the Setup process, use the safe recovery and safe detection options.

Using Custom Setup Mode

Microsoft's Windows 95 development team has done an admirable job of establishing compatibility with a wide variety of peripheral components, but there's no way to test all combinations of PC hardware, and in some cases two devices that work fine by themselves can cause problems when used in the same system.

Installing Windows 95 for special setups is straightforward if you have the appropriate information ready before you begin. The Custom setup option enables you to specify application settings, network configuration options, and device configurations, and it gives you more control over the installation of Windows 95 components.

> **CAUTION**
>
> The Custom installation mode puts a lot of power in your hands. If you're uncertain how to configure non-standard hardware devices or network components, let Windows do the job automatically, or ask the hardware vendor or a technical support representative for step-by-step instructions.

Before you begin, know the exact name and model number of any add-in cards or devices in your system. If the manufacturer supplied Windows 95 device driver files on a floppy disk, have that handy. Write down any custom settings for the peripheral if applicable, including IRQs and logical memory addresses (see the peripheral documentation).

To use Windows 95 Setup in Custom mode, proceed with the installation as before, but select Custom instead of Typical from the Setup Options dialog box and click Next to proceed. When you choose this option, Setup follows the same general process as in a Typical installation, with the addition of a few extra dialog boxes, such as the Analyzing Your Computer dialog box shown in Figure 2.11.

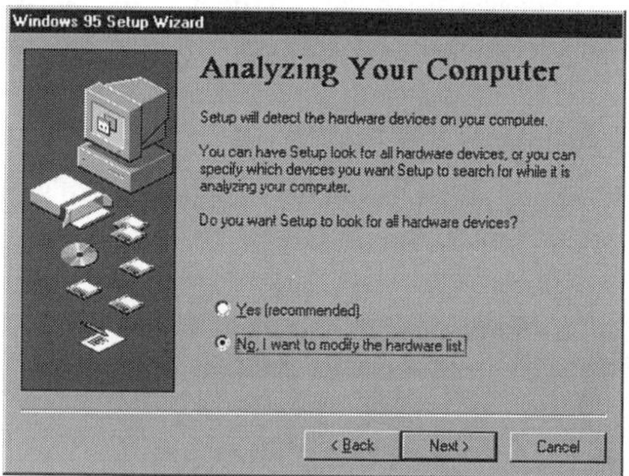

FIG. 2.11
If you know that you'll need to provide custom drivers for one or more installed devices, select the bottom option in this dialog box.

If you know you have nonstandard or unsupported devices in your installation, select the No, I Want to Modify the Hardware List option. Then click Next to proceed. Setup displays a screen like the one in Figure 2.12.

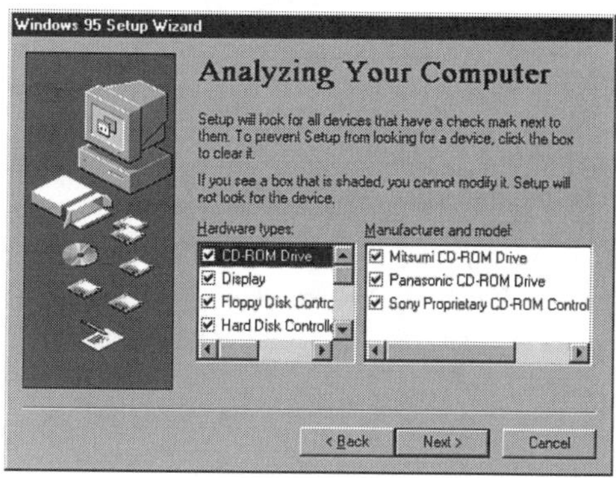

FIG. 2.12
Select the device type in the left window and the specific device name in the right. Changing the item on the left changes the list on the right.

Here's where you need detailed information about your system, as mentioned earlier. If you know that you have an unusual peripheral, look for it here. Setup guides you through installing any special drivers for the device at the appropriate time.

If your device doesn't appear in the lists here, it means one of two things: either Windows 95 already includes 32-bit support for the device, or the device is not supported with built-in Windows drivers. If Setup didn't detect your device earlier in the installation, you need to tell it to install it now. If it was detected, and the Windows installation didn't work, you can tell Windows to skip it this round. You can manually install the device later by using the Add New Hardware option in Control Panel.

When you've selected all the device types you want configured, click Next to proceed. After completing its analysis of your selected equipment, Setup displays the Select Components dialog box. See "Adding and Removing Windows Components," earlier in this chapter.

When you've selected all of the Windows 95 components you want to install, click Next to proceed. The remainder of the installation depends on what hardware and software component options you've selected. Setup attempts to locate your devices and prompts you when it needs additional information such as device driver files. In the next section, we look at an example of this; specifically, the basic steps to install network support under Windows 95.

Installing Windows 95 Network Features

If you've selected network support, the Custom Setup option next displays the Network Configuration dialog box shown in Figure 2.13.

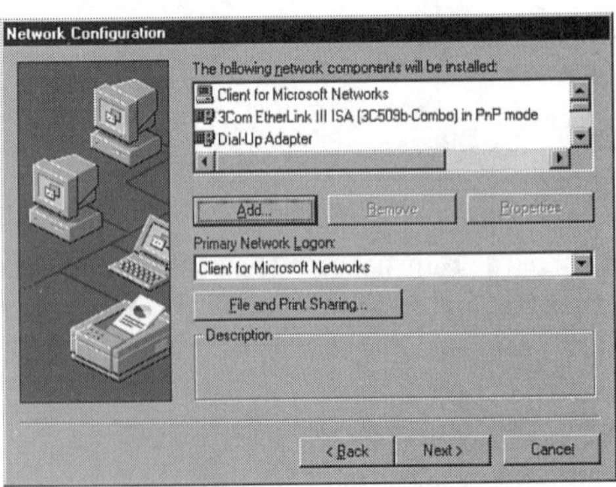

FIG. 2.13
You can install network support for multiple adapters and protocols from this one Setup screen.

To begin configuring your network options, click Add. Setup displays the Select Network Component Type dialog box (see Figure 2.14).

When you select the component type you want to install, Setup displays another selection dialog box for that component classification. For example, if you select Protocol and then click Add, Setup displays the Select Network Protocol dialog box shown in Figure 2.15.

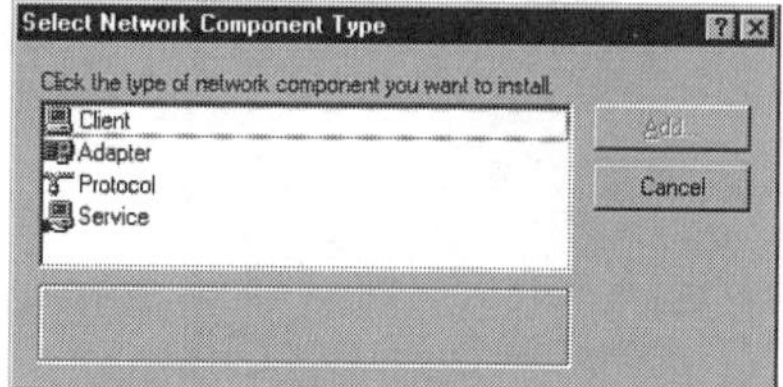

FIG. 2.14
Click the network component type you want to install.

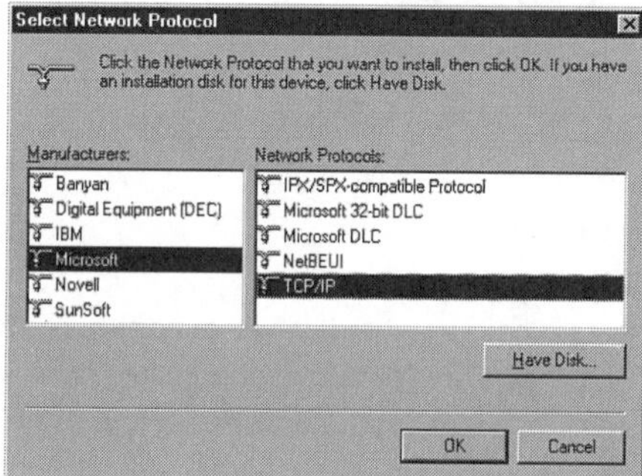

FIG. 2.15
Select the protocol publisher in the left list, and then select the specific protocol type in the right list.

When you've selected the appropriate network components—protocols, network adapter, client software, and services—you can either click OK (to let Setup determine if Windows 95 has native drivers for these types) or click Have Disk to install your own drivers.

Setup might make assumptions about other network support components based upon the adapter type you select. For example, selecting most standard Ethernet cards results in Setup selecting clients and protocols for both NetWare and Microsoft network types.

Using Safe Recovery

If Setup fails during your installation, it has the capability to recover gracefully. Setup Safe Recovery automatically skips problem configuration items so the installation can finish and then enables you to go back to the problem and correct it (see Figure 2.16).

Safe Recovery also can be used to repair a damaged installation. If you run Setup after a complete Windows 95 installation, it first asks whether you want to confirm or repair your installation or whether you want to completely reinstall Windows 95.

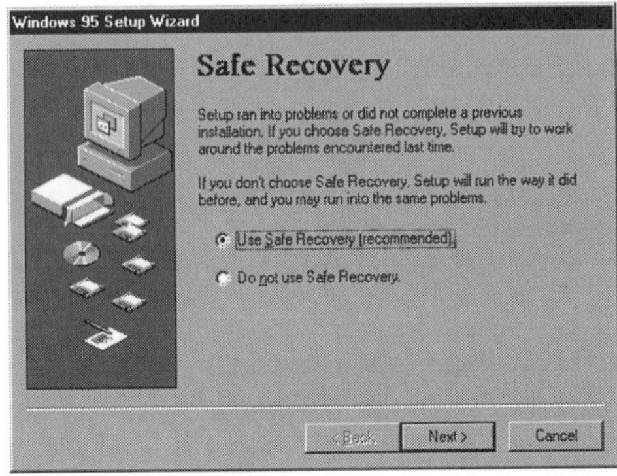

FIG. 2.16
Use Safe Recovery if Setup does not complete normally; you also can use this option to repair damage that occurs after a complete installation.

Using Safe Detection

Windows 95 Setup looks for system components in a variety of ways. Setup can detect communication ports, display adapters, processor type, drive controllers, sound cards, and network adapters. Setup also looks for system hardware resources such as IRQs, DMA channels, and I/O addresses to avoid conflicts between devices. Setup can detect both newer Plug and Play devices and older "legacy" peripherals.

Safe Detection works on four classes of devices:

- Sound cards
- Network adapters
- SCSI controllers
- CD-ROM controllers

One problem with such auto-detection routines is failure during the detection process itself. Plug and Play devices basically identify or announce themselves to the system, but older adapters require interactive tests to locate them and confirm operation. Whereas most devices respond well to this, some don't. In addition, if there's any duplication of IRQ, DMA, or I/O addresses between devices, your system might lock up when Setup inadvertently trips over the conflicting settings.

Windows 95 Setup can recover from such failures. Setup keeps track of the process of testing devices during installation and knows at what point a device failed. When you restart it, Setup knows not to touch that subsystem again until corrections have been applied, such as loading 16-bit device drivers if the 32-bit native Windows 95 drivers have failed. ●

CHAPTER 3

Configuring Windows 95

In this chapter

Installing and Configuring Printers

Windows 95 has greatly simplified the installation of printers. If you have a Plug and Play printer and computer, it can be as simple as connecting the printer to the computer, starting Windows 95, and following the directions in a few Wizard boxes. Even if you don't have Plug and Play components, the Add Printer Wizard takes you through the installation process step by step. After you've installed your printer, turn to Chapter 5, "Controlling Printers," to learn how to work with printers in Windows 95.

The printer installation process depends largely on the make and model of your printer. The following sections describe how to fully install a printer—with an emphasis on printer differences.

Installing a New Printer

Before you install a printer, you should follow these preliminary steps:

- Determine your printer's make and model (for example, Hewlett-Packard 4).
- Refer to the printer manual, or print a test page by using the printer's test feature, to find the amount of RAM contained in your printer (for example, 2M).
- Identify the type of communications interface required to connect your printer to the computer (for example, serial, parallel, or a special interface).
- Identify any special features or functions supported by your printer, such as PostScript compatibility. Some printers are multimode and may require installation as two separate printers (such as the HP LaserJet IV with PostScript option).
- Find the location of a suitable port on your computer to connect your printer. The selected port must correspond to the same port type as required by your printer (that is, serial to serial, parallel to parallel).

This information is required by the Windows Add Printer Wizard later in the installation process.

Installing a Printer with the Add Printer Wizard The Windows 95 print architecture incorporates a printer installation wizard to step you through the labor-intensive chore of installing a printer.

To use the Add Printer Wizard, follow these steps:

1. Open the Start menu and choose Settings, Printers. If the control panel is open, double-click the Printer folder. The Printers window appears and shows each installed printer as an icon (see Figure 3.1). Don't worry if you have no installed printers yet: The window also includes the Add New Printer icon. The program associated with the Add New Printer icon is the Add Printer Wizard.

   If there are no printers installed, the Add New Printer Wizard will automatically be loaded.

2. Double-click the Add New Printer icon to start the Add Printer Wizard. Windows displays the initial Wizard screen.
3. Choose Next. Windows displays the Add Printer Wizard screen shown in Figure 3.2.

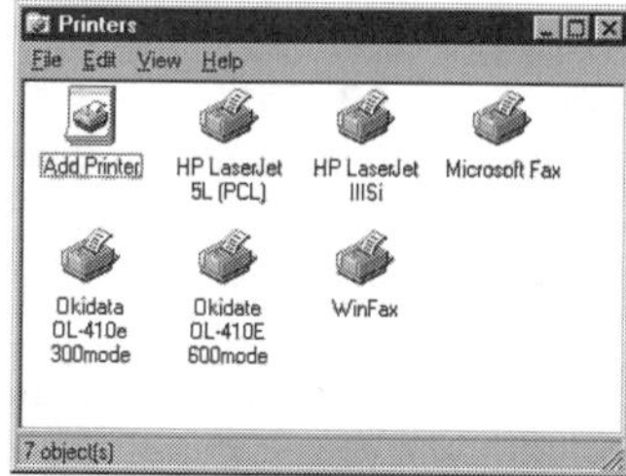

FIG. 3.1
Start a printer installation by opening the Printer folder.

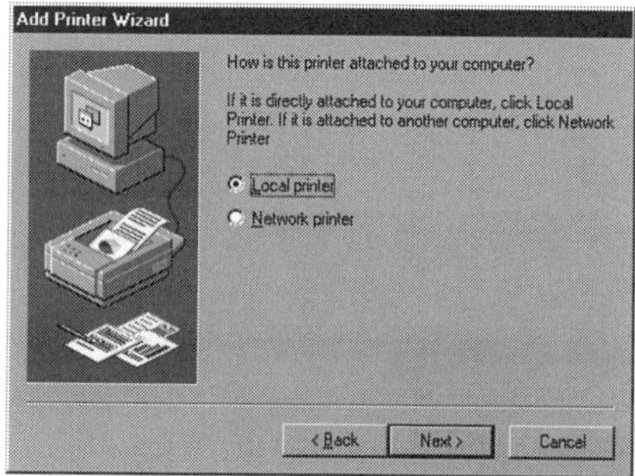

FIG. 3.2
The Add Printer Wizard steps you through the printer installation procedure by first asking whether you are installing a local or network printer.

4. Choose the Local Printer option to install a printer attached directly to your computer. Choose Next. The screen shown in Figure 3.3 appears.

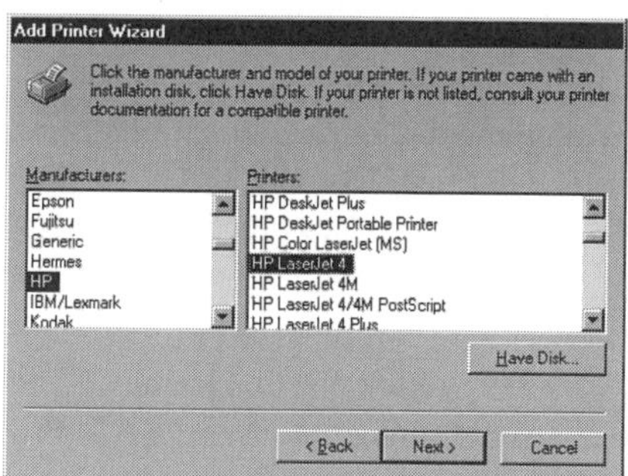

FIG. 3.3
Select the make and model of the printer you are installing from the lists provided.

5. Locate the make and model of your printer by scrolling through the wizard's screen lists (Windows 95 has drivers that support over 300 printers). Select the appropriate options, then choose Next to display the screen shown in Figure 3.4.

   If you're adding a printer after initial installation, you need the Windows 95 installation disks or CD. Windows will ask for these if it does not have an existing driver available. You also can use a manufacturer's disk to install custom printer drivers.

   If you are installing a new driver for an existing printer, click the Have Disk button and locate the new driver in the Install From Disk dialog box. Choose OK.

Scroll the screen on the far left to select your printer's manufacturer, and then select the appropriate printer model. If your printer isn't on the list, you can install your printer by choosing either the generic printer or the Have Disk button. If your printer came with its own software driver, insert the disk from your printer manufacturer and choose the Have Disk button to complete the requirements of this screen.

Many laser printers are Hewlett-Packard compatible and many dot-matrix printers are Epson compatible. If you can't get a driver or the generic driver doesn't work well, try one of the commonly emulated printers.

NOTE If your printer is not listed, you should contact your printer manufacturer for an updated driver. Choose a generic printer until you get an updated driver version.

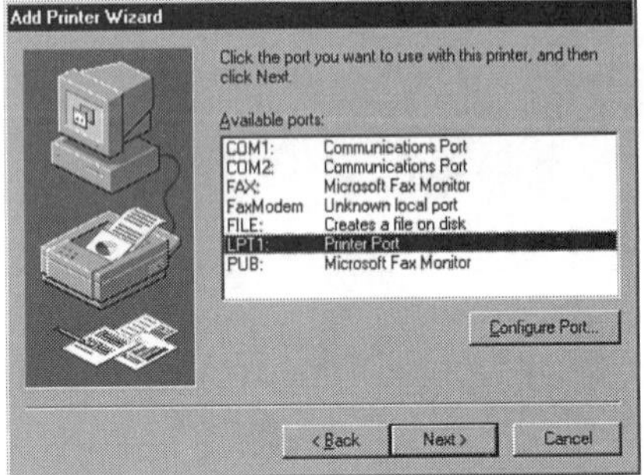

FIG. 3.4
Select the printer port to which you want to attach the printer.

6. Provide the printer port information. The wizard screen shown in Figure 3.4 displays ports based on the survey Windows did of your computer hardware. You may have several COM and LPT ports. Refer to the list of information you compiled before you started the installation and choose the port to which you want to attach the printer. The port selected in Figure 3.4 is LPT1, a very typical selection.
7. Click the Configure Port button. The wizard displays the Configure Port window (see Figure 3.5). The window contains a check box that enables Windows 95 to spool your MS-DOS print jobs. This is the only configuration in the Add Printer Wizard for the LPT1 port. This check box should always be selected to enable MS-DOS printing, unless your MS-DOS applications prove to be incompatible with Windows 95 printing. Put a check in the Check Port State Before Printing check box if you want Windows 95 to determine whether the printer port is available prior to starting the print job.

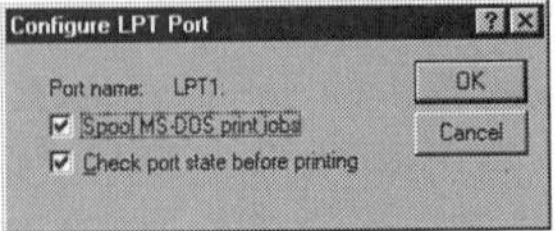

FIG. 3.5
Configure your parallel printer port to enable MS-DOS applications to use the same driver.

8. After you configure the port, choose OK and Next to open the dialog box shown in Figure 3.6. Use this dialog box to name the new printer and define it as your default printer, if desired. In the Printer Name field, type the name of the printer. The name can be up to 128 characters long and can contain spaces and nonalphanumeric symbols. The printer's name should include location or ownership.

NOTE If you have access to two printers of the same type, add unique identifiers to their names, such as "HP LaserJet 4 Room 5, Building 10" and "HP LaserJet 4 Room 25, Building 15."

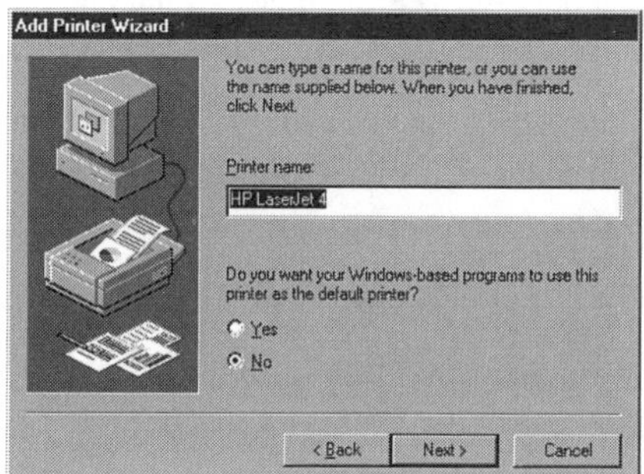

FIG. 3.6 The printer name and default status are specified by using this wizard screen.

9. Choose Yes to set this printer as the system default. By setting this printer as your default, you instruct all applications to use this printer, unless you tell the application to use a different printer. (You can set the default to any other installed printer at any time.) Click Next to continue. The final wizard screen appears (see Figure 3.7).

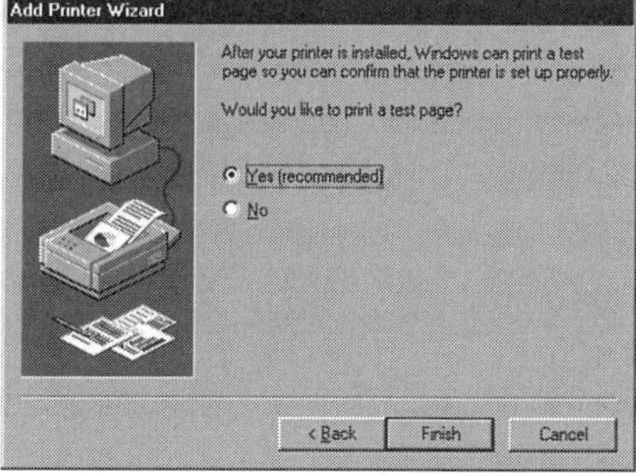

FIG. 3.7 Printing a test page is the final step in configuring and testing your printer installation.

10. Specify whether you want to print a test page. Printing one will test the overall operation of the printer based on the settings you just entered. Choose Yes and click Finish to print the test page.

NOTE The test page contains information specific to your printer, its configuration, and the drivers that Windows will use to interface with it. After this page is printed, save it for future reference. If others use your computer, you might have to return to a known installation configuration someday.

You also can get information on your printer by using the MSINFO32.EXE utility located in the \Program Files\Common Files\Microsoft Shared\MSInfo folder. Run this utility and click Printing in the left pane of the Microsoft System Information window to view information on all installed printers.

Installing a Plug and Play Printer Plug and Play printers interact with Windows to automatically configure printers by using a dialog box transparent to the user. Many printer manufacturers have cooperated with Microsoft to make configuration easier and to automatically update the software when you make changes to the printer hardware configuration.

If your printer is Plug and Play compatible, see Chapter 7, "Plug and Play and Legacy Device Installation," for an explanation of how Plug and Play devices are installed.

Renaming an Existing Printer Use the Printers folder to rename printers named during installation. The Printers folder displays all installed printers; their individual names are located immediately below the printer's icon (refer to Figure 3.1).

To rename a printer after it is installed, follow these steps:

1. Open the Start menu, choose Settings, Printers, and the Printers folder appears. If the Control Panel is open, double-click the Printers folder.
2. Select the desired printer and choose File, Rename or right-click the printer name and choose Rename. You can also click the printer name, wait a second, and click a second time. Windows creates a text box around the printer name and highlights it.
3. Change the name by typing a new name or editing portions of the existing name.
4. When you finish, press Enter. The new printer name is used throughout the Windows operating system.

See "Changing Settings and Properties with the Right Mouse Button," **p. 613**

Deleting an Existing Printer You can delete an installed printer from the Printers folder that displays all installed printers as icons. To delete a printer from the Printers folder, follow these steps:

1. Select the printer you want to delete and press the Delete key or right-click the printer and choose Delete. Windows opens a dialog box and asks if you're sure you want to delete the printer.
2. Choose OK; the printer is now deleted. Windows then asks whether it can remove the associated software from your hard disk.

CAUTION

If you have a similar printer that could use the same drivers, do not remove the software. Deleting the associated software might remove that driver from use by other printers.

3. Choose OK to remove the deleted printer's software driver.

The printer and its driver are now removed. Windows signifies this event by removing that printer icon from the Printers folder.

NOTE If you plan to reattach this printer in the future, do not remove the software drivers. This can save you time when reattaching the printer.

NOTE If a new driver becomes available for your printer, you can update your existing driver by using the Add Printer Wizard. A new driver can add new capabilities, correct bugs, or increase the performance of your printer. In step 5 of the steps in the section "Installing a Printer with the Add Printer Wizard," choose the Have Disk button to specify the location of the new driver, and then continue as if adding a new printer.

One source for new drivers is the printer manufacturer. Most manufacturers have a private BBS or a site on CompuServe or the Internet where you can download updated drivers. Check your printer manual for online addresses. You also can find updated drivers in the Windows 95 Driver Library (W95DL), which is available at several online locations:

CompuServe: **GO MSL**

Microsoft Download Service (MSDL): (206) 936-6735

Internet (anonymous FTP): **ftp.microsoft.com** (SOFTLIB/MSLFILES directory)

World Wide Web: **http://www.microsoft.com/windows/software**

Configuring Your Printer

By now, you have installed one or more printers for use by Windows 95 applications. Both Windows and MS-DOS applications can use these resources without further effort. The initial installation of the printer created a default configuration. You might want to make changes to that configuration. Because few default configurations satisfy all printing requirements, you might want to change the printer's configuration frequently.

If you change printer settings frequently, you can install duplicate printers and configure each printer with its own set of properties. This eliminates repeated property changes.

NOTE Windows 3.1 provided a setting to change the priority of background printing. This feature does not appear in Windows 95. However, the print spooler in Windows 95, which uses 32-bit device drivers and DLLs, handles background printing much more smoothly than does the spooler in Windows 3.1, eliminating the need to optimize the background printing settings.

Options for Your Printer Printer properties are preset during installation of the printer. The preset values for the many variables might not meet your current printing needs. You might also have to make changes to meet special printing needs or to solve any performance problems that arise.

Like many other printing issues discussed in this chapter, the exact options available depend on the capabilities of your printer. The following discussion focuses on the basic procedures so you must adapt these to fit your specific printer.

To change printer options, open the Printer properties sheet (see Figure 3.8). Use one of these two methods:

- If the Print Manager is open for the printer whose options you want to change, choose Printer, Properties.
- Open the Printer control panel and select the printer whose options you want to change. Choose File, Properties or right-click the printer icon and choose Properties from the shortcut menu.

This sheet has several tabbed pages. The settings on each page depend on the manufacturer, printer model, and printer options.

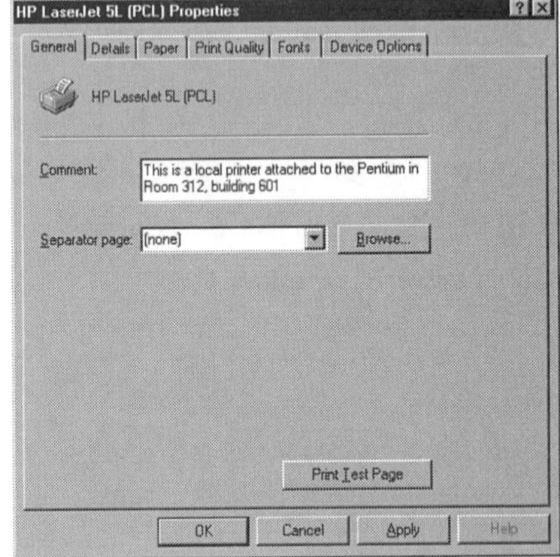

FIG. 3.8
Use the General tab page of the Printer properties sheet to get and specify basic information about the printer.

The Printer properties sheet typically contains the following information. (The details of these tabs will change with different printers.)

- **General page**. Enables you to identify your printer, print a test page, and choose a separator page to separate print jobs of different users. Each page includes a user name and job-specific information such as date, time, and file name.
- **Details page**. Contains controls to attach or change ports, add or delete ports, change time-out periods, and specify how Windows will process print files. Use the Details page to configure enhanced metafile printing and the spooler.
- **Sharing page**. Enables a printer to be shared with other workstations attached to your computer over a network.
- **Paper page**. Provides several controls that set the printer's default paper handling, orientation, and number of pages to be printed.

- **Graphics page**. Sets the resolution, halftone capabilities, scaling, and other options that define how the printer treats graphic files.
- **Fonts page**. Enables you to adjust how fonts are treated by Windows for this printer. Configurable fonts include printer, cartridge, and software fonts.

Be certain to accurately configure the available printer memory. An incorrect value in this variable can change the speed of your printouts or cause your printer to time-out or fail during printing sessions.

- **Device Options page**. Configures the options associated with the printer's hardware, such as the printer memory capacity settings, page protection, and other device-specific options. The number and type of controls are specific to the printer's make, model, and hardware.

TROUBLESHOOTING

I've always been able to set the number of copies I print from the control panel of my printer. When I print in Windows 95, however, I always get one copy no matter how I set the printer. In Windows 95, the settings in your programs for the number of copies to be printed overrides the setting on your printer. To print multiple copies, change the setting in the program you are printing from.

I'd like to be able to print multiple copies from WordPad, but this option is not available. WordPad and Paint do not support printing multiple copies, so if your printer does not support printing multiple copies, this option will not be available.

When I try to print a page, I receive the message, "Not enough memory to render page." If your printer has bidirectional communication with your computer, there may be a problem with the amount of memory the printer driver detected. To have Windows 95 recheck the printer for memory, follow these steps:

1. With the printer online, open the Start menu and choose Settings, Printers.
2. Right-click the icon for the printer you want to check and choose Properties.
3. Select the Device Options tab and choose the Restore Defaults button.
4. Click OK.

Printing with Color Microsoft uses licensed Image Color Matching (ICM) technology from Kodak to create an image environment that treats color consistently from the screen to the printed page. The Windows ICM goal is to be able to repeatedly and consistently reproduce color-matched images from source to destination.

ICM provides more consistent, repeatable quality among various brands of printers and scanners and provides a higher quality color rendering (the term *color* includes grayscale rendering). To fully benefit from ICM technology, choose a color printer that is compliant with Kodak's ICM specifications.

Setting Color Printing Properties Figure 3.9 shows the Graphics page of the Printer properties sheet for a color printer. The controls on this page allow you to configure your printer to produce the best color possible.

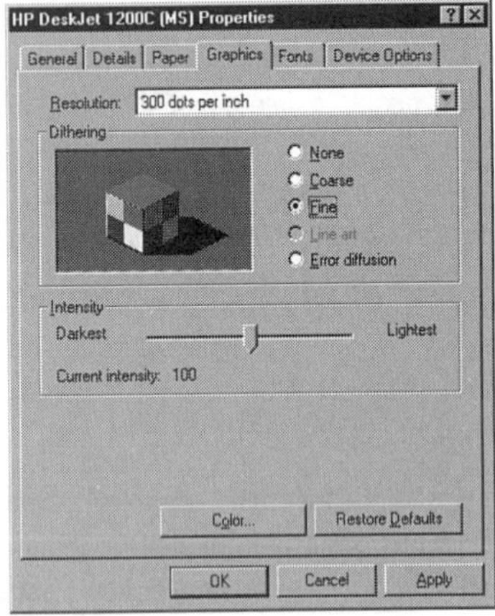

FIG. 3.9
The Graphics page of the Printer properties sheet for a color printer lets you adjust color and output quality.

- **Resolution.** This drop-down list box specifies the number of dots per inch (dpi) that the printer can produce. The higher the dpi, the clearer the graphics.
- **Dithering.** This error-correcting tool, used by Windows 95, more accurately represents an object's color and grayscale.
- **Intensity.** This brightness control lightens or darkens a printout to more accurately reflect its screen appearance and to compensate for deficiencies in toner or paper quality.

To access the color settings for a color printer, click the Color button. Use the Graphics—Color dialog box to set ICM compliance alternatives (see Figure 3.10).

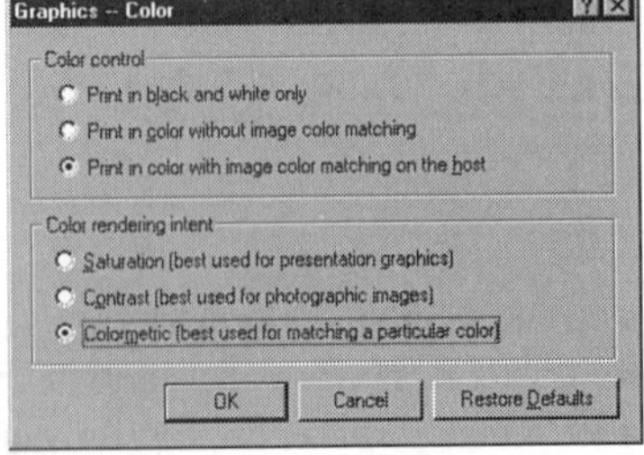

FIG. 3.10
Display this box by choosing the Color button on the Graphics page.

Use the color settings to adjust the level of compliance of your printer with the ICM standards. The dialog box is also useful for trial-and-error adjustment of color printer output quality. Following is a list of the settings:

- **Color Control.** A macro command that enables you to direct the printer to print only black and white or to specify whether you want ICM technology.

- **Color Rendering Intent.** Provides the best ICM settings for three of the major uses of color printing: presentations, photographs, and true color screen display printing. Select the choice that works best for your purpose.

Configuring the Printer Port In addition to configuring settings that affect the printer itself, you can make a few configuration changes to the port to which the printer is attached. These options vary depending on which port you use to print. The most common printing port is an LPT port, usually LPT1 (or LPT2, if you have a second LPT port). You might have to change the printer port if you attach a printer to a serial port or add a printer switch.

Follow these steps to change the configuration options for port LPT1:

1. Open the Start menu and choose Settings, Control Panel.
2. Double-click the System icon.
3. Windows displays the System Properties dialog box. Choose the Device Manager tab to configure printer ports (see Figure 3.11).

FIG. 3.11
The Device Manager tab of the System properties sheet identifies the port, its present state of operation, and the hardware configuration being used.

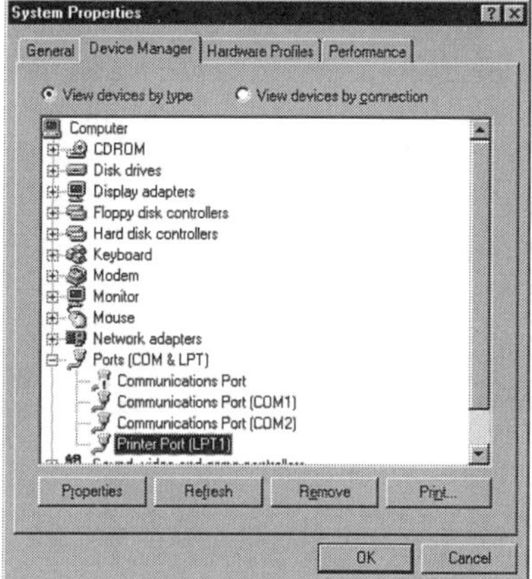

4. Double-click the Printer Ports icon to show the attached ports. Choose the printer port whose configuration you want to change, such as LPT1 or COM1. For this example, choose LPT1. If your printer is attached to another parallel port or a COM (serial) port, choose that port instead.
5. Click Properties. The Printer Port properties sheet shown in Figure 3.12 appears. Note that Printer Port Properties are divided among three tabs: General, Driver, and Resources.

OSR2

NOTE If you have the OEM Service Release 2 (OSR2) version of Windows 95 installed, the General tab shown in Figure 3.12 will look slightly different. The Device Usage box will consist of a simple check box that allows you to disable the device, in this case, the printer port, for the current hardware configuration.

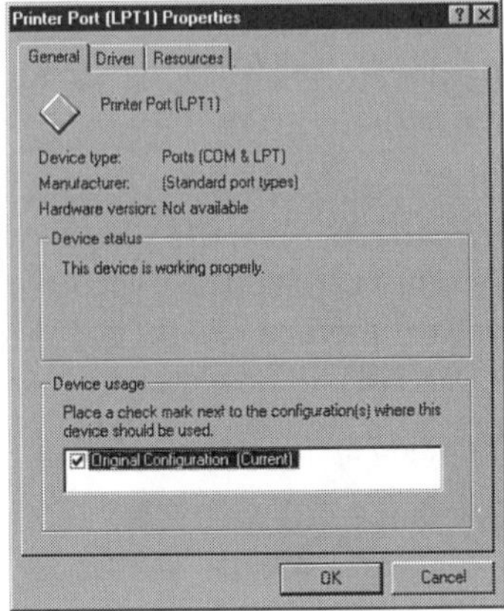

FIG. 3.12
The General page of the Printer Port properties sheet provides current status and information about the port's hardware.

6. Choose the Driver tab.
7. Verify that the driver file selected on the Driver page is the most current printer driver available (see Figure 3.13). Note that the VXD extension signifies a 32-bit virtual driver that can be expected to provide the best performance. If you have a driver with a DRV extension, you are not using a 32-bit driver. Check with your printer manufacturer for the latest version.

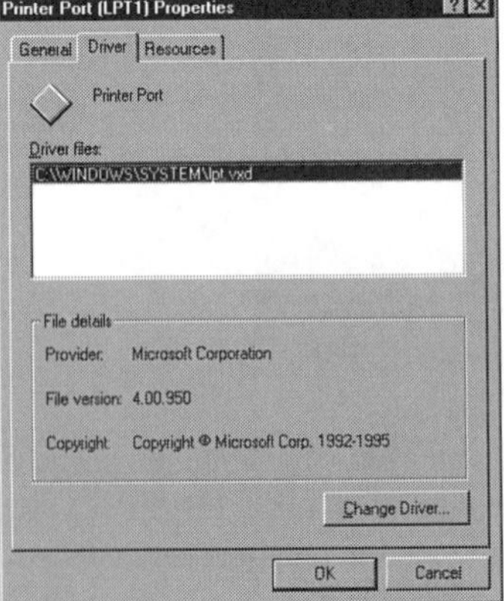

FIG. 3.13
The Driver page of the Printer Port properties sheet provides the name and version of the currently installed port driver.

8. To install a different driver, click Change Driver. Windows displays the Select Device dialog box shown in Figure 3.14. Use this dialog box to load a new driver from either a vendor-supplied disk or to choose a previously installed driver. If you have a vendor-supplied disk that contains the new port driver, choose Have Disk.
9. Windows displays an instruction window that directs you to insert the manufacturer's disk in Drive A. The window also allows you to browse and select a driver from another location. Windows requests a vendor disk so insert the appropriate vendor disk and click

OK. Otherwise, click Cancel to stop the installation process. Windows installs the vendor software and links it to the selected printer port.

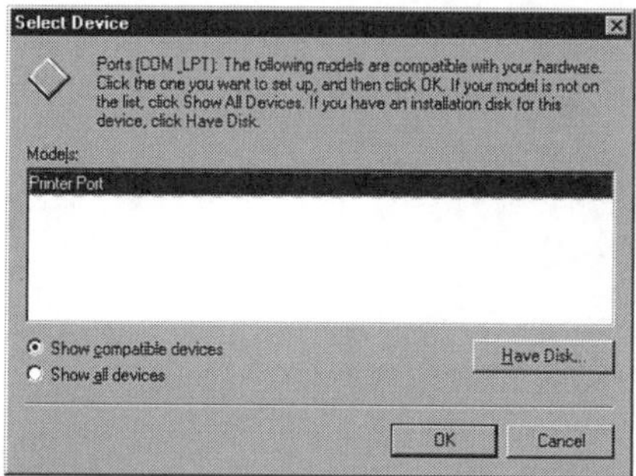

FIG. 3.14
Select a new or existing printer port driver.

Part I Ch 3

If you have the OSR2 version of Windows, the Driver tab appears as shown in Figure 3.15, and the procedure for installing a different driver differs from the steps just outlined. To install a new driver in OSR2, follow these steps:

1. Click the Update Driver tab to display the Update Device Driver Wizard dialog box shown in Figure 3.16.
2. Leave the Yes option selected to have Windows search for an updated driver. Click Next.

   or

   Select the No option and click Next to select the driver from a list.
3. If you selected the Yes option in step 2, click Finish when Windows 95 finds the driver.

   If an updated driver is not found, click Other Locations in the Update Device Driver Wizard and change to the location where the updated driver is located.

   If you selected the No option in step 2, select the correct items from the Manufacturer and Models lists and click Finish.

You will be prompted to insert the disk or CD-ROM on which the updated driver is located, if you haven't done this already. The wizard will search for the driver and install it on your computer. Select Yes when you are prompted to restart the computer to complete the setup.

The Resources page contains detailed information about the printer port's addresses and any configuration conflicts. Review this information to verify that Windows has properly installed the driver. In the background, Windows cross-checked the port's configuration with the system startup settings. Windows can and does spot configuration problems, but doesn't necessarily notify the user. The resources contain the Input/Output Range of addresses. The addresses of the LPT1 port are shown under the Setting column. If a device uses an interrupt, that interrupt is also shown. If Windows spots a problem, it will designate that a conflict exists and list the information in this window. You can then choose alternative configurations to test other configurations.

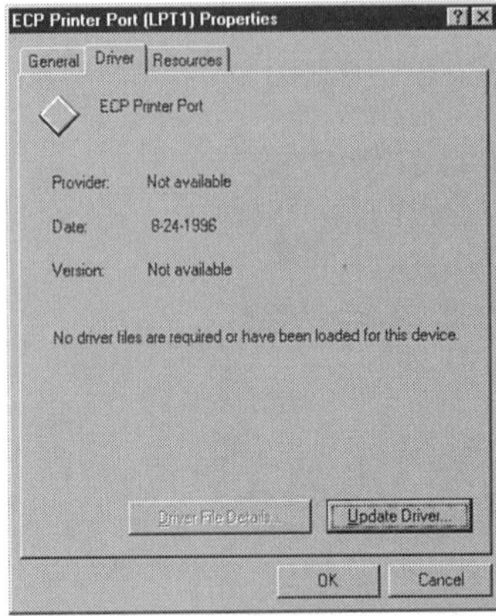

FIG. 3.15
The Driver page as it appears in the OSR2 version of Windows 95.

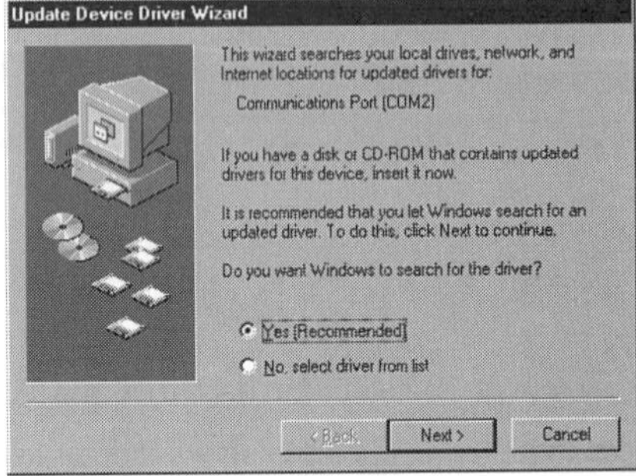

FIG. 3.16
Use the Update Device Driver Wizard to search for and install updated drivers.

To configure the printer port, click the Resources tab. The critical information is the Conflicting Device List (see Figure 3.17). This list contains all items that conflict with your printer port. When installing new hardware, always verify that its address and interrupts do not conflict with existing hardware properties.

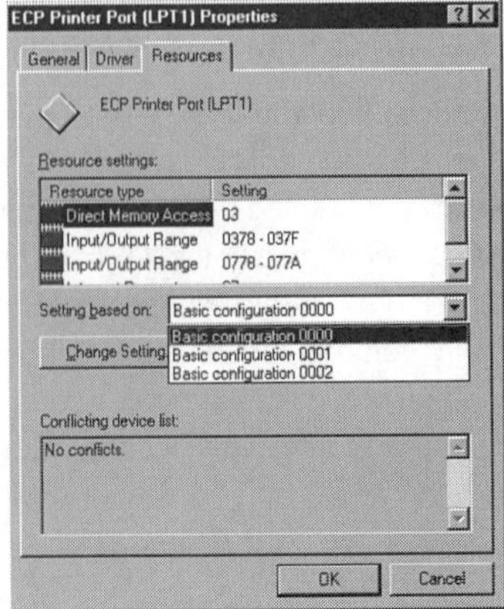

FIG. 3.17
The Resources page of the Printer Port properties sheet displays detailed hardware information vital to port operation and the diagnosis of communications problems.

You should normally choose Use Automatic Settings. If you have any conflict problems, the Settings Based On list box provides several optional configurations that Windows can use to configure the printer port.

To use this control, first clear the Use Automatic Settings check box and then use the Settings Based On option to select from a list of Windows configurations (see Figure 3.17). Each configuration shows the port configured to different devices and interrupts. As each configuration is considered, problems associated with the new configuration are shown in the Conflicting Device List information box at the bottom of the page.

NOTE Carefully review the hardware properties for all devices to identify potential conflicts. Windows cannot discover and display all problems in normal operation. Use the Device Manager to check for conflicting devices because it can prevent problems later. ■

Most printer installations do not require changes to the printer port settings. However, unusual address conflicts from older equipment or Enhanced Capability Ports (ECP) technology provide more configuration options. The number of possible decisions and potential conflicts between pieces of hardware increase as the number of options increase. Select OK to complete the port configuration.

Using PC Card Devices

Many notebook computers contain one or two special bus slots called *PC Card slots* (formerly PCMCIA slots) that accommodate adapters (the size of a credit card) for various functions. Although initially only flash memory cards were available in PCMCIA format, today many types of devices—including modems, hard disks, network cards, sound cards, and other devices—are available in PC Card/PCMCIA format. In addition, PC Card docking stations enable you to use PC Card devices in desktop computers, making it possible, for example, to use the same PC Card modem in a notebook and a desktop computer.

NOTE There are three official types of PC Card slots, referred to as Type I, Type II, and Type III. The specification for a fourth type of slot—Type IV—is being finalized by the PCMCIA organization (Personal Computer Memory Card International Association). One of the primary differences between the types of PC Card slots is that each higher-numbered slot accommodates a thicker PC Card than the previous slot. PC Card hard disks, for example, generally require a Type III slot, but modems can be installed in a Type I or Type II slot. Most of today's newer notebook computers can accommodate one Type III device, or two Type II devices (or any combination of two Type I and Type II devices). ■

The primary advantage of PC Card devices for portable computer users is that these devices make it possible to expand the capabilities of portable computers in the same way you can expand desktop systems, enabling you to add optional hardware to the portable computer. Windows 95 improves on the PCMCIA support in DOS and Windows 3.x by providing 32-bit device drivers to support the PC Card controllers in most computers. This makes it possible for Windows 95 to support a wide variety of PC Card devices without requiring 16-bit, real-mode drivers that slow down the system and use conventional memory.

Another improvement for PC Card devices in Windows 95 is expanded support for ***hot swapping,*** which is the ability to remove and insert PC Card devices in the computer without turning off the computer. If you need to temporarily remove your hard disk card to use a modem, for example, you first use the PC Card object in the Control Panel to turn off the hard disk card. Then, you remove the hard disk card from its slot and insert the modem. Windows 95 disables the hard disk driver(s) temporarily and enables the modem drivers.

See "Installing Plug and Play Hardware," **p. 168**

The Windows 95 OEM Service Release 2 (OSR2) has several PC Card enhancements. OSR2 supports the newer PC Card 32 (Cardbus) cards, which provide 32-bit I/O using a 33MHz bus, similar to the PCI bus architecture found on desktops. These cards enable much higher data transfer than the original 16-bit cards, up to 132M/second versus a maximum of 20M/second with 16-bit cards. For applications that demand high data throughput, such as video conferencing over a Fast Ethernet network, the need for this technology becomes apparent. Another benefit is that CardBus cards use less power (3.3 volts), extending battery life.

OSR2 also supports multifunction network/modem and Global Positioning Satellite (GPS) PC Cards. To learn how to obtain and install OSR2 see Chapter 2, "Installing and Upgrading Windows 95."

Installing PC Card Support

Each computer with PC Card slots or a PC Card docking station includes a PC Card controller that enables the CPU to communicate with the PC Card bus. This controller requires a set of drivers that enable the operating system (in this case, Windows 95) to communicate using the PC Card bus. In addition, each PC Card device requires a device-specific driver that enables the device to function and communicate with the operating system. If you are using a PC Card network card, for example, Windows 95 requires a set of drivers for the PC Card slot itself and a separate driver for the network card.

When you install Windows 95, Setup automatically detects your computer's PC Card controller and installs support for it. Setup does not, however, enable the 32-bit PC Card controller drivers. Setup takes this approach because some portable computers require that you continue to use 16-bit drivers (which come with the portable computer) to control the PC Card slots.

NOTE Windows 95 supports 32-bit drivers for systems based on either an Intel PCIC-compatible PC Card controller or Databook PC Card controller.

In addition to enabling 32-bit PC Card support (if your computer supports it), you must install the drivers for the PC Card devices you'll be using. In many cases, Windows 95 can install these devices automatically using Plug and Play, even on systems without a Plug and Play BIOS. To install a PC Card modem, for example, simply insert the modem in its slot. Windows 95 detects the new device and starts the Add New Modem Wizard to install the modem driver.

Enabling 32-Bit PC Card Support After you install Windows 95, you must use the PC Card object in the Control Panel to enable 32-bit support for your PC Card controller. Enabling 32-bit support provides better overall system performance and more effective memory use. In addition, enabling 32-bit PC Card support is required to support Plug and Play installation of PC Card devices and hot swapping.

NOTE When Windows 95 enables 32-bit PC Card support, your existing 16-bit real-mode PC Card drivers are disabled. If you are installing Windows 95 from a network server, you must have local access to the Windows 95 source (cabinet) files. Therefore, you must have a set of Windows 95 floppy disks or have a CD-ROM connected to your portable PC to enable Windows 95 to read the 32-bit driver files for the PC Card controller. Optionally, you can copy the Windows 95 cabinet files from the network server to your portable computer's hard disk prior to enabling 32-bit support. ■

To enable 32-bit PC Card support for your computer, follow these steps:

1. Verify that you have local access to the Windows 95 cabinet files, as explained in the previous note.
2. Open the Start menu and choose Settings, Control Panel.
3. Double-click the PC Card (PCMCIA) program icon. The first time you open this object, the PC Card (PCMCIA) Wizard appears (see Figure 3.18).

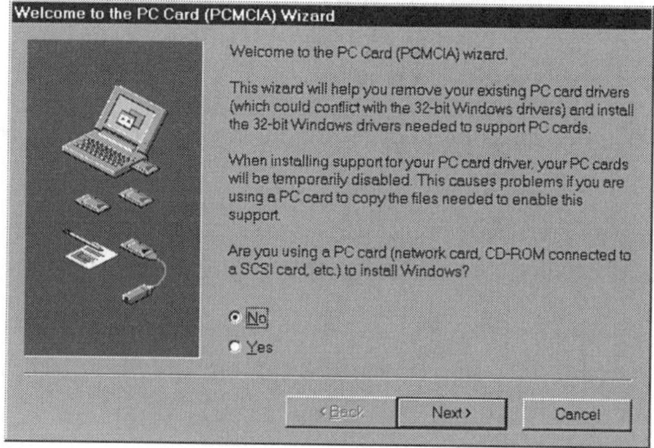

FIG. 3.18 The opening dialog box of the PC Card (PCMCIA) Wizard checks to see whether you are using a PC Card to install the new PC Card drivers.

4. Choose No and then Next to inform the Wizard that you are not setting up Windows 95 from a network server.
5. If the PC Card Wizard detects existing real-mode PC Card drivers, it displays a dialog box that enables you to view the drivers and control the way the wizard handles the existing drivers. If you want the wizard to automatically remove the drivers, choose the No option button and then choose Next. If you want to view and verify the deletion of the existing real-mode PC Card drivers, choose Yes and then choose Next.
6. If you select Yes, the wizard displays a set of dialog boxes that show the device entries it will delete in CONFIG.SYS, AUTOEXEC.BAT, and SYSTEM.INI. (Figure 3.19 shows the dialog box for the CONFIG.SYS file.) If you do not want the wizard to delete a specific driver from one of these files, clear the line in the appropriate dialog box by clicking it, and then choose Next.

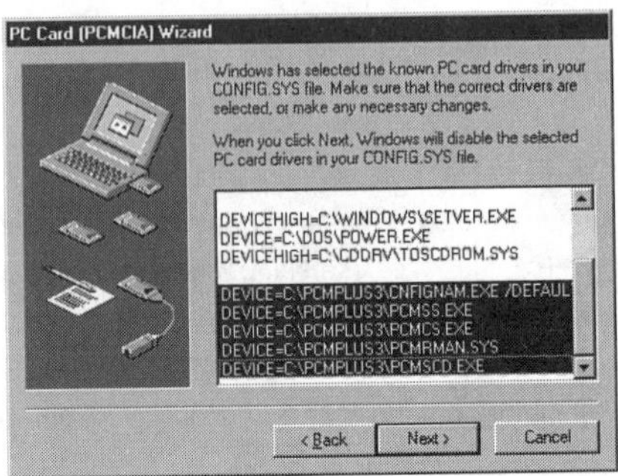

FIG. 3.19
To verify your drivers, choose Yes.

7. After the PC Card Wizard removes the real-mode drivers (if any) as directed by you, it displays a final dialog box that prompts you to choose Finish to complete the PC Card setup process and enable 32-bit PC Card support. Choose the Finish button to complete the process. Windows 95 shuts down your computer so the change can take effect.

Installing PC Card Devices After you enable 32-bit PC Card support, Windows 95 can typically install PC Card devices automatically. If you insert a network card in the computer, for example, Windows 95 detects the new card and automatically installs the necessary drivers for the card. If, for some reason, Windows 95 does not automatically recognize your PC Card device, you must manually install support for it.

To manually install a PC Card device other than a modem or network adapter, use the following procedure:

1. Insert the new PC Card device in the appropriate slot. (Check the PC Card device's manual to determine if the device must be installed in a specific slot.)

NOTE If you are installing a PC Card network adapter, use the Network object in the Control Panel to install it. If you are installing a PC Card modem, use the Modems object in the Control Panel. ■

2. Open the Control Panel and double-click the Add New Hardware program icon to start the Add New Hardware Wizard. Then choose Next.
3. Choose Yes and then Next to enable the wizard to automatically detect your new PC Card device.
4. If the wizard is unable to detect the new device, the wizard displays a hardware selection dialog box similar to the one shown in Figure 3.20. Choose the type of device you are installing and choose Next.
5. From the Manufacturers list, choose the manufacturer of the device you are installing. Then, from the Models list, choose the device model. If your manufacturer or model is not listed and you have a driver disk for the device, choose Have Disk and then follow the prompts to direct the wizard to the directory on the floppy disk where the necessary files are located.

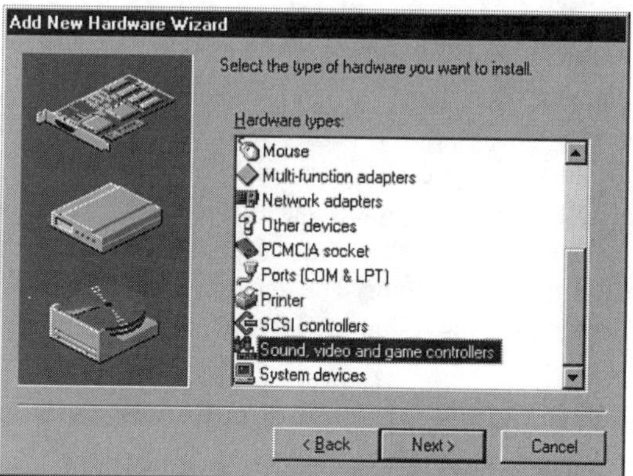

FIG. 3.20
Choose the type of device you are installing and then choose Next.

6. After you have selected the correct manufacturer and model, choose OK to complete the setup process.

See "Installing a Plug and Play Modem," **p. 69**

Hot Swapping PC Cards

Windows 95 enables you to remove a PC Card device and replace it with another without turning off the system. This capability enables you to quickly swap PC Card devices. Before you remove a device, however, you should first shut it down. To do so, choose the PC Card object in the Control Panel. Windows 95 displays a PC Card (PCMCIA) properties sheet, which displays information about the computer's PC Card slots and any currently inserted devices.

To remove a PC Card device from the system, first select the device from the list on the Socket Status tab and then choose Stop. Windows 95 shuts down the device and temporarily disables its drivers (the socket is listed as empty). You then can remove the PC Card device.

Insert the new device in the proper slot. If you have previously installed support for the device, Windows 95 detects the device and automatically enables its drivers. If you have not used the device in the computer previously, Windows 95 detects the new hardware and automatically installs support for the device.

TROUBLESHOOTING

The System Agent reports the ScanDisk error message, "Check was stopped because of an error," but the ScanDisk log file does not show an error. This occurs if you created a ScanDisk with a PC Card or docking station disk drive and later removed that drive. To resolve that problem, delete the existing ScanDisk task and schedule separate new ScanDisk tasks for permanent and removable drives.

Installing and Configuring Your Modem

Modems and the technology that they use—serial communications—have been a problem for Windows since Version 1.0. In Windows 95, however, Microsoft finally got it right—and then some. The operating system now incorporates a rich, reliable, full-featured communications subsystem that is capable of operating today's fastest modems. Windows 95 is an extensible system that works well with tomorrow's communications devices, such as ISDN adapters, parallel-port modems, and cable modems. These forthcoming devices work at speeds beyond even the fastest of today's modems. Windows 95 can handle all these devices at the same time.

Understanding the Windows 95 Communications System

In the past, getting good performance from modems running with Windows often meant changing the part of Windows that controlled all the serial ports and, therefore, controlled the modems. Various companies supplied these ***enhanced communications drivers***, which were sold with high-speed modems, by themselves, or with communications programs. (Often, you couldn't get the modem working without a special driver.) Although literally thousands of enhanced communications drivers were available, all of them worked by taking over control of the modem and serial ports in Windows.

Windows 95 doesn't need these third-party drivers to make communications fly. The sophisticated Plug and Play communications subsystem in Windows 95 is designed to automatically recognize, install, and configure modems when they are installed. Even if you have a standard modem that does not support Plug and Play, Windows provides a Wizard to help you install and configure the modem.

Whichever type of modem you choose to install, Windows can use it to communicate more reliably and with better data throughput than ever before. The three reasons for this are:

- New 32-bit TAPI communications system for 32-bit applications
- Improved 16-bit communications driver for older 16-bit programs
- Support for the new 16550-compatible UART (Universal Asynchronous Receiver Transmitter) chips found in new modems and modern serial ports

Windows uses these features to give you more control over your communications with your modem and to make your modem do a better job for you. Windows also has special capabilities for 32-bit communications programs far beyond the capabilities of its predecessor. You learn more about TAPI (Telephony Applications Programming Interface) capabilities in the section "Working Smarter with TAPI and 32-Bit Windows Programs," later in this chapter.

▶ **See** "How Plug and Play Works," **p. 71**

OSR 2 **NOTE** Microsoft has updated the Unimodem driver that was released with the original Windows 95. The new Unimodem V driver supports voice modems, including VoiceView and AT+V modems. Voice modems enable you to switch back and forth between voice and data communication and can perform telephony functions such as answering and forwarding calls and recording messages.

For more information on the Unimodem V driver and instructions on how to download it, visit the following Web site:

http://www.microsoft.com/kb/articles/q139/3/83.htm

If you have the OEM Service Release 2 (OSR2) version of Windows 95, the new Unimodem V driver is already installed on your system. For more information on OSR2, see "Installing the Windows 95b (OSR2) Service Release," in Chapter 2. ■

Installing a Plug and Play Modem

Like other devices that support this new technology, Plug and Play modems communicate with Windows to cooperate in setting themselves up. These modems always contain the serial communications port and modulator/demodulator/dialer on the same card, so that Windows can configure them to work together at the same time.

See "Understanding Plug and Play Hardware," p. 170

Many Plug and Play modems are located on PC Cards (formerly known as PCMCIA cards). These cards can support full Plug and Play functionality, including hot swapping.

NOTE ISA stands for Industry Standard Architecture. ISA cards are the familiar add-in peripheral cards that have been used in PCs since IBM set the standard. ■

Some Plug and Play modems may be on ISA cards. These cannot benefit from hot swapping because they are designed to be fixed inside the computer and not removed during operation.

Make sure any internal ISA card modem you buy includes the modern 16550 type of UART chip. All PC Card modems already do. If you're buying a serial port card to put in an ISA slot, check to make sure you're buying one with the 16550 chip or a compatible.

NOTE Internal modems consist of three main functional sections. The Serial Communications Port handles communications with your computer. The Modulator/Demodulator handles communications over the phone lines with another modem. The Dialer handles communications with the telephone network and gets your call connected.

External modems don't contain the Serial Communications Port–they attach to one that is built into your computer.

Plug and Play modems add another section that identifies the modem's capabilities and resource needs to Windows 95 setup. ■

During Windows setup, information is exchanged between your modem and the system. This is what happens, automatically, when Windows comes to the part of setup in which your modem will be configured.

1. Windows searches through all the system's input-output (I/O) ports and finds the Plug and Play circuits on the modem.
2. The system assigns the card an identification number, which Windows stores in its information files.
3. Windows asks the modem about its speeds and specifications. The modem gives the information to Windows Setup.
4. Setup then assigns a communications port number (COM1, COM2, and so on) and resources to be used by the port. These resources are an interrupt and an I/O address. If the Plug and Play modem is on a PC Card, Windows also assigns a memory address to the modem.

Plug and Play in Action If a Plug and Play modem is installed in your computer before you install Windows, the modem setup occurs automatically. This section examines what happens if you have a PC Card modem installed in PC Card slot 1 when you install Windows 95.

First, Windows configures the PC Card slots. The PC Card Wizard appears during installation (see Figure 3.21).

CAUTION

Notice in Figure 3.21 that the wizard warns you that it is about to disable all PC Cards while it works. If you're installing Windows from a CD-ROM connected through a PC Card, Setup will fail. For a workaround, use floppy disks for this portion of Setup, or copy all the Windows 95 CAB files to your hard disk from the CD-ROM before you disable the PC card.

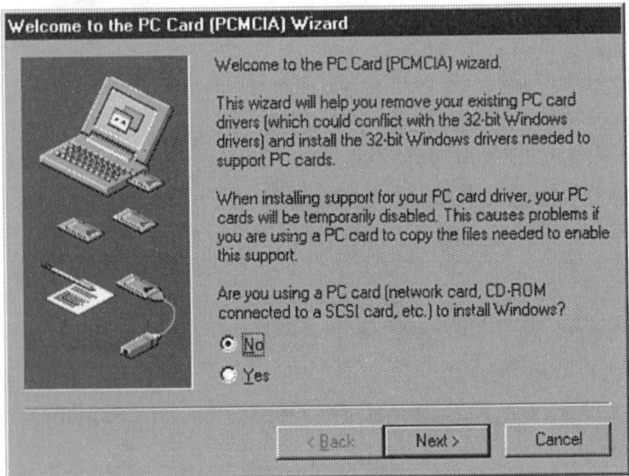

FIG. 3.21
The PC Card Wizard begins installing your PC Card modem.

Next, Windows proposes removing the old DOS-based 16-bit Card and Socket Services drivers from the CONFIG.SYS, AUTOEXEC.BAT, and SYSTEM.INI files. To review the changes before proceeding, choose Yes and then click the Next button. Figure 3.22 shows the real-mode 16-bit drivers in CONFIG.SYS. They are the last five lines in the file. For best results, you should permit the wizard to remove the old drivers. Click Next to accept the changes. After the wizard processes CONFIG.SYS, it processes the next two files in the same way.

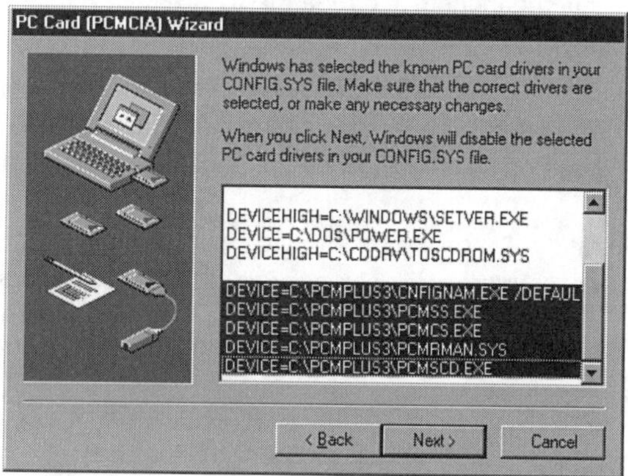

FIG. 3.22
Real-mode drivers in CONFIG.SYS that will be removed by Windows 95.

NOTE Technically speaking, the statements are not actually removed from the file. Instead, the wizard *comments out* (switches off) the statements by inserting a "REM-Removed By PC Card Wizard" statement at the beginning of each line in which the drivers are referenced.

When the wizard finishes setting up the PC Card slots, it installs the 32-bit protected-mode Card and Socket Services driver software for them. These drivers control all the Plug and Play features.

After the drivers are installed, you need to restart Windows to activate the new drivers. Click Finish in the wizard dialog box, close any other applications that you may have running, and click Yes when you're ready to shut down.

Windows loads with the 32-bit drivers enabled for the first time. Now it can "see" (and therefore configure) the modem in your PC Card slot. Using the new, protected-mode 32-bit Card and Socket Services, Windows can install any modem in your PC Card slot. In Figure 3.23, Windows detected a new modem and installed the software drivers for it automatically.

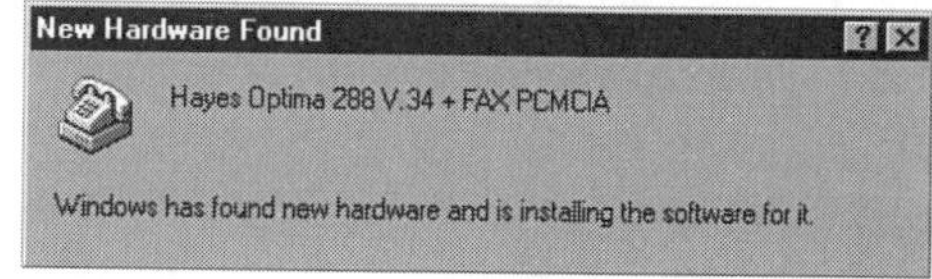

FIG. 3.23
Windows Setup finds your modem.

Your Plug and Play modem is now installed. Next, the modem must be configured to allow all advanced features in Windows to operate, which is discussed in the "Advanced Settings" section later in this chapter. The following section explains what Windows really did, via the wizard.

How Plug and Play Works The Windows user interface for the installation of the Plug and Play modem is the Setup Wizard. The wizard does all the setup work, and a lot happens behind the scenes.

What has actually happened during the Plug and Play modem installation is this:

1. Windows asks the modem to identify itself and the modem responds. Windows installs the software to run the modem and then the wizard tells you its job is complete and your modem is installed.
2. Windows installs the Unimodem driver for any modems that support AT (Attention) commands. Most modems do. Windows then looks in its database of INF files. If information is found on the specific modem, it installs the modem mini-driver.

NOTE Windows assigns the IBM-compatible standard communications port names to ports and modems. The names will be assigned in order, using the standard resources:

Port Name	I/O Port Resource
Com1	3F8
Com2	2F8
Com3	3E8
Com4	2E8

CAUTION

If Windows finds a modem configured to a base address that is not listed in the previous table, it will assign COM5 to that modem. Programs designed for Windows 3.1 or DOS may not be able to work with a modem on this port. The workaround is to change the nonstandard address in Device Manager control panel.

▶ **See** "Understanding the Device Manager," **p. 183**

TROUBLESHOOTING

I can't get the modem to install. First, check Device Manager to see whether the hardware communications port exists and is working properly. If the Port doesn't exist in Device Manager's list of ports, follow the steps in the section "Installing a Legacy Modem" later in this chapter to install the communications port. A legacy modem is a modem that does not incorporate the Plug and Play standards. Turn your external modem off and then on again. If you are using an internal modem, shut down Windows, turn off the computer, and try again.

Installing a Legacy Modem

Legacy modems don't have the hardware in them to identify themselves to Windows 95 setup. They can't tell Windows about their capabilities or their resource requirements. Legacy modems are not Plug and Play devices. They can, however, be either internal or external modems.

▶ **See** "Installing Legacy (Non-PnP) Hardware," **p. 174**

An *internal modem* is one that fits into a slot in the computer bus and contains the serial port on the modem.

An *external modem* does not contain the serial port. The external modem connects via cable to the serial port inside the computer.

Windows considers the serial port to be a separate device from the modem, even if you have an internal modem, in which both the modem and the serial port are on the same add-in card. Windows configures these devices separately. You should be aware of the process that Windows uses to perform the configurations.

If you're trying to install an internal modem, Windows may act differently with different modems. You may be able to install the serial port at the same time you install the modem. If Windows cannot detect and initialize the port, however, you may have to use the Add New Hardware option in the Control Panel to set up the port.

In Windows 95, you can install a legacy modem in any of the following ways:

- Use the Add New Hardware Wizard.

- Click the Modem icon in Control Panel.
- Start a 32-bit program that uses a modem. If no modem is installed, Windows suggests you install one.

The following procedure uses the Add New Hardware Wizard to install the modem. Follow these steps:

1. Open the Start menu and choose Settings, Control Panel.

2. Double-click the Add New Hardware icon. The Add New Hardware Wizard window appears.
3. Click Next.
4. You should allow Windows to try to find your modem by itself, so choose Yes when the wizard asks if you want Windows to detect it automatically. You'll see a progress report during the detection process.

   If Windows can, it sets up the serial port and the modem at the same time. Windows may not find the modem when it finds the port. In that case, run Add New Hardware Wizard again.

   The report from the Add New Hardware Wizard, shown in Figure 3.24, indicates that Windows has found a new Communications Port. View this report by clicking the Details button.
5. Click Finish.
6. When you are prompted, restart the computer.

After Windows restarts, look in Control Panel's Device Manager. On the Resources page, you'll see that a new Communications Port, COM3, has been added (see Figure 3.25).

NOTE Many times Windows will not find the port and the modem on the same pass through the installation process. Don't be concerned—follow the next steps. ■

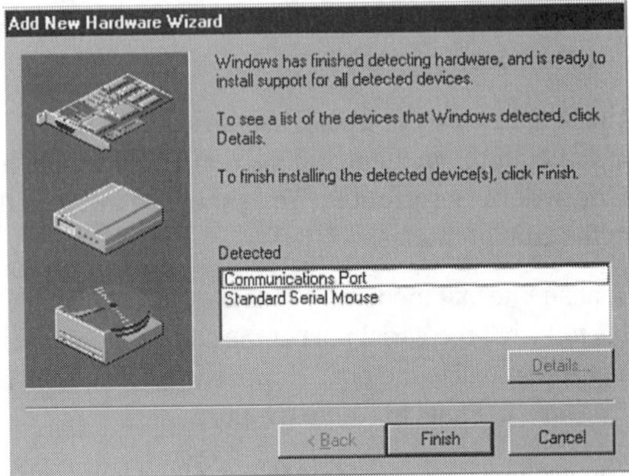

FIG. 3.24
This report from the Add New Hardware Wizard shows two new devices detected.

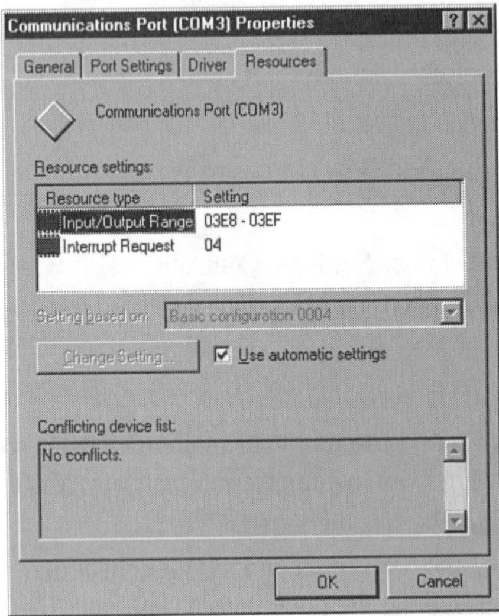

FIG. 3.25
The new communications port and its resources.

In this common example, Windows could not detect and install the port and modem in one step. Therefore, you need to visit the Control Panel again. Now that COM3 is working properly, Windows should be able to detect and install the modem connected to that port.

Double-click the Modems icon in the Control Panel. When the Install New Modem Wizard starts, choose Other.

In the next dialog box, the wizard asks for another chance to detect the modem. Click Next but don't tell the wizard what modem you have because you want to see whether Windows can find out if the port is working. Figure 3.26 shows the window that appears just before automatic modem detection.

At the end of the modem installation process, Windows reports that it found the modem attached to COM3 (see Figure 3.27). Because the reported type matches the type that is installed, you have finished the installation of the standard legacy modem. To close the dialog box, click Next.

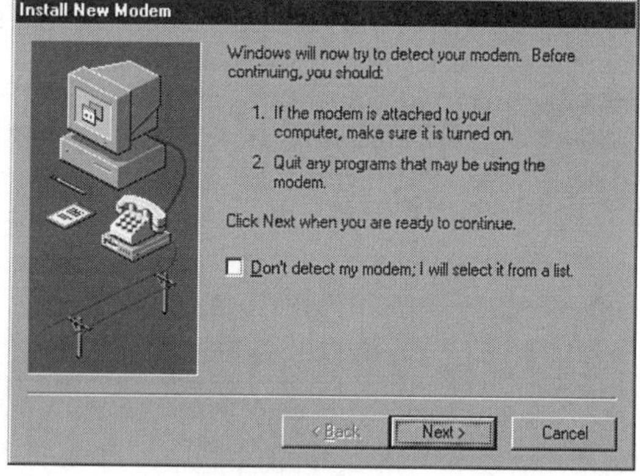

FIG. 3.26
The Modem Installation Wizard set to auto-detect your modem.

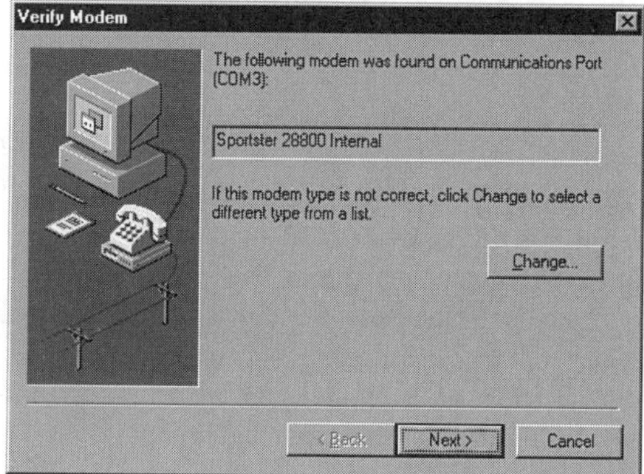

FIG. 3.27
The Modem Wizard has detected the new modem.

NOTE Windows chooses slow port speeds by default. If you have a fast computer, change the port speeds in the Modems Properties Control Panel to the modem's maximum speed. See "Configuring Your Modem," later in this chapter.

TROUBLESHOOTING

When I use the modem, another program—or the entire system—locks up or crashes. How do I fix it? This problem usually results from an interrupt conflict. Two devices may be trying to use the same interrupt. If you have a serial mouse on COM1, which uses Interrupt 4, and you set up a modem on COM3, which by default also uses Interrupt 4, a conflict will exist.

Use Device Manager to look for a modem or mouse icon that has a yellow exclamation point. Double-click the icon and choose Resources. If a conflict is listed, Windows offers to start the Hardware Conflict Troubleshooter. This program can help you resolve interrupt conflicts by reassigning resources such as interrupts.

Understanding the Unimodem Driver

Most of the modems on the market use a variation of the AT command set, which Dennis Hayes developed for the original Smartmodem in 1980. The command set has evolved over the years, and each manufacturer has its own set of proprietary extensions for advanced features. Still, the most basic commands are the same for all modems that use AT commands. The fact that this lowest common denominator of commands exists for the vast majority of modems allowed Microsoft to write a universal modem driver—the Unimodem driver.

Table 3.1 shows the basic AT commands used by the Unimodem driver.

Table 3.1 Modem Commands for Unimodem Driver

AT Command	Function
AT	Attention
ATZ	Reset modem
ATD	Dial modem
ATI	Identify modem
ATH	Hang up modem
ATO	Go off hook in originate mode

Once the Unimodem driver is talking to the modem, these commands provide enough functionality for the driver to interrogate the modem, find its manufacturer and model number, and try to find a match in its modem database. If a match is found, the driver tells Windows to install the mini-driver that matches the modem. This mini-driver works with the modem to enable advanced features such as data compression and error correction. These features are likely to be implemented differently by each manufacturer.

Even without a mini-driver, the Unimodem driver can make a partially Hayes-compatible modem dial, connect, and disconnect. Modems that are running with only the Unidriver will be shown in Control Panel as a Standard modem.

Using Drivers Provided by Modem Manufacturers

You may encounter a modem that comes with a Windows 95 driver disk. This disk indicates that Windows 95 has no appropriate mini-driver, or the modem has features that are not supported by the Unimodem driver.

To install the modem with its own driver software, follow these steps:

1. Double-click the Modem icon in Control Panel.
2. Choose Add.
3. Choose PC Card or Other, as appropriate.

4. Choose Don't Detect My Modem, I Will Select It.
5. Now choose Have Disk.
6. Insert the manufacturer's driver disk into the proper disk drive when you are prompted, and then choose OK.

Your modem's drivers are installed in Windows and the modem's special features are enabled.

Configuring Your Modem

Now that your hardware is installed, you can configure Windows to work cooperatively with it. Windows can take some information from you and supply that information to communications programs to allow them to function more effectively.

Windows automatically collects the following information from you:

- Your location
- Your area code
- Access number(s) needed to get an outside line
- Type of dialing used at this location (tone or pulse)

This information, however, is not enough to make your modem operate at peak efficiency and at maximum data-transfer rates. You should tell Windows other things about your modem, including the following:

- Maximum port speed (computer to modem)
- Default data-formatting properties
- How to handle situations involving no dial tone
- How long the modem should try to connect before stopping
- Whether to use error control and compression for robust and fast communication
- Your modem's error control and compression features
- What kind of flow control to use with your modem
- How to handle low-speed connections
- How to record a log file of the modem's interaction with the system to be used in troubleshooting
- How to manually send extra AT commands to the modem during initialization

The following sections explain these items.

General Properties Use the Modems Control Panel to select the modem that you are working with, and then choose Properties. The Modem properties sheet, which has two sheets, appears. The General properties, as shown in Figure 3.28, contains settings that can make your modem work better when the proper values are selected.

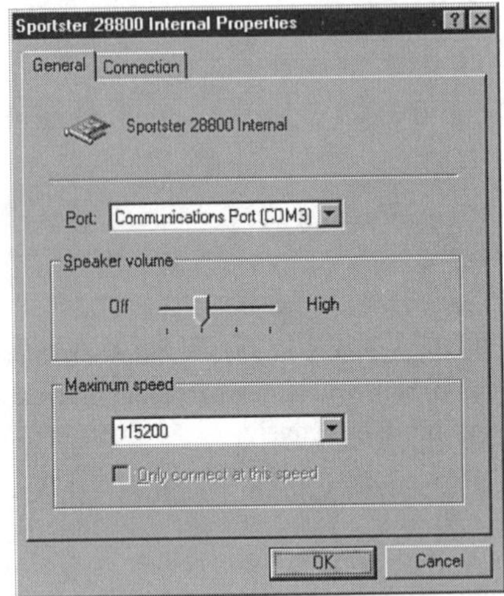

FIG. 3.28
The General page of a modem's properties sheet displays basic information about your modem.

Port The Port option shows the communications port to which Windows assigned the modem. If the modem is an internal Plug and Play type, in which Windows can configure the serial port, you may have a choice in setting which communications port to use with the modem. If other communications ports are used, or if the modem cannot be configured by Windows (you must use jumpers to set its port and address), you will not be able to change the communications port assigned to this modem.

Speaker Volume The Speaker Volume control is a handy way to tell 32-bit Windows 95 communications programs how loud to set the volume of the modem's speaker.

The volume control slider works with modems that have physical speakers and with modems (such as PC Cards) that rely on the computer's speaker for their sound. If the volume control is grayed out, the modem has no speaker and no way of using the speaker in the computer. (Many ISDN Terminal Adapters will have the Speaker Volume grayed out.)

NOTE DOS and 16-bit Windows communications programs ignore the Speaker Volume setting; instead, they set modem volume themselves. These older programs set the volume themselves because when they were written, the operating system had no way to keep track of your preferences.

Maximum Speed The Maximum Speed parameter is extremely important. This setting has nothing to do with the speed at which your modem connects to another modem—it represents the speed at which your *computer* connects to your modem.

Why is this important? Any modem that operates at 9600 bps (formerly referred to as the baud) or faster typically supports data compression. The International Telecommunications Union (ITU), the professional society that sets worldwide communications standards, has established four data compression standards. Your modem may support one or all of these standards.

Table 3.2 shows the standards, the modem speed associated with each standard, and the port speed that you should use with your modem. These general guidelines work for almost all modems.

Table 3.2 Modem Port Speed Settings

Modem Speed	ITU Standard	Port Speed
9600	v.32	19,200
14400	v.32bis	57,600
19200	v.32ter	57,600
28800	v.34	115,200

NOTE You may not be able to set the port speed as high as 115,200 on older, slower computers. These computers may not have the right type of serial port hardware, which is based on the type 16550A chip. In such a case, use 57,600.

When two modems that are using one of the ITU standards (or one of the older, but still widely used Microcom MNP compression standards) connect, the modems examine the data that they are sending to see whether it can be compressed. If so, the modems compress the data. Sending compressed data raises the effective speed of the modem. Modem speed can approach the speed of the port if the data can be greatly compressed.

See "Advanced Settings," **p. 81**

Compression works only if the port speed is fast enough to feed the data to the modem as quickly as the modem needs it. If a 14,400 v.32bis modem compresses data into half the space that the data takes up on disk, the port must feed data to the modem at least twice as fast as the 14,400 connect speed. Setting the port to 57,600 allows for the high-speed data feed to the modem and also takes care of some overhead for processing.

Only Connect at This Speed Check this box if you don't want your modem to adjust its speed to match the speed of the modem on the other end. Checking this box allows only high-speed connections between two high-speed modems.

Sometimes bad conditions on the telephone line can make two high-speed modems connect at low speeds. Checking this box prevents the low-speed connection from taking place. In that case, you will have to keep trying the call until the modems can connect at the highest speed.

Connection Properties To define the default modem settings used for new connections, open the Connection page of the Modems Control Panel, as shown in Figure 3.29.

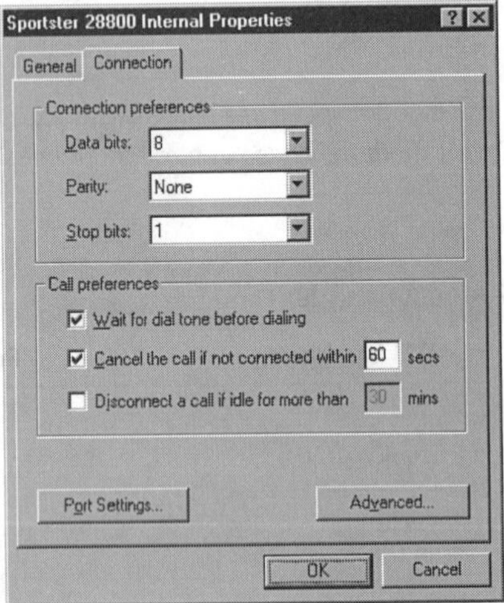

FIG. 3.29
Use the Connection page to set your default modem connection settings.

Connection Preferences The default settings—8 bits, no parity, and 1 stop bit—work for most online services, BBSs, remote access and remote control programs, data transfer services, dial-up networking, and so on. Change these settings only if the resource you are dialing requires different values.

Wait for Dial Tone Before Calling When this option is enabled, Windows cancels the connection if no dial tone is present when the modem tries to dial. Under normal circumstances, this option should be checked; however, uncheck it if you have any of the following situations:

- You have to dial the phone manually for your modem.
- You are using a phone system with a dial tone that your modem fails to detect.
- You want to speed up the dialing process by a few milliseconds so that the modem does not wait for a dial tone before dialing.

Cancel the Call If Not Connected Within X Seconds If the modem you are calling does not answer within 60 seconds, a problem may exist. When you choose this option, you are notified if your call did not connect so that you can check to see whether you have the right phone number. If 60 seconds is not long enough, type a longer duration in the text box.

Disconnect a Call If Idle for More than X Minutes This option can save you money if you use commercial online services regularly. If you get interrupted or called away from your computer, Windows disconnects from the service so you won't continue to accumulate expensive online charges.

Advanced Settings At the bottom of the Connection page is the Advanced button. When you click this button, you see the dialog box shown in Figure 3.30.

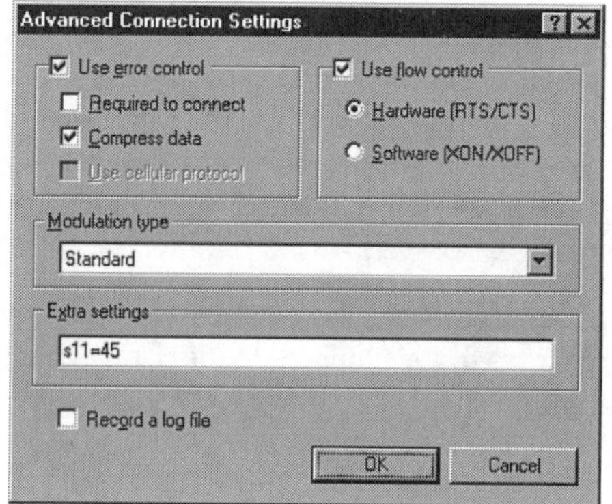

FIG. 3.30 Use the Advanced Connection Settings dialog box to configure modem error control, flow control, modulation, log files, and additional settings.

The Use Error Control, Compress Data, and Use Flow Control options in the Advanced Connection Settings dialog box work with one another and with the port speed setting in the General page of the Modem properties sheet.

Your choices in Advanced Connection Settings will determine if your modem will work as fast, and as reliably, as intended by its manufacturer.

Error Control For modems with data speeds of 9,600bps or faster, Windows turns on the Use Error Control option automatically. When using error control, such as V.42 or MNP 4, the receiving modem verifies data when it arrives. If a bad data transmission is detected, the receiving modem requests the data again.

When modems connect, they negotiate the highest level of error control and compression. If you don't want error control or compression, simply uncheck the Use Error Control check box. To insist that connections use error control, check the Required to Connect check box.

Check the Use Cellular Protocol check box if you use a cellular modem. The cellular error control protocol offers more robust connections for mobile communications moving between cells.

If your modem supports compression, such as the V.42bis or MNP 5 compression standards, choose the Compress Data option. MNP 5 offers 2X compression. MNP 5 doesn't sense when it is sending previously compressed data, such as a ZIP or GIF file, and results in slower effective throughput. Better, V.42bis offers 4× compression and senses when data has already been compressed. Refer to your modem manual to see what level of compression your modem supports.

Flow Control Use flow control to throttle data between your computer and the modem. If data buffers on either side become full, the receiving side will notify the sender to hold off for a moment. If you do not use flow control, data collisions occur resulting in garbled or illegible information.

In the Use Flow Control section of the dialog box, check the Use Flow Control check box and choose Hardware if you are using an internal or PC Card modem. You also should choose Hardware when using an external modem rated at 9,600bps or faster, but be sure you are using a hardware-handshaking cable that includes the necessary lines for the Request To Send/Clear To Send (RTS/CTS) handshake. If you don't choose Hardware, high port speeds can cause data overrun errors, and result in excessively slow throughput.

Choose Software if you cannot use Hardware flow control. Software flow control (also referred to as XON/XOFF flow control) uses byte sequences in the data of the connection, and can cause problems when transmitting binary files.

Modulation Type The Modulation Type setting controls how Windows handles connections at 300 and 1200bps. If you connect with an old modem at 300 or 1200bps, you have to decide whether to use U.S. or European standards. Bell works with American modems and CCITT V.21 works with modems in the rest of the world. If you want to connect to a CCITT V.21 or V.22 modem, make sure that your modem can use these standards.

NOTE American and European modems used different standards until 9600bps modems became popular. At that time, American manufacturers adopted the standards set by the CCITT (in English, the International Telegraph & Telephone Consultative Committee) and its successor, the ITU (International Telecommunications Union). Now modems all over the world can communicate at 9600bps and faster. ■

Extra Settings If you need to send the modem an AT command that Windows does not include automatically in its initialization procedure, type the command in the Extra Settings box.

Windows hides extra settings away in this obscure location because Windows architects believe the operating system should handle all details of communicating with the modem. The user should be isolated from sending raw AT commands. Because each brand of modem implements the AT command set differently, an AT command that works on one 28.8 Kbps modem may not work the same on any other brand of modem.

However, if you are certain about your modem's implementation of the AT command set, Extra Settings is the place to send additional commands at modem initialization time, just before the modem dials out.

For example, if you want to turn off the speaker completely on a Hayes modem, enter ATM0 (that's a zero after the M) in the Extra Settings dialog box.

Using Log Files If you repeatedly have trouble making a connection, tell Windows to keep a record of the commands that it sends to the modem and the replies from the modem. This record can be useful in troubleshooting the problem. You can look for responses from the modem that contain the word "ERROR" and see what commands caused the errors. To activate this feature, choose the Record a Log File option.

NOTE The log file is stored in the Windows directory as MODEMLOG.TXT. You can use Notepad to examine the log file.

When you are done making your choices in the Advanced Connection Settings dialog box, click OK. This returns you to the Modem properties sheet.

Understanding Your Modem and Your Telephone System

Dialing Properties is a new concept for Windows 95. Dialing Properties gives you a way to control how your calls are dialed. You can create and choose from a list of dialing locations, each of which can be in a different area code or country. Windows will still dial the modem properly. Finally, the system knows how to do these things!

Dialing Properties also works with your modem to tell it whether you need to dial an access code to get an outside line. It allows you to make a calling card call with your modem. Dialing Properties can disable call waiting so that your modem calls won't be interrupted by an incoming call. With Dialing Properties, you can also tell your modem whether it can use touch tones on your phone line or if the modem must use rotary pulse dialing.

To control Dialing Properties, choose Dialing Properties from the Modem properties sheet.

The preceding sections explain how some of the properties settings for your modem control the way that the modem call is made. So far, the only actual dialing parameter that you've given the modem is whether to use tone or pulse dialing.

Many of the things that a modem needs to do to complete a call depend on where you and your computer are. A modem that's being used at home, for example, usually dials differently from a modem that's being used in a hotel room or at the office. Knowing the phone number of the computer that you want to dial with the modem isn't enough—you also have area codes and outside line codes to deal with. In addition, you may want to make a credit card call.

These issues used to be problems. Windows 95, however, collects information from you so that communications programs handle these issues in a seamless, elegant fashion.

Figure 3.31 shows the Dialing properties sheet where you specify location information. This information tells your modem how to work wherever you go with your computer. If you are using your modem at home, where you don't need to dial a code for an outside line but do have the call-waiting feature, your settings may look like the ones shown in Figure 3.31.

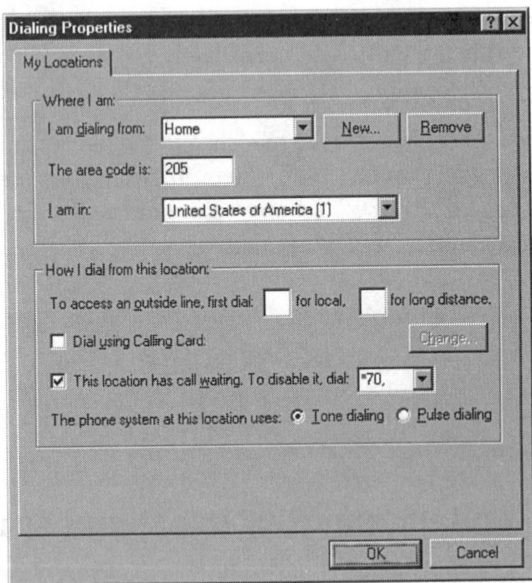

FIG. 3.31
You can set location information in the Dialing properties sheet.

Suppose, however, that you're working in a hotel room in Washington, D.C.; that you need to dial 9 to get an outside line (or 91 to get a long distance outside line); and that you want to charge the call to a credit card.

To make a credit card call, you need to check the Dial Using Credit Card box. Your Dialing Properties settings would look like the ones shown in Figure 3.32.

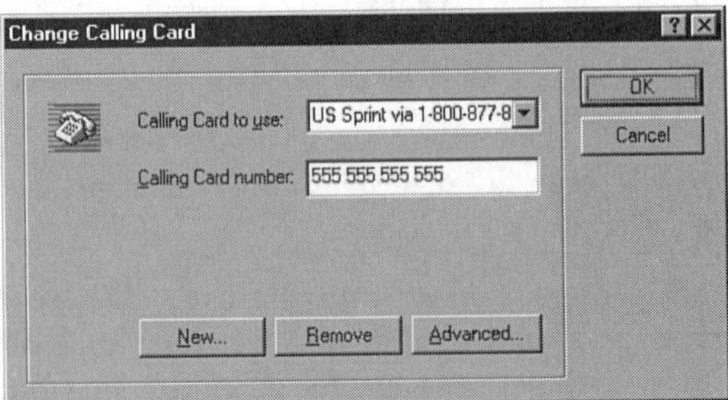

FIG. 3.32
Making a calling card call with your modem is easy.

In the Dialing properties sheet, Windows has created your first Location for you, based on information you gave Setup during Windows installation. Windows has named this the Default Location.

Create additional locations by choosing New on the Dialing properties sheet. Name the Location and fill out the country and area code for the Location. You also can remove a location by choosing Remove.

▶ **See** "Working Smarter with TAPI and 32-Bit Windows Programs," **p. 88**

When you use a communications program that is TAPI-aware and Windows 95-aware, you can specify your location before dialing. Examples of programs that take advantage of Locations are Windows HyperTerminal; Windows Phone Dialer; the Microsoft Network online service; Microsoft Exchange; and any of Exchange's MAPI modules, such as CompuServe Mail and Dial-Up Networking.

To learn more about Microsoft Exchange and MAPI modules that use modems, see Chapter 27, "Using Microsoft Exchange and Windows Messaging."

Getting Your Modem to Dial After you define your modem settings, you need to test the modem to verify that it dials properly. Phone Dialer, an accessory that comes with Windows 95, is a good program to perform the test. Run Phone Dialer by opening the Start menu, and choosing Programs, Accessories, Phone Dialer. Figure 3.33 shows the main Phone Dialer dialog box.

FIG. 3.33
Use Phone Dialer to test dial your modem.

When you tell Phone Dialer to dial the number shown in the Number to Dial box, it knows how to handle the area code. Because you defined your location in Dialing Properties, Phone Dialer knows if you are dialing a number in the same area code as your computer; in that case, it leaves off the area code and dials the call as a local call, as shown in Figure 3.34. Phone Dialer also knows whether to dial 1 before the number, based on what you define as your dialing properties. When you must dial 1 and the area code for long distance calls in your same area code, select the Dial as a Long Distance Call check box in the Dialing properties sheet.

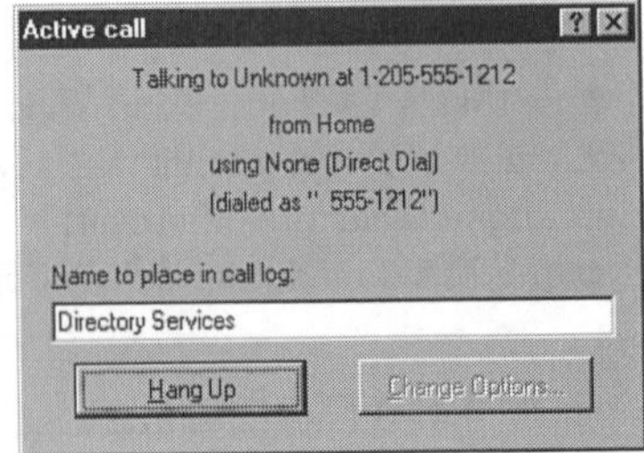

FIG. 3.34
When calling in the same area code, Windows dials only seven digits.

TROUBLESHOOTING

The modem won't dial. In the Modems Control Panel, check to see whether the modem displayed matches your model. If not, choose Add New Modem to install your modem. If any modems that are not in your system appear in the Control Panel, delete their entries.

In the System Control Panel, choose Device Manager. Choose Modems, select your modem, double-click to display the properties sheet, and click the General tab. The page shown in Figure 3.35 indicates that the device is used in the current configuration and that it is working properly.

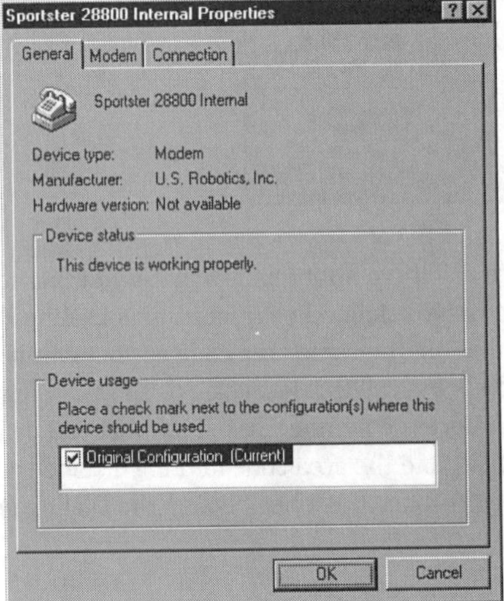

FIG. 3.35
Use Device Manager to see if your modem is working properly.

Make sure that the communications port is set correctly. Click the Modem tab, shown in Figure 3.36, and check the port name and port speed.

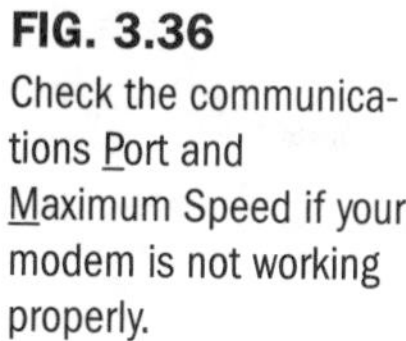

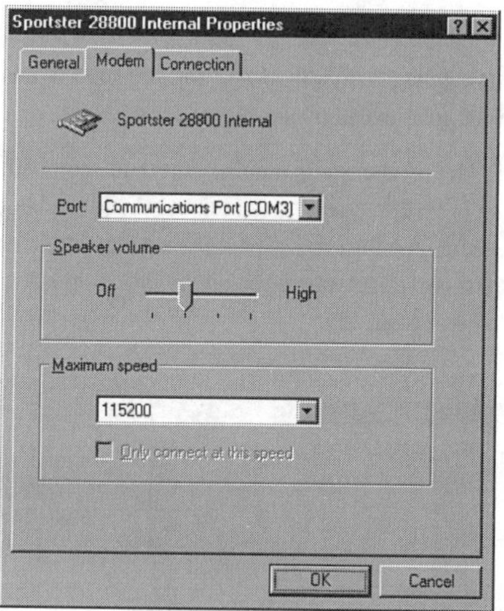

FIG. 3.36
Check the communications Port and Maximum Speed if your modem is not working properly.

Make sure the port name matches the port that your application wants to use. If the port is set to COM2, for example, make sure your application is trying to use the modem on COM2.

You also can try lowering the port speed. Perhaps your serial port hardware does not support the selected speed. Try a range of speeds between the data speed of your modem and the maximum speed. Use the highest setting that works reliably.

If these suggestions do not work, use Windows built-in diagnostic tool that tests the communication from your computer to the modem. To use the modem diagnostic tool, start the Modems Control Panel. When the Modem properties sheet appears, click the Diagnostics tab.

Select your modem and choose More Info. Windows issues a series of interrogatory commands to the modem and notes the responses. Figure 3.37 shows sample results. Use the results to verify that the modem is responding to Windows commands. Also, some modems respond with their model number. Cross-check this with your modem settings. Refer to your modem reference manual for the meaning of the responses.

TROUBLESHOOTING

My modem connects, but it doesn't stay connected. If your phone line has call waiting, incoming calls may be throwing you offline. Use Dialing Properties to disable call waiting. You reach the Dialing properties sheet by choosing Dialing Properties from the Modem properties sheet.

If that doesn't work, flow control may be set incorrectly. For 9600bps and faster modems, make sure that flow control is set to Hardware.

To get to the flow control setting, use Control Panel, double-click the Modem icon, and then choose Properties. Click the Connection tab and then choose Advanced.

continues

continued

Also check all cables for quality by swapping them with cables that you know to be good; swap serial cables for external modems as well as your regular phone cables.

My Windows 95 application keeps dialing the wrong number. Check to see whether the Dialing Location properties are set correctly. To do this, open the Control Panel and double-click the Modem icon. Then click Dialing Properties. Make sure the entry in I Am Dialing From matches your location, and that the area code and country shown match where you are as well. If they don't, Windows 95 programs will be dialing phone numbers incorrectly.

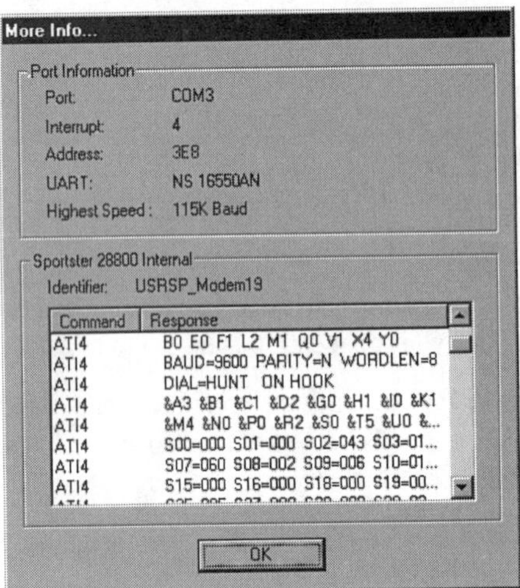

FIG. 3.37
Use Modem Diagnostics to show modem responses to basic information commands.

Working Smarter with TAPI and 32-Bit Windows Programs

Telephony Applications Programming Interface, or TAPI, lets your modem do more for you in Windows 95.

TAPI uses all the information that you gave Windows during the modem configuration process to set up not only your modem, but also all the 32-bit Windows 95 communications programs. Phone dialer, HyperTerminal, Microsoft Exchange, and Dial-Up Networking all share one modem because of TAPI. Communications programs that are written specifically for Windows 95 talk to TAPI, which issues appropriate commands to the modem. *Device independence* is the way Windows uses TAPI for all communications, instead of making each communications program learn to talk to every other modem. Device independence frees the program developer from having to know everything about your modem.

TAPI provides the following major benefits, which were covered earlier in the section "Understanding Your Modem and Your Telephone System."

- The capability to define locations to make dialing effortless
- Support for 16550A UART chips for better throughput

In addition, TAPI provides the following benefits, which are the subject of the following sections:

- Sharing of modems by applications
- Sharing fax modems over a network

Sharing a Modem Under TAPI You know the problem from Windows 3.1: Your system has one modem, which is used for data and for faxes, and you want to leave the modem under the control of the fax program so that the modem is ready for incoming faxes. When you try to make a data call with the modem, however, an error message appears, telling you that the port is already in use. You have to disable the fax program, use the data program, and re-enable the fax program.

Now suppose that you are using Windows 95. At 3 p.m., Microsoft Fax is waiting for an incoming fax to arrive. At the same time, the CompuServe Mail driver in Microsoft Exchange is scheduled to check CompuServe to see whether any new mail has arrived. Without missing a beat, TAPI allows the mail driver to use the modem; then TAPI hands modem control back to Microsoft Fax. The importance and convenience of this cooperation cannot be overstated.

TROUBLESHOOTING

My Windows 95 communications programs work fine, but I can't access the modem with a DOS or old Windows communications program. How can I make my legacy communications programs work? You ran into the TAPI gotcha. TAPI works only if all the communications programs you will be using are TAPI-aware, 32-bit, Windows 95 programs. If Microsoft Fax is waiting for an incoming fax or Dial-Up Networking is waiting for an incoming call, DOS and old Windows programs cannot access the modem; this capability is reserved for TAPI-enabled Windows 95 applications.

Sharing a Fax Modem over a Network TAPI allows any user on a Windows 95 network to send faxes via another network user's fax modem. The user who has the fax modem enables the modem as a shared device; TAPI does the rest.

NOTE Data modems cannot be shared over a network. ■

Understanding File Transfer Errors

Errors occur in file transfers with DOS and old Windows programs. Fortunately, you can track them down and fix them.

If you're using DOS and Windows 3.1 communications programs, you've probably upgraded from Windows 3.1 to Windows 95. There are settings in the old Windows 3.1 SYSTEM.INI file that can cause problems in your new installation of Windows 95.

To correct these problems, some manual editing of SYSTEM.INI may be necessary. You can use NOTEPAD.EXE to perform these tasks.

In the [boot] section of your SYSTEM.INI file, make sure there is a line that states COMM.DRV=COMM.DRV. If it doesn't, edit it so it does.

This will make sure Windows 95 is using its own communications driver for older, 16-bit programs.

In the [386Enh] section, make sure a line exists that says DEVICE=*VCD. If you don't see DEVICE=*VCD, type it on a line by itself anywhere in the [386Enh] section. Use NOTEPAD.EXE to do this.

Next, set the FIFO buffer to 512 bytes. Determine the communications port that you're using with these DOS and old Windows programs. If the port is COM2, for example, add the line COM2BUFFER=512 in the [386Enh] section of your SYSTEM.INI file. Use the same syntax for other ports. You can add COM2BUFFER=512 on a line by itself, anywhere in the [386Enh] section of SYSTEM.INI. You can use NOTEPAD.EXE to do this. ●

CHAPTER 4

Configuring Multimedia Windows 95

In this chapter

Optimizing Video and Animation

Windows 95 has certainly given a boost to digital video. The 32-bit architecture of Windows 95 helps streamline video playback and eliminate pesky resource problems. Better yet, Windows 95 puts video capability directly into the operating system, which means that virtually anyone who has Windows 95 is able to work with AVI files.

At the core of Windows-based video is the Media Control Interface, or MCI. MCI is an architecture that gives programs a standard, script-based interface to Windows multimedia resources, such as the Media Player, video playback windows, and audio controls. In addition, MCI enables programmatic control of video and audio so that development tools like Visual Basic, or even application macro scripts, can invoke and control video playback and editing. MCI is also at the core of object linking and embedding (OLE) video clips, where video clips are played within OLE-aware documents such as spreadsheets.

Beyond MCI and the familiar Media Player interface, users will notice that the device and video compression drivers needed to work with video are all preinstalled in Windows 95. As a result, you can distribute AVI video files to virtually any Windows 95 user and be assured that the file can be played back.

Working with the Video Tools in Windows 95

Windows 95 puts a wealth of video-centric tools into the hands of PC users. To help you get up to speed, here is a rundown of their operation.

The Video Properties Box The properties sheet for AVI files displays valuable data that can help you optimize video playback. Right-click any AVI file in an Explorer or Browser window, and select Properties from the context menu. You'll see a tabbed sheet that opens to the General page. Here, you're able to browse all the usual file information, like file name, size, and creation date.

Click the Details tab. Here you'll see the length of the video clip, the audio compression and fidelity, as well as the compression scheme, resolution, color depth, and frame rates of the clip (see Figure 4.1). It even provides the data rate, in KB/Sec (kilobytes per second), so you can tell if your CD-ROM drive is up to the task of playing the clip.

You also can preview the AVI file from the properties sheet. Click the Preview tab and you'll see the opening frame of the video (see Figure 4.2). To view the video, click the play button or drag the slider control to move through the clip.

Using the Windows 95 Media Player The Media Player is the multimedia headquarters for Windows 95 and closely resembles the application found in Windows 3.1. One key exception: This Media Player is a 32-bit application with all the advantages and benefits that implies.

Media Player supports a wide variety of formats such as Video for Windows video (AVI), sound (WAV), MIDI (MID), animation (FLC and FLI), and CD audio. It also accepts driver updates that let it support a variety of other formats including QuickTime for Windows MOV files, MPEG video files, and other media types.

To play videos with Media Player, double-click an AVI file in an Explorer or Browser window. Media Player loads the AVI file and immediately starts playing it.

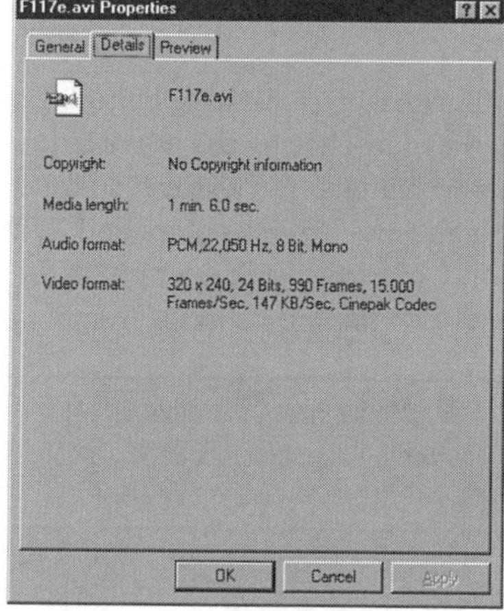

FIG. 4.1
The Details page reveals information such as data rates, color depth, and resolution.

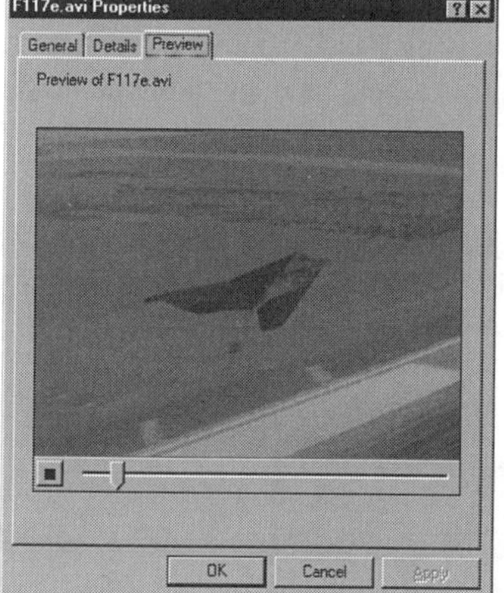

FIG. 4.2
The Preview page lets you sample AVI files.

NOTE The numbered hot key for selections beneath the Device menu vary depending on what multimedia drivers are loaded onto your system. ■

You can open an AVI file from Media Player by following these steps:

1. Choose Device, then click the Video for Windows option.
2. Select an AVI file in the Open dialog box, then click Open.
3. Click the play button in Media Player (see Figure 4.3).

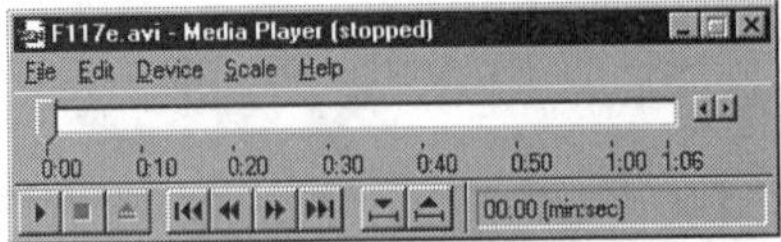

FIG. 4.3
The Windows 95 Media Player uses simple, VCR-like controls.

When a video is playing, the play button changes to a pause button. You can stop the video by clicking the stop button or pause the video by clicking the pause button. To fast forward or rewind the video, click the double-arrow buttons. You also can advance to the beginning and end of a clip or section of video by clicking the Previous Mark and Next Mark controls. Finally, the Scroll Forward and Scroll Backward buttons just to the right of the slider bar allow you to do single-frame playback, which is great for finding a specific frame.

When you double-click a video file to play it with Media Player, the video appears in a window without the Media Player controls. You can call up the Media Player controls while watching a video by double-clicking the movie's title bar.

Sizing Video Windows Media Player gives you the option of playing back a video clip at various sizes. Although you can stretch a video window by grabbing it by the edge, doing so may distort the original image.

Most AVI clips measure either 320×240 or 160×120 pixels, an aspect ratio of 4:3. To change the video window size while preserving the aspect ratio, go to Media Player's properties sheet by choosing Device, Properties.

Click the Windows drop-down list box to see the available selection of window sizes for video playback (see Figure 4.4). You can select from Double original size, 1/16 of screen size, 1/4 of screen size, 1/2 of screen size, and Maximized. The monitor image in the Video properties sheet shows an approximation of what the resized video will look like, complete with blocky pixelation.

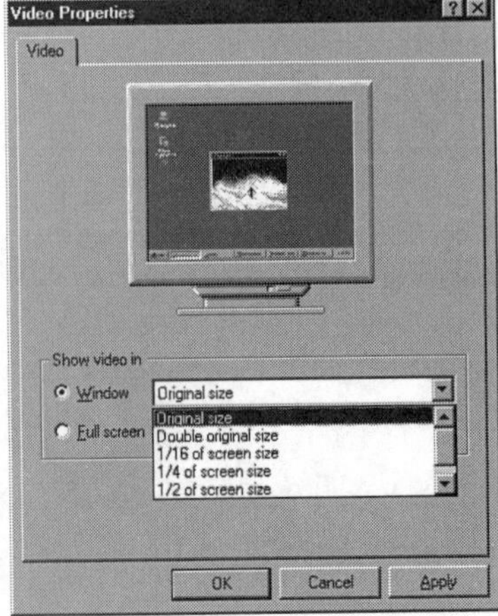

FIG. 4.4
Expand and shrink video windows from the Video properties sheet.

You can vary the size of a video in four increments by selecting Ctrl+1 (normal) through Ctrl+4 (full-screen), while the movie's window is selected.

Unless you have video-enhancing hardware and drivers for Windows 95, you usually get the best results by playing videos at Original size. Stretching or shrinking video forces the CPU to do additional processing, causing lost frames.

TIP If you want the best full screen video, click the Full screen option button and not the Maximized setting on the drop-down list. Windows 95 can streamline video playback when it does not have to manage graphical user interface (GUI).

Working Scale Settings When Media Player plays a video clip, it uses a frame- or time-based scale to measure progress. This scheme lets you find specific points in the video so you can easily edit, play, or copy selected parts of video files. For example, a frame-based scale lets you perform frame-accurate video editing and tracking. To have Media Player display the scale by frames, choose Scale, Frames. To have the scale expressed in minutes and seconds, choose Scale, Time. The display beneath the video progress slider bar changes to reflect the new setting. You can even do this while a clip is playing.

Setting Playback Options You can customize the look and function of a video window during playback with Media Player. For instance, you can set a video to play back continually so that it starts again at the beginning once it finishes playing. Choose Edit, Options (or press Ctrl+O) to see the Options dialog box (see Figure 4.5).

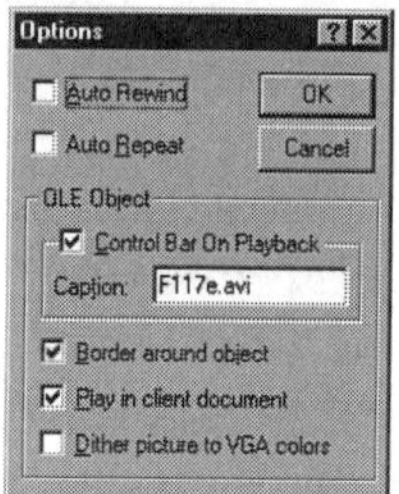

FIG. 4.5
You can control the look and behavior of video clips in the Media Player's Options dialog box.

When checked, the controls in this dialog box allow you to do the following:

- **Auto Rewind** queues the video clip back to the beginning after the clip finishes playing.
- **Auto Repeat** forces the clip to play in a loop until the user stops playback.
- **Control Bar On Playback** puts start/stop and slider bar controls on video files embedded into other applications using the OLE object linking and embedding technology of Windows.

- **Caption** lets you change the text that appears in the control bar on OLE-embedded video clips.
- **Border around object** draws a border around an embedded video while it plays.
- **Play in client document** lets the embedded video run inside the OLE application document without invoking a separate video window.
- **Dither picture to VGA colors** if the color in a video clip looks distorted.

Controlling the Volume If a clip is too loud for your tastes, you can adjust the volume by choosing Device, Volume Control. The Windows 95 Volume Control dialog box appears with slider controls to handle the volume, balance, and mute settings for all the various audio inputs and outputs.

You also can adjust volume by clicking the speaker icon located in the taskbar, invoking a slider control that adjusts volume.

Inserting Video Objects in a Document You can use Media Player to cut and paste a portion of a video into a document. You can then play the video by double-clicking it. To copy a portion of a video to your document, do the following:

1. Position the trackbar thumb on the starting frame of the portion of the video you want to copy.
2. Click the Start Selection button.
3. Position the trackbar thumb on the last frame of the portion you want to copy.
4. Click the End Selection button.
5. Select Edit, Copy Object to copy that portion of the video to the Clipboard.
6. Open the document and paste the video clip by choosing Edit, Paste.

When you double-click the object in the document, the video clip plays.

If you want to deselect the clip, select Edit, Selection from Media Player's menu. Then select None and click OK.

Media Player Secrets There are many features in Media Player that you won't find in the interface or the Help file. Some of these features can help you understand and take advantage of video on your multimedia PC.

For example, pressing Ctrl+F5 when the Media Player application is open invokes the Send MCI String Command dialog box. From here, you can enter a variety of powerful text commands to play, adjust, or get information on video files. Here's a quick list of Media Player secrets:

- **Count frames**: Media Player tracks how many frames drop during playback. To see how many frames dropped after a clip has played, press Ctrl+F5 to invoke the MCI String Command dialog box (see Figure 4.6). Type **status frames skipped** in the Command box and click Send. You'll see how many frames were dropped during video playback.

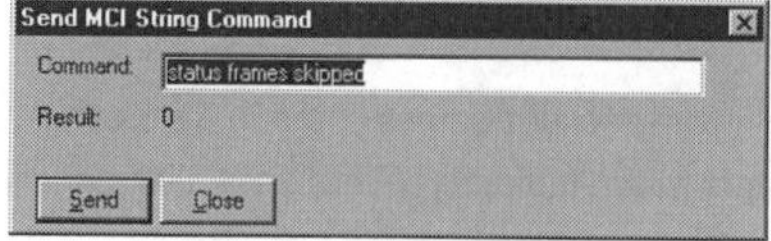

FIG. 4.6
Use the status frames skipped MCI call to see how many frames were dropped during playback.

- **More MCI command tricks**: You can type other commands in the Command dialog box that appears after pressing Ctrl+F5. For example, to pause a video, press Ctrl+F5 and type **pause**. You also can type **stop**, **play**, and **close** in the MCI String Command dialog box.
- **Drag-and-drop video**: Media Player won't look at your CD-ROM drive for video by default, thus forcing you to do lots of pointing and clicking. Take a shortcut by dragging the icon of an AVI file in a Browser or Explorer window onto the Media Player application. You'll now see the mouse cursor with a plus sign. Release the button and the file opens and begins playing right away in the background.
- **Compact video playback**: With a video window open, double-click the Media Player application title bar. You'll get a consolidated video window (without a separate Media Player window) that includes pause buttons, a start/stop button, and a slider bar (see Figure 4.7).

FIG. 4.7
The consolidated video window saves screen space.

- **Change video size**: This tip is particularly useful when using the compact playback window. Expand a video window to full screen by pressing Ctrl+4 and return to original size by pressing Ctrl+1. Ctrl+2 doubles the window size and Ctrl+3 quadruples it.

TROUBLESHOOTING

When I attempt to play an .AVI file, I see a message like, "Video not available, cannot find 'vids:cvid' decompressor." This is an indication that the codec needed to play this movie is not installed. Open the Control Panel and double-click the Add/Remove Programs icon. In the Windows Setup page, click Multimedia and then click Details. Select the Video Compression check box and choose OK. Close the Add/Remove Programs page to install the codecs.

continues

continued

If you want to play a movie compressed with specialized hardware or a third party codec, you'll have to install the appropriate hardware or contact the manufacturer for a specialized decompressor.

When I attempt to play an .AVI file, I see a message like, "MMSYSTEM266: The device could not be loaded. Verify the driver is installed correctly." You need to reinstall several Multimedia files that have been lost or corrupted. Unfortunately, the Add/Remove Programs tool won't capture them if you simply reinstall the Multimedia components. Instead, you need to run the Windows 95 Setup from within Windows 95 by selecting Run from the Start menu and typing **Setup**. When prompted, choose to copy all the Windows files again.

Using ActiveMovie With the release of Internet Browser 3.0, Microsoft introduced ActiveMovie technology to Windows multimedia. ActiveMovie gives Windows the capability to play back all standard video and audio formats, including MPEG and QuickTime. (See "Understanding Video File Formats and Compression," in the next section for more on video file formats.) ActiveMovie also supports ActiveMovie Streaming Format (ASF). This enables audio and video files to begin playing immediately instead of waiting until the entire multimedia has downloaded. Another benefit of ActiveMovie is that the DirectX technology, discussed later in this chapter, is integrated into ActiveMovie, allowing enhanced video playback on systems that have the hardware to take advantage of this technology.

ActiveMovie is available in two ways, depending upon your version of Windows and Internet Explorer. If you want to use Internet Explorer 3, download Internet Explorer 3 from the Microsoft Web site. As you do, you are given the option of also installing ActiveMovie. If your computer has the OEM Service Release 2 version of Windows 95 (OSR2) installed, ActiveMovie is incorporated into Windows.

ActiveMovie is the default player in the OSR2 release of Windows 95 and is the player used to play back videos when you double-click a video file. Even if your computer uses OSR2 you can still open Media Player from the Accessories, Multimedia submenu in the Start menu and use it to play your video files. Note that Media Player will not play back MPEG files.

The advantage to Media Player is that it gives you much more control over your playback, as described in the previous sections. The ActiveMovie component that comes with OSR2 and Internet Explorer 3.0 only has Play, Pause, and Stop controls.

To use ActiveMovie, double-click the video file you want to view in My Computer or Explorer or click Start, Programs, Accessories, Multimedia, ActiveMovie Control. The ActiveMovie control appears on screen with the Open dialog box overlaying it. Select the file you want to view and choose Open. You can pause and stop the video as it plays and view the elapsed time in the box at the bottom of the viewer.

NOTE If you have a newer computer, purchased after the fall of 1996, it probably came with the OSR2 version of Windows installed. If not, there are ways to upgrade to OSR2. To find out more about the OSR2 release of Windows 95 and how to install it on your computer, see "Installing the Windows 95b (OSR2) Service Release," in Chapter 2. ■

ON THE WEB

To download ActiveMovie from the Web, visit the following URL:

http://www.microsoft.com/IE/download

Understanding Video File Formats and Compression

Digital video puts excessive strain on the most powerful PCs. Video files consist of a long string of color images, which are played one after the other in rapid succession to create the illusion of fluid motion. For digital video, 30 frames per second is considered full motion, although many video clips are recorded at 15 or 24 frames per second to ease playback. Also, don't forget the work that goes into synchronizing the audio that goes with each video image.

Some standard file formats and compression technologies were needed to enable digital video. Standards, however, could not overcome the challenge of managing so much data. For that, technologies had to be created that took the pressure off the PC's CPU. In 1992, Video for Windows 1.0 helped establish some key standards. More recently, the PC platform has embraced the elements needed to enhance video.

Understanding Video File Formats To handle this flood of data, video file formats were needed that gave the PC a place to start. Today, there are a variety of video formats. Among those you are most likely to encounter are: Video for Windows (AVI), QuickTime for Windows (MOV), MPEG (MPG), and Motion JPEG (MJG). These video formats are described next.

Audio Visual Interleave—AVI The standard video file format for Windows is called *AVI*, which stands for Audio Visual Interleaved. AVI is the most common Windows video file format and can be played back on virtually any PC running Windows 3.11 or later.

As the name suggests, the audio data and video data are meshed together in the file, allowing systems to synchronize sound and images. Ironically, video playback is slaved to the audio track, ensuring that you always hear all of the audio, even if your system drops video frames. Although you can still make sense of a video that drops even a majority of its frames, the loss of audio data makes it impossible to understand what's being presented. For this reason, even when frames are lost, the soundtrack goes on uninterrupted—except in extreme cases.

AVI video files can be compressed using a variety of schemes, including Intel's Indeo, Radius' Cinepak, and Microsoft's Video 1. Whereas each of these produces a video with distinctive characteristics, the AVI format itself is unchanged. You can play the video, provided that you have the proper decompression driver (Windows 95 ships with all of these).

Apple's QuickTime Video for Windows—MOV Apple made a splash in the video world with its QuickTime technology, which multimedia developers snatched up for use in their titles. When Apple developed QuickTime for Windows, it immediately became a force on the PC because so many multimedia titles used QuickTime as their video format. QuickTime for Windows files generally carry the MOV extension. Although Windows 95 does not ship with QuickTime drivers, a large percentage of multimedia titles use QuickTime video so they will install the drivers during setup.

Like AVI files, QuickTime MOV files can be compressed using a variety of compression schemes, although Radius' Cinepak is generally the most popular. The QuickTime drivers include tools for handling decompression, so as long as you have QuickTime installed, you should be able to play back MOV files (see Figure 4.8).

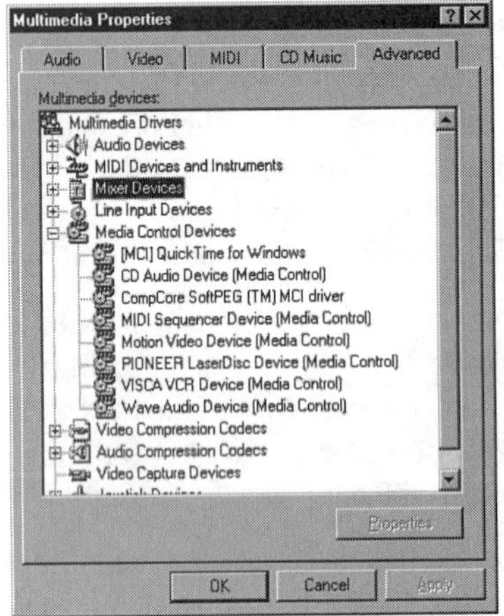

FIG. 4.8
Select the Advanced tab of the Multimedia properties sheet to see if QuickTime for Windows is installed.

NOTE To see if your system is QuickTime-ready, click the Multimedia icon in the Control Panel; then click the Advanced tab, and click the plus sign next to Media Control Devices. You should see an entry called (MCI) QuickTime for Windows. If you don't, you need to install QuickTime before MOV files can be played. ■

The Next Big Thing in Video—MPEG MPEG video is being hyped as the next big thing in multimedia. Unlike Video for Windows and QuickTime for Windows, MPEG is both a file format and a codec scheme. MPEG videos are crunched down to a very small size using the MPEG compression scheme, which does all sorts of mathematics and interframe comparisons. The result is video of much higher visual quality than other schemes, yet uses a tiny 150 kilobits per second (kb/sec) of data—low enough to run off a single-speed CD-ROM drive. But MPEG is very complex, and high-end PCs have only recently reached the level where they can play back MPEG video without expensive add-in cards.

NOTE As with QuickTime, you can check the Advanced page of the Multimedia properties sheet for MPEG drivers. Click the plus sign next to Media Control Devices and look for an entry that refers to MPEG. ■

To get MPEG playback capability, you need one of several MPEG software players. Xing, Mediamatics, and CompCore all sell MPEG player software that you can purchase. In addition, many graphics boards come with MPEG player software as part of their bundle. Those with Pentium-75 or slower machines should buy a dedicated MPEG add-in board to get acceptable MPEG performance.

OSR 2

NOTE If you have the OEM Service Release 2 (OSR2) version of Windows installed on your system, you now have MPEG playback capability with the new ActiveMovie application. OSR2 comes with several MPEG codecs. ■

Understanding Video Compression Schemes (codecs) The only way digital video can be played on a PC is to reduce the amount of data required to store and move it. Video compression/decompression algorithms, referred to as *codecs*, do just that, reducing streams of full color images into compact code. Your system's CPU must decode the compressed video before it can be displayed to screen, a time-consuming task that often results in dropped frames.

NOTE Don't confuse video codecs with video file formats. A file format like AVI or MOV can often be compressed using a number of codecs. For example, AVI files can be compressed using Indeo, Cinepak, Video1, and TrueMotion codecs, just to name a few. ■

Unlike file compression utilities like PKZip or Stacker, video compression schemes actually throw out a good deal of image data to achieve compact file sizes. For this reason, video codecs are referred to as "lossy," whereas file compressors are referred to as "lossless."

NOTE Whereas lossless compression schemes like PKZip achieve compression ratios of about 2:1, lossy video compression schemes can shrink files sizes by 100 times or more, for ratios of 100:1. ■

Video codecs save a great deal of space by discarding redundant data. For example, MPEG only saves changes that occur between video frames instead of storing all the data in every single frame. In addition, codecs can discard color, brightness, and other visual data because much of the detail is not actually visible to the human eye. However, most software codecs, such as Indeo and Cinepak, must throw out a great deal of visual information to achieve data rates of about 300 Kbps. The result is grainy video and visual artifacts such as banding and color distortion.

Before your system can decompress a video file, you need to have a driver installed that lets the system know how to do it. To see if you have drivers installed to handle, for example, Cinepak video, go back to the Multimedia properties sheet in Control Panel's Multimedia icon. Click the Advanced tab and then click the plus (+) sign next to Video Compression Codecs. You'll see a list of installed codecs (see Figure 4.9).

Among the most common video codecs are:

- Indeo
- Cinepak
- Video 1
- RLE
- TrueMotion
- MPEG
- Motion JPEG

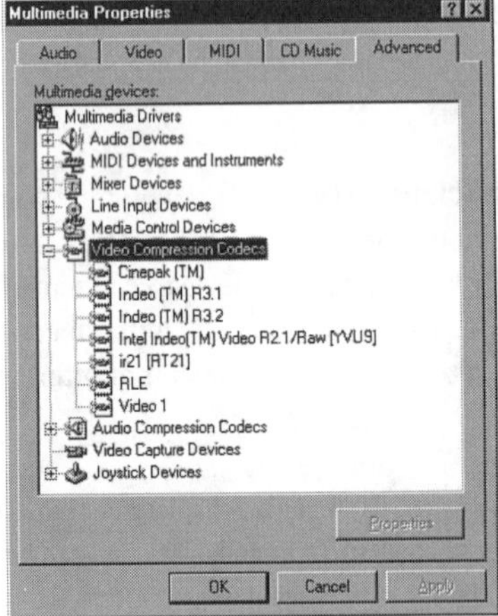

FIG. 4.9
Windows 95 comes standard with several codecs, although you can install more.

Intel Indeo 3.2 Intel's Indeo codec was among the first on the PC and is among the most prevalent. Indeo 3.2 is included with Windows 95, making it a universal playback compression scheme. To play an Indeo-compressed AVI file, you need to open the file from Media Player. Media Player automatically detects the codec used to compress the file and invokes the Indeo driver to decode it. Indeo is generally favored for video clips that contain less motion and activity that are used for clips such as interviews and speeches.

Radius Cinepak 8.02 Cinepak was developed by Radius and is also bundled with Windows 95. The Cinepak codec is popular with title vendors because it is able to compress high action sequences without too much loss of visual quality and CPU effort. However, the latest release of Indeo (3.2) has largely closed the performance gap. Cinepak-compressed files can be found in both Video for Windows and QuickTime for Windows files.

Microsoft Video 1 Microsoft Video 1 was included in the first Video for Windows release in 1992, but it lacks the sophistication to handle rich, full-color video. Although the Video 1 codec works well for animation and other simple video compression tasks, it is limited to 8-bit color and lacks interframe compression.

MPEG The original release of Windows 95 did not include support for MPEG. However, the OSR2 release of Windows does include MPEG codecs and ActiveMovie, a video player that is capable of playing back MPEG files. Users of the original version of Windows 95 can get MPEG playback by purchasing a separate playback utility from companies like Xing, CompCore, and Mediamatics, or they can download ActiveMovie from Microsoft's Web site.

Many graphics boards come bundled with MPEG playback software. Check your board's software for MPEG video drivers.

OSR 2

NOTE If your system has the Windows 95 OEM Service Release 2 (OSR2) version of Windows installed, the new ActiveMovie technology, which was released with Internet Browser 3.0, is now incorporated into Windows. You can use ActiveMovie to play back all the standard video and audio formats, including MPEG. ActiveMovie is the default multimedia in OSR2 instead of Media Player. You can also download ActiveMovie as a separate component. See "Using ActiveMovie," earlier in this chapter, for more information on ActiveMovie.

The secret to MPEG is its complex interframe compression, where only changes between frames are stored in the MPEG video file. The problem is that this scheme requires a lot of processing horsepower, which is why it takes a Pentium-90 PC (or better) to handle MPEG adequately in software. Older systems can play back MPEG video using an add-in card, such as the RealMagic Rave or Number Nine MPEG-Plus, to handle the decompression.

The Editor's Choice—Motion JPEG Motion JPEG, like MPEG, is both a file format and a codec. Actually, Motion JPEG is an outgrowth of the JPEG (Joint Photographic Experts Group) file format, which is a popular still-image compression scheme for files posted on the Internet. Motion JPEG's main appeal is to video artists and editors because every frame is compressed individually. By contrast, MPEG compression stores only the changes that occur between frames of video—so if you want to go back and edit a frame, it's likely that some visual data is missing.

Video capture boards such as the Reveal VideoStudio Pro and miroVideo DC-20 capture to Motion JPEG format. Files compressed to Motion JPEG format often look better than QuickTime or Video for Windows clips but require more CPU and greater data bandwidth. The files, however, can be recompressed to AVI or MOV, although video quality will likely degrade.

The Future of Codecs: MPEG-2 New codecs are constantly being developed and updated to meet the needs of digital video. MPEG-1, for example, has a big brother by the name of MPEG-2, which is a broadcast-quality compression scheme used with DSS services such as DirecTV. MPEG-2 excels where MPEG-1 breaks down—for instance, in the display of high action sequences where the efficiencies of interframe compression are lost. But MPEG-2 requires 10 times the bandwidth of MPEG-1—as much as 1.5Mbps—meaning that current CD-ROM drives are unable to keep up. In addition, MPEG-2's large file sizes mean that CD-ROM discs could only hold scant minutes of MPEG-2 video. For this reason, MPEG-2 is likely to remain a consumer video codec until PC users adopt super-density compact discs with several gigabytes of storage capacity.

The Future of Codecs: Indeo Video Interactive Perhaps more relevant is Intel's Indeo Video Interactive, also known as Indeo 4.0. This intriguing codec breaks with the past by adopting a wavelet-based compression scheme that reduces access times and visual artifacts. Intel has claimed—and some independent CD-ROM title developers have confirmed—that Indeo 4.0 can challenge MPEG video for visual quality. However, like MPEG, Indeo 4.0 needs a Pentium CPU to handle the complex decompression. It's also unclear if Indeo 4.0 can actually match MPEG quality at the low 150 Kbps data rate that MPEG maintains.

Indeo 4.0 provides powerful streaming and branching technologies that enable video to be used in interactive games. For example, multiple video streams can be played on a single display—providing, say, a simultaneous rear view video while the player looks forward. The format also enables much faster access so video can be employed in fast action games without annoying delays. These features could turn Indeo 4.0 into *the* codec for Windows 95.

Finally, Indeo 4.0 includes powerful chromakey and overlay support. For example, Indeo 4.0 videos do not have to be constrained to a video window. Instead, video images can float on the Windows desktop and interact with other Windows elements. These features provide exciting new opportunities for hobbyists and publishers alike.

Windows Video Primer: DirectVideo and Other Nifty Things in Windows 95

To lessen the load, video files are compressed down to smaller sizes to conserve disc space, ease bus traffic, and enable higher frame rates. In fact, without compression, video playback would be impossible on even the most powerful PCs. Compression has its own costs because the CPU must take time to decode the encoded video stream.

There's more to playing digital video than simply decompression. The CPU also must handle a variety of other tasks to turn an encoded pile of bits into a smooth train of images that make video:

- **Decompression**: The encoded video file is reassembled by the CPU using the appropriate driver, such as an Indeo, Cinepak, or MPEG decoder. Some compression/ decompression schemes require a great deal of computing power but yield better looking images at lower data rates.
- **Color space conversion**: To save disc space, the color data in video files is usually saved using a compact format called YUV, which is optimized to the sensitivities of the human eye. This YUV color data must be converted to the standard RGB (Red, Green, Blue) format recognized by graphics cards and monitors. Color space conversion can take up to 30 percent of the CPU processing time during video playback.

NOTE YUV represents luminance, hue, and saturation and is a method for composing color video signals that was originally applied to television broadcasting. The main advantage of YUV color is that it is much more compact than the RGB format used by computers.

- **Image scaling**: This step occurs when the user changes the size of the video window from its original size. Often, 320×240 pixel videos are displayed at full screen to ease viewing. However, the CPU must calculate and create all the new pixels that appear in the image, which further strains the system. In addition, the image that results appears blocky and pixelated because the CPU simply replicates pixels to fill in the larger window.

Improved Video Performance The big problem with video is that it's, well, *big*. Really big. Consider: A modest video saved at 320×240 pixels and 15 frames per second would push 3M of data per second through your system if played uncompressed. Even with compression, video floods your system with data, taxing your CD-ROM drive, clogging the system bus, and pushing your processor to the limit. When these demands outstrip your PC, Windows has no choice but to drop frames to keep up.

A number of recent performance enhancements make it possible for Windows 95 to play back 320×240 video files at 30 frames per second. Even better, these videos can be stretched up to 640×480 pixels and beyond, and still enjoy smooth motion, provided you have the right drivers and multimedia hardware installed. Among the enhancements are:

- **DirectDraw**. DirectDraw allows accelerated access to the memory on your graphics card, key for pushing 30 frames of video each second. In essence, DirectDraw is a graphics shortcut that lets video software talk directly to your graphics hardware, eliminating Windows' slow graphics engine. DirectDraw also provides pixel scaling and color-space conversion features.
- **DirectVideo**. The second half of Microsoft's video-improvement plan, DirectVideo opens the door to hardware-accelerated video under Windows 95. DirectVideo lets inexpensive graphics hardware take over key video playback tasks from the CPU by providing an interface into DirectDraw.

NOTE Like other DirectX components, DirectDraw and DirectVideo both ship separately from the Windows 95 operating system. Most users will get DirectDraw and DirectVideo when they install software that uses DirectX technology, such as games or titles.

With the OEM Service Release 2 version of Windows 95 (OSR2), the DirectX technology is incorporated directly into Windows 95.

- **CDFS**. The CD File System improves throughput from the CD-ROM by providing an optimized, 32-bit, protected-mode file system. The result is improved performance of CD-ROM drives in Windows 95, which reduces dropped frames. CDFS also takes some of the burden off the system CPU, allowing it more time to decompress video files (see Figure 4.10).
- **Multitasking**. Windows 95's preemptive multitasking minimizes pauses and delays during video playback. These breaks in the continuity can ruin the viewing experience. Video can continue to play even while other processes, such as display of separate graphics, run in the background.

Enhanced CD-ROM and file management benefit all aspects of your computer's performance, but DirectDraw and DirectVideo are aimed squarely at improving multimedia and video. The good news is that you don't need to throw out your existing graphics hardware to play games and software using Direct X technologies. However, you will enjoy much better video playback if your graphics card includes the proper drivers and video-intelligent hardware.

DirectVideo works by first checking the graphics card and finding out what video-accelerating features, if any, are supported in the hardware. Windows then knows to send key tasks, like color space conversion and pixel scaling, straight to the graphics card, if it is properly configured. If the card lacks enhanced video support, all the video-handling tasks are sent straight to the system CPU.

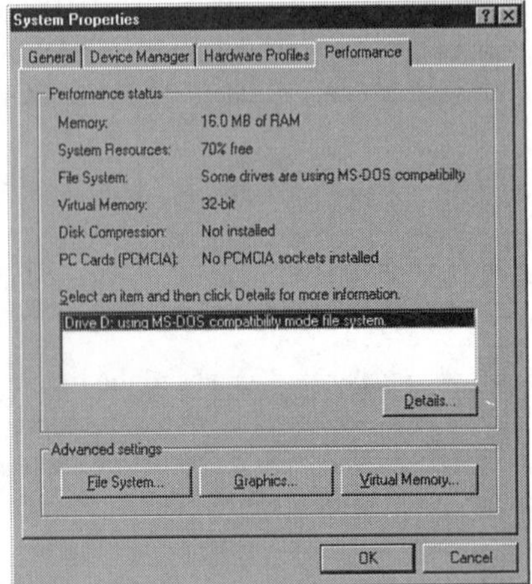

FIG. 4.10
Windows 95 may not recognize your CD-ROM drive and use slower compatibility-mode drivers. Check the Performance page of the System properties sheet to see if your CD-ROM drive is not fully optimized.

NOTE The newest graphics hardware does little good without the proper drivers. Otherwise, Windows 95 sends all the video tasks straight to the system CPU, even if you have a video-accelerating card. In fact, Windows 95 can fail to install the specific driver you need. Check the installed driver from the Display properties sheet by clicking the Change Display Type button. ■

Older graphic boards lack video enhancing hardware; you won't see much improvement in video performance even with DirectVideo installed. However, most mid-range graphic boards sold since the release of Windows 95 are video-savvy. Of course, you'll need DirectDraw and DirectVideo drivers to let Windows 95 know that the multimedia features are there. Contact your graphics card vendor and make sure you have the latest DirectVideo-enabled drivers.

CAUTION

If you only have 16-bit drivers for multimedia graphics boards, such as the Jazz Jakarta or miroVideo 20TD, Windows 95 will probably be unable to provide the full functionality that these boards had under Windows 3.1. Contact the board's vendor to get 32-bit drivers.

New Developments in Windows 95 Video Windows 95 delivers many improvements to desktop video playback, but Microsoft has announced a limited road map of features, functions, and new video types that should enhance the quality of CD-ROM games and titles. This section gives you a sneak peek at what to expect next.

Among the key technologies promised by Microsoft are:

- Surround Video
- WinToon

Surround Video Microsoft's Surround Video, a scheme similar to Apple's QuickTime VR, lets developers build 360-degree, photo-realistic scenes. Users will be able to interact with on-screen objects, images, and videos as they traverse immersive scenes.

Surround Video scenes consist of a series of photographs stitched together into a 360-degree panorama, allowing users to turn and view an entire scene. Games can use Surround Video to put photo-realistic backgrounds behind interactive elements. Surround Video is actually even better suited for creating virtual tours built from actual photos.

For users, Surround Video is something that comes as part of the games and other software they purchase.

Installing and Configuring Sound Options

Just as digital video has improved over the last three years, PC audio has come a long way. The original Sound Blaster board delivered audio quality about on par with that of a dashboard AM option. Today, sound boards have evolved to handle CD-quality sound, reproduce realistic MIDI scores, and even create compelling 3-D audio for games and titles. Most importantly, the majority of PCs sold now include installed sound boards.

In the past, intractable audio conflicts and difficult installations made PC-based audio difficult to manage. Windows 95 has improved the situation, providing a set of standard interfaces and applications that make working with audio easier than before. In addition, Windows 95 reduces the amount of CPU processing needed to play back audio, which enhances game play.

In this section, you will be introduced to some basic concepts about audio files. You will also learn how to install and configure a sound board and how to use the sound tools that come with Windows 95.

MIDI and WAV Sound Files

Your system has the capability to utilize two types of audio files:

- Digital audio (WAV files)
- MIDI (musical instrument digital interface)

Windows 95 includes built-in support for both MIDI and WAV waveform audio. However, you need to install an additional sound device, such as an add-on board, before you can realize these capabilities.

WAV, or sound wave, files take up a great deal of disk storage space compared to MIDI files because WAV files record the entire sound to your hard disk. Although WAV files take up more disk space than MIDI files, the sound is generally better. MIDI doesn't save the entire sound but keeps a record of how the sound is played. The MIDI file then consults the "instructions" when you want to play the sound back and attempts to reproduce that original sound as best it can—sometimes not very successfully if you are using a less expensive 8-bit sound card.

You can use MIDI files to great effect when integrated into a computer-based presentation, for example. On the other hand, you can attach simple WAV files to electronic-mail for distribution to a third party on a network.

MIDI uses either FM synthesis or wave table synthesis to reproduce the required sound. FM synthesis uses artificial sounds that are similar to the required sound, and wave table synthesis uses actual stored samples of sounds from real instruments.

With sampled sound, a small example of the instrument's sound is stored. When sound from that type of instrument needs to be reproduced, the sample is retrieved and it undergoes various changes, such as pitch variation, in order to reproduce a relatively accurate rendition.

Because a MIDI file essentially contains just the instructions on how to play a specific sound, the method of reproducing that sound depends on the quality of the sound board that will be playing it. When it comes to sound boards, what you pay for is what you get. A low-cost, 8-bit board is going to give you a low-quality sound reproduction. On the other hand, if you invest in a high-end, 16-bit board with extensive wave table synthesis capabilities and a good set of speakers, you are probably going to get great sound reproduction.

NOTE Many new PCs are billed as "multimedia-ready" with built-in CD-ROM and sound board capabilities, but these PCs rarely contain high-end sound cards. What you often get is average-quality sound, which is adequate for the average user. If you want a new PC capable of playing back recording-quality sound, buy a PC with a built-in CD-ROM drive and then add a high-end sound board of your choice. ■

Recording sound to your hard drive takes a great deal of disk space. Therefore, Windows 95 offers two groups of sound-compression technologies, or codecs (coders/decoders). The first technique enables the compression of voice data, such as TrueSpeech. The second method enables you to compress a type of high-quality musical sound. These capabilities, for example, allow for the use of voice compression during recording, which lets the resulting sound file be compressed in real-time, that is, as it is recorded.

Another sound capability, called *polymessage MIDI support*, enables Windows 95 to handle multiple MIDI instructions at the same time. The result is that less processor resources are required, which frees up the CPU for other operations.

Sound Blaster and Windows

Creative Labs' Sound Blaster family of add-on audio boards has become something of an industry standard among multimedia PCs. If you don't have a Sound Blaster board installed, you probably have one that is Sound Blaster-compatible.

CAUTION

Boards that are advertised as Sound Blaster-compatible are not always true to their claim. The result can be distorted or inadequate sound reproduction. However, most games or CDs that fall under the multimedia label probably support Sound Blaster. Check the packaging thoroughly and if the retail outlet is unable to verify compatibility, don't be afraid to contact the manufacturer directly.

Because of Sound Blaster's popularity, even Windows 95 comes with a compatible driver for supporting Sound Blaster programs. But if you don't want Sound Blaster, Windows 95 includes a less popular alternative in the form of the Microsoft Windows Sound System. Windows 95's built-in audio supports capabilities required for Microsoft's own sound specifications.

Even if you use MS Windows Sound System, you are still going to need an audio board, or at least a "multimedia-ready" PC with enhanced sound capabilities and speakers, for listening to and recording CD-quality sound. The average built-in PC speakers are totally inadequate for the task.

Configuration of Sound Options

Any number of things can lead to sound features not working properly. Many elements need to be configured properly in relation to one another. Any time one element doesn't function properly (especially with respect to the next step in the sound playing or recording process), audio problems are likely to result. This section describes how proper configuration can help you avoid sound problems.

Many times the problems are the result of hardware conflicts or wrong settings for specific components, such as IRQs or DMA channels. Hardware conflicts occur when two hardware devices want to use the same system resources. Fortunately, Windows 95 includes a very useful feature called the *Device Manager*, which keeps a centralized graphical registry of all system resources as they relate to the different PC components. As a result, you can more easily locate hardware problems in Windows 95 than you could in the previous DOS/Windows combination.

Sound problems are often the result of an error in installing a new sound device and are likely caused by wrongly assigned resources. The next section discusses the installation of a sound board using Windows 95's extremely useful Add New Hardware Wizard, which reduces the possibility of conflicts.

TROUBLESHOOTING

I get no sound at all, and when I do it is distorted. Common settings problems, such as an IRQ conflict or a wrong DMA channel selected, can result in no sound coming out at all. A wrong DMA driver setting may also result in distorted WAV file playback.

Distorted sound can also result from using sound files stored on a compressed disk. If the files with distorted sounds are located on a compressed disk, try playing them from a disk that is not compressed, if possible, and see if that makes a difference. If it does, you may want to decompress your disk if you are working a lot with sound files.

To define the hardware settings, you need to configure groups of pins, called *jumpers*, on the audio board. Jumpers are essential to the smooth running of the audio board and you must configure them according to available settings as defined by Windows 95 before installing the board. Jumper configuration can vary depending on the board being installed. As a result, a thorough reading of the documentation accompanying your new board is a must.

Adding a Sound Board

The first step in configuring sound is to install a suitable audio board. Thankfully, Windows 95 simplifies the installation of sound cards by recommending a hardware configuration for you via the Add New Hardware Wizard.

Windows 95 has made installation easier by implementing the Plug and Play standard and by providing an Add New Hardware Wizard. Microsoft designed its new Plug and Play standard to make it easier to add hardware components to existing PCs. If you are installing a sound card that conforms to the Plug and Play standard, it may be as simple as installing the card and turning on your computer. Windows should recognize the device and install its device drivers.

If you are installing a legacy sound card that is not Plug and Play, the Add New Hardware Wizard will still simplify the process by recommending a hardware configuration that does not conflict with devices already installed in your computer. The wizard takes you through the installation of a hardware device step by step.

CAUTION

You might want to use the sound board's own installation program instead, because the wizard can run into problems identifying the correct interrupts for some components.

As an example of the process as it relates to sound devices, this section reviews the installation of a Sound Blaster board. In this case, the Sound Blaster 16 AWE-32, using the Add New Hardware Wizard.

You can access the Add New Hardware Wizard through the Control Panel feature or by choosing "sound cards, setting up" from the Help Topics Index page. This example takes you through the Control Panel option.

CAUTION

With virtually all sound boards, installation problems may occur when you try to install enhanced utilities that come with the board, *after* you have installed the component using Windows 95's Add New Hardware Wizard. This is because hardly any option allows you to install the utilities separately from the drivers. However, this may be necessary because Windows 95 will have already installed the board without including the separate software utilities.

▶ **See** "Installing Legacy CD-ROM Drives," **p. 125**

CAUTION

Some cards come with CD controllers already built in. When this happens, you need to install it in Windows 95 and then configure the CD portion at the same time you install the sound card.

1. Don't install the card itself until the Add New Hardware Wizard has recommended specific resource settings.
2. Open the Start menu; then choose Settings, Control Panel.
3. Double-click the Add New Hardware icon. The Add New Hardware Wizard appears (see Figure 4.11).

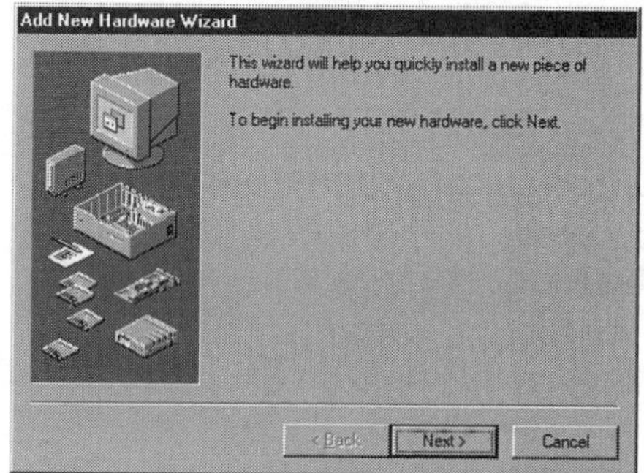

FIG. 4.11 The Add New Hardware Wizard eases the pain of adding hardware components by taking you through the installation step by step.

4. Click Next. The wizard then asks you whether you want Windows 95 to search for new hardware (see Figure 4.12).

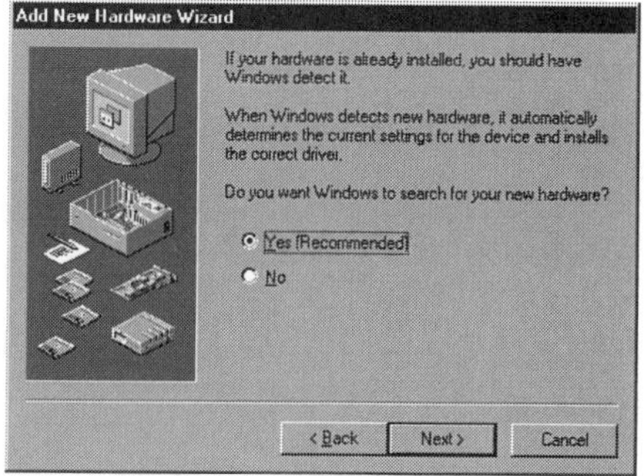

FIG. 4.12 You can choose to have Windows 95 automatically search for new hardware.

5. At this point, select the No option button as, in this case, we are only going through the steps to install sound devices.
6. Click Next. The Hardware Types list appears (see Figure 4.13).
7. Select the type of hardware device you want to add from the wizard's Hardware Type list box. In this case, select Sound, Video and Game Controllers, and then click Next. The hardware Manufacturers and Models lists appear for the device you selected (see Figure 4.14).
8. Click the sound board manufacturer's name in the left window. A list of products that Windows 95 is familiar with appears in the right window.
9. Select the board you want to add. In this case, Creative Labs Sound Blaster 16 or AWE-32.

You may need to install a driver from a floppy disk. If that is the case, you need to take a couple of extra steps. Don't click Next yet, but continue with step 10. If you don't need to install a driver from a floppy disk, go to step 13.

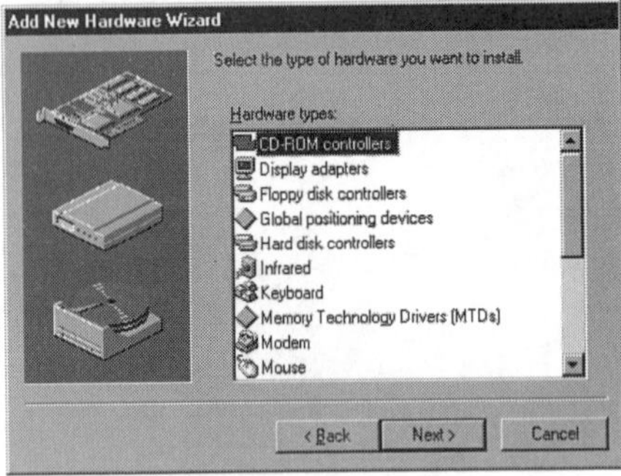

FIG. 4.13 Select the type of hardware you want to install from the wizard's Hardware Type list.

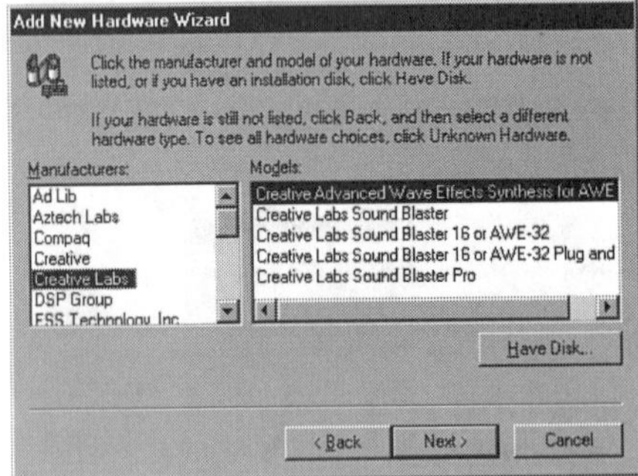

FIG. 4.14 Select the manufacturer and hardware model you want to add from these lists.

10. From the Add New Hardware Wizard dialog box, click Have Disk. The Install From Disk dialog box appears (see Figure 4.15).

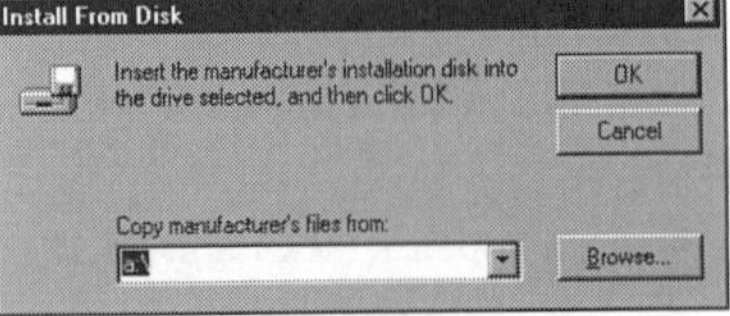

FIG. 4.15 You need to insert the installation disk into the selected drive to install a new device driver from a floppy disk.

11. Specify the directory and disk where the manufacturer's files should be copied from.
12. Click OK. The Install From Disk dialog box disappears and you are back to the Add New Hardware Wizard.
13. Now you can click Next. The wizard window changes to display the settings it wants you to use for the new board (see Figure 4.16). This list of settings is important; it is based on available settings as defined in the Windows 95 Device Manager Registry.

FIG. 4.16
The Add New Hardware Wizard gives you the settings to use for your new board based on what settings are available.

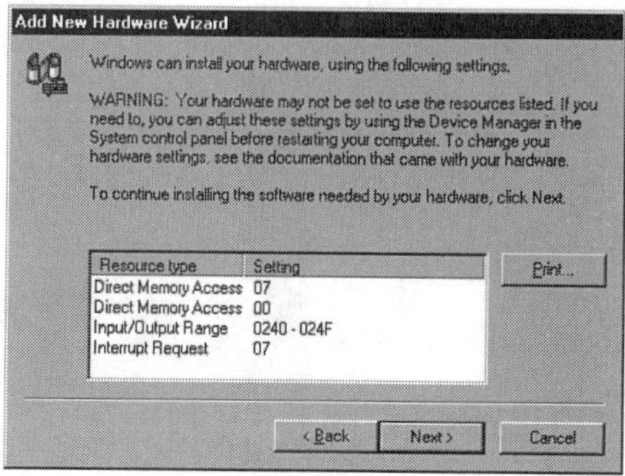

14. Write down these settings or print them out. The new board should have these settings before you install it.
15. Insert the floppy disks containing the drivers that the wizard requests.
16. Shut down your PC.
17. Configure the new sound card according to the settings given during the wizard process. See the documentation that comes with your sound board on how to make changes to I/O configuration settings, as well as IRQ and DMA changes.
18. Install the sound card, using instructions that came with the card.

NOTE You also can install the sound card prior to running the Add New Hardware Wizard and then choose Yes to the question, "Do you want Windows to search for your new hardware?" However, this method is less reliable when installing legacy devices. ■

Adding or Changing Hardware Drivers Anytime you add a component or peripheral to your PC, you need to make sure a software driver is also installed. The driver acts as a liaison between the computer operating system and the device so that they can communicate. You may need to change drivers if an updated one becomes available. With Windows 95, you can add or change hardware device drivers using Device Manager, which is the centralized registry of system properties and configurations. Follow these steps to update a sound card driver:

1. Open the Start menu; then choose Settings, Control Panel.
2. Open the System control item in the list box.
3. When the System properties sheet appears, click the Device Manager tab (see Figure 4.17).
4. Click the plus sign next to Sound, Video and Game Controllers.
5. Double-click the specific hardware device you are interested in, in this case, your sound card.

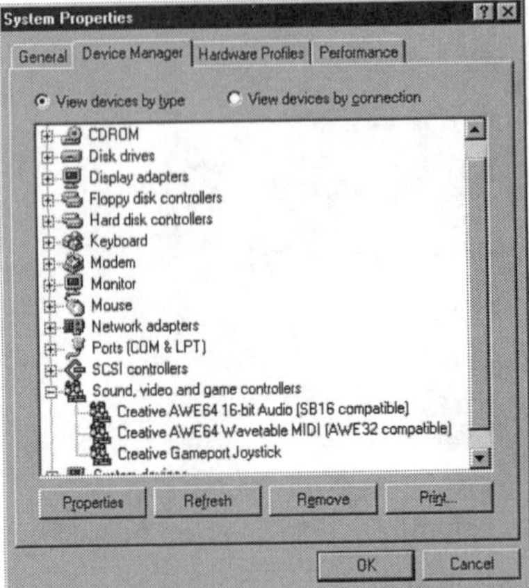

FIG. 4.17
Device Manager enables you to change driver settings.

6. In the properties sheet that appears, click the Driver tab (see Figure 4.18).

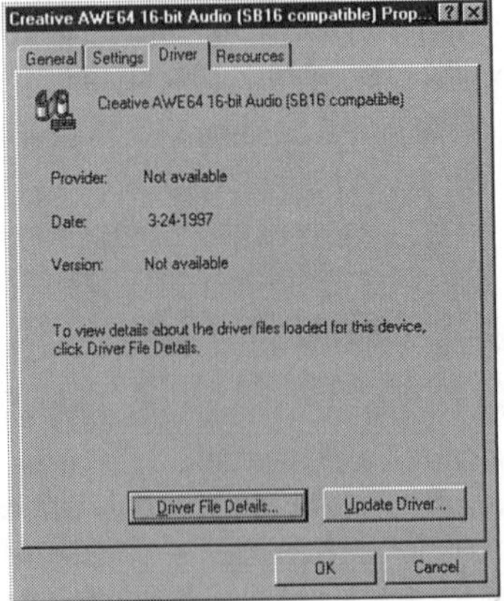

FIG. 4.18
The Driver page for your sound card (in this case, Sound Blaster AWE32) enables you to change drivers.

7. Click Change Driver, and the Select Device dialog box appears. A list details the models compatible with your hardware. Make sure the Show Compatible Devices option is selected. If the hardware model you want to set up is not on the list, you should select the Show All Devices option (use this category with caution, as it includes drivers that are, by definition, incompatible with your hardware). The list changes to show all such devices.
8. Click the device you want to set up, and then click OK.

   The Select Device dialog box disappears, leaving the Driver page showing the driver files and their correct directory path.
9. Click OK to return to the Device Manager device type list.
10. Click OK to exit from System Properties.

If you have the OSR2 version of Windows, the Driver tab appears as shown in Figure 4.19, and the procedure for installing a different driver differs from the steps just outlined.

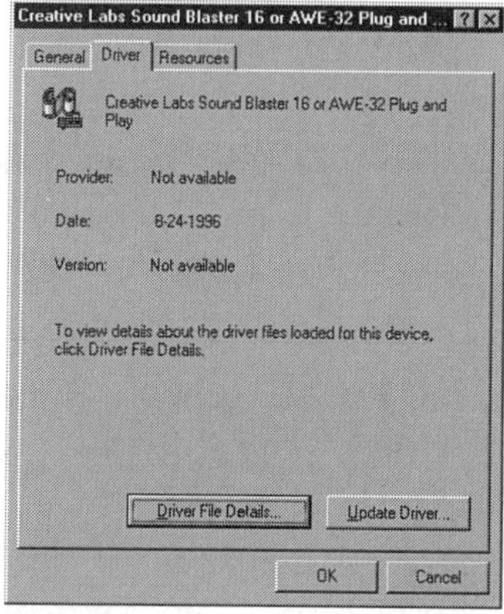

FIG. 4.19
The Driver page as it appears in the OSR2 version of Windows 95.

To install a new driver in OSR2, follow these steps:

1. Click the Update Driver tab to display the Update Device Driver Wizard dialog box shown in Figure 4.20.

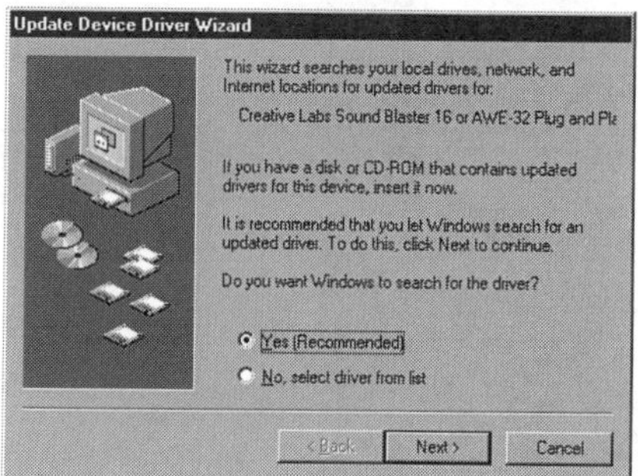

FIG. 4.20
Use the Update Device Driver Wizard to search for and install updated drivers.

2. Leave the Yes option selected to have Windows search for an updated driver. Click Next. Click Finish when Windows 95 finds the driver. If an updated driver is not found, click Other Locations in the Update Device Driver Wizard and change to the location where the updated driver is located.

   or

   Select the No option and click Next to select the driver from a list. Select the correct items from the Manufacturer and Models lists and click Finish.

You will be prompted to insert the disk or CD-ROM on which the updated driver is located, if you haven't done this already. The wizard will search for the driver and install it on your computer. Select Yes when you are prompted to restart the computer to complete the setup.

TROUBLESHOOTING

I get a hissing during playback of sound files. If you hear a hissing during the playback of a sound file, the file may be recording in 8 bits and playing back in 16 bits. The 16-bit board doesn't realize that the 8-bit file isn't the same high quality as a 16-bit file, so playing the file with expectations of higher sound quality emphasizes the lower detail.

Setting Up a MIDI Instrument One of the added features of a relatively high-quality sound board is the capability to plug a MIDI instrument into a MIDI port and play sampled sound. Here is a quick overview of setting up a MIDI instrument:

1. Plug the instrument into the sound card's MIDI port.
2. Open the Start menu; then choose Settings, Control Panel.
3. Double-click the Multimedia icon.
4. In the Multimedia properties sheet that appears, click the MIDI tab (see Figure 4.21).

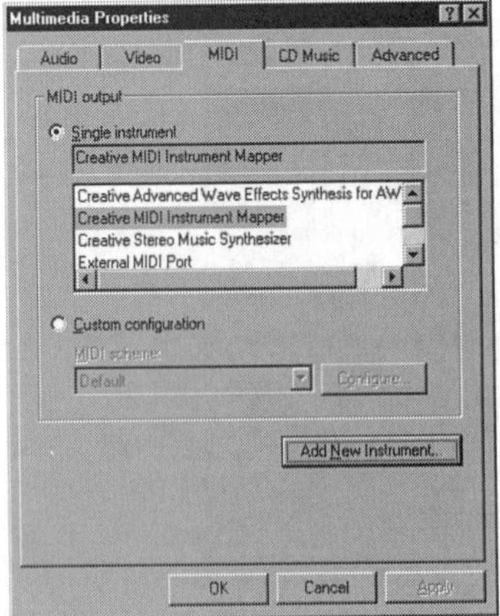

FIG. 4.21
Configure your new MIDI instrument using the Multimedia properties sheet.

5. Click Add New Instrument.
6. Follow the on-screen instructions to install the instrument.
7. Choose Single Instrument on the MIDI page.
8. Select the instrument you just installed and click OK. Your new MIDI instrument is now installed.

Moving a MIDI Instrument to Another Sound Board You can move MIDI instruments between sound boards using these steps:

1. Open the Start menu; choose Settings, Control Panel.
2. Double-click the Multimedia icon.
3. On the Multimedia properties sheet, click the Advanced tab (see Figure 4.22).

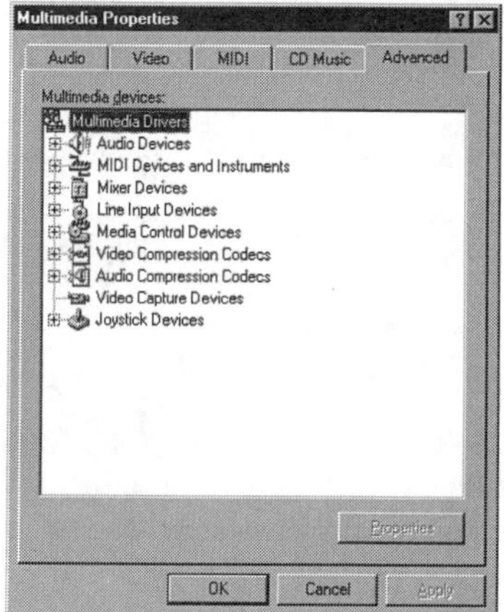

FIG. 4.22 The Advanced page in the Multimedia properties sheet is where you specify the MIDI instrument you want to move.

4. Click the plus sign next to MIDI Devices and Instruments. A sublist of devices appears under MIDI Devices and Instruments.
5. From the resulting list (see Figure 4.23), click the plus sign next to the sound board your MIDI instrument was connected to.

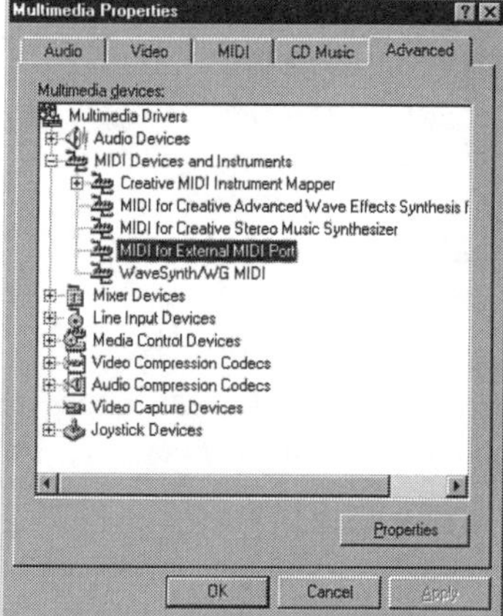

FIG. 4.23 Clicking the plus sign next to MIDI Devices and Instruments brings up a list of devices.

6. Click the instrument you want to move, and then click Properties.
7. Click the Detail tab.

8. From the MIDI Port list, select the name of the sound board to which you want to connect the instrument.
9. Connect your MIDI instrument into the new sound board you just specified, using the appropriate port, according to the instructions that come with your sound board.

Windows 95 Sound Accessories

Windows 95 has some useful sound accessories related to the recording and playing of sound, either from audio CDs or specially recorded files.

CD Player enables you to play audio CDs from your CD drive while you are working in another application. CD Player offers many of the controls found in stand-alone audio CD players and looks and operates much the same way. In addition, CD Player enables you to edit your play list for each CD, and the program remembers that list each time the disc is inserted.

Sound Recorder is a very rudimentary digital recording system. This feature enables you to make small, recorded files that you can edit and mix into other sound files (although these capabilities are somewhat limited).

Using CD Player CD Player enables you to play audio CDs in the background while you are working in another application. To access CD Player follow these steps:

1. Open the Start menu; then choose Programs, Accessories.
2. Choose Multimedia and then choose CD Player.

If you have used a stand-alone audio CD player, the controls on CD Player should be quite familiar (see Figure 4.24).

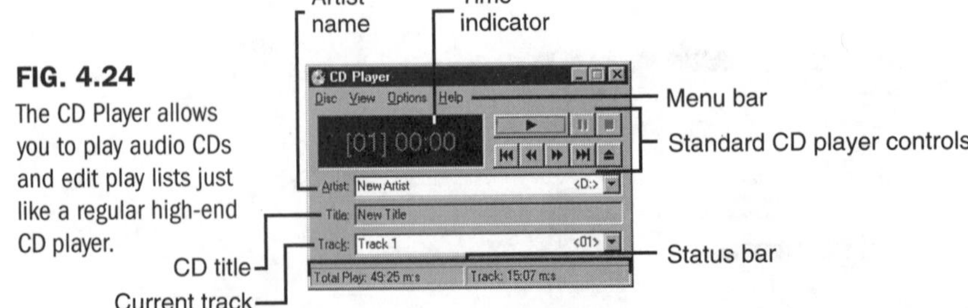

FIG. 4.24
The CD Player allows you to play audio CDs and edit play lists just like a regular high-end CD player.

CD Player includes a number of advanced functions that you access from the menu bar, such as Random Order, Continuous Play, and the ability to edit your play list.

The main CD Player screen offers four menus: Disc, View, Options, and Help. The Disc menu offers two options:

- Edit Play List enables you to edit your personal play list (see Figure 4.25).
- Exit closes the CD Player window and turns off the audio CD at the same time.

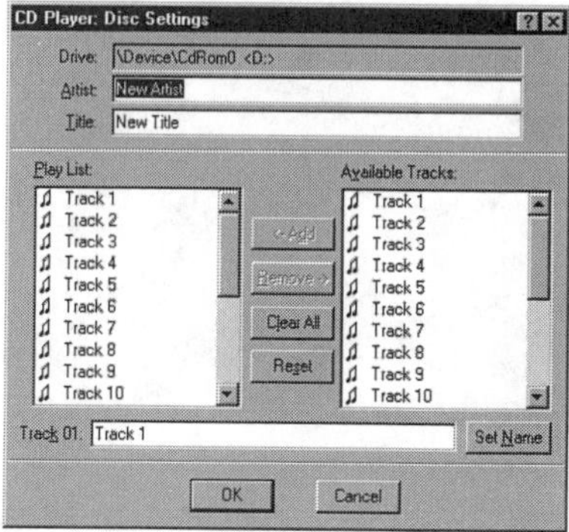

FIG. 4.25
You can customize each CD's play list by choosing the Edit Play List option from the Disc menu.

The View menu offers three sets of options. The first enables you to customize the general CD Player screen:

- Toolbar enables you to display or remove the toolbar. There are seven icons on the toolbar:
  - Edit Play List enables you to edit your play list.
  - Track Time Elapsed tracks the time elapsed since the start of the track.
  - Track Time Remaining lets you know how much time is remaining on the track.
  - Disc Time Remaining shows you how much time is left on the audio CD currently playing.
  - Random Track Order plays the track in random order.
  - Continuous Play starts the CD over again after the last track has played.
  - Intro Play plays the beginning 10 seconds of each track before moving to the next one.
- Disc/Track Info enables you to display or remove the CD disc and track information at the bottom of the general CD Player screen.
- Status Bar enables you to display or remove the status bar at the bottom of the window.

The second set of options on the View menu enable you to change the time displayed in the time indicator window:

- Track Time Elapsed shows how much time has elapsed on the current track.
- Track Time Remaining shows how much time is left on the current track.
- Disc Time Remaining shows how much time is left on the current CD.

The third set on the View menu has a single option:

- Volume Control enables you to set the control levels for volume, wave, and MIDI (see Figure 4.26).

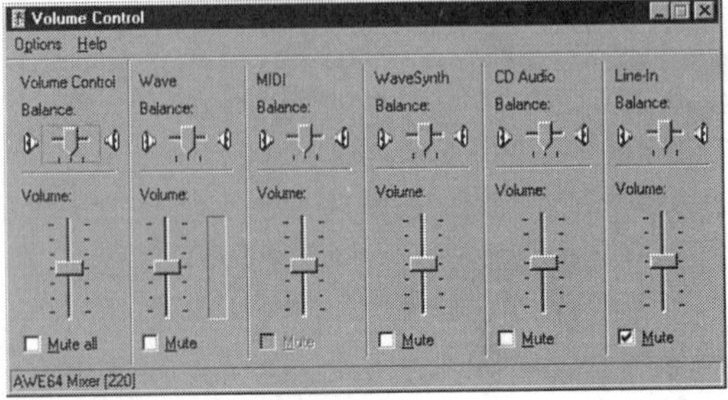

FIG. 4.26
In addition to controlling volume, you can also set WAV and MIDI file balance via the Volume Control option in the View menu.

The Options menu offers four options:

- Random Order enables you to play tracks from different CDs in random order, which can be especially useful if you have more than one CD drive.
- Continuous Play enables you to repeat the track.
- Intro Play plays the first ten seconds of each track.
- Preferences enables you to set preferences for the CD Player (see Figure 4.27).

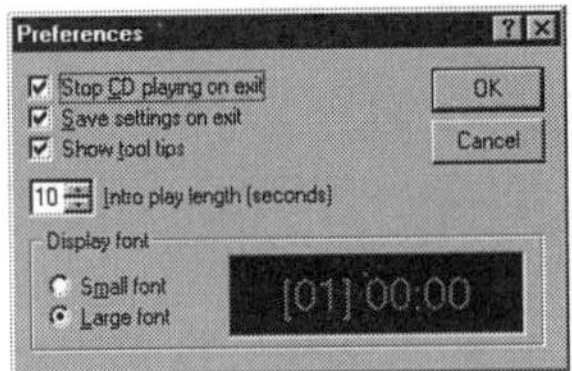

FIG. 4.27
Preferences enables you to set general preferences for CD Player, such as the length of the introduction for each track in seconds, when you choose Intro Play from the Options menu.

The Help menu offers two options:

- Help Topics offers help concerning CD Player (see Figure 4.28).
- About CD Player lets you know how much memory is being used.

Editing a Play List A play list is a list of tracks from an audio CD that you want to play. With CD Player, you can specify the tracks you want played from a CD and the order in which they should run.

You can change the play list by first choosing the Edit Play List from the Disc menu in CD Player. The CD Player: Disc Settings dialog box appears (refer to Figure 4.25).

The left window shows the desired Play List and the right window lists all Available Tracks on the audio CD. To remove a track from the Play List, highlight it and choose Remove. To add a track to the Play List from the Available Tracks list, highlight it and click Add.

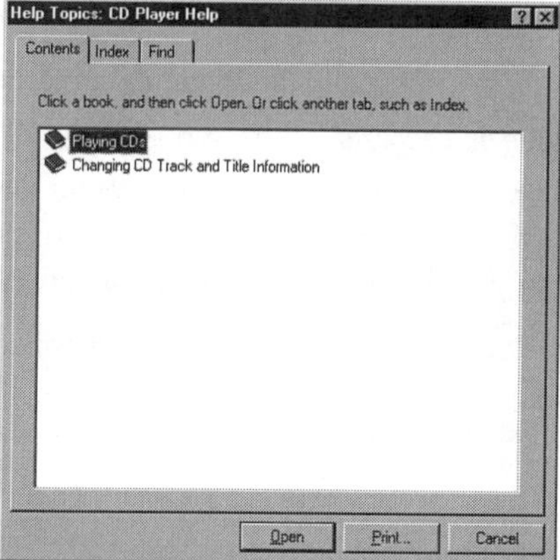

FIG. 4.28
Find help by topic with the Help Topics index option.

Using Sound Recorder The Sound Recorder feature in Windows 95 provides an introduction to the world of digital recording. Using Sound Recorder you can record small sound files to your hard drive to include in multimedia presentations or attach to documents for distribution among colleagues. You can even e-mail the file across your in-house local area network or the Internet. Sound Recorder does not have the advanced features of high-end digital recorders, but it does provide features suitable for most users' needs.

This section provides an overview of the basic features of Sound Recorder. To access Sound Recorder, you do much the same as you do to access CD Player:

1. Open the Start menu; then choose Programs, Accessories.
2. Choose Multimedia.
3. Choose Sound Recorder to open the Sound Recorder dialog box (see Figure 4.29).

CAUTION

Most sound cards have both line and microphone inputs, and attaching a powered microphone–like the one that comes with the Windows Sound System–to the wrong input can damage your speakers. Microphone inputs are amplified because they expect a much lower signal than line inputs, so test your connection at a low volume to be sure you won't overdrive the system.

FIG. 4.29
Sound Recorder enables you to record sounds for future playback.

The Sound Recorder display shows several important bits of information:

- **Position.** Your current location in a sound file, akin to a cursor in a Word document.
- **Length.** Total size of the file, in seconds.
- **Visual Wave display.** A graphic representation of the sound sample. More sophisticated sound editors allow you to edit start and end points in this display and show "clipping limits," where the sound will distort from over-amplification.

The *control buttons* control such operations as fast forward and rewind, like a regular tape recorder.

TROUBLESHOOTING

When I play video and sound files together, they appear out of step with each other. If you are trying to play video with sound and it isn't synchronized, you again may have a computer that isn't fast enough. You can try improving performance and adding RAM, but if you have an older, slower processor and a relatively slow hard drive, you may need to think about upgrading to a new PC with faster video capabilities built in.

The File menu contains a number of familiar and self-explanatory options, as well as two not-so-common ones. Revert enables you to undo a deleted section of a sound file, and Properties enables you to change the properties of the file and change the quality of the recording (see Figure 4.30).

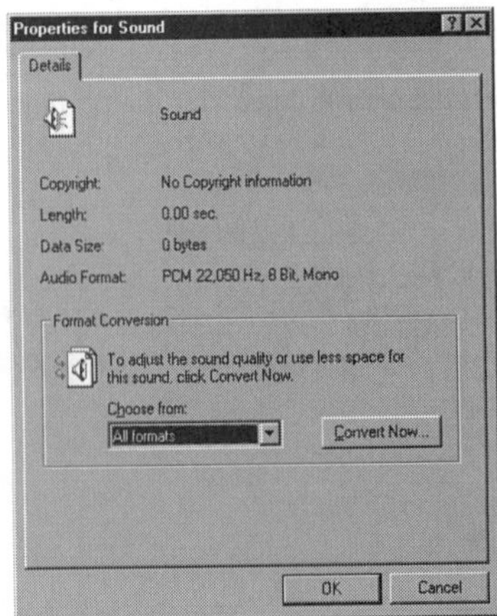

FIG. 4.30 The Properties option from the File menu enables you to change the quality of the recording by changing the format.

NOTE The Revert command works only if you have *not* saved the sound file you partially deleted.

The Edit menu offers a variety of options, some of which may sound familiar but actually accomplish tasks not normally associated with those commands:

- Copy copies a sound (used in conjunction with paste).
- Paste Insert inserts a sound into a document.
- Paste Mix inserts a mixed sound file.
- Insert File enables you to insert a file into another file at the point where you position the slider.
- Mix with File enables you to mix another file with the file playing at the point where you position the slider.
- Delete Before Current Position deletes everything before a specified point, once you have moved the slider to the point in the sound file where you want to cut.
- Delete After Current Position deletes everything after a specified point, once you have moved the slider to the point in the sound file where you want to cut.
- Audio Properties opens the Audio properties sheet, from where you can change various properties, such as volume, for both recording and playback (see Figure 4.31).

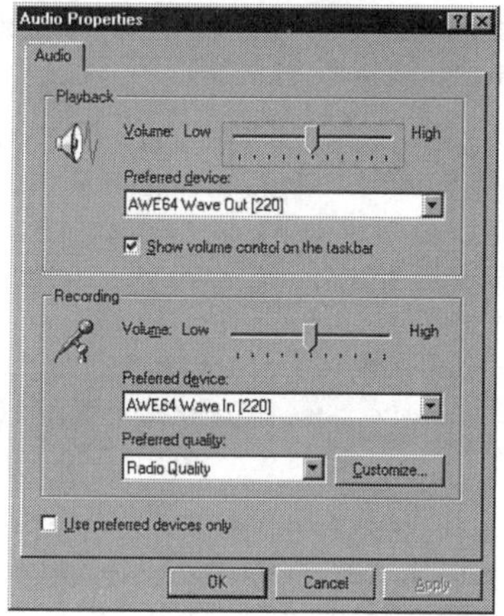

FIG. 4.31 Change recording and playback specifications, such as volume level and designated reproduction device, using the Audio Properties option.

The Effects menu offers options that allow for effects to be added to the sound file:

- Increase Volume [by 25%] increases the volume of a sound file.
- Decrease Volume decreases the volume of a sound file.
- Increase Speed [by 100%] increases the speed of a sound file.
- Decrease Speed decreases the speed of a sound file.
- Add Echo adds an echo to a sound file.
- Reverse plays a sound file in reverse.

TIP You cannot change the speed of a sound file, or add an echo to a sound file, if it is compressed.

See "Compressing a Disk," p. 355

The Help menu offers two options:

- Help Topics accesses the Sound Recorder Help section of the general Windows 95 Help Topics feature.
- About Sound Recorder lets you know who the product is licensed to, how much memory the PC contains, and how much is currently being used.

Common Problems with Sound

Many problems can occur when you are trying to get sound capabilities working on a PC because of the complexity of the operation between the system and the components. Windows 95's Plug and Play and easy-to-use Device Manager Registry help keep track of available IRQs and I/O addresses, but things can still go wrong.

One of the most problematic and intimidating steps required in installing sound devices, or any hardware for that matter, is figuring out available IRQ, DMA, and I/O settings that you can use. If you get the setting wrong and use one that is already assigned to another device, the sound component you are adding will not work properly.

Fortunately, the Device Manager Registry keeps track of which device is using what resources. This feature is useful because when you want to add a new hardware component, you can just start the Add New Hardware Wizard, which takes you step by step through installing the device. During the installation process, the wizard gives you suggested free I/O, IRQ, and DMA settings that you should use for the new device, such as a sound board. You take those settings and configure your board or hardware component to match the settings before you install it. The new device should now work because Windows 95 figured out what free settings to give you in the first place. For more information, refer to the "Adding a Sound Board" section earlier in this chapter.

Should hardware conflicts occur, Windows 95 includes the Help option from the Start menu plus an especially useful feature: the Hardware Conflict Troubleshooter. You access the step-by-step Troubleshooter by choosing "hardware, troubleshooting conflicts" from the Help Topics Index. If you have a hardware conflict, start the troubleshooting wizard and it will take you through an investigative process that should resolve most hardware conflicts, or at least identify the conflict.

Installing and Using a CD-ROM Drive

The CD-ROM has become nearly as essential to computing as the floppy drive; more so, in fact, when you consider that e-mail has effectively replaced floppies around the office and software is increasingly shipped on CD rather than disk, making the CD-ROM a more common sight than the floppy disk for many people. Most new computers, in fact, ship with a CD-ROM drive already installed. Demand for CD-ROM software titles has mushroomed and vendors are rushing to satisfy the demand.

Most multimedia applications rely on such a quantity of sounds, videos, and images that they would not be possible without this ubiquitous little silver disc. A multimedia encyclopedia like Encarta, for instance, consumes about 600M—the equivalent of 500 floppy disks! Also, software vendors ship software on CD for economic reasons: A single CD-ROM is significantly less expensive to press—less than a dollar—than a handful of floppy disks.

Increasingly, popular software packages, such as Microsoft Office, ship on CD as well. Installing an application as large as Office is much quicker from CD-ROM: Swapping disks can take more than 90 minutes, whereas a CD-ROM installation is done in about 15 minutes.

In this section, you learn how to install and configure a CD-ROM drive and how to use your CD-ROM.

Installing Plug and Play CD-ROM Drives

In Chapter 7, "Plug and Play and Legacy Device Installation," you learn what Plug and Play is and how to install Plug and Play devices. Installing a Plug and Play CD-ROM adapter is similar to installing other Plug and Play devices. They are simpler to install than legacy CD-ROM adapters because you don't have to worry about IRQ, DMA, and I/O port settings. Driver configuration is automatic, too.

Windows will take care of the details: It identifies the hardware, identifies the resource requirements, creates the configuration, programs the device, loads the 32-bit device drivers, and notifies the system of the change. It will appear in My Computer the next time you boot Windows.

Installing Legacy CD-ROM Drives

Installing legacy CD-ROM drives is not as easy as installing Plug and Play drives. However, Windows Add New Hardware Wizard greatly simplifies the task. This wizard looks for clues in your computer that tell it what hardware is installed. Some clues include the following:

- Signatures or strings in ROM
- I/O ports at specific addresses that would indicate a specifically known hardware class
- Plug and Play devices that will report their own ID
- Drivers loaded in memory before you run Setup
- DEVICE=lines in the CONFIG.SYS that indicate specific device drivers to the wizard

▶ **See** "Installing Legacy (Non-PnP) Hardware," **p. 174**

CD-ROM Types Supported Windows supports three types of CD-ROM drives: SCSI, IDE, and proprietary CD-ROM drives.

- **SCSI**. Often pronounced *skuzzy*, a Small Computer System Interface adapter allows you to connect multiple pieces of hardware to a single adapter: scanners, hard drives, CD-ROM drives, and others. SCSI devices are known for their speed.
- **IDE**. An Interface Device Electronics adapter, commonly integrated into the motherboard, provides an interface for your floppy and hard disks. CD-ROM drives made for IDE adapters are less expensive than drives made for SCSI adapters.

- **Proprietary**. Some CD-ROM manufacturers, such as Sony and Mitsumi, sell drives that require a proprietary adapter. These drives require you to use an open slot for the adapter.

CAUTION

When buying a Plug and Play adapter, be wary of packaging that says "Plug and Play Ready" on the box. You may be up for an expensive upgrade when you are ready to use this adapter in a Plug and Play computer. Verify that it is truly a Plug and Play device before you purchase it.

Installing the CD-ROM on an Existing Adapter If you install your CD-ROM drive to an existing adapter that Windows already recognizes, you do not need to do anything else. All you have to do is complete the physical installation and connect the drive and cables as described in your manufacturer's documentation. Your CD-ROM drive will appear in your device list the next time you boot Windows.

Installing a CD-ROM and Adapter By installing the driver for your new CD-ROM adapter before actually installing the hardware, you can let Windows suggest a configuration that does not conflict with existing devices in your computer. Therefore, make sure that you have not installed your adapter in your computer before following these steps.

▶ **See** "Adding or Changing Hardware Drivers," **p. 113**

NOTE If you are installing one of the popular combination sound/CD-ROM adapters, install the sound card device drivers as described in "Adding a Sound Board," earlier in this chapter before continuing installation as described in this section.

TIP If you are absolutely sure that your CD-ROM adapter will not conflict with existing devices in your computer, go ahead and install the adapter and allow Windows to automatically detect it.

To install a legacy CD-ROM adapter and drive in your computer, follow these steps:

1. Open the Control Panel and double-click the Add New Hardware icon. The Add New Hardware Wizard opens.
2. Click Next. The wizard allows you to choose between automatically detecting new hardware and manually installing new hardware. Select No and click Next.
3. Choose your adapter from the dialog box shown in Figure 4.32.
4. Select a manufacturer from the Manufacturers list and a specific model from the Models list (see Figure 4.33). Make sure that your selection matches your adapter exactly. Click Next. The wizard displays information about the recommended settings for this device.
5. Click Print to output the recommended settings to the printer or write them down on paper. You'll use these settings to configure your hardware before installing it in your computer.

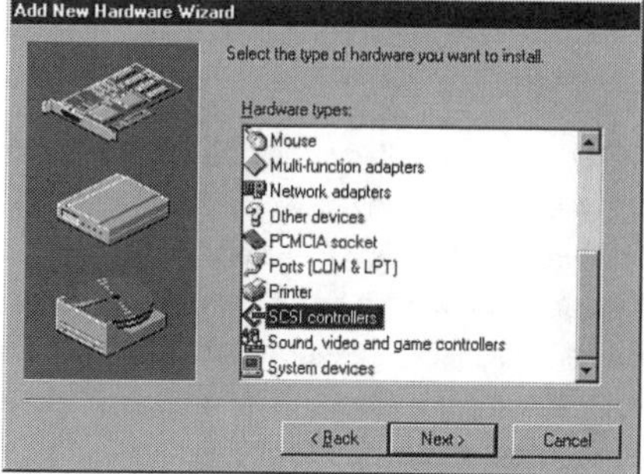

FIG. 4.32
Select either CD-ROM Controllers or SCSI Controllers from the list, depending on which type of adapter you are installing.

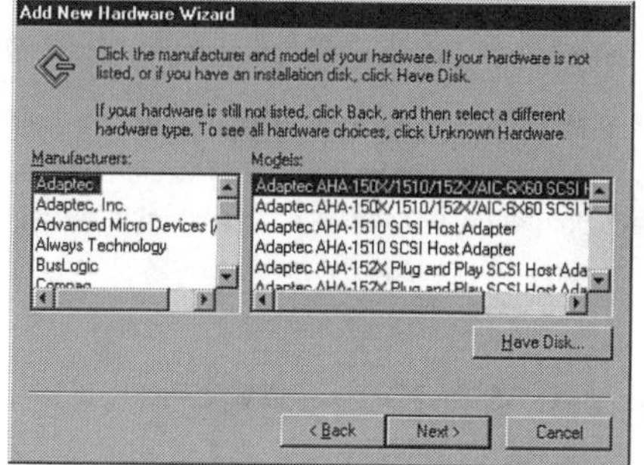

FIG. 4.33
Select a manufacturer and model. If your exact adapter doesn't appear in these lists, you'll need a disk from the manufacturer.

6. Click Next; then click Finish, and Windows installs the necessary drivers on your computer.
7. After Windows has installed the drivers, shut down Windows and turn off your computer.

   ▶ **See** "Installing Legacy Cards After Setting Up Drivers," **p. 180**

8. Configure and install the CD-ROM adapter and drive using the instructions provided by the manufacturer and the settings recommended by Windows. For additional information on setting an adapter's I/O address, IRQ line, and DMA address, see Chapter 7, "Plug and Play and Legacy Device Installation."

NOTE If you are installing a separate sound card, don't forget to connect the audio output of the CD-ROM drive to the audio input of the sound card. See your manufacturer's instructions for more information. ■

Congratulations! You have successfully installed your CD-ROM adapter and can start enjoying the benefits right away.

▶ **See** "Using CD Player," **p. 118**

TROUBLESHOOTING

I successfully installed my CD-ROM (I can see the files on the CD-ROM using the Explorer), but it won't play audio CDs. First, check the volume by clicking the Volume icon in the system tray. Then, run Media Player, select Device, and make sure that there is a menu entry that says CD Audio. If not, install the MCI CD Audio driver. Otherwise, if your CD-ROM plays but you can't hear the music, plug your speakers or headphones into the external audio jack of the CD-ROM. If you hear music using the external audio jack but not through your sound card, your CD-ROM is not properly connected to your sound card. Connect your CD-ROM to your sound card by following the manufacturer's instructions.

I tried to connect my CD-ROM to the sound card but the cable doesn't fit both cards. You'll need a new cable that is capable of connecting your CD-ROM drive to your sound card. If you are using commonly available hardware, contact the manufacturer and they can provide you with a cable.

My computer dies during setup after installing my new CD-ROM adapter. Restart your computer. Run Setup again and it will ask you if you want to use Safe Recovery to continue the installation. Choose Safe Recovery and click Next. Continue using the steps described in this section. Setup will skip the portions of the hardware detection that caused the failure.

Optimizing CD-ROM Drives in Windows 95

Windows 95 incorporates a new file system specifically designed and optimized for CD-ROM drives. CDFS (CD File System) is a 32-bit, protected-mode file system that provides the following benefits:

- Replaces MSCDEX, which loads in conventional memory, with a driver that occupies no conventional memory.
- Improves performance of your applications by providing 32-bit, protected-mode caching. Your multimedia applications run more smoothly.
- Requires no configuration. CDFS is a dynamic cache.

The CD-ROM cache is separate from your disk cache because it is specifically optimized for use with a CD-ROM drive. Windows normally caches the CD-ROM to memory. However, when Windows needs more memory for your applications, it swaps the cache to the hard drive instead of discarding it altogether. The next time Windows needs that particular data, it reads it from the hard drive instead of the CD-ROM. This significantly improves performance as reading data from the hard drive is about ten times faster than reading data from the CD-ROM.

To optimize your CD-ROM, use the following steps:

1. Right-click My Computer and select Properties.
2. Click the Performance page of the System Properties property sheet, click File System, and select the CD-ROM tab. A CD-ROM tab appears.

3. Drag the Supplemental cache size slider to the setting indicated here.

Installed RAM	Cache Size
Up to 8M	114K
8M to 12M	626K
12M and over	1138K

4. Select the type of CD-ROM in the Optimize Access Pattern For list, and then click OK.

Using Your CD-ROM Drive

With a few exceptions, using your CD-ROM drive in Windows is no different than using any other drive. Figure 4.34 shows the D drive icon in My Computer as a CD-ROM. You access it in My Computer or Explorer just like the other drives in your computer: Double-click the icon to open its folder, or right-click to display its context menu.

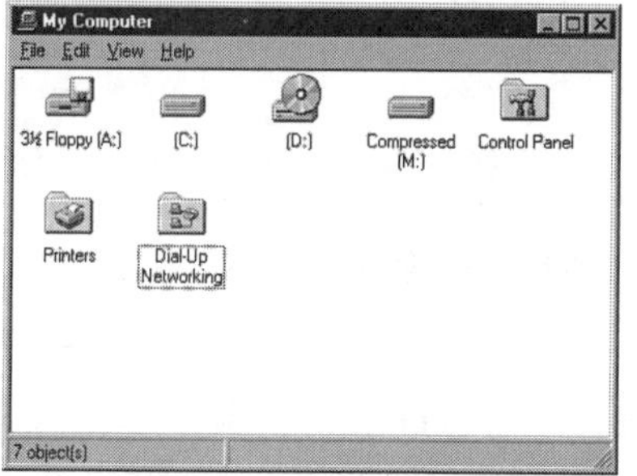

FIG. 4.34 Double-click the CD-ROM icon to open it in a folder. Right-click it and select Properties to see its size or share it.

TROUBLESHOOTING

I have a CD-ROM installed in my machine but it doesn't show up in My Computer or the Explorer. If you are using an external CD-ROM drive, make sure that it is turned on. At times, Windows may skip detecting your CD-ROM drive when you install Windows for the first time. In this case, use the Add New Hardware Wizard to allow Windows to automatically detect your CD-ROM as described in "Installing Legacy CD-ROM Drives" earlier in this chapter. If your CD-ROM drive still does not show up in My Computer, right-click My Computer and select Properties. Click the Device Manager page, select your CD-ROM, and click Properties. A description of the problem and a possible solution is displayed in the Device Status area. If your CD-ROM does not appear in the Device Manager at all, consult the manual that came with your CD-ROM for more troubleshooting information or call the vendor's support line.

▶ **See** "Troubleshooting Hardware Installation," **p. 183**

Playing a CD-ROM Automatically Windows automatically detects when you insert a CD-ROM into the drive. As a result, it displays the label of the CD-ROM next to the drive letter in My Computer. When you remove the CD-ROM, it clears the label.

▶ **See** "Adding and Removing Windows Components," **p. 21**

Some CD-ROMs for Windows 95 are set up to automatically run when they are inserted into the CD-ROM drive. If Windows detects an AutoPlay CD-ROM, it runs the appropriate program on the disk. The Windows 95 CD-ROM is a good example. After you have installed Windows 95, reinsert the CD-ROM in the drive. Almost immediately, a window opens, which gives you the opportunity to add or remove Windows components by clicking Add/Remove Software.

In the future, software vendors will use AutoPlay as a significant marketing tool (or "Spin and Grin," as Microsoft calls it). However, AutoPlay is more than a marketing tool. AutoPlay simplifies installation for countless first-time users who would otherwise spend hours figuring out how to install these products. In the future, installation instructions for many programs using Spin and Grin will simply say, "Insert this CD in your drive and follow the on-screen instructions."

To disable AutoPlay, hold down the Shift key while inserting a CD-ROM in the drive.

TROUBLESHOOTING

Windows doesn't automatically recognize a CD-ROM when I insert it. I have to refresh My Computer or Explorer to see the CD-ROM's contents. Right-click My Computer, select Properties, select the CD-ROM in the device list, click the Properties button, and select the Settings page of the properties sheet. Make sure the Auto Insert Notification option is checked.

Sharing Your CD-ROM Drive on a Peer-to-Peer Network If other users on your peer-to-peer network don't have a CD-ROM drive, you may want to share yours. Sharing your CD-ROM drive is similar to sharing any other drive on your computer.

With Windows 95 file-sharing for Novell Networks, you can share a CD-ROM drive with other Novell clients, even though Novell is a client/server network.

However, there are two considerations when sharing a CD-ROM drive

- If a user *maps* to your shared CD-ROM drive and no disc is in it, a message appears that says "X:\ is not available."
- You are sharing a drive, not a particular CD-ROM title. Therefore, if you share the drive with the Windows 95 CD-ROM in it, and then change the disc, you will be sharing the new disc.

Installing a Software Application from a CD-ROM Drive Installing software from a CD-ROM drive is similar to installing from floppy disk, but it's a lot easier. You can double-click the Add/Remove Programs icon in the Control Panel or run the Setup program on the CD-ROM directly. For Windows 95 applications, you should install using the Control Panel. For legacy software (software written for older versions of Windows), either method is appropriate.

In addition to installing an application using the preceding methods, some software is AutoPlay-enabled as described earlier in this chapter. In this case, insert the CD-ROM in the drive and follow the instructions. For information on partial installations, see the section "Partial Installation," later in this chapter.

▶ **See** "Installing Applications in Windows 95," **p. 628**

TROUBLESHOOTING

When I try to install a program from a CD-ROM using the Control Panel, it complains that Windows was unable to locate the installation program. Your CD-ROM did not have a SETUP.EXE or INSTALL.EXE file in its root directory. Click Browse to search the CD-ROM for another setup program such as WINSTALL.EXE or try to run the program directly if there is no setup program.

I successfully installed a program from a CD-ROM on my hard drive. When I run the program now, I get an error that says File not found. Or, if I try to use Help, the Help window pops up and displays an error that says Help file not found. First, make sure that you have inserted the CD-ROM you used to install the program in the drive because the program is probably looking for program or data files on the CD. If you still get the error message, make sure that the CD-ROM is still assigned to the same drive letter it was when you installed the program. If it is not, you will need to reassign the drive or reinstall the program. You can change the drive letter to which the CD-ROM is assigned by selecting the CD-ROM drive in the Device Manager, clicking the Properties button, and clicking the Settings page of the property sheet. Select a new drive letter in the Start Drive Letter list box.

Complete Installation Some applications automatically do a complete installation. All of the files required to run the program are copied to the hard drive. This is typical of applications that don't require a large amount of space, but are distributed on CD-ROM for convenience. Also, some applications, that by default install only partially, will give you the opportunity to do a complete install when performance is important.

Partial Installation Other applications enable you to do a partial installation. In this case, only core components are copied to the hard drive, whereas other files such as data or help files are left on the CD-ROM. The advantage to this method is that you don't lose a significant amount of hard drive space to store the application. However, the disadvantage is that you must place the CD-ROM in the drive to run the application, and the application will run slower than if you installed it to your hard drive.

Running Applications from the CD-ROM Drive

A very limited number of applications can be run directly from the CD-ROM drive. Many multimedia preview discs exist that contain programs you can run directly on the CD-ROM. However, the performance of applications that are run directly from the CD-ROM is poorer than if you copy the files to your hard drive because a quad-speed CD-ROM transfers data at about 600K per second, whereas a hard drive can transfer data up to 5M per second. See the HoverHavoc game on your Windows 95 CD-ROM in \Funstuff\Hover for an example of an application you can run directly from the CD-ROM.

If the CD-ROM contains a SETUP.EXE file in the root directory, you probably can't run the application from the CD-ROM.

Although programs generally can't be run directly from the CD-ROM, many other types of files can be used directly:

- **Data Files.** Data files include clip art, bitmaps, documents, and other files that you don't use often and would normally occupy a lot of space on your hard drive. You can use these files directly from the CD-ROM or copy them individually to your hard drive.
- **Font.** A collection of fonts that you install via the Control Panel. Once the font is installed, you don't need the CD-ROM in the drive to use the font.
- **Multimedia.** Some CD-ROMs are packed with sounds and videos you can preview directly from the CD-ROM. For example, see the Funstuff directory on your Windows 95 CD-ROM.

  ▶ **See** "Using CD Player," **p. 118**
- **Audio CD.** Your favorite audio CD. You can play audio CDs on your computer as you work in other applications.

Double-click \Funstuff\Video\Goodtime.avi on your Windows 95 CD-ROM to see a great example video!

CHAPTER 5

Controlling Printers

In this chapter

Printing from Applications

When you print from an application under Windows 95, you use the same commands and techniques available under previous versions of Windows; however, there have been changes. You find that application printing now takes less time, the operating system releases your resources quicker, and the color/gray scale found in the printer output is substantially more consistent and accurate. However, many details of the printing architecture are transparent to application users.

Basic Windows 95 Printing Procedure

Depending on the application from which you are printing, you may have some slightly different printing options. In this section, we look at the printing options available to all applications written for the Windows 95 operating system. The two most common Windows 95 applications are WordPad and Paint, included with Windows 95. The options you see in these applications are the same as the options in many Windows 95 applications.

To print from an application, perform the following steps:

1. Open the file you want to print.
2. Choose the printing command. In most Windows applications, do this by choosing File, Print. Figure 5.1 shows a typical Print dialog box. The controls in this dialog box let you specify the portion of the file you want to print and the printer designated to complete the job.

NOTE Most Windows applications that have toolbars also have a button for printing (similar to the one shown here). In some applications (such as Word, Excel, and other MS Office applications), clicking the Print button immediately prints the document using the current print settings–there are no dialog boxes to go through. Other applications open the Print dialog box shown in Figure 5.1 after you click the Print button.

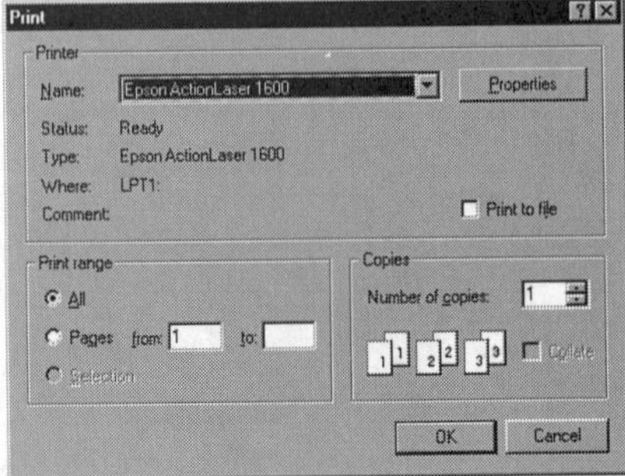

FIG. 5.1
A typical application's Print dialog box lets you send a print job to a specific printer.

3. Determine whether the printer shown in the Name box is the printer you want to use for this document. If it is not the desired printer, click the drop-down arrow for this box and select the desired printer.
4. Specify the number of copies you want to print by clicking the up and down arrows on the Number of Copies control. You may also select the default setting and type a number to replace the default number 1.
5. By default, most applications choose All as the print range. If you want to print something other than the entire document, you must define the print range. To do this, choose one of the three option buttons in the Print Range box:
   - **All.** Prints all pages contained within the document.
   - **Selection.** Prints only those portions of the document you selected using the selection features of the application.
   - **Pages.** Prints the page range you specify in the boxes located to the right of the option button. Specify a beginning page in the From box and an ending page in the To box.

NOTE The Selection option is not available in all applications. In applications that do have this option, it is available only when you select part of the document.

Some applications allow you to specify more complicated ranges. See "Applications with Special Print Options," later in this chapter.

The sheets-of-paper icons next to the collate option show whether or not the printer collates the print job.

6. If you print more than one copy of the document, you can have the copies collated (each copy of the multipage document prints completely before the next copy of the document). To collate copies, select the Collate check box. If you don't select this option, all the copies of each page are printed together (for example, four copies of page 1 print and then four copies of page 2). The Collate option is not available in all applications.

   ▶ **See** "The Print Manager," **p. 137**

7. To output the printer information to a print file, select the Print to File check box. Print files were used in earlier versions of Windows to store print jobs, but Windows 95 uses Deferred Printing to create its own spooled print file, eliminating the need to check this box. Print files also are used for transferring printouts between computers with dissimilar applications.
8. To begin printing, choose OK. If you change your mind and don't want to print, click Cancel to return to the document without making any changes or starting the print job.

This basic printing procedure applies to most applications, even if their Print dialog boxes are slightly different than the one shown in Figure 5.1. Some applications have additional options, as discussed in the next two sections.

NOTE If you plan to print to a file frequently, set up a bogus printer. For example, set up a second PostScript printer to create EPS files. Use the Options, Printer Setup command (or the Printers application in Control Panel) to install a new printer; accept the current driver if you already have a PostScript printer installed or add the PostScript driver if you don't have one installed. Follow the preceding procedures to direct this printer's output to an EPS file. When you're ready to print from the application, choose File, Print Setup to select the bogus printer and print. ■

Applications with Special Print Options

Some applications take the basic printing features in Windows 95 and add a few features of their own. This section looks at some of the additional features you may find in other programs, with Word 97 as an example. Although these features vary from application to application, this section should give you an idea of what to look for.

Figure 5.2 shows the Word 97 Print dialog box.

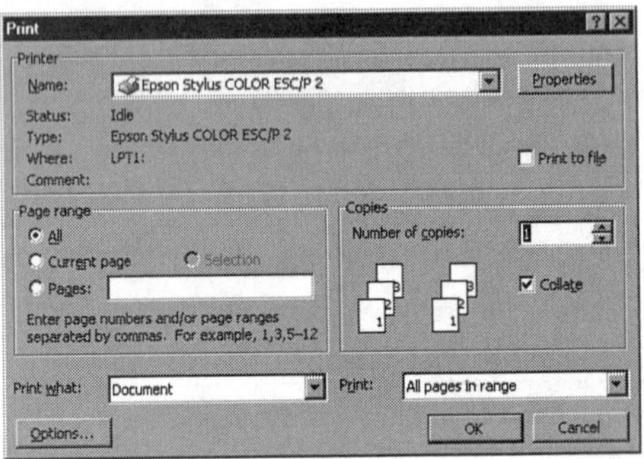

FIG. 5.2
The Print dialog box in Word 97 includes several enhancements not found in the standard Windows 95 Print dialog box.

Here is a quick summary of some of the additional (and different) options provided by this application compared to the standard Windows 95 printing options:

- The Current Page option in the Page Range section. When you select this option, Word prints the page in which the insertion point is currently located.
- An enhanced Pages option. This enhanced option allows you to specify a page range in the variable box located to the right of the Pages label. The range can be individual pages separated by a comma, a page range separated by a hyphen, or both: for example, 1,2,4–8,10. In this example, pages 1, 2, 4, 5, 6, 7, 8, and 10 are printed.
- The Print What drop-down list. In Word, you can select to print the document itself or other information such as summary information, annotations, and styles.
- The Print option. From this drop-down list, you select to print odd, even, or all pages in the range.
- The Options button. When you click this button, Word displays the Options dialog box, opened to the Print tab. Use this dialog box to set printing options specific to Word.

NOTE For a more complete discussion of Word's printing features, see Que's *Special Edition Using Word 97, Bestseller Edition*. ■

Keep in mind that the options described here are not the same in all applications.

Windows 3.1 Applications with Special Print Options

The other common type of Print dialog box you may encounter is from a Windows 3.1 application that has a customized dialog box, such as the one for Word 6 shown in Figure 5.3.

FIG. 5.3
The Word 6 dialog box is still styled like a Windows 3.1 dialog box.

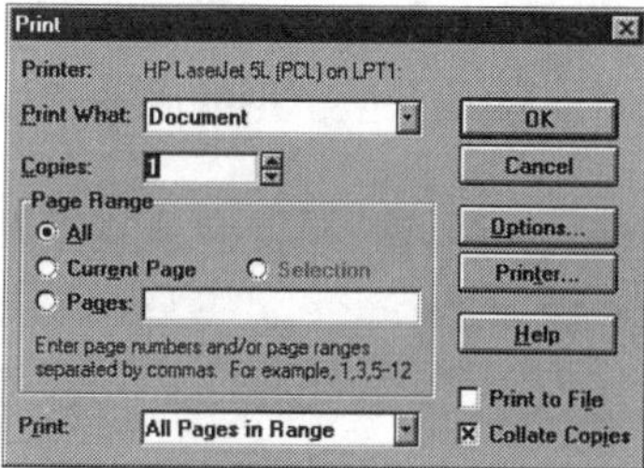

Most options in this dialog box are the same as those shown in Figures 5.1 and 5.2. However, there are some differences:

- There is no status entry or comment field that describes the printer's current activity.
- You select a different printer by clicking the Printer button and selecting from a dialog box instead of choosing a printer from a drop-down list.
- There is no Properties button.

As with the other printing options discussed in this chapter, the options displayed in the Print dialog box vary from application to application.

Managing Print Jobs

Like Windows 3.1, Windows 95 offers the option of printing directly to the configured port or using its Print Manager. For most applications, the Print Manager provides facilities to better manage the printing of documents.

The Print Manager

To start the Print Manager, open the Start menu and choose Settings; then choose Printers and double-click the icon for the printer you want to manage in the Printer control panel (see Figure 5.4). Depending on the printers you have installed, your control panel will differ from the one shown in the figure.

If you have a shortcut to your printer on your desktop, you can open its control panel by double-clicking the shortcut icon. To create a shortcut for your printer, see "Create a Desktop Printer Icon," later in this chapter.

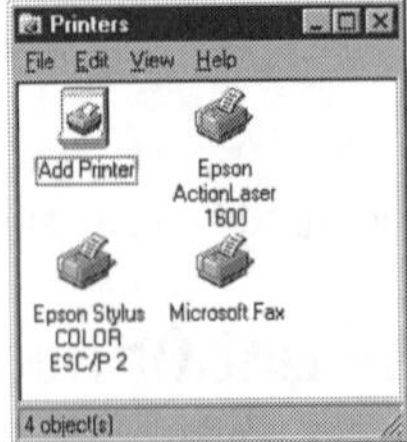

FIG. 5.4
The Printer control panel has icons for each of your installed printers as well as the icon to add a new printer.

Unlike Windows 3.1, Windows 95 uses a separate Print Manager for each printer. Therefore, make certain that you choose the correct Print Manager to view the status of your print jobs.

The Print Manager shown in Figure 5.5 displays the current printer status for each print job.

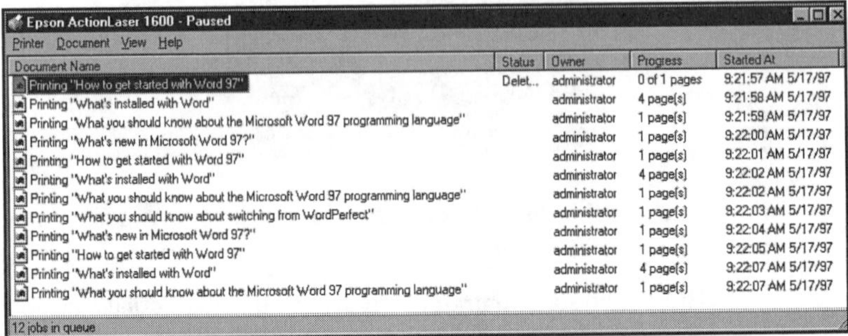

FIG. 5.5
Each printer has its own Print Manager; make sure that you select the correct printer from the Printer control panel for the print jobs you want to check.

The printer status includes the following information:

- The Document Name section shows the name of each application that has submitted a print job as well as the name of each document job in the print queue.
- The Status column describes the current condition of each print job, such as paused or spooling.

  ▶ **See** "Managing Print Files and Sharing," **p. 961**

- The Owner column gives the user's name associated with each document. A print job on your printer may belong to someone else when you share your printer.
- The Progress column shows the relative progress of each job in the print queue. The progress of each job monitors the printing of each document and provides information concerning the number of pages printed and the number of pages left to print.

By default, print jobs are listed in the order they entered the queue. You can sort them according to name, status, owner, progress, or start time by clicking the appropriate column heading.

- The Started At column provides the time and date when each job entered the queue. This is important for those users with deferred print jobs.

Controlling Printing

The Print Manager coordinates and schedules the printing of files received from your applications. These applications may be Windows-based or MS-DOS-based.

The Print Manager pull-down menus provide you with the following capabilities, all of which the next several sections describe:

- Pause Printing
- Purge Printing
- Work Offline
- Set Printer as Default
- Change a Printer's Properties
- Pause a Selected Document's Printing
- Cancel a Selected Document's Printing
- View the Status Bar
- Access Windows Help

▶ **See** "Managing Print Files and Sharing," **p. 961**

NOTE If you are using a network printer, you can cancel only your own print jobs. You cannot pause printing, even of your own documents. Canceling someone else's print jobs or pausing printing requires network supervisor rights.

Pausing Printing Pausing a printer temporarily stops print jobs from being sent to a printer. Once you restart a paused printer, all pending print jobs start and sequentially enter the printer queue. This feature is useful when changing toner or performing printer maintenance.

To pause printing, choose Printer, Pause Printing. The Print jobs pause and the Print Manager's title bar displays `Paused`.

To restart printing, choose Printer, Pause Printing again, which is now prefaced by a check mark. The Pause Printing check mark disappears and printing resumes.

Purging Print Jobs The Purge Print Jobs command permanently removes all queued print jobs. Choose Printer, Purge Print Jobs. The documents listed by the Print Manager disappear.

TROUBLESHOOTING

The printer started my print job and the Purge Print Jobs command won't stop it. Purging print jobs stops Windows 95 from sending print jobs to the printer. However, it does not purge the print jobs currently being processed by the printer. You may have to reset the printer to terminate unwanted printing.

Working Offline Windows 95 enables you to initiate a print job without being physically attached to a printer. This feature is known as Deferred Printing, or Working Offline. Deferred Printing is available for network printers and laptop users with docking stations. Deferred Printing tracks deferred print jobs and releases them under configuration control when the computer is connected to the printer locally or networked, or attached through a docking station.

The Work Offline command is only available for laptop computers and network printers. Use the Pause Printing command to delay printing on a computer that uses a local printer. See the section "Pausing Printing" earlier in this chapter for more information on that option.

▶ **See** "Using Your Laptop with a Docking System," **p. 190**

▶ **See** "Printing on a NetWare Network," **p. 956**

▶ **See** "Printing on a Microsoft Network," **p. 958**

NOTE The spooler must be turned on for you to use Deferred Printing.

To configure a printer to work offline, choose Printer, Work Off-Line. A check mark appears in front of the Work Off-Line command. The Printer is now configured to work offline and defer printouts. The Print Manager changes its title to read "User Intervention Required." This information is then placed in the status line of each print job being sent to this printer. The Print manager defers printouts until you change the status of the Work Off-Line flag.

To change the status of the Work Off-Line flag, choose Work Off-Line for a second time. The check mark disappears and the deferred printouts are sent to the printer.

The taskbar normally displays a clock at the lower right of the screen. This box also displays a printer when a document is being printed. If deferred documents are pending, the icon changes to include a question mark circled in red.

▶ **See** "Printing on a NetWare Network," **p. 956**

▶ **See** "Printing on a Microsoft Network," **p. 958**

To print documents that have been deferred, follow these steps:

1. Physically connect the target printer to the system by putting the laptop in the docking station or connecting to the network printer.
2. From the Print Manager window, choose Printer. Then choose the Work Off-Line option to remove its check mark.
3. Verify that printing begins immediately to the target printer and that the deferred print jobs are no longer displayed by the Print Manager.

Setting a Default Printer If you have more than one printer available (either locally or on a network), you can choose the printer to be used as the default. The default printer is used by all applications unless you choose another printer from within the application.

To set a printer as the default, start that printer's Print Manager and then choose Printer, Set as Default. A check mark appears next to the Set as Default command on the pull-down menu, signifying that this printer is now the Windows default printer.

To remove the printer as the system default, select the Set as Default option again to reset the flag. Alternatively, from the Print Manager of another printer, select the Printer, Set as Default command. Windows allows only one default printer.

Pausing a Document You may pause a document to stop the Print Manager from sending it to the printer. Pausing suspends processing of the print job, but it does not stop the document from being spooled. The Print Manager displays a list of documents being printed; any paused print jobs are labeled "Paused."

To pause a document, choose one or more documents from the list of documents in the print queue. (Choosing a document highlights the document's entry in the Print Manager.) Choose Document, Pause. The selected documents now display a `Paused` status.

To release a paused document, choose the paused documents from the list of documents in the print queue. Choose Document, Pause. The selected documents no longer display a "Paused" status.

Canceling a Document from Printing You also can permanently remove selected documents from the list of documents being printed. To cancel documents, choose one or more documents from the documents in the print queue; then choose Document, Cancel.

CAUTION

Once you cancel a document, Windows immediately removes that document from the print queue. You do not receive a confirmation prompt. You might try Pause first and make certain that you want this document's printout terminated.

Turning the Status Bar Off and On The status bar lists the status of the print queue and contains the number of print jobs remaining to be printed. To turn off the display of the status bar, choose View, Status Bar. Repeat this action to turn the status bar display back on. The Status Bar option is a standard Windows toggle control: if the option is not preceded by a check mark, the status bar is not visible.

Closing Print Manager

To close the Print Manager, choose Printer, Close; or click the Close button.

Closing the Print Manager in Windows 95 does not purge the associated print jobs (unlike Windows 3.1). Printing continues based on the Print Manager's settings.

To rearrange the print queue, select a document, drag it to the correct queue position, and drop it. Dragging and dropping a document in the print queue works only with documents that are not currently being printed.

Drag-and-Drop Printing from the Desktop

A new feature of the Windows 95 operating system is the capability to print a document without first opening the associated application or the File Manager. Using desktop icons, you can quickly run print jobs from the desktop.

In earlier versions of Windows, printing used a four-step operation: open an application, load a file, initiate printing, and finally shut down the application after printing. Windows 95 uses a two-step printing procedure that is quick and convenient. However, before you can print from the desktop, you must take certain steps to set up your system.

Create a Desktop Printer Icon

Before you can drag-and-drop documents to desktop icons, you must first create the icons. Although some icons are automatically created during Windows setup, printer icons are not.

To create a shortcut icon for a printer, follow these steps:

1. Open the Start menu, choose Settings, and then choose Printers. You also can open the Printers folder by double-clicking the Printers icon in the Control Panel window. The Printer's folder is now open.
2. Select the desired printer, drag it onto the desktop, and release it.
3. Windows displays a question window that asks permission to create a shortcut (see Figure 5.6). Answer Yes and Windows creates the shortcut icon. If you answer No, the icon disappears from the desktop.

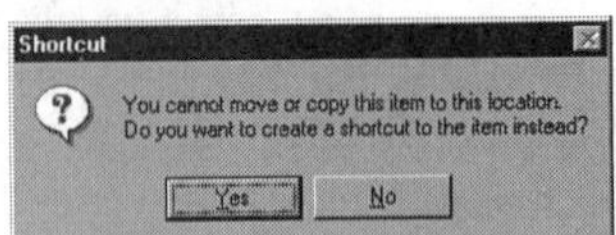

FIG. 5.6 A Windows question window asks your permission to create a shortcut.

After you create the shortcut to the printer, you can modify it by creating a shortcut key or changing the icon. Chapter 10, "Navigating and Controlling Windows," discusses modifying shortcuts.

Print from the Desktop

Once you create a shortcut icon on the desktop for your printer, you can print any document from the desktop.

To print from the desktop, follow these steps:

1. Open any folder (either in My Computer or Windows Explorer) that contains a printable document.

2. Select that document by using the left mouse button.
3. While holding down the left mouse button, drag the document's icon from its folder to a printer desktop icon. Don't worry: This action makes no changes to the file.
4. When the document icon is on top of the printer desktop icon, release the mouse button.

TIP Make sure that the document is associated with an application and that the application is available to Windows, or your printing will be terminated.

Windows starts the associated application configured to handle that file type. Windows executes that application's print command. Once the printing has been committed to the background print spooler, Windows releases the associated application, closes it, and background prints the spooled files.

Why all the fuss about such a simple control function? Consider the time it saves you: If you have to print documents quickly, simply point, click, and drag the document to the printer; then you can go back to your other applications. Windows delivers hard copy with minimum effort. Also, if you use more than one printer, you can create a shortcut for each of the printers you use. Then, instead of having to open the application and select the printer you are connected to, you can simply drag and drop the document on to the correct printer icon.

Another way to quickly print a file is to add a shortcut for your printer to the Send To folder (which is in the Windows folder). You can then right-click a file in the Explorer or a folder window, choose Send To, and choose the printer from the Send To list. If you have multiple printers or multiple configurations for the same printer, add shortcuts for each one to the Send To folder.

Desktop Printing of Multiple Documents

Using Windows, you can print several files at once by dragging them to the shortcut icon on the desktop. Follow these steps to print several files at once:

1. Select several documents to print by dragging around them, or by holding down the Ctrl key and clicking the documents.
2. Drag the selected documents to the desktop printer icon.
3. Drop the documents on the icon.
4. The message window shown in Figure 5.7 displays. Select Yes to print. Select No only if you want to stop all documents from printing.

Windows starts each of the applications associated with the selected documents and begins printing.

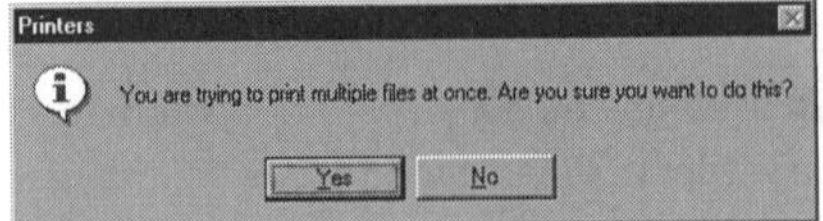

FIG. 5.7
A message window asks permission to print the multiple documents.

You can select and print multiple documents created by using different applications.

NOTE Before trying to print multiple documents, check whether your system has the resources (enough memory) to support the number of applications Windows has to open to print the files. A quick check would be to start the applications prior to printing and look for an out-of-memory or other diagnostic message that indicates Windows cannot support the application load. ■

Printing from MS-DOS Applications

Windows provides support for printing from MS-DOS applications in much the same way it does for printing from Windows applications. The print stream is spooled using the RAW setting for the print spooler. The result is a faster return to MS-DOS applications and the ability to mix Windows and MS-DOS print streams (avoiding contention problems that occurred under Windows 3.1).

Under Windows 3.1, MS-DOS applications could not access the Windows printing facilities. In the past, printing from a DOS application was neither robust nor fail-safe. When printing simultaneously from both Windows and MS-DOS applications, you often received notice of a printer conflict. In most cases, this caused either the MS-DOS application or the Windows application to stall, and you had to reboot.

The major change Windows 95 brings to MS-DOS applications is direct access to the Windows print spooler. MS-DOS applications no longer compete for a share of the printer; you can actually use the Print Manager to queue your MS-DOS printouts with those of Windows applications.

When you print from an MS-DOS application in the Windows environment, the DOS application spools print jobs to the 32-bit print spooler, which takes the output destined for the printer port and spools it before printing. Windows automatically installs the print spooler for MS-DOS applications; the spooler is transparent to users. Although your MS-DOS printouts automatically use the 32-bit spooler, they cannot be processed into Enhanced Meta Files.

Printing from a Docking Station

Every time you start Windows, it performs an inventory check of all attached hardware. Windows also provides a choice of configurations during startup, if there is more than one configuration. You must choose one of the selections from this list.

You can configure Windows to work offline when the PC is undocked and online when the PC is docked. You can set the system configurations for the printer port to be configured only when the laptop is attached to the docking station. You also can configure the port to be automatically unavailable when the system is being used as a laptop.

Configuring a Hardware Profile

A hardware profile specifies whether Windows will use or not use a specific peripheral. Hardware profiles provide a tool that you can use to specify the hardware configurations to operate your system. You change and create the hardware configurations through the Control Panel's System icon.

Because the printer is not a system resource, it is not part of the hardware configuration. However, the printer is attached to the system through the LPT1 port. This port *is* a system resource and can be configured to be available when the computer is in a docking station. You can configure the port as unavailable when you use the system as a laptop.

Use the following steps to create the hardware profile:

1. Open the Start menu; choose Settings and then choose Control Panel.
2. Double-click the System icon. The System Properties dialog box appears.
3. Choose the Hardware Profiles tab. The tab contains a text window with a single item: Dock 1. When Windows is first installed at a docking station, it creates the Dock 1 setting in the text window.
4. Select the Dock 1 setting and click Copy.

NOTE Windows will automatically detect most docking stations and create a Dock 1 profile. Even if you initially install Windows on a laptop, Windows checks the system components each time it starts and creates profiles automatically when it finds changes.

5. Change the name of the newly created configuration from *Dock 1* to *Lap Top* or some other name that indicates that the laptop is not in its docking station. Click OK.
6. Choose the Device Manager tab from the System Properties dialog box.
7. Select the port (COM or LPT) from the Device Manager tab.
8. Choose the printer's port (LPT1). The Printer Port (LPT1) Properties dialog box that appears contains a Device Usage block with a hardware configuration window (see Figure 5.8). The Device Usage block now contains two hardware configurations: the initial Dock 1 and the new Lap Top. The two items are check box controls. A check in the Dock 1 box directs Windows to include port LPT1 in its hardware configuration whenever a docking station has been detected.
9. Check the Dock 1 box. Don't check the Lap Top box.
10. Reboot your Windows system. During initial bootup, Windows asks for a configuration. Choose Lap Top.

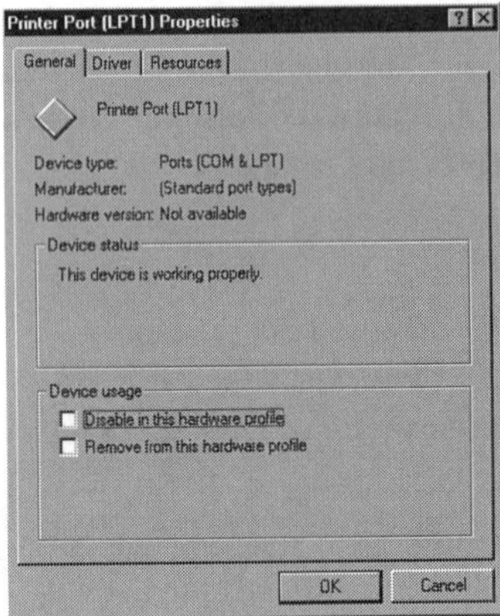

FIG. 5.8
The Printer Port Properties dialog box showing the currently configured hardware profile.

To verify that you have configured the hardware profile correctly, do not change the hardware and follow these steps:

1. After Windows starts, open the Start menu; choose Settings and then choose Control Panel.
2. Double-click Device Manager.
3. Select the port (COM or LPT) from the Device Manager tab.
4. Note that the printer port is now offline, signified by a red X through the port's icon. Printing now results in a diagnostic message that the printer is not attached. The Print Manager deletes all print files. Therefore, you must set the printer to Work Off-Line so that the system will save all print files.

Repeat the process first by rebooting Windows, this time selecting the Dock 1 configuration setting. The printer port returns. The saved print files can then be released for printing.

Common Printer Problems

You install a printer only on occasion. But you troubleshoot printer problems frequently. The most useful tool in identifying and correcting printer problems is a thorough knowledge of your printer's installation and properties. During installation, test your printer and the wide range of properties available to better identify a starting point for dissecting most problems.

Windows provides fundamental troubleshooting aid with Bi-Directional Printer Communication. If a printer can talk to its drivers, many potential causes for problems can be routinely identified.

Advance preparation is always an excellent safeguard against any PC problem. The following checklists can be useful when you are diagnosing a local printer problem.

Before the Problem: Initial Preparation

Following initial installation of the printer, perform these steps:

1. Make a test-page printout and save the resulting printout for future use. The test page can contain important configuration information including the current printer driver, memory size, and port information. On PostScript printers, it will contain version level and settings.
2. If your printer can perform a self test, make a printer self-test printout. For most printers, this test page contains the printer's internal configuration. This information may contain the number of pages printed, memory size, a list of configured options, and internal software revision level. Save the printout for future use. This information may be useful in describing your printer to its manufacturer at a later date, for upgrading or troubleshooting.
3. Note the proper configuration of your printer's indicators: the Ready or Online light and the display status.
4. Make a record of your printer's internal menu settings for paper size, orientation, interface, and so on.
5. Record the installation results and the information from the Printer Properties screens.

Diagnosing the Problem: Basic Troubleshooting

For a local printer, perform the following steps to start diagnosing a problem:

1. Verify that all cabling is free of nicks, tears, or separations.
2. Verify that all cabling is fully inserted and locked at both the PC and the printer ends.
3. Verify that the printer is online and that all proper indicators are lit (for example, that the Online or Ready indicators are lit).
4. Verify that the printer is properly loaded with paper and that there are no existing paper jams.
5. Verify that the printer has toner (laser), ink (inkjet), or a good ribbon (dot-matrix).
6. Verify that cabinet doors and interlocks are closed and locked.
7. Verify that the printer's display, if available, shows a normal status.
8. Verify that the Windows printer driver can communicate with the printer using the Printer Properties screens. You should be able to print a test page to verify communication. If you cannot print a test page, Windows generates a diagnostic message providing you with a starting point to diagnose the problem.
9. Verify that the Windows Printer Properties screens display the same information that was contained in the Properties screens when you installed the printer.
10. Attempt to print to the errant printer by using another application and a different type of print file (for example, print a text file or a graphics file).

Troubleshooting Tools

If the basic troubleshooting steps listed in the preceding section fail, Windows comes with three important tools you can use to further investigate printer problems. The first tool is Windows 95's new Help file. Initiate the Help file from the Print Manager's Help menu. Then select the Troubleshooting icon.

The Troubleshooter steps you through several of the most probable causes of printing problems (see Figure 5.9). Primarily, this tool verifies that the printer can communicate with the PC. If basic communication is lost, none of the software tools can provide any real assistance. You must resort to hardware exchange until you resolve which component or components are defective. However, with the exception of toner and paper problems, most printing problems are not hardware failures; the problems are primarily software settings or corrupted printer drivers.

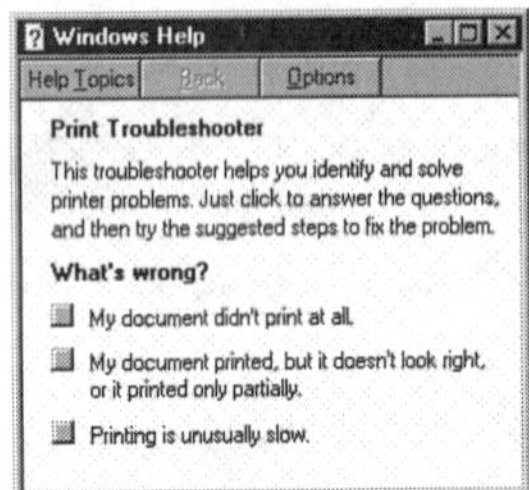

FIG. 5.9
The Windows Print Troubleshooter assists you in isolating problems by using logical fault-isolation techniques.

The Windows 95 Print Manager provides a diagnostic tool that can aid you during the process of equipment interchange. The diagnostic screen shown in Figure 5.10 is usually the first indication you receive that a printer fault has occurred. The information on this screen varies (Windows provides as much detail as possible about the problem). The increased amount of information is a result of the Bidirectional Communications between the PC and the printer. For those printers without bidirectional capability, you will receive a standard "Unable to print" diagnostic.

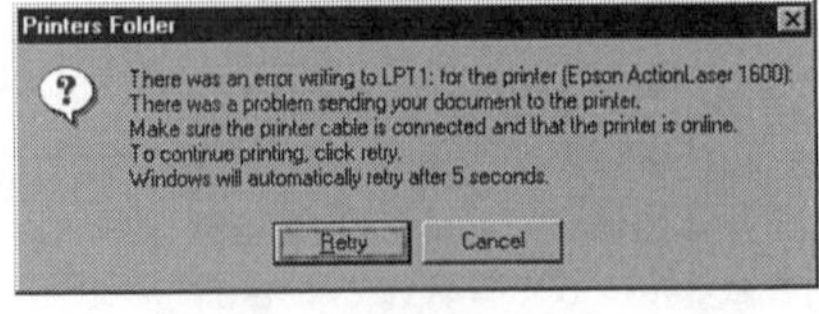

FIG. 5.10
The Print Manager diagnostic reports problems as they are found and continues until either the problem is fixed or the print job is canceled.

If you click the diagnostic's Retry button, Windows continues to monitor the printer's status at approximately five-second intervals. If you click the Cancel button, the diagnostic discontinues and the Print Manager pauses the print file.

The third troubleshooting tool is the Enhanced Print Troubleshooter, shown in Figure 5.11. This software application steps you through your problem by asking you questions concerning the problem. As you answer each question, Windows provides you with a range of possible alternatives to help you narrow in on the potential source of the problem. Clicking the hot buttons next to the most accurate answer brings up another screen with additional insight and questions. This tool is a Windows 95 executable file named EPTS.EXE.

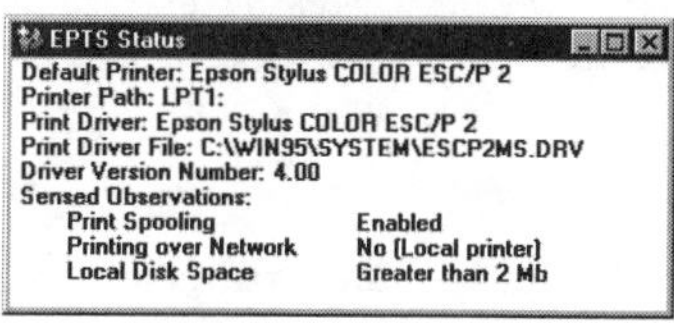

FIG. 5.11
The Enhanced Print Troubleshooter steps you through a printer problem using plain English-language prompts.

Most Common Printer Problems

The most common printing problems are printing supplies running out or a change that has recently taken place in either the printer or the operating system. In any event, a checklist is an excellent place to start because it lets you consider each possible problem. The most common problems, in order of probability, are listed here:

- **The printer is either not selected or is not the default.**

  Make the printer the system default using the Print Manager's Printer menu.

- **The printer doesn't appear to be turned on.**

  Verify that the printer has been plugged in and that the power is in the on position.

- **The printer does not begin printing even though my PC says that I am printing a document.**

  If your system is attached to more than one printer, make sure the appropriate printer is being printed to by checking the Print Manager of each attached printer to find the current print job.

- **The printer is offline.**

  Set the printer online.

- **The printer is out of paper.**

  Reload the printer's paper supply.

- **The printer is out of toner.**

  Reload the printer's supply of toner.

- **The printer is out of ink.**

  Reload the printer's ink cartridge.

- **The printer's ribbon is no longer functional.**

  Remove and replace the printer's ribbon with a new one.

- **The printer's door is open or has a failed interlock.**

  Check for open doors or covers.
- **The printer cable is not properly connected to either the printer or PC.**

  Replace or reseat the cable.
- **The Printer is not connected to the correct port.**

  Remove the cable and connect it to the appropriate port.
- **The printer's software configuration has changed or the drivers have been corrupted.**

  Delete and reinstall the printer.
- **New hardware has been added to either the printer or the PC and a conflict has resulted in addressing or interrupts.**

  Review the installation records of the printer and reconfigure it if required.
- **Additional software has been added to Windows that changed the printer's configuration files.**

  Check the printer's configuration for driver files that have changed using the printed test page created during installation.
- **An application has indicated that it can no longer print to a corrupted print driver and to the selected printer.**

  Delete and reinstall the printer.
- **The operating system has been stalled during a print operation.**

  Reboot Windows 95 and verify printer operation, by printing a test document.
- **A printout stops halfway through printing a large detailed graphic.**

  Using your application, set the print quality to draft. If the graphic printout completes, check your printer's documentation to possibly increase the amount of memory in your printer. If it doesn't complete, run a printer self-test to print a test page.
- **A printer with a cartridge option does not report that the cartridge is installed.**

  Turn the printer off and then check to verify that the cartridge is properly seated. Turn the printer on and test it again.
- **A hardware problem may have occurred in either the PC or printer that stops during the printing of a document.**

  Reinitiate printing the document. If it fails again, review the installation records of the printer and note any changes.

CHAPTER 6

Working with Fonts

by William S. Holderby

In this chapter

Understanding Fonts

Individual fonts belong to a family of similar fonts that share various characteristics such as style, size, and special effects. For example, a Times Roman font is really more than a single entity because a character set is associated with the font. To review fonts, you should first understand a few terms:

- *Font size* is the definition of how large or small a font character is displayed or printed. Sizes are normally described in points; there are approximately 72 points in an inch.
- *Font style* consists of bold, normal, italic, or bold italic. The style determines how the characters belonging to a font are displayed.
- *Font effects* defines color, special instructions (such as an underline or strikethrough), and in some cases, gradient grayscale fill for outlined fonts.

The presence of serifs is important to you as a design issue because the serifs add a decorative "complication" to characters. This means that if you create a document with sections of very small characters (for instance, less than 7 or 8 points), you'll want to use a sans serif font to make it easier to read. Also, many designers feel that sans serif is the appropriate font type for headlines.

- *Serif fonts* have projections (serifs) that extend the upper and lower strokes of the set's characters beyond their normal boundaries. The Courier font is an example of a serif font. Sans serif fonts, such as Arial, do not have these projections.
- *Font spacing* refers to the space between characters on the screen or printed page. Fixed-spaced fonts have the same space between each character. Courier is a fixed-spaced font. Proportional-spaced fonts, such as Arial, adjust the inter-character space based on the shape of the individual characters.
- *Font width* describes the width of individual characters. These widths can be fixed, normal, condensed, or expanded. In Windows, certain fonts are fixed, such as the OEM font. Other fonts use variable width to display characters that are out of proportion.

Font technology can seem complex and confusing because of the large number of fonts in use and the advantages touted by various vendors. The introduction of TrueType fonts, which provide standard font choices in all your Windows applications, has eliminated much of the confusion. Windows 95 supports numerous other font technologies from many vendors, including Adobe, Bitstream, and other software suppliers.

▶ **See** "Reviewing Types of Fonts," **p. 155**

32-Bit TrueType Font Rasterizer

Microsoft has included a new *rasterizer* that improves the time it takes to create TrueType fonts. A rasterizer prepares a TrueType font for either display or printing from a file that contains a mathematical model of the fonts characters. The Microsoft 32-bit TrueType Font Rasterizer was developed as part of the new Windows 32-bit printing architecture. A scalable font such as TrueType can be made larger or smaller without losing its distinctive shape and appearance, that is, the appearance of a character shown in size 6 is identical to the same font character at size 18. The Rasterizer creates new sizes and parameters to use in displaying font characters of different sizes, orientations, and effects (for example, Arial 12 Bold, Italic). With Microsoft Plus! installed, you can smooth display mode curves and reduce the jagged effects of font enlargement by selecting the Smooth Edges of Screen Fonts option in the Plus! tab of the Display Properties dialog box. With this option selected, the rasterizer uses a technique called *anti-aliasing* to render a smoother font.

In Windows 95, a single file—the TTF file—replaces the FOT and TTF TrueType font families. The TTF file contains all the information needed to create fonts of different sizes and complexity.

If you upgraded to Windows 95 from Windows 3.x, you can remove all the files with an extension of FOT. This will give you a little bit of additional disk space (the files aren't very large but if you have a lot of fonts, there can be quite a few of them). The .FOT files are in the Windows\System subdirectory.

Registry-Based Font Support

In Windows 3.1, fonts were identified and loaded using INI files. Windows 3.1 dutifully loaded each font during startup. The time Windows 3.1 took to start increased as more and more fonts were loaded into the system. In addition, the number of fonts available was restricted under Windows 3.1.

Windows 95 attaches fonts through the Registry. Because Windows has immediate access to these fonts, as needed, it no longer has to load all of them, thereby reducing time and overhead. The Registry also provides better management and enables access to many more fonts. Windows uses the Registry instead of the INI files to configure software options for Windows access. The Registry provides a systematic structure and interface that is available to all software regardless of manufacturer.

Changing to Registry-based fonts provides the following benefits:

- The number of fonts that Windows can configure is limited only by available disk space. The number of fonts you can simultaneously use and print in the same document is approximately 1,000.
- Registry-based fonts create an environment where more than one person can use your PC hardware. Each user can individually configure a unique environment, which can include individual font selection.
- Improved font handling through the universal Registry enables an efficient standard access for both Windows and applications.

Windows 3.1 used initialization files to identify which font files were available for use. Most 16-bit Windows applications use the WIN.INI file to identify which fonts are installed. Under Windows 95, 32-bit applications use the system Registry to access installed fonts. Windows still maintains the WIN.INI file to stay compatible with the 16-bit applications.

Required Fonts for Windows

The number of fonts that Windows 95 requires is defined by the applications that you plan to run under the operating system. If you are primarily interested in word processing, then 10 to 12 scalable fonts are more than adequate. A page of text may require only one or two fonts for emphasis. If you plan to use CAD (computer-aided design), desktop publishing, or imaging applications, consult these packages for their special requirements. Because fonts provide an additional dimension you can use to create special effects or to distinguish a particular area of a document, CAD or desktop publishing documents may require a large number of fonts.

The following list describes the standard Windows fonts that are shipped with the operating system:

- *System fonts* are used by Windows to draw menus and controls and to create specialized control text. System fonts are proportional fonts that Windows can size and manipulate quickly. Therefore, Windows uses these fonts to save time when it creates your screen environment.
- *Fixed-width fonts* are included with Windows 95 to maintain compatibility with earlier versions of Windows 2.0 and 3.0.
- *OEM fonts* are provided to support older installed products. The term *OEM* refers to Original Equipment Manufacturers. This font family includes a character set designed to be compatible with older equipment and software applications.

Fonts You Should Keep

Unlike Windows 3.1, Windows 95 does not slow down when loaded with additional fonts. However, these extra fonts do take up valuable disk real estate. You should carefully weigh the value of these fonts before you load them on your system. Microsoft has optimized the font-handling drivers for the TrueType font family, but you still may use other fonts. The decision about which fonts to keep depends on which applications you use.

The only way to make this determination is to experiment by adding, changing, displaying, printing, and eventually deleting unneeded fonts. Experiment with all the fonts on both the display and printed page before you make this decision.

NOTE Experimenting with other font families from various manufacturers provides you with a wide range of optional selections. You can add other font families to Windows, such as fonts from Adobe. However, Adobe fonts require more Windows resources because they require the Adobe Type Manager (ATM) to be running. You may want to look for TrueType fonts that will serve your needs if your applications don't specifically require ATM. ■

Reviewing Types of Fonts

Some fonts are designed to be compatible with special printing devices. These fonts use mathematical outline descriptions to create their character set. The resulting characters can be scaled and rotated. However, fonts designed for special printers are often difficult to display. To solve this problem, Adobe has created the Adobe Type Manager (ATM), a Windows application that converts Adobe PostScript printer fonts into displayable characters for use by Windows 95 applications.

NOTE Many printer vendors have designed custom software drivers to support their printers. Your printer manufacturer may have special Windows 95 handler software. ■

These output devices involve different font handling technology and drivers:

- PostScript printers use PostScript meta file printing that is similar to, but not compatible with, Windows Enhanced Meta Files (EMF).
- Dot-matrix printers range from older, very simple models to newer Near Letter Quality (NLQ) printers. Many of the older dot-matrix printers did not support downloading of soft fonts, and some of the newer printers may provide better results using proprietary drivers.
- Hewlett-Packard PCL printers use various levels of HP's Printer Control Language (PCL). For example, the Laserjet II supported level 4, and Laserjet III supports level 5 PCL. Both Windows and HP provide up-to-date drivers that provide the best font settings.
- Plotters primarily use vector fonts as plotter software converts plotter outputs into a series of straight lines.
- Specialized OEM printers may use proprietary fonts to create unique symbols or increase the speed of graphic character creation. Most of the specialized printers provide optimum performance when they are interfaced with their manufacturer's proprietary drivers.

NOTE If your printer came with special drivers, check with the manufacturer for the latest updated Windows 95 driver. ■

Windows supports three font *technologies* by default. A technology determines how a font is created, stored, and what device limitations it has. The three font technologies supported by Windows are:

- **Raster fonts.** Fonts that are bitmapped for fast display. These fonts are created in specific sizes and rotation angles.
- **Vector fonts.** Fonts that are created from mathematical line models, each character consisting of a series of lines (vectors). Vector fonts are an outgrowth of plotter technology. Pen Plotters are used extensively in Computer Aided Design (CAD) to create line drawings.

- **TrueType fonts.** Scalable, rotatable fonts created from mathematical models. These fonts are a compromise between displayable and printable fonts.

The following sections discuss these and some other font technologies.

Raster Fonts

The name *raster fonts* describes a font set that was designed primarily for the raster display. You cannot scale raster fonts in odd multiples or rotate them effectively. Raster fonts consist of arrays of dots and are stored in bitmap files with the extension FON. Raster fonts need separate files for each point size, resolution, and display device. Therefore, each raster font file has a letter designating its targeted device:

D = printer

E = VGA display

F = 8514 display

The Courier raster font has three files associated with it: COURD.FON for the printer font, COURE.FON for the VGA font, and COURF.FON for the fonts optimized for the 8514 display. Each raster file is optimized for its intended display device and contains attribute-specific information:

- Font type
- Font character set
- Font sizes
- Font optimized resolution

You can scale raster fonts in even multiples up to the point where they no longer appear smooth. By their nature, bitmaps that are expanded too far lose their orderly appearance and smoothness. However, these fonts are quickly displayed and reduce the Windows screen refresh time.

Raster fonts are printable only if the chosen font set is compatible with your printer's horizontal and vertical resolution.

NOTE Not all printers can print raster fonts acceptably. Before you combine any font type with your printer, you should first test the compatibility. You can test the appearance of printed fonts by creating a page of text using that font type and then printing that page. Another way to test printed fonts is print the font family from the Control Panel's Font folder shown later in this chapter.

Five raster fonts are supplied with Windows 95, and several other vendors supply additional font sizes. The supplied raster fonts are MS Serif, MS Sans Serif, Courier, System, and Terminal.

Vector Fonts

Vector fonts are derived from lines or vectors that describe each character's shape. You can scale vector fonts to any size or aspect ratio. The characters are stored as a set of points and interconnecting lines that Windows 95 can use to scale the font to any required size. These fonts are very applicable for plotting and CAD. As with the raster fonts, vector fonts are stored in FON files.

The way Windows 95 treats this font type is to rasterize the various characters by using function calls to the Graphics Device Interface (GDI). The number of calls required for each font increases the display time required to create the characters and to refresh the display. The fonts are useful for CAD and desktop publishing because they are readily extensible. Large vector font sizes maintain the same aspect ratio as smaller sizes. Windows 95 supplies three vector fonts: ROMAN, SCRIPT, and MODERN. Additional fonts are available from several sources, including CAD and desktop publishing software vendors.

TrueType Fonts

TrueType fonts use *scalable* font technology. Scalable fonts have many advantages over raster fonts and have greatly simplified the use and management of fonts. Scalable fonts are stored in files that contain both the outline information and the ratios necessary to scale the font. Windows uses this information to render the fonts, that is, to produce the dots needed to display and print the font.

Windows 95 supplies many TrueType fonts, including Arial (ARIAL.TTF), New Courier (COUR.TTF), Times New Roman (TIMES.TTF), and Swiss (TT0007M_.TTF). Because TrueType fonts are included with Windows, scalable fonts are available to all users at no extra cost. A market still exists for Adobe PostScript Type 1 fonts, because these fonts are the standard in the typesetting world. For most users, however, TrueType fonts are more than sufficient.

Other Fonts

In addition to raster, vector, and TrueType fonts, other fonts exist that perform specialized services. Your printer may have an entire set of fonts or may be configured with font sets through the use of font cartridges or additional cards. The following list describes additional Windows 95 fonts:

- **System fonts.** 8514SYS.FON and VGASYS.FON.
- **OEM fonts.** 8514OEM.FON and VGAOEM.FON.
- **Fixed fonts.** 8514FIX.FON and VGAFIX.FON.
- **MS-DOS legacy fonts.** Several MS-DOS-compatible font files for DOS applications to use while running in the Windows 95 environment. These files provide backward compatibility to the real-mode DOS environment. Files included are CGA40WOA.FON, CGA80WOA.FON, DOSAPP.FON, EGA40WOA.FON, and EGA80WOA.FON. Although these fonts are primarily used for application display, the DOSAPP.FON is a good choice for printing.

- **Printer soft fonts.** Depending on your printing hardware, you may download soft fonts to your printer. Downloading fonts reduces the time taken by the printer to process printouts. You download soft fonts once to speed up subsequent print jobs.

Installing and Deleting Fonts

During the Windows installation process, Windows loads its standard suite of font files onto the system disk. Windows and your applications use these files as default fonts. You have the option of installing and deleting fonts from your system to change the look of your desktop environment, word-processing, spreadsheet applications, or for use by special application needs, such as CAD.

CAUTION

Be careful when deleting seemingly useless font sets. Deleting certain sets such as fixed, OEM, or system fonts may drastically alter the look and proportion of your Windows desktop and applications. When you delete fonts, you may see applications and even Windows dialog boxes change appearance. Even though Windows substitutes existing fonts to replace deleted ones, you may not like the substitution. Make sure you have a backup copy of all fonts you delete, as you may want to replace them for aesthetic reasons.

Installing New Fonts

Windows enables you to quickly install new fonts using the Control Panel; you can install fonts from the Windows disks or from vendor supplied disks. This procedure installs new Fonts into Windows Registry for use by both Windows and applications.

1. Open the Start menu and choose Settings; then choose Control Panel. Double-click the Fonts folder in the Control Panel. Windows displays the Fonts window that contains a list of all the fonts currently registered by the system (see Figure 6.1).
2. You can display the list as individual icons with the name of each font below the icons. Or you can display a detailed list that contains the name of the font, the name and extension of the font file, the size of the file, and the date of its creation. To change the look of this list, choose View and then choose Large Icons, List, or Details. See Figure 6.1 for an example of Details view.

NOTE On occasion, you may want to look at the list of font types displayed without their many variations, such as Bold. You may choose this option in conjunction with other View menu selections by choosing View, Hide Variations (Bold, Italic, and so on). ■

3. Choose Files, Install. Windows displays the Add Fonts dialog box, shown in Figure 6.2.
4. Using the Drives and Folders controls, choose the location of the font you want to install. This location may be a directory on the hard drive or a manufacturer's floppy disk.
5. Windows displays a roster in the List of Fonts window. Select the font or fonts to add. If these fonts are in a location other than the Windows font directory, you may have the

files automatically copied to this directory by checking the Copy Fonts to Windows Folder box at the bottom of the Add Fonts dialog box.

6. Click OK to add the selected font(s). Windows installs the new fonts and enters them in its Registry.

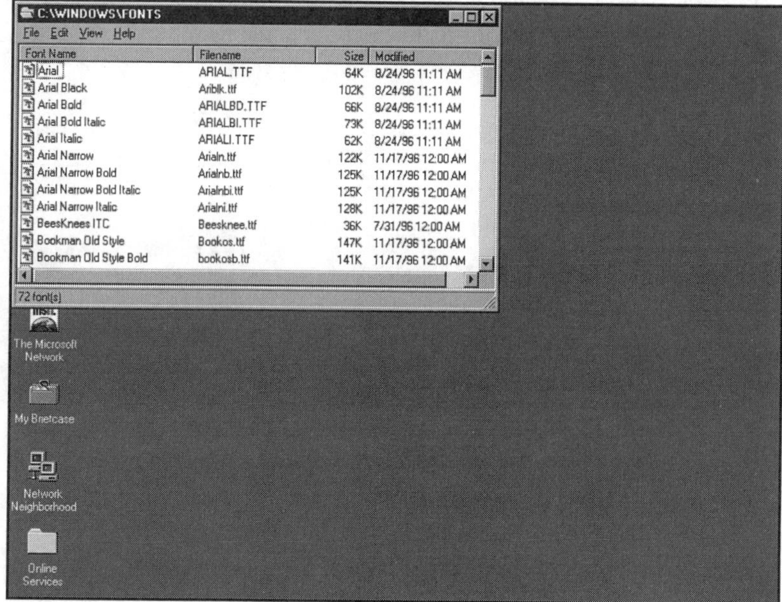

FIG. 6.1
The Fonts window shows which fonts are loaded along with their file name, size, and configuration date.

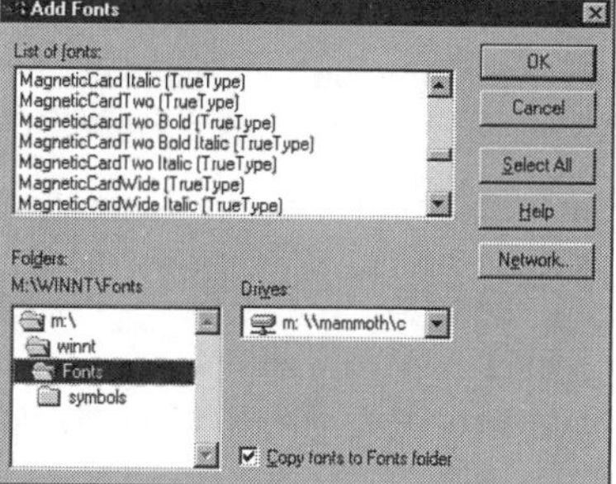

FIG. 6.2
The Add Fonts dialog box provides the controls needed to add a new font to Windows 95.

Deleting Fonts from the Hard Disk

Windows also enables you to quickly delete installed fonts from the Control Panel. The following procedure deletes unwanted fonts and removes them from the Windows Registry.

1. Open the Start menu and choose Settings; then choose Control Panel. Double-click the Fonts folder in the Control Panel. In the Fonts window, Windows displays the fonts currently registered by the system (refer to Figure 6.1).

2. Highlight the font or fonts to delete.
3. Choose File, Delete.

If you mistakenly delete fonts, you may recover them from the Recycle Bin.

4. Windows displays a warning asking if you want to delete these fonts. Choose Yes. Windows shows the font being sent to the Recycle bin as it removes the deleted fonts from the Registry.

NOTE For faster deletion, you can also delete fonts by dragging and dropping them from the Fonts Folder into the Recycle bin, using the Windows Explorer. ■

Using TrueType Fonts

TrueType fonts are an integral part of Windows 95 and many font styles come bundled with the operating system, as described earlier. TrueType scalable fonts offer several advantages over previous font technologies:

- A single font file can print and display the font over a wide range of point sizes. Raster files require many font files to cover the same range of sizes.
- The same font file can render both screen display and printer output. Raster fonts require a screen font and printer font file for each font set.
- The technology for scalable fonts has standardized the production of fonts, bringing the cost of font production way down.
- You can use the same font with any printer that has a Windows printer driver. Individual printer manufacturers don't need to worry about creating fonts for their printers.
- By using the same font file to render both the screen and printer fonts, the match between what you see on your screen and the printer output is very close.

TrueType fonts have certain limitations, however. The anti-aliasing technology described earlier in this chapter needs a 256-color mode or higher, requiring more complex and higher-priced hardware. For specific printing applications and CAD applications, PostScript fonts repeatedly provide better printing results. In addition, not every printer is compatible with TrueType fonts, causing some printers to treat TrueType fonts as graphics and thus reducing printer speed.

Windows enables you to easily identify your TrueType fonts. Open the Fonts windows in the Control Panel. Choose View, Large Icon to display your fonts as icons. TrueType fonts are designated with an icon containing the letters T_T. In the List and Details view, TrueType fonts are shown prefaced by a smaller icon showing T_T. In the Details view, TrueType fonts also are denoted by their file type TTF. Other font types are shown as file type FON.

If you work with many MS-DOS applications, note that TrueType and other fonts are also distinguishable by their file extensions. TrueType fonts have the TTF extension; other font types have the FON extension.

Adding or Removing TrueType Fonts

You add or delete TrueType fonts the same way you add or delete other font types. To add or remove TrueType fonts, use the previously described Add a Font or Delete a Font procedures, selecting only fonts with TTF file extensions.

Using Windows 3.1 TrueType Fonts

In Windows 3.1, each TrueType font was maintained by two files, TTF and FOT. Windows 95 eliminates the need for an FOT by implementing faster font creation. You can add your existing TrueType fonts to Windows 95 by specifying the TTF file when adding a font. Windows will not ask for a separate FOT file and accepts Windows 3.1 TrueType fonts as well as fonts created from most existing applications.

Using Only TrueType Fonts

To select only TrueType fonts in your applications, you can set the appropriate font option. Microsoft has integrated TrueType fonts into the Windows operating system. If you want to only use TrueType fonts in your applications, follow this procedure:

1. Choose the Fonts folder from the Control Panel. Windows displays the Fonts folder containing a list of the registered fonts.
2. Choose View, Options.
3. Choose the TrueType tab in the Options dialog box (see Figure 6.3).

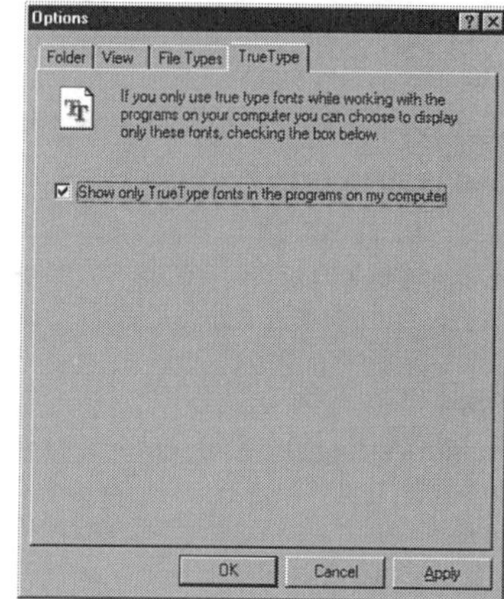

FIG. 6.3 To configure only TrueType fonts for applications, check the box in the Options dialog box that reads Show Only TrueType Fonts in the Programs on My Computer.

4. Check the box that reads Show Only TrueType Fonts in the Programs on my Computer. Now, only TrueType fonts are shown as available to applications.

Using Other Font Configurations

Each printer in your Windows 95 system is configurable through its Printer Properties pages. The printer property options vary from printer to printer. Many printers support downloaded soft fonts. And many of these printers support TrueType fonts as downloaded soft fonts or support printing them as graphics. You can set these options on the appropriate Printer Properties Fonts page, but you should understand the ramifications of any changes you make.

Downloading TrueType fonts as soft fonts stores the fonts in your printer. If your printer has adequate memory to store fonts, downloading speeds up the printing operation. If the printer is unable to store these fonts, you usually receive a "memory overflow" error on the printer following the download. Printing TrueType fonts as graphics increases your printing time, but on some printers, it substantially improves the look and quality of the printed font.

PostScript printers provide an option to substitute PostScript fonts for TrueType fonts by use of a Font Substitution Table. The Printer Properties Fonts page for those printers enables you to change which fonts are substituted by changing the table.

Managing Fonts in Windows 95

In Windows 95, fonts are a managed resource. Applications can quickly access fonts through standardized registration, making your fonts quickly available for viewing, printing, comparing, sorting, adding, and deleting.

Previewing and Printing Font Samples

Before you use a font, you may want to preview it or print a sample before committing it to a document. Windows provides quick access to this information by performing the following steps:

1. In the Control Panel, double-click the Fonts folder. Windows displays the Fonts window containing the list of registered fonts.
2. Select the font you want to view and choose File, Open; or double-click the font to view it. Windows displays the font in various sizes (see Figure 6.4).

You also can print a sample from the Fonts folder by selecting the font and choosing File, Print.

3. To print the sample page, choose Print.
4. When you are done previewing and printing the font, choose Done.

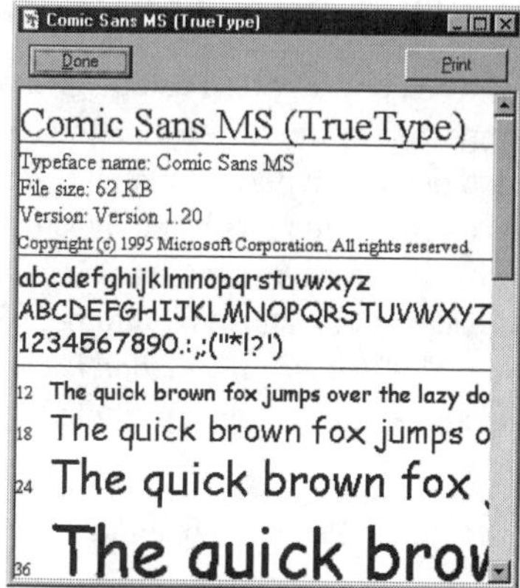

FIG. 6.4
A sample of a font type showing sizes and font detail information.

Showing Font Properties

Fonts, like most other Windows objects, have properties. The properties include version information that may contain important information for purposes of upgrading your fonts. Although at present there is no way to change these font properties, you can view the information contained in these screens in the following procedure.

1. Double-click the Fonts icon in the Control Panel. Windows displays the Fonts window containing the list of registered fonts.
2. Select the font you want to view.
3. Choose File, Properties. Windows displays a properties sheet like the one shown in Figure 6.5. The properties sheet contains version and management information for each font type registered by Windows.

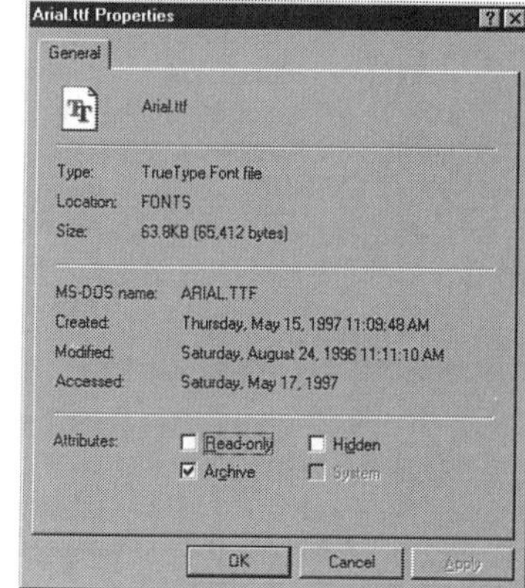

FIG. 6.5
A properties sheet for the Arial TrueType font provides file and configuration information.

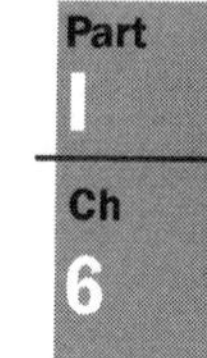

Viewing Fonts by Similarity

Fonts are distinguished by their differences, but they also can be grouped by similar features. Grouping fonts by similarity may be important to you when you find subtle differences in the text in a document or when your printed document doesn't match the display. Substituting a similar font may correct this problem. You will find fonts listed by similarity, except where Windows has insufficient Panose information to make a comparison. *Panose* refers to a Windows internal description that assigns each font a Panose ID number. Windows uses several internal descriptions to categorize fonts. The Panose information is used to register a font class and a means to compare similar font features. You can group similar fonts by following this procedure.

1. Double-click the Fonts icon in the Control Panel to open the Fonts folder with a list of registered fonts.
2. To change the way the fonts are displayed, choose View, Details, List, or Large Icons.
3. To see which fonts are similar to a specific font, choose View, List Files by Similarity. Windows redisplays the Font list as shown in Figure 6.6.
4. Open the List Fonts by Similarity To drop-down list, and select a font from the list to use as a master against which you test other fonts for similarity. The list now shows all fonts with an assessment of their similarity to the master font. Fonts are shown as being very similar, fairly similar, not similar, or no Panose information available.

You can test the similarity of other fonts by selecting the "List Fonts by Similarity to" control and choosing another font type.

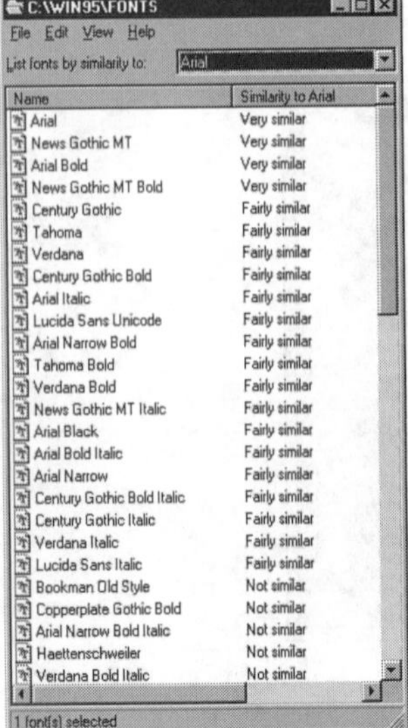

FIG. 6.6
This list shows how closely other font types match the Arial font.

Installing Printer Fonts

Printer fonts reside in the printer as a cartridge or within the printer's memory. You can install printer fonts through Windows or through installation applications that usually accompany your printer. Follow these steps to install printer fonts using Windows:

1. Open the Print Manager for the selected printer.

   ▶ **See** "The Print Manager," **p. 137**

2. Choose Printer, Properties.
3. Choose the Fonts tab on the properties sheet. See the Printer Properties Fonts page shown in Figure 6.7. Note that each printer type is supported by a different set of Properties pages, which depend on the make, model, and hardware configuration of the printer.

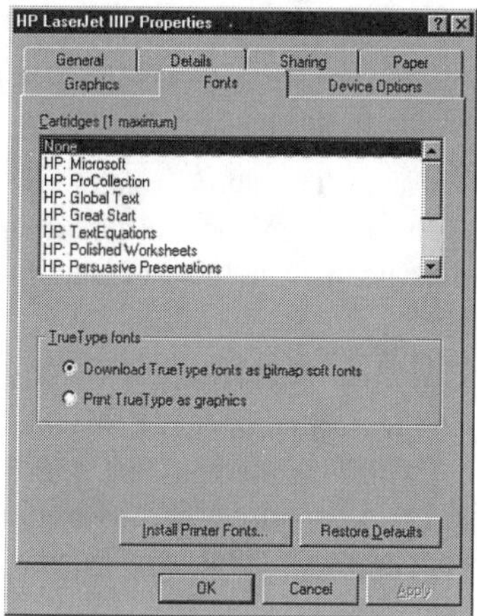

FIG. 6.7 The Printer Properties Fonts page displays the available font options for the selected printer and allows you to install new printer fonts.

4. Choose Install Printer Fonts. A dialog box similar to the one in Figure 6.8 appears. The printer fonts installer for your printer may look different from the one shown in the figure, but all installers perform similar functions.

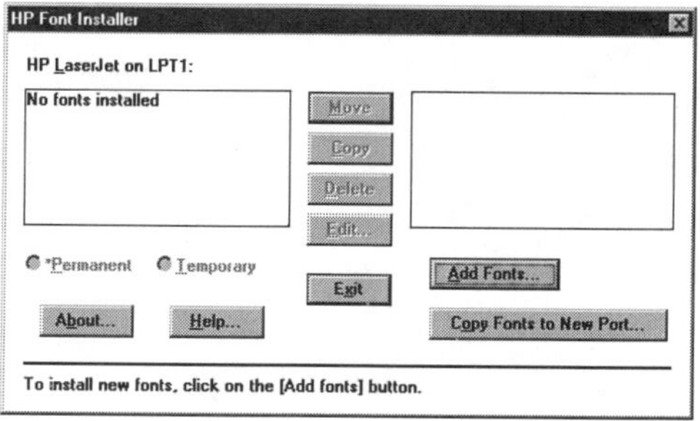

FIG. 6.8 The HP Font Installer dialog box.

NOTE The HP Fonts Installer shown in Figure 6.8 cannot be used to download TrueType fonts to HP Printers. PCL printers can download only PCL-compatible fonts. Be certain that your printer and the fonts being specified for download are compatible. Refer to the installer's help file for more information on compatible fonts. ■

5. Select the fonts to be installed in the list on the right side of the Font Installer dialog box.
6. Choose Copy to move the selected fonts to the left window.
7. Choose Add Fonts to register the printer's fonts. A dialog box appears, asking for the location of the fonts. This box provides a Browse button to enable you to find the disk location of the fonts to be installed.
8. Identify where the font files are located and click OK to enable Windows to install the selected fonts.

Downloading Fonts as Permanent or Temporary

Most Printer Properties Fonts pages include a set of option button controls that enable you to select whether a font is to be temporarily or permanently downloaded.

Download frequently used fonts as permanent. This allows you to print faster. However, permanent downloaded fonts limit the amount of printer memory available for printing. Therefore, to stay within normal printer memory limits, keep the number of fonts you specify as permanent to three of four.

Downloading fonts as temporary does not store the font in the printer's memory until it is needed. The font is loaded only temporarily in the printer before a document is printed and removed after the printing is completed. This increases printing time, but it also increases the amount of available printer memory and reduces print overrun errors. Downloading fonts as temporary is the default setting and works well with most applications. ●

CHAPTER 7

Plug and Play and Legacy Device Installation

In this chapter

TROUBLESHOOTING

When I use the Add New Hardware Wizard, it fails to detect a device upgrade for an unsupported device. What am I doing wrong? If you have upgraded a sound card or other device that uses Windows 3.1 drivers, the new sound card may not be detected by the Add New Hardware Wizard. This occurs because Windows 95 is still seeing the reference to the older card's 16-bit drivers in the SYSTEM.INI file. To resolve the problem, you must go into SYSTEM.INI with a text editor, such as NOTEPAD.EXE, and remove the lines referring to the 16-bit drivers. Run the Add New Hardware Wizard, and the new sound card or other device should be set up correctly.

This chapter helps you understand how Plug and Play works—and more importantly, what to do when it doesn't. You learn how to use the Add New Hardware Wizard and other tools to work with peripherals that are not Plug and Play-compliant. You also learn how to handle conflicts.

Installing Plug and Play Hardware

Plug and Play can make adding peripherals easy for users of all levels of expertise. With the proper hardware, installing peripherals can be as simple as plugging in an add-in card and starting up the PC. This section guides you through the steps involved in setting up a Plug and Play device. You also learn how Plug and Play technology works.

How Windows 95 Plug and Play Works

Because it addresses so many components in the PC, Plug and Play is a complex technology. Plug and Play enables all parts of the PC to communicate to each other, from the low level BIOS to the various add-in cards. When Windows 95 starts, the operating system and PC go through a series of steps to establish configurations, arbitrate conflicts, and record changes.

The Components of Plug and Play To understand how Plug and Play works, you have to know what elements are involved. Four major technologies work together under Plug and Play:

- **System BIOS (basic input/output system).** The system BIOS is the low-level code that boots your system, detects the hard disk, and manages basic operations. Plug and Play systems employ a specially tuned BIOS that has the intelligence to detect hardware and manage configuration changes.

NOTE Under the Plug and Play specification, PnP BIOSes are identified as Plug and Play BIOS version 1.0a or later. To find out what BIOS version you have, look for the BIOS information on your monitor at the beginning of the bootup process. ■

- **Operating system.** The operating system interacts with the BIOS and hardware, playing a critical role in Plug and Play. Windows 95 is the first Plug and Play operating system, but Microsoft intends to bring the technology to Windows NT in the future.

- **Hardware peripherals.** To be Plug and Play-compliant, adapter cards and other hardware must include circuitry that stores configuration data and allows interaction with other PnP components. PCI add-in cards, by definition, are PnP-compliant, while ISA and EISA cards must be specifically designed for PnP. External peripherals such as modems or printers can be PnP as well.
- **Device drivers.** Drivers let your peripherals talk to Windows 95. Under Windows 95's Plug and Play, hardware must employ 32-bit *virtual device drivers* (called VxDs), as opposed to the 16-bit, real-mode drivers used under DOS/Windows 3.x.

NOTE The 32-bit VxDs for most devices are supplied by the hardware vendors. If the appropriate driver is not available on the Windows 95 CD-ROM or disks, contact your peripheral manufacturer to get the latest PnP-compliant drivers.

Walking Through the PnP Process Each time you boot up the system, a series of steps occurs that launches the Plug and Play process. All the hardware on the system is checked at boot time, so if new hardware has been installed, it will be detected and the appropriate steps taken by the PnP system.

The list below details the steps that Windows 95 goes through during system startup:

1. The system BIOS identifies the devices on the motherboard (including the type of bus), as well as external devices such as disk drives, keyboard, video display, and other adapter cards that are required for the boot process.
2. The system BIOS determines the resource (IRQ, DMA, I/O, and memory address) requirements of each boot device. The BIOS also determines which devices are legacy devices with fixed resource requirements and which are PnP devices with flexible resource requirements. Note that some devices don't require all four resource types.

NOTE Microsoft uses the term *legacy device* to refer to older hardware peripherals that do not comply with the Plug and Play specification. As a general rule, any ISA card bought before 1995 is probably a legacy device.

3. Windows 95 allocates resources to each PnP device, after allowing for legacy devices with fixed resource assignments. If many legacy and PnP devices are in use, Windows 95 may require many iterations of the allocation process to eliminate all resource conflicts by changing the resource assignments of the PnP devices.
4. Windows 95 creates a final system configuration and stores the resource allocation data for this configuration in the registration database (the Registry).
5. Windows 95 searches the \WINDOWS\SYSTEM directory to find the required driver for the device. If the device driver is missing, a dialog box appears asking you to insert into drive A the manufacturer's floppy disk containing the driver software. Windows 95 loads the driver into memory and then completes its startup operations.

Note that Windows 95 makes educated guesses about the identity and resource requirements of legacy devices. Windows 95 includes a large database of resource settings for legacy devices, allowing it to detect and configure itself to a variety of existing hardware. However, this detection is not perfect, and it forces dynamic PnP peripherals to be configured around the static settings of legacy hardware.

Understanding Plug and Play Hardware

Of course, Windows 95 Plug and Play works best on systems properly equipped to support it. This section helps you to determine if your existing PC is Plug and Play-ready; and if not, what you can do to upgrade it. This section also can help you to determine whether a new system you plan to buy is PnP-compliant.

Determining Whether Your PC Supports Plug and Play So is your PC Plug and Play? To make that claim, a system must have a BIOS that conforms to Plug and Play version 1.0a or later. Vendors generally began building Plug and Play into motherboards at the beginning of 1995, so older PCs probably won't support direct PnP features.

NOTE Even if your BIOS is PnP-compliant, you won't have a true Plug and Play system until all the peripherals in your system are PnP, too. Remember, legacy devices force Windows 95 to make educated guesses about their requirements and their resources can't be dynamically allocated. ■

How can you find out if your Windows 95 system is PnP-ready? Go to Windows 95's System Properties sheet and do the following:

1. Click the Device Manager tab of the System Properties sheet to display Devices by Type. (Click the View Devices by Type option button if necessary.)
2. Double-click the System Devices icon in the device list to expand the System Devices list.
3. If your PC supports Plug and Play, you see a Plug and Play BIOS entry (see Figure 7.1). The I/O Read Data Port for ISA Plug and Play Enumerator item appears regardless of whether your PC is Plug and Play.

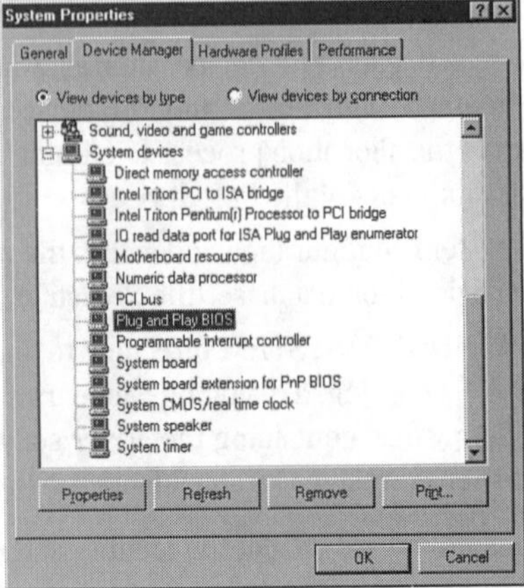

FIG. 7.1 Check the System Devices list to determine whether your PC has Plug and Play BIOS.

4. Double-click the Plug and Play BIOS icon to open the properties sheet for the Plug and Play BIOS.
5. Click the Driver tab to display the device driver (BIOS.VXD) that Windows 95 uses to connect to the PnP feature of your system BIOS (see Figure 7.2).
6. To leave the sheet, click OK, and then click OK on the System properties sheet.

FIG. 7.2
Click the Driver tab to check the properties of Windows 95's Plug and Play BIOS device driver.

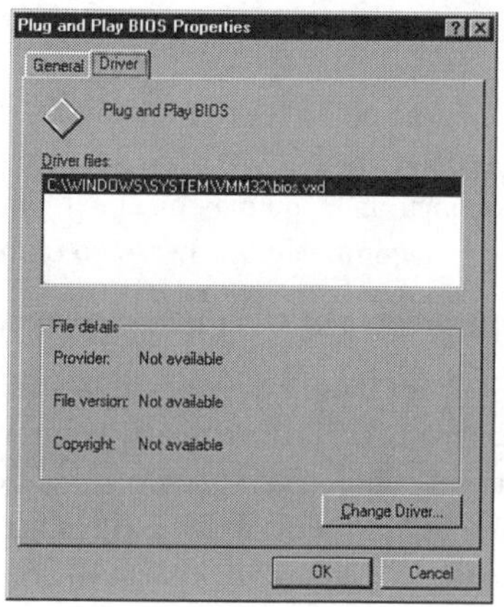

What does a Plug and Play BIOS do exactly? As the cornerstone of PnP functionality, the BIOS adds three major enhancements to conventional PC BIOSes:

- *Resource management* handles the basic system resources: direct memory access (DMA), interrupt requests (IRQs), input/output (I/0), and shared memory address ranges. Resource management allows various devices to access limited system resources without causing conflicts. The Plug and Play BIOS resource manager configures boot devices on the motherboard and any PnP devices in the system.
- *Runtime management* of configuration is available with PnP. PnP BIOS includes the capability to reconfigure devices after the operating system loads. This feature is particularly important for notebook PCs that have PCMCIA (also known as PC Card) devices that you can change at will. Previously, the operating system considered all devices detected by the BIOS to be static, which required restarting the system anytime a PC Card or other device was swapped out.
- *Event management* detects when devices have been removed or added to the system while the computer is running. PnP BIOS 1.0a provides event management, such as detecting when your notebook PC is connected to a docking adapter. (Note that installing or removing desktop add-in cards while the PC is running is not a safe practice.) Event management relies on runtime management to reconfigure the system.

CAUTION

Some brands of computers whose motherboards were produced in 1994 display messages during the boot process, indicating that the motherboard supports Plug and Play. Many of these motherboards, however, have early versions of the PnP BIOS, which do not conform to the 1.0a specification. Even if your computer displays a PnP message during the boot process, check Device Manager for the Plug and Play BIOS entry to verify that you have PnP BIOS 1.0a.

Upgrading to Plug and Play If you have an older 486 or Pentium PC, you may not be able to take advantage of Plug and Play. The problem is that the BIOS in these systems was written before there was a PnP standard to support. Still, you may be able to upgrade your PC to support PnP, so that future installations of PnP-compliant hardware go more smoothly.

Generally, there are three options for upgrading an older PC to a Plug and Play BIOS:

- **Flash the BIOS.** This is an option for those systems with a Flash BIOS, a nonvolatile memory chip (NVRAM) that retains BIOS instructions when the power is turned off. Updating a Flash BIOS is as easy as running an upgrade utility from a floppy disk. The utility writes a newer BIOS to the NVRAM chip, effectively turning your PC into a PnP system. Contact your system vendor for an updated Flash BIOS.
- **Replace the BIOS chip.** If your system is two years old or more, you probably don't have a Flash BIOS. But you may be able to replace the BIOS chip, which is often seated into a socket on the motherboard. You'll need to call your PC or motherboard vendor about a PnP BIOS upgrade kit, which lets you pull the existing BIOS chip(s) and plug in the replacement(s).
- **Replace the motherboard.** This is the most radical (and expensive) approach, but it's the only solution if the BIOS chip is soldered directly onto the motherboard and is not Flash-upgradable. You need to make sure the new motherboard fits in your system's chassis and accepts your existing add-in cards, memory, and processor.

NOTE While a motherboard upgrade can update older BIOSes to Plug and Play, it may make more sense to wait to purchase a new system. A new PC comes with updated peripherals, such as a larger hard drive and faster graphics board, which improve overall system performance.

Purchasing a Plug and Play System Owners of older PCs may have to do a little investigating to determine if their systems support Plug and Play, but newer systems should be PnP-compliant right out of the box. Now that Microsoft has committed to bringing PnP to its other Windows operating system—Windows NT—the presence of PnP on Intel-compatible PCs becomes even more important.

Making sure you have a PnP-ready PC is not difficult. Generally, any machine that displays the "Designed for Windows 95" logo is PnP-compliant. Lacking that logo, look for the following:

- **Plug and Play BIOS 1.0a or later.** Also make sure that the system uses a Flash BIOS, because future updates to the PnP specification or other system architectures may require a BIOS upgrade.
- **PCI bus expansion slots.** Unlike ISA peripherals, all PCI cards are PnP-compliant. Even in non-PnP systems, PCI cards arbitrate configuration among themselves and offer the further convenience of being software-configurable. Also, the VESA Local Bus (VLB) standard is on the wane as Pentium systems replace 486s, which makes VLB peripherals harder to find.

You should also check if the ISA peripherals installed in the PC, such as sound boards or modems, are PnP-compliant. Remember, the presence of non-PnP or legacy hardware in your system makes the task of hardware configuration more difficult and prone to failure. You should also check on the CD-ROM and fixed disks to ensure that they are designed for the specification.

TROUBLESHOOTING

Why does my PCI graphics card show an IRQ conflict in the System properties sheet? Under Plug and Play, PCI cards can share IRQs; however, Windows 95 does not support PCI cards that try to share IRQs with non-PCI devices. While Windows 95 display drivers do not require IRQ resources, PCI graphics cards request an IRQ in order to maintain full compatibility. As a result, all PCI graphics cards attempt to assign an IRQ. You must use Device Manager to assign a new IRQ setting to the device that is conflicting with the PCI graphics card.

Why does Device Manager show a resource conflict with a PCI-to-ISA bridge? There is no conflict here. If your Plug and Play BIOS reports both a PCI and an ISA bus, the Device Manager may report a conflict with that component. Users see an exclamation point in a yellow circle next to the PCI-to-ISA bridge entry in Device Manager. However, the PCI and ISA buses both work normally; there is no actual conflict. If you want, you can contact your hardware vendor to see if an updated Plug and Play BIOS is available that will only report a PCI bus.

Installing Plug and Play Hardware

If you've been through a few nightmarish upgrades, you'll find installing a PnP adapter card into a PnP-compliant PC to be a refreshing experience. To install both a new card and its 32-bit VxD driver, do the following:

1. Turn off power to the PC.
2. Open the case and install the adapter card, following the instructions provided with the card.
3. Close the case and turn on your PC.
4. Insert the driver software floppy disk in your A or B drive, if requested, and follow the steps for installing the driver software.
5. Restart Windows 95, if requested.

It's that easy. If the driver for your card is included with Windows 95, you may not need the card's floppy disk; Windows 95 automatically sets up the driver for your device. (Note that in this case, you may need to put the Windows 95 CD-ROM or requested floppy disk into the appropriate drive so the bundled VxD can be loaded.)

Windows 95 and your hardware may both provide a 32-bit VxD for your device. Compare the dates of the driver files using Explorer, and install the more recent file.

The same basic procedure applies for PnP-compatible external devices, such as printers, scanners, or external modems. If your PC has PnP-compliant serial and parallel ports, you will follow a procedure similar to the one in the preceding list. When you add or change a peripheral device, you don't need to open the PC, and in some cases (modems, for example), a new driver is not required.

▶ **See** "Using Your Laptop with a Docking System," **p. 190**

Installing Legacy (non-PnP) Hardware

As a Plug and Play operating system, Windows 95 may eventually make even complex upgrades a simple matter of plugging in a card and booting to a new configuration. But the existence of millions of add-in cards and external peripherals with no PnP support means that day is still sometime in the future. Understanding this, Microsoft has gone to great effort to ensure that non-PnP peripherals are adequately supported under the new regime.

The effort seems to have paid off. While installing legacy devices can still be tricky, the experience is simpler and less hazardous than under 16-bit Windows 3.x. This section shows you how to install legacy devices.

How Windows 95 Operates with Legacy Hardware

Windows 95 cannot fully automate the configuration of legacy devices; however, it does interact with non-PnP devices to ease the process. Detection routines, for example, allow Windows 95 to recognize popular add-in cards such as Creative Labs Soundblaster boards, even though they lack PnP capability. The System Properties sheet, meanwhile, provides a one-stop shop for determining hardware conflicts, editing resource setting values, and optimizing performance. Finally, Windows 95's automated handling of PnP devices makes managing the remaining legacy hardware that much easier.

Almost all PC adapter cards require at least one interrupt request (IRQ) level and a set of I/O base memory addresses for communication with your PC's processor. Some cards require one or more DMA (Direct Memory Access) channels for high-speed communication with your PC's RAM. IRQs, I/O memory, and DMA channels collectively are called *device resources.*

Legacy adapter cards use the following two methods for setting device resource values:

- *Mechanical jumpers* that create a short circuit between two pins of a multipin header. Jumpers are commonly used to designate resource values for sound cards, and they must be set to match the resource settings of Windows 95. If jumper settings do not match those set in Windows 95, the device will not operate.

- *Nonvolatile memory (NVM)* for storing resource assignments. Nonvolatile memory—such as electrically erasable, programmable read-only memory (EEPROM)—retains data when you turn off your PC's power. Network adapter cards and sound cards commonly use NVM. Usually, you must run a setup program for the card to match the board settings to those of the operating system.

NOTE PCI adapter cards do not have jumpers or nonvolatile memory to designate resource values. Instead, the system BIOS and Windows 95 automatically allocate resources needed by PCI adapter cards during the boot process.

The following sections describe how Windows 95 deals with a variety of legacy adapter cards. Later chapters of this book describe in detail the installation process for specific device types, such as modems, CD-ROM drives, and sound cards.

▶ **See** "Installing and Configuring Your Modem," **p. 68**

▶ **See** "Installing and Configuring Sound Options," **p. 107**

▶ **See** "Installing and Using a CD-ROM Drive," **p. 124**

Legacy Device Detection During Windows 95 Setup

When you run Windows 95's setup program, Windows 95 attempts to detect all the hardware devices in your PC, including legacy devices, such as ISA sound cards and network adapters. It then installs 32-bit protected mode drivers for peripherals for which updated drivers are available. However, Windows 95 often keeps references to real-mode (16-bit) device drivers in the CONFIG.SYS and AUTOEXEC.BAT files, which are used when the system runs DOS software in DOS-only mode.

If Windows can't identify the legacy device, you need to install the device manually. This procedure is described in the section "Installing Legacy Cards After Setting Up Drivers," later in this chapter.

Setting Resource Values for Legacy Adapter Cards

You must set the IRQ, I/O base address, and DMA channel parameters of a new adapter card to values that do not conflict with the resource values that are already assigned to system devices, PCI slots, or other legacy adapter cards. One of the problems with the basic design of IBM-compatible PCs is that only 16 interrupts are available, and the majority of these interrupts are likely to be in use. Therefore, your choice of IRQs is limited.

NOTE The word "base" in *I/O base address* refers to the location at which the block of I/O addresses for the adapter card begins. The actual number of address bytes occupied by the I/O system of the adapter card varies with the type of card. I/O addresses are separated by 16 bytes, and most adapter cards require fewer than 16 bytes of I/O address space.

Table 7.1 lists the PC's IRQs and most common use of each interrupt level.

Table 7.1 Interrupt Assignments and Options for ISA Cards Installed in 80×86-Based PCs

IRQ	Function	Most Common Use
0	Internal timer	Dedicated; not accessible
1	Keyboard	Dedicated; not accessible
2	Tied to IRQ9	Dedicated; see IRQ9
3	Second serial port	COM2 and COM4; usually assigned to a modem
4	First serial port	COM1 and COM3; usually for a serial mouse
5	Second parallel printer	Often used for bus mouse, network, and scanner cards
6	Floppy disk drives	Dedicated; do not use
7	First parallel printer	Used by some scanner cards; otherwise available
8	Time-of-day clock	Dedicated; not accessible
9	IRQ2 on 80×86 computers	IRQ2 is rerouted to IRQ9; often shown as IRQ2/9
10	Unassigned	Good choice for sound card, if offered
11	Unassigned	Not a common option; use if 12 is assigned
12	Usually unassigned	Sometimes dedicated to an IBM-style mouse port
13	80×87 coprocessor	Dedicated; do not use even if an 80×87 is not installed
14	Fixed-disk drive	Dedicated; do not use
15	Usually unassigned	Used for secondary disk controller, if installed

Assigning IRQs is a real shell game, with many legacy devices being limited to just two or three specific IRQ numbers. In addition, many ISA boards won't support high IRQ numbers (any setting above IRQ9), which further limits your options.

When you install a new legacy device, you should assign it the highest IRQ number that it will support, leaving the lower IRQs for cards that don't support interrupts above IRQ9 or IRQ10. The Soundblaster 16 audio adapter card, for example, supports only IRQ2/9, IRQ5 (default), IRQ7, and IRQ10.

Virtually all PCs come with two serial port devices (COM1 and COM2) and one parallel port (LPT1) device. COM1 is usually occupied by the serial mouse, unless your PC has a separate IBM PS/2-compatible mouse port that requires an assignable interrupt. The default interrupt for the Soundblaster and most MPC-compatible audio adapter cards is IRQ5, the same setting preferred by many network adapters. Although IRQ5 is assigned to the second parallel printer

(LPT2), few users have two printers, and printers seldom require an interrupt—so IRQ5 is a good candidate when space gets tight.

If you can't get sound on a networked PC, it may be that the network and sound cards are conflicting. IRQ5 is the preferred setting for both network adapters and sound cards, which makes this problem very common.

NOTE Most legacy PC adapter cards use jumpers to set resource values. Cards that store resource settings in nonvolatile RAM require that you run their setup applications to set IRQ, I/O base address, and DMA channel (if applicable). If the setup program unavoidably installs real-mode drivers for the device, don't forget to disable the real-mode drivers by adding temporary REM prefixes before restarting Windows 95. See the section "Changing Resource Settings," later in this chapter. ■

Installing Adapter Cards with Automatic Detection

The easiest way to install a new legacy card in a Windows 95 system is to use the Add New Hardware Wizard's automatic detection feature to identify your added card. The wizard also can determine if you have removed a card. Auto-detection is best suited for PCs that have few or no specialty adapter cards, such as sound and video capture cards.

The following steps describe the automatic-detection process in installing a Creative Labs Sound Blaster AWE 32 card:

1. Set non-conflicting resource values for your new adapter card, using jumpers or the card's setup program.
2. Shut down Windows 95, and turn off the power on your PC.
3. Install the new adapter card in an empty ISA slot, and make any required external connections, such as audio inputs and speaker outputs for sound cards.
4. Turn the PC power on, and restart Windows 95.
5. Launch Control Panel, and double-click the Add New Hardware icon to start the Add New Hardware Wizard (see Figure 7.3).

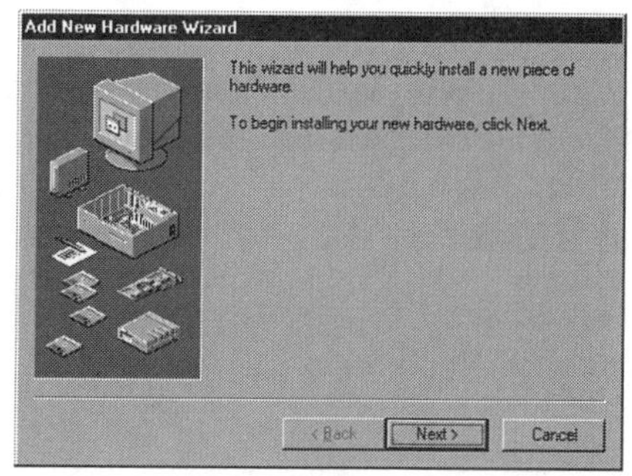

FIG. 7.3
The Add New Hardware Wizard provides a step-by-step guide to installing new devices into your PC.

6. Click the Next button. The next wizard dialog box appears. You can choose manual or automatic hardware detection and installation. Accept the default Yes (Recommended) option (see Figure 7.4).

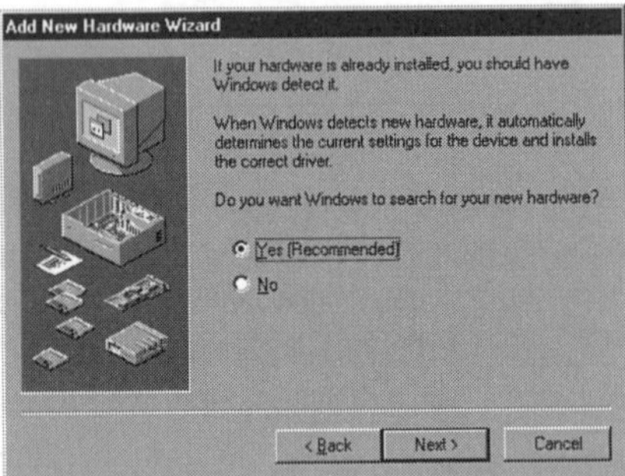

FIG. 7.4 The Add New Hardware routine lets you choose between automatic or manual hardware detection. Be warned that automatic selection can take a while, particularly on slower machines.

7. Click the Next button to display the wizard's warning that the detection process may take several minutes.
8. Click the Next button to start the detection process. After a few minutes of intense disk activity, often interspersed with periods of seeming inactivity, the wizard advises you that detection is complete (see Figure 7.5).

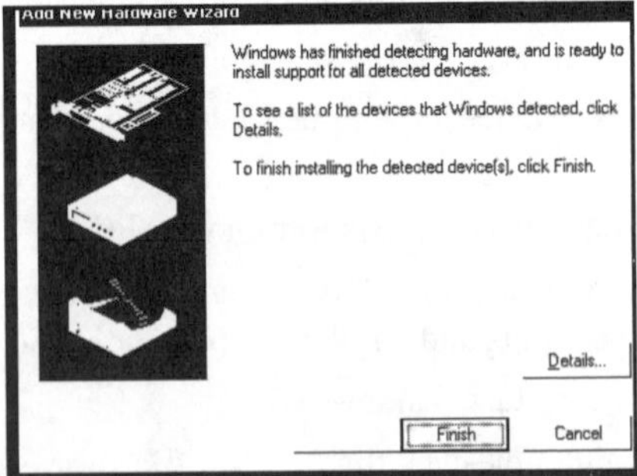

FIG. 7.5 The Wizard has finally finished the detection process.

9. Click the Details button to display what the wizard detected. Figure 7.6 shows that the Sound Blaster AWE-32 was detected.

   If the wizard does not detect your newly installed card, you must install the card manually. Click Cancel to terminate the automatic detection process.

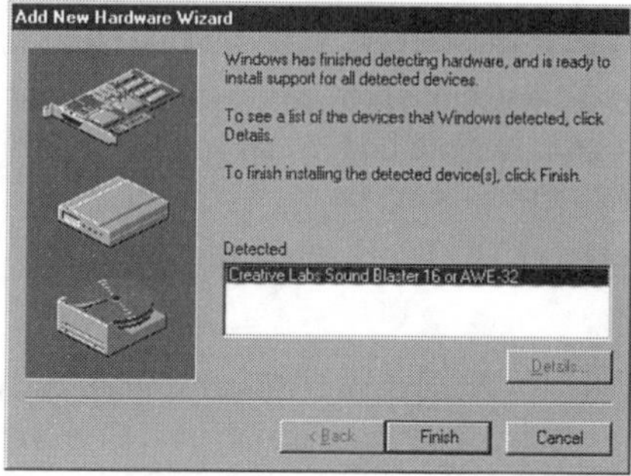

FIG. 7.6
The wizard detected the Sound Blaster AWE-32 sound card.

10. Click the Finish button to install the required drivers from the Windows 95 CD-ROM or floppy disks. The message box shown in Figure 7.7 indicates the expected medium—in this case, the Windows 95 CD-ROM.

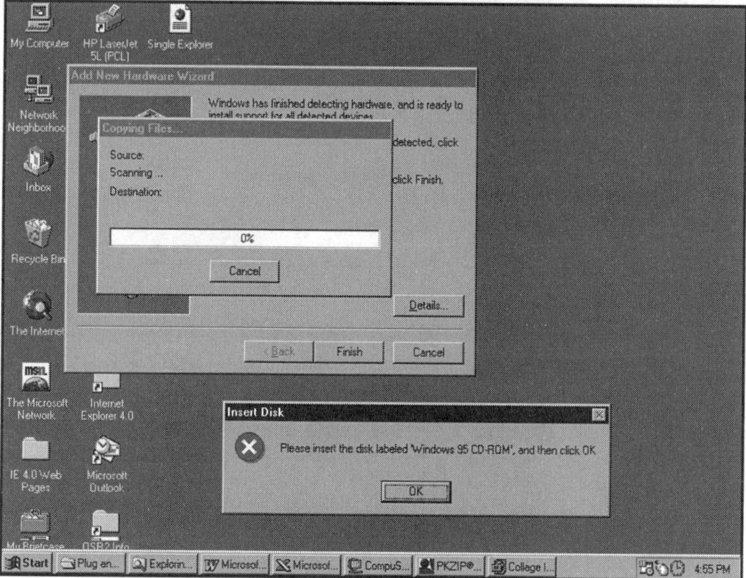

FIG. 7.7
If the driver software isn't available on your hard drive, Windows 95 prompts you to install the media that contains the drivers.

11. Insert the Windows 95 CD-ROM into the drive, and click OK to install the drivers.
12. If Windows 95 can't find the required device driver file in the expected location, you will be prompted to browse for the necessary files.
13. When driver installation is complete, a message box advises you that system settings have changed and asks whether you want to restart Windows 95. Click Restart Now so that your driver change takes effect.

Installing Legacy Cards After Setting Up Drivers

The alternative to automatic device detection is to install the new adapter card *after* you install its driver software. The advantage to this method is that you can determine in advance resource settings that don't conflict with existing devices.

The following steps describe the process of reinstalling the drivers for the Sound Blaster AWE-32 card:

1. Launch the Add New Hardware Wizard from Control Panel, and click the Next button in the opening dialog box to display the wizard dialog box. Here you choose between manual and automatic hardware detection and installation (refer to Figure 7.4).
2. Choose the No option to select manual installation; then click the Next button to display the wizard's Hardware Types dialog box (see Figure 7.8).

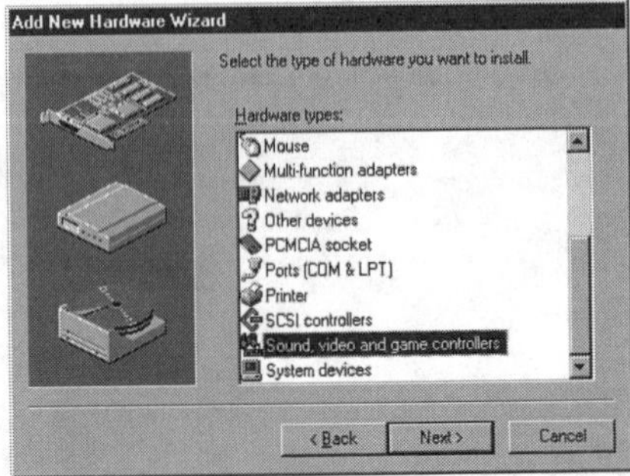

FIG. 7.8 The Add New Hardware Wizard's Hardware Types dialog box lists a variety of adapter card categories.

3. Select the card type in the Hardware Types list; then click the Next button to display the Manufacturers and Models dialog box (see Figure 7.9).

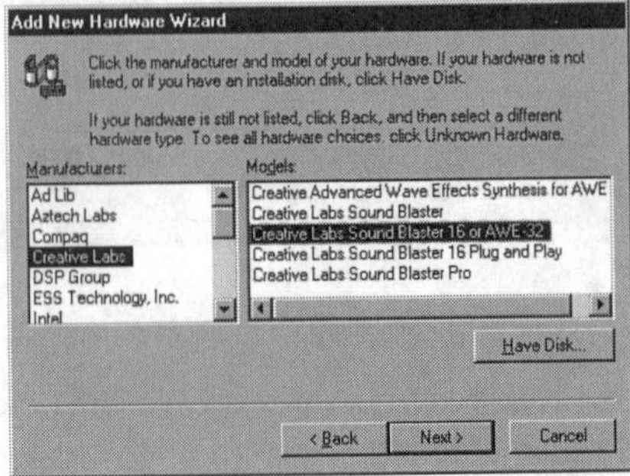

FIG. 7.9 The Wizard dialog box lists manufacturers and models of devices for whose drivers are included with Windows 95.

4. Make the appropriate selections in the Manufacturers and Models list boxes; then click the Next button to display the default settings for the new device.

NOTE If you don't see the manufacturer or model in the list boxes, you need a floppy disk or CD-ROM that contains Windows 95 drivers for your device (Windows 3.1 or later drivers won't work). If you have the required Windows 95 drivers, click the Have Disk button to install the drivers from floppy disk or CD-ROM. If you don't have Windows 95 drivers, click the Cancel button to terminate the installation. ■

5. Windows 95 can't determine what resource value settings you made for your new or replacement adapter card, so the default settings for the device appear in the wizard's Resource Settings dialog box (see Figure 7.10). You should write down or print these default settings.

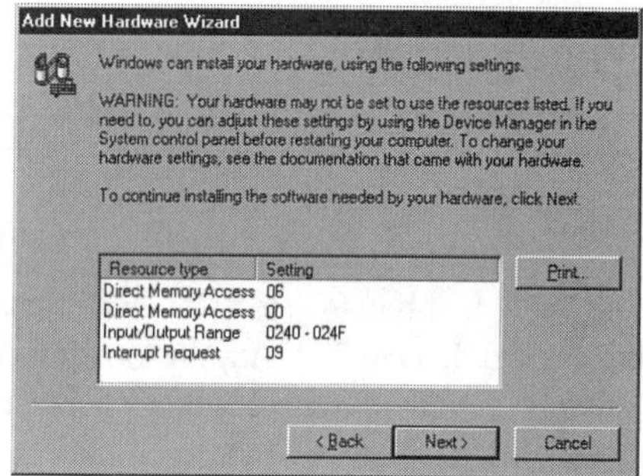

FIG. 7.10
Default values for the Sound Blaster AWE-32 card appear when you open the Resource Setting dialog box.

6. Click the Next button to display the System Settings Change message box (see Figure 7.11).

   If the default settings in the preceding step correspond to the resource settings of your card, click the Yes button to shut down Windows 95. If you haven't installed the card (which is the normal situation for manual device detection), turn off the power to your PC, install the card, turn the power back on, and restart Windows 95 with the new card activated.

   If any of the resource values in the preceding step are incorrect, or you receive a "resource conflict" message, click the No button in the System Settings Change message box so that you can alter the resource values as necessary.

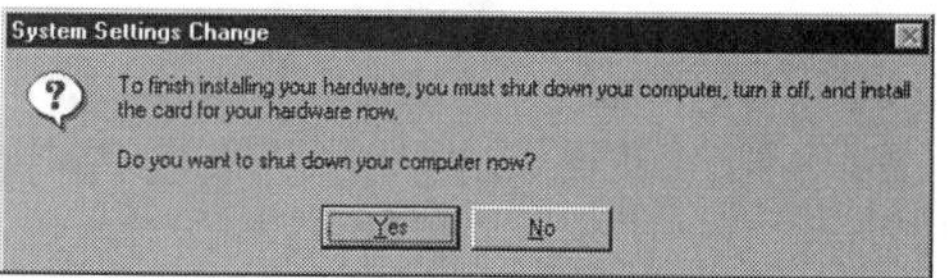

FIG. 7.11
The System Settings Change message box gives you the option to restart Windows 95.

7. Open Control Panel's System Properties sheet, click the Device Manager tab, and expand the entries for the type of device that you're installing. Exclamation points superimposed on the device's icon(s) indicate that the device is not yet fully installed or has been removed from your PC.

8. If you're replacing a card, entries for both cards appear in the Device Manager list. To remove the old entry, select the entry and click the Remove button. A message box requests that you confirm the removal process (see Figure 7.12).

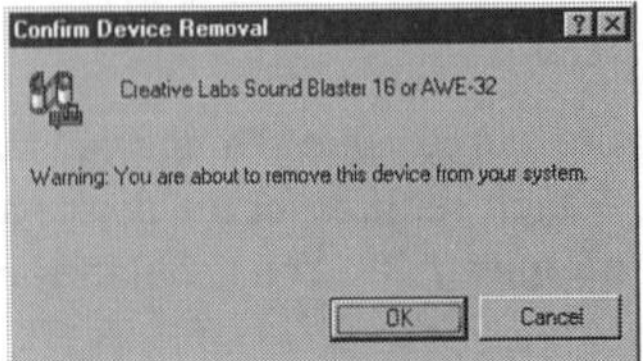

FIG. 7.12 Windows 95 asks for confirmation before you remove a device from the Device Manager.

9. Double-click the entry for the new adapter card to display the Properties sheet for the device.
10. In the Resource Settings list box, select the resource whose value you want to change; then click the Change Settings button to display the Edit Interrupt Request dialog box for the resource.
11. Use the spin buttons of the Value text box to select the value that corresponds to the preset value for your adapter card. If a conflict with the existing card occurs, the card that has the conflicting value is identified in the Conflict Information text box (see Figure 7.13).

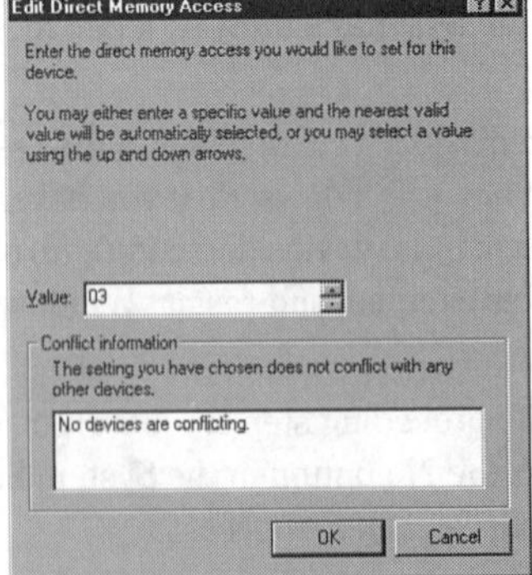

FIG. 7.13 Change the IRQ setting for the new adapter card to avoid a conflict.

12. Change the Value setting to a value that displays No devices are conflicting in the Conflict Information box; then make the corresponding change in the card, using the jumpers or nonvolatile RAM. (Turn off power to your PC before making jumper changes.)
13. After making all the changes necessary to remove resource conflicts, click OK to close the resource's Edit Input/Output Range dialog box, and then click OK to close the Properties page for the specific device.
14. Click OK to close the System Properties sheet.
15. Shut down and restart Windows 95 so that your new settings take effect.

The process of manually installing a legacy device described in the preceding steps appears to be complex, but it is a much more foolproof method than the one used by Windows 3.x. For example, the capability to detect potential resource conflicts before the new setting is locked in helps eliminate many problems associated with installing new devices under Windows 3.x.

NOTE Windows 95 includes drivers for an extraordinary number of popular devices but not for low-volume products, such as digital videocapture and MPEG-1 playback cards. Most manufacturers of specialty legacy devices should provide 32-bit protected-mode drivers for Windows 95. You can find updated Windows 95 drivers on manufacturer's forums on CompuServe, America Online, and Microsoft Network, as well as on World Wide Web sites. ■

Removing Unneeded Drivers for Legacy Devices

If you remove a legacy device from your PC and don't intend to reinstall it, it's good Windows 95 housekeeping to remove the driver for the device from the Device Manager list. Follow these steps to remove the Device Manager entry for permanently removed adapter cards:

1. Double-click Control Panel's System icon to open the System Properties sheet.
2. Click the Device Manager tab, and double-click the icon for the hardware type of the device removed to display the list of installed devices. An exclamation point superimposed on a device icon indicates a removed or inoperable device.
3. Click the list item to select the device you want to remove, and then click the Remove button.
4. Confirm that you want to remove the device by clicking OK in the Confirm Device Removal message box.

If you have more than one hardware configuration, a modified version of the Confirm Device Removal message box appears. Make sure the Remove from All Configurations option button is selected; then click OK to remove the device and close the message box.

Troubleshooting Hardware Installation

Windows 95 is clearly superior to Windows 3.x when it comes to installing and managing hardware, but it is not perfect. The peaceful coexistence that Windows 95 tries to foster between PnP and legacy devices can break down into bitter conflict, particularly when new legacy hardware is being installed. But Windows 95 does provide a wealth of tools for managing these conflicts when they occur. This section helps you troubleshoot hardware installation problems under Windows 95, with tips for using the Device Manager and other tools.

Understanding the Device Manager

The Device Manager displays all the system components in hierarchical format, allowing you to dig down to individual devices and subsystems. In essence, the Device Manager is the user interface for the Windows 95 Registry. But unlike working in the Registry, the Device Manager is designed to avoid the kind of catastrophic crashes that making changes in the Registry can cause.

The Device Manager gives you quick access to hardware configurations for virtually all the devices in your PC. To open the Device Manager, double-click the System icon in Control Panel and click the Device Manager tab. You will see a list of items, some with a plus (+) sign to the left. This plus sign indicates that more detailed device information is available. Selecting the plus sign expands the display to show any listings below that item.

The Device Manager displays hardware information from two separate perspectives, by device type and by device connection. By default, Device Manager opens with the View Devices by Type option button selected (see Figure 7.14). In this mode, similar devices are grouped under a single item, such as the entry under Ports (COM & LPT). Clicking the View Devices by Connection option button shows the same information, but now most of the devices appear under the Plug and Play BIOS item (see Figure 7.15).

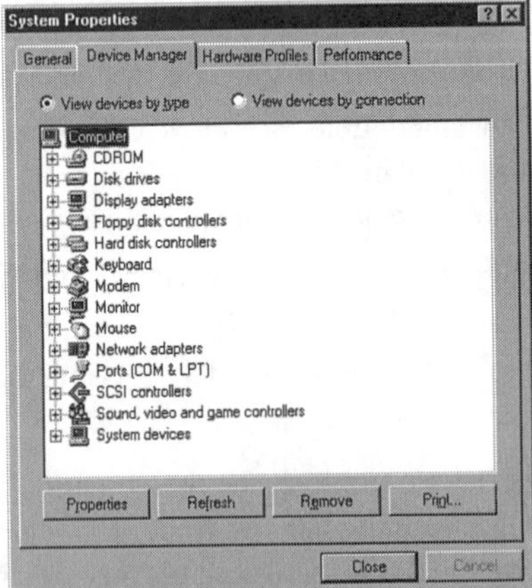

FIG. 7.14
The Device Manager showing devices listed by type.

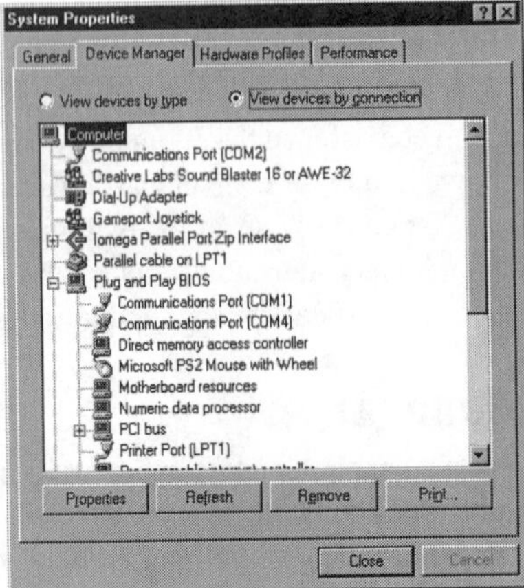

FIG. 7.15
The second option button lets you view components by their physical connections in the system.

To access the configuration for a sound card, do the following:

1. Go to the Device Manager page of the System Properties sheet.
2. Click the plus (+) sign found next to the Sound, video, and game controllers item.
3. Click the specific sound hardware item that appears on the sheet.
4. Click the Properties button to display the tabbed properties sheet for the sound hardware device.

Changing Resource Settings

After you are at the General page of a device's properties sheet, you can access the IRQ, I/O address, and DMA resource settings by clicking the Resources tab. Here you see the resources that are currently assigned to that device. Any conflicts are indicated with an asterisk next to the resource having a problem.

To change the resource settings for a device, do the following:

1. In the Resource Settings box, click the resource item you want to view or edit.
2. Click to clear the Use Automatic Settings check box (see Figure 7.16).

FIG. 7.16
Before you can make changes to device settings, you must disable the Use automatic settings item.

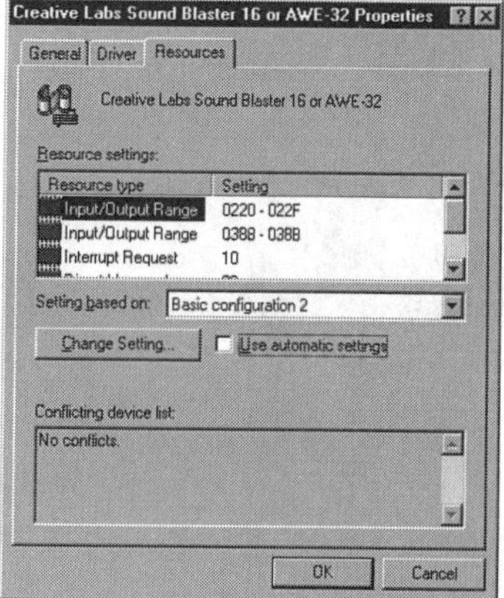

3. Click the enabled Change Setting button.
4. In the Resource Edit dialog box, click the spinner buttons to switch among system resources.

NOTE Device Manager shows all the resources, indicating those that are already in use by another peripheral. Be sure you don't create a conflict by assigning a resource to a device that is already being used by another device.

TROUBLESHOOTING

Why do I get a Resource Conflict message when I install a Plug and Play adapter card? Most PC adapter cards require at least one I/O base address and one or more interrupts. (The section "Setting Resource Values for Legacy Adapter Cards" describes I/O base addresses and interrupts.) Most adapter cards support only a few of the available I/O base addresses and interrupts. If you already have several legacy adapter cards in your PC, you may have a situation where the I/O base addresses or, more likely, the interrupts supported by the new card are occupied by existing legacy cards. In this case, you need to change the settings of one or more of your legacy cards to free the required resource(s) for use by your new card.

The worst-case condition occurs in PCI-bus PCs where all of the available interrupts are assigned before you install the new card. (In many PCI-bus PCs, PCI slots consume one interrupt each, whether or not the slot is in use.) The only solution in this instance is to free an interrupt by reconfiguring your PC's system BIOS to reassign an interrupt from an unused PCI slot. Obviously, this action will disable that slot, rendering it useless. If your system BIOS does not permit reconfiguration, you must remove an existing adapter card to free an interrupt.

You can get an effective roster of system settings by double-clicking the Computer icon at the top of the Device Manager tree. Doing so brings up the Computer Properties sheet, which features two tabs: View Resources and Reserve Resources (see Figure 7.17).

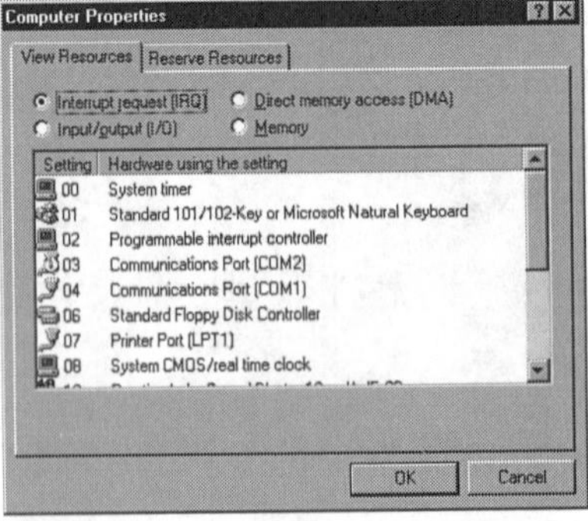

FIG. 7.17 The Computer Properties sheet provides a bird's-eye view of your system resource status.

The View Resources tab displays these four option buttons that cause the page to display the status of key system resources:

- Interrupt Request (IRQs)
- Input/Output (I/O)
- Direct Memory Address (DMA)
- Memory

Clicking the option button brings up a list of occupied settings and the devices that are using them.

NOTE The View Resources page of the Computer Properties sheet is an excellent place to get an overview of your system's resource status.

The Reserve Resources page lets you view any resources that have been excluded from use by hardware devices (see Figure 7.18). You also can use this page to reserve resources.

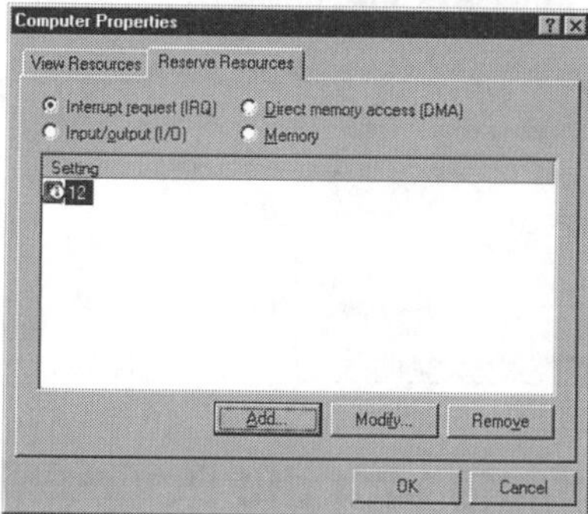

FIG. 7.18
The Reserve Resources page lets you set aside key resource settings to avoid conflicts.

TROUBLESHOOTING

Why does my system hang during shutdown? This problem can occur when a system BIOS expects a PS/2-style mouse port to occupy IRQ12, but a software-configured PnP adapter occupies it instead. You need to change the software-configurable device in Device Manager to another IRQ number. You might also consider reserving IRQ12 in Device Manager, so Plug and Play does not later assign a device to that resource. Also consider getting a BIOS upgrade that allows you to make full use of IRQ12.

Follow these steps to reserve IRQ12 (some older BIOSes won't recognize an IRQ12 device unless it is a PS/2 mouse):

1. Click the Reserve Resources tab.
2. Click the Interrupt Request (IRQ) option button.
3. Click the Add button to bring up the Edit Resource Setting sheet (see Figure 7.19).
4. Use the spinner controls to select the IRQ you want to change.

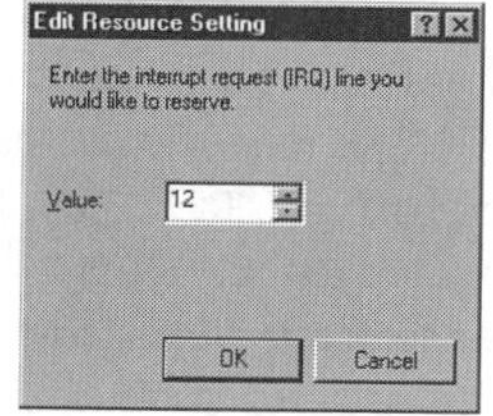

FIG. 7.19
Set the resource to reserve in the Edit Resource sheet.

5. Click OK to change the settings.
6. If a device is currently logged into the IRQ being reserved, the Resource Conflict Warning sheet will apprise you of the possible problem and ask for confirmation (see Figure 7.20).

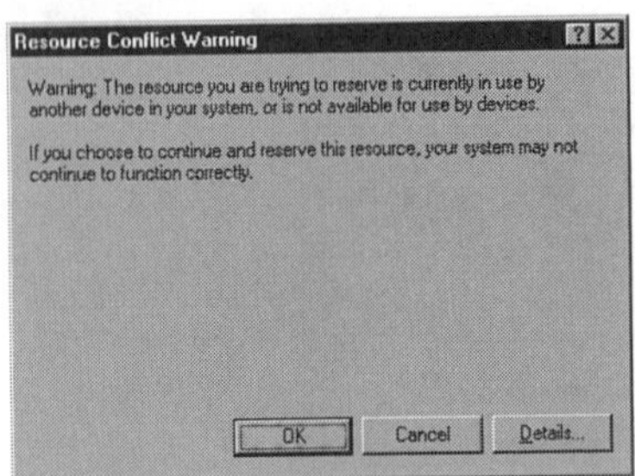

FIG. 7.20
If Windows 95 detects a device already using the resource being reserved, it will warn you and ask for confirmation.

Checking for Resource Conflicts with the Device Manager

The Device Manager is an excellent tool for resolving hardware resource conflicts, allowing you to see if any devices are experiencing a conflict. Device Manager displays an exclamation point or a strikethrough symbol through the icon of any item with a conflict, allowing you to quickly zero in on problems. The symbols indicate different situations:

- **Exclamation point inside a yellow circle.** Indicates a device that is experiencing a direct conflict with another device.
- **Red X symbol.** Indicates a device that is disabled, either due to a conflict or by user selection.

Unfortunately, it is not possible to cover all the various things that can go wrong during hardware installation under Windows 95. Many problems are the result of interactions between specific types of hardware. If you discover a problem with hardware you are installing, you should seek guidance from the vendor, since they should know about potential driver updates and other fixes that can help resolve the problem.

TROUBLESHOOTING

I can't get my second IDE drive to appear in My Computer or Explorer. Most PCs with recent system BIOSes automatically detect an additional drive connected to the primary IDE controller as a primary slave drive. If you have an older BIOS, you need to use the PC's BIOS setup application to specify the type of drive installed (number of cylinders, number of heads, landing zone, and other drive parameters). If you connect a third drive to a PC with a recent BIOS, you need to enable the secondary IDE controller in the BIOS setup program so BIOS can recognize the drive. IDE CD-ROM drives connected to sound cards usually can be installed as secondary, tertiary, or quaternary IDE drives. Use the default (secondary) setting for an IDE CD-ROM if you don't have a secondary IDE controller in your PC; if your PC has a secondary IDE controller, use the tertiary I/O base address and interrupt for the CD-ROM.

CHAPTER 8

Special Features for Notebook Users

In this chapter

Quick Overview

Many business professionals want to take their office with them. Portable technology and Windows 95 make a hard-to-beat combination. Portable PCs enable you to work nearly anywhere, and Windows 95's features for portable computing—which include 32-bit support for PC Card (PCMCIA) devices, file synchronization, Dial-Up Networking, remote mail, and more—make Windows 95 a perfect operating system for your portable PC. Not only does Windows 95 make it easy for you to take your work with you, but features such as Dial-Up Networking and remote mail enable you to keep in touch with coworkers and access disk and printer resources in your main office from anywhere in the world.

Windows 95 delivers PC Card, Plug and Play, disk compression, power management, and support for port replicators and docking stations all complement portable PC hardware. Windows 95 architectural enhancements conserve battery power and manage configuration changes, which helps extend the life of older portables. Dial-Up Networking enables you to access your office file server(s) using your modem and to send e-mail to and receive e-mail from coworkers. Windows 95 keeps users organized as well. Using an advanced file synchronization system called Briefcase and a deferred printing option, roaming users remain "in sync" with their desktop environments (and vice versa).

To help you understand how to get the most from Windows 95's features for portable computing, this chapter explores the following topics:

- Using a docking system
- Using a direct cable connection to share resources
- Using power management
- Using Dial-Up Networking
- Synchronizing files with Briefcase
- Using mouse trails

Using Your Laptop with a Docking System

With Windows 95, *hot-docking support* integrates hardware and software for quick and easy docking. Docking and undocking can occur when the power is on or off. Windows 95 automatically detects any configuration changes and manages any conflicts or file disruptions. Windows 95 also loads and unloads hardware drivers as required. To undock your PC when Windows 95 is running, open the Start menu and choose Eject PC. Windows 95 reconfigures the system automatically for the undocked configuration and then prompts you to remove the PC from the docking station.

Creating and Modifying Hardware Profiles

Windows 95 enables you to create multiple hardware profiles to accommodate different hardware configurations, such as when your PC is docked and when it is undocked. Windows 95 automatically creates two hardware profiles for you: one for the docked configuration and a second for the undocked configuration. Windows 95 detects which profile is required at startup and automatically uses the correct one.

NOTE If your portable PC contains a Plug and Play BIOS, Windows 95 does not have to use multiple hardware profiles to accommodate hot docking. Instead, the Plug and Play BIOS can detect which devices are available, and Windows 95 can configure the system accordingly.

If you want to change an existing profile or create a new one, you can do so through the Control Panel. Use the following procedure to create a new hardware profile:

1. Open the Start menu and choose Settings, Control Panel.
2. Choose the System object to display the System properties sheet.
3. Click the Hardware Profiles tab to display the Hardware Profiles page (see Figure 8.1).

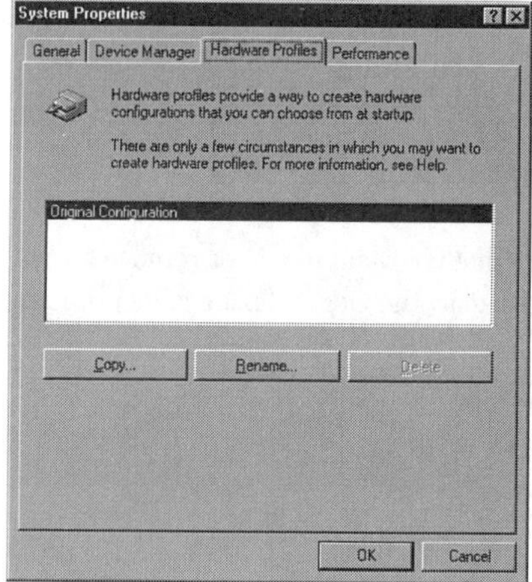

FIG. 8.1
The Hardware Profiles page enables you to modify and create hardware profiles.

4. Select the hardware profile you want to use as a basis for the new profile, and then choose Copy. Windows 95 displays a Copy Profile dialog box in which you specify the name for the new hardware profile (see Figure 8.2).

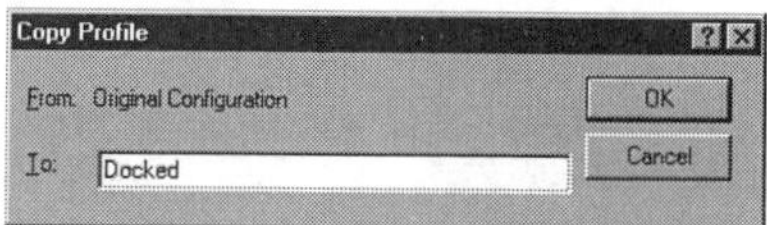

FIG. 8.2
Specify a name for the hardware profile.

5. Enter a name for the new profile and choose OK. The new hardware profile appears in the Hardware Profiles list.

In some cases, you might want to modify a hardware profile. If Windows 95 is unable to properly detect the hardware in a particular configuration, for example, you can modify the profile to add and remove hardware from the profile.

To modify a hardware profile, use the following procedure:

1. Open the Control Panel and double-click the System icon. Then click the Device Manager tab to display the Device Manager properties sheet (see Figure 8.3).

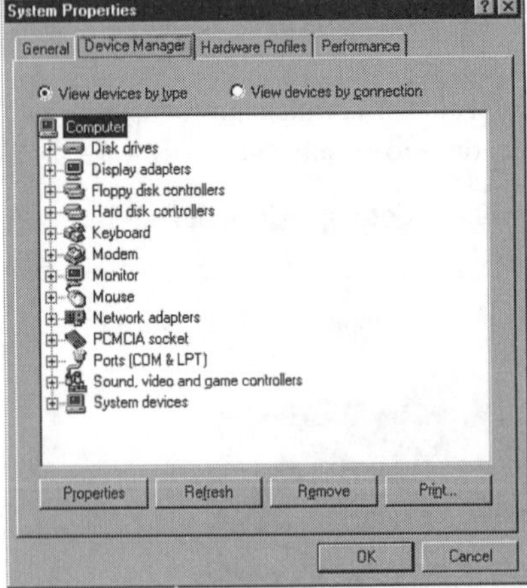

FIG. 8.3
Use the Device Manager page to modify a hardware profile.

2. Select the hardware device that you want to add or remove from a particular profile, and then choose Properties to display the General page of its properties sheet (see Figure 8.4).

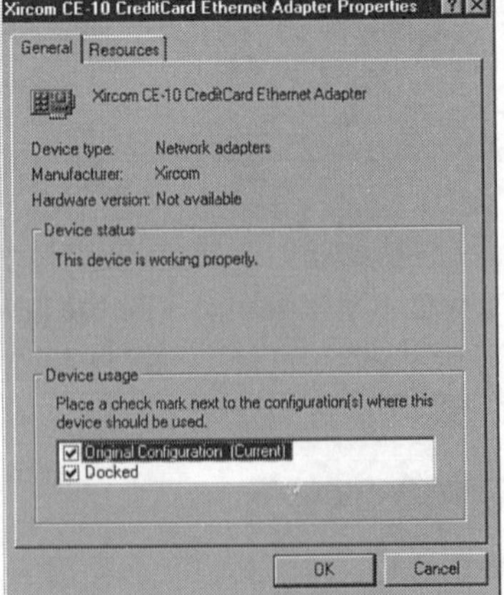

FIG. 8.4
Use the Device Usage list to add and remove hardware from a profile.

3. At the bottom of the device's General page is a Device Usage list that defines which profiles use a device. Place a check in the check box beside a hardware profile to enable the device for that profile. Clear the check box to disable the device for that profile.
4. Choose OK to apply the changes.

When you start the system, Windows 95 detects the hardware configuration you are using and automatically applies the appropriate hardware profile. If the hardware profiles are so similar that Windows 95 cannot determine which profile to use, Windows 95 displays a menu containing a list of the available profiles and prompts you to select the profile to be used.

Working with Different Configurations Most hardware settings in Windows 95 are stored relative to the current hardware profile. Changes that you make to a device's settings are applied to the current profile, but not to other hardware profiles. Therefore, it's possible to maintain different settings for the same device in two or more different hardware profiles. For example, you might use a display resolution of 640×480 in one profile, but use 800×600 in a different profile. Such is probably the case when you are using an external monitor with your PC. You probably use 640×480 with the portable's LCD display and a higher resolution with the external monitor.

To configure unique settings for a device, first start Windows 95 using the hardware profile in which you want the changes to be made. If you want to use a high-resolution mode with an external monitor, for example, select the hardware profile you normally use with the external monitor (or create a profile for use with the external monitor as explained in the previous section). After you start Windows 95 with the appropriate hardware profile, change the settings for the device. The changes are applied to the current hardware profile and do not affect other profiles you have created.

TROUBLESHOOTING

My LCD monitor is not working properly. Windows 95 might not automatically select the LCD monitor type when you are using your portable PC's internal LCD display. Therefore, you should check the monitor type in the hardware profile that is used when you are working with the internal display. To set the monitor type, right-click the desktop and choose Properties. Click the Settings tab to display the Settings page. Choose Change Display Type to display the Change Display Type dialog box. Choose the Change button to display the Select Device dialog box. Choose the Show All Devices option button, choose Standard Monitor Types from the Manufacturers list, and then choose the appropriate Laptop Display Panel selection from the Models list.

Using Deferred Printing

When your portable PC is docked, you probably have access to a printer connected to the docking station or that is available across the network. When your PC is not docked, however, it is unlikely that you'll have access to a printer. Windows 95 addresses that problem through *deferred printing*. When you print a document, Windows 95 places the document in the printer's queue, where it remains even when you turn off your computer.

▶ **See** "Controlling Printing," **p. 139**

When you dock your computer, Windows 95 senses that the printer is available and begins spooling the document to the printer. Windows 95 automatically handles deferred printing. You simply print the document, and when the printer becomes available, Windows 95 begins sending the document to the printer.

Sharing Local Resources via Parallel or Serial Connection

A growing number of portable users also have a desktop system. They regularly transfer files between systems by using either a floppy disk or a direct parallel or serial cable, and a third-party application to handle the transfer. Windows 95 includes a feature called Direct Cable Connection that integrates the same capability within Windows 95; essentially, you can use a serial or parallel cable to network together your portable and desktop PCs, creating a small peer-to-peer network. The two computers then can access each other's files and other resources (such as a fax modem) as if they were joined by a traditional network interface.

In a direct cable connection, one computer acts as the host (server) and the other computer acts as a guest (client). The host PC also can act as a gateway, enabling the client to access the network to which the host is connected. The host can serve as a gateway for NetBEUI or IPX/SPX protocols but cannot serve as a gateway for TCP/IP.

Setting Up Direct Cable Connection

If you select the Portable option when you install Windows 95, Setup installs Direct Cable Connection on your PC. If you use a different option or deselected the Direct Cable Connection option during Setup, you must install it. To add Direct Cable Connection, use the following procedure:

1. Open the Start menu and choose Settings, Control Panel.
2. Choose the Add/Remove Programs object.
3. Click the Windows Setup tab to display the Windows Setup page.
4. Select Communications from the Components list, and then choose Details.
5. Place a check beside Direct Cable Connection, and then choose OK.
6. Choose OK again to cause Windows 95 to add Direct Cable Connection to your PC.

NOTE If Direct Cable Connection is already checked in the Components list, the software is already installed on your PC. ■

After installing the Direct Cable Connection software, you must connect the two computers with an appropriate cable. You can use either a parallel or null-modem serial cable to connect your two PCs. The types of cables you can use for the connection include the following:

- Standard 4-bit null-modem cable, and LapLink and InterLink cables made prior to 1992.
- Extended Capabilities Port (ECP) cable. To use this type of cable, your parallel port must be configured as an ECP port in your system BIOS.
- Universal Cable Module (UCM) cable, which supports connecting together different types of parallel ports. You can use a UCM cable to connect together two ECP ports for fastest performance.

As previously indicated, configuring your parallel ports as ECP ports provides the best performance. To use ECP, however, your PC's ports must be ECP-capable, and the ports must be configured as ECP ports in the system BIOS. Older PCs do not contain ECP-capable parallel ports.

The final step in setting up the Direct Cable Connection is to ensure that both the guest and host computers use the same network protocol. You can use the NetBEUI, IPX/SPX, or TCP/IP protocols. In addition, you must use an appropriate network client, such as Client for NetWare Networks or Client for Microsoft Networks. The host computer must run either the File and Printer Sharing for Microsoft Networks service or the File and Printer Sharing for NetWare Networks service.

Setting Up the Host

In a Direct Cable Connection between two PCs, one PC acts as the host and the other PC acts as the guest. The first step in enabling the connection is to configure the host. To do so, use the following procedure:

1. Open the Start menu and choose Programs, Accessories, Direct Cable Connection. Windows 95 displays the dialog box shown in Figure 8.5.

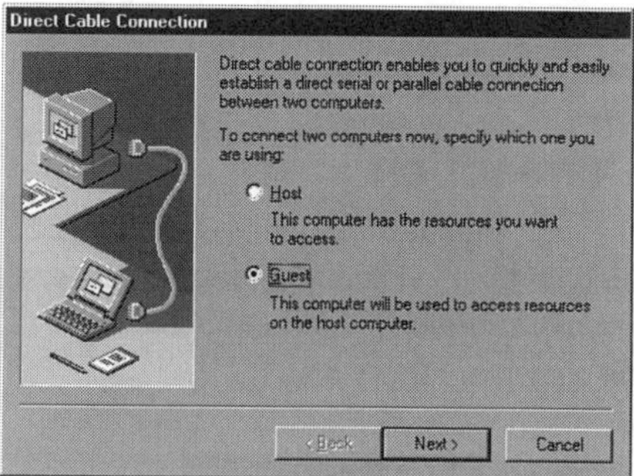

FIG. 8.5 Choose whether the PC will act as host or guest.

2. Select the Host option button and then choose Next >. Windows 95 displays the dialog box shown in Figure 8.6.

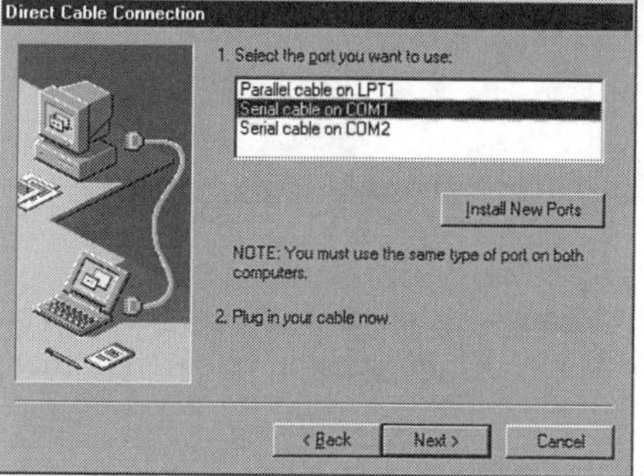

FIG. 8.6 Select the port to be used by the connection.

3. Choose the port you want to use on the host for the connection. You can choose one of the host's parallel or serial ports. After selecting the port, choose Next >.
4. Specify whether you want to use password protection to prevent unauthorized access to the host. To use password protection, enable the Use Password Protection check box. Then choose Set Password, which displays a simple dialog box in which you enter the password that must be provided by the guest computer to access the host. When you've specified the desired password settings, choose Finish to complete host setup.

Setting Up the Guest

After configuring the host, you're ready to configure the guest computer. To do so, use the following procedure:

1. On the guest computer, open the Start menu and choose Programs, Accessories, Direct Computer Connection.
2. From the Direct Cable Connection dialog box, choose Guest and then Next >.
3. Choose the port on the guest PC through which the connection will be made, and then choose Next.
4. Choose Finish to complete the setup.

Before you begin sharing files using the Direct Cable Connection, you must share a directory in which the files will be transferred. To set up sharing, refer to Chapter 36.

Using the Direct Cable Connection

When you want to begin using your mini-network connection, you need to start the Direct Cable Connection software on both the host and the guest computers. On the host, open the Start menu and choose Programs, Accessories, Direct Cable Connection. Windows 95 displays a dialog box similar to the one shown in Figure 8.7.

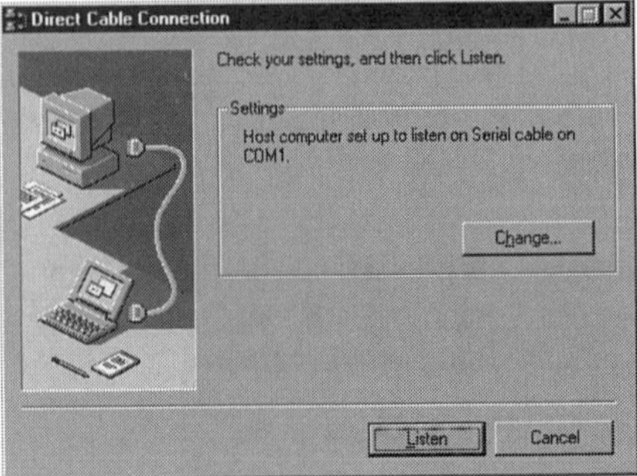

FIG. 8.7
Choose Listen to set up the host for the connection.

If the settings you specified previously are correct, choose Listen to place the host computer in listen mode to listen for a connection by the guest. If you need to change the password or port settings, choose Change.

▶ **See** "Setting Up a Windows 95 Peer-to-Peer Network" **p. 841**

After placing the host computer in listen mode, start the Direct Cable Connection software on the guest computer. Open the Start menu and choose Programs, Accessories, Direct Cable Connection. Windows 95 displays a dialog box similar to the one shown Figure 8.7, except that the Listen button is replaced by a Connect button. Choose Connect to connect to the host and begin using the connection.

Using Power Management

Most portable PCs (and an increasing number of desktop PCs) support some form of power management that allows the PC's devices to be shut down to conserve power while the computer remains on. Power management, for example, can power down the hard disk when the disk is not being used, conserving battery power. When the system is idle, power management can shut down the display and even CPU to further conserve power. Windows 95 integrates power management into the operating system and adds features to the interface that enable you to easily take advantage of power management.

In order for your PC to use power management, the PC's BIOS must include support for power management, and power management must be enabled in the PC's BIOS.

If you have a newer portable computer that has the APM 1.2 BIOS, you may want to consider installing the Windows 95 OEM Service Release 2 (OSR2) update. OSR2 supports the features of the new APM BIOS, including wake-up on ring for modems, power down of PC Card modems that are inactive, and notebooks with multiple batteries. See Chapter 2, "Installing and Upgrading Windows 95," for more information on OSR2.

If your portable PC supports power management and power management software (such as MS-DOS's POWER.EXE) is enabled when you install Windows 95, Setup adds support for power management automatically. If power management software was not enabled during Setup, you must enable power management yourself through the Control Panel. The following steps explain how to enable power management:

1. Open the Start menu and choose Settings, Control Panel.
2. Choose the System object.
3. Click the Device Manager tab, and then double-click the System devices item to expand the System devices tree.
4. Select the Advanced Power Management support item and choose Properties.
5. Click the Settings tab to display the Settings page shown in Figure 8.8.
6. Place a check in the Enable Power Management Support check box and then choose OK.
7. Choose OK to close the System properties sheet. Windows 95 prompts you to restart the computer for the change to take effect.

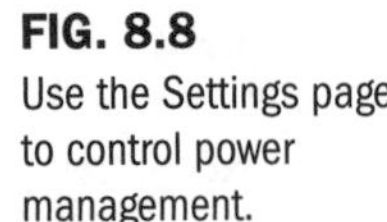

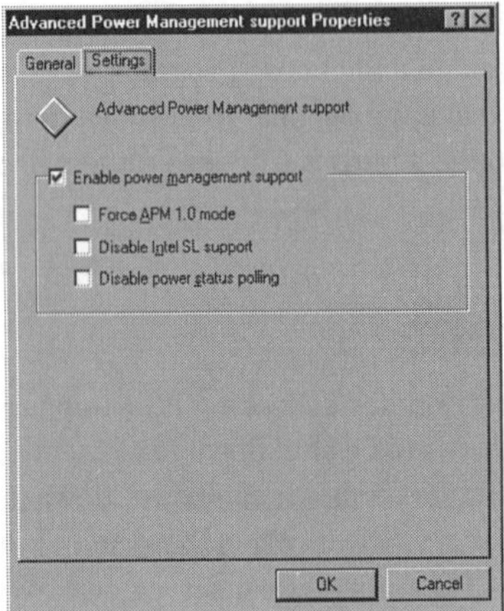

FIG. 8.8
Use the Settings page to control power management.

The other options on the Settings page control the way power management works. These options include:

- **Force APM 1.0 Mode.** Enable this option if your PC's power management features do not work properly. This option causes Windows 95 to use an APM 1.1 BIOS in 1.0 mode, which overcomes problems with some portable PCs.
- **Disable Intel SL Support.** If your computer uses the SL chipset and stops responding at startup, enable this option.
- **Disable Power Status Polling.** Enable this option if your PC shuts down unexpectedly while you use it. This option prevents Windows 95 from calling the APM BIOS to check battery status, consequently also disabling the battery meter in the tray.

Setting Power Management Options

The Power icon in the Control Panel enables you to specify options that control power management features. Double-clicking the Power icon in the Control Panel displays the Power properties sheet shown in Figure 8.9. The large SL button appears on the Power page of the sheet only if your PC uses an SL processor.

▶ **See** "Setting SL Options," **p. 200**

The Power Management list enables you to specify the level of power management your system uses. You can select from the following options:

- **Standard.** Choose this setting to use only the power management features supported by your PC's BIOS. Additional features such as battery status monitoring are not enabled when you choose this feature.
- **Advanced.** Choose this setting to use full power management support, including features provided by Windows 95 in addition to those provided by your PC's BIOS. These include battery status monitoring and power status display on the tray.
- **Off.** Choose this setting to turn off power management.

FIG. 8.9
Use the Power page to set power management options.

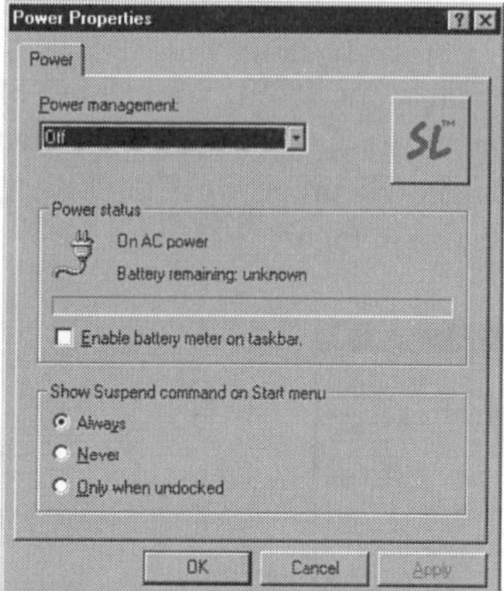

Additional options on the Power page control whether or not the Suspend command appears in the Start menu. Choose Always if you want the Suspend command always displayed on the Start menu. Choose Never if you do not want it to appear on the Start menu, even when the system is undocked. Choose Only when Undocked if you want the Suspend command to appear on the Start menu only when the PC is not connected to a docking station.

TIP When you want to place the PC in suspend mode, open the Start menu and choose Suspend. Windows 95 will immediately place the PC in suspend mode. If you have files open across the network, you should first save or close the files before placing the PC in suspend mode to avoid losing data.

The Power page also displays information about battery status and enables you to turn on or off the power status indicator on the tray. To view the amount of power remaining in your battery, rest the cursor on the power indicator on the tray for a second, and Windows 95 will display a ToolTip listing battery power remaining. Or double-click the power indicator to display a Battery Meter dialog box similar to the one shown in Figure 8.10.

FIG. 8.10
The Battery Meter dialog box shows power remaining.

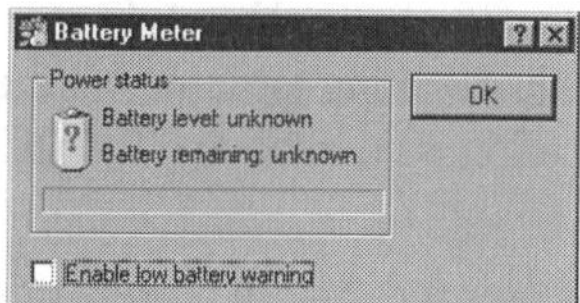

NOTE As you can see in Figure 8.10, Windows 95 cannot always detect the amount of power remaining in the battery. This is often due to the way in which the batteries used in portable PCs drain their charges. The voltage remains fairly steady through the battery's cycle and then begins to drop rapidly as the battery nears the end of its useful charge.

Setting SL Options

If your PC uses an Intel SL processor such as the 486SL, you can use SL-specific options to control additional power management features. As previously explained, an SL button appears on the Power page on systems containing an SL processor. Choosing the SL button displays the SL Enhanced Options dialog box shown in Figure 8.11.

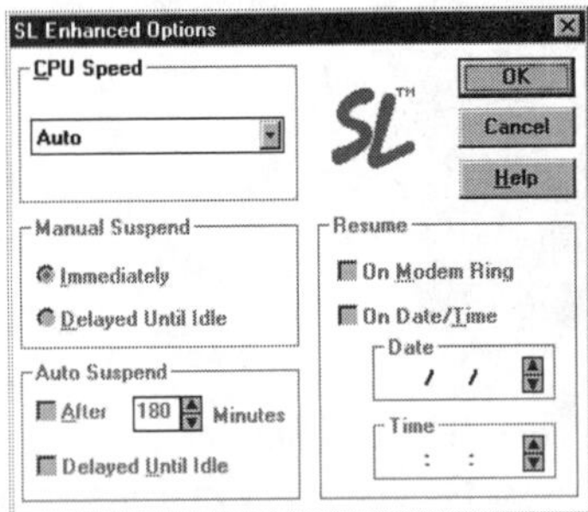

FIG. 8.11
The SL Enhanced Options dialog box controls SL-specific power options.

The following list explains the groups in the SL Enhanced Options dialog box:

- **CPU Speed.** This drop-down list enables you to control how the CPU is managed. Choose Auto to cause the CPU to run at full speed but power down whenever possible to conserve power. Choose 10 percent, 25 percent, or 50 percent to run the CPU at a specific reduced speed. Choose 100 percent to run the CPU at full speed and prevent the CPU from powering down.
- **Manual Suspend.** The two settings in this group control the way the system powers down when you press the Suspend button, close the display (on a notebook PC), or choose Suspend in the Start menu. Choose Immediately in the Manual Suspend group to cause the PC to suspend immediately when you press the PC's Suspend button or close the display. Windows will suspend all applications even if they are currently processing. Choose the Delayed Until Idle option to cause Windows to wait for all applications to finish processing before it powers down the PC. Some applications appear to Windows to be processing when they actually are just waiting for input, so the system might not enter suspend mode if such an application is running and the Delayed Until Idle option is selected.
- **Auto Suspend.** This option controls how the system powers down automatically after a specified period of time with no keyboard or mouse activity. The After option lets you specify an amount of time after which the system powers down automatically. The Delayed Until Idle option causes the system to power down automatically only if there are no active applications. These settings don't affect the screen, hard disk, or other devices individually. Instead, they control shutdown of the entire system, including the CPU.
- **Resume.** These settings control how the system resumes after it has been suspended. The On Modem Ring option, if enabled, causes the system to resume if a call comes in to

a line that is connected to the PC's modem. The On Date/Time option enables you to specify a specific date and time at which the system will resume.

TROUBLESHOOTING

The Windows 95 marketing literature describes more power management features than are available on my laptop computer. Older computers do not have BIOSes that are compatible with APM. Some newer computers have known incompatibilities with the APM 1.1 specifications. Consequently, some or all of Windows 95's Advanced Power Management features might not be available.

Using Dial-Up Networking

Windows 95 expands and improves on the remote access client in Windows for Workgroups, integrating remote access almost seamlessly within the Windows 95 interface. With the remote access features in Windows 95—collectively called *Dial-Up Networking*—you can connect to a remote computer to access its files and printer(s). If the remote computer is connected to a network and you have the necessary access rights on the remote LAN, dialing into the server is just like connecting locally to the network. You can use the shared resources of any computer on the network, send and receive e-mail, print, and perform essentially any task remotely that you can perform with a workstation connected directly to the network.

▶ **See** "Creating a Connection," **p. 204**

NOTE A Windows NT server can act as a TCP/IP gateway, routing TCP/IP traffic for your dial-in PC. If your office network is connected to the Internet, for example, you can dial into a server to gain access to the Internet from home. To use this capability, you must install the TCP/IP network protocol and bind it to the dial-up adapter. The Windows NT server's Remote Access Server service must also be configured to allow TCP/IP dial-in and route TCP/IP traffic. ■

If you did not install Dial-Up Networking when you installed Windows 95, you must now do so with the following procedure:

1. Open the Start menu and choose Settings, Control Panel, and then click the Add/Remove Programs icon. Then choose the Windows Setup tab to display the Windows Setup dialog box.
2. Double-click the Communications item to display the Communications dialog box.
3. Place a check in the Dial-Up Networking check box, and then choose OK. Choose OK again and Windows 95 installs Dial-Up Networking on your PC.

Before you can begin using Dial-Up Networking, you must install the dial-up adapter and network protocol required by the remote server. The following section explains how to set up Dial-Up Networking.

Setting Up Dial-Up Networking

Setting up Dial-Up Networking requires four steps: installing the dial-up adapter, installing the network protocol(s) used by the remote server, installing a network client, and installing an appropriate file and printer sharing service.

The dial-up adapter is a special driver supplied with Windows 95 that acts as a virtual network adapter, performing much the same function that a typical hardware network adapter performs. Instead of handling network traffic across a network cable, the dial-up adapter handles network traffic through your PC's modem.

To install the dial-up adapter, follow these steps:

1. Open the Control Panel and choose the Network object.
2. In the Configuration page of the Network property sheet, choose Add.
3. Choose Adapter from the Select Network Component Type dialog box, and then choose Add. Windows 95 displays the Select Network Adapters dialog box shown in Figure 8.12.

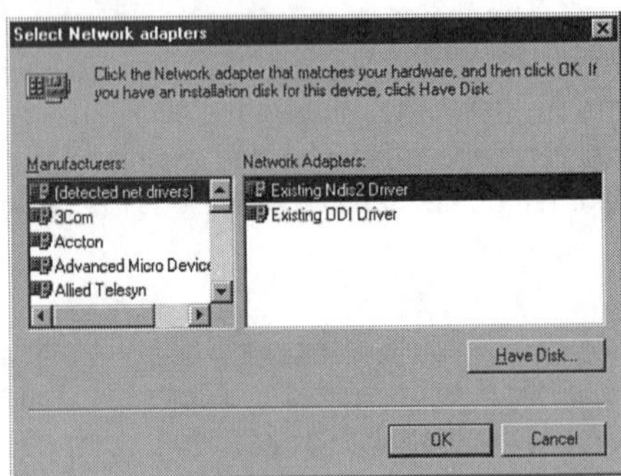

FIG. 8.12 You must install the dial-up adapter before you can use Dial-Up Networking.

4. From the Manufacturers list, choose Microsoft.
5. From the Network Adapters list, choose Dial-Up Adapter, and then choose OK. Windows 95 will add the dial-up adapter to your system.

After you install the dial-up adapter, you must install at least one network protocol to be used for the dial-up connection. The protocol you select depends on the protocol used by the remote server. On Microsoft-based networks, the protocol used typically is NetBEUI. On NetWare-based networks, the protocol typically used is IPX/SPX. If you are connecting to a remote network that uses TCP/IP, you should install the TCP/IP protocol.

To install a protocol and bind it to the dial-up adapter, use the following procedure:

1. Open the Control Panel and double-click the Network icon.
2. From the Configuration page, choose the Add button.
3. Choose Protocol from the Select Network Component Type dialog box, and then choose Add.
4. From the Manufacturers list, choose Microsoft.

5. From the Network Protocols list, choose the appropriate network protocol. Then choose OK.

In addition to a network protocol, you also might need to install a network client. The network client enables your PC to access files and printers on the remote server and network. If you are connecting to a Microsoft network-based computer or network, you should install the Client for Microsoft Networks client. If you are connecting to a NetWare system, you should install the Client for NetWare Networks client.

If you are using TCP/IP to gain access to the Internet through a dial-up server, and do not want to have access to the remote server's files or shared resources on the LAN to which the server is connected, you do not need to install a network client.

To install a network client and bind it to the dial-up adapter, use the following procedure:

1. Open the Control Panel, double-click the Network icon, and then choose Add from the Configuration page.
2. From the Select Network Component Type dialog box, choose Client; then choose Add.
3. From the Manufacturer's list, choose Microsoft, choose the appropriate client from the Network Clients list, and then choose OK.
4. In the Configuration property page, select Dial-Up Adapter from the list of installed network components. Then choose Properties to display the Dial-Up Adapter properties sheet.
5. Choose the Bindings tab to display the Bindings page shown in Figure 8.13.

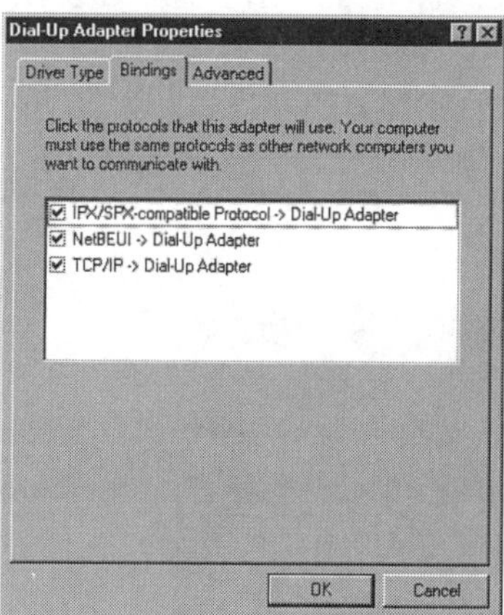

FIG. 8.13
Use the Bindings page to bind a network protocol to the dial-up adapter.

6. Place a check beside the network protocols you want to use with the dial-up adapter, and then choose OK. Choose OK again to close the Network dialog box.

Your PC is now configured to act as a Dial-Up Networking client. Making a connection is explained in the following section.

▶ **See** "Installing and Configuring Your Modem," **p. 68**

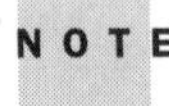

NOTE If you have not already installed your modem, do so before continuing. Your modem must be installed in order to use Dial-Up Networking.

Creating a Connection

To create a new Dial-Up Networking connection, first open My Computer, and then choose the Dial-Up Networking folder. The Dial-Up Networking folder contains an object named Make New Connection that starts a wizard to help you create Dial-Up Networking connections. The following steps help you start the wizard and create a Dial-Up Networking connection:

1. Open the Dial-Up Networking folder and double-click the Make New Connection object. Windows 95 displays the Make New Connection Wizard box shown in Figure 8.14.

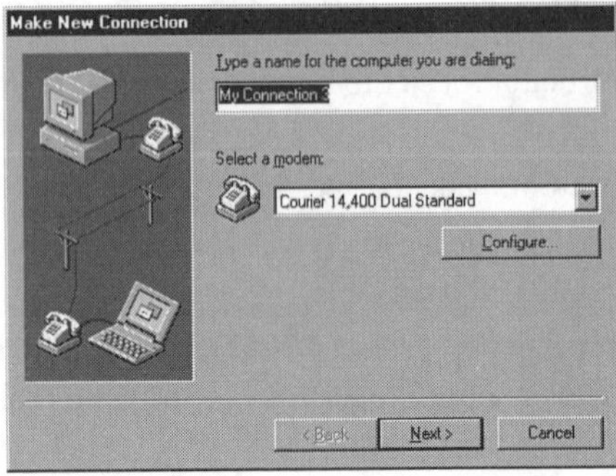

FIG. 8.14 The Make New Connection Wizard helps you create Dial-Up Networking connections.

2. By default, the wizard names the connection My Connection. Highlight the name and enter a name that describes the remote system to which you are connecting. This is the name that will appear under the connection's icon in the Dial-Up Networking folder.
3. Use the Select a Modem drop-down list to choose the modem you want to use for the Dial-Up Networking connection, and then choose Next. The dialog box changes to the one shown in Figure 8.15.

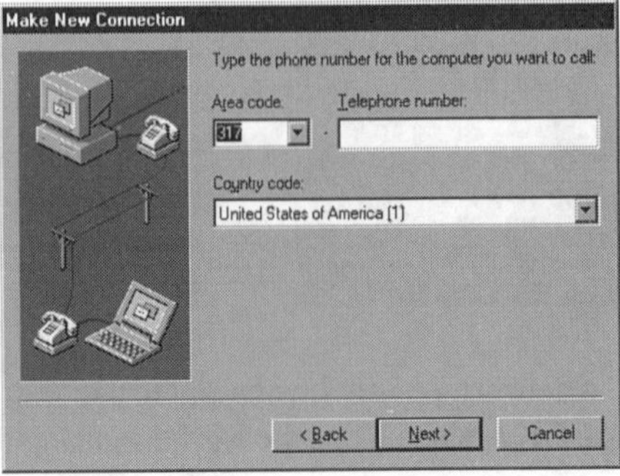

FIG. 8.15 Specify the phone number for the remote connection.

4. Enter the area code and telephone number in the appropriate text boxes.
5. Use the Country Code drop-down list to choose the country in which the remote system is located, and then choose Next.
6. Choose Finish to create the connection and add its icon to the Dial-Up Networking folder.

Connecting to a Remote System

Connecting to a remote system through a Dial-Up Networking connection is simple. Open the Dial-Up Networking folder, and then double-click the icon of the server to which you want to connect. Windows 95 displays a dialog box for the Dial-Up Networking connection similar to the one shown in Figure 8.16.

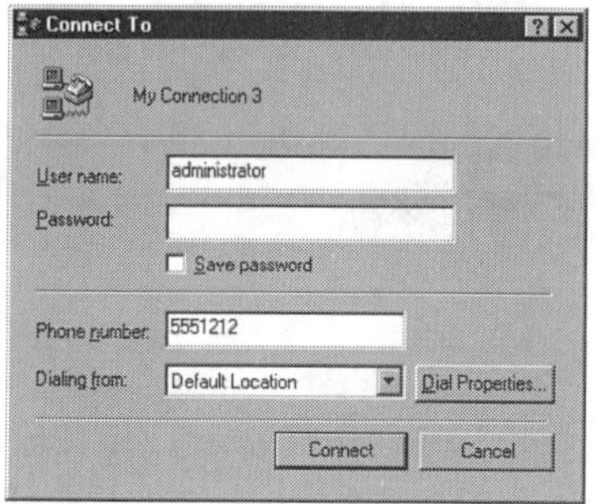

FIG. 8.16
You can verify and change settings prior to making the connection.

In the User Name and Password text boxes, enter the account name and password required by the remote server. If you want Windows 95 to save the password so you don't have to enter it each time you use the Dial-Up Networking connection, enable the Save Password check box.

Next, verify that the phone number and dialing location specified in the connection are correct; then choose Connect. Dial-Up Networking dials the remote server and attempts to connect and log on using the name and password you have provided. After the connection is established, you can begin using the shared resources of the remote server and the shared resources of other computers on the remote network as if your PC were connected locally to the network.

A new feature in Dial-Up Networking in the OSR2 release of Windows 95 is *scripting*. Scripts are text files consisting of commands, parameters, and expressions that automate the process of making a connection with a remote system using Dial-Up Networking. The script contains the information that you would normally have to enter manually to make a connection with another computer. Once you create a script, you can assign the script to the appropriate Dial-Up Networking connection in the Scripting tab of the properties sheet for that connection. Once you do this, the script will be executed automatically every time you dial the connection.

To learn how to create a script for automating your Dial-Up Networking connections, open the file SCRIPT.DOC in WordPad. SCRIPT.DOC is located in the WINDOWS folder. A complete description of the scripting language and instructions on how to create a script file are included in this document.

Using Infrared to Communicate with Devices

One of the nuisances you face when moving around with laptop computers is the extra burden of carrying cables, network adapters, and PC Cards. In a temporary office, you have to get out cables, pull out printers, crawl around on the floor routing cables, and install drivers before you can finally print. Then you leave a few hours later.

Most of these nuisances go away if you use a laptop computer with IrDA in an office with IrDA-compatible equipment. IrDA is an abbreviation for the Infrared Developers Association—an industry association that has agreed on communication standards between infrared devices. The IrDA standard ensures that devices from different hardware and software manufacturers will work together.

Infrared communication enables you to communicate between hardware devices without a cable of any type. Instead, a beam of infrared light substitutes for a serial cable that carries data.

CAUTION

Always remove any previously installed infrared drivers before upgrading or changing to a new driver. You will need to do this if you upgrade to a newer infrared driver or if you change IR adapters in your computer.

Installing IrDA Support

Before you go to the effort of downloading the IrDA software upgrade, make sure your computer will support it. After you examine the Device Manager for IrDA software and the IRQ it uses, follow the steps listed in the section "Installing the Infrared Monitor Software" to install the Infrared Monitor.

Checking for IrDA Hardware and Its IRQ Before upgrading your Windows 95 software, check your computer manufacturer's manuals to make sure your computer is IrDA-compliant. If you are unsure, look on the back of your laptop for a small blackish-maroon window approximately 1/2" by 1". It may be next to a wave or signal icon. This is the infrared window.

Check in System Properties for IrDA-compliant hardware by opening the Start menu and choosing Settings, Control Panel. Double-click the System program. Select the Device Manager tab, and then select the View Devices by Type option. Click the Ports (COM & LPT) icon in the hierarchy. Check if there is a Generic IRDA Compatible Device item. This listing will be there if an IrDA device is built in to your computer.

With Generic IRDA Compatible Device selected, click the Properties button. Select the General tab from the Generic IRDA Compatible Device properties sheet. Look at the Device Status check box for the message, "This device is working properly." If you see a message indicating a problem with your IrDA device, check the hardware manuals from your computer's manufacturer for support.

With the properties sheet still displayed, select the Resources tab to check which Interrupt Request (IRQ) the IrDA device uses. Write down the IRQ listed under Resource Settings. COM2 and COM4 correspond to IRQ 3 and are usually assigned to a modem. COM1 and COM3 correspond to IRQ 4 and are usually assigned to a serial mouse.

Installing the Infrared Monitor Software Infrared communication capability was not in the original release of Windows 95 but was added with Service Pack 1 during the first quarter of 1996. For a small shipping and handling fee, you can have Service Pack 1 shipped to you by calling Microsoft at 1-800-426-9400.

ON THE WEB

You can download components of Service Pack 1 for free by visiting this Microsoft software upgrade Web site.

http://www.microsoft.com/windows/software.htm

When you are at Microsoft's software upgrade page, select the hyperlink for Service Pack 1, and then download the file W95IR.EXE into its own folder. This self-extracting file, approximately 300K in size, contains the IrDA installation software.

Since the release of Service Pack 1, Microsoft has released another Windows update, called OEM Service Release 2 (OSR2). Included in this update is a newer version of the IrDA driver, IrDA 2.0. In addition to supporting data transfer between two computers and printing to an IrDA-compliant printer, you can now connect to a local area network (LAN) using an IrDA device. See "Installing the Windows 95b (OSR2) Service Release," in Chapter 2 for more information on OSR2.

You don't have to obtain the complete OSR2 update to take advantage of the newer IrDA driver. You can download the IrDA 2.0 driver from the following Microsoft Web site:

http://www.microsoft.com/windows/software/irda.htm

The newer driver is also called W95IR.EXE, and you can use the following procedure to install either version of the driver.

To install the IrDA upgrade you received from Microsoft, make sure you have uninstalled any previous IrDA drivers. Then follow these steps:

1. Double-click the W95IR.EXE file to expand the files it contains.
2. Double-click RELNOTES.DOC to open it in WordPad. Read the release notes for information that may apply to your computer. Close the release notes when you are done.

3. Double-click the SETUP.EXE file that came from the W95IR.EXE file. Messages will flash while a setup database is built and when Windows detects your infrared hardware. The first Add Infrared Device Wizard appears (see Figure 8.17). Click Next.

FIG. 8.17
The Add Infrared Device Wizard installs the software for infrared communication.

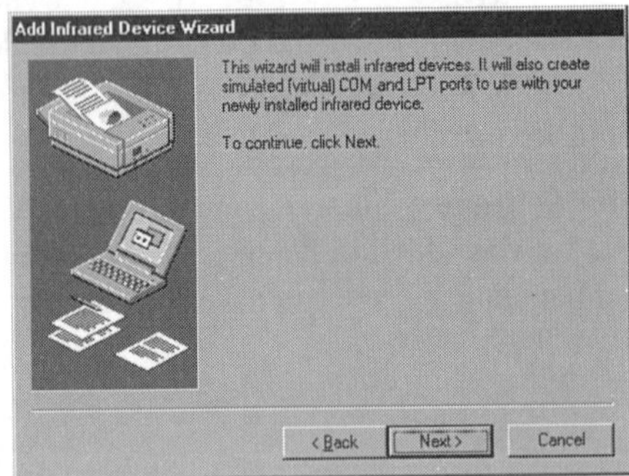

4. Select the manufacturer and model of your IrDA hardware from the lists in the second wizard dialog box shown in Figure 8.18. If your computer has a built-in IrDA port, choose (Standard Infrared Devices) from the Manufacturers list, and then click Next.

FIG. 8.18
Select the manufacturer and model for your IrDA device.

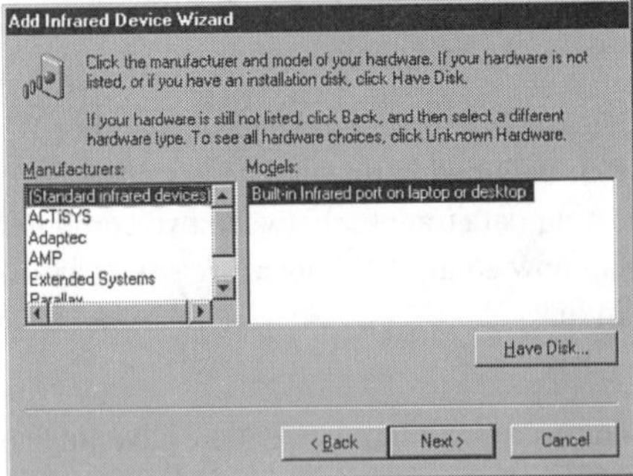

5. Select the COM port that the IrDA device uses. It may be automatically detected, as shown in Figure 8.19. If not, select a COM port using the IRQ information you saw in the Device Manager. Then click Next.

TIP If you are unsure which COM port to use during installation, take a guess at one that appears unused. If your IrDA communication does not work, uninstall it, and reinstall it using the other COM port.

6. Change the simulated Infrared Serial (COM) port or Infrared Printer (LPT) port if you do not want to use these simulated ports. Figure 8.20 shows the simulated infrared port sheet. Select whether you want to use the default simulated ports or enter new simulated ports, and click Next.
7. Click Finish to complete the installation.

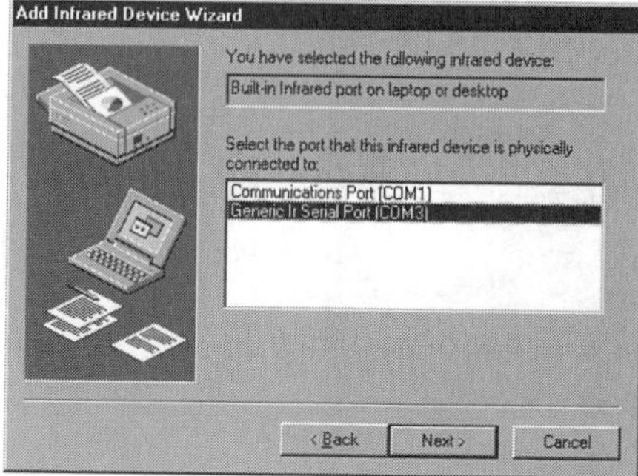

FIG. 8.19
Select the COM port used by your IrDA device.

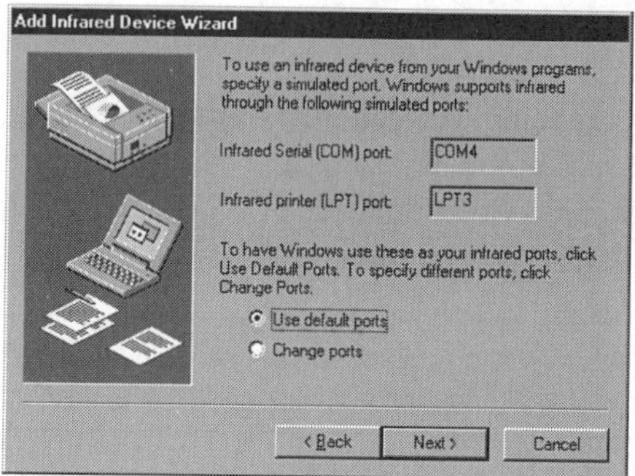

FIG. 8.20
Change the simulated infrared serial and printer ports or accept the defaults.

Starting and Controlling Infrared Communications Support

The Windows 95 Infrared Monitor program must be running if you want your computer to check its surroundings for other IrDA devices, such as printers and network connections. While it is running, the Infrared Monitor sends out an infrared beam and checks for responses every few seconds. If the Monitor gets a response from another IrDA device, it keeps a log that the device is available and indicates whether a driver for that device is loaded.

The Monitor also tracks which devices are currently communicating with your computer and the quality of that communication. You can see the quality level and communication status by opening the Infrared Monitor whenever it is working. Figure 8.21 shows communication in progress with a Hewlett-Packard (HP) printer. Use the Monitor to change the communication rate and enable or disable communication with devices in range.

Starting the Infrared Monitor and Turning On Communication To start the Infrared Monitor, open the Start menu and choose Settings, Control Panel. When the Control Panel appears, double-click the Infrared program. The Infrared Monitor sheet appears.

If you selected the Display the Infrared Icon in The Taskbar option from the Preferences tab of the Monitor, an Infrared icon will appear at the right side of the taskbar. Double-click this icon to display the Infrared Monitor sheet.

FIG. 8.21
This Status tab shows that data is being sent to an HP LaserJet 5P printer and that the communication rate is good at 115.2 Kbps.

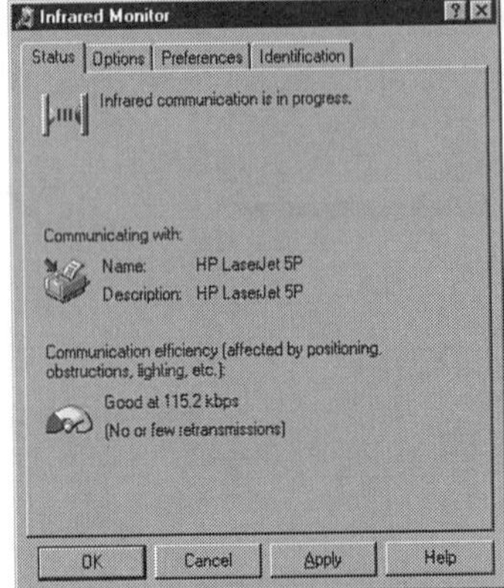

When the Infrared Monitor is running, you can turn communication on and off with a right mouse click. To turn on infrared communication, right-click the Infrared icon on the taskbar, and then check the Enable Infrared Communication On check box. Turn off infrared communication by clearing the Enable Infrared Communication On check box.

The Search For and Provide Status For Devices in Range option and the Enable Software Install For Plug and Play Devices in Range option are turned off when infrared communication is turned off.

Changing the Infrared Monitor Settings To change the Infrared Monitor settings, display the Infrared Monitor by double-clicking the Infrared icon on the taskbar, or by double-clicking the Infrared program in the Control Panel.

Figure 8.22 shows the Status tab when no devices are detected; Figure 8.23 shows the Status tab when an IrDA-compatible printer is within range.

FIG. 8.22
The Status tab shows if devices are in range and the quality of their communication.

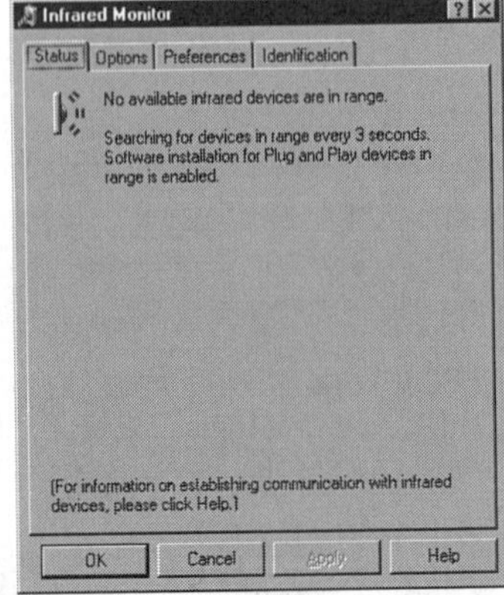

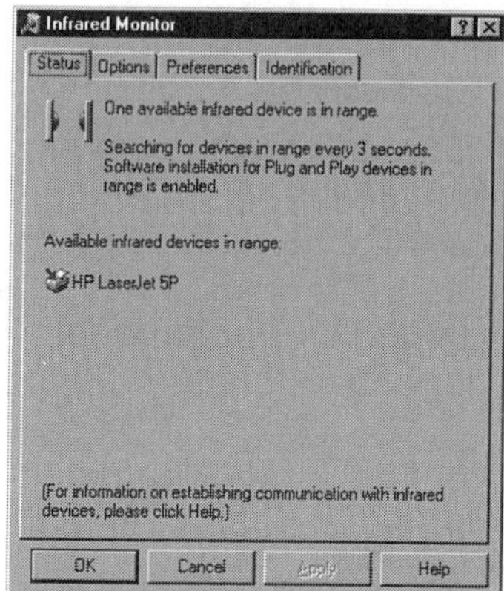

FIG. 8.23 The Status tab shows that an IrDA-compatible printer is in range.

Figure 8.24 shows the Options tab. The following table describes its options.

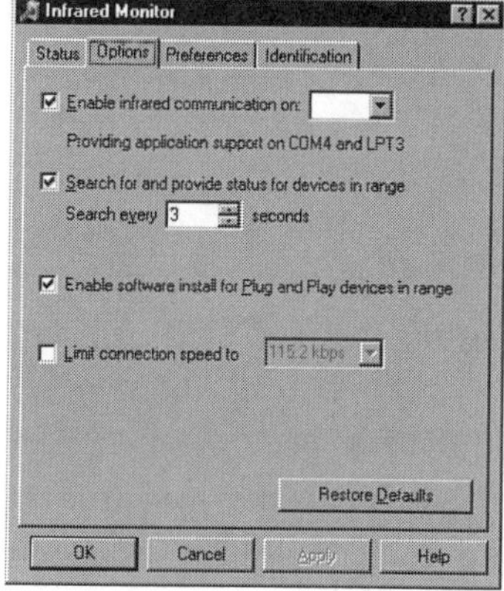

FIG. 8.24 The Options tab enables or disables infrared communication.

Option	**Description**
Enable Infrared Communications On	Enables infrared communication when selected and specifies which physical port is being used. You can choose between the physical COM ports you have available.
Search For and Provide	This must be selected if you want Status For Devices In Range devices to detect one another.
Search Every *x* Seconds	Specifies how frequently devices search for one another.
Enable Software Install for Plug and Play Devices in Range	When selected, Plug and Play devices will automatically install their drivers when the computer is within range. If the driver is already installed, it is not reinstalled. You will probably want to leave this deselected most of the time.

continues

continued

Option	Description
Limit Connection Speed To:	The Infrared Monitor attempts to transmit at the highest possible speed, but this may cause lower effective transmission rates if a large number of retries are required. In some cases, a lower speed may improve the effective transmission rate.

Figure 8.25 shows the options available on the Preferences tab. The following table describes those options.

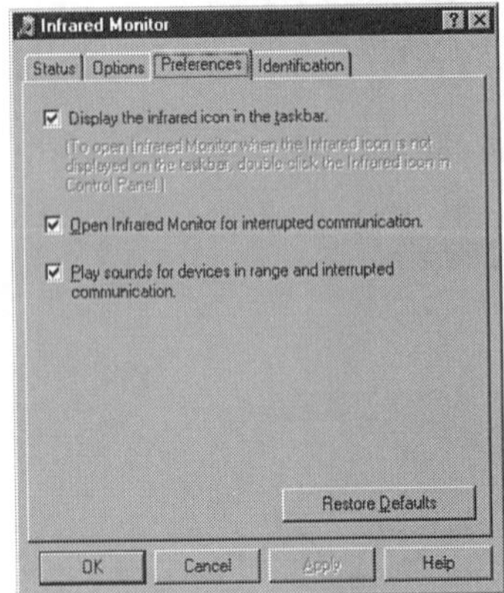

FIG. 8.25
The Preferences tab specifies personal options about how the Infrared Monitor appears.

Option	Description
Display the Infrared Icon in the Taskbar	Select this check box to display a small Infrared icon in the taskbar. Right-click the icon for controls, or double-click it to display the Infrared Monitor.
Open Infrared Monitor for Interrupted Communication	When selected, a warning message displays when infrared communication is interrupted. The message box closes when communication resumes.
Play Sounds for Devices in Range and Interrupted Communication	When selected, a sound plays when communication is interrupted. If you have a sound card, you can customize these sounds by double-clicking the Sounds program in the Control Panel and selecting the sounds to play for infrared events.

Figure 8.26 shows the options available on the Identification tab. The following table describes these options.

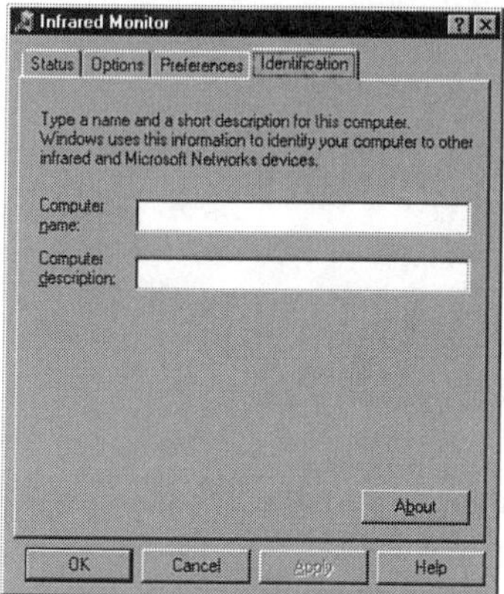

FIG. 8.26
Use the Identification tab to specify a network name and description for your computer.

Option	Description
Computer Name	Specify the name you want for your computer to be identified by on the network.
Computer Description	Specify the description for your computer to help in identifying it on a network.

Finding and Monitoring the Status of Infrared Devices

For infrared devices to communicate, they must be turned on and oriented so they send infrared light to each other. The infrared windows on the devices must be facing each other within an approximate 30-degree cone. They should be from six inches to nine feet apart. Most devices are designed for a range of three to nine feet.

To check the status of communication between two devices, open the Infrared Monitor by double-clicking the Infrared icon on the taskbar, or by double-clicking Infrared in the Control Panel. Select the Options tab. Select the Enable Infrared Communication On check box, select the Search For and Provide Status For Devices In Range check box, and then click Apply.

If the transmission quality is poor, lower the transmission speed by selecting a smaller number from the Limit Connection Speed To: list. Normally, infrared communication occurs at the highest possible speed. In cases of a poor link, a lower transmission rate may actually improve throughput by decreasing retries.

Installing Software for Your Infrared Device

Some Plug and Play IrDA devices will install the appropriate driver on your computer when your computer comes within range. Figure 8.27 shows the dialog box that displays when an IrDA computer comes within range of a Hewlett-Packard 5P printer.

To install software for an infrared device, follow these steps:

1. Right-click the Infrared icon on the taskbar.
2. Select the Enable Plug and Play check box.

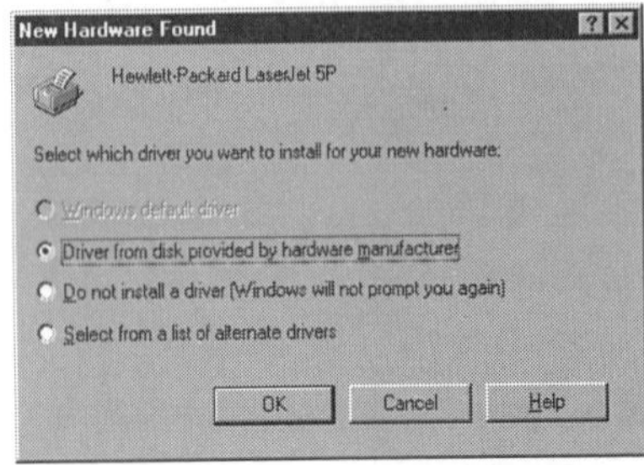

FIG. 8.27
Windows indicates when it is within range of a device for which it does not have a driver.

You also can display the Infrared Monitor sheet and check the Enable Software Install For Plug And Play Devices In Range check box. If you want to prevent unwanted drivers from being installed on your computer, leave this check box clear.

If the IrDA device is not Plug and Play-compliant, you'll need to install the driver for that IrDA device. This driver should be on a disk that came with the device.

If the IrDA device is not Plug and Play-compliant, click Start, Settings, Control Panel; then double-click the Add New Hardware program. Keep the infrared windows of the devices in range and run the Add New Hardware Wizard, or manually install the drivers using manual selections from the Add New Hardware Wizard.

▶ **See** "Installing Legacy (non-PnP) Hardware," **p. 174**

Using Infrared for Direct Cable Connection

You can use infrared to transfer files with Direct Cable Connection. The infrared communication acts the same as communication via a serial or parallel cable. Make sure that infrared is enabled in both devices. Then turn on Direct Cable Connection by opening the Start menu and choosing Programs, Accessories, Direct Cable Connection. Follow the Direct Cable Connection procedures described earlier in this chapter.

Printing with an Infrared Printer

Printing to an infrared printer is the same as printing to any other printer. However, you do need to make sure that the infrared windows on the devices are within an angle of 30 degrees and within six inches to nine feet of the printer.

If you have not assigned the printer to an infrared port, follow these steps:

1. Open the Start menu and choose Settings, Printers.
2. Right-click the Printers icon and choose the Properties sheet.
3. Select the Details tab.
4. Select Infrared from the Print to the Following Port list.

Connecting to a Network Using IR

If you have installed IrDA 2.0, which is the latest version of the infrared driver, you can now connect a computer with an IR device to a local area network (LAN) that is equipped with an IrLan access point device. The IrLan device takes the place of the network adapter that you would normally use in a computer to connect to a network. Check the release notes that come with the IrDA driver for a list of IrDA 2.0-compliant IrLan access devices.

To establish an IR connection with a network equipped with an IrLan device, turn on the IrLan device and run the Infrared Monitor, as described in "Starting the Infrared Monitor and Turning On Communication," earlier in this chapter. Once the IR connection is established, you can double-click the Network Neighborhood icon to view files and folders on the network.

Removing Infrared Support

You must remove infrared support from your computer before upgrading to new or different infrared support. You may need to upgrade if you change the infrared adapter in your computer, or if you upgrade from Infrared Support for Windows v1.0 that was released in Service Pack 1 during the first quarter of 1996.

To remove infrared support, follow these steps:

1. Open the Start menu and choose Settings, Control Panel; then double-click the Add/Remove Programs program.
2. Select the Install/Uninstall tab.
3. Select Infrared Support for Windows 95 Version 1.0 from the list.
4. Click the Add/Remove button.

Troubleshooting When Infrared Communication Fails

If you have trouble with infrared communication and you know the Infrared Monitor is on and the communication is enabled, follow this checklist to search for possible problems:

- Make sure all non-IrDA communication has stopped. Non-IrDA communication prevents IrDA communication.
- Both devices should be IrDA-compliant.
- Check that infrared is on and enabled in both IrDA devices.
- The search option must be turned on by selecting the Search For and Provide Status For Devices in Range check box on the Options tab of the Infrared Monitor.
- Check that the search interval is long enough so the devices can detect each other. Set the Search Every X Seconds box for approximately three seconds on the Options tab. The Search For and Provide Status For Devices in Range check box must be selected.
- Check that the devices are between six inches and nine feet apart and their infrared windows are pointing at each other and within a 30-degree cone. Check that the infrared windows are clean.
- Make sure sunlight is not shining on either infrared window.

http://www.microsoft.com/windows/software/irda.htm

Maintaining Laptop and Desktop Files with Briefcase

Many users of portable PCs also use a desktop system and often need to juggle files between the two systems. You might, for example, have a set of reports you are preparing with your desktop system and you need to move those files to your portable to work on them while you are out of town. Windows 95 includes a Briefcase feature that simplifies the task of synchronizing the files on your desktop and portable PCs, helping you keep track of which copy of the file(s) is most current.

The following is a simplified example of how you might use the Briefcase:

- You create a Briefcase (which appears as a typical folder) on your portable PC.
- You copy one or more files to the Briefcase using a direct cable connection to your desktop PC or through your docking station's network connection.
- You work on the documents contained in the Briefcase while you are away from the office, modifying and updating the files.
- While you are away from the office, a coworker modifies one of the files on your desktop system that you copied to your Briefcase.
- When you return to the office, you reconnect your portable to your desktop PC, and then open the Briefcase on your portable.
- You use the Briefcase to update the files. The Briefcase informs you which files have been modified and enables you to easily copy the files from the Briefcase to their original locations on the desktop PC. The Briefcase also informs you that a file on your desktop PC (the file modified by your coworker) has changed and gives you the option of updating your copy in the Briefcase.

The Briefcase also can detect when the original and Briefcase copies of a file have been changed. The Briefcase then prompts you to specify which copy of the file should be retained. The Briefcase also supports *reconciliation* of the two copies of the file. This means that if the document's source application supports reconciliation, the Briefcase uses OLE to communicate with the source application and merge the two files together, retaining the changes made in each copy of the file.

NOTE Because the Briefcase is a new feature, few applications currently support reconciliation, but the number of applications that support it should grow as developers take advantage of this new feature. ■

You are not limited to creating a Briefcase on your portable PC. In fact, you can create a Briefcase on a floppy disk or your desktop PC. You might find a Briefcase useful for synchronizing files on which multiple users on the network collaborate. And you are not limited to creating a single Briefcase—you can create as many as you like. For example, you might create a separate Briefcase for each project on which you are currently working.

▶ **See** "Synchronizing Files with a Floppy Disk," **p. 219**

NOTE Placing a Briefcase on a floppy disk is useful if you do not have the necessary cable to connect your desktop and portable PCs using Direct Cable Connection, or your docking station is not connected to the network. Simply create the Briefcase, and then move it to a floppy disk. Drag files from your desktop PC to the Briefcase; then move the Briefcase disk to your portable and begin working on the files. ■

Creating a Briefcase

If your PC does not already include a Briefcase on your desktop, you can easily create a new Briefcase. To create a Briefcase, follow these steps:

1. Decide where you want the Briefcase to be created (on the desktop, in a floppy disk folder, in a folder on the hard disk, and so on).
2. Right-click in the location in which you want the Briefcase created. If you want the Briefcase created on the desktop, for example, right-click the desktop.
3. From the pop-up menu, choose New, Briefcase. Windows 95 will create a Briefcase and add an icon for it in the location you have selected.
4. If you want to rename the Briefcase, click the Briefcase icon to select it; then click the Briefcase's description. Type a new description and press Enter.

As previously explained, you can create as many Briefcases as you like. By default, Windows 95 creates a Briefcase called My Briefcase on your desktop. You can rename the default Briefcase to suit your preferences.

Placing Files in the Briefcase

Although the Briefcase is a special type of folder, it behaves almost identically to a standard directory folder. You can move or copy files to a Briefcase in the same way you move or copy files to any folder. Simply open the folder in which the files are located, and then drag them to the Briefcase. Hold down the Ctrl key while dragging to copy the files, or hold down the Shift key to move the files. If you prefer, you can open Explorer (open the Start menu and choose Programs, Windows Explorer) and drag the files from Explorer into the Briefcase.

▶ **See** "Copying and Moving," **p. 619**

In addition to using standard file copying and moving techniques to place files in the Briefcase, you also can use Send To to place files in the Briefcase. Locate the file(s) you want to place in the Briefcase; then right-click one of the files. From the pop-up menu, choose Send To, and then choose the Briefcase to which you want to send the selected file(s). Windows 95 will copy the file(s) in the Briefcase.

TIP If you right-drag a document to the Briefcase, the pop-up menu includes an item labeled Make Sync Copy. Choose this option to create a copy of the object in the Briefcase.

Synchronizing Files

If you travel or work at home on your portable with files copied to your Briefcase from your desktop PC, Briefcase can keep your files updated. When your PC is undocked or you are working remotely, use your files as you normally would, opening and saving them in the Briefcase. When you return to the office desktop or remote network, first reconnect your portable to your desktop system or network, or insert the Briefcase floppy disk in your desktop PC. Then simply open the Briefcase and choose Briefcase, Update All. Briefcase displays a dialog box similar to the one shown in Figure 8.28.

FIG. 8.28
Briefcase prompts you to specify how modified files should be handled.

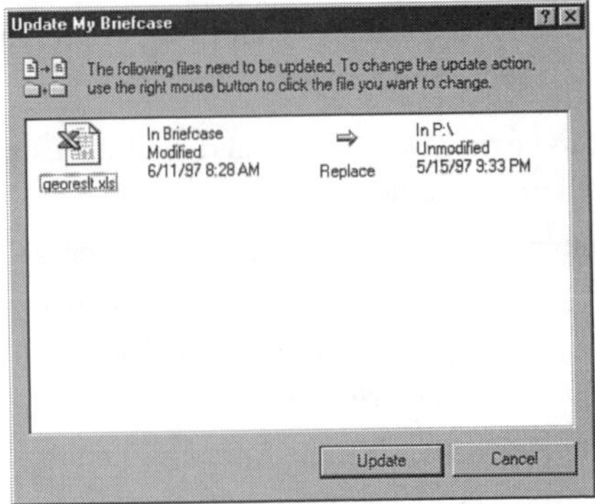

The left column lists the name of the file, and the second column lists the status of the file in the Briefcase. The third column specifies the update action that occurs if you do not choose a different action. The fourth column indicates the status of the original copy of the file.

If the update actions listed for each file are appropriate, click Update to update the files. To change the update action for a file, right-click the file. Briefcase opens a dialog box as shown in Figure 8.28. Choose the appropriate update action, and Briefcase changes the action for the file. When all of the files are set the way you want them, click Update.

NOTE If you update a file on a network server, you have no guarantee that another user won't modify the file after you have updated it, placing it once again out of sync with your Briefcase copy. If you again update the files in the Briefcase, however, the Briefcase will indicate that the original copy of the file located on the network server has changed.

TIP To select a group of files in the Briefcase, hold down the Ctrl key and click each file you want to update.

If you prefer to update only a few of the files in the Briefcase, simply select the files you want to update, and then choose Briefcase, Update Selection. Briefcase lists in the Update My Briefcase dialog box only those files you have selected.

After your selection of files is complete, choose Briefcase, Update Selection to update the selected files. You also can right-click a file in the Briefcase to open a dialog box, and then choose Update from the context menu to update the selected file(s).

Synchronizing Files with a Floppy Disk

You can move a Briefcase to a floppy disk to simplify transferring files between your portable and desktop PCs. To move your Briefcase to a floppy disk, follow these steps:

1. If you do not yet have a Briefcase on the desktop PC, create one. Right-click the Windows 95 desktop, and then choose New, Briefcase.
2. Open the My Computer folder and position the folder so you can see the Briefcase icon.
3. Open the folder containing the files you want to place in the Briefcase, and then right-drag the files from their folder to the Briefcase icon. From the context menu, choose Make Sync Copy.
4. Place a formatted disk in the desktop PC's floppy disk drive.
5. Right-drag the Briefcase from the desktop to the floppy drive icon in My Computer, and then choose Move Here.
6. Remove the floppy disk containing the Briefcase and insert it in the portable's floppy disk drive.
7. On the portable, work on the files in the Briefcase, opening and saving them in the Briefcase.
8. When you're ready to synchronize the files, place the floppy disk containing the Briefcase in the desktop PC's floppy disk drive. Open My Computer; then open the floppy disk folder. Right-drag the Briefcase from the disk folder to the desktop, and choose Move Here.
9. Open the Briefcase, and then synchronize the files as explained in the previous section.

Synchronizing Files with a Network

You can use a Briefcase to help you synchronize files on a network server on which you collaborate with other users. The process for working with the Briefcase and synchronizing files is the same as for a desktop PC/portable PC scenario. Create the Briefcase on your desktop, and then copy the files from the network server to the Briefcase. Edit the files in the Briefcase. When you're ready to synchronize them again with the original files on the server, open the Briefcase, and synchronize the files as previously explained.

Checking the Status of Briefcase Files

The update status of each file is listed in the Briefcase folder if you use Details to display the contents of the Briefcase as a detailed list. To configure the Briefcase to display a detailed list, choose View, Details.

You also can view the status of files in the Briefcase by selecting the files and choosing Briefcase, Update Selection. You also can view the status of individual files in the same way. In addition, you can use a file's pop-up menu to view its status. With the Briefcase open, right-click the file or folder that you want to check. Choose Properties to display the file's properties sheet. Then choose the Update Status tab to display the Update Status page shown in Figure 8.29.

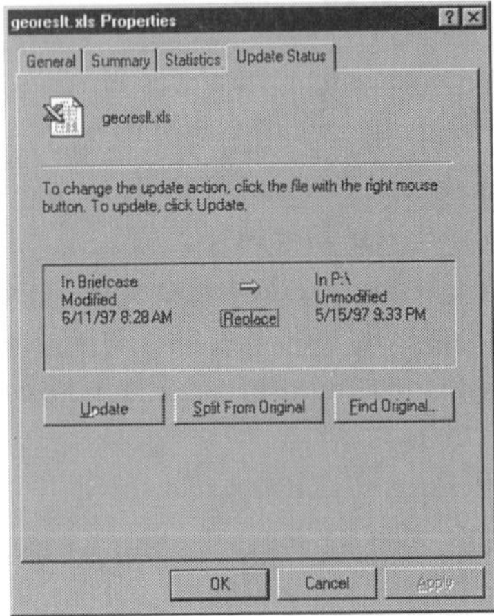

FIG. 8.29
A file's property sheet shows its update status.

If you want to check the status of all your Briefcase files, choose Briefcase, Update All. A status window pops up, enabling you to view the status of all files in the Briefcase. Choose Update to update the files, or Cancel to close the dialog box without making any changes.

Splitting the Briefcase File from the Original Files

Occasionally, you might want to disassociate (or split) a file in the Briefcase from its original. Splitting a file removes the link between the two files. To split a file, first open the Briefcase and select the file you want to split. After selecting the file, choose Briefcase, Split From Original. After a file is split from an original, it is labeled an orphan and can no longer be updated.

LCD Screen Mouse Trails

Pointing device features are also enhanced with the mobile user in mind. Switching between integrated pointing devices—track ball or clip-on mouse—to a desktop mouse (Plug and Play-compatible) is now automatically detected and enabled by Windows 95. Installing a serial, Plug and Play mouse amounts to plugging it in, and the system enables its use.

Like Windows for Workgroups, Windows 95 also adds a few special features that make it easier to see the cursor on a passive-matrix LCD panel, which many portable PCs use for their displays (active-matrix panels have much better image quality, and consequently it is much easier to see the cursor on an active-matrix LCD). The following sections explain these features.

Using Mouse Trails

When you move the cursor on a passive LCD display, the display typically cannot update fast enough to adequately display the pointer as it moves across the display. This makes it difficult to see the cursor. To alleviate the problem, you can turn on *mouse trails*. When mouse trails is enabled, a set of "ghost" pointers trail the pointer as it moves across the display. This makes it much easier to locate the cursor.

To enable mouse trails, open the Start menu and choose Settings, Control Panel. From the Control Panel, select the Mouse icon, and then click the Motion tab to display the Motion properties page shown in Figure 8.30.

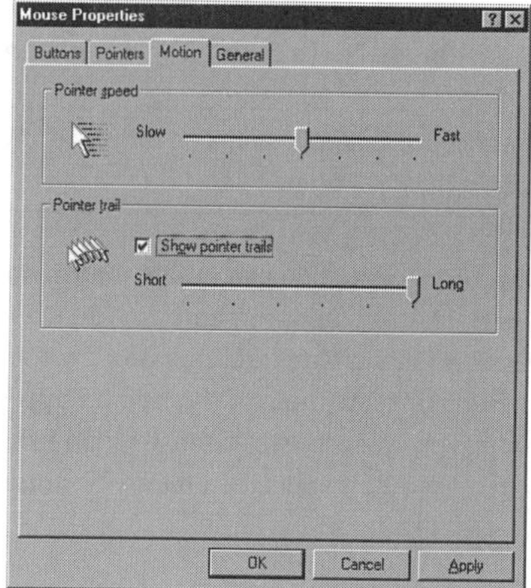

FIG. 8.30 Use the Show Pointer Trails check box to turn on mouse trails.

Place a check in the Show Pointer Trails check box to enable mouse trails. Use the accompanying slider control to specify the length of the mouse trail; then choose OK to apply the changes.

NOTE If you are using the new Microsoft IntelliMouse that came on the market when Microsoft Office 97 was released and have installed the Microsoft IntelliPoint 2.0 software, there is another option that helps you locate the mouse pointer on a laptop screen. The Sonar view, when enabled, produces a series of concentric circles around the mouse pointer when you press and release the Ctrl key. To enable this feature, open the Mouse properties sheet from the Control Panel, select the Visibility tab, and check the Show Location of Pointer When You Press the Ctrl Key option. To locate the pointer, press and release the Ctrl key. ■

Using Large Pointers

In addition to using mouse trails, you also might want to increase the size of the pointer you use on your portable to make it easier to see. Windows 95 enables you to create pointer schemes much like you create desktop color schemes, saving the pointer schemes by name. Windows 95 includes a small selection of predefined schemes, two of which use large pointers that are much easier to see on a passive LCD panel than the standard Windows 95 mouse pointers.

NOTE If you did not install the optional pointers when you installed Windows 95, you must install them before you can use the large pointer schemes. To do so, open the Control Panel and choose the Add/Remove Programs icon. Double-click Accessories, and then scroll through the Accessories list to find the Mouse Pointers item. Place a check beside Mouse Pointers and choose OK. Choose OK a second time to add the pointers to your system.

To use a large pointer scheme, open the Control Panel and choose the Mouse icon; then choose the Pointers tab to display the Pointers properties page. From the Schemes drop-down list, choose either the Windows Standard (Large) or Windows Standard (Extra Large) scheme. Then choose OK. Windows 95 immediately begins using the new pointers.

To add a new scheme, customize as many pointers as you want; then click Save As on the Pointers property page to identify the new scheme.

In addition to using a predefined scheme, you also can create your own custom schemes. Display the Pointers properties page as described earlier, and then select the pointer you want to change. Choose Browse, and Windows 95 displays a dialog box from which you can select a pointer file. When you select a pointer file, a sample of the pointer appears in the Preview box. When you have selected the pointer you want to use, choose Open to select the pointer and return to the Pointers page. Choose Save As to specify a name for your new pointer scheme.

PART II

Navigation Skills

CHAPTER 9

Understanding the Windows 95 Interface

by Ron Person and Ed Bott

In this chapter

Understanding the Most Important Screen Elements in Windows 95

This chapter gives you "the big picture" to help you understand Windows 95. If you're a new user, you'll want to get a feel for the important concepts and see where you are going. If you're an experienced Windows user, you'll want to compare this new version of Windows with previous versions. And if you are a power user or consultant, you'll want a quick introduction to ways you can customize and troubleshoot Windows 95.

People who have used previous versions of Windows should read this chapter so that they can quickly grasp what has changed.

After reading this chapter, you should have a good idea what sections of the book to read to start learning about Windows 95. Throughout this chapter, you'll find recommendations for three different approaches to learning, based on whether you are an inexperienced Windows user, an experienced Windows user, or a power user.

Throughout this chapter, important concepts are broken up by experience level. Rather than repeat basic concepts for each experience level, you should read the concepts from the inexperienced user level up to your level.

The appearance of the Windows 95 screen, shown in Figure 9.1, is completely different from MS-DOS or previous versions of Windows. The backdrop of the screen is the desktop. On the desktop, you'll find icons that represent programs, documents, and special system folders. The taskbar, Quick Launch toolbar, and Start button along the bottom of the screen enable you to launch programs and switch between running applications. Because it's so easy to customize Windows 95, don't be surprised if your desktop layout looks different from the one shown in the figure.

Beginning Users of Windows 95

If you are unfamiliar with previous versions of Windows, the important things to notice are as follows:

- Each item on the screen does something when you select, launch, or right-click the item.
- Icons represent programs, documents, or shortcuts. Shortcuts are pointers to a program, document, disk drive, printer, or other resource.
- You use the taskbar and Start button shown at the bottom of Figure 9.1 to start and switch between programs.
- Running programs appear in three ways: as a button on the taskbar, in a window on the screen, or filling the entire screen.

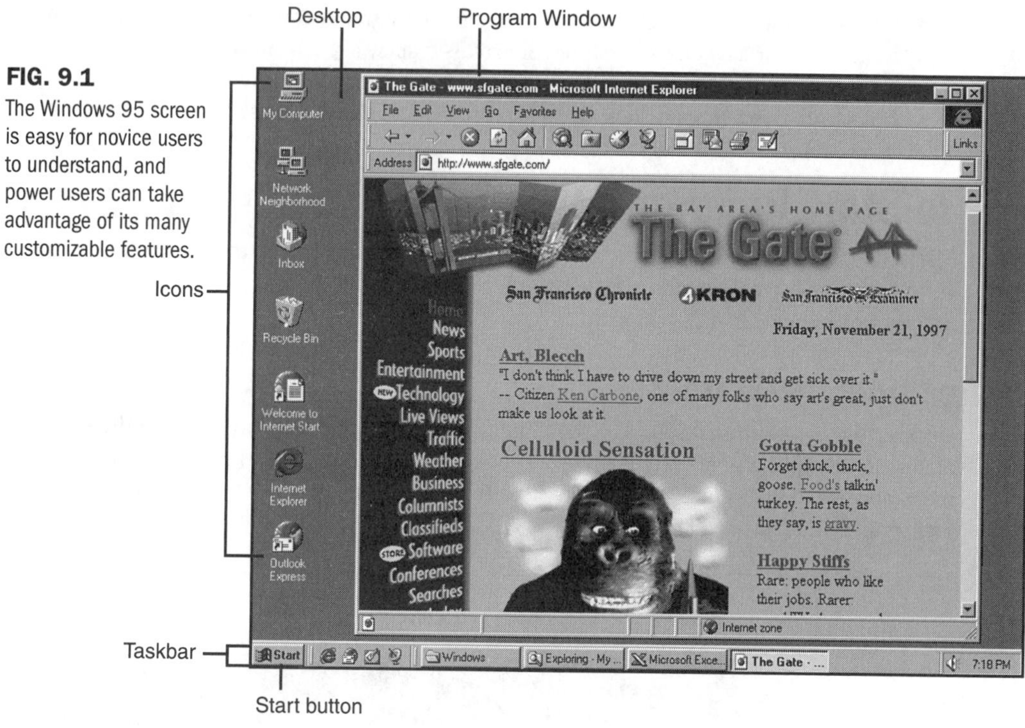

FIG. 9.1
The Windows 95 screen is easy for novice users to understand, and power users can take advantage of its many customizable features.

▶ **See** "Learning the Parts of the Windows Display," **p. 246**

▶ **See** "Starting Applications from the Start Menu and Taskbar," **p. 249**

▶ **See** "Creating Shortcut Icons on the Desktop to Start Programs," **p. 252**

▶ **See** "Customizing the Mouse," **p. 801**

▶ **See** "Making Windows Accessible for the Hearing, Sight, and Movement Impaired," **p. 804**

Experienced Users of Windows 3.*x*

If you are familiar with previous versions of Windows or consider yourself a power user, the important things to notice are as follows:

- You can customize much more of Windows. To customize, right-click an item, choose Properties, and then change options on the property sheet for the item.
- The Program Manager is gone. In its place are icons that appear on the Start menu, which pops up when you click the Start button shown at the bottom of Figure 9.1.
- You can drag icons on the desktop to any location, and they stay there. You can even place folders (the Windows 95 term for directories) on the desktop.

- Shortcut icons on the desktop act as pointers to programs or documents that you don't want to put directly on the desktop. Shortcuts display a small curved arrow at their lower-left corner. Double-clicking a shortcut icon opens the document or program. Deleting a shortcut icon does not delete the file to which it points.

How to Start Programs and Open Documents

Microsoft has made it much easier to start programs with Windows 95 than it was in previous versions of Windows. Depending on your experience level and the task, you can start programs or documents in different ways.

Starting from the Start Menu

Clicking the Start button displays a menu like the one shown in Figure 9.2. Notice the small arrows to the right of some menu items; as you move the pointer over these menu items, a new menu appears to the right. Follow these cascading menus until you see the program or document you want to open and then click it.

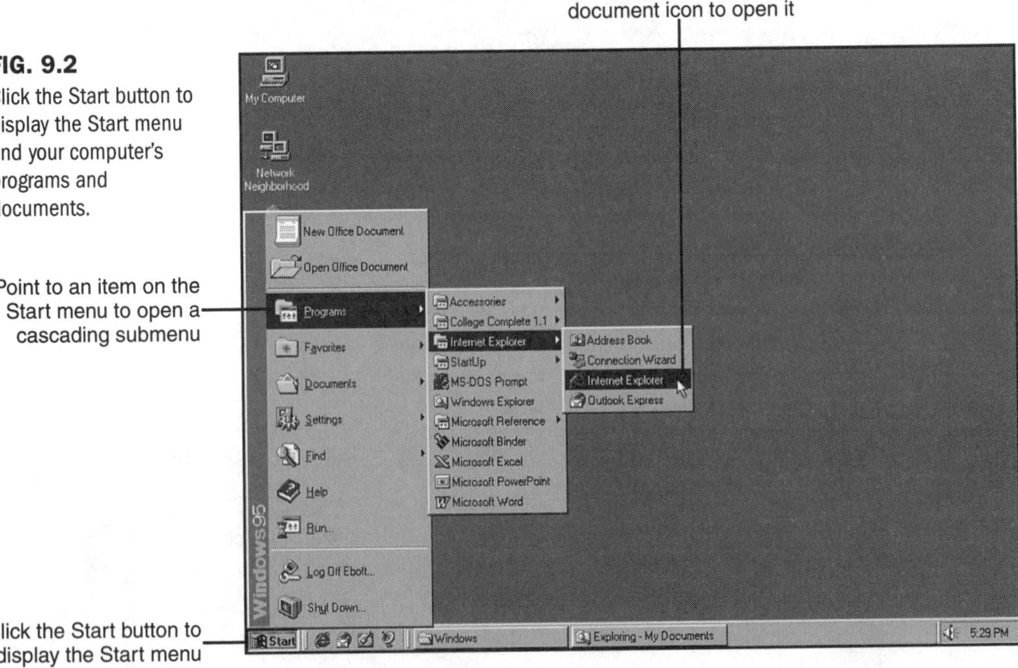

FIG. 9.2
Click the Start button to display the Start menu and your computer's programs and documents.

Beginning Users of Windows 95 If you are unfamiliar with previous versions of Windows, the important things to notice are as follows:

- To see which programs are installed on your computer, click the Start button and choose Programs.

- To open a document you've worked with recently, click the Start button and choose Documents; then click the entry on the menu to the right.
- To find documents or programs, click the Start button and choose Find, Files or Folders.
- When you're ready to quit using Windows and turn off your computer, click the Start button and choose Shut Down.

▶ **See** "Starting a Program from the Start Menu," **p. 250**

▶ **See** "Quitting Windows Applications," **p. 257**

Experienced Users of Windows 3.*x* If you are familiar with Windows 3.1 or Windows for Workgroups 3.11, the important things to notice are as follows:

- You no longer need to use Program Manager; if you migrated from Windows 3.*x*, your existing Group windows now appear as submenus off the Programs item of the Start menu.
- Click the Start button to see your programs and the documents you've used most recently.
- Go directly to the Control Panel or printer settings from the Settings item on the Start menu.
- To add a favorite program to the top of the Start menu, where it's easier to access, drag the program icon from the Start menu and drop it on the Start button.
- You also can drag icons for your favorite programs and drop them onto the Quick Launch bar for even easier access.

▶ **See** "Launching Applications at Startup," **p. 241**

▶ **See** "Customizing the Start Menu," **p. 767**

Power Users with Extensive Windows Experience If you are a power user and are very experienced with Windows, the important things to notice are as follows:

- Cascading menus on the Start menu might seem to slow you down. You can make the Start menu much easier to use by adding your own submenus and reorganizing programs and documents on the menu.
- With IE4's Windows Desktop Update in place, you can directly drag and drop items from the Programs menu and use right-click shortcut menus to adjust properties of any item on the Start menu.
- You can add shortcuts to programs, documents, or folders to the Quick Launch bar. You also can add any folder as a custom toolbar alongside the taskbar.
- Change the properties of programs so that they open as a button on the taskbar, as a window, or maximized to fill the screen.

▶ **See** "Controlling How Startup Programs Appear," **p. 243**

▶ **See** "Customizing the Taskbar," **p. 762**

▶ **See** "Managing Windows after an Application Failure," **p. 258**

Starting from Shortcuts

Shortcuts are icons that point to files, folders, disk drives, and other resources on your computer (see Figure 9.3). When you double-click a shortcut, it starts the target file defined in the shortcut's properties; the target might be a program, a document, a folder or drive, even a printer or a location on the World Wide Web. You can create and save shortcuts just about anywhere: on the Start menu, on the Windows desktop, on the Quick Launch toolbar, in folders, and even in email messages.

When you drag one or more icons and drop it on a shortcut icon, the effect is the same as if you had dropped the object onto the target. To take advantage of that capability, create a shortcut to a folder and place it on your desktop; then, you can drag a file onto the folder shortcut to move or copy the file to that folder.

FIG. 9.3
Double-click a shortcut icon to open the program or document.

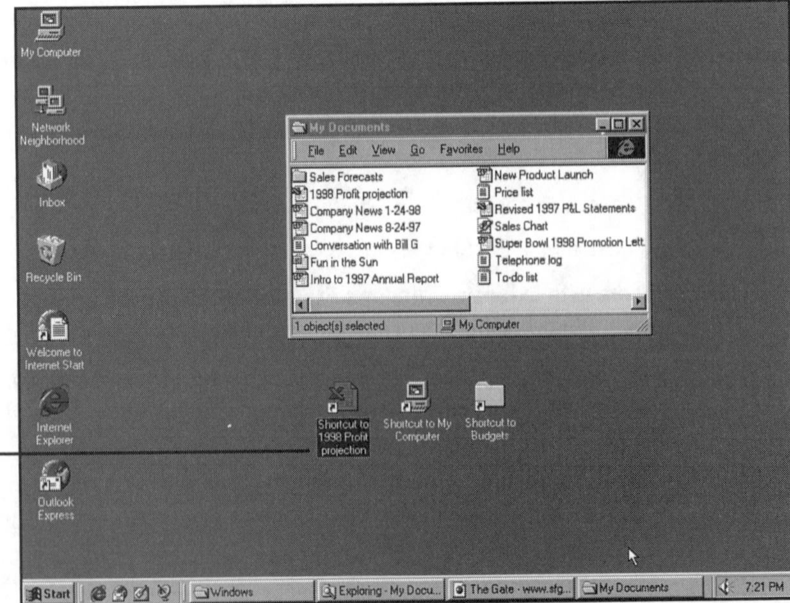

Shortcut icons have a small curved arrow in the lower-left corner

Beginning Users of Windows 95 If you are unfamiliar with previous versions of Windows, the important things to notice are as follows:

- Shortcuts point to documents, programs, folders, or other objects stored elsewhere.
- When you launch a shortcut, the effect is the same as if you had opened the target to which it refers.
- You can delete a shortcut icon without deleting the file or folder that it represents.

▶ **See** "Starting Programs from a Shortcut Icon," **p. 252**

Experienced Users of Windows 3.*x* If you are familiar with Windows 3.1 or Windows for Workgroups 3.11, the important thing to notice is that you can create a shortcut for any program, document, folder, disk drive, printer, or other resource by holding down the right mouse button and dragging the icon to a new location on the desktop or in a folder.

▶ **See** "Creating Shortcut Icons on the Desktop to Start Programs," **p. 252**

Power Users with Extensive Windows Experience If you are a power user who is very experienced with Windows, the important things to notice are as follows:

- You can create shortcuts that automatically run procedures or programs. For example, you can create a shortcut to a Microsoft Word document or Excel spreadsheet that automatically runs a macro when opened. The Windows 95 Backup program also enables you to create shortcuts that automatically back up selected files.
- To customize a shortcut, right-click the shortcut icon, choose Properties, and then click the Shortcut tab. Among other things, this property sheet enables you to define keyboard combinations that automatically launch the shortcut, change the target file to which the shortcut points, specify how a program runs, and change its icon.

▶ **See** "Modifying and Deleting Shortcuts," **p. 256**

Starting Programs from an Explorer Window

You can open any drive or folder to manage the program and document files on your computer. Use the Windows Explorer to see a hierarchical display of all the drives and folders available to you. You can also open a drive icon in the My Computer window to see all the folders on that drive and then continue opening folders until you find the file for which you're looking.

As Figure 9.4 shows, every program file has a distinctive icon, and if you examine its properties, you'll see that its file type is Application.

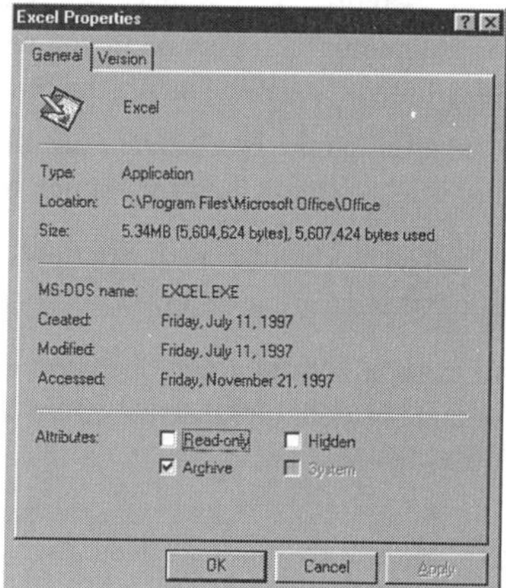

FIG. 9.4
Right-click a program icon and choose Properties to see more information about the program; the Version tab offers even more details.

If you're not sure where to find a specific program on your hard disk, click the Start button and choose Find, Files or Folders. Click the drop-down arrow to the right of the Look in box and choose Local hard drives; then click the Advanced tab and choose Application from the drop-down list labeled Of type. Click Find Now to begin the search; the results look like the list in Figure 9.5.

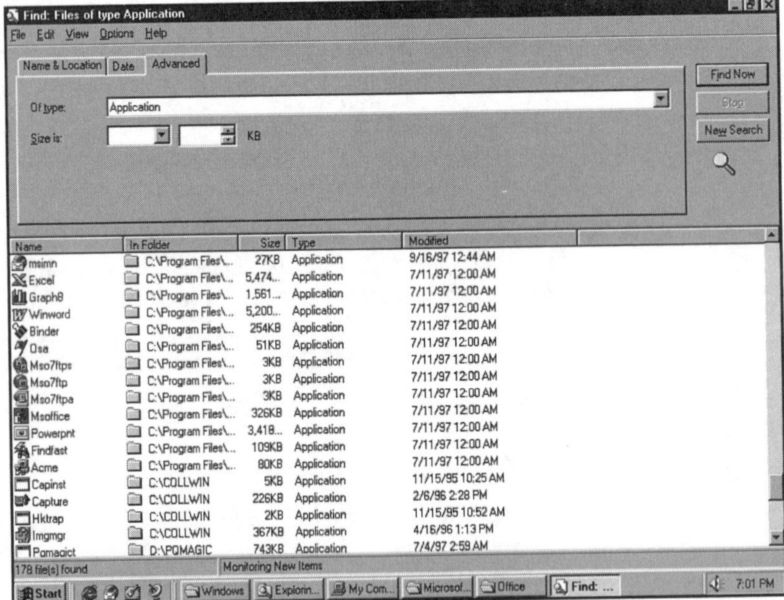

FIG. 9.5
Use the Windows Find utility to search for Application files if you're not certain where a program is stored.

Beginning Users of Windows 95 If you are unfamiliar with previous versions of Windows, the important things to notice are as follows:

- You should use the Start menu to open programs whenever possible. Open documents from within the program. If you're looking for a document you worked with recently, you might find it on the Documents submenu, located just off the Start menu.
- If there is a program that you can't find on the Start menu, use the Find utility to search for program files. When you find the program you want, launch the program's icon.

Experienced Users of Windows 3.*x* If you are familiar with Windows 3.1 or Windows for Workgroups 3.11, the important things to notice are as follows:

- If you are familiar with opening program or document files in the File Manager, you already know how to open programs or documents from within My Computer or the Explorer. Find the file and double-click it.

- You can tell Windows to associate a given file type with its matching application so that opening a file of that type launches the associated application and loads the file. Most file types are automatically registered, but you can manually register a file or change a file type's registration by choosing View, Options; select the File Types tab and either add a new type or edit an existing type.

▶ **See** "Using Windows Explorer to View Files and Folders," **p. 282**

▶ **See** "Managing Files and Folders," **p. 293**

Power Users with Extensive Windows Experience If you are a power user and are very experienced with Windows, the important thing to notice is that you can open multiple files at the same time from within an Explorer window; to select multiple files, hold down the Ctrl key as you click each file. Right-click any of the selected files and choose Open from the shortcut menu.

Customizing Windows with Property Sheets

Property sheets serve two crucial functions in Windows 95: They provide important information about objects such as files, folders, and Windows components, and they typically offer an interface where you can change information or adjust settings and preferences. Virtually every object you see on the Windows screen has an associated dialog box that enables you to inspect its properties—the dialog box in Figure 9.6, for example, enables you to adjust the amount of space you set aside to protect files from inadvertent deletion. To display a property sheet, right-click an icon or onscreen object and then choose Properties from the shortcut menu.

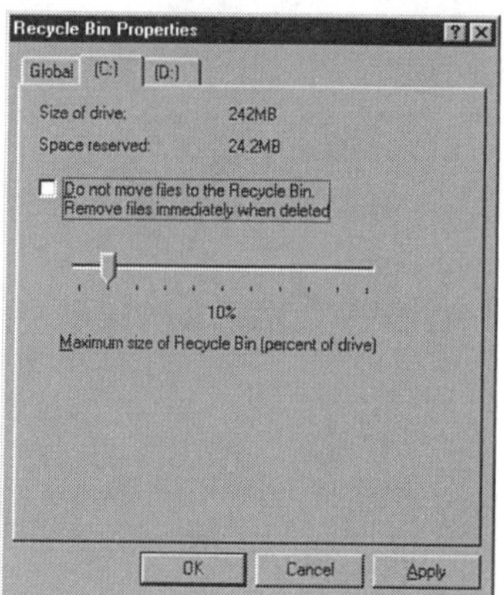

FIG. 9.6
Property sheets like this one offer information about an item and enable you to change the way the item behaves.

Beginning Users of Windows 95

If you are unfamiliar with previous versions of Windows, the important things to notice are as follows:

- You can view a description and change the behavior of many items by displaying property sheets.
- Because Open and Save dialog boxes are extensions of the Windows Explorer, you often can see a document's properties even when working with applications. Just choose File, Open or File, Save, right-click the document icon in the dialog box, and choose Properties.

▶ **See** "Changing Settings and Properties with the Right Mouse Button," **p. 613**

Experienced Users of Windows 3.*x*

If you are familiar with Windows 3.1 or Windows for Workgroups 3.11, the important things to notice are as follows:

- You don't have to go through the Control Panel to customize many items anymore. Get in the habit of right-clicking unfamiliar objects, and you'll quickly see what you can do with shortcut menus and property sheets.
- To quickly open dialog boxes that enable you to customize Windows, right-click the item you want to change, such as the desktop, and then choose Properties from the shortcut menu. This technique works for many common Windows objects, including the following: the Windows desktop (opens Display Properties); My Computer (System Properties); Network Neighborhood (Network Properties); Internet Explorer (Internet Properties). The taskbar, Quick Launch bar, and most icons in the notification area at the right of the taskbar offer property sheets, as well.

▶ **See** "Customizing the Desktop Colors and Background," **p. 780**

▶ **See** "Changing the Screen Resolution, Font Size, and Color Palette," **p. 794**

Power Users with Extensive Windows Experience

If you consider yourself a power user and are very experienced with Windows, the important things to notice are as follows:

- You can create logon profiles that change Windows hardware configuration, depending on a selection at startup. This is useful when you use a portable computer on the road and as a desktop computer.
- You can use logon information (usernames and passwords) to identify different users on a network or a standalone computer. When you enable user profiles, Windows starts up with the custom settings associated with that user's account.

▶ **See** "Reviewing Your Computer's System Information," **p. 812**

▶ **See** "Changing Custom Settings for Each User," **p. 809**

How to Manage Files

In Windows 95, every file, program, shortcut, drive, and folder has a corresponding icon. To move, copy, delete, and otherwise organize icons, you open one or more windows showing the contents of a drive or folder and then drag the icons from place to place. To display the contents of a drive or folder, choose from two basic types of windows. Although they look different, both are actually variations of the Windows Explorer.

NOTE In this chapter (and throughout this book), we assume that you've installed the Windows Desktop Update included with IE4. That update replaces the original Windows Explorer with the newer IE4 version shown here.

For the simplest view of drives and folders, right-click My Computer and choose Open from the shortcut menu. The resulting window shows each drive (and some special system folders) as large icons. When you open a drive window and then open a folder from that window, the files appear as program or document icons (see Figure 9.7). You can move these icons between folders or make copies in another folder. Network Neighborhood displays network servers and resources in the same way.

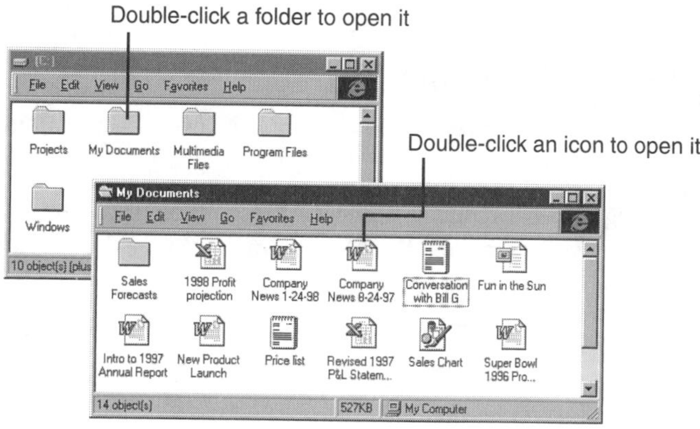

FIG. 9.7
My Computer displays the contents of your computer in windows that contain folders and program/document icons.

Those default windows show the contents of only one drive or folder at a time. But the Windows Explorer also offers a second view that enables you to see all the drives and folders on your system, on your corporate network, and even in web pages you've browsed recently. To see this comprehensive view, right-click My Computer and choose Explore. The resulting Explorer window (see Figure 9.8) includes two panes. On the left, the tree-style All Folders pane shows the hierarchy of folders; when you click the plus sign to the left of an icon, the tree expands to show the folders within that drive or folder. The right pane displays the contents of the drive or folder that has been selected in the left pane.

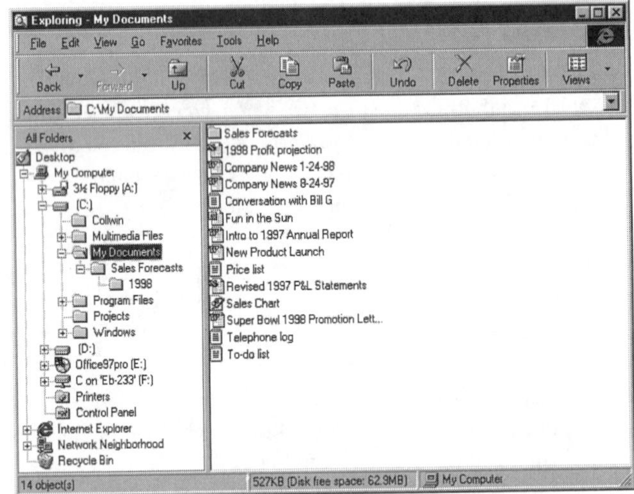

FIG. 9.8
To see the hierarchy of drives and folders on your system, look in the All Folders pane at the left of the Explorer window.

You also can open Windows Explorer by using its shortcut in the Programs group on the Start menu.

Beginning Users of Windows 95

If you are unfamiliar with previous versions of Windows, the important things to notice are as follows:

- Opening the My Computer window is the simplest way to see the contents of drives and folders on your computer. Open a new window to see the contents of drives and folders.
- Use these simple windows to copy and delete files.
- To create your own folders in a window, choose File, New, Folder.

▶ **See** " Managing Files with My Computer and Windows Explorer," **p. 279**

Experienced Users of Previous Windows Versions

If you are familiar with previous versions of Windows, the important things to notice are as follows:

- To manage files, open simple drive and folder windows, including My Computer and Network Neighborhood, or use the hierarchical panes in Windows Explorer.
- Windows Explorer is the best way to see relationships between drives and folders—how folders are grouped inside other folders.
- Right-click any file, drive, or folder icon to see shortcut commands for copying, deleting, printing, and other available actions.

- You can change the displays in a simple folder window or in the right-hand Contents pane of an Explorer window to show large icons, small icons, lists of names, or lists of details about all files.
- In all its views, Windows Explorer enables you to open special system folders, such as Control Panel and Printers. Use these folders to change computer and printer settings.

See "Managing Files and Folders," **p. 293**

See "Working with Long Filenames," **p. 318**

See "Improving Performance with Disk Defragmenter," **p. 352**

Power Users with Extensive Windows Experience

The more you work with Windows, the more ways you'll find to work with different views of Windows Explorer. Important things to notice are as follows:

- Opening Windows Explorer enables you to see more file and folder information at a glance.
- To quickly move or copy files between two folders, open each folder in a separate window, right-click an empty area of the taskbar, and choose Tile Vertically.
- With the right command-line switches, you can create Explorer-style views in which the left pane shows only folders on an individual drive. To create this "rooted" Explorer view of your C: drive, for example, right-click an empty area of the desktop and choose New, Shortcut. Enter the following command in the Command line box:

```
explorer.exe /e,/root,c:\
```

See "Customizing Explorer's Appearance," **p. 291**

See "Using Explorer with Shared Resources on a Network," **p. 320**

See "Monitoring Your System," **p. 371**

CHAPTER 10

Navigating and Controlling Windows

by Ron Person and Ed Bott

In this chapter

Starting and Quitting Windows

What you learn in this chapter will help you operate Windows and any Windows application. This chapter describes the parts of the Windows screen, how to use the keyboard and mouse, and how to start Windows and applications. You learn that there are many different ways to start an application. This chapter not only describes these different methods but also tells you which ways you might prefer to use, depending on your experience and the type of task you are doing.

If you have not yet installed Windows and Internet Explorer 4.0, turn to Chapter 2, "Installing and Upgrading Windows 95," to learn how. After you install Windows, it starts automatically every time you turn on your computer. If your computer requires real-mode drivers, you might see a series of text messages as the drivers load. Also, if your PC supports multiple hardware configurations—enabling you to choose between the screen on a portable PC and a desktop monitor, for example—then you might see a text menu that enables you to choose between configurations. After you make your choice, Windows starts.

When Windows starts, you might see a logon dialog box that requires you to enter a username and password. If the computer is connected to a network, your username and password log you on to the network and give you access to network resources. Windows also uses the logon information to load custom user profiles that enable multiple users on a single PC to personalize their working environment and save those settings.

After you've successfully passed the logon dialog box, Windows displays the desktop with My Computer, Recycle Bin, and Network Neighborhood icons. You might also see a My Briefcase icon and shortcut icons created by prior users. The taskbar usually appears at the bottom of the screen, although it might appear in another location or not at all.

The first time you start Windows or Internet Explorer, you see a Welcome message. To prevent this message from automatically appearing each time you start Windows, clear the Show this Welcome Screen check box.

CAUTION

Do not turn off your computer until you correctly exit Windows and it displays a message saying that it is safe to turn off the computer. Incorrectly exiting Windows might result in the loss of data.

If you plan to turn off your computer, you should always correctly exit Windows. Windows and Windows applications store some data in memory, and using the Windows Shut Down process makes sure that you write those files to your hard disk. To exit Windows correctly, follow these steps:

1. Save the data in the applications in which you are working. If you forget to do so, most Windows applications ask whether or not you want to save open documents when you exit the application.

2. Exit any DOS applications that you are running.
3. Open the Start menu and choose Shut Down. The dialog box shown in Figure 10.1 displays.

FIG. 10.1
The Shut Down menu choice enables you to power off the computer, restart Windows, or restart the computer in MS-DOS mode.

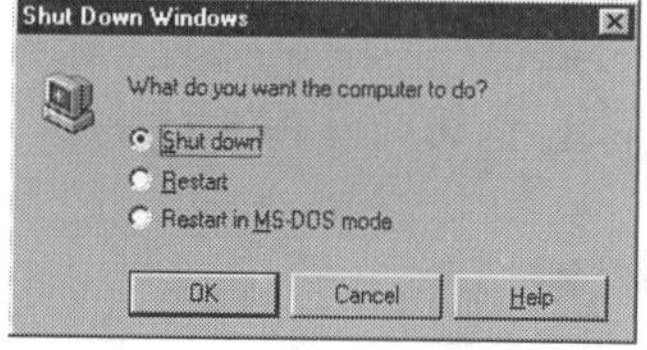

4. Choose the Shut down option.

If you share a computer with other users and have enabled user profiles, you must log on with your username and password to use your customized desktop and other features. The Windows Desktop Update installed with IE4 moves this option to a new location on the Start menu. When you've finished working, open the Start menu and choose Log off username. That option closes all open programs and presents the logon dialog box again.

5. Click the OK button.
6. Turn off your computer when you see the message that says that it is safe to do so.

Do not turn off the computer hardware until you see a message saying that you can safely do so. If you've reconfigured your computer in the current session, this message might take a minute or two to appear. Under some circumstances, the computer might hang at this step and you will never see the "OK to shut down" message. In that case, watch the hard-disk light and listen to make sure all hard disk activity has stopped before you turn off the computer.

Launching Applications at Startup

If you work with certain programs each time you use your computer, you can tell Windows to start these programs automatically when you turn on your computer. You can even tell Windows how you want the program to appear at startup—either in a window, maximized, or minimized—so that it appears as a button in the taskbar.

You also can specify that Windows opens certain documents at startup. In this case, Windows starts the program associated with the document in addition to opening the document.

Running Programs on Startup To specify the programs you want to run at startup, add them to the Startup folder. The easiest way to do this is with the Taskbar Properties dialog box, which has a wizard that guides you through the process step by step. Any programs you add to the Startup folder appear in the Startup menu, which is a submenu of the Programs menu.

With IE4's Windows Desktop Update installed, you can drag shortcuts directly into the Startup folder on the Start menu.

To specify programs that you want Windows to run at startup, follow these steps:

1. Open the Start menu and choose Settings, Taskbar & Start Menu.
2. Click the Start Menu Programs tab to display the dialog box shown in Figure 10.2.

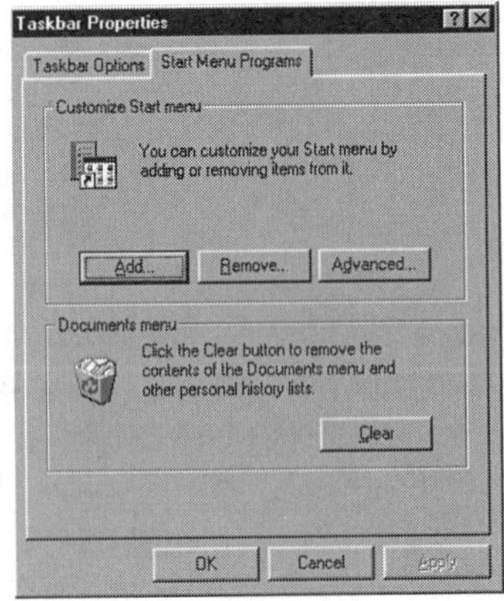

FIG. 10.2
Use the Start Menu Programs page to specify programs to run at startup.

3. Click the Add button to open the Create Shortcut dialog box.
4. If you know the exact filename and path of the program, enter it here. Otherwise, click the Browse button, locate the program, and click the Open button.
5. Choose Next.
6. In the Select Program Folder dialog box, choose the Startup folder and click Next.
7. Accept the default title for the program shortcut, or type a new title in the text box. The name you enter appears in the Startup menu.
8. Click Finish.
9. Repeat steps 3 through 8 to add more programs to the Startup folder, or choose OK if you are finished adding programs.

Waiting for programs to start automatically can be frustrating. If you'd rather get straight to work, tell Windows to ignore programs in the Startup folder by holding down the Shift key as Windows loads. This option affects only the current session.

To remove a program from the Startup folder, follow these steps:

1. Open the Start menu and choose Programs, Startup.
2. Right-click the entry for the program you want to remove.
3. Choose Delete from the shortcut menu.

Specifying Documents to Open at Startup If you regularly work with particular documents each time you use your computer—for example, if you work on the same budget worksheet every day—you can tell Windows to open such documents automatically at startup. For Windows to open a document automatically, the document must be associated with a program. For many programs, Windows automatically associates the documents it creates with the program. This association enables you to open a document and the program that created it simultaneously.

▶ **See** "Registering a New File Type," **p. 773**

To specify a document to open at startup, follow the same procedure outlined in the preceding section, "Running Programs on Startup," except that in step 4, you select a document rather than a program. After you do so, the program associated with the document automatically runs at startup and the specified document opens.

Controlling How Startup Programs Appear After specifying that a program run at startup, you can tell Windows how you want the program to display when it starts. By default, Windows runs the program in a normal window. However, you also can choose to have the program run *maximized*, so that it fills the screen, or *minimized*, so that it appears as a button on the taskbar.

To control how a program appears on startup, follow these steps:

1. Add the program to the Startup folder, as described in the section "Running Programs on Startup."
2. Click the Start button and choose Programs, Startup. The cascading menu of all programs in your Startup folder appears to the right.
3. Right-click the icon for the program shortcut you want to adjust, and then choose Properties.
4. Select the Shortcut tab.
5. Select one of the three options from the drop-down list labeled Run, as shown in Figure 10.3.
6. Choose OK.

Starting Windows After Technical Problems Occur

Normally, Windows starts when you turn on your computer. When it doesn't, there are two troubleshooting techniques you can use. A startup disk enables you to start your computer if problems with hardware or the boot sector prevent you from booting by using the hard disk. If the system boots, but you have problems starting Windows, the problem might be caused by faulty drivers, corrupt startup files, or a damaged Windows Registry. In all cases, the first troubleshooting step is to start Windows in *Safe mode*, which enables you to bypass the problem and access the tools you need to repair the damage.

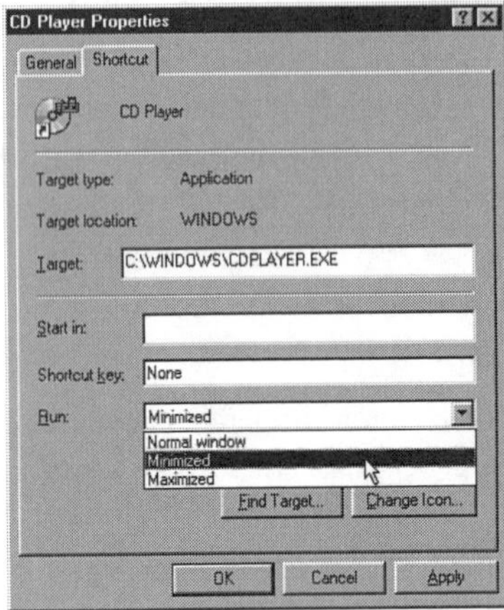

FIG. 10.3 Use this setting to configure how an application—the CD Player, in this example—will run on startup.

Creating a Startup Disk If you have trouble starting Windows, you might need to use a startup disk to start your computer. For example, if you inadvertently delete a file that Windows needs for startup, you must start Windows with the startup disk in your disk drive and then remedy the problem so that you can start Windows normally.

When you install Windows, you have an opportunity to create a startup disk, which you should label and always keep on hand. If you didn't create the startup disk during installation or have misplaced the disk, you can create one after Windows is installed. Make sure to do so now, before you need the disk. Otherwise, if you have problems starting Windows, you won't be able to get into Windows to create the startup disk. (You might, however, be able to use another computer to create a startup disk.)

To create a startup disk, follow these steps:

1. Open the Start menu and choose Settings, Control Panel.
2. Open the Add/Remove Programs option.
3. Click the Startup Disk tab, as shown in Figure 10.4.

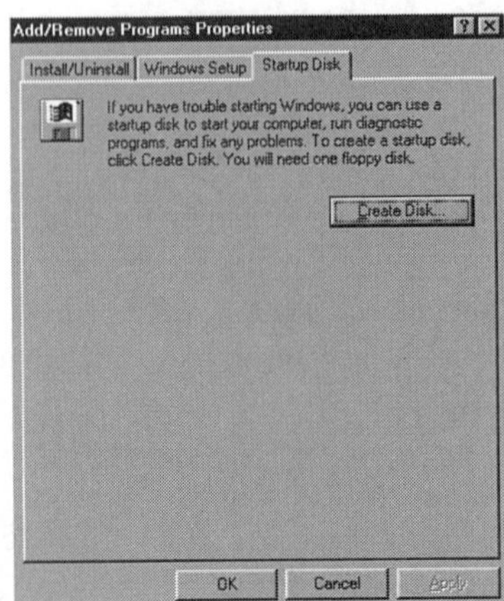

FIG. 10.4 Use this button to create a startup disk, enabling you to start your computer when the hard disk won't boot properly.

4. Insert a disk in your A: drive. This is the drive from which your computer attempts to boot if a disk is in the drive. The contents of this disk will be deleted.
5. Choose Create Disk and follow the instructions as they appear onscreen. To create the startup disk, you must have access to your original Windows CD-ROM (or the equivalent files on a local hard disk or network location).
6. Click OK.

Store your startup disk somewhere safe and easy to remember. If you have a portable computer, store your startup disk in the computer's case.

▶ **See** "Configuring a Startup Disk," **p. 38**

To use the startup disk, insert it in the disk drive and reboot the computer. You can now diagnose and correct the problem that is preventing your computer from booting normally.

Starting Windows in Safe Mode If Windows 95 refuses to start properly, or if the video adapter or another piece of hardware does not operate correctly, use *Safe mode* to diagnose and correct the problem. This special startup mode bypasses your normal startup files and uses simple default settings that enable you to start Windows under almost any circumstances short of catastrophic hardware failure. For example, if you install the wrong driver for a new video adapter, you might not be able to see the display when you restart Windows. Restarting Windows in Safe mode uses the default VGA driver, which enables you to see the screen, open Control Panel, and set up the correct driver.

▶ **See** "Getting Help," **p. 258**

Default Safe mode settings use a generic VGA monitor and Microsoft mouse drivers, with no network options and only those device drivers necessary to start Windows. When you start Windows in Safe mode, you cannot access any CD-ROM drives, printers, or other optional hardware devices. But you can at least access Windows and then diagnose and correct the problem.

To start Windows in a different mode, follow these steps:

1. Turn on the computer and the display monitor. Watch the text messages as your computer boots and Windows prepares to start. Be ready to press the F8 key.
2. When the message "Starting Windows" appears onscreen, press F8 to display the Windows 95 Startup Menu. Safe Mode is choice 3 and Safe Mode with Network Support is choice 4.
3. Type the menu number for Safe Mode or Safe Mode with Network Support. Press Enter.

To skip the Startup Menu and begin directly in a mode, start your computer and press one of the key combinations in the following table when the message "Starting Windows" appears.

Key Combination	Operating Mode
F5	Loads HIMEM.SYS and IFSHLP.SYS, loads DoubleSpace or DriveSpace if necessary, and then runs Windows 95 WIN.COM. Starts in Safe mode.
Shift+F5	Loads COMMAND.COM and DoubleSpace or DriveSpace if necessary. Starts at command prompt.
Ctrl+F5	Loads COMMAND.COM and starts in Safe mode without loading compression drivers.
F6	Loads HIMEM.SYS and IFSHLP.SYS. Processes the registry, loads COMMAND.COM, loads DoubleSpace or DriveSpace if necessary, runs Windows 95 WIN.COM, loads network drivers, and runs NETSTART.BAT. Starts in Safe mode with network support.

A message informs you that Windows is running in safe mode and that some of your devices might not be available. The words **Safe mode** appear at each corner of the screen.

▶ **See**"Checking Performance Settings," **p. 817**

Learning the Parts of the Windows Display

Windows computer screens display many graphical elements. Learning the names of these graphic elements or icons is important because you'll see these terms throughout this book. Likewise, you need to be familiar with these elements and icons because you can invoke a command for Windows or a Windows program by clicking the mouse pointer on many of them.

Figure 10.5 shows a Windows desktop that contains multiple applications, each in its own window. The figure identifies the parts of a typical Windows screen.

In the desktop shown in Figure 10.6, the Start button appears in the lower-left corner. This button provides one of the easiest ways to start programs, open documents you have recently used, or adjust system settings. (The Start button and taskbar might appear along different edges of the screen if a previous user has moved them.) Click the Start button to open the Start menu. The keyboard equivalent is Ctrl+Esc. If you have a Windows-compatible keyboard, pressing the Windows key (marked with the Windows logo) opens the Start menu.

▶ **See** "Customizing the Taskbar," **p. 762**

Across the bottom of the screen is the taskbar, which displays a button for every running program and open window. To switch to another window, click its taskbar button. Note that IE4 changes the behavior of taskbar buttons in a subtle way: Normally, when you click a taskbar button, Windows 95 brings the selected window to the foreground, and clicking the same button again has no effect. With IE4's Windows Desktop Update installed, however, clicking a taskbar button a second time minimizes the window associated with that button. Each time you click a taskbar button, the window toggles between its minimized and restored or maximized state.

To use the keyboard to switch between running programs, hold down the Alt key and press Tab. When the correct icon is highlighted, release the keys.

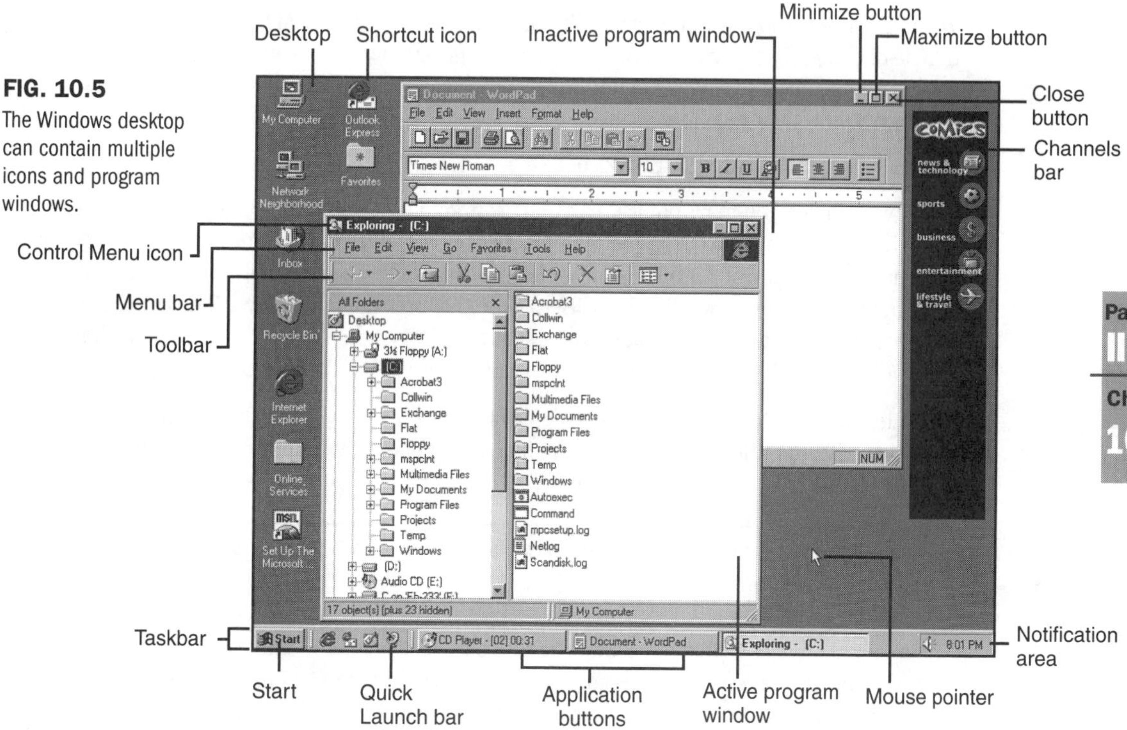

FIG. 10.5
The Windows desktop can contain multiple icons and program windows.

TROUBLESHOOTING

Pressing Alt+Tab just seems to alternate between two applications. That's not a bug; it's a feature. The first choice in the list of running applications is always the window that was previously active. To switch to another window, hold down the Alt key and then press and release the Tab key. You will see a bar displaying an icon for each running application and open window. As you continue to hold down the Alt key, each tab of the Tab key selects the next icon in the list. When the correct icon is selected, release both the Alt and the Tab keys.

The taskbar might appear in a different location on your screen. You can move the taskbar by dragging it to another location. You can also hide the taskbar when it is not in use by customizing your screen, as described in Chapter 31, "Customizing the Taskbar and Start Menu."

▶ **See** "Moving the Taskbar," **p. 762**

With the mouse pointer, you can control Windows applications quickly and intuitively. The mouse pointer enables you to choose commands, select options, and move onscreen items. When you move the mouse, the mouse pointer moves synchronously. At different locations on the screen, the mouse pointer changes shape to indicate that it has capabilities specific to its current location. For example, when the pointer passes over a window border, it changes to a two-headed arrow to indicate that you can use the mouse to resize the window.

You use five actions to affect onscreen items that are under the tip of the pointer: clicking, double-clicking, right-clicking, dragging, and right-dragging. The actual techniques you use to select and open items vary, depending on whether you've selected the Classic Windows 95 interface or the Web-style interface.

▶ **See** "Single-Click or Double-Click?" **p. 274**

Windows enables you to run more than one program at the same time. Each program appears in its own window, with a corresponding taskbar button. When programs are in windows, the program in the topmost window is the *active* program in the *active* window. By default, the color of the active window's title bar differs from that of inactive windows. The active window receives your keyboard commands. One of the advantages of Windows is that even while you are working with the active program in the active window, other programs can be working.

The title bar at the top of each window displays the name of the application in the window. After you save a file, the title bar also shows the filename. (The active window is the one on top; it contains the currently running application.)

Throughout this book, the letter that you press in combination with Alt to open a menu command is underlined, as in File.

The menu bar, which is directly under the title bar, displays the menu names. Windows applications use the same menu headings for common functions (such as File, Edit, Window, and Help), which makes it easier for you to learn new applications. To open a menu, click its name with the left mouse button, or press Alt and then the underlined letter in the menu name.

Icons are small, graphic representations. To reduce the clutter of a filled desktop, you can minimize windows so that they appear as icons on the taskbar. Even if it's not currently displayed in a window, an application is still running if the taskbar displays its icon.

Using the Mouse and Keyboard on the Desktop

In Windows 95, the mouse offers the most obvious way to perform almost every action, but you can choose keyboard alternatives for those tasks, as well. The most efficient Windows strategy is a combination of mouse clicks and keyboard shortcuts—the exact mix depends on your skills as a touch typist.

▶ **See** "Customizing the Mouse," **p. 801**

▶ **See** "Customizing the Keyboard," **p. 802**

This section explains the basic techniques you need to know to perform Windows tasks with the mouse. Windows users routinely use the mouse to select text, objects, menus and menu commands, toolbar buttons, and dialog box options, and to scroll through documents. To perform such tasks, you need to know how to point and click with the mouse.

To click items by using the mouse, follow these steps:

1. Move the mouse so that the tip of the mouse pointer, usually an arrow, is on the menu, command, dialog box item, graphics object, or a position within the text. (When moved over editable text, the pointer changes to the shape of an I-beam.)
2. With a single, quick motion, press and release the left mouse button.

Throughout this book, this two-step process is called ***clicking***. Clicking the mouse button twice in rapid succession is called ***double-clicking***. Double-clicking produces an action different than clicking. In a word processing application, for example, you often click to position the insertion point but double-click to select a word.

You also can use the mouse for ***dragging***. Dragging selects multiple text characters or moves graphic objects such as windows.

To drag with the mouse, follow these steps:

1. Move the mouse so that the tip of the pointer is on the object or at the beginning of the text that you want to select. (When over text, the pointer appears as an I-beam.)
2. Press and hold down the left mouse button.
3. Move the mouse while holding down the mouse button. If you are dragging a graphical object, the object moves when you move the mouse. If you are selecting text, the highlighted text area expands as you move the mouse.
4. Release the mouse button.

Windows 95 makes extensive use of the right mouse button. When you place the tip of the pointer on most screen objects and click the right mouse button, Windows displays a shortcut menu with commands specific to that object. For example, right-clicking a filename produces a shortcut menu containing commands such as Copy, Delete, and Rename. The right mouse button also works when dragging; for example, you can select one or more icons in a folder window and hold down the right mouse button while dragging them onto the desktop. When you release the button, a shortcut menu appears.

Starting Applications from the Start Menu and Taskbar

Most of the work that you do on your computer consists of opening a program, using the program to create or modify a document, saving the document as a file, and then closing the program. Windows is designed to make these routine tasks as simple as possible.

This section describes the different methods for starting programs by using the Start menu, shortcuts, and the Windows Explorer. You also learn what to do if a program fails to start properly or locks up when you are using it.

Starting a Program from the Start Menu

The Start menu is the jumping-off point for most common Windows tasks. You can open the Start menu at any time, from within any program, with one mouse click. From the Start menu, you can open programs, customize the look and feel of Windows, browse your list of favorite web sites, find files and folders, get Help, and shut down your computer.

The simplest way for a new Windows user to open a program is to use the Start menu. When you install a Windows application, the installation program usually places programs in the Programs menu or on a submenu within the Programs menu. You can open the program simply by selecting it from a menu (see Figure 10.6).

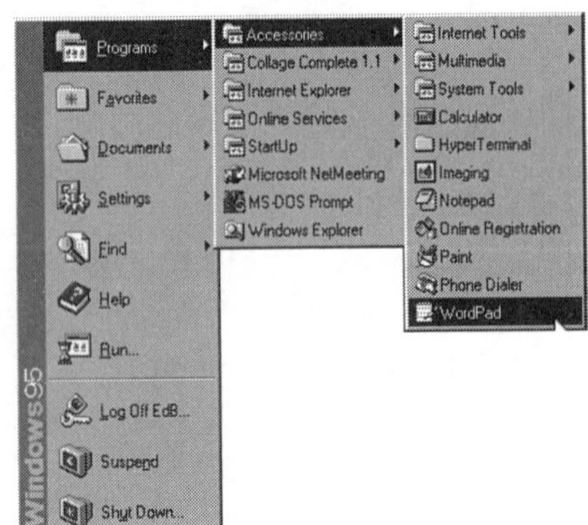

FIG. 10.6
Select a program—WordPad, in this example—from one of the menus that cascade out from the Start menu.

NOTE If you upgraded from Windows 3.*x* to Windows 95, the Group windows that appeared within the Program Manager are converted to submenus under the Programs choice in the Start menu. 

TROUBLESHOOTING

The taskbar isn't visible. This problem most likely has one of two causes. You might have inadvertently resized the taskbar to be zero rows high. Move the mouse pointer to the edge of the window where the taskbar should appear; when it turns to a two-headed arrow, click and drag to make the taskbar visible. Also note that some programs written for older versions of Windows cover the taskbar so it is difficult to switch between applications or click the Start button. Even when you can't see the taskbar, you can switch between applications by holding down the Alt key and pressing Tab. A bar appears with icons for each application. Press Tab until the application you want is selected; then release both keys.

To simultaneously display the taskbar and open the Start menu, press Ctrl+Esc.

To start a program by using the Start menu, follow these steps:

1. Click the Start button in the taskbar to open the Start menu.

   If you have customized your computer with the Auto hide option, you might not see the taskbar and Start button at the bottom of your screen. If you see a gray line at one edge of the screen, move the pointer to that edge to display the taskbar. With the keyboard, you can press Ctrl+Esc to display the taskbar and open the Start menu.

2. Point to Programs on the Start menu. The Program menu appears to the right.
3. To find the program that you want, you might have to move through a series of submenus. If the Programs menu doesn't list the program that you want to start, click the folder that contains the program.
4. Point to the program that you want to start, and click.

If you are using a keyboard and do not have a mouse available, open the Start menu by pressing Ctrl+Esc. Use the up and down arrow keys to move up and down the menu; the right and left arrows enable you to move back and forth between the Start menu and submenus. Press Enter to run the currently highlighted menu item. Press Esc to close the Start menu.

▶ **See** "Switching between Applications," **p. 623**

▶ **See** "Customizing the Start Menu," **p. 767**

If you are familiar with Windows and want to make your programs more accessible, you can add the programs that you use most frequently to the Start menu. As we'll see later in this chapter, you can also create a shortcut icon on the desktop to start an application.

Opening a Document from the Start Menu

The Documents choice on the Start menu lists the 15 files you have worked on most recently (see Figure 10.7). To open a document in this list, click its entry. Windows automatically starts the associated application, if it is not already running, and opens the document.

FIG. 10.7
The Start menu maintains a list of the documents with which you've worked most recently. Click one to load it and its associated application.

All the choices on the Documents submenu are actually shortcuts stored in the Windows\Recent folder. Every time you open a document, Windows adds a new shortcut to this list until the total reaches 15, at which point it deletes the oldest item on the list. If you move a document, the shortcut on the Documents menu might not work any longer. As with items on the Programs menu, you can right-click any document shortcut, inspect its properties, move or copy the shortcut, or delete it. To clear the Documents list, click the Start button and choose Settings, Taskbar & Start Menu. Select the Start Menu Programs tab on the Taskbar Properties sheet and choose the Clear button. Click OK to close the Properties sheet.

Starting Programs from a Shortcut Icon

Another method for starting programs is to create shortcuts for the programs that you use most frequently. These shortcuts can appear as icons on your desktop or on the Quick Launch bar. To run a program or open a window, you use its shortcut icon. If you don't like using menus to start your programs, you might prefer using shortcuts. In both cases, however, there are drawbacks. To access shortcut icons on the desktop, you have to first clear any open windows out of the way; if a program is maximized, you cannot see the shortcuts. And although the Quick Launch bar is useful, it reduces the amount of space available for taskbar buttons, making it harder to see at a glance which programs are open.

Creating Shortcut Icons on the Desktop to Start Programs

To create a shortcut for a program on your desktop, follow these steps:

1. Using the Windows Explorer or My Computer, locate the program for which you want to create a shortcut. See Chapter 12, "Managing Files with My Computer and the Windows Explorer," to learn how to browse files and folders.

Drag a file from My Computer or the Windows Explorer onto the desktop with the right mouse button. Drop the file and select Create Shortcut(s) Here to create a shortcut icon on the desktop.

2. Right-click the program icon and choose Copy from the pop-up shortcut menu.
3. Right-click any empty space on the desktop and choose Paste Shortcut.

The icon now appears on your desktop. You can drag the icon to any location. Refer to Figure 10.8, which shows a shortcut from the desktop. (You can always tell a shortcut icon at a glance, because a small arrow appears beneath the icon.)

▶ **See** "Registering a New File Type," **p. 773**

FIG. 10.8
To start an application, double-click its shortcut icon.

You also can create a shortcut for a document. Find the document in Windows Explorer or My Computer and create a shortcut for the document, as described in the preceding steps. If the document is associated (or registered) with a program, you can start the program and open the document by double-clicking its shortcut.

TROUBLESHOOTING

Double-clicking a shortcut icon no longer opens the document or program. The file to which the shortcut points has probably been moved or deleted. Windows attempts to find the target file when it has been moved; if this process fails, Windows displays its best guess as to the right file and gives you an opportunity to search for the target file. The easiest way to correct this problem is to delete and then re-create the shortcut. You can also edit the shortcut's properties directly: Right-click the shortcut icon and choose Properties. Click the Shortcut tab. Enter the file (including the complete path) in the Target box.

Starting Programs by Using Quick Launch Shortcuts

When you first install Internet Explorer 4.0 with the Windows Desktop Update, four shortcut icons appear on the Quick Launch bar, just to the right of the Start menu. You can add program or document shortcuts to the Quick Launch bar by dragging and dropping. The results are shown in Figure 10.9.

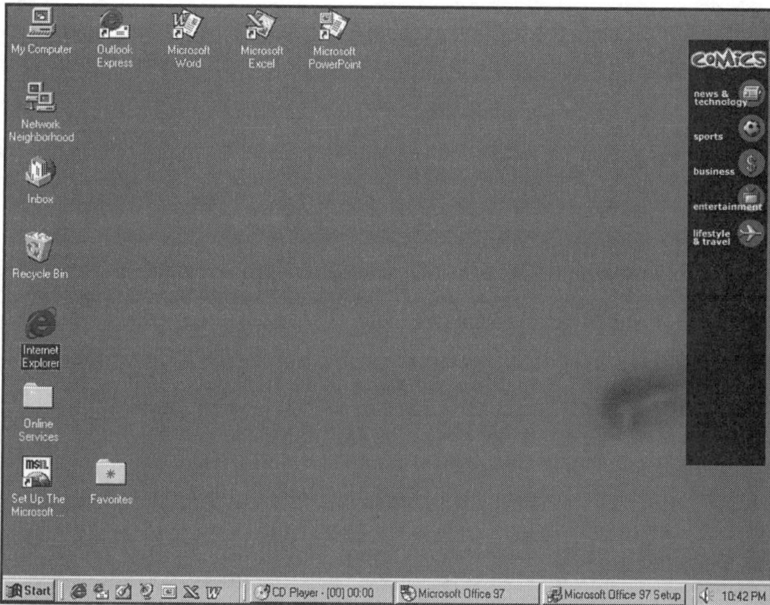

FIG. 10.9
Add shortcuts to your favorite programs or documents on the Quick Launch bar.

Here's how to add a new shortcut to the Quick Launch bar:

1. Select the program icon in a Windows Explorer or My Computer window.
2. Drag the icon onto the Quick Launch bar. You'll see a thick, dark I-beam to indicate where the shortcut icon will appear.
3. Drop the icon onto the Quick Launch bar. Windows creates a shortcut; the original icon remains intact.
4. To rearrange icons on the Quick Launch bar, drag and drop. To delete a shortcut icon, right-click the icon and choose Delete.
5. If you can't see all the shortcuts on the Quick Launch bar, it's easy to expand the space available. Point to the divider between the Quick Launch bar and the taskbar until the mouse pointer turns to a two-headed arrow and then drag to resize the bar. Grab the top of the toolbar and drag up to stack the Quick Launch bar on top of the taskbar.

If the Quick Launch bar is not visible, right-click any empty space on the taskbar and choose Toolbars, Quick Launch. A check mark next to the menu choice means the toolbar should be visible.

Setting the Properties for a Shortcut Icon

You can change how a shortcut icon acts and how it appears by changing its properties. On the Properties sheet, you can find information such as when a shortcut was created. You also can make a variety of changes such as those listed here:

- Change the file that the shortcut opens.
- Make an application start in a folder you specify.
- Add a shortcut key that activates the shortcut.
- Indicate whether you want the document or application to run minimized, maximized, or in a window.
- Change the icon used for a shortcut.

To display the Properties sheet and set the properties for a shortcut icon, follow these steps:

1. Right-click the shortcut icon.
2. Click the Properties command to display the General page of the Shortcut Properties sheet shown in Figure 10.10.

   On the General page, you can read where the LNK file for the shortcut is stored, as well as when it was created, modified, and last used. You also can change its file attributes.
3. Click the Shortcut tab to see the Shortcut page shown in Figure 10.11.

   At the top of the page, you can read the type of shortcut and the folder in which it is located. In the figure, the shortcut is to Microsoft Excel application in the Office folder.
4. If you want a different file to start from the shortcut, click the Target edit box and type the folder and filename.

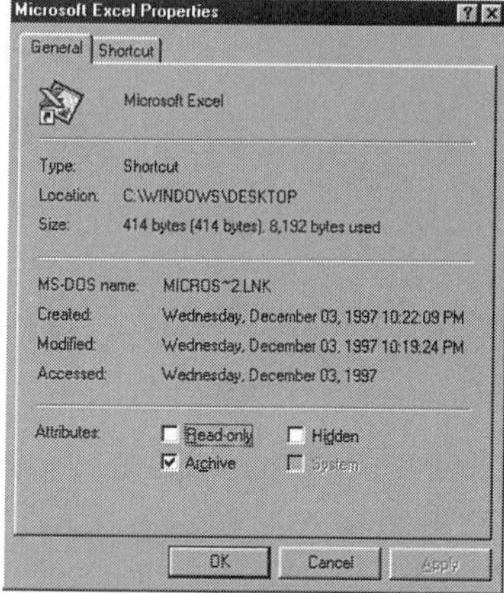

FIG. 10.10
The General page shows you file information about the shortcut icon.

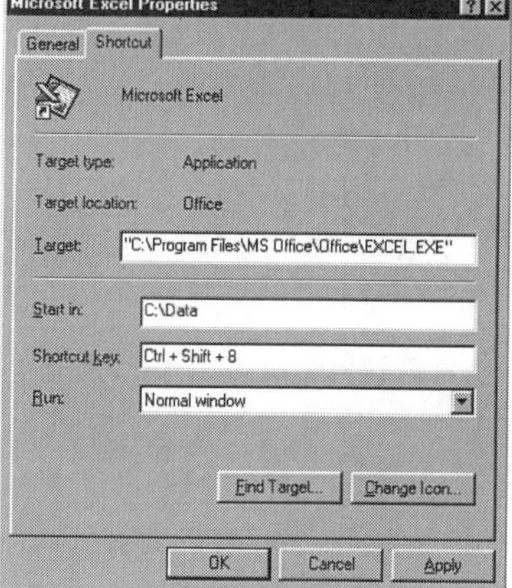

FIG. 10.11
The Shortcut page enables you to specify the file, startup folder, shortcut key, and icon used by a shortcut.

If you are unsure of the location, click Find Target to open a My Computer window in which you can look for the file and folder you want. After you find the folder and file, close the My Computer windows and type the name in the Target edit box.

5. To specify a folder containing the file or files necessary for operation, click the Start In edit box and enter the drive and folders.

TIP You can press a shortcut's key combination to run the shortcut's program or document even when another program is active.

6. To specify a shortcut key combination that will activate this icon, click the Shortcut Key edit box and then press the key you want as the shortcut key. The key combination must be a letter or a number, plus any two of the following three keys: Ctrl, Alt, and Shift. (If you simply press a letter or number, Windows defaults to Ctrl+Alt+*key.)* You can also use

any Function key, with or without the Ctrl, Alt, and Shift keys. You cannot use Esc, Enter, Tab, the Spacebar, Print Screen, or Backspace. To clear the Shortcut Key edit box, select the box and press the Spacebar.

To use this shortcut key, press the key combination you selected.

CAUTION

Shortcut keys you create take precedence over other access keys in Windows. Be careful not to inadvertently redefine a system-wide key combination that you use in other Windows applications.

7. To specify the type of window in which the application or document runs, click the Run drop-down list. Select from Normal Window, Minimized, or Maximized.
8. To change the icon displayed for the shortcut, click Change Icon to display the Change Icon dialog box shown in Figure 10.12. The Change Icon dialog box displays a scrolling horizontal list of icons stored in files with the extensions EXE, DLL, and ICO.

FIG. 10.12
You can select the icon you want for your shortcut.

9. Select the icon you want and then choose OK.
10. Click the OK button to make your changes and close the Shortcut Properties sheet. Click Apply to make your changes and keep the Shortcut Properties sheet open for more changes.

NOTE When selecting icons for a shortcut, you don't have to restrict yourself to the icons in the file to which the shortcut points. You can select an icon from any other DLL, EXE, or ICO file. To see other icon files from the Change Icon dialog box, click the Browse button.

Modifying and Deleting Shortcuts

If you want to modify the name that appears under a shortcut icon, right-click the icon and choose Rename. (To rename shortcuts on the Programs menu or in the Quick Launch folder, use the Windows Explorer to open those folders.) The pointer changes to an I-beam and the entire name is selected. Begin typing to completely replace the name, or click to position the insertion point where you want to add or change text. After you edit the name, press Enter or click on an empty portion of the desktop or taskbar to register the change.

CAUTION

Be careful when deleting shortcuts from the desktop. When you delete a shortcut for a file, you delete only the shortcut, not the file. When you delete an icon that represents a file, however, you delete the file. You can always tell whether an icon represents a shortcut because an arrow appears beneath the icon.

If, for example, you drag a document from My Computer to the desktop with the left mouse button, the icon actually represents the file; if you then delete the icon, you also delete the file. Make sure that you know what you are doing before you delete an icon on your desktop.

Starting Programs and Documents from Windows Explorer or My Computer

You can use the Windows Explorer to find any file on your computer. (Note that the My Computer icon on the desktop opens a simplified version of the Explorer.) After you find the file, you also can use Windows Explorer to start the program or document. If the file is a program file, you can start the program by double-clicking its file in Windows Explorer. If the file is a document, you can start its associated application and open the document simultaneously. If the application is already running, Windows opens the document in that application.

To quickly access Windows Explorer, right-click the Start button and choose Explore.

TROUBLESHOOTING

Double-clicking a file in Windows Explorer doesn't open the file. An Open With dialog box displays, asking which program should be used to open the file. Windows does not recognize the application to use when opening the document you double-clicked. Windows displays the Open With dialog box so you can select the application to open. If you check the box labeled Always use this program to open this file, Windows records the information about this application so it can open the same application the next time you double-click this type of document.

Quitting Windows Applications

Most Windows applications operate the same way. To quit a Windows application, follow these steps:

1. Activate the application by clicking the application's window or by holding down the Alt key and pressing Tab until you have selected the application.

2. Click the Close button, or choose File, Exit.

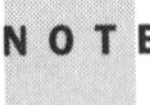

NOTE Throughout this book, instructions such as "Choose File, Exit" mean that you click the File menu (or press Alt+F) and then click the Exit command (or press X).

If the application contains documents that you have modified since the last time you saved them, most applications prompt you to save your changes before the application quits.

Managing Windows After an Application Failure

Windows 95 significantly improves on how failed or misbehaving applications are handled. Windows 95 continuously polls the applications to see if they are running and responding. When an application fails to respond, Windows 95 displays the [Not Responding] dialog box. In this dialog box, you can click the End Task button to close down the application. You lose all changes to data in the application since the last time you saved. Click Cancel to return to the application.

If the application misuses memory or has a fatal error that causes the application to crash, other applications in Windows are not usually affected. When an application fails to respond—if clicks or keystrokes get no response, for example—press Ctrl+Alt+Del to display the Close Program dialog box.

The troublesome application shows the phrase **[Not responding]**. To continue working in Windows on your other applications, you must shut down this application. Select the application and click End Task. If you click Shut Down or press Ctrl+Alt+Delete again, all applications and Windows 95 shut down.

Getting Help

Windows 95, its accessories, and most Windows applications offer extensive Help screens to help you find information on procedures, commands, techniques, and terms. Many applications even include numbered lists of steps in Help to guide you through complex procedures. The tools in Windows Help enable you to search for topics, print Help information, annotate the Help screens with your own notes, and copy information from the Help screens to the Clipboard for use in other applications.

When you install Internet Explorer 4.0, it adds its own Help system, which uses a different interface. Although there are similarities in the look and feel of the two Help systems, the IE4 version is notable for its use of HTML-based pages and links.

Many Windows accessories and applications use the Windows Help engine. Each application's Help screens differ, however. You can learn how to use the application's Help system by opening the Help menu (from the application's menu bar) and choosing a command similar to How to Use Help.

Using Windows Help

You start Windows Help by opening the Start menu and choosing Help. Figure 10.13 shows the Contents tab of the Help Topics window. This is the Help window for Windows 95; other Windows applications provide Help windows that look different.

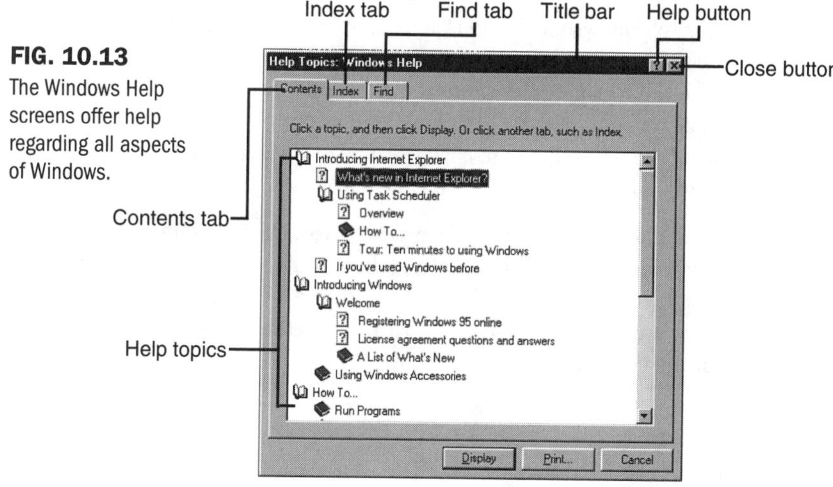

FIG. 10.13 The Windows Help screens offer help regarding all aspects of Windows.

Table 10.1 describes the parts of the Help Topics window.

Table 10.1 Parts of the Help Topics Window

Part	Description
Title bar	Includes the Control Menu icon at the top left (you can choose either Move or Close), the Help button (use it to display pop-up help, discussed later in the chapter), and the Close button
Contents tab	Displays the available Help topics
Index tab	Enables you to search through the available Help topics
Find tab	Enables you to search for specific words or phrases in the Help system
Close	Closes the selected book icon on the Contents page
Open button	Opens the selected book icon on the Contents page
Display button	Displays the selected Help item from the Index or Contents page
Cancel button	Closes Help
Print button	Displays the Print Current Topic dialog box, from which you can print the selected topic

The Help Topics window uses the standard Windows controls: scroll bars (as needed), the Close button, and the application Control menu button in the upper-left corner.

NOTE To start Help from within a Windows application, press the F1 key. Help then displays for the active application or window.

Using Pop-Up Help In many Windows applications, a question mark button (?) appears at the top-right corner of some dialog boxes and windows. You can use this button to pop up detailed information about how to use the dialog box or window. If you're not certain how to use a data-entry box within a dialog box, for example, click the Help (?) button; when the mouse pointer turns to a question-mark-and-arrow combination, click the data-entry box. A pop-up window displays Help information about the item on which you clicked.

You can use pop-up help throughout Windows 95. To inspect hardware, for example, you can right-click the My Computer icon, choose Properties, and then click the Device Manager tab of the System Properties dialog box. To learn how the list of hardware devices works, click the Help (?) button and then click anywhere in the list of hardware. Figure 10.14 shows the pop-up window that tells you about the list in the Device Manager.

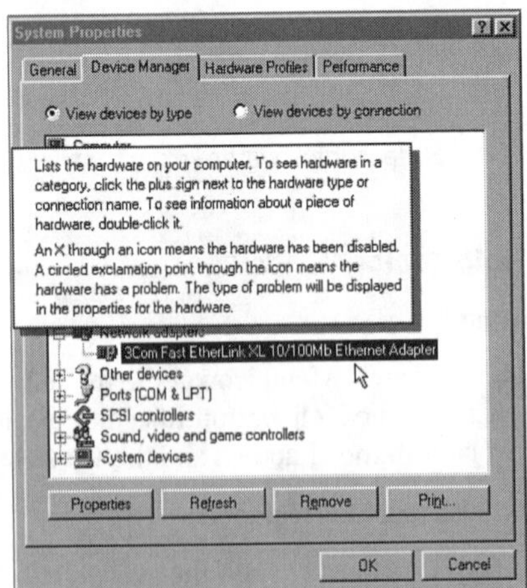

FIG. 10.14 To view a pop-up Help window describing a control on a Properties sheet or dialog box, click the Help (?) button, and then click any control.

Using the Contents Page The Contents page of the Help Topics window lists Help topics that are available in the Windows application in which you chose Help. Topics are categorized into books. Each Help topic icon first appears as a closed book. When you open a book, you see page icons. Displaying a page icon reveals the Help contents for that topic.

Figure 10.15 shows a Help window's contents. In addition to a list of steps, the window also contains a shortcut button. Clicking that button immediately displays the Password Properties dialog box that the Help screen discusses. You can keep the Help window open as you work in the Password Properties dialog box. Many of the topics include tips and tricks that offer shortcuts and other time-saving techniques.

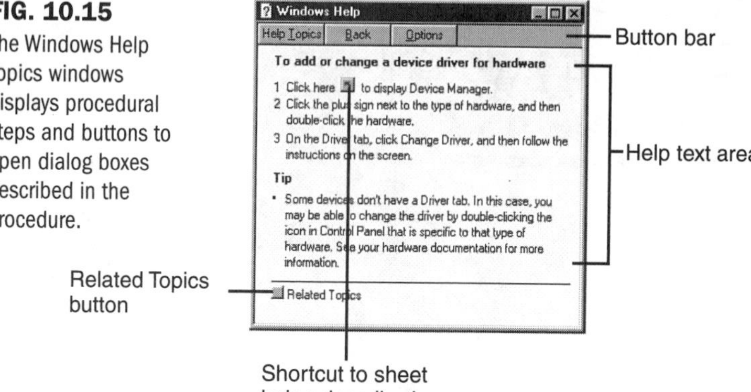

FIG. 10.15
The Windows Help Topics windows displays procedural steps and buttons to open dialog boxes described in the procedure.

To display a Help window about one of the topics on the Contents page, follow these steps:

1. Open the Start menu and choose Help.
2. Click the Contents tab.
3. Scroll through the list of topics to locate the topic you want.
4. Double-click a book to display its contents. The contents of the topic display as page icons.
5. Double-click a page icon to display its contents, or select the topic and choose Display. The Help topic displays in a window sized to fit its contents. You can resize the window to make it easier to work in your application.

Using the Help Window After you select a Help topic from either the Contents or Index tab, the Help window appears. Table 10.2 describes the toolbar buttons in the Help window.

Table 10.2 Help Toolbar Buttons

Button	Description
Help Topics	Displays the Help Topics window. Options include Copy, Print, and Keep Help on Top.
Back	Moves the Help window back to the previous topic.
Options	Displays a menu of commands enabling you to use the contents of the Help window in different ways. The following sections in this chapter describe these commands.
Related Topics	Displays a list of related Help topics.

Using the Index Page The Index Help page provides a search feature that finds the topic that you want (see Figure 10.16). For example, if you want to learn about adding shortcuts to the desktop, you can type **sho**. The selection bar moves through the list of index entries to **shopping on the Web**. The more letters you type, the closer you get to the topic name.

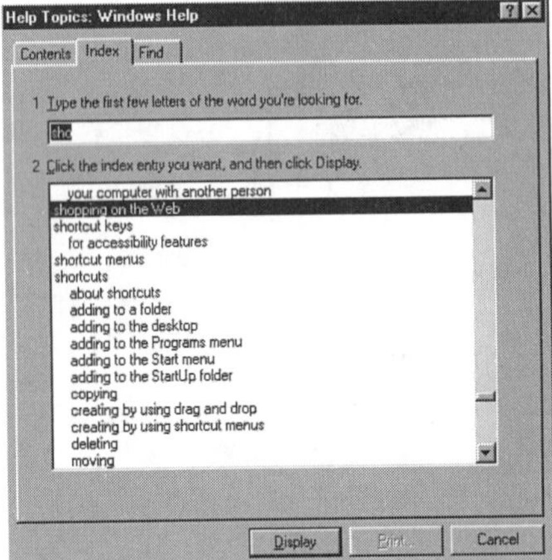

FIG. 10.16
Find a Help topic with the Windows Help Index.

To use the Help Index, follow these steps:

1. Open the Start menu and choose Help.
2. Click the Index tab.
3. Click the text box and type the name of the subject on which you want Help. As you type, the selection bar moves through the list of topics.
4. When you select your topic, double-click it, or click it and choose Display. The Help screen displays.

Finding Words and Phrases With the Contents and Index panes, you're at the mercy of the Help system author. In both cases, you choose from a preset list of topics that might or might not include the topic you're seeking. When that happens, use the Find pane to search the entire Help file for specific words or phrases.

NOTE The first time you use the Help Index, Windows creates an index file. This process takes a few seconds, and the resulting index occupies disk space (more than 500KB for the main Windows Help file). The results are worth it, however, as this index significantly speeds up searches.

To search for detailed information in a Help file, follow these steps:

1. Open Help for Windows or a Windows application and click the Find tab.
2. Begin typing in the text box at the top of the dialog box. By default, Windows starts searching immediately. (Click the Options button to change this setting.) Enter a single word or phrase.
3. If you want, select one or more words in the middle box to narrow your search.
4. Help topics appear in the list at the bottom of the dialog box. Scroll through the list of topics, highlight any that look promising, and then click the Display button.
5. Click Clear to erase the contents of your search and begin again.

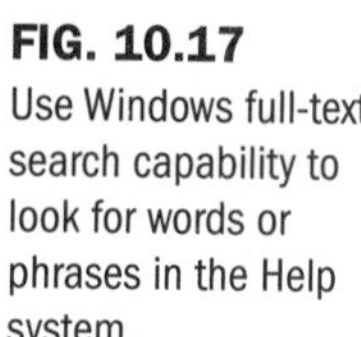

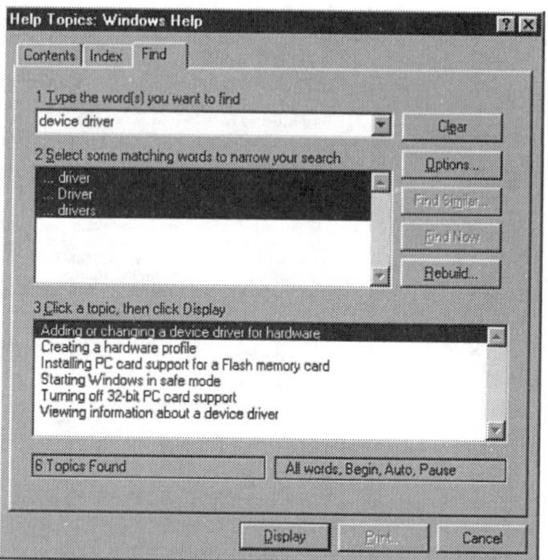

FIG. 10.17
Use Windows full-text search capability to look for words or phrases in the Help system.

Jumping Between Topics You can easily jump between Help topics by returning to either the Contents or Index tab. After you finish reading a Help window, if you want to search for help about another topic, simply click the Help Topics button in the Help window.

When more information related to the topic that you're viewing is available, the Help window includes a Related Topics button. Click the Related Topics button to see a list of related topics. The Topics Found window displays and lists the additional related topics. Click the topic that you want and click Display to view the topic's Help.

Printing a Help Topic Often, having a printed copy of the Help topic in which you are interested can help you understand the topic more clearly. When the topic for which you want information is in the Help window, choose the Options button and then Print Topic to display the Print dialog box. Click OK to print.

NOTE Some of the handiest information that you can print or copy from Help is an application's shortcut keys. If you didn't get a shortcut keystroke template for your application, look in the application's Help contents for a topic similar to Keyboard Shortcuts. Copy these topics (by pressing Ctrl+C) to a word processor, reorganize them, and print them. Alternatively, you can print the topics directly from Help. You can then copy the contents at a reduced size and paste them onto three-by-five cards. ■

Using Internet Explorer Help

Although IE4 and Windows 95 work well together, they don't share a single help system. When you choose Help, Contents and Index from the Internet Explorer menu (or from the equivalent menus of other IE4 applications, including Outlook Express), you'll see a slightly different Help system, as shown in Figure 10.18.

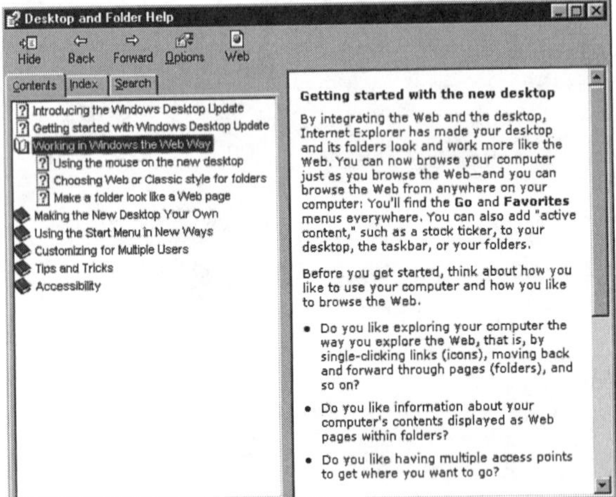

FIG. 10.18
Although it's similar to its Windows counterpart, the Help system in IE4 behaves differently, thanks to HTML and hyperlinks.

Unlike Windows Help, which forces you to jump back and forth between the Help Topics window and individual Help screens, IE4 Help uses an Explorer-style two-pane view that makes it easier to find answers. Entries in the left pane function like web-style hyperlinks; when you click a link, the contents display in the right pane.

Like its Windows counterpart, Internet Explorer Help offers three ways to find information: The Contents tab organizes Help into broad topics; the Index tab provides an extensive alphabetical list of topics; and the Search tab enables you to hunt for a word or phrase. Click the tab to view each different pane.

Because information in IE4 Help is contained in compiled HTML pages, you can create shortcuts to Help screens to which you'd like to refer later. Right-click the page in the right Help pane and then choose Create Shortcut. Windows places the newly created shortcut on the desktop.

After you find the Help topic for which you're looking, use the Hide button to clear away the list of topics in the left pane. Use the Show button to reveal the list again.

Customizing Help

Help is more than just a list of procedures or word definitions. You can print Help screens, copy screens into word processors, and even add notes to Help windows so that Help becomes customized to the kind of work that you do.

Adding Custom Notes to Help Topics You can customize Help information in a Windows application to make Help information more useful to you or to coworkers. For example, when users view a Help window on document formatting, you might want them to see information about your company's default settings. Or, you might want to supplement a built-in Help window that describes how to create mailing labels with a note that includes the names of templates for mailing labels. To add such information, you use *annotations*.

To indicate that a Help window has annotated text, Windows displays a paper clip icon next to the topic.

To create an annotation, follow these steps:

1. Display the topic that you want to annotate.
2. Click the Options button and then choose Annotate. The Annotate dialog box, a small notepad, appears.
3. Type the notes that you want to save regarding this Help topic.
4. Choose the Save button.

A paper clip icon appears to the left of the topic title in the Help window. Whenever you want to read an annotation, just click the paper clip icon.

To remove an annotation, click the paper clip icon. When the Annotate dialog box appears, choose the Delete button.

Copying Help Information to Another Application You can create a collection of Help topics by copying Help information and pasting this data into a word processor document file. You can copy and paste into another application any information that you see in a Help window. The information transfers as editable text.

▶ **See** "Using the Windows Clipboard," **p. 822**

To copy the entire contents of a Help window, choose the Options button and then the Copy command. To copy a portion of the window, select the text and press Ctrl+C. To paste this information into another Windows application, such as a word processor, open the other application, position the insertion point wherever you want to paste the information, and choose Edit, Paste, or press Ctrl+V.

To copy information from Internet Explorer Help, you must select text and then right-click and choose Copy.

Finding Help, Support, and Resources

Windows is one of the most popular software applications ever written. Therefore, much support is available for Windows. The following sections describe resources that can help you get the most from Windows.

An extensive listing of telephone, email, and Internet-based help and support is available in the Appendix, "Additional Help and Resources."

Getting Telephone Support Use the following telephone numbers to get technical support or produce sales information about Windows or Windows applications.

For questions specific to Windows installation, Windows Explorer, or Windows accessories, call Microsoft Corporation's Windows support line at (206) 635-7000. For customer service and product upgrade information, call (800) 426-9400.

If Windows or Windows applications came preinstalled on your computer, check the documentation included with the computer; your license will probably require that you contact the hardware vendor who supplied your equipment to get technical support for the preinstalled software.

▶ **See** "Getting Telephone and FAX Support for Windows 95 and Microsoft Products," **p. 1002**

Getting Help over the Internet Microsoft provides two Internet sites that you can access for free software, updates, technical papers, and device drivers. From within your Internet browser, you can access the Microsoft FTP site with this URL:

ftp://ftp.microsoft.com/

You can access the same information by using your browser on the World Wide Web with this URL:

http://www.microsoft.com/support

▶ **See** "Online Technical Support," **p. 1003**

Consultants and Training Microsoft Solution Providers develop and support applications written for the Windows environment with Microsoft products. They are independent consultants who have met the strict qualifying requirements imposed by Microsoft.

Microsoft also certifies training centers. A certified training center has instructors who have passed a competency exam and use Microsoft-produced training material.

You can find the Microsoft Solution Providers and training centers in your area by calling the following number:

1-800-SOL-PROV

▶ **See** " Referrals to Consultants and Training," **p. 1008**

CHAPTER 11

The Overview of the Windows Desktop Update

by Ed Bott

In this chapter

Internet Explorer 4.0 isn't just a web browser; an optional component called the Windows Desktop Update makes radical changes in the interface that Microsoft introduced in the original version of Windows 95.

Some users love the new interface, whereas for others it requires a period of adjustment. Fortunately, you have an exceptional degree of control over the new interface. This chapter explains how to install and remove the Windows Desktop Update, what changes it makes, and how you can select the interface that helps you be most productive.

Installing the Windows Desktop Update

When you install Internet Explorer 4.0 on top of Windows 95, you can choose to install a component called the Windows Desktop Update, which dramatically alters the Windows interface. If you're familiar with the original Windows 95 interface, you will notice the following changes when you install the Windows Desktop Update:

- An enhanced taskbar includes a new Quick Launch toolbar and changes in the way taskbar buttons work.
- An enhanced Start menu, with a new menu item for Web Favorites plus new options on the Find menu; it also gives you the capability to edit or rearrange program shortcuts directly.
- New folder and desktop options, including a choice of single-click or double-click navigation.
- Many, many small improvements to the original Windows interface, which collectively make file management more productive.
- The Web view option enables you to display the contents of drives and folders as part of a customizable web page.
- The optional Active Desktop setting enables you to add web pages and HTML components to the Windows desktop.

NOTE Because the names are so similar, it's easy to confuse the Windows Desktop Update and the Active Desktop. In fact, even some Microsoft marketing pieces use the two names interchangeably. The two are not the same, however; in fact, the Active Desktop is one small part of the Windows Desktop Update. You can find detailed information about the Active Desktop in Chapter 21, "Working with Web Subscriptions and the Active Desktop." ■

Adding the Windows Desktop Update from a CD-ROM

If you chose not to install the Windows Desktop Update when you originally set up Internet Explorer 4.0, it's easy to add this option later. Follow these steps if you installed IE4 from a CD-ROM:

1. Put the CD-ROM disc in your drive. It should start automatically; if it doesn't, open the My Computer window and double-click the drive icon.

2. When the Internet Explorer 4.0 CD-ROM dialog box appears, click the second option—Install Internet Explorer 4.0 Add-On Components.
3. This step opens your web browser and loads the Active Setup control. When you see the dialog box that asks if it's OK to determine which components are installed on your computer, click Yes.
4. The Component Download page lists all the options available and tells you which ones are already installed on your computer. Check the box to the left of the Windows Desktop Update option, as shown in Figure 11.1, and click Next.

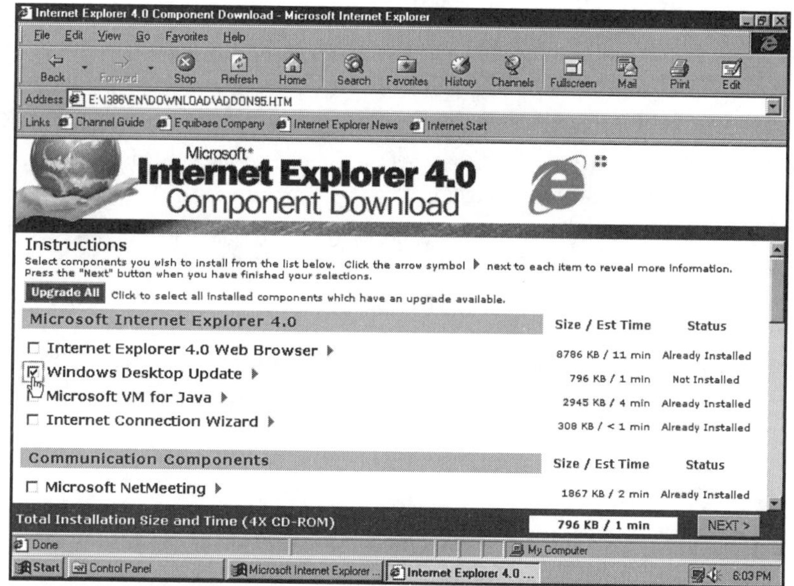

FIG. 11.1
Use IE4's Active Setup program to add the Windows Desktop Update if you didn't install it originally.

5. On the Component Confirmation page, click the Install Now button.
6. After the installation process is complete, restart your computer.

Installing the Windows Desktop Update from the Web

If you originally installed IE4 from Microsoft's web site, the procedure for adding the Windows Desktop Update is slightly different:

1. Click the Start button and choose Settings, Control Panel.
2. Open the Add/Remove Programs option.
3. In the bottom half of the Add/Remove Programs dialog box is a list of software installed on your computer. Choose Microsoft Internet Explorer 4.0 from this list and click the Add/Remove button.
4. In the Internet Explorer 4.0 Active Setup dialog box (see Figure 11.2), select the option labeled Add the Windows Desktop Update component from web site.

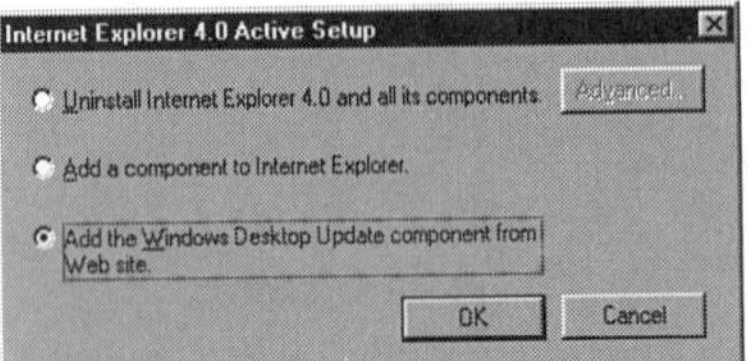

FIG. 11.2
Use the Add/Remove Programs option to add the Windows Desktop Update after IE4 is already installed.

5. Internet Explorer connects to the IE4 Active Setup page on Microsoft's web site. When you see the dialog box that asks if it's okay to determine which components are installed on your computer, click Yes.
6. On the Component Download page, check the box to the left of the Windows Desktop Update option and click Next.
7. On the Component Confirmation page, choose a download site and click Install Now.
8. After the installation process is complete, follow the prompts to restart your computer and make the changes.

▶ **See** "Keeping Your Copy of Windows 95 Up to Date," **p. 21**

NOTE Although the Windows Desktop Update is an optional component of Internet Explorer 4.0, we highly recommend it for all Windows 95 users. The only situations in which you should not install the Windows Desktop Update are in corporate environments in which management has expressly prohibited its use. Throughout this book, we assume you have installed the Windows Desktop Update.

Removing the Windows Desktop Update

It's easy to remove the Windows Desktop Update without uninstalling the Internet Explorer 4.0 web browser. When you remove the Windows Desktop Update component, the following changes take place to the Windows interface:

- The taskbar and Start menu revert to the design introduced with the original version of Windows 95. There's no Quick Launch toolbar, and you must open the Start menu folder to move or edit program shortcuts—you can't directly edit these items.
- Active Desktop options are no longer available, and the Web tab and other enhancements to the Display Properties dialog box are also missing.
- When you open the My Computer window or choose Windows Explorer from the Programs menu, you see the original version of Explorer, which uses a small toolbar and does not include web-browsing capabilities.
- The single-click option is no longer available on the Windows desktop.
- The Channel Bar is visible on the desktop, but it looks slightly different, because the title bar and Close button are always visible. A check box on the Advanced tab of the Internet Options dialog box enables you to control whether or not the Channel Bar displays at startup.

Although removing the Windows Desktop Update breaks the integration between the Windows shell and Internet Explorer, you can still use the newer Explorer for file management. Open a copy of Internet Explorer and type any file specification (**C:**, for example, or **My Computer**) in the Address bar. To open the new version of the two-pane Explorer, right-click any folder or drive icon in the Internet Explorer window and choose Explore. Note that you cannot customize folder options in this version of Explorer, nor can you see an Internet Explorer icon in the All Folders pane.

To remove the Windows Desktop Update, first make sure no other programs are running, and then follow these steps:

1. Click Start and choose Settings, Control Panel.
2. Open the Add/Remove Programs option.
3. In the bottom half of the Add/Remove Programs dialog box is a list of software installed on your computer. Choose Microsoft Internet Explorer 4.0 from this list and click Add/Remove.
4. In the Internet Explorer 4.0 Active Setup dialog box (see Figure 11.3), select the option labeled Remove the Windows Desktop Update component.

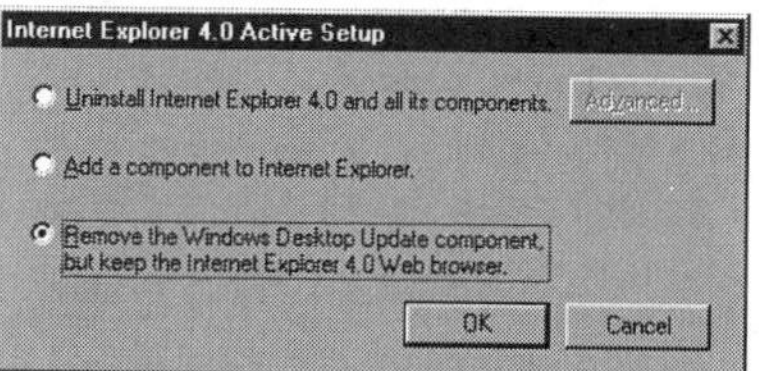

FIG. 11.3 Use this option to remove the Windows Desktop Update without uninstalling the Internet Explorer 4.0 web browser.

5. An additional dialog box warns you that uninstalling the Windows Desktop Update changes the format of the Recycle Bin and makes it impossible to recover files currently stored there. If necessary, open the Recycle Bin and restore any files you want to preserve.
6. Click OK to continue. After a brief interval, the Active Setup program removes the Windows Desktop Update component. You do not need to restart your system to continue.

Classic or Web—Choosing a Navigation Style

With the Windows Desktop Update installed, you have several important interface choices to make. To see the available options, open My Computer or an Explorer window and choose View, Folder Options. On the General tab, you see the dialog box shown in Figure 11.4.

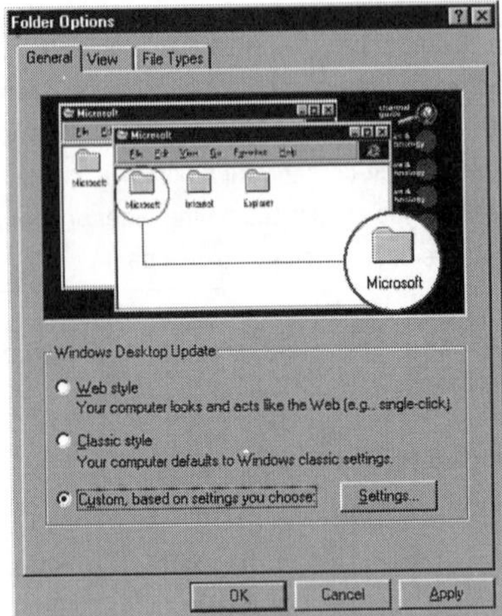

FIG. 11.4
Choose your interface: The Classic Windows 95 style, one that resembles a web browser, or a mix of the two.

TROUBLESHOOTING

I've opened Explorer, but I can't find the Folder Options choice on the View menu. First make sure you've installed the Windows Desktop Update. If that component is installed and you still don't see the menu choice, you're probably viewing a web page in the Explorer window, in which case the View menu offers an Internet Options choice instead. Click the Address bar, type **C:**, and press Enter. You should now be able to select Folder Options.

Choose one of the following three interface options:

- Web style sets the Windows desktop and folder options to resemble your web browser. Icons are underlined, like hyperlinks on a web page. You point at icons to select them and single-click to open folders and launch programs.

▶ **See** "Using an HTML Page as Your Desktop," **p. 499**

- Classic style resembles the original Windows 95 interface. You single-click to select icons and double-click to open folders and launch programs.
- Custom enables you to mix and match interface options. After you choose this option, click Settings to choose from four options in the Custom Settings dialog box, as shown in Figure 11.5.

Although the Custom Settings dialog box looks daunting, it actually follows a simple organization. Each of the four options includes two choices. If you choose the top item in each list, you end up with web style; choose the bottom option in all four cases and you end up with Classic style.

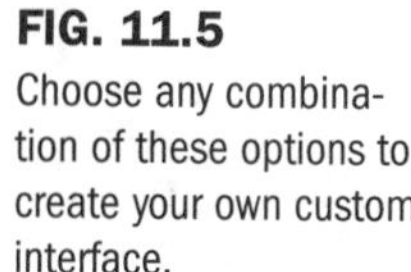

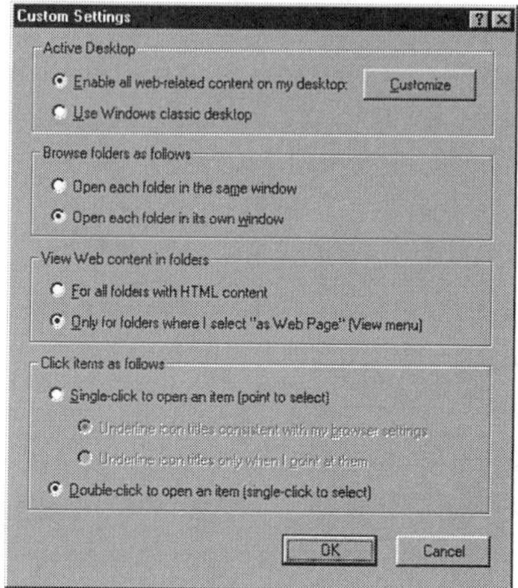

FIG. 11.5
Choose any combination of these options to create your own custom interface.

Turning on the Active Desktop

Choosing the option labeled Enable all web-related content on my desktop has the same effect as checking the Active Desktop's View As Web Page option. Clicking the Customize button has the same effect as opening the Display Properties dialog box and clicking the Web tab. Choosing Use Windows classic desktop turns off the Active Desktop. For a full discussion of your Active Desktop options, see Chapter 21.

Choosing a Browsing Style

In the Classic Windows 95 interface (pen each folder in its own window), the original window remains open when you display the contents of a new drive or folder; if you drill down through multiple folders and subfolders, the result is a screen full of windows. Choose Open each folder in the same window to display the contents of each new drive or folder in the same window with which you started, replacing the contents that were there previously.

▶ **See** "Two Views of Windows Explorer," **p. 280**

Viewing Web Content in Folders

With the Windows Desktop Update installed, Explorer enables you to view any folder as a web page, using a standard folder template or a custom HTML page you create. Web view adds a banner to the top of the folder window and an info pane along the left side of the window; the file list appears below the banner on the right side of the window. Choose the top option to use Web view with all folders; the bottom option enables you to selectively turn on Web view. For a full discussion of Web view, including details on how to create your own custom HTML folder templates, see Chapter 14, "Managing Files Using Web View."

Single-Click or Double-Click?

The most important interface choice you will make is how you use the mouse to select icons and open folders or launch programs. By default, the Windows Desktop Update takes a conservative approach, preserving the familiar double-click style introduced in the original Windows 95 interface. To change this option, choose Web style or open the Custom Settings dialog box and choose Single-click to open an item (point to select). The first time you choose this option, you see a warning dialog box like the one in Figure 11.6.

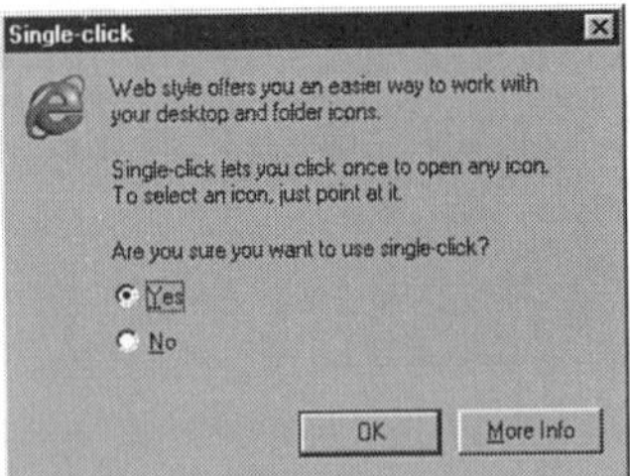

FIG. 11.6
Because the single-click interface is a radical change, Windows asks you to confirm your choice when you first select it.

Why the warning? Because when you choose the web-style interface, you change the way Windows handles some of its most basic tasks. Table 11.1 offers a side-by-side comparison of how you deal with files and folders by using the two navigation styles.

Table 11.1 Differences in Navigation Styles

Task	Web style	Classic style
Select an icon	Point to the icon.	Click the icon.
Open an icon	Click the icon.	Double-click the icon.
Select a group of adjacent icons	Point to the first icon, and then hold down the Shift key and point to the last icon.	Click the first icon, hold down the Shift key, and click the last icon.
Select multiple icons	Hold down the Ctrl key and point to individual icons.	Hold down the Ctrl key and click individual icons.
Drag and drop	Point to an icon, press and hold down mouse button, and drag icon to new location (same as Classic style).	Point to an icon, press and hold down mouse button, and drag icon to new location.

TROUBLESHOOTING

I've chosen the single-click option, but Windows ignores me when I adjust the option to underline icons only when you point at them. When you choose the single-click option in the Custom Settings dialog box, you also have the choice to underline all icon titles, just as Internet Explorer does, or to underline icons only when you point at them. If you select the top choice in all four Custom options, Windows shifts your choice to web style and ignores your underlining preferences. The only way to force Explorer to accept this change is to select the bottom (Classic) choice in one of the first three options in this dialog box.

Customizing Other Folder Options

Installing the Windows Desktop Update adds an assortment group of advanced folder options, as well. To adjust these settings, choose View, Folder Options, and click the View tab; you see a series of items in the bottom of the dialog box, as shown in Figure 11.7.

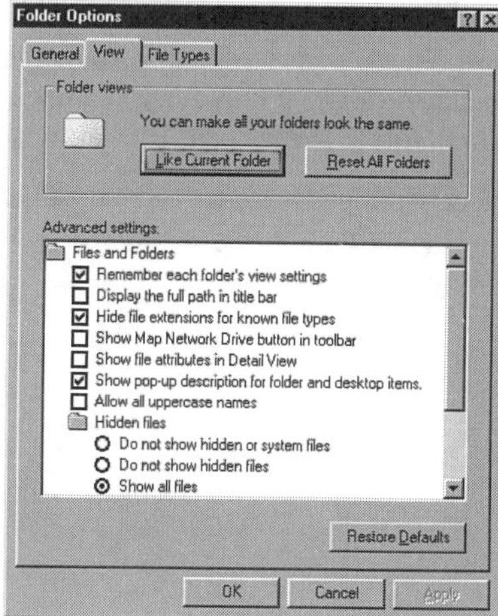

FIG. 11.7
These are the default settings for advanced folder options.

Part II Ch 11

Table 11.2 lists the effect of each of these settings.

Table 11.2 Effects of the Default Settings

Option	Effect When Checked
Remember each folder's view settings	Saves the icon view of folder windows; also saves size and position when using multi-window browsing option. Does not apply to two-pane Explorer windows. See "Changing the Way a Folder's Contents Appear" in Chapter 12.
Display the full path in title bar	Shows full DOS-style path (e.g., C:\Windows\System) in folder windows. Handy when comparing subfolders with identical names in different parts of Explorer tree.

continues

Table 11.2 Continued

Option	Effect When Checked
Hide file extensions for known file types	Uncheck this box to show all file extensions, even when file type is registered. See "Associating Files with Programs" in Chapter 13.
Show Map Network Drive button in toolbar	Adds two buttons to Standard toolbar; check if you regularly assign drive letters to shared network folders.
Show file attributes in Details view	Adds a column at the far right of Details view. See "Changing the Way a Folder's Contents Appear" in Chapter 12.
Show pop-up description for folder and desktop items	Displays ScreenTips when you point to My Computer and other desktop items; experienced users should uncheck this box.
Allow all-uppercase names	Normally, Windows capitalizes only the first letter of all filenames (for example, Abc); uncheck this box to allow file and folder names like ABC.
Hidden files	Select whether to display hidden and/or system files. See "Changing the Way a Folder's Contents Appear" in Chapter 12.

PART III

Working with Files and Folders

CHAPTER 12

Managing Files with My Computer and Windows Explorer

by Ed Bott

In this chapter

Two Views of Windows Explorer

The most basic building block of Windows is the icon. Every object you work with has its own icon—files and folders, drives and network servers, programs, printers, and shortcuts to web pages. Program icons are as distinctive as product logos, data files use standard icons that help you group related files easily, and system objects use icons that are intended to illustrate their main function. They're all organized into folders and subfolders in a strict hierarchy.

Whenever you view or manage icons and folders, you use a program called the Windows Explorer in one of its two views. Right-click a drive or folder icon, and shortcut menus enable you to choose between the two faces of Explorer: Click Open, and the contents of the drive or folder you selected appear in a simple window; choose Explore, and you see a more complex view, with one pane that shows all the resources available to you and another that displays the selected folder's contents. As soon as they learn how Explorer works, most Windows users incorporate both views as part of their working style.

Viewing Resources in My Computer

For a simple, uncluttered view of all the resources on your computer, find the My Computer icon on the desktop and open this window. The resulting display looks something like the one shown in Figure 12.1.

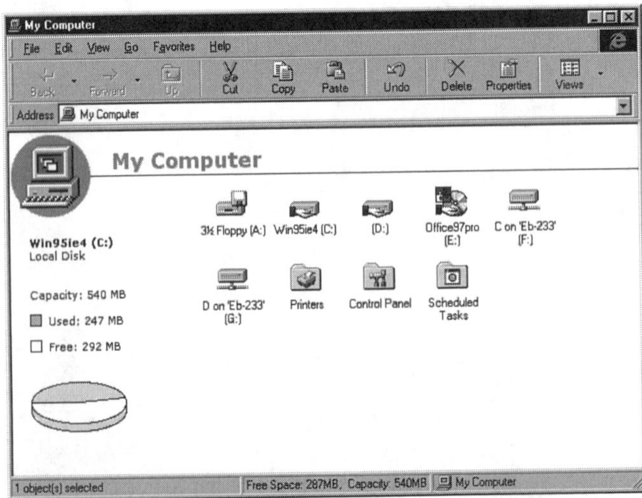

FIG. 12.1
The My Computer window offers a simple way to view local resources, including drives, printers, and other hardware.

Microsoft's interface designers created My Computer as the primary file-management interface for novice users, but even Windows experts will find it ideally suited for some file management tasks. Because the My Computer window displays the amount of free disk space, for example, it's a convenient way to see at a glance how much total storage is available on your system.

To see the maximum amount of information about drives in the My Computer window, choose View, Details. Click the Free Space heading to sort drives in order of available storage space.

Browsing the Contents of a Folder

Unlike the Windows Explorer, which shows you the outline-style hierarchy of all drives and folders on your system, starting with the My Computer window shows you the contents of one folder at a time. To view the contents of drives and folders from the My Computer window, open a drive icon, a folder within that drive, and then a folder within that folder. Keep drilling down in this fashion until you find the folder for which you're looking.

The easiest way to go back up through the hierarchy of folders is to use the Up button on the Standard toolbar. (If the toolbar is hidden, choose View, Toolbars, Standard Buttons to make it visible.)

What happens to the current folder window when you open a drive or folder icon by starting with the My Computer window? If you've chosen web style, the contents of the folder you selected replace the contents of the current window, so you're always working with a single window. If you've selected Classic style, on the other hand, the My Computer window remains open and a new drive or folder window appears. For each folder you open, you will see a new folder window, as in Figure 12.2.

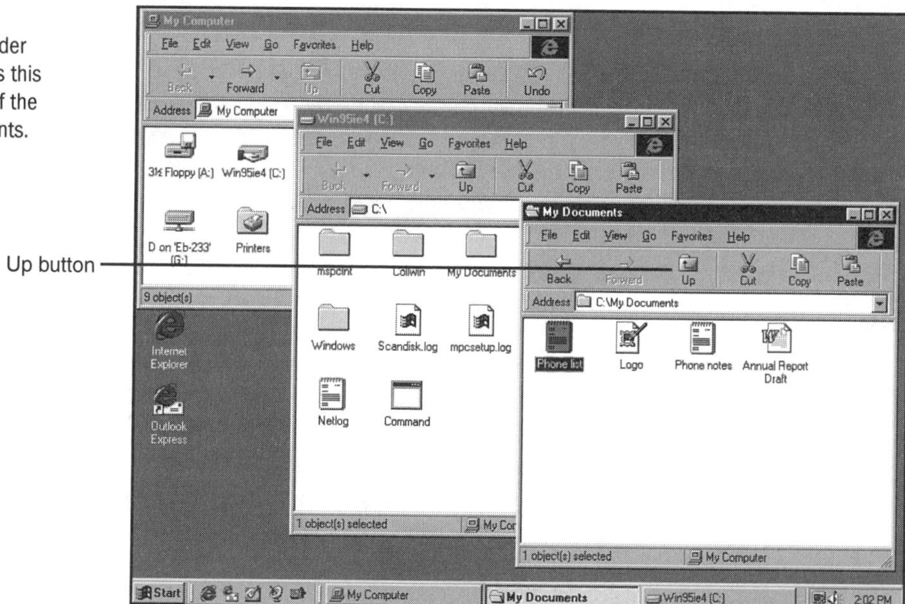

FIG. 12.2 Opening a folder window shows this simple view of the folder's contents.

Using the multiple-window option results in unnecessary and confusing clutter when you delve several folders deep. But sometimes you want to open two or more windows at once so you can move or copy icons from one folder to another. Windows enables you to specify whether each new folder uses the same window or opens in a separate window. To adjust the default behavior of folder windows, you must use the Custom settings in the Windows Desktop Update.

▶ **See** "Customizing Other Folder Options," **p. 275**

The settings you choose in the Folder Options dialog box determine whether new folder windows replace the current window or open a new one. You can also hold down the Ctrl key and double-click a folder or drive icon to override this default setting at any time. If you've chosen the single-window option, this procedure opens a new window; if you normally open a new window, this technique replaces the contents of the current window. Note that this option requires you to hold down Ctrl and double-click even if you've chosen the web-style single-click option.

NOTE When you view the contents of a floppy disk, Windows will not automatically update the display when you change disks. Likewise, if another user adds, renames, or deletes files in a shared network folder, these changes do not automatically appear in an open window on your system. Under these conditions, you need to *refresh* the display to see the most up-to-date contents. In Windows Explorer, point to the icon for the drive or folder and click to refresh the window. You can also choose View, Refresh, or press F5. ■

Using Windows Explorer to View Files and Folders

When you right-click a drive or folder icon and choose Explore from the shortcut menu, Windows opens the two-paned view of Explorer, with a tree-style All Folders pane on the left and a contents pane on the right. The title bar begins with the word *Exploring,* followed by the currently selected drive or folder. As the example in Figure 12.3 shows, the left pane includes every available resource, including local and network drives, system folders, and even Internet shortcuts.

There are many ways to open the Windows Explorer—Open the Start menu and choose Programs, Windows Explorer. Right-click the Start button or the My Computer icon and choose Explore. Type **Explorer** in the Run dialog box or at an MS-DOS Prompt. Create a shortcut on the desktop or on the Quick Launch bar.

As noted earlier, the two-paned Explorer uses the same program code as the single-pane folder window, adding only the All Folders pane. When you use the Explore command to open a new window, you can show or hide this pane by choosing View, Explorer Bar, All Folders. This technique enables you to quickly switch between Internet pages, folder windows, and Explorer windows. Curiously, if you start with a folder window or by opening an Internet shortcut, the All Folders pane is not available.

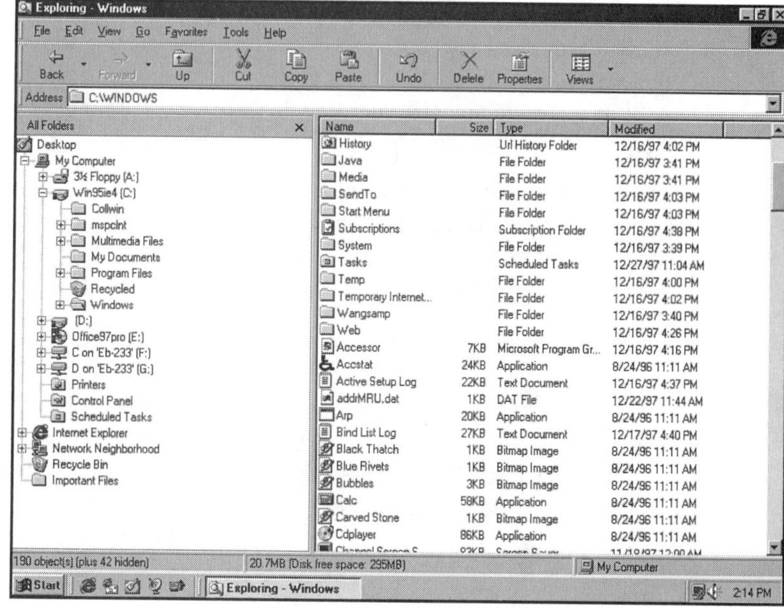

FIG. 12.3
The Windows Explorer uses these two panes to enable you to quickly navigate through local, network, and Internet resources.

Understanding the Explorer Hierarchy

When you use the two-pane Explorer view, it's easy to see the organization of drives, folders, and system resources in the left-hand All Folders bar. If the Address bar is visible, you can see a compact version of the same tree in a folder window. Click the arrow at the right of the Address bar to see a drop-down list like the one in Figure 12.4.

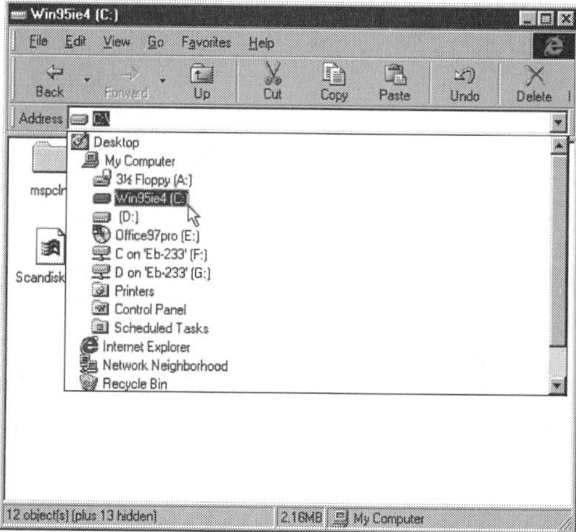

FIG. 12.4
The Address bar enables you to jump to different drives or system folders even when the All Folders pane is hidden.

If you've used MS-DOS or earlier versions of Windows, the hierarchy of a local drive is easy to understand: Each drive can contain one or more folders, starting with the root folder. Windows and Windows applications create folders to store program and data files, and you can create folders within folders to organize your files. In the case of data and program files, folders and subfolders are directly equivalent to MS-DOS directories and subdirectories.

Windows also uses folders to display objects that do not correspond to directories on a hard disk. Look at the All Folders pane or the drop-down list in the Address bar, and you can see that Explorer organizes available resources using a consistent hierarchy. The Desktop icon is always at the top of the list, which includes the following objects:

- *My Computer* displays icons for all local drives, any shared network drives that have been mapped to a drive letter, and the Printers, Control Panel, Scheduled Tasks, and Dial-Up Networking folders.
- *Network Neighborhood* shows icons for all servers and workstations in your network.
- *Internet Explorer* displays shortcuts for web pages you've added to the Active Desktop, as well as pages you've browsed recently.
- *Recycle Bin* shows files you've deleted recently.
- Any folders you create on the desktop appear at the bottom of the All Folders pane and the drop-down Address list.

If you have set up custom profiles for individual users of your computer, you can create folders, files, and shortcuts that appear on the desktop or Start menu. You can find the All Users folder within the Windows folder; any objects you create in the Desktop or Start Menu folders here will be visible to anyone who logs on to the computer.

Using Explorer Menus and Toolbars

When you browse files and folders by using Explorer, you have access to a consistent set of menus and toolbar buttons. When you select system folders, additional menu choices and buttons appear to reflect special options available in those folders. For example, when you view the contents of the Subscriptions folder, two new toolbar buttons enable you to update subscriptions, whereas Briefcase folders add menu choices and toolbar buttons that enable you to synchronize files.

▶ **See** "Maintaing Laptop and Desktop Files with Briefcase," **p. 216**

Navigating Through the Explorer Hierarchy

With the help of the Windows Explorer, it's easy to display the contents of any drive or folder. When you click an icon in the All Folders pane, the contents of that folder appear in the right pane.

By default, each branch of the tree-style listing in the All Folders pane is collapsed when you first open the two-pane Explorer view—all you see are the top-level icons for drives and system folders. A plus sign to the left of an icon means there are additional folders beneath it; click the plus sign to expand that branch and see additional folders. When you expand the folder listing, the plus sign turns to a minus sign; click to collapse that branch again. Figure 12.5 shows a typical display, with the contents of the Accessories folder visible in the right pane.

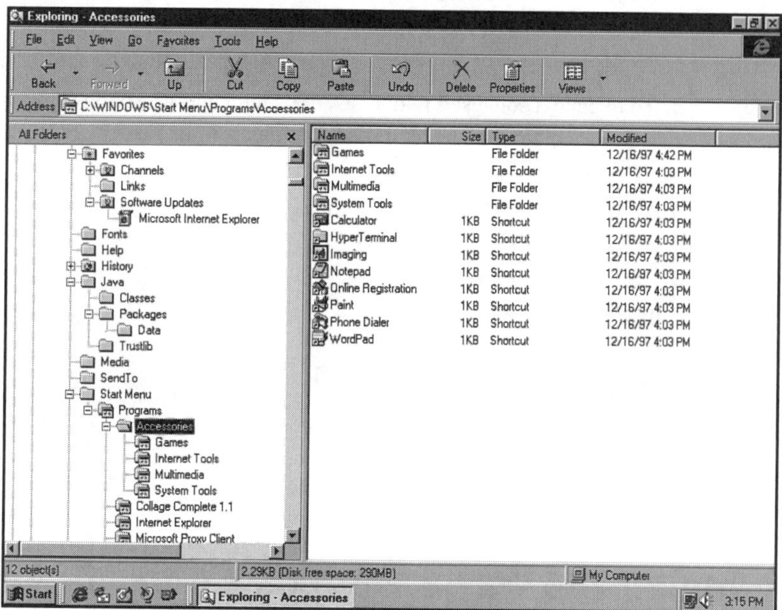

FIG. 12.5
Click the plus sign to expand a branch of the tree; click the minus sign to collapse the listing again.

TROUBLESHOOTING

You see a plus sign to the left of a drive icon, but when you click the icon, the plus sign disappears. Windows is behaving exactly as designed. When you first open the two-pane Explorer view, Windows checks the contents of all local hard drives and adds the plus sign when it detects subfolders; however, it does not automatically check for subfolders on removable drives (such as floppy disks) or network connections, because doing so might slow down the performance of your system. Instead, it places the plus sign next to each of those icons and waits until you select the icon before checking to see whether there really are any subfolders. If there are none, it removes the plus sign, as you've seen.

To display the contents of a different folder, select its icon in the All Folders pane. As you move from folder to folder, you can use the Back and Forward buttons to quickly return to folders you visited previously.

You can also use the keyboard to navigate through file and folder listings in Explorer. Here's a partial listing of useful keyboard shortcuts:

- Use the Tab key (or F6) to move from pane to pane; as you press Tab, the selection moves from the All Folders pane to the contents pane, to the Address bar, back to the All Folders pane, and so on.
- When the focus is in the All Folders pane, pressing the up and down arrow keys moves through the list of folders, without expanding collapsed branches. The contents of the selected icon automatically appear in the right pane as you move through the list.
- To move to the parent of the currently selected folder, press the Backspace key.
- To expand a collapsed folder, select its icon and press the right arrow key or the plus (+) key on the numeric keypad. Use the minus (-) key on the numeric keypad to collapse a branch.
- Press the star (*) key on the numeric keypad to expand all branches of the currently selected icon.
- To quickly move to the Address bar and open the drop-down list of top-level icons, press F4.

CAUTION

Be careful when using this shortcut! Pressing the * key when the Desktop or Network Neighborhood icon is selected can result in a very long delay as Explorer checks the contents of every available network drive.

Changing the Way a Folder's Contents Appear

Display options enable you to control how icons appear in an Explorer window. You can choose the size, arrangement, and order of icons, and you can also specify whether Explorer should show or hide system files. All of the options described in this section work the same in folder windows or in the right contents pane of Windows Explorer.

Icons, List, or Details: Choosing a View

Windows enables you to choose from four different arrangements of icons when displaying the contents of a folder. Each view has advantages and disadvantages under different circumstances. To apply a new view to the folder currently displayed, choose View, and then select one of the following choices:

- *Large Icons* view uses full-sized icons (32 pixels on each side), which enable you to easily distinguish between different types of icons. Labels appear along the bottom of each icon. You can position icons anywhere within the folder. This view is most practical for folders that contain few icons, such as My Computer; it's an impractical choice when you want to find a handful of files in a folder that contains hundreds of icons.
- *Small Icons* view displays icons that are one-fourth the size of those in the Large Icons view (16 pixels on each side); labels appear to the right of each icon. Initially, Small Icons

view arranges icons in rows from left to right, but you can move icons anywhere within the folder. This view is useful when you want to select a large number of icons in one motion.

- *List* view uses the same size icons and labels as Small Icons view. In List view, however, Windows arranges icons in columns, starting at the top left of the contents window; when the column reaches the bottom of the window, Windows starts a new column to the right. You cannot rearrange the position of icons in this view.
- Use *Details* view to see maximum information about objects in any window. From left to right, each row in this view includes the file icon, name, size, type, and the date the file was last modified. Note that these details change slightly for different types of windows; the My Computer window, for example, shows the total size and amount of free space in place of the last two columns. You cannot move or reposition icons in Details view.

The Views button on the Standard toolbar enables you to cycle through all four views of the current folder. Each time you click, the view changes to the next option. Use the drop-down arrow at the right of the Views button to choose a view.

Arranging File and Folder Icons

When you use either Large Icons or Small Icons view, Windows enables you to move icons anywhere within the folder. You can cluster your favorite icons in one location and move the others to a far corner, for example, or just rearrange the order in which the icons appear. Two options enable you to control the arrangement of icons within a folder.

If you prefer to have all your icons lined up neatly at all times, choose View, Arrange Icons, Auto Arrange. A check mark appears next to this menu choice to indicate that it is in use with the current folder. You can still move icons into any order you want, but other icons will shift position to make room for the icons you move. When you resize a folder window with this option turned on, the rows of icons automatically reposition so that you can see them properly within the window.

If you prefer to arrange icons yourself but want them to snap to position along an imaginary grid, rearrange the icons and then choose View, Line Up Icons. This option enables you to leave empty spaces within the folder window, and if you resize the window, some icons might not be visible—you need to use the scroll bars to move them into view.

CAUTION

These icon-arranging options apply to the Windows desktop, as well. Right-click any empty desktop area and choose Line Up Icons to straighten up the display of icons on the desktop. Avoid checking the Auto Arrange option on the Windows desktop, however. Most users prefer to position desktop icons in predictable locations; letting Windows automatically arrange desktop icons lines them up in columns, from top to bottom and left to right, without regard for wallpaper and Active Desktop items. That can make it difficult to work with desktop icons.

Sorting Files and Folders

Windows enables you to sort the contents of any folder by using one of four menu choices. These options work the same in folder windows and in the contents pane of an Explorer window. To sort files within a folder, follow these steps:

1. Display the contents of the folder.
2. Choose View, Arrange Icons from the pull-down menus or right-click in any empty space within the contents pane and choose Arrange Icons from the shortcut menu.
3. Choose one of the following options from the submenu:
   - *by Name* Sorts in ascending alphabetical order by filename, with folders grouped at the top of the list.
   - *by Type* Sorts in ascending alphabetical order by file type (note that this does not sort by file extension; Windows uses the registered name of the file type to determine sort order).
   - *by Size* Sorts folders first in ascending alphabetical order by name and then arranges files by size, with smallest files at the top of the list.
   - *by Date* Sorts folders by date, in descending order, and then sorts files the same way; in both cases, newest files appear at top of list.

The easiest way to sort files and folders is to switch to Details view. When you click the column headings in Details view, Windows sorts the folder's contents by the column you selected. Click again to sort in reverse order—something you cannot do in any other view.

Saving Folder Display Options

When you use the two-pane Windows Explorer, the view options you choose apply to all folders you display in the contents pane. If you choose Large Icons view for one folder, all folders adopt that view until you choose a different view.

When you use folder windows, however, Windows enables you to save separate view options for each folder. As you move from folder to folder, the view changes to reflect the settings you last used. If you prefer to set all folder windows to a single view, follow these steps:

1. Open any folder window and choose View. Select Large Icons, Small Icons, List, or Details. If you want to use Web view for all folders, choose View, as Web Page.
2. Choose View, Folder Options, and click the View tab. You see the dialog box shown in Figure 12.6.
3. In the box labeled Folder views, click the button labeled Like Current Folder.
4. When you see the confirmation dialog box, click Yes.
5. Click OK to save your changes.

Note that using this option does not save the sort order of windows, nor does it save toolbar settings.

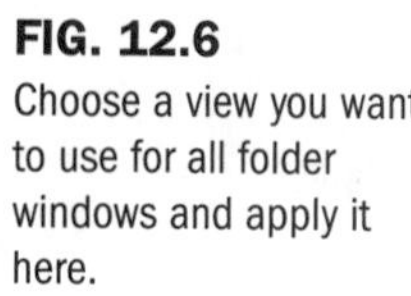

FIG. 12.6
Choose a view you want to use for all folder windows and apply it here.

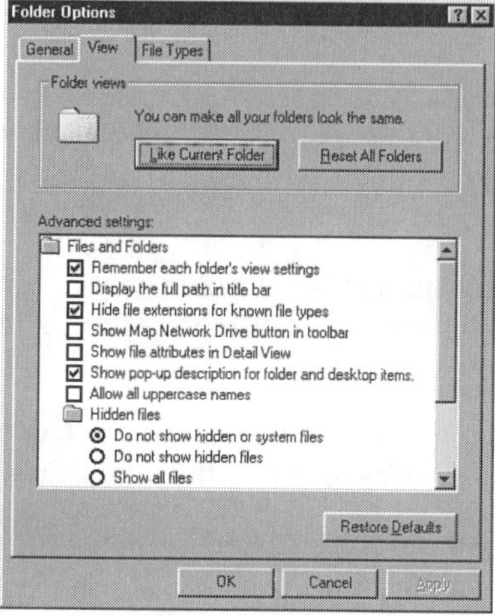

To restore folder windows to their default view settings, choose View, Folder Options, click the View tab, and click the button labeled Reset All Folders. This restores the My Computer, Control Panel, Fonts, and other system folders to their default Large Icons view.

Displaying or Hiding Different File Types

Files and folders created under MS-DOS or Windows enables you to set four special attributes. These settings enable you to prevent inadvertent damage to important files. To see the attributes for a given file or folder, select its icon and choose Properties from the shortcut menu. Click the General tab to see the current settings for the following four attributes:

Attribute	Description
Read-only	Prevents changes to files and folders with this attribute set. Note that setting a folder's read-only attribute does not affect files in that folder.
Hidden	Prevents the display of files using Windows Explorer or MS-DOS `DIR` command.
Archive	If this attribute is checked, the file has been changed since it was last backed up. The MS-DOS `XCOPY` command and most backup programs use the Archive attributes to perform partial backups.
System	Prevents the display of files and folders required by the system.

For the most part, Windows and Windows applications adjust file attributes automatically. The one circumstance under which you might want to manually adjust file attributes is to set a crucial workgroup file as read-only.

CAUTION

Setting the Read-only or System attribute for an object doesn't make it impossible to delete that file or folder; it only adds a warning dialog box to the process. If the file is truly important, make sure you have a backup copy stored in a safe location.

By default, Windows hides a tremendous number of files to prevent accidental changes or deletions that can cause the system to stop working properly. Look at the left side of the status bar in any Explorer window to see how many hidden files are in the current folder.

If you're confident of your ability to work with hidden and system files without causing your computer to crash, adjust Explorer's options to display those files. Follow these steps:

1. Open Windows Explorer or any folder window and choose View, Folder Options.
2. Click the View tab and find the entry labeled Hidden files in the Advanced settings box.
3. Select the Show all files option, as shown in Figure 12.7.

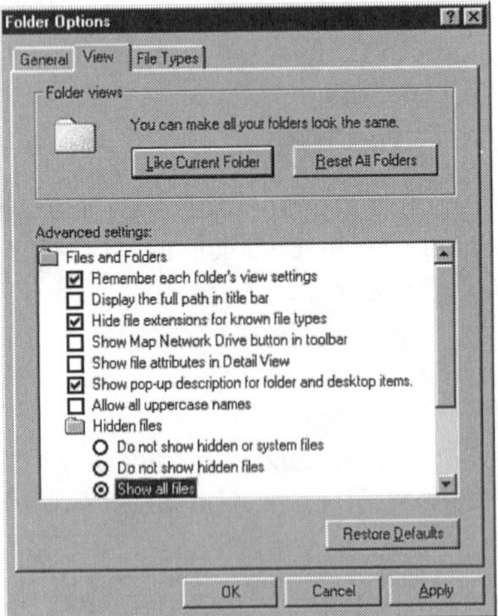

FIG. 12.7
Use this option to make hidden and system files visible.

4. Click OK to save your changes and close the Folder Options dialog box.

When you choose to make hidden files visible, you can easily distinguish them in Explorer windows—they appear in Explorer as grayed-out icons. You might need to press F5 or choose View, Refresh to make these files appear.

CAUTION

There's generally a good reason why Windows sets some files as hidden or system. If you need to change that attribute temporarily (to edit MSDOS.SYS, for example) be sure to change the attribute back when you're finished.

If you use the menus or the Ctrl+A keyboard shortcut to select all files in a folder that contains hidden files, you see a warning message like the one in Figure 12.8. There is no way to manage hidden files from Explorer unless you make them visible.

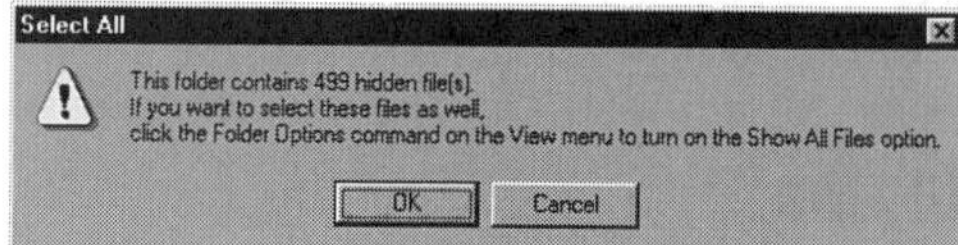

FIG. 12.8
Before you can select all the files in this folder, you must make hidden files visible.

You can use Explorer to change the Read-only, Hidden, and Archive attributes of a file or folder. Right-click the icon, choose Properties, and check or uncheck the appropriate box. Explorer will not enable you to change a file's System attribute, however. If you must perform that task, open an MS-DOS Prompt window and issue the command **ATTRIB –S *filename***. For more information about the `ATTRIB` command, type **ATTRIB /?** at the MS-DOS Prompt.

TIP Do you want to see information about file attributes every time you switch to Details view? Open Explorer and choose View, Folder Options. Click the View tab and scroll through the list of Advanced settings. Check the option labeled Show file attributes in Detail View, and click OK.

Customizing Explorer's Appearance

Like most parts of Windows, Explorer contains a wide array of customization options.

Changing the Width of Panes

To change the proportions of the two panes when using Windows Explorer, point to the vertical dividing line between the panes. When the pointer changes to a two-headed arrow, click and drag in either direction. Release the mouse button when the panes are the desired size.

Changing the Width of Columns

In Details view, Windows uses columns to display information about files, folders, and system objects. To change the width of columns, point to the dividing line between column headings. When the pointer changes to a two-headed arrow, click and drag in either direction. Double-click the dividing line to the right of a column heading to automatically resize the column to match the widest entry in the list.

TROUBLESHOOTING

One or more columns are missing when you switch to Details view. It's possible you resized a column to zero width. To restore the default column widths, click anywhere in the contents pane, and then hold down the Ctrl key and press the + key on the numeric keypad.

Showing and Hiding the Status Bar

The status bar shows important information about the number and size of objects in the current folder, and it works the same in folder windows and in the two-pane Explorer view. To show or hide this screen element, choose View, Status Bar. A check mark next to this menu choice means the status bar should appear at the bottom of the window.

Showing and Hiding Toolbars

By default, the Address bar and the Standard Buttons toolbar (with text labels) appear when you open the two-pane version of Explorer. You can use both screen elements with folder windows, as well. To show or hide either element, choose View, Toolbars, and check or uncheck the Standard Buttons and Address Bar menu choices.

There's no way to customize the buttons on these toolbars, but if you want maximum room to work with files and folders you can hide the text labels on the Standard Buttons toolbar. Choose View, Toolbars, and then remove the check mark from the Text Labels menu choice. The result looks like the window shown in Figure 12.9.

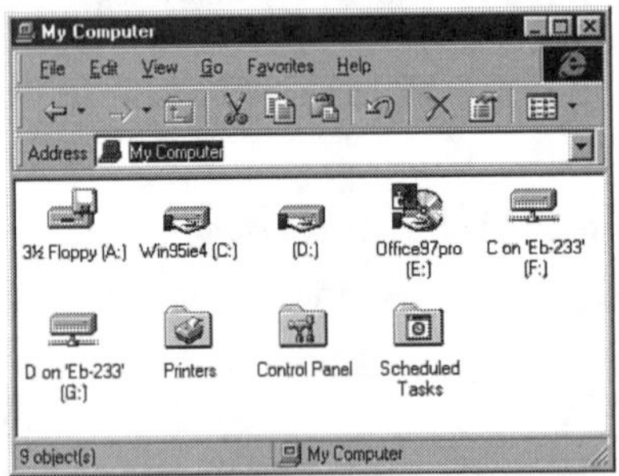

FIG. 12.9
To conserve Explorer space, hide the text labels that normally appear under the toolbar buttons.

Opening Explorer at Specific Folders or Files

The full two-pane Explorer view can be overwhelming, particularly when you just want to reorganize files among a handful of subfolders in a single location. The solution is to create shortcuts for each task. It's possible to launch a copy of Explorer that opens at the location where you want to work. Even better is to restrict the display of objects in the left pane so that it includes only the drives or folders with which you want to work.

If you create a shortcut with only the command `explorer`, you will open the default two-pane Windows Explorer, with all resources visible in the All Folders pane. To reduce the clutter, you need to use command-line switches along with the Explorer command.

Specifically, follow the command with the `/e` switch to force it to open in two-pane mode (use `/n` to specify a single-pane window instead). Normally, Explorer uses the desktop as the root of the All Folders pane, but you can specify any drive or folder to fill this role. When you do, the display becomes much less confusing. Use the `/root,object` switch to restrict the scope of the All Folders pane to the object you specify. In place of the *object*, substitute the name of a network server (in UNC format), a local drive, or a folder.

ON THE WEB

For a detailed explanation of all the options you can use when creating an Explorer shortcut, read the Microsoft Knowledge Base article "Command-Line Switches for Windows Explorer." You'll find it at

http://premium.microsoft.com/support/kb/articles/q130/5/10.asp

To open a two-pane Explorer window that includes only files and folders on the C: drive, for example, follow these steps:

1. Right-click any empty desktop space and choose New, Shortcut. The Create Shortcut Wizard appears.
2. In the box labeled Command line, enter the following command (the spacing and punctuation are crucial):

   explorer /e,/root,c:
3. Click Next, and name the shortcut Explore Drive C.
4. Click Finish. The shortcut appears on the desktop.
5. Open the shortcut to verify that it works. Move or copy the shortcut to another location if you want.

Managing Files and Folders

Although many Windows applications offer basic file management functions, Explorer is the tool you will use most often to organize your files. Regardless of which view you choose, Explorer enables you to create new folders, copy and move files between folders, delete files, and rename files.

Selecting Files and Folders

Before you can perform any action on an object, you must first select it. The procedures for selecting files, folders, and other icons vary, depending on the folder and desktop options you've chosen. If you've chosen the Classic (double-click) interface, you click each icon to select it. If you've chosen the web-style (single-click) interface, on the other hand, simply point at a file to select it. Objects change color to indicate that you've selected them.

▶ **See** "Customizing the Desktop Colors and Background" to adjust the color of selected items with the Display Properties dialog box, **p. 780**

To select multiple icons that are adjacent to one another in a folder window or on the desktop, select the first object, and then hold down the Shift key and select the last object. All the icons in between the two will be selected as well.

To select multiple icons that are not adjacent to one another, select the first one, and then hold down the Ctrl key and select additional objects. To deselect an icon, continue holding down the Ctrl key and select it again.

You can also use marquee selection to quickly select a group of adjacent files by using the mouse. Use this technique to draw an imaginary rectangle around the group of files, as in Figure 12.10—point to one corner of the rectangle, hold down the left mouse button and drag the selection to the opposite corner. This technique works regardless of which icon view you've selected.

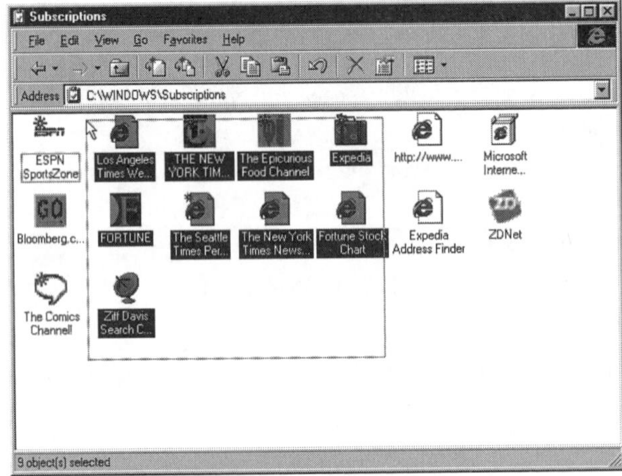

FIG. 12.10
As you draw this rectangle around a group of icons, watch the dotted line. All files within the box are selected.

You can also select multiple icons by using the keyboard. In a two-pane Explorer window, press Tab to move the focus into the contents pane, and then use the arrow keys to move through the list to the first item you want to select. To select a group of adjacent icons, hold down the Shift key and use the arrow keys to move through the list. To use the keyboard to select a group of icons that are not adjacent to one another, select the first file, and then hold down the Ctrl key and use the arrow keys to move through the list; press the Spacebar for each file you want to select.

To quickly select all the files in a folder, choose Edit, Select All (or press Ctrl+A). To remove all current selections, click any empty space, another object in the folder window, or the desktop.

There's a lightning-fast way to select all but a few icons within a folder. This technique comes in handy when you want to archive or delete most of the files in a folder, keeping only a small number of items. Select the objects you plan to keep, and then choose Edit, Invert Selection. You can now use any of the standard Windows techniques to move, copy, or delete the selected objects.

Renaming a File

To rename a file or folder, first select its icon, and then use any of the following options to select the name for editing:

- Press the F2 key.
- Choose File, Rename.
- Right-click the icon and choose Rename from the shortcut menu.

When the label text is selected, type the new name. To save the name, press Enter or click any empty space on the desktop or in a folder window.

Renaming Multiple Files

There is no way to rename more than one file at a time by using Explorer. To accomplish this task, you must open an MS-DOS Prompt window and use the REN (Rename) command.

To rename multiple files with long filenames, use this procedure:

1. Open the Start menu and choose Programs, MS-DOS Prompt.
2. At the MS-DOS prompt, type **CD *pathname*** to switch to the directory that contains the files you want to rename. It might take several repetitions to reach the correct drive and directory.
3. Type **REN *oldname.ext newname.ext***. If either name contains a space, enclose the name and extensions in quotation marks. Press Enter.
4. Use the ? wild card character to match any single letter in the filename; use the * wild card to substitute for any group of characters. For example, if you start with the following group of files:

   05 Sales Forecast.xls

   06 Sales Forecast.xls

   07 Sales Forecast.xls

   08 Sales Forecast.xls

   Enter this command at the MS-DOS prompt to rename them in one operation:

   REN "?? Sales*.*" "?? Mrktg*.*"

   The result will be four files named:

   05 Mrktg Forecast.xls

   06 Mrktg Forecast.xls

   07 Mrktg Forecast.xls

   08 Mrktg Forecast.xls

Creating New Folders

To create a new folder, follow these steps:

1. Select the icon for the drive or folder in which you plan to create the new folder.
2. Right-click the icon or any empty space in the contents pane and choose New, Folder.
3. The new folder has a generic name; to replace it with a more meaningful name, just start typing. When you finish, press Enter to record the new name.

▶ **See** "Working with Long Filenames" to learn the rules for naming folders, **p. 318**

Moving and Copying Files and Folders

With Explorer, the easiest way to move and copy files is not always the surest. When you select one or more objects, hold down the left mouse button, and drag them from one location to another, the results can vary dramatically. The exact effect depends on the location and the type of file. Every time you drag and drop files by using Explorer, one of three things happens:

- When you drag an object from one location to another on the same logical volume, Explorer moves the object. On local drives, each logical volume uses the same drive letter, so dragging a group of icons from C:\Windows\Temp to the Windows desktop moves them to the new location.
- When you drag an object from one logical volume to another, Explorer makes a copy of the file. If you drag a group of icons from C:\Data and drop them on the icon for a floppy disk (A:) or a shared network folder, Explorer leaves the original files untouched and creates copies in the new location.
- When you drag a program file from one location to another, regardless of location, Explorer creates a shortcut, leaving the original file untouched.

There are solid logical reasons for this default behavior, but the results can be confusing for novice users. Even experienced Windows users can sometimes stumble over these rules. For example, if you drag multiple program icons from a folder onto the desktop, Explorer creates a group of shortcuts; but if you select even one icon that isn't a program, you get a move or a copy instead.

The best way to predict what Explorer will do when you drag and drop icons is to examine the mouse pointer before you release the mouse button. If you see a plus sign just to the right of the pointer, as in Figure 12.11, you can expect a copy; a small arrow next the pointer means you'll get a shortcut, and a plain pointer means you're about to move the selected objects. If the pointer you see doesn't match the result you intend, press Esc before releasing the mouse button to abort the move or copy.

FIG. 12.11
The small plus sign next to the mouse pointer means you're about to make a copy of this icon.

For maximum control over the results of drag-and-drop operations, select one or more objects and hold down the right mouse button when dragging. When you release the button, Windows pops up a shortcut menu like the one in Figure 12.12. The default action appears in bold type, but you can choose any of the three actions or cancel the whole operation, if you prefer.

FIG. 12.12
When you hold down the right mouse button while dragging files, Windows enables you to choose the result you prefer from this shortcut menu.

Dragging and Dropping Files Between Folders The easiest way to move or copy files between folders is to open two folder windows and arrange them side by side. Follow this procedure to let Windows position two folder windows automatically:

1. Minimize or close all open windows. The easiest way to accomplish this task is to click the Show Desktop button on the Quick Launch toolbar.
2. Open both folder windows so that they're visible on the desktop.
3. Right-click any empty space on the taskbar and choose Tile Windows Vertically from the shortcut menu. Windows arranges both windows so that each occupies exactly half the display.

If you inadvertently left an extra window open on the desktop before attempting this procedure, right-click an empty space on the taskbar, choose Undo Tile, and try again.

To move or copy files from one folder window to another, select the icon or icons and drag them to any empty space in the destination folder.

To quickly copy one or more files to a floppy disk, select the icon(s) in an Explorer window, right-click, and choose Send To from the shortcut menu. Choose the floppy drive from the submenu.

Dragging and Dropping Files in Explorer View To move or copy files by using the two-pane Explorer view, follow these steps:

1. Open Windows Explorer. In the All Folders pane, select the icon for the folder that contains the files you want to move or copy.
2. In the contents pane, select the icon or icons to move or copy.
3. Hold down the right mouse button and drag the icon(s) on top of the folder icon in the left pane. If the icon for the destination folder is not visible, let the mouse pointer hover over the parent icon for a second or two; the branch expands automatically.

4. When the pointer is over the icon for the destination folder, release the mouse button.
5. Choose the appropriate action—Move, Copy, or Create Shortcut(s)—from the menu that appears.

Using Cut, Copy, and Paste Explorer offers one final option for moving and copying files that doesn't involve dragging and dropping. Use the Windows Clipboard to cut, copy, and paste files between folders and drives in exactly the same way you copy text and graphics between documents. These techniques work equally well in Explorer windows, folder windows, email messages, and on the Windows desktop.

To copy, move, or create shortcuts by using the Clipboard, follow this procedure:

1. Select the file or files.
2. To copy a file from one folder to another, use the Copy command; to move a file, use the Cut command. Any of the following mouse or keyboard techniques will work:

   Choose Edit, Copy or Edit, Cut.

   Right-click the selected icon and choose Copy or Cut.

   Press Ctrl+C (Copy) or Ctrl+X (Cut).

   Click the Copy or Cut buttons on the Explorer toolbar.

3. Display the contents of the destination folder and use any of the following commands to complete the move or copy:

   Choose Edit, Paste.

   Right-click the folder icon or the contents pane and choose Paste.

   Right-click the folder icon or the contents pane and press Ctrl+V.

   Click the Paste button on the Explorer toolbar.

Copying Disks

It's impractical to copy an entire hard disk or CD-ROM, but it's ridiculously easy to copy a floppy disk. Windows includes a utility that handles the whole process in two passes—one for the source (original) disk, the second pass for the destination (copy) disk. To copy a floppy, make sure you have a formatted disk that's the same size as the original you plan to copy, and then follow these steps:

1. Insert the original disk in the floppy drive.
2. Open the My Computer window or Windows Explorer, right-click the floppy drive icon (normally A:), and choose Copy Disk. If you have only one drive that handles the selected disk format, the same drive letter will appear in the Copy from and Copy to areas of the dialog box. If you have more than one such drive, select the destination drive in the Copy to box; if this is a different drive, insert the destination disk in that drive.
3. The Copy Disk dialog box (see Figure 12.13) appears. Click Start, and Windows reads the entire contents of the disk into memory.

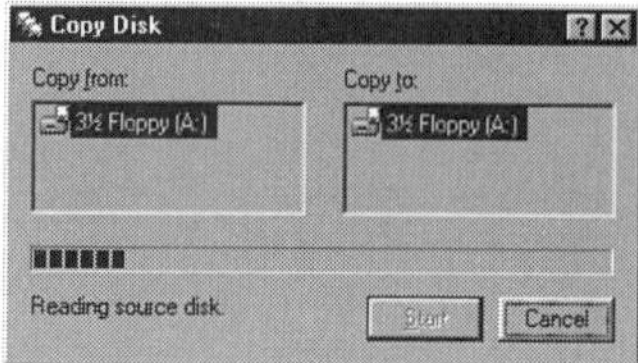

FIG. 12.13
Follow the prompts to duplicate a floppy disk.

4. If you're copying from one physical drive to another, Windows handles the operation in one pass. On most systems, where there is only a single floppy drive, you see a prompt when the Copy from phase is complete. Remove the original disk, insert the destination disk into the drive, and click OK.
5. Windows transfers the stored data to the destination disk; if the disk requires formatting, that happens automatically. When the copy is complete, you see a message at the bottom of the Copy Disk dialog box.
6. To copy another floppy, remove the destination disk, insert another source disk, and repeat steps 3–5. When you finish, click Close.

CAUTION

Windows will erase a destination disk without prompting you, which can be disastrous if the destination disk contains important data. If you store important files on floppy disks, always use the write-protect tab to prevent accidental erasure.

Deleting Files and Folders

To delete one or more files or folders, select the icons and then use any of the following techniques:

- Press the Del key.
- Choose File, Delete from the pull-down Explorer menu.
- Right-click and choose Delete.
- Drag the icon(s) and drop them on the Recycle Bin icon.
- To delete files completely without using the Recycle Bin, hold down the Shift key while you press the Del key or choose Delete from the right-click shortcut menu.

Normally, when you delete one or more files or folders, Windows pops up a Confirm File Delete dialog box. You can turn off the dialog box that asks whether you're sure you want to send the files to the Recycle Bin; when you bypass the Recycle Bin, though, you must deal with the dialog box shown in Figure 12.14.

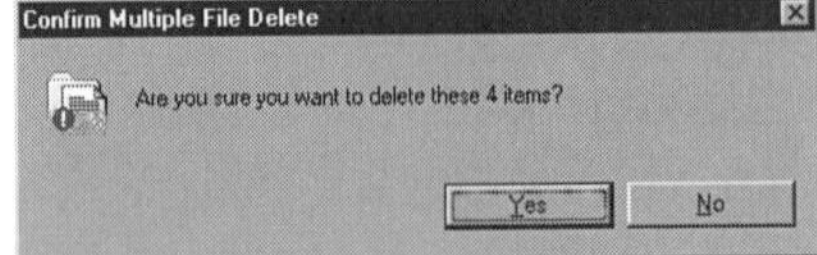

FIG. 12.14
When you bypass the Recycle Bin, Windows forces you to deal with this dialog box.

CAUTION

When you delete a folder, you also delete all files and subfolders within that folder. Check the contents carefully before you trash an entire folder.

Undoing Changes

Windows enables you to undo the last three actions you perform when working with the Windows Explorer. If you inadvertently delete a file, move it to the wrong location, or make a mistake when renaming a file or folder, click the Undo button on the Standard Buttons toolbar or press Ctrl+Z.

It's not always easy to tell exactly what Undo will accomplish, and there's no Redo option to restore your original action. Within an Explorer window, look at the top of the Edit menu to see what Windows can undo; likely choices include Undo Delete, Undo Move, and Undo Rename.

Although it's not obvious, the Undo shortcuts work if you make a mistake on the Windows Desktop as well. If you inadvertently move or delete a desktop file by mistake, press Ctrl+Z immediately to recover.

Using the Recycle Bin

The Windows Recycle Bin can't prevent every file-management disaster, but it can help you recover when you inadvertently delete a crucial file. When you delete a local file by using the Windows Explorer, it doesn't actually disappear; instead, the Recycle Bin intercepts and stores it. The file remains there until you empty the Recycle Bin or it's displaced by a newer deleted file. As long as that file remains in the Recycle Bin, you can recover it intact.

CAUTION

The Recycle Bin is far from perfect, and every Windows user should be aware of its limitations. When you use a network connection to delete files on another computer or when you delete files on a floppy disk or other removable media, they are not saved in the Recycle Bin. Likewise, using the DEL command from an MS-DOS Prompt removes the files permanently, without storing safe copies in the Recycle Bin. And when you overwrite a file with another file of the same name, the old file does not go into the Recycle Bin. If these limitations disturb you, check out Norton Utilities and other third-party programs, which can expand the capabilities of the Recycle Bin to cover some of these situations.

Recovering a Deleted File To recover a deleted file, open the Recycle Bin (you can find its icon in the My Computer folder and on the desktop). Browse its contents until you find the file or files fo which you're looking. To return the file to its original location, right-click and choose Restore from the shortcut menu. To restore the file to an alternate location, such as the Windows desktop, drag the icon or icons to the location where you want to restore them.

Changing the Size of the Recycle Bin By default, the Recycle Bin sets aside 10 percent of the space on every local hard disk for storing deleted files. If your hard disk is nearly full, that might be too much; on the other hand, if you have ample disk space, you might want to reserve more space for the Recycle Bin. On systems with more than one drive, you can choose different Recycle Bin settings for each drive.

To adjust the Recycle Bin's appetite, follow these steps:

1. Right-click the Recycle Bin icon and choose Properties from the shortcut menu. You see a dialog box like the one in Figure 12.15.
2. Each drive will have its own tab in the dialog box. Use the option at the top of the Global tab to specify whether you want to configure the drives independently or use one setting for all drives.
3. Use the slider control on the Global tab to change the percentage of disk space reserved for the Recycle Bin (adjust this setting on each of the dialog boxes for individual drives). You might choose any setting between 0–100 percent, although the most realistic settings are between 3–20 percent.
4. To stop using the Recycle Bin completely, check the box labeled Do not move files to the Recycle Bin.
5. To avoid seeing the confirmation dialog box every time you move a file to the Recycle Bin, clear the check mark from the box labeled Display delete confirmation dialog box.
6. Click OK to save your changes and close the dialog box.

FIG. 12.15
The default setting uses 10 percent of hard disk space for storing deleted files; use this dialog box to adjust this setting.

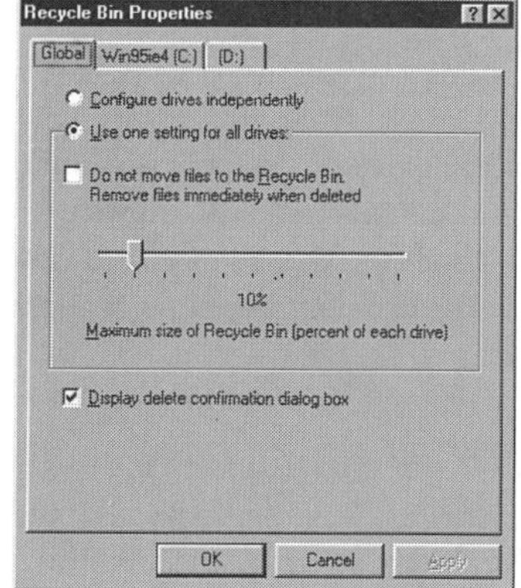

Emptying the Recycle Bin Under normal circumstances, you shouldn't need to delete the Recycle Bin. When it fills up, Windows automatically deletes the oldest files to make room for new files you delete. If you run short of hard disk space—when installing a new program, for example—you might need to clear out the Recycle Bin to make room. To delete all files from the Recycle Bin, right-click its icon and choose Empty Recycle Bin.

Previewing a Document with Quick View

Even the most compulsive file-naming system can't tell you exactly what's in every file on your hard drive. By using Windows Explorer, you can examine a file's name, type, size, and the date it was last modified. But to see the contents of a file, you must open it with its associated application—or use Windows' Quick View utility to peek inside.

To view the contents of a file, right-click the file and choose Quick View. When you do, you see a window like the one in Figure 12.16.

▶ **See** "Keeping Your Copy of Windows 95 Up to Date" to install Quick View, **p. 21**

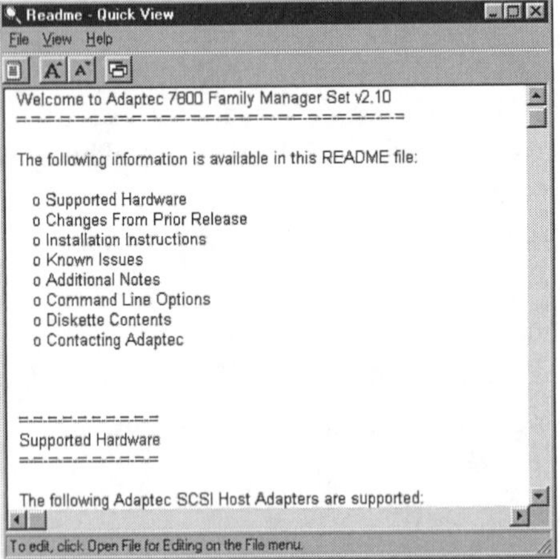

FIG. 12.16
Use the Quick View utility to see the contents of a file without opening it.

Although Quick View is useful, it's far from perfect. It supports a limited number of file types, for example, and you can't copy the file's contents to the Windows Clipboard or print the file. The Quick View version included with Windows 95 enables you to view simple text and graphics files and those created by some word processing programs; it doesn't support Office 97 applications, unfortunately.

ON THE WEB

If you use Quick View regularly, consider purchasing the full commercial version from its developer, Inso software. Quick View Plus adds support for hundreds of file types, including Office 97. It also enables you to copy text and graphics to the Windows Clipboard or send a file directly to a printer without having to open the application. For more details, go to

http://www.inso.com

Using Shortcuts

The files you use most often are scattered across your hard disk in a variety of folders. When you set up a new program, its files go in their own folders, and you organize data files by using whatever system makes most sense—by project, date, or department, for example. If you had to root through folders and subfolders every time you wanted to open a document or launch a program, you'd hardly have any time to get work done.

So how do you maintain an orderly filing system and still keep programs and documents close at hand? The solution is to use shortcuts. As the name implies, shortcuts are pointer files that enable you to access a file without moving the file or creating a copy of it. You can create shortcuts for almost any object in Windows, including programs, data files, folders, drives, Dial-Up Networking connections, printers, and web pages. Windows uses shortcuts extensively: Every item in the Programs folder on your Start menu is a shortcut, for example, and every time you save a web address to your Favorites folder, you create an Internet shortcut. Learning how to create and manage shortcuts is a crucial step in mastering Windows.

How Shortcuts Work

Shortcuts are small files that contain all the information Windows needs to create a link to a *target file*. The shortcut uses the same icon as the target file, with one crucial difference: a small arrow in the lower-right corner that identifies the icon as a shortcut rather than the original.

When you right-click a shortcut, the available menu choices are the same as if you had right-clicked the target file. Opening the shortcut has the same effect as opening the target file.

Shortcuts are a tremendous productivity aid. If you have a document file stored six subfolders deep, for example, you can create a shortcut icon and store it on the desktop, where it's always accessible. The target file remains in its original location.

You can create many shortcuts to the same file. For your favorite programs, you might create shortcuts on the desktop, on the Start menu, and on the Quick Launch bar. Each shortcut takes up a negligible amount of disk space (typically no more than 500 bytes), even if the original file occupies several megabytes of disk space.

What happens when you attempt to launch the target file by using its shortcut icon? Windows is intelligent enough to re-establish the link to the target file even if you've moved or renamed the original, following these steps:

1. Windows looks at the static location (the filename and path), whether the file is stored locally or on a network.
2. If that file no longer exists, Windows checks to see whether you've renamed the file, looking in the same folder for a file with the same date and time stamp but a different name.

3. If that search fails, Windows checks to see whether you moved the file, looking in all subfolders of the target folder and then searching the entire drive. (On a network location, the search extends to the highest parent directory to which you have access rights.) If you move the target file to a different drive, Windows can't find it, and the shortcut breaks.
4. If Windows can't find the target file, it tries to identify the nearest matching file, and you see a dialog box like the one in Figure 12.17. Confirm the choice if it's correct; otherwise, choose No, and then delete the shortcut and re-create it by using the correct file.

▶ **See** "Starting Programs from a Shortcut Icon," **p. 252**

▶ **See** "Using Internet Shortcuts," **p. 456**

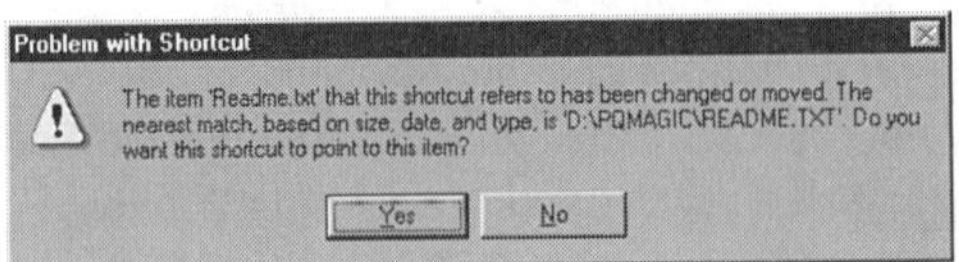

FIG. 12.17 If Windows can't locate the target file for a shortcut, it suggests the closest matching file.

Creating a New Shortcut

The easiest way to create a new shortcut is with the help of the Create Shortcut Wizard. Follow these steps:

1. Right-click an empty space on the Windows desktop and choose New, Shortcut. You see the dialog box shown in Figure 12.18.

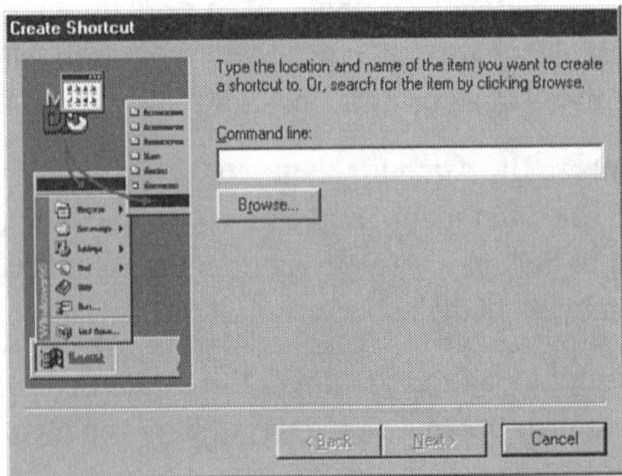

FIG. 12.18 Creating a new shortcut is a two-step process with this wizard.

2. Click the Browse button and select the document or program file from the Browse list. To create a shortcut to a drive or folder, you must type its name directly in the box labeled Command line. Include the full path, if necessary. Click Next.
3. Give the shortcut a descriptive name and click Finish. Test the shortcut to make sure it works correctly.

You can also create a shortcut from an icon. Select the icon in an Explorer window, hold down the right mouse button, and drag the icon to the desktop or another folder. Choose Create Shortcut(s) Here from the menu that pops up.

▶ **See** "Setting the Properties for a Shortcut Icon," **p. 254**

Deleting a Shortcut

To delete a shortcut, use any of the techniques described earlier in this chapter. When you delete a shortcut, you remove only the link to the target file. The target file remains intact in its original location. ●

CHAPTER 13

Advanced File Management Techniques

by Ed Bott

In this chapter

Associating Files with Programs

When you attempt to open an icon, Windows checks the file's extension against a database of registered file types to determine what action it should take. A registered file type can have multiple actions, all of which are available on the right-click shortcut menus; Windows uses the default action when you launch the icon. If Windows does not recognize the file type, it offers a dialog box that enables you to choose which application to use with the file you've selected.

File extensions have been around since the very first version of DOS. Beginning with the first release of Windows 95, Microsoft began tracking file types, as well. File types are inextricably linked to file extensions, but the relationship isn't always easy to understand. Here are the essential facts you need to know:

- File types typically have friendly names (HTML Document), whereas extensions are typically three or four letters (HTM or HTML).
- File types are visible in their own columns when you choose Details view in the Windows Explorer; extensions for registered file types are hidden by default. You can also inspect a file's properties to see which file type is associated with it. The extension for an unregistered file type is always visible in the Explorer list.
- Every file type has an associated icon, which appears when you view files of that type in the Windows Explorer or a folder window.
- Every unique file extension is associated with one and only one file type. After you install Microsoft Word, for example, Windows associates the DOC extension with the Microsoft Word Document file type.
- A file type, on the other hand, can be associated with multiple extensions. The HTML Document file type works with the HTM and HTML extensions, for example, and JPEG images can end with the extension JPE, JPEG, or JPG.
- As the previous examples illustrate, a file extension can be more than three letters long.
- Windows common dialog boxes (File Open and File Save As) include a drop-down list that enables you to choose a file type; Windows adds the default extension for the file type automatically when you save a document.
- A Windows filename might contain more than one period. Windows defines the extension as all characters that appear after the last period in the filename.

Most application programs handle the details of registering file types and associations when you install them. Creating a file type manually or editing an existing file type is a cumbersome and difficult process best reserved for expert users as a last resort.

TROUBLESHOOTING

Your document appears to have the correct extension, but when you try to open it, the wrong application launches. You or another user tried to add or change the file extension manually, by adding a period and the extension. The associated program added its own (hidden) extension as well, resulting in a filename such as Letter.doc.rtf. To see the full name, including extension, choose View, Folder Options, click the View tab, and remove the check mark next to the option labeled Hide File Extensions for Known File Types. The file extension is now visible and editable. Be sure to restore this option after you repair the problem file.

Viewing File Associations

To see a list of all registered file types, open the Windows Explorer or any folder window (including My Computer). Choose View, Folder Options, and click the File Types tab. You will see a list like the one in Figure 13.1.

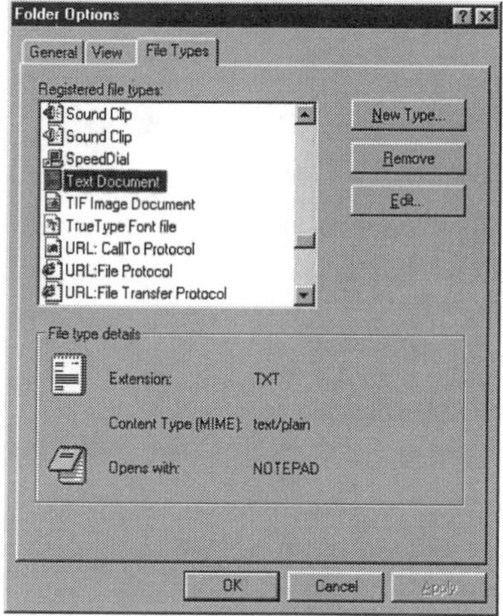

FIG. 13.1
Use this list of registered file types to see which applications are associated with different file types.

The list is arranged in alphabetical order by file type. As you scroll through the list, note that the details in the dialog box change. For each entry in the list, you can view the registered file extensions, the MIME details, and the name of the associated application.

CAUTION

Multipurpose Internet Mail Extensions (MIME) are the standards that define how browsers and mail software should handle file attachments. Do not adjust these settings in the File Types dialog box unless you are certain the changes will produce the correct result. Unnecessary tinkering with these settings can result in unreadable mail and web pages.

Changing File Associations

Windows enables you to associate only one program with each action for each file type. In most cases, when two applications claim the right to edit or open a given file type, the one you installed most recently claims that file type as its own. When a newly installed program "hijacks" a file type, you might want to restore the association with the older application. There are two ways to accomplish this goal:

- Reinstall the original program. The setup process typically edits the Windows Registry and adjusts file associations. If the setup program was written correctly, you will not lose any custom settings or data.
- Edit the file type directly, changing the associated program to the one you prefer. To do so, follow these steps:

    1. Open the Windows Explorer or any folder window (including My Computer) and choose View, Folder Options. Click the File Types tab.
    2. Select the file type you want to change and click the Edit button. The Edit File Type dialog box appears (see Figure 13.2).

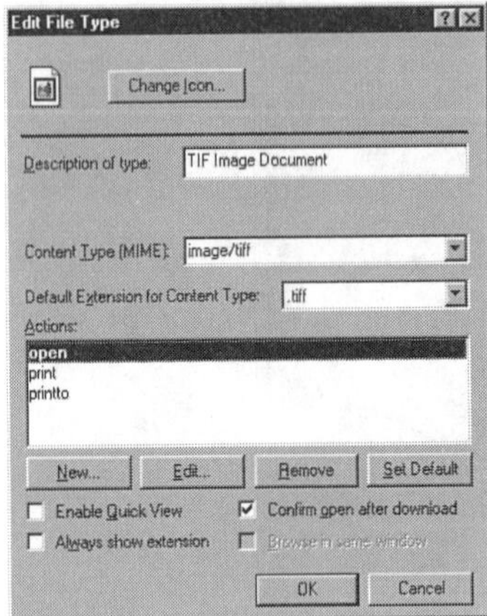

FIG. 13.2 Exercise caution when manually editing file types. A wrong setting in this dialog box can hinder your ability to work with common document types.

    3. Select an entry from the Actions list—the default action is in bold type—and click the Edit button. The dialog box shown in Figure 13.3 appears.

FIG. 13.3 Change the program listed here to adjust how Windows works with a given file type.

Editing action for type: Saved Search

Action: open

Application used to perform action: C:\WINDOWS\Explorer.exe

OK | Cancel | Browse...

Use DDE

DDE Message: [OpenFindFile("%1", %I)]

Application: Folders

DDE Application Not Running:

Topic: AppProperties

CAUTION

Note that some actions require Dynamic Data Exchange (DDE), an extremely complex process that passes information between multiple programs; if you see these options listed, exit this dialog box and don't attempt to edit the action by hand.

4. Click the Browse button and find the executable (EXE) file for the program you want to use with the selected action. Click Open to insert the filename into the box labeled Application Used to Perform Action.
5. Click OK to close the Edit Action dialog box and save your change.
6. Repeat steps 3–5 for other actions you want to change. When you've finished, click OK to close the Edit File Type dialog box, and click OK again to close the Folder Options dialog box.

Three options in the Edit File Type dialog box are worth noting here:

- Choose an action and click the Set Default button to make this the default action for the file type. The previous default action still appears as a choice on right-click shortcut menus.
- Check the box labeled Enable Quick View to control whether or not you see a Quick View choice on the shortcut menu for the selected file type.
- Check the box labeled Always Show Extension to display the file's extension in all Explorer and folder windows. This setting is useful if you regularly change the extensions of certain types of documents (such as RTF documents created by Office 97) but don't want to clutter the Explorer window with other extensions.

CAUTION

It's possible to completely eliminate a file type or an action associated with this file type. Generally, however, this drastic step is not recommended. The settings for each file type take up a trivial amount of space in the Windows Registry, and removing a file type can cause installed programs to fail.

Using an Alternate Program to Open a Registered File Type

You might have several programs at your disposal to view or edit a particular type of file. For example, FrontPage Express and Microsoft Word both enable you to edit HTML files. Unfortunately, Windows forces you to associate one and only one program with the default action for each registered file type. However, you can override that default decision at any time and choose which program you want to use for a given file icon. Follow these steps:

1. Select the document icon, hold down the Shift key, and right-click. The shortcut menu that appears includes a new Open With choice, not found on the default menu.
2. Choose Open With from the shortcut menu. The dialog box shown in Figure 13.4 appears.

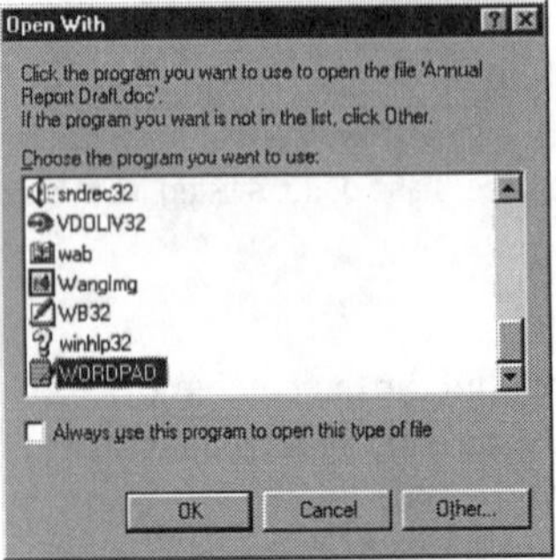

FIG. 13.4
Use this dialog box to open a document with the application of your choice instead of the default program.

3. Scroll through the list and find the program you want to use. Note that the list shows only the short names of executable files (Winword, for example) rather than the long name of the application (Microsoft Word).
4. If the program appears in the list, select its entry. If you can't find its entry, click the Other button, browse for the program's executable file, and then click Open.
5. Before you click OK, note the check box labeled Always Use This Program to Open This Type of File. By default, this box is unchecked. Do *not* add a check mark unless you want to change the program associated with the Open action for this type of file.
6. Click OK to open the document.

▶ **See** "Customizing the Shortcut (Right-Click) Menu," **p. 772**

Opening an Unrecognized File Type

When you attempt to open the icon for an unrecognized file type, Windows displays an Open With dialog box similar to the one shown in Figure 13.4. Note that there are two crucial differences between this dialog box and the one that appears with a recognized file type. These changes are designed to let you quickly create a new file type for the unrecognized type:

- This Open With dialog box includes a text box at the top. Enter the name of the new file type here.
- By default, there is a check mark in the box labeled Always Use This Program to Open This Type of File. Remove this check mark if you don't want to create a new file type.

If you inadvertently create a new file type by using this dialog box, it's easy to remove it. Open the Folder Options dialog box, click the File Types tab, select the newly created file type, and click the Remove button.

Finding Files

On a hard disk with a capacity measured in gigabytes, it's possible to store tens of thousands of files in hundreds or even thousands of folders. So it shouldn't be surprising that you occasionally lose track of one of those files. Fortunately, Windows includes a handy utility that enables you to hunt down misplaced files, even if you can't remember the file's exact name. You can search for a portion of the name or use other details, including the size and type of the file, the date it was created, or a fragment of text within the file.

Finding a File or Folder by Name

To begin searching for a file on a local disk or on a shared network drive, click the Start button and choose Find, Files or Folders. If the Windows Explorer is open, choose Tools, Find, Files or Folders. You see a dialog box like the one in Figure 13.5.

FIG. 13.5
Use the Find utility to search for any file, anywhere on your computer or across a network.

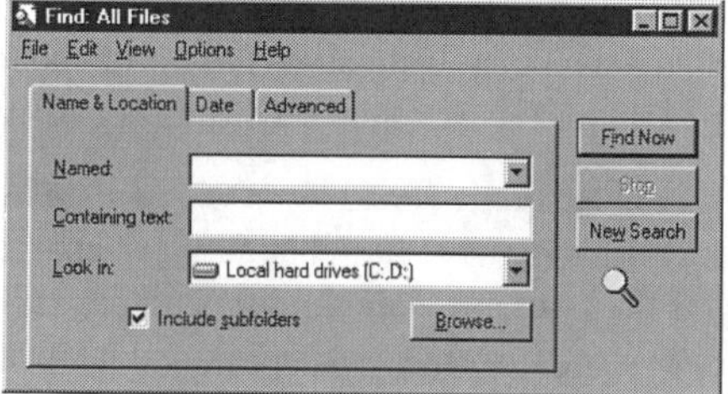

The most common type of search enables you to look for a file when you remember all or part of the name.

1. Click the box labeled Named and enter all or part of the filename. (The file extension is not necessary.)

DOS-style wildcards (* and ?) are not required in the Named box, but they can be extremely useful in helping you reduce the number of matches. For example, if you enter the letter **b**, Windows returns all files that include that letter anywhere in the name. On the other hand, **b*** finds only files that begin with that letter, and **b???.*** returns only files that begin with the letter *b* and contain exactly four characters, not counting the extension.

2. Tell Windows in which drives and folders you want to look. If you opened Find from the Windows Explorer, the Look In box includes the name of the currently selected drive or folder; otherwise, this entry shows the location you specified when you last used Find. Enter a folder name directly (C:\Data, for example), or click the Browse button to choose a folder name, or use the drop-down Explorer-style list to select any of the following default locations:
    - The Windows Desktop
    - The My Documents folder
    - Any local or mapped network drive
    - Local hard drives
    - My Computer (searches all local hard drives, as well as floppy and CD-ROM drives)

You can specify multiple locations in the Look In box. Enter the full path, including drive letter or UNC-style server and share name, for each location. Separate the entries in this list with semicolons. For more information about UNC-style names, see "Understanding the UNC (Universal Naming Convention)," in Chapter 39, "Connecting Windows 95 to Windows NT Server 4.0."

3. To search in all subfolders of the location you selected, place a check mark in the box labeled Include Subfolders.
4. Click Find Now to begin searching.

The more details you provide, the more restrictive the results will be. But don't provide too much information, or there's a good chance that you will miss the file for which you're looking, especially if the spelling of the filename is even slightly different from what you enter.

Windows compares the text you enter in the Named box with the names of every file and folder in the specified location, returning a result if that string of characters appears anywhere in the filename. Entering **log** as the search parameter, for example, will turn up all files that contain the words *log, logo, catalog,* or *technology,* as in Figure 13.6. Search results appear in a pane at the bottom of the Find dialog box.

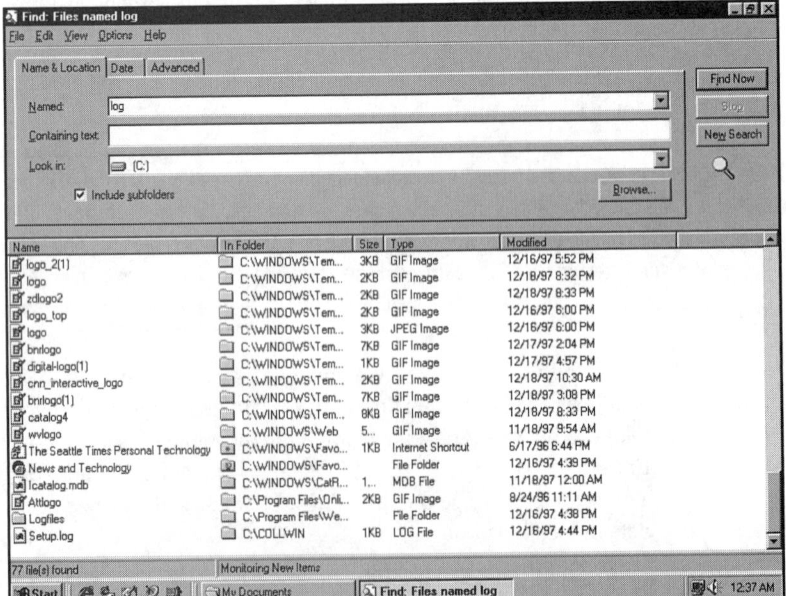

FIG. 13.6 The Find utility returns all filenames that include the characters you enter. Click any column heading to sort the results.

By default, the results list appears in Details view; right-click the results pane and use the shortcut menu to change to a different view. Click column headings to sort results by name, size, type, the date the files were last modified, or the folder in which the files are stored. Click again to sort in reverse order.

After you've completed a Find, look at the status bar at the bottom of the window. The message `Monitoring New Items` means that Windows continues to watch your actions and updates the results list automatically as you create, rename, move, and delete files that match the specified criteria.

Advanced Search Techniques

The Find utility is fast and extremely effective, even when you haven't the vaguest idea what the target file is named. Advanced options enable you to search by using other criteria.

If you have a general idea of when you created a file or when you last edited it, click the Date tab and narrow the search by date. Spinners enable you to specify ranges of dates by day or month: To find all files you worked with yesterday or today, for example, click the Find All Files option, choose Modified from the drop-down list, and choose the option During the Previous 1 Day(s). You can also specify a range of dates here, as illustrated in Figure 13.7.

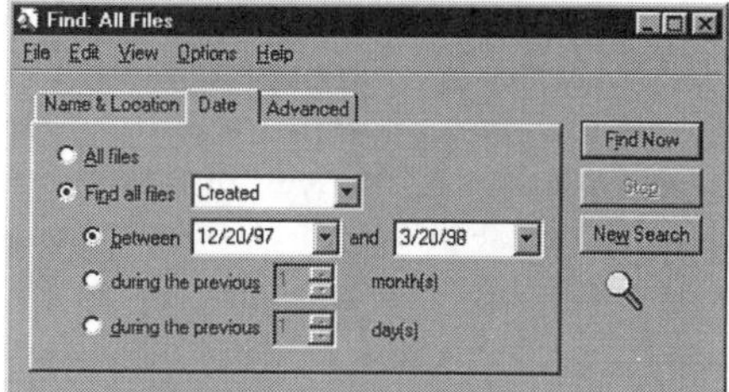

FIG. 13.7 Narrow down your search by entering a range of dates.

You can type dates into this dialog box, but it's far easier to use the built-in calendar controls that appear when you click drop-down arrows in date boxes, as shown in Figure 13.8. Click the month heading to produce a menu of months; click the year to reveal a spinner control that enables you to quickly adjust the year.

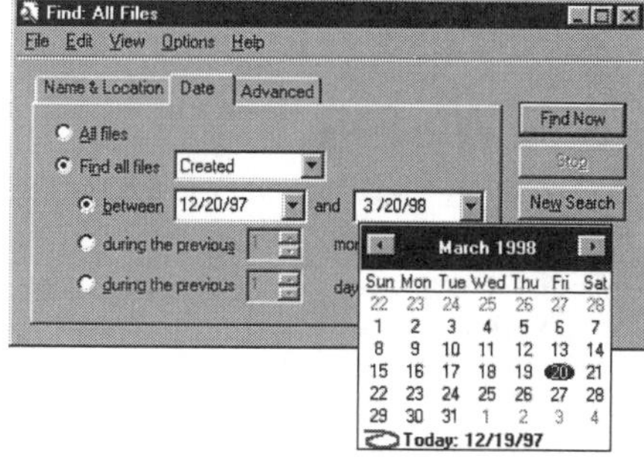

FIG. 13.8 This calendar appears automatically when you click the drop-down arrow.

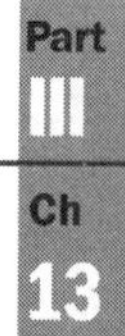

Click the Advanced tab to search for files by type and by size, as shown in the example in Figure 13.9. Note that this dialog box enables you to select only registered file types. Because it requires you to enter size parameters in kilobytes, be sure to multiply by 1000 when specifying megabytes.

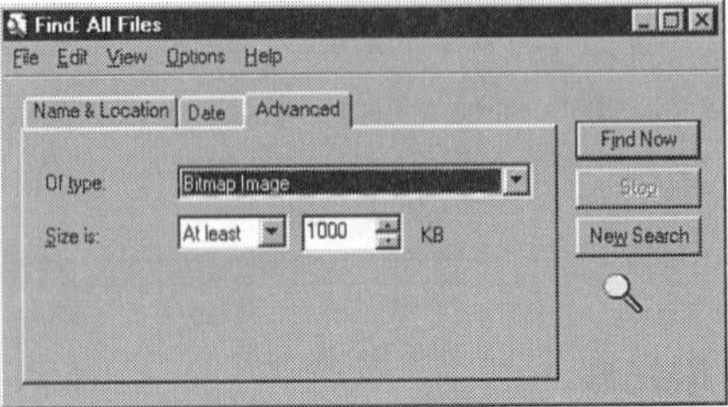

FIG. 13.9
This set of search criteria enables you to hunt down large graphics files.

Use the Find utility to organize and archive files. For example, you can search for all Microsoft Word files modified more than 6 months ago, and then move the results to a backup disk or to a network folder. You also can use advanced Find parameters to search for files larger than 1MB in size. If you leave all boxes blank and check the Include Subfolders option, the resulting list will include all files on your computer, up to a maximum of 10,000. You can sort that list to find files of a certain type or size.

With the help of the Find utility, you also can search for text within files. Obviously, it won't do you much good to search for common words such as "the," but if you remember a specific phrase that appears in a lost document, you can have Windows track down all files that contain that phrase. To look for a draft of your company's annual report, for example, click the Name & Location tab and enter *annual report* in the box labeled Containing Text. Click the Find Now button to begin searching. Note that text searches can take a very long time, especially on large hard disks or across a network.

Combine settings from the Find dialog box to narrow down your search for a specific file. For example, you might order Windows to search for a Microsoft Word document that contains the phrase *annual report* and was last modified in February, 1998. With those specifics, you have a good chance of finding the file for which you're looking, even if you can't remember what you named it.

If the search didn't find the file for which you were looking, modify the criteria and click the Find Now button again. To clear all criteria and start from scratch, click the New Search button.

Managing Files from the Find Window

Because the Find dialog box is actually a specially modified version of the Windows Explorer, you can use the results pane for virtually any file management task. Right-click any icon to display shortcut menus that include file management options, or drag items from the results pane and drop them anywhere, including a folder window, the Windows Explorer, the desktop, or an email message.

Use the File menu or right-click for these choices:

- Open
- Quick View
- Send To

- Cut and Copy (available only from shortcut menu)
- Create Shortcut
- Delete
- Rename
- Properties

The Find utility includes an extremely powerful feature that's so well hidden even many Windows experts don't know it exists. Select any file in the results pane and choose File, Open Containing Folder. This choice, available only from the main menu and not from the right-click shortcut menus, opens a folder window for the folder containing the file you selected.

Saving and Reusing a Search

If you find yourself performing the same search regularly, save the search criteria as an icon so that you can reuse it later. To save a search, follow these steps:

1. After you've completed your search, choose File, Save Search. You won't be prompted for a name or location; instead, Windows automatically creates a saved search icon on the desktop.
2. Close the Find window and locate the new Saved Search icon on the desktop. The icon has a descriptive name drawn from the title bar of the search. Rename the icon, if you want. You also can copy or move the icon to any other location, including the Start menu.
3. To reuse a saved search, double-click its icon and click the Find Now button.

CAUTION

When you reuse a saved search, the results are not up-to-date. The Options menu in the Find dialog box includes a Save Results menu item, but checking this option might not have the effect you expect. Save Results keeps the search results pane open with the names of the files you found. The next time you use that saved search, the results pane reappears, but the contents will not reflect files you've added, deleted, or renamed since you last used the search. To update the list, click the Find Now button.

Working with Compressed Files

File compression utilities make it possible to pack large files into small spaces. They also enable you to store large numbers of files in a single archive. Windows 95 users typically encounter compressed files in one of two formats:

- Setup files for Windows 95 and other Microsoft products are stored in Cabinet format—you can recognize these files by the .Cab extension. Microsoft's Setup program processes cabinet files automatically, without requiring any utilities.
- The Zip compression format is a widely used standard for distributing files over the Internet. Windows does not include support for Zip files.

Windows includes a command-line utility that enables you to pull one or more compressed files out of a cabinet. This capability is useful when you need to replace a lost or corrupted system file without reinstalling Windows. This Extract tool also enables you to list the files in a cabinet so you can determine the exact location of the file for which you're looking. To see detailed instructions on this command, open an MS-DOS Prompt window, type **EXTRACT /?**, and press Enter.

ON THE WEB

If you regularly work with cabinet files, you'll appreciate the CabView utility, included as part of the Windows 95 PowerToys collection. It enables you to open cabinet files from any Explorer or folder window and manage the compressed files as though they were in a folder. You can find CabView at

http://www.microsoft.com/windows95/info/powertoys.htm

Although there are many utilities that enable you to work with Zip files, the best by far is WinZip, from Nico Mak Computing. Download the shareware version from

http://www.winzip.com

Working with Long Filenames

Windows enables you to create names for files and folders using up to 255 characters. Legal filenames might contain spaces and most special characters, including periods, commas, semicolons, parentheses, brackets ([]), and dollar signs. You are not allowed to use the following characters when naming a file or folder:

```
:  '  " \  /  *  ?  ¦
```

How Windows Generates Short Filenames

Because Windows 95 maintains backward compatibility with older operating systems and applications, the file system automatically generates short filenames from long names you create. Although this process happens in the background, it's important to understand how the rules work.

When you save a file by using Windows 95 or a 32-bit Windows application, Windows checks the filename you enter. If the name is a legal MS-DOS compatible name, with no spaces or other illegal characters, no more than 8 characters in the name, and no more than 3 characters in the extension, the short filename is the same as the long filename.

If the long filename contains spaces or other illegal characters or is longer than 8 characters, Windows uses the following rules to create a short filename:

1. Remove all spaces and other illegal characters, as well as all periods except the rightmost one.
2. Truncate the long filename to six characters, if necessary, and append a tilde (~) followed by a single-digit number. If this procedure duplicates an existing filename,

increase the number by one: ~1, ~2, ~3, and so on. If necessary, truncate the long filename to five characters, followed by a tilde and a two-digit numeric tail.

3. Truncate the file extension to the first three characters. If the long filename does not include a period, the short filename will have no extension.
4. Change all lowercase letters to capital letters.

CAUTION

Several books and computer magazines have published details for adjusting a Registry setting (NameNumericTail) that controls the way in which Windows automatically generates short filenames from long filenames you create. Do not make this change! The result can seriously affect the operation of some Windows accessories that depend on the Program Files folder. For more details on this problem, open **http://support.microsoft.com** and search for Knowledge Base article Q148594.

There is no way for the user to change the automatically generated short filename. To see the MS-DOS compatible name for any file, right-click its icon, choose Properties, and click the General tab.

Using Long Filenames with Older Windows and DOS Programs

If you use 16-bit Windows programs, you cannot see long filenames in common dialog boxes such as File Open and File Save As. Instead, you see the truncated short version of all filenames. You see the same results if you use the old-style Windows File Manager, as in Figure 13.10.

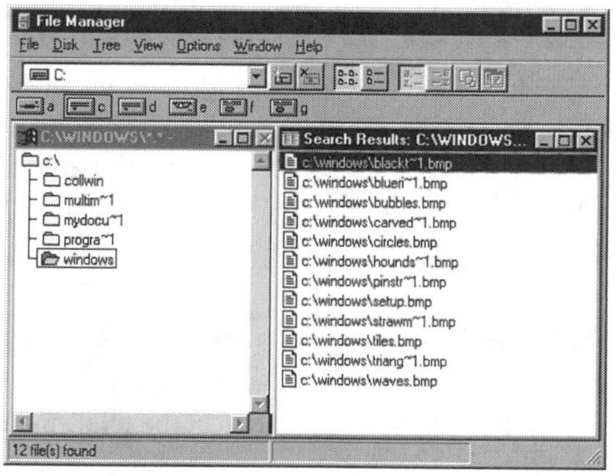

FIG. 13.10
When you view files by using 16-bit Windows programs, you see only the short filenames and not their long equivalents.

Through a process called *tunneling*, Windows enables you to preserve long filenames even when you edit them by using older programs. If you create a file and give it a long name by using Windows or a 32-bit Windows program, and then edit and save it by using a 16-bit program, Windows preserves the long filename.

Working with Long Filenames at an MS-DOS Prompt

When you open an MS-DOS Prompt session within Windows 95, Windows recognizes long filenames and enables you to work with them directly. By default, directory listings display the DOS-compatible short name at left and the long name at right, as shown in Figure 13.11.

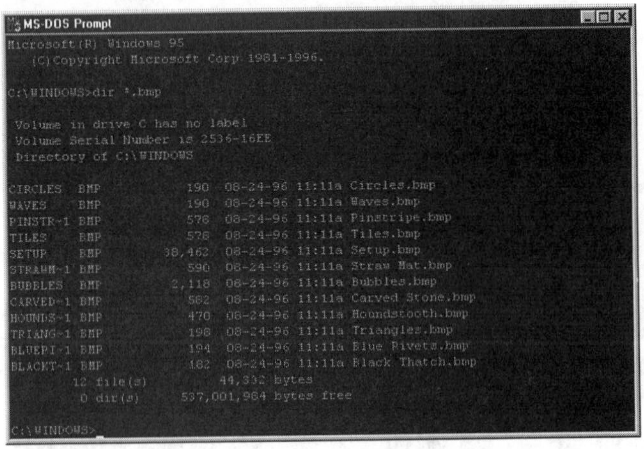

FIG. 13.11
Enter DIR in an MS-DOS Prompt session to see long and short filenames.

```
MS-DOS Prompt
Microsoft(R) Windows 95
   (C)Copyright Microsoft Corp 1981-1996.

C:\WINDOWS>dir *.bmp

 Volume in drive C has no label
 Volume Serial Number is 2536-16EE
 Directory of C:\WINDOWS

CIRCLES  BMP           190  08-24-96 11:11a Circles.bmp
WAVES    BMP           190  08-24-96 11:11a Waves.bmp
PINSTR~1 BMP           576  08-24-96 11:11a Pinstripe.bmp
TILES    BMP           576  08-24-96 11:11a Tiles.bmp
SETUP    BMP        38,462  08-24-96 11:11a Setup.bmp
STRAWM~1 BMP           590  08-24-96 11:11a Straw Mat.bmp
BUBBLES  BMP         2,118  08-24-96 11:11a Bubbles.bmp
CARVED~1 BMP           582  08-24-96 11:11a Carved Stone.bmp
HOUNDS~1 BMP           470  08-24-96 11:11a Houndstooth.bmp
TRIANG~1 BMP           198  08-24-96 11:11a Triangles.bmp
BLUERI~1 BMP           194  08-24-96 11:11a Blue Rivets.bmp
BLACKT~1 BMP           182  08-24-96 11:11a Black Thatch.bmp
        12 file(s)         44,332 bytes
         0 dir(s)     537,001,984 bytes free

C:\WINDOWS>
```

To manage files from an MS-DOS prompt, you might use either the long or short versions. If you want to display, rename, copy, or move a file by using a long filename that contains one or more spaces, be sure to enclose the entire name and path in quotation marks.

Using Explorer with Shared Resources on a Network

The Windows Explorer enables you to view and manage files and folders across the network, provided you have a working network connection and sufficient permissions. Use the Network Neighborhood to view all available network resources or map shared resources to drive letters to make them easier to work with. If you know the exact name of the shared resource, you can enter it directly into any common Windows dialog box.

Using Network Neighborhood to View Shared Resources

Icons for other computers, including Windows workstations and network servers, appear in the Network Neighborhood. You typically see some or all of the following icon types when you open the Network Neighborhood:

- Windows workstations
- Windows NT servers
- NetWare and other servers
- Windows workgroups (which in turn contain icons for other workstations)

When you open a computer icon in Network Neighborhood, you see all the named shares available on that computer. These might be individual drives, folders, printers, or fax modems. Before you can browse shared files and folders or print to a shared printer, you must have permission to use that resource. To connect with a shared resource, follow these steps:

1. Open the Windows Explorer and click Network Neighborhood.
2. Click the plus sign to the left of the computer name; available shares appear in a list below the computer icon, as in Figure 13.12.

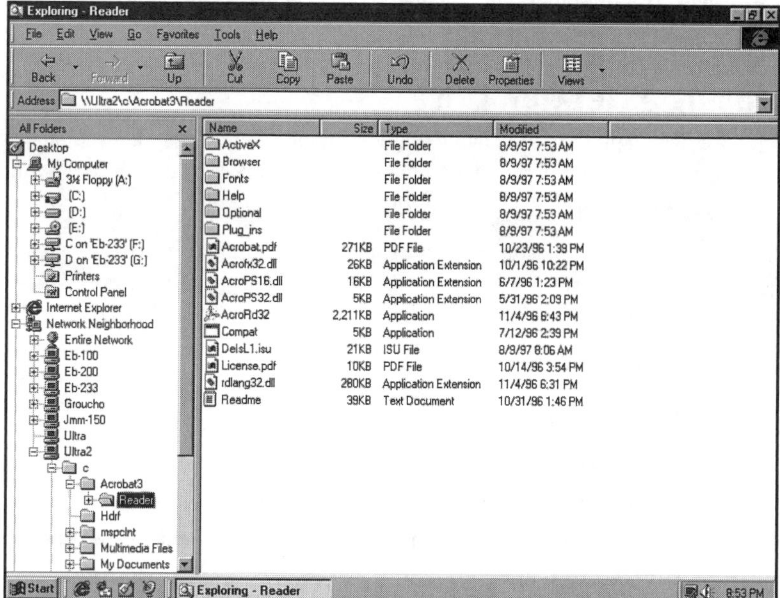

FIG. 13.12
The Network Neighborhood displays all shared resources available on other workstations and servers.

3. Select a share name from the list; its contents appear in the right-hand pane.
4. Open a document, launch an application, or perform other file management tasks as though you were working with a local file or folder.

TROUBLESHOOTING

When you attempt to connect to a shared drive or folder on a Windows NT server, you're asked to supply a password for *servername*\IPC$. Your computer has successfully created an interprocess communication (IPC) connection with the NT resource, but your username and password are not recognized by the NT domain controller. You must log off and log on again by using an account that is valid on the domain.

▶ **See** "Sharing Windows 95 Peer-to-Peer Resources," for more information about sharing resources on your computer with other network users, **p. 855**

Opening Shared Folders with UNC Names

In Windows programs and in the Start menu's Run dialog box, you can specify any file by entering its Universal Naming Convention (UNC) pathname. To use a UNC name, you must follow this syntax:

```
\\computername\sharename\path
```

For example, if a co-worker whose computer is named BillG has created a shared folder named Budget, you can browse his shared files by entering \\Billg\Budget in the File Open dialog box and pressing Enter. You can also create a shortcut to a shared network drive or folder by using the UNC name of the resource.

Mapping a Network Drive

Drive mapping, as the name implies, enables you to assign a virtual drive letter to a shared network resource. When you map a network drive, you refer to it by using the drive letter, just as though it were a local drive on your own computer.

There are two reasons why you might want to map drive letters. First, it makes working with files more convenient; instead of browsing through the Network Neighborhood, you can simply choose a drive letter from the drop-down Drives list in a common dialog box. Second, some older programs (and even some components of Windows 95) do not enable you to browse network resources directly; in these cases, the only way to access a shared file or folder is to first map it to a drive letter.

To map a shared drive or folder, follow these steps:

1. Open the Network Neighborhood in a folder window or the Windows Explorer, and open the server or workstation icon to display available shared resources on that computer.
2. Right-click the share icon and choose Map Network Drive from the shortcut menu. The dialog box shown in Figure 13.13 appears.

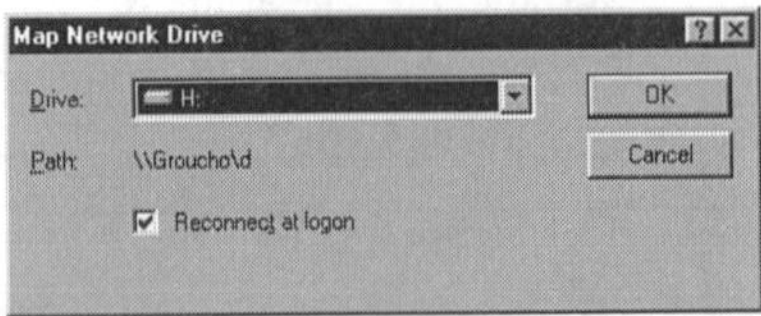

FIG. 13.13
Mapping a shared folder to a drive letter is the only way to use network resources with some programs.

3. Select an available drive letter from the drop-down Drive list.
4. If you want Windows to automatically reestablish the drive mapping every time you start your computer, check the box labeled Reconnect at Logon. If you want the mapping to be temporary, clear this box.
5. Click OK to map the drive to the selected letter. The mapped drive letter is now available in all common dialog boxes. You can also display its contents directly by typing the drive letter and a colon in the Run dialog box on the Start menu.

NOTE All mapped drives appear in the My Computer window alongside the icons for local drives. The label for a mapped drive includes the share name, server name, and drive letter.

To remove a drive mapping, follow these steps:

1. Right-click the Network Neighborhood icon and choose Disconnect Network Drive. A list of mapped drives appears.
2. Choose the mapped drive from the Drive list.
3. Click OK to disconnect. You will not see a confirmation dialog box before disconnecting.

Finding a Computer on Your Network

Large networks can include hundreds of computers across different domains and workgroups. On large networks, even opening the Network Neighborhood and displaying all the icons in it can take minutes. To find a specific computer without browsing through the entire network, follow these steps:

1. Click the Start button and choose Find, Computer. The Find Computer dialog box appears (see Figure 13.14).

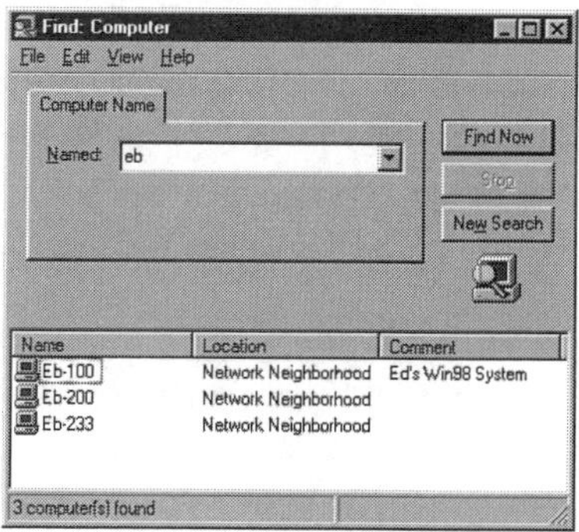

FIG. 13.14 To avoid long delays when you open the Network Neighborhood, search for a computer name instead.

2. In the box labeled Named, enter all or part of the computer name for which you're searching.
3. Click the Find Now button. The list of matching computer names appears in the results pane at the bottom of the dialog box.

TIP Right-click a computer name and choose Properties to see more information about the computer, including the name of the workgroup or domain to which it belongs and the operating system it uses.

Managing Files from an MS-DOS Prompt

There are things you can do from an MS-DOS prompt that you can't do any other way, and for some people it's the most efficient way to work. By using the DIR command and MS-DOS wildcards, for example, you can quickly display a filtered list of files within a given folder and redirect the output to a text file. It's the only way to quickly rename a group of files by using wildcards, and it's the fastest way to change the extension (and thus the file type) of some types of documents without having to adjust Windows Explorer preferences.

To see command-line switches for DIR and other MS-DOS commands, type the command followed by **/?** at the MS-DOS prompt. If the instructions scroll off the top of the screen before you can read them, add **| MORE** to the end of the command.

Starting an MS-DOS Prompt Session

To open an MS-DOS Prompt session within Windows, open the Start menu and choose Programs, MS-DOS Prompt.

Note that an MS-DOS Prompt session behaves differently from the command prompt that appears when you restart your computer in MS-DOS mode. Here are some key differences:

- The MS-DOS Prompt session enables you to work with long filenames. In MS-DOS mode, you see only the short 8.3-style names.
- The MS-DOS Prompt session can run in a window or in full-screen mode. When you start in MS-DOS mode, on the other hand, you are limited to full-screen display.
- All network resources are available to an MS-DOS Prompt session; accessing those resources in MS-DOS mode requires that you load real-mode network drivers.
- You can launch any Windows or MS-DOS program or batch file from the MS-DOS Prompt window. When you restart in MS-DOS mode, you can run MS-DOS programs only.

To switch between a windowed MS-DOS Prompt and a full-screen display, press Alt+Enter.

To close an MS-DOS Prompt window, type **EXIT** at the prompt and press Enter.

Using the Windows Clipboard with the MS-DOS Prompt

There's a special set of procedures for copying text to and from an MS-DOS Prompt window. These procedures are particularly useful when you need to copy a lengthy file name, complete with its full path. Follow these steps:

1. Open an MS-DOS Prompt window. If the MS-DOS Prompt session opens in full-screen mode, press Alt+Enter to force it into a window.
2. Click the control-menu icon at the far-left edge of the title bar; you see the pull-down control menu shown in Figure 13.15.

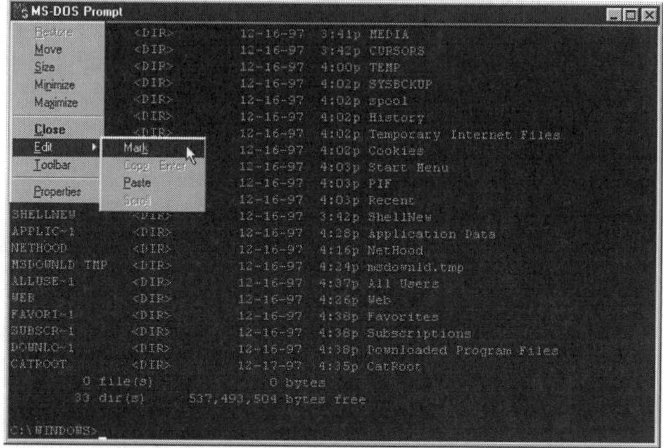

FIG. 13.15
Use this pull-down menu to cut, copy, and paste text between an MS-DOS window and the Windows Clipboard.

3. Choose the Edit command; a cascading menu appears to the right.
4. To copy part or all of the screen, choose Mark. This switches the mouse pointer into Mark mode, which enables you to select any rectangular portion of the MS-DOS screen.
5. When you've marked the section you want to copy, press Enter. Whatever you marked is now available on the Windows Clipboard; you can paste it into the MS-DOS window or into any Windows program.
6. To paste text from the Clipboard into your MS-DOS window, position the insertion point at the right spot in your DOS screen. Click the control-menu icon on the title bar and choose Edit, Paste from the pull-down menu.

▶ **See** "Using the Windows Clipboard," **p. 822**

Using Universal Naming Convention Pathnames

In Windows programs and in the Start menu's Run dialog box, you can specify any file by using its Universal Naming Convention pathname. In an MS-DOS Prompt window, however, these names are not recognized. To list or manage shared files across the network from an MS-DOS Prompt, you must first map the share to a drive letter. Use the procedures outlined earlier in this chapter.

To map a drive letter at the MS-DOS prompt, type **NET USE *driveletter:* *servername**sharename*** (substitute the appropriate drive letter, server name, and share name). For more details about this command, type **NET USE /?** and press Enter. ●

CHAPTER 14

Managing Files Using Web View

by Ed Bott

In this chapter

What Is Web View?

Ordinarily, Explorer displays files, folders, and other system objects as icons in a window. You can choose between large and small icons or arrange them in a list or in a column-oriented Details view. A separate Web view option, independent of the icon arrangement you've chosen, enables you to add web-style information panels around the display of icons.

When you open Explorer, you can choose to view the contents of any folder as a web page. When you do, the display changes to resemble the one in Figure 14.1.

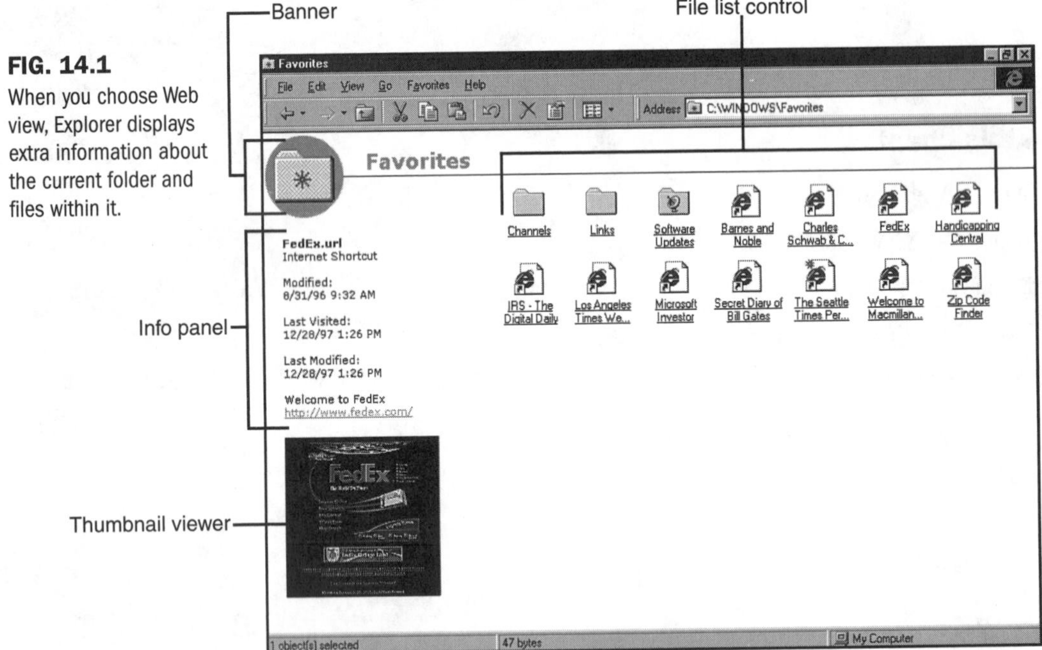

FIG. 14.1
When you choose Web view, Explorer displays extra information about the current folder and files within it.

The default web page view includes four standard elements:

- A banner identifies the title of the current folder.
- An info panel displays details about the folder and the currently selected file(s).
- Thumbnail images of certain file types appear below the contents pane, making it easier to identify the file's contents at a glance.
- The file list is contained in an ActiveX control embedded within the folder window.

Web view works in folder windows and in the contents pane of a two-pane Explorer window.

Using Web View with Folders

If you've selected web-style navigation, Web view is turned on for all folders by default. If you've selected Classic-style navigation, Web view is disabled for all folders by default. With custom settings, you can choose whether to enable or disable Web view by default.

▶ **See** "Choosing a Browsing Style," **p. 273**

Regardless of the global settings, you can turn Web view on or off for any folder. The Web view menu choice is a toggle: If Web view is on, choose View, as Web Page to restore the current folder window to a normal Explorer view. Setting this option for one folder window does not have any effect on other folder windows. If you turn on Web view by using the two-pane Explorer view, however, your preferences apply to all folders you view in the current Explorer window.

Displaying Thumbnails and File Information

When you choose Web view and select any file, the info panel at the left side of the window displays that file's name, its file type, the date it was last modified, and its size. If you select a folder icon, the info panel shows the name only.

When you select multiple files, the details in the info panel change. You see a count of the number of items you've selected, as well as the total combined size of the selected files (useful if you're planning to move or copy files to another folder), and a column listing the name of each selected file.

Below the info panel, the default Web view template includes a thumbnail image of certain file types. Only a handful of file formats appear as thumbnails in Web view: Document files, Bitmap, GIF, and JPEG images, and web pages in HTML format (if the file is stored locally or if a copy of the page is in the browser's cache). If you create a document with one of the applications in the standard edition of Microsoft Office 97, you can see detailed information about the file, along with a thumbnail image of the document, as in Figure 14.2.

If you're an Office 97 user, taking advantage of Web view requires some extra effort. By default, Word and Excel files do not display thumbnail images unless you choose File, Properties, click the Summary tab, and check the box labeled Save preview picture. Likewise, the info panel displays the name of the author and other file properties but only if you went out of your way to add that information on the Summary dialog box.

Can you turn on thumbnails for a given file type? Unfortunately, the answer is no. In theory, any application can add thumbnail support if the developer integrates its file formats with the WebViewFolderContents object; that's the ActiveX control that adds Web view capabilities to the Windows Explorer. If an application includes this feature, it should appear automatically, without requiring extra effort on your part.

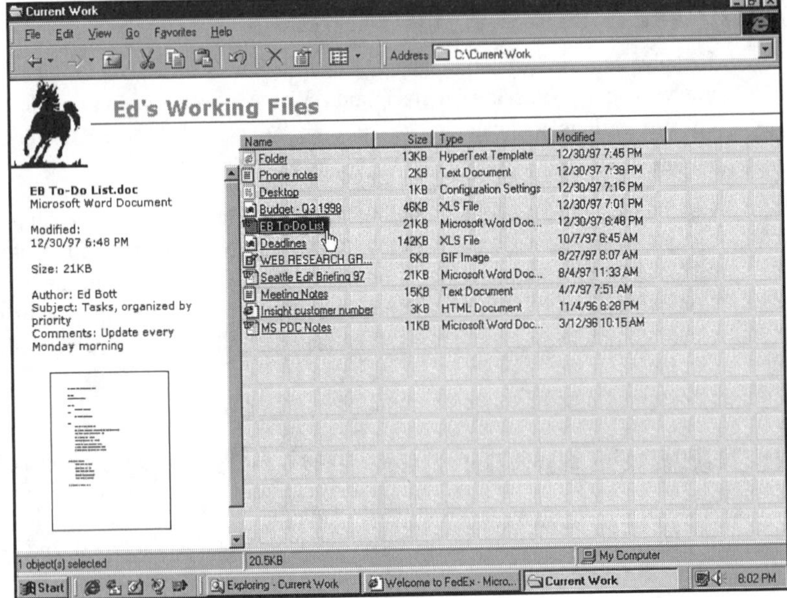

FIG. 14.2
If you use Office 97, extra information you save with documents appears in the Web view info pane.

TROUBLESHOOTING

You've turned on Web view, but you can't see a thumbnail view in some folders. The folder window you're using might be too small. Maximize the folder and see if thumbnails return. When you restore the drive or folder to a window, try resizing it and watch the changes in Web view as it decreases in size. The banner along the top becomes more compact, and the thumbnail viewer goes away when the window reaches a certain size.

Using Web View with System Folders

A handful of system folders use custom Web view templates. When you display the My Computer folder in Web view, for example, you see a display like the one in Figure 14.3.

NOTE Although it's easy to forget this fact, the Windows desktop is just another Explorer folder minus the window borders, menus, and toolbars. When you turn on the Active Desktop and display web content on the desktop, you've actually told Windows to display the desktop folder in Web view. Internet Explorer 4.0 automatically generates a custom Web view template—Desktop.htt—every time you customize your Active Desktop settings. Although it's theoretically possible to find this template and edit it manually, this practice is not recommended. ■

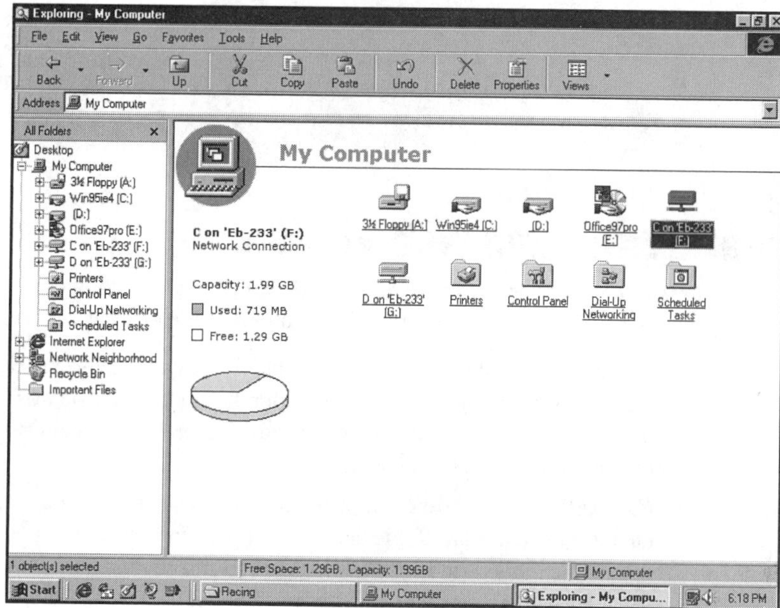

FIG. 14.3
You can see detailed drive information when you turn on Web view in the My Computer folder.

Other system folders that include custom Web view templates include Control Panel and Printers. Table 14.1 lists the built-in web templates you can find in a typical Windows 95 installation. All of these templates are stored in the Windows\Web folder.

Table 14.1 Built-In Web Templates

Template file	Description
Controlp.htt	Displays help text in the Info panel when you select individual Control Panel icons. Includes hyperlinks to two Microsoft web pages.
Folder.htt	The default template Windows uses when you customize Web view options for a folder. Editing this file does not change folders you have already customized.
Deskmovr.htt	Provides support for Active Desktop objects. Do not edit this file.
Mycomp.htt	Displays information about selected local and network drives; also displays help text for system folders.
Printers.htt	Offers instructions for setting up a new printer; selecting printer icon displays the number of messages in print queue.
Safemode.htt	Contains information and troubleshooting links for resolving problems when Active Desktop crashes.

CAUTION

Before editing any of the default templates in the Windows\Web folder, be sure to create backup copies. This precaution enables you to recover the original HTML files if you want to start over.

Creating Custom Web Views

There's no particular magic to Web view. When you display a folder's contents and choose View, as Web Page, you instruct Explorer to look in the current folder for two files:

- *Desktop.ini* lists shell objects that enable the folder to interpret HTML code and display files in a defined region within the folder. It also includes pointers to custom HTML templates and background images for the folder. If this file does not exist in the current folder, Explorer uses default settings.
- *Folder.htt* is a HyperText Template file that defines scripts, objects, and HTML code that enable files to display. If this file does not exist in the current folder, Explorer uses the default file in the Windows\Web folder. You can customize this template file, and you can use a file with a different name by specifying it in Desktop.ini.

Windows includes a wizard that enables you to customize the look of a folder by editing the Web view template.

CAUTION

There's no way to force users to open a folder by using Web view. If you've designed a custom web page to help other users of your PC navigate in a particular folder or to simplify file access for coworkers on a network, your work will only pay off if they use Web view. If they access the custom folder by using a version of Windows that does not include the Windows Desktop Update, they cannot view your changes.

Using the Web View Wizard

To customize the appearance of a folder in Web view, choose View, Customize this Folder. That action launches the wizard that appears in Figure 14.4.

As wizards go, this one is fairly crude. When you choose Create or edit an HTML document, the wizard launches Notepad and loads the HyperText Template specified in Desktop.ini. If this is the first time you've used the wizard in a given folder, it copies the Folder.htt template file from the Windows\Web folder.

After you finish editing the file in Notepad, you can close the Customize this Folder dialog box and return to the folder to see your changes.

The second option enables you to add a background graphic behind the file list control on the Web view folder. You can use any file in any standard graphic format, including Bitmap, JPEG, or GIF.

FIG. 14.4
Use this wizard to edit the Web view template or add a background graphic to a folder.

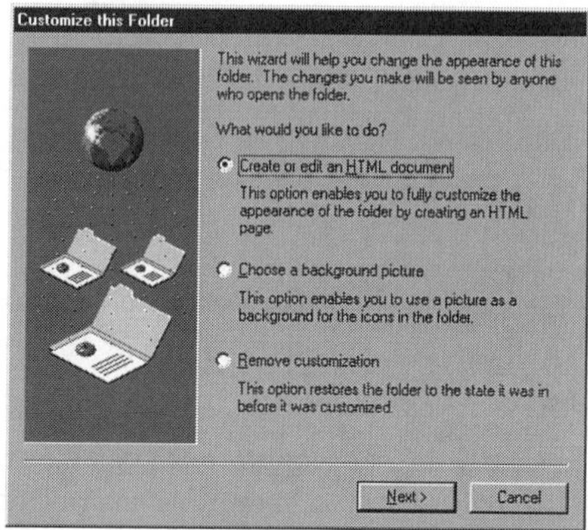

Start the Customize this Folder Wizard and follow these steps:

1. Select Choose a background picture. Click the Next button.
2. The next dialog box (see Figure 14.5) displays a list of graphics files from the \Windows folder. Click the Browse button to choose a different folder, if necessary.

FIG. 14.5
Choose a background image to appear behind the file list control in Web view. Pick a light image that won't obscure icons.

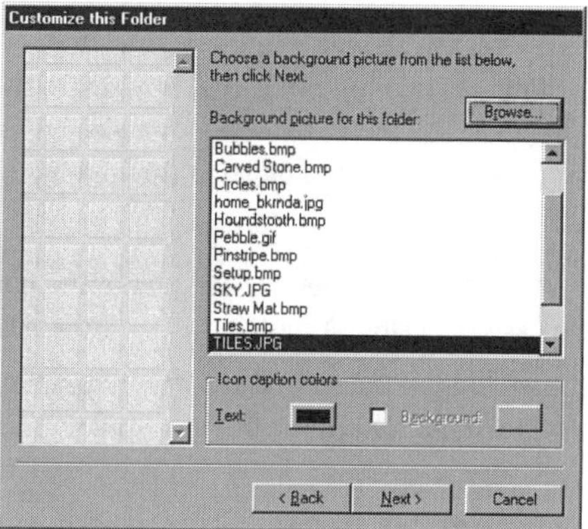

3. As you click graphics files in the list, the contents of the file appear in the preview window at the left of the dialog box. If the graphic is small, Windows tiles the image to fill the preview box.
4. After you've selected an appropriate graphic file, click the Text button to choose a contrasting color for icon labels that will appear on top of the graphic. You might also want to check the Background box and adjust the color that appears behind the icon labels.
5. Click Next to record your changes, and then click Finish to close the wizard. You might need to press F5 to refresh the folder's contents and see your changes.

If you must use a graphic behind the file list control, choose a light image, preferably in a shade of gray. Dark or detailed images such as photographs can make it difficult to see icons in the file list.

Editing a HyperText Template

You need to be fluent in HTML, and you won't be able to fall back on the WYSIWYG editor in FrontPage Express. By default, when you choose to customize the HyperText Template file for a folder, Windows dumps you into the most rudimentary HTML editor imaginable—Notepad.

▶ **See** "Using Notepad," **p. 756**

Some sections of folder.htt are strictly for web experts; don't edit the scripts that display file information, for example, unless you're sure you know what you're doing. But even an inexperienced editor can safely edit the following sections of the default folder template. (All these procedures assume you have used the Customize this Folder Wizard to open folder.htt for editing in Notepad.)

NOTE Future updates to Windows and Internet Explorer might include more complex templates for customizing folders. In that case, you might need to adjust the instructions that follow to deal with the revised HTML code. ■

Changing the Banner In the default Web view template, the banner includes a graphic and text that identifies the current folder. The blue circle that appears to the left of the banner is called out in the <style> section, near the top of the folder.htt file. Additional HTML code near the end of the file instructs an ActiveX control to position the folder icon over the blue circle. To change the banner, follow these steps:

1. On the line that begins with `#Banner`, delete all the text in the parentheses after `URL`, beginning with the prefix `res://`. Do not delete the parentheses.
2. With the insertion point positioned between the parentheses, enter the URL of an icon-sized graphics file. Note that a file URL must begin with **file:///** followed by the full path and name of the file.
3. To completely remove the blue circle, replace all text between the word `background:` and the final curly brace with the word **window**, as in the line that begins with `#MiniBanner`.
4. To delete the folder icon that appears over the blue circle, choose Search and enter the following text in the box labeled Find what: This is our awesome icon extractor. Click the button labeled Find Next.
5. Press Esc to close the Find dialog box, and delete or comment out the three lines after the search text, between `<object id=` and `</object>`.
6. By default, the banner text uses the name of the folder itself. To change this text, search for the section that begins with `<!-- start normal banner -->`, and count down six lines. Delete `%THISDIRNAME%` and replace it with your preferred text. Repeat this step in the section that begins with `<!-- start mini banner -->`.
7. Save the file by using the default name, and press F5 to refresh the contents and see the new image in place.

Adding Web Links to a Custom Folder View The default folder template includes a section where you can add your own hypertext links to web pages or files. (Open Control Panel and turn on Web view to see examples of these links.) To customize this section, open folder.htt and follow these steps:

1. Choose Search and enter the following text in the box labeled Find what: **A FEW LINKS OF YOUR OWN**. Click the button labeled Find Next.
2. The HTML code in this section includes two sample URLs. Replace the two sample URLs with your own link, and replace the link text (Custom Link 1 and Custom Link 2) with your own label.
3. To create additional links, copy the two lines that follow the first sample link and paste them below the second sample. Repeat for any additional links and customize as in step 2.
4. Delete the comment tags above and below the links to make them visible in Web view. When finished, the code should look like the sample in Figure 14.6.

FIG. 14.6
Edit the HyperText Template to add links that appear in Web view. Note that links can include web pages, folders, or filenames.

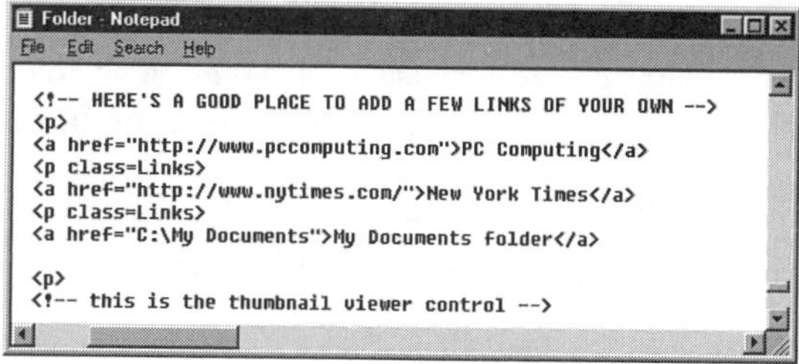

5. Close Notepad, saving the file with the default name. Press F5 to refresh the folder view and see the links in place.

Removing Custom Web View Settings

If you've customized a folder's Web view template and you're not happy with the results, use the wizard to delete your changes and start over. The procedure is simple:

1. Choose View, Customize this Folder.
2. Select the option labeled Remove Customization and click the Next button.
3. You will see a dialog box warning you that you're about to delete folder.htt and remove custom settings from desktop.ini. Click Next to continue.
4. Click Finish to close the wizard. You will see the default Web view settings for the current folder.

Advanced Customization Options

There's no limit to the amount of customization that a skilled HTML author can perform. As noted earlier, you can create your own HyperText Template file using any name. Store it in the folder you want to customize, and then open Desktop.ini and enter the name of your custom HTML file after the entry `PersistentMoniker=`.

Remember, both Desktop.ini and Folder.htt are hidden files. To edit either one without using the wizard, you might need to adjust Explorer's options to show hidden files. See "Changing the Way a Folder's Contents Appear" in Chapter 12, "Managing Files with My Computer and Windows Explorer," for more details.

Although most users will specify an HTML file in Desktop.ini, it's also possible to call out a web page in this file. This option is not officially supported, but it works just the same. You can point a folder to a page on the Internet or on your Intranet. The effect is a bit baffling: Although the Address bar displays the name of the folder, the Explorer window shows the web page listed in Desktop.ini.

To use the file list control in a custom web page, open the default Folder.htt file, copy the file list code to the clipboard, and paste it in your custom HTML document. Look for this block of code:

```
<object
classid="clsid:1820FED0-473E-11D0-A96C-00C04FD705A2">
</object>
```

You might need to add a Position statement to place the control where you want it to appear on the page.

ON THE WEB

For ideas on how to create useful custom Web view pages, check out the following article on the Microsoft SiteBuilder Network:

http://www.microsoft.com/workshop/prog/ie4/folders.htm

CHAPTER 15

Working with Disks and Disk Drives

In this chapter

Understanding What Your Disk Drive Does

You use *magnetic storage* to store applications and data for long periods of time or when the computer is turned off. Magnetic-storage media include *floppy disks* and *hard disks*. Floppy disks are removable and don't contain much space. Hard disks are internal to the computer and have much larger amounts of space.

The hard disk you store your data and programs on does not have to reside in the computer at your desk. If you are connected to a network, you can access information stored on the hard disk in the *file server*, the computer that serves the *clients* on the network. When you start an application or open a data file, the computer places a *copy* of the information stored in magnetic storage (on floppy disks or a hard disk) into electronic memory (RAM). If power is lost, the magnetic copy still is available.

You save the work you do in your programs in magnetic *files*, which are stored on a floppy disk or hard disk. Over time, you may have hundreds or even thousands of files. Searching for a specific file among the thousands of files can be very time-consuming.

Large computers and network file servers have multiple hard disks, each disk with its own drive letter. Figure 15.1 shows a hard disk drive (see the icon for drives C), a floppy disk drive (see the icon for drive A), a removable disk drive (drive E), and a CD-ROM drive (drive F). Each disk acts as a separate filing cabinet and can have its own unique folder organization.

NOTE Some drives may have more than one letter, depending on the controller versus drive size. If the drive is larger than the controller or BIOS can read, it can be partitioned as two drives. It is still only one piece of hardware, but software sees it as two drives. It also is possible for a drive to have more than one letter if it is compressed. In this case, the software doing the compression addresses the drive with one letter, and all other software accesses it using another drive letter, which is controlled by the compression software. ■

FIG. 15.1
The My Computer window displays all the resources on your computer, including all the floppy disk drives and hard drives.

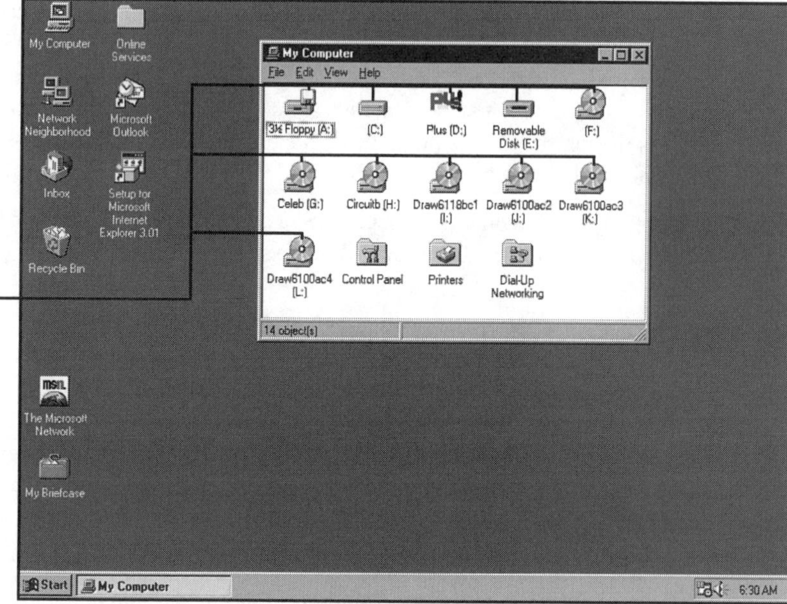

The FAT32 File System

The FAT file system is the system used by DOS to keep track of the storage of files on disks. Files are stored in units called *clusters*, which in turn are made up of sectors. Each sector is 512 bytes, but the size of a cluster varies, depending on the size of the hard disk. The FAT or File Allocation Table is used to keep track of which clusters belong to which files. Thus, although a file may be made up of many clusters scattered across your hard disk, the FAT table keeps track of the clusters so your applications will "see" the clusters as one file.

The original version of Windows 95, as well as DOS, uses a file system called FAT16, a 16-bit file system. There are two major drawbacks to the FAT16 file system in this age of larger and larger hard disks. First, FAT16 can only support single disk volumes (partitions) of up to 2G. With larger hard disks, you are forced to partition your drive into 2G or smaller volumes. Second, the cluster size increases dramatically as you increase partition size. A 2G partition, for example, uses 32K clusters, which means a small file, such as a shortcut on your desktop that is typically around 1K in size, will use 32K of disk space. This results in very inefficient use of hard disk space, especially if there are many small files on your hard disk. This storage waste is called *slack*. The smaller the cluster size, the less *slack* there is.

Microsoft has introduced a new file system called FAT32 with the Windows 95 OEM Service Release 2 (OSR2). The FAT32 file system supports single disk volumes (partitions) up to 2 terabytes in size and uses much smaller clusters. For partitions up to 8G, FAT32 uses 4K clusters, resulting in much more efficient file storage.

A drawback to the FAT32 file system is that FAT32 disks can only be accessed by the OSR2 version of Windows 95. FAT32 partitions are not recognized by MS-DOS, Windows 3.x or the original release of Windows 95. At this time, Windows NT is also unable to access a FAT32 disk, although Microsoft states that they are still determining if Windows NT will support FAT32 in the future. The upshot of this limitation is that you cannot dual-boot from a FAT32 disk using any of these operating systems.

For more information on how to obtain OSR2 and install FAT32 on your computer, see Chapter 2, "Installing and Upgrading Windows 95."

The Windows 95 File System

A major architectural change in Windows 95 is the installable file system, which has a new 32-bit, protected-mode Virtual File Allocation Table file system (VFAT) as its primary file system. With the installable file system, Windows 95 can manage multiple files systems, which makes it easy to connect to network computers using different file systems, such as HPFS (OS/2's file system) and NTFS (the Windows NT file system). Note that Windows 95 will not handle HPFU and NTFS on a local hard drive.

VFAT, the primary file system in Windows 95, was actually an optional file system introduced in Windows for Workgroups 3.1. VFAT in Windows 95 has been improved and has many advantages over the original FAT file system used in MS-DOS:

- Faster file accessing and improved multitasking because of the 32-bit, protected-mode data path.
- Improved, dynamic, protected-mode disk caching (VCACHE) for improved performance and stability. Also works with CD-ROMs and network drives.
- No conventional memory used by disk cache driver (VCACHE versus older SmartDrive).
- Cache memory is allocated dynamically, based on available free memory and read/write activity.
- Support for long file names (up to 255 characters).
- Capability to read and write long file names supported by other file systems, such as NTFS and HPFS.
- Support for FAT partitions and short (8.3) file names for backward compatibility.

Formatting Disks

You usually cannot use new disks until you format them (but some disks come already formatted). *Formatting* prepares disks for use on a computer. Formatting is similar to preparing a blank book for use by writing in page numbers and creating a blank table of contents. If a disk contains data, formatting it completely erases all existing data. Part of the process of formatting is checking for bad areas on the disk's magnetic surface. All bad areas found are identified so that data is not recorded in these areas.

The 32-bit multitasking environment in Windows 95 makes it possible to format disks in the background as you go about your work in other applications. This capability is a real time-saver.

Formatting a Floppy Disk

TIP If you attempt to open an unformatted floppy disk in My Computer or Windows Explorer, you will be asked if you want to format the disk. The Format dialog box immediately displays.

To format a floppy disk, follow these steps:

1. Insert the floppy disk to be formatted in the disk drive.
2. Right-click the icon for the drive in a folder window or in the Windows Explorer, and then choose Format. The Format dialog box appears (see Figure 15.2).

   In a folder window, you also can select the drive icon and choose File, Format.

NOTE If you are working in the Windows Explorer, there is no File, Format command; instead, right-click a floppy disk drive icon in the left pane of the Explorer, and select Format from the shortcut menu.

TIP To bypass having to open the Explorer or My Computer, create a shortcut to your floppy disk drive on the desktop. To format a floppy disk, right-click the disk icon, and choose Format from the shortcut menu. You also can copy a floppy disk using the Copy Disk command on the shortcut menu.

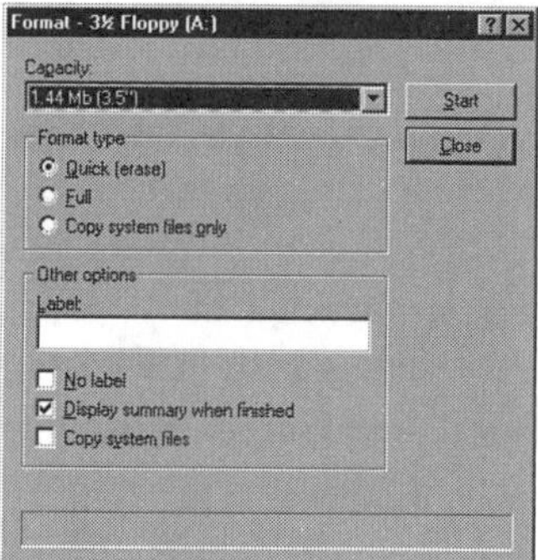

FIG. 15.2 Set up a formatting operation in the Format dialog box.

3. Select the size of the floppy disk from the Capacity drop-down list.
4. Select the type of format you want from the Format Type options:

Option	Description
Quick (Erase)	Formats the disk without scanning it for bad sectors first. Speeds up formatting, but you should be sure that the disk is undamaged.

continues

continued

Full	Checks for bad sectors on the disk before formatting and marks them so that these areas are not used.
Copy System Files Only	Adds the system files to the disk without formatting it so that the disk can be used to start the computer.

5. If you want to assign a label to the disk, type the label in the Label text box. Otherwise, select the No Label option.
6. Select the Display Summary When Finished option if you want to see a screen of information about the disk after it is formatted (see Figure 15.3).

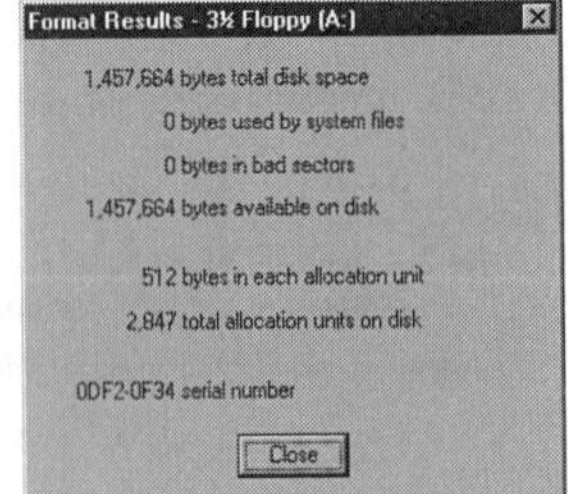

FIG. 15.3
You can get information about a formatted disk in the Format Results message box.

The Format Results message box tells you how much total disk space there is, how many bytes are used by system files and bad sectors, and how many bytes are available.

If you want to switch to another application while formatting a disk, select the Display Summary option so the Format Results dialog box will notify you when the formatting is completed.

7. If you want to use the disk to start the computer, select the Copy System Files option. Do not use this option unless you need to, because system files use storage space on the disk that can otherwise be used for data.
8. Choose Start. The progress of the formatting operation appears at the bottom of the Format dialog box.
9. To format another disk, insert a new disk and repeat steps 3 through 8.
10. When you finish formatting disks, choose Close.

CAUTION

When you format a disk, you remove all the information from the disk. You should check a disk for important files before formatting.

TROUBLESHOOTING

Windows will not format a disk drive. A dialog says there are files open but all applications and documents on the drive are closed. Windows 95 prevents you from formatting a disk that has a file open or a disk that is open in My Computer or the Windows Explorer. Close any documents or applications that are open on that disk, and close any My Computer or Windows Explorer windows open into the disk.

CAUTION

Drives that have been compressed with DriveSpace or another compression software must be formatted from DriveSpace or the appropriate compression software.

Formatting Your Hard Disk

Before you can use a new hard drive, you need to format it as if it has not been formatted before. You also may want to format a hard drive that has been used and is cluttered with data or other operating systems. Formatting does more than just erasing old data, it magnetically scrubs the disk so that the files do not exist.

If you purchased a preassembled computer that contains a hard disk and the computer starts and runs Windows or DOS, then you do not need to format the hard disk. If, however, you install additional hard disks in your computer, you may need to format them before you can use them.

CAUTION

You should format a disk that contains confidential or secret information before giving the computer to someone who should not have access to that data. The erase or delete commands only remove a file's name and location from a disk's table of files. The data still exists on the disk until it is overwritten by another file. Formatting erases the name and location table and magnetically erases the actual data.

Using FDISK to Partition a New Hard Drive An essential part of formatting a hard drive for data is *partitioning*. You must create at least one partition on your hard disk, but you can create more than one partition. You can define these additional partitions as DOS partitions or as non-DOS partitions on which you can install other operating systems. To run Windows 95, you need to create at least one DOS partition, and if want to start Windows 95 from this disk, you must also define this partition as a primary DOS partition and as the active partition. If you don't use the entire disk for the primary DOS partition, you can create an extended DOS partition from the remaining space and divide this partition into logical drives. Use the FDISK program that comes with DOS and Windows 95 to accomplish all these tasks.

If you are installing a new hard disk as your primary drive, place the Windows 95 Startup disk in the drive A and turn on your computer. Windows sees the new drive and asks if you want to allocate all of the unallocated space on your drive. Answer "yes" and it will run FDISK behind the scenes and restart your computer. After the restart, it formats the new partition automatically.

Your other alternative is to boot to DOS Mode by pressing F5 during startup and running FDISK from the DOS Prompt. When you type FDISK at the DOS prompt, it puts a menu on the screen. Be sure to check to see that the drive that you want to partition is the selected drive. Option 5 on the menu allows you to select a different drive. After you confirm that you have the correct drive selected, choose option 1 from the menu. This option creates a DOS partition on your drive and asks if you want to use the entire drive for your DOS partition. The most common answer is "yes." Once the DOS partition is created, your computer will restart and be ready for the formatting of the drive.

As you can see by the two choices of partitioning a hard drive, Windows 95 has made this step much easier.

Formatting an Uncompressed Hard Drive from MS-DOS To format an uncompressed drive from the MS-DOS prompt, type **Format *d:***, where *d*: is the drive letter of the drive that you want to format.

Formatting an Uncompressed Hard Drive from Windows Before you format an uncompressed hard drive, make sure you have backed up or copied any file that you may need again. Once the formatting process begins, you cannot retrieve previous data from the drive.

To format a hard drive, follow these steps:

1. Close all documents and applications on the drive you want to format. Close any windows from My Computer that look at that drive. Collapse all folders in Windows Explorer for the hard drive you want to format.
2. Open My Computer and select the icon for the drive you want to format. Choose File, Format.
   or
   Open Windows Explorer, and right-click the hard drive icon you want to format. Choose Format.

   The Format dialog box displays as shown in Figure 15.4.
3. Select the option you want for formatting your disk:

Capacity	Click the drop-down list arrow to select a different capacity for the drive.
Format Type	
Quick (erase)	Erases all the files, but does not use ScanDisk to check for bad areas of the disk. The disk must be formatted to use this command. If you think your disk may have bad areas or has shown erratic behavior, be sure to run ScanDisk after the Quick format.

Full	Prepares a disk for use. All files are completely removed. Diskettes are checked for bad sectors, but hard disks are not. If this is a new hard disk or a disk that has shown erratic behavior, be sure to run ScanDisk after the Full format.
Copy System Files Only	Does not format the disk but it does copy system files to the disk so the floppy or hard disk can be used to start the computer.
Other Options	
Label	Creates a magnetic label on the disk, which appears in the title bar of My Computer and Windows Explorer.
No label	Disables the label so the disk will not have a label.
Display Summary When Finished	Displays a report when formatting is complete that shows the space available on the disk, the room taken by system files, and the number of bad sectors.
Copy System Files	Copies system files onto the disk after formatting. Select this check box if you need to use this floppy or hard disk to start the computer.

FIG. 15.4
You can use the Format dialog box to do a full format, erase files, and copy system files onto a disk.

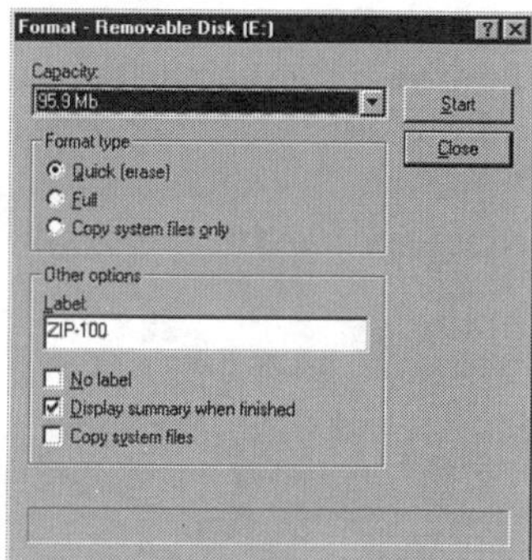

4. Choose OK. A dialog box displays telling you that all files on the disk will be destroyed. Are you sure you want to format this drive? Choose OK to format or Cancel to stop.
5. If you choose OK, you will see the Format dialog box showing you the progression of the file format, as shown in Figure 15.5.
6. When formatting is complete, the Format Results dialog box displays the properties of the formatted drive (see Figure 15.6).
7. Choose Close to close the Format Results dialog box; then choose Close to close the Format dialog box.

▶ **See** "Using FDISK to Partition a New Hard Drive," **p. 343**

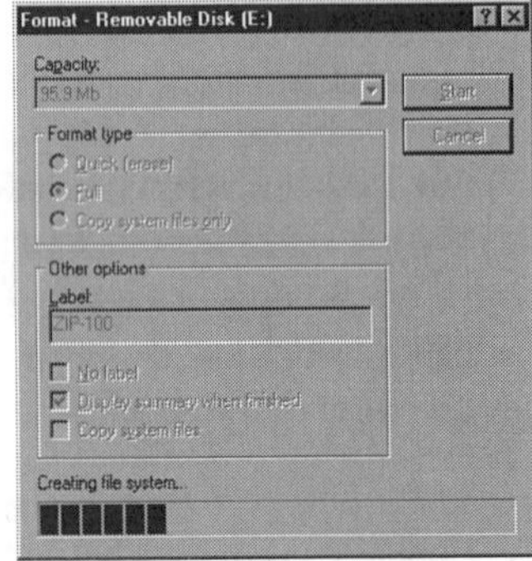

FIG. 15.5
A progression bar at the bottom of the dialog box shows you the progress of disk formatting.

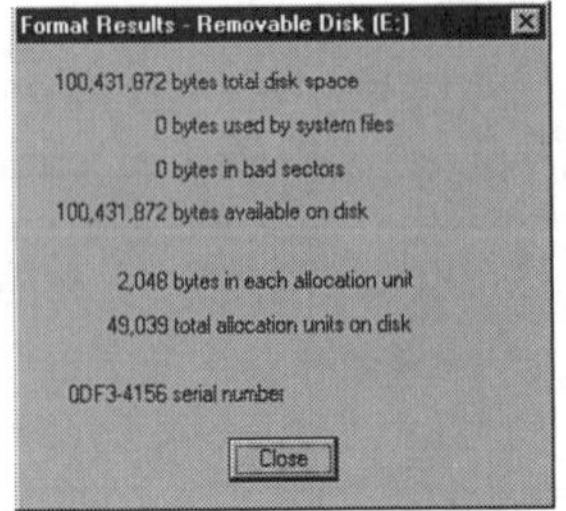

FIG. 15.6
The Format Results dialog box displays a report on disk statistics when formatting is complete.

If My Computer or Windows Explorer does not display the icon for the hard drive you want to format, then you may need to recheck the drive connections to the drive adapter, or partition the hard drive using the FDISK command. You also need to check setup to be sure the proper drive type is selected.

▶ **See** "Using ScanDisk to Check for Disk Damage," **p. 348**

CAUTION

You cannot format the hard disk containing Windows while Windows is running. If you need to format the hard disk containing Windows, you will need either a disk copy of MS-DOS with the FORMAT command or a set of the Windows 95 upgrade disks that contains a disk for formatting hard disks.

The system files, FDISK, and Format are created on the Startup disk that Windows 95 asks if you want to create during the install. It is *highly* recommended that you create the Startup disk.

Formatting an Uncompressed Drive from the Windows Startup Disk If you want to reformat the drive that has Windows 95 installed on it, you must use the Windows startup disk. Reformatting the drive that has Windows 95 on it is an extreme measure, since it will erase everything on the drive and you will have to reinstall Windows 95 and all your applications. In some cases, this may be necessary, for example, if your installation of Windows is corrupted beyond repair. Also, some users like to periodically back up their entire system and then reformat their hard drive and reinstall Windows 95 and their applications. This "spring cleaning" can rid your hard disk of files you are no longer using and often improves the performance of your system.

To format the drive that has Windows 95 installed on it, follow these steps:

1. Insert the startup disk in drive A and restart the computer.
2. Type **format *drive_letter*** at the command prompt.

   If you are formatting the boot drive (drive C), type **format C: /s**. The /s parameter will add the system files to the disk.
3. Press **Y** when the warning message appears.
4. When the formatting is completed, you can add a volume label if you want. Then press Enter to complete the formatting.
5. Remove the startup disk and restart the computer.

When you restart your computer, drive C: will have only the files needed to boot the computer. You will then have to reinstall Windows 95 and all your applications. See Chapter 2, "Installing and Upgrading Windows 95," to learn how to install Windows 95.

Naming Your Drive with a Volume Label

Although you may be accustomed to putting a paper label on disks, both hard disks and floppy disks can have magnetically recorded labels, known as ***volume labels***. Volume labels can help you identify disks. You can read the volume label for a disk by looking at the disk's properties.

In the preceding section, you learned how to create a volume label when you format a disk. If you want to create or change a volume label on a previously formatted disk, follow these steps:

1. Open the Explorer or the My Computer window.
2. Select the drive with the volume name you want to change.
3. Choose File, Properties. Alternatively, right-click the drive and choose Properties from the shortcut menu. The Properties sheet appears, as shown in Figure 15.7.

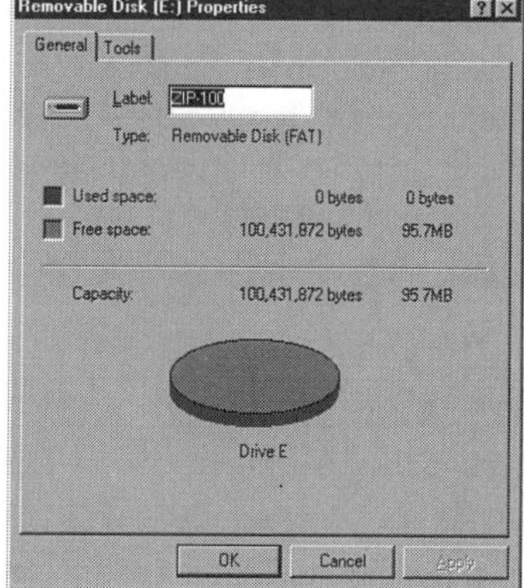

FIG. 15.7
Enter a volume label for a disk in the Properties sheet.

You can view the name of a disk by right-clicking the disk icon in the My Computer or Explorer window and selecting the Properties command.

4. Type the name you want to give the disk in the Label text box and click OK.

   If there is already a name in the box, select it first and then type a new name. The Properties sheet also gives you information on the total size of the disk (in bytes), how much space is used, and the amount of remaining space.

Using ScanDisk to Check for Disk Damage

In an ideal world, you would never have to worry about errors occurring on your hard disk or floppy disks. This not being the case, Windows 95 comes with a program called ScanDisk you can use to check for, diagnose, and repair damage on a hard disk or floppy disk. Part of your routine hard disk maintenance, along with defragmenting your hard disk as described in the next section, should be to periodically run ScanDisk to keep your hard disk in good repair.

In its standard test, ScanDisk checks the files and folders on a disk for logical *errors*; if you ask it to, ScanDisk also automatically corrects any errors it finds. ScanDisk checks for *cross-linked* files, which occur when two or more files have data stored in the same *cluster* (a storage unit on a disk). The data in the cluster is likely to be correct for only one of the files and may not be correct for any of them. ScanDisk also checks for *lost file fragments*, which are pieces of data that have become disassociated with their files. Although file fragments may contain useful data, they usually can't be recovered and just take up disk space. You can tell ScanDisk to delete lost file fragments or save them in a file.

You also can have ScanDisk check files for invalid file names and invalid dates and times. When a file has an invalid file name, you may not be able to open it. Invalid dates and times can cause problems when you use a backup program that uses dates and times to determine how current a file is.

You can run a more thorough test, in which ScanDisk checks for both logical errors in files and folders and also scans the surface of the disk to check for physical *errors*. Physical errors are areas on your disk that are damaged and shouldn't be used for storing data. If ScanDisk finds bad sectors on your hard disk, any data in them can be moved to new sectors, and the bad sectors are marked so that data is not stored in them in the future.

To check a disk for errors, follow these steps:

1. Open the Start menu and choose Programs, Accessories, System Tools, and ScanDisk. The ScanDisk window appears, as shown in Figure 15.8.
2. Select the drive you want to check in the Select the Drive(s) You Want to Check for Errors box.
3. To check only for logical errors in the files and folders on the selected disk, make sure to select the Standard option.

To check for logical errors and to scan the disk for physical errors, select the Thorough option.

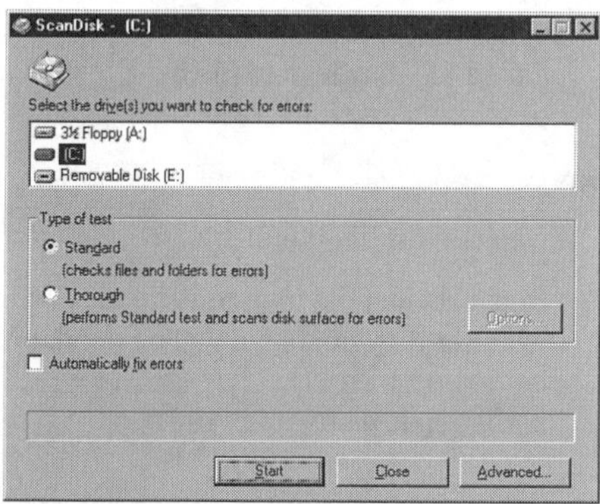

FIG. 15.8
Use ScanDisk to check your hard disk for logical and physical errors and repair any damage.

4. Click the Advanced button to change the settings used for checking files and folders for logical errors. The ScanDisk Advanced Options dialog box appears (see Figure 15.9). Use this dialog box to change the options in Table 15.1.

Table 15.1 ScanDisk Advanced Options

Display Summary Options	
Option	**Function**
Always	A summary with information about your disk and any errors found and corrected appears whenever you run ScanDisk.
Never	A summary never appears when you run ScanDisk.
Only If Errors Found	A summary shows only if Windows detects errors.
Log File Options	
Replace Log	Saves the details of a ScanDisk session in a log file named SCANDISK.LOG in the top-level folder on drive C. Replaces any existing file with the same name.
Append to Log	Saves the details of a ScanDisk session, appending the information to the end of SCANDISK.LOG.
No Log	The results of the ScanDisk operation are not saved to a log file.
Cross-Linked Files Options	
Delete	Deletes cross-linked files when such files are found.
Make Copies	A copy is made of each cross-linked cluster for each of the cross-linked files.

continues

Table 15.1 Continued

Option	Function
Ignore	Cross-linked files are not corrected in any way. Using a cross-linked file may lead to further file damage and may cause the program using it to crash.
Lost File Fragments Options	
Free	Deletes lost file fragments, freeing up the space they use.
Convert to Files	Converts lost file fragments to files, which you can view to see whether they contain data you need. Files are given names beginning with FILE (for example, FILE0001) and are stored in the top-level folder of the disk.
Check Files For Options	
Invalid File Names	Checks files for invalid file names. Files with invalid file names sometimes cannot be opened.
Invalid Dates and Times	Checks files for invalid dates and times, which can result in incorrect sorting and can also cause problems with backup programs.
Check Host Drive First	If the drive you check has been compressed using DoubleSpace or DriveSpace, ScanDisk checks the host drive for the compressed drive first. Errors on the host drive often cause errors on the compressed drive, so it is best to check it first.

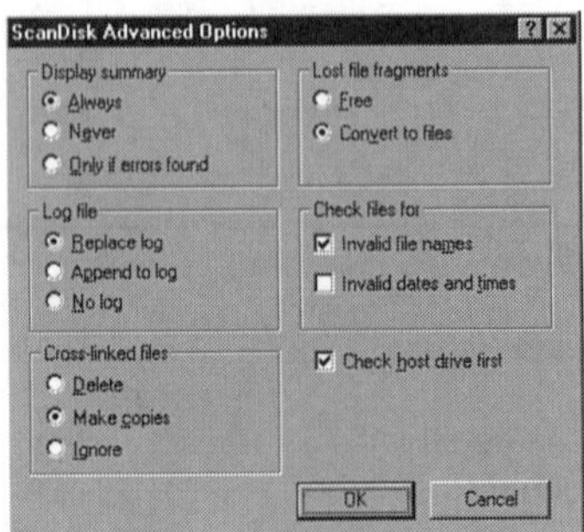

FIG. 15.9
You can change the settings ScanDisk uses to check files and folders for logical errors in the ScanDisk Advanced Options dialog box.

5. If you selected the Thorough option, choose Options to change the settings used to scan the disk for physical errors. The Surface Scan Options dialog box appears (see Figure 15.10). Use this dialog box to change the following options:

Option	Function
System and Data Areas	Scans the entire disk for physical damage.
System Area Only	Scans only the system area of the disk for physical damage. This is the disk area that contains files used to start the computer and hold the operating system.
Data Area Only	Scans only the data area of the disk for physical damage. The data area contains application and data programs. Use this if Windows behaves erratically, even if you have reinstalled it.
Do Not Perform Write-Testing	If this option is not selected (the default), ScanDisk reads and writes every sector to verify both read and write functions. If you select this option, ScanDisk does not write-verify the sectors.
Do Not Repair Bad Sectors in Hidden and System Files	ScanDisk will not move data from bad sectors in hidden and system files. Some programs look for hidden system files at specific locations and will not work if data in these files is moved.

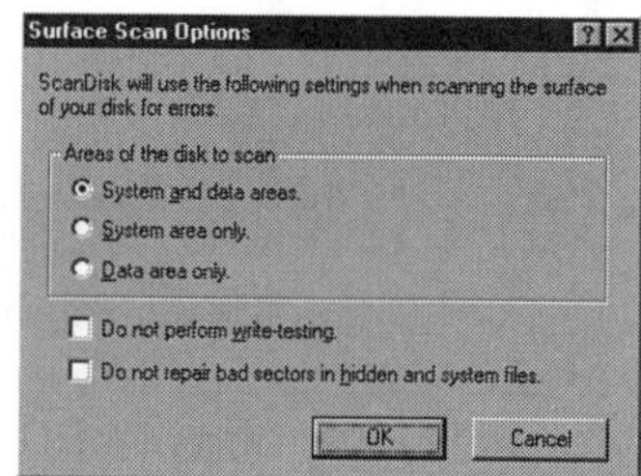

FIG. 15.10
You can change the settings ScanDisk uses to scan the disk for physical errors.

6. Select the Automatically Fix Errors option if you want ScanDisk to automatically fix any errors it finds without first reporting the errors.

   If you don't select this option, ScanDisk informs you when it finds an error, and you can determine how ScanDisk fixes it.

7. Choose Start to begin the test. The progress of the test appears at the bottom of the ScanDisk dialog box. You can halt the test by choosing Cancel. If you told ScanDisk to scan your disk for physical errors, the test can take several minutes. When the test is complete, a summary report like the one in Figure 15.11 may appear, depending on the options you selected in the ScanDisk Advanced Options dialog box. Click Close to close the Results dialog box.

8. Choose Close to exit ScanDisk.

▶ **See** "Improving Performance with Disk Defragmenter," **p. 352**

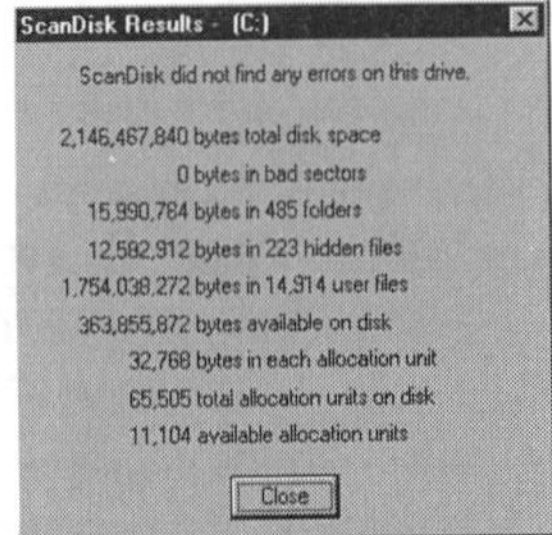

FIG. 15.11
The results of a ScanDisk operation appear in the ScanDisk Results dialog box.

TROUBLESHOOTING

Whenever Windows retrieves a file, the hard disk light seems to come on a lot. It even sounds like the hard disk is chattering. The more we use the computer, the worse this problem gets. ScanDisk didn't show any problems with the disk. The problem is probably not with the physical quality of your hard drive's magnetic surface, which is what ScanDisk checks. The problem is more likely that files on the hard disk are fragmented. Fragmented disks have pieces of files scattered all over the disk. Rather than reading a file at one location in one quick continuous movement, the read-head on the drive must skitter around on the disk searching for all the pieces that belong to a file. Once fragmenting is bad, it gets worse. This is why your computer seems to be slowing down the more you use it. Windows comes with a defragmenting utility that will reorganize your files on the disk so they are contiguous and can be read quickly.

Improving Performance with Disk Defragmenter

Information written to a hard disk is not necessarily stored in a *contiguous* (adjacent) block. Rather, fragments of information are more likely spread across the disk wherever the system can find room. The more you use the hard disk, the more fragmented the disk becomes. Obviously, the drive takes more time to hunt for information located in several places than it takes to fetch the same information from a single location. Because of this extra time, disk fragmentation can slow the computer's operation considerably.

The Windows Disk Defragmenter can significantly improve file access time by restructuring files into contiguous blocks and moving free space to the end of the disk.

To optimize the performance of your hard disk, use Disk Defragmenter on a regular basis to defragment your hard disk.

To defragment a disk, follow these steps:

1. Open the Start menu and choose Programs, Accessories, System Tools, and Disk Defragmenter. The Select Drive dialog box appears (see Figure 15.12).

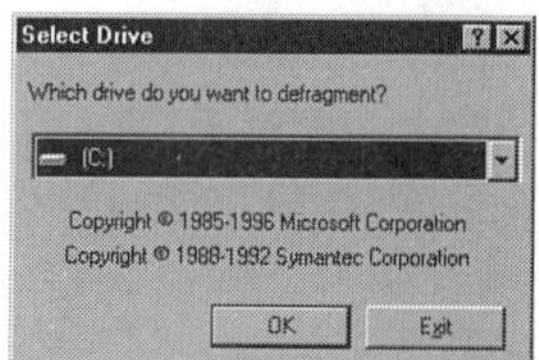

FIG. 15.12
Select the drive you want to defragment in the Select Drive dialog box.

2. Select the drive you want to defragment from the Defragment Which Drive drop-down list and choose OK. The Disk Defragmenter dialog box appears, as shown in Figure 15.13. The percent fragmentation of the selected drive appears in the dialog box. You are also informed whether defragmentation will improve performance.

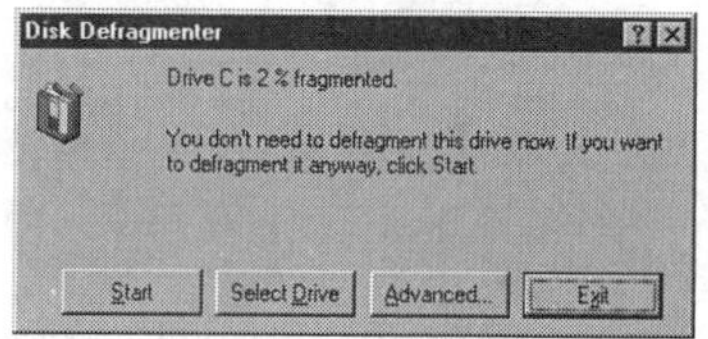

FIG. 15.13
The Disk Defragmenter dialog box tells you how fragmented your drive is and whether defragmenting it will improve its performance.

3. To change the Disk Defragmenter options, choose Advanced. The Advanced Options dialog box appears (see Figure 15.14). Use this dialog box to change the following options:

Option	**Function**
Full Defragmentation (Both Files and Free Space)	Defragments all the files on the selected disk.
Defragment Files Only	Defragments only the files on your hard disk, without consolidating the free space.
Consolidate Free Space Only	Only consolidates the free space on the selected disk without defragmenting the files.
Check Drive for Errors	Checks the files and folders on the drive for errors before defragmenting.
This Time Only. Next Time, Use the Defaults Again	Uses the selected options for this defragment operation only.
Save These Options and Use Them Every Time	Saves the selected options and uses them each time you run Disk Defragmenter unless you change them again.

Select the desired options and click OK. You return to the Disk Defragmenter dialog box.

4. Choose Start. The progress of the defragmentation operation appears in the Defragmenting dialog box (see Figure 15.15).

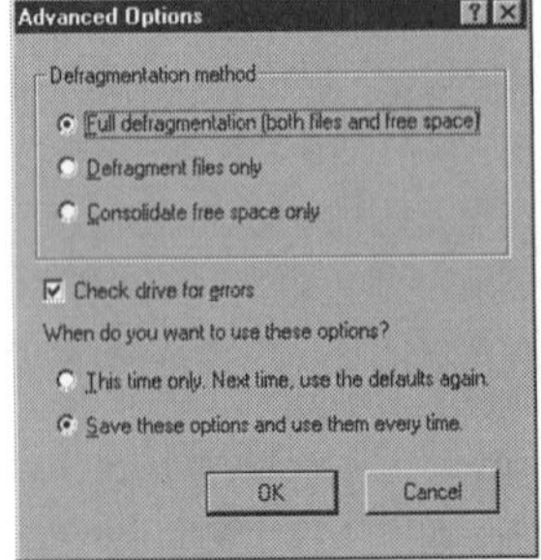

FIG. 15.14
Change the way Disk Defragmenter works in the Advanced Options dialog box.

FIG. 15.15
Monitor the progress of the defragmentation operation in the Defragmenting dialog box.

5. When the defragmentation operation is complete, choose Exit to close the Disk Defragmenter, or choose Select Drive to defragment another drive.

Defragmenting a hard disk can take a long time. Although you can continue working on your computer during the defragmentation operation, you will notice a significant slowdown in your computer's operation. Also, every time you make a change that affects the FAT, the defragmenting process has to be restarted. For these reasons, try to run the Disk Defragmenter during a time when you do not need to use the computer, for example, before you leave work for the day.

You can pause the defragmentation operation if you need to use your computer before defragmentation is completed and you don't want performance slowed down. Choose Pause from the Defragmenting dialog box to pause Disk Defragmenter. To resume defragmentation, choose Pause again. You can also cancel the defragmentation operation by choosing Stop. Choose Show Details to open a window that displays the details of the defragmentation operation. To close the window, choose Hide Details.

Compressing a Disk

If you are like many computer users, you may reach the limits of the storage space on your computer as you install new programs and generate more and more data files. You've probably also discovered that new releases of Windows programs seem to take up more and more room on your hard disk. One solution is to install a new hard disk in your computer. But if you have limited finances, or you work with a laptop in which it is not possible to add another hard disk, you have another option. Windows 95 comes with a program called DriveSpace that enables you to squeeze more storage space from your existing hard drive. DriveSpace is a software solution to your hardware problem. DriveSpace works by compressing the files on your hard disk so that they take up less room. When you need to use a file, DriveSpace automatically decompresses it. The compression and decompression of files happens transparently—you are not even aware that it is happening. You will notice very little delay in file access when you use DriveSpace.

Microsoft Plus!, the companion software released at the same time as Windows 95, comes with DriveSpace 3, an enhanced version of DriveSpace. DriveSpace 3 offers superb disk compression that improves on Windows 95 DriveSpace in several ways:

- Handles disks up to 2G (versus 512M for the original DriveSpace).
- Works with smaller units of data (512-byte sectors versus 32K byte clusters), improving storage efficiency.
- Supports two new higher levels of compression (HiPack and UltraPack).
- Has settings for specifying what type of compression to use and when to use it.
- Adds a Compression tab to the Properties sheet for floppy and hard disks.

In this section, we assume you have installed Microsoft Plus! on your computer and will use DriveSpace 3.

OSR 2 DriveSpace 3 is included with the OEM Service Release 2 (OSR2) version of Windows 95, so if you have OSR2 installed on your computer, you do not have to install Microsoft Plus! to have access to DriveSpace 3. However, if the hard drive you want to compress has the FAT32 file system installed (see"The FAT32 File System," earlier in this chapter), you cannot compress the drive. FAT32 drives cannot be compressed using DriveSpace3.

NOTE The Windows 95 DriveSpace is compatible with both DoubleSpace, which was included with MS-DOS 6.0 and 6.2, and DriveSpace, which was included with MS-DOS 6.22. You can work with compressed drives of either type, and the two types of compressed drives can coexist on the same computer.

Disk Compression

Despite the name, disk compression doesn't actually compress your hard disk, which is a physical entry, nor does it increase the physical capacity of your disk. What it really does is use software magic to increase the capacity of your hard disk in two ways.

First, disk compression software increases the capacity of your hard disk by reducing the smallest storage unit to 512 bytes, rather than the much larger clusters (8-64K) used in the native DOS environment. This improvement in storage efficiency goes a long way toward reducing the wasted space that occurs when you save a lot of small files.

The second component of disk compression involves the use of a software algorithm that looks for patterns in a data file and codes repeating patterns in a way that takes up less space. Many types of files have lots of repeating information and can be compressed to less than 60 percent of their original size.

The Facts About Disk Compression

DriveSpace 3 is an optional program that you can install when you install Microsoft Plus! or you can install it at a later time. To see if you have DriveSpace 3 available, open the Start menu and choose Programs, Accessories, System Tools. If DriveSpace 3 is not listed in the System Tools menu, you will need to install it using your Microsoft Plus! software (or your Windows 95 CD-ROM if you are using the OSR2 version of Windows 95).

When you run DriveSpace 3, it creates a compressed drive on your existing hard disk. The compressed drive is actually a file, not a physical hard drive, called a *compressed volume file* (CVF). The CVF is stored on a physical, uncompressed drive, called the *host drive*. The CVF is assigned a drive letter, just like a physical drive and can be accessed like any other drive. The file that DriveSpace creates on your hard drive is a hidden, read only, system file, thus is it not acted upon by most normal DOS commands. From the user's point of view, the only difference after running DriveSpace is that the original drive has a lot more free space and there is a new drive, the host drive.

As a rule of thumb, DriveSpace 3 will add 50 to 100 percent more capacity to your disk. The amount of actual compression depends upon the types of files stored on the disk. Some files such as text files or certain graphics files compress significantly, while other files such as an application's EXE file may barely change.

You can run DriveSpace 3 in one of two ways. Typically, you use DriveSpace 3 to compress your entire existing drive to free up more storage space. You can run DriveSpace 3 to compress your C drive, for example, which then becomes a compressed volume file on the host drive H. You also can use DriveSpace 3 to compress a specified amount of the free space on your hard drive to create a new, empty compressed drive. The rest of the hard drive is not compressed. If, for example, you have 80M of free space on your drive C, you can use DriveSpace 3 to compress 25M of the free space to create a new drive D with roughly 50M of free space. You then have 55M free on drive C and 50M on drive D for an effective 105M of free space.

NOTE If you have installed the FAT32 file system on your computer using the Windows 95 OEM Service Release 2 update, you cannot compress your hard disk. DriveSpace 3 does not support compression of FAT32 partitions. ■

▶ **See** "Changing the Estimated Compression Ratio for Your Compressed Drive," **p. 364**

TROUBLESHOOTING

Large files will not copy onto the compressed drive. The available free space displayed for compressed drives is only an estimate. It is based on the average compression for all files on your disk. If the file you try to save does not compress as much as the average, then it may not fit in the available space.

Compressing a Drive with DriveSpace 3

Remember that compressed disks can be slow—the greater the compression, the slower your system's performance is likely to be. Also, compressing your system's primary hard disk can take a long time, during which you can't work with your system.

Use the following steps to compress a disk with DriveSpace 3:

1. Open the Start menu and click Programs, Accessories, System Tools, and DriveSpace. The DriveSpace 3 window appears (see Figure 15.16).

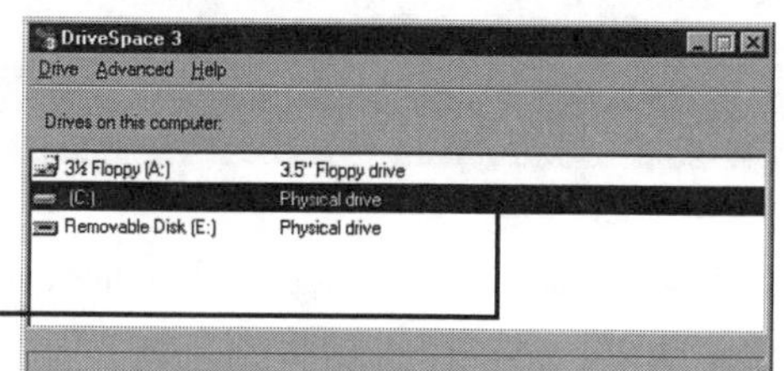

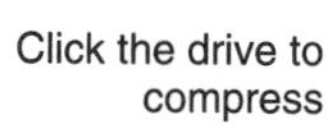

FIG. 15.16
The DriveSpace 3 window displays the available drives on your system.

2. Click the drive that you want to compress.

NOTE If you previously compressed a hard disk with DoubleSpace or DriveSpace (for Windows 95 or for earlier DOS versions), you can select the disk and then choose Drive, Upgrade to convert the disk to DriveSpace 3 format. ■

3. Choose Advanced, Settings. The Disk Compression Settings dialog box appears (see Figure 15.17).
4. Click the option button for the compression method you want to use:
    - No Compression does not compress the disk.

- No Compression, Unless Drive Is at Least X% Full only compresses the disk after it's more full than the percentage you specify.
- Standard Compression compresses the disk contents by approximately a 1.8:1 ratio.
- HiPack Compression compresses the disk contents by up to 2.3:1.

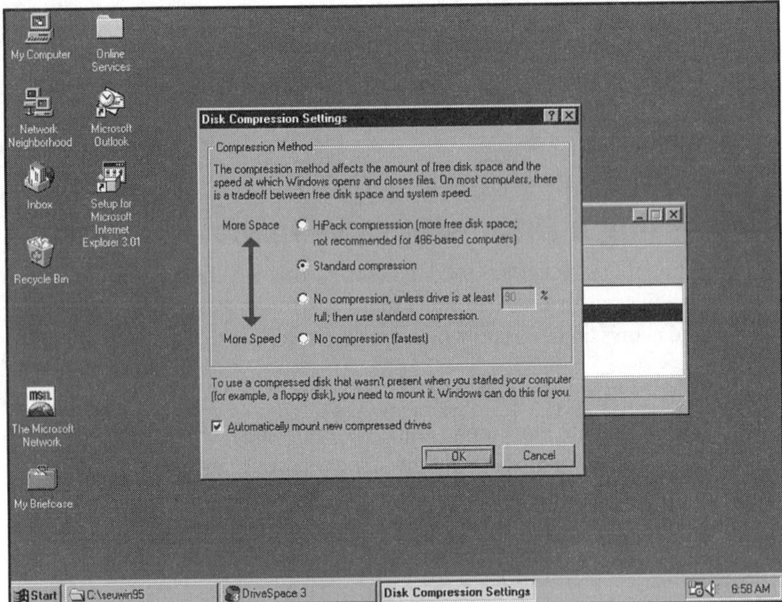

FIG. 15.17 Choose your preferences for compression settings.

NOTE As always, the compression ratio on your hard drive depends on the type of files being compressed. Leave the Automatically Mount New Compressed Drives option checked, especially if you are compressing a floppy disk. This will ensure that the compressed disk is automatically mounted when you insert it in the disk drive. Mounting establishes a connection between a drive letter and the CVF, so the files in the CVF can be read.

5. Click OK to close the Compression Settings dialog box and accept the specified compression method.
6. Choose Drive, Compress. The Compress a Drive dialog box appears (see Figure 15.18), informing you of the estimated results of the compression operation—that is, how much free space and used space the disk will have after compression.
7. Click Options. The Compression Options dialog box appears (see Figure 15.19). Use it to specify a drive letter and free space for the Host drive where DriveSpace 3 will store compressed information about the drive.

   You should only need to change these first two options if your system connects to a network that uses drive H for another purpose. If you compress a floppy disk you might use on another computer that doesn't have DriveSpace 3, click to select the Use

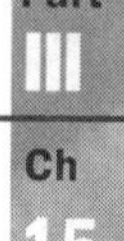

DoubleSpace-Compatible Format check box; note that you do need to select this option for Windows 95 systems without DriveSpace 3 or for systems using DriveSpace from a DOS 6.X version. Click OK to accept the Compression Options you set.

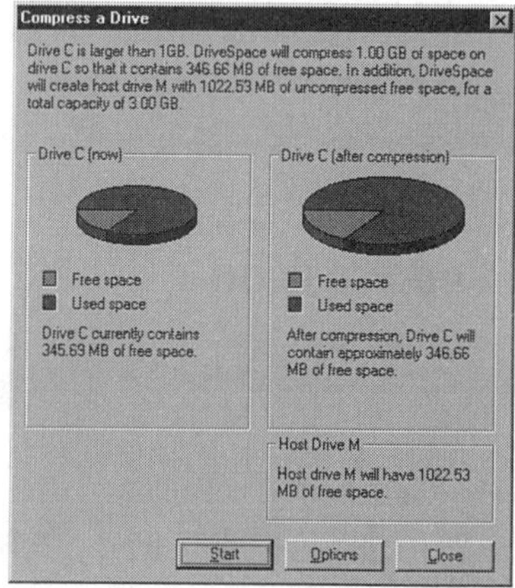

FIG. 15.18 The Compress a Drive dialog box displays information on the size of the selected disk and how much space there will be after running DriveSpace.

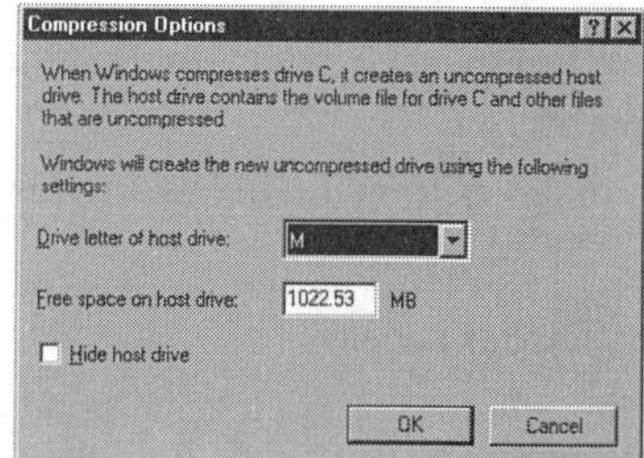

FIG. 15.19 Change the options used for compressing a drive in the Compression Options dialog box.

8. Click the Start button in the Compress a Drive dialog box. The Are You Sure? dialog box appears, asking you to confirm the compression operation (see Figure 15.20).

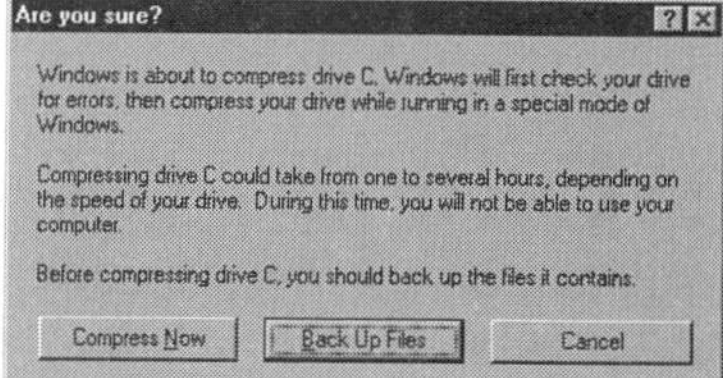

FIG. 15.20 Back up your files before you run DriveSpace by choosing the Back Up Files button.

9. Click the Back Up Files button to make a backup copy of the files on the disk before you compress it. This is an important safety measure; skipping it isn't recommended.
10. DriveSpace 3 runs the backup utility installed to work with your system. Follow any on-screen instructions to complete the backup process.

11. When the backup finishes, click Continue to compress the disk. DriveSpace 3 compresses the disk and then redisplays the Compress a Drive dialog box to report on the compression results.
12. Click Close to complete compressing the disk.
13. A Restart Computer dialog box appears asking if you want to restart your computer. Choose Yes to restart, No to continue working.

    Do not set up new software, change system settings, or run MS-DOS programs until you restart your computer.

Returning a Drive to Normal Compression

DriveSpace also enables you to decompress a drive. Before you decompress a drive, make sure that there will be enough space on the drive to hold all the files on the drive after it is decompressed.

When you choose to decompress a drive and there is not enough room, you get an error dialog box that tells you how much data you have, how much free space you need, and how much data you need to delete or move off of which drive.

To decompress a drive, follow these steps:

1. Open the Start menu and choose Programs, Accessories, System Tools, and DriveSpace 3. The DriveSpace 3 window appears.
2. Select the drive you want to decompress from the Drives on This Computer list.
3. Choose Drive, Uncompress.
4. Choose Start. A confirmation dialog box appears.
5. If you haven't backed up your files, choose the Back Up Files button to open Backup. See Chapter 16, "Backing Up and Protecting Your Data," for detailed information on how to back up your files.
6. Choose Uncompress Now to start the decompression operation. The progress of the decompression operation appears at the bottom of the Uncompress a Drive dialog box.
7. When the message box informing you that the drive has been decompressed appears, choose OK.

Setting Up Your Floppy or Hard Disk to Read Compressed Files

When you work with compressed, removable storage media (such as floppy disks), you must mount the compressed drive if it wasn't present when the computer started. Mounting a drive links a drive letter with a compressed volume file (CVF) and enables your computer to access the files on the compressed volume files.

To mount a compressed drive, follow these steps:

1. Open the DriveSpace 3 window and select the drive you want to mount in the Drives on This Computer list. For example, if you want to read a floppy disk in drive A and the floppy disk has DriveSpace or DoubleSpace compression, then you would select the A drive.

2. Open the Advanced menu and choose Mount.
3. Select the compressed volume file you want to mount. Once you mount a drive, it shows up in the Drives on This Computer list as a compressed drive.

You can select an option so that newly compressed devices automatically mount. Choose Advanced, Settings. Select the Automatically Mount New Compressed Devices option and choose OK. Windows now automatically mounts new compressed devices so that you don't have to mount the compressed device each time you insert it in the computer.

To unmount a compressed drive, follow these steps:

1. Open the DriveSpace 3 window and select the compressed drive you want to unmount from the Drives on this Computer list.
2. Choose Advanced, Unmount.
3. When the message box appears informing you that the operation is complete, choose OK.

Compressing Part of Disk

You don't have to compress your entire hard disk; you can compress some or all of the free space on your hard disk to create a new compressed drive. To create a new compressed drive from part of a hard disk, follow these steps:

1. Open the DriveSpace 3 window and select the drive with the free space you want to use to create a new compressed drive. You cannot select a compressed drive.
2. Choose Advanced, Create Empty. The Create New Compressed Drive dialog box appears, as shown in Figure 15.21.

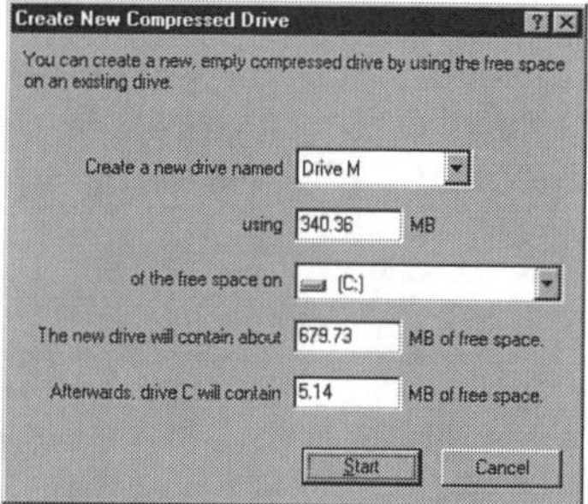

FIG. 15.21 Create a new compressed drive using the free space on your hard disk.

3. Accept the default name for the new drive or select an alternative name from the Create a New Drive Named drop-down list.
4. Enter the amount of free space (in megabytes) you want to use to create the new drive in the Using text box. If you enter a value here, the amount displayed in the new drive will contain about...MB of free space text box changes to reflect how much free space will be created in the new drive.
5. Select the drive that has the free space you want to use to create the new drive from the Of the Free Space On drop-down list.

6. If you know how much free space you want the new drive to have, enter that figure in the New Drive Will Contain About...MB of Free Space text box. If you enter a value here, the amount displayed in the Using text box automatically adjusts to show how much free space on the selected drive will be used for the new drive.

   The amount of free space that will be left on the uncompressed drive is displayed in the Afterwards, drive *letter* will contain...M of free space text box.

7. Choose Start.
8. When the message box appears informing you that the operation is complete, choose OK.

Deleting a Compressed Drive

Deleting a compressed drive is something you want to think seriously about before doing. Deleting a compressed drive removes all the data from the compressed drive returning the drive to a blank decompressed state. One reason for deleting a compressed drive is so that you can remove the physical drive from your computer and have it accessible by any MS-DOS computer. If you only want to return the compressed data to its decompressed form and retain the data on the drive, then use the decompress feature.

▶ **See** "Returning a Drive to Normal Compression," **p. 360**

When you delete a compressed drive, Windows 95 deletes the compressed volume file (CVF) that contains all the compressed data and application files. (The contents of the CVF file are what looks like a compressed disk drive.) The CVF has the name DRVSPACE.000 and is located on the Host drive. You can't manually delete the DRVSPACE.000 file because it has a system attribute. (You can remove the system attribute and then manually delete the file, but deleting the compressed drive is better.)

In addition to deleting the CVF file, deleting a compressed drive also removes from the DRVSPACE.INI file the line ACTIVATE DRIVE= for the drive represented by the CVF. If you have only one compressed drive on your hard disk, then you will also be asked whether you want to delete the DriveSpace driver, DRVSPACE.BIN. You can delete this driver if you do not have other compressed drives on this drive.

CAUTION

When you delete a compressed drive, you lose all the information stored on that drive, so be sure that you have backed up or moved any files you need on this drive before deleting it.

TROUBLESHOOTING

An overzealous novice removed the system attribute from the DRVSPACE.000 file and deleted it. Is there a way to recover the data that was on the compressed drive? If the user has not saved files to that disk after deleting DRVSPACE.000, you may be able to recover the drive. Use an undelete utility to restore the deleted DRVSPACE.000 file, and then exit Windows and restart.

To delete a compressed drive, follow these steps:

1. Open the DriveSpace 3 window and select the compressed drive you want to delete from the Drives on This Computer list.
2. Choose Advanced, Delete.
3. When the confirmation message box appears, choose Yes.
4. A message box appears asking if you want to delete the DriveSpace driver. Choose Yes if this is the only compressed drive on your computer and you will not be using compressed floppy disks. Choose No if you have other compressed drives or if you will be using compressed floppy disks.
5. When the message box appears informing you that the operation is complete, choose OK.
6. You will be prompted to restart Windows 95 or continue. Switch to any open applications and save the documents; then choose Yes. If you choose No, you cannot change system settings, install applications, or use MS-DOS until you restart.

   ▶ **See** "Setting Up Your Floppy or Hard Disk to Read Compressed Files," **p. 360**

If you are in doubt about whether to delete the driver for DriveSpace, remember that it is much easier to reinstall than it is to deinstall the driver. You can remove it now and add it back at any time using the procedure to mount a compressed drive.

Adjusting the Size of the Free Space on a Compressed Drive

You can adjust the distribution of free space between a compressed drive and its host. When you increase the free space on the compressed drive, you decrease the free space on the host drive, and vice versa. To adjust the free space on the compressed and host drives, follow these steps:

1. Open the DriveSpace 3 window and select either the compressed drive or its host from the Drives on This Computer list.
2. Choose Drive, Adjust Free Space; the Adjust Free Space dialog box appears (see Figure 15.22).

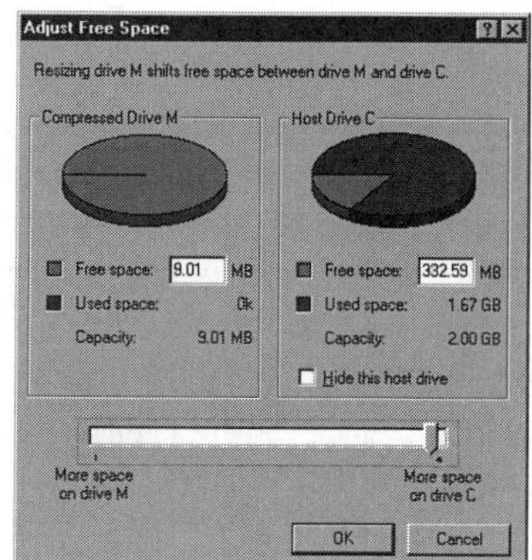

FIG. 15.22
Adjust the distribution of free space between a compressed drive and its host in the Adjust Free Space dialog box.

3. Drag the slider to change the distribution of free space between the compressed and host drives. The pie charts will reflect the amount of free space and used space.
4. Choose OK.

   A message box shows you the amount of free space on the compressed and host drives when the operation is complete.
5. A Restart Computer dialog box appears asking if you want to restart your computer. Choose Yes to restart, No to continue working.

   Do not set up new software, change system settings, or run MS-DOS programs until you restart your computer.

TROUBLESHOOTING

There seems to be enough space on the hard disk to store some very large video and sound files, but even after resizing the compressed drive there still isn't enough space. Some files, such as application, video, and music files, may not compress very much. The estimated free space on a compressed drive, however, is calculated from the average amount of compression for all files on the drive. As a consequence, files that look like they may fit, may not.

Changing the Estimated Compression Ratio for Your Compressed Drive

DriveSpace 3 contains a command that enables you to change the estimated compression ratio. This does not change how tightly data is compressed on your hard drive. It is just an estimate used by Windows 95 to calculate how much free space remains on your hard drive. The remaining free space, as calculated by the estimated compression ratio, is then used in Windows 95 dialog boxes to give you an estimate of how much drive space remains. Changing the compression ratio to a larger number would not compress files tighter but would give you a very misleading idea of how much free space remains.

In general, do not change the compression ratio to more than a two-to-one (2:1) ratio.

You may want to change the estimated compression ratio in order to see a more accurate calculation of the free space available on your compressed drive. There is a reason that you can calculate this number more accurately than Windows 95. Windows 95 calculates the estimated compression ratio from an average of the actual file size and the compressed file size for all files on the drive. Every time a file is saved or erased, Windows 95 recalculates the estimated compression ratio and then uses that number to calculate the estimated free space remain.

The problem with accepting the estimated compression ratio is that Windows 95 has no idea what types of files you store on the hard disk. Since you are familiar with the types of files you store, you can estimate a better compression ratio. This gives you a better idea of the amount of free space available.

To understand the problem, you must know that different files compress by different amounts. Files such as text files and some graphics files contain a lot of repetitive information that can be tightly compressed into a small space. Other files such as an application's EXE files or a video's JPEG or MPEG files have little room for compression and may not change significantly in size.

If you have just installed many application files on a compressed drive with few data files, then Windows 95 will calculate a low compression ratio. Conversely, if your compressed drive has few application or multimedia files, then the estimated compression ratio will be higher. As long as you continue saving and removing the same type of files, Windows 95 will report a fairly accurate estimated free space. But if you change the type of files you save, the estimated free space will be wrong because the new files compress to a different amount.

If you will not be adding more application or multimedia files to your compressed drive, but you will be adding a lot more data files, then you may want to increase the estimated compression ratio to get a more accurate reading of free space. Conversely, a drive that has stored word processing files may have much less space available than it appears to have when you begin storing sound, video, and application files on it.

CAUTION

What you see is not necessarily what you get when dealing with compression ratios. Some files such as EXE application files or JPEG and MPEG video files compress very little. This means that even though the estimated free space may be 15M, it's doubtful that 12M of JPEG, MPEG, or EXE files would fit because they do not compress as tightly as other files have.

To adjust the compression ratio, follow these steps:

1. Open the DriveSpace 3 window and select the compressed drive whose compression ratio you want to adjust from the Drives on This Computer list.
2. Choose Advanced, Change Ratio; the Compression Ratio dialog box appears (see Figure 15.23).

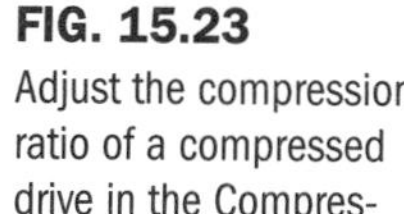

FIG. 15.23
Adjust the compression ratio of a compressed drive in the Compression Ratio dialog box.

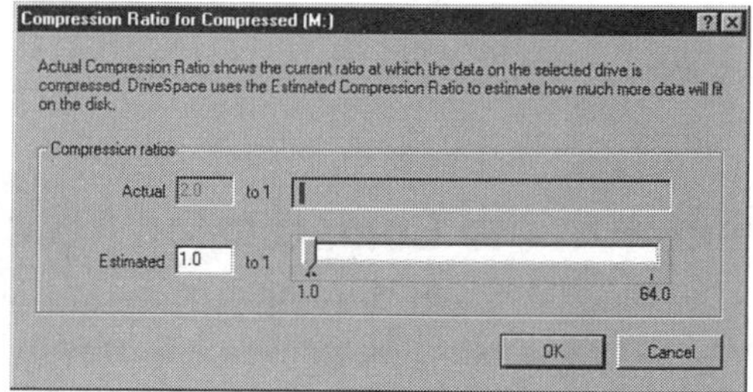

3. Drag the Estimated Compression Ratio slider to adjust the compression ratio.
4. When the message box appears informing you that the operation is complete, choose OK.

Viewing the Properties of a Compressed Drive

You can view the properties of a compressed drive or its host using the Drive Properties command. You can find out the name of the compressed volume file and what drive it is stored on, the amount of free and used space on the drive, and the compression ratio if it is a compressed drive.

To view the properties of a drive, follow these steps:

1. Open the DriveSpace 3 window and select the drive whose properties you want to view from the Drives on This Computer list.
2. Choose Drive, Properties. The Compression Information dialog box appears, as shown in Figure 15.24.

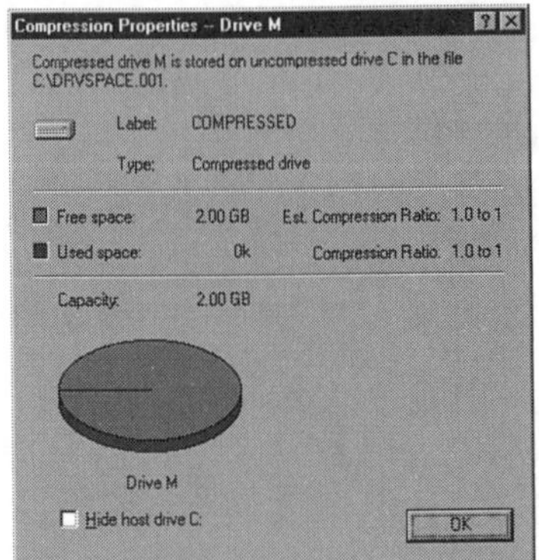

FIG. 15.24 View the properties of a compressed drive or its host in the Compression Information dialog box.

3. You can select the Hide Host Drive option to hide the display of this drive when the drive contents display in the Explorer or My Computer window and in some dialog boxes such as Open and Save As. If you select this option, a message box informs you that you cannot use the data or free space on the drive. Choose Yes to confirm that you want to hide the drive.

   You can use the DriveSpace Properties dialog box to unhide the host drive if you change your mind at a later time.
4. Choose OK.

Improving Compression with the Compression Agent

Compression Agent is a tool that comes with Microsoft Plus! that provides even higher levels of compression and, used in conjunction with DriveSpace 3, allows you to optimize the balance between maximizing disk space and performance. You can specify that particular files and folders are compressed using one of two high compression formats (UltraPack or HiPack) or not at all.

Compression Agent, unlike DriveSpace, doesn't compress files as they are used. Instead, it compresses your files when you run the program. Because it can take a long time to compress your files using the Compression Agent, it is best to run the program when you are not working. You can use the System Agent, discussed in the next section, to schedule the Compression Agent to run after work hours.

To run the Compression Agent, follow these steps:

1. Open the Start menu and click Programs, Accessories, System Tools, and Compression Agent. The Compression Agent dialog box appears (see Figure 15.25).

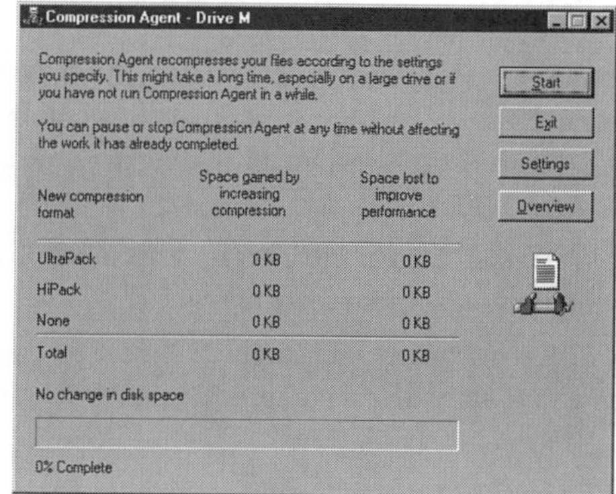

FIG. 15.25
The Compression Agent dialog box is used to set up and run Compression Agent.

2. Click Start to run Compression Agent using the default settings. Compression Agent will recompress the drive file by file, using the best compression method for each file.
3. To change the settings used by Compression Agent, click the Settings button. The Compression Agent Settings dialog box appears (see Figure 15.26).

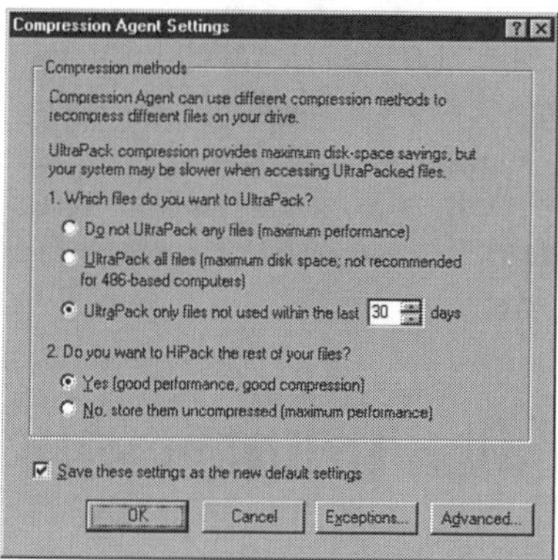

FIG. 15.26
You can specify which compression method you want used on which files in the Compression Agent Settings dialog box.

4. Specify which files you want to UltraPack in the first set of options:
   - Select the Do Not UltraPack Any Files option to maximize performance.
   - Select the UltraPack All Files option to maximize space. Packing and unpacking files using this method is slow, so it is recommended for Pentium systems only.

- Select the UltraPack Only Files Not Used Within the Last Days option to specify that only those files that have not been modified in a specified number of days be UltraPacked.

5. Specify whether or not to HiPack the remaining files in the second set of options:
   - Select Yes to HiPack the remaining files. This option yields a good balance between performance and space-savings.
   - Select No to leave the remaining files uncompressed. Use this option if you want to maximize performance.
6. The Compression Agent can reduce the compression method used for files you have used recently (as specified in step 4). You can override this option when disk space starts to get low by clicking Advanced and specifying a setting in the Advanced Settings dialog box.

   Select the Leave all UltraPacked files in the UltraPack format option if you want files UltraPacked even if you have used them recently.
7. If you want to specify different compression settings for particular files or folders, click the Exceptions button and specify which compression method you want to use for which files and folders.
8. Click Start to run the Compression Agent using your settings.

By manipulating the settings used in both DriveSpace 3 and in Compression Agent, you can fine-tune the balance between performance and disk space, depending on your priorities. For example, to maximize performance while still gaining the benefits of disk compression, you can turn off compression in DriveSpace's Disk Compression Settings dialog box and run the Compression Agent at night to compress your files.

After you choose the settings you want in the Compression Agent, use the System Agent as described in the section "Running Disk Performance Utilities with the System Agent" to run the Compression Agent and recompress the specified disk.

Even when you tell DriveSpace not to compress files, you save space. This is because DriveSpace 3 uses sectors (512 bytes) instead of clusters (32K in size on a 1G drive) as the minimum storage unit. This significantly improves storage efficiency.

Running Disk Performance Utilities with the System Agent

Microsoft Plus! for Windows 95 provides the System Agent, a program that enables you to schedule when to run the system maintenance utilities discussed in this chapter. The System Agent can run other programs, as well, and notify you when your hard disk is low on space.

By default, the System Agent is enabled after you install Plus! This means that each time you start Windows 95, the System Agent starts automatically and runs in the background, only becoming active when it needs to start a scheduled program or notify you of low disk space. Even though System Agent is active by default, it isn't fully set up. After you install System Agent, it automatically places Low Disk Space Notification, ScanDisk for Windows (Standard Test), Disk Defragmenter, and ScanDisk for Windows (Thorough Test) programs in the System Agent. You need to manually tell the System Agent which other programs to run, when to run them, and which program features to use.

To schedule programs with the System Agent, use the following steps:

1. Open the Start menu and choose Programs, Accessories, System Tools, System Agent. The System Agent window opens (see Figure 15.27).

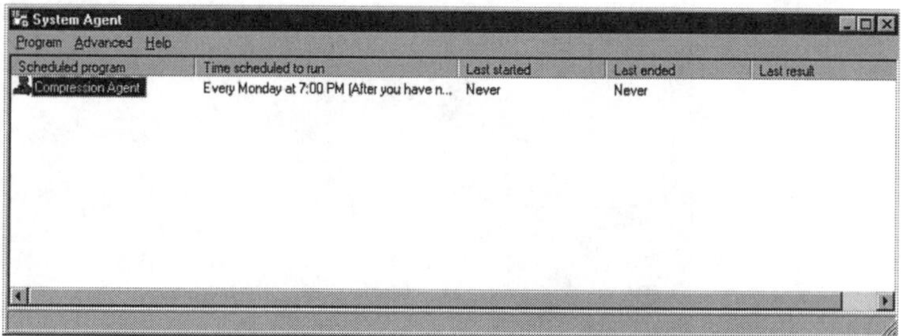

FIG. 15.27 The System Agent window lists the currently scheduled programs.

2. Choose Program, Schedule a New Program. The Schedule a New Program dialog box appears (see Figure 15.28).

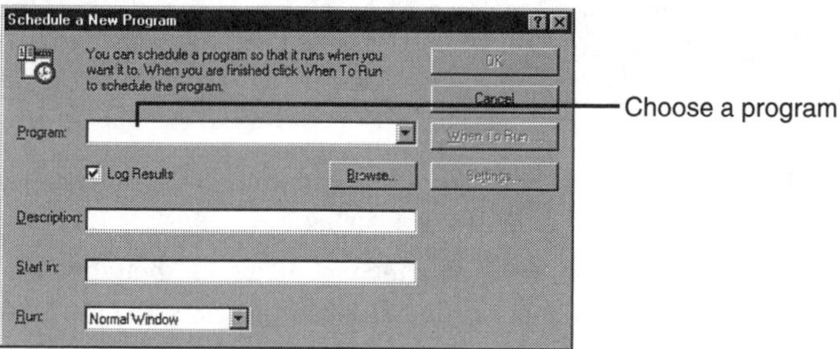

FIG. 15.28 Use the Schedule a New Program dialog box to select programs for System Agent to run according to the schedule you set.

3. Click the drop-down list arrow to open the Program list. Choose a program from the list that appears. You can choose ScanDisk for Windows, Disk Defragmenter, Compression Agent, or Low Disk Space Notification. If you want to run a program other than one of these, click Browse, select the program to run in the Browse dialog box, and then click OK. No matter what method you use, the selected program appears as the Program choice.
4. If you want, you can edit the Description for the program and the Start In folder, which specifies the folder containing files the program needs to run.
5. Open the Run drop-down list and specify whether you want the program to run in a Normal Window, Minimized, or Maximized.

Schedule time-consuming programs such as Disk Defragmenter for a time you won't normally use your computer. Then, leave your computer on during that time, and System Agent will handle the task for you.

6. To specify the schedule for the program, click the When to Run button. The Change Schedule of... dialog box appears (see Figure 15.29).

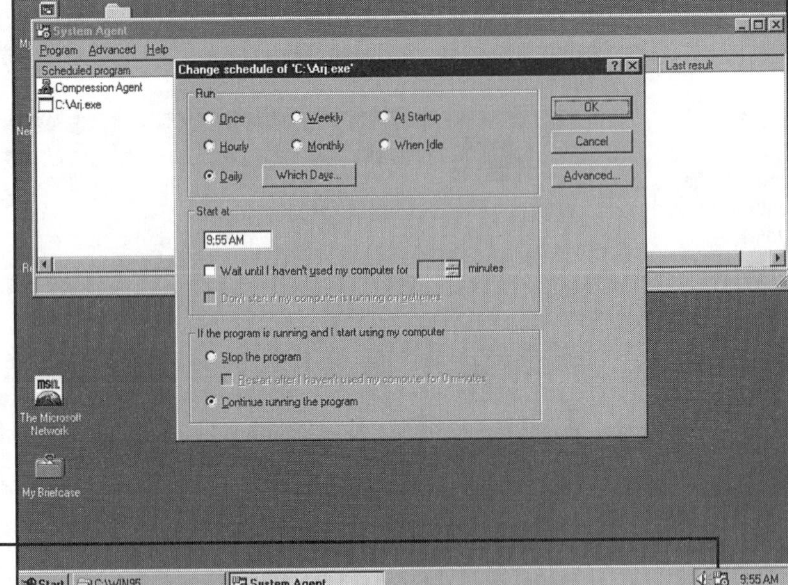

FIG. 15.29
Use the Change Schedule dialog box to set up a schedule for the selected program.

This icon in the status area of the taskbar lets you know that Windows 95 loaded System Agent

7. Click a Run option, such as Weekly or Monthly. Your choice here affects the options available in the Start At area of the dialog box.
8. Specify the options you want in the Start At area. Although there might be other options depending on your choice in step 7, you always need to enter a starting time. Also, you can specify a number of minutes to tell System Agent to wait if you're using your computer when the scheduled program runtime occurs.
9. Choose whether System Agent should Stop the Program or Continue Running the Program should you start using your computer when the scheduled program is running. Stopping the program can protect against data loss while running system utilities.
10. Click Settings to accept your changed schedule of options and to control which features the selected program uses when the System Agent runs the program. The Scheduled Settings dialog box that appears varies depending on the selected program.
11. Specify the settings you want for the selected program; then click OK to close the Scheduled Settings dialog box.

12. Click OK again to finish scheduling the program. System Agent adds the program to the list of scheduled programs.

NOTE Remember that you can schedule the same program to run at different times with different settings. For example, you can schedule a standard ScanDisk check once a week, plus a thorough check once a month. ■

Although you can use the Program menu choices to make changes to the schedule and settings for one of the listed programs, it's faster to simply right-click the program you want to make changes for. A shortcut menu appears, from which you can choose the following:

- Choose Properties to change things such as the program startup folder and settings (click the Settings button in the dialog box that appears).
- Use the Change Schedule option to adjust how often System Agent runs the program.
- Choose Run Now to run the program immediately, using the settings you specified.
- Choose the Disable option to prevent the listed program from running at the designated time but leave the program on the list; choose Disable again to reinstate the program's schedule.
- Choose Remove to delete the selected program from the System Agent list; confirm the deletion by clicking Yes at the warning that appears.

The Advanced menu in System Agent offers two commands for controlling System Agent itself. Toggle the Suspend System Agent option off whenever you want to stop all your regularly scheduled programs from running; then toggle this choice back on when you need to. The Stop Using System Agent choice completely stops the System Agent operation; after you use this option, System Agent no longer loads when you start Windows, and you have to select System Agent from the System Tools Shortcuts to start using it. To close System Agent after setting it up, choose Program, Exit.

If you have installed Internet Explorer 4.0, you will not find System Agent in your System Tools menu. System Agent is upgraded to the Task Scheduler when you install Internet Explorer 4.0, and the System Agent item in the System Tools menu is replaced with the Scheduled Tasks folder icon. To learn how to use the Task Scheduler, see Chapter 23, "Using FrontPage Express and Internet Components."

Monitoring Your System

Windows 95 comes with an application called System Monitor that enables you to monitor the resources on your computer. You can see if you have the System Monitor installed by opening the Start menu, clicking Programs, Accessories, System Tools, and checking for the System Monitor item. If you do not see it on the menu or if it does not start, then you need to rerun Windows 95 and reinstall the System Monitor. Chapter 2 describes how to install and reinstall Windows 95.

You can see information about the 32-bit file system, network clients and servers, and the virtual memory manager, among other things. Most of this information is highly technical in nature and useful only to advanced users. You can display the information in either bar or line charts or as numeric values. To open the System Monitor, open the Start menu; choose Programs, Accessories, System Tools, and System Monitor. The System Monitor window appears, as shown in Figure 15.30.

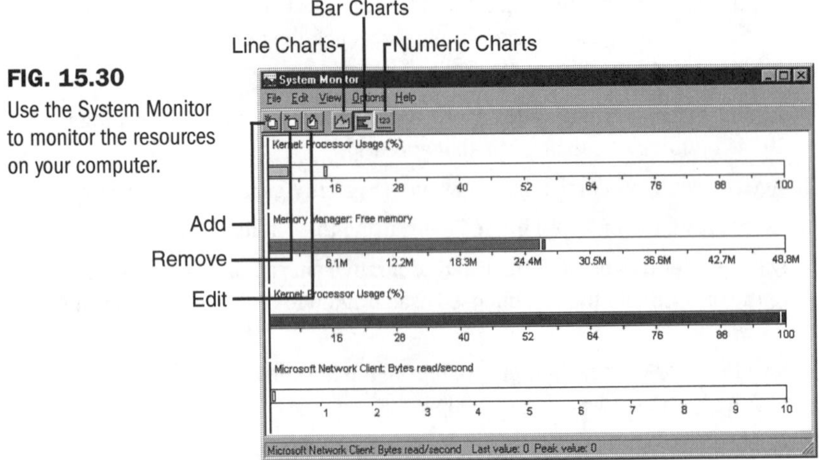

FIG. 15.30
Use the System Monitor to monitor the resources on your computer.

To monitor an item in System Monitor, follow these steps:

1. Select the item you want to monitor by choosing Edit, Add Item; alternatively, click the Add tool. The Add Item dialog box appears (see Figure 15.31).

   You can obtain information on what an item is by selecting the item and clicking Explain. When you select an item in the right box, the explain button becomes an option.

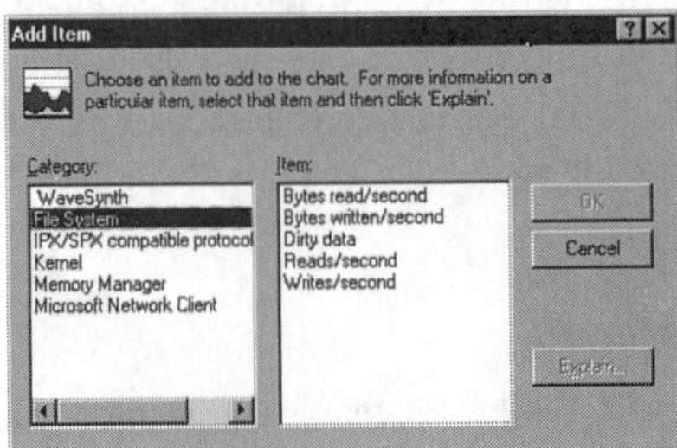

FIG. 15.31
Select the items you want to monitor in the Add Item dialog box.

2. Choose OK.
3. Repeat steps 1 and 2 to add additional items to the window.

To remove an item from the window, follow these steps:

1. Choose Edit, Remove Item; alternatively, click the Remove tool.
2. Select the item you want to remove and choose OK.

You can edit an item that is being monitored, changing its display color and the scaling used in its chart. To edit an item, follow these steps:

1. Choose Edit, Edit Item, or click the Edit tool, to display the Edit Item dialog box.
2. Select the item you want to edit and choose OK. The Chart Options dialog box appears, as shown in Figure 15.32.

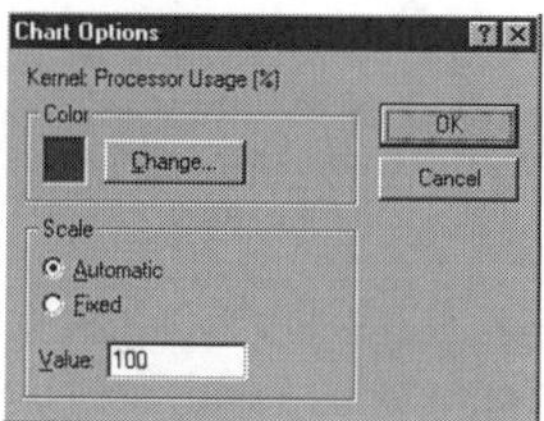

FIG. 15.32 Change the display of an item being monitored in the Chart Options dialog box.

3. Choose Change to change the color of the item.
4. Select Automatic to let System Monitor set the maximum value on the Y-axis.

   or

   Select Fixed and type a value in the Value text box to set your own maximum value for the Y-axis.
5. Choose OK.

You can display the items being monitored as either a line or bar chart or as a numeric value. To change the display, open the View menu and choose Line Charts, Bar Charts, or Numeric Charts; alternatively, click the appropriate tool on the toolbar.

If you want the System Monitor window to stay on top of other windows, even when you work in another program, open the View menu and choose Always on Top. This is handy if you want to monitor some resource as you work in a program. You can shrink the window so that it doesn't take up too much room. Choose the View, Always on Top command again when you don't want the System Monitor window to stay on top of other windows. You can also hide the title bar so that all the System Monitor window is devoted to displaying the chart: Choose the View, Hide Title Bar command. To redisplay the title bar, double-click the chart or press Esc.

Pressing Esc also will hide the title bar if pressed when the title bar is visible.

You can adjust the frequency at which the chart updates by choosing the Options, Chart command and moving the slider to change the update interval. If you are on a network, choose File, Connect to connect to a different computer.

NOTE You can quickly find out how much free disk space there is on a hard disk or floppy disk. Select the disk you want to check in either the Explorer or My Computer, and choose the File, Properties command (alternatively, right-click the desired disk and choose Properties from the shortcut menu). The amount of free space on the disk appears in the Properties dialog box.

Improving Memory Use with Virtual Memory

Your computer has a certain amount of physical memory (RAM) installed. Typically, computers running Windows have at least 4M of RAM, and often 8M or more. The more memory you have, the more programs you can run at the same time and the faster your system operates. However, with Windows 95, you can use a special area of the hard disk as an extension of RAM, called *virtual memory*, to increase the amount of memory available to programs. Using virtual memory, you can run more programs at the same time than is normally possible using only the RAM on the system.

When RAM is tight, Windows begins to move *pages* of code and data from RAM to the hard disk to make more room in RAM. Windows uses a *least-recently used* technique to move pages of memory to the disk, selecting first the pages of code and data not recently accessed by a program. If a program requires a piece of data no longer in physical memory, Windows retrieves the information from disk, paging other information from memory to disk to make room. To programs running in Windows, no difference exists between RAM in the system and virtual memory on the disk.

When you install Windows 95, it automatically determines how much hard disk space to use for virtual memory, depending on the amount of free disk space. In most cases, you should let Windows determine the settings used for virtual memory on your computer. Unless you know what you are doing, changing the settings manually can adversely affect the performance of your computer. If you do want to specify your own virtual memory settings, follow these steps:

1. Open the Start menu and choose Settings, Control Panel.
2. Double-click the System icon to display the System Properties dialog box; select the Performance tab.
3. Click the Virtual Memory tab to display the Virtual Memory dialog box shown in Figure 15.33.
4. Select the Let Me Specify My Own Virtual Memory Settings option.
5. If you want to use a different hard disk for virtual memory than already specified, select a new disk from the Hard Disk drop-down list. The amount of free space on the hard disk appears next to the drive letter.

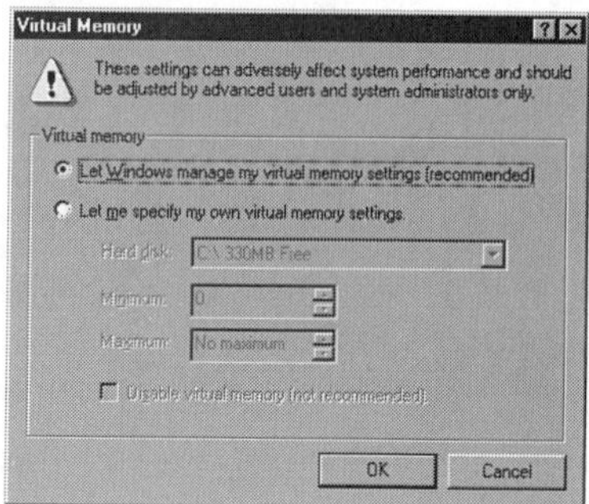

FIG. 15.33
You can let Windows manage your virtual memory settings or specify your own in the Virtual Memory dialog box. Microsoft recommends you let Windows manage virtual memory settings.

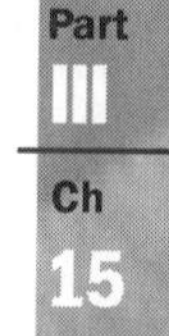

6. Specify the minimum amount (in megabytes) of hard disk space you want Windows to use for virtual memory in the Minimum text box.
7. Specify the maximum amount of memory (in megabytes) you want Windows to use for virtual memory in the Maximum text box.
8. Choose OK.

The Virtual Memory dialog box contains a Disable virtual memory (not recommended) check box at the bottom. This turns off all use of virtual memory and is not recommended. ●

CHAPTER 16

Backing Up and Protecting Your Data

by Ron Person

In this chapter

Backing Up Your Files

As you know, there is more information stored on your hard drive than you can possibly fit on a single floppy disk. The Windows Backup program automatically overcomes this problem by creating a duplicate image of your hard disk's data on a magnetic tape or by spreading an image across multiple floppy disks—as many as necessary to back up your data. During the backup operation, Windows fills each disk in the set to capacity before requesting the next disk. The collection of all these duplicate files and folders is the *backup set*.

As hard disks grow in capacity, it becomes more and more laborious to use floppy disks to back up your data. A much more convenient method is to use a tape backup system. You can fit much more data on a magnetic tape and may be able to back up your entire hard drive with one tape. With tape backups, you also avoid the inconvenience of having to sit at your computer swapping floppy disks. In fact, you can initiate the backup when you leave for lunch; when you return, it will be done.

CAUTION

You put the entire concept of having secure data at risk if your backups are not kept in a safe location, physically separate from the original data. For a small company, the physical location for the backup set can be a safe deposit box or the president's house. For a large company, there are services that pick up tapes and store them in disaster-proof vaults. I know of two instances in which the backups were lost along with the original system. In one case, a thief stole the backup floppy disks that sat next to the computer. In the other case, the fire that destroyed the legal firm's computers also destroyed their backups, which were in a closet in an adjacent room.

NOTE In the last few years, several new options for backing up large amounts of data have appeared on the market. The ubiquitous Iomega Zip Drive is a very convenient way to back up moderate amounts of data (a Zip disk can hold 100M of data). Iomega's Jaz Drive disks can hold up to 1G, ideal for today's large-capacity hard drives. Removable disk media such as these are much faster than tape drives and more convenient to use. Software for backing up your hard drives come with both of these products. For more information, visit Iomega's Web site:

http://www.iomega.com/

NOTE Backup does not install as part of a typical or minimum installation. If Backup is not installed and you want it, refer to Chapter 25, "Installing, Running, and Uninstalling Windows Applications," on how to add programs. On the Windows Setup page of the Add/Remove Programs Properties sheet, look for Backup in the Disk Tools items in the Components list.

To start the backup program, open the Start menu and click Programs, Accessories, System Tools, and Backup. When you first start Backup, you may see a Welcome to Microsoft Backup dialog box that describes the process of making backups. You can select the Don't Show This Again check box if you do not want to see this dialog box again. Backup will also try to detect a tape backup device when you first run it. And you may see a message box that says "Backup has created a Full System Backup file set for you." This means that until you specify otherwise, Backup marks all files and folders to be part of the backup. It is a very good idea to do a Full System Backup at least once a week or once a month, depending on the value of your data and how often program configurations change.

Create a Full System Backup occasionally. It has all the configuration and registry files necessary to rebuild your system from a disaster.

Once you are past these initial dialog boxes, the Backup dialog box appears, as shown in Figure 16.1.

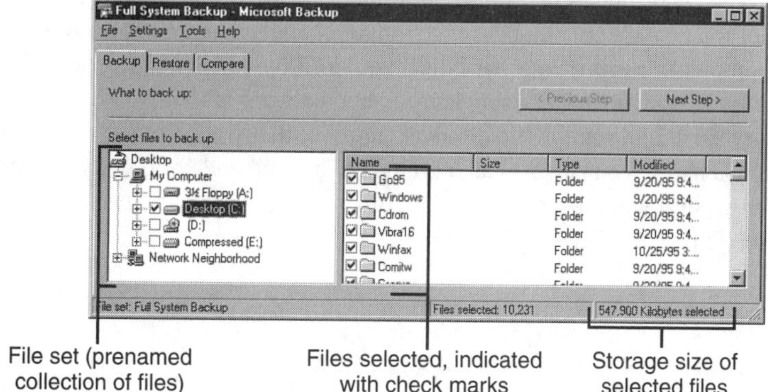

FIG. 16.1
Windows Backup creates duplicate copies of files and folders, compares backups to original files, and restores duplicate files and folders.

Windows divides the three basic functions of Backup into tabs in the Backup dialog box:

- **Backup.** Copies one or more files and folders from your hard disk.
- **Compare.** Compares the files in a backup set to make sure that they match the source files on the hard disk.
- **Restore.** Copies one or more files from your backup set to the hard disk or to another floppy disk.

In addition to these major functions, you can access several other operations from the pull-down menus:

- The File menu enables you to load and save setup files that define settings to be used when backing up and restoring files. The File menu also enables you to print a list of files contained in a backup set.
- The Settings, File Filtering command enables you to filter the folders or file types you want to include in a backup set (this command is discussed in detail later in this chapter). Using the Settings, Options command, you can set various options for each of the major functions, as well as options that affect the program generally.
- The Tools menu contains commands for working with tapes.

Understanding Backup

Before you implement a backup strategy, you need to understand the difference between *full* and *incremental* backups, the two types of backups that you can perform with Windows Backup. When you carry out a full backup, all files and folders on the selected drive are backed up. With a full backup set, you can completely restore your system to its original state in the event of a catastrophe. The disadvantages to a full backup are that it can take a lot of time and storage space if you have many files on your hard drive. The first step of your backup strategy, however, should include a full backup.

With an incremental backup, only those files that have changed since the last full or incremental backup (whichever was last), using the same backup set, are backed up. Typically, you start a backup cycle with a full backup and then periodically perform an incremental backup, using a different set of floppy disks or a new tape, for each incremental backup. Each incremental backup set will contain only those files that have changed since the previous backup. If you need to completely restore your hard disk, you need the full backup set and all the incremental backup sets. The advantage of using incremental backups is that it takes much less time and less space than a full backup. The disadvantages are that you must use a new set of disks (or a new tape) each time you perform an incremental backup and restoring your hard disk is more complicated, since you need to use each of the incremental backup sets, in addition to the full backup set, to be sure that you get the most recent version of a file.

CAUTION

To back up all the files you need to completely restore your system, including essential system files used by Windows 95, you need to use the *Full System Backup Set*. This is the only way to safely back up all the files you need to rebuild your system after a catastrophe. Selecting the drive you want to back up in the Select Files to Back Up pane *will not* back up important system files needed to fully restore your system.

An Overview of How to Back Up Your Hard Disk

Backup makes it easy to name different sets of backup files so that you don't have to select the files and folders each time. When you aren't using your computer (at lunch time, when you return phone messages, or when you leave work), you can start a backup.

Here is the general procedure for creating a backup:

1. Have enough formatted floppy disks or tapes to store the backup.
2. Start Windows Backup.
3. Select the name of a backup set you previously created. Alternatively, manually select the drives, files, and folders you want to back up.
4. Select the Next Step button; then select the destination to which you want to back up. This can be to a tape, to a floppy disk drive, or to another hard disk.
5. Start the backup.

When Backup finishes, you should store the backup media in a safe location physically separate from the computers.

For an extensive list of tape drives compatible with Backup, choose Help, select the Contents tab, and then select the Using Tapes for Backup item. You will also find a list of drives that are not compatible with Backup.

Windows Backup supports the following tape drives and backup devices:

- Hard disks
- Network drives
- Floppy disks
- QIC 40, 80, and 3010 tape drives connected to a primary floppy disk controller
- QIC 40, 80, and 3010 tape drives, manufactured by Colorado Memory Systems and connected to a parallel port

Backup supports compression using the industry standard QIC-113 format. It can read tapes from other backup programs that use the same format with or without compression. Full backups can be restored to a hard disk of another type.

Preparing a Backup Schedule

When you back up important or large amounts of data, it's important to have a backup schedule and a rotation plan for the backup tapes.

Creating a full backup is important to preserving your entire system. Full backups take care of merging Registry settings and the file replacements necessary when restoring a Windows system.

Basically, the backup schedule for most businesses should consist of a full system backup followed by partial or differential backups spread over time. Should your computer ever completely fail, you can rebuild your system using the full backup (which restores Windows, the system Registry, all applications, and their data files as they existed on a specific date). You can then use the partial or differential backups (which store only changed files) to bring the restored system back to its current status. Do a full system backup once a week and a differential backup daily.

Some companies create a full system backup every day. At the end of the week, the tapes are taken to an off-site vault and a new set of tapes are started. Multiple sets of backup tapes are used and rotated between the on-site and off-site storage locations.

CAUTION

Never use one set of tapes for all your backups. If you have only one set of tapes, composed of a full backup and partials, creating another backup means that you overwrite one of the previous backups. Should the

continues

continued

tape fail or the computer fail during backup, you might be left with no backups capable of restoring your system.

Backing Up Files

Whenever you frequently work with the same files and settings, save them as a file set.

Running a backup operation consists of selecting the files you want to backup, specifying the destination for the backup files, and starting the backup. The files that you select for backup will be stored in a single backup file with the extension QIC. To perform a backup, follow these steps:

1. Open the Start menu, click Programs, Accessories, System Tools, and Backup.
2. Select the drive containing the files you want to back up. To select the drive, click the check box for the drive in the left pane of the Backup window.

   In Figure 16.1, local drive C is selected. The files and folders on the drive appear in the right pane. You can expand and collapse the hierarchical display in the left pane by clicking the plus (+) and minus (–) signs next to the folders.
3. Select the files and folders you want to back up. If you want to back up using a file set you have previously named, choose File, Open File Set and select the file set you want to back up.

   ▶ **See** "Saving File Sets," **p. 386**

   You can select all the files in a folder by clicking the check box next to the folder's name in the left pane of the Backup dialog box.

   To view the files and folders inside a folder, in the left pane, open the folder containing the folders or files you want to view, and then in the left pane click the name of the folder whose contents you want to see; its contents appear in the right pane. You can then select individual files or folders inside that folder.

   To select the entire drive, click the box next to the drive in the left pane.

   If you select a folder with many files, a File Selection dialog box momentarily appears, notifying you that file selection is in progress; the box displays the number of files and their total size as the selection progresses.

   The total number of files currently selected and their cumulative size appears in the status bar at the bottom of the window.
4. When you finish selecting the files and folders you want to back up, click the Next Step > button.
5. Select the destination for the backup files (see Figure 16.2).

   If you select a tape drive, the volume name for that tape appears in the Selected Device or Location box. If you select a disk drive, this box shows the drive letter or path, such as A:\.

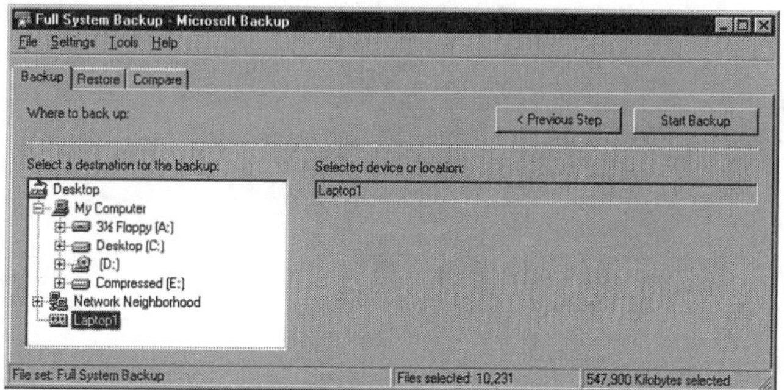

FIG. 16.2
Select the destination for the files you want to back up.

6. Save the file settings for this backup set if you will be doing this backup frequently (see "Saving File Sets," later in this chapter, for more information on saving backup sets).
7. Click the Start Backup button.
8. Type a name for the backup set in the Backup Set Label dialog box that appears (see Figure 16.3). This will be the name of the file containing all the files you have selected for backup.

   If you want to prevent unauthorized people from restoring the backup and stealing your data, click the Password Protect button in the Backup Set Label dialog box and enter a password.

   The name you enter for the backup set is used by you and the computer to identify the data if you ever need to restore or compare it. You can use meaningful names that include spaces, symbols, and numbers. You may want to use a name such as *Accounting, full backup 5/10/95.*

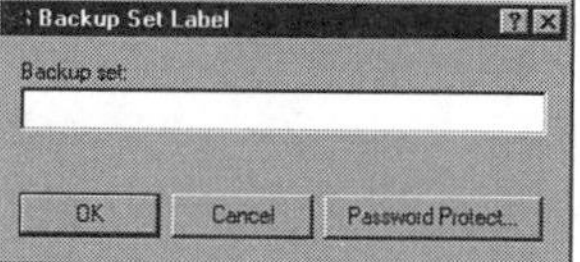

FIG. 16.3
Name the backup set in the Backup Set Label dialog box.

CAUTION

Do not forget the password you assign to your backup set. Without it, there is no way to use your backup.

When you have specified a backup label and an optional password, choose OK. The Backup message box appears (see Figure 16.4), showing you the progress of the backup operation. You can cancel the operation by choosing the Cancel button.

If you are backing up to floppy disks, a message box prompts you when you need to insert the next disk, if necessary.

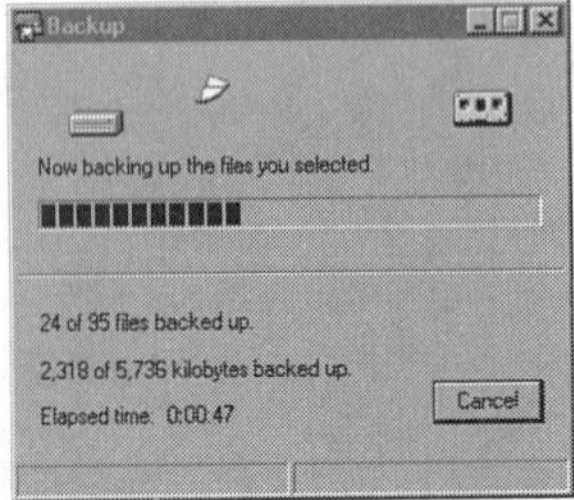

FIG. 16.4
You can monitor the progress of a backup operation in the Backup message box.

9. When the message box appears informing you that the backup operation is complete, click OK. Click OK again to return to the Backup dialog box.

TROUBLESHOOTING

I tried to back up my hard disk on to my Iomega Zip drive with no success. Is there a way to use Windows Backup with my Zip drive? Windows Backup does not support disk spanning with the Zip drive. In other words, if your backup set requires more than one Zip disk, Backup won't work. You can use the backup software that comes with your Zip drive to back up an entire disk onto Zip disks.

The Task Scheduler, available with Internet Explorer 4, will run single copy commands or batch files of copy commands at times that you schedule. To learn more about the Task Scheduler see "Using the Task Scheduler," in Chapter 22.

Using Backup to Create an Archive The Backup program is a handy way to archive files. Suppose that you want to make room on your hard disk by deleting some files you are not currently using but want to use at a later date. Use Backup to archive the files to floppy disks or a tape; then delete the files from the hard disk. If you need the files later, use the restore function to put them back on your hard disk.

▶ **See** "Restoring Files," **p. 392**

Using Backup to Copy Files to Another Computer Another use for Backup is for transferring folders and files to another computer. The benefit of using Backup for this task is that it takes care of spreading the files across multiple floppy disks when necessary, and it preserves the arrangement of folders, so that you can duplicate your folder organization on another computer. If you purchase a laptop, for example, you can use Backup to transfer the information on your desktop computer to the laptop, including the arrangement of your folders.

Scheduling Backups Using System Agent

You can schedule your backups to run automatically when you are not working with your computer using the System Agent that comes with Microsoft Plus! for Windows. The System Agent has a default schedule for running some of the disk utilities that come with Windows 95, so you can schedule additional programs to run at specified times. To schedule Backup to run automatically, follow these steps:

1. Create a backup set following the steps outlined in "Saving File Sets," later in this chapter.

   Before you save the backup set, choose Setting, Drag and Drop, and clear the Confirm Operation Before Beginning and Quit Backup After Operation is Finished options. Choose OK.
2. Exit Backup.
3. Click Start, Programs, Accessories, System Tools, and System Agent.
4. Choose Program, Schedule a New Program.
5. Type the following in the Program text box:

   "C:\Program Files\Accessories\Backup.exe" C:\Program Files\Accessories*setname.set*

   Setname.set is the name of the backup set you created.
6. Choose the When to Run button and schedule when you want Backup to run.
7. Exit System Agent.

Be sure to leave your computer running if you have scheduled Backup to run after you leave work. You can create two different schedules, one that does a full backup, perhaps once a week, and another that does daily incremental backups.

Changing Backup Settings and Options

You can change several settings and options that affect your backup operations. To change the settings and options for the backup operation, follow these steps:

1. Open the Settings menu and choose Options.
2. Click the Backup tab to display the Settings–Options dialog box shown in Figure 16.5.

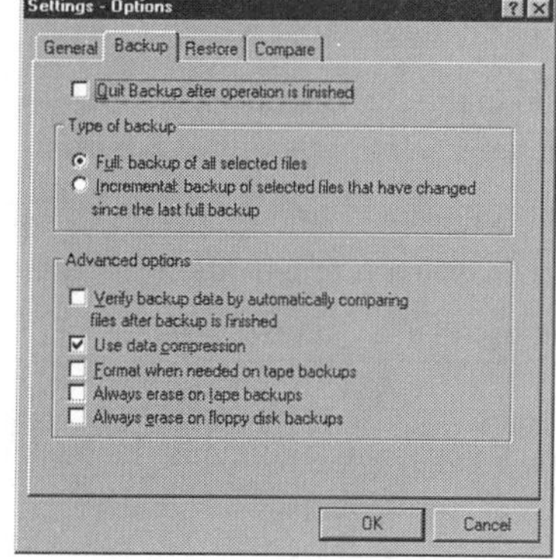

FIG. 16.5
Use the Backup tab in the Settings–Options dialog box to change the settings and options that affect the way backup operations work.

3. Change or select from the following options and then choose OK.

Option	Function
Quit Backup After Operation Is Finished	Closes Backup when the backup operation is completed.
Full: Backup of All Selected Files	Backs up all selected files, regardless of whether file has changed since the last backup.
Differential: Backup of Selected Files that Have Changed Since the Last Full Backup	Only backs up selected files that have changed since the last full backup.
Verify Backup Data by Automatically Comparing Files After Backup Is Finished	Compares each file that is backed up with the original file to verify accurate backup.
Use Data Compression	Compresses files as they are backed up to allow more files to be backed up on a tape or floppy disk.
Format when Needed on Tape Backups	Automatically formats an unused tape before backup operation. This only works on tapes that have not already been formatted.
Always Erase on Tape Backups	Erases the tape on backup. When this option is not selected, backups are added to the tape if there is room.
Always Erase on Floppy Disk Backups	Automatically erases floppy disks before they are used in a floppy disk backup operation. When this option is not selected, backups are added to the floppy disk if there is room.

Saving File Sets

If you back up the same set of files regularly, you can save the settings for that file set. Saving backup settings saves you the trouble of reselecting the files and destination each time you want to back up the files. To save a file set, follow these steps:

1. Open the Backup dialog box and in the Backup tab, select the files you want to back up, as described earlier in this chapter. Click the Next Step > button.
2. Select the destination for the backup files from the Select a Destination list.
3. Choose File, Save As. The Save As dialog box appears (see Figure 16.6).
4. Type a name for the backup set in the File Name text box.
5. Choose the Save button.
6. Choose the Start Backup button if you want to continue the backup operation and create a backup using the file set you just specified.

FIG. 16.6
Name your file set with a recognizable name for what it contains and when it was created.

If you make changes to an existing file set, choose the File, Save command to save the file set with the same name without opening the Save As dialog box.

To open a file set for use in a backup operation, follow these steps:

1. Open the Backup dialog box; then click the Backup tab. Choose File, Open File Set to display the Open dialog box shown in Figure 16.7.

FIG. 16.7
Open a file set to use in a backup or restore operation from the Open dialog box.

2. If you cannot see the file set you want to open, open the folder that contains the file set.
3. Select the file set and choose Open.

The file set is opened, and the files named in this file set are selected in the Backup dialog box.

Filtering Folders and File Types Included in Backup Operations

Backup's file-filtering commands enable you to filter out specific folders and types of files so that they are not included in the backup set. These commands can save you a lot of time when you create a file set to be backed up.

You may not want to include all the files on your hard disk in a backup operation. In some cases, you may want to back up all but a few folders; it is easier to specify the folders you *don't* want to include in the backup set than to select all the folders you do want to include. You may not want to include program files in your daily backups because you can always reinstall your programs if your system crashes. You can dramatically reduce the number of disks you use in a backup if you limit the file set to data files only.

To exclude from a backup files of a specific type or date, follow these steps:

1. Choose Settings, File Filtering. The File Filtering—File Types dialog box appears, as shown in Figure 16.8.

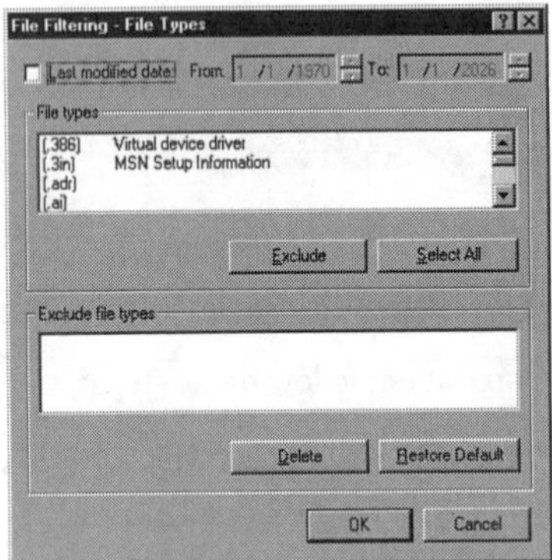

FIG. 16.8
You can exclude files of a specific type or files with specific dates.

2. To exclude files modified between two dates, select the Last Modified Date check box. Enter From and To dates that *exclude* the files you do not want copied. Click the insertion point in the date segment you want to change, and then click the up or down spinner arrow to change the date.

   For example, if you want to exclude files before November 30, 1995, enter a From date of **1/1/1970** and a To date of **11/30/95**.

If you want to exclude all but a few of the file types in the File Types list, click Select All, hold the Ctrl key, and click the types of files you don't want to exclude.

3. To exclude specific file types from the backup operation, select the types of files you want to exclude from the File Types list and click Exclude. Continue to select file types and click the Exclude button until all the file types you want to exclude appear in the Exclude File Types list at the bottom of the dialog box.

   To select all of the file types in the list, click Select All.

4. To delete a file type from the list in the Exclude File Types box, select the file type and click Delete.
5. To clear the Exclude File Types box, click Restore Default.
6. When you finish making your selections, choose OK.

Changing the General Settings in Backup

You can change two options in Backup that affect the backup, restore, and compare functions. To change these options, choose Settings, Options. Select the General tab to display the Settings—Options dialog box shown in Figure 16.9.

- Select the Turn on Audible Prompts option if you want to hear beeps from your computer's speaker during backup, compare, and restore operations.
- Select the Overwrite Old Status Log Files option to replace the old status log with the new one generated by the current backup. The status log records errors and completions of file backups.

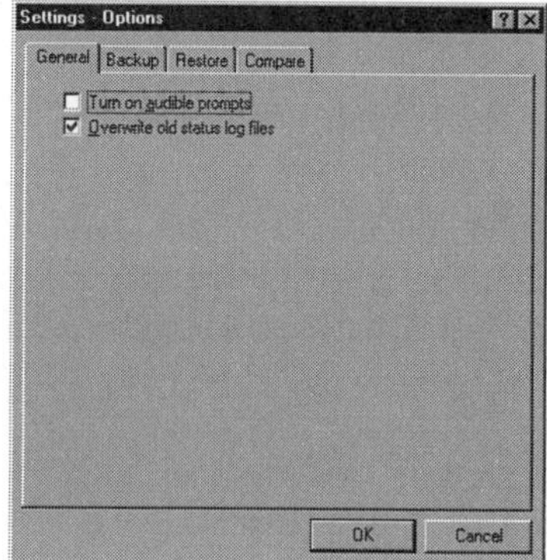

FIG. 16.9
Use the General tab in the Settings–Options dialog box to change the settings and options that affect the way Backup's operations work.

Backing Up with a Simple Drag and Drop

Once you understand the importance of backing up files and see how easy it is to do, you will back up frequently. There is an easy way to back up your files if you created file sets (as described earlier in this chapter). You can drag a file set and drop it onto the Backup icon, or you can double-click a file set name. Either of these actions immediately starts the backup. With the appropriate settings, the entire backup operation can go on in the background, and you can continue to use the computer for other tasks.

Backing up data is so important that if you are an experienced Windows user, you may want to set up other users' computers with drag-and-drop backup so that they can easily protect their data.

To prepare Backup for drag-and-drop operation, follow these steps:

1. Choose Settings, Drag and Drop to display the Drag and Drop dialog box shown in Figure 16.10.

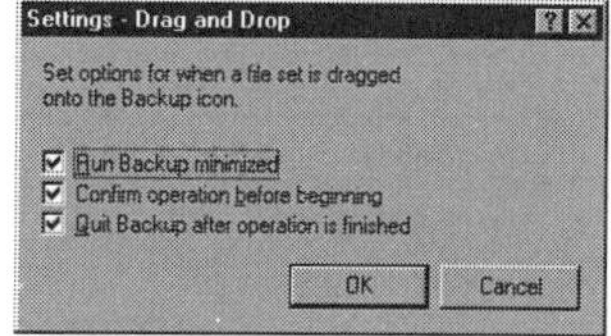

FIG. 16.10
Change the Backup settings to make drag-and-drop backup operate in the background while you work.

2. Change or select from the following options and then choose OK.

Option	Function
Run Backup Minimized	After dragging a file set onto the Backup icon, the Backup window minimizes.
Confirm Operation Before Beginning	Displays a message showing which files will be backed up. Asks you to confirm that you want the files backed up.
Quit Backup After Operation Is Finished	Quits Backup after the file set is backed up.

If Backup is operating in the background, you don't see it as a window on-screen. If you need to stop a backup that is in the background, display the title bar and click the Backup button. A dialog box displays the current backup status and gives you the opportunity to cancel the backup.

NOTE If you have multiple file sets, but you don't want them all as Shortcuts on your desktop, you can still start them quickly to do a backup. In the Windows Explorer or My Computer window, double-click the name of the file set you want to back up. You are prompted whether you want to make a backup; the backup runs with the settings specified for that file set.

Before you can create backups with a drag-and-drop procedure, you must display the Backup program icon. You can open the Program Files/Accessories folder in a window in the Windows Explorer or My Computer. A more convenient method is to create a shortcut to BACKUP.EXE and display it on your desktop.

If you also want a quick way to find and display the SET files that specify your file sets, create a shortcut to the directory containing the SET files. You can do this by using the Find command (available on the Start menu) to find all files that end with SET. Create a new folder and drag the SET files into the new folder. Now create a shortcut to this folder and put that shortcut on the desktop (see Figure 16.11).

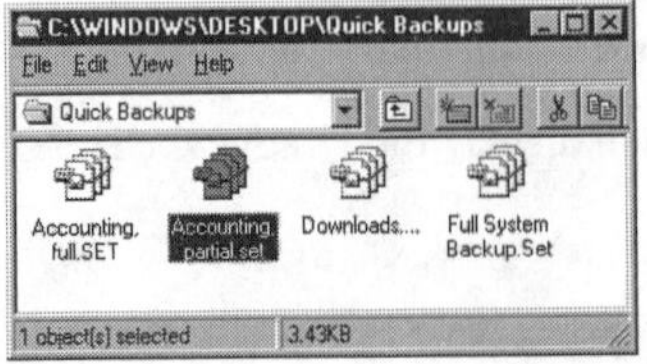

FIG. 16.11 Once drag and drop is enabled, backing up is as easy as dropping a file-set icon onto the Backup shortcut.

NOTE Normally, Windows stores the file sets in the Program Files\Accessories folder. If you are unsure where your backup file sets are stored on your hard disk, open the Start menu and choose Find. Search for all files ending with .SET by entering ***.SET** in the Named box.

To back up a file set, you only need to double-click the shortcut to the folder containing the file sets. This opens the folder containing the file sets as a Window on your desktop. Figure 16.11 shows such an open folder. Now drag the file set you want to back up onto the shortcut to BACKUP.EXE and drop it. You are prompted whether you want to continue with the backup operation. Respond by clicking Yes or No.

Formatting and Erasing Tapes

If you use tapes to do your backups, Backup includes two tools for working with tapes. When you purchase a new tape, you must format the tape before you can use it, just as you format a floppy disk. The Format Tape command formats a tape for you. If you want to erase the contents on a tape before you use it for a new backup operation, you can use the Erase Tape command.

To format a tape, follow these steps:

1. Insert the tape in the tape drive.
2. Open the Backup dialog box and choose Tools, Format Tape. If the Format Tape command is grayed out, choose the Redetect Tape command, which enables Backup to detect the tape.
3. When the Format Tape dialog box appears (see Figure 16.12), type a name for the tape and choose OK. You use this name to identify the tape relative to other tapes you use.

Formatting begins. The progress of the formatting operation appears in the Format Tape dialog box. Formatting a tape can take a long time; you may want to start the formatting operation when you are going to be away from your desk for an extended period.

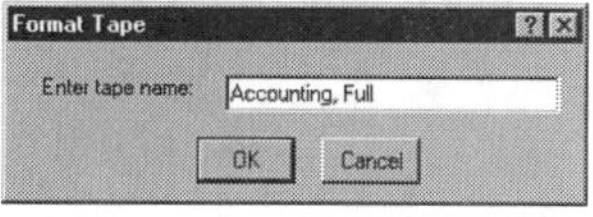

FIG. 16.12
Enter a name for the tape you want to format in the Format Tape dialog box.

4. When the message box appears telling you the operation is complete, choose OK; choose OK again to return to the Backup dialog box.

To erase a tape, follow these steps:

1. Insert the tape in the tape drive.
2. Open the Backup dialog box and choose Tools, Erase Tape. If the Erase Tape command is grayed out, choose the Redetect Tape command, which enables Backup to detect the tape.
3. Choose Yes when the confirmation message box appears. The progress of the erase operation appears in the Erase dialog box.
4. When the message box appears telling you the operation is complete, choose OK. Choose OK again to return to the Backup dialog box.

Restoring Files

If you're lucky, you may never have to use Backup's restore function. When you do need it, however, it's as easy to use as the backup function. You can restore all the files from a backup set or select specific files or folders to restore. You can also choose where you want to restore the files.

To restore files, follow these steps:

1. Open the Backup dialog box and click the Restore tab (see Figure 16.13).
2. Select the drive containing the backup files from the left panel of the window. In Figure 16.13, the tape drive has been selected as the backup source.

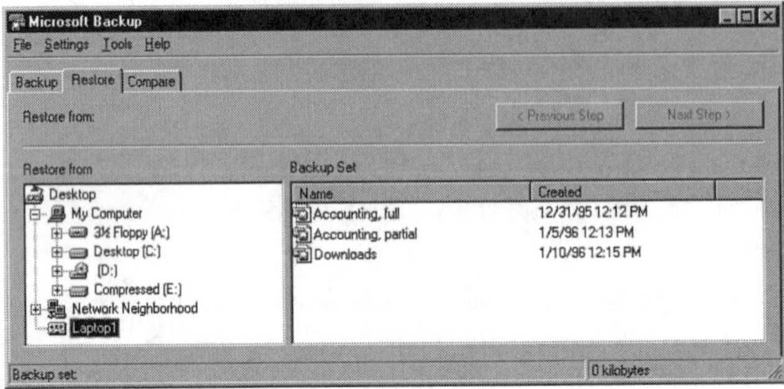

FIG. 16.13
In the Restore tab of the Backup dialog box, select the files you want to restore.

3. Select the backup set containing the files you want to restore from the right pane. If you have more than one backup file on a floppy disk or tape, select the one containing the files you want to restore. A single backup file, with the extension QIC, contains the files you backed up.
4. Click the Next Step button.
5. Select the folders or files you want to restore as shown in Figure 16.14.

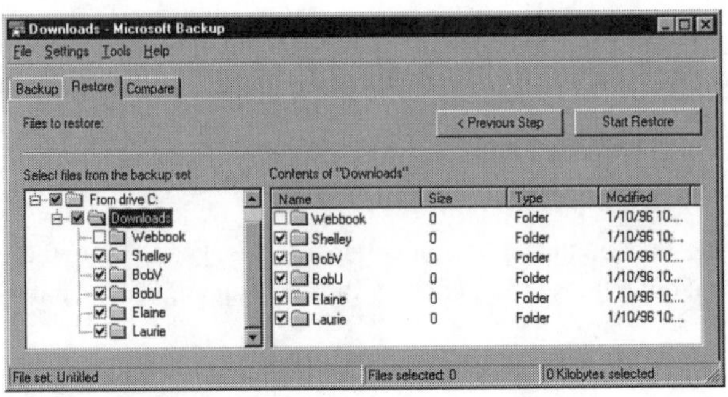

FIG. 16.14
You can select all or part of a backup set when you restore.

6. Click the Start Restore button. The Restore message box appears, showing you the progress of the restore operation (see Figure 16.15).

By default, the files are restored to their original location. You can choose to restore the files to another location by changing one of the restore options, as described next.

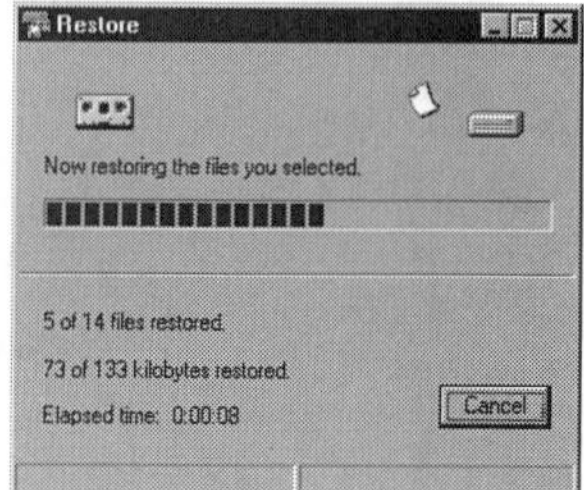

FIG. 16.15 The Restore message box informs you about the progress of the restore operation.

7. When the Operation Complete message box appears, choose OK.

Restoring Files to Other Locations You can restore files to a locations other than their original location (the location from which they were initially backed up). To restore files to an alternate location, follow these steps:

1. Choose Settings, Options.
2. Click the Restore tab.
3. Select the Alternate Location option and choose OK.
4. Perform steps 1 through 6 of the restore procedure described in the preceding section (stop just before you have to click the Start Restore button).
5. Click the Start Restore button. The Browse for Folder dialog box appears (see Figure 16.16).

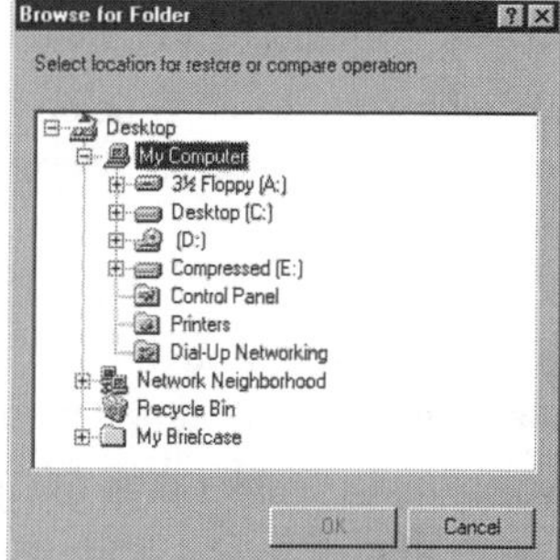

FIG. 16.16 Select the location to which you want to restore files from the File Redirection box.

6. Select the location to which you want to restore the files and choose OK.
7. When the Operation Complete message box appears, choose OK.

Changing Restore Settings and Options You can change several settings and options that affect your restore operations. To change the settings and options for the restore function, follow these steps:

1. Choose Settings, Options.
2. Click the Restore tab to display the dialog box shown in Figure 16.17.

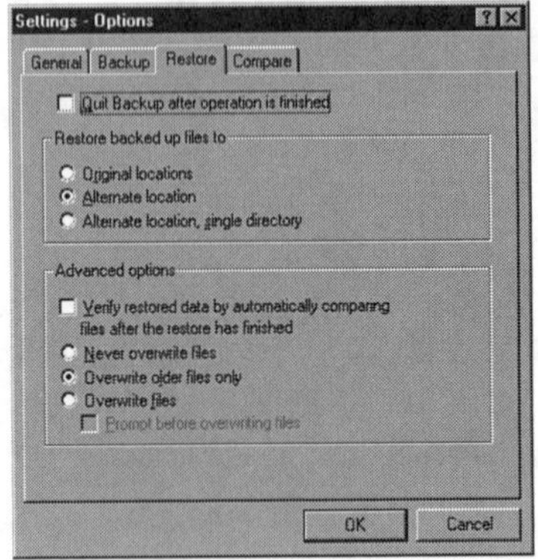

FIG. 16.17 Use the Restore tab in the Settings–Options dialog box to change the settings and options that affect the way restore operations work.

3. Change or select from the following options and then choose OK.

Option	Function
Quit Backup After Operation Is Complete	Closes Backup when the restore operation is completed.
Original Locations	Restores files to their original locations.
Alternate Location	Restores files to an alternate location. (See "Restoring Files to an Alternate Location" earlier in this chapter.)
Alternate Location, Single Directory	Restores files to a single directory at an alternate location. Doesn't duplicate original folder structure.
Verify Restored Data by Automatically Comparing Files After the Restore Has Finished	Compares each file to the file on disk or tape after it is restored to check for accuracy of restore.
Never Overwrite Files	Files that are already on the destination location are not overwritten during a restore operation.
Overwrite Older Files Only	Only files that are older than the files in the backup set are overwritten during a restore operation.
Overwrite Files	All files are overwritten during a restore operation. Use the Prompt Before Overwriting Files check box to specify whether you want to be prompted before a file is overwritten.

Verifying Backup Files

The first time you use a series of disks or a tape for a backup, or any time you want to be absolutely sure of your backup, you should do a comparison. When you compare backups to the original files, you verify that the backup copies are both readable and accurate. To perform a compare, follow these steps:

1. Open the Backup dialog box and click the Compare tab.
2. From the left pane of the dialog box, select the device containing the backup files you want to compare (see Figure 16.18).

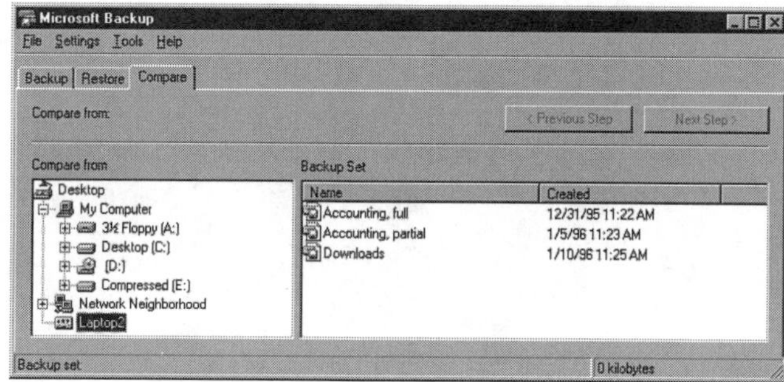

FIG. 16.18
Use the Compare function to verify the accuracy of your backup operations.

3. From the right pane, select the backup set containing the files you want to compare.
4. Click the Next Step button.
5. Select the files or folders you want to compare to the original files.
6. Click the Start Compare button. The Compare message box informs you of the progress of the compare operation.
7. Choose OK when the Operation Complete message box appears; choose OK again to return to the Backup dialog box.

Changing Compare Settings and Options

You can change several settings and options that affect your compare operations. To change the settings and options for the compare function, follow these steps:

1. Choose Settings, Options.
2. Click the Compare tab to display the dialog box shown in Figure 16.19.
3. Change or select from the following options and then choose OK.

Option	Function
Quit Backup After Operation Is Finished	Closes Backup when the compare operation is completed.
Original Locations	Compare files to files at their original locations.

continues

continued

Option	Function
Alternate Location	Compares files to files at an alternate location.
Alternate Location, Single Directory	Compare files to files in a single directory at an alternate location. Doesn't look for duplicates of the original folder structure.

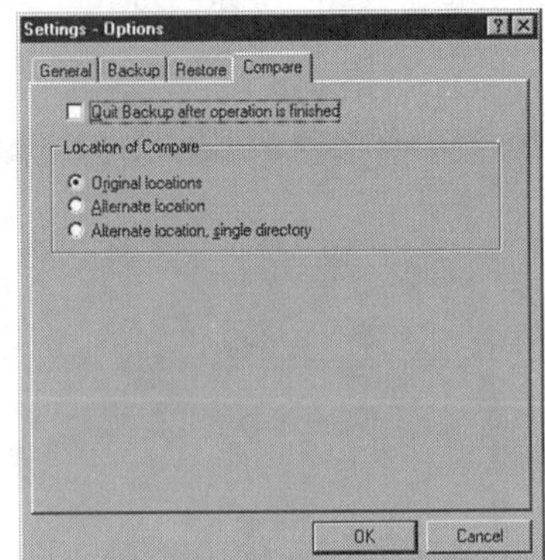

FIG. 16.19
Use the Compare tab in the Settings–Options dialog box to change the settings and options that affect the way compare operations work.

Protecting Your Files from Viruses

You need to take measures to protect your computer from viruses, a scourge of the modern day computer world. In addition to backing up your system regularly, you should obtain an antivirus program and make a habit of using it on a regular basis to protect your files against infection, especially if you frequently introduce files onto your hard disk from outside sources.

Understanding How Viruses Damage Your Computer

A computer virus is a program designed to do damage to either your computer or your computer's data. Viruses make copies of themselves and spread from one computer to another.

There are three ways in which viruses can be transmitted between computers:

- Loading and running infected software
- Booting up with an infected floppy disk
- Opening a document or template file that has a macro virus attached to it

It used to be the case that viruses were only transmitted by one of the first two routes. With the arrival of macro viruses, it has become much more difficult to insulate your system from viruses. Now you can get a virus by simply opening an infected Word for Windows or Excel document or template file. If there is a macro virus attached to the document, all the documents you open from that point on will become infected with the virus. If you commonly exchange documents with other users, you must take precautions against this new type of virus.

The best approach for protecting against viruses is to install one of the available antivirus programs. Used correctly, a good antivirus program can protect against the vast majority of known viruses before they damage your computer. Symantec's Norton Anti-Virus for Windows and McAfee Associates VirusScan are well-respected virus protection programs.

ON THE WEB

Both Symantec and McAfee Associates provide virus-definition updates that you can download from their Web sites to protect your system against the many new viruses that are constantly arriving on the computing scene. Visit the following Web sites for more information on these products.

http://www.symantec.com

http://www.mcafee.com

PART IV

Working with the Internet

CHAPTER 17

Establishing a Dial-Up Internet Connection

by Ed Bott

In this chapter

Do you want to connect to the Internet from home? Does your office network lack Internet access? There are literally thousands of Internet service providers and online services scattered throughout the world that will gladly give you a dial-up account—for the right price, of course. Windows 95 supplies all the software you need to make a fast, reliable Internet connection. All you need to add is a modem or other connecting device.

Using the Internet Connection Wizard

The first time you open the Internet icon on the desktop, you launch the Internet Connection Wizard (see Figure 17.1); after you run through its initial setup steps, the Internet icon starts Internet Explorer.

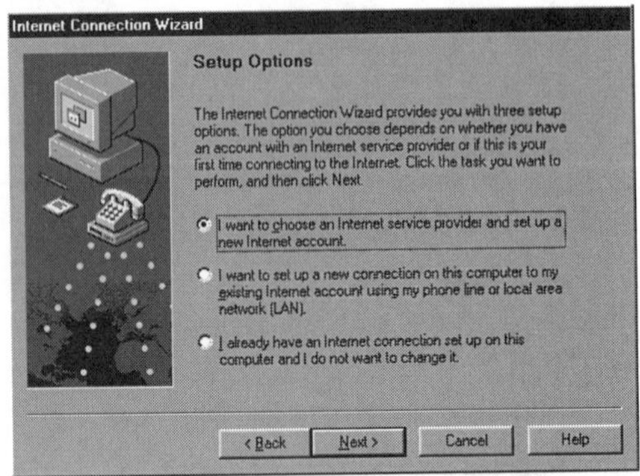

FIG. 17.1
These three options are just a small sampling of what you can do with the Internet Connection Wizard.

The Internet Connection Wizard is a remarkably versatile piece of software. After you get past the initial explanatory screen, you have three choices:

- You can sign up for a new Internet account; the Internet Connection Wizard offers a referral list of Internet service providers in your area.
- You can set up an existing Internet account for access through Windows 95, either over the phone or through a network.
- You can tell the Internet Connection Wizard to use your existing Internet connection. If you're comfortable with TCP/IP and networking, this is a reasonable choice.

The Internet Connection Wizard isn't just a one-time deal, either. You can make the wizard reappear at any time by following these steps:

1. Right-click the Internet icon on the desktop.
2. Choose Properties and click the Connection tab. The dialog box shown in Figure 17.2 appears.
3. Click the button labeled Connect.

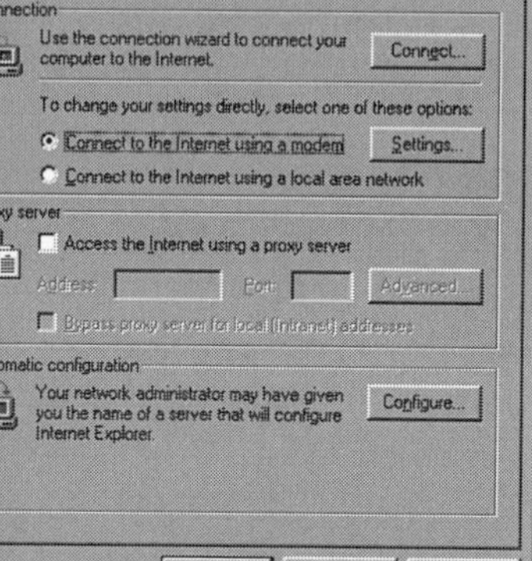

FIG. 17.2 Want to use the Internet Connection Wizard again? Click the Connect button on this dialog box.

Don't underestimate the Internet Connection Wizard. Although it's easy to stereotype it as a tool for beginners, this tool is useful for experts as well, and it handles nearly every imaginable task when it comes to setting up and managing Internet connections.

Because of the sheer number of choices available when you run the Internet Connection Wizard, it's pointless (and probably impossible) to try to explain or illustrate every step in order. But this is a partial list of what you can use it for:

- Install and configure a modem (or set up a LAN connection for Internet access instead).
- Adjust the dialing settings you use, including the local area code and the prefixes you use to access outside lines.
- Create and edit Dial-Up Networking connection icons for one-button access to the Internet.
- Use right-click shortcut menus to adjust advanced Internet settings.
- Enter and edit account information you use to connect with an Internet service provider.

NOTE If you have not yet installed Dial-Up Networking, the Internet Connection Wizard installs these system services automatically. You need your original Windows CD-ROM or disks, and you need to restart the computer to complete the installation. ■

Installing and Configuring a Modem

There are two obvious prerequisites to any dial-up connection: You need a modem (or another type of connecting device, such as an ISDN adapter) and you need a phone line. If you haven't set up a modem previously, the Internet Connection Wizard includes a series of steps that automatically installs modem drivers and configures your modem. You can also use the Modems option in Control Panel to add a new modem or to configure an existing one.

Although most dial-up connections use only one modem at a time, you can install multiple communication devices. The system depicted in Figure 17.3, for example, includes an analog modem and an ISDN adapter—you can assign only one such device to each Dial-Up Networking connection.

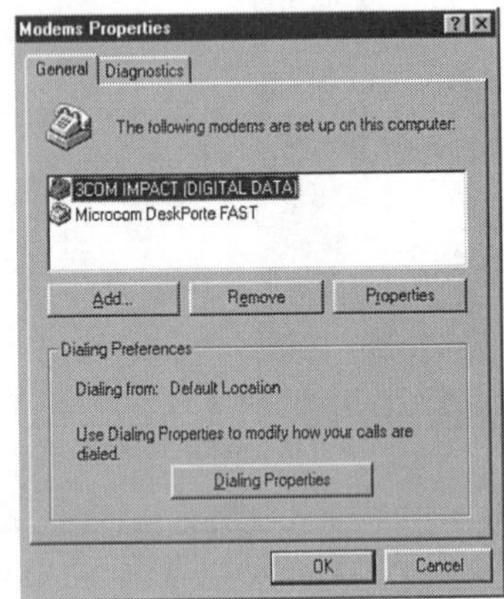

FIG. 17.3
This system includes two communication devices–a 3COM ISDN adapter and a Microcom analog modem. Both are available for dial-up connections.

▶ **See** "Installing and Configuring Your Modem," **p. 68**

Adding a New Analog Modem

Windows 95 does a super job of identifying and configuring the correct modem type from a list of hundreds of choices. If your modem is Plug and Play compatible, Windows should detect it automatically, install the correct drivers, and configure all relevant settings. For modems that don't take advantage of Plug and Play detection, you might have to do the installation and configuration duties manually.

▶ **See** "Using PC Card Devices," for step-by-step instructions to install PC Card modems for mobile computers, **p. 63**

To add a new modem, follow these steps:

1. Open the Modems option in Control Panel.
2. If you have not previously set up a modem on this system, the Install New Modem Wizard appears. If you are adding a new modem, click the Add button.
3. In the Install New Modem dialog box, click the Next button to enable Windows to detect your modem. If you've downloaded a driver or the manufacturer supplied a driver on disk, and you're certain that this driver is more up-to-date than the built-in Windows drivers, select the option to skip detection, click Next, and skip to step 5.
4. If Windows detected your modem properly, click Finish to install the driver. Skip over all additional steps.

5. If you bypassed the detection process, you see a list of available modem drivers. If Windows did not correctly detect your modem, click the Change button to display this same list. Choose the modem manufacturer from the list on the left and the model name from the list of modems on the right. If you have an updated Windows 95 driver, click the Have Disk button and specify the location of the driver.
6. Select the port to which the modem is attached. Most desktop PCs have two serial ports (COM1 and COM2), and a mouse is often attached to one; you might need to check the system documentation or the label on the physical port to verify which port the modem is using.
7. Click Finish to install the driver and configure the modem.

If you can't find a compatible Windows 95 driver for your modem, select (Standard Modem Types) from the top of the Manufacturers list and choose the generic model that most closely matches your modem's speed. You will lose any advanced features included with your modem, but this procedure enables you to send and receive data at the modem's rated speed.

Configuring an Analog Modem

After you've installed drivers for an analog modem, it should be configured correctly. Still, it can't hurt to double-check settings to guarantee that the device is properly set up for maximum performance. A series of nested dialog boxes includes options for adjusting drivers, connection speeds, port assignments, and hardware-specific connection settings, including control over the volume of the modem's built-in speaker.

To set basic modem options, open the Modems option in Control Panel, select the modem whose settings you want to adjust, and click Properties. A dialog box like the one shown in Figure 17.4 appears; click the General tab.

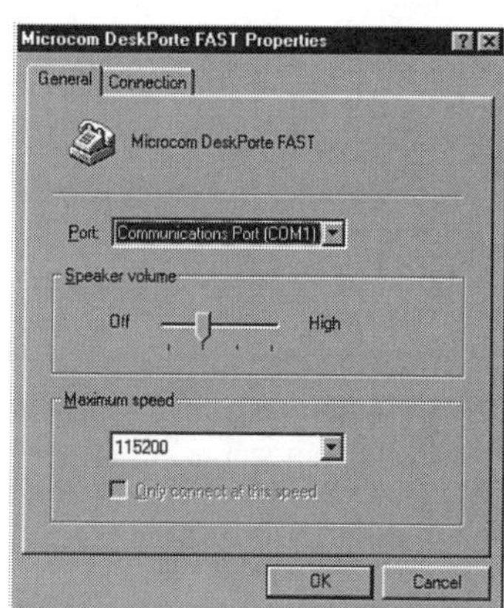

FIG. 17.4
Use this properties sheet to adjust the volume of the modem's internal speaker and its maximum speed.

Three basic options are available here:

- Note that this dialog box displays the port the modem is configured to use. To switch the modem to another port, use the drop-down Port list.
- This is also the place to adjust the modem's speaker. The slider control uses four positions: From left to right, they are Off, Low, Medium, and High. For most circumstances, the Low setting is the best, because it enables you to hear the dial tone and handshaking sounds and retry a connection when your modem and the one at the other end are not communicating correctly.
- Don't be confused by the Maximum speed control at the bottom of this dialog box. This setting controls the internal speed at which your computer communicates with the modem, and on most Pentium-class computers, that speed is invariably faster than the transmission speed of the modem itself. Previous versions of Windows typically set this value too low. On most Pentium PCs, you can safely set the port speed to 115,200 bps. Reduce this setting only if you experience persistent data errors when sending and receiving. Avoid the check box labeled Only connect at this speed.

To set general connection options, click the Connection tab. You'll see a dialog box like the one in Figure 17.5.

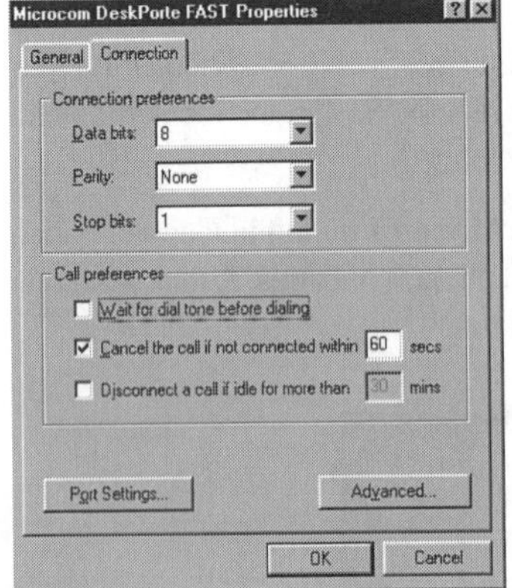

FIG. 17.5
Avoid the temptation to tinker with these connection settings; for the majority of circumstances, the default settings work best.

You can adjust four settings here:

- The connections preferences section at the top of the dialog box specifies settings for data bits, parity, and stop bits. These settings are typically used for modem-to-modem communications rather than PPP or SLIP connections. It should not be necessary to adjust these settings for Internet access.
- Under the heading Call preferences, note the check mark in front of the box labeled Wait for dial tone before dialing. If your phone system uses a dial tone that differs from the standard U.S. dial tone, Windows mistakenly believes the line is dead and refuses to dial until you clear this box. Likewise, voice-mail systems that alter the normal dial tone to a "stutter" signal can confuse Windows unless you clear this box.

- The 60-second timeout is sufficient for most domestic calls. If you regularly dial in to servers that require lengthy connect times, you should increase this value to avoid timeout errors.
- The Disconnect option at the bottom of the dialog box enables you to specify the amount of time that the connection can be idle before Windows disconnects automatically. This setting is appropriate only for modem-to-modem connections; for Internet connections, use the timeout settings defined by the Internet Explorer Connection Manager.

Finally, you can set hardware-specific options that control the basic functioning of your modem. Click the Advanced button to see the dialog box shown in Figure 17.6.

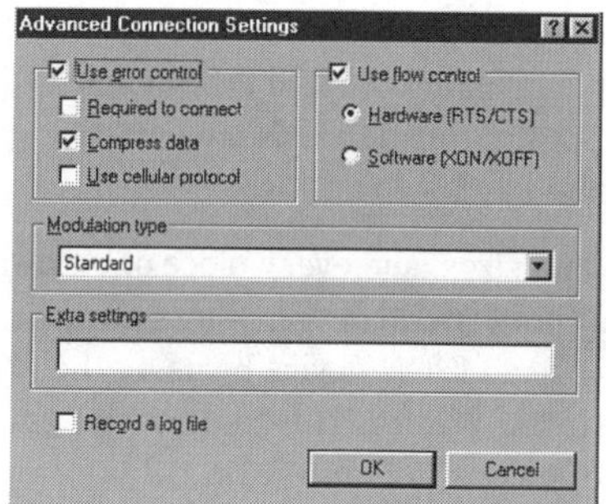

FIG. 17.6
Adjust these advanced connection settings only if you understand the consequences of your actions. Unnecessary tinkering here can actually reduce data transmission speeds.

Four advanced options are available in this dialog box:

- Error control options reduce the risk that noisy phone lines will cause data corruption. Most modern modems support both data compression and error control. The modem information file should set these options for your specific modem. The Use cellular protocol box enables the MNP10 error control protocol for use with some (but not all) cellular modems.
- Flow control governs the integrity of the connection. By default, Windows 95 enables hardware flow control, and most modern modems support this mode for best performance. Change this setting to software flow control only if the manufacturer of your modem recommends it.
- Do not change modulation type unless it is specifically recommended by the manufacturer of your modem.
- If necessary, click the Extra Settings box and add AT commands that enable or disable a particular feature of your modem or adapter. For example, S0=5 tells your modem to answer automatically after 5 rings. Check your modem documentation for AT commands applicable to your hardware.

ON THE WEB

Zoom Telephonics offers a comprehensive source of information about modem technology and the AT command set; browse its listings at

http://www.modems.com

Configuring an ISDN Adapter

Most home and small-office dial-up connections use conventional analog lines. In some areas, you can use the Integrated Services Digital Network (ISDN) to establish high-speed digital connections. Compared with analog lines, ISDN circuits offer significant advantages: Connection times are practically instantaneous, for example, unlike analog lines that require 20 seconds or more to establish a connection. Speeds are typically 2–5 times faster than most analog modems. Because the connection is digital from end to end, you won't lose data because of noise on the line—something that can't be said for the typical analog connection. And each ISDN line includes two digital data channels and one analog data channel, enabling you to talk on one line while simultaneously sending and receiving data on a digital channel.

ISDN technology has its share of disadvantages as well. Generally, these lines cost more—sometimes many times more than an analog line. Not all ISPs support ISDN, and those that do often charge a premium for its use. Configuring an ISDN connection can be a nightmare as well, and the technology is difficult and filled with jargon.

ISDN hardware comes in all shapes and sizes, and every piece of hardware uses a different setup routine. Some devices install as network adapters, others as modems, and still others as routers on a network. When you choose an ISDN device by using the Add Hardware option in Control Panel, Windows installs the ISDN Wizard. This tool enables you to configure the technical details of your ISDN line, as we've done in Figure 17.7.

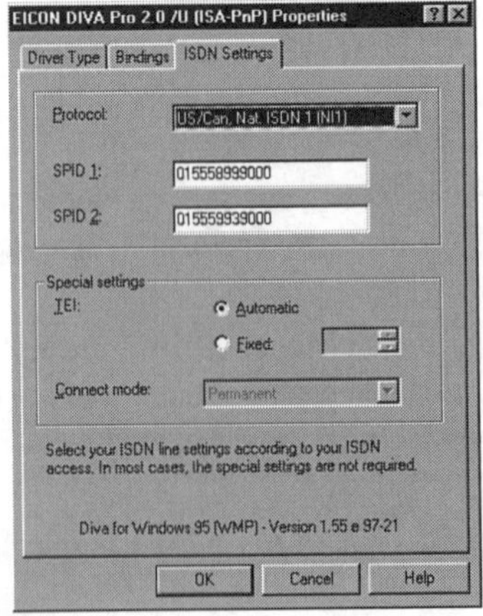

FIG. 17.7
Although some ISDN adapters emulate modems, this device from Eicon Systems looks like a network card to Windows 95.

ON THE WEB

For more information about ISDN technology, check out Dan Kegel's detailed page:

http://www.alumni.caltech.edu/~dank/isdn/

For details on how to order ISDN plus links to updated ISDN software for Windows 95, try Microsoft's Get ISDN page:

http://www.microsoft.com/windows/getisdn/about.htm

Although the ISDN Wizard makes setup somewhat easier than it used to be, the process is still complex. When connecting an ISDN line, get detailed instructions from the manufacturer of the adapter and from the phone company—and follow those instructions to the letter. At a minimum, you need to know the Service Provider IDs (SPIDs) and telephone numbers for each channel, as well as the switch type used in the telephone company office. Some ISDN hardware includes a utility that enables you to upload this information to the adapter itself.

When you successfully install your ISDN adapter, it appears as a choice in the Dial-Up Networking Wizard.

Other High-Speed Access Options

Telephone companies are no longer the only sources of access to the Internet. There are an increasing number of high-speed alternatives to traditional dialup access that use different types of wires—and in some cases no wires at all.

Hughes Network systems sells a small satellite dish called DirecDuo, which enables Internet access at speeds of up to 400Kbps, as well as several hundred channels of TV programming.

Not to be outdone, many phone companies are rolling out systems that use Digital Subscriber Line (DSL) technology to provide Internet access at speeds in excess of 1MB per second, while enabling you to use the same line for voice calls.

Some cable TV companies now offer Internet access over the same cable you use to receive television signals. Depending on the system configuration, these solutions can deliver data at speeds of up to 10MB per second, roughly on a par with local area network performance.

Windows 95 does not offer built-in support for any of these cutting-edge technologies, but third parties offer hardware and Windows drivers that work well. If you plan to use any of these services, be sure to ask the provider for detailed instructions on how to access the service from Windows 95.

Configuring a Connection to an Existing Internet Account

Windows 95 uses a service called Dial-Up Networking (DUN) to connect your system to the Internet over telephone lines. The Internet Connection Wizard automatically installs DUN if necessary. Individual connection icons within the Dial-Up Networking folder contain all the information you need to connect with the Internet. You'll find the Dial-Up Networking folder in the My Computer window; to open this system folder from the Start menu, choose Programs, Accessories, Dial-Up Networking.

If you already have an account with an Internet service provider, the wizard's step-by-step procedures can create a Dial-Up Networking connection with a minimum of clicking and typing. The default settings assume you're making a standard PPP connection, with IP address and DNS settings assigned dynamically.

1. Start the Internet Connection Wizard and choose the option to set up a new connection to an existing account. Click Next to continue.
2. Choose the option to connect by using your phone line and click Next.
3. Choose the modem you want to use with this connection and click Next. (If you haven't set up a modem, you can to do so here.)
4. You can choose an existing connection icon if there are any in your Dial-Up Networking folder. In this case, select the option to create a new icon and click Next to continue.
5. Enter the dial-in phone number of your Internet service provider and click Next.
6. Enter your username and password and click Next.
7. The wizard asks whether or not you want to adjust advanced settings for the connection. For standard PPP connections where you don't need to specify an IP address or DNS servers, select No and click Next.
8. Give the connection a descriptive name, as in Figure 17.8, and click Next.

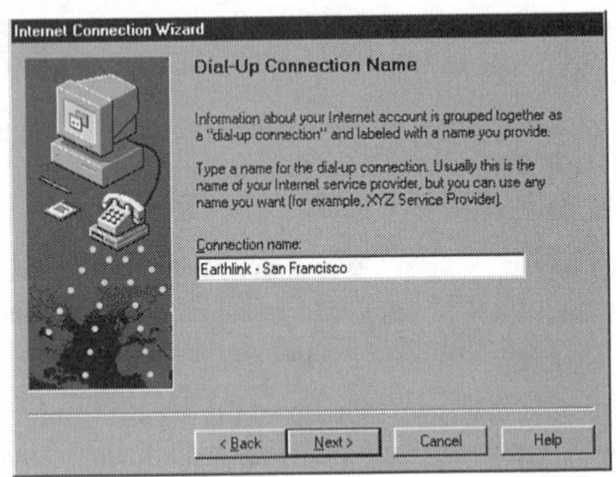

FIG. 17.8 The default connection icon uses a generic name. Add location info, as we've done here, to make the icon's purpose easier to identify.

9. If you need to set up mail and news accounts or a directory server, the wizard includes separate steps to help with each of these tasks. (See Chapter 22, "Using Outlook Express for Email and News," for instructions on how to set up these accounts.) When you reach the end of the wizard, click Finish to create the Dial-Up Networking connection icon.

Adjusting Advanced Settings

The Internet Connection Wizard includes an option to adjust advanced connection settings. If your Internet service provider uses a SLIP connection or requires scripting, or if you need to enter a fixed IP address and specify addresses for DNS servers, select Yes in the Advanced Settings dialog box (see Figure 17.9) and fill in the four boxes that follow.

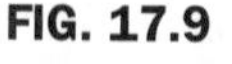

FIG. 17.9
When you select Yes in this dialog box, the Internet Connection Wizard takes a brief detour into advanced configuration options.

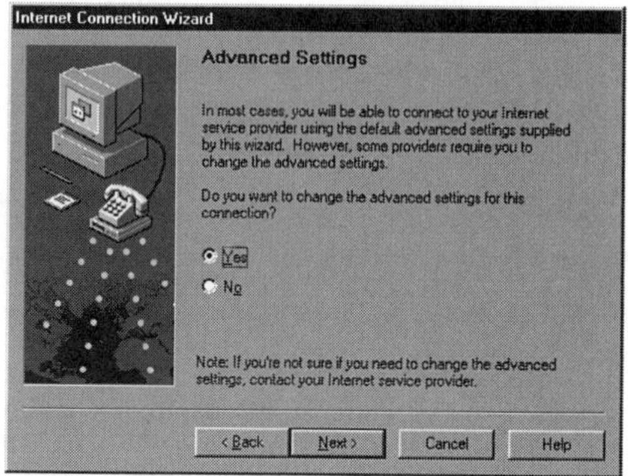

Part IV Ch 17

Advanced settings include the following:

- *Connection type* Choose PPP or SLIP connection.
- *Logon procedure* Select the manual option to bring up a terminal window when connecting, or specify a logon script.
- *IP Address* If your ISP provides a fixed IP address, enter it here.
- *DNS Server Address* If your ISP requires you to specify primary and backup name servers, enter their IP addresses here.

Using Multilink Options for Faster Connections

Most dial-up Internet connections are a simple one-modem, one-line system, and transmission speed is limited by the slower of the two modems on either end of the connection. Under specialized circumstances, though, you can use two or more connecting devices to increase the speed of a dial up connection. These so-called multilink connections require the following conditions:

- You must have multiple devices to bind together into a single virtual connection.
- Each device requires its own driver software.
- Each device needs access to a separate analog phone line or a channel on an ISDN line.
- The dial-up server at the other end of the connection must support multilink PPP connections.

NOTE Before you can create a multilink connection, you might need to upgrade the Dial-Up Networking software components included with Windows 95 and OSR2 to version 1.1 or later. This upgrade first appeared in the Microsoft ISDN Accelerator Pack and is also available in the Dial-Up Networking 1.2 Upgrade. See "Available Updates for Windows 95," in Chapter 2, "Installing and Upgrading Windows 95," for instructions on how to download and install these and other updates. ■

The most common use of multilink connections is to join two 56KB or 64KB channels on an ISDN line to create a 112KB or 128KB connection. It's also possible to use multiple analog modems to dial in to a Windows NT Remote Access Server. An emerging technology called Shotgun, from Diamond Multimedia, might enable you to accomplish the same goal by using two standard analog modems and two phone lines.

To enable multilink options on an existing connection, follow these steps:

1. Open the Dial-Up Networking folder, right-click the connection icon you want to modify, and choose Properties from the shortcut menu.
2. Click the General tab and click the Settings button in the box labeled Set additional devices. The dialog box shown in Figure 17.10 appears.

FIG. 17.10
If your Internet service provider supports multilink PPP, use these settings to combine two modems to create a faster virtual connection.

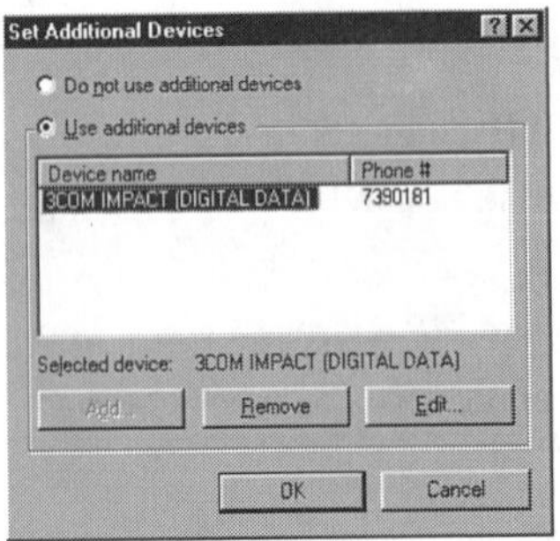

3. Select the option labeled Use additional devices. The grayed-out buttons at the bottom of the dialog box become available.
4. Click the Add button and choose a modem or ISDN adapter from the drop-down list. If no choices are available, click Cancel to set up your additional hardware, and then continue.
5. Enter a separate phone number for the additional device, if required. The hardware documentation and service provider can supply more details about your specific configuration.
6. Select any entry and use the Remove or Edit buttons to modify entries in the list.
7. Click OK to save your changes.

Creating and Editing Logon Scripts

Today, most commercial Internet service providers use logon servers that communicate easily with Windows Dial-Up Networking connections. Some older providers, however, or noncommercial dial-up sites might require additional keyboard input that the Windows connection can't provide. In these cases, you need to create a logon script for use with the Dial-Up Networking connection; when you open a connection icon whose configuration details include a script, Windows opens a terminal window and sends the additional commands. The script might operate unattended in the background, or it might stop and require that you make an entry in the terminal window.

NOTE Script support is not included as part of the version of Dial-Up Networking in the original release of Windows 95. If you want built-in scripting support and you're not using OSR2, you must update the DUN files to version 1.1 or later. See "Available Updates for Windows 95," in Chapter 2, for instructions on how to download and install these and other updates.

Script files are simple text files that end in the extension SCP. You can find these four general-purpose scripts in the Program Files\Accessories folder:

- Cis.scp establishes a PPP connection with CompuServe.
- Pppmenu.scp logs on to a server that uses text menus.
- Slip.scp establishes a SLIP connection with a remote host machine.
- Slipmenu.scp establishes a SLIP connection on a menu-based host.

TIP Some scripts require editing before use; in that case, it's prudent to back up the script file you plan to modify before you make any change.

To assign a script to a connection icon, follow these steps:

1. Open the Dial-Up Networking folder, right-click the icon, and choose Properties from the shortcut menu.
2. Click the Scripting tab. The dialog box shown in Figure 17.11 appears.

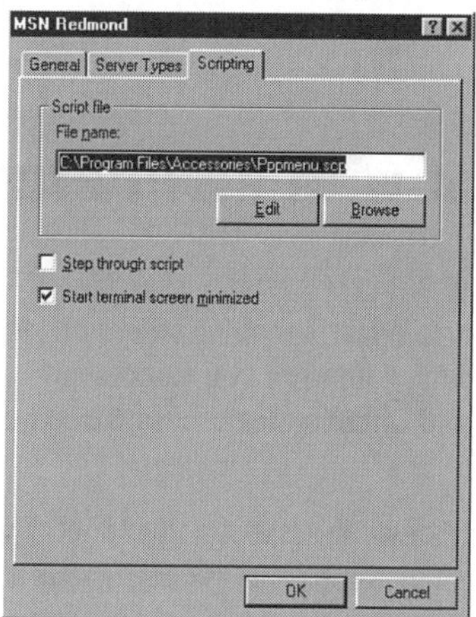

FIG. 17.11 Choose a logon script from this dialog box. Click the Edit button to open Notepad and edit the script.

3. Click the Browse button and navigate to the Accessories folder. Select a script from the list and click Open.
4. If you need to modify the script, click the Edit button. The script opens in Notepad; be sure to save your changes before closing the editing window.
5. To avoid being distracted by the script as it runs, check the box labeled Start terminal screen minimized.

6. To tell Windows that you want the script to pause after each step so you can see where modifications are needed, check the box labeled Step through script.
7. Click OK to save your changes.

When you open a Dial-Up Networking connection with a script attached, the terminal window shown in Figure 17.12 appears. If you've selected the Step through script option, you also see the Automated Script Test window.

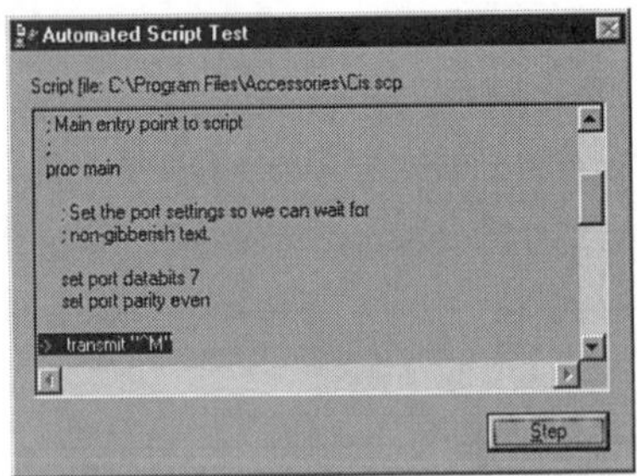

FIG. 17.12 Use the step option to walk through a logon script one step at a time for debugging purposes.

Normally, the terminal window doesn't accept keyboard input. If you need to respond to a prompt, check the box labeled Allow keyboard input. When the script has finished processing, you might need to click Continue to complete the connection.

NOTE For detailed documentation of the dial-up scripting language, look in the Windows folder for a Wordpad file named Script.doc.

Setting Up a New Account with an Internet Service Provider

The top option on the Internet Connection Wizard enables you to choose an Internet service provider and set up a new Internet account. Although you can research available ISPs and sign up for an account on your own, this wizard offers a quick, hassle-free way to change service providers or set up a new account.

Using the wizard is a straightforward process. You specify the country you live in, the area (or city) code, and any necessary dialing instructions. The wizard installs a handful of required software components, including support for TCP/IP and Dial-Up Networking. During the setup and configuration process, the wizard might restart your system one or more times. Although the wizard manages the details of shutting down and restarting, you'll have to respond to dialog boxes like the one in Figure 17.13 to move the installation process along.

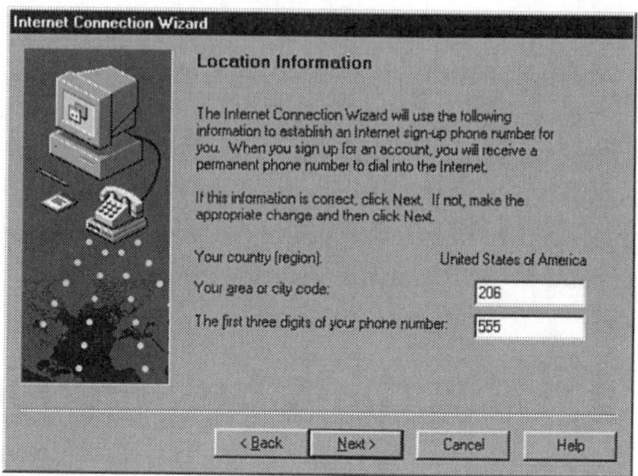

FIG. 17.13
The Internet Connection Wizard's automatic signup option requires almost no intervention except for input in this dialog box.

Eventually the wizard makes two phone calls. The first is to Microsoft's Internet Referral Server, which uses your area (or city) code and the first three digits of your phone number to identify Windows 95-compatible Internet service providers available in your area and language. Because Microsoft regularly updates the roster of eligible service providers, the exact choices you see will vary; the list should resemble the one shown in Figure 17.14.

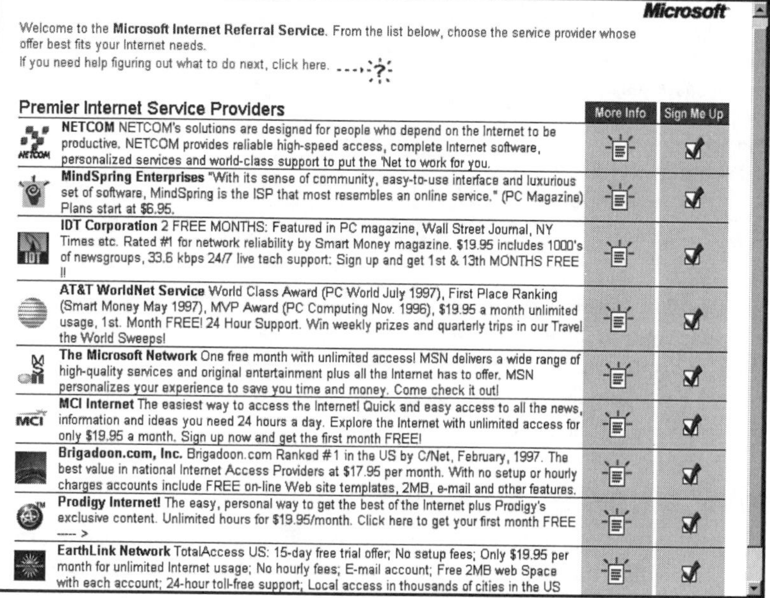

FIG. 17.14
The Microsoft Referral Server generates this list of available Internet service providers just for you, based on your location and operating system.

If the summary information isn't enough to help you decide, click the More Info icon to the right of a listing for extra details about that company's services. When you're ready to choose, click the Sign Me Up icon to the right of the entry you've selected. The Internet Connection Wizard makes a second phone call, this one to the provider you've chosen. Each provider's signup procedure varies, but in general you have to supply your name, address, and credit-card information. The wizard takes care of the remaining details, including setting up Dial-Up Networking connection icons and installing any necessary access software.

Managing Dial-Up Networking Connections

Windows stores every connection icon you create in the Dial-Up Networking folder. Although you can make copies and shortcuts for use elsewhere, the only way to create or manage these icons is to open the Dial-Up Networking folder (see Figure 17.15). You can find it in the My Computer folder or inside the Accessories folder on the Start menu.

NOTE Believe it or not, some Microsoft documentation calls these icons *connectoids.*

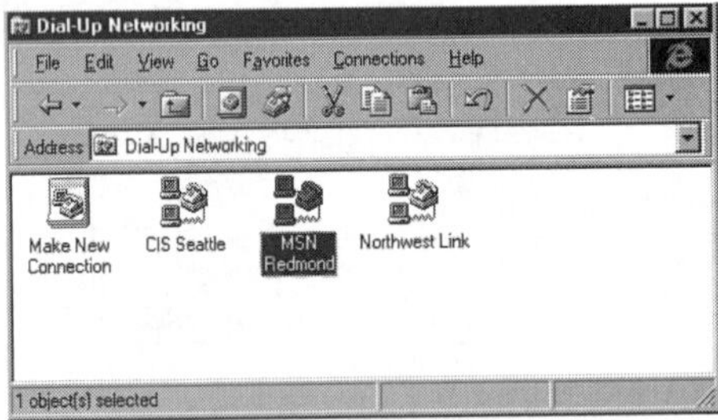

FIG. 17.15 Open the Dial-Up Networking folder to create or manage your connection icons. Note the additional Create and Dial icons in the toolbar.

Like the Desktop, Control Panel, and Printers folders, the Dial-Up Networking folder is a special system folder and doesn't have a corresponding MS-DOS–style directory. You can make this folder more accessible, however; open the My Computer window and drag the Dial-Up Networking icon onto the Quick Launch bar, or drag the icon onto the Start button to create a shortcut at the top of the Start menu.

Adding a New DUN Connection

As we've seen, the Internet Connection Wizard creates connection icons as part of the process of configuring your Internet connection. If you're comfortable working directly with connection icons, you can create them from scratch using a two-step wizard in the Dial-Up Networking folder. Follow these steps:

1. Open the Dial-Up Networking folder and open the Make New Connection icon.
2. In the Make New Connection Wizard, give the connection a name and select a modem or other communication device. Click Next.

3. Enter the area (or city) code, country code, and phone number of the server you want to dial. Click Next.
4. Click Finish to save the connection in the Dial-Up Networking folder, where you can edit it later.

> **CAUTION**
>
> Although this is a quick way to create a Dial-Up Networking icon, the default settings almost always require editing. For example, by default these connections use three different protocols; for most Internet connections, only TCP/IP is needed.

Adjusting Properties of an Existing Connection Icon

Regardless of how you create a Dial-Up Networking connection icon, you can change its properties at any time. Open the Dial-Up Networking folder, select an icon, right-click, and choose Properties. You'll see a multi-tabbed dialog box like the one in Figure 17.16.

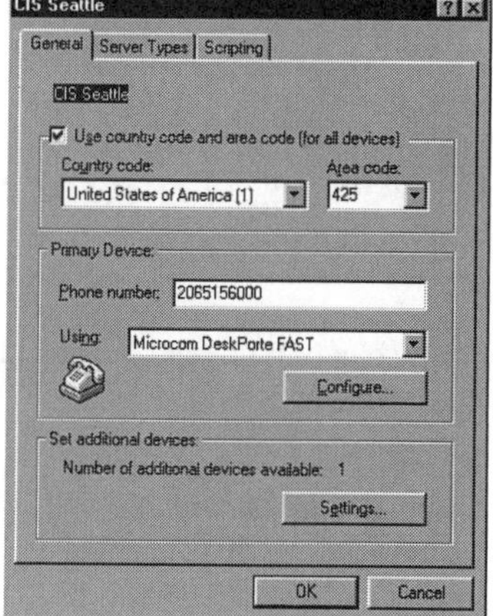

FIG. 17.16
Use this dialog box to change the phone number or modem associated with a connection.

On the General tab, you can adjust the area code, country code, and phone number for any connection. You can also change the modem or other connecting device you use with the connection.

Click the Server Types tab to adjust properties specific to the server with which you plan to connect. Figure 17.17 shows the choices available.

In the drop-down list labeled Type of Dial-Up Server, you find five choices. Select PPP for the overwhelming majority of cases. If you're dialing in to a Unix server with a shell account, you might need to choose SLIP or CSLIP.

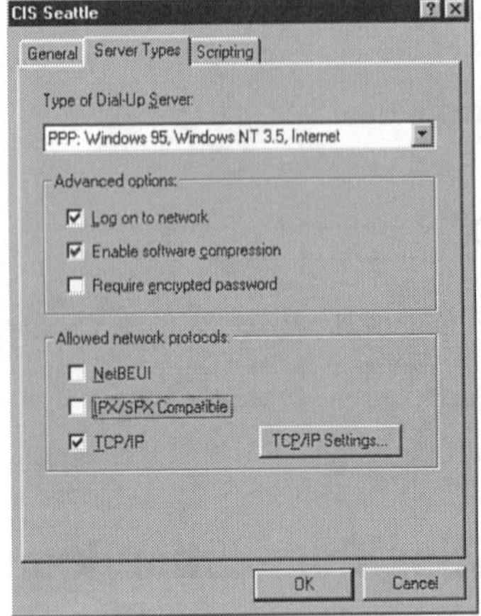

FIG. 17.17
If your ISP uses any nonstandard settings, you need to adjust them here.

NOTE PPP stands for Point-to-Point Protocol. SLIP is short for Serial Line Interface Protocol. PPP has largely replaced SLIP as the standard way to remotely access Internet service providers, thanks to its better error checking and its capability to handle automatic logons.

Unless your ISP recommends that you change settings in the Advanced options area, leave them alone. The defaults are optimized for standard PPP connections. For example, most ISPs support Password Authentication Protocol (PAP) or the Challenge-Handshake Authentication Protocol (CHAP); if you check the box labeled Require encrypted password, you won't be able to log on.

For Internet access, improve performance by clearing the check marks in front of NetBEUI and IPX/SPX in the list of Allowed network protocols. TCP/IP is all you need, unless you're dialing in to a Windows NT server.

Finally, click the TCP/IP Settings button to check the configuration details of your connection. You see a dialog box like the one in Figure 17.18.

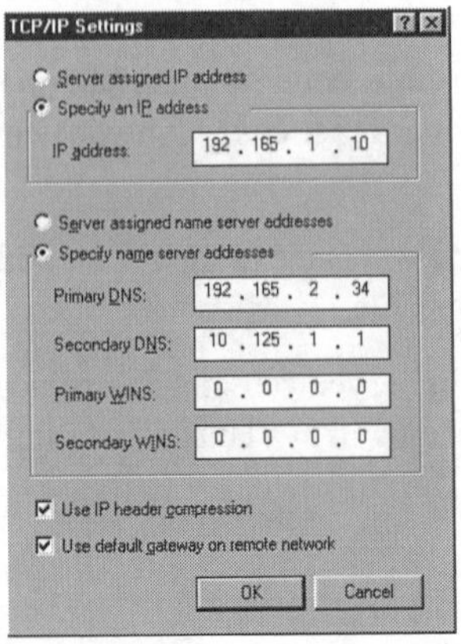

FIG. 17.18
If your ISP has assigned you a static IP address, enter it here, along with the addresses of DNS servers.

The default settings for a Dial-Up Networking connection assume you're dialing into a network that assigns you an IP address automatically each time you connect, without requiring that you specify DNS servers. On networks that use static IP addresses, these options enable you to fill in your IP address and the addresses of DNS servers. For access to an ISP, leave the WINS server entries blank, and don't change the default gateway or IP header compression unless your ISP specifically recommends it.

Creating a Shortcut to a Dial-Up Connection Icon

Although connection icons can only exist in the Dial-Up Networking folder, you can create shortcuts to those icons and use them anywhere you like. To place a shortcut on the desktop, open the Dial-Up Networking folder, select an icon, right-click, and choose Create Shortcut. You can also right-drag a connection icon to any folder or onto the Start menu and choose Create Shortcut(s) Here from the menu that appears when you release the icon.

Moving or Copying Connection Icons

When you right-click a connection icon, there are no Cut, Copy, or Paste menus. But you can share these icons with other users or copy them to other machines, if you know the undocumented technique. When you drag a connection icon out of the Dial-Up Networking folder and drop it in any legal location, including the desktop or a mail message, Windows creates a special Dial-Up Networking Exported File, with the DUN extension.

Although these exported files resemble shortcuts, they behave differently. There's no shortcut arrow, for example; when you right-click a Dial-Up Networking Exported File and choose Properties, you see an abbreviated properties sheet in place of the normal shortcut information. If you drop one of these files in the Dial-Up Networking folder of another machine running Windows 95, however, it works just as though you'd created the connection from scratch. This is an excellent technique for quickly giving other users access to Dial-Up Networking without forcing them to go through the process of creating a connection icon from scratch.

Renaming and Deleting Connection Icons

To rename a connection icon, open the Dial-Up Networking folder, select the icon, right-click, and choose Rename. To delete a connection icon, select the icon, right-click, and choose Delete.

Using Locations to Control Dial-Up Connections

Each time you use a Dial-Up Networking connection icon, you have the option to specify what location you're dialing from. Settings for each location include the area (or city) code for that location, as well as prefixes required to reach an outside line or to dial long distance, calling card information, and much more. Locations are especially useful for owners of portable PCs; by selecting an entry from a list, you can tell Windows to dial the access number for your ISP's server when you're at home, but to use a dialing prefix, area code, and calling card number when you're on a business trip.

Even if you always dial in from your home or office, though, you can still take advantage of multiple "locations." This is especially true if your Dial-Up Networking calls sometimes incur long-distance or toll charges or if your telephone company requires special dialing procedures for nearby area codes.

To set up dialing locations for the first time, open the Modems option in Control Panel and click the Dialing Properties button. To adjust dialing options on-the-fly each time you make a dial-up connection, click the Dial Properties button to the right of the phone number in the Connect to dialog box. Regardless of which technique you use, you see a dialog box like the one in Figure 17.19.

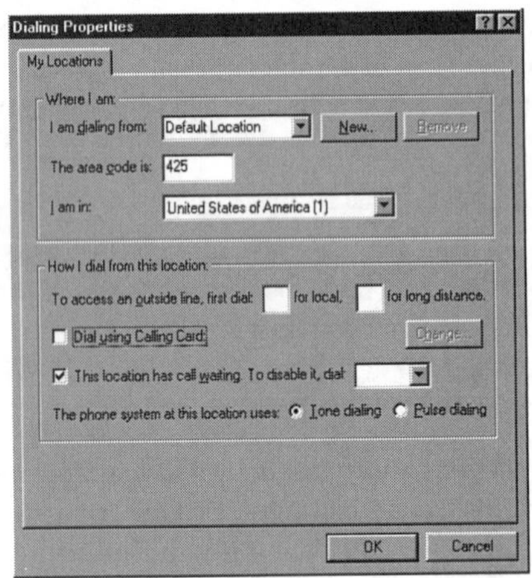

FIG. 17.19
Don't be fooled by the name—you can use dialing locations to define dialing prefixes and area code preferences or to bill your calls to a telephone credit card.

If your ISP has multiple access numbers and you sometimes get a busy signal on your local number, you might want to call a number outside your area code. In many areas, that call is inexpensive late at night but prohibitively costly during business hours. Follow these steps to set up a "location" that enables you to charge the daytime calls to a less expensive credit card.

Follow these steps to set up a new location called Credit Card Call from Home:

1. Open the Modems option in Control Panel and click the Dialing Properties button.
2. Click the New button, enter a name (Credit Card Call from Home, in this example), and click OK to the message box that confirms you've created a new location.
3. Enter the area code for the location. Your default area code should already be in this box.
4. Check the box labeled Dial using Calling Card.
5. Select your calling card from the drop-down list; if you're using a prepaid card or your telephone card isn't in the list, click the New button, give the entry a name, and then click the Advanced button to enter information about the card. (Use the Help button at the top of the dialog box for information about these codes; the Copy From button enables you to use another card's settings as a template for the new card.) Click OK.

6. If the card format you selected requires a number, enter it in the text box labeled Calling Card number, as shown in Figure 17.20. Click OK.

FIG. 17.20
Use this dialog box to set up access options for a telephone calling card.

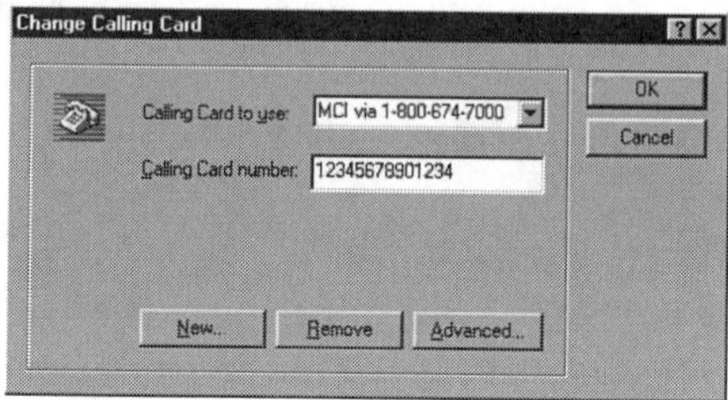

7. Verify that your area code, country setting, and access prefixes are set correctly, and then click Close to save your dialing settings.

Now, whenever you want to call a Dial-Up Networking connection by using a telephone calling card, select the appropriate location in the Connect To box and Windows automatically punches in the correct sequence of tones.

Because Dialing locations work with all TAPI applications, you can reuse calling card settings with the Windows 95 Phone Dialer (found in the Accessories group) and other communication programs, as well.

Would you prefer not to use dialing properties at all? When you create a Dial-Up Networking connection icon, clear the check mark from the box labeled Use area code and Dialing Properties. Then enter the phone number exactly as you want Windows to dial it, complete with any prefixes, area and city or country codes, and calling card numbers.

Using the Microsoft Network for Internet Access

Although it started out with the launch of Windows 95 as on online service competing with America Online and CompuServe, today The Microsoft Network (MSN) is a curious hybrid. Partly an entertainment medium, with "channels" of content ranging from the Disney Blast to Microsoft Investor, it's also a low-cost Internet service provider with worldwide coverage and a variety of access plans.

Naturally, Microsoft makes it easy to install the MSN access software and sign up for a trial account. Look on the Windows desktop for an icon called Set Up the Microsoft Network. If you choose this option, it loads nearly 4MB of software and calls a Microsoft server to establish your account. Although MSN uses many of the same components as Windows 95, most notably Internet Explorer 4.0, it also adds its own distinctive touches, including a custom Connection Manager.

A typical MSN setup makes these changes to your system:

- It replaces the Internet Explorer dialer with its own Connection Manager.
- MSN automatically configures email and news accounts with the username you chose at startup.
- It changes the icon in Outlook Express and Internet Explorer from the stylized Explorer logo to MSN's logo.
- When you connect to MSN, you see an additional icon in the taskbar's notification area. Right-click that icon to pop up a cascading menu with access to all of MSN's services.
- MSN makes other subtle changes throughout the operating system, including installing and configuring a handful of multimedia players.

If you use MSN to access the Internet but aren't fond of its interface, you can have the best of both worlds. When you install MSN, it adds a connection icon to the Dial-Up Networking folder. Use that icon to connect, and you will bypass all of the MSN interface changes. Even if you uninstall the MSN software completely, you can still access your MSN account with this connection icon; for your username, enter MSN/*username*, and dial your local MSN access number.

Using Other Online Services

Increasingly, online services are resembling Internet service providers, both in the services they offer and the rates they charge. When you open the Online Services folder on the Windows desktop, you have access to shortcuts that enable you to connect with America Online (AOL), AT&T WorldNet, CompuServe (which is now owned by AOL), and Prodigy Internet. On some systems, you might see a different collection of shortcuts, including one that points to the now-defunct CompuServe WOW! service.

The icons in the desktop folder are shortcuts to much larger setup files stored on the Windows 95 CD-ROM. You can use these icons to open a new account or to enable access to an existing account with one of these services.

For more details about each of the online services, including technical support numbers, see the text file in the Online Services folder.

Connecting to the Internet

After you've created a Dial-Up Networking icon that contains your connection settings, Windows 95 gives you three choices for establishing a connection:

- Open the Dial-Up Networking folder and use that icon to manually connect to the Internet. This option gives you maximum control over when and how you connect to the Internet.

- Set up Internet Explorer to automatically open a Dial-Up Networking connection whenever you attempt to access a web page. By default, this option requires you to respond to a confirmation dialog box before actually dialing. This is your best choice when you share a single line for voice and data calls.
- Use advanced settings in the Dial-Up Networking folder to make a hands-free connection, without requiring confirmation from you, whenever you attempt to access any Internet resource. This option is best if you have a dedicated data line and don't want any interruptions from Windows.

Making a Manual Connection

To connect to the Internet manually, follow these steps:

1. Select the connection icon and open it. A dialog box like the one in Figure 17.21 appears.

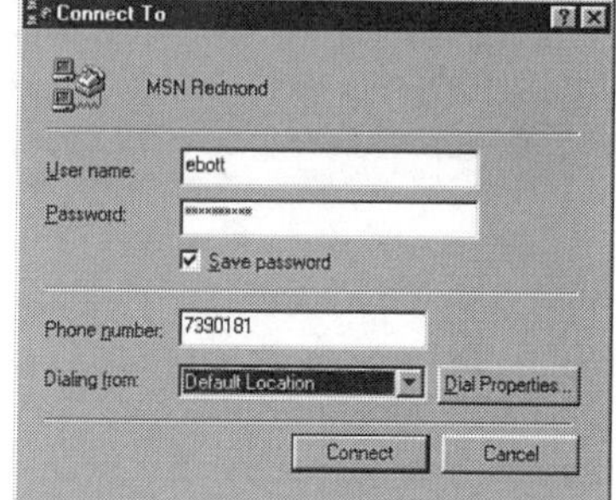

FIG. 17.21 Regardless of the settings you defined in the connection icon, this dialog box enables you to temporarily change phone number, username, location, and other settings.

2. Check your username and enter a password, if necessary. To store the password for reuse, check the box labeled Save password.
3. Check the entry in the Phone number box; if the format is incorrect, choose a new location or edit the number to include the required prefixes.
4. Click the Connect button.

After you complete those steps, Windows opens a modem connection and attempts to dial the number. You see a series of status messages, such as the one in Figure 17.22, as the connection proceeds.

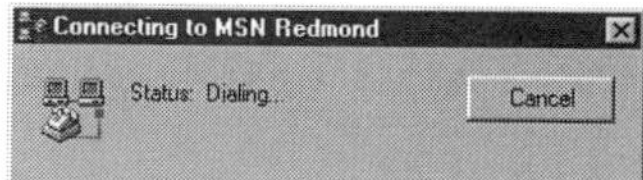

FIG. 17.22 Status messages such as this can help you identify problems when making an Internet connection.

After you successfully complete the connection, you see an informational dialog box, such as the one in Figure 17.23. At the same time, a Dial-Up Networking icon appears in the notification area to the right of the taskbar.

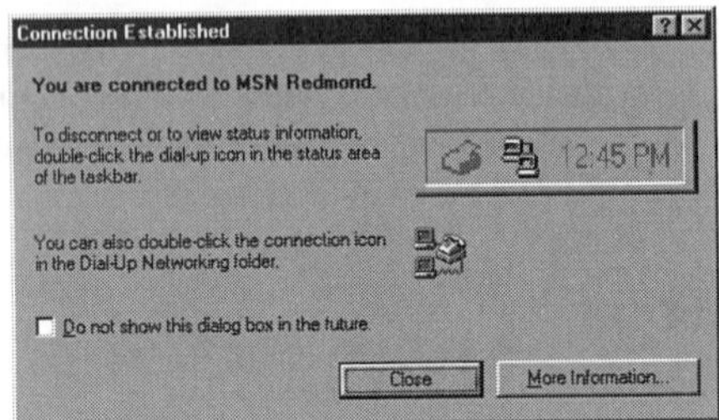

FIG. 17.23
If you'd prefer not to see this dialog box after every completed connection, check the option just above the Close button.

NOTE If the status messages and taskbar icon on your screen look different from the ones you see here, it's probably because you're using the original release of Windows 95. Dial-Up Networking updates in OSR2 and in the ISDN Accelerator Pack add the enhancements you see here. See Chapter 2 for instructions on how to update Dial-Up Networking on your system. ■

Monitoring Connection Status

Whenever you have an open connection to the Internet, Windows 95 offers you a variety of ways to check its status. Right-click the icon in the notification area, for example, and choose Status to see a display showing the total time this connection has been open, as well as the total number of bytes you've received and sent, as in Figure 17.24.

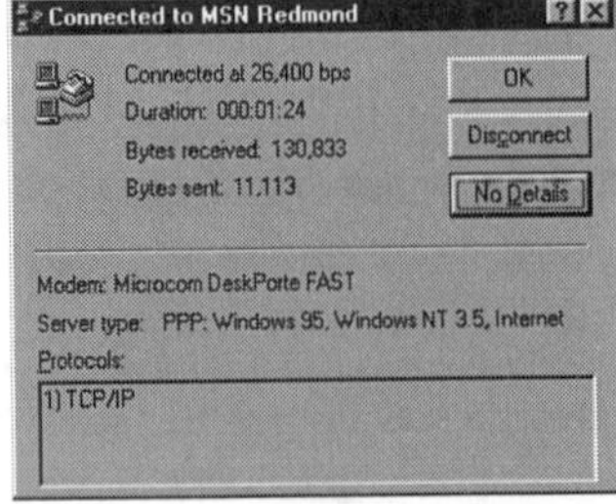

FIG. 17.24
To eliminate the display of connection information in the bottom of this status window, click the No Details button.

To see status information at a glance without opening a dialog box, point to the icon in the notification area; after a few seconds, a ScreenTip appears.

Closing Your Internet Connection

When you've finished working with your Internet connection, you have three options to close it:

- Right-click the icon in the notification area and choose Disconnect.
- Right-click the connection icon in the Dial-Up Networking folder and choose Disconnect (note that the same menu is available if you right-click a shortcut to a connection icon). This technique is useful if the taskbar icon is not available for any reason.
- If the connection status dialog box is open, click the Disconnect button.

Connecting (and Disconnecting) Automatically

Internet Explorer includes a component called Connection Manager, which can automatically establish an Internet connection whenever you attempt to access a web page. You can configure Connection Manager to pause for confirmation or to dial automatically.

NOTE Connection Manager does not work with other Internet programs. If you want Outlook Express to dial automatically each time you check your mail, you must set up separate dialing options by using that program. See Chapter 22 for details on how to set up an automatic mail and news connection.

To set up Connection Manager, open the Internet Options dialog box and click the Connection tab. Choose the option labeled Connect to the Internet using a modem, and then click the Settings button. The dialog box shown in Figure 17.25 appears.

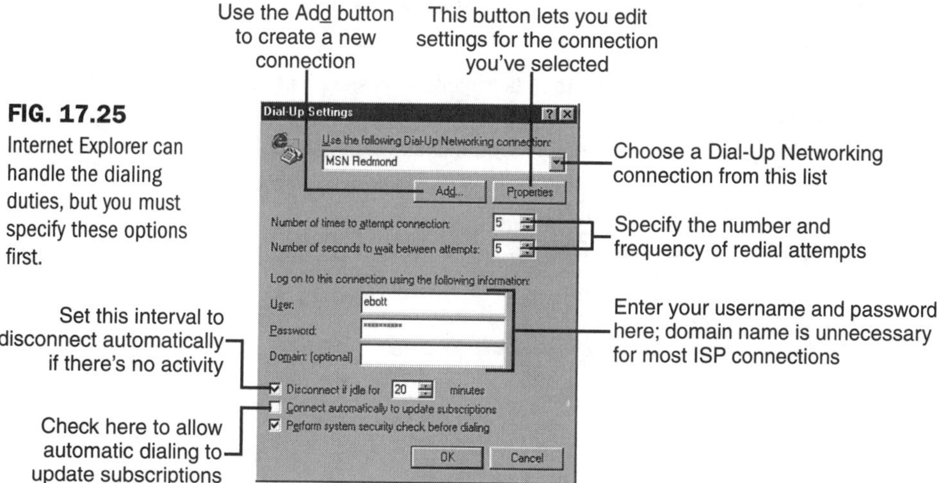

FIG. 17.25 Internet Explorer can handle the dialing duties, but you must specify these options first.

After you've configured all Connection Manager options, click OK to close the Dial-Up Settings dialog box, and click OK again to close the Internet Options dialog box. Open Internet Explorer and try to access a web page. If you don't have an open Internet connection, you see a Dial-up Connection dialog box like the one in Figure 17.26.

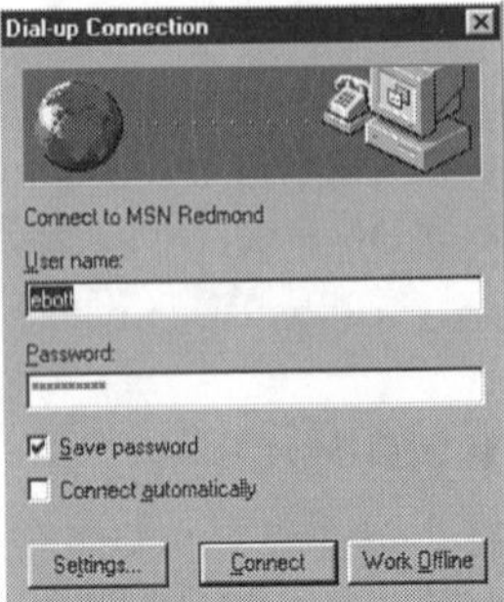

FIG. 17.26
By default, Connection Manager prompts you before trying to make a dial-up connection.

Here are some tips for getting maximum benefit out of Connection Manager:

- Check the Save password box to store your password in the Windows cache. Uncheck this box if you don't want other users to be able to access your Internet account.
- If you see the Connection Manager dialog box but you're not ready to connect, click the Work Offline button.
- Check the box labeled Connect automatically if you have a dedicated data line and you don't need to confirm your action each time you dial.

The Disconnect if idle option automatically closes your dial-up connection if there's been no activity for the amount of time you specify. The default value is 20 minutes, but you can reset the idle time to any value between 3 and 59 minutes.

If you're working with a web page when the idle timer expires, Internet Explorer won't suddenly close the connection. Instead, you'll see a warning dialog box like the one in Figure 17.27. You have 30 seconds to respond before Connection Manager shuts down access to the Internet.

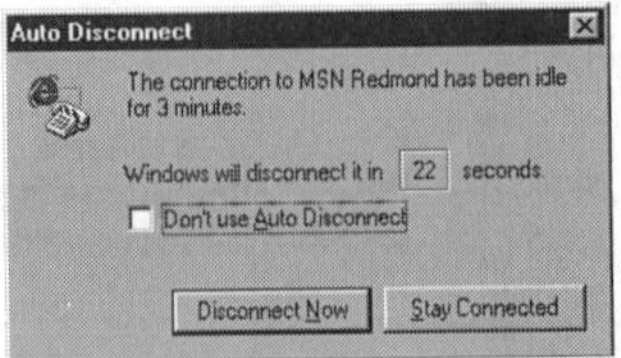

FIG. 17.27
You will receive fair warning before Connection Manager shuts down an open connection.

The Auto Disconnect dialog box gives you these options:

- Click the Disconnect Now button to close the connection immediately.
- Click the Stay Connected button to reset the timer and continue working with Internet Explorer.
- Check the Don't use Auto Disconnect box to disable this feature until you reset it. This has the same effect as clearing the check box in the Dial-Up Settings dialog box.

CAUTION

Some sites can keep an Internet connection open indefinitely. For example, pages that automatically refresh every few minutes do this, as will sites that deliver streaming data such as RealAudio. Don't expect Internet Explorer to hang up automatically if you leave one of these pages open and then walk away from your computer.

Making a Hands-Free Manual Connection

If you prefer not to use the Connection Manager, open the Internet Options dialog box and configure Internet Explorer to connect by using a local area network. You have to connect manually by using a Dial-Up Networking connection icon before attempting to access a web page. To turn this into a single-click process, follow these steps:

1. Open the Dial-Up Networking folder.
2. Open the connection icon you want to automate, and enter your username and password. Check the Save password box.
3. Click Connect. When the status dialog box appears, click Cancel to abort the connection and return to the DUN folder.
4. Choose Connections, Settings.
5. Clear the check marks in front of the box labeled Prompt for information before dialing and Show a confirmation dialog after connected, as shown in Figure 17.28.

FIG. 17.28
Use these settings to bypass all dialog boxes when you click a connection icon.

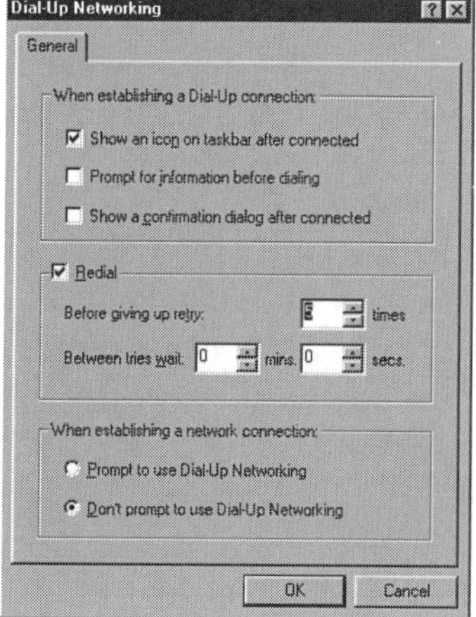

6. Check the Redial box and set automatic retry options if desired.
7. Click OK to save your changes.

CHAPTER 18

Web Browsing with Internet Explorer 4.0

by Ed Bott

In this chapter

What Is Internet Explorer 4.0?

Internet Explorer 4.0 delivers all the basic functionality you've come to expect from a web browser. It enables you to gather information from servers located on your company's intranet or on the World Wide Web. It displays text and graphics in richly formatted pages, runs scripts, accesses databases, and downloads files. With the help of Internet Explorer 4.0, you can establish secure, encrypted sessions with distant servers so that you can safely exchange confidential information, such as your credit-card number, without fear that a third party will intercept it.

Internet Explorer 4.0 also does things that previous web browsers couldn't. It enables you to establish security zones, for example, so that you can tightly restrict the capability of unknown web servers to interact with local computers and network resources. Using subscriptions, you can transfer web-based information automatically to a desktop or notebook PC and then view those pages even when you're not connected to the Internet.

IE4 looks different, too. You can use the versatile Explorer bar—a simple frame that locks in place along the left edge of the browser window—to organize your Favorites list, search for information on the web, or browse pages stored in your local cache. Because the browser shares code with the Windows Explorer, you can display the contents of a folder on your local PC or network and then jump to a web site in the same window. And there are dozens of configuration options to make the interface more comfortable.

To open Internet Explorer and display your home page, click the Internet icon on the desktop or the Quick Launch bar. Figure 18.1 shows the default browser window.

Decoding URLs

Before you can open a web page, you must specify its location, either by clicking a shortcut or link that points to the file or by entering its full name and path in the Address bar. For an HTML document stored on your local PC or a network server, use the familiar [drive]:\filename or \\servername\sharename\filename syntax. For web pages stored on a web server on the Internet, you need to specify a Uniform Resource Locator, or URL.

NOTE Some otherwise credible sources insist that URL actually stands for Universal Resource Locator, but the organizations that set Internet standards agree that U is for Uniform. Opinion is evenly divided on whether to pronounce the term "earl" or spell out the letters U-R-L. ■

As Figure 18.2 shows, each URL contains three essential pieces of information that help Internet Explorer find and retrieve information from the Internet.

- The prefix tells Internet Explorer which protocol or retrieval scheme to use when transferring the document. The prefix is always followed by a colon. Standard web pages use the http: prefix, whereas secure web pages use https:. The URL for a file stored on an FTP server uses the prefix ftp:. Internet Explorer automatically adds the http: and ftp: prefixes if you type an otherwise valid web or FTP address.

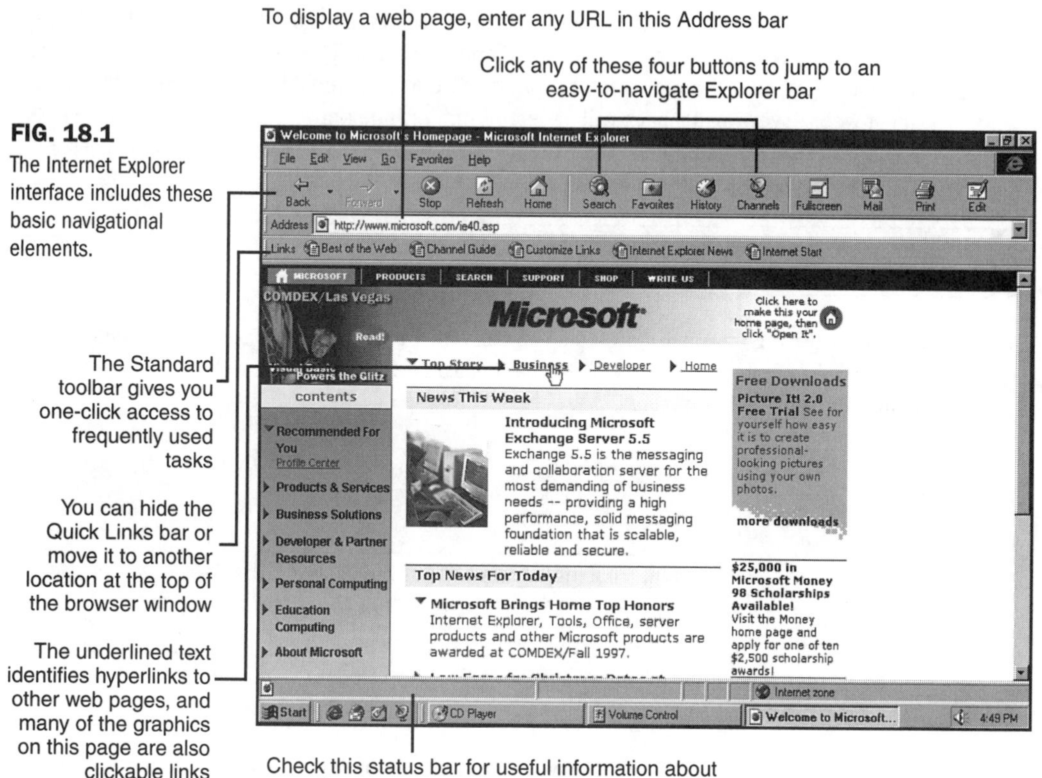
To display a web page, enter any URL in this Address bar
Click any of these four buttons to jump to an easy-to-navigate Explorer bar
The Standard toolbar gives you one-click access to frequently used tasks
You can hide the Quick Links bar or move it to another location at the top of the browser window
The underlined text identifies hyperlinks to other web pages, and many of the graphics on this page are also clickable links
Check this status bar for useful information about the current page, especially as it loads

FIG. 18.1
The Internet Explorer interface includes these basic navigational elements.

Part
IV
Ch
18

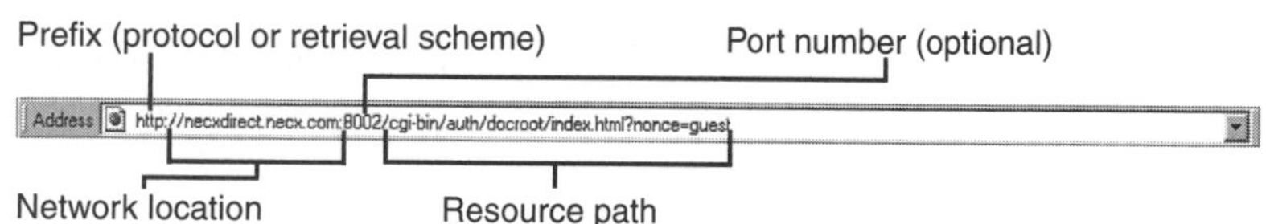
Prefix (protocol or retrieval scheme)
Port number (optional)
Address
http://necxdirect.necx.com:8002/cgi-bin/auth/docroot/index.html?nonce=guest
Network location
Resource path

FIG. 18.2
Every URL is different, but these three components help define the location of all sorts of web resources.

- The network location, which appears immediately to the right of the prefix, identifies the Internet host or network server where the document is stored: **www.microsoft.com**, for example. Note that you must separate the prefix from network location in URLs with two forward slashes. This part of an URL might also include a username and password for connecting with resources on servers that require you to log on. If the server requires connection over a nonstandard TCP port number, you can add a colon and the port information at the end of this entry.

- The resource path defines the exact location of the web page or other resource on the specified server, including path, filename, and extension. This entry begins with the first forward slash after the network location. If you don't include a resource path in the URL, most web servers load a page called default.htm or index.htm. Two special characters define parameters that appear after the path: ? indicates query information to be passed to a web server, and # identifies a specific location on the page.

To display a blank page in your web browser, use the URL **about:blank**.

There are a surprising number of prefixes you can type in the Address bar. Each uses its own protocol or retrieval method to gather information. Table 18.1 provides a detailed listing of the most generally used URL prefixes.

Table 18.1. Legal URL Prefixes

Prefix	Description
about:	Displays internal information about the browser. IE4 uses this prefix to display some error messages, including about:NavigationCanceled.
file:	Opens a local or network file. Used in other browsers but not required with IE4 when the Windows Desktop Update is installed.
ftp:	Connects with a server running the File Transfer Protocol.
gopher:	Connects with a server running the Gopher or Gopher+ Protocol.
http:	Retrieves information from web servers using Hypertext Transfer Protocol.
https:	Creates a connection with a secure web server and then encrypts all page requests and retrieved information over Secure Hypertext Transfer Protocol.
mailto:	Launches the default email client and begins composing a message to the address named in the URL.
news:	Connects with a Usenet news server by using the default news reader.
nntp:	Connects with a Usenet news server by using the NNTP access.
res:	Resource within a binary file; IE4 uses information with DLL files to display some help information.
telnet:	Launches the system's default Telnet client to create an interactive session with a remote host computer.
wais:	Connects with Wide Area Information Servers that contain large databases.

Working with Web Pages

The basic building blocks of the World Wide Web are simple text documents written in HyperText Markup Language, or HTML. To communicate with the web server where a given page is stored, your browser uses HyperText Transfer Protocol, or HTTP.

Every time you open an HTML document, Internet Explorer interprets the formatting tags and other coded instructions in that document and displays the fully formatted results in your browser window. A single web page might contain text, graphics, links to other pages and to downloadable files, and embedded objects, such as ActiveX controls and Java applets. When you load that web page, it might in turn load dozens of additional linked files, especially graphic images.

HTML pages can incorporate scripts that cause specific actions to take place in response to a trigger event—for example, clicking a button to submit data from a web-based form for processing by a web server. Dynamic HTML instructions enable the contents of the browser window to change as you work with the page.

To see the underlying HTML code for the current web page, choose View, Source. Internet Explorer uses its basic text editor, Notepad, to display HTML source, as shown in Figure 18.3.

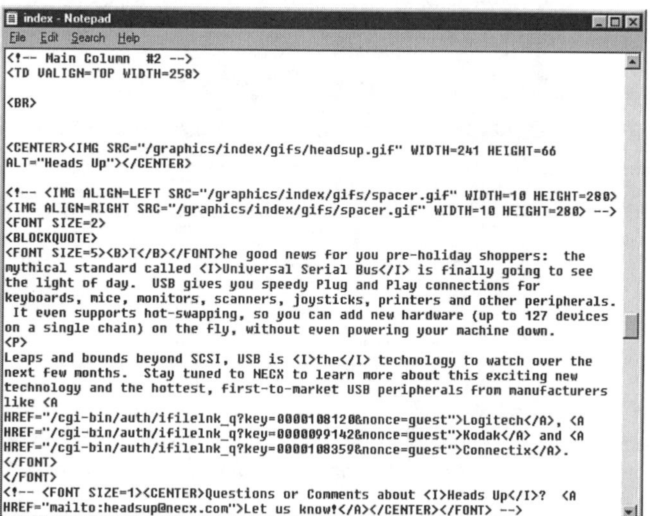

```
index - Notepad
File Edit Search Help
<!-- Main Column  #2 -->
<TD VALIGN=TOP WIDTH=258>

<BR>


<CENTER><IMG SRC="/graphics/index/gifs/headsup.gif" WIDTH=241 HEIGHT=66
ALT="Heads Up"></CENTER>

<!-- <IMG ALIGN=LEFT SRC="/graphics/index/gifs/spacer.gif" WIDTH=10 HEIGHT=280>
<IMG ALIGN=RIGHT SRC="/graphics/index/gifs/spacer.gif" WIDTH=10 HEIGHT=280> -->
<FONT SIZE=2>
<BLOCKQUOTE>
<FONT SIZE=5><B>T</B></FONT>he good news for you pre-holiday shoppers:  the
mythical standard called <I>Universal Serial Bus</I> is finally going to see
the light of day.  USB gives you speedy Plug and Play connections for
keyboards, mice, monitors, scanners, joysticks, printers and other peripherals.
 It even supports hot-swapping, so you can add new hardware (up to 127 devices
on a single chain) on the fly, without even powering your machine down.
<P>
Leaps and bounds beyond SCSI, USB is <I>the</I> technology to watch over the
next few months.  Stay tuned to NECX to learn more about this exciting new
technology and the hottest, first-to-market USB peripherals from manufacturers
like <A
HREF="/cgi-bin/auth/ifilelnk_q?key=0000108120&nonce=guest">Logitech</A>, <A
HREF="/cgi-bin/auth/ifilelnk_q?key=0000099142&nonce=guest">Kodak</A> and <A
HREF="/cgi-bin/auth/ifilelnk_q?key=0000108359&nonce=guest">Connectix</A>.
</FONT>
</FONT>
<!-- <FONT SIZE=1><CENTER>Questions or Comments about <I>Heads Up</I>?  <A
HREF="mailto:headsup@necx.com">Let us know!</A></CENTER></FONT> -->
```

FIG. 18.3
Because HTML documents are strictly text, you can view the underlying source code in the bare-bones Notepad editor.

When you install Microsoft's full-strength web-page editor, FrontPage, it adds an Edit button to the Internet Explorer toolbar. Click this button to begin editing the current web page in FrontPage.

Working with Hyperlinks

Hyperlinks are HTML shortcuts that activate with a single click. Clicking a link has the same effect as typing its URL into the browser's Address bar. The specific action depends on the prefix: a link with the http: prefix, for example, enables you to jump from page to page. Other prefixes typically found in links carry out specific actions: A link can enable you to begin executing a script (javascript:), download a file (ftp:), begin composing a mail message (mailto:), or open Outlook Express to read a linked newsgroup message (news:).

On a web page, the clickable portion of a hyperlink can take several forms. Text links appear in color (blue, by default) and are underlined. A web page designer can also attach a link to a picture or button on the screen. Internet Explorer changes the shape of the pointer when it passes over a link. To see additional information about a link, look in the status bar or inspect its properties. Some web pages, such as the one in Figure 18.4, include pop-up help text for the image under the pointer; the status bar shows where the link will take you.

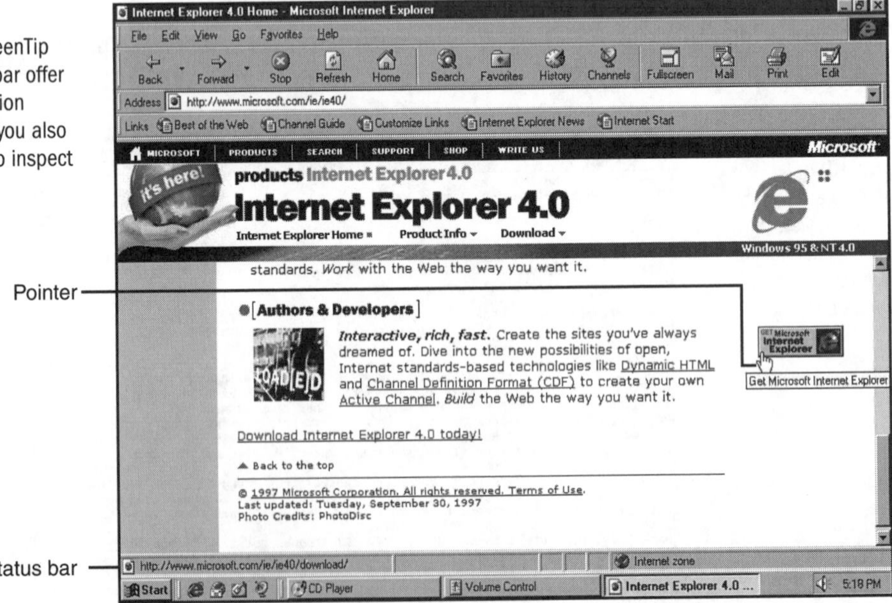

FIG. 18.4
The pop-up ScreenTip and the status bar offer helpful information about this link; you also can right-click to inspect its properties.

TROUBLESHOOTING

I clicked a link, but nothing happened. Clicking a link might fail to have the desired effect, often because the author left out a crucial portion of the web address or simply mistyped it. You can sometimes open the link anyway, although it might take several extra steps: Right-click the link and choose Properties; select the link text from the Properties dialog box and press Ctrl+C to copy it to the Windows Clipboard. Close the property sheet and then paste the URL into the Address bar; edit as needed, and press Enter.

To copy the underlying URL in text format from a link to the Windows Clipboard, right-click the link and choose Copy Shortcut. For a link that's attached to a graphic, choose Copy only if you want to copy the image itself to the Clipboard.

Normally, clicking a link replaces the page displayed in the current window. To open the linked page in its own window without affecting the current page, right-click the link and choose Open in New Window.

Starting Internet Explorer

The browser window opens automatically when you click a hyperlink or an Internet shortcut. To open Internet Explorer and go directly to your home page, use the Internet Explorer icon on the desktop or on the Quick Launch bar.

You can have two or more browser windows open at one time—a technique that's handy when you're gathering and comparing information from multiple sources. To open a new browser window, use any of these three techniques:

- Choose File, New, Window. The new window displays the same contents as the current browser window.
- Press Ctrl+N. This keyboard shortcut has the same effect as using the File menu. In both cases, the new browser window "remembers" previously visited sites, so you can use the Back button just as you would in the original window.
- Click the Launch Internet Explorer Browser button in the Quick Launch toolbar. The new window opens to your home page.

Navigating Internet Explorer

There are at least six ways to display a web page in the current browser window:

- Type an URL in the Address bar, or choose a previously entered URL from the drop-down list, and press Enter.
- Type an URL in the Run box on the Start menu.
- Click a link on an HTML page.
- Open an Internet shortcut on the desktop, in a folder, in the Favorites list, or in a mail message.
- Click a shortcut on the Links bar.
- Use the Back and Forward buttons, the File menu, or the History list to return to previously viewed pages.

Using the Address Bar

You can click the Address bar and painstakingly type a full URL to jump to a particular web page, but Internet Explorer 4.0 includes several shortcut features that reduce the amount of typing required for most web addresses.

There's no need to start with a prefix when you enter the address of a valid Internet host. For example, when you type

www.microsoft.com

the browser automatically adds the http:// prefix. If the address you enter begins with ftp, it adds the ftp:// prefix.

> **CAUTION**
>
> There's an important distinction between the forward slashes used in URLs and the backslashes used in local files and in UNC names that refer to network resources. If you enter **servername** in the Address bar, you see a list of all the shared resources available on a network server, whereas //servername jumps to the default HTML page on the web server with that name.

If you type a single word that doesn't match the name of a local web server, Internet Explorer automatically tries other addresses based on that name, using the common web prefix www and standard top-level domains—.com, .edu, and .org. To tell Internet Explorer to automatically add www to the beginning and com to the end of the name you typed, press Ctrl+Enter.

Using AutoComplete to Fill in the Blanks

As you move from page to page, Internet Explorer keeps track of the URL for every page you've visited. Each time you begin to type in the Address bar, Internet Explorer checks the History list and attempts to complete the entry for you, suggesting the first address that matches the characters you've typed. You can see the results of this AutoComplete feature in Figure 18.5. Note that the characters you type appear on a plain white background, while the suggested completion is highlighted.

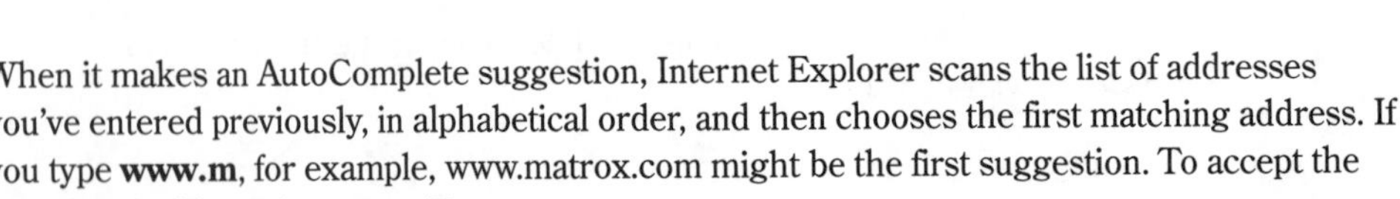

FIG. 18.5
The AutoComplete feature suggests the first address that begins with the characters you've typed.

When it makes an AutoComplete suggestion, Internet Explorer scans the list of addresses you've entered previously, in alphabetical order, and then chooses the first matching address. If you type **www.m**, for example, www.matrox.com might be the first suggestion. To accept the completed address, just press Enter.

If the suggested address isn't the one you want, you have two alternatives: If you continue typing, Internet Explorer revises its suggestion based on the new text you type. In the previous example, if you press **i** so that the contents of the Address bar read www.mi, Internet Explorer might suggest www.microsoft.com.

What do you do if there are dozens of pages in your History list that begin with the same domain name? After AutoComplete makes its first suggestion, use the down arrow to cycle through every entry in your History list that begins with that string of text. When you reach the right address, press Enter to load that page.

You can simply ignore AutoComplete suggestions and continue typing the address. If you find the feature more confusing than helpful, turn it off. Choose View, Internet Options, click the Advanced tab, and clear the check mark from the box labeled Use AutoComplete.

Navigating with the Mouse

Click the Back button to jump to pages you previously visited, and then click the Forward button to return. When you right-click either button (or use the arrow at right), a list of the nine most recent pages appears, as seen in Figure 18.6. (The same list of up to nine pages also appears at the bottom of the File menu.)

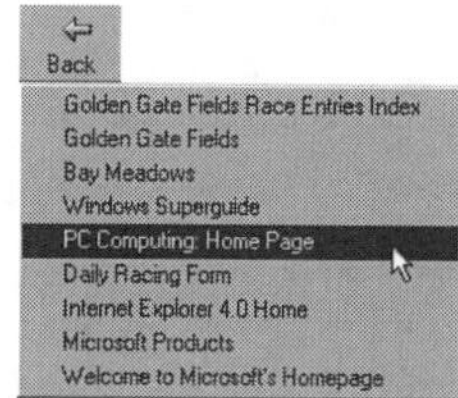

FIG. 18.6
Right-click or use this drop-down arrow for a faster alternative to repeatedly clicking the Back or Forward button.

If you own a Microsoft IntelliMouse, use the wheel (located between the buttons) to take advantage of three navigational shortcuts:

- Hold down the Shift key and roll the wheel downward to return to the previously viewed page; hold down Shift and move the wheel up to go forward again.
- Roll the wheel up or down to scroll three lines at a time through a web page (the Advanced tab of the Internet Options dialog box enables you to adjust this setting).
- Click the wheel to turn on continuous scrolling. When you see the indicator, move the pointer and the page scrolls automatically in that direction, like a Teleprompter. The further you move the pointer, the faster the page scrolls. To resume normal scrolling, click the wheel again or press Esc.

Virtually every object on a web page is accessible via shortcut menus. Right-click to inspect properties, copy or print an image, or add a page to your Favorites list, for example.

Working with Frame-Based Pages

Frames are an effective way for clever designers to make web pages more usable. Unlike ordinary pages, which fill the browser window from border to border, frame-based pages split the window into two or more zones, each with its own underlying HTML code and navigation controls. The most common use of frames is to add a table of links along one side of the browser window, with pages displayed in the frame on the other side; because the frame containing the list of links is always visible, it's easy to quickly move through the site without constantly hitting the Back button. Not surprisingly, Microsoft's developer pages (see Figure 18.7) make good use of frames.

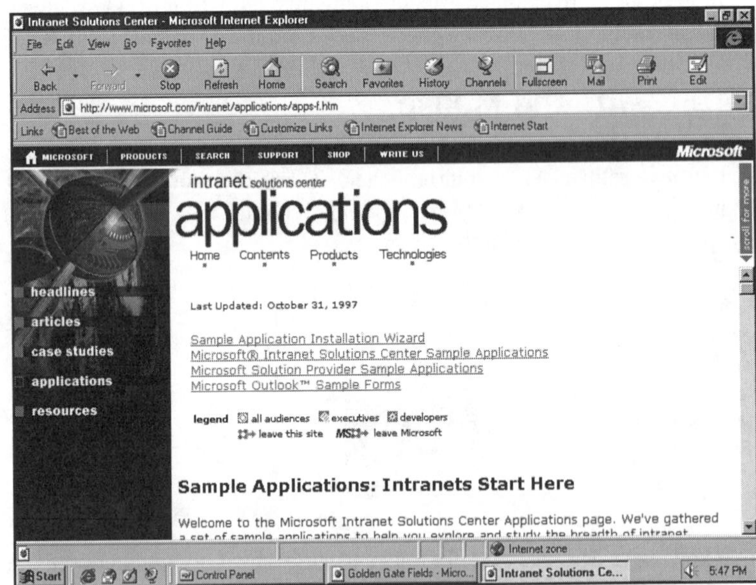

FIG. 18.7
Look carefully and you will see four frames in this page. In addition to the obvious navigation area at left, there are two frames along the top. The main browser window is a frame with its own scroll bar.

Working with frames takes practice. The Back and Forward buttons, for example, don't work as they do with an ordinary HTML page. To move back and forth within a frame, right-click within the frame itself and click the Back or Forward menu choices. Likewise, to view the source code for a frame, you need to right-click the area of interest and choose View Source from the shortcut menu. When you save or copy a frame-based page, make sure you select the portion of the document you want and not just the small master document that contains pointers to the frames! See Chapter 19, "Finding, Organizing, and Saving Web-Based Information," for advice on printing frame-based pages.

Navigating with the Keyboard

For most people, most of the time, the mouse is the best way to navigate with Internet Explorer. But the web browser also offers superb keyboard support, which is important for users who have physical disabilities that make it difficult or impossible to use a mouse. Keyboard shortcuts are also a useful way to accelerate web access for skilled typists who prefer to keep their hands on the keyboard while they work.

Most of the movement keys in Internet Explorer 4.0 work as they do elsewhere in Windows. Home and End go to the top and bottom of the current page, for example. The Up and Down arrow keys move through the page, and the Page Up and Page Down keys move up and down in bigger jumps.

You can use shortcut keys to choose commands and view documents. Many of the pull-down menus include pointers to keyboard alternatives. The following table lists the most useful keyboard shortcuts in Internet Explorer.

To do this...	Press this
Go to the next page	Alt+Right Arrow
Go to the previous page	Alt+Left Arrow, Backspace
Display a shortcut menu for a link or object	Shift+F10
Move forward between frames	Ctrl+Tab
Move back between frames	Shift+Ctrl+Tab
Move to the next link on a page	Tab
Move to the previous link on a page	Shift+Tab
Activate the currently selected link	Enter
Refresh the current page	F5
Stop downloading a page	Esc
Open a new location	Ctrl+O
Open a new browser window	Ctrl+N
Save the current page	Ctrl+S
Print the current page or active frame	Ctrl+P

Using Image Maps

One popular navigational aid on some web pages is the image map. Instead of assigning links to a series of graphic objects or buttons, a web designer can create links to specific coordinates of a single large image. The image map in Figure 18.8, for example, enables you to jump to linked pages by using a map of Houston, Texas. How do you know when you're working with an image map? Watch the status bar at the bottom of the browser window as the mouse passes over the image—if you see coordinates, as in this figure, there's an image map under the pointer.

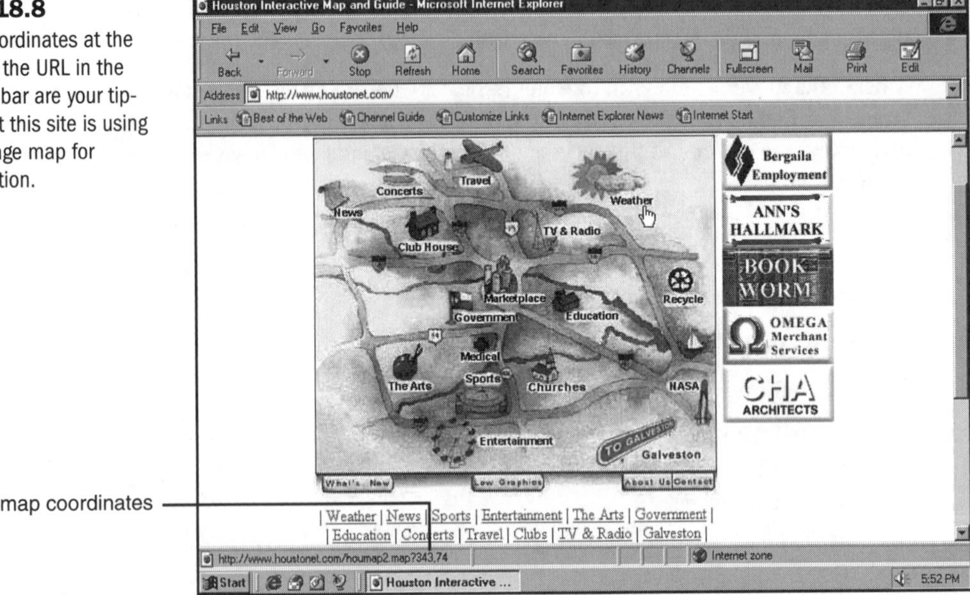

FIG. 18.8
The coordinates at the end of the URL in the status bar are your tip-off that this site is using an image map for navigation.

Image maps are clever and useful jumping-off points on web sites. Their only drawback is that they require the use of the mouse—there's no way to use an image map with the keyboard.

Gathering Information from the Status Bar

Each time your browser makes a connection with a web server, valuable information appears on the status bar along the bottom of the screen. The status bar (see Figure 18.9) shows the following:

- The status of the current download—look for an hourglass over a globe as a page loads, and a full-page icon when the download is complete.
- The status of objects currently loading, including linked graphics, ActiveX components, and Java applets. This area also counts down the number of items that have not yet been downloaded.
- Point to a link to see its associated URL in the status bar; use the Advanced tab of the Internet Options dialog box to switch between full URLs (**http://www.microsoft.com/default.asp**) and friendly names (Shortcut to default.asp at **www.microsoft.com**).
- A blue progress bar shows what percentage of the entire page has been loaded.
- Look for a padlock icon to indicate when you're viewing a page over a secure connection or using international language support; when you print a page, you will see a printer icon here.

- The security zone for the current page appears at the far right of the status bar. To learn how to use the security zones, see Chapter 20, "Internet Explorer 4.0 and Security."

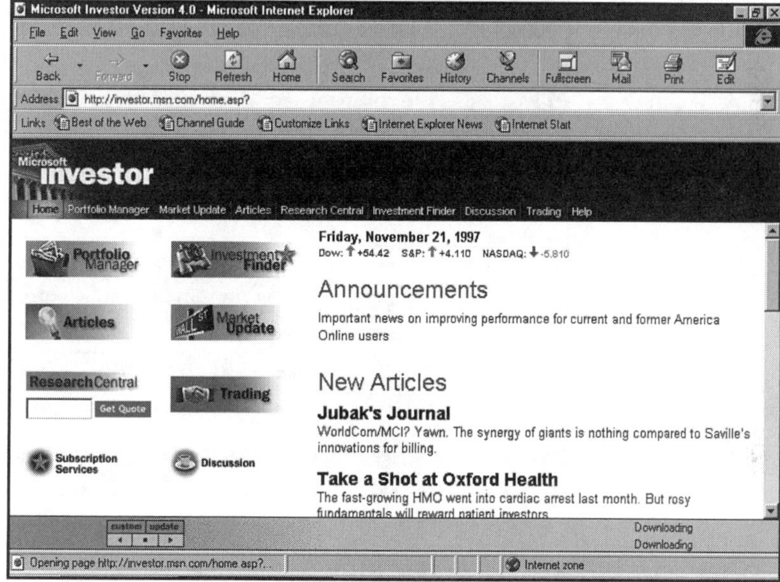

FIG. 18.9 You can find important information about the status of the current page here.

Stopping Downloads and Reloading Pages

The Refresh button is especially valuable when viewing frequently updated pages, such as weather information, traffic maps, or stock quotes, to guarantee that the version you see is the most recent and not a stale copy from the Internet Explorer cache. You should also click the Refresh button when a download fails in the middle of a page or when one or more objects on a page fail to load, as in the example in Figure 18.10.

TIP You don't have to refresh the entire page if a small portion of the page failed to load. Look for a red X or broken image icon, indicating a linked file that failed to load. To refresh just that portion of the page, right-click and choose Show Picture.

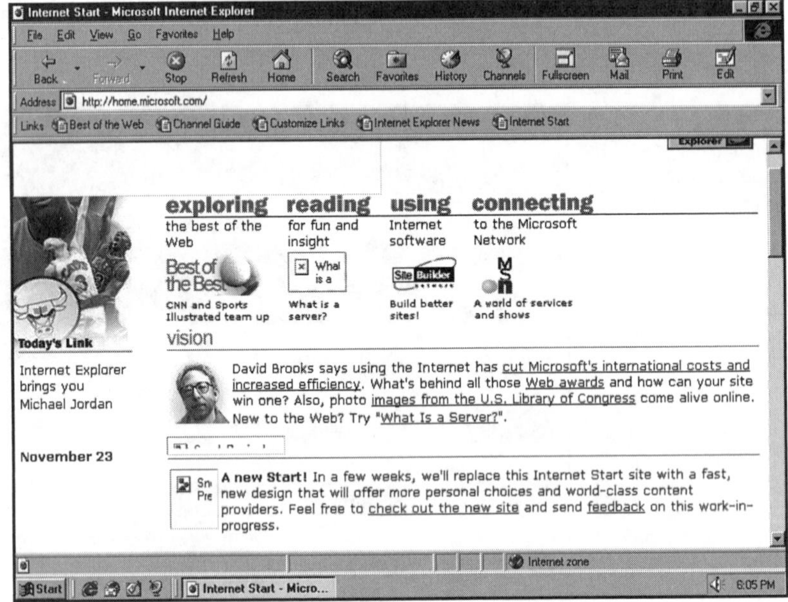

FIG. 18.10
The icon in each empty box means that a graphic file failed to load. Click Refresh to reload the entire page, or right-click to download just one image.

Setting Your Home Page

Every time you start Internet Explorer, it loads the page you designate as your home page. By default, Microsoft takes you to home.microsoft.com, where you can follow links to assemble a home page based on your own interests. You can designate any web page as your home page; if you're connected to a company intranet, you might prefer to set a local page to load automatically at startup.

To reset your home page, load the page you want to use, choose View, Internet Options, and click the General tab (see Figure 18.11). Click Use Current to set the current page as your home page. Click Use Default to restore the default Microsoft home page. Click Use Blank to replace the home page with a blank page that loads instantly.

When choosing a home page, make sure it's readily accessible, to avoid delays when you start your browser. Better yet, use FrontPage Express to construct your own home page, with links to favorite sites inside your intranet and on the World Wide Web. See Chapter 23, "Using FrontPage Express and Internet Components," for more details on how to use FrontPage Express.

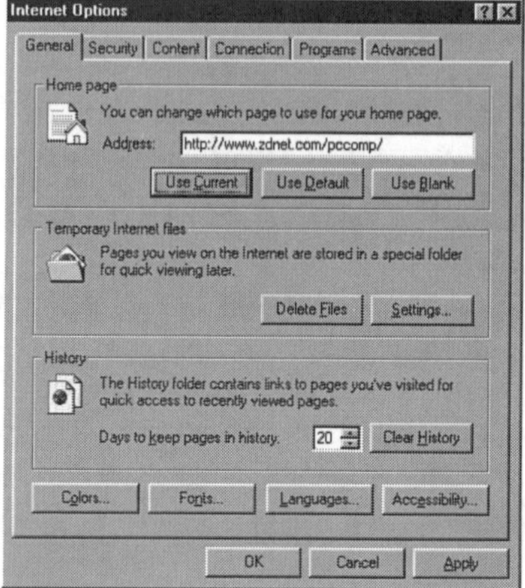

FIG. 18.11
Choose your preferred home page and then navigate to this dialog box to designate that page to run every time you start Internet Explorer.

Increasing the Size of the Browser Window

Pieces of the Internet Explorer interface can get in the way of data, especially on displays running at low resolutions. There are several ways to make more space available for data in the browser window. Most involve hiding, rearranging, or reconfiguring these optional interface elements.

The simplest way to reclaim space for data is to hide the toolbars and status bar. To hide the status bar, choose View and click Status Bar; to eliminate one or more of the three built-in toolbars, right-click the menu bar and remove the check marks from Standard Buttons, Address Bar, or Links.

You can also rearrange the three toolbars, placing them side by side or one on top of the other. You can even position any toolbar alongside the menu bar. To move a toolbar, click the raised handle at the left and then drag the toolbar to its new position. Drag the same handle from right to left to adjust the width of the toolbar.

Want to cut the oversize buttons on the browser window down to size? Choose View, Internet Options, click the Advanced tab, and check the option to use the smaller Microsoft Office-style buttons instead; next, choose View, Toolbars, and clear the check mark from Text Labels. The results should resemble what you see in Figure 18.12.

To configure Internet Explorer for the absolute maximum viewing area, load any page, and then click the Full Screen button. This view, shown in Figure 18.13, hides the title bar, menu bar, Address bar, and Links bar. The Standard buttons toolbar shrinks to its smallest setting, and even the minimize and close buttons in the upper-right corner adjust their size and position.

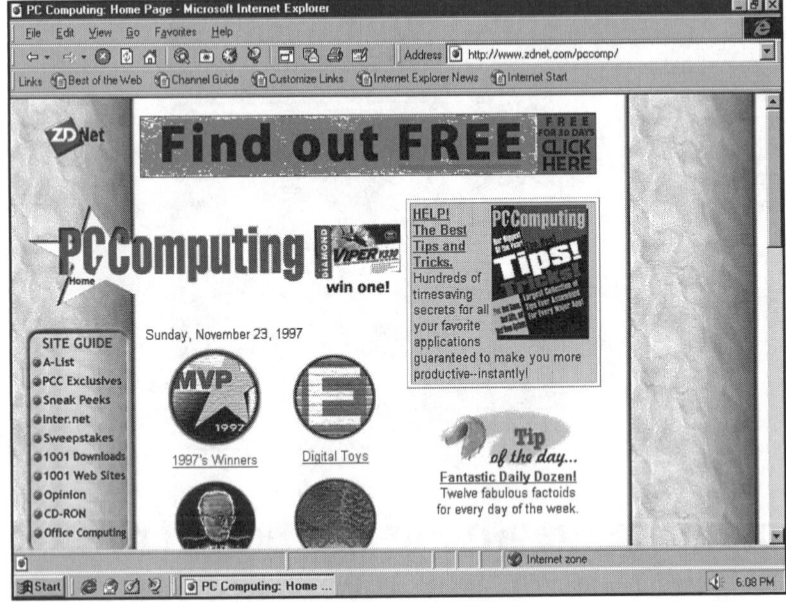

FIG. 18.12
These smaller buttons, without labels, fit comfortably alongside the Address bar to make room for more data in the browser window.

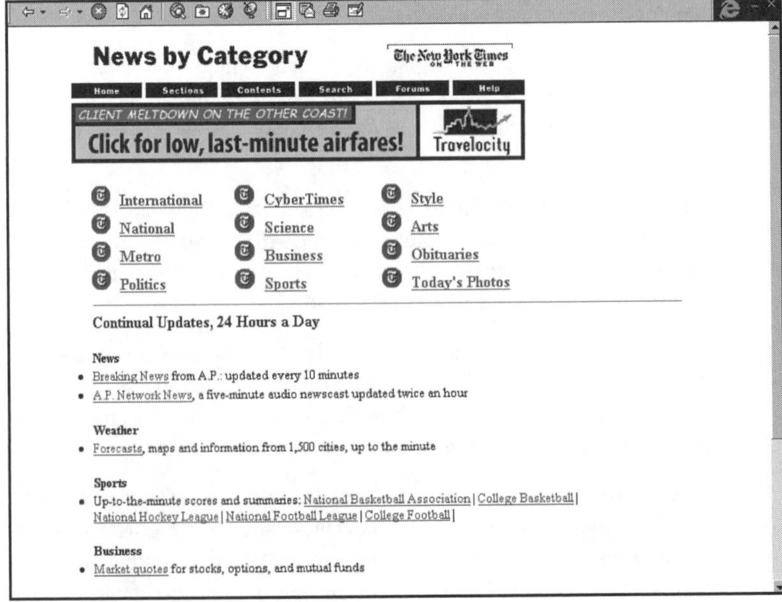

FIG. 18.13
Click the Full Screen button to expand the Internet Explorer browser window to its maximum size.

TIP

If you prefer the extra screen real estate you get with Full Screen view, you can configure IE4 to automatically open all web pages this way. You can also configure IE4's Channels to appear by default in Full Screen view. To set up either option, choose View, Internet Options, click the Advanced tab, and check the boxes labeled Launch browser in full screen window or Launch Channels in full screen window.

In Full Screen view, right-clicking the toolbar enables you to add the menu bar, Address bar, or Links bar to the same row. The Auto Hide choice on the same shortcut menu enables every last piece of the interface to slide out of the way; to make the toolbar reappear, move the mouse pointer to the top edge of the screen.

To switch back to normal view, click the Full Screen button again.

Adjusting Fonts and Colors to Make Web Pages More Readable

Can you change the look of a web page? That depends on decisions the designer of the page made when creating it. Some web pages use only generic settings to place text on the page. Sophisticated designers, on the other hand, use web templates, called cascading style sheets, to specify fonts, colors, spacing, and other design elements that control the look and feel of the page. You can specify fonts and colors you prefer when viewing basic web pages; advanced settings enable you to ignore style sheets as well.

The primary benefit is for people with physical disabilities that make it difficult or impossible to read the screen. To adjust any of these settings, choose View, Internet Options and then click the General tab.

If you're curious about how a web designer created the specific look of a page, use the View Source option to inspect the HTML code. If you like a particular look, you might be able to copy and paste the code to adapt the design for use in your own web page.

To adjust the default fonts, click the Fonts button. Besides selecting from a limited assortment of options for proportional and fixed fonts, you can also change the size that Internet Explorer uses for basic web pages from its default Medium. Choose smaller settings to pack more information onto the screen; use larger values to make text easier to read.

Click the Colors button to change the default values for text and backgrounds on basic web pages. By default, Internet Explorer uses the Window colors you defined by using the Windows Display; with the Standard Windows settings—that means black text on a white page. To change the defaults, you must change that system-wide setting or click the Clear the Use Windows Colors check box and specify different Text and Background colors, as shown in Figure 18.14. Internet Explorer also enables you to reset the colors for links here.

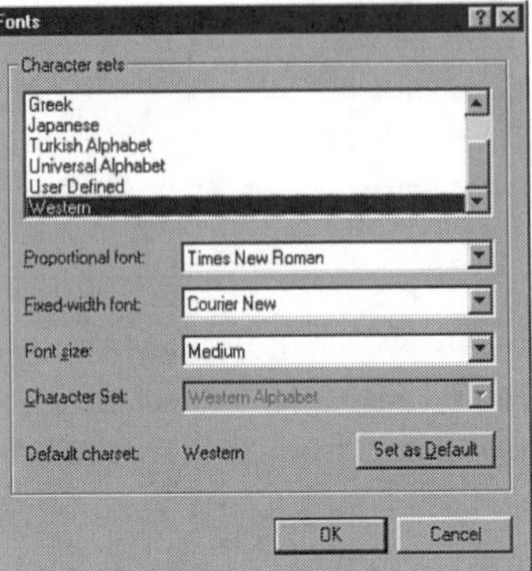

FIG. 18.14
Setting alternate font choices affects only basic web pages—those that don't use style sheets.

Changes you make to default fonts and colors do not apply to pages that use style sheets, unless you make one final adjustment. Click the Accessibility button and check the appropriate boxes to tell the browser to ignore colors, font styles, and font sizes specified in style sheets.

You can increase or decrease default font sizes exclusively for pages you open in the current session. Choose View, Fonts, and select one of the five relative sizes from that menu. This change applies only when viewing pages that use standard fonts, and Internet Explorer will return to normal settings if you close and then reopen the browser window. When you adjust font sizes, be aware that pages can look odd and, in some cases, can even become unreadable. If you find yourself using this feature regularly, go to the Advanced tab on the Internet Options dialog box and check the option to add a Fonts button to the Standard toolbar.

Viewing Web Pages in Other Languages

Do you frequently find yourself browsing pages created by designers using an alphabet that's not the same one used in your Windows language settings? Before Internet Explorer can display foreign-language pages, you must use the IE4 setup program to install Multi-Language Support for the appropriate languages. You will find a Pan-European add-on that enables most Western European languages to display correctly. There are Japanese, Korean, and Chinese add-ins as well.

After you've installed the additional font support, you should be able to see pages in any of those alphabets, as shown in Figure 18.15.

If you regularly view web pages that are designed to display in your choice of languages, tell IE4 which one you prefer. Choose View, Internet Options and click the Languages button on the General tab. Add support for the appropriate languages, and place your preferred language at the top of the list.

FIG. 18.15
If you try to view foreign-language web pages, you might see only a garbled mess (right); you need to add fonts for the extra languages to see them correctly (left).

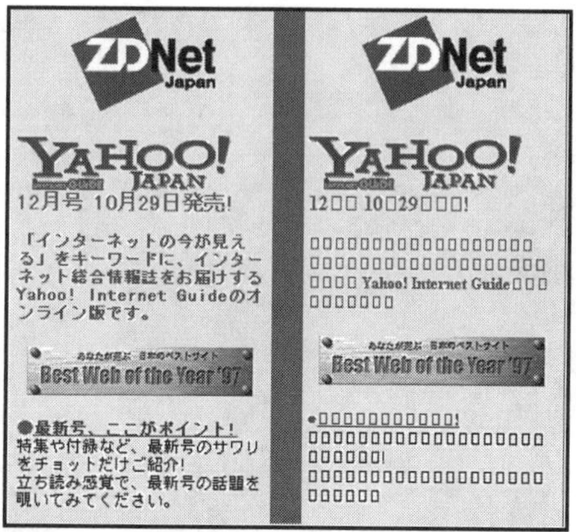

Configuring IE to Work with Other Programs

When you first install Internet Explorer, it includes most of the capabilities you need for browsing basic web pages and handling other types of data, such as streaming audio and video. IE4 enables you to dramatically expand its capabilities by using a variety of add-in programs. Some install themselves automatically, with your permission, whereas others require that you run a separate setup program.

Installing and Using Add-ins and Plug-ins

Core components of Internet Explorer enable you to view text formatted with HTML, as well as graphics created in supported formats, including JPEG and GIF images. To view other types of data, you must install add-in programs that extend the capabilities of the basic browser. Add-ins can take several forms:

- ActiveX controls offer to install themselves automatically when needed. Depending on your security settings, Internet Explorer can refuse to install ActiveX add-ins, or you might have to click a confirming dialog box. ActiveX controls can perform a practically unlimited variety of functions; examples range from simple data-viewing panels to sophisticated analytical engines for tracking stock quotes. MSNBC's home page, shown in Figure 18.16, includes an ActiveX control that automatically turns current headlines into entries on a cascading menu, making it easier for you to navigate through the day's news. For a detailed discussion of ActiveX and Java security issues, turn to Chapter 20.

There's no need to seek out ActiveX controls. Pages that require add-ins will offer to install the control when you need it, and most controls download in a matter of minutes, even over relatively slow connections.

- Java applets download and run each time you access the page containing the helper program. The security settings for Java applets prohibit them from interacting with local or network resources except on the machine where they originated, and you can't install them permanently, as you can ActiveX controls.

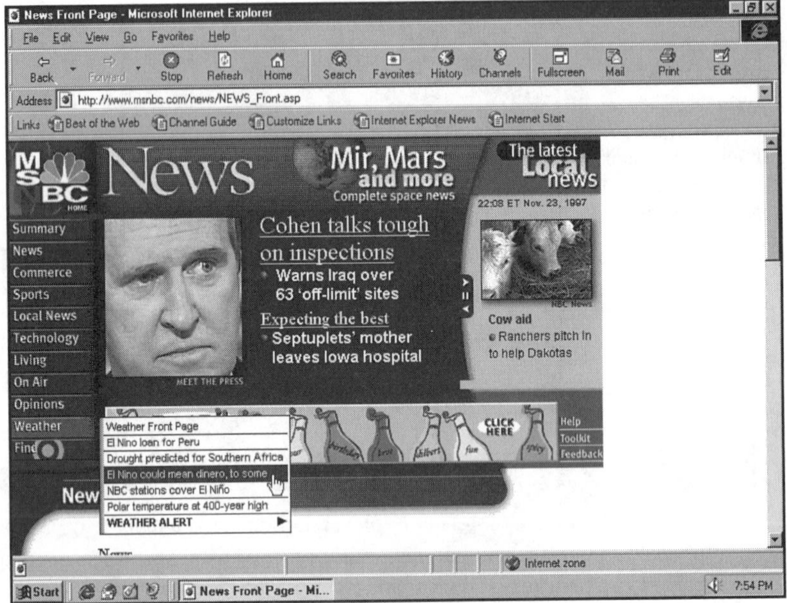

FIG. 18.16
This ActiveX control on MSNBC's home page enables you to browse news headlines and jump to linked pages by using cascading menus.

- Other add-in programs use standard installation routines and can often run on their own. The two must-have add-ins for Internet Explorer are RealNetworks' RealPlayer, which enables your browser to receive live audio and video broadcasts over the Internet, and Adobe's Acrobat Reader (see Figure 18.17), which enables you to display and print richly formatted documents, complete with graphics, columns, and other design elements that go far beyond HTML. Both are free (in fact, RealPlayer 4.0 is included with IE4); upgrades to more powerful versions are available for a price.

ON THE WEB

To download the most recent streaming audio and video player from RealNetworks, start at

http://www.real.com

To find the most recent version of Adobe's Acrobat reader, follow the links from

http://www.adobe.com

Tuning In to the Internet with NetShow 2.0

One of the most intriguing uses of Internet bandwidth is to deliver so-called streaming media. Unlike conventional sound and video files, which require that you download the entire file before beginning to play it back, streaming media begins playing as soon as the first bits reach your browser. With streaming media, radio stations can "broadcast" their signals over the Internet, making it possible for sports fans, for example, to follow the exploits of their hometown heroes no matter how far they roam.

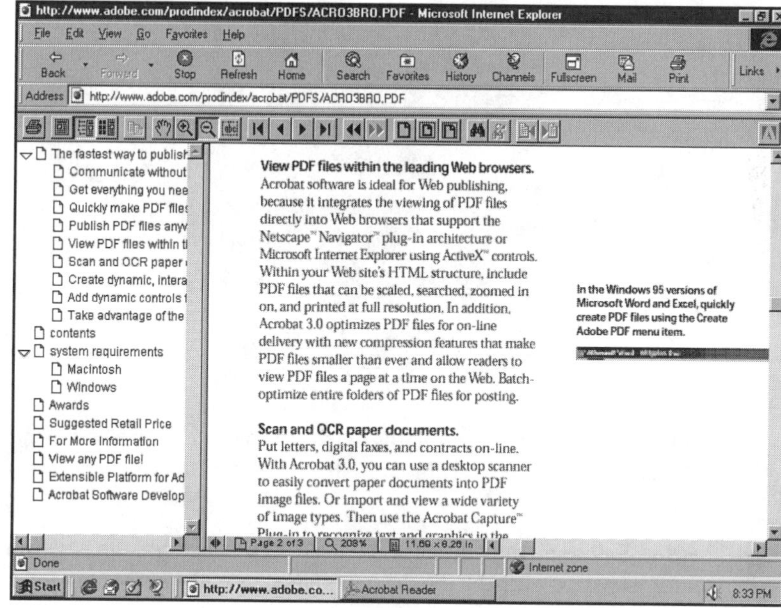

FIG. 18.17
When you view a formatted document by using the Adobe Acrobat Reader, it takes over the browser window and adds its own toolbars.

Streaming media can consist of audio, video, or both. On a normal dial-up connection at 28.8KB, audio typically works well, but video signals are unbearably choppy because the pipe between server and client simply can't deliver data fast enough. Video broadcasts are more practical on company intranets, where network cables can deliver data fast enough to handle broadcast-quality signals.

Internet Explorer includes two useful streaming-media players—RealPlayer and NetShow. For video broadcasts, the NetShow player can function as an ActiveX control, with the viewing screen embedded in the HTML page, or it can run as a standalone application, with its own menus and VCR-style controls. (See Figure 18.18 for an example of the NetShow player in action.)

FIG. 18.18
With its menu bar and VCR-style controls, the NetShow player looks like a standard Windows application. If only the video window is visible, right-click to set options.

NetShow includes several useful customization options. To access the NetShow properties sheet, right-click the image window or the player controls and choose Properties. You will see a dialog box like the one in Figure 18.19.

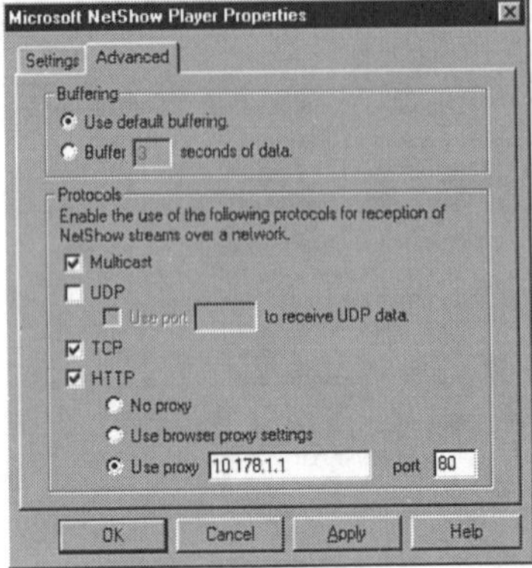

FIG. 18.19 Use the settings on the Advanced tab to configure NetShow to work through a proxy server.

Click the Settings tab to shrink the video window to half-size or expand it to double the default size. Another drop-down list on this tab enables you to choose full controls, simple controls, or none at all.

Use the options on the Advanced tab to configure NetShow on a network that uses a proxy server. You need to check the documentation from the server to see which TCP and/or UDP ports are required.

Basic title information appears on the General tab, whereas the Details and Statistics tabs display information about the current connection.

Setting Default Mail and News Clients

The Mail button on the Standard toolbar launches your default email program. Links that begin with the news: prefix fire up your default news reader. If you have more than one program that can work with Internet Explorer, you can control which one starts up when it's needed. To switch between Outlook 97 and Outlook Express as your default mail program, for example, choose View, Internet Options, click the Programs tab, and choose the preferred program from the drop-down lists shown in Figure 18.20.

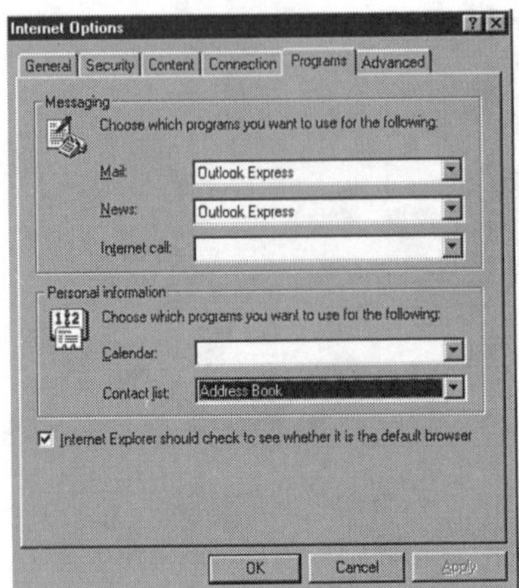

FIG. 18.20 To switch from one helper program to another, use the drop-down arrow to the right of each entry. Only programs specifically written to work with Internet Explorer appear in these lists.

Speeding Up Web Connections

Tuning Internet Explorer for speed and responsiveness involves inevitable tradeoffs between rich content and quick results. Elaborate graphics, video clips, sound files, and other large elements add fun and extra dimensions to the web, but waiting for those elements to download over a slow connection quickly becomes frustrating.

Selectively filtering out some types of downloadable content can reduce the amount of time it takes to load a page the first time. Intelligently managing the browser's cache makes it much faster to access pages a second or subsequent time. Of course, even the most careful configurations can't overcome traffic jams on the Internet.

Browsing Without Graphics

When slow downloads are a problem, the most common culprit is a page that's overstuffed with graphics, sound, and video files, which take time to download. To turn Internet Explorer into a lightning-fast, text-only browser, follow these steps:

1. Choose View, Internet Options and click the Advanced tab.
2. Scroll down to the Multimedia branch of the tree.
3. Remove the check marks from all boxes in this section, as shown in Figure 18.21.
4. Click OK to apply your changes.

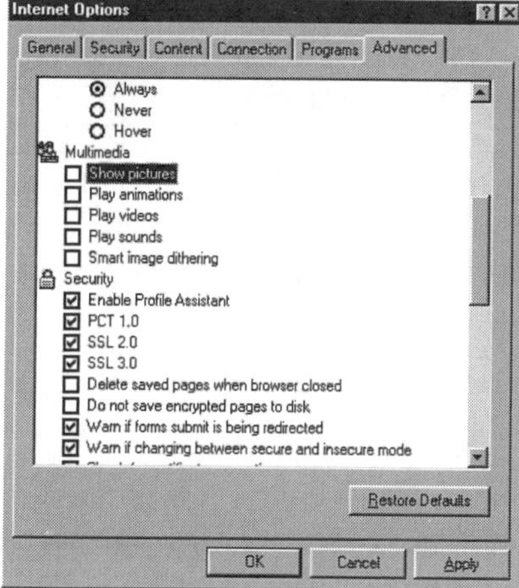

FIG. 18.21
Clear all the check boxes in the Multimedia section to transform Internet Explorer into a speedy text-only browser.

With multimedia options turned off, Internet Explorer shows generic icons, empty boxes, and simple text labels where you normally see images. It also ignores any sound files, animations, or video clips embedded in the page. Some sites work perfectly well without images; Fortune magazine, for example, offers an all-text page (see Figure 18.22) that loads quickly and doesn't require any graphic images.

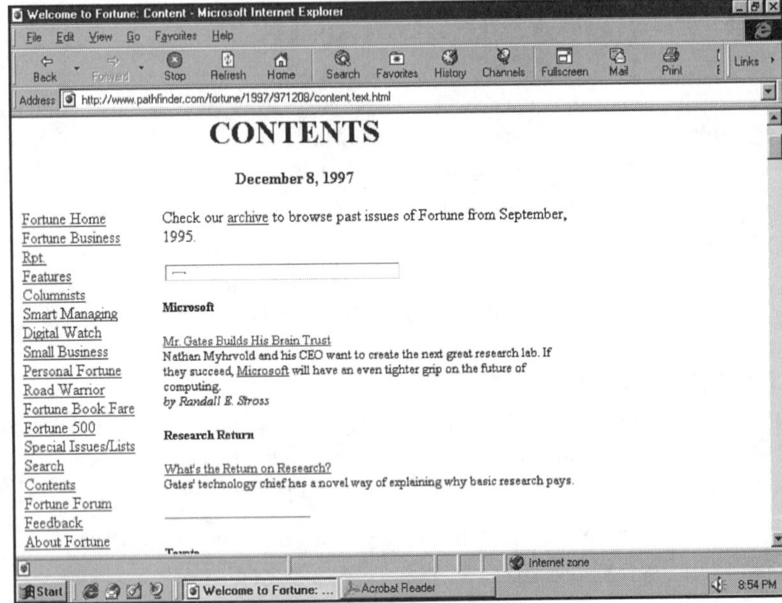

FIG. 18.22
Who needs graphics? Even without images for its buttons, this all-text page is eminently readable, thanks to excellent labels.

Although turning off the browser's capability to load image and multimedia files can dramatically improve performance, it can also block important information. On sites that use image maps as their only navigation tool, for example, there's literally no way to get around without displaying that image. To selectively show a picture after downloading the text-only page, right-click and choose Show Picture from the shortcut menu.

One of the most useful Internet Explorer Power Toys adds a Toggle Images button to the Standard toolbar. If you want to speed up downloads by selectively turning off the display of images, without having to continually open and close dialog boxes, this add-in is essential. You'll find it at

http://www.microsoft.com/ie/ie4/powertoys

Managing the Browser's Cache

With or without graphics, the best way to improve performance is to make sure the browser's cache is correctly configured. Each time you retrieve a new web page, Internet Explorer downloads every element and stores a copy of each one in a cache directory on your hard disk. The next time you request that page, the browser first checks the cache; if it finds a copy of the page, it loads the entire document from fast local storage, dramatically increasing performance.

When the cache fills up, Internet Explorer throws out the oldest files in the cache to make room for new ones. To increase the likelihood that you will be able to load a cached copy of a page instead of having to wait for it to reload from the Internet, adjust the size of the cache. Choose View, Internet Options, and click the General tab (see Figure 18.23) to find all the controls you need to fine-tune the web cache.

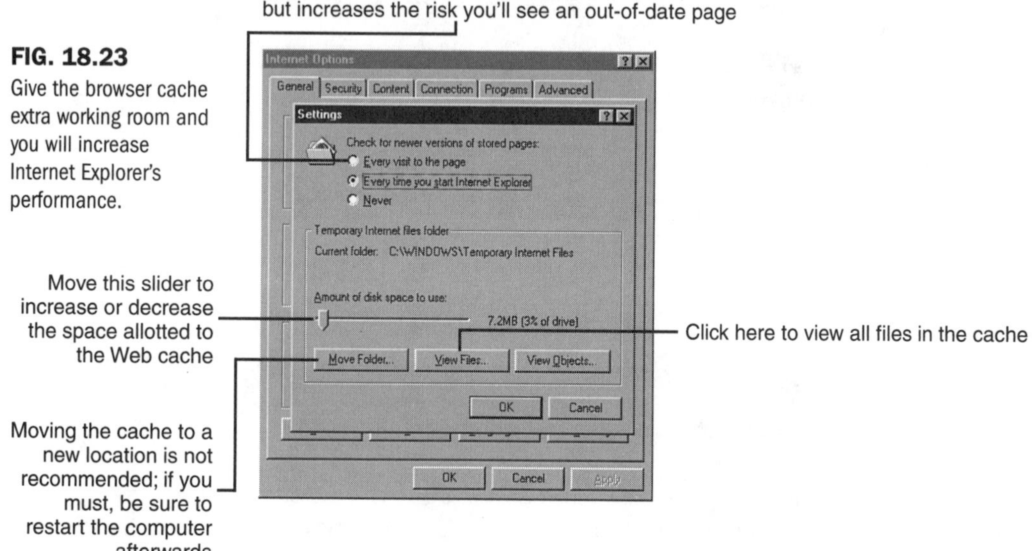

FIG. 18.23
Give the browser cache extra working room and you will increase Internet Explorer's performance.

CAUTION

If you tell Internet Explorer you never want to check for a more recent version of cached pages, your browser will seem remarkably faster. Beware, though—for pages that update frequently, such as news headlines or stock quotes, you will have to work to see the most recent version. If you choose this setting, get in the habit of clicking the Refresh button to make sure the page is up-to-date.

When should you click the Delete Files button? This action completely empties the Temporary Internet Files folder and can have a noticeable negative impact on how fast your favorite pages load. Under ordinary circumstances, Internet Explorer manages the size of the cache by itself. You might need to clear the cache manually, though, if a corrupt cached file is causing Internet Explorer to crash or if you've run out of disk storage and you need to make room for crucial files.

Viewing Cached Files and Objects

Normally, you use the History Explorer bar to browse full pages stored in the browser cache. But you can also view the individual objects in the cache—HTML pages, graphics, ActiveX controls, and even cookie files. Click the View Files button in the Settings dialog box to see a full listing, like the one shown in Figure 18.24.

The Temporary Internet Files folder is unlike any other folder you will see in Windows. Notice the column headings, for example, which track the time a file was last created. Double-click column headings to re-sort the list—that's particularly useful for finding and deleting large files that are cluttering up the cache. Use right-click shortcut menus to inspect the properties of stored objects and open, copy, or delete them.

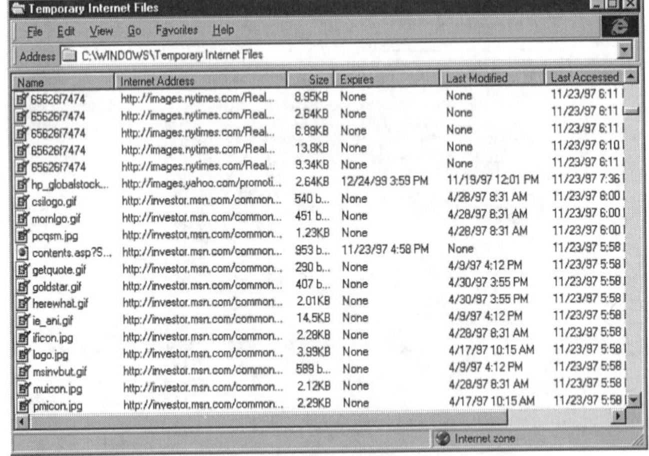

FIG. 18.24
The Temporary Internet Files folder holds a copy of every object you've viewed in the browser recently. Right-click to open, copy, or delete any file.

NOTE Where are cached pages really stored? Windows organizes all cached files by using a maze of hidden folders inside the Temporary Internet Files folder. These folders have randomly generated cryptic names like 25NMCE84; shell extensions in Windows pull the contents of all these folders together into a single display in the Temporary Internet Files folder. Although you can use the DOS Attrib or Windows Find commands to see these files in their actual locations, avoid the temptation to move or delete these hidden objects. Use Internet Explorer's View Files button to manage them instead. ■

CHAPTER 19

Finding, Organizing, and Saving Web-Based Information

by Ed Bott

In this chapter

Using Internet Shortcuts

Regardless of where you find a web page—on a corporate intranet or on a distant server—inside, it's nothing more than a document file. And just as you use conventional shortcuts to organize documents stored locally, Internet shortcuts are the most effective way to organize web-based information. When you inspect the properties of an Internet shortcut, you see a page of settings such as the one in Figure 19.1.

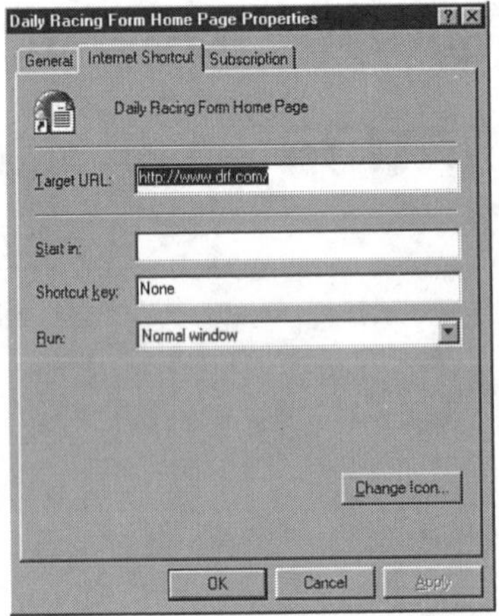

FIG. 19.1
The target for an Internet shortcut is an URL rather than a local or UNC file specification.

Internet shortcuts behave just like other shortcuts. You can add Internet shortcuts to the desktop or Start menu, move them between folders, send them to other people in mail messages, or rename the shortcut without affecting the target to which it points. See Chapter 10, "Navigating and Controlling Windows," for more details about working with shortcuts.

If you start the Create Shortcut Wizard and enter a valid URL in the Command line box, Windows creates an Internet shortcut. You can drag that shortcut into the browser window or the Address bar to open the target page or drop it into the Favorites folder or Links bar to make the page more readily accessible.

It's easy to create a shortcut that points to the web page you're currently viewing in the browser window. Just choose File, Send, Shortcut to Desktop. After the shortcut is on your desktop, you can rename it, modify its properties, move it to another folder, or send it to a friend or coworker in an email message.

Using the Favorites Folder to Organize Your Favorite Web Sites

If you've used a web browser before, you're already familiar with the concept of saving pointers to web sites you visit frequently. Netscape Navigator calls them bookmarks, whereas prior versions of Internet Explorer saved shortcuts to web pages in a Favorites folder. Internet Explorer 4.0 also enables you to collect Internet shortcuts in a Favorites folder, but the user interface for working with Favorites is dramatically different.

NOTE This chapter assumes you've installed Internet Explorer 4.0 and enabled the Windows Desktop Update. If you're still using Internet Explorer 3.0, turn to Chapter 2, "Installing and Upgrading Windows 95," for instructions on how to upgrade Windows with IE4.

Click the Favorites button to open the Favorites Explorer bar; this frame along the left border pushes the main browser window to the right. When you choose an entry from the Favorites list, the page you selected appears in the browser window, as in Figure 19.2.

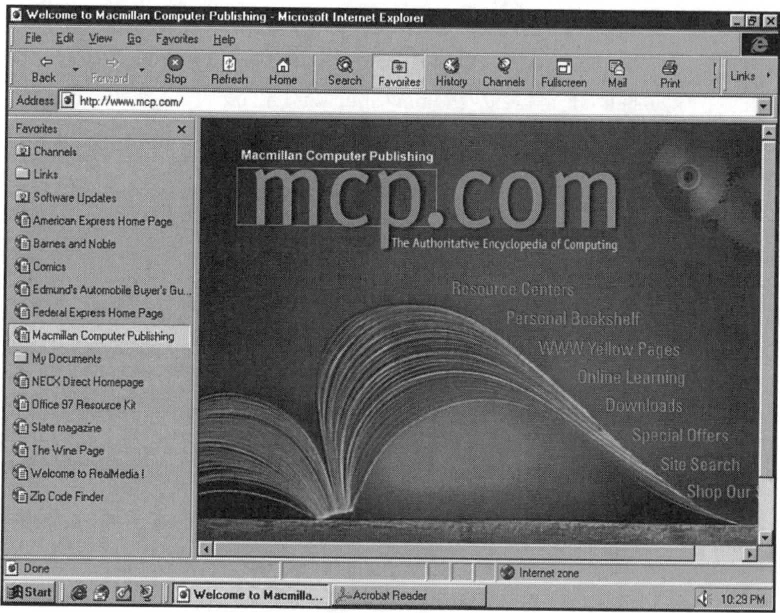

FIG. 19.2
Click a shortcut in the Explorer bar at left, and the target page appears in the browser window at right. Arrows at the top and bottom of the Favorites list enable you to scroll to additional entries.

The Favorites folder is located within the Windows folder; if you've enabled multi-user settings, each user with a profile on the computer receives a personal Favorites folder. The contents of the Favorites list appear in alphabetical order on the pull-down Favorites menu and in the Explorer bar.

Although the Favorites folder is most useful with Internet shortcuts, you can move any object there, including files, folders, and shortcuts to documents or programs. Clicking a document or program shortcut in the Explorer bar usually launches the associated application in its own window.

Adding a Web Page to the Favorites Folder

To add the current page to the Favorites list, use one of these two techniques:

- Drag the page icon from the left of the Address bar and drop it into the Favorites Explorer bar.
- If the Explorer bar is not visible, choose Favorites, Add to Favorites.

You can also use shortcut menus to create new entries in the Favorites folder. Follow this simple procedure:

1. Right-click any blank space or text in the current page.
2. Choose Add to Favorites from the shortcut menu; you'll see a dialog box like the one in Figure 19.3.
3. Give the shortcut a descriptive name, if you want, or use the default page title.
4. Click the Create in button and choose a subfolder in the Favorites list.
5. Click OK to create the new shortcut and close the dialog box.

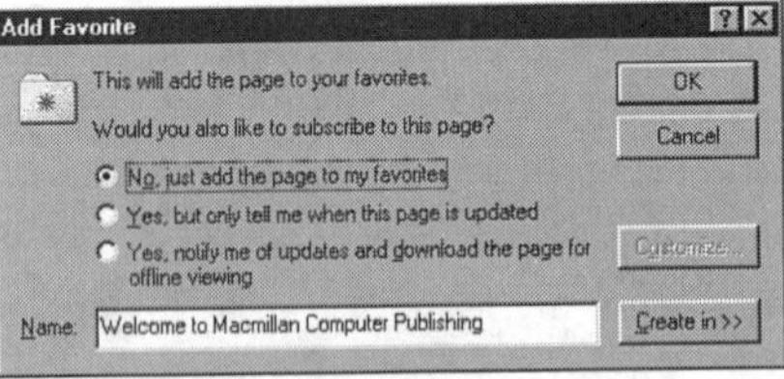

FIG. 19.3
When you create a new entry in the Favorites folder, give it a new name, if necessary, to help you identify the page later.

If the current page contains a link to a page you'd like to add to your Favorites folder, you can use the same technique without having to open the page. Point to the link, right-click, and then follow the preceding steps.

▶ **See** "Working with Web Subscriptions and the Active Desktop" for more information about subscribing to your favorite web sites, **p. 497**

Deleting and Renaming Favorites

To delete an Internet shortcut in the Favorites folder, point to the shortcut, right-click, and choose Delete. To rename an Internet shortcut, point to its entry in the list, right-click, and choose Rename. Edit the name of the shortcut and press Enter to save your changes.

Using Subfolders to Organize Favorites

As you add items to the Favorites folder, the list can quickly become too long to work with comfortably. When you reach that point, use subfolders to help organize the Favorites list. You can create an unlimited number of subfolders in the Favorites folder, and you can even add new folders within those subfolders.

With the Favorites Explorer bar open, it's easy to move one item at a time from folder to folder. However, you can't use the Explorer bar to create new folders or to move more than one shortcut at a time. For these more serious organizing tasks, choose Favorites, Organize Favorites; that opens the dialog box shown in Figure 19.4, which includes the full set of tools you need.

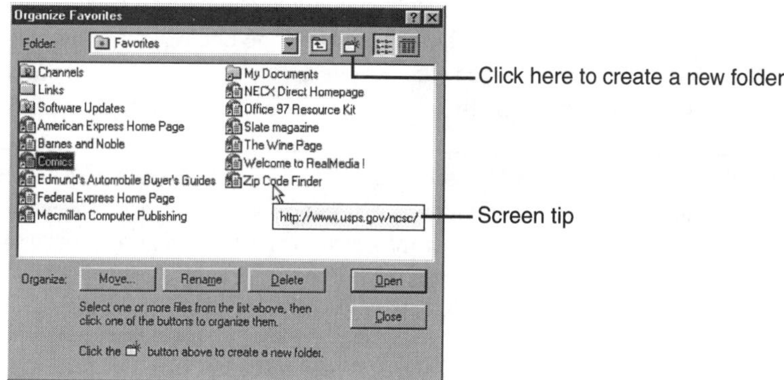

FIG. 19.4
Use the buttons along the bottom of this dialog box to organize your Favorites folder. Right-click or use Screen Tips like this one to gather more information about a shortcut.

Moving shortcuts to a new folder is a simple process, as long as you perform the steps in the right order. Open the Organize Favorites dialog box and do the following:

1. Click the New Folder button; the new folder appears at the end of the current folder list, with a generic name selected for editing.
2. Type a name for the new folder and press Enter.
3. Select one or more shortcuts from the Favorites list and click the Move button.
4. In the Browse for Folder dialog box, click the name of the folder you just created.
5. Click OK to make the move, and click Close to return to Internet Explorer.

You can also drag and drop Internet shortcuts within the Organize Favorites dialog box. If your collection of Favorites is relatively small, you probably will find it easier to rearrange them this way than by using the complicated procedure just outlined.

Folders appear in alphabetical order at the top of the Favorites Explorer bar. To see the contents of a folder, click its entry—the list of shortcuts in the folder appears just below the folder icon, also in alphabetical order. Click the folder icon again to close it.

For fastest access to the Favorites folder, click the Start menu. The cascading Favorites menu appears between the Programs and Documents choices.

Changing or Adding Quick Links

Although the Favorites folder is a convenient way to organize web pages, it still takes a couple of clicks and some scrolling to find a particular page. For the handful of sites you visit most frequently, use the Links bar instead. The shortcuts on this toolbar are never more than a click away, and you can easily arrange them for fast, convenient access.

To show or hide the Links bar, right-click the menu bar and click Links. When you first start Internet Explorer, there are five shortcuts on the Links bar, all pointing to pages at Microsoft. In less than five minutes, you can give the Links bar a complete makeover and dramtically boost your productivity in the process.

Do you really need all those Microsoft pages on the default Links bar? Not likely. The Internet Start link, for example, is completely unnecessary; anytime you want to jump to **www.microsoft.com**, just click the spinning Explorer logo in the upper-right corner of the browser window. The Customize Links button leads to a simple Help screen that tells you how to change links; after you learn the technique, you can safely delete this link!

There's no limit to the number of shortcuts you can add to the Links bar. To keep navigation simple, though, you'll probably want to limit the number of links to 10 or 12. On the Links bar in Figure 19.5, for example, there are nine shortcuts; adding one more would push the last link off the screen. When that happens, left and right arrows appear at either side of the Links bar to aid in scrolling.

To give your Links bar a makeover, follow these steps:

1. Right-click Links you don't plan to keep and choose Delete from the shortcut menu.
2. To add the current page to the Links bar, drag the icon from the left side of the Address bar and drop it alongside any existing link. The shortcut icon tells you when it's okay to drop.
3. Click the Favorites button and drag shortcuts from the Favorites folder to the Links bar.
4. To rearrange the order in which links appear, grab an icon and move it to its new location. Other links will shift left or right to make room for it.
5. To rename a link, open the Favorites Explorer bar, click Links, right-click the entry you want to change, and choose Rename.

The width of each shortcut on the Links bar is defined by its label. The shorter the name, the more links you can use. "FedEx," for example, takes up much less space than "Federal Express Home Page," without sacrificing any meaning.

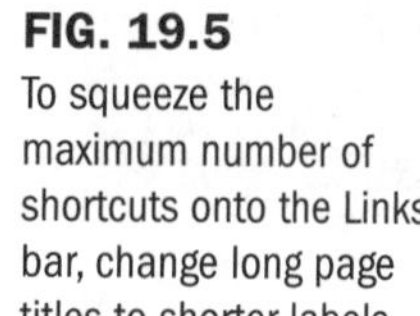

FIG. 19.5
To squeeze the maximum number of shortcuts onto the Links bar, change long page titles to shorter labels.

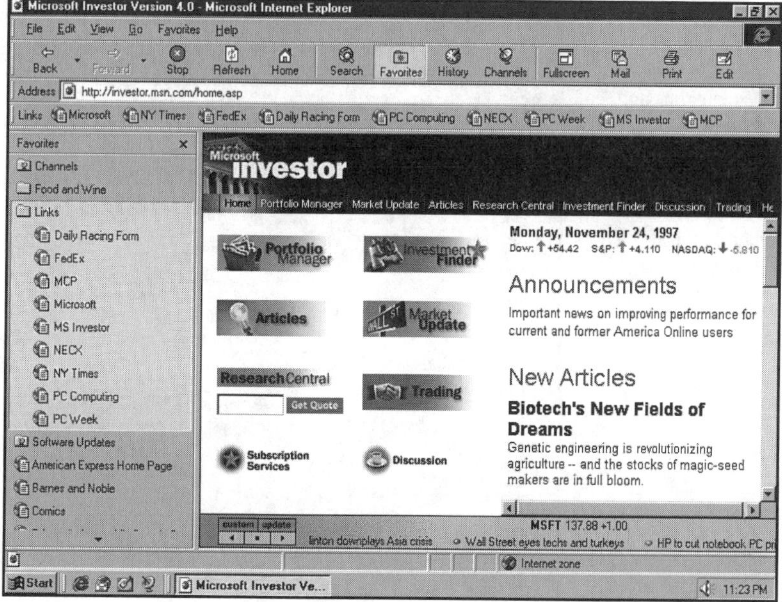

Using the Search Bar to Find Information on the World Wide Web

How many pages are there on the World Wide Web? No one can say for sure, but the number is at least 50 million, probably more than 100 million, and growing every day. How do you find specific information in the billions of words and hyperlinks on all those pages? That's where search engines come in.

Internet Explorer offers easy access to several popular search engines through an Explorer bar that works much like the Favorites bar. When you click the Search button, an Explorer bar like the one in Figure 19.6 takes over the left side of the screen.

Finding information on the web is a two-step process: First, you have to choose a search engine that's appropriate for the type of information for which you're looking; then you have to construct your search so the pages for which you're looking appear at the top of the list.

Choosing the Right Search Engine

In general, search engines can be divided into two types. Category-based sites like Yahoo! organize the Internet by category. Indexed search engines, such as Excite and Alta Vista, use web robots to gather text and create searchable databases of information. Most popular search sites now combine both techniques on their home pages.

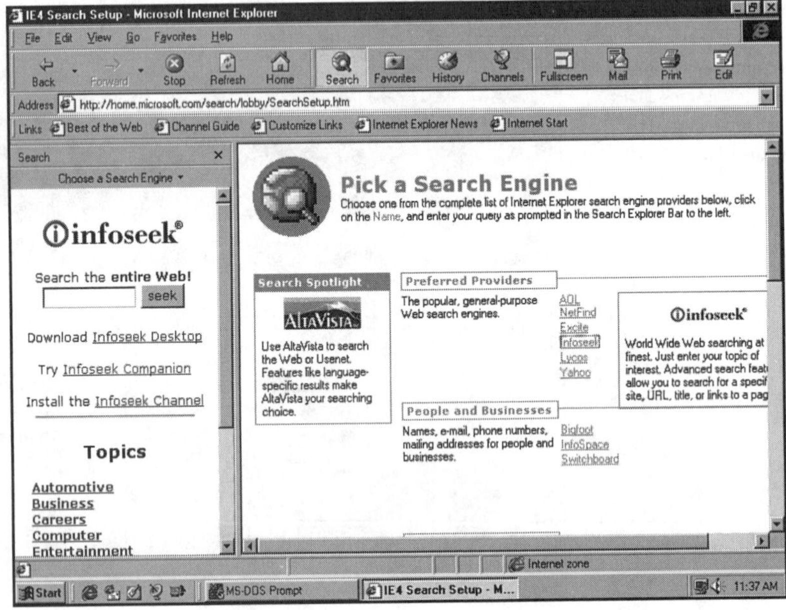

FIG. 19.6
Pick a search engine from the drop-down list in the Explorer bar, and then enter the text for which you're looking. Click links in the search results to view pages in the window at right.

Category searches are ideal for broad, open-ended questions, while indexed sites are better for finding specific facts. In either case, getting the right results takes practice and some basic understanding of how the search engine works. To avoid playing favorites, Internet Explorer picks one of five search engines at random each time you click the Search button. You can accept that choice, or study Table 19.1 and make your own selection by using the drop-down "Select provider" list.

Table 19.1 Popular Internet Search Engines

Name	URL	Description
AOL NetFind	**www.aol.com/netfind**	America Online calls on a huge database of reviews to help you find people, companies, places, and information. Powered by Excite technology, it's open to non-AOL members as well.
Excite	**www.excite.com**	If you can't find it by using Excite, it probably isn't on the Internet. Click "Channels" to find information by topic, or use its massive database to search the entire web.
Infoseek	**www.infoseek.com**	Enter text or click topic links to find information. Jump to InfoSeek's main page to try its impressive capability to process plain-English questions.

Name	URL	Description
Lycos	**www.lycos.com**	One of the oldest search engines around, Lycos began as a research project at Carnegie Mellon University. Today it offers Yahoo!-style category lists and superb international support.
Yahoo!	**www.yahoo.com**	The original category-based search engine now uses AltaVista's indexing software to do keyword searches as well. Make sure you choose the correct search method before sending your request.

Don't like any of the built-in search options? Then choose List of all Search Engines from the drop-down list in the Search bar. That option opens Microsoft's all-in-one search page, with links to dozens of general-purpose and specialized search sites.

Performing the Search

After you've selected a search engine, follow these steps to carry out your search:

1. If you see a category that's relevant to your search, click that link. Otherwise, enter the text for which you're looking in the search box.
2. If the search engine provides any options, check them carefully. For example, do you want to search the web, Usenet newsgroups, or both?
3. Click the button that submits your request to the search engine.
4. A list of search results will appear in the Search bar, as in the example in Figure 19.7. Scroll through the list and click any links that look promising. The page will appear in the browser window to the right of the Search bar.
5. Use the Next button at the bottom of the results list to see more entries in the results list.
6. If the search request didn't produce the correct results, change your search or choose a different search engine and try again.

Part IV Ch 19

There's no need to click the Search button if you simply want to look for a keyword or two. If you type **find**, **go**, or **?** in the Address bar, followed by one or more words, Internet Explorer's AutoSearch feature submits your request to Yahoo! for processing, returning results in the main browser window.

If you've found a favorite search engine, you can tell Internet Explorer to take you to that site instead of Yahoo! each time you use AutoSearch. To make the change, you first have to download Microsoft's Tweak UI utility, one of the unofficial PowerToys for Windows 95. You will find all the PowerToys, with full instructions for their use, at

http://www.microsoft.com/windows95/info/powertoys.htm

After installing Tweak UI, open Control Panel and start the utility; click the General tab and use the drop-down list to change the default search engine.

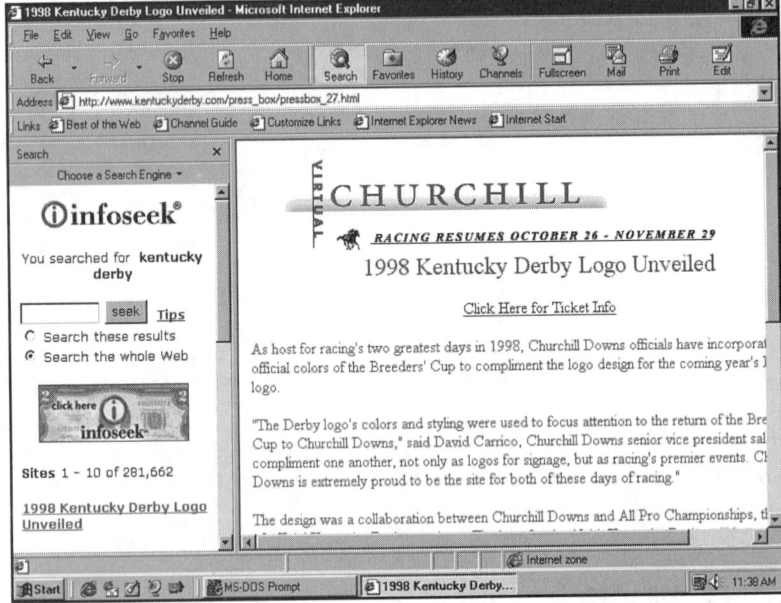

FIG. 19.7
This search produced a staggering 281,662 matches. Use the Next button to move through the list ten links at a time, or return to the top of the Search bar and refine the search.

Tips and Techniques for More Successful Searches

How can you guarantee better results when you search the web? Try these techniques:

Visit the major search sites often. They regularly add new features and upgrade search interfaces. If you use only the Internet Explorer Search bar, you won't see those improvements.

Learn how to combine search terms by using the logical operators AND, OR, and NOT to narrow the results list. Every search engine uses a slightly different syntax for these so-called Boolean queries; check the help pages at the search engine's site. The default operator is usually OR, which means if you enter two or more words, the search engine returns any page that contains any of the words; use an ampersand or AND or quotation marks to be more specific.

Don't stop at simple searches. Some search engines enable you to specify a range of dates to search, for example, to avoid being bombarded with stale links. Others enable you to specify or exclude a particular web server.

Saving a Successful Search

When you find a search that you think you will want to reuse, follow these steps to save it:

1. Right-click anywhere in the Search bar and choose Properties.
2. Select the entire URL that appears on the General tab, right-click, and choose Copy from the shortcut menu. Click OK to close the Properties dialog box.
3. Select the entire contents of the Address bar, right-click, and choose Paste.

4. Press Enter to load the page whose URL you just copied.
5. Create a shortcut to the current page, either on the desktop or in the Favorites folder, and give it a descriptive name.

Searching for Information on the Current Page

A web page can consist of a single paragraph, or it can run on for tens of thousands of words. Internet Explorer's Find feature enables you to search for words or phrases on the current page or within a selected frame. To begin, press Ctrl+F and enter your text in the Find dialog box shown in Figure 19.8.

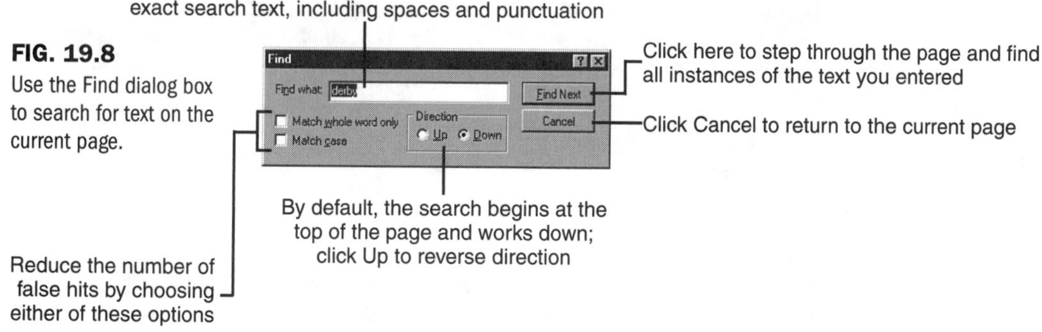
Enter a word or phrase here; IE searches for your exact search text, including spaces and punctuation
Find
Find what: derby
Find Next
Cancel
Match whole word only
Match case
Direction
Up
Down
Click here to step through the page and find all instances of the text you entered
Click Cancel to return to the current page
By default, the search begins at the top of the page and works down; click Up to reverse direction
Reduce the number of false hits by choosing either of these options

FIG. 19.8
Use the Find dialog box to search for text on the current page.

Note that the Find dialog box searches only text that actually appears on the page; it won't look at hidden text or HTML tags in the source for the page. To search for hidden text or tags, choose View, Source and use Notepad's Search menu.

Looking for text on frame-based pages can produce unexpected results if you're not careful. On these pages, the Find feature searches only in the current frame, not in all frames visible in the browser window. Before you open the Find dialog box and enter your search text, make sure you click the frame in which you want to search.

Using the History Bar to Revisit Web Sites

In addition to the cache in the Temporary Internet Files folder, Internet Explorer keeps a record of every URL you load. This History list is indispensable when you want to return to a page you visited recently but can't remember its address. If you've enabled multiple user settings on your Windows 95 PC, each user who logs in gets a private History folder. See Chapter 18, "Web Browsing with Internet Explorer 4.0," for more information about how you can manage the Temporary Internet Files folder.

Click the History button to open an Explorer bar similar to the one in Figure 19.9. The History bar looks and acts just like the Favorites bar, snapping into position along the left edge of the browser window and pushing the main viewing window to the right.

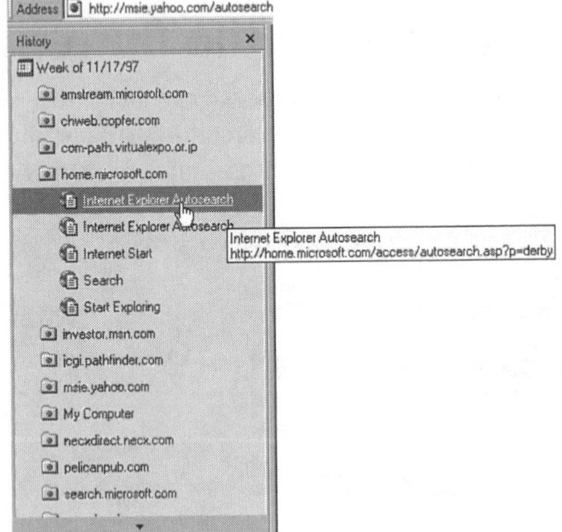

FIG. 19.9
Every time you visit a web page, it receives an entry in this History list. If you can remember when you saw the page, you can find it here.

NOTE From the Windows Explorer, you can examine the History list by double-clicking the History icon. Individual shortcuts are not actually stored in the History folder, however; instead, Internet Explorer uses an internal database to manage the collection of shortcuts, with a single data file for each day. The entire collection is organized in one or more hidden folders. Although it's possible to view these hidden files from a DOS prompt, there's no way to see their contents without using Explorer's system extensions.

Navigating Through the History Folder

By default, the History folder keeps a shortcut to every page you've accessed for the past 20 days. When you click the History button to open the Explorer bar, you see the list of shortcuts organized by day, with the most recent day's collection at the bottom of the list. Click the entry for any day to see the list of shortcuts for that day, with a single entry for each resource location. Click any of these entries again to see a shortcut for each page within that domain. When you click an Internet shortcut in the History list, Internet Explorer loads the page in the browser window at the right.

TIP To increase or decrease the size of the History list, choose View, Internet Options and change the number of days to keep pages in history. Use the spinner control on the General tab to select a number between 0 and 999. Choosing 0 clears the History list every day, although you can still recall any page you visited earlier in the same day.

Although you cannot directly add an Internet shortcut to the History list, you can copy an entry from the History list to a variety of places—the desktop, the Start menu, the Favorites folder, or an email message, for example. Drag a shortcut from the History list to any legal destination, or use the right-click menu to copy the shortcut to the Windows Clipboard.

Clearing Out the History

Internet Explorer enables you to empty the History folder completely or to delete entries one at a time. Clearing out the History folder can reclaim a modest amount of disk space, and it can also make the list easier to navigate. But a more practical reason to remove items from this list is for privacy reasons—to keep another user from seeing the list of sites you've visited recently.

- To clear a single shortcut from the list, point to the shortcut, right-click, and choose Delete.
- To remove a group of shortcuts, point to the entry for a given web location or day, right-click, and choose Delete.
- To empty all entries from the History folder, choose View, Internet Options, click the General tab, and click the button labeled Clear History.

Browsing the Web Offline

Internet Explorer's cache and History folders work together exceptionally well when you choose to work offline. With the History folder visible in the Explorer bar, you can choose File, Work Offline, and view any files stored in the cache, even if you have no current connection to the Internet.

When you work with Internet Explorer offline, a network icon with a red X appears in the status bar along the bottom of the browser window. Except for that indicator, you can browse pages in the History cache just as if you were working with a live Internet connection. When you point to a link that isn't cached locally, the pointer changes to the shape shown in Figure 19.10. Before you can view the selected page, you must open an Internet connection.

Part IV Ch 19

FIG. 19.10
This pointer appears when you work offline and attempt to access a page that isn't stored in the web cache.

For details on how to work offline with subscriptions and Internet channels, see Chapter 21, "Working with Web Subscriptions and the Active Desktop."

Printing Web Pages

Successfully transferring a web page to paper can be as simple as clicking a button, although complex page designs require some preparation for best results.

To print a full web page that doesn't include frames, click the Print button on the Standard toolbar. This action sends the current page to the printer without displaying any additional dialog boxes. Internet Explorer scales the page to fit on the standard paper size for the default printer. The entire web document prints, complete with graphics, even if only a portion of the page is visible in the browser window.

By default, Internet Explorer ignores any background images or colors when printing. That behavior is by design, because most of these decorations simply make printed text harder to read. To add background images or colors to printed pages, choose View, Internet Options, click the Advanced tab, and check the appropriate box in the Printing section. Be sure to reverse the process after printing.

Arranging Frames on the Printed Page

For more complex pages, especially those that include frames, choose File, Print (or press Ctrl+P). That opens the Print dialog box, shown in Figure 19.11) and enables you to specify how you want to arrange the page on paper. See Chapter 5, "Controlling Printers," for more details on configuring and using a printer.

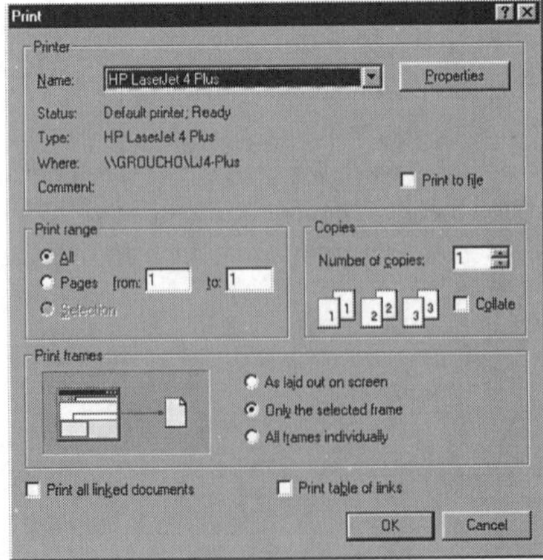

FIG. 19.11
Watch the display at the left of the Print frames box to see how a frame-based page will appear when printed.

Follow these steps for maximum control over any printed page:

1. Choose the area to be printed. The Selection option is grayed out unless you've selected a portion of the page.
2. Choose the number of copies to print. The default is 1.
3. Tell Internet Explorer how to deal with frames—print a single frame, print the page as it appears onscreen, or print each frame on a separate page.

4. Choose either of the two options at the bottom of the dialog box to specify whether and how linked pages print.
5. Click OK to send the page to the printer. An icon on the status bar confirms that the page has gone to the printer.

CAUTION

An option at the bottom of the Print dialog box enables you to print all linked documents along with the current page. Exercise this option with extreme care, because printing indiscriminately in this fashion can consume a ream of paper with a single click.

Adding Headers and Footers to a Printed Web Page

To control most options that Internet Explorer applies before printing a web page, choose File, Page Setup. Using this dialog box (shown in Figure 19.12), you can change the orientation, margins, and paper specifications for the current page. More important, though, you can specify a header and footer to print on each page.

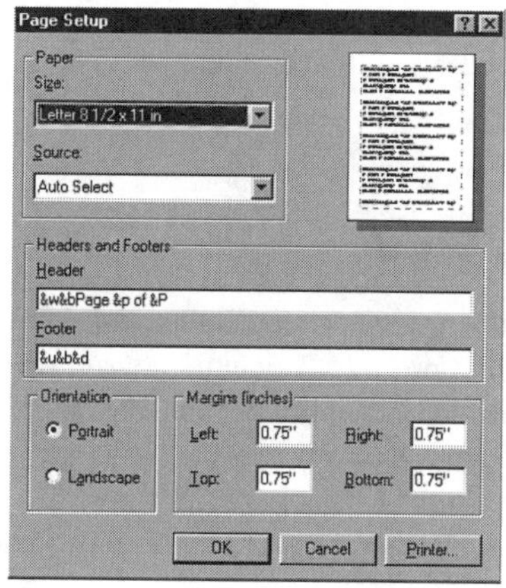

FIG. 19.12 Use these formatting codes to specify a header and footer to appear on each page you print. Internet Explorer saves the format you enter here as your default.

You can enter any text as part of the header or footer; in addition, Internet Explorer uses a set of arcane codes, each prefixed by an ampersand, to add information about the current page to the header or footer. Table 19.2 lists each of these codes:

Table 19.2 Custom Header/Footer Variables

To Print This	Enter This Code
Window title	**&w**
Page address (URL)	**&u**

continues

Table 19.2 Continued

To Print This	Enter This Code
Date (short format)	**&d**
Date (long format)	**&D**
Time (default format)	**&t**
Time (24-hour format)	**&T**
Single ampersand	**&&**
Current page number	**&p**
Total number of pages	**&P**
Right-align following text	**&btext**
Center Text1, right-align Text2	**&btext1&btext2**

NOTE If you can't remember the codes for headers and footers, click the question mark icon in the title bar of the Page Setup dialog box and point to the Header or Footer box. Watch out for a bug in the documentation, though: Any text you add after the characters &b will be right-aligned, not centered, in the header or footer.

Saving and Editing Web Pages

Only the simplest web pages consist of a single, simple document. More often, the page you see in your browser consists of one or more HTML documents and several linked images. There's no way to save all the elements on the entire page in one smooth operation. Instead, when you choose File, Save As, Internet Explorer saves the underlying HTML document and ignores any images or pages that are linked to that page. (You can also choose to save the current page as a plain-text document instead of an HTML-formatted page.)

To save graphics, frames, and other files linked to the current page, right-click each one and choose Save Target As from the shortcut menu. Right-click any link and use the same menu choice to save a linked page without opening it.

With the help of a handy Internet Explorer keyboard shortcut, you can turn any web graphic into wallpaper for your desktop. When you find an image you'd like to install on the desktop, right-click and choose Set As Wallpaper. For more ways to customize the Windows desktop, refer to Chapter 32, "Customizing the Desktop Settings."

Because Internet Explorer includes a basic HTML Editor, you can also load a web page directly from your browser into FrontPage Express. Using the web browser, open the page you want to edit, and then click the Edit button on the Standard toolbar. You can also create a shortcut to the current page, right-click that shortcut icon, and choose Edit. For more information about creating and editing your own web pages with FrontPage Express, see Chapter 23, "Using FrontPage Express and Internet Components."

Downloading Files from FTP Sites

One of the most common ways to distribute files of all types over the Internet is with FTP servers. Unlike web servers, which are specifically designed to work with graphically intense hypertext documents, FTP servers use File Transfer Protocol (FTP) to move files between computers. Internet Explorer is capable of acting as a basic FTP client.

To connect directly to an FTP site by using your web browser, enter the name of the site in the Address bar. Because FTP servers don't include graphic support, the display in the browser window will be as austere as the one in Figure 19.13.

FIG. 19.13
Don't expect fancy graphics or menus when you connect to an FTP site. Although this listing is plain, it's easy to find your way around.

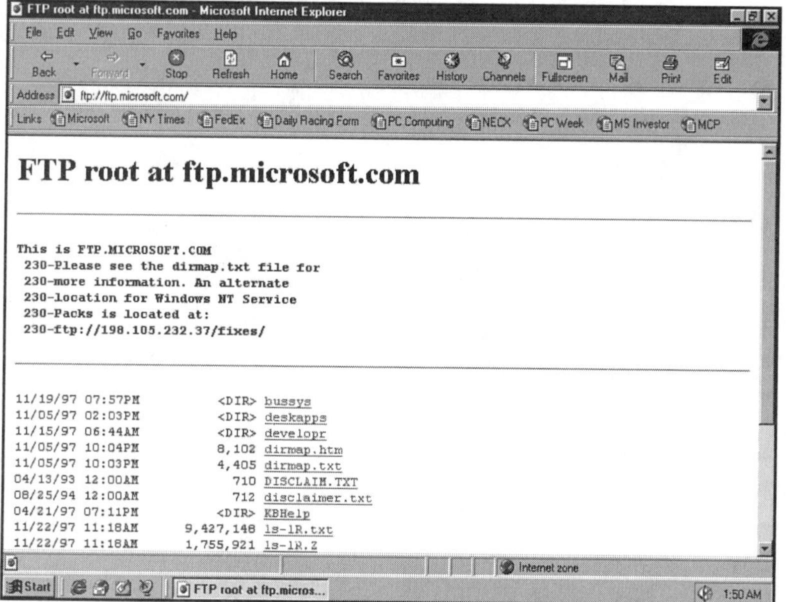

Click any link in the FTP window to begin downloading that file. When you click a link to a file stored on an FTP server, Internet Explorer handles the details of logging on to that server and negotiating the details of file transfer. If Internet Explorer connects to the FTP server, you'll typically see the dialog box shown in Figure 19.14. Choose the option labeled Save this program to disk, and then designate a name and destination for the downloaded file to begin the transfer.

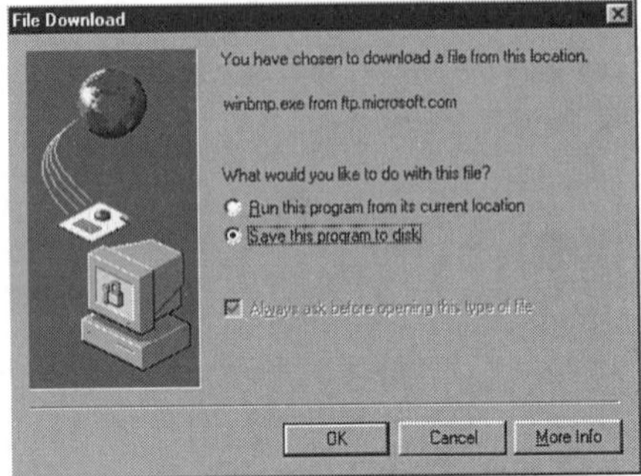

FIG. 19.14 Under most circumstances, you will want to save a file rather than run it directly from an FTP server.

Based on the size of the file and the speed of your current connection, Internet Explorer attempts to estimate the time remaining on your download. This process isn't always successful; in particular, it fails when the FTP server at the other end of the connection fails to report crucial information about the file you've chosen to download. In those cases, the dialog box you see tells you how much of the file has been downloaded so far.

When downloading a file of any sort with IE4, a dialog box appears, like the one in Figure 19.15, which might include an estimate of the amount of time remaining for the file to download.

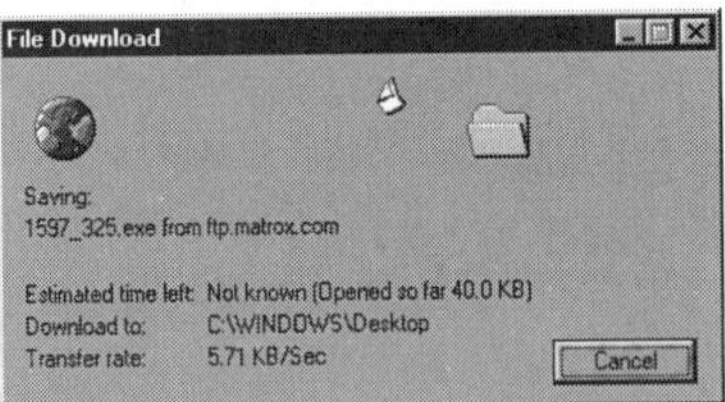

FIG. 19.15 This progress dialog box appears whenever Internet Explorer downloads a file to your computer.

If you minimize the Download dialog box, you see the progress of your download in the label and ScreenTip of the Taskbar button. You can close the browser window or switch to another page without interrupting the download.

Logging on to Password-Protected FTP Servers

Many FTP servers enable anonymous access without a designated username and password. Microsoft, for example, uses its FTP server to freely distribute patches and updates for Windows and other products. Internet Explorer handles anonymous logons easily. Other FTP servers, however, might refuse to enable logon unless you enter valid account information; this is especially true of corporate sites intended for use only by employees and other authorized users. Because Internet Explorer does not properly respond to password prompts from FTP servers, you must construct a custom URL to connect to a password-protected FTP server. Click the Address bar and enter the URL in the following format:

ftp://<username>:<password>@<ftp_server>/<url-path>

Substitute the proper username, password, and FTP server address in the example.

Using Windows 95's FTP Client

Because Internet Explorer offers only the most basic FTP capabilities, it is incapable of connecting properly with some FTP servers. If you encounter such a server, use the Windows 95 command-line FTP client instead. Follow these steps to download a file from **ftp.microsoft.com**; the same techniques should work with any site:

1. Click Start and choose Run.
2. In the Open box, type **ftp** and press Enter.
3. At the ftp> prompt, type **open ftp.microsoft.com**.
4. Enter **anonymous** as the username; although any password will do on an anonymous FTP server, the widely accepted custom is for you to enter your email address as the password.
5. Use the **cd** command to navigate to the proper directory, and **ls** or **dir** to list the contents of the current directory.
6. If the file you want to download is a binary (non-text) file, enter **type I** and press Enter.
7. Type **get *filename*** to begin the download.
8. When your FTP session is finished, enter **close** to disconnect from the server and **quit** to close the FTP window.

For rudimentary help with FTP commands, type **help** at the FTP> prompt.

ON THE WEB

If you use FTP regularly, consider a shareware FTP client like FTP Explorer, available from **www.ftpx.com**.

CHAPTER 20

Internet Explorer 4.0 and Security

by Ed Bott

In this chapter

Setting a Security Policy

Windows 95 and Internet Explorer 4.0 include a broad set of security tools. Before you can properly configure these options, however, you need to establish a security policy. This policy should balance the need to protect sensitive data against the undeniable value of open access to information and the wealth of information available on the world's largest network. Different environments have different security requirements, as well: With a dial-up Internet connection at home, you might not worry about the risk of break-ins, but on a corporate network, firewalls and other sophisticated security precautions are a must.

These elements should be central to any security policy:

- *Authentication* When you connect to a web site, how do you know who's really running that server? When you download and run a program, how do you know that it hasn't been tampered with or infected with a virus? When extremely sensitive information is involved, you might want to insist on secure connections guaranteed by digital certificates.
- *Encryption* Certain types of data—usernames and passwords, credit card numbers, and confidential banking information—are too sensitive to be sent "in the clear," where they can be read by anyone who can intercept the packets. For these transactions, only secure, encrypted connections are acceptable.
- *Control over executable content* The Internet is filled with programs and add-ins that can expand the capabilities of your browser. Unfortunately, poorly written or malicious add-ins can carry viruses, corrupt valuable data, and even expose your network to unauthorized break-ins. On most networks, administrators try to limit the potential for damage by restricting the types of files that users can download and run.

ON THE WEB

Microsoft publishes regular security news, advisories, and updates for Windows and Internet Explorer users; find the latest announcements at

www.microsoft.com/security

Configuring Internet Explorer to Use a Proxy Server

With ordinary dial-up Internet connections, client machines connect directly to web or FTP servers, making it possible for a would-be hacker to break into the network. To minimize that risk, most corporate networks include a firewall—a secure gateway made up of one or more systems that sit between the network and the Internet at large. Firewalls restrict the ability of outsiders to connect with machines inside the network, while enabling legitimate users to access resources on the Internet. This combination of hardware and software is designed to intercept and filter packets of information, letting through only those that meet strict standards of security.

Carefully isolated machines called proxy servers are crucial components of most corporate firewalls. When a client computer inside the firewall requests a service from the Internet—a web page, for example, or a file on an FTP server—the proxy server intercepts the request and handles the transaction. To the server on the other end of the connection, the request looks as though it came from the proxy server; there's no possibility of a direct (and possibly compromised) connection between it and the host machine inside the firewall.

ON THE WEB

Want more information about firewalls? You'll find links to the definitive Firewalls FAQ and mailing list at

www.greatcircle.com

Before Internet Explorer 4.0 can use a proxy server, you must specify its name or IP address. Some proxies (Microsoft Proxy Server 2.0 or later, for example) can automatically configure client machines; in that case, you need to enter the name of the machine that contains the configuration files.

Users on corporate networks might find that many of the options described in this chapter are unavailable. That's usually a sign that the network administrator has used Microsoft's Internet Explorer Administration Kit to enforce security policies from a central server. In that case, most security settings (and many other options, for that matter) will be grayed out and inaccessible. See your Network Administrator if you need to change one of these settings.

Follow these steps to set up Internet Explorer for use with a proxy server:

1. Choose View, Internet Options, and click the Connection tab. A dialog box like the one in Figure 20.1 appears.

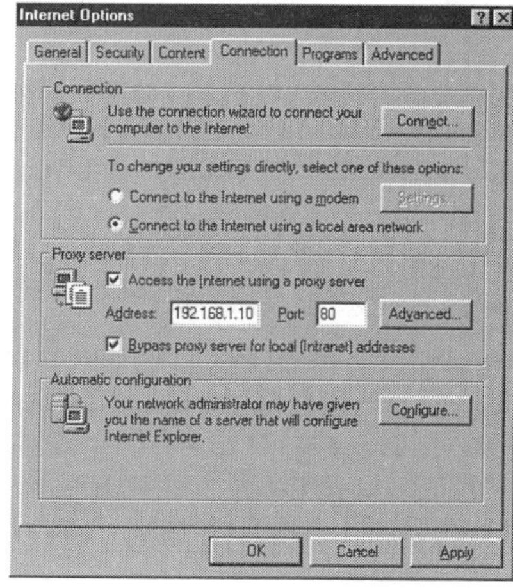

FIG. 20.1
Check the Access box and enter the name or IP address of your proxy server. Port 80 is the standard setting for virtually all web proxies.

2. Check the box labeled Access the Internet Using a Proxy Server.
3. If your network includes a server that can automatically configure Internet Explorer, click the Configure button, enter the full URL of the server, and click OK. No additional configuration is necessary.
4. If your network does not include an auto-configuring proxy server, click the Address box and enter the name or IP address of the proxy machine.

NOTE When configuring a proxy server, you can use either the server's name or its IP address. The effect is identical no matter which technique you use. The administrator in charge of the proxy server can supply information about your network's configuration.

5. Click the Port box and enter the name of the TCP port that the proxy server uses. In the overwhelming majority of cases, this will be port 80, the standard for web traffic.
6. If your network uses separate proxy servers to handle other protocols, click the Advanced button to open the dialog box shown in Figure 20.2. Enter those settings here.

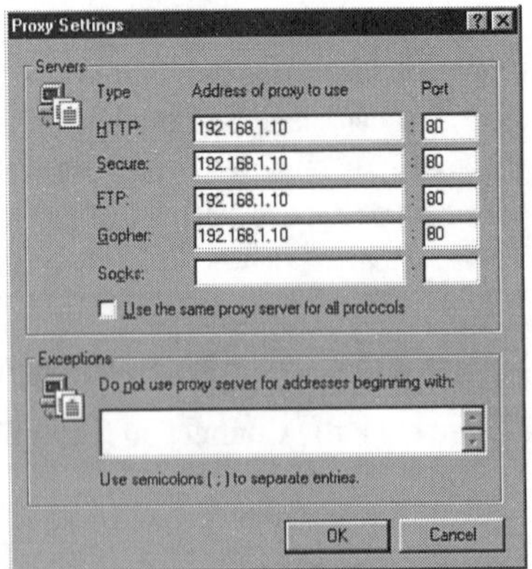

FIG. 20.2 Click the Exceptions box and specify URLs that you want to access directly, without using the proxy server.

7. Your network administrator might provide direct access to some sites and block access through the proxy server. If instructed to do so, click the Exceptions box and enter the names of any domains that do not require access through the proxy server. Be sure to enter a protocol prefix (typically http:// or https://) for each address. Use semicolons to separate entries in this list.
8. Click OK to close the Advanced dialog box.
9. Click OK to close the Internet Options dialog box and begin using the proxy server.

On most corporate networks, you should check the box labeled Bypass Proxy Server for Local (Intranet) Addresses. The proxy's safety features shouldn't be necessary inside the firewall, and routing intranet requests through the proxy hurts performance without improving security.

Establishing and Maintaining Internet Security Zones

Internet Explorer 4.0 includes dozens of security settings. Applying each of those options to individual web sites would be impractical; instead, the system enables you to group sites into four security zones, each with its own high, medium, or low security settings. Initially, as Table 20.1 shows, all sites are divided into two groups: those inside your company's intranet and those on the Internet. As part of a comprehensive security policy, you can designate specific web sites as trusted or restricted, giving them greater or less access to machines inside your network.

Table 20.1 Security Zones at a Glance

Security Zone	Default Locations Included in Zone	Default Security Settings
Local intranet zone	Local intranet servers not included in other zones; all network paths; all sites that bypass proxy server	Medium
Trusted sites zone	None	Low
Internet zone	All web sites not included in other zones	Medium
Restricted sites zone	None	High

As you move from one address to another with Internet Explorer, the system checks to see to what zone the address has been assigned and then applies the security settings that belong to that zone. If you open a web page on a server inside your corporate intranet, for example, you can freely download files and work with ActiveX controls or Java applets. When you switch to a page on the Internet, however, your security settings might prevent you from using any kind of active content or downloading any files.

There are three built-in security levels, plus a Custom option that enables you to pick and choose security settings for a zone. Table 20.2 summarizes the security options available when you first start Internet Explorer 4.0.

Table 20.2 Default Security Levels

Security Level	Default Settings
High	ActiveX controls and JavaScript disabled; Java set to highest safety level; file downloads prohibited through browser; prompt before downloading fonts or logging on to secure site.

continues

Table 20.2 Continued

Security Level	Default Settings
Medium	ActiveX enabled for signed controls only, with prompt before downloading; file and font downloads permitted; Java set to medium safety level; all scripting permitted; automatic logon to secure sites.
Low	All ActiveX controls enabled, but prompt before using unsigned code; Java set to low safety; desktop items install automatically; file and font downloads permitted; all scripting permitted; automatic logon to secure sites.
Custom	Enables user or administrator to select security settings individually.

Adding an Internet Domain to a Security Zone

Initially, Internet Explorer includes every external web site in the Internet zone. Over time, you will identify some sites that are extremely trustworthy, such as a secure server maintained by your bank or stockbroker; on these sites, you might want to relax security settings to enable maximum access to information and resources available from that domain. Other sites, however, might earn a reputation for transferring unsafe content, including untested software or virus-infected documents. On a network, in particular, you might want to tightly restrict access to these unsafe sites.

To add the addresses for specific web sites to a given security zone, open the Internet Options dialog box and click the Security tab; the dialog box shown in Figure 20.3 appears.

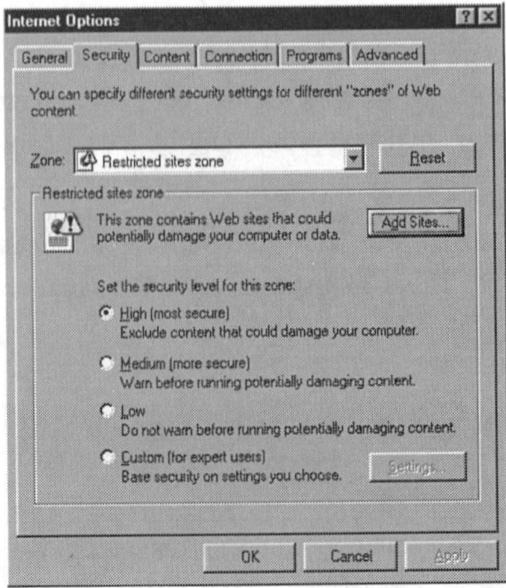

FIG. 20.3 Adding a web site to the Restricted Sites zone enables you to tightly control the site's capability to interact with your PC and network.

By definition, the Internet zone includes all sites not assigned to other zones; as a result, you can't add sites to that zone. Follow these steps to assign specific sites to the Trusted Sites or Restricted Sites zones:

1. Open the Internet Options dialog box and click the Security tab.
2. Choose a zone from the drop-down list at the top of the dialog box.
3. Click the Add Sites button.
4. Enter the full network address of the server you want to restrict in the text box and click the Add button.

   Be sure to include the prefix (http://, for example), but don't add any address information after the host name—Internet Explorer applies security settings to all pages on that server.
5. Repeat steps 3 and 4 to add more server names to the selected zone.
6. Click OK to close the dialog box.

To remove a web server from either the Trusted Sites or Restricted Sites zone, click the Add Sites button, select the address from the list, and click the Remove button. Any addresses you remove from a zone once again belong to the default Internet zone.

Some special considerations apply when adding sites to the Trusted Sites or Local Intranet zones.

- By default, only secure sites (those with the htpps:// prefix) can be added to the Trusted Sites group. To add other sites, clear the check box that reads Require Server Verification (https:) for All Sites in This Zone.
- To add sites to the Local Intranet zone, you'll have to go through one extra dialog box, as shown in Figure 20.4. Clear the middle check box if you want resources that you access without using the proxy server to fall into this group by default. Click the Advanced button to add sites to the Local Intranet zone.

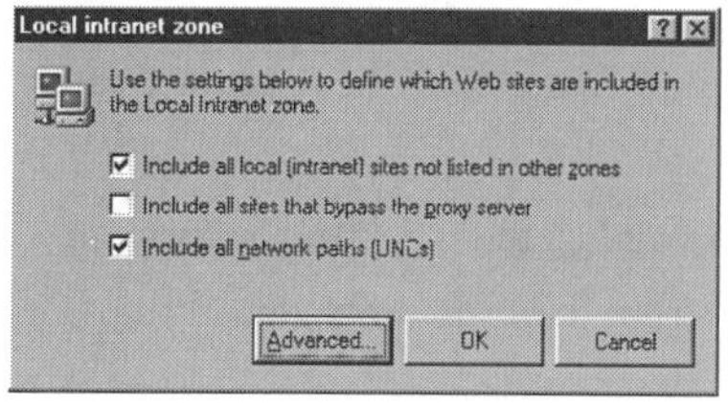

FIG. 20.4 Clear one or more of these check boxes to move sites from the Local Intranet zone to the default Internet zone.

Part IV

Ch 20

The status bar always displays the security zone for the current page. After you add a site to a security zone, load the page to confirm that the change was effective.

Changing Security Settings by Zone

When you first run Internet Explorer 4.0, all web pages use the same Medium security settings, but it doesn't have to stay that way. If your intranet is protected by a reliable firewall and you use ActiveX components developed within your company, you might want to reset security in the Local Intranet zone to Low. Likewise, if you're concerned about the potential for damage from files and programs on the Internet, you can reset security for the Internet zone to High.

To assign a different security level to any of the four built-in zones, follow these steps:

1. Open the Internet Options dialog box and click the Security tab.
2. Choose the appropriate zone from the drop-down list.
3. Click the High, Medium, or Low option button.
4. Click OK to save your new security settings

When you choose the High option for the Internet zone (or use custom options to choose similar security settings), don't be surprised if many pages don't work properly. Because ActiveX controls are disabled by default, for example, you're likely to see dialog boxes like the one in Figure 20.5 when you load an ActiveX-enabled page or attempt to download and play a streaming audio file.

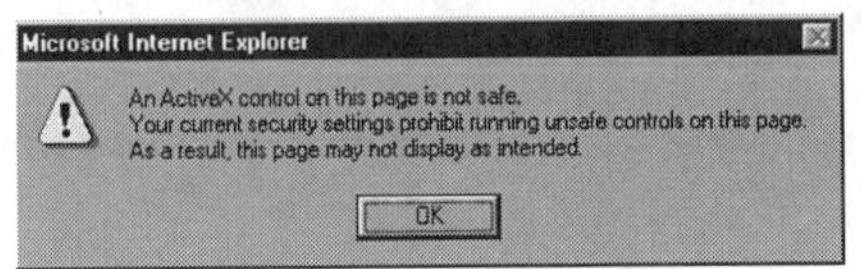

FIG. 20.5
With the security level set to High, many forms of rich content won't work. Instead of hearing multimedia files, for example, you see a dialog box like this one.

Setting Custom Security Options

If none of the built-in security levels is quite right for the policy you've established, you can create your own collection of security settings and apply it to any of the four security zones. Instead of choosing High, Medium, or Low, use Internet Explorer's Custom option to step through all the security options, choosing the ones that best suit your needs. Follow these steps:

1. Open the Internet Options dialog box and click the Security tab.
2. Choose the appropriate zone from the drop-down list.
3. Click Custom.
4. The Settings button, which is normally grayed out, should now be available. Click it, and the Security Settings dialog box shown in Figure 20.6 appears.
5. Scroll through the list and choose the options that best apply to your security needs. If you're not sure what an option means, right-click one and choose What's This for context-sensitive help.
6. After you've finished adjusting all security settings, click OK to apply the changes to the selected zone.

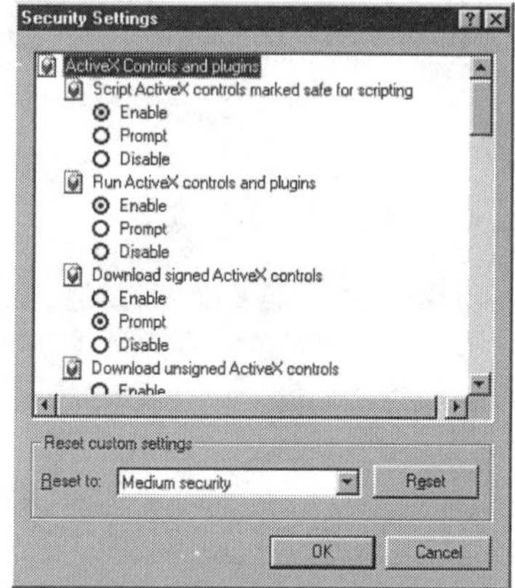

FIG. 20.6
Internet Explorer includes a long list of security settings for each zone. Use context-sensitive help for a concise explanation of what each one does.

Have you experimented with security settings to the point where you're afraid you've done more harm than good? Just start over. Open the Security Settings dialog box, choose a security level in the Reset to box, and click Reset. That restores the custom settings to the default security settings for that level and enables you begin fresh.

Restricting ActiveX Controls

The single most controversial feature of Internet Explorer 4.0 is its support for ActiveX controls. ActiveX technology, an extension of what was known in previous versions of Windows as Object Linking and Embedding (OLE), commonly refers to component software used across networks, including the Internet. Internet Explorer 4.0 uses ActiveX components in the browser window to display content that ordinary HTML can't handle, such as stock tickers, cascading menus, or Adobe Acrobat documents. An ActiveX chart control, for example, can take a few bits of data from a distant server and draw a chart at the speed of the local PC, instead of forcing you to wait while downloading a huge image file. The Microsoft Investor page (see Figure 20.7) offers a particularly rich example of this capability to quickly gather and manipulate data.

When you view a page that includes an ActiveX control, you don't need to run a setup program and restart your browser—the program simply begins downloading and then offers to install itself on your computer. That's convenient, but automatic installation also enables poorly written or malicious applets free access to your computer and network. Internet Explorer security options enable you to take control of ActiveX components and apply security settings by zone: You can completely disable all such downloads, or you can rely on digital certificates to decide which components are safe to install.

FIG. 20.7
An ActiveX control on this page makes it possible to quickly analyze and display complex data such as stock prices.

Customizing ActiveX Security Settings

Whenever Internet Explorer encounters an ActiveX control on a web page, it checks the current security zone and applies the security settings for that zone:

- The default Medium security settings disable any unsigned ActiveX controls and prompt you before downloading and installing those that have a valid certificate.
- The most drastic ActiveX security option completely disables any components you encounter in a given security zone. To enable this setting in the Internet zone, set the security level to High.
- When security is set to Low, the browser runs any ActiveX control. Signed controls download and install automatically; Internet Explorer prompts you before using an unsigned control.

CAUTION

Low security settings put your computer and network at risk. The only circumstance in which we recommend this setting is the Local Intranet zone, to enable access to trusted but unsigned ActiveX controls developed by other members of your organization.

In zones in which some or all ActiveX controls are disabled, Internet Explorer downloads the prohibited control but refuses to install it. Instead, you see an error message like the one in Figure 20.8.

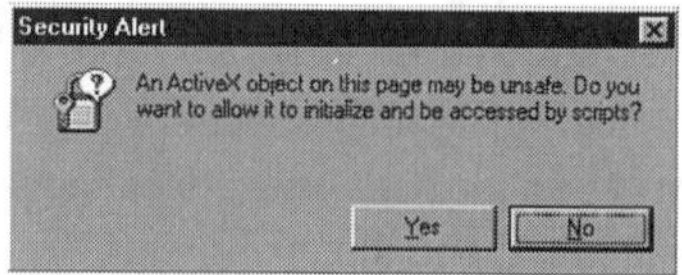

FIG. 20.8
Unless you set security options to Low, you see this dialog box anytime you encounter an unsigned ActiveX control. With High security, all ActiveX components are disabled.

Table 20.3 shows default ActiveX settings for each security zone. If you don't see a mix of options appropriate for your security policy, choose a zone and use Custom settings to redefine security levels.

Table 20.3 ActiveX Security Settings by Zone

Security Setting	Option	High	Medium	Low
Download unsigned ActiveX controls	Prompt			X
	Disable	X	X	
	Enable			
Script ActiveX controls marked safe for scripting	Prompt			
	Disable			
	Enable	X	X	X
Initialize and script ActiveX controls not marked as safe	Prompt		X	X
	Disable	X		
	Enable			
Download signed ActiveX controls	Prompt		X	
	Disable	X		
	Enable			X
Run ActiveX controls and plug-ins	Prompt			
	Disable	X		
	Enable		X	X

Custom security settings offer a way to take advantage of only the ActiveX controls you specifically approve, while prohibiting all others. Choose the Custom security level for the Internet zone, click Settings, and enable two options: Run ActiveX Controls and Plug-Ins, and Script ActiveX Controls Marked Safe for Scripting. Disable all other ActiveX security settings. With these security settings, currently installed ActiveX controls will function normally. When you encounter a new page that uses an ActiveX control, it will refuse to install; you can choose to install it by temporarily resetting the security options for that zone.

Using Certificates to Identify People, Sites, and Publishers

Internet Explorer uses digital certificates to verify the publisher of an ActiveX control before determining how to handle it. This feature, called Authenticode, checks the ActiveX control for the existence of an encrypted digital signature; IE4 then compares the signature against an original copy stored on a secure web site to verify that the code has not been tampered with. Software publishers register with Certifying Authorities such as VeriSign, Inc., who in turn act as escrow agents to verify that the signature you're viewing is valid.

ON THE WEB

For more information about how Authenticode uses digital signatures and Certifying Authorities, go to

http://www.verisign.com/developers/authenticodefaq.html

If Internet Explorer cannot verify that the signature on the ActiveX control is valid, you will see a Security Warning dialog box like the one in Figure 20.9. Depending on your security settings for the current zone, you might be able to choose to install the control anyway.

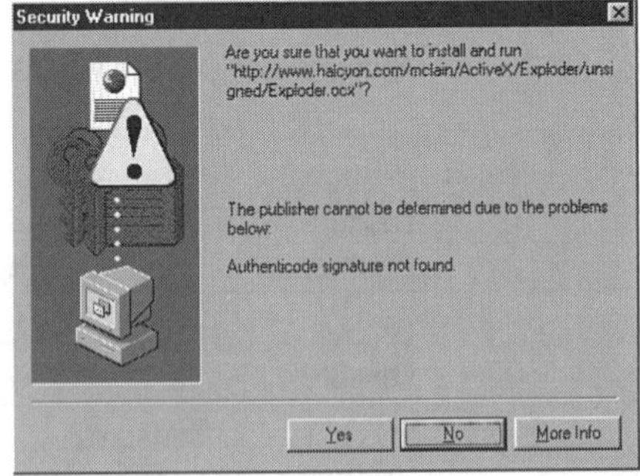

FIG. 20.9 You see this warning when Internet Explorer can't verify that a certificate is valid. Click Yes to install the software anyway or No to check again later.

If the Certifying Authority verifies that the signature attached to the control is valid, and the current security zone is set to use Medium settings, you see a dialog box like the one in Figure 20.10.

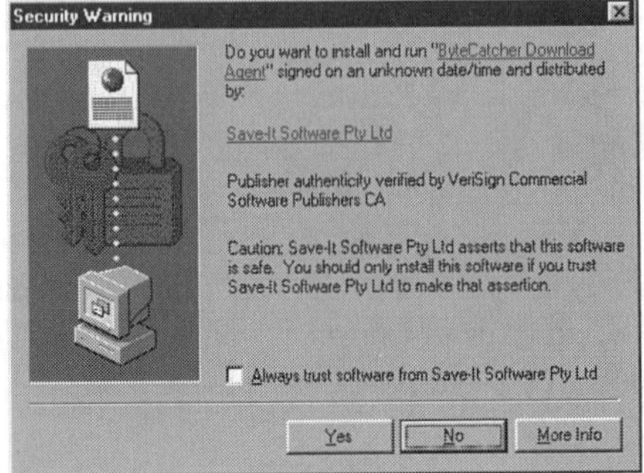

FIG. 20.10 Use the links on this certificate to see additional information about the publisher of ActiveX controls you download.

The Security Warning dialog box confirms that the signature is valid. In addition, it offers links that you can follow for more information about the publisher and gives you the option to add that publisher to a list of trusted sites:

- Click here for detailed information about the publisher, gathered from its certificate. If the applet or control is requesting permission to access system resources, an additional link will appear. Detailed Help is available.
- Click here to see additional information about the applet or control. This link typically points to a web site run by the software publisher.
- Choose Yes to install the software, and No to abort the installation.
- Check this box to add the certificate to your list of trusted publishers. Future downloads accompanied by certificates on your trusted publishers list will install automatically, without requiring your approval.
- Click here for general information about certificates and ActiveX security.

NOTE To view the full list of trusted publishers and certifying authorities, click the Content tab and look in the Certificates box.

CAUTION

A valid certificate provides no guarantee that a signed ActiveX control is either bug-free or safe. The certificate simply identifies the publisher with reasonable certainty. Based on that identification and the publisher's reputation, you can decide whether or not to install the software, and in the event something goes wrong, you know who to call for support.

Managing ActiveX Components on Your Computer

Every time Internet Explorer adds an ActiveX control, it downloads files to the local computer and makes adjustments to the Windows Registry. Unlike conventional programs, you can't use the Control Panel's Add/Remove Programs applet to remove or update components. But there is a way to manage this collection. Follow these steps:

1. Choose View, Internet Options and click the General tab.
2. In the box labeled Temporary Internet files, click the Settings button. The Settings dialog box appears.
3. Click the View Objects button to open the Downloaded Program Files folder. You see a list of all installed ActiveX controls and Java class libraries, as in Figure 20.11. If you're not sure what a control does, right-click and choose Properties to see additional information.
4. To delete one or more components, right-click the entry or entries and choose Remove from the shortcut menu. This step deletes each component's executable file and clears out any Registry settings as well.

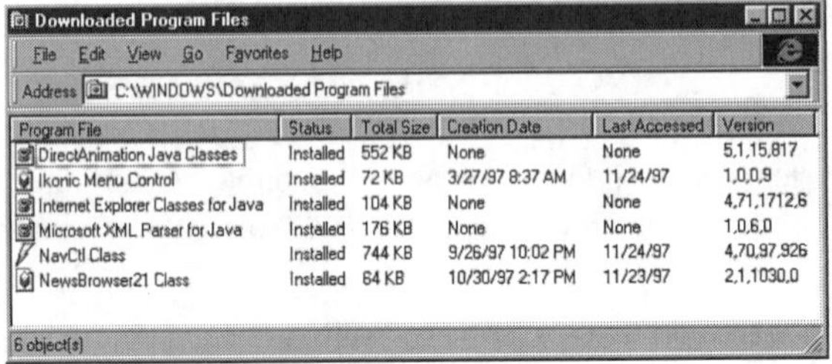

FIG. 20.11
All installed ActiveX controls appear in this folder. Use the right-click shortcut menus to inspect the file's properties, update it, or remove it.

5. To update one or more components with the most recent versions, right-click the entry or entries and choose Update from the shortcut menu. This step checks the original source for each file (usually an Internet address), replaces the component with new versions, and updates applicable Registry settings as needed.
6. Close the Downloaded Program Files window and click OK to close the Settings dialog box.

Limiting Java Applets

Like ActiveX controls, Java applets extend the capabilities of Internet Explorer by displaying and manipulating data and images in ways that HTML can't. There's a significant difference between ActiveX and Java, though: Java applets run in a virtual machine with strict security rules. The Java Security Manager (sometimes referred to as the "sandbox") prevents applets from interacting with resources on your machine, whereas ActiveX controls are specifically designed to work with files and other applications.

Unlike ActiveX controls, Java applets are not stored on your machine. Instead, every time you access a Java-enabled page, your browser downloads the applet and runs the program in the Java virtual machine. When you've finished with the applet, it disappears from memory, and the next time you access the page, you have to repeat the download. Over slow links, large Java applets can take excruciatingly long times to load, although the results can be impressive, as the example in Figure 20.12 shows.

Internet Explorer's Security Settings dialog box enables you to control specific aspects of the Java interface. Like the security settings for ActiveX controls, you can assign ready-made Low, Medium, or High options to Java applets or disable Java completely. There's even a Custom option, although most of its settings are meaningful only to Java developers. To adjust Java security, follow these steps:

1. Choose View, Internet Options, and click the Security tab.
2. Choose a zone from the drop-down list and click Custom.
3. Click Settings.
4. Scroll through the Security Settings dialog box until you reach the Java section.
5. Choose one of the five safety options.

6. If you select the Custom option, a new Java Custom Settings button appears at the bottom of the dialog box. Click this button, and the Custom Permissions dialog box appears (Figure 20.13).

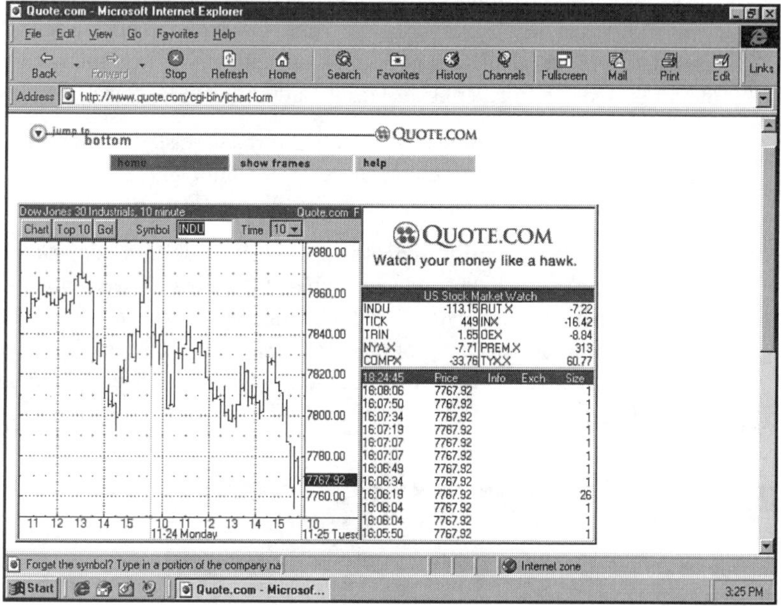

FIG. 20.12 This stock-charting page is an excellent illustration of the rich capabilities of Java applets.

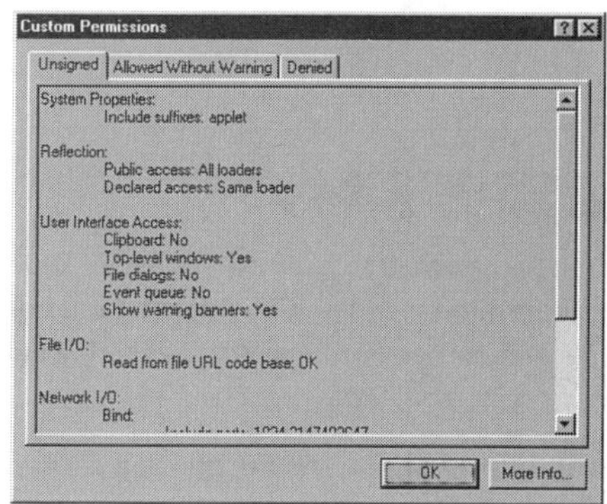

FIG. 20.13 Concerned about security with Java applets? Internet Explorer enables you to tightly control the Java virtual machine, but only an experienced Java developer will be able to work comfortably with these options.

7. To change permissions in this dialog box, click the Edit button.
8. Close all three dialog boxes to apply the changes you've made.

ON THE WEB

Earthweb's Gamelan site is the best place on the Internet to look for applets and information about the Java language.

www.gamelan.com

Blocking Dangerous Scripts and Unsafe File Downloads

In addition to its capability to host embedded controls and applets, Internet Explorer supports simple scripting, using JavaScript and VBScript. With the help of scripts, web designers can create pages that calculate expressions, ask and answer questions, check data that users enter in forms, and link to other programs, including ActiveX controls and Java applets.

Although the security risks posed by most scripts are slight, Internet Explorer gives you the option to disable Active scripting, as well as scripting of Java applets. You'll find both options in the Security Settings dialog box when you choose Custom settings.

A far more serious security risk is the browser's capability to download and run files. Although the risk of executing untrusted executable files is obvious, even document files can be dangerous. Any Microsoft Office document, for example, can include Visual Basic macros that are as powerful as any standalone program. To completely disable all file downloads, select the built-in High security level. With this setting turned on, you'll see a dialog box like the one in Figure 20.14 whenever you attempt to download a file from a web page.

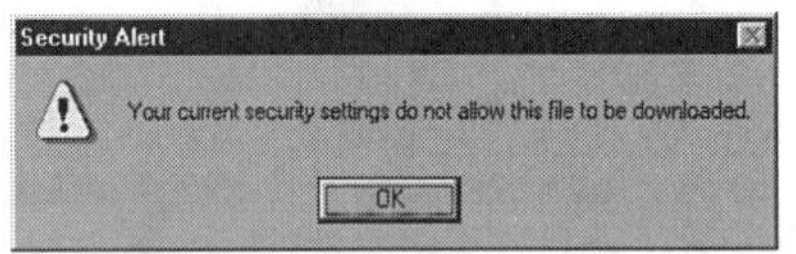

FIG. 20.14 With the security level set to High, no file downloads are allowed. When you attempt to download any file, including programs and documents, you will see this dialog box instead.

Working with Secure Web Sites

When is it safe to send confidential information over the Internet? You should transmit private information, such as credit card numbers and banking information, only when you can establish a secure connection using a standard security protocol called Secure Sockets Layer (SSL) over HTTP.

To make an SSL connection with Internet Explorer 4.0, the web server must include credentials from a designated Certification Authority. The URL for a secure connection uses a different prefix (https://), and Internet Explorer includes two important indications that you're about to connect securely: You'll see a warning dialog box each time you begin or end a secure connection and a padlock icon in the status bar, as in Figure 20.15.

After you negotiate a secure connection, every bit of data is encrypted before sending and decrypted at the receiving end; only your machine and the secure server have the keys required to decode the encrypted packets. Because of the extra processing time on either end, loading HTML pages over an SSL connection takes longer.

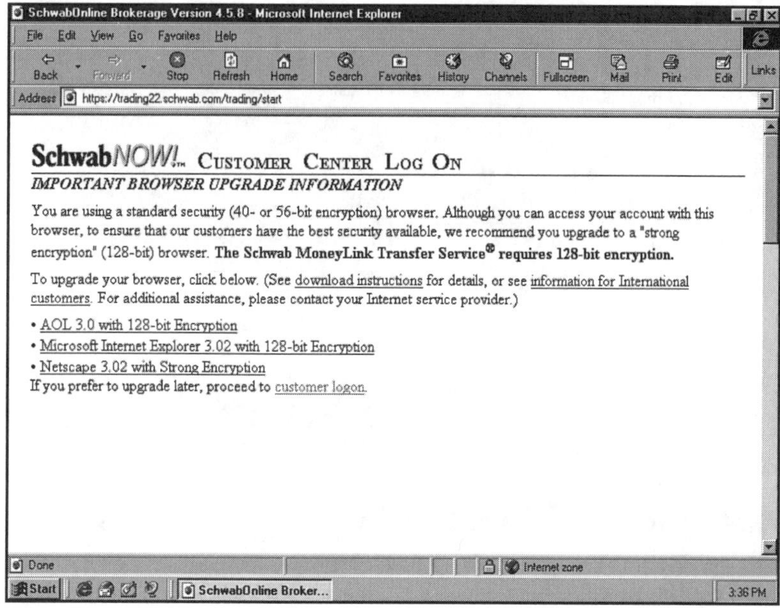

FIG. 20.15
The padlock icon and the https:// prefix tell you that the data you just sent was encrypted for safety's sake. Internet Explorer also warns you when you switch between secure and insecure connections.

ON THE WEB

For more information on certificates for commercial web servers, visit

www.verisign.com/microsoft

Although the built-in encryption capabilities of Internet Explorer 4.0 are powerful, one option can help you ensure even greater security. Because of United States government export restrictions, the default encryption software uses 40-bit keys to scramble data before transmission. That makes it difficult to decode, but a determined hacker can break 40-bit encryption in relatively short order. A much more powerful version of the encryption engine uses 128-bit keys, which are nearly impossible to crack; some banks and brokerage firms require the stronger encryption capabilities before you can access personal financial information online.

At this writing, the 128-bit security software is available only in the United States and Canada, although Microsoft has won permission to make this code available through banks and financial institutions overseas as well. To check which version you have, find a file called Schannel.dll, normally stored in the \Windows\System folder. Right-click the file icon, choose Properties, and then inspect the Version tab, as in Figure 20.16.

The weaker, 40-bit encryption code includes the words "Export version" on the Properties tab. The stronger 128-bit security engine includes the label "for Domestic use only." You can download the 128-bit upgrade, as long as you do so from a machine that is physically located within the United States or Canada. You'll find complete download instructions for the 128-bit upgrade at

http://www.microsoft.com/ie/ie40

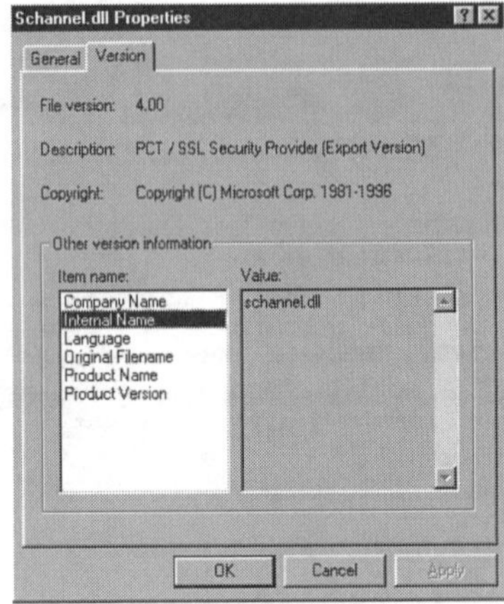

FIG. 20.16
If your copy of Internet Explorer includes the Export version of this security code, your commercial transactions are not as safe as they could be.

How Safe Are "Cookies"?

When you view a page in your web browser, some servers give you more than you asked for—quietly, without your knowledge, they record information about you and your actions in a hidden file called a "cookie." In more formal terms, these data stores are called client-side persistent data, and they offer a simple way for a web server to track your actions. There are dozens of legitimate uses for cookies: Commercial web sites use them to keep track of items as you add them to your online shopping basket; the *New York Times* web site stores your username and password so you can log in automatically; still other sites deliver pages tailored to your interests, based on information you've entered in a web-based form.

The first time you access a cookie-enabled server, the server creates a new cookie file in the Temporary Internet Files folder. That record contains the server's domain name, an expiration date, some security information, and any information the webmaster chooses to store about the current page request. When you revisit that page (or access another page on the same site), the server can read and update information in the cookie record. Although information stored in each cookie is in plain text format, most sites use codes, making it nearly impossible to decipher exactly what's stored there.

If you're troubled at the thought of inadvertently sharing personal information with a web site, you can disable cookies completely, or you can direct Internet Explorer to ask your permission before setting a cookie. To control your cookie collection, follow these steps:

1. Choose View, Internet Options, and click the Advanced tab.
2. Scroll to the Security heading and find the section labeled Cookies (see Figure 20.17).
3. Choose the option you prefer: Disable All Cookie Use or Prompt Before Accepting Cookies.
4. Click OK to record the new security settings.

FIG. 20.17
If you'd prefer not to share personal information with web sites using hidden "cookie" files, change this default option.

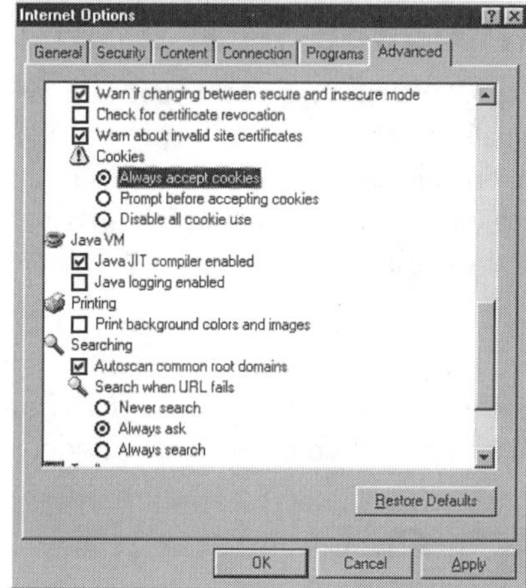

Should you be overly concerned about cookies? The privacy risks are minimal, thanks to strict security controls built into your web browser that limit what the server can and cannot do with cookies. They can't be used to retrieve information from your hard disk or your network; in fact, a server can only retrieve information from a cookie that it or another server in its domain created. A cookie can track your movements only within a given site—it can't tell a server where you came from or where you're going next.

Many web designers set cookies simply because that's the default for the server software they use; the information they collect gathers dust, digitally speaking. So when you ask Internet Explorer to prompt you before accepting a cookie, be prepared for a barrage of dialog boxes like the one in Figure 20.18. Try saying no; the majority of web sites work properly without cookies.

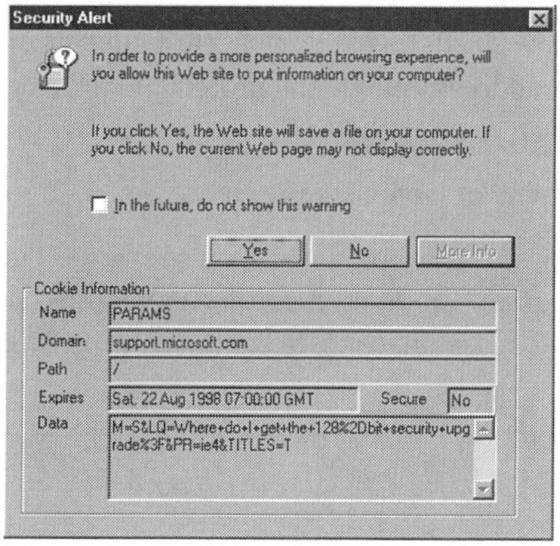

FIG. 20.18
You can ask Internet Explorer to warn you before it accepts a cookie; click the More Info button to see the contents of the proposed cookie file, as shown here.

Simplifying Online Purchases with Microsoft Wallet

A new feature in Internet Explorer 4.0 makes it possible to conduct safe transactions over the Internet without having to continually reenter your credit card and address information. The Microsoft Wallet enables you to store address and credit card information in encrypted form on your hard disk. When you encounter a web site that enables payments from the Microsoft Wallet, select a credit card and address from the lists you created earlier and then complete the transaction.

You can add multiple addresses and credit card entries to the Address Selector and Payment Selector lists. By entering separate home and work addresses, for example, as in Figure 20.19, you're free to order products and services for shipment to either address.

FIG. 20.19
With multiple entries in the Microsoft Wallet Address Selector, you can easily tell a merchant where you want to receive goods you order over the Internet.

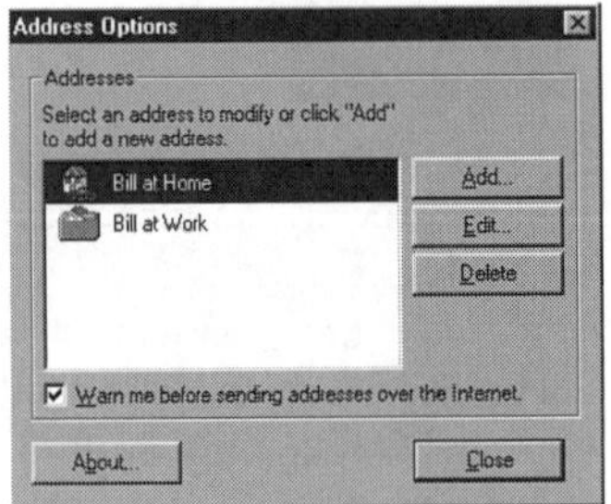

To add credit card information to the Payment Selector, follow these steps:

1. Choose View, Internet Options. Click the Content tab.
2. Click the Payments button to open the Payment Options dialog box.
3. Click the Add button and choose a payment method—Visa, Mastercard, American Express, or Discover—from the drop-down list.
4. Use the wizard (see Figure 20.20) to enter credit card information, select a billing address (or create a new address entry), and protect the information with a password.
5. To add another credit card, repeat steps 3 and 4.
6. Click Close to exit the Payment Options dialog box.

Note that address information is not encrypted—anyone with access to your computer can view, edit, or delete this information. Credit card details, on the other hand, are password protected; if you forget your password, you have to delete the entry from the Payment Selector and re-enter it.

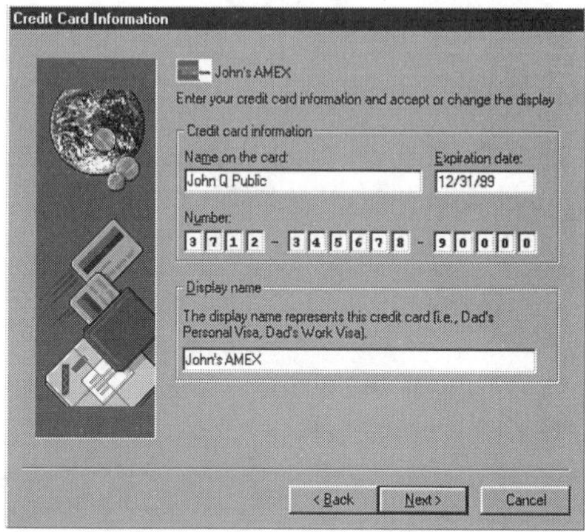

FIG. 20.20
The display name you enter here identifies this card when you use the Microsoft Wallet. The following screen enables you to protect this information with a password.

Controlling Access to Undesirable Content

Not every site on the Internet is worth visiting. Some, in fact, are downright offensive. That can represent a problem at home, where children run the risk of accidentally stumbling across depictions of sex, violence, and other inappropriate content. It's also potentially a problem at the office, where offensive or inappropriate content can drain productivity and expose a corporation to legal liability in the form of sexual harassment suits.

Internet Explorer includes a feature called the Content Advisor, which uses an industry-wide rating system to restrict the types of content that can be displayed within the borders of your browser. Before you can use the Content Advisor, you have to enable it: Choose View, Internet Options, click the Content tab, and click the Enable button. You'll have to enter a supervisor's password before continuing. After you've handled those housekeeping chores, you'll see the main Content Advisor window, shown in Figure 20.21.

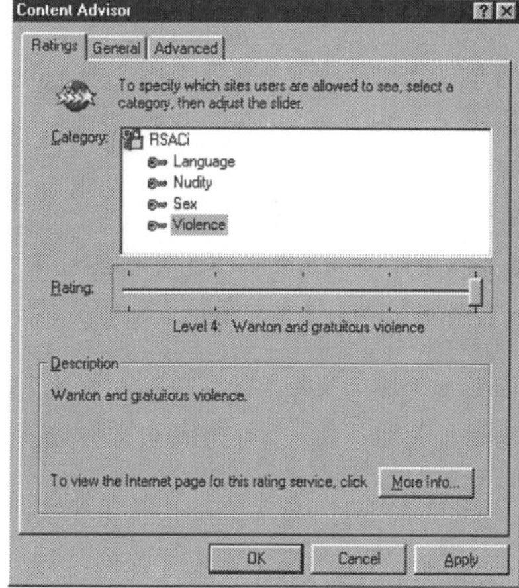

FIG. 20.21
Use the Content Advisor's ratings system to restrict access to web sites that contain unacceptable content.

The Content Advisor interface is self-explanatory: You use slider controls to define acceptable levels of sex, violence, language, and nudity. After you click OK, only sites whose ratings match your settings are allowed in the browser window.

Surprisingly, many adult sites adhere to the rating system, and an increasing number of mainstream business sites have added the necessary HTML tags to their sites as well. Unfortunately, many mainstream business sites don't use these ratings; as a result, you'll want to avoid setting the option to restrict unrated sites. ●

CHAPTER 21

Working with Web Subscriptions and the Active Desktop

by Ed Bott

In this chapter

Adding Web Content to the Active Desktop

The Active Desktop represents a key change to the Windows interface. Whereas the classic Windows 95 interface uses the desktop simply as a holding area for icons, the Active Desktop treats the entire Windows desktop as if it were a web page. You can still store icons there, but you can also add live web pages, components written in HTML, ActiveX controls, and Java applets. To see the Active Desktop in operation, look at Figure 21.1.

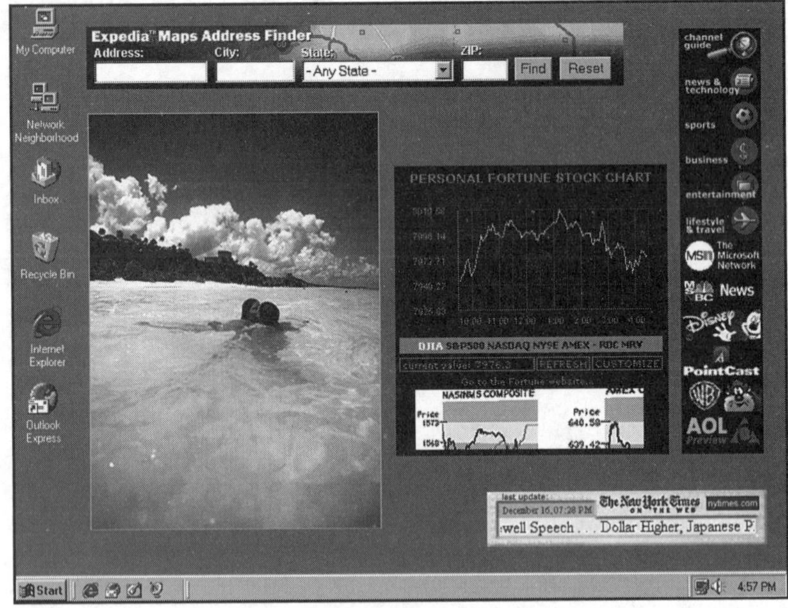

FIG. 21.1
Add live web content, including the headline and stock tickers shown here, to the Active Desktop.

NOTE Don't confuse the Active Desktop with the Windows Desktop Update. The Windows Desktop Update, an optional part of Internet Explorer 4.0, makes sweeping changes to the Start menu, taskbar, Explorer, and other parts of the Windows interface. The Windows Desktop Update offers a number of options, including the choice of web style: single-click navigation or the traditional double-click style. The Active Desktop is one choice in the Windows Desktop Update, but even if you choose to disable web-based content on the desktop, the other changes in the Windows Desktop Update remain in place. ■

When you choose web style as your preferred interface, the Active Desktop is automatically enabled. If you choose Classic style, on the other hand, the Active Desktop is automatically disabled, and your desktop looks and acts like Windows 95.

▶ **See** "Classic or Web—Choosing a Navigation Style," **p. 271**

You can enable or disable the Active Desktop at any time, regardless of which navigation style you've chosen. Follow these steps:

1. Right-click any empty space on the desktop and choose Active Desktop from the shortcut menu.
2. To enable or disable the Active Desktop, select the View As Web Page option. A check mark appears in front of this menu choice when the Active Desktop is enabled.
3. To hide or show individual web items, select Active Desktop, Customize My Desktop. Uncheck items on the web tab of the Display Properties dialog box to prevent them from displaying on the Active Desktop. Restore an item's check mark to once again show it on the Active Desktop.

What good is information on the Active Desktop if your application windows cover it up? To quickly clear away all windows, use the Show Desktop button on the Quick Launch toolbar.

Using an HTML Page as Your Desktop

If you're a skilled web page designer, it's a trivial task to create a custom page that organizes essential information and links. In corporate settings, using a standard HTML-based background page can be an excellent way to ensure that every user has access to the same crucial information on the intranet. Windows 95 enables you to specify an HTML page as the desktop background, just as previous versions of Windows enabled you to use a graphic image as wallpaper.

You can use any HTML editor, including FrontPage Express, to create your background page. Think of this page as the base layer of the Active Desktop: Standard desktop icons sit on top of this layer, and you can add other web elements as well. The HTML page you use as your Windows background can include hyperlinks, graphics (including a company logo), tables, HTML components, and ActiveX controls.

▶ **See** "Using FrontPage Express," **p. 570**

After you've created the background page, save it to local or network storage. To begin using the page as your desktop background, follow these steps:

1. Right-click any empty space on the desktop and choose Properties.
2. In the Display Properties dialog box, click the Background tab (see Figure 21.2).
3. Click the Browse button to display the Browse dialog box. Select the HTML file you want to use as the desktop, and then click Open.
4. Click Apply to see your new background immediately.
5. Click OK to close the Display Properties dialog box.

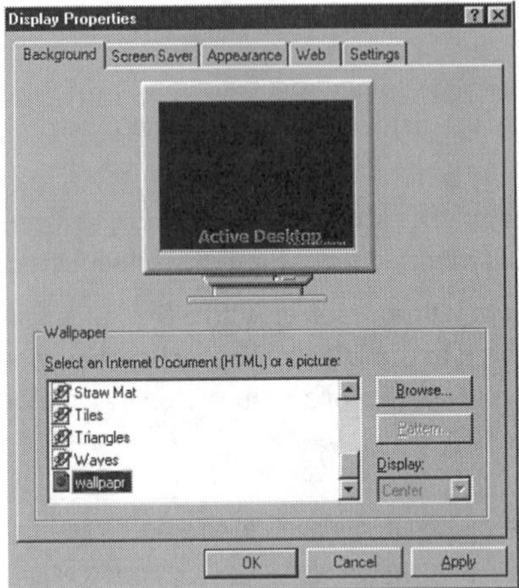

FIG. 21.2
Create a custom web page and use it in place of wallpaper to make a truly custom interface.

Displaying Objects on the Active Desktop

Enabling the Active Desktop enables you to use the Windows desktop to display a wide variety of content. You can add the following:

- An HTML page as the Windows background; unlike wallpaper, this background can contain text, hyperlinks, images, and HTML code.
- One or more web pages, each in its own self-contained region.
- Web components, including ActiveX controls and Java applets.
- Active Channels, which enable you to download prepackaged collections of web content for offline browsing.
- Pictures, stored locally or from a web server.

Adding a New Web Page to the Active Desktop

Before adding a new web page to the Active Desktop, create an Internet shortcut to the page. Then follow these steps:

1. Right-click any empty space on the desktop and choose Properties from the shortcut menu. The Display Properties dialog box appears. Select the web tab to display the dialog box shown in Figure 21.3.
2. Click the New button. (Choose No if you're prompted to connect to Microsoft's gallery of Active Desktop components.)
3. If you know the exact file name or URL of the item you want to add, enter it. Otherwise, click the Browse button.
4. The Browse dialog box displays only files you can add to the Active Desktop—typically images and Internet shortcuts. Select the item you want to add and click Open.

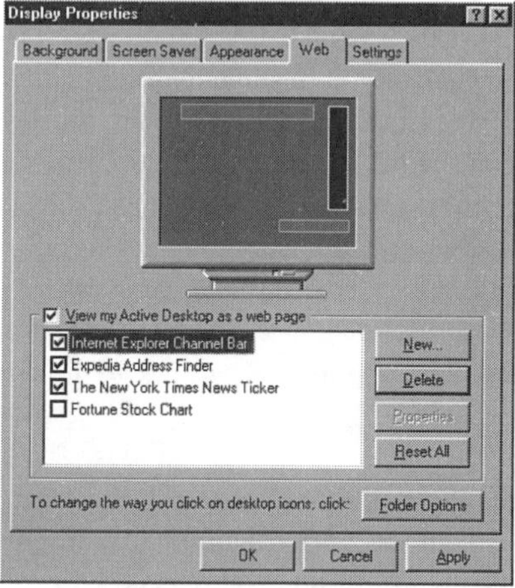

FIG. 21.3 Enter a filename or web address to add pictures or entire web pages to your Active Desktop.

5. Click OK. If you entered an Internet shortcut, you see the dialog box shown in Figure 21.4. Click the Customize Subscription option if you need to enter a password or reschedule updates. Click OK to continue.

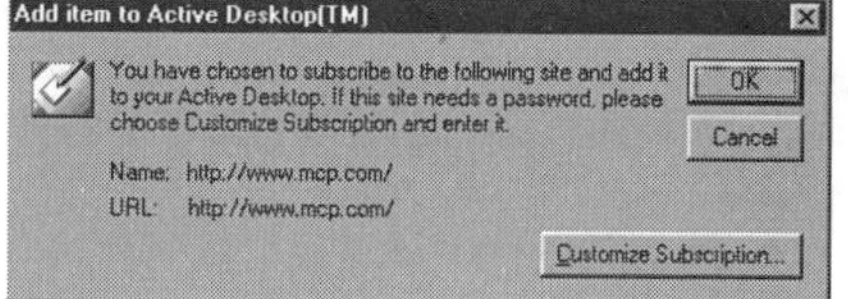

FIG. 21.4 Use this button to customize login and update options for web pages on the Active Desktop.

6. The new object appears in the list at the bottom of the web tab. Note that the screen display at the top of the dialog box shows the approximate position of each desktop item. Click Apply to display the new item and add another. Click OK to save your changes and close the dialog box.

There's a far easier way to add a new element to the Active Desktop. First, view the web page or open the graphic file in the browser window; size the window so that you can see a portion of the desktop. To add a web page, hold down the right mouse button and drag the icon from the left of the address bar onto the desktop. To add a picture to the Active Desktop, right-drag the image onto the desktop. Choose Create Active Desktop Item (or Image) Here.

To move or resize objects on the Active Desktop, let the mouse pointer hover over the object until a gray border appears around the object. Click the thick bar at the top of the object and drag it to a new location. Use the borders to resize the windows itself. Scroll bars appear if the object is larger than the window you've created.

Placing a Picture on the Active Desktop

The Classic Windows 95 interface enables you to add one graphic, centered or tiled, as wallpaper on the Windows desktop. Using the Active Desktop, you can add multiple pictures to the desktop and rearrange them as you see fit. You can use saved image files, such as a family picture or a postcard of your favorite tropical resort. Or, you can select a web-based image that is regularly updated, such as a weather or traffic map.

NOTE The Active Desktop supports three standard graphic file formats: Windows Bitmap (BMP), GIF, and JPEG File Interchange Format (JPEG). GIF and JPEG are the most common graphic formats on the Internet.

For photographs and other images that remain static, your best strategy is to create the Active Desktop item from a file stored on your local drive. Linking to a graphic file on a web site forces the browser to try to update the file for no good reason. To save an image you find on a web page, right-click the image and choose Save Picture As from the shortcut menu. Give the picture a meaningful name, and store it where you will be able to find it later.

▶ **See** "Saving and Editing Web Pages," **p. 470**

CAUTION

Images and other original elements on most web sites are protected by copyright. Displaying an image file on your personal desktop is generally considered acceptable, but reusing a copyrighted graphic on a commercial web site without permission could land you in court.

Adding a Component to the Active Desktop

Unlike web pages, which sometimes have to be forced into service as an Active Desktop object, components are made for this very purpose. A component can be a simple scrap of HTML, or it can include an ActiveX control or a Java applet. Some components are actually mini-programs that you can customize to match your own preferences.

▶ **See** "Restricting ActiveX Controls," **p. 483**, and "Limiting Java Applets," **p. 488**

ON THE WEB

Microsoft's Active Desktop Gallery includes an assortment of interesting desktop components, including a useful search box, stock tickers, and several clocks. Browse the entire collection at

http://www.microsoft.com/ie/ie40/gallery

Adding a new component to your Active Desktop is simple. In most cases, the web page designer includes an Add to Active Desktop button, like the example shown in Figure 21.5. Click this button to download and install the component.

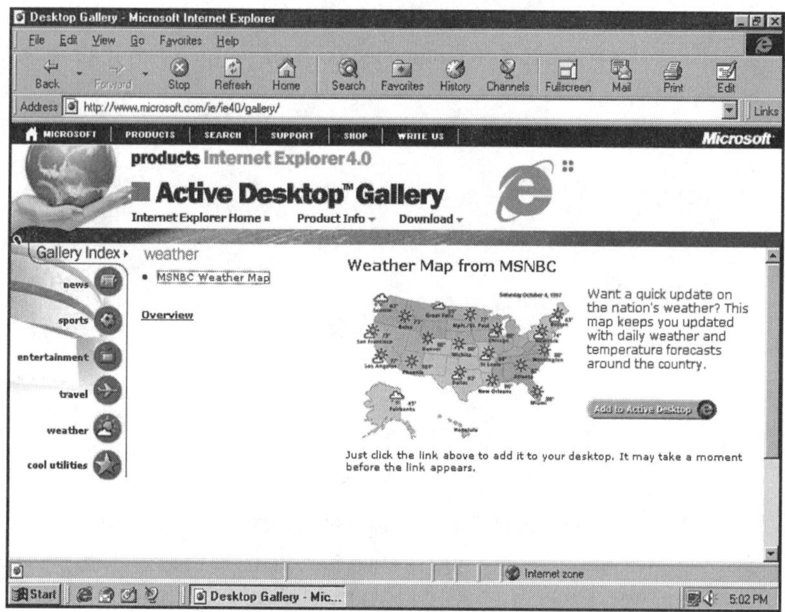

FIG. 21.5
Choose a component such as this weather map from Microsoft's gallery, and then click the button to add it to your desktop.

Hiding, Removing, and Editing Objects

You don't have to display every installed component, picture, and web site on your Active Desktop. Hide objects you use infrequently so that they remain available when you need them. To display, hide, remove, or edit objects on the Active Desktop, right-click the desktop, and then choose Properties. Select the web tab in the Display Properties dialog box.

- To hide an object, clear the check box next to its entry. The object remains in your list of installed objects.
- To remove an object from the list, select the object and click Delete. The object is permanently removed from your system.
- To adjust the subscription settings for the object, click the Properties button.

Click OK to accept your changes.

Using Subscriptions to Download Web Pages

When you subscribe to a web site, you instruct IE4 to regularly visit the site in search of new content. Don't let the term *subscription* mislead you; there's no fee associated with the process. Subscriptions are simply a way for you to automatically search for and download content from your favorite sites.

If you can load a web page into the browser window, you can subscribe to it. You can specify the amount of information to download from the site, although this capability is limited and might not produce the results you're expecting.

You can also subscribe to Active Channels—prepackaged collections of web content that include a site map and a recommended schedule for updates. With the help of Channel Definition Format (CDF) files, a webmaster can assemble just the information you need, and not a page more.

CAUTION

With an IE4 subscription, you can instruct the browser to retrieve a given page and all pages linked to it, to a depth of as many as three pages. On web sites that contain large collections of files, this "web crawling" can cause an unacceptable performance hit. For this reason, some sites ban web crawlers, and you will find that your subscriptions to these sites won't update correctly.

Subscribing to Web Sites

To subscribe to a web site, you start by adding it to your Favorites list. Follow these steps:

1. Open the web page in the browser window.
2. Choose Favorites, Add to Favorites. Rename the shortcut, if you want, and choose a folder. Note that the Add Favorite dialog box includes two subscription options, as shown in Figure 21.6.

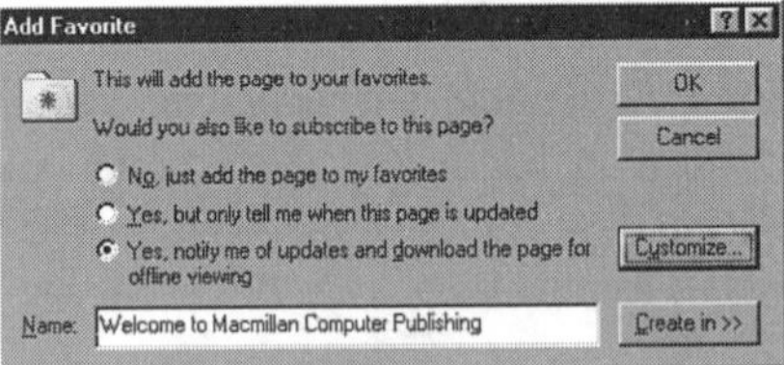

FIG. 21.6
Choose one of these options to add a web page to your Subscriptions list.

When you subscribe to a web site, IE4 adds a shortcut in your Favorites folder and in the Subscriptions folder. Deleting the shortcut in the Favorites folder does not delete your subscription, nor does deleting a subscription remove the entry from your Favorites list. The property sheet for an Internet shortcut includes extra tabs when you've subscribed to that site.

3. If you simply want IE4 to notify you when new content is available on this page, choose Yes, But Only Tell Me When This Page Is Updated. Click OK to accept these settings and skip all remaining steps.
4. To set up a subscription that automatically downloads content from the specified web site, choose Yes, Notify Me of Updates and Download the Page for Offline Viewing.
5. Default subscription settings download only the specified page; the update is scheduled daily at 1:00 a.m. To accept these settings, click OK and skip all remaining steps.
6. If the web site to which you're subscribing requires a password for access, or if you want to adjust any other subscription properties, click the Customize button. That launches the Subscription Wizard, as shown in Figure 21.7.

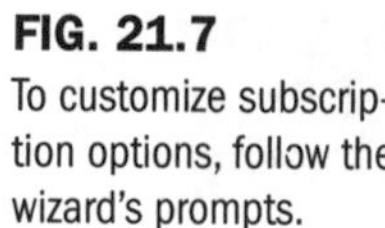

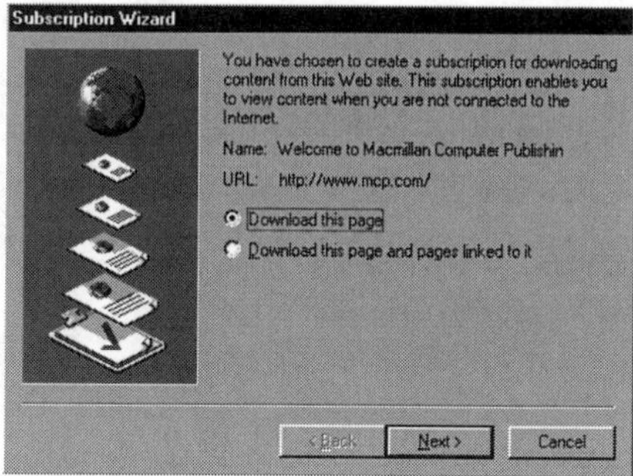

FIG. 21.7
To customize subscription options, follow the wizard's prompts.

The wizard includes four options (for further details on each of these options, see the following section):

- Download pages linked to the specified page. Choose a number between 1 and 3.
- Ask IE4 to send you an email message when the page is updated.
- Adjust the schedule IE4 uses to update this subscription. Choose daily, weekly, monthly, or custom options.
- Enter a username and password if the site requires it.

7. When you've finished the Subscription Wizard, click OK to add the entry to your Subscriptions list.

Managing Subscriptions

Internet Explorer maintains your list of subscribed sites in the \Windows\Subscriptions folder. Special extensions to the Windows Explorer enable you to view subscription details, edit update schedules, and delete sites when you no longer want to subscribe.

To open the Subscriptions folder, choose Favorites, Manage Subscriptions. You see a window like the one in Figure 21.8.

Select one or more sites from the list and use the right-click shortcut menus to open, copy, delete, or update the selection. Select a single site and choose Properties to adjust the subscription's settings.

Customizing Subscriptions

By default, each subscription downloads one page, once a day, around 1:00 a.m. For most subscriptions, you probably will want to change those defaults. Most often, you will want to increase the amount of content that IE4 downloads, as well as the update schedule.

You can adjust all the following options when you first create a subscription, using the Subscription Wizard. To change a subscription's properties after, open the Subscriptions folder, right-click the entry for the site, and choose Properties from the shortcut menu. Select the Subscription, Receiving, or Schedule tabs and make any of the following changes.

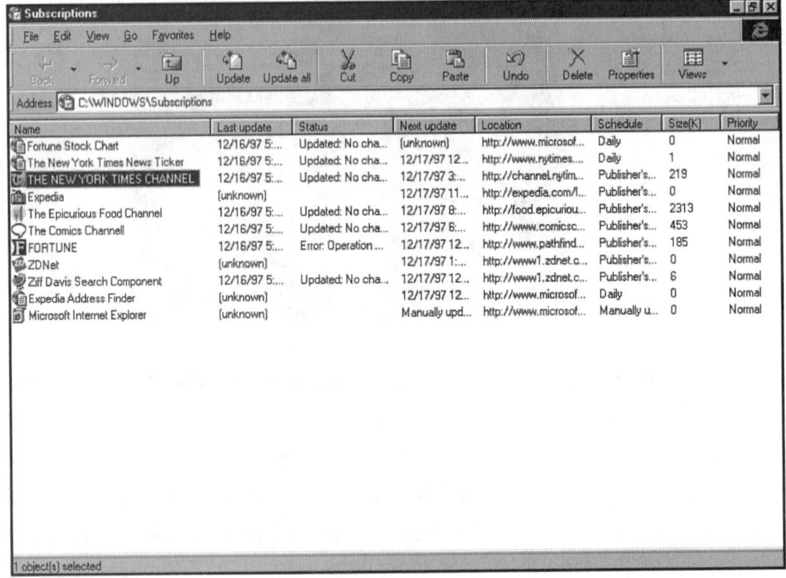

FIG. 21.8
Switch to Details view to see information about each entry in the list, including error messages from the last update attempt.

Controlling the Size and Depth of Subscriptions Chances are you want to see more than one page for your favorite web sites. On the front page of a newspaper like the *Los Angeles Times*, for example, you usually find links to the day's top stories. When you go to those pages, you find links to still more stories.

As part of the settings for each subscription, you can tell IE4 to follow all the links on the subscribed page. For subscriptions you plan to read offline, it's crucial that you enter a number large enough to gather the information you need. But it's also important to monitor the amount of material that IE4 has to download. The number of pages needing updating can increase dramatically with each additional layer. If you don't set the right limits when setting up a subscription, the downloaded content might consume all the space in your Temporary Internet Files folder.

If you typically read only one portion of a web site, don't start at the site's home page; instead, pick the site that contains the links you plan to follow. On highly structured sites, this page might be deep within the site. You might not be able to do this with an active server page or a page that was created in response to your query.

To define exactly which pages IE4 will download with each update, follow these steps:

1. Right-click the site's entry in the Subscriptions folder, and then choose Properties.
2. Select the Receiving tab. You'll see a dialog box like the one in Figure 21.9, with the lower option selected in the Subscription Type box.

FIG. 21.9
If you opt to download a subscription for offline viewing, click the Advanced button to adjust how much content to retrieve.

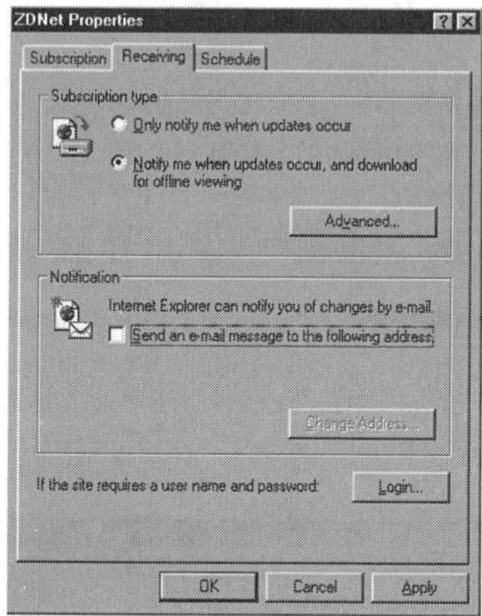

3. Click the Advanced button. The Advanced Download Options dialog box appears (see Figure 21.10).

FIG. 21.10
Balance these options to download the right amount of content without consuming too much disk space.

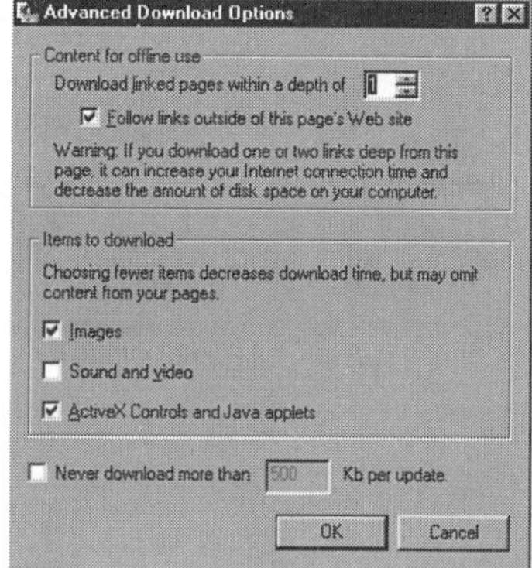

4. To download pages linked to the main page in your subscription, adjust the Download Linked Pages option. Enter a number between 1 and 3. To restrict the download to pages on the main site, clear the check box labeled Follow Links Outside of This Page's Web Site.
5. To restrict the total amount of content downloaded with each update, check the box labeled Never Download More Than *x* KB Per Update. Enter a limit in kilobytes (the default is 500KB).
6. To further limit downloads, review the list of options in the center of the dialog box. By default, IE4 gathers image files, ActiveX controls, and Java applets, while not retrieving sound and video files.

CAUTION

Many web pages use images to help with navigation and to supply information. Don't restrict image downloads unless you're certain a site is useful in text-only mode.

7. Click OK or select another tab to further customize the subscription.

Specifying a Format for Update Notifications How do you know when there's been a change in a web site to which you subscribe? Look at any Internet shortcut, on the desktop, in the Favorites bar, in the Channel Bar, or in the Subscriptions window: A red gleam in the upper-left corner of an icon means there's new content, as in Figure 21.11.

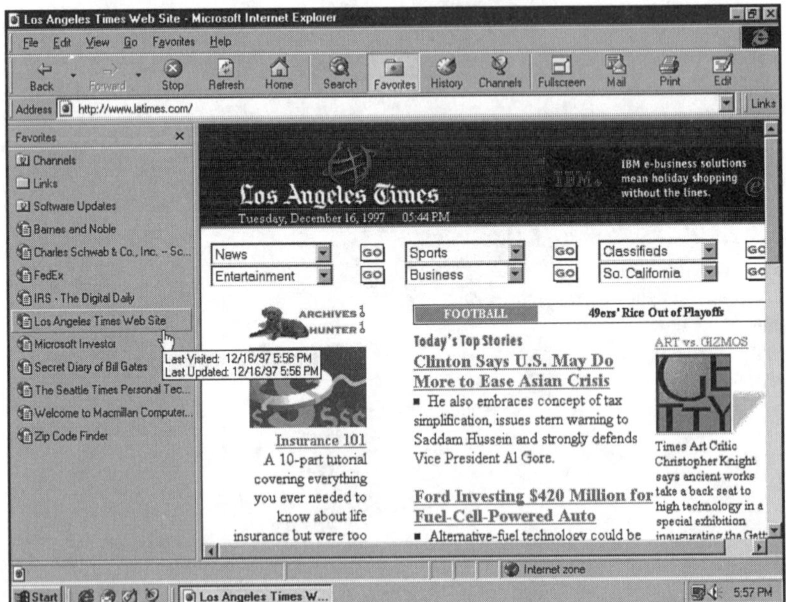

FIG. 21.11
The star in the upper-left corner of two icons means the latest update turned up new material.

If you prefer a more emphatic notice, ask IE4 to send you an email message every time it notices a change in a web site to which you subscribe. The email message can be a simple notice with a hyperlink, or it can contain a copy of the updated HTML page.

To set up email updates, follow these steps:

1. Select an entry in the Subscriptions folder, right-click, and choose Properties.
2. Click the Receiving tab.
3. Choose one of the two Subscription types at the top of the dialog box. If you select the option to download content for offline viewing, IE4 sends you the page via email.
4. Check the box labeled Send an Email Message to the Following Address. If necessary, click the Change Address button and enter or change the address and server information.
5. Click OK to close the dialog box and save your changes.

By default, IE4 updates your subscriptions once a day, at 1:00 a.m. You can adjust the update interval, if you want, or set the subscription for manual updates only. You can also specify whether IE4 dials your Internet connection automatically.

To adjust a subscription's update schedule, open the Subscriptions folder and select the Schedule tab. You see a dialog box like the one in Figure 21.12.

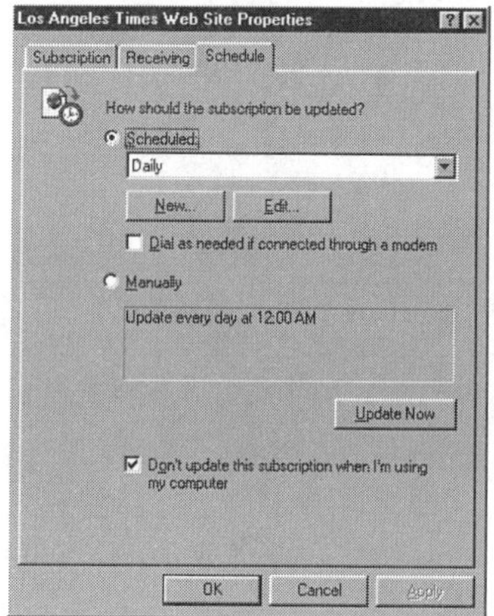

FIG. 21.12 Use these options to control how and when IE4 updates your subscriptions.

To use a regularly scheduled interval, choose the Scheduled option and select Daily, Weekly, or Monthly from the drop-down list. Click the Edit button to adjust the details of this schedule. For example, if you subscribe to an online magazine that appears every Friday at midnight, you can tell IE4 to update your subscription each Friday morning at 5:00 a.m., before you arrive at work.

Network administrators might be horrified at the thought of thousands of users requesting web updates on the hour. IE4 attempts to minimize that problem by randomly varying the exact time for each update by up to 30 minutes in either direction. To take maximum control over how users work with Internet Explorer 4.0, make sure you check the Internet Explorer Administrator's Kit, available from Microsoft. For more information about the most current release of IEAK, try **http://ieak.microsoft.com/**.

You can also create a custom schedule, using a dizzying variety of options. For example, if you have a favorite business-oriented site, you can set a subscription to update once an hour, from 8:00 a.m.–5:00 p.m., every weekday. You can update a subscription every Monday, Wednesday, and Friday. You can even specify that a site update at 9:00 a.m. on the second Tuesday of every other month. When you save a custom schedule, you can reuse the schedule with other subscriptions, as well.

To create a custom schedule for updates, follow these steps:

1. Select an entry in the Subscriptions folder, right-click, and choose Properties.
2. Click the Schedule tab and click the New button. The Custom Schedule dialog box (see Figure 21.13) opens.

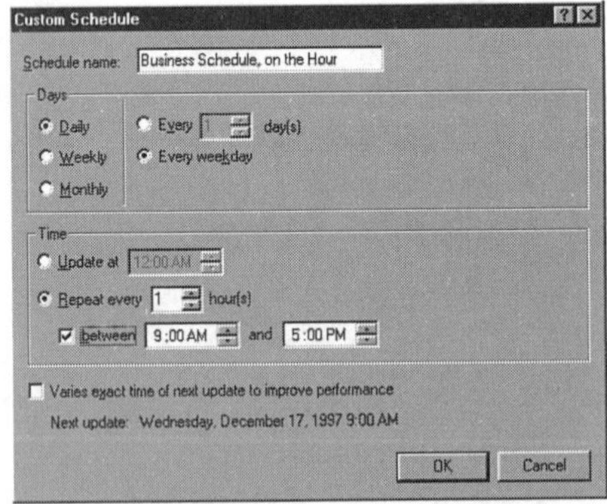

FIG. 21.13
Be sure to give each custom schedule a descriptive name, so you can reuse the schedule with other subscriptions.

3. Choose the day or days to update. Select Daily, Weekly, or Monthly and adjust the available options that appear to the right.
4. Choose the time or times to perform the update. Options enable you to repeat the update throughout the day; if the exact time of each update is not important, check the option to vary the exact time of each update to avoid causing network congestion.
5. Give the schedule a descriptive name and click OK.
6. Set two final options to tell Internet Explorer whether it should automatically dial up your Internet connection or update a subscription when you're working with your computer.
7. Click OK to save your changes.

Updating Subscriptions Manually IE4 enables you to manually update all your subscriptions with the click of one button. This capability is especially useful if you are about to leave on a trip and you want to make sure your notebook computer contains the most current versions of all your web subscriptions. You can also update an individual site if you know there's new content and you don't want to wait for the next scheduled update.

To manually update all subscriptions, follow these steps:

1. Verify that you have a working Internet connection. If necessary, open a Dial-Up Networking connection.
2. If the Subscriptions folder is open, click the Update All button.
3. If the Subscriptions folder is not open or the toolbar is not visible, choose Favorites, Update All Subscriptions.

4. If you have a lengthy list of subscriptions to update, the process can take a long time. The Downloading Subscriptions dialog box (see Figure 21.14) displays the status of the operation, including any error messages that might appear. To cancel all further updates, click Stop. To skip over one site's update and proceed with the next site, click Skip. Click the Hide button to move this dialog box out of the way and continue working. You can close the browser window or view other sites while the update process continues.

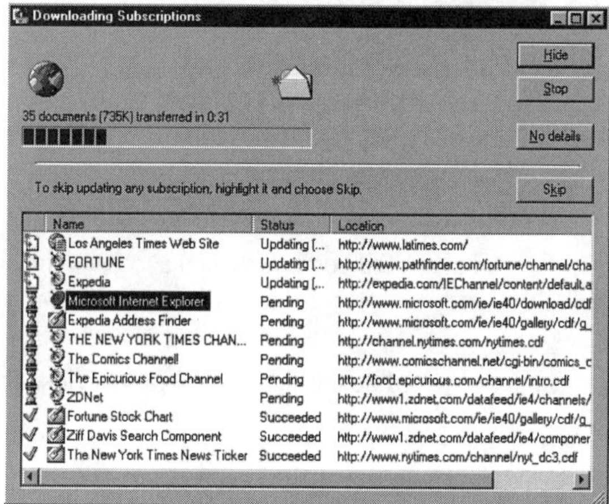

FIG. 21.14
If you don't see this full status window, click the Details button.

To update an individual subscription, follow these steps:

1. If the Subscriptions folder is open, click the Update button.
2. If the Subscriptions folder is not open or the toolbar is not visible, choose Favorites, Manage Subscriptions.
3. Right-click the name of the site you want to update and choose Update Now.

If you subscribe to a site that rarely changes or one you rarely visit, you can tell IE4 to update that subscription only when you manually choose to do so. Right-click the subscription icon and choose Properties. Click the Schedule tab and choose the option labeled Manually. The Update Now button at the bottom of this dialog box also enables you to refresh the subscription with the most current content.

Subscribing to Password-Protected Sites Sites such as the *Wall Street Journal* (**http://www.wsj.com**) require you to enter a username and password before browsing the site. If you're using IE4 interactively, you can type the information directly into a login box. When you subscribe to a password-protected site, IE4 enables you to include the login information so that you can get the information you're looking for automatically.

You do not have to subscribe to the specific page that includes the login screen. You can subscribe to a page above the login screen and specify a depth of delivery that reaches below the login screen. When IE4 reaches the page that requests your user ID and password, it supplies them and continues updating the subscription.

To enter a username and password for use with a web subscription, follow these steps:

1. If you are initially creating the subscription, click the Login button. If you are editing an existing subscription, right-click its entry in the Subscriptions folder, and then click Properties. Click the Schedule tab and click the Login button to display the Login Options dialog box (see Figure 21.15).

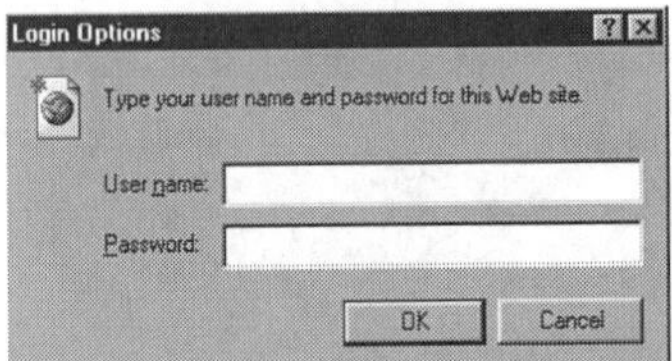

FIG. 21.15
Enter login information here for IE4 to gain access to password-protected sites when updating a subscription.

2. Enter the username and password you use to gain access to the site. Make sure both entries are spelled correctly and that the case (the mix of upper- and lowercase letters) is correct.
3. Click OK to return to the Schedule tab. Click OK again to close the dialog box and save your changes.

After setting up a subscription to a password-protected site, it's always a good idea to verify that it works. Update the subscription manually; if the update fails because of an incorrect username or password, try logging in manually to make sure the site is working and the information you enter is correct. Then edit the subscription's username and password to match those you've tested.

Speeding Up Subscription Updates

If you're about to hit the road and you're running short on time, two shortcuts can dramatically reduce the time it takes to update all the subscriptions on your notebook. First, cut the update list to the bare minimum. Choose Favorites, Manage Subscriptions, and hold down the Ctrl key as you select the sites you want to update. When you're finished, right-click and choose Update Now from the shortcut menu.

To speed the update process even more (and save precious disk space), tell IE4 to concentrate on text and ignore large graphics and media files. Note that some sites use images for navigation, and at other sites images might contain important information; as a result, the pages you end up with when you use this technique might be of limited use. Still, when time is short, you can follow these steps:

1. Open the Subscriptions dialog box.
2. Right-click each site you plan to update, choose Properties, and click the Delivery tab.
3. Click the Advanced button to open the Advanced Download Options dialog box.
4. In the Items to Download box, clear the check mark next to the options labeled Images, Sound and Video, and ActiveX Controls and Java applets.

5. Repeat steps 2–4 for each subscription you plan to update.
6. Select the group of icons to update, right-click, and choose Update.

Subscribing to Active Channels

Channels are prepackaged subscriptions. Instead of indiscriminately delivering web pages to your hard disk, a webmaster can put together a collection of pages, just as a newspaper publisher assembles a daily paper. When you subscribe to an Active Channel, you download a single file, created by using the Channel Definition Format (CDF). Channel files typically include multiple HTML files, graphics, a map of the web site (including links to pages not included in the CDF file), and a publisher's recommended schedule for updates.

By default, Internet Explorer 4.0 adds a Channel Bar to your desktop, with shortcuts to dozens of brand-name channels. Note that you don't have to subscribe to view the content in a channel.

The Channel Bar contains an Internet shortcut that takes you to Microsoft's Active Channel Guide. Browse through this lengthy list by category, or search for keywords by using the built-in search button. The Active Channel Guide, shown in Figure 21.16, is updated frequently.

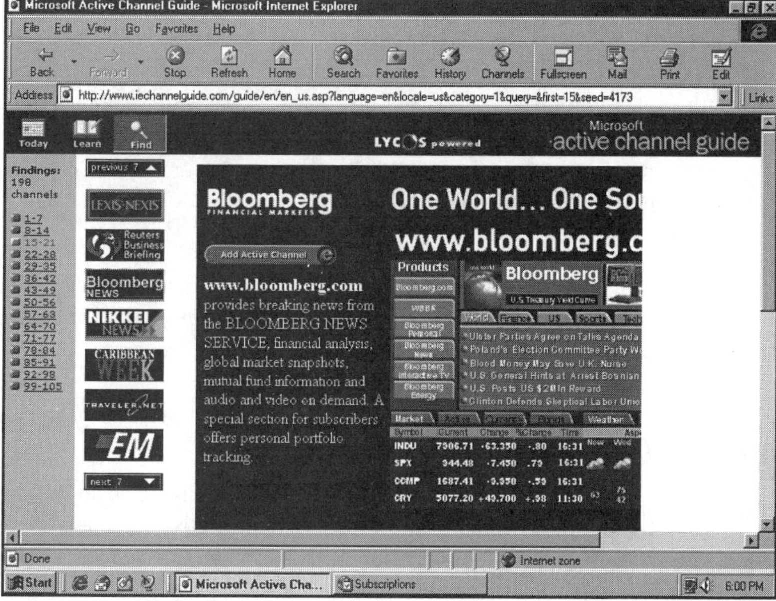

FIG. 21.16
Microsoft maintains this exhaustive list of channels to which you can subscribe.

ON THE WEB

If you inadvertently delete the Channel Guide shortcut from the Channel Bar, don't worry. You'll find the latest list of Active Channels at

http://www.iechannelguide.com

Adding a Channel to the Channel Bar

Most channels include an Add Active Channel button that enables you to add its shortcut to the Channel Bar. When you add a channel to the Channel Bar, you typically have the option to subscribe to the channel, using the publisher's recommended schedule or a custom schedule of your choosing; if there's no Add This Channel button on the preview pane in the Channel Guide, right-click and choose Subscribe from the site icon at left.

Viewing Channels

When you click a shortcut in the Channel Bar on the Windows desktop, Internet Explorer opens in full-screen mode, with the Channel Bar visible along the left side of the browser window.

Although the Channel Bar in the browser window includes the same sites as its desktop counterpart, the two bars behave differently. In the browser's bar, for example, the icon for each channel is black and white until the mouse pointer passes over it. When you click a shortcut, the channel's home page opens in the pane to the right. If the CDF file for that channel includes a site map, clicking the channel button opens the list of available pages.

You can view channels as ordinary web pages, as desktop components, or in full-screen mode. To specify whether IE4 should use full-screen mode for all channels, choose View, Internet Options, click the Advanced tab, and check the option labeled Launch Channels in Full Screen Window.

Some channels include a screen-saver view, as well. You might see this option during the initial Channel setup. To enable, disable, or adjust the Channel screen saver at any time, right-click the desktop, choose Properties, click the Screen Saver tab, and choose the Channel Screen Saver option.

▶ **See** "Having Fun with the Screen Saver," **p. 791**

When you view a channel in full-screen mode, the Channel Bar slides off the screen when you read the page; it reappears when you move the pointer to the left edge of the screen. If you're running at a high screen resolution, use the pushpin icon to lock the Channel Bar in place, as we've done in Figure 21.17.

Browsing Channels Offline

To view channels and other subscriptions without making an active Internet connection, choose File, Work Offline. Like all subscriptions, Active Channels share the Temporary Internet Files with pages you browse interactively. When the cache fills up, IE4 pitches the oldest pages to make way for the newest ones.

▶ **See** "Browsing the Web Offline," **p. 467**

If you encounter frequent error messages when you attempt to update or view subscriptions, you might have used all the available space in your Temporary Internet Files folder. To make room for more content, increase the size of the web cache.

▶ **See** "Managing the Browser's Cache," **p. 452**

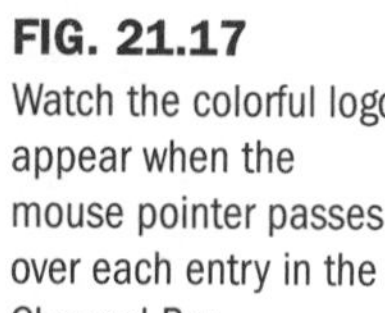

FIG. 21.17
Watch the colorful logo appear when the mouse pointer passes over each entry in the Channel Bar.

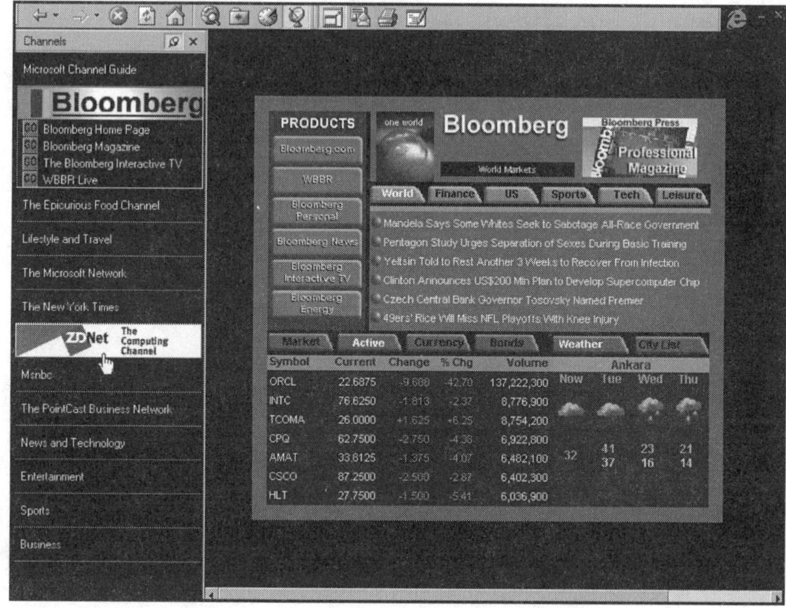

N O T E Don't be surprised when you discover that some channels actually provide only a table of contents and links. Although these sites can give you a good idea of what's available when you go back online, you won't find enough information to justify keeping a subscription to this sort of channel.

Managing the Channel Bar

The Channel Bar appears on the desktop when you install Internet Explorer 4.0. It also appears as an Explorer bar within the browser window when you click the Channels button.

By default, the Channel Bar includes built-in shortcuts to channels delivered by some well-known companies, including Disney, America Online, and MSNBC (see Figure 21.18). There are also shortcuts to categories—news, entertainment, and business, for example—which include shortcuts to additional channels.

Although the Channel Bar initially gets a place of honor on the Windows desktop, it's really just another HTML component on the Active Desktop. That means you can customize its look and feel to suit your computing style. After you've sampled the selection of built-in channels and subscribed to a handful, give your Channel Bar a makeover, as we've done in Figure 21.19. You can customize the Channel Bar by doing the following:

- To move the Channel Bar to a different location on the desktop, click any empty desktop space and let the mouse pointer hover over the top of the bar until the gray sizing handle pops up (see Figure 21.19). Click and drag to a new location.

FIG. 21.18
Out of the box, the Channel Bar includes these preset selections. You can change the collection of shortcuts and rearrange the Channel Bar itself.

- To resize the Channel Bar, aim the mouse pointer at the bar and wait for a thin gray border to appear. Click any border and drag to change the size and orientation. Note that as the size of the bar changes, shortcuts on the bar reorder themselves automatically.
- To add or delete channels from the bar, right-click any channel icon and choose Delete from the shortcut menu.

CAUTION

Be careful before deleting any of the category icons on the Channel Bar. If you've subscribed to a channel within that category, you lose easy access to the channel.

- To rearrange channels on the bar, simply drag them to the location you prefer. Other shortcuts on the bar rearrange themselves automatically.
- To remove the Channel Bar from the desktop, let the mouse pointer hover over the top of the bar until the gray sizing handle pops up. Click the X in the top right corner.

FIG. 21.19
After deleting unnecessary channels and changing its size and orientation, this Channel Bar looks vastly different from its default settings.

The Channel Bar on the desktop is identical to the one that appears in the browser window. When you add or remove channels from one, the other changes accordingly. If you'd rather use the Windows desktop for other items, close the Channel Bar there and use the Channels button on the Internet Explorer toolbar when you want to work with channels.

CHAPTER 22

Using Outlook Express for Email and News

by Ed Bott

In this chapter

Should You Switch to Outlook Express?

Every version of Windows 95 has a desktop icon labeled Inbox. In the original version of Windows 95, this icon launched a program called the Exchange Inbox. Microsoft promised that this "universal inbox" would be capable of storing email from just about anywhere, as well as faxes, voice mail, and other types of data. If you've used Exchange Inbox, though, you know it's hard to configure, slow, and notoriously buggy; the fax components in particular are a usability nightmare.

▶ **See** "Using Microsoft Exchange and Windows Messaging," **p. 667**

▶ **See** "Using Fax, Address Book, and Phone Dialer" **p. 705**

Since the original release of Windows 95, Microsoft has updated the Exchange Inbox program slightly. The new version, which is included with every copy of OSR2, was renamed Windows Messaging. The update fixed several bugs (and added a few new glitches), and the new name was supposed to help dispel confusion with Microsoft Exchange Server, Microsoft's mail server package for businesses.

Although Windows Messaging is right on the Windows desktop, Microsoft no longer recommends that you install it. The program is now officially an "orphan," replaced by the new Windows default mail program, Outlook Express. Microsoft also sells a full-featured mail package called Outlook 97 (an Outlook 98 upgrade is due in mid-1998). If you currently use Exchange Inbox or Windows Messaging, should you switch to Outlook Express? The correct answer depends on how the rest of your mail system works:

- If you have been using Exchange Inbox or Windows Messaging to gather email exclusively through industry-standard Internet mail servers, you should switch to Outlook Express. It's simple to set up and much easier to use, and it does a superb job of handling Internet mail.
- If you send and receive email by using a Microsoft Exchange server on a corporate network, you must use an Exchange-compatible client program. Acceptable options include the Exchange Inbox, Windows Messaging, Outlook 97 (included with Microsoft Office 97), or Outlook 98. In this situation, Outlook Express is an option only if your Exchange Server uses the IMAP format.
- If you use Microsoft Fax or another MAPI-compatible application, it will not work with Outlook Express. (MAPI stands for *messaging application program interface*, a Microsoft standard for communication between email applications. Outlook Express supports only Simple MAPI, which enables programs such as Word and Excel to use Outlook Express for sending messages.) For full MAPI compatibility, you must use an Exchange-compatible mail client.

Starting Outlook Express

When you choose either the Standard or Full installation of Internet Explorer 4.0, you also install Outlook Express—there's no way to avoid adding Outlook Express on initial Setup. You can, however, uninstall the program if you decide you prefer other mail and news clients. (To uninstall Outlook Express, open Control Panel, choose Add/Remove Programs, click the Install/Uninstall tab, choose Microsoft Outlook Express, and click the Add/Remove button.)

To find the shortcut for Outlook Express, click the Start button, choose Programs, and look in the Internet Explorer group. You also can find shortcuts to Outlook Express on the desktop and in the Quick Launch bar.

The first time you run Outlook Express, it prompts you to select a location for storing data files (see Figure 22.1). By default, the program creates Outlook Express and Address Book folders in \Windows\Application Data\Microsoft, with separate Mail and News folders within the Outlook Express folder. If your computer is configured to enable multiple users to log on with their own settings, the default folders appear under \Windows\Profiles*profilename*.

▶ **See** "Changing Custom Settings for Each User," **p. 809**

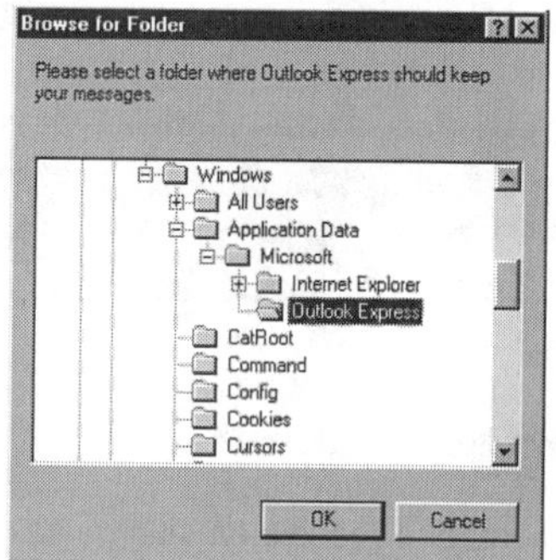

FIG. 22.1
To avoid problems later, accept this default data location when you first set up Outlook Express.

Your best choice is to accept the default location that Outlook Express offers. What if you want to move these data files after setting up Outlook Express for the first time? There's no simple way to accomplish this chore. First you have to use the Windows Explorer to move the data folders and then open the Registry Editor, find HKEY_CURRENT_USER\Software\Microsoft\Outlook Express, double-click the Store Root value, and change that value to reflect the new location.

CAUTION

Think twice before using the Registry Editor, and always make a backup. Incorrectly editing the Windows Registry can result in data loss and cause programs to fail to start and run properly.

After you've configured Outlook Express, running the program takes you to the Start Page (see Figure 22.2), which enables you to move quickly between your Inbox, newsgroups, and your address book.

TIP You can bypass the Outlook Express Start Page and jump straight to your mail. Choose Tools, Options, click the General tab, and check the box labeled "When starting, go directly to my Inbox folder."

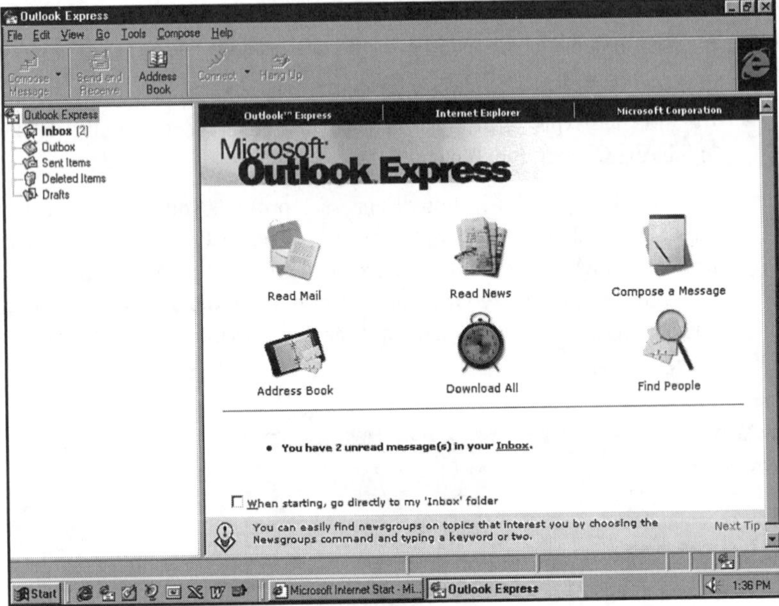

FIG. 22.2
From this Start Page, you can jump to your email inbox, follow threaded discussions on an Internet newsgroup, or search for address information.

Configuring Outlook Express

Before you can use Outlook Express to send and receive email, you must supply some basic configuration information. At a minimum, you have to enter the name and type of the mail server that stores and forwards your messages, along with the username and email address associated with your mail account. Before you can access newsgroups with Outlook Express, you need to enter similar configuration information, including your username and email address, as well as the name of the news server you plan to use.

The Internet Connection Wizard handles all Outlook Express setup details, although you can also configure accounts manually. If you did not use the wizard when you first set up IE4, or if you skipped the mail and news steps, the Internet Connection Wizard will run automatically the first time you use Outlook Express.

If you receive Internet mail from multiple sources—from a corporate server and a personal account with an Internet service provider, for example—you need to establish separate Outlook Express mail accounts for each one. Each news server requires its own news account, as well. There's no limit to the number of mail and news accounts you can set up in Outlook Express.

Setting Up a Default Mail Account

When you first launch Outlook Express, the program prompts you to set up a default mail account by using the Internet Connection Wizard.

Follow the Wizard's prompts to enter the following information:

- *Your name* This is the display name that appears in the From field when you send a message. Most people enter their real name; you might want to add a company affiliation or other information to help mail recipients identify you more readily.
- *Your email address* When recipients reply to messages you send, this is the address their mail software uses.
- *Mail server information* As Figure 22.3 shows, you must fill in addresses for incoming and outgoing mail servers, even if a single server does both jobs. Be sure to specify the mail protocol your incoming server uses: POP3 (the default setting) or IMAP.

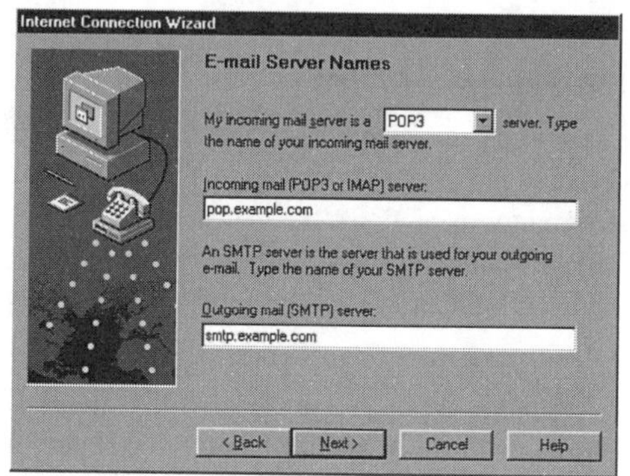

FIG. 22.3 You must enter names for the servers that handle incoming and outgoing mail. In most cases, the same server handles both chores.

NOTE Outlook Express supports three widely used mail standards. The overwhelming majority of Internet service providers transfer email by using servers that run *Simple Mail Transfer Protocol (SMTP).* To download messages from an SMTP server, most mail clients use version 3 of *Post Office Protocol (POP3).* A newer standard, *Internet Message Access Protocol (IMAP),* is less widely used.

- *Logon information* Enter the account name you use to log on to the mail server. If you enter a password in this dialog box, Outlook Express stores the password and uses it each time you check mail; for extra security, leave the password box (shown in Figure 22.4) blank and you will be asked to enter it each time you check for mail. The Secure Password Authentication option is rarely used by Internet service providers; if you receive mail over The Microsoft Network, however, you should check this box.
- *A friendly name for the account* This is the label that appears in the Accounts list.
- *Connection type* Tell Outlook Express whether you access the Internet through a LAN or over a dial-up connection.

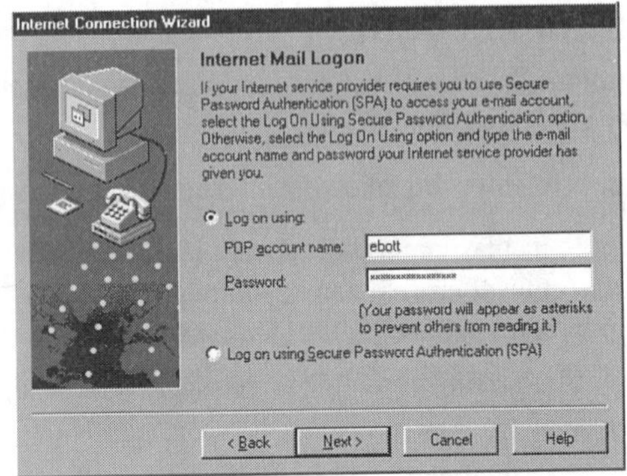

FIG. 22.4 Leave this password box blank if you want to keep other users from accessing your mail. Outlook Express asks for your password each time you connect to the server.

NOTE To configure additional mail accounts, choose Tools, Accounts. Click the Add button, choose Mail, and the relevant portions of the Internet Connection Wizard will run again.

Setting Up One or More News Servers

Outlook Express is more than email; it's also a full-featured news-reading client that enables you to download and read messages from newsgroup servers, post replies, and manage locally stored messages. With a few minor exceptions, the user interface is the same one you see when you send and receive mail, and the program uses the same system services to help you compose and send messages to public or private newsgroups. See "How Newsgroups Work," later in this chapter.

Before you can read newsgroup messages, you must provide Outlook Express with the name of a news server to which you have access. Most Internet service providers offer a news feed to their customers. If your ISP's name is acme.com, for example, you'll probably find a news server at news.acme.com. The Microsoft Network provides newsgroup access on servers at msnnews.msn.com and netnews.msn.com. Microsoft's public newsgroups are available from msnews.microsoft.com. If you have access to a private news server, it might require that you log on with an account name and password.

ON THE WEB

If your ISP or corporate site does not maintain a news feed, try connecting to a public-access news server. You get what you pay for, of course; most sites are slow and unreliable for serious news access. You'll find a well-maintained list of public news servers at these addresses:

http://www.findit.mcmail.com/public.htm

http://www.jammed.com/~newzbot/sorted-group.html

http://www.geocities.com/SiliconValley/Pines/3959/usenet.html

http://www.jammed.com/~newzbot/sorted-group.html

As with mail accounts, setting up a news account with the Internet Connection Wizard is a simple fill-in-the-blanks process. The wizard appears the first time you click the Read News icon on the Outlook Express Start Page, or when you choose Tools, Accounts, click the Add button, and choose Mail.

You have to enter a name and email address for each news account. Enter the name of your news server when prompted (see Figure 22.5), and check the option at the bottom of this dialog box if the server requires you to log on with a username and password.

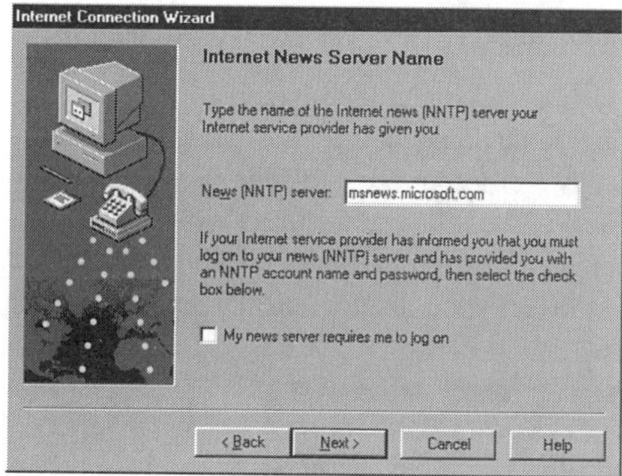

FIG. 22.5
You must supply the name of a news server before accessing newsgroups with Outlook Express.

Give the account a friendly name to help identify it in the account list. The default entry is the server name, but a descriptive name such as "Microsoft public newsgroups" is easier to understand than msnews.microsoft.com.

You don't have to be truthful when entering your name and email address. In fact, some experienced newsgroup participants never use their real address when posting, because it's too easy for unscrupulous marketers to skim addresses from newsgroup participants and target them for unsolicited email, or Spam.

Managing Mail for More Than One User

On many Windows 95 computers, one user will gather mail from one or two Internet mail accounts. But Outlook Express enables you to manage mail in more complex environments, with multiple users of the same computer by using the mail software to access separate mail accounts.

Before multiple users can store messages in separate mailboxes, you must open the Users option in Control Panel and enable multi-user settings. Each user who logs on to Windows with a separate username and password creates separate data files for addresses and messages when they use Outlook Express.

Adjusting Properties for an Existing Mail or News Account

To change the settings for a mail or news account after you've set it up by using the Internet Connection Wizard, click Tools, Accounts, select the entry you want to change, and click the Properties button. With minor exceptions, the options for mail and news accounts are identical.

The first account you create in the mail and news group becomes the default account for that category. That's an important distinction, because it determines which information appears on screen when you click the Read Mail or Read News icon on the Start Page, and it defines which SMTP server Outlook Express uses when sending messages. To change default mail or news accounts, select the account and click the Set as Default button.

For both types of accounts, use the General tab (see Figure 22.6) to change the friendly name for the account or to edit personal information. This dialog box enables you to add the name of your organization and specify a different reply-to address. For example, if you send a message by using your corporate mail account but prefer to receive replies via your personal Internet mail account, enter the personal address in the Reply address box; when recipients reply to your message, their mail software should automatically insert the preferred reply-to address.

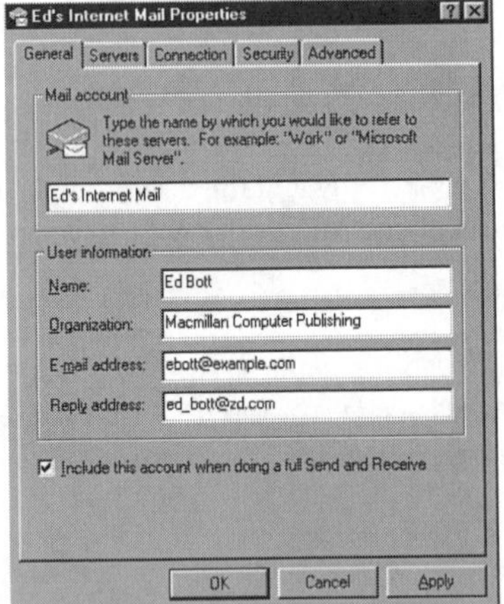

FIG. 22.6
Edit the reply-to address for a mail or news account if you want to receive replies at an address other than the one from which you send messages.

The Server tab enables you to change the name or logon settings for mail and news servers. The Advanced tab enables you to adjust timeout settings (sometimes necessary over very slow connections) and break apart lengthy messages (required by some mail servers running older software). Do not adjust these settings unless specifically instructed to do so by the server's administrator.

Selecting Connection Options

For each Outlook Express mail and news account, you can specify how you prefer to connect to the Internet—over a LAN, manually, or by using a modem. If your computer is permanently connected to a network with Internet access, you can set all your accounts for LAN access and be done with it. But on machines with dial-up Internet access, particularly notebook computers, you should pay close attention to these settings.

Each time you create a new account, you have a chance to specify connection properties. To adjust these settings after you've created an account, choose Tools, Accounts, select the account name, click Properties, and click the Connection tab. You'll see a dialog box like the one in Figure 22.7.

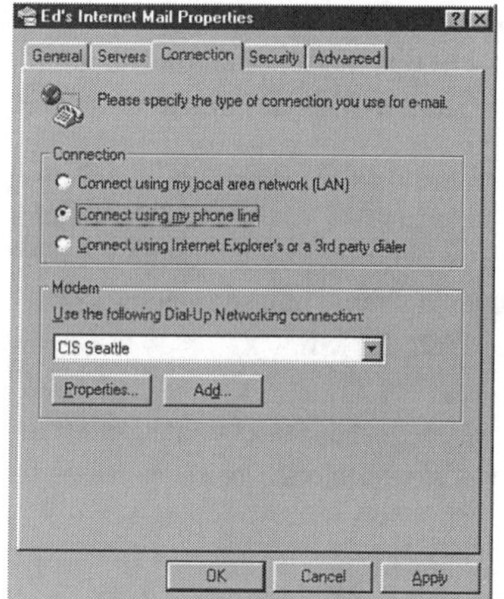

FIG. 22.7
The choice shown in this dialog box enables Outlook Express to dial your Internet service provider automatically every time you access a mail server.

The following explains the difference between the three connection options:

- *Connect using my local area network (LAN)* The LAN option assumes you have a full-time connection to the Internet through a local area network. Unless you choose to work offline, Outlook Express checks for mail every 30 minutes. To change the interval for checking mail, choose Tools, Options, click the General tab, and use the spinner control.
- *Connect using my phone line* Choose a Dial-Up Networking connection from the list at the bottom of this dialog box, or click the Add button to create a new one; Outlook Express dials this connection whenever you attempt to access a mail or news server. Use this option if you do not use the IE4 dialer (for example, if you access the web through a proxy server) but you must use a dial-up connection for email.
- *Connect using Internet Explorer's or a 3rd party dialer* Outlook Express uses the connection settings you specify for your web browser. This is your best choice if you use the same phone line for voice calls and Internet access because Internet Explorer and Outlook Express can share the same connection.

Notebook users might want to create multiple copies of mail and news accounts, each with a different connection type, to handle different working environments. For example, you would specify a LAN connection when you're connected to the office network but use the IE4 dialer to make a manual connection when you're working in a hotel room.

Choosing HTML or Plain Text as Your Message Format

Each time you compose a message by using Outlook Express, you choose whether to use plain text only or to add graphics, colors, and rich text formatting by using HTML. If most of your messages go to users of Outlook Express or other HTML-compatible mail programs, rich text formatting can make your messages livelier and more readable. With HTML formatting, your messages look and behave like web pages; you can specify fonts and their sizes, change text colors, use paragraph styles, and control text alignment. You can add background colors and graphics, bulleted and numbered lists, and hypertext links to other web pages.

All that fancy formatting is lost, though, if your correspondents use email software that can't interpret HTML. They see a plain text version of your message, along with a file attachment that they can open in a web browser. In fact, there's a good chance they will be annoyed to receive HTML messages, because even a simple one-sentence message typically occupies 1KB or more of disk space when translated into HTML.

NOTE Users of Netscape mail products can send and receive HTML-formatted mail as well, although you might notice minor differences in the look of messages sent between Netscape and Microsoft clients. ■

Outlook Express enables you to set separate default formats for mail and news messages, and it enables you to override those settings on individual messages. Unless you're certain that the overwhelming majority of your email recipients can handle HTML attachments, your best bet is to choose plain text for mail messages. Likewise, on newsgroups where people use a variety of news reader clients, it's good manners to specify plain text as your default format.

To adjust the default settings, follow this procedure:

1. Choose Tools, Options, and click the Send tab. You see the dialog box shown in Figure 22.8.

FIG. 22.8
Using these default settings, all your mail messages go out in HTML format, with plain text the preferred format for news messages.

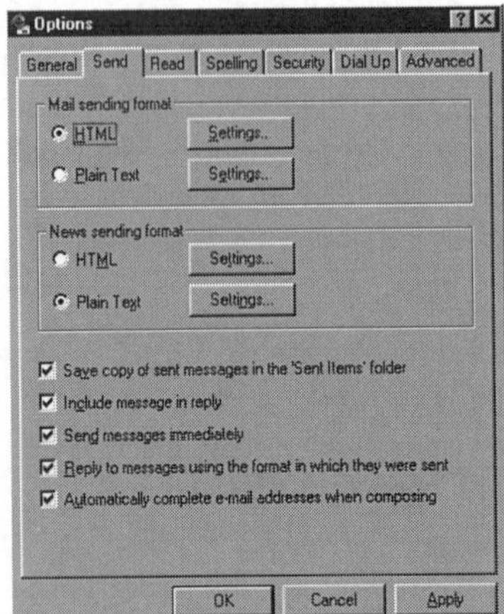

2. In the box labeled Mail sending format, select HTML or Plain Text as the default format for mail messages.
3. In the box labeled News sending format, select HTML or Plain Text as the default format for messages you post to newsgroups.
4. After you specify a format, the Settings button enables you to specify additional formatting options. These additional choices are shown in Figure 22.9.

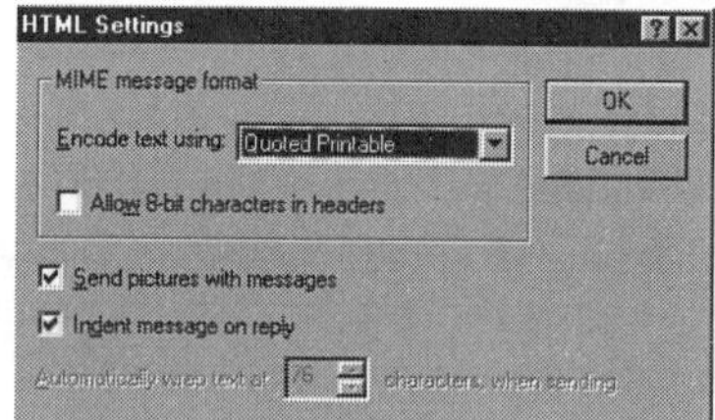

FIG. 22.9
If recipients complain about stray characters (especially equals signs) in text messages, try changing text encoding from Quoted Printable to None.

TROUBLESHOOTING

Some recipients complain that all the paragraphs appear as a single long line or that the messages are filled with equals signs. Mail format options control how Outlook Express encodes your messages by using Multi-Purpose Internet Mail Extensions, (MIME). Quoted-Printable MIME replaces line endings and special characters (such as accented vowels) with an equals sign and an optional numeric code. This technique enables you to send some formatting information by using ASCII characters. Your recipients are seeing this encoding through a mail reader that isn't fully compliant with the MIME standard. If they're unwilling to switch to another mail client, choose Tools, Options, click the Send tab, and click the Settings button to the right of the mail format you've chosen. Change the text encoding option to None and the problem should disappear; unfortunately, you also lose the ability to use extended ASCII characters. To read more about options for composing individual messages, see "Composing a New Message," later in this chapter.

Exchanging Data with Other Mail Programs

If you currently use another email package and plan to switch to Outlook Express, the process is simple and straightforward. Outlook Express can import address books and archived messages from the following popular mail clients:

- Eudora Pro or Eudora Light (version 3.0 or earlier)
- Netscape Mail (versions 2 or 3)
- Netscape Communicator
- Microsoft Internet Mail

- Microsoft Exchange Inbox
- Windows Messaging

In addition, you can import messages from Microsoft Outlook 97 or Outlook 98. (See the following section for detailed instructions on how to transfer address information from Outlook 97 to Outlook Express.)

Migrating from Exchange or Outlook 97

Do you currently use the Exchange Inbox email program that Microsoft introduced with Windows 95? In versions of Windows 95 sold after late 1996, this program might go by the name Windows Messaging. Outlook 97 and Outlook 98 both use the Windows Messaging system services and the same format for messages and Personal Address Books. If you use any of these programs, Outlook Express will offer to convert your messages and addresses the first time you run the program, as shown in Figure 22.10.

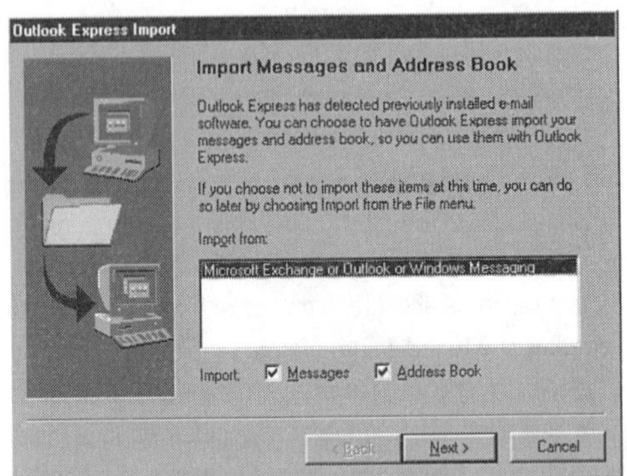

FIG. 22.10
Switching from the older Exchange Inbox to Outlook Express can be as easy as clicking OK in this dialog box.

Converting data from most mail programs is a simple process, but there's one notable exception: To transfer your Contacts folder from Outlook 97 to the Windows Address Book in Outlook Express, you need to go through a cumbersome two-step conversion process. The first step is to export the Contacts information into an Exchange-compatible Personal Address Book (PAB); then you can import the PAB into Outlook Express. Follow these steps:

1. Open Outlook 97, choose File, Import and Export, and select Export to a file. Click the Next button.
2. Following the wizard's prompts, select the Contacts folder, click Next, and choose Personal Address Book from the list of export formats. Click Next again.
3. When you click Finish, Outlook 97 copies the information to the Personal Address Book in your current profile.

4. Next, open Outlook Express, choose File, Import, Address Book, and select Microsoft Exchange Personal Address Book from the list of available formats. (This choice is available only if you have Windows Messaging or Outlook 97 installed and you have created a Personal Address Book.)
5. Click the Import button to finish the process. Your collection of email addresses and other contact information will appear in the Windows Address Book.

Restoring Outlook Express as the Default Mail Client

Note that you can set up more than one mail program on a system running Windows 95. When you install another mail program, however, it might take over as the default email program that starts when you click the Mail icon on IE4's Standard toolbar or click a mailto: hyperlink on a web page. To restore Outlook Express as the default mail client, follow this procedure:

1. Start Outlook Express, choose Tools, Options, and click the General tab.
2. Check the option labeled Make Outlook Express my default e-mail program.
3. When you check that box, the grayed-out option below it becomes available. Check Make Outlook Express my default Simple MAPI client if you want Outlook Express to start up when you choose File, Send from an application's menu. This option prevents Windows Messaging or Outlook 97 from performing this function.

Importing Data from Another Mail Program

When you choose File, Import, Outlook Express offers a cascading menu with three additional choices. The Address Book and Messages options are self-explanatory; the third choice, Mail Account Settings, enables you to reuse the information (server and logon names, for example) that you've entered for one mail account when setting up another. When importing messages or addresses, Outlook Express first asks you to specify the mail program, and then checks data-file locations specified for that program in the Registry. If Outlook Express can't find the program on your system, you see a dialog box that enables you to specify the location.

Each import option steps you through a series of dialog boxes, with slightly different choices that depend on the mail program or data type you start with. If you choose to import data from a text file with comma-separated data, for example, you have to specify which Outlook Express fields should receive each column of data in your text file. As Figure 22.11 shows, Outlook Express makes a reasonable guess at mapping fields in your text file to those in your Address Book. You can manually adjust the relationship between fields; check the box to the left of each field to include or remove it from the import operation. Click the Change Mapping button to see a drop-down list of available Outlook Express fields.

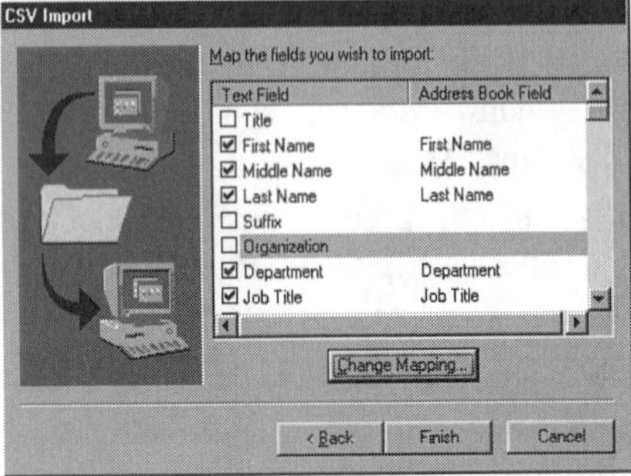

FIG. 22.11
Outlook Express doesn't recognize the Organization label in this text file; click the Change Mapping button to tell the program that its data belongs in the Company field.

You can use the Import choices to bring in messages or addresses even if there's already data in your Address Book or message store. When the program detects that a record you're trying to import already exists in your Address Book, you see a dialog box like the one in Figure 22.12, at which point you can choose whether to keep the existing entry or replace it with the new data.

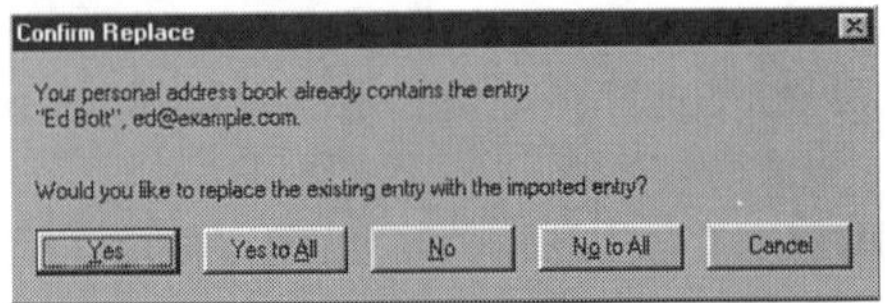

FIG. 22.12
Click Yes to All to completely replace matching records in your Address Book with new data from an import file.

Exporting Data to Another Program

Unfortunately, Outlook Express isn't nearly as cooperative when it comes to moving messages and address information back to competing mail programs. When you choose File, Export from the Outlook Express menu, you can easily move information into Outlook 97 or Microsoft Exchange. To transfer addresses into other programs, you first have to convert the information into a text file with comma-separated values and then find the corresponding import feature in the destination program. There's no easy way to move messages from Outlook Express into another mail client.

Reading Messages in Outlook Express

When you first click the Read Mail or Read News icon on the Outlook Express main screen, you see a display much like the one in Figure 22.13.

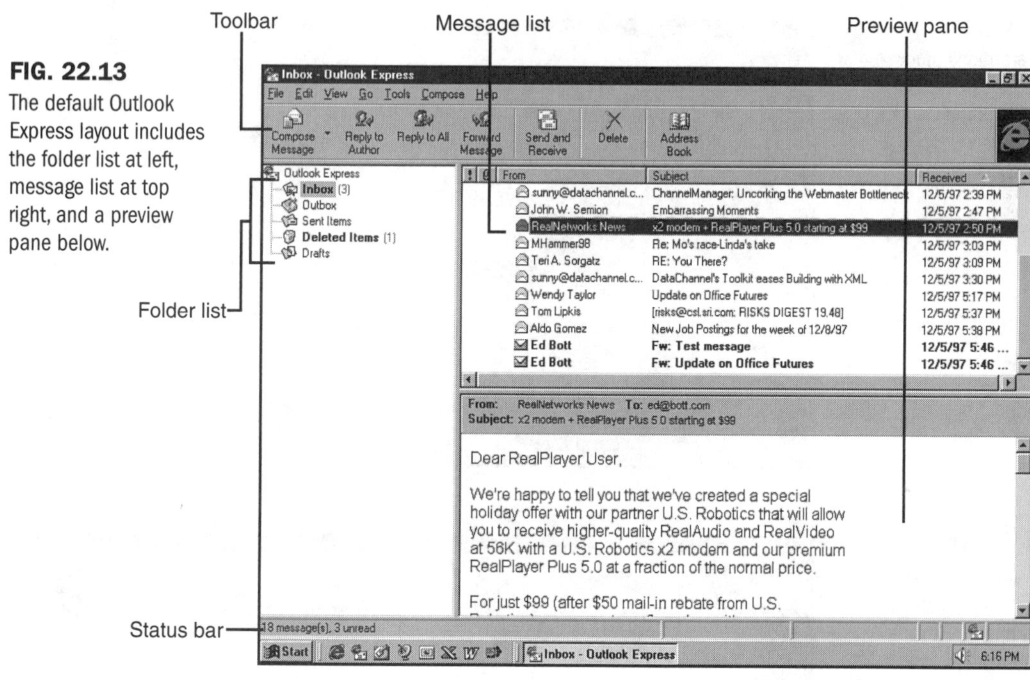

FIG. 22.13
The default Outlook Express layout includes the folder list at left, message list at top right, and a preview pane below.

The folder list at the left of the screen includes the default mail folders, any additional folders you've created, all news servers you've set up, and any newsgroups to which you've subscribed. The right side of the screen includes the column-oriented message list, which shows the contents of the currently selected folder or server. Below is a preview pane that shows the contents of the currently selected message. There's a customizable toolbar at the top and a status bar at the bottom of the window.

Two optional parts of the Outlook Express screen—the Outlook Bar and the folder bar—are hidden by default. The message list is always visible; there's no way to make it disappear. Using a few menu choices, and check boxes, though, you can show, hide, and rearrange virtually every other aspect of the Outlook Express interface.

Changing the Layout

To alter the basic look of Outlook Express, choose View, Layout. You see a dialog box like the one in Figure 22.14.

These settings rearrange the Outlook Express interface so that it closely resembles the Outlook 97 interface, as shown in Figure 22.15. The Outlook Bar at left shows all the default folders plus any top-level folders you've created; it doesn't include icons for subfolders you create. The Outlook Bar also includes icons for news servers and subscribed newsgroups. Just above the message list is the drop-down folder bar, which shows all folders in an Explorer-style hierarchy.

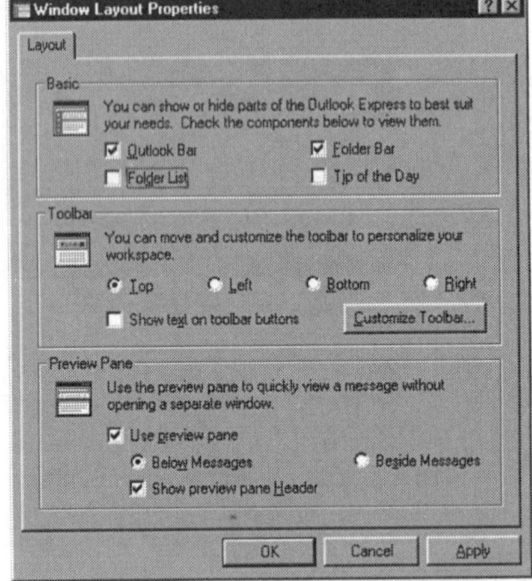

FIG. 22.14
These options produce a layout that closely resembles the Outlook 97 interface.

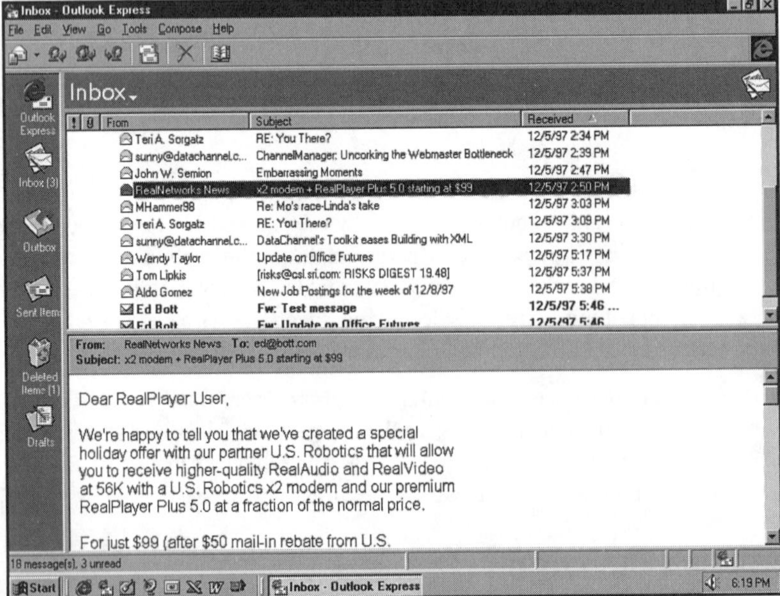

FIG. 22.15
The Outlook Bar at left resembles the one in Outlook 97, with one difference—you can't change the order of icons.

Using the Preview Pane

As you move between messages in the message list, the contents of the currently selected message appear in the preview pane. Use the layout options to change the appearance and behavior of this pane:

- To toggle the preview pane on and off, choose View, Layout and click the Use preview pane check box.

- To move the preview pane, choose the Below Messages or Beside Messages option.
- To show or hide the address and subject line in the preview pane, check the box labeled Show preview pane Header.
- To change the size of the preview pane, point to the bar between the message list and the preview pane until it turns to a double-headed arrow, and then click and drag.

Each entry in the message list appears first in bold to indicate you haven't yet read it. The unread status changes when you open the message or allow it to appear in the preview pane for more than a few seconds. To filter the message list so it shows only those messages you haven't yet read, choose View, Current View, Unread Messages.

Navigating Through Folders

After you move past the Start Page, the Outlook Express message list always shows the contents of the currently selected folder, newsgroup, or news server. To move from folder to folder, use one of these three navigational tools:

- Click any icon in the folder list to switch to the contents of the message list.
- If the folder bar is visible, the name of the currently selected folder, server, or newsgroup appears just above the message list. Click that folder name to unfurl a drop-down folder list. The down arrow to the right of the name provides a visual clue; after you make your selection, the list snaps out of the way again.
- Click any icon in the Outlook Bar to show the messages stored in that folder.

To view or adjust the properties of any icon, right-click the icon and choose from the shortcut menu.

Use one of three Internet links at the top of the Outlook Express Start Page to launch Internet Explorer, jump to Microsoft's home page, or navigate to the Outlook Express start page on the web. The icon for the Outlook Express Start Page is always available at the top of the folder list, folder bar, or Outlook Bar.

Sorting the Message List

To sort the contents of the message list, click any column heading. Choose View, Columns to add or remove columns and change the order of those that are displayed. (Note that different types of objects provide different choices of columns.) Click the border between two column headings and drag to adjust column widths.

To group mail or newsgroup messages by using threads, choose View, Sort By, and toggle the Group Messages by Thread setting.

Opening Individual Messages

Double-click any item in the message list to open it in its own window, as shown in Figure 22.16.

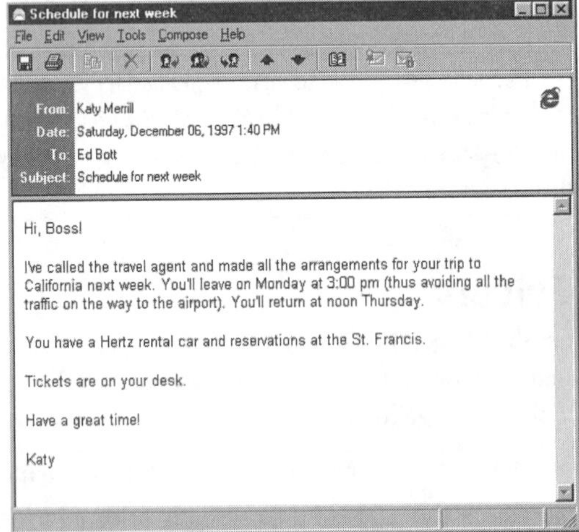

FIG. 22.16 This full message window offers more space than the preview pane. Maximize the window and use the up or down arrows to navigate without the message list.

Icons on the message window toolbar enable you to save, print, or delete the current message.

It's possible to navigate through your entire message list without switching back and forth between the message list and the message window:

1. Open any message in its own window. Maximize the window if you want to see as much of the message as possible without having to use the scroll bars.
2. To move to the next message in the list, click the up arrow on the toolbar. Click the down arrow to move back to the previous message
3. To move to the next unread message in the list, press Ctrl+U.
4. In threaded message lists, such as those found in newsgroups, press Ctrl+Shift+U to move to the next unread thread.
5. To move or copy a message to a folder, choose File, Move To Folder or File, Copy to Folder. To delete a message, click the delete button on the toolbar.

Changing the Way Plain Text Messages Look

When you receive an HTML-formatted message, the formatting codes in the message itself control how it looks in the preview pane and in individual message windows. If the message doesn't specify font information, Outlook Express uses default fonts and sizes to control the display of proportional fonts (used for general text) and fixed fonts (used for tabular material that must line up precisely).

When you receive a plain-text message, Outlook Express displays it by using the default proportional font and the default font size. On most systems, that means plain-text messages appear in Arial, using the Medium size setting (12 point). Follow these steps to change the font and size to improve readability or to see more text in a message window.

1. Open any plain-text message and choose View, Fonts. Select the size you prefer from the five available choices. Note the size and close the message window.
2. From the main Outlook Express window, choose Tools, Options.
3. Click the Read tab, and then click the Fonts button in the box labeled Font Settings
4. To change fonts, use the drop-down list labeled to Proportional font. (Adjusting the Fixed-width font setting affects only HTML-formatted messages.)
5. To change to the default font size you noted earlier, use the drop-down list labeled Font size.
6. Click OK to save your changes. You might need to close and restart Outlook Express to see the font changes in both the preview pane and individual message windows.

Customizing the Outlook Express Toolbar

To change the look of the Outlook Express toolbar, choose View, Layout; use the check boxes to move the toolbar to either side or to the bottom of the window. Hide the text labels to dramatically reduce the amount of space the toolbar takes up. To add, remove, and rearrange buttons, click the Customize Toolbar button; you can also open this dialog box, shown in Figure 22.17, by right-clicking the toolbar and choosing Buttons from the shortcut menu.

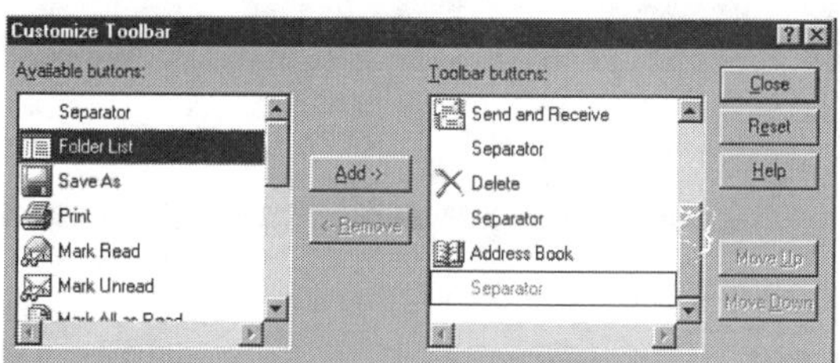

FIG. 22.17
Use the Add and Remove buttons to rearrange the toolbars for mail and news windows.

Note that there are separate toolbars for mail and news windows, so you have to customize them individually. You can't customize toolbars used in Outlook Express message windows or those in the Windows Address Book.

TIP If you use the folder list regularly but don't want to sacrifice the screen real estate it demands, add the Folder List button to your toolbar. It acts as a toggle, revealing or hiding the folder list so you can have more room for the message list and preview pane and still navigate between folders without having to wade through pull-down menus.

Using the Windows Address Book

Outlook Express organizes email addresses by using a module called the Windows Address Book. Each contact record includes fields that enable you to track additional details about a person, including home and business addresses and phone numbers. The Windows Address Book also enables you to create group records so you can send email to several individuals by entering an alias instead of a lengthy list of addresses.

Address-book information is stored in a single file with the .wab extension. Each user profile on a machine can contain its own Address Book file, but there is no way to maintain multiple address books within a single profile.

NOTE Although the Windows Address Book appears to be an integrated part of Outlook Express, it's actually a separate application called Wab.exe. If you use the Address Book frequently, you might want to create a shortcut to this program and place it on the Start menu or the Windows desktop. ■

To open the Windows Address Book, click the Address Book icon on the Outlook Express toolbar. As in an Explorer window, you can choose one of four different views for the contents of the Address Book. In the default Details view (see Figure 22.18), click a column heading to sort the records by the values in that field—click again to sort in reverse order.

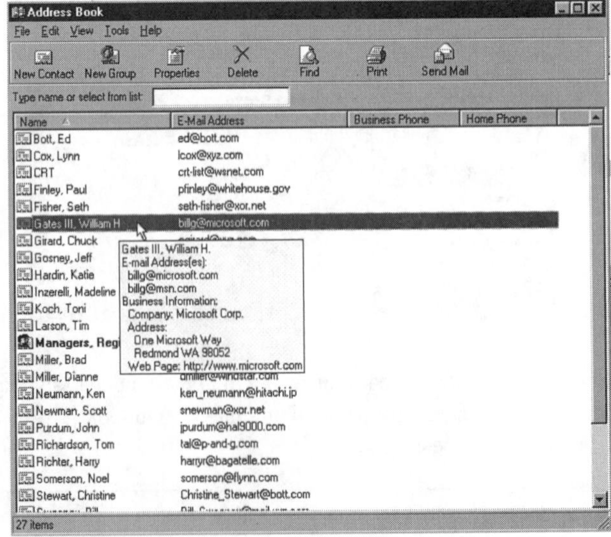

FIG. 22.18 As the mouse passes over each Address Book entry, a ScreenTip displays the contents of that record.

- To open an individual record, double-click the item or select it and click the Properties button.
- To delete a record, select it and click the Delete button.

- To copy the text from a contact record to the Windows Clipboard, right-click the item and choose Copy from the shortcut menu.
- To begin composing a message to a recipient whose email address is in your Windows Address Book, select the person's record and click the Send Mail button.

Creating and Editing Address Book Entries

To create a new record from scratch, click the New Contact button and begin filling in fields on the Personal tab. As Figure 22.19 shows, you can enter more than one email address for a contact. Choose one address and click the Set as Default button to tell Outlook Express to use that email address when you click the Send Mail button.

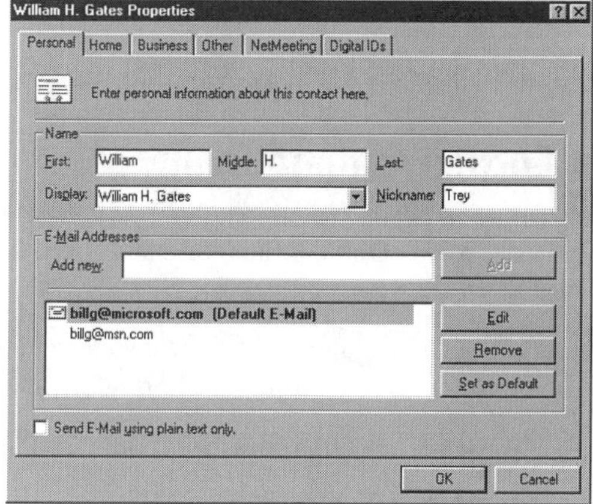

FIG. 22.19
You can enter multiple email addresses in a contact record—personal and business addresses, for example.

Note as you enter information in the First, Middle, and Last fields that the value in the Display field automatically fills in as well. This field is what you see under the Name heading when you look at the Address list. The drop-down Display list enables you to choose from several defaults, but you can enter anything you like here, including a descriptive name like "Caterer," "Travel agent," or "Boss."

Creating Mailing Groups

A mailing group (also known as an alias) enables you to send messages to multiple people without having to enter each name in the message. When you enter the name of a mailing group in the address box of a message, Outlook Express substitutes the names that make up that group before sending the message. To create a mailing group, follow these steps:

1. Click the New Group button.
2. Enter a name for the mailing group in the Group Name box. The name may be up to 255 characters long, and may contain spaces and special characters.
3. Click the Select Members button. A dialog box containing names from your Address Book appears.

4. Click a name in the list and then click the Select button to add that person's entry to the list. Continue adding names individually, or hold down the Ctrl key to select more than one name at a time. Use the New Contact button to add an entry to the list.
5. When you've finished adding names to the group, click OK.
6. Add notes about this group in the field at the bottom of the Group Properties dialog box, if you want, and then click OK.

A mailing group can contain group entries, as well as individual names. You can use this feature to avoid updating multiple groups. For example, you might create separate mailing groups for each department in your company: Accounting, Sales, Marketing, and so on. Then create an All Employees list consisting of each of the department lists. When a new employee joins the company, update the department list and the master list will automatically update as well.

To see all the groups in your Address Book, choose View, Groups List.

Adding Address Book Entries Automatically

The easiest way to create contact records in your Windows Address Book is to copy email addresses from messages you receive. Outlook Express enables you to add contact records one at a time or automatically.

For one-at-a-time addressing, open a message, right-click any name in the From, To, or CC fields, and then choose Add to Address Book from the shortcut menu, as shown in Figure 22.20.

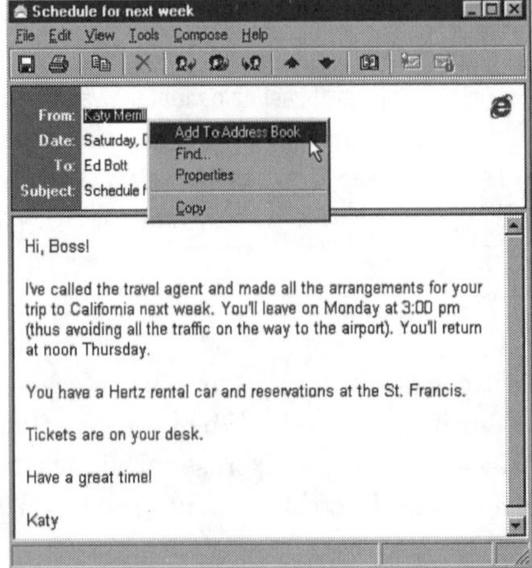

FIG. 22.20
Right-click any address and use the shortcut menu to add the name and address to your Windows Address Book.

You can automatically create a new entry in your Windows Address Book whenever you reply to a message. Choose Tools, Options, click the General tab, and check the box labeled "Automatically put people I reply to in my Address Book."

Finding People by Using Public Directories

What's the best way to find someone's email address? Copying it from an email or a business card is still the surest way to be certain your message will reach its destination. But the next best technique is to use a public directory server. When you click the Find button on the Windows Address Book toolbar, you see a dialog box like the one in Figure 22.21.

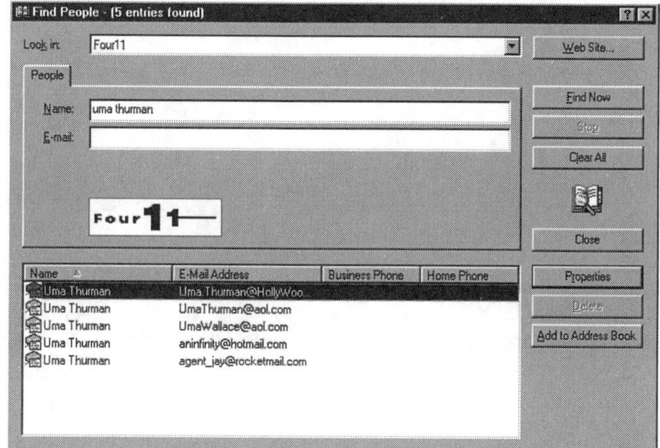

FIG. 22.21
Use a public directory server to track down email addresses and add them to your address book.

Outlook Express gives you a choice of several public servers that use the Lightweight Directory Access Protocol (LDAP), an Internet standard for exchanging directory information. Select a server in the Look in box, and then click the Name box and enter all or part of the name for which you're searching. Click Find Now to begin the search.

ON THE WEB

For more information about how LDAP works, check this web site, managed by the university that invented the protocol:

http://www.umich.edu/~dirsvcs/ldap/index.html

Matching records appear in a list at the bottom of the Find People dialog box. Select a name and click the Properties button to view more information about that directory entry. Right-click and choose Send Mail to begin composing a message to that person. Click Add to Address Book to save the contact's name and address in your Windows Address Book.

Composing a New Message

To begin a new mail or news message from scratch, click the New Message button or press Ctrl+N. You see a blank New Message window like the one in Figure 22.22.

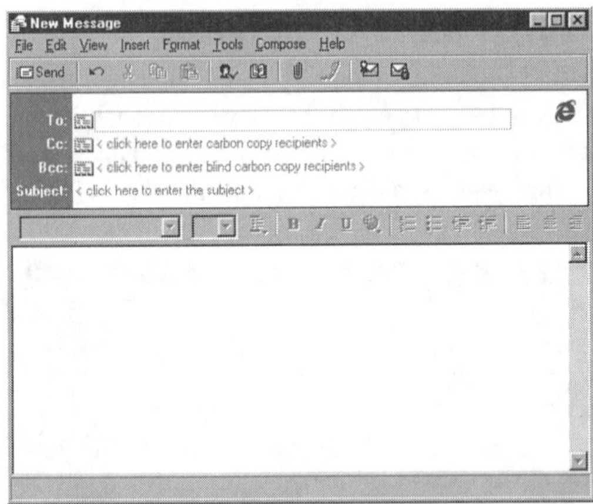

FIG. 22.22
Follow these prompts to begin addressing and composing a message.

Addressing a Mail Message

Although you can simply begin typing your message within the New Message window, it's easier to start by filling out the address box. Enter the main recipient(s) for the message on the To: line, and then use the Tab key to move to the Cc:, Bcc:, and Subject lines before tabbing into the body of the message.

Click the small address-card icon at the beginning of any line in the address box to open a special window on your Windows Address Book. This Select Recipients dialog box, shown in Figure 22.23, enables you to pick names from a list and add them to the address box.

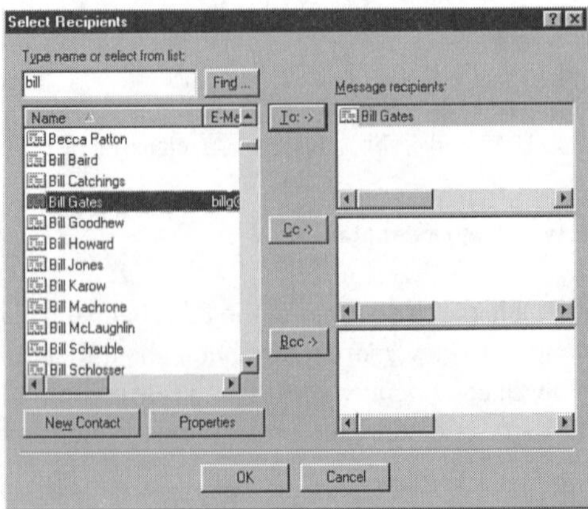

FIG. 22.23
Click the small index-card icon at the beginning of any address line to open this view of the Windows Address Book.

Use other buttons in this dialog box to create a new contact and add it to the list, to see more details about an address-book entry or to find an address on a public directory server. To clear a name from any of the three message recipient boxes, select the name, right-click, and choose Remove from the shortcut menu. When you've finished adding recipients, click OK to return to the New Message window.

Checking a Recipient's Address

You don't need to use the Windows Address Book to add recipients. Simply type one or more valid email addresses and continue—be sure to separate address entries with a semicolon or comma.

If you know a name is in your address book, enter a few characters from the first or last name. Outlook Express fills in matching names as you type; this AutoComplete feature works almost exactly like its equivalent in Internet Explorer. When the correct name appears in the address box, press Enter to add the address and a semicolon, with the insertion point positioned for you to add another address. Press Tab to move to the next address field.

CAUTION

Check the contents of the address box carefully before sending a message. If you type even a single incorrect character here, the AutoComplete feature might insert the wrong address, and you might wind up sending a sensitive or personal message to someone other than the recipient you intended.

If you don't like this AutoComplete feature, turn it off. Choose Tools, Options, click the Send tab, and uncheck the box labeled Automatically complete email addresses when composing. Even with this feature disabled, you can still enlist the help of the Address Book in completing addresses; just type a few characters from the first or last name, and then click the Check Names button (see Figure 22.24). If only one address-book entry matches the characters you typed, that entry will appear in your address box; if there's more than one match, you have to pick the correct address from a dialog box. After Outlook Express has verified that the address is valid, it adds a link to that address entry; you know the process was successful when you see the underline beneath each address entry.

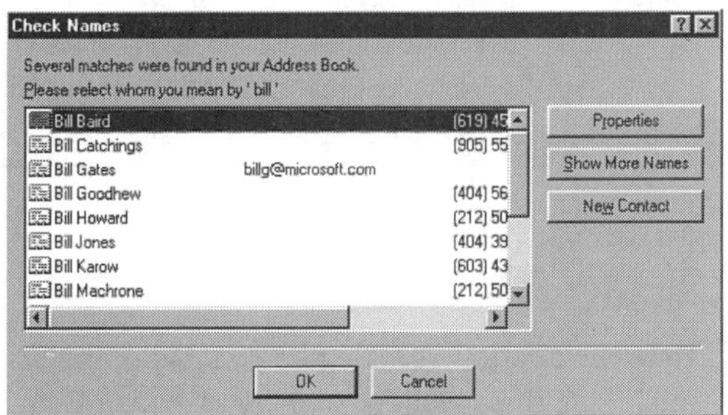

FIG. 22.24
The Check Names button returns address records that contain the characters you typed in any position.

Composing the Message

If you've chosen HTML format for your message, the formatting toolbar appears just above the box in which you enter the message text. Use the toolbar buttons to change font and paragraph formatting, colors, and alignment. The three rightmost buttons, shown in Figure 22.25, insert a rule, a hyperlink, or a graphic image.

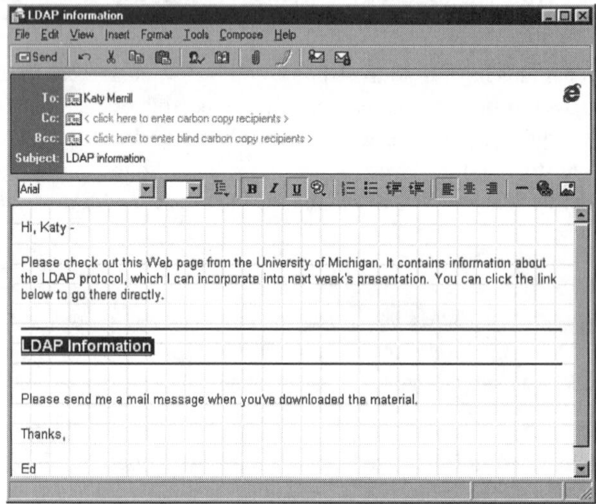

FIG. 22.25
Use these formatting buttons to control the look of an HTML message. Buttons at the far right enable you to insert this rule and hyperlink.

The New Message window includes most of the features you expect from a formatting editor, including the capability to specify fonts, colors, and alignment; there's even a multi-level undo (press Ctrl+Z to roll back changes you've made or text you've typed).

TROUBLESHOOTING

You tried to check the spelling of your message, but the Tools, Spelling, command was grayed out and unavailable. Outlook Express does not include its own spell-checking module; instead, it "borrows" the spell checker from other Microsoft applications, such as Word and Works. You must install one of these applications before you can check the spelling of an Outlook Express message.

To create a hyperlink in a message, follow these steps:

1. Select any piece of text or a graphic image.
2. Click the Insert Hyperlink button. A dialog box enables you to choose from an assortment of formats, including the default http:// for web pages, ftp:// for file locations, and mailto:// for mail links.
3. Type the URL and click OK to assign the link to the object you selected. Notice that the hyperlink appears underlined in your message.

Changing Message Formats

To change the format of a message from HTML to plain text and vice versa, choose the appropriate entry from the Format menu. You can use the General tab of a contact record to specify that an addressee always receive messages in plain text. By default, when you respond to a message, Outlook Express uses the same format as the original. When you reply to an HTML-formatted mail message, your reply uses the same format unless you specifically tell Outlook Express not to do so.

Giving Messages a Consistent Look

When you create a message from scratch, you start with a blank slate. They also lack basic information that you take for granted when you print correspondence on letterhead, such as your name, company name and logo, your job title, and your phone number. Outlook Express offers two features that help you apply a consistent look to your messages and supply some of this missing information.

With HTML-formatted messages, use templates called *stationery* to add background graphics, fonts, paragraph formatting, and other standard elements to mail and news messages. Use *signatures* with all kinds of messages, including text messages, to add standard information at the end of every message you create.

Using Signatures For daily use, especially in a business setting, creating a standard signature makes sure important information goes out with every message you send. A signature might include your name, return email address, company affiliation, and telephone number. At some companies, employees routinely add a disclaimer stating that the views expressed in email messages are personal opinions and do not represent the company.

To set up a personal signature, choose Tools, Stationery, click the Mail or News tab, and click the Signature button. You can compose a simple text signature, like the one in Figure 22.26. You can store your signature in a text file if you prefer, or use FrontPage Express to add graphics and formatting codes, and then store the result in an HTML file. To use a file as your signature, choose the File option and specify its location.

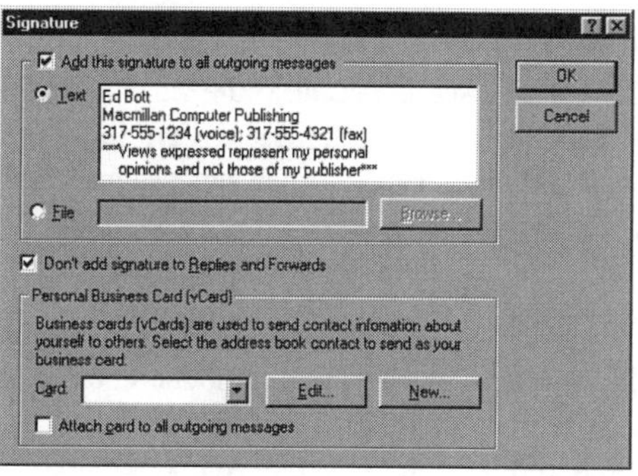

FIG. 22.26 Netiquette dictates that signatures should be short and to the point. At five lines, this signature is long enough.

Check boxes on the Signature dialog box enable you to specify whether you want Outlook Express to automatically add the signature to every message you create. There's also an option to skip signatures on replies and forwarded messages. Leave both check boxes blank if you prefer to add a signature only to selected messages.

To add a signature to a message while composing it, choose Insert, Signature.

Applying a Look with Stationery Outlook Express includes a collection of HTML templates called stationery. These starter documents typically incorporate background graphics, standard fonts, and a few styles. To see and use the sample stationery, choose Compose, New Message using, and then select an entry from the cascading menu.

Most of the sample stationery, built around personal themes, including party invitations and greeting cards, is inappropriate for business use. But it might supply some ideas for stationery you can create for your own use. For example, you might use a company logo as a background graphic, and add your signature in a formatted block of text set off from the main text by an HTML rules.

To modify one of the sample stationery formats, follow these steps:

1. Choose Tools, Stationery. Choose the option labeled This stationery, and then click the Select button to open a list of stationery installed on your computer.
2. Pick a format that includes the basic elements you want in your custom stationery. Use the Preview window to see what each stationery type looks like.
3. Click the Edit button to launch FrontPage Express with the selected stationery type.
4. Add text and graphics, and make any other formatting changes.
5. Save the document with a descriptive name in the same folder with the other stationery samples. (By default, these are in \Program Files\Common Files\Microsoft Shared\Stationery.) Close FrontPage Express.
6. Select the stationery you just created and click OK.

To use a stationery file for all mail or news messages you compose, make sure its name is selected in the Stationery box. To compose a plain-text message without using the default stationery, choose Compose, New Message using, No Stationery.

Exchanging Address Information with vCards

When you meet a new business contact in person, you exchange business cards. To send the digital equivalent of a business card in an email message, Outlook Express uses the vCard format. When you attach a vCard to your mail or news messages, recipients with a vCard-compatible address book (the Windows Address Book or Netscape Communicator, for example) can merge the attachment into their personal address book, creating a new record that includes all your address information.

Before you can send a vCard, you have to create a personal record in the Windows Address Book, and then tell Outlook Express to use that card as your business card. Choose Tools, Stationery, and click the Signature button to choose your card.

> **CAUTION**
>
> You can set an option in the Signature dialog box that automatically adds your electronic business card to every mail message. Think twice before you check that box, though. Your regular correspondents probably won't appreciate the extra disk space consumed by every one of those redundant business card attachments, and correspondents without a vCard-compatible address book will probably also resent the useless attachments. It's far better to selectively attach business cards, by choosing Insert, Business Card.

Composing a News Article

Composing a message to a newsgroup uses tools that are virtually identical to those you use to create mail messages, with one major exception: Instead of picking addresses from your Windows Address Book, choose Tools, Select Newsgroups (or click the news server icon to the right of the To: in the address box). You see a dialog box like the one in Figure 22.27, which you can use to fill in one or more newsgroup names in the address box.

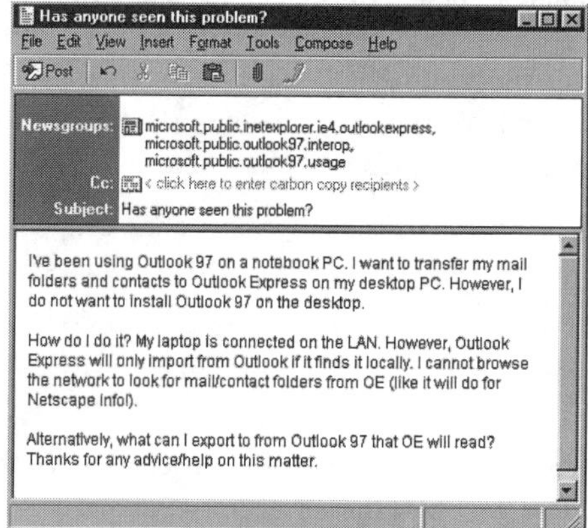

FIG. 22.27
Posting the identical message to multiple newsgroups, as in this example, is generally considered bad Netiquette.

Before posting a question to a newsgroup, see if it's already been answered in a FAQ—a list of frequently asked questions. It's the fastest way to get answers, and you'll also avoid being flamed for not reading the FAQ. The mother of all FAQs, with upwards of 900 files, is news.answers. There, you'll find information ranging from the laughably trivial (every cult TV program ever made, along with more information on body piercing than any human should need), to the deadly serious (you can read about a half-dozen religions or find detailed information on organ transplantation, depression support groups, and other sober topics).

Sending Your Message

After you've finished addressing and composing your message, you have a variety of options for actually launching it on its way.

- To send a mail message immediately by using the default mail account, click the Send button.
- To post a newsgroup message immediately, click the Post button.
- To choose which mail account to use when sending a message, choose File, Send Message Using, and pick the account from the cascading menu.
- To tell Outlook Express you want to choose when to send a message, choose File, Send Later.
- To save a mail message in the Drafts folder so you can work on it later, choose File, Save.

Working with File Attachments

In addition to formatted text and graphics, you can attach a file to any message you compose by using Outlook Express. Binary files, such as images and programs, can safely travel across the Internet but only if you encode them into ASCII text before sending. When an incoming message includes an attachment, Outlook Express and other MIME-compatible mail clients are capable of converting the encoded text back into binary files.

To add a file attachment to a message you're composing, click the paper clip icon on the tool bar. You can also attach one or more files by dragging them from an Explorer or folder window into the message window.

CAUTION

Not all mail client software is capable of decoding all attachment formats. If you're certain the recipient uses Outlook Express or another modern, MIME-compatible program, you should have no problem exchanging attachments. If you're not certain what mail software the recipient uses, try sending a small test attachment to verify that the process works before you send important files via email.

To view or save a file attachment in a message you've received, look for its icon.

- In the preview pane, click the paper clip icon at the right of the preview header to see a list of attached files. Choose an item from the list to open it; you can't save an attachment from the preview pane.
- In a message window, look for file icons in a separate pane just below the message text, as in Figure 22.28. Double-click to launch the file, or use right-click shortcut menus to save the file to your local hard disk or a network location.

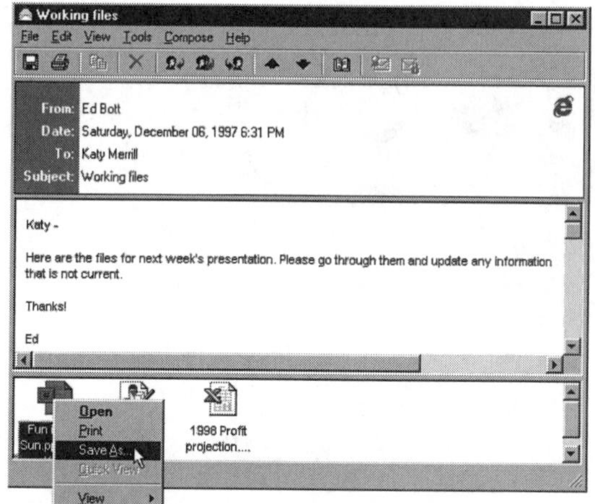

FIG. 22.28
Right-click its icon to open, save, or print a file attachment. When composing a message, you can also right-click to add or remove files.

TROUBLESHOOTING

Your recipients report that file attachments appear as gibberish in messages they receive from you. Your recipient is probably using a mail client that is not fully MIME-compatible. If you can't convince them to change mail clients, try re-sending the attachment by using the Uuencode format instead of MIME encoding. You must send the message as plain text; choose Tools, Options, click the Send tab, and click the Settings button opposite the Plain Text option to adjust the format for outgoing attachments. Many older mail clients that don't handle MIME formatting can process Uuencoded attachments just fine. If that still doesn't work, there are free and shareware Uudecode programs that can help convert UUencoded text to its original binary format.

Sending and Receiving Mail

Exchanging messages with a mail server is an interactive process. A mail server will not automatically send messages to your computer; to begin the transfer process, your mail client has to send a request to the server. Outlook Express can poll for mail at regular intervals, or you can send and receive messages on demand by clicking a button.

Collecting Mail Automatically

If you have a LAN connection, Outlook Express automatically checks for new messages and sends outgoing mail every 30 minutes. To check for mail more or less frequently, follow these steps:

1. Choose Tools, Options, and click the General tab. You'll see the dialog box shown in Figure 22.29.

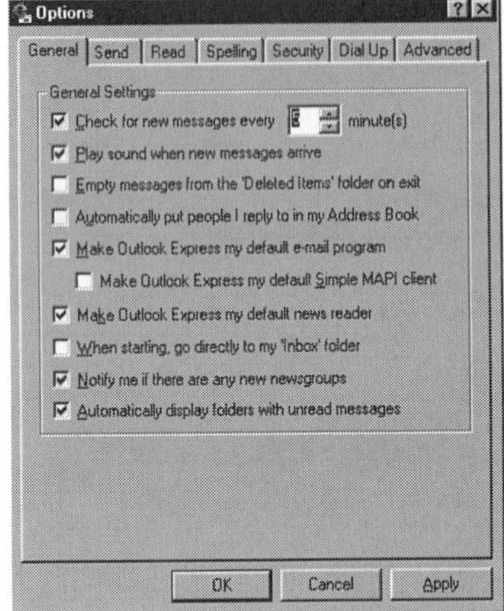

FIG. 22.29
On a LAN connection, Outlook Express checks for new mail every half-hour. To pick up messages more frequently, adjust this setting to 5 or 10 minutes instead.

2. Make sure there's a check mark in the box labeled Check for new messages every *x* minute(s).
3. Use the spinner control to adjust how often Outlook Express sends and receives mail. This number must be in the range of 1 (every minute) to 480 (every 8 hours).
4. Click OK to make the change effective.

How do you know when new mail has arrived? Outlook Express gives you two cues when you've received mail. A letter icon appears in the notification area at the right of the taskbar, and the program also plays a sound. If you find the sound disturbing, it's easy to kill the noise. Choose Tools, Options, click the General tab, and remove the check mark for that option.

You can also choose a different sound file to play when new mail arrives. Open the Control Panel and use the Sounds applet to assign a different .wav file to the New Mail Notification event.

▶ **See** "Changing the Sounds Associated with Windows Events," **p. 800**

As Outlook Express checks for mail, look in the status bar for messages that display the results of the connection attempt. Double-click the icon at the far right to display a dialog box with more details, including any error messages you might have received.

Delivering the Mail Manually

Of course, you can check for new messages anytime by using the Send and Receive button. This technique works even if Outlook Express is set to check messages at regular intervals. The Send and Receive command automatically connects with every mail account and your default news account. To add or remove a server from this group, follow these steps:

1. Choose Tools, Accounts and select the account from the list.
2. Click the Properties button to display the account's property sheet.

3. Click the General tab and check or uncheck the setting labeled Include this account… (the exact wording is different for mail and news accounts). A check mark means Outlook Express automatically checks for messages when you click the Send and Receive button.
4. Click OK to make the change effective, and then close the Accounts dialog box.

If you have multiple mail providers and you want to connect with only one of them, regardless of the default settings, choose Tools, Send and Receive from the menus. Outlook Express presents a cascading menu that enables you to choose which mail providers you want to connect with.

Checking the Mail When You're Out of the Office

Outlook Express enables you to file and save all the messages you send and receive. But what happens when you need to read your email from a machine other than the one you normally use? This might be the case if you normally use an office PC but occasionally check your email from home or the road. If you use the default settings, you end up with a collection of messages on different PCs.

The cure is to adjust the account settings on your "away" PC so that it downloads messages but does not delete them from the mail server. Later, when you return to the office, you can connect to the server and download all the messages, saving and filing the important ones.

You must specifically set this option for each account you intend to check. Choose Tools, Accounts, select the account, and click the Properties button. Click the Advanced tab, and then check the Delivery options shown in Figure 22.30.

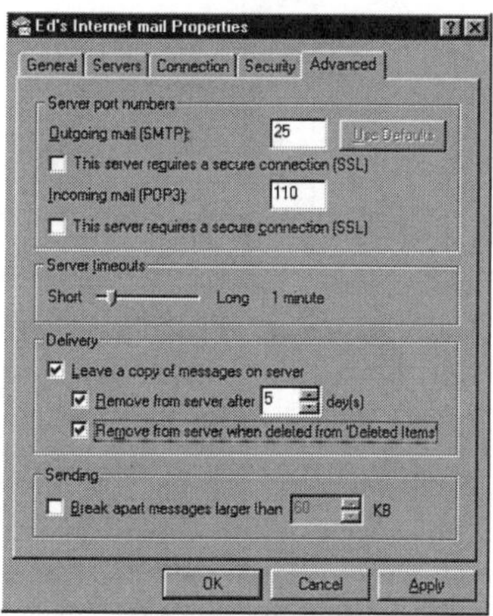

FIG. 22.30
If you check your mail when you're away from the office, tell Outlook Express to leave messages on the server so that you can retrieve them when you return to work.

The other two Delivery options help you avoid cluttering up the mail server by automatically deleting messages after a set number of days or when you delete them from your "away" machine.

Replying to Messages You've Received

The simplest way to compose a message is to reply to one you've received. The format for replies varies slightly between mail and news messages.

Replying to a Mail Message

When you select a message and click the Reply button, Outlook Express opens a New Message window, selects the same format as the message to which you're responding, fills in the To: line with the sender's address from the original message, adds Re: to the beginning of the original Subject line, and positions the insertion point at the top of the message. When you click the Reply to All button, Outlook Express picks up every addressee from the To: and Cc: lines in the original message and adds them to your new message.

By default, all replies include the full text of the original message, with a separator line between your reply and the original text. How that message appears depends on the format of your reply.

- With HTML-formatted messages, all graphics are included and the original text is indented
- With plain-text messages, each line of the original text begins with the ">" character.

Choose Tools, Options, and click the Send tab to adjust these defaults, as shown in Figure 22.31.

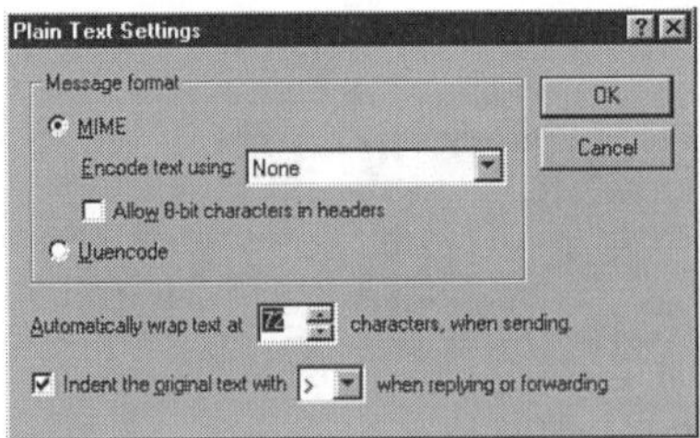

FIG. 22.31
If you routinely reply to replies, lower the default text wrap to 72 characters. That lessens the chance that your prefix character will cause lines to wrap inappropriately.

To change the default setting so all replies start with a blank message, uncheck the Include message in reply option.

Replying to a Newsgroup Message

When reading newsgroup messages, you have a choice of two reply buttons. Click Reply to Group to begin composing a message to the current newsgroup; just as with a mail message, your reply includes the original posting, although the format of the separator text is different.

To reply in a private email to the person that posted the original newsgroup message, click the Reply to Author button. Although there's no Reply to All button, that option is available: Choose Compose, Reply to Newsgroup and Author to post your reply to the newsgroup *and* send a copy to the author via email.

CAUTION

Check the email address carefully when responding to newsgroup postings. Many newsgroup contributors deliberately corrupt the reply-to address in their messages to frustrate junk emailers. You might need to edit stray characters or words to see the real address.

Forwarding Messages

You have two choices when you forward a message you've received to another person. Select the message and click the Forward button to open a New Message window containing the original message; the message will use the same indent settings as if you had chosen to reply to the sender. Enter one or more addresses, add any comments of your own, and click the Send button.

You can also forward an email message as an attached file—choose Compose, Forward as Attachment. That's the correct choice when you want another person to see the message exactly as you saw it, without prefix characters or other reply formatting.

Organizing Messages with Folders

By default, Outlook Express includes five top-level mail folders. There's no way to delete these basic mail folders, which perform the following crucial functions:

- All incoming messages hit the *Inbox* first; use the Inbox Assistant to file or process messages automatically as they arrive.
- Mail that you've sent goes to the *Outbox* until the next time you exchange messages with your mail server.
- By default, a copy of every message you send goes to the *Sent Items* folder. To change this setting, choose Tools, Options, click the Send tab, and uncheck this option.
- When you delete a message, Outlook Express moves it to the *Deleted Items* folder. An option on the General tab enables you to empty this folder each time you exit. By default, though, this folder stays full until you right-click its icon and choose Empty Folder.
- The *Drafts* folder stores messages you've composed and saved but haven't yet sent.

NOTE You can't organize newsgroup messages by using mail folders, although you can drag a newsgroup message from the message list and copy it into a mail folder.

Creating a New Folder

You can add an unlimited number of top-level mail folders and subfolders to Outlook Express. The easiest way to create a new folder is to follow these steps:

1. If the folder list is not visible, choose View, Layout; check the box labeled Folder list and click OK.
2. Select the folder in which you want to create the new subfolder. To create a new top-level folder, choose the Outlook Express icon at the top of the folder list.
3. Right-click the icon you selected and choose New Folder from the shortcut menu.
4. Enter a name for the new folder. (This dialog box also enables you to use the tree at the bottom of this dialog box to change the location in which the new folder will be created).
5. Click OK to create the new folder.

Moving or Copying Messages Between Folders

To move messages, drag them from the message list and drop them on the folder icon in your folder list. To copy messages to a folder while leaving the original file intact, hold down the Ctrl key as you drag the messages.

If you use folders extensively, use right-click shortcut menus in the folder list to move and copy messages. As Figure 22.32 shows, these commands enable you to create a new folder on-the-fly. Better yet, add the Move To button to the toolbar for instant access to this dialog box.

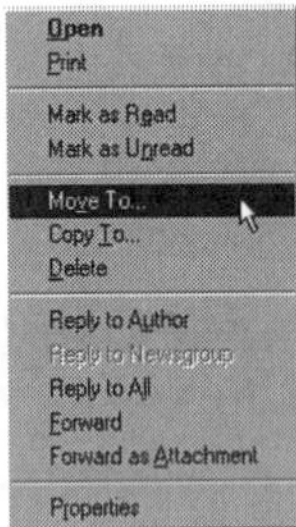

FIG. 22.32
Use the New Folder button to create a folder and move or copy messages from the same dialog box.

Adding a new top-level folder creates a matching shortcut on the Outlook Bar. If you create a folder within an existing folder—under the Inbox, for example—it will appear in the folder list but not on the Outlook Bar.

Moving, Renaming, and Deleting Folders

Open the folder list and simply drag folder icons to move them from one location to another. Right-click and use the shortcut menus to delete or rename a folder. You can freely move, delete, or rename any folders you've created, but you can't change any of the five default mail folders.

Compacting Folders to Reduce the Size of Your Mail File

As you receive new messages and organize them into folders, the size of your mail file grows. When you move and delete messages, Outlook Express removes the messages but leaves the empty space in the mail file. Over time, this can cause your mail folders to waste a significant amount of space. To eliminate wasted space in a single folder, select its icon and choose File, Folder, Compact. To remove slack space from every mail folder, choose File, Folder, Compact All Folders.

After you compact your mail folders, it's a good idea to back up all your mail files. Click the Start Menu, choose Find, Files or Folders, and search for the data files for each folder; these files use the extension .mbx, whereas a matching index for each file has the same name but the .idx extension. Folders you create go by the name Folder1.mbx, Folder2.mbx, and so on.

Using the Inbox Assistant to Process Mail Automatically

In some busy organizations that live and die by email, it's not uncommon for workers to receive dozens or even hundreds of messages per day. Managing that torrent of messages can be a full-time job, but Outlook Express can do at least part of the work. The secret is a tool called the Inbox Assistant, which enables you to define rules for Outlook Express to follow when you receive new mail.

Defining Rules for Processing Mail

To define rules that automate mail processing, choose Tools, Inbox Assistant. Click the Add button and a dialog box like the one in Figure 22.33 appears.

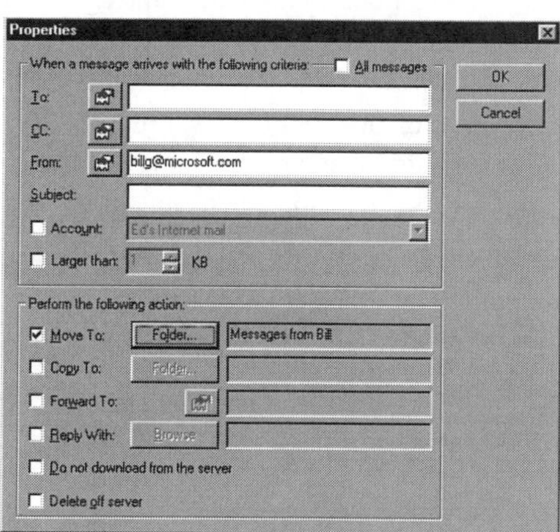

FIG. 22.33
To create a mail processing rule, define one or more criteria in the top of this dialog box, and then select an action to be performed when a message meets that condition.

Each rule consists of two parts: a set of criteria and a matching action. Each time a message arrives in your Inbox, Outlook Express compares it with the conditions defined in your Inbox Assistant rules; when it finds a match, it performs the action defined for that rule.

You can define a variety of conditions to trigger mail actions:

- Search for text in the address box or in the subject line
- Look for messages that come through a specific mail account
- Check the size of each incoming message
- Apply the rule to all messages

NOTE If you're familiar with filtering options in other mail programs, such as Eudora Pro, you might be disappointed in the limitations of the Inbox Assistant. For example, you cannot define complex "or" conditions—when you specify multiple criteria, Outlook Express acts only on messages that meet all those criteria. Nor can you check the text of the message itself or see whether a message has a file attachment. The Inbox Assistant doesn't accept wildcards; it simply checks the text you enter against the text in the messages it receives; when it finds a match, it applies the rule. ■

When a message meets the conditions you define, you can order Outlook Express to move or copy it to a folder, forward it to another recipient, reply automatically with a saved message, leave the message on the server, or delete the message from the server.

The following list and Figure 22.34 shows some rules you might find useful for weeding out junk mail and helping to identify important messages.

- Automatically move mail sent by a VIP or from your company's domain (mcp.com, for example) to a special "Read Me Now" folder.
- Look for messages where your name is in the CC field and move them to a "Read Me Later" folder.
- Move messages to the Deleted Items folder if the subject contains key junk-mail phrases ("make money fast," for example) or if the message was sent by someone from whom you do not want to receive mail (this feature is often called a "bozo filter").
- When you're out of the office on business or on vacation, use an Inbox Assistant rule to forward all your mail to an assistant and send an advisory message to the sender.
- If space on your notebook computer is tight, tell Outlook Express not to download messages that are larger than a specified size—say, 100KB.

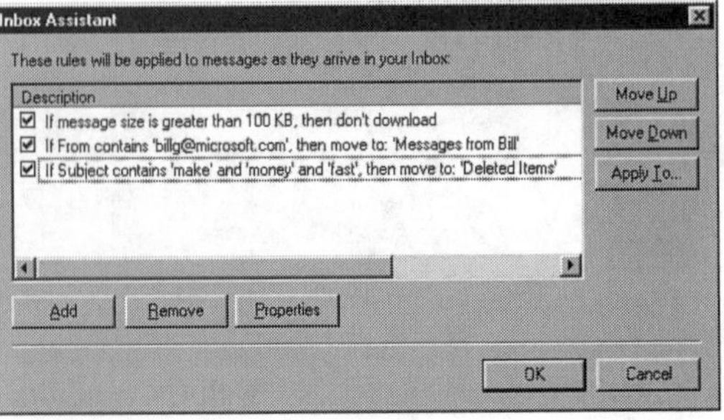

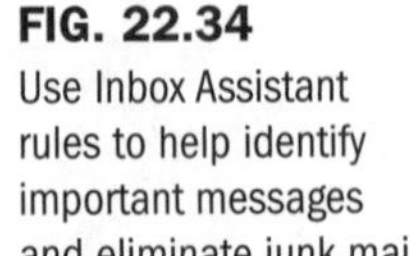
FIG. 22.34
Use Inbox Assistant rules to help identify important messages and eliminate junk mail.

Changing Inbox Assistant Rules

Note that rules are applied in the order in which they appear in your list. If two or more conditions apply to the same message, the Inbox Assistant can apply only the first rule. This type of conflict between rules can produce effects you didn't anticipate.

- To adjust the order in which the Inbox Assistant applies rules, select a rule from the list and use the Move Up and Move Down buttons.
- To completely eliminate a rule, select it and click the Remove button.
- To temporarily disable a rule without eliminating it, clear the check box to the left of its entry in the list.
- To change the conditions or actions associated with a rule, select it and click the Properties button.

To clean up a cluttered mail folder, select a rule, click the Apply To button, and pick a folder from the dialog box that pops up. The Inbox Assistant processes all the messages in that folder and any subfolders.

Enhancing Email Security

By its very nature, an ordinary email message is as insecure as a postcard. It takes only the most rudimentary technical knowledge to "spoof" a message so that it appears to be coming from someone other than the actual sender. In fact, a favorite hacker trick is to send bogus mail messages that appear to have come from famous individuals such as Bill Gates. And because email travels in packets across the Internet, it's theoretically possible for anyone to intercept a transmission, read a message sent to someone else, and change the contents of that message.

Outlook Express includes two features that enhance email security, although neither offers foolproof protection from a skilled and determined data thief. *Encryption* enables you to encode the contents of a message so that only a recipient with a matching code key can decipher the text. A *digital signature* tacked on to the end of a message guarantees that the message originated from the sender and has not been tampered with in transit.

Before you can use either security feature, you first have to acquire a digital certificate from a certifying authority and add it to Outlook Express. You also need to enable that certificate for every mail account with which you plan to use it, as in Figure 22.35.

ON THE WEB

Internet Explorer 4.0 includes a special offer for a free Class 1 digital ID from VeriSign, Inc. Read full details at

http://digitalid.verisign.com

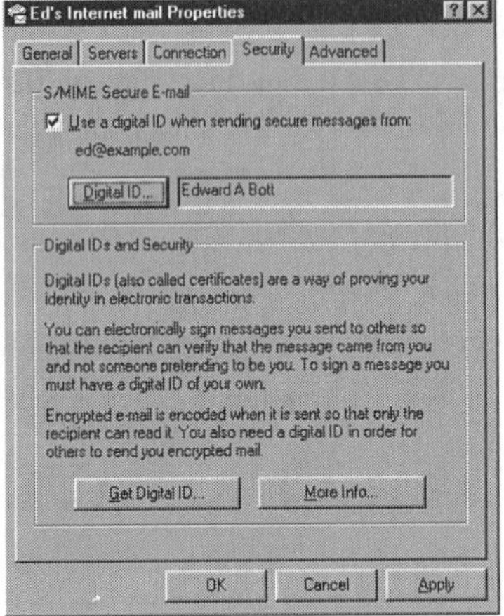

FIG. 22.35
Before you can encrypt or digitally sign an email message, you need to enable a certificate like this one. Click the button at the bottom of the dialog box for more information.

To install your digital ID, follow the instructions provided by the certificate provider. The certificate includes two parts: a ***public key***, which you distribute freely to others, and a ***private key*** that only you have access to. Anyone can encrypt a message by using your public key, and after they've done so, only you can unscramble it by using the private key.

Sending a Digitally Signed Message

To add a digital signature to a message, click the Digitally sign message button on the toolbar in the New Message window. A red icon in the lower-right corner of the address box tells you this is a signed message.

CAUTION

Outlook Express includes the option to digitally sign and/or encrypt all your messages. Don't activate this feature unless you're certain that most of your correspondents use mail software that can accept digital certificates. For the overwhelming majority of email users, it's best to choose secure email options one message at a time.

Encrypting a Message

To scramble a message so that only a trusted recipient can read it, click the Encrypt message button in the New Message window. A blue padlock icon in the address box lets you know the message is encrypted. You must have a copy of the recipient's public key before you can encrypt a message to that person. (You can ask a correspondent to send you her public key; you can also find public keys on some directory servers.)

ON THE WEB

Pretty Good Privacy, Inc. has one of the best online sources of information about encryption and secure email. You can find it at

http://www.pgp.com/privacy/privacy.cgi

Reading a Signed or Encrypted Message

Anyone can encrypt a message and send it to you, as long as he has a copy of your public key. When you receive the encrypted message, Outlook Express uses your private key to unscramble the text so you can read it. When you receive a digitally signed message, you see an introductory message like the one in Figure 22.36.

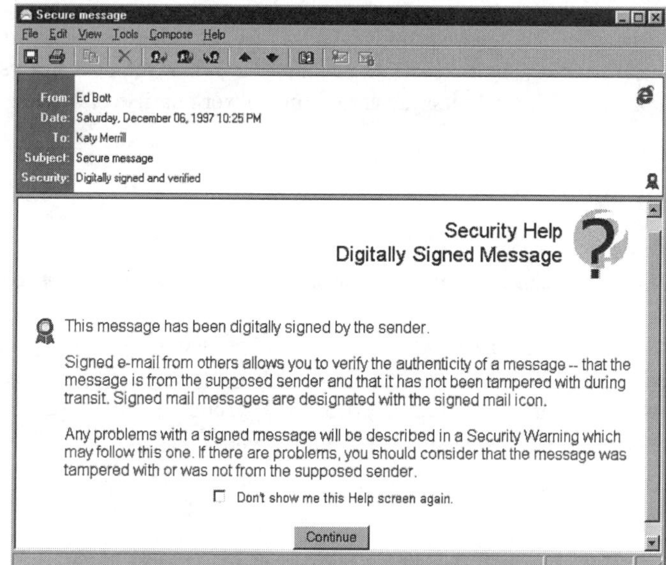

FIG. 22.36
Outlook Express offers this help screen when you receive a digitally signed message. Note the additional information in the address header, too.

Working with Newsgroups

Although newsgroup messages appear in the same window as mail messages, the mechanics of downloading and managing newsgroup messages are dramatically different. Unlike mail messages, which are addressed directly to you, newsgroup messages are posted on public servers for all to see. You probably don't want to read every message in busy newsgroups, which can get hundreds of new messages per day.

Getting the maximum benefit from Internet newsgroups takes careful setup and management. Before you start, you have to identify potentially useful or interesting newsgroups.

How Newsgroups Work

Newsgroups are nearly as old as the Internet itself. They get only a fraction of the publicity that goes to the newer and flashier World Wide Web, but that doesn't mean they're less useful. On the contrary, public peer-support newsgroups can be an excellent source for quick answers to thorny software and hardware support questions. Newsgroups are also popular among hobbyists ranging from BMW enthusiasts to cat owners, and moderated newsgroups are important gathering places for computer and science professionals.

Don't be misled by the name—newsgroups have nothing to do with the *New York Times* or CNN. They function more like public bulletin boards, organized by topic, where individuals post messages (sometimes called *articles*) that anyone with access to that group can read and reply to. Just as web servers use HyperText Transfer Protocol, or HTTP, to communicate, news servers use Network News Transfer Protocol, or NNTP, to share information.

The oldest collection of newsgroups is called Usenet, a distributed network of servers that continually exchange messages with one another. When you post a newsgroup article to your local news server, it works its way across the network until every Usenet news server has a copy.

ON THE WEB

For the definitive description of what Usenet is and isn't, read this web page:

http://www.netannounce.org/news.announce.newusers/archive/usenet/what-is/part1

Not all Usenet news servers carry all newsgroups, and it's up to the manager of a news server to decide when older messages "expire" and drop off the server. The past few years have seen a steady increase in the number of private newsgroups as corporations have seen how easy it is for employees to communicate by using these easy-to-use forums.

CAUTION

Don't expect to find useful information in a newsgroup just because the name sounds appealing. As the Internet has grown, newsgroups have become increasingly vulnerable to Spam—posts (usually commercial in nature) that are unrelated to the stated purpose of a newsgroup and simply serve to clutter the listings of articles. On some once-popular newsgroups, the only traffic these days consists of variations on chain letters and enticements to visit X-rated web sites.

Viewing the Full List of Newsgroups

The first time you connect to a news server, Outlook Express offers to download a list of all the newsgroups available there. On a well-stocked server, that can represent thousands of newsgroups. Click the Newsgroups button to view the complete list of groups available on a news server (note that not all news servers carry all newsgroups). If you've defined multiple accounts, make sure you select the correct server from the list at the left of the window.

Deciphering a Newsgroup Name

Newsgroups use a dotted naming convention like those found elsewhere on the Internet, with strict hierarchies that identify what subscribers can expect to find in each one. To read a newsgroup name, follow the hierarchy from left to right as it goes from general to specific. In Usenet newsgroups, for example, the first entry is the top-level domain. The following table lists many (but not all) of the most common top-level domains.

Top-Level Newsgroup Domain	Description	Sample
comp	general computer subjects	comp.os.ms-windows.networking.tcp-ip
rec	hobbies, the arts, pop culture	rec.music.beatles
soc	social issues and world culture	soc.culture.irish
sci	science-related, many highly specialized	sci.space.policy
gov	government newsgroups	gov.us.fed.congress.documents
news	newsgroup administrative issues	news.newusers.questions
misc	Miscellaneous, often commercial groups	misc.taxes.moderated

There are a variety of unofficial newsgroup hierarchies as well, including the infamous alt category. When people complain about pornography on the Internet, they're talking about newsgroups whose names begin with alt.sex and alt.binaries.pictures.erotica.

There are also local newsgroups, whose top-level domain identifies a geographic region (try ba.food for San Francisco Bay Area restaurant recommendations, or nyc.jobs for employment in the Big Apple), as well as private groups intended for subscribers of Internet service providers like Netcom.

Microsoft now provides its first level of technical support through newsgroups in the microsoft.* hierarchy. You'll find them on **msnews.microsoft.com**, and an increasing number of Internet service providers are replicating the Microsoft news feed to their own news servers.

Finding a Specific Newsgroup

On Microsoft's public news servers, there are nearly 600 separate groups. Some well-stocked Usenet news servers include more than 15,000 distinct newsgroups. Instead of scrolling through the full Newsgroups list to find relevant ones, use the text box at the top of the dialog box to show only groups whose names contain certain letters or words. If you're looking for information about Outlook Express, for example, type the word Outlook to see a filtered list like the one in Figure 22.37.

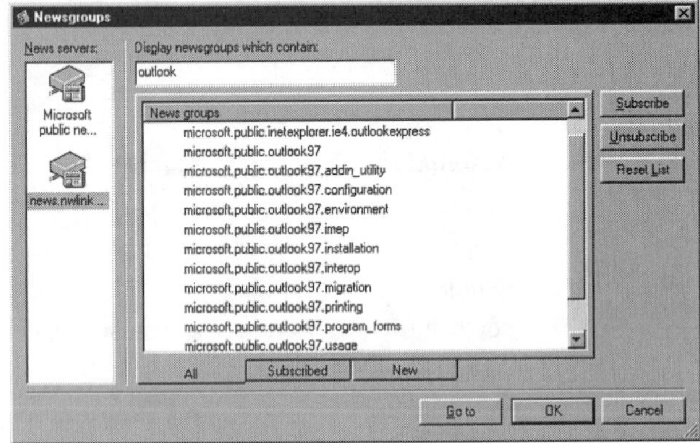

FIG. 22.37
After you've found the newsgroup you're looking for, double-click its name to add it to your list of subscribed groups.

ON THE WEB

You can't use Outlook Express to search the contents of a newsgroup for specific information, but web-based news archives like Deja News (**http://www.dejanews.com**) can handle that task. Use Deja News to search for messages and threads that match your interests; if you find a wealth of information in a particular newsgroup, use Outlook Express to go there directly.

Refreshing the List of Newsgroups

On Usenet servers in particular, it's common for new groups to appear and old ones to disappear regularly. If you suspect that there are new groups available on a server, do the following:

1. Select the news server icon in the folder list.
2. Click the Newsgroups button to show the list of all newsgroups.
3. Click the Reset List button to update the master list. This operation might take some time, especially over a slow Internet connection.
4. After you've refreshed the list, click the New tab along the bottom of the newsgroups list to see only new groups.

Managing Newsgroup Subscriptions

Don't be confused by the buttons to the right of the Newsgroups list. Subscribing to a newsgroup doesn't cost anything, and it doesn't require that you send any information about yourself to a news server. In Outlook Express, subscriptions are simply a way of managing the newsgroup list to show only your favorite groups.

Follow these steps to manage your newsgroup subscriptions:

1. Select the news server icon in the folder list, and then click the Newsgroups button.
2. Click the All tab at the bottom of the dialog box to see the full list of newsgroups.
3. Select at least one name from the list; to select more than one name at a time, hold down the Ctrl key as you click.
4. Use the Subscribe button to add a newsgroup to your personal list. An icon appears to the left of the newsgroup name.
5. Use the Unsubscribe button to remove a newsgroup from your personal list. (You can also double-click an entry in the Newsgroups list to toggle the subscribed icon.)
6. Click the Subscribed tab at the bottom of the Newsgroups list to see only the list of newsgroups you've selected. Icons for all subscribed newsgroups appear under the news server icon in your folders list, as shown in Figure 22.38.

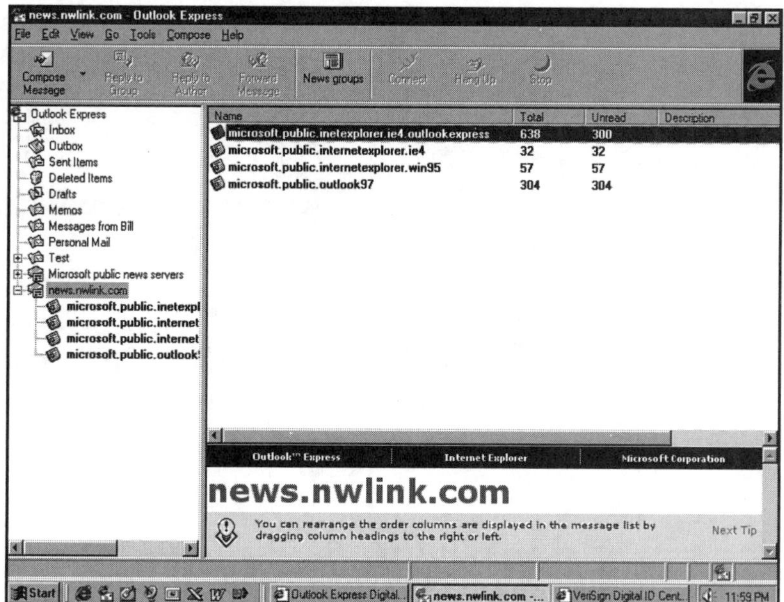

FIG. 22.38
When you select a news server in the folder list at left, the list at right shows only newsgroups to which you've subscribed.

You needn't subscribe to a newsgroup to see its contents. Select a name from the Newsgroups list, and then click the Go to button to open the newsgroup. Use the choices on the Tools menu to manage subscriptions for the newsgroup you're currently viewing.

Downloading and Reading Newsgroup Messages

Before you can read the messages in a newsgroup, you have to download them from the server to your computer. That process is not as straightforward as it sounds. For starters, you can't tell from the newsgroup list how many messages are currently available for each newsgroup. Some obscure groups generate only a handful of messages, but popular groups can contain thousands of messages at one time, with some containing binary attachments or graphic files that occupy significant amounts of disk space. Downloading every message without first checking the newsgroup's contents is clearly a bad idea.

To make newsgroup traffic more manageable, Outlook Express distinguishes between message headers and bodies. Regardless of the size of the message itself, the header contains only the subject line, the author's name, and the message size. By default, when you open a newsgroup for the first time, Outlook Express connects with the server and asks it to transfer the 300 most recent subject headers.

Look at the status bar shown in Figure 22.39 to see how many headers were left on the server. To download more headers, choose Tools, Get Next 300 Headers. Outlook Express always chooses the most recent headers that have not yet been downloaded.

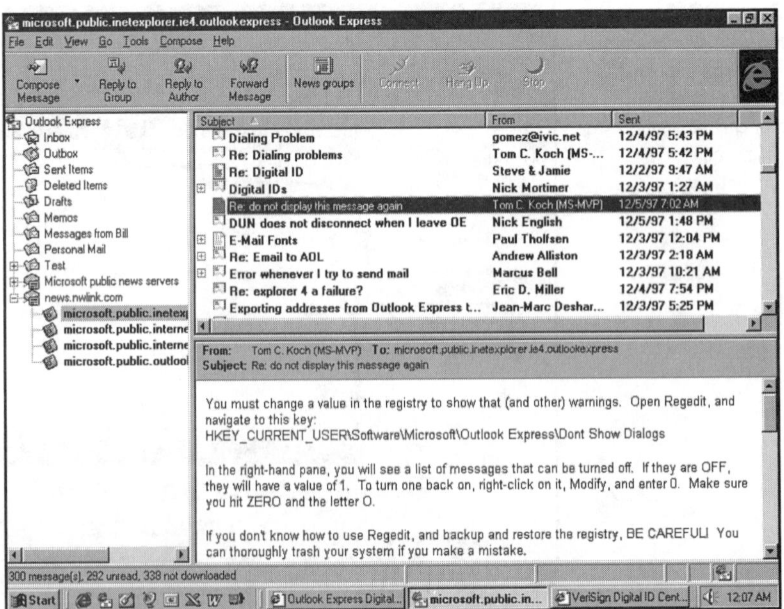

FIG. 22.39
The status bar tells you how many message headers you've downloaded from the total available on the server.

TIP To adjust the number of headers Outlook Express retrieves on each pass, choose Tools, Options and increase or decrease the number shown on the Read tab.

Navigating Through Newsgroups

The window in which you read news messages works much the same as the mail window, with a single notable exception: Outlook Express organizes news messages so that you can follow a discussion that might take place over days or even weeks.

Newsgroups facilitate *threaded conversations*, in which one user posts a message and others reply to that message. News servers keep track of the links between original posts, replies, and replies to replies. By default, Outlook Express maintains these threads, regardless of the sort order you've chosen for messages in a given newsgroup. These messages remain grouped together even when the reply title begins with the Re: prefix.

Replies to a message are indented below the original message, and replies to replies are indented further. To see all the messages in a thread, click the plus sign to the left of the message header that begins the thread. To collapse the thread so you see only the first header, click the minus sign to the left of the thread.

Navigating through threads with the keyboard is fast and easy. Use the up and down arrows to move through the list of messages. In the default view, where all message threads are collapsed, the up and down arrow moves from thread to thread. To work with threads from the keyboard, use the right arrow to expand and the left arrow to collapse each thread.

If messages are not grouped together properly, choose View, Sort By, Group Messages by Thread.

Reading Messages Online

As long as the connection between Outlook Express and the news server is active, you can read messages by opening a message window or by using the preview pane. When you select a header, Outlook Express automatically retrieves that message from the server and adds it to your file. When you double-click to open a message window, or if you keep the preview pane open for more than five seconds, the header text changes from boldface to normal type, indicating that you've read the message.

If you'd prefer to keep your connection open while you scroll through the headers and retrieve only those messages that look most interesting, choose Tools, Options, click the Read tab, and clear the check mark from the box labeled Automatically show news messages in the Preview Pane. As Figure 22.40 shows, with this option set you must select a header and tap the Spacebar to retrieve a message.

Working Offline for Maximum Efficiency

The most efficient way to work with large newsgroups is offline. Outlook Express enables you to download a batch of headers, and then scroll through the list and mark the ones you want to download. The next time you connect to the server, Outlook Express will retrieve the marked messages, which you can read anytime.

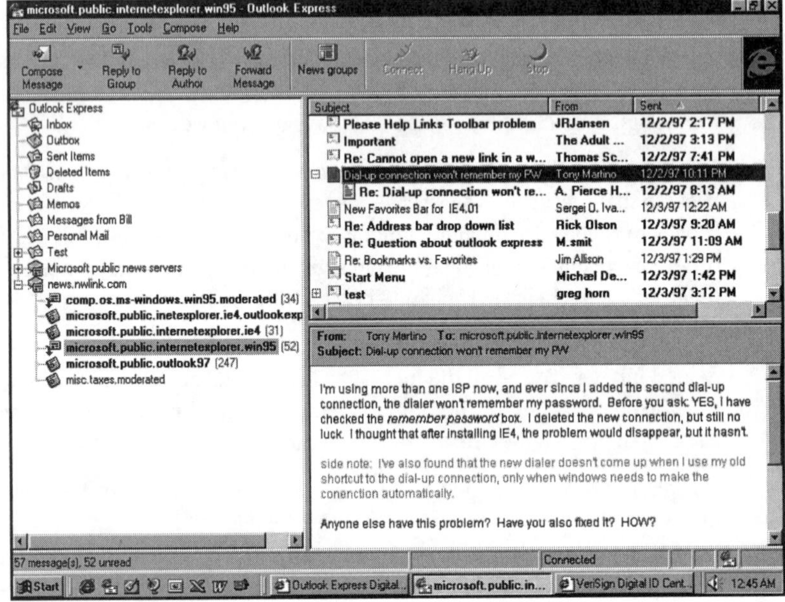

FIG. 22.40
Note the different icons in this list: Downloaded messages show a full page, and the corner is turned down after reading.

Follow these steps to work offline:

1. To begin working offline, choose File, Work Offline.
2. When you see a message header you want to read, mark it for retrieval. You can use the right-click shortcut menu, but it's easier to select one or more message headers and press Ctrl+M.
3. To select an entire thread for retrieval, make sure the thread is collapsed, with a plus sign visible to the left. Select the first message in the thread and press Ctrl+M. The icon to the left of a message header that has been marked for retrieval changes, as Figure 22.41 shows.
4. To remove marks, select one or more marked messages and choose Tools, Mark for Retrieval, Unmark.
5. To go online again, choose File and clear the check mark from the Work Offline choice.
6. To retrieve all marked messages, choose Tools, Download this Newsgroup. In the dialog box that appears, check the option labeled Get marked messages, as shown in Figure 22.42.

Reestablishing Connections with a News Server

Unless you've set up your news account to hang up immediately after downloading messages or headers, the connection will remain active while you work with messages and headers. By default, Outlook Express disconnects from the server after a minute; when that happens, the text in the status bar changes and you see a dialog box like the one in Figure 22.43.

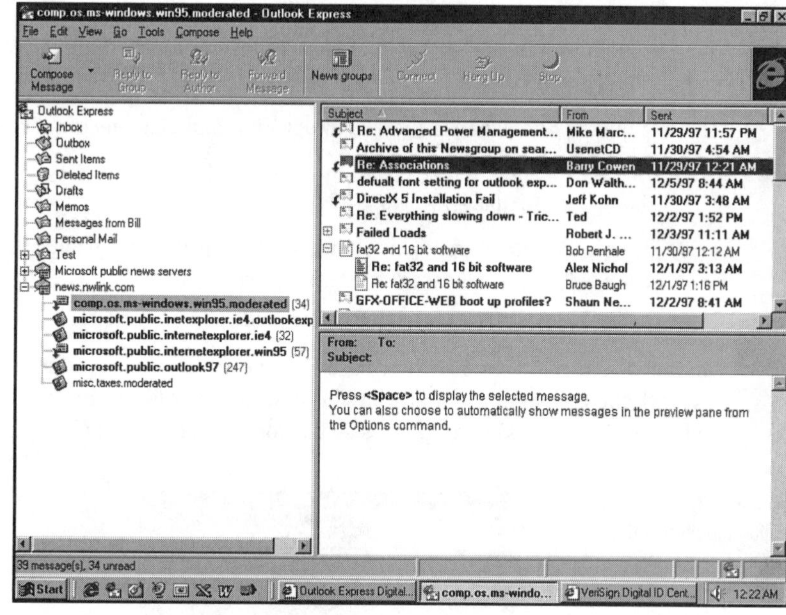

FIG. 22.41
The tiny arrow to the left of some headers means they've been marked for retrieval the next time you connect with the news server.

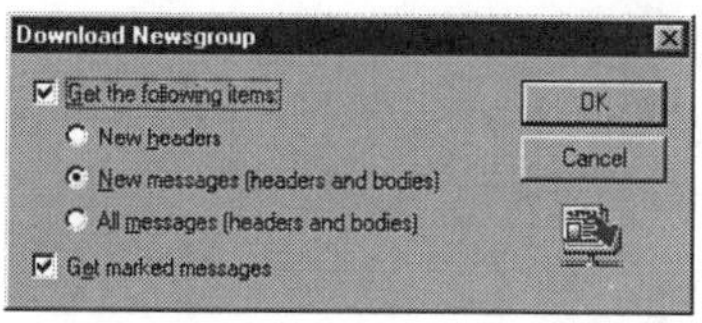

FIG. 22.42
Check the option at the bottom of this dialog box to retrieve messages whose headers you've marked.

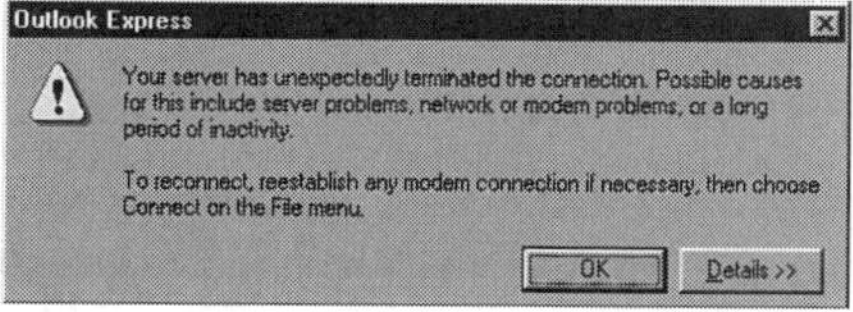

FIG. 22.43
After a period of inactivity, you might lose your connection to the news server. To reconnect, choose File, Connect, or press F5.

If you're using a dial-up connection, you might need to redial at this point. Click the Connect button or choose File, Connect to redial the server. If you're connected through a LAN, you can reestablish the connection by pressing the Refresh key, F5.

Using Filters to Make the News More Readable

After a while, the sheer bulk of downloaded headers and messages from some newsgroups is overwhelming, and navigation can become nearly impossible. To cut the display down to manageable proportions, use filters to show only messages that meet specific criteria. Outlook Express includes three built-in filters, or you can create your own.

News filters are analogous to mail-processing rules created by the Inbox Assistant. Unlike those rules, however, newsgroup filters can't move or forward messages or reply automatically on your behalf to messages.

To use a built-in filter, choose View, Current View and pick one of these three choices:

- *Unread Messages* Use this filter to quickly pick up new messages, especially when they're part of older threads.
- *Downloaded Messages* This choice works especially well after you've marked a widely scattered group of messages for offline reading.
- *Replies to My Posts* For active participants in a busy newsgroup, this filter is essential.

You can also create your own filter based on one or more rules, which can be used in conjunction with the built-in filters. To create the rules for your filter, choose Tools, Newsgroup Filters, and then click the Add button. You see a dialog box like the one in Figure 22.44.

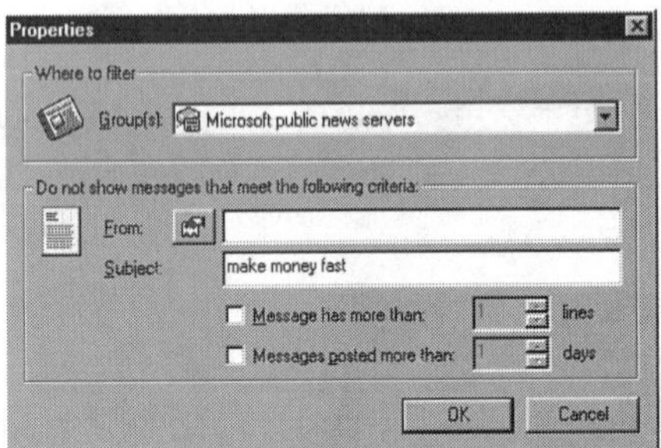

FIG. 22.44
Use filters to reduce the amount of clutter in crowded newsgroups. This filter, for example, hides all "Make Money Fast" postings.

You can apply filters to a single newsgroup or server or to every server. Filters enable you to suppress messages from specific individuals or domains or messages with a key word or phrase in the subject line. You can also hide messages that are too old or too big.

To apply all active filters to the current display, choose View, Current View, and make sure Filtered Messages is checked.

To temporarily disable a single rule, clear the check box next to its entry in the Filters list. To change the order in which rules are applied, use the Move Up and Move Down buttons. To edit a rule, select its entry and click the Properties button. To eliminate a rule permanently, click the Remove button.

Controlling Message Downloads for Each Newsgroup

Eventually, as you develop experience, you will build up a list of favorite newsgroups, each with its own characteristics. Outlook Express enables you to create different settings for each one so that you can download messages or headers according to your preferences.

To set up each newsgroup, open the folder list, right-click a newsgroup entry, and choose Properties. The General tab provides information about the number of messages and headers;

click the Download tab (see Figure 22.45) to tell Outlook Express whether you want only headers or full messages each time you download a newsgroup.

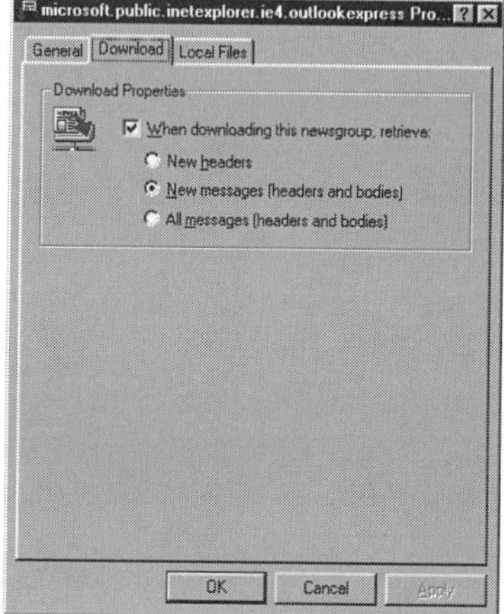

FIG. 22.45 Be careful with this option; downloading extremely active newsgroups can consume more disk space than you think.

After you've set your preferences for each newsgroup to which you're subscribed, use one of the Download choices from the Tools menu to gather mail and news. Figure 22.46 shows the status screen you see if you choose Download All Messages.

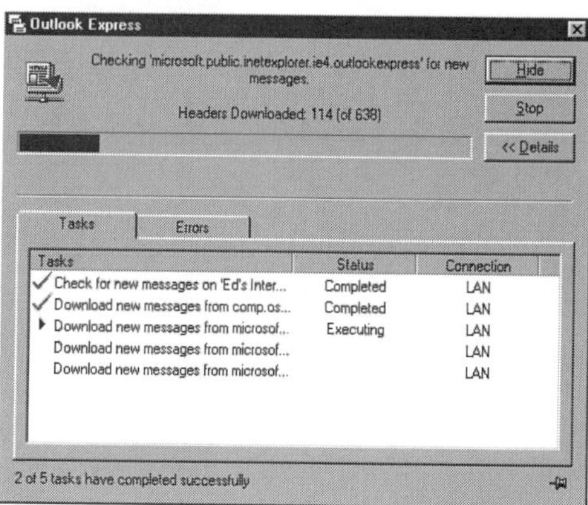

FIG. 22.46 Watch this status screen for details as Outlook Express gathers mail and news from all your accounts.

CHAPTER 23

Using FrontPage Express and Internet Components

by Paul Sanna, Barry Gross, Ron Person, and Bob Voss

In this chapter

Using FrontPage Express

Anyone who has had to interrupt his work to go to a seminar will appreciate the third application—NetShow. It provides the capability to get training or seminars on demand. NetShow can be used for broadcasting audio, video, and illustrated audio (sound combined with sequenced images) over the web or an intranet. Microsoft is already using it on the web to deliver multicast videos and on-demand training.

FrontPage Express is a perfect web page editor for creating the HTML pages you need to create your own Active Desktop or to customize web views of folders. Though not as robust as the full-featured FrontPage 97, FrontPage Express is very capable. With FrontPage Express, you are can create all but the most advanced web page designs.

What Is FrontPage Express?

FrontPage Express is a WYSIWYG *HTML* (HyperText Markup Language) editor that enables you to create or modify HTML-encoded documents that are normally viewed with web browsers such as Internet Explorer or Netscape Navigator. WYSIWYG stands for *what you see is what you get*. This means that you see the finished version of your web page as you develop it.

NOTE HTML is the language used to develop all web pages. For a web browser, such as Internet Explorer 4.0, to display a web page, the browser must read and interpret HTML, which tells the browser what text, images, sounds, video, and other content to display, as well as where and in what format on the page. You use FrontPage Express to create the HTML for you. Some browsers might not understand the latest addition to HTML; some browsers extend HTML by incorporating browser-specific extensions to HTML. ■

FrontPage Express provides all the tools for entering and editing text, images and hyperlinks, and for formatting all the elements on your web page. FrontPage Express enables you to design your web pages as they will be viewed and handles all the underlying HTML coding automatically. FrontPage Express also provides an interface that enables you to view and edit the HTML code of your documents directly. It even includes a Personal Home Page Wizard to help you create your own home page. If you are familiar with Microsoft Word, it isn't difficult to start using FrontPage Express to create your own web pages.

Starting FrontPage Express

You can start FrontPage Express from within Internet Explorer 4.0 or from the Start menu. To start FrontPage Express from the Windows 95 desktop, open the Start menu and choose Programs, Internet Explorer, FrontPage Express. The FrontPage Express window appears, as shown in Figure 23.1.

You also can start FrontPage Express by clicking the Edit icon on the right side of the Internet Explorer 4.0 standard toolbar. This opens Internet Explorer's current document in FrontPage Express for editing. To display the standard toolbar, choose View, Toolbars, Standard Buttons from the Internet Explorer 4.0 menu.

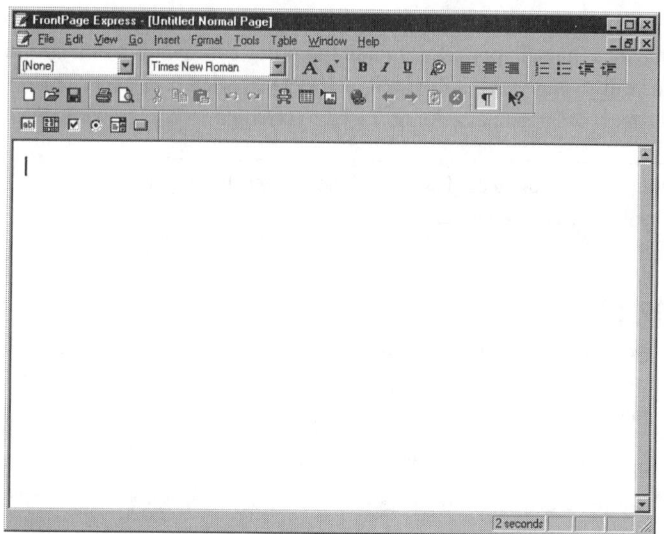

FIG. 23.1
FrontPage Express starts with a new blank document, ready for you to begin editing.

Creating a New HTML Document with FrontPage Express

When you start FrontPage Express, it begins with a blank untitled normal page. You probably will want to create a title for your page; the title appears in the caption of the Internet Explorer window when the page is viewed. Assign a title to your new HTML document by following these steps:

1. Choose File, Page Properties or right-click the document window and choose Page Properties.
2. Select the General tab.
3. Enter your title in the Title text box (see Figure 23.2).
4. Choose OK.

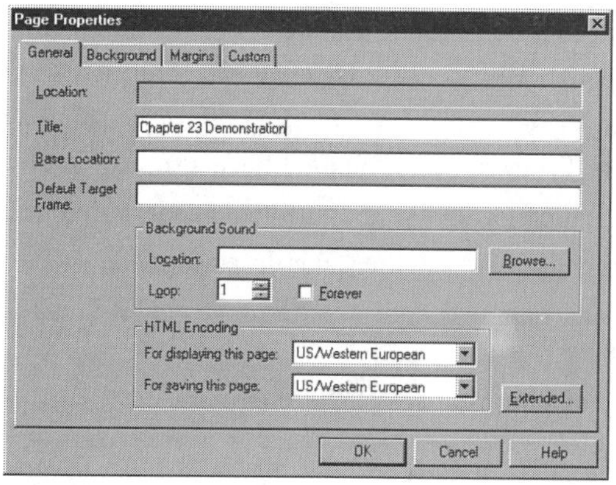

FIG. 23.2
Specify a title for your HTML document in the General tab of the Page Properties dialog box.

After you have titled your new web page, begin building the web page by entering text, inserting images, tables, hyperlinks, and all the other components that comprise a web page. You can format your page to give it the look and feel you want it to have. The following sections guide you through the specific tasks required to create a web page with FrontPage Express.

If you want to learn how to use FrontPage Express to modify or create web views of files and folders, read Chapter 14, "Managing Files Using Web View."

Formatting Text

Type text or copy and paste it from another document. Text in your HTML document can be formatted similarly to formatting text in a Word processing document. To specify the font characteristics for your text, follow these steps:

1. Select the text that you want to format.
2. Choose Format, Font to open the Font dialog box (see Figure 23.3).

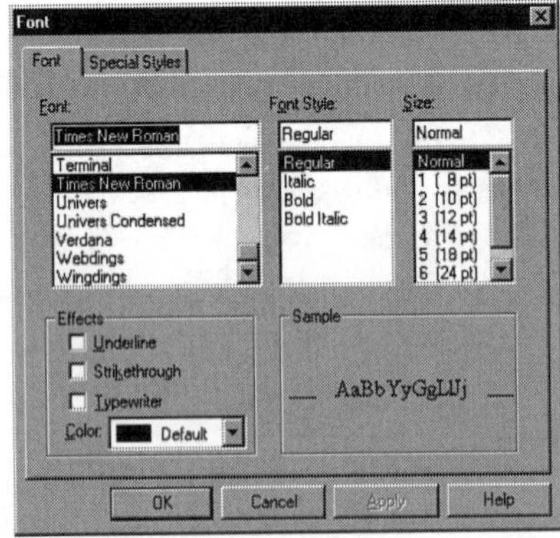

FIG. 23.3
Use the Font dialog box to select the font, font style, and size of the selected text.

3. Select the font you want to use from the Font list box.
4. Select a font style in the Font Style list box.
5. Select the size for the font in the Size list box.
6. If you want to format your text with additional effects, check the Underline, Strikethrough, or Typewrite boxes in the Effects group.

   The Typewriter option formats your text with a fixed-width font.
7. Select a color for your text from the Color drop-down list.

   You can preview all your selections in the Sample box and make changes before you close the dialog box.
8. When you finish making your selections, choose OK.

You can also do most of your text formatting with the FrontPage Express Format toolbar. The toolbar includes tools for selecting a font, increasing and decreasing font size, applying font styles, and choosing a font color.

Formatting Paragraphs with FrontPage Express

The HTML code used to create web pages includes specific styles used for paragraphs. Each style appears as predefined by the specific browser displaying the web page. These styles are used for many different types of paragraphs, ranging from body text to definitions to bulleted lists to heading levels.

Each of these styles displays text as defined in the browser. For example, Internet Explorer might display a specific style differently than Netscape Navigator. Browsers do produce similar results, though. For example, Normal is used for body text; Bulleted List indents paragraphs and precedes them with a bullet; Numbered List indents paragraphs and numbers them; Heading formats each line appropriate to its topic level.

To set the paragraph format, click the paragraph and choose Format, Paragraph or right-click the paragraph and choose Paragraph Properties. The Paragraph Properties dialog box appears, as shown in Figure 23.4.

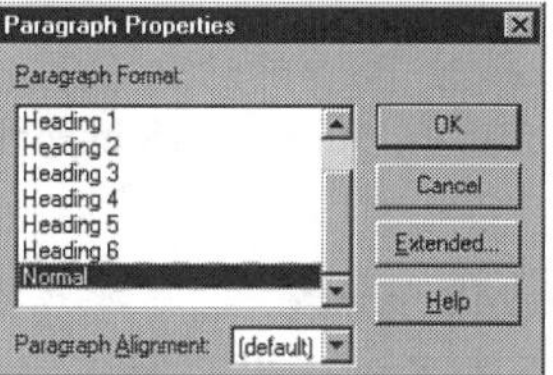

FIG. 23.4
The Paragraph Properties dialog box sets the predefined style for a paragraph.

You can select a paragraph format and set the paragraph alignment in the Paragraph Properties dialog box. Select one of the following paragraph formats from the Paragraph Format list box:

Table 23.1 Paragraph Formatting Styles

Format	Use
Address	A special HTML style generally used to specify the author of a document, a method for contacting the author (for example, an email address), and/or the date when the page was last modified.
Bulleted List	Displays paragraphs with left indentation with each paragraph preceded by a bullet. The bullet type can be changed.
Defined Term	Creates a left-aligned title line for the term being defined. Pressing Enter at the end of the defined term creates a new line with the Definition style.

continues

Table 23.1 Continued

Format	Use
Definition	A left-indented paragraph that follows a line with the Defined Term style. Pressing Enter creates the next paragraph with the Defined Term style.
Directory List	A form of bulleted list that is intended for use with short entries.
Formatted	This style generates text in a fixed-width font, which is useful when you want to present information in columns and rows but do not want to create a table.
Heading 1-6	Heads appear in different size and prominence. These styles are generally used to indicate topic heading levels.
Menu List	A bulleted list for use with short entries.
Normal	Standard text used in the body of the document.
Numbered List	Paragraphs display with left indentation and are sequentially numbered. Numbering style can be changed. The number is incremented for subsequent paragraphs with this style.

The Paragraph Alignment drop-down menu at the bottom of the Paragraph Properties dialog box enables you to set paragraph alignment to left, center, or right to display that paragraph in the corresponding screen location.

The FrontPage Express Format toolbar shown in Figure 23.5 speeds the paragraph formatting process. If the toolbar is not selected, display it by clicking View Format Toolbar. Set paragraph alignment by clicking one of the three alignment icons immediately to the right of the color palette icon. Paragraph formatting can be set by using the drop-down style menu at the far left of the Format toolbar. Format paragraphs with line numbering or bullets by clicking the Numbered List or Bulleted List buttons on the Format toolbar.

Remove Bulleted List or Line Numbering format by reformatting the paragraphs with Normal style.

Customizing the Bullet or Numbering Style

You also can quickly create numbered and bulleted lists by clicking the numbered list icon or bulleted list icon in the right-hand grouping of the Format toolbar.

To change the numbering or bulleting of lists, choose Format, Bullets, and Numbering to open the List Properties dialog box (see Figure 23.6). You can also open the dialog box by right-clicking a list in your HTML document and choosing List Properties.

FIG. 23.5
Quickly change paragraph styles by choosing a new style from the Change Style box on the Format toolbar.

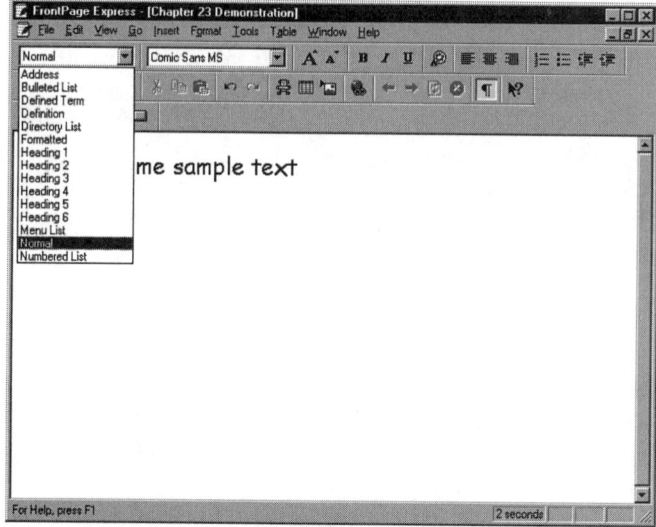

FIG. 23.6
Change the formatting of a list in the List Properties dialog box.

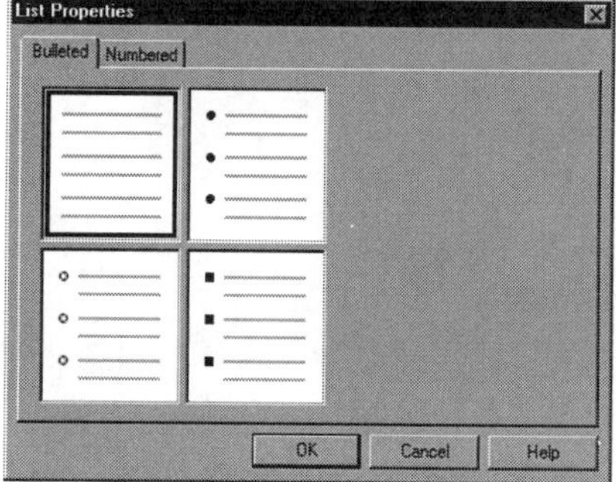

Selecting the Bulleted tab enables you to choose various bullet styles, whereas selecting the Numbered tab enables you to specify the number or letter to start from, as well as various numbering or lettering schemes.

Trying to insert a normal paragraph in the midst of a numbered list can be frustrating. If you format the inserted paragraph as Normal, the rest of the numbered list starts its numbering from 1 rather than the next number in the sequence. Prevent this by inserting your paragraph and giving it the Normal style. To format the paragraph where you want numbering to restart, click Format Bullets and Numbering, select the Numbered tab, choose the number where you want the list to restart from the Start At box, and click OK.

Two additional tools on the Format toolbar are the Decrease Indent and Increase Indent tools, located at the far right of the toolbar. Each time you click one of these tools, you increase or decrease the indentation for the selected paragraph.

Creating Color or Image Backgrounds

You can add a color to the background of your web page in FrontPage Express. If you don't specify a background, the viewer's browser displays your page with the default background (usually plain gray or white if the user hasn't changed the default). By specifying an image as your background, the browser repeats the image to fill the background area (known as *tiling*). The background image file should be in either the Graphical Interchange Format (GIF) or the Joint Picture Experts Group (JPEG) file format. These are the formats widely supported by graphics-capable web browsers.

Follow these steps to specify a color as your document's background:

1. Choose Format, Background or right-click the document, choose Page Properties, and select the Background tab.
2. Click the Background color drop-down list to select a color. You can select one of the sixteen standard colors (see Figure 23.7) or select Custom to open the standard Color dialog box.
3. Choose OK when you have finished your color selection.

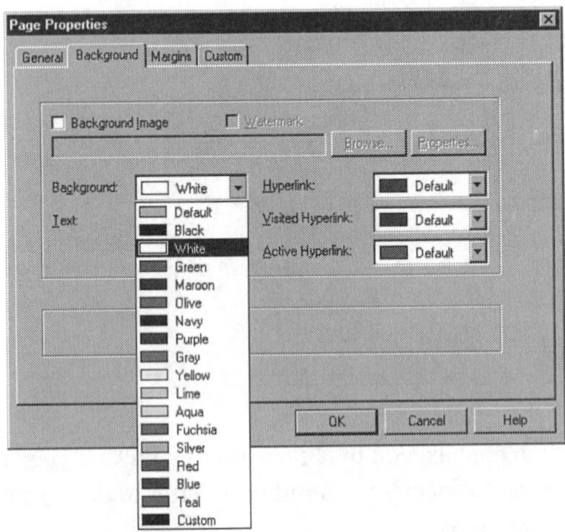

FIG. 23.7 Specify a background color for your HTML document in the Background tab of the Page Properties dialog box.

To specify an image as your document's background, follow these steps:

1. Choose Format, Background or select the Background tab in the Page Properties dialog box.
2. Select the Background Image check box.
3. Choose Browse to open the Select Background Image dialog box.
4. Select the Other Location tab to use a graphics file on your local drive or network. Select the From File option button and specify the path to your local background image file or

choose Browse to locate the file on your hard disk. Select From Location and enter the URL to use a graphic file on your intranet.

Select the Clip Art tab to use backgrounds supplied by any Microsoft product installed on your computer. Select Backgrounds from the Category list. Select the background you want.

5. Click OK to return to the Background tab.
6. If want the background to appear to remain fixed as the viewer scrolls down the page, select the Watermark check box.
7. Click OK.

You will now see your document set against the tiled image as a background.

Adding Images

FrontPage Express supports a wide range of image file formats for insertion into your HTML documents. Practically speaking, however, there are only two image formats—GIF (.gif) and JPEG (.jpg)—in wide use on the web. However, FrontPage Express automatically converts images from the following file formats:

- Bitmap (.bmp)
- TIFF (.tif)
- Windows metafile (.wmf)
- Sun Raster (.ras)
- Postscript (.eps)
- PCX (.pcx)
- Targa (.tga)

When you insert an image that is not in the GIF or JPEG format, FrontPage Express first converts it to the GIF format (for images with 256 or fewer colors) or the JPEG format (for images with more than 256 colors). When you save your HTML document, FrontPage Express prompts you to save your image file in the new format if a conversion took place.

To insert an image into your HTML document from a file, follow these steps:

1. Choose Insert, Image from the menu to open the Image Properties dialog box (see Figure 23.8).
2. Enter the path to image file you want to insert in the From File text box or choose the Browse button to locate the file on your hard disk.
3. Choose OK.

You can insert images that are objects in other open Windows applications into a FrontPage Express document by using drag-and-drop or copy-and-paste methods. When you save your HTML document, you are prompted to save these image files along with your document.

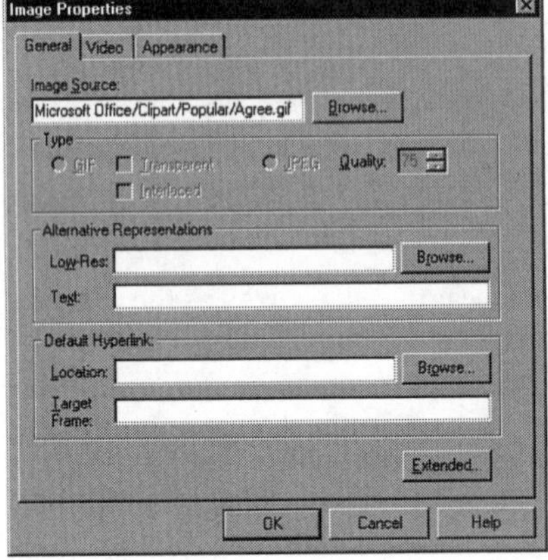

FIG. 23.8
Insert images into your HTML document in the Image Properties dialog box.

ON THE WEB

You can find web resources of free art at the following:

http://www.microsoft.com/gallery

http://www.clipart.com

http://the-tech.mit.edu/KPT/bgs.html

http://www.barrysclipart.com/mdex.html

http://sunsite.unc.edu/gio/iconbrowser/

http://home.eurocontrol.fr/~christin/index.html

http://www.hq.nasa.gov/office/pao/Library/photo.html

Controlling the Properties of an Image

Once an image is inserted into your HTML document, you can customize its properties by using the Image Properties dialog box. To customize an image, click the image to select it and choose Edit, Image Properties or right-click the image and choose Image Properties. The Image Properties dialog box appears. There are three tabs in the Image Properties dialog box. The General and Appearance tabs contain options that are related to graphic images. To learn about an option, click the Help button at the bottom of the Properties dialog box.

You can resize images in the FrontPage Express document window by clicking the image to select it and then moving your mouse cursor over one of the resizing anchors at the borders of the image, where the mouse pointer changes to a two-sided arrow. Click and drag the mouse to change the dimensions of the image.

Adding Horizontal Lines

You can create horizontal lines of various sizes and colors to provide separation between sections of your document. Choose Insert, Horizontal Line to add a horizontal line to your document. To adjust the properties of the line, right-click the line and choose Horizontal Line Properties to open the Horizontal Line Properties dialog box (see Figure 23.9). You can specify the line width either as a Percent of the browser window or as an absolute length in Pixels. The height of the line can be set in increments of one pixel. The alignment of the line can be set to Left, Center, or Right. The color of the line can be specified by using the drop-down color menu in a manner similar to setting Background color described in the "Creating Color or Image Backgrounds" section. The last check box directs the browser to display a Solid line rather than a shaded line if the default color is selected.

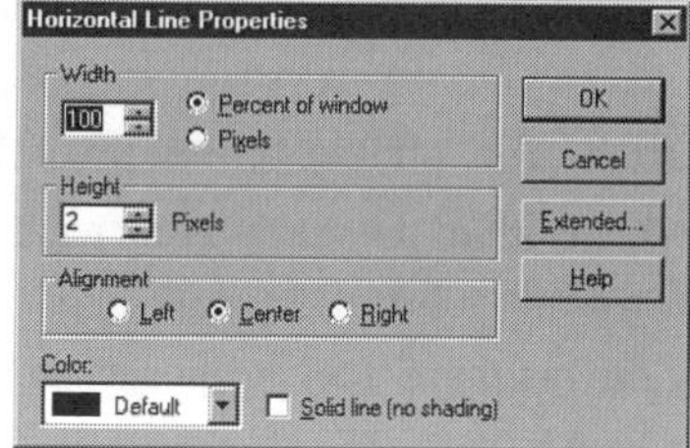

FIG. 23.9 Set horizontal line properties in the Horizontal Line Properties dialog box.

Add a Marquee

A marquee is a region of scrolling text that your can use in your document to draw the viewer's attention. Marquees are normally located in the top or bottom portion of documents. To add a marquee, follow these steps:

1. Choose Insert, Marquee to open the Marquee Properties dialog box (see Figure 23.10).

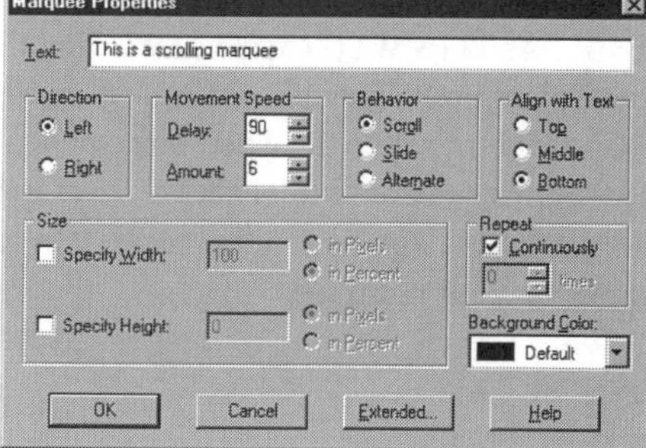

FIG. 23.10 Set marquee properties in the Marquee Properties dialog box.

2. Enter the line of text that you want to scroll across the screen in the Text field of the dialog box.
3. Select either Left or Right as the Direction for scrolling.

4. Set the Movement Speed Delay time in milliseconds.

   The Delay time sets the time between each successive step in the direction that the text is moving.

5. Set the Amount setting to specify the amount of movement in pixels of each step that the text takes on the screen.

6. Select Scroll in the Behavior box if you want the text to move across the screen and then start scrolling again.

   Or, select Slide if your want your text to move across the screen and then remain in place after it reaches the opposite side.

   Or, select Alternate to cause your text to reverse directions each time it reaches the opposite side of the screen.

7. Select one of the options in the Align with Text box to specify how text around the marquee is aligned.

   Adjacent text can be aligned with the Top, Middle, or Bottom of the marquee.

8. Select Specify Width to specify the width of the marquee as an absolute number of pixels or as a percentage of the browser window size.

9. Select Specify Height to specify the height of the marquee as an absolute number of pixels or as a percentage of the browser window size.

10. Select Continuously to repeat the marquee motion continuously or specify a number of times for the motion to be repeated.

11. Select a Background Color for the marquee area from the drop-down list.

12. Choose OK.

You can also resize a marquee in the FrontPage Express document window by clicking the marquee to select it and then moving your mouse pointer over one of the resizing anchors at the borders of the image, where the mouse pointer changes to a two-sided arrow. Click and drag the mouse pointer to change the dimensions of the marquee.

One limitation of FrontPage Express's WYSIWYG capabilities is that the actual scrolling action of a marquee cannot be previewed within the FrontPage Express document window. FrontPage Express simply denotes the marquee text within a dashed box, set against the marquee background color. You need to view your document in Internet Explorer to preview the animated effects. First, save your file in FrontPage Express and then open it in Internet Explorer to preview the actual text motion within your marquee.

Adding Background Sound

You can add background sound to your web page that plays when the page opens, providing the computer viewing the page has sound capability. To add background sound, follow these steps:

1. Choose Insert, Background Sound to open the Background Sound dialog box.

2. Select the From File option button and specify the path to the sound file on your hard disk or choose Browse to locate it.

The following sound file formats are supported: *.wav, *.mid, *.midi, *.aif, *.aifc, *.aiff, *.au, and *.snd.

3. Choose OK.

ON THE WEB

To download free sound files for use in your web pages, go to the following:

http://www.microsoft.com/gallery

Adding Hyperlinks

Perhaps the most powerful aspect of HTML comes from its capability to link designated text or an image to another document or resource anywhere on the World Wide Web. A viewer's browser can highlight the designated text or image with color and/or underlines to indicate that it is a hypertext link, or hyperlink for short. Normally the textual or graphical representation of the hyperlink reveals sufficient information about the destination so a viewer can decide whether or not to click the link to follow it to its destination. Additionally, the mouse pointer usually changes shape when it passes over a hyperlink.

The destination of a hyperlink is encoded as a *Uniform Resource Locator* (URL). A URL gives the address of a resource on the World Wide Web and also identifies the protocol used to transfer the resource, such as *HTTP* (Hypertext Transfer Protocol) or *FTP* (File Transfer Protocol). The general format for a URL is *protocol://hostname/path_to_resource.*

To add a hyperlink from your document to a resource on the World Wide Web, follow these steps:

1. Enter the text or insert the image that will serve as the hyperlink.

   This hyperlink serves as the pointer in the viewer's browser and is clicked to activate the URL that is attached to the hyperlink.

2. Select the text and choose Insert, Hyperlink to open the Create Hyperlink dialog box (see Figure 23.11).

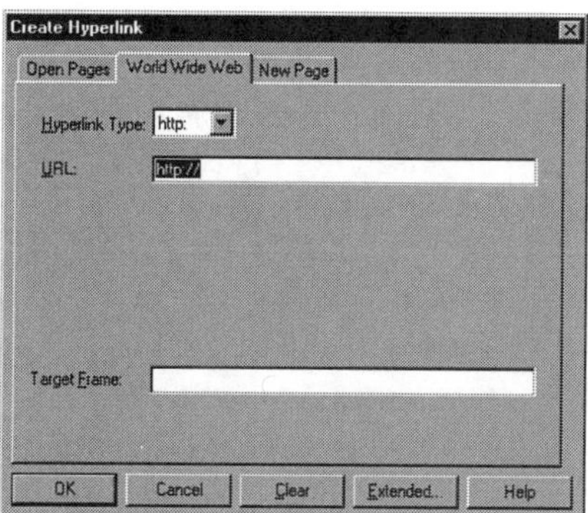

FIG. 23.11
Insert a hyperlink into your document by using the Create Hyperlink dialog box.

3. Select the World Wide Web tab to insert a link to a resource on the web.
4. Select the type of hyperlink from the Hyperlink Type drop-down list:

Type	Explanation	Format of path designation
file:	file on local hard disk	file://drive_designator/path_to_file
ftp:	File Transfer Protocol	ftp://ftp.hostname/path_to_resource
gopher:	Gopher protocol	gopher://gopher.hostname/path_to_resource
http:	Hypertext Transfer Protocol	http://www.hostname/path_to_resource
https:	Secure Hypertext Transfer Protocol	https://www.hostname/path_to_resource
mailto:	Electronic mail	mailto:mailbox_name@host
news:	Usenet news	news:newsgroup_name
telnet:	Telnet login	telnet://hostname
wais:	Wide Area Information Server	wais://hostname/path_to_resource

5. Enter the path to the web resource serving as the destination for the hyperlink in the URL text box.
6. Choose OK.

FrontPage Express automatically retrieves the URL of the web resource open on your browser when the Create Hyperlink dialog box opens. Before inserting a hyperlink in your FrontPage Express document, open Internet Explorer, go to the destination where you want to link, and switch to your FrontPage Express document. Select the anchor for the link and choose Insert, Hyperlink and notice that the URL field automatically fills in. Choose OK to finish.

If you used a textual anchor for your hyperlink, you will now notice that the text appears blue. Text that serves as a hyperlink is normally displayed as a special color to alert the viewer that it is a hyperlink. You can control how your hyperlinks will be colored via the Background tab of the Page Properties dialog box (see Figure 23.12). Choose File, Page Properties or right-click anywhere in your document window and choose Page Properties to open the Page Properties dialog box.

FIG. 23.12
Set the display colors for your hyperlinks in the Background tab of the Page Properties dialog box.

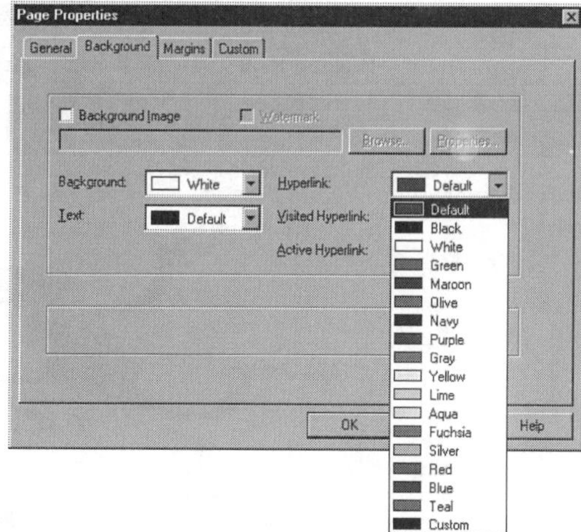

There are three categories for setting the way a hyperlink will be displayed in a viewer's browser:

Name	Description	Default Color
Hyperlink	A hyperlink the viewer has never activated. before	blue
Visited Hyperlink	A hyperlink the viewer has previously. activated	purple
Active Hyperlink	A hyperlink the viewer is currently pointing to (for example, a hyperlink changes to this color when the user moves the mouse over it).	red

Use the drop-down color menus to set colors for the three types of links and choose OK.

Adding Tables

One of the most important design features available in an HTML editor is the capability to create and manipulate tables. Figure 23.13 shows a table that has been inserted within a web page by using FrontPage Express. The table has six rows and four columns. The columns have been merged for the first two rows, where the title and the logo appear. Although you can format borders around tables, the dashed lines shown here are invisible when the page appears in the browser.

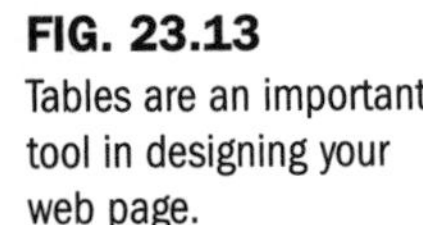

FIG. 23.13
Tables are an important tool in designing your web page.

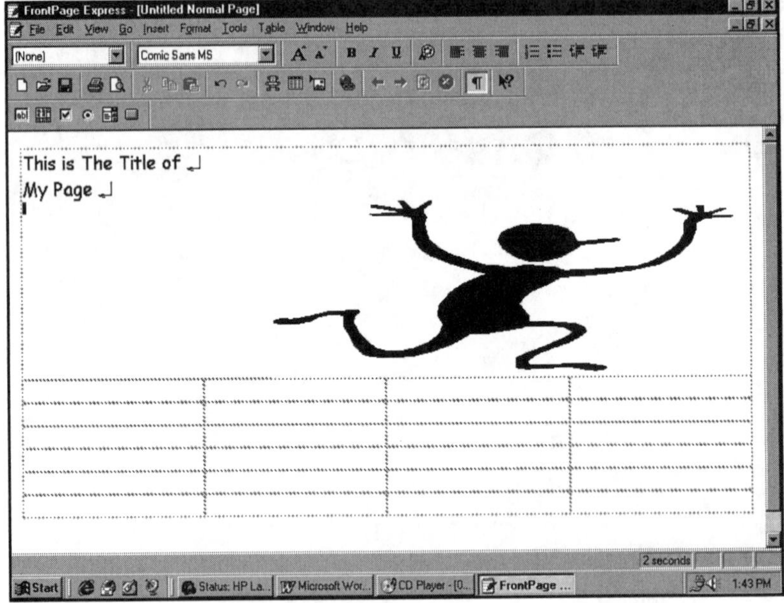

Tables are an easy way to create ordered rows and columns of graphics, text, and hyperlinks. Tables can even be used to create newsletter-like column formats. If you have browsed the web very much, you are familiar with how many sites arrange material in three columns, left column links, middle column text content, right column advertisements, or graphics. This type of layout is nearly impossible without the use of tables.

Tables, though, solve one of the tough design problems in web page design, positioning text and graphics accurately. You can use a table simply to place text or graphics at a specific position on the page, even if there is other presentation of row/column information on the page. While the new Cascading Style Sheets (CSS) enable very accurate positioning of text and graphics, CSS is not supported by a wide base of browsers. Nearly all browsers support tables, however, so you can be assured that your web page will appear approximately the way you want in most browsers.

Many of the examples in Chapter 14, "Managing Files Using Web View," were created by using tables as design grids in which text, graphics, and hyperlinks were placed.

To create a table in your web page, follow these steps:

1. Move the insertion point to where you want to place the table.
2. Click Table Insert Table to display the Insert Table dialog box shown in Figure 23.14.
3. Enter the number of rows and columns you want in the Rows and Columns boxes.

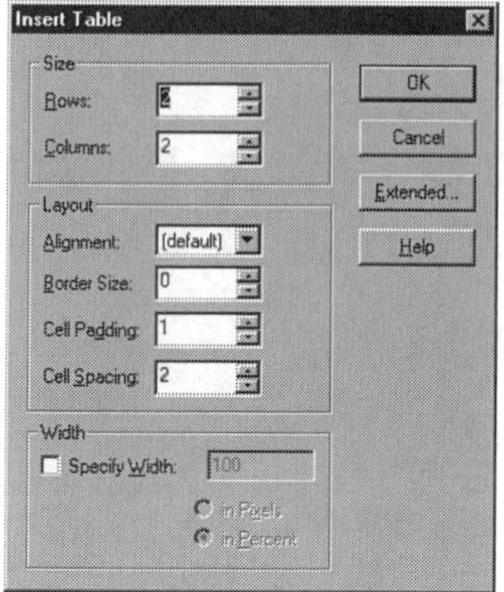

FIG. 23.14
Insert a table with a specific size, alignment, and border spacing with the Insert Table dialog box.

4. Select the Layout of the table by using the following options:

Options	Description
Alignment	Select the horizontal alignment of the entire table on the page. Default is the original alignment.
Border Size	Border width in pixels. Use 0 to create an invisible border in most browsers.
Cell Padding	Sets the padding in pixels between the cell contents and the left edge of the cell. This applies to the entire table and cannot be set for one cell. Default padding is 1.
Cell Spacing	Sets the spacing in pixels between cells in a table. The default is 2.

5. If you want to specify a width for the entire table, select the Specify Width box and enter the width measured in pixels or percent of the page width. In most cases you should use 100 percent so that the table will resize for the browser displaying the page.
6. Click OK.

FrontPage Express inserts a table at the insertion point in the web page. If you used zero pixels for the border width, the border appears as a dashed line so you can see it. It will not appear in the browser.

To insert items such as text, graphics, or hyperlinks in a cell within a table, click the cell in which you want the element, and then type or choose a command from the Insert menu. You can format one or more cells within a table by dragging across the cells, rows, or columns you want to format and then clicking a command from the Format menu.

Format individual cells or rows or columns of cells by selecting the cells and then clicking Table, Cell Properties. The Cell Properties dialog box appears, as shown in Figure 23.15. Select the formatting changes you want. To adjust the widths of columns, it is usually easiest to set the table width to 100 percent, and then adjust the column widths so the total percentage of all column widths equals 100 percent. If the column widths do not total 100 percent, it is difficult to predict the appearance.

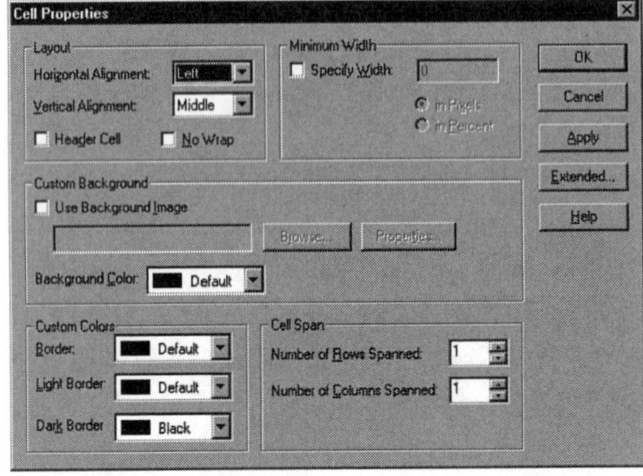

FIG. 23.15
Format the properties of single or groups of cells with the Cell Properties dialog box.

Format the entire table by moving the insertion point inside the table and then clicking Table, Table Properties. The Table Properties dialog box appears, as shown in Figure 23.16. Select the formatting changes you want and then click OK.

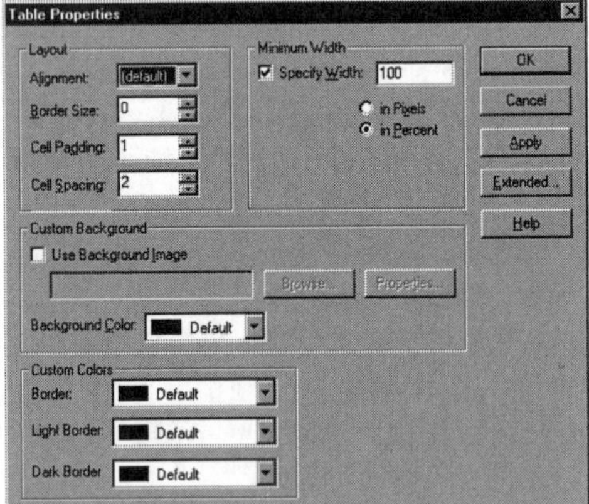

FIG. 23.16
Modify or format an entire table with the Table Properties dialog box.

Viewing the HTML Coding of Your Documents

Up to now, you have been using FrontPage Express as a WYSIWYG editor. You can, however, view and edit the HTML code for a document in FrontPage Express. To see the code for an HTML document, follow these steps:

1. Choose View, HTML to open the View or Edit HTML dialog box (see Figure 23.17). The HTML code for the active FrontPage Express page displays.
2. Select the Original option to view the page as it was last saved.

   Or, select the Current option to view the page in its current state.

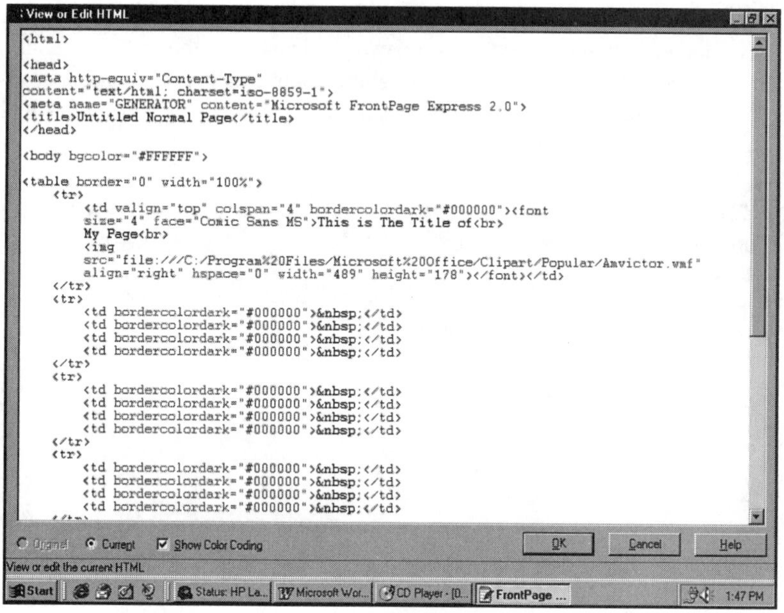

FIG. 23.17
You can view and edit the HTML code for a web document in FrontPage Express.

```
<html>

<head>
<meta http-equiv="Content-Type"
content="text/html; charset=iso-8859-1">
<meta name="GENERATOR" content="Microsoft FrontPage Express 2.0">
<title>Untitled Normal Page</title>
</head>

<body bgcolor="#FFFFFF">

<table border="0" width="100%">
    <tr>
        <td valign="top" colspan="4" bordercolordark="#000000"><font
        size="4" face="Comic Sans MS">This is The Title of<br>
        My Page<br>
        <img
        src="file:///C:/Program%20Files/Microsoft%20Office/Clipart/Popular/Amvictor.wmf"
        align="right" hspace="0" width="489" height="178"></font></td>
    </tr>
    <tr>
        <td bordercolordark="#000000"> </td>
        <td bordercolordark="#000000"> </td>
        <td bordercolordark="#000000"> </td>
        <td bordercolordark="#000000"> </td>
    </tr>
    <tr>
        <td bordercolordark="#000000"> </td>
        <td bordercolordark="#000000"> </td>
        <td bordercolordark="#000000"> </td>
        <td bordercolordark="#000000"> </td>
    </tr>
    <tr>
        <td bordercolordark="#000000"> </td>
        <td bordercolordark="#000000"> </td>
        <td bordercolordark="#000000"> </td>
        <td bordercolordark="#000000"> </td>
```

3. To view the text of the HTML tags, parameter names, parameter values, and document content in different colors, check the Show Color Coding text box.
4. When you finish viewing or editing the text, choose OK.

You can directly edit the HTML code in the dialog box, but if you plan to do a significant amount of HTML coding (rather than relying on FrontPage Express's WYSIWYG interface), a number of HTML editors are available that are more suited to this task than FrontPage Express.

Using NetMeeting

The interconnectivity that the Internet brought to computer users around the world has given birth to a new type of software called *collaboration software*. Collaboration software enables multiple users to work together in real-time from disparate locations, communicating by voice, video, and data exchange by using a local area network (LAN), WAN (wide area network), an intranet, or the Internet. NetMeeting is the latest version of Microsoft's contribution to this arena. NetMeeting has many powerful features that enable users to exchange ideas over the Net, make joint decisions, collaborate on editing a document or refining a budget, and to just stay in touch.

NetMeeting enables you to conference with other NetMeeting users using data, audio, and video exchange. NetMeeting gives priority to audio communication so that, depending on the available bandwidth, the speed of data and video exchange will be varied as necessary to maintain a high quality audio connection.

Figure 23.18 shows a NetMeeting conference in progress. The Current Call tab (shown in the left edge of the screen) lists the two participants in the conference. In Figure 23.19, you can see Microsoft Excel being used as a shared application. In this case, because the person who is sharing the application is not collaborating, the person viewing the application cannot work in the application.

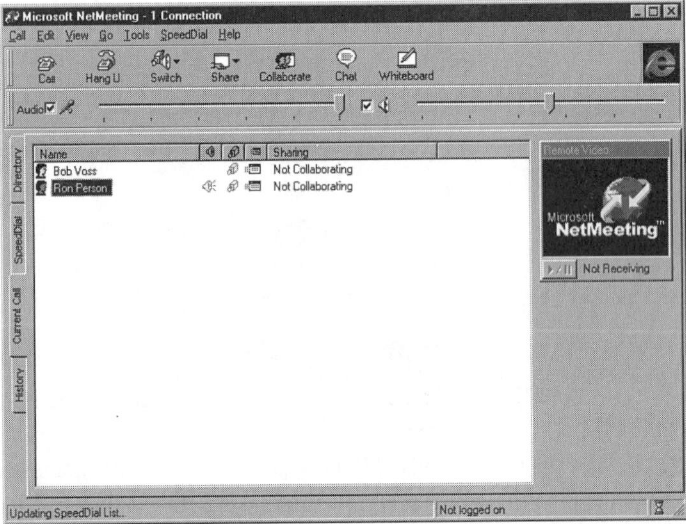

FIG. 23.18
The Current Call tab in NetMeeting lists the participants who are currently involved in a call.

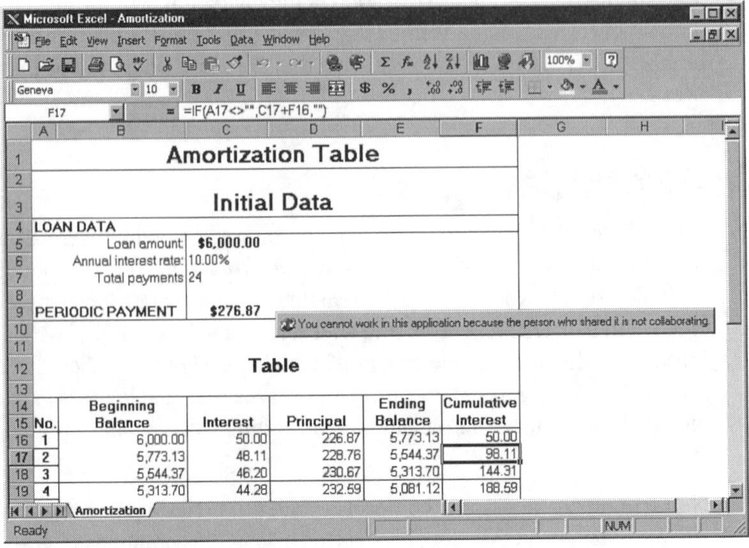

FIG. 23.19
You can share an application in a NetMeeting conference so that multiple users can view and work on a document.

Data Conferencing

NetMeeting is capable of multipoint data conferencing, meaning that multiple users can exchange data with each other simultaneously. With NetMeeting you can exchange data with other participants in a conference in several ways:

- *Shared applications* Participants can share an application that resides on the computer of just one of the participants. All participants can watch as one person works in the application, editing data, highlighting important aspects of a document, or demonstrating a feature of the application. At any time, the person sharing the application can opt to collaborate with other participants so that they can work in the application as well, even if they don't have the application on their computers.
- *Shared clipboard* Participants in a conference can share data via a common clipboard, so information from an application on one participant's computer can instantly be copied and pasted to an application on another participant's computer. One participant, for example, can contribute data from a document on his/her computer to the document being worked on in a shared application.
- *Whiteboard* Imagine an electronic whiteboard that you can "walk up to" at any time during a data conference to use just as you use a whiteboard in an ordinary conference room. This is exactly what the Whiteboard in NetMeeting enables you to do. Use the Whiteboard to sketch out an idea, draw a diagram, or make a list of points for a meeting. Essentially a drawing program, Whiteboard has tools for drawing, moving objects, pointing to or highlighting areas on a page, or turning to a new page. All participants in a conference can view and work on the Whiteboard.
- *Chat* This feature enables participants to exchange text messages. This is useful for jotting down shared meeting notes or for communicating when one or more of the participants in a conference lacks audio capability. You can even exchange private messages with selected participants in a conference.
- *File transfer* Most persons are familiar with transferring data files as a mode of data exchange. NetMeeting enables you to transfer data files in the background while you are in conference. You can transfer a file to a selected participant or to all the participants in the conference, who can then choose to accept or reject the file. You can, for example, work collaboratively on a document in a data NetMeeting session, using a shared application on your computer, and then send each participant a copy of the edited file at the end of the conference.

NOTE Although you can transfer files in the background during a NetMeeting data conference, be aware that file transfer is slow in comparison to normal file transfer using a regular communications package. The reason for this is that NetMeeting is working with a limited bandwidth and has to divide up that bandwidth with the other forms of exchange that are happening simultaneously. File transfer is not given the highest priority. If you know you want to transfer a file to the participants in a planned conference, you can save time by sending them the file ahead of time (or after the conference is over).

Video Conferencing

If two or more of the participants in a NetMeeting conference have video hardware that is compatible with Video for Windows, you can exchange visual data. You can see each other as you carry on a meeting or use your video capabilities to show another participant a prototype of a product you are working on, a diagram or schematic, or the view out the window of your corner office. Video and audio conferencing in NetMeeting are point-to-point, meaning you can see and talk to only one person at a time. In a meeting with several participants, you can select a person's name from the list in the Current Call window.

NOTE Although you can see and speak to only one participant with NetMeeting at the time of this writing, H.323 conference servers and gateways are currently being developed that will enable multiple users to exchange audio and video data. ■

You can dynamically resize the My Video window during a video conference to change the size of the image sent to the other user. You can also move the My Video and Remote Video windows, which normally reside in the Current Call window, to any location on your desktop, and pause and resume the transmission of video data by using buttons in the video windows. Even if you don't have the hardware needed to send video images, you can still receive them from other participants in a conference.

Audio Conferencing

You might not need or have the capability for transmitting video images but would still like to enhance your NetMeeting sessions with real-time voice exchange. NetMeeting enables you to do this with ease. You can engage in point-to-point voice communication with other NetMeeting users. NetMeeting supports both half-duplex (one person speaking at a time) or full-duplex (both people speaking simultaneously) calls. It enables you to adjust the sensitivity of your microphone, tune your audio by using the Audio Tuning Wizard, and turn off your microphone if you want to interrupt audio transmission.

Ways to Use NetMeeting

NetMeeting opens up limitless possibilities for cooperating over the Internet:

- *Technical support* Use your intranet and NetMeeting to provide remote technical support to end users in your company. The user can call the technical support person, establish a NetMeeting connection, and watch as the support person diagnoses the problem. In many cases, this can save technical support staff a visit to the person needing help. The regular telephone can be used for verbal communication during the support session.
- *Meetings* You can host a meeting with one or more participants. After you have all established a connection via an ILS (Internet Locator Server) (described later in the "How NetMeeting Works" section), you can exchange data by using a shared application, the shared Clipboard, the Whiteboard, and Chat. You can also exchange audio and video data to liven up the meeting.

- *Collaborative Editing* Several people can work together editing a document that appears in a shared application. You can, for example, involve people from several locations in the editing of an annual report or a budget. Each participant would be able to work on the actual document, using the shared application that resides on one of the participant's computer.

ON THE WEB

For a complete overview of the features of NetMeeting and to download NetMeeting to your computer, visit the following web site:

http://www.microsoft.com/netmeeting/corp/corpfeatures.htm

How NetMeeting Works

This section is only meant to give you an overview of how NetMeeting works. To learn more about the details of how to use NetMeeting, refer to the Help topics in NetMeeting.

The first step in establishing a connection in NetMeeting is to find the participants. This is done by using a directory server called the Microsoft Internet Locator Server, or ILS. The ILS helps you find the people with which you want to communicate, and once that is accomplished and a connection is established, the ILS drops out of the picture. The ILS is not involved in the communication between callers. Microsoft currently has several directory servers online that you can use to link to other users, or you can set up your own ILS by using the software that is part of the Microsoft Internet Information Server package. If your company has its own Intranet, for example, you would benefit by having your own ILS for users of the Intranet.

Figure 23.21 shows the listing for one of Microsoft's directory servers. In this case, the list has been filtered to show only those users who have categorized their user information for business use only. The list shows everyone who is currently connected to that server and running NetMeeting. A red asterisk next to a name indicates that the person is currently involved in a call. To call someone on the list, double-click the name. The person receiving your call will see a dialog box on his screen and have the choice of accepting or rejecting your call. If someone calls you, you also will see the same dialog box and can reject or accept the call.

CAUTION

The first time you connect to one of Microsoft's directory servers, you might be in for a shock. You will quickly discover that many NetMeeting users are looking for a different kind of meeting than you are and you might be offended by the remarks you see in the Comments field of the Directory window. Normally, you can avoid offensive material on the web by picking and choosing the sites to which you link. NetMeeting is a different story. When you connect to a directory server in hopes of finding someone with whom to hold a NetMeeting session, you are entering a new world that reflects a wide range of human behavior and tastes. Prepare yourself!

FIG. 23.21
The Directory tab displays a listing of everyone connected to selected directory server.

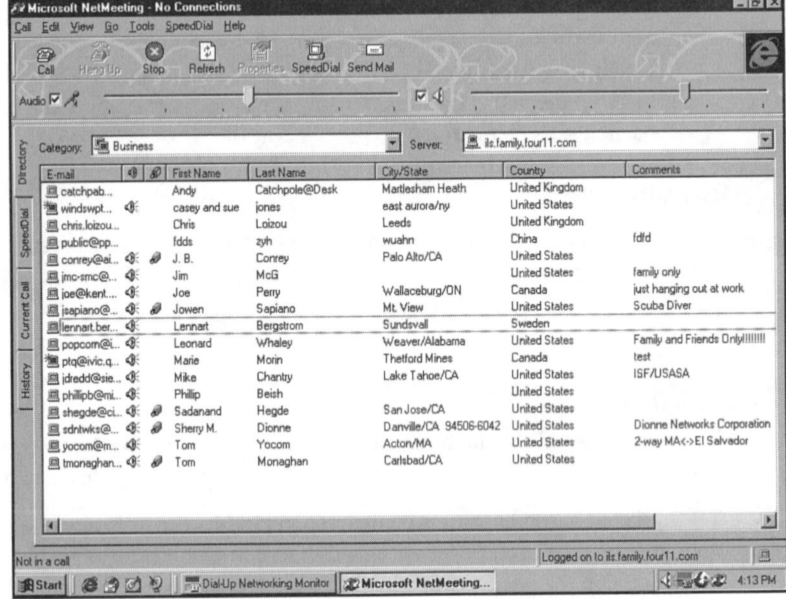

After you establish communication with another NetMeeting user, you can use all of the features of NetMeeting to conference with the other user. Even if you are not capable of audio and video communication, you can still share applications, exchange data by using the shared clipboard, exchange messages by using Chat, and transfer files. To find out how to use the features of NetMeeting, refer to the Help topics in the Help menu.

Introducing NetShow

Another new component of Internet Explorer 4.0 is NetShow, Microsoft's application for broadcasting multimedia content over the Internet and intranets. NetShow incorporates some exciting new technologies that take the broadcasting of rich multimedia presentations to a new level.

From the user's point of view, the most exciting development is the use of media streaming technology. Instead of having to first download a multimedia file before it can be played back, NetShow delivers a continuous stream of data that can be played back almost immediately. The data isn't actually stored on the computer—it is simply played back as it arrives and then discarded. The benefit of media streaming is obvious. You no longer have to suffer through the interminable wait as a large multimedia file downloads before you can view the file. You start viewing the file right away and stop viewing the file if it is not what you want. In addition, streaming content can also be delivered to the desktop from the Internet, such as audio from radio stations, online training and classes, and more.

Another benefit of NetShow is the capability to *multicast*. NetShow can be used to multicast multimedia content, which means a single multimedia file can be sent to multiple users, rather than the same file being sent multiple times to reach the same users. This decreases the amount of data traffic on a network.

NetShow can be used for broadcasting audio, video, and illustrated audio (sound combined with sequenced images). NetShow has three components: NetShow server, NetShow client, and the NetShow authoring and production tools. NetShow server resides on a Windows NT 4.0 server and does the job of broadcasting multimedia files to clients, either live or on demand (from stored content). NetShow client is the player that enables the user to play multimedia content sent by the server. As soon as a user clicks a link to a file, the player starts and the file is played back.

The NetShow authoring and production tools are used to create multimedia content that takes advantage of NetShow's technologies, including tools for creating ASF files—files that use the new Active Streaming Format standard, which enables media streaming.

Using NetShow Client

Using the client piece of NetShow is simple. First, be sure you run the full install of Internet Explorer 4.0. This way, NetShow is automatically installed onto your system, along with all of the other optional Internet components. Next, browse the web as you normally would, but pay particular attention to those sites that advertise cybercasting of NetShow contents, such as:

- Radio station netcasts
- Press conferences
- Training

When you click an event or content that is being cybercast over NetShow, the NetShow client automatically starts, and the content begins to play on your system.

ON THE WEB

Microsoft provides a schedule of NetShow cybercasts that include both audio and video components:

http//www.microsoft.com/netshow/

PART V

Working with Applications

CHAPTER 24

Application Management Fundamentals

by Ron Person

In this chapter

Working in the Windows Environment

Windows uses concepts that, for many people, make computers easier to use. The basic organizational concept is that all applications run on a desktop and that each application runs in its own window. Windows can run multiple applications, just as you might have stacks of papers on your desk from more than one project. You can move the windows and change their size just as you can move and rearrange the stacks of papers on your desk.

▶ **See** "Making Windows Accessible for the Hearing, Sight, and Movement-Impaired," **p. 804**

▶ **See** "Understanding Data Linking," **p. 833**

▶ **See** "Cutting, Copying, and Pasting Data," **p. 823**

Just as you can cut, copy, and paste parts between papers on your real desktop, Windows enables you to cut or copy information from one application and paste the information into another. Some Windows applications even share live information; when you change data in one application, Windows automatically updates linked data in other applications.

The process for making entries, edits, and changes to text, numbers, or graphics is similar in all Windows applications. The basic procedure is as follows:

1. Activate the window that contains the desired application.
2. Select the text, number, or graphics object that you want to change. You can select items with the mouse or the keyboard.
3. Choose a command from the menu bar at the top of the application.
4. If a dialog box appears, select options to modify how the command works. Then execute the command by choosing the OK button.

An *application window* is the window that contains an application. *Document windows* appear inside application windows and contain documents. In many (but not all) applications, you can have several document windows open at a time. You switch between them by pressing Ctrl+F6 or by selecting from the Window menu the document that you want.

The Control menu contains commands to control a window's location, size, and status (open or closed). Each application and each document window within the application window has its own Control menu. The application Control menu appears at the left edge of the application's title bar. The document Control menu appears at the left edge of the document's title bar (if the document window is smaller than a full screen) or at the left edge of the menu bar (if the document window is a full screen). To open an application Control menu, click the application Control menu icon (the icon at the top-left corner of the program window), or press Alt+spacebar. To open a document Control menu, click the document Control-menu icon (the icon in the upper-left corner of a document window) or press Alt+hyphen (-).

To maximize a window so it fills the screen, click the Maximize button, a square window icon in the window's top-right corner (see Figure 24.1). You can also minimize a window and place it on the taskbar. To do so, you click another icon in the window's upper-right corner, the Minimize button, which looks like an underline representing the taskbar (see Figure 24.1).

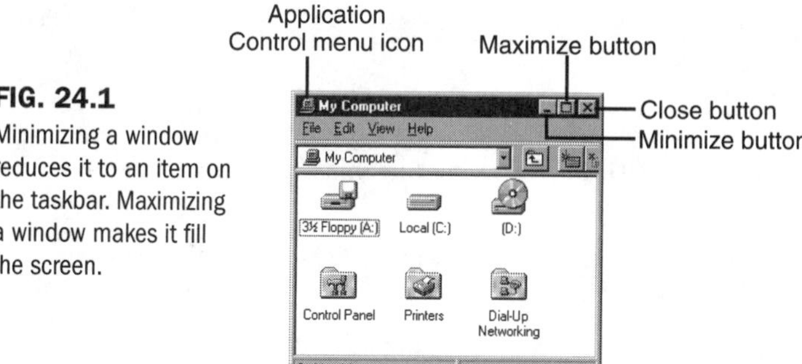

FIG. 24.1
Minimizing a window reduces it to an item on the taskbar. Maximizing a window makes it fill the screen.

TIP To minimize all windows with one command, click a clear area in the taskbar with the right mouse button and choose Minimize All Windows.

TIP To restore all minimized windows with one command, click a clear area in the taskbar with the right mouse button and choose Undo Minimize All.

When you minimize a program, its window shrinks to become an icon and name on the taskbar. The program still runs even though it is not in a window. To make a program on the taskbar appear in a window, click the program in the taskbar. (To use the keyboard to activate a program, press Alt+Tab repeatedly until you have selected the appropriate program, and then release the keys.)

You can resize a window by dragging its window border with the mouse, or by choosing the Size command from the Control menu. You can move a window without resizing it by dragging its title bar with the mouse, or by choosing the Move command from the Control menu.

▶ **See** "Customizing the Mouse," **p. 801**

▶ **See** "Customizing the Keyboard," **p. 802**

Table 24.1 introduces keystrokes that perform certain actions. You may want to refer to this table as you read through the book or begin working with Windows 95.

Table 24.1 Keystrokes to Control Windows

Keystroke	Action
Alt+Esc	Activates the next application window.
Alt+Tab	Displays a program bar showing open programs as icons. Each press of Alt+Tab selects the next icon. Releasing Alt+Tab activates the program selected in the program bar.

continues

Table 24.1 Continued

Keystroke	Action
Alt+Shift+Tab	Moves the selection through the program bar in the opposite direction of Alt+Tab. Releasing Alt+Shift+Tab activates the selected program.
Ctrl+F6	Activates the next document window (if an application has multiple document windows open).
Ctrl+Esc	Displays the Start menu. Press the up or down arrow keys to select from the menu.
Alt+spacebar	Displays the Control menu for the active program icon or window. Use the Control menu to change the location, size, and status of the program window.
Alt+hyphen (-)	Displays the Control menu for the active document window within the program. Use this Control menu to change the location, size, and status of the document window.

Using Menus and Dialog Boxes

Every properly designed Windows application operates in a similar way. As you will learn, you can move and resize all windows the same way in every Windows application. You can also execute commands the same way in all Windows applications.

You can choose a command from a menu by using the mouse or the keyboard (also, many time-saving shortcuts exist for choosing commands). If a command requires information from you before executing, a dialog box appears when you choose the command. In the dialog box, you use the mouse or the keyboard to choose options or enter values that control the command.

▶ **See** "Making Windows Accessible for the Hearing, Sight, and Movement-Impaired," **p. 804**

Choosing Menus and Commands

When you click a menu, a list of commands drops down under the menu, as shown in Figures 24.2 and 24.3. If you're not sure where to find a command, try browsing through the menus by clicking them until you find the command that you want. Many applications use similar commands for similar actions—a practice that makes learning multiple Windows applications easier.

To choose a menu or command with the mouse, move the tip of the pointer over the menu or command name and click the left mouse button. To choose a menu or command with the keyboard, press Alt+*letter* where *letter* is the underlined letter in the menu. When the menu appears, press the key for the underlined letter in the command (you don't have to hold down the Alt key while you do this). For example, to choose the File menu's Open command, hold down the Alt key, press F, and then press O.

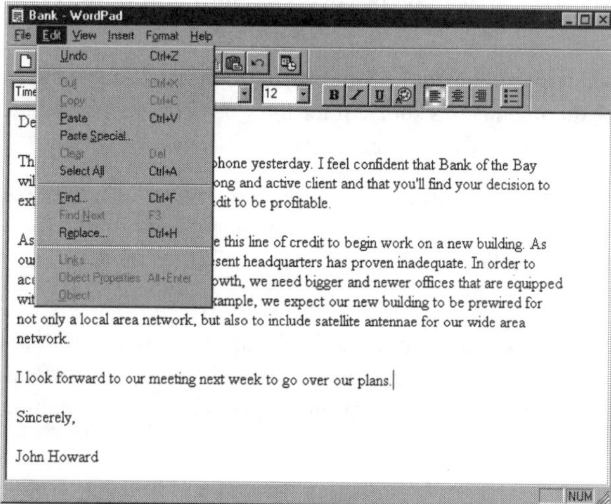

FIG. 24.2
WordPad's Edit menu displays shortcut keys.

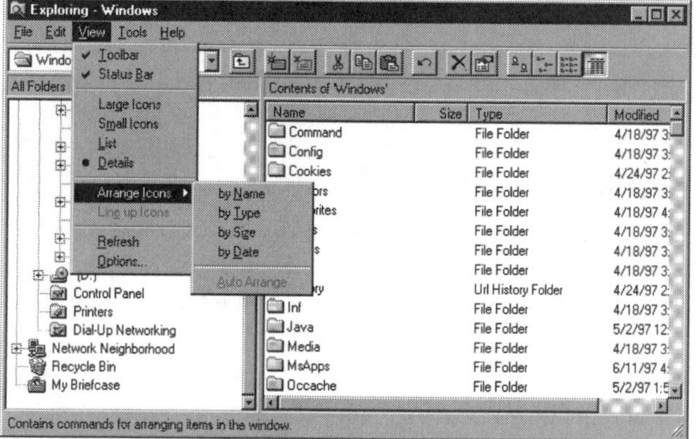

FIG. 24.3
In the Explorer, when you choose View, Arrange Icons, you see a submenu that displays additional commands.

You can choose commands that appear in a menu in solid black (bold) type. You *cannot* choose commands that appear in gray in a menu, even though you can see them. Gray commands or options are *disabled*. Commands or options appear in bold only when they are available, or *enabled*. For example, the Edit menu's Copy command appears in bold type only when you have selected something to copy.

Command names followed by an ellipsis (...) display an additional dialog box or window from which you can choose options or enter data. If you choose Edit, Find... from a Windows application, for example, a dialog box appears in which you type the word that you want to find.

Commands with a check mark to the left are commands that toggle on and off. A check mark indicates that the command is on; no check mark indicates that the command is off.

Commands with key combinations listed to the right have shortcuts. In Windows Explorer, for example, the Edit menu lists a shortcut for the Copy command, Ctrl+C. Therefore, to copy a file, you can choose Edit, Copy or press Ctrl+C.

Commands with an arrowhead next to them, as in Figure 24.3, have submenus that list additional commands. In the Explorer, the Arrange Icons command in the View menu has an arrowhead to its right, indicating that a submenu will show the ways in which you can arrange icons.

If you don't want to make a choice after displaying a menu, click the pointer a second time on the menu name or click outside the menu. If you are using the keyboard, press Esc to exit a menu without making a choice. Continue to press Esc until no commands or menus are selected.

NOTE If a dialog box appears on screen and you aren't sure what to do, you can escape without making any changes. Click the Cancel button or press the Esc key to cancel the current dialog box and ignore any changes to options.

Most Windows applications have an Undo command. If you complete a command and then decide that you want to undo it, check whether the Edit menu includes an Undo command.

Selecting Options from Dialog Boxes

Commands that require more information before they work, display a *dialog box*—a window similar to those shown in Figures 24.4 and 24.5. Dialog boxes like the one in Figure 24.4 have areas in which you enter text (such as the File Name text box) or select from a scrolling list of choices (see the Save In list of disks and folders in Figure 24.4). Many applications also include drop-down list boxes with lists that appear only when you select the box and press the down arrow key, or click the down arrow on the right side of the text box.

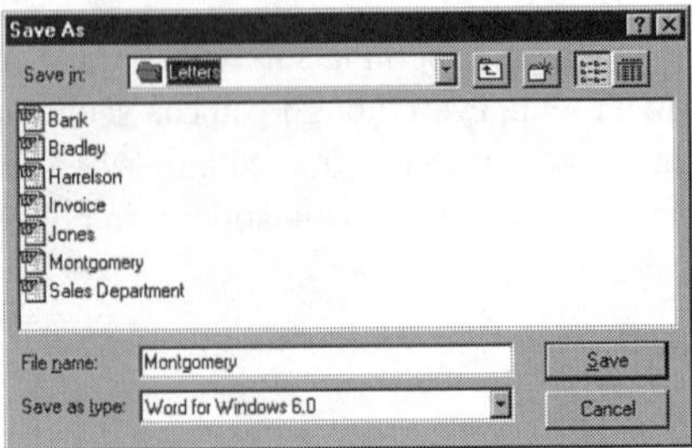

FIG. 24.4
The Save As dialog box is similar among Windows programs.

Figure 24.5 shows that dialog boxes can have round *option* buttons and square *check boxes*. The option buttons are clustered in a group labeled Hidden Files. When options are in such groups, you can choose only one of them. Check boxes act independently of other check boxes so you can select as many of them as you want. After you select options or make text entries, you accept the contents of the dialog box by choosing the OK button or cancel them by choosing the Cancel button.

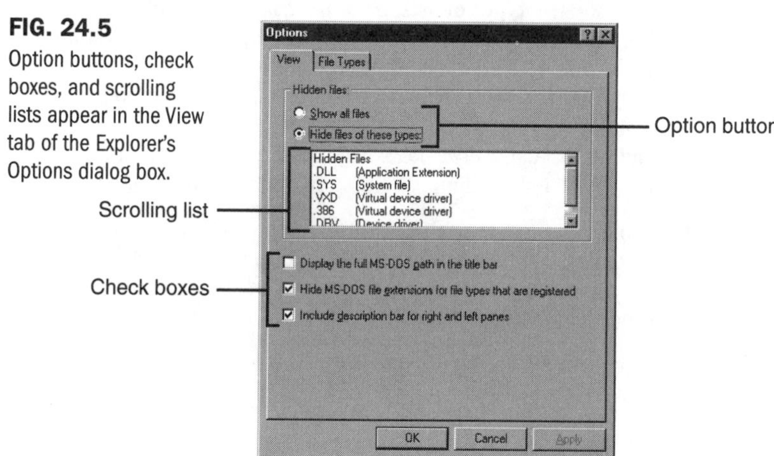

FIG. 24.5 Option buttons, check boxes, and scrolling lists appear in the View tab of the Explorer's Options dialog box.

If a dialog box hides something that you want to see on-screen, you can move the dialog box with the mouse by dragging the dialog box by its title bar to a new position. With the keyboard, press Alt+spacebar to open the dialog Control menu and then choose Move. A four-headed arrow appears. Press any arrow key to move an outline of the dialog box. Press Enter when the outline of the dialog box is where you want to place the dialog box. (Before you press Enter, you can cancel the move by pressing Esc.)

Figure 24.6 shows other types of controls used in dialog boxes, and Table 24.2 summarizes them.

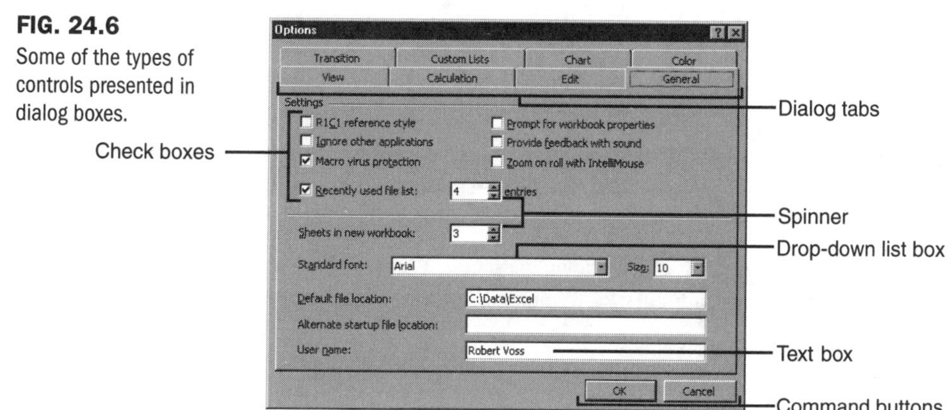

FIG. 24.6 Some of the types of controls presented in dialog boxes.

Table 24.2 Types of Dialog Box Controls

Control	Use
Text box	Move the pointer over the text box until it changes to an I-beam shape, then click. Type text entries manually. If you make a mistake, press the Backspace or Delete key to erase characters.
List box	You will see two types of lists. *Scrolling lists* show a columnar list of choices (refer to Figure 24.5). Click the up or down arrow on the right side of the list to scroll through the list, and then click the item that you want. The selected item appears in highlighted text (and might also appear in the text box above the list). The second type of list, a *drop-down list*, like the one shown in Figure 24.6, displays its scrolling list after you click the down arrow.
Option button	Click one option from within a group of option buttons. (You can select only one option button in each group.) The selected option button has a darkened center. To remove a selection, select a different option in the same group.
Check box	Click a check box to turn it on or off. Check boxes are square and contain an X when selected. You can select more than one check box at a time.
Spinner	Click the up or down arrow on the right side of a spinner to make the number change in increments of one.
Command button	Click a command button to complete the command, cancel the command, or open an additional dialog box for more alternatives.
Dialog tab	Click a dialog tab to see another grouping of options.

Using the Mouse in Dialog Boxes To select an option button or check box, click it. Clicking a blank check box selects it by putting an X in it. Clicking a check box that already has an X removes the X. To turn off an option button, click one of the other option buttons in the group.

To choose command buttons such as OK, Cancel, Yes, or No, click them.

▶ **See** "Editing Text in Text Boxes," **p. 607**

To select from a scrolling list box, click in the list box and then scroll through the list by clicking the up or down arrow in the scroll bar at the right side of the list box. To jump through large sections of the list, click in the scroll bar's shaded area. For long moves, drag the scroll bar's square to the new location. When the desired selection appears in the list box, click that selection.

Some Windows applications use drop-down list boxes. When closed, these list boxes look like the Printer list box shown in Figure 24.7 when closed; when open, they look like the same list box as shown in Figure 24.8. To select from a drop-down list box, click the down arrow on the text box's right side. When the scrolling list appears, select from it the same way that you select from any scrolling list box: Click the item that you want.

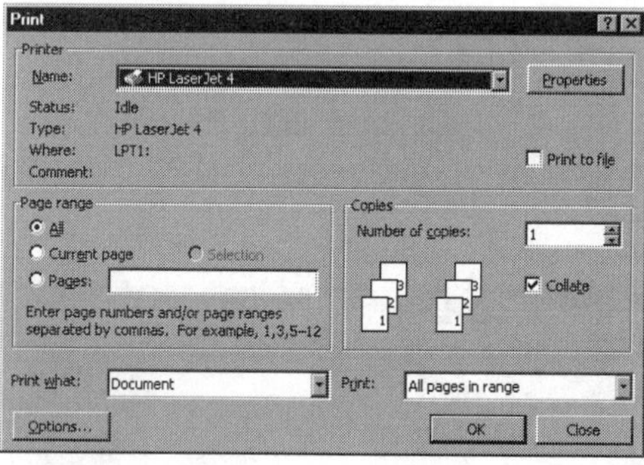

FIG. 24.7
The Printer drop-down list box when closed.

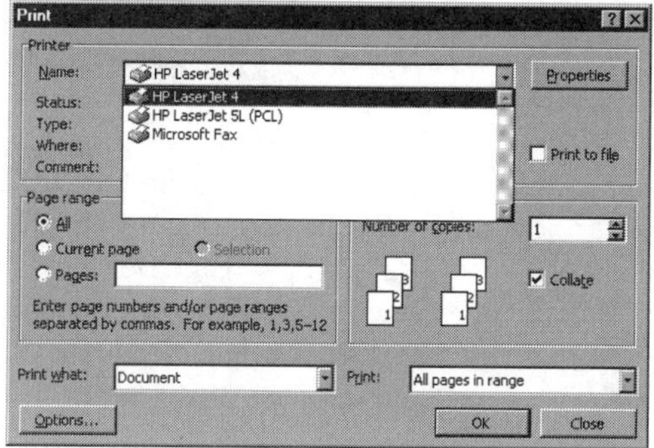

FIG. 24.8
The Printer drop-down list box when open.

NOTE In some dialog boxes, double-clicking an option button or an item in a list selects that option and simultaneously chooses the OK command button. In the Open dialog box, for example, you can double-click a file name to select and open the file. Experiment with the dialog boxes in your applications to determine whether double-clicking is a viable shortcut.

Using the Keyboard in Dialog Boxes Some drawing or graphics applications require that you use the mouse. In most Windows applications, however, you have the same functionality available from either the keyboard or the mouse. You might find that in some situations using the keyboard to control Windows is faster or more convenient.

To access a group of option buttons with the keyboard, you press Alt+*letter*, where *letter* is the underlined character that appears in an option's label. If the individual options do not have an underlined letter, press Alt+*letter*, where the underlined *letter* is in the title of the option group; then use the arrow keys to select an option.

To select a check box, press Alt+*letter*, where *letter* is the underlined character in the check box's label. Each time that you press Alt+*letter*, you toggle the check box between selected and deselected. An X appears in the check box when the box is selected. You also can toggle the active check box between selected and deselected by pressing the spacebar.

To make an entry in a text box, select the text box by pressing Alt+*letter*, where *letter* is the underlined character in the name of the text box. Press Alt+N, for example, to select the File Name text box in the Save As dialog box shown in Figure 24.9. Type a text entry or edit the existing entry by using the editing techniques described in the upcoming section "Editing Text in Text Boxes."

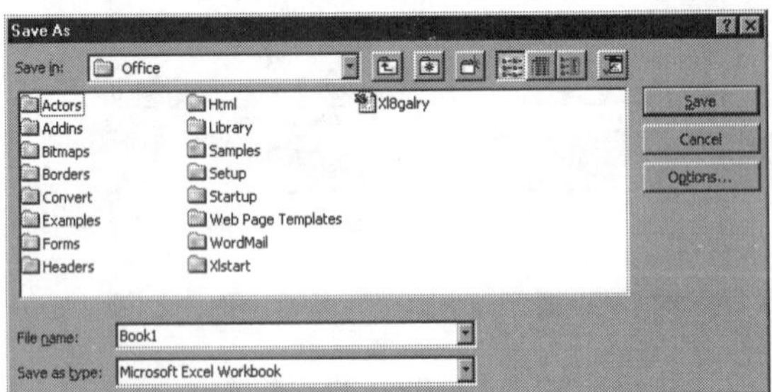

FIG. 24.9
The Save As dialog box's File Name text box when selected.

To select from a list of alternatives in a scrolling list box, select the list box by pressing Alt+*letter*, where *letter* is the underlined character in the name of the list box. When the list box is active, use the up or down arrow key or Page Up or Page Down to move through the list. The text is selected and displayed in reversed type. (To use the keyboard to display a drop-down scrolling list, press Alt+*letter* to activate the list and then press Alt+down arrow to drop the list. Then select items by pressing the up or down arrow keys.)

To select a command button, press Alt+*letter*, or if no letter is underlined, press Tab or Shift+Tab until a dashed line encloses the name of the button that you want. Press the spacebar to select the active button indicated by the dashed enclosure. At any time, you can select the command button that appears in bold type (usually the OK button) by pressing Enter. Press Esc to choose the Cancel button and escape from a dialog box without making any changes.

Changing Folders in Save As and Open Dialog Boxes When you save a file on your hard disk, Windows places the file in a folder in your hard disk. Folders are analogous to the file drawers and file folders that you use in your office to help you organize and locate your papers. You can locate files more easily if you store related files together in a folder. For example, you can store all the business letters that you create with your word processor in a folder named LETTERS and all your proposals in a folder named PROPOSALS.

Don't store the files that you create in the folders that store your program files. If you ever have to reinstall or upgrade a program, you might lose files that you store in the program folders. Also, these folders are already full of files, and it is difficult to find yours. Create your own folders, and folders within folders, to store your files.

The first time that you use the File, Open, or File, Save As command in a program, the application usually assumes that you want to open or save a document in that program's folder. Usually, however, you want to open or save a file in one of your own folders. You must tell the program where the file that you want to open is located or where you want to save a file—whether that location is a different folder, a different drive on your hard disk, or a disk inserted in Drive A or B. To switch folders or drives, use the appropriate list boxes in the Open and Save As dialog boxes, as discussed in the following paragraphs.

The selected folder appears in the Look In drop-down list (see Figure 24.10). You can display this list to select another drive.

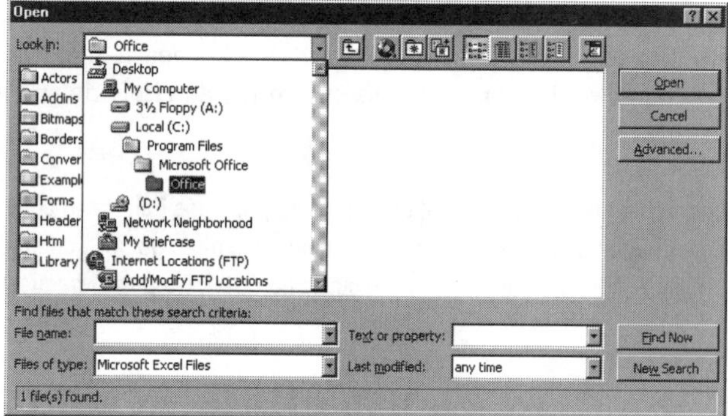

FIG. 24.10
Open the Look In drop-down list to select a different drive in the Open and Save As dialog boxes.

The list box includes all the folders in the current folder. An icon that resembles a file folder represents each folder. If you want to open a file in a folder contained within another folder, you first must open the folder containing the folder with the file. You can do so by double-clicking the folder icon.

To change disk drives or folders in the Open or Save As dialog boxes, follow these steps:

1. Display the Look In drop-down list by clicking its drop-down arrow, and then select the drive that you want.

2. To select a folder, double-click the folder icon. You can also click the Up One Level button to move up one level in the folder structure.
3. Select the file from the list, or type the file name in the File Name text box.
4. Choose Open or Save.

Editing Text in Text Boxes You can use the text-editing techniques that you learn in this section in all Windows applications. Although the editing techniques described are specifically for the text boxes that appear in dialog boxes, they also apply to editing text in other locations in Windows applications.

To use a mouse when editing text in a text box, you position the pointer over the text where you want to place the insertion point, and then click. When moving over editable text, the pointer changes from an arrowhead to an I-beam shape. To select multiple characters, drag across the characters.

While positioned in a text box, you can press left or right arrow keys to move left or right, End to move to the end of the text, and Home to move to the beginning of the text.

To delete a character to the right of the flashing insertion point, press Delete. Press Backspace to delete a character to the left of the insertion point.

Replace existing text with new text by selecting the text that you want to replace and then typing the new text. Select text with the mouse by dragging the I-beam across the text as you hold down the mouse button. To select text with the keyboard, move the insertion point to the left of the first character that you want to select, press and hold down Shift, and press the right arrow key.

NOTE When editing text in an application, you usually can use Edit menu commands such as Undo, Copy, and Paste. Although these commands often do not work in dialog boxes, the keystroke equivalents Ctrl+C (to copy), Ctrl+X (to cut), and Ctrl+V (to paste) frequently do work.

Controlling the Size and Position of Windows

Just as you move papers on your desktop, you can move and reorder windows on-screen. In fact, you can resize windows, expand them to full size, shrink them to a small icon to save space, and restore them to their original size.

The easiest way to resize and reposition application or document windows is with the mouse. As you will see, you can simply drag title bars or edges to move windows or change their size.

As you move the mouse pointer over edges of application or document windows, the pointer changes shape. Each shape, shown in Table 24.3, indicates the type of window change that you can make by dragging that edge or corner. Before you can move a window, it must be active—that is, the window must be on top. To activate a window, you can click it or press Alt+Tab until you select the application.

Table 24.3 Pointer Shapes Used When Moving or Resizing Windows

Shape	Pointer	Mouse Action
↔	Left/right	Drag the edge left or right
↕	Up/down	Drag the edge up or down
↘	Corner	Drag the corner in any direction

Using Taskbar Shortcuts to Arrange Windows

There are times when you want to quickly arrange a few applications on your desktop so that you can compare documents, drag and drop between documents, and so on. Manually moving and resizing each window is a tedious job, so Windows 95 has a few shortcuts that can make this type of work easier.

When the taskbar has a lot of application buttons, the titles may be too truncated to read. Pause the pointer over a button to see a pop-up title.

First, you can make your desktop easier to work on by minimizing all applications so that they appear as buttons on the taskbar. To do this quickly, right-click a blank area of the taskbar. When the shortcut menu appears, click Minimize All Windows.

If you want to compare documents in two or three applications, minimize all applications except the two or three you want to work with and then right-click a gray area of the taskbar. When the shortcut menu appears, click either Tile Horizontally or Tile Vertically. Your applications will appear in adjacent windows that fill the screen as shown in Figure 24.11.

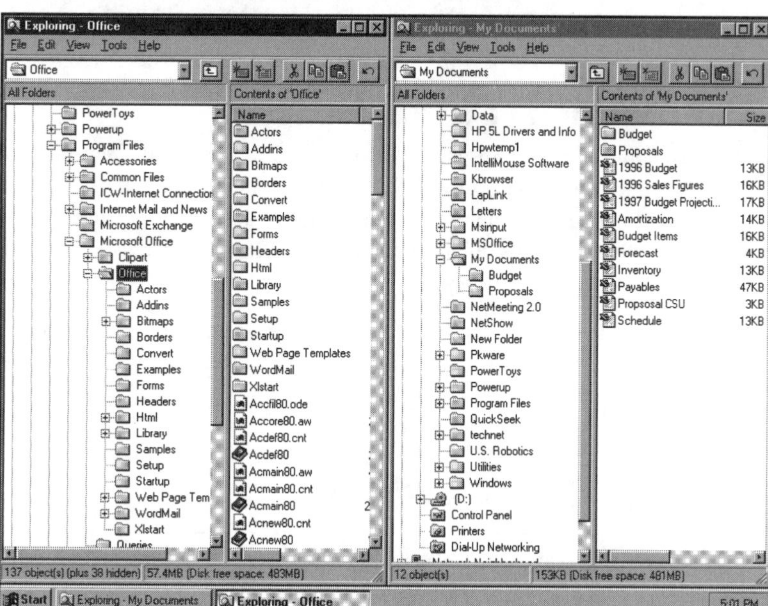

FIG. 24.11
Tiling application windows horizontally or vertically makes it easy to compare documents or to drag and drop contents.

If you want to be able to quickly see all the application title bars so that you can click title bars to switch between many application windows, right-click in the gray area of the taskbar. When the shortcut menu appears, click Cascade. The windows will arrange as shown in Figure 24.12.

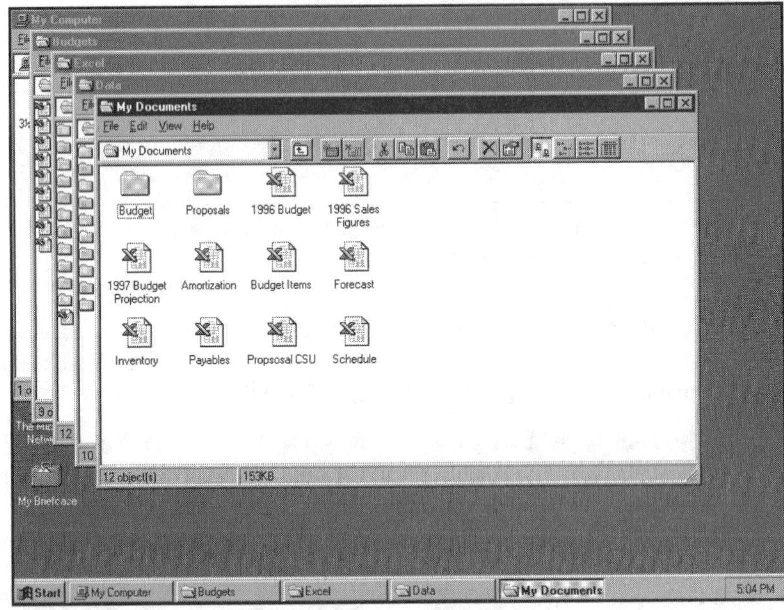

FIG. 24.12
Cascading application windows overlays them so that you can see each title bar. It is then easy to move among windows by clicking the title bars.

Moving a Window or a Desktop Icon

If an application window is not maximized (does not fill the screen), you can move the application's window. Move the pointer over the application's title at the top of its window, hold down the left mouse button, and drag the window to its new location. Windows displays an outline that indicates the application's position. When you release the mouse button, the window moves to its new position.

To drag document windows within the application, you use the same technique. As long as the document is within a window, you can drag its title bar. You can more easily arrange some documents within the application by choosing Window, Arrange All. This command puts document windows in predefined layouts.

Changing the Size of a Window

You cannot size a maximized window—a window that fills the screen—because you cannot make it any larger.

To change the size of a window with the mouse, you first activate the window by clicking it. Move the pointer to one edge or corner of the window until the pointer changes to a two-headed arrow (refer to Table 24.3). Press and hold down the mouse button, and then drag the double-headed arrow to move the edge or corner of the window to resize it. The moving edge appears as an outline until you release the mouse button.

To move two edges at once with the mouse, move the pointer to the corner of a window so that the pointer becomes a two-headed arrow tilted at a 45-degree angle. Drag the corner to its new location and release the mouse button.

Learning About Drag and Drop

After becoming proficient at operating Windows and its programs with commands, you will want to learn some of the faster, but less obvious, methods of controlling Windows and its programs. One of the most powerful methods is *drag and drop*.

The term *drag and drop* specifies exactly the action that the method uses. You click an object, such as a folder, and then hold down the mouse button as you drag the object to a new location. You drop the object by releasing the mouse button.

▶ **See** "Drag-and-Drop Printing from the Desktop," **p. 142**

▶ **See** "Backing Up with a Simple Drag and Drop," **p. 389**

For drag-and-drop methods to work, each Windows object has to know how to behave when dropped on other Windows objects. For example, if you drag the icon of a file in Windows Explorer and drop it on the icon for a program, the program starts and loads that file.

Figure 24.13 illustrates how you can use drag and drop to make frequently used folders more accessible. Instead of tediously having to find the folder each time in Windows Explorer, you can put a shortcut icon on the desktop that enables you to open the folder directly. To create a shortcut icon with drag and drop, follow these steps:

1. Double-click the My Computer icon to open its window. Make sure that the window does not fill the screen.
2. Double-click the local drive icon for your computer.
3. Click a folder that you frequently use, then hold down the right mouse button and drag the folder out of the window and over the desktop.

   In Figure 24.13, the user has dragged the Budgets folder to the desktop.
4. Release the right mouse button. A menu appears over the folder on the desktop as shown in Figure 24.13.
5. Choose the Create Shortcut(s) Here command.

TIP You can tell at a glance that an icon is shortcut by the small arrow at the lower-left corner.

The Shortcut to Budgets icon, shown in Figure 24.14, remains on the desktop even after you close the My Computer windows. You can open the folder at any time by double-clicking the shortcut icon.

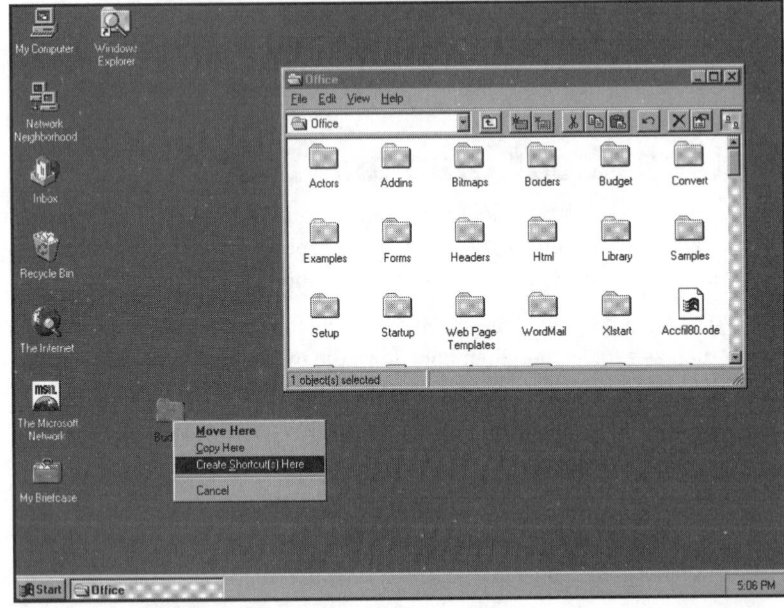

FIG. 24.13
The user has dragged the reverse-colored Budgets folder (by holding down the right mouse button) and dropped the folder to the desktop. When you release the mouse button, a shortcut menu appears.

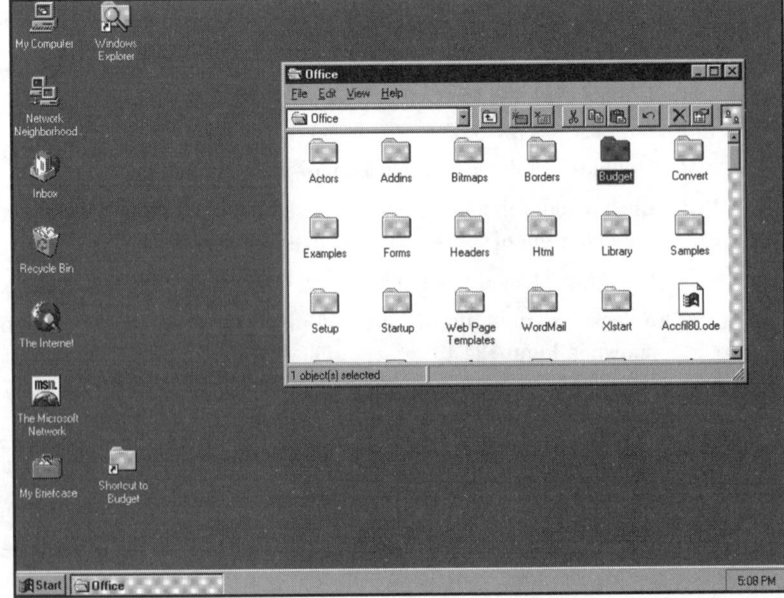

FIG. 24.14
Choosing the Create Shortcut(s) Here command produces a shortcut icon on the desktop that you can click to start the application.

CAUTION

When dragging and dropping a file or folder, make sure that you use the right mouse button and choose Create Shortcut(s) Here from the shortcut menu. This creates a shortcut icon while leaving the original file or folder in its original location. If you delete the shortcut icon, the original file or folder remains intact. If you delete an original icon (which you create by dragging with the left mouse button) from your desktop, Windows deletes the original file or folder along with the icon. If the file is important, this causes a disaster and a lot of interoffice panic.

NOTE Drag-and-drop features are available only with Windows applications that are compatible with Object Linking and Embedding (OLE). ■

You can use the drag-and-drop method to save time in many ways. You can move and copy files and folders, which makes reorganizing the contents on your computer easy. You can drag a shortcut for your printer onto your desktop, drag documents from My Computer or Windows Explorer, and then drop them onto the printer icon, which prints the documents. With applications compatible with the OLE 2 specifications, you can even drag and drop objects from one application to another. For example, you can drag a table from a spreadsheet into a word processing document.

Throughout this book, you accomplish your computer tasks by using drag-and-drop methods. Always look for ways to use these methods for saving time and trouble.

Changing Settings and Properties with the Right Mouse Button

One important Windows concept is that most objects that you see on-screen have *properties* related to them. Properties can include such characteristics as an object's appearance and behavior.

You can change some properties, but others are *read only*—you can view them, but cannot change them. For example, changeable properties of the Windows desktop include the types of patterns and wallpapers used as backgrounds and the color of different screen elements. Read-only properties that you can see but not change include a file's size or a program's version number.

You can experiment to find properties in Windows, the Explorer, and most Windows 95 applications. To see an object's properties, point to the object and click the right mouse button (that is, you *right-click* the object). A properties sheet appears, or a menu displays a Properties command. For example, you can place the pointer's tip on most objects, such as the desktop or a file, and then click the right mouse button. From the menu that appears, select the Properties command.

NOTE Don't be afraid to experiment when you look for properties. To discover how you can customize Windows, right-click files, taskbars, and so on. If you do not want to change the object's properties, press the Esc key or click the Cancel button in the properties sheet that appears.

To see the properties that you can change on the desktop, right-click the desktop and then choose the Properties command. The Display properties sheet shown in Figure 24.15 appears. In this dialog box, you can change the display's background, color, and screen saver, as well as display adapter settings. To learn how to change these settings, see Chapter 32, "Customizing the Desktop Settings." Click the Cancel button to remove the dialog box without making changes.

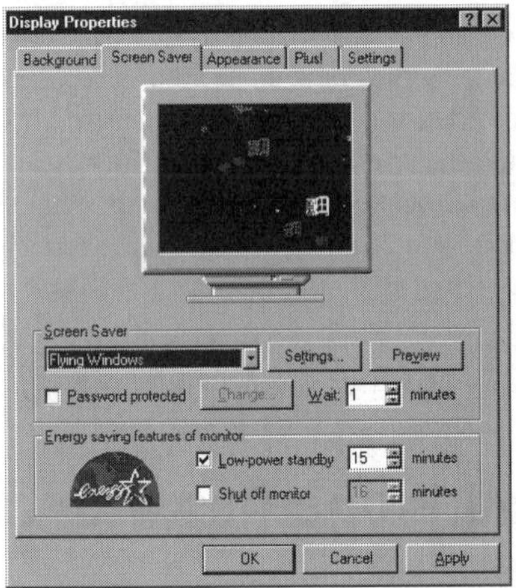

FIG. 24.15 Right-click the desktop and then choose Properties to see the desktop properties. The Screen Saver page, shown here, enables you to choose one.

If you want to change how the taskbar operates, right-click a blank area of the taskbar and then choose the Properties command. The Taskbar properties sheet is displayed. On this sheet, you can add or remove applications from the Start menu, or change when and how the taskbar is displayed. Chapter 31, "Customizing the Taskbar and Start Menu," describes this properties sheet and how to customize the taskbar. Click the Cancel button to remove the dialog box without making changes.

Working with Applications

Many operations are similar among Windows applications. Nearly all Windows applications, for example, start with the File and Edit menus. The File menu includes commands for opening, closing, saving, and printing files. The Edit menu includes commands for cutting, copying, pasting, and other editing actions specific to the application. The procedures you use to control menus and select items in dialog boxes are the same in nearly all Windows applications.

Opening, Saving, and Closing Documents

When you create or edit a document and then save the document, you create a *file* that Windows stores in a magnetic recording on disk. The file contains all the information necessary to re-create the document in your program. When this book uses the term *file*, it usually refers to the information stored on the computer's hard disk or on a removable disk.

When first started, many applications present a new, empty document: It's a blank page if the application is a word processing, graphics, or desktop publishing application; it's an empty worksheet if the application is a spreadsheet application. If you finish working on one file, you can start a new file by choosing File, New. Your application might ask you for information about the type of new file to start.

To open an existing file, choose File, Open. An Open dialog box similar to the one shown in Figure 24.16 appears. In the Look In drop-down list, select the drive that contains your file. The Look In drop-down list displays your computer's drives as icons. Click the drive you want to look in. In the Look In box, select the folder that contains your file and then choose OK to display the list of files in that folder. From the files presented, select the one that you want to open and then choose OK or press Enter.

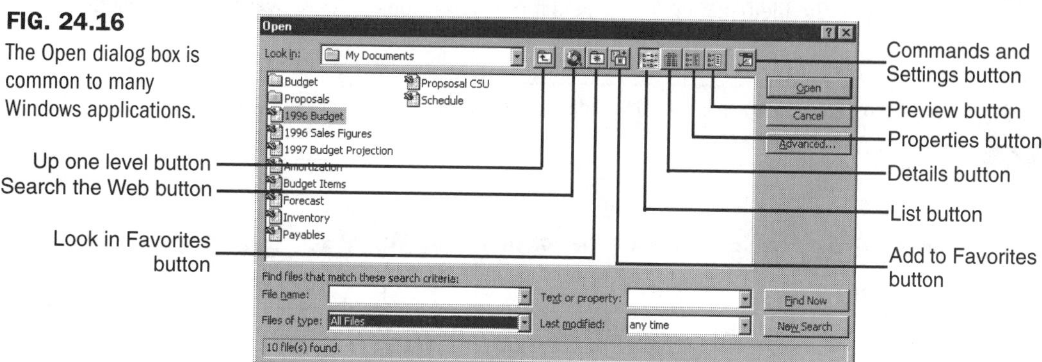

FIG. 24.16
The Open dialog box is common to many Windows applications.

TIP Double-click a file name in the Open dialog box to open that file.

You can do far more in a Windows 95 Open dialog box than meets the eye. Click a button at the top of the dialog box to get the result you want. Table 24.4 lists the buttons and their results.

Table 24.4 Open Dialog Box Buttons

Button	Result
Up One Level	Moves up to the next higher folder
Search the Web	Opens the Search page of your Internet browser

continues

Table 24.4 Continued

Button	Result
Look in Favorites	Displays a list of favorite or frequently used files
Add to Favorites	Adds the selected file to the Favorites list
List	Displays files in a list view
Details	Displays files with all file details shown
Properties	Displays a file or folder's properties
Preview	Displays the contents of a file using QuickView
Commands and Settings	Displays a shortcut menu from which you can print, sort, or search for files and map to a network drive

Explore with your right mouse button by clicking files or folders to see some of the things you can do to files and folders. When you right-click a file or folder, a shortcut menu appears with various commands from which you can choose. The specific commands on the menu can vary, depending on the file type. Table 24.5 lists the basic options that are available for most file types.

In some applications, you can open multiple documents by selecting the files with Ctrl+click and then clicking the Open button.

Table 24.5 Shortcut Commands for Files and Folders

Command	Result
Open	Opens the file.
Open Read Only	Opens the file as a read-only document that must be saved to a different file name.
Print	Prints the file.
Quick View	Displays a preview of the file.
Send To	Copies the file to a shortcut folder, floppy disk, or mail or Fax address.
Cut	Removes the file or folder from its location in preparation to paste it elsewhere.
Copy	Copies the file or folder in preparation to copy it elsewhere.
Paste	Pastes a file or folder that has been cut or copied. (This command appears only when a file or folder has been cut or copied to the Clipboard.)

Command	Result
Create Shortcut	Creates a shortcut to the file or folder.
Delete	Deletes the selection(s).
Properties	Displays the file or folder's properties.

The File menu contains two commands for saving files: Save As and Save. Choose one of these commands the first time that you save a file. They tell Windows where to save the file and enable you to name your file. If you choose File, Save As, you can create a new version of an existing file by specifying a new name for the file. The Save As dialog box is often similar to the Open dialog box shown in Figure 24.16. In the Save As dialog box, you must specify the drive and folder to which you want to save your file and name the file.

After you type the file name in the File name text box, choose Save or press Enter to save the file. After you name your file, you can choose File, Save to save it without changing its name or location. The File, Save command replaces the original file.

To close a document, you often can choose File, Close. If you choose File, Exit, you exit the application. When you close or exit a Windows application, you might be prompted to save any changes that you made since you last saved your document.

Scrolling in a Document

Most applications include scroll bars at the right and bottom edges of the screen, as shown in Figure 24.17. You can use the vertical scroll bar at the right to scroll up and down in your document. You can use the horizontal scroll bar to scroll left and right. To scroll a short distance, click the arrow at either end of a scroll bar, and you will scroll in the direction that the arrow points. To scroll a longer distance, click in the gray area next to the arrow or drag the scroll bar box to a new location. In many applications, the scroll bars are optional; if you want more working space, you can turn them off.

FIG. 24.17
To scroll through a document, use the scroll bars on the window's right and bottom sides.

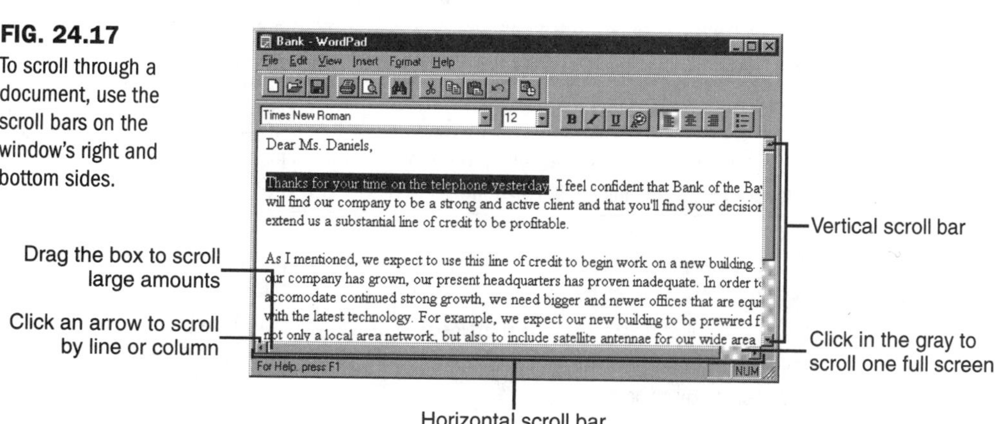

To scroll with the keyboard, you can press the arrow keys to move a character or line at a time, or press the Page Up or Page Down keys to move a screen at a time. With most applications the Home key scrolls you to the left margin, and the End key takes you to the end of the line or the right side. Holding down the Ctrl key while pressing any other scrolling key extends the scroll: Ctrl+Home, for example, takes you to the beginning of your file; Ctrl+End takes you to the end of the file; Ctrl+left arrow or Ctrl+right arrow moves you a word at a time rather than a character at a time. Most applications have many shortcuts for scrolling.

If you use the scroll bars to scroll, the insertion point does not move—it remains where it was before you scrolled. If you use the keyboard to scroll, the insertion point moves as you scroll.

Using Simple Editing Techniques

Editing text and objects is similar in all Windows applications. When you work with text, in your document or in a dialog box, the mouse pointer turns into an I-beam when you move it over editable text. You can use the I-beam to move the insertion point and select text. The flashing vertical insertion point is where the text that you type appears. (The insertion point is equivalent to the cursor in DOS applications.)

Although the pointer changes to an I-beam over editable text, you cannot edit at the location until you click the mouse button.

You can use the mouse or the keyboard to move the insertion point. To use the mouse, position the I-beam where you want the insertion point in the text and click the left mouse button. (If you cannot see the insertion point, it might be under the I-beam. Move the mouse a little to move the I-beam.) To use the keyboard to move the insertion point, press the arrow keys.

▶ **See** "Cutting, Copying, and Pasting Data," **p. 823**

▶ **See** "Understanding Data Linking," **p. 833**

To insert text at the insertion point, you simply type. Most applications push existing text to the right to make room for the new text (although some applications enable you to select an overtype mode, which replaces existing text as you type). To delete text to the left of the insertion point, press the Backspace key. To delete text to the right of the insertion point, press the Delete key.

Most applications contain an "oops" function: the Edit, Undo command. This command undoes your most recent edit (or more edits, depending on the program).

CAUTION

If you accidentally press the Insert key, you turn on Overtype mode, which types new text over existing text. If this happens, press the Insert key again. Some applications display "OVR" or a similar indicator in the status bar to show when they are in Overtype mode.

Selecting Text and Objects

You can sum up one of the most important editing rules in all Windows applications with three simple words: select, then do. You must select text or an object before you can do anything to it. If you don't select first, the application doesn't know where to apply your command.

To select text and objects, you can use the mouse or the keyboard. To select text with the mouse, position the I-beam at the beginning of the text that you want to select, click and hold down the left mouse button, drag to the end of the text that you want to select, and release the mouse button. To select text with the keyboard, position the insertion point at the beginning of the text that you want to select, press and hold down the Shift key, use arrow keys to move to the end of the text that you want to select, and then release the Shift and arrow keys. The selected text appears in reverse type, as shown in Figure 24.17.

Many shortcuts exist for selecting. Some of the following shortcuts apply to text in many Windows documents and dialog boxes:

- To select a word with the mouse, double-click the word.
- To select a word using the keyboard, hold down Ctrl+Shift while pressing the left or right arrow key.
- To select a length of text with the mouse, you can drag until you touch the end of the screen, which causes the screen to scroll.

  To select a length of text with the keyboard, position the I-beam where you want to start the selection, hold down the Shift key, and scroll to the end of the selection by using any keyboard scrolling technique.

After you select a word, you can change its appearance. For example, you might make the word bold or change its font. In most applications, typing replaces the selection, which enables you to replace text by selecting it and typing the new text. If you select a graphic, you can resize it or apply formatting.

To use the mouse to select an object such as a picture, click the object. (To select multiple objects, hold down Shift while you click each one in turn.) To select an object with the keyboard, position the insertion point beside the object, hold down Shift, and press an arrow key to move the object in the direction indicated by the arrow key. Selected objects, such as graphics, usually appear with *selection handles* (small black boxes) on each side and corner. These handles are used to resize and move objects.

Copying and Moving

After selecting text or an object, you can use the Edit menu to copy or move the selection. The Edit menu commands, that all Windows applications use to copy and move, are Cut, Copy, and Paste. The Edit, Cut command removes the selection from your document, and Edit, Copy duplicates it. Both commands transfer the selection to the Clipboard, a temporary holding area. The Edit, Paste command copies the selection from the Clipboard and into your document at the insertion point's location. Your selection remains in the Clipboard until you replace it with another selection.

To copy and paste between documents and dialog boxes, try using the shortcut keys described in this section.

To copy a selection, choose Edit, Copy; then move the insertion point to where you want to duplicate the selection, and choose Edit, Paste. To move a selection, choose Edit, Cut; then move the insertion point to where you want to move it, and choose Edit, Paste. Many shortcuts exist for copying and moving. Ctrl+X usually cuts a selection, Ctrl+C copies a selection, and Ctrl+V usually pastes the Clipboard's contents. Many Windows applications also take advantage of the Windows drag-and-drop feature, which enables you to use the mouse to drag a selection to its new location and drop it into place.

Because all applications running under Windows share the Clipboard, you can move or copy a selection between documents and between applications as easily as you can move and copy within a file. The next two sections explain how to switch between documents and applications.

Switching Between Document Windows

In many (but not all) Windows applications, you can easily open more than one document and switch between the documents in the same application. Use these techniques when you want to copy or move information from one document to another. To open multiple documents, choose File, Open each time for a different document. If your application doesn't support multiple documents, it closes the current file, asking whether you want to save any changes that you made since you last saved.

If your application supports multiple documents, each document opens in its own document window as shown in Figure 24.18. Multiple document windows have a document Control menu to control the active document window's size and position.

The document Control menu appears to the left of the document title bar, or if the document is displayed as a full screen, to the left of the menu bar. You can click the document Control-menu icon to display the Control menu. This menu enables you to change the window's size or close the document. If you are using the keyboard, press Alt+hyphen (-). There is, however, an easier way to control document windows than through the document Control menu.

A faster way to control documents in Windows is to use the buttons that appear at the top right corner of each document, as shown in Figures 24.19 and 24.20. If the document fills the application window, the Restore Document button appears to the right of the menu bar as shown in Figure 24.19.

If a document is in its own window, three buttons appear at the top right corner of the document's title bar, as shown in Figure 24.20. Click one of these buttons to reduce the document to an icon, enlarge the document to fill the application window, or close the document.

Reducing a document window creates an icon in the application window such as that shown in Figure 24.21. Notice that this icon has three buttons that you can click to restore the document to a window, enlarge it to full screen, or close it.

FIG. 24.18
When documents are in their own windows, you can switch between them quickly by clicking the one you want active.

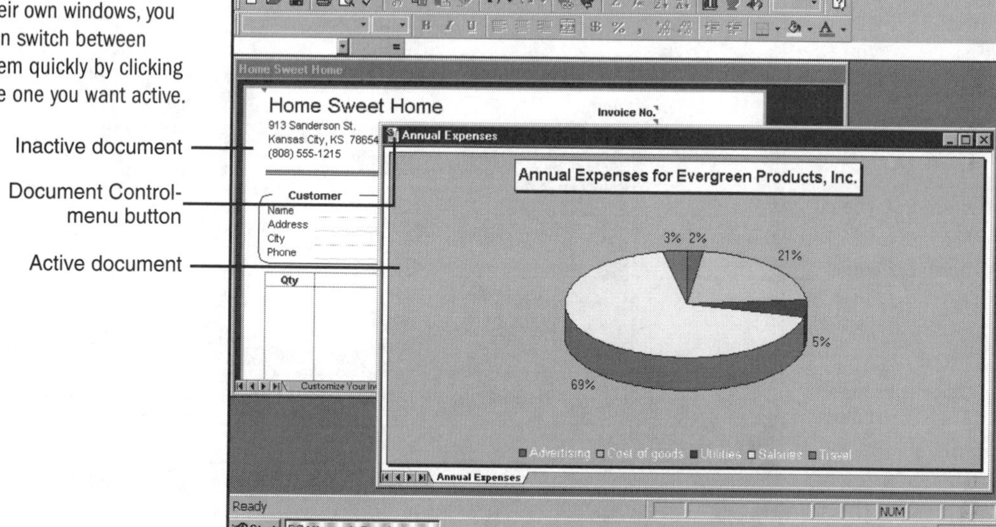

FIG. 24.19
Maximized documents fill the entire program window.

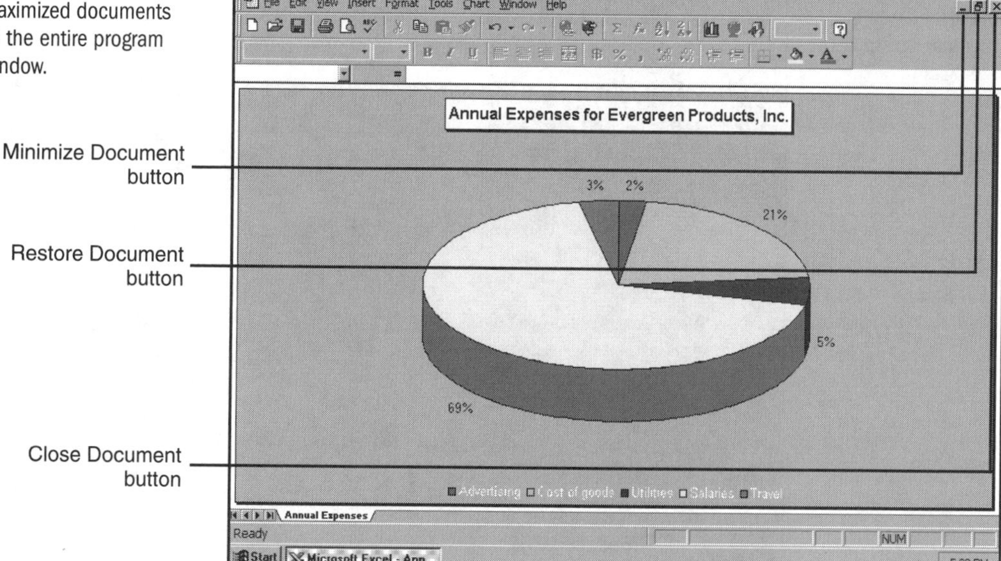

Part V
Ch 24

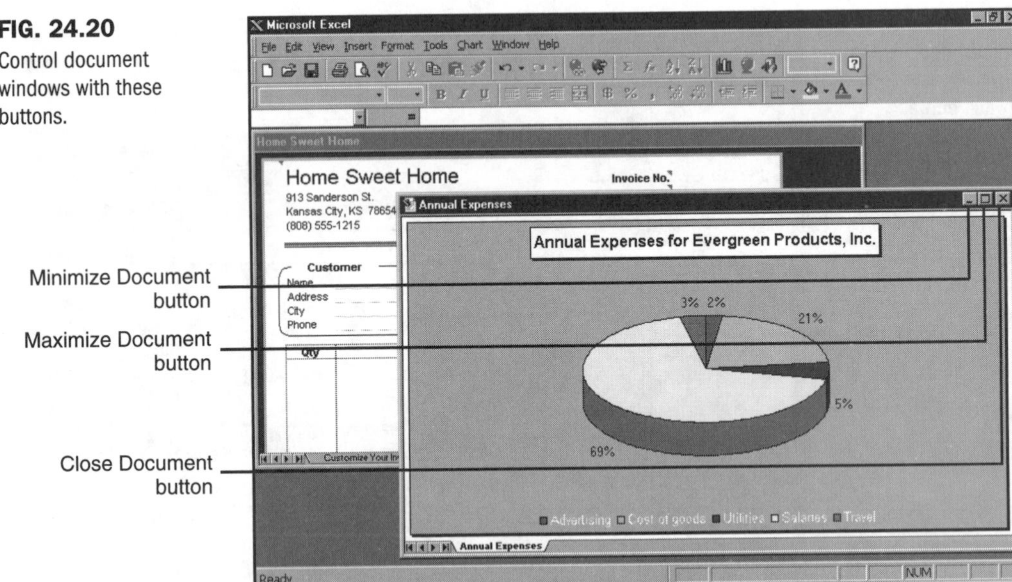

FIG. 24.20
Control document windows with these buttons.

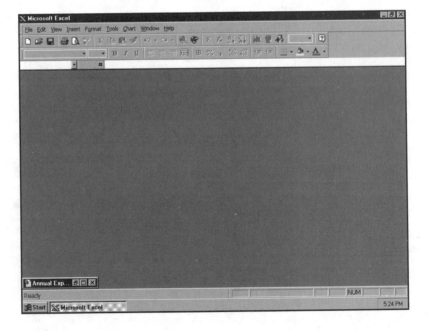

FIG. 24.21
Documents reduced to icons require less space in the program's window.

Switching Between Applications

When you run several applications, you need an easy way to switch between them. If the taskbar is visible, you can switch to another application by clicking the application's button in the taskbar. If you cannot see the taskbar, press Ctrl+Esc to display it and open the Start menu.

Another way to switch between applications is to hold down the Alt key and press Tab. When you first press Alt+Tab, a bar with open applications appears, as shown in Figure 24.22. Continue holding the Alt key to keep the bar on screen. Each time you press Alt+Tab, the next application on the bar is selected. A box encloses the icon of the active application. Press Shift+Alt+Tab to move the selection to the application to the left. Release Alt+Tab when you have selected the application that you want to activate.

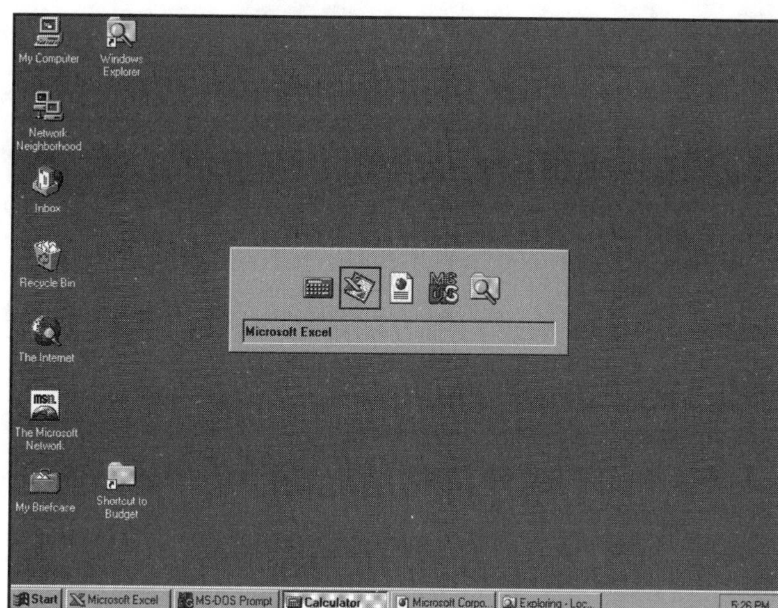

FIG. 24.22
Press Alt+Tab to switch to another open application.

To switch between document windows with the mouse, click the window that you want to activate. If the window that you want to activate is not visible, you might have to move or size the active window on top. (To move a window, drag its title bar; to size a window, drag its border.) To use the keyboard to switch between document windows, open the Window menu and select from the list of open windows the document that you want. ●

CHAPTER 25

Installing, Running, and Uninstalling Windows Applications

by Michael O'Mara

In this chapter

Understanding How Windows Runs Applications

Windows 95 can run applications designed specifically for Windows 95. It also can run most older Windows 3.1 applications, DOS-based applications, and applications designed for Windows NT. Windows 95 no longer requires the traditional CONFIG.SYS, AUTOEXEC.BAT, and INI files for configuration information. However, for backward-compatibility, Windows 95 can use settings from INI files and can maintain its own versions of CONFIG.SYS and AUTOEXEC.BAT in order to support loading real-mode device drivers.

Although Windows 95 can run various kinds of applications successfully, it provides different kinds of support for each category of application. Windows applications fall into one of two general categories: 32-bit applications (designed for Windows NT and Windows 95) and 16-bit applications (designed for Windows 3.1 and earlier versions). This section describes how Windows 95 runs these programs. Chapter 26, " Installing, Running, and Uninstalling MS-DOS Applications," discusses DOS-based applications.

Support for Win32 Applications

Windows 95 offers several significant advantages over Windows 3.1. Some advantages such as preemptive multitasking and multithreading support are available only to 32-bit applications.

Support for long file names is one feature of Windows 95's 32-bit operating system that is available to any application designed to make use of it. Of course, all Windows 95 applications will let you create file names containing up to 255 characters, allowing you to assign files names such as "First Quarter Sales Results" instead of "1QSALES." Theoretically, program developers can adapt 16-bit applications to use long file names as well. However, don't expect many older Windows applications to add long file name support; the programmers are likely to concentrate on converting the application to full-fledged 32-bit status instead of spending time on minor upgrades.

Most applications benefit from Windows 95's 32-bit architecture, which makes memory addressing more efficient. In addition, Windows 95 runs each 32-bit application in its own memory space. Ordinarily, such details are of interest only to programmers. However, these advantages have a side effect that all users will appreciate. If a 32-bit application hangs or crashes, the problem is isolated, confined to the application's own address space, and thus unlikely to affect other running applications. You can simply exit the problem application and, without even rebooting, have Windows 95 clean up the affected memory.

Advantages of Preemptive Multitasking and Multithreading Despite appearances, our computers can't really perform multiple tasks from several different applications all at the same instant. Generally, computers perform only one or two tasks at a time, but they can do so very fast. Therefore, if the applications are designed to break operations into small tasks, the operating system can switch between tasks from several applications so quickly that it seems that all the applications and their processes are running simultaneously.

Programmers had to design Windows 3.1 applications to surrender control of the CPU voluntarily at various points of execution, enabling Windows to switch to another task. This scheme is called *cooperative multitasking*. However, some applications were more cooperative than others. If an application was reluctant to share CPU capacity with other applications, Windows 3.1 couldn't do much about it.

Preemptive multitasking, on the other hand, enables the Windows 95 operating system to take control away from one running task and pass it to another task, depending on the system's needs. The system doesn't have to wait for an application or process to surrender control of the CPU before another application can take its turn.

With preemptive multitasking, Windows 95 doesn't depend on the foresight of application programmers to ensure that an application performs multitasking successfully. Windows 95 has more power to arbitrate the demands of various running applications.

Multithreading enables an application to create and run separate concurrent *threads* or processes and thus handle different internal operations. Each process gets its own share of Windows 95's multitasking resources. For example, a word processing application might use one thread to handle keyboard input and display it on-screen. At the same time, a separate thread can run in the background to check spelling while another thread prints a document.

Some Windows 3.1 applications implement their own internal multithreading, with varying degrees of success. Now, Windows 95 makes multithreading an integral feature of the operating system, available to all 32-bit applications.

Increased System Resources Windows 95 doesn't remove the limitation on System Resources that was common in Windows 3.1, but the improvement is dramatic. The system limits on some kinds of programming information that Windows 3.1 severely restricted are now unlimited. Windows 95 still limits other kinds of programming information, but those limits are significantly higher than in Windows 3.1. As a result, you can run more applications, create more windows, use more fonts, and so on—all without running out of system resources. For instance, as I write this, I have two very large, resource-hungry applications running, plus a communications program, a personal organizer, Explorer, and CD Player. That's more than enough to exhaust system resources in Windows 3.1 and precipitate a flurry of error messages. But in Windows 95, I still have more than 80 percent of the available system resources free.

NOTE With 32-bit applications in Windows 95, rarely will you have the "Not Enough Memory" error (which occurred frequently in Windows 3.1).

Support for Windows 3.1 Applications

Most Windows 3.1 applications run in Windows 95 without modification or special settings. Microsoft claims that 16-bit Windows applications run at least as well in Windows 95 as in Windows 3.1.

Windows 3.1 applications continue to use cooperative multitasking; they cannot use Windows 95's preemptive multitasking and multithreading. However, 16-bit applications can benefit from the advantages Windows 95 derives from 32-bit device drivers and improved printing throughput due to multitasking at the operating system level.

Windows 3.1 applications running in Windows 95 all run in the same virtual machine and share the same address space—just as they do when running in Windows 3.1. As a result, they don't share the same crash protection as Windows 95 applications. If one 16-bit application hangs or crashes, it's likely to affect other 16-bit applications that are running at the same time. In other words, any application failure that would have required rebooting or restarting Windows 3.1 will require you to shut down all the 16-bit applications you're running. However, a failure of a 16-bit application should not affect 32-bit applications, and Windows 95 probably can clean up after an errant 16-bit application without requiring a reboot to recover System Resources and clear memory.

Installing Applications in Windows 95

To install any Windows application, you usually use a setup program or install utility. Installing DOS-based applications is a different matter (and the subject of Chapter 26, "Installing, Running, and Uninstalling MS-DOS Applications"). These setup programs for Windows applications take care of all the details of installing the application. You don't have to concern yourself with creating directories, copying files, and integrating the application into Windows. That's good, because installing sophisticated applications can be complex. A manual installation of a major software suite is beyond the capabilities of the average user, and a dreaded chore for even the most advanced user.

▶ **See** "Installing MS-DOS Applications," **p. 656**

What Does Setup Do?

A typical setup or installation program begins by prompting you for some information and then installs the application automatically. The better setup programs provide feedback during installation to keep you informed of what it's doing to your system and the progress of the installation. Depending on the complexity of the application you are installing, the setup program might give you an opportunity to select various options and customize the installation. The program might limit your input to accepting or changing the path where you install the application, selecting whether to install various optional components, or specifying configuration settings for the new application.

After receiving your input, the setup program proceeds to perform some or all of the following steps automatically:

- Search for an existing copy of the application it's about to install and switch to upgrade mode if appropriate.
- Scan your system to determine whether your hard disk has enough room for the necessary files and perhaps check for the existence of special hardware or other system requirements.
- Create directories and copy files. Often, the setup program must expand files that are stored in a compressed form on the distribution disks.
- Create a shortcut that you can use to launch the application.
- Add a folder and/or shortcuts to your Start menu.
- Update Windows' configuration files.
- Update the Windows Registry.
- Register the application as an OLE server.
- Register the application's file types so Windows can recognize the file-name extensions for the application's document and data files.
- Install fonts, support utilities, and so on.
- Configure or personalize the application.

What If There's No Setup Program?

A few Windows programs don't include a setup utility to install the application—the developer just didn't supply one. Such an application is probably a small utility program for which installation consists of copying a couple of files to your hard disk and perhaps adding a shortcut to your Start menu to launch the application. You'll probably find instructions for installing the application in an accompanying manual or README file.

The installation instructions may assume that you're installing the program in Windows 3.1, not Windows 95. Fortunately, this isn't a serious problem. Most of the procedures for installing an application in Windows 3.1 work equally well in Windows 95. For instance, although Windows 95 supplies new tools for managing files, the underlying process of creating directories (folders) and copying files is the same in both versions of Windows. Also, for backward-compatibility, Windows 95 includes full support for WIN.INI and SYSTEM.INI files, so any additions that you're instructed to make to those files should work as expected.

There are two common manual installation procedures that you must adapt for Windows 95. First, if the Windows 3.1 installation instructions require that you create a file association in File Manager, you must substitute the Windows 95 equivalent of registering a file type. Second, instead of creating a program item in Program Manager, you add a program to the Start menu.

Using Windows 3.1 Applications in Windows 95

According to Microsoft, Windows 95 features full backward-compatibility with 16-bit Windows 3.1 applications, and thus you can install and use your Windows 3.1 applications in Windows 95 without modification. And in fact, with only rare exceptions, Windows 3.1 applications do indeed run successfully in Windows 95.

For a current list of programs with known incompatibility problems with Windows 95 and suggested fixes or workarounds, read the file PROGRAMS.TXT in the Windows folder. You can also search for compatible software programs at the following site on the Internet:

http://www.microsoft.com/windows/thirdparty/compat.htm

If you encounter a compatibility problem with a legacy application—an older application designed for a previous version of DOS or Windows—running in Windows 95, check with the application's developer for a patch or workaround for the problem. In some cases, perhaps the only solution is an upgrade to a new, Windows 95 version of the application.

Installing Windows 3.1 Applications

You install Windows 3.1 applications in Windows 95 the same way that you do in Windows 3.1. You simply insert the first disk of the program's installation disks in your floppy disk or CD-ROM drives, run the Setup program, and follow the prompts and instructions.

The installation instructions for most Windows 3.1 applications direct you to use the Run command to start the setup program and begin installing the application. The instructions might mention that you can find the Run command on the File menu in either Program Manager or File Manager. However, in Windows 95, you find the Run command on the Start menu.

NOTE You might prefer a different technique for launching the Setup program. Open the My Computer window and double-click the drive icon for the drive that contains the installation disk. Then locate the Setup program's icon and launch the program by double-clicking it.

When you use this technique, you need not type the command in the Run dialog box to start the Setup program. The technique also lets you scan the disk for README files before installing the application. ■

Of course, the setup program for a legacy application will be tailored to Windows 3.1 instead of Windows 95. For example, the installation program will probably offer to create Program Manager groups (see Figure 25.1) and update INI files. Fortunately, you can just accept those options when the program offers them. Windows 95 will intercept Program Manager updates and automatically convert them to Start menu shortcuts. Windows 95 also transfers WIN.INI and SYSTEM.INI entries into the Registry.

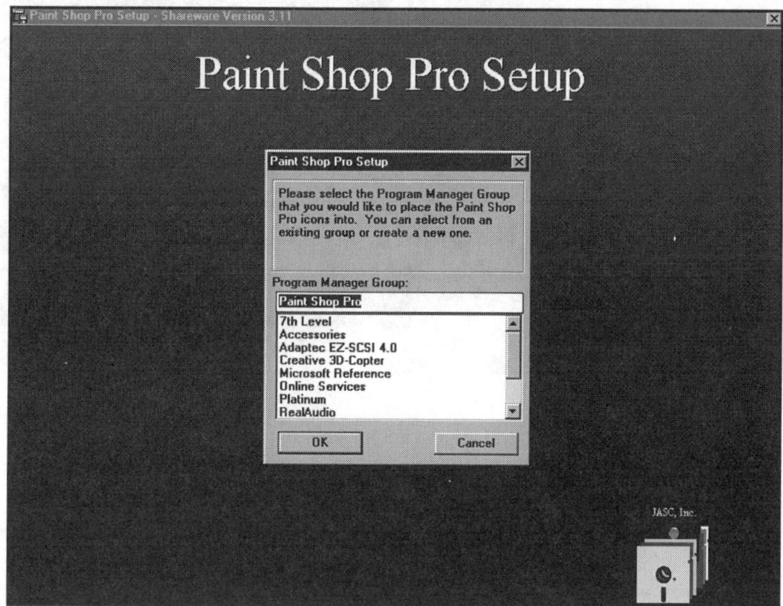

FIG. 25.1
Windows 95 translates some actions of a Windows 3.1 application's Setup program into their Windows 95 equivalent.

If you install Windows 95 as an upgrade to Windows 3.1, the Setup program should take care of such issues. The Windows 95 Setup program automatically transfers information about your existing applications to the Registry when you install Windows 95 into your existing Windows 3.1 directory. As a result, you shouldn't have to reinstall applications.

Running Windows 3.1 Applications

After installing a Windows 3.1 application in Windows 95, you can launch and run the application just like any other Windows application. Windows 95 changes the application's appearance automatically, giving it the new Windows look (see Figure 25.2). The application window's title bar will have the new format, complete with the new style of Minimize, Maximize, and Close buttons, and most buttons and other window elements will take on the new three-dimensional look.

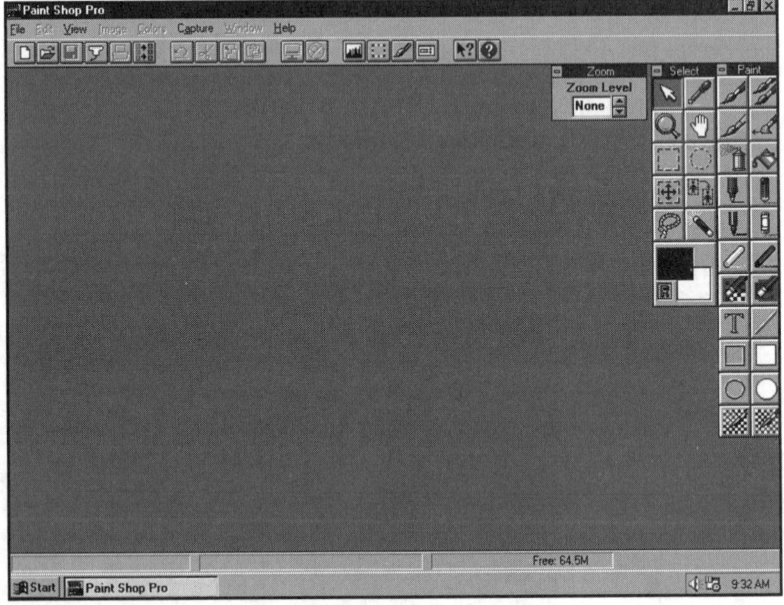

FIG. 25.2 Running a Windows 3.1 application in Windows 95 gives the program an automatic facelift. However, despite the change of appearance, the application performs the same as in Windows 3.1.

Beneath the superficial appearance changes, the application works the same as it did under Windows 3.1. The application might benefit from some Windows 95 performance improvements, such as more efficient printing. However, to take maximum advantage of the features and capabilities of Windows 95's 32-bit operating system, you must upgrade to a new version of the application. In the meantime, you should be able to continue using your 16-bit Windows 3.1 applications effectively and efficiently.

Installing Windows 95 Applications in Windows 95

The basic technique for installing Windows 95 applications is essentially the same as installing other Windows applications; you run Setup (or Install) and follow the prompts. The Setup program takes care of all the details of installing the application. However, the Run feature is located in the Start menu in Windows 95.

One new feature of Windows 95 is an optional way to start an application's setup program: a new Install Programs Wizard accessible via the Add/Remove Programs icon in the Control Panel. The Add/Remove Programs dialog box provides a common starting point for adding and removing Windows applications and Windows system components and accessories.

When you're ready to run the Install Programs Wizard and use it to install a Windows application, follow these steps:

1. Open the Start menu and choose Settings, Control Panel. This opens the Control Panel window shown in Figure 25.3.

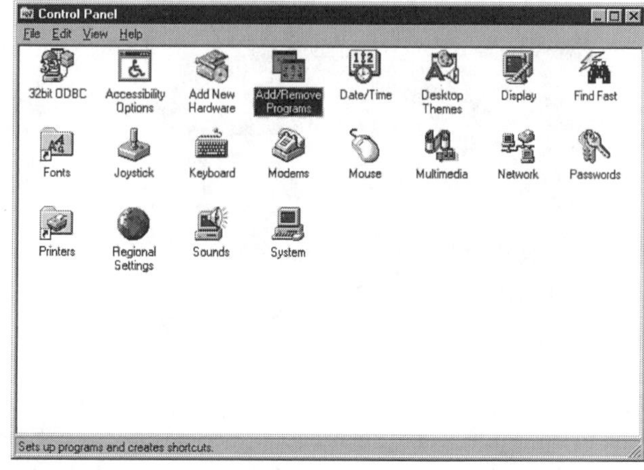

FIG. 25.3
The Windows 95 Control Panel contains a new wizard to make installing applications easier.

2. In the Control Panel window, double-click Add/Remove Programs to open the Add/Remove Programs properties sheet shown in Figure 25.4. By default, the Install/Uninstall tab should be active.

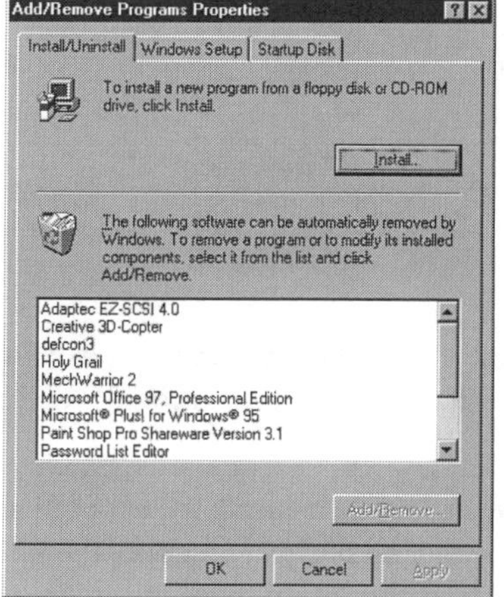

FIG. 25.4
The Add/Remove Programs Properties dialog box is the master control for adding and removing applications.

3. To start the Install Program Wizard, choose Install.
4. When the Install Program from Floppy Disk or CD-ROM dialog box appears, insert the application's distribution disk (the first floppy disk or compact disc) in the appropriate drive and click Next.
5. The wizard searches the disk's root directory for an installation program (usually named SETUP.EXE or INSTALL.EXE) and displays the command line in the Run Installation Program dialog box (see Figure 25.5).

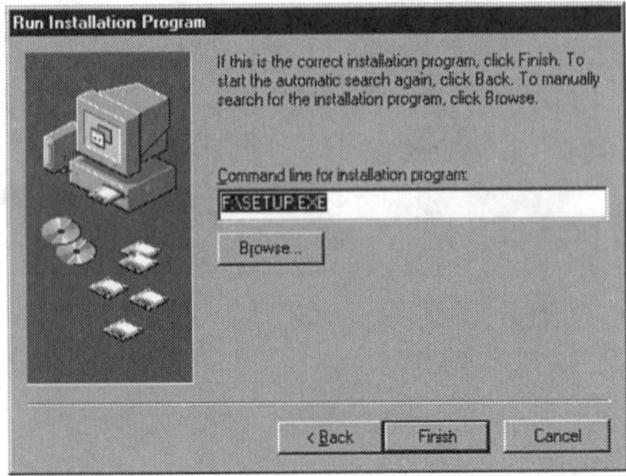

FIG. 25.5
Usually the wizard finds the application's setup program on the disk.

6. If the wizard fails to find the setup program (perhaps because it is in a subdirectory) or you want to run a different setup program (perhaps from a network drive), you can choose Browse and select a different file in the Browse dialog box (see Figure 25.6). Choose Open to insert the selected file name in the wizard.

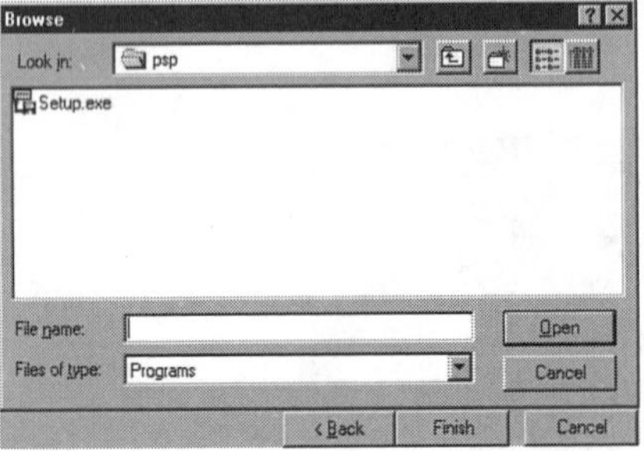

FIG. 25.6
If the wizard needs help locating the setup program, you can browse for the correct file.

7. After the correct command line for the setup program appears in the Run Installation Program dialog box, click Finish to start the setup program and begin the application installation.

The application's setup program then proceeds to install the application. You'll probably need to respond to several prompts during the installation process. If the setup program includes a Windows 95-compatible uninstall feature, the wizard notes this and adds the new application to a list of programs that you can remove automatically. (The section "Removing Windows Applications," later in this chapter, discusses this new feature in more detail.)

NOTE You also can use the Install Programs Wizard to install Windows 3.1 applications. However, using the wizard for this purpose yields no significant advantage. Windows 3.1 setup programs lack the special features that let you use the Add/Remove Programs control panel to remove the applications later. ■

Running Applications

After you install your application's and Windows' accessories, Windows 95 gives you many options for launching them. You can use any of the methods to run any application. The technique that you choose depends on your personal preferences, working style, and what you're doing at the time.

The various methods for launching applications are discussed in more detail in Chapter 10, "Navigating and Controlling Windows," and Chapter 12, "Managing Files with My Computer and Windows Explorer." The following is a summary of the techniques:

- Choose the application's shortcut from the Start menu.
- Create and use a shortcut on the desktop.
- Right-click the application's icon in Windows Explorer or the My Computer window; then click Open in the context menu.
- Double-click the application's icon in the My Computer window or Windows Explorer.
- Choose the Run command from the Start menu, and then type the path and file name of the application's executable file.
- Choose the Run command from the Start menu. Then drag an EXE file from My Computer or Network Neighborhood, and drop the file into the Run dialog box.
- Use the Windows 3.1 Program Manager, and then run the application by double-clicking its program item.

NOTE Windows 95 includes updated versions of both Program Manager and File Manager. The optional 3.1 interface will add applications to the Program Manager during installation. If you opt for the Windows 3.1 interface, you also can add program items to the Program Manager manually.

If you want to start Windows 95 in the Program Manager, you need to install Window 95 using the Custom option. Choose User Interface in the Computer Settings dialog box and then choose Change. Select Windows 3.1 (Program Manager) and choose OK. If you have already installed Windows 95, add a shortcut to PROGMAN.EXE to the \WINDOWS\STARTUP folder. PROGMAN.EXE is located in the \WINDOWS\ folder.

- Open a document or data file associated with the application. When you open a file, Windows launches the application automatically and then opens the file in that application. There are as many ways to open files as there are ways to launch applications. For instance, you can open files in Explorer, by choosing a recently used file from the Documents submenu on the Start menu, or by double-clicking a shortcut on your desktop.
- Finally, for a bizarre twist, try this method of launching a Windows application. You can open a MS-DOS window and type the command to start the application at the DOS prompt. You would expect to get an error message saying the program requires Windows to run. But, instead, Windows 95 launches the Windows application for you.

Removing Windows Applications

Installing a Windows application can be a complicated venture. Windows applications are often tightly integrated with the operating system. Installing such applications not only requires copying the application's files into the application's own directory, but also adds numerous support files to your Windows directory and changes Windows' settings. Fortunately, nearly all applications provide setup programs to automate the installation process.

Removing an application can be similarly complicated. Finding all the support files and settings added or changed during the application's installation can be nearly impossible. Fortunately, many application setup programs now offer an uninstall option to automate the process when you need to remove the application from your system.

Windows 95 takes this welcome trend a step further by adding a facility to remove applications. That facility is in the same Control Panel dialog box that you use to install applications and Windows components.

Removing Applications Automatically

Windows 95's Add/Remove Programs Wizard adds to the capability of individual setup programs by tracking an application's components in the Registry. This lets Windows delete an application's files and settings but still identify and retain any files that another application might share and use.

NOTE Only applications that provide uninstall programs specifically designed to work with Windows 95 appear in the list of applications that Windows 95 can remove automatically.

To uninstall an application automatically, start by opening the Control Panel and double-clicking the Add/Remove Programs icon. This opens the Add/Remove Programs properties sheet—the same sheet you used to install the application (see Figure 25.7).

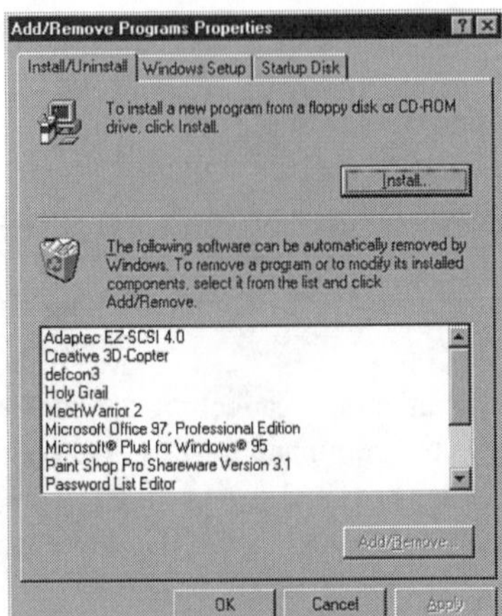

FIG. 25.7
In the Add/Remove Programs properties sheet, you can remove applications as well as install them.

The lower portion of the dialog box lists applications that you can remove. To remove an application, select it from the list and choose Remove. After you confirm that you want to remove the program, Windows runs the selected application's uninstall program.

Removing Applications Manually

If you want to remove an application from your system, just hope that it's one that Windows can remove automatically. Removing an application manually can be difficult, and possibly dangerous.

Remove Files from the Application Directory Getting rid of the files in an application's own directory is fairly straightforward. In fact, that should probably be the first step in removing an application manually.

Many applications install support files in the Windows directories. It's nearly impossible to tell what application added which files, and to make matters worse, several applications can share the same files. If you ignore the files in the Windows directories when you remove an application, you can leave numerous orphaned files on your system needlessly consuming hard disk space. However, if you make a mistake and delete the wrong file or one that another applications also uses, you might render the other application unusable.

If you find support files in your Windows directory that you think are unnecessary, copy them to a separate folder before you remove them. If you don't encounter any problems after a few months, you can delete that folder.

Remove Shortcuts and Folders from the Start Menu After you remove an application's files from your hard disk, you want to get rid of any shortcuts that pointed to the application. To delete a shortcut icon from your desktop, simply drag and drop the shortcut onto the Recycle Bin icon on your desktop. The Recycle Bin is like a trash can that stores deleted files until the Bin reaches a certain capacity.

To remove the application from the Start menu, click the Start button and choose Settings, Taskbar. Then in the Taskbar properties sheet, click the Start Menu Programs page. Next, choose Remove to open the Remove Shortcuts/Folders dialog box (see Figure 25.8).

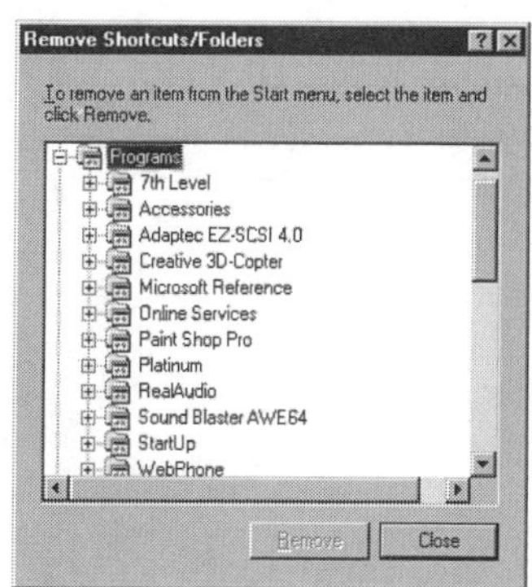

FIG. 25.8
After removing an application, you open the Remove Shortcuts/ Folders dialog box to remove the application's folder and shortcuts from your Start menu.

The Remove Shortcuts/Folders dialog box, like the Windows Explorer, displays a hierarchical list of folders and files. To expand the display and show a folder's contents, you can click the plus sign beside the folder. Select the folder or shortcut that you want to delete, and then choose Remove. To remove other items, repeat the process as necessary. When you finish removing items, click Close.

Remove File Associations After you remove an application, you can remove any associations that might have existed between file extensions and the defunct application. After all, you don't want Windows to try to launch the nonexistent application when you double-click a document file.

To remove the link between a file extension and an application, start by opening the My Computer window. Next, choose View, Options to open the Options dialog box; then click the File Types tab. You then see the screen shown in Figure 25.9. Scroll down the Registered File Types list and select the file type that you want to delete; then choose Remove. Windows asks you to confirm your choice. If you answer Yes, Windows abolishes the registration of that file type.

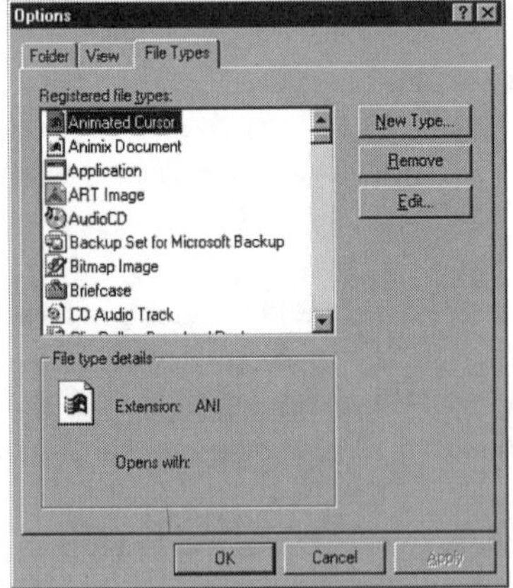

FIG. 25.9
Using the Options dialog box to remove a file type registration is easier and safer than editing the Registry directly.

There are several commercial utilities available for helping you uninstall applications, including MicroHelp's UnInstaller, Quarterdeck's CleanSweep 95, and Vertisoft's Remove-It for Windows 95. Be sure to get the Windows 95 versions of these programs that are designed to modify the Registry when you uninstall a program. These utilities will also uninstall Windows 3.x programs.

CHAPTER 26

Installing, Running, and Uninstalling MS-DOS Applications

by Dick Cravens

In this chapter

Understanding How Windows 95 Works with MS-DOS Applications

Applications that simply would not run under earlier versions of the Windows MS-DOS Prompt now perform admirably. For applications that still won't run under the new Windows, a special mode helps you run them quickly and easily from within Windows, and then automatically returns you to your Windows session when you're finished.

The following are some of the improvements in Windows 95 for supporting MS-DOS applications:

- Better local reboot support
- Zero conventional memory usage for protected-mode components
- Consolidated setup for MS-DOS-based applications
- Toolbar support for windowed MS-DOS applications
- Graceful shutdown for windowed MS-DOS sessions
- Long file name support, with full backwards compatibility for "8.3" format file names
- Execution of Windows programs from the MS-DOS session
- The ability to open documents from the command line
- Better control over MS-DOS window fonts
- User-scalable MS-DOS session windows
- Improved Cut, Paste, and Copy commands for integrating MS-DOS and Windows application information
- Universal Naming Convention (UNC) path name support
- Spooling of MS-DOS-based print jobs

Windows 95 makes dealing with MS-DOS/Windows integration quicker and easier than ever and makes working with MS-DOS applications similar to working on a machine running only MS-DOS. In addition, MS-DOS emulation under Windows 95 gives the user many of the other benefits of Windows 95: the graphical user interface, multitasking, enhanced printing support and networking support.

Conventional Memory in Windows 95

An added bonus of the overall design of Windows 95 is the greater conservation of conventional memory (that below the 640K mark). Windows 95 replaces DOS-based drivers, which cannot be loaded above the first 1M of memory, with virtual device drivers (VxDs). VxDs are protected-mode drivers that can be loaded above 1M, thereby freeing up space in the conventional (up to 640K) and upper memory areas (between 640K and 1M). You can then use HIMEM and EMM386 to load any real-mode device drivers and TSRs (terminate-and-stay resident) programs into the upper memory area to free up conventional memory for DOS applications. Some MS-DOS applications simply couldn't run under Windows 3.1. By the time mouse, network, SCSI, and other necessary drivers were loaded, there simply wasn't enough RAM below 640K. Windows 95 alleviates this situation by checking each driver specified in your installation against a "safe list" of known drivers, and loading approved ones in extended memory, or substituting equivalent drivers.

For example, if your PC is on a NetWare network and uses a SCSI CD-ROM drive, the SMARTDrive disk cache, DriveSpace disk compression, and an MS-DOS mouse driver, you can save more than 250K in conventional memory using the MS-DOS system in Windows 95.

CAUTION

Don't run MS-DOS or Windows 3.1 file system utilities in a Windows MS-DOS session or you may corrupt files or lose long file names. Examples of this type of software are MS-DOS disk defragmenter and unerase or undelete utilities. Windows comes with many of these utilities, so use the Windows versions instead (don't just boot to MS-DOS to use your older utilities; some of them will corrupt the Windows 95 long file name system).

Starting the MS-DOS Prompt Session

Getting started with MS-DOS under Windows is as simple as selecting a menu item. To begin a session, follow these steps:

1. Open the Start menu and choose Programs. Windows displays a submenu.
2. Choose the MS-DOS Prompt menu item. Windows opens the MS-DOS Prompt window, as shown in Figure 26.1.

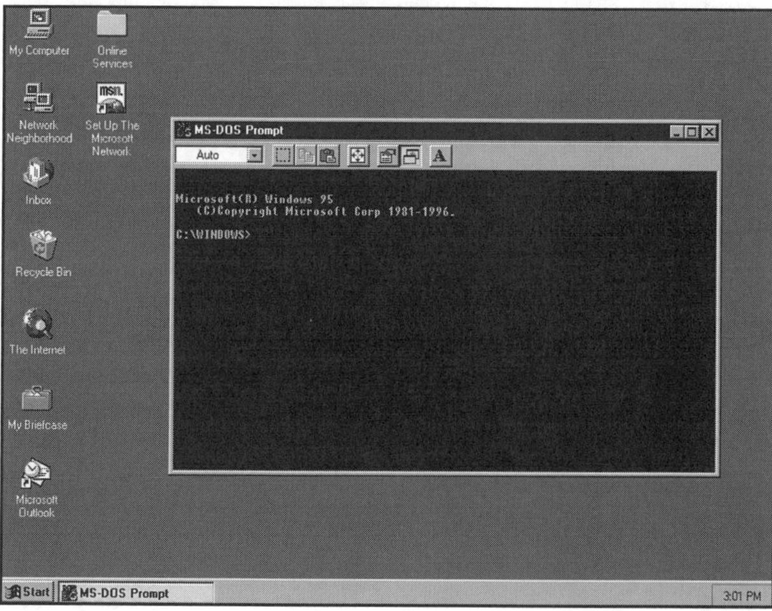

FIG. 26.1
The MS-DOS Prompt window where you can execute DOS commands.

Ending MS-DOS Prompt Sessions

You can still run DOS batch files, either from the command line, the Run command in the Start menu, or from within Windows, using a shortcut. In Windows 95, you can modify the properties of the BAT file using the properties sheet. Right-click the shortcut and select the Program tab. You can select what mode you want the DOS session to run in (normal window, maximized, or minimized) and assign a shortcut key. You also can specify that the DOS window be closed when the batch file is finished running.

You also can specify a batch file that will be run whenever you start a particular DOS program. Open the properties sheet for the DOS program, select the Program tab, and type the full path and name for the batch file in the Batch File text box.

Now that you've started an MS-DOS Prompt session, practice closing it before you move on to the finer points of operation. To close the MS-DOS Prompt window, follow these steps:

1. Click in the MS-DOS Prompt window to bring it to the foreground.
2. Find the flashing cursor near the MS-DOS command prompt. At the flashing cursor near the MS-DOS command prompt, type **exit**.
3. Press Enter, and Windows closes the MS-DOS Prompt session window.

Don't leave MS-DOS Prompt sessions open any longer than necessary. Every session takes a big chunk out of available CPU time, slowing down your entire Windows performance in all applications.

NOTE As with most other procedures under Windows, several other ways to close an MS-DOS Prompt session are available. As alternatives, try each of the following:

- Double-click the MS-DOS icon in the top-left corner of the MS-DOS Prompt session window.
- Click the MS-DOS icon; then choose Close from the menu.
- Click the Close icon in the upper-right corner of the MS-DOS Prompt window.
- Right-click anywhere in the MS-DOS Prompt window title bar. Windows displays a menu from which you can choose Close.

Ending Sessions with Running Applications

Windows also allows you to close sessions that have applications open; but by default, it warns you if the application is running or has open files.

Besides giving you options for more gracefully ending a session, Windows 95 improves on previous versions by performing better session cleanup, releasing memory, and deallocating system resources much more consistently.

To close an active session, simply follow the same procedures for closing a session with just an MS-DOS Prompt that you used earlier. This time, however, Windows displays the warning dialog box shown in Figure 26.2.

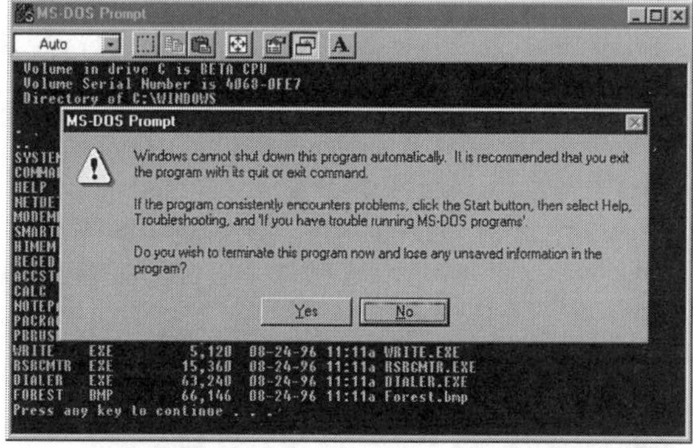

FIG. 26.2
Windows warns you if you try to exit an MS-DOS session while an application is active.

If you choose No, Windows returns you to the MS-DOS Prompt session, and you can exit the program before you close the MS-DOS session.

Otherwise, choose Yes and Windows shuts down the MS-DOS session and terminates the running application. It's not recommended that you close sessions this way, since you will lose any information that was not saved in the program, but you can do it in an emergency (for example, if the application is hung and simply won't *let* you exit gracefully).

TROUBLESHOOTING

My MS-DOS application simply won't respond and none of the close procedures you list are working. What can I do to shut down this unresponsive application and get back to work? Will I lose all my data in other applications? Use the classic "three-fingered salute," Ctrl+Alt+Del, after which Windows 95 displays the Close Program dialog box. Windows 95, however, does a good job of recovering from application failure because it gives you a choice of which task to shut down instead of assuming the one in the foreground is the culprit. After you select the application task to deal with, you have the choice of ending the errant task, shutting down the entire computer, rebooting using Ctrl+Alt+Del again, or canceling.

You learn a way to override the Windows warnings about closing an active MS-DOS Prompt session later in this chapter.

▶ **See** "Miscellaneous Properties," **p. 661**

Controlling the MS-DOS Prompt Session

Now that you know the basics for working in a DOS window, you are ready to learn about the ways you can work with and control your DOS sessions.

Change the MS-DOS session from full screen to windowed and back again by pressing Alt+Enter.

Using the MS-DOS Prompt Toolbar

Windows MS-DOS sessions have a variety of interface controls. The toolbar will be familiar to you if you've been using the Windows Explorer. Figure 26.3 shows the MS-DOS Prompt toolbar and its controls.

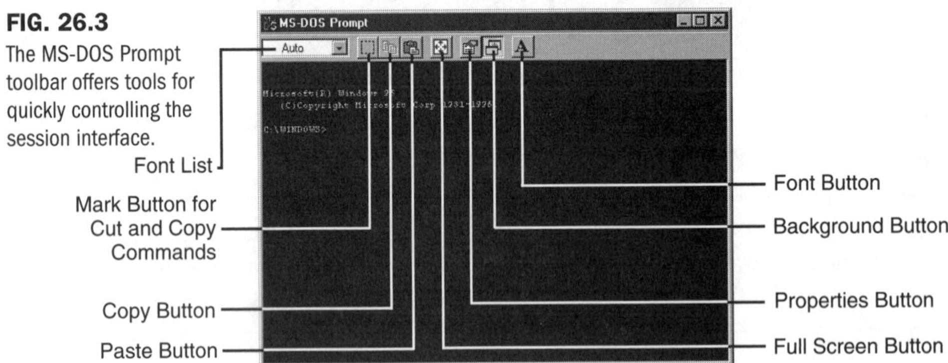

FIG. 26.3 The MS-DOS Prompt toolbar offers tools for quickly controlling the session interface.

To continue running a DOS application in the background when you switch to another application, click the Background button on the Prompt toolbar. If you are downloading a file using a DOS-based communications application, for example, you will want to enable background operation. Normally, you will not want to run the DOS application in the background, so that you free up all system resources for the foreground application.

Controlling the MS-DOS Prompt Interface

Windows offers TrueType scalable fonts in addition to the familiar system fonts, allowing on-the-fly resizing of the entire session window. To try the new font features, open an MS-DOS session and perform the following steps:

1. Click the toolbar's Font list, then choose TT7×14 (the TrueType font for TT7×14 resolution). The window should now appear as shown in Figure 26.4 (assuming you're using 800×600 Super VGA display resolution).
2. Grab the window borders in the lower-right corner and resize the window. Notice that the vertical and horizontal window scroll bar controls appear on the window, but the text in the window remains the same, as shown in Figure 26.5.

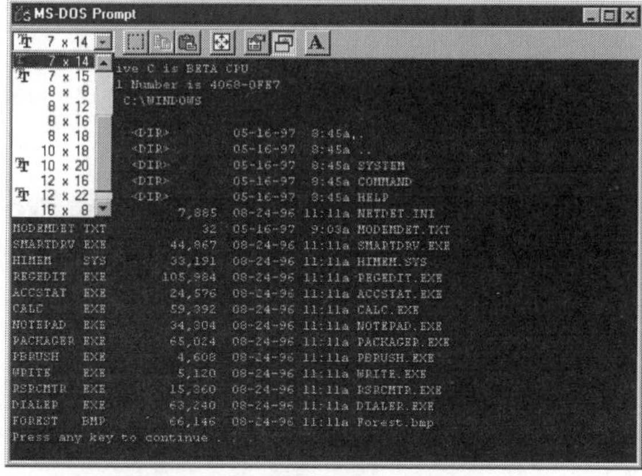

FIG. 26.4
You can use the toolbar to control TrueType fonts in your MS-DOS Prompt session.

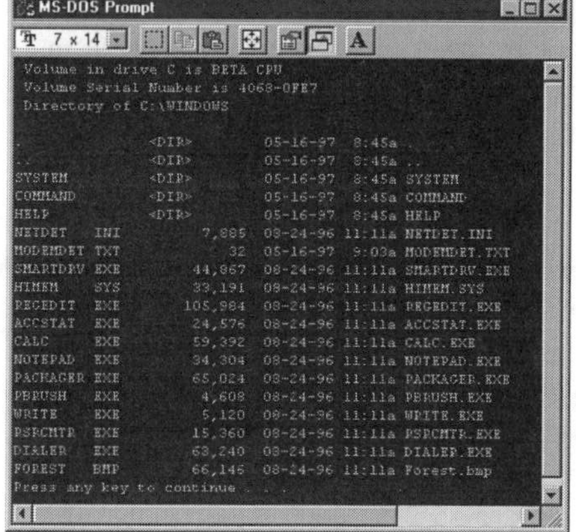

FIG. 26.5
Windows supports dynamic resizing of the MS-DOS Prompt window. You can access any hidden areas of the session using standard scroll bar controls.

3. Repeat the procedure in step 1 to select the 4×7 font mode. Notice that the text in the window is much smaller, and the window has shrunk to match (see Figure 26.6). Grab the window borders again and try to enlarge the window; notice how it is limited to a maximum size.

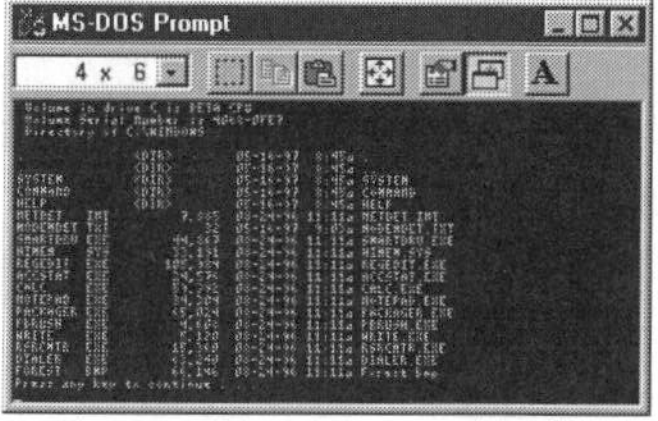

FIG. 26.6
If you choose a font that allows full viewing of the MS-DOS Prompt session, Windows won't let you resize the window larger than the session.

4. Repeat the procedure in step 1 to select Auto mode. The window does not change.
5. Grab the window borders in the lower-right corner and resize the window. Notice how Windows alters the font on-the-fly. When you change the window size again, the font adjusts automatically to the nearest available size.

Using the Windows Clipboard with the MS-DOS Prompt

Windows offers even easier access to the data in your MS-DOS session, via the toolbar. Copying information from your session into a Windows application is quick and easy. Follow these steps to try it out:

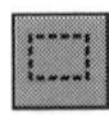

1. Using the mouse, click the Mark tool and select text in your MS-DOS application.
2. Click the Copy tool on the MS-DOS Prompt toolbar. Windows places a copy of the text in the Clipboard.
3. Using the mouse, click your Windows application (for example, Notepad) to make it active. Position the cursor where you want to insert the text and then choose Edit, Paste from the Notepad menu. Notepad displays the text copied from your MS-DOS session window.

TROUBLESHOOTING

I used to be able to use the mouse to highlight text in an MS-DOS session and then press Enter to copy the text to the Clipboard, but now it doesn't work. This still works under Windows 95, but it simply isn't enabled by default. You can use the mouse to select and copy text if the application you're running supports it (for example, EDIT), but the MS-DOS Prompt itself won't (for example, you can't mark and copy the results of the dir command that MS-DOS writes to your window). If you use the toolbar on your MS-DOS sessions, just click the Mark tool on the toolbar before you select the text. If you've set up your MS-DOS sessions so the toolbar doesn't show, then you can tell Windows 95 to enable the QuickEdit feature.

To enable this feature, simply click the window system icon (the MS-DOS icon in the upper-left corner) and choose Properties and then choose the Misc tab when the properties sheet appears. Check the QuickEdit box under the Mouse section, click OK, and you're ready to go.

To copy information from a Windows application to an MS-DOS application, select and copy the information in the Windows application and then choose the Paste tool on the Prompt toolbar. You also can right-click the MS-DOS window title bar and choose Edit, Paste if you don't have the toolbar displayed. You can use this method to paste information into a DOS application or onto the DOS command line.

Using Long File Names

One of the most bothersome limitations of the MS-DOS environment has been the 8.3 file name format. Windows 95 supports longer file names, and the MS-DOS Prompt offers support for them, too. To see how this works, follow these steps:

1. Using My Computer, create a new folder called Incredibly Long Folder Name on the root of Drive C, as shown in Figure 26.7.

FIG. 26.7 You can use up to 255 characters in a file or folder name.

2. Using the Start menu, open an MS-DOS Prompt. At the prompt, type **dir c:***. The MS-DOS window displays the folder listing for the root of Drive C (an example is shown in Figure 26.8).

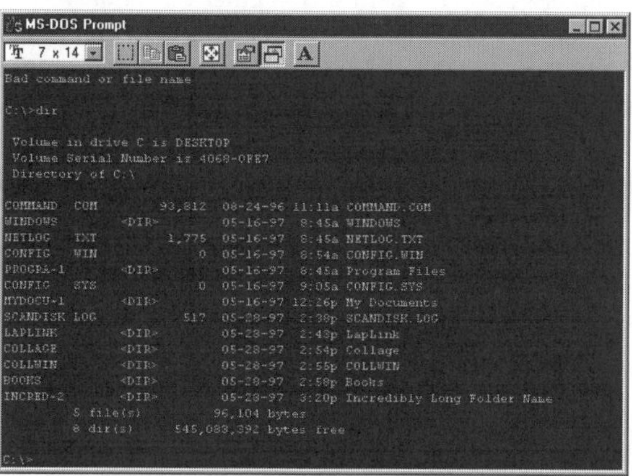

FIG. 26.8 The MS-DOS Prompt session supports and displays both long and short file and folder (directory) names.

Notice the dual display of both the 8.3 format and long format folder names. Windows and MS-DOS coordinate both naming systems, but not without a price—the 8.3 format name uses the tilde character (~) to show the inevitable truncation. Even under Windows, some long names may be shortened using the ellipsis characters (…) when space is at a premium.

To ensure complete backwards compatibility, Windows still uses file extensions, even though they are not displayed in the Windows Explorer or on the Desktop. If you rename a file from the Windows environment, it does not change the hidden file name extension. Windows still uses the extension for file associations with applications and viewers.

NOTE Not all applications support long file names just because Windows does. It's doubtful that any MS-DOS application will support long file names because most were written prior to this version of Windows. Most 16-bit Windows applications won't support longer file names until their first release after Windows 95, if then. Some software companies will probably wait for the first release of their application as a true 32-bit program to include this feature.

Many of the native MS-DOS commands in Windows 95 have been enhanced to provide support for long file names. For example, the dir and copy commands both support long file names.

You can use long file names at the DOS command prompt if they don't include spaces. If they do include spaces, enclose the file name in quotes. For example:

```
CD "MSOFFICE\WINWORD\BUSINESS LETTERS"
```

Using Universal Naming Convention Path Names

More and more PCs are on *local area networks* (*LANs*). Most shared resources on a LAN are stored on *servers*, or PCs dedicated for a particular network task, such as printing, file storage, or database storage.

Gaining access to other PCs on the network, whether server or workstation, can be a tiresome process of mapping the other machine to a virtual drive letter on your system. The Windows 95 MS-DOS Prompt offers a way around this with *Universal Naming Convention (UNC)* support. This is a fancy way of saying that you can view, copy, or run files on another machine without having to assign it a drive letter on your computer. It also means that if you are running short of logical drive letters, you can get to servers that you use only intermittently, with a simple command from the MS-DOS Prompt.

For example, if you want to run an application called SHARED.EXE in the folder STUFF on server FRED1, you can enter the following at the command prompt:

```
\\fred1\stuff\shared.exe
```

You also can use this feature with any legal MS-DOS command. For example, to see the contents of the folder STUFF, use the familiar dir command as follows:

```
dir \\fred1\stuff
```

This yields a standard folder listing of the contents of that area of the server.

NOTE Although the MS-DOS prompt in Windows 95 supports UNC names, be aware that some DOS and Windows 3.1x applications do not support UNC.

Printing from the MS-DOS Prompt

The biggest change in printing support for MS-DOS applications comes in the form of better conflict resolution and print job queuing. Windows handles printer port contention between MS-DOS and Windows applications by shuttling all MS-DOS print tasks to the same printer management utility used by Windows applications.

▶ **See** "Printing from MS-DOS Applications," **p. 144**

Understanding MS-DOS Mode

Although you will be able to run most DOS applications without any difficulties from within Windows, you may run into problems with some poorly designed MS-DOS applications—some MS-DOS applications demand total control over system resources and access hardware in the most direct way, bypassing "standard" Windows methods.

Windows 95 accommodates a poorly behaved application to the best of its capability, via *MS-DOS mode*. This mode is the equivalent to the Real mode present in older versions of Windows, with some "real" improvements.

MS-DOS mode works by giving the errant MS-DOS application the entire system for the duration of the session. Windows removes itself from memory, and leaves only a small "stub" loader in preparation for its return to control of your system.

▶ **See** "Advanced Program Settings," **p. 658**

To use this mode, the user sets a property in the Advanced Program Settings dialog box. When the MS-DOS application runs, Windows literally shuts down, loads the application, and then returns automatically when the application is finished. This process can be slow and cumbersome, but it's faster and more convenient than exiting Windows manually, using the dual-boot option, and reloading Windows.

Knowing When to Use MS-DOS Mode

Before you decide to enable MS-DOS mode for an application, try these other options:

- Confirm that you've optimized the MS-DOS session settings for that application. Check the program's documentation for special memory requirements or other unusual needs. You may be able to adjust MS-DOS support in Windows to make the application work in a standard MS-DOS session.
- Try running the application in full-screen mode, using the Alt+Enter key sequence.

If either of the preceding methods works, you will have a faster, more convenient alternative, allowing you the full benefit of multitasking and other features in Windows, all of which disappear during the MS-DOS mode session.

Setting Up an Application to Run in MS-DOS Mode

Whenever possible, Windows 95 determines that an application needs to run in MS-DOS mode and closes down all other applications and switches to this mode automatically. Unless you specify otherwise, you'll be warned when Windows is about to switch to MS-DOS mode.

In some cases, you may have to manually configure an application to run in MS-DOS mode. If you try to run such an application, you get an error message telling you that you can't run the application in Windows. If this happens, you should manually configure the application to run in MS-DOS mode, using the following steps:

1. If you haven't created a shortcut for the application, create one now. You can only modify the settings of a DOS application using a shortcut.
2. Right-click the shortcut for the application and choose Properties.
3. Select the Program tab and choose Advanced to display the Advanced Program Settings dialog box.
4. Select the Prevent MS-DOS-based Programs from Detecting Windows option.
5. Choose OK.

Double-click the shortcut icon to try running the application. If the application still doesn't run, follow these steps:

1. Open the Advanced Program Settings dialog box again, as covered in the last steps.
2. Select the MS-DOS Mode option.
3. Choose OK.

Try running the application again. If it still doesn't run, you have to modify the configuration for the MS-DOS mode, using the following steps:

1. Open the Advanced Program Settings dialog box. The dialog box appears as in Figure 26.9.
2. Select the Specify a New MS-DOS Configuration option.

   Selecting this option allows you to override the default settings for the MS-DOS-mode session.
3. Modify the lines in the CONFIG.SYS for MS-DOS Mode and AUTOEXEC.BAT for MS-DOS Mode windows as needed to allow this application to run.

   The changes you make here affect only this application. In this way, you can customize each application that must run in MS-DOS mode.
4. If necessary, choose the Configuration button and select from the options in the Select MS-DOS Configuration Options dialog box and choose OK.

   Be aware that when you choose from among the options in this dialog box, you remove the entries that already appear in the CONFIG.SYS and AUTOEXEC.BAT text boxes.

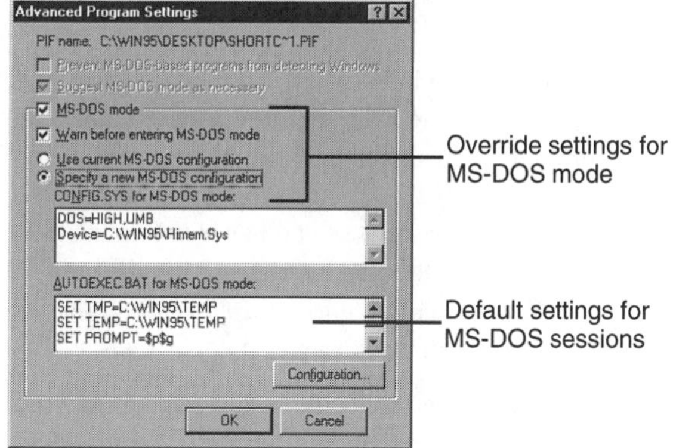

FIG. 26.9
Windows allows you to override the default settings for MS-DOS mode support. You can even run a special CONFIG.SYS and AUTOEXEC.BAT file for each application.

CAUTION

Use the Direct Disk Access option with great care. It is possible for an MS-DOS application to destroy long file name support when you select this option.

5. Choose OK twice to close the dialog boxes.

If there are programs or drivers that you want to load for all your MS-DOS mode sessions, edit the file named DOSSTART.BAT that is located in your \Windows folder. For example, if you want to have access to your CD-ROM drive in your MS-DOS sessions, include a line that will enable the CD-ROM.
For example:

```
MSCDEX.EXE /D:MSCD0001 /M:12
```

MSCDEX is included with Windows 95 and is located in the \Windows\Command folder. You also need to include a line in your CONFIG.SYS file that loads the CD-ROM real-mode driver. This driver is not loaded into memory when you're running Windows 95.

Part V Ch 26

TROUBLESHOOTING

I set my main MS-DOS Prompt to run in MS-DOS mode, and now whenever I start it, Windows shuts down completely! How can I set it back if I can't get to the properties? You can access the properties of any program or file from the Windows Desktop without running the program or opening the file. When Windows restarts after the MS-DOS Mode session, locate the icon for the MS-DOS Prompt program (in the WINDOWS\START MENU\PROGRAMS folder) with the Windows Explorer and right-click the icon to get the menu that offers the Properties function.

When the properties sheet opens, go to the Program page and choose the Advanced button, which opens the Advanced Program Settings dialog box, as shown earlier in Figure 26.9. Simply uncheck the MS-DOS Mode box and choose OK twice to close the properties sheet and return to the Desktop. See "Configuring Your MS-DOS Application" later in this chapter.

Using PIF Files

Some MS-DOS applications running in Windows 3.1 required special settings kept in a Program Information File (PIF). Creating PIFs required a lot of knowledge and time as well as a modicum of luck. Windows 95 reduces that mess by using the same mechanism for MS-DOS applications and data that's now used for Windows files: the properties sheet. With a simple right-click of the mouse, you can directly view and alter the entire gamut of controls for your MS-DOS application. No separate editor, no hunting for the PIF, and then confirming that it's the correct one. Although Windows 95 still uses PIF files, the properties sheet provides a unified means of viewing the PIF properties for a given application.

One of the more confusing issues under Windows 3.1 was the need to create a PIF file for each MS-DOS application that required custom settings. Windows 95 takes care of that chore automatically—all you need to do is view the properties for your MS-DOS application.

To view an example properties sheet for an MS-DOS application, follow these steps:

1. Using the Windows Explorer, find the Windows folder and then open the Command folder.
2. Select EDIT.COM in the file list in the right pane of Explorer.
3. Right-click to open the shortcut menu and choose Properties. Windows displays the Edit properties sheet, as shown in Figure 26.10.

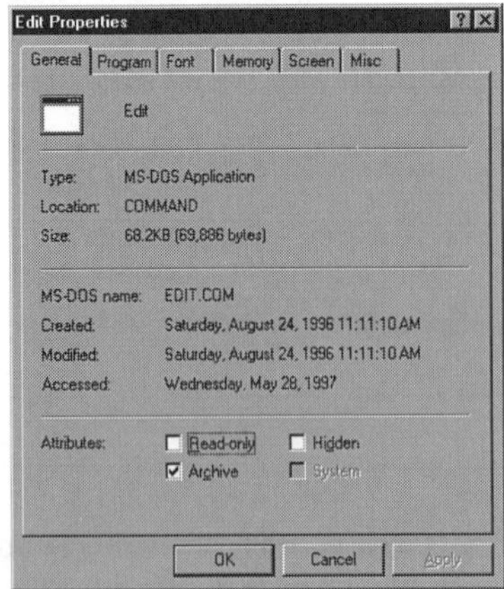

FIG. 26.10
The properties sheet for MS-DOS applications has several tabs unique to the needs of the MS-DOS environment.

If you're mystified by some of the terms and control types you see here, don't worry. The section "Configuring Your MS-DOS Application," later in this chapter, shows examples of how these controls can help you maximize the performance of Windows when you run MS-DOS applications.

Graphic-Intensive Applications

One great example of the enhanced MS-DOS support available under Windows 95 is the capability to run some applications in graphics mode in a window. Although this doesn't sound like a big trick, remember that earlier versions of Windows don't support this at all—you are forced to run MS-DOS graphics-mode applications full screen.

Why would you want to take advantage of running MS-DOS applications in a window? For some of the same reasons you like Windows applications: the capability to quickly and easily move back and forth between applications and the capability to easily cut and paste information between programs.

Also, in earlier versions of Windows, moving from a full-screen MS-DOS application in graphics mode back to Windows involves a time lag during which the display has to reset for a completely different video mode and resolution; some monitors handle this gracefully, but most don't. Running your MS-DOS program in a window avoids this altogether.

NOTE Windows 95 contains the capability to self-configure for many popular MS-DOS programs. These configurations are derived from research with the applications used the most and are stored in a file called APPS.INF. When you install an MS-DOS application, Windows checks to see if it's registered in the APPS.INF database. If the application is listed in the APPS.INF file but no PIF file exists, Windows uses the information to create a PIF for future use.

Although this new capability is wonderful, be aware that not all MS-DOS applications are supported. Not all applications follow the "official" guidelines for MS-DOS hardware access. (Some programmers break or bend the rules to gain faster performance; for example, writing directly to the video hardware versus using the MS-DOS service calls for video.) Hence, Windows 95 can't support them in a windowed, virtualized MS-DOS environment. The same application may run perfectly full screen because there are fewer layers of virtualization for Windows to provide. Game programs are a great example of this scenario, which constantly attempt to use the system timer, video, and sound resources as directly as possible.

How do you know if your application will run in graphics mode in a Windows 95 window? The best test is to try it. Follow these steps to test your program:

1. Locate the icon for the MS-DOS graphics program you want to test and double-click it to start the program. Windows starts the program in full-screen mode unless you've configured it otherwise or if the program was installed with a windowed default. If the program opens in a window, press Alt+Enter to return to full-screen mode.
2. If the program supports both Character and Graphics modes, activate the program feature that requires graphics mode (such as Page or Print Preview).
3. When the screen has reformatted for graphics display, press Alt+Enter to return to windowed display mode.
4. If Windows can't support the application in this mode, you will see the warning box displayed in Figure 26.11.

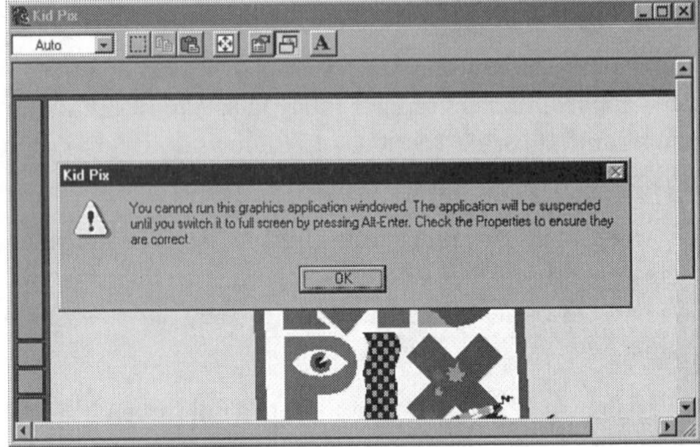

FIG. 26.11 Although Windows now offers improved support for MS-DOS graphics mode, some applications still don't work in a window.

Improved Memory Protection

Windows 95 offers a higher level of memory protection for the entire system and specifically for MS-DOS applications. This reduces the chance of programs writing to each other's memory space. You can specify special protection for conventional system memory by checking the Protected check box on the Memory property page, as shown in Figure 26.12.

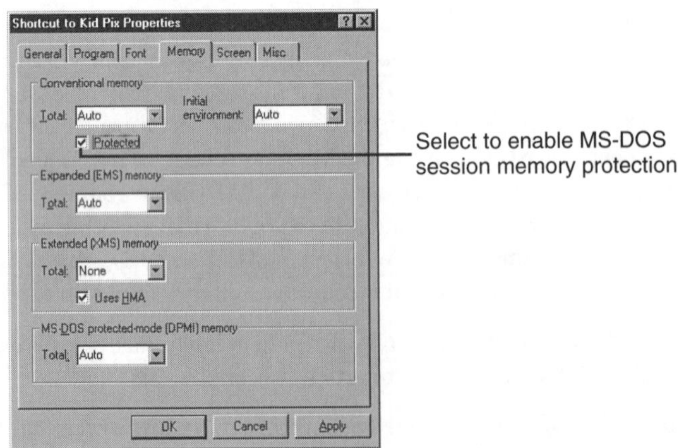

FIG. 26.12 Windows 95 allows you to protect conventional memory from errant applications via the Protected setting on the Memory property page.

Although it might seem logical to enable this option by default for all MS-DOS applications, enough overhead is involved in tracking this for each session that it's really best to turn it on only for those applications that have proven that they require it.

Enhanced Virtual Machine Support

MS-DOS application support requires the presence of a virtual MS-DOS environment, or *virtual machine.* Windows 95 offers many improvements over the virtual-machine model used in previous versions of Windows.

The virtual-machine support in Windows 3.1x required an existing real-mode MS-DOS environment. The method Windows 3.1x used to create this environment, although it worked, had two major shortcomings: It wasted system memory and restricted the customization of individual virtual MS-DOS sessions. Program Information Files (PIFs) allowed the user to alter some parameters of the memory model for each successive virtual-machine session, but the overall settings could not be altered once Windows 3.1 was started.

Windows 95 offers many improvements over this model. Because Windows 95 doesn't require a complete, existing real-mode MS-DOS environment before it runs, you can control almost every aspect of the virtual MS-DOS environment because it is more "truly" virtual. You can even run batch files within the session to customize the environment for your application's needs.

Windows 95 also offers better management of MS-DOS session closings. Under Windows 3.1, not all system memory and resources were released when a virtual-machine session ended. This resulted in a slow erosion of performance with the eventual inability to open additional applications and requiring the user to restart Windows.

Enhanced Local Reboot Support

Windows 95 improves over Windows 3.1 in how it handles programs that do not respond (or *hang*). In Windows 3.1, a program that did not respond was handled with a local reboot that theoretically affected only the errant program and its data. Under Windows 3.1's local reboot, the Ctrl+Alt+Del key sequence didn't restart the machine; it closed the misbehaving application and theoretically left Windows and all other applications fat and happy.

Local reboot had two main problems:

- Users didn't always know which application was hung, so when they used Ctrl+Alt+Del, Windows often closed the wrong one (sometimes offering to shut itself down!).
- Windows 3.1 didn't always respond quickly to the Ctrl+Alt+Del command, and the user "sat" on the keys, resulting in a complete machine reset. (A single Ctrl+Alt+Del would bring up a blue screen warning that a second Ctrl+Alt+Del would reset the system; often this screen would flash by as the system crashed and restarted, making history of any unsaved data.)

Windows 95 improves on this scenario by putting a menu between you and data loss. A single Ctrl+Alt+Del displays the Close Program dialog box.

If an application creates a problem or freezes, Windows now indicates that it is "not responding," and you have the choice of ending that task or completing an orderly shutdown of the entire system. Although this doesn't totally insulate your computer from errant applications, it does drastically improve your ability to control otherwise disastrous circumstances.

Installing MS-DOS Applications

Now that you have explored the basic concepts, tools, and techniques behind MS-DOS Prompt session support under Windows 95, look at the steps required to install and configure an MS-DOS application.

NOTE You can install any application in the following two ways:

- Locate and run the installation program for the application.
- Create a folder for the application and copy the files to that folder.

Although Windows can handle complete installations of true Windows applications, it relies on structures and capabilities that are simply not present in most MS-DOS applications. Thus, you need to set up application shortcuts and Start button menu items manually. ■

Using MS-DOS Application Installation Programs

Most professionally written MS-DOS applications have an installation or setup program that handles the details of installation for you. Besides simply creating a storage area for the application and moving the files to it, these installation programs perform the additional operating system configuration chores that may be necessary for successful operation.

NOTE MS-DOS installation programs that are Windows-aware may handle some of the preceding tasks for you, but most won't—you'll have to handle some of the tasks yourself. How do you know what alterations to make? Look for the documentation for the manual program installation instructions in the program folder. Often this is a simple text file, labeled README.TXT or INSTALL.TXT. ■

▶ **See** "Installing Applications in Windows 95," **p. 628**

Installing MS-DOS Applications from the MS-DOS Prompt

You can find and run your MS-DOS application installation program from the Windows Explorer or the Start button Run command. However, you should, instead, go directly to the MS-DOS Prompt session and install your application directly or else your application may not have a structured installation program. In either case, Windows certainly allows you this level of control.

Using an Installation Program from the MS-DOS Prompt Running the installation program from an MS-DOS Prompt is just like doing it on a machine that's running only MS-DOS. Follow these steps to begin:

1. Open a new MS-DOS session from the Start menu.
2. At the MS-DOS Prompt, enter the command to start the installation program (for example, **a:\install.exe**) and press Enter.
3. When the installation program is finished, close the MS-DOS session manually or run the application.

▶ **See** "Ending MS-DOS Prompt Sessions," **p. 642**

Installing MS-DOS Programs Manually from the MS-DOS Prompt Some MS-DOS applications don't have installation programs at all. This is most common with shareware applications or small utility programs.

To install your application manually, follow these simple steps:

1. Open a new MS-DOS session from the Start menu.
2. At the MS-DOS Prompt, enter the command to create a folder for your program (for example, **md c:\myprog**) and press Enter.
3. Enter the command to copy the program to the new folder, such as **xcopy a:*.* c:\myprog**. MS-DOS copies the files to the new folder.

NOTE You may need to alter the preceding routine slightly if your application comes as a compressed archive (such as a ZIP or an ARJ file). Usually, all this means is an additional step for decompression once the files are copied. ■

Configuring Your MS-DOS Application

Before you explore the myriad options for customizing the MS-DOS environment for your application, there's one point that needs to be stressed: The odds are very good that your program will run perfectly without any reconfiguration at all. Microsoft has done a truly admirable job in observing the reality of how people use MS-DOS applications under Windows, and it is reflected in the design of Windows 95 MS-DOS defaults. Preset configurations for the most popular MS-DOS applications are stored in Windows, awaiting your installation of the program. So before you begin messing around with all the options, be smart and run the program a few times. The old adage truly applies: If it ain't broke, don't fix it. See "Graphic-Intensive Applications," in this chapter about the APPS.INF file.

Understanding and Configuring MS-DOS Application Properties

You've already been introduced to the Windows properties sheet. Now you should take a closer look at specific property options and how they relate to your application.

General Properties The General properties page is primarily informational, with minimal controls other than file attributes (see Figure 26.13).

The only real controls exposed in the General properties page are the file attribute settings. These are used mainly to protect documents (by setting the read-only attribute), and you shouldn't alter them unless you have a specific reason.

NOTE A running MS-DOS application displays only six properties tabs. (The General tab is not shown when the program is in use.) ■

Program Properties The Program properties page gives you control over the basic environment your application starts with (see Figure 26.14).

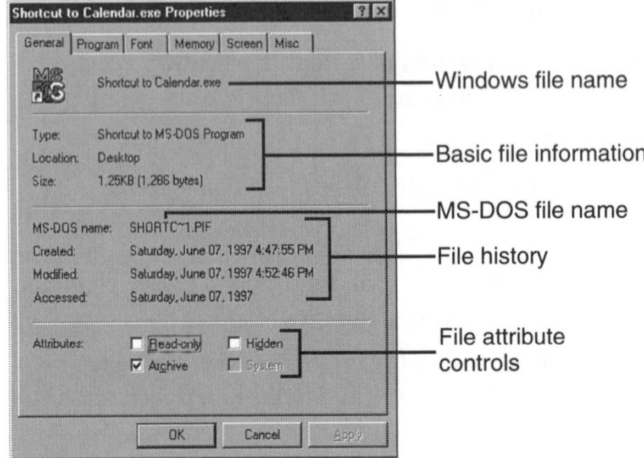

FIG. 26.13
The General properties page gives you most of the basic information about the file and easy access to control of the file attributes.

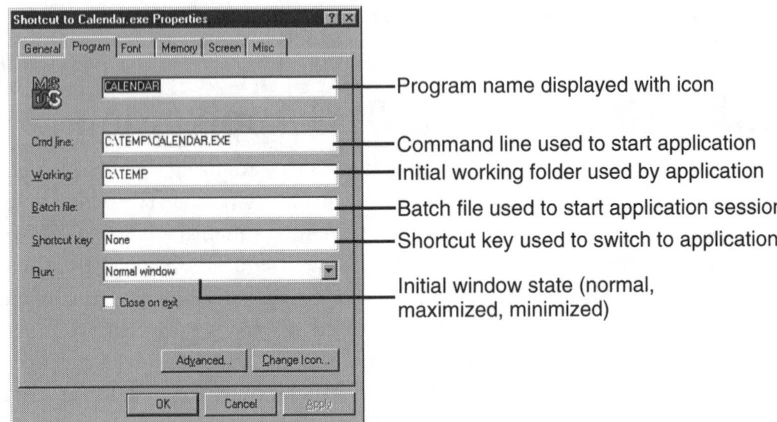

FIG. 26.14
The Program properties page allows you to alter the variables used to name and start the application.

Advanced Program Settings Clicking the Advanced button in the Program properties page opens the Advanced Program Settings dialog box, shown in Figure 26.15.

If you need to run your application in MS-DOS mode, here's where you can enable it. You can even set up custom CONFIG.SYS and AUTOEXEC.BAT values for your session. If you click the Specify A New MS-DOS Configuration option button, you can edit the special CONFIG.SYS and AUTOEXEC.BAT values right in this dialog box.

If you click the Configuration button, you will see the dialog box displayed in Figure 26.16.

All the settings under the Advanced dialog box should be altered only if your MS-DOS application simply won't run in a standard session with the default settings. For that matter, don't even enable MS-DOS mode unless your application demands it.

▶ **See** "Knowing When to Use MS-DOS Mode," **p. 649**

FIG. 26.15
The Advanced Program Settings dialog box enables you to define the precise mode and environment for your MS-DOS session.

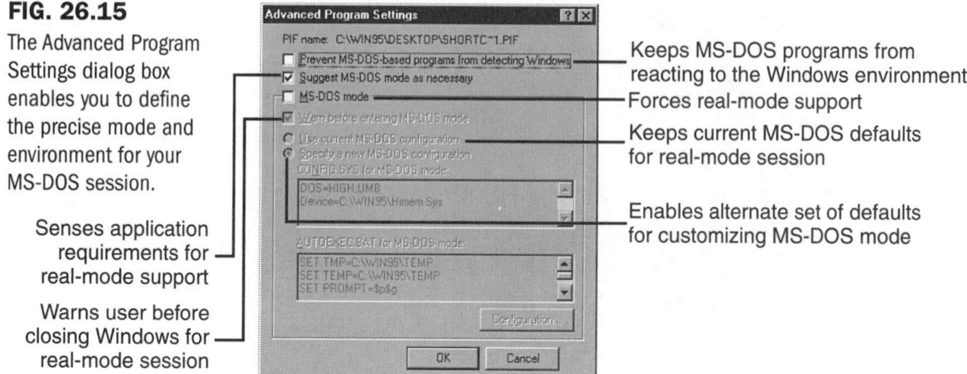

FIG. 26.16
The Select MS-DOS Configuration Options dialog box lets you control expanded memory, disk caching, disk access, and command-line editing.

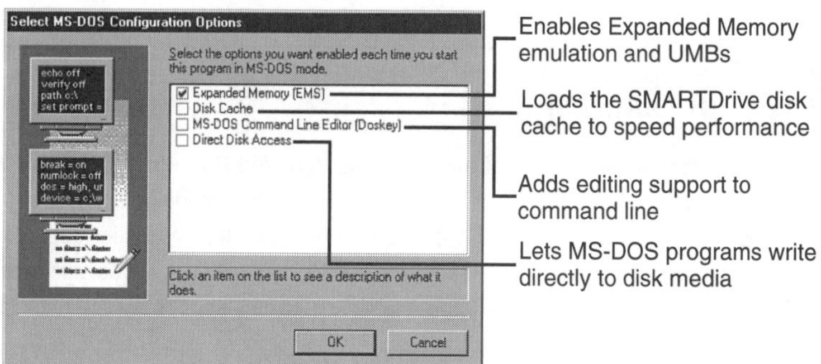

Changing MS-DOS Application Icons If you click the Change Icon button shown in Figure 26.14, the Change Icon dialog box appears (see Figure 26.17).

FIG. 26.17
The Change Icon dialog box lets you customize the icon for your MS-DOS application.

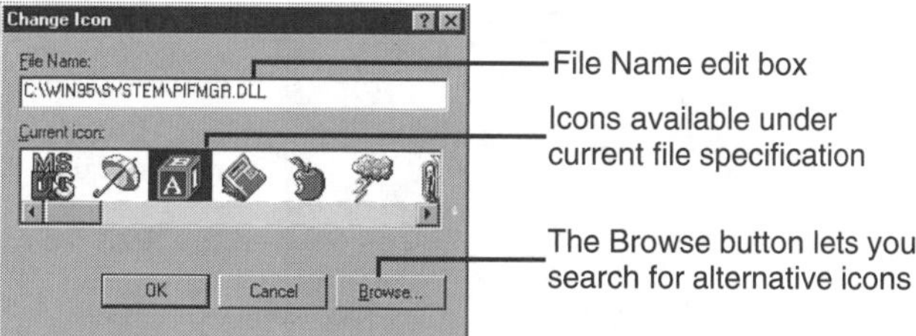

It's likely that your MS-DOS application won't come with any icons. Windows 95 shows you the icons in the file PIFMGR.DLL when you choose Change Icon. You can choose icons from other applications simply by specifying them in this dialog box.

Font Properties The Font properties page is primarily informational with minimal controls other than file attributes (see Figure 26.18). It works just like the Font list control on the MS-DOS session toolbar.

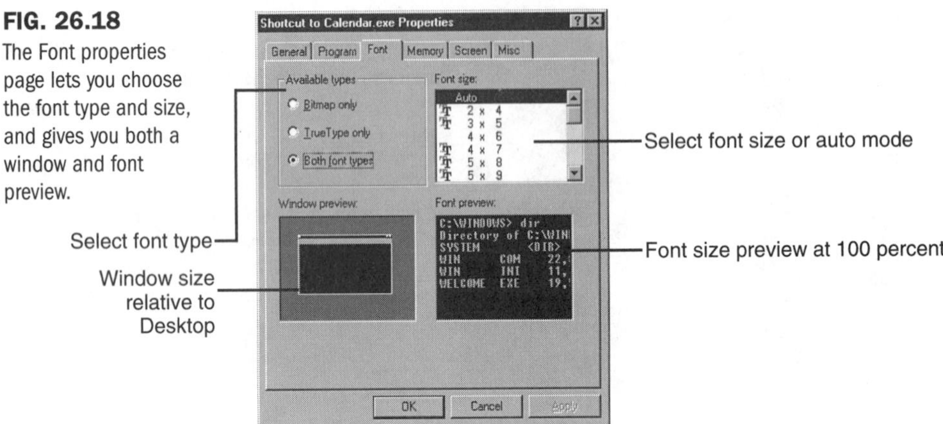

FIG. 26.18
The Font properties page lets you choose the font type and size, and gives you both a window and font preview.

TROUBLESHOOTING

When I selected a TrueType font for the display in an MS-DOS window, the font did not change on the screen. If you are running a DOS application in graphics mode, you cannot change the font because DOS graphics applications handle fonts directly. If the application supports text mode, you can switch to text mode (from within the application) and then you will be able to switch screen fonts. The other alternative is to run the application in full-screen mode (press Alt+Enter) and then change the fonts.

Memory Properties The Memory properties page makes simple work of the traditional maze of MS-DOS memory management (see Figure 26.19). With a few mouse clicks, you can configure your application memory precisely as needed.

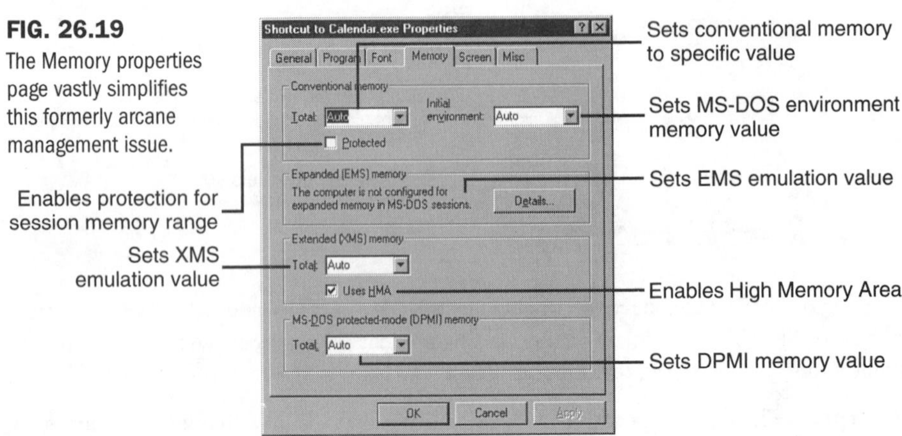

FIG. 26.19
The Memory properties page vastly simplifies this formerly arcane management issue.

Several dozen books have been written on the subject of MS-DOS memory management. Let's keep it simple: If your application works without altering these values, *do not change them.* If your application doesn't work with the default settings, *consult the documentation* to determine what the appropriate settings are. *Then* you can alter the values in this dialog box. Proceeding in any other way, unless you have considerable experience with the techniques involved, can severely inhibit the performance of your system.

▶ **See** "Improved Memory Protection," **p. 654**

Screen Properties The Screen properties page lets you control the appearance of the MS-DOS session (see Figure 26.20).

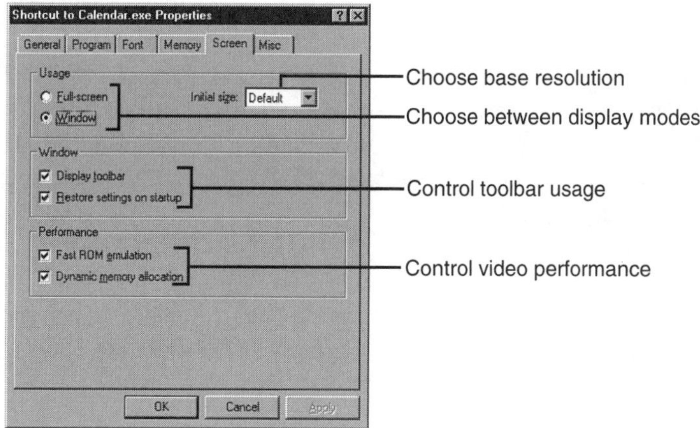

FIG. 26.20
The Screen properties page gives you control of the size, type, and performance of the MS-DOS interface.

You may find that certain MS-DOS programs (especially those running in graphics mode) respond poorly to the video emulation used in windowed mode. If so, try defeating the performance defaults by unchecking the Fast ROM Emulation and Dynamic Memory Allocation options. Fast ROM Emulation tells the Windows 95 display driver to mimic the video hardware to help display MS-DOS programs faster. Dynamic Memory Allocation releases display memory to other programs when the MS-DOS session isn't using it. If you experience strange display problems with your MS-DOS programs, try changing these settings.

Miscellaneous Properties The Misc properties page covers the remaining configuration items that don't fit under the other categories (see Figure 26.21).

- The *Allow Screen Saver* control lets your default Windows screen saver operate even if your MS-DOS session has the foreground.
- *Always Suspend* freezes your MS-DOS application when you bring another application (either MS-DOS or Windows) to the foreground. If you have an application that must perform time-sensitive operations (such as a communications program), make sure to disable this option.

- *Idle Sensitivity* tells your MS-DOS program to yield the system to other applications if it really isn't doing anything important. A word processor, for example, won't have a problem letting go of the system clock when you're not using it. A communications program, however, may need to respond quickly, so you want to set its idle sensitivity to Low.
- The *Mouse* controls enable *QuickEdit* mode (letting you mark text using just the mouse) and *Exclusive Mode* (the MS-DOS application has control of the mouse cursor when the application is in the foreground, even if you try to move the mouse out of the MS-DOS window).
- The *Warn If Still Active* item in the Termination box tells Windows to notify you before the MS-DOS session is closed. It's really best to leave this enabled, unless you are absolutely certain that the MS-DOS program will never, ever have open data files when you close it.
- The *Fast Pasting* setting simply tells Windows that your MS-DOS program can handle a raw data stream dump from the Windows Clipboard. Some MS-DOS programs clog at full speed, so if you paste to your MS-DOS application and you consistently lose characters, turn this one off.
- *Windows Shortcut Keys* allows you to override the standard quick navigation aids built into the Windows environment, just for your MS-DOS session. (Some MS-DOS programs think they can get away with using the same keys, and something has to give—Windows!) By default, Windows "owns" these shortcuts, but you can lend them to your MS-DOS application by unchecking them here.

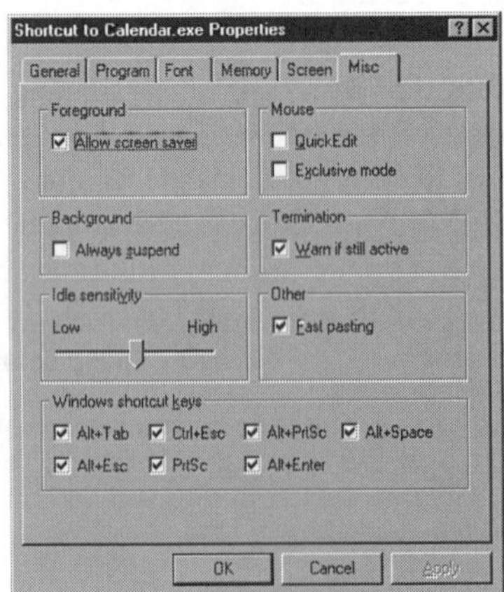

FIG. 26.21
The Misc properties page controls screen saver, mouse, background operation, program termination, shortcut key, and editing options.

Running Installed MS-DOS Applications

Windows comes set up with a default MS-DOS Prompt configuration designed to run the vast majority of applications. Although your application may have special needs, odds are it will work fine if you start it from within a running MS-DOS Prompt session.

To start your application from an MS-DOS Prompt session, follow these steps:

1. Open a new MS-DOS Prompt session from the Start menu.
2. At the MS-DOS Prompt, enter the command to move to the folder of the program you want to start (for example, **cd \wp60**) and press Enter. The MS-DOS Prompt now shows the current folder, as shown in Figure 26.22.
3. At the MS-DOS Prompt, enter the command to start your application (for example, **wp**) and press Enter. The MS-DOS Prompt window now displays the application you've started, as shown in Figure 26.23.

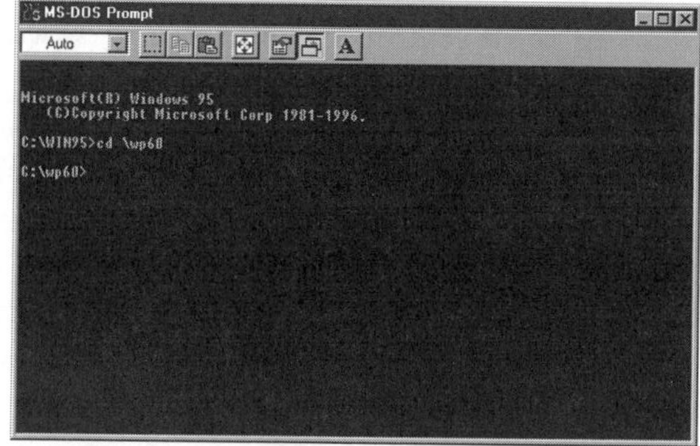

FIG. 26.22
Once you're in the MS-DOS Prompt session, all the basic MS-DOS commands can be used to start your application.

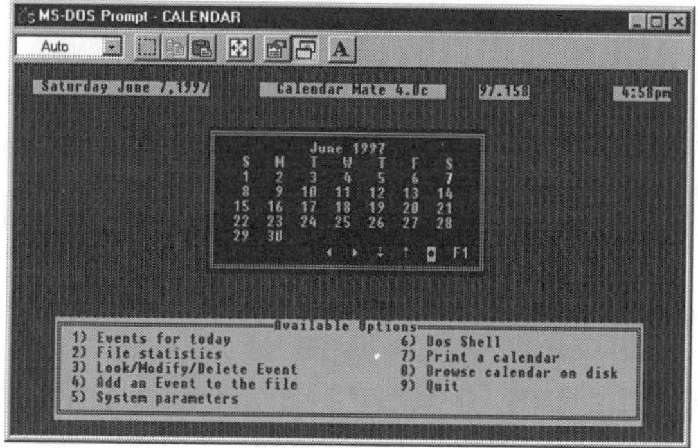

FIG. 26.23
Once your application starts, Windows displays it in the MS-DOS Prompt window space. Note that the window title reflects the command name of the program running.

Although running an application from within the MS-DOS Prompt window works well and seems familiar to the veteran command-line user, it's not really the most convenient method under Windows.

In addition to the default Windows MS-DOS Prompt, Windows 95 offers four other ways to start an application:

- Windows Explorer
- The Start button Run option

- The Start button Programs menu
- The Application shortcut

If you want the opportunity to enter optional (or even required) command-line parameters when you run a DOS application, follow these steps:

1. Right-click the shortcut icon for the application and choose Properties.
2. Select the Program tab and add a question mark to the end of the path in the Cmd Line text box.
3. Choose OK.

Now when you double-click the shortcut, a text box will appear in which you can input the startup parameters for the application.

These startup methods work just like they do for their Windows counterparts.

Removing MS-DOS Applications

If you decide to remove your MS-DOS application from your computer, there are two easy ways to do it:

- Use the MS-DOS Prompt dir and deltree commands
- Use the Windows Explorer and Recycle Bin

CAUTION

Regardless of which technique you use, make sure that you don't have any data stored with the application you're removing. Some applications allow you to store your documents or data files in the same folder as the application code itself. Although this is inherently poor design, it still happens; and if you don't tell the application to save your files to another folder or directory, you may be very sorry after you've deleted the program itself.

Using MS-DOS Commands to Remove an MS-DOS Application

Perhaps the most straightforward way to remove an MS-DOS application is to use the MS-DOS tools themselves. To do this, follow these steps:

1. Open MS-DOS Prompt session from the Start menu.
2. At the MS-DOS Prompt, type the command **dir c:*appdir* /p** (where *appdir* is the folder in which your doomed application awaits its final moments). In this example, you'll use **c:\wp60 /p**. The MS-DOS Prompt session displays a folder listing similar to that shown in Figure 26.24.

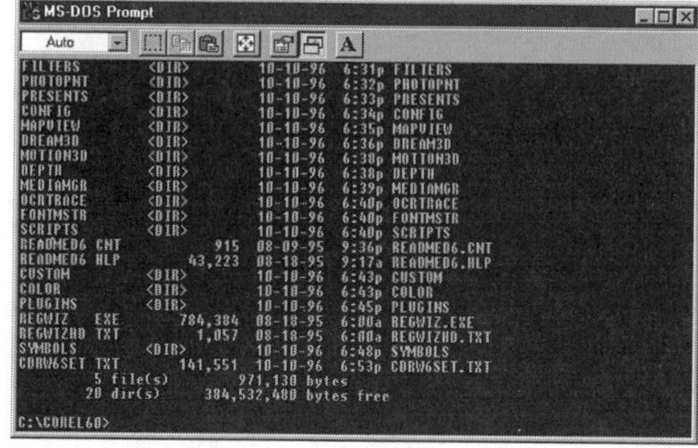

FIG. 26.24
The `dir` command shows the contents of the folder you want to delete. The `/p` switch displays the listing one page at a time. Simply press any key to continue through the listing.

3. Look for any files that contain your personal data (be sure to check in any subfolders). If necessary, copy or move these files to another location.
4. After you've saved any personal data, delete the application. At the MS-DOS Prompt, type **deltree c:*appdir*** (where *appdir* is the folder containing the application to be deleted) and press Enter. MS-DOS displays a message asking you to confirm the deletion. If you're absolutely sure, type **y** and press Enter. MS-DOS deletes the application folder and all subfolders.

Using the Explorer to Remove an MS-DOS Application

An even simpler way to remove an MS-DOS application is to use the Explorer and the Recycle Bin. It's really as simple as locating the application folder, checking it for your personal data, and then dragging it to the "trash."

For complete instructions on using the Explorer to remove an application, see Chapter 12, "Managing Files with My Computer and Windows Explorer."

Cleaning Up Shortcuts and the Start Menu

Be sure to remove shortcuts to applications after you've removed the application itself. If you don't, Windows will still try to load the application and ask you to help find it when it can't—a real hassle. If you've placed the shortcut on your Desktop, simply drag it to the Recycle Bin.

If you used the Control Panel Add/Remove Programs feature discussed in Chapter 16 to add the shortcut to the Start menu, just follow the removal steps outlined in that chapter.

▶ **See** "Removing Windows Applications," **p. 636**

ON THE WEB

Check out a shareware utility called Start Clean, written by Firas El-Hasan, which is available at the following Internet site:

http://users.aol.com/felhasan/startcln.htm

This utility scans your system and removes any items in the Start menu folder that are no longer linked to programs.

CHAPTER 27

Using Microsoft Exchange and Windows Messaging

by Brady P. Merkel, Gordon Meltzer, Peter Kent, and Ken Poore

In this chapter

Overview of Windows Messaging Features

So that you know how to set up Windows Messaging during the installation process, you should have some detailed information about what Windows Messaging can do. Knowing about the capabilities will help you to make the right installation and setup choices.

NOTE When Microsoft originally released Windows 95, the messaging component was named Microsoft Exchange. Since Microsoft used that same name to identify their server product, they decided to rename the client component *Windows Messaging*. For the purpose of simplicity, the term *Windows Messaging* is used to refer to the original Microsoft Exchange and the recent name change. Where appropriate, an icon in the margin identifies new features in Windows Messaging.

You call on Windows Messaging when you want to compose a fax. You visit Windows Messaging again when you want to send a message to a colleague down the hall, to anyone in your enterprise, or possibly, anyone connected to the Internet. When one of those folks replies, the message will appear in your Inbox, no matter where it originated. Faxes sent to your fax card head for the Windows Messaging Inbox, too.

Your messages do not have to be just plain text, either. Because Windows Messaging supports rich text format, you can view and create messages using any font on your system, at any size, in any color. The first time you see a mail message that has made it around your workgroup, and each member has contributed his thoughts in a different color, you will begin to appreciate the power of Windows Messaging.

More important than rich text is the ability to work with Object Linking and Embedding (OLE). Your messages can contain OLE documents created in applications that are OLE servers, such as Microsoft Word for Windows, Microsoft Excel, or any of the many OLE server applications.

The inclusion of Windows Messaging in Windows 95 confirms the notion that email is now a standard feature of personal computing. Integration with the operating system and applications enables you to easily take full advantage of all the usefulness of email in increasingly complex networked environments.

Clients and Servers

The introduction of this chapter noted that Windows Messaging was a central communications client. The word *client* is so important in Windows Messaging, and in Windows 95 generally, that it needs to be explained along with its complementary counterpart, the *server*.

For the purposes of programs such as Windows Messaging, a server is a program, running on a network, that holds information accessible by users on the network. These users employ programs called clients to get at the server-based information.

If the server is a mail or fax server, it provides a place to store mail and fax messages for all the clients (users) on the network. This is the kind of server to which the Windows Messaging client connects.

The Universal Inbox

Discussions of Windows Messaging have commonly referred to the "Universal Inbox." The Inbox function is a very important part of Windows Messaging, as this section explains.

You use Windows Messaging to communicate, and a large part of communication is finding out what others have to say. You may receive messages by fax or email. In Windows 95, these received messages are directed to Windows Messaging, where they can be conveniently read. Windows Messaging is called a *universal* Inbox because all messages, both fax and email, no matter where they come from, go to your Windows Messaging Inbox.

Windows 95's designers decided that collecting all these messages in one place would be more convenient for users. All of those messages can now be set up to communicate through the universal inbox of Windows Messaging, eliminating the need to use different messaging packages to read your email and faxes.

Microsoft Workgroup Email

If your computer connects to a local area network (LAN), Windows Messaging is the program you will use to send and receive email with your workgroup colleagues. Windows 95 contains a Microsoft Mail Postoffice so you can set up an email system on your workgroup network.

Once you have a Postoffice installed, Windows Messaging collects all email addressed to you. You can then read, reply to, and forward them, all while using the Windows Messaging program. Other accessory programs, installed on your network, will let Windows Messaging send and receive email over networks wider than your workgroup LAN.

▶ **See** "Installing the Workgroup Postoffice," **p. 702**

Online Service Mail Systems

The Microsoft Network (MSN) is an online service, similar in concept to CompuServe and America Online. Each of these provides email to its members as a service.

Windows Messaging provides a way to dial into online services and quickly retrieve any email waiting for you. You also can use Windows Messaging to send email to other service members.

Rich Text Format

Windows Messaging supports rich text format (RTF). This means you can create messages using any font on your system. You also can change the text's size and use different colors. These text-formatting capabilities let you personalize your messages, and they can be quite useful when messages route to various people for comment. Individuals can use different colors, typefaces, and type sizes to help set off each set of comments.

OLE Support

OLE allows you to put part of one document into another. Every major Windows applications publisher has used this capability. You can highlight a section of a document, copy it into the Windows Clipboard, and paste-link or paste-embed it into another program. The original program might be a spreadsheet, and the target program might be a word processor. It does not matter, as long as the source program is an OLE server, and the target program is an OLE client. Most major programs are both.

NOTE The data you copy and paste-link or paste-embed is called an *OLE object*. Often in Windows 95, OLE objects have an associated icon. You can drag the icon into other programs, or drop it on the Windows desktop. In other cases, the OLE object simply appears in its original format, such as rows from a spreadsheet. ■

Windows Messaging extends your powers to work with OLE objects by allowing you to drop them into mail messages you compose.

Most Windows applications are OLE-enabled. Although Microsoft Word and Excel were mentioned in the section "Overview of Windows Messaging Features," any OLE object can be embedded in a message and sent with that message. For more information on using OLE, see Chapter 34, "Simple Ways of Sharing Data Between Applications."

Installing and Configuring Windows Messaging

If your computer arrived with Windows 95 already installed on it, you may have Windows Messaging already available. If you are upgrading a previous version of Windows to Windows 95, you can install Windows Messaging during your initial installation or afterward. After the first few steps, however, the process is the same. The following sections explain how to install and configure Windows Messaging.

NOTE Windows Messaging requires a minimum of 6M of memory in your system to run. For good performance, plan to have at least 8M. Windows Messaging also takes 10M of space on your hard drive for required files. The basic program files take 3.7M of disk space. Because Windows Messaging can work with all sorts of data, you should allow a few megabytes for your incoming messages, too. It is easy to end up with 5M or more of faxes and email. ■

Deciding Whether to Use Windows Messaging

Before you load Windows Messaging, you must first determine whether you really need it. Just because you use email does not mean that you will always benefit from using Windows Messaging. Windows Messaging has powerful features and integrates into Windows 95; however, Windows Messaging can require some detailed configuration and maintenance, and it does occupy some of your system resources.

To help you make your decision, consider these questions:

- Do you want to share email with others in your workgroup?
- Do you have more than one email address on different online services such as CompuServe or an Internet service provider?
- Does your current email program poorly manage received messages or have an inadequate address book?
- Do you read email on a laptop computer that is occasionally connected to the network?
- Does more than one person use your computer to read email?
- Do you have a fax modem and want to send and receive faxes?

If you answered *yes* to any of these questions, chances are you will benefit from using Windows Messaging. Conversely, if you are happy with your current email program and only connect to one online service to send and receive email, then you might want to skip loading Windows Messaging altogether. Of course, the choice is still yours, and you can always load Windows Messaging, try it, and delete it later if you don't seem to get much out of it.

Installing Microsoft Exchange During Windows 95A Setup

When upgrading a previous version of Windows to the initial release of Windows 95 (not OSR2), you can install Microsoft Exchange during the Windows 95 setup. The Windows 95 Setup Wizard displays the Get Connected dialog box, shown in Figure 27.1. In this dialog box, you can choose to install The Microsoft Network online service, Microsoft Mail for use on workgroup networks (LANs), and the Microsoft Fax service.

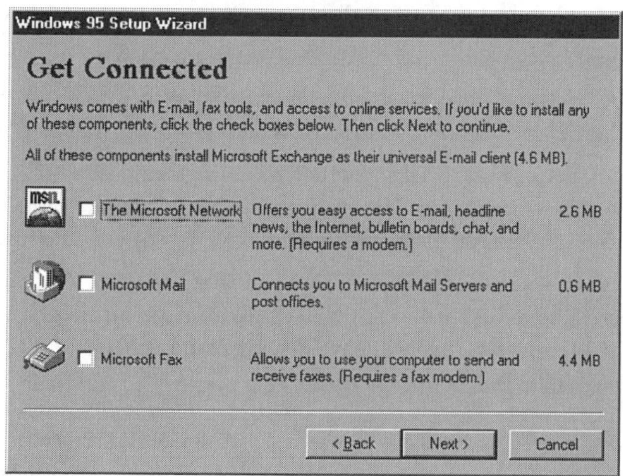

FIG. 27.1
The Get Connected dialog box is the first step to installing Microsoft Exchange.

You can install any or all of these three connectivity components. (You can always add them later, too.) MSN, Microsoft Mail, and Microsoft Fax all require Microsoft Exchange to work, so when you choose any of them, Microsoft Exchange is installed for you.

It is also possible to install Microsoft Exchange without installing any of these items; for instance, if you want to use Microsoft Exchange for Internet email. To do so, you must choose a Custom installation—you can then select Microsoft Exchange from a list of optional components.

Adding Microsoft Exchange After Windows 95A Is Installed

If you did not install any of the connectivity components during your Windows 95 installation, or your computer did not arrive with Windows Messaging already installed, you can still add Windows Messaging.

If you are upgrading to the original version of Windows 95, you can install Microsoft Exchange.

Follow this procedure to install Microsoft Exchange:

1. Double-click the Inbox icon on your desktop. You will see the Inbox Setup Wizard.

NOTE If you have installed a Microsoft Exchange service and now want to install one or more other services, you will not be able to use this procedure. This procedure works only when no Windows Messaging services have been installed. To install Microsoft Fax or The Microsoft Network, open the Start menu and choose Settings, Control Panel. Then double-click the Add/Remove Programs icon, click the Windows Setup tab, and select the item from the list of components. To install Microsoft Mail or Internet Mail, right-click the Inbox icon, choose Add, and select the service you want to install. ■

2. Choose one or more of the information services offered to you. The services are The Microsoft Network, Microsoft Mail, and Microsoft Fax. (To make this example most useful, what happens when you choose all three will be covered, too.)
3. After selecting the information services you want, choose OK.
4. The Inbox Setup Wizard asks you to insert your Windows 95 CD-ROM or floppy disk. Insert the CD or disk and choose OK. Windows then installs the needed files.
5. The Inbox Setup Wizard asks whether you have used Microsoft Exchange before. Because you are setting up Microsoft Exchange for the first time, choose No. Then choose Next. Windows displays the message box shown in Figure 27.2.
6. The services you selected in step 2 are checked, along with Internet Mail. If you plan to use Microsoft Exchange for receiving email from an Internet service provider (other than The Microsoft Network), leave this check box checked. If you are not going to use Internet email, deselect this check box.

NOTE The Microsoft Network has a level of service that provides full Internet access, and it also allows users at *all* levels to send and receive email across the Internet. However, the Internet Mail service referred to by the Inbox Setup Wizard is intended for use with other Internet service providers, not with The Microsoft Network. ■

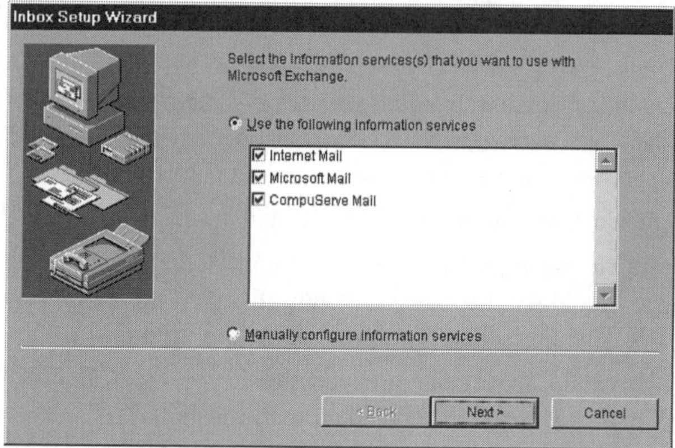

FIG. 27.2
The Inbox Setup Wizard offers you a choice of services.

7. Choose Next to begin configuring your services.

The basic setup of Microsoft Exchange is done, but the Inbox Setup Wizard continues, setting up each of the services you have selected. Read the following sections to configure the individual communications services you just chose to use with Microsoft Exchange.

TROUBLESHOOTING

I followed the procedure in the section, "Adding Microsoft Exchange After Windows Is Installed" but could not get Windows Messaging to install correctly. The Inbox Setup Wizard may run into problems—it may even "crash" while setting up your information. For instance, you may get a message telling you that the wizard was unable to complete something and to click the Finish button to end the procedure. If this happens to you, double-click the Inbox icon and the wizard should start again.

Upgrading to OSR2 Windows Messaging

If you run the initial release of Windows 95 with Microsoft Exchange, you can upgrade to Windows Messaging. The update is available for free from Microsoft's Web site (connect time charges may apply). In Windows Messaging, Microsoft improved the client startup time, includes the Microsoft Mail service, and fixed several problems with the Internet Mail service.

Follow this procedure to upgrade to Windows Messaging:

1. Connect to Microsoft's Web site and download the Windows Messaging self-installer. The self-installer is available **http://www.microsoft.com/windows95/info/updates.htm**. Download the update file and save it into a temporary folder. If you want the United States version, download **exupdusa.exe**, which is a little over 3M in size.

2. Run the file you downloaded. A dialog box appears and asks you to review the license agreement. Click Yes to accept the terms of the agreement.
3. A dialog box appears welcoming you to the Windows Messaging installation program. The dialog box warns you that the installation may fail if shared files are currently in use. Close all other running applications and then click Continue.
4. In the next dialog box, enter your name and organization. Click OK.
5. Windows Messaging Setup checks for required disk space and copies files. If all goes well, you should see the dialog box indicating that the installation was successful. Click OK. The upgrade to Windows Messaging is done.

If you used Microsoft Exchange before, you should see that Windows Messaging is very similar. In fact, Windows Messaging should automatically inherit your Microsoft Exchange profile settings. To check your settings or add new services, right-click the Inbox icon on the desktop and select Properties.

Configuring Microsoft Mail

If you chose to install Microsoft Mail or if you add Microsoft Mail after upgrading to Windows Messaging, you see the dialog box shown in Figure 27.3. (If you did not choose to install Microsoft Mail, you can skip this section.)

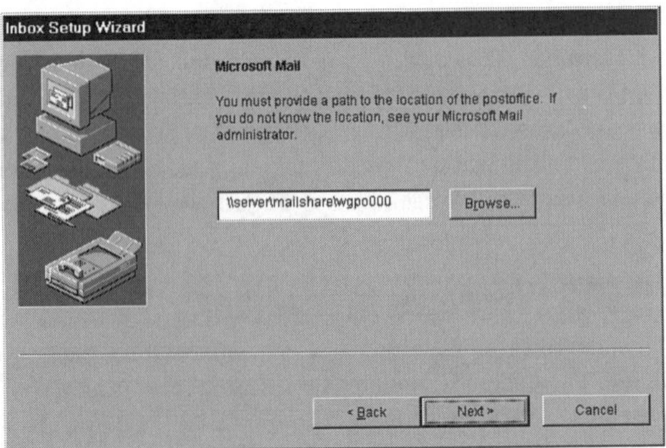

FIG. 27.3
You need to specify a Postoffice location to use Microsoft Mail.

Microsoft Mail requires that one of the computers on the workgroup LAN be set up as a Postoffice. You may have a network administrator who has already done this. If so, ask the administrator for the path to the Postoffice. Then put the path to the Postoffice in the text box shown in Figure 27.3 (click the Browse button and search for the path if necessary), and choose Next.

When the administrator creates a Postoffice, a folder called WGPO000 is created. For example, if the administrator creates a folder called Mail and tells the Microsoft Workgroup Postoffice Admin Wizard to place the Postoffice there, the wizard places the WPGO000 folder inside the Mail folder. You must specify where the WPGO000 folder is. In this example, you would enter **C:\MSMAIL\WGPO000**, not C:\MSMAIL.

If you don't have an administrator to set up your Postoffice, turn to the "Installing the Workgroup Postoffice" section later in this chapter. Then return to this section.

You are shown a list of people who have been given access to the Postoffice. Select your name from this list (if it's not on the list, ask the administrator to add it). The Inbox Setup Wizard then asks for your password. Again, ask your administrator what password he used when creating your account, and carefully type that into the text box. Then choose Next.

The wizard has finished setting up Microsoft Mail, and you are ready to use it on your workgroup LAN.

Configuring Internet Mail

If you chose to install Internet Mail, you see the dialog box shown in Figure 27.4. (If you did not choose to install Internet Mail, skip this section.) The first step is to specify your Internet access method.

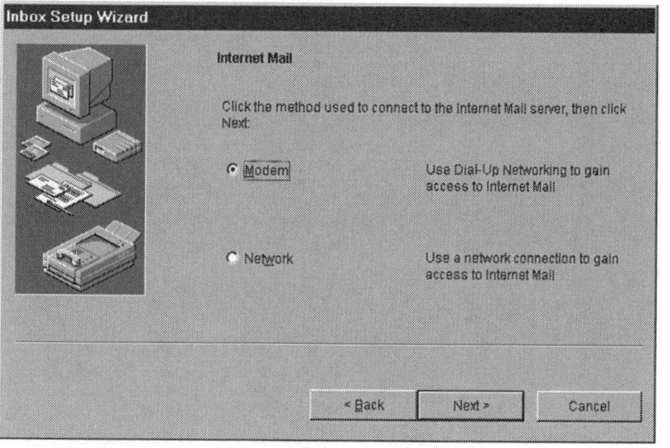

FIG. 27.4
Choose an access method to the Internet for your Internet Mail.

NOTE In order to use Internet Mail, you must have the TCP/IP protocol installed on your computer. If it is not, you will see a message reminding you to install it. To install TCP/IP, open the Start menu and choose Settings, Control Panel; double-click the Network icon and choose Add; select Protocol and choose Add; select Microsoft and TCP/IP, and then choose OK.

Internet Access Method The wizard offers Modem and Network options for Internet access. If you connect to the Internet by modem and Dial-Up Networking, follow these steps:

1. Choose Modem, and then choose Next.
2. Now select the connection you created in Dial-Up Networking that dials your Internet service provider.

   If you have not created a connection yet, choose New and create a connection. (Chapter 17, "Establishing a Dial-Up Internet Connection," provides detailed instructions for creating a connection.)

NOTE If you have not yet installed the TCP/IP software, the Wizard skips step 2; it doesn't ask you which service provider to use. Later, you can specify a service provider by choosing Tools, Services on the main Windows Messaging menu, clicking Internet Mail, choosing Properties, and clicking the Connection tab.

3. Choose Next.

If you connect to the Internet via your LAN, choose Network and then choose Next.

Selecting Your Internet Mail Server Now tell the wizard about your Internet Mail server. Either you can tell the wizard the Name of the server where your Internet mail is stored, or you can tell the wizard its IP Address. Figure 27.5 shows an example, with a mail-server name filled in. When you are finished, choose Next.

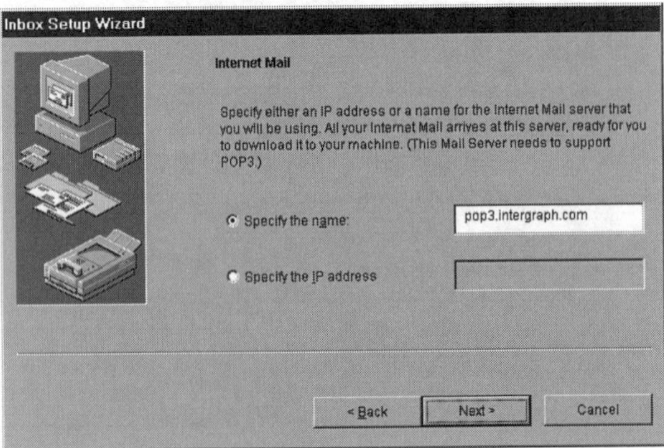

FIG. 27.5
Enter your Internet Mail server information.

Internet Mail Transfer Method You can choose Off-line or Automatic mail transfers:

- Off-line lets you use Remote Preview to view only incoming mail headers. You selectively decide which messages to download to your inbox, based on the header contents.
- Automatic instructs Windows Messaging to connect to your Internet Mail server and retrieve all new mail into your inbox automatically. The Automatic option also automatically sends any outbound Internet mail you have created.

Make your choice, and then choose Next.

Your Internet Email Address Next, the wizard wants you to fill in your email address in the form *user@domain*. Enter this in the text box called Email Address. Also, put your full name in the text box called Your Full Name. When you are finished, choose Next.

Internet Mailbox Information The Inbox Setup Wizard needs the Mailbox Name and Password you use to access your account in your Internet Mail server. Enter them in the text boxes provided and then choose Next.

Internet Mail is now set up and ready to use with Windows Messaging.

Completing Your Microsoft Windows Messaging Installation

Now that you have set up the various services you selected, the Wizard finishes off the more general Windows Messaging settings. First, it asks you which Personal Address Book it should use.

You probably have not created a Personal Address Book (assuming that you are installing Windows Messaging for the first time), so simply choose Next.

You see a similar dialog box, this time asking where your Personal Folder file is. This file stores all your messages. Choose Next to accept the file that the Wizard is suggesting.

NOTE It is common for network-based email users (especially if you are using the Microsoft Mail service) to have personal folders exceeding 50M. When backing up your system, be sure to specify the directory in which you have placed your files containing your address book and personal folders (see Chapter 16, "Backing Up and Protecting Your Data"). Also, be sure to exit Microsoft Windows Messaging before running the backup; otherwise, the backup may skip your personal folders file because Windows Messaging has it open.

Next, the wizard may ask whether you want to run Windows Messaging automatically every time you start Windows. This choice requires some thought; Windows Messaging uses many system resources and can affect performance in low-memory configurations. If you are going to use Windows Messaging only on a dial-up basis, such as with The Microsoft Network or an Internet service provider, choose No.

TIP If you connect to a LAN, start Windows Messaging automatically every time you start Windows so that you will not miss any email from workgroup members.

Running Windows Messaging at Windows startup wastes system resources if you do not need to use Windows Messaging services constantly. If you do not expect much email and use Windows Messaging and its communications services infrequently, select the Do Not Add Inbox to StartUp Group check box.

If your messaging needs require constant connectivity or periodic automatic logon to an online service to check for new mail, choose to Add Inbox to the StartUp Group.

To complete the installation, choose Next. The Inbox Setup Wizard displays a final dialog box confirming that Windows Messaging is set up to work with all the communications services you selected (see Figure 27.6).

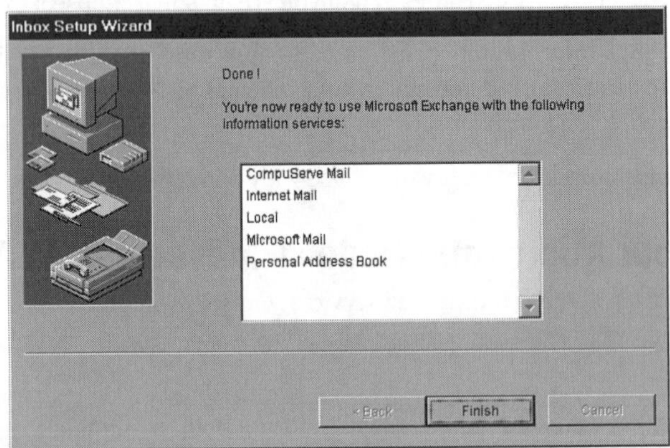

FIG. 27.6 The Inbox Setup Wizard confirms that the setup of services is complete.

Choose Finish. After this long setup and configuration process, you are ready to start using Microsoft Windows Messaging. (The Windows Messaging window opens automatically immediately after the wizard closes.)

Using the CompuServe Mail Service

The universal inbox of Windows Messaging is designed to be a flexible, modular mail system, able to access many different mail services across many different networking and dial-up connections. Earlier in this chapter, you read how to install the service that allows you to send and receive mail over the Internet. CompuServe has a similar add-in module that allows Windows Messaging to be the inbox for CompuServe mail as well.

Installing the CompuServe Mail Service

You must first add the service to Windows Messaging in order for you to use it. Follow these steps:

1. The CompuServe mail connector is not included with Microsoft Windows Messaging, so you first need to obtain the latest version of CompuServe Mail for Windows Messaging from CompuServe. After logging into CompuServe, use **GO CISSOFT** and select CompuServe Mail for Microsoft Windows Messaging (Win 95). Then choose to download the file (CSMAIL.EXE)—it's a free download.
2. CSMAIL.EXE is a self-extracting archive. Once downloaded, copy it into its own directory and run CSMAIL.EXE to extract the setup files. Next, run the extracted SETUP.EXE to start the installation.

3. Follow the instructions provided by the setup program. When the program asks if you would like the service to be installed into your default profile, select Yes. After the service is installed, you are prompted to enter your Name, CompuServe ID, and Password.

Configuring the CompuServe Mail Service

Once installed, you may never need to change how the service is configured. However, if your password changes, or if you would like to set up the service to connect to CompuServe on a scheduled basis, you have to reconfigure it.

Follow these steps to change your CompuServe Mail settings:

1. Open the Start menu and choose Settings, Control Panel.
2. In Control Panel, double-click the Mail icon.
3. Choose the CompuServe Mail Service and select Properties. You will see the tabbed dialog box shown in Figure 27.7. The tabs contain the following configuration settings:
    - **General.** Choose this tab to update your Name, CompuServe ID, or Password.
    - **Connection.** Choose this tab to change the Phone Number to access CompuServe, the modem you use to connect, or the Network type (such as Tymnet or SprintNet). You also can select what type of connection you have to CompuServe. Choose Windows Modem Settings if you are using a modem to connect to CompuServe. Choose Winsock Connection if your computer is connected to the Internet. Choose Direct Connection if you have a communications port (for example, COM1) directly wired into CompuServe.
    - **Default Send Options.** Choose Send Using Microsoft Exchange Rich-Text Format if you want to preserve all the rich text formatting (fonts, colors, and so on) in your email message. Setting the Release Date holds outgoing messages in your outbox until the date specified; if not set, all mail is sent as soon as possible. The Expiration Date is the date that mail is deleted in your recipient's mailbox.
    - **Advanced.** The Create Event Log option generates a mail message in your inbox each time you connect to CompuServe. The log details how many messages were retrieved and sent, and notifies you if there was a problem connecting. Setting Delete Retrieved Messages removes messages from your CompuServe mailbox when Windows Messaging successfully retrieves them. The Change CompuServe Dir option tells the service where your CompuServe access program (for example, WINCIM) resides on your system. Use Schedule Connect Times to set up when Windows Messaging should automatically connect to CompuServe and retrieve and send mail messages.

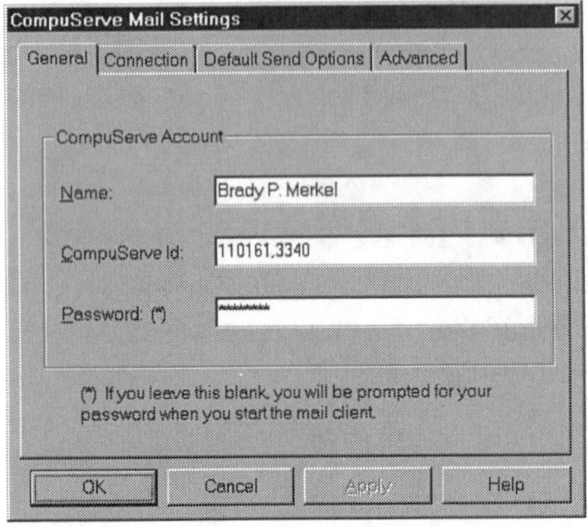

FIG. 27.7
Use the General tab on The CompuServe Mail Settings property sheet to configure your CompuServe account information.

Creating and Sending Mail Messages

After you configure one or more information services, you can create and send a message with the Windows Messaging client. If Windows Messaging were perfect, it would have a universal composition screen in which you could compose any type of message for any type of recipient and for any delivery method. Because of the differences between fax recipients and electronic-mail recipients, however, you have to decide whether to compose a mail message or a fax.

This section explains how to create and send an email message to members of a work-group LAN.

Creating a Mail Message

How to send an email message to a member of your workgroup LAN will be explained first. You'll be working with the message form discussed earlier in this chapter. Remember that you'll have all the power of rich text formatting and OLE available when you create your email message.

TIP: To quickly email a file from within Explorer, right-click the file name and select Send To, Mail Recipient.

If the Windows Messaging window is not open, start the Windows Messaging program by double-clicking the Inbox icon on the desktop. Then choose Compose, New Message. If you prefer to use the toolbar, click the New Message button. Windows Messaging opens the New Message window.

Figure 27.8 shows the initial blank composition window, which is the New Message form, or window. You will see this form frequently while you work in Windows Messaging. Now you can work on your message.

FIG.27.8
Use the New Message window to compose messages.

You also can get to the New Message window by pressing Ctrl+N in the main Windows Messaging window.

Choosing a Recipient

When you click To in the New Message window, your Personal Address Book pops up, showing the list of recipients that you have created. Select the names of the people to whom you want to send your message; you can select names for the To box and names for the Cc box.

You may want to send a blind carbon copy, called a Bcc. The blind copy will be sent to any recipients on the Bcc list. The recipients of the original message and any Cc recipients will not know a copy has gone to the Bcc recipient. The New Message form does not show the Bcc text box by default. You can display this text box by choosing View, Bcc Box.

Entering Text

Start with the Subject box and type the subject of the message.

Pressing Tab takes you to the main message-entry space, where you can write what you have to say. Start entering text now.

Enter your text for the message first and format it later.

Formatting Message Text

If you use a word processor, you should see a remarkable similarity between the word processor and the menus and toolbars of the New Message form. The toolbars and menus give you the option of choosing the following formatting options for your message text (the options are listed as they appear on the toolbar, from left to right):

- Font (limited to the fonts on your system)
- Font Size (as small or large as the TrueType font scaler can handle)
- Bold
- Italic
- Underline
- Text Color
- Bullets
- Indents
- Text Alignment (left-align, center, and right-align)

You can combine these options to create messages in rich text format. Whenever you use fonts in varying sizes, colors, and alignments, or other formatting options, you add depth to your communications.

Sending Files and OLE Objects with Windows Messaging

You are not limited to text messages, or even rich text format messages. One of the most useful capabilities is including files and objects in messages. When you use files and objects in your messages, you can add a lot of extra content to those messages with very little work.

Practically any file on your system can be included in a message. You can send text files, graphics files, and files created by the applications you have. However, if you do send an application file (such as a spreadsheet or database file), be sure that your recipients also have the same applications so they can read what you send them.

NOTE If you want to send a file to a user who retrieves mail from an online service such as CompuServe and who may not be using Windows Messaging to read mail, you should not send the file as an OLE object. Send it as a file instead. Few email programs other than Windows Messaging can interpret an embedded OLE object in an email message. On the other hand, most email programs, including those on nearly all online services, have no difficulty detecting an attached file and can deliver it properly to your recipient. ■

Follow these steps to insert a file (also known as an *attachment*) into a mail message:

1. After opening up a New Message window by choosing Compose, New Message, choose your recipients and type in the subject of the message. Go to the body of the message and choose Insert, File. A file selection dialog box appears (see Figure 27.9).

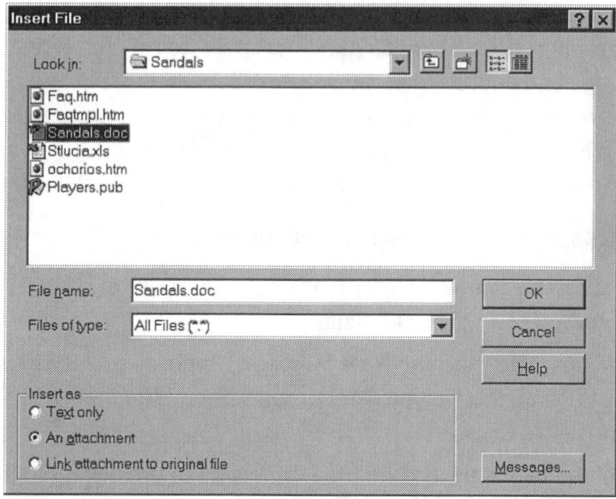

FIG. 27.9
Use the Insert File dialog box to insert files into mail messages.

2. Browse through your file system and select the file you want to include inside the message.
3. Use the options in the Insert As section at the bottom of the dialog box to choose how you would like to insert the file into your message:
   - If your message is a straight text file, you can insert the file directly into the mail message, dumping the contents of the file right into the body of your message. Select the Text Only option in the Insert As section at the bottom of the dialog box. Press the OK button to import the text file's content into your mail message.
   - If you are inserting a file containing something other than straight text, you must insert it as an attachment. This preserves the file as a separate item in your mail message. The recipients of the message can save the file to their disk when they read your message, or they can choose to double-click the File icon in the mail message and launch the application associated with the type of file you sent them.
   - Related to the previous method of attaching the file and using the mail message as a means to transfer it around, you can choose to send the recipients a link to the file. This only works, however, if you and all your recipients are on a network that can access the file through Network File sharing. To learn how to send links, continue reading the next section.

Sending File Links with Windows Messaging

Windows 95 introduced a powerful feature called *shortcuts*, which are simple links to files elsewhere on the system or network. You can place shortcuts on your desktop, in other directories, or on the Start menu so you can have quick access to what the shortcut points to. You also can send shortcuts in mail messages.

The benefit of doing this is that you are not actually inserting the entire file into your mail message: you are merely inserting a link, or shortcut, to the file. When your recipients receive your mail message and double-click the inserted link, their application resolves the shortcut to the file on your system, connects to your machine, and accesses the file directly over the network. Sending a link is useful if the file to send is very large or may be accessed by several people simultaneously, like a Microsoft Access database file (.MDB file).

Follow these steps to send a file link in a mail message:

1. Verify that the file you want to send is on a shared drive, accessible to all the recipients to whom you want to send the file link.
2. Choose Insert, File from the New Message window's menu. Browse through the file system and locate the file you want to send. Select the file—its name will appear in the File Name field.
3. In front of the file name, type in the UNC name of the network share containing this file. If the file is in a subfolder of the share, be sure to include it in the UNC (see Figure 27.10).

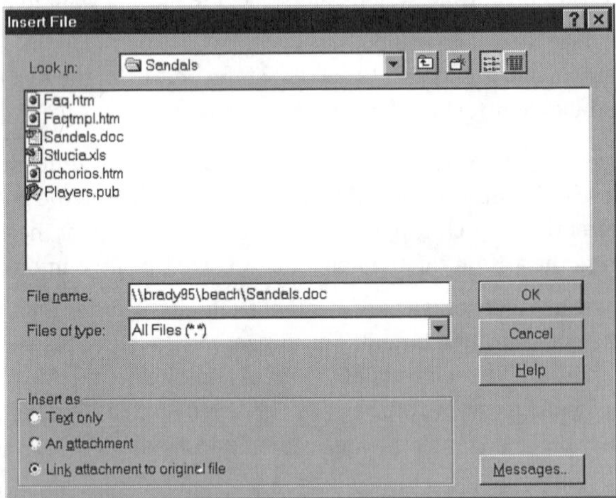

FIG. 27.10
Instead of embedding large files in messages, send links.

4. In the Insert As box at the bottom of the dialog box, choose to insert the file as Link Attachment To Original File.
5. Choose OK.

NOTE You can send links to Internet sites in mail messages. In Internet Explorer, choose File, Create Shortcut, when displaying the page you want to mail to someone else. Then in your mail message, choose Edit, Paste to insert the link.

If you are only going to send types of files that are common and built into Windows 95, you should send them as embedded OLE objects. This way, the recipient only has to double-click the object and Windows 95 automatically knows how to view it.

You can insert the following types of Windows 95 objects into your messages:

- Audio Recorder
- Bitmap images
- Media clips
- Microsoft Word documents or pictures
- MIDI sequences
- Packages
- Paintbrush pictures
- QuickTime movies
- Video clips
- Wave sounds
- WordPad documents

Each application on your system that is an OLE server can create OLE objects that you can place in your messages, so the preceding list is not exhaustive.

Follow these steps to insert an OLE object in a mail message:

1. In Windows Messaging, choose Insert, Object. The list of available object types appears (see Figure 27.11).

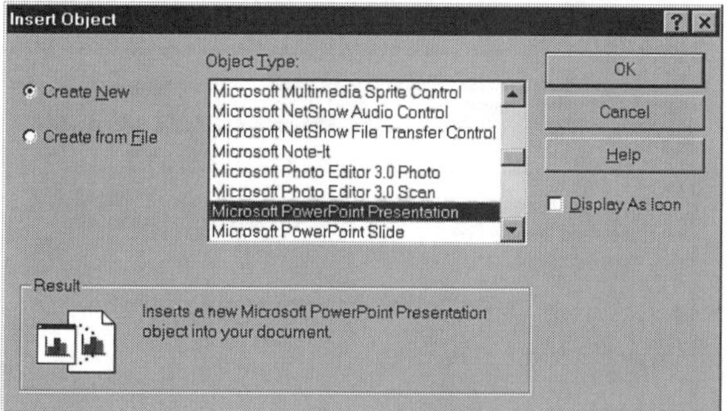

FIG. 27.11
Use the Insert Object dialog box to choose an OLE object type to insert in a message.

If you want your OLE option to appear as an icon, select the Display As Icon option while in the Insert Object dialog box. Leave this check box cleared if you want the data—the spreadsheet rows, word processing text, picture, or whatever—displayed rather than the icon. (Some objects—sounds, for instance—can't be displayed, so their icons display automatically.)

2. Select the type of object you want to include in your message, and then choose OK. Select Wave Sound, for example, to insert a sound recording in the message. The application used to create the object starts. In the case of a Sound Wave object, the Sound Recorder applet starts.

NOTE Notice that the OLE server application that opens has a special kind of title bar. Instead of saying Sound Recorder, for instance, the title bar would say Sound Object in Mail Message. The OLE server applications also have slightly different menus and options from when they run normally. The File menu in Sound Recorder, for example, has a new option: Exit & Return to Mail Message.

3. Use the application to create the object that you want to mail. In this case, record the audio that you want to send with your mail, and then choose File, Exit & Return to Mail Message. The application disappears, leaving the Wave Sound icon in your message.

If you are inserting a form of data that can be displayed, and if you didn't choose the Display As Icon check box in the Insert Object dialog box, you see the actual data rather than the icon. You can move this data, or the icon, around in your message, and you can give the icon a more useful name than the default name (Bitmap Image).

When recipients get a message containing an icon, they must double-click the icon. This starts the application that created the OLE object. The object is then played or displayed (see Figure 27.12).

FIG. 27.12
Use RTF and OLE to compose effective messages.

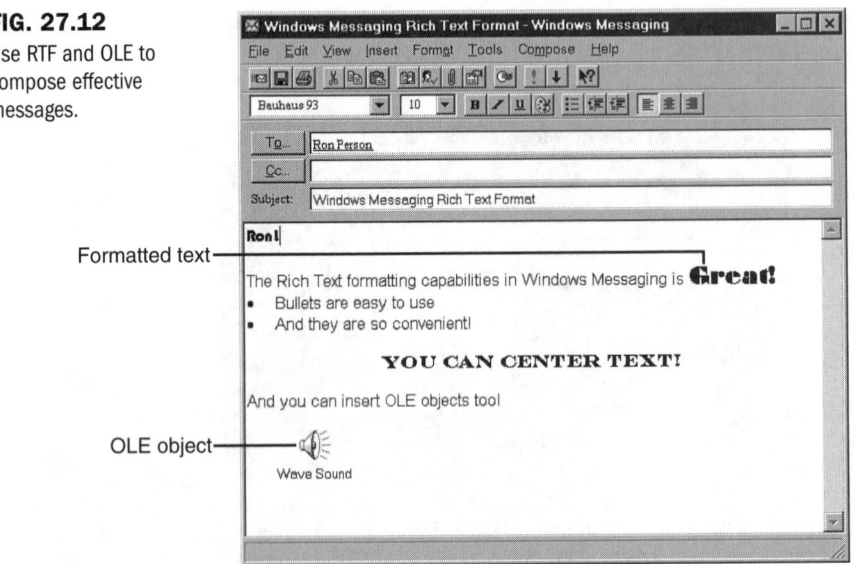

When you insert objects in messages, rename the icon, including text such as "Click here to play," to make the icon's intended function obvious to the receiver. To rename the icon, right-click it, choose Rename, and then type the new name in the text box over the old name. Press Enter when you finish.

Embedding an object or file in a message is an example of OLE at work in Windows Messaging.

Many applications today have a File, Send command that creates a new email message and automatically embeds the document you are working on in the new email message.

Finishing and Sending Your Mail Message

Once you have written your message and added any formatting or OLE objects that you want, there are a few more options you may want to select.

Choose Tools, Options, and then click the Send tab. The following list describes the items on the Send page:

- **Font.** Select the font typeface and size you prefer for new messages.
- **Read Receipt and Delivery Receipt.** Request that a receipt be sent back when the message has been delivered to or read by the recipient.
- **Sensitivity.** Set the sensitivity ranking such as Normal, Personal, Private, or Confidential to your message.
- **Importance.** Choose whether you want High, Normal, or Low priority for your message. You also can choose the High/Low icons to perform this task.
- **Save a Copy in 'Sent Items' Folder.** Saves a copy of all of your outgoing messages in the Sent Items folder.
- **Use Simplified Note on Internet mailto: and file.send.** Use a simple compose window when sending quick messages from a Web browser.

Close the Properties box. To send your message, choose File, Send, or click the Send button.

TROUBLESHOOTING

I sent a Microsoft Mail message on my workgroup network, but the message was not received. Make sure that only one Postoffice is installed for your workgroup and that the Postoffice is located in a shared folder that everyone in the workgroup can access.

Using Remote Mail

When you are not connected to a network or your online service and need to read your email, Remote Mail can help you download specific mail messages and optimize your modem connect time. Remote Mail is best used when you expect either a large number of messages to be waiting in your inbox, or you anticipate large messages with attachments that you don't want to download all at once. Remote Mail enables you to connect to your email service, look at the headers of all the mail in your inbox, and choose which mail messages you want to download and read. This section shows how easy Remote Mail is to use.

Setting Up Remote Mail

Most add-in mail services for Windows Messaging support using Remote Mail in addition to the usual way Windows Messaging transfers mail. Some Windows Messaging add-in services require more configuration than others to set up Remote Mail. Some services, such as the CompuServe Mail Service for Windows Messaging, require no set up at all—you can use Remote Mail any time without any additional configuration. The Microsoft Mail service, however, has several options important to configuring Remote Mail.

To use Remote Mail with a Microsoft Mail Postoffice, you need to configure the connection and delivery options of Microsoft Mail. However, you must first have a Dial-Up Networking connection established to connect you to the machine where the Postoffice resides.

▶ **See** "Using Dial-Up Networking," **p. 201**

To set up Remote Mail for Microsoft Mail, follow these steps:

1. Open the Start menu and choose Settings, Control Panel.
2. Double-click the Mail icon.
3. Choose the Microsoft Mail service and click Properties.
4. On the Connection page, select which type of connection you use to access your Microsoft Mail Postoffice:
    - If you are sometimes connected to a LAN and sometimes using a modem to read mail (if you are using a laptop, for instance), choose Automatically Sense LAN or Remote. Windows Messaging figures out how you are connected and uses the right connection type.
    - If you are always on the LAN, select Local Area Network (LAN). You will probably not use Remote Mail if you are always connected to the LAN where your Microsoft Mail Postoffice resides. However, you can still use Remote Mail if you have a slow network connection to the mail server or do not want mail to be automatically delivered to your inbox.
    - If you always use a modem to send and receive mail, choose Remote Using a Modem and Dial-Up Networking.
    - If you do not want to connect via a LAN or a modem, choose Offline. You can compose mail while not connected and reconnect later, if needed.

5. Choose the LAN Configuration page.
6. If you are connected to the LAN and still need to use Remote Mail, choose the Use Remote Mail option. Mail will only be delivered and sent when you use Remote Mail.
7. Choose the Remote Configuration page. These settings are used only when you use a modem to read mail remotely (see Figure 27.13).

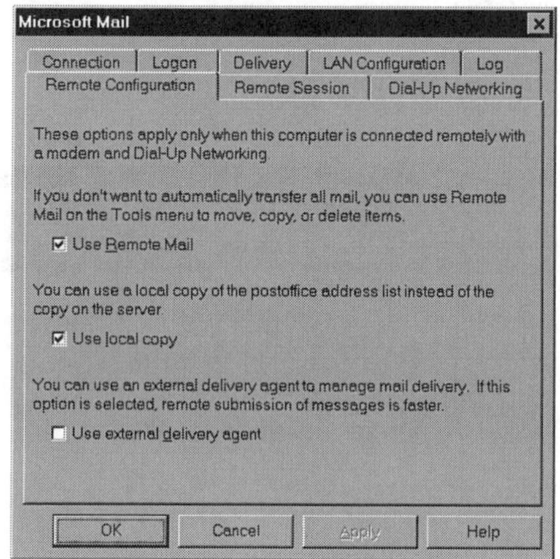

FIG. 27.13
The Remote Configuration Page sets up your Microsoft Mail Service to use Remote Mail.

8. Choose the Use Remote Mail option. This enables Remote Mail for the Microsoft Mail Service.
9. If you want to keep a local copy of the Postoffice's Address List on your machine so you can select Postoffice mail addresses while not actually connected to the Postoffice, choose the Use Local Copy option. You can later download a copy of the Address Book and store it locally.
10. If you want to connect to your Postoffice automatically during your Windows Messaging session, choose the Remote Session page and choose When This Service Is Started. You can set up scheduled connections to your Postoffice by clicking the Schedule Mail Delivery button. Otherwise, by default, you will only connect to your Postoffice when you choose.
11. If you use Dial-Up Networking to connect to your Postoffice, on the Dial-Up Networking page, select which Dial-Up Networking Connection you use to connect to your Postoffice.

Once configured, Remote Mail is very easy to use. The next section explains how to use Remote Mail after it's configured.

Sending and Receiving Mail Using Remote Mail

Once you configure your mail services to use Remote Mail, the process of connecting to your email service, sending, selecting, and downloading mail is very easy.

Remote Mail uses a separate window for viewing the headers of mail messages waiting on the remote email service. When you initially connect to your mail service, you will usually have Remote Mail retrieve the headers of all your new mail, as well as send out what is in your outbox. After completing that and disconnecting, you will review the headers of all your new messages, choosing which ones you would like to download and read. Finally, you reconnect to your mail service and retrieve the messages you have selected. Here are the steps you would typically take to access your mail using Remote Mail:

1. From the Windows Messaging menu, choose Tools, Remote Mail, Microsoft Mail. This displays the dialog box shown in Figure 27.14.

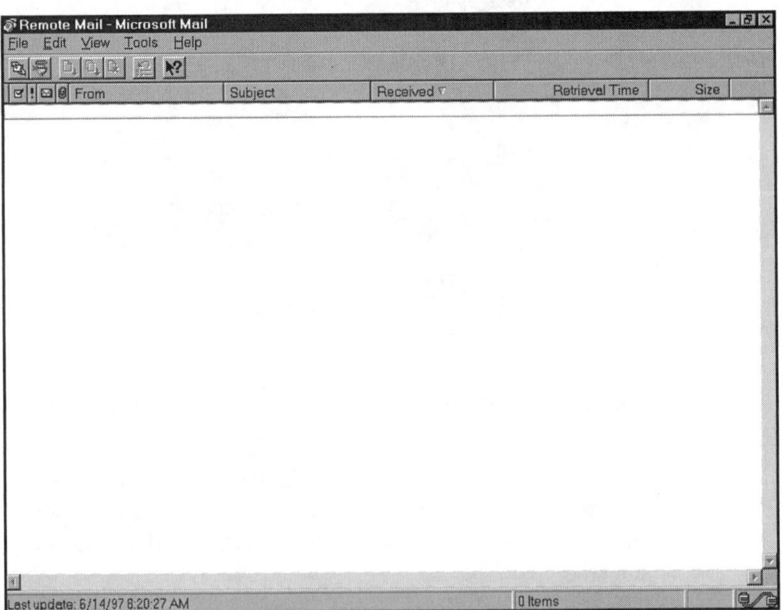

FIG. 27.14 Use the Remote Mail window to select which messages you want to receive from your Postoffice.

2. Click the Connect icon or select Tools, Connect. The Connect to Server dialog box in Figure 27.15 appears.

Connect to Server

When Mail connects to the server it will perform the selected actions. Actions can be turned on or off by checking the appropriate box

- [x] Send mail
- [x] Receive marked items
- [x] Update view of mail headers
- [ ] Download address lists
- [ ] Disconnect after actions are completed

OK Cancel Help

FIG. 27.15 You can do several different tasks when updating the list of message headers.

3. While retrieving the waiting message headers, you also can choose the following options:
    - Send Mail takes any messages in your outbox addressed to a mail recipient in the Postoffice and sends them.
    - Receive Marked Items retrieves the messages you have selected from your header list. The first time you enter the Connect dialog box, you will probably not have chosen to retrieve any messages.
    - Update View of Mail Headers checks for new messages.
    - Download Address Lists downloads a local copy of the Postoffice's Address List. This will enable you to select Postoffice mail recipients when you are not connected to the Postoffice. If you think your copy of the address list is out-of-date, you should choose this option. Depending on the number of people in your Postoffice, this could add several minutes to your connection time.
    - Disconnect After Actions Are Completed terminates your modem connection after your headers are downloaded.
4. Click OK to start the transfer. A dialog box with a gauge will keep you informed of what is transpiring during your connection. After a few moments, depending on how many options you've selected, the Remote Mail dialog box will display the headers of the messages waiting in your Postoffice inbox (see Figure 27.16).

FIG. 27.16
The list of waiting messages appears after updating the message headers.

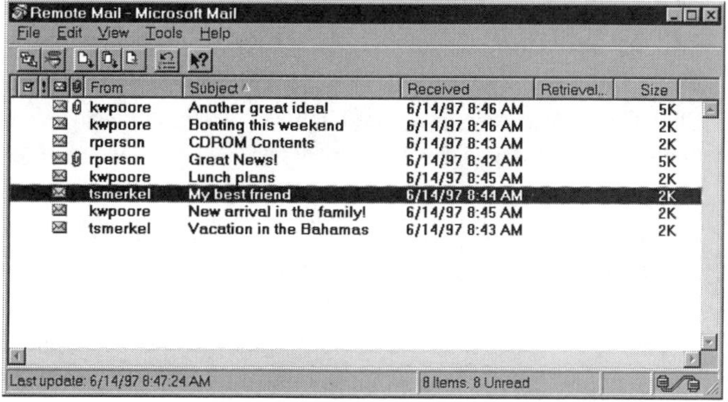

5. Now you can select which messages you need to retrieve from your Postoffice inbox. When you select which messages to retrieve, you have three options from which to choose (each of these options is also available by right-clicking the message header and choosing it from the pop-up menu):
    - Click the Mark to Retrieve button, or choose Edit, Mark to Retrieve, from the menu to retrieve the message and remove it from the Postoffice. The next time you update the message headers, you will not see this message in your Postoffice.
    - Click the Mark to Retrieve a Copy, or choose Edit, Mark to Retrieve a Copy, to retrieve a copy of the message, but also keep it in your Postoffice. The message will be marked as "read" and will not be bolded when you update your headers again.

If you use both a notebook computer and a computer that is connected to your Postoffice over a LAN, choose to Retrieve a Copy of your mail messages. Messages will stay in your Postoffice inbox so you can access them from your LAN-based computer later.

- Click the Mark to Delete button or choose Edit, Mark to Delete to delete messages without reading them (see Figure 27.17).

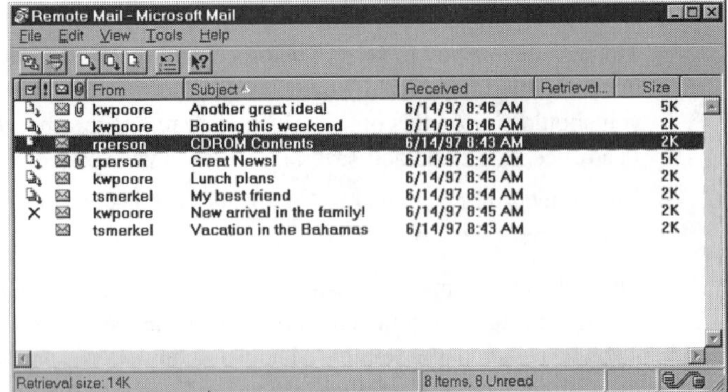

FIG. 27.17
Choose the messages to retrieve from your Postoffice using Remote Mail.

6. Click the Transfer Mail button or choose Tools, Transfer Mail. A dialog box similar to the Update Headers dialog box seen earlier appears; only this time with the Send Mail, Receive Marked Items, and Update View Of Mail Headers selected by default.
7. Click OK to process your marked items and refresh your view of the waiting message headers. All messages marked for retrieval are placed in your Windows Messaging Inbox where they can be accessed as usual.
8. If you did not choose to disconnect from the Postoffice automatically and you're finished with Remote Mail for now, you should click the Disconnect button or choose Tools, Disconnect to end your connection with the Postoffice.
9. You can either close the Remote Mail window by selecting File, Close, or select your main Windows Messaging window and continue working with both windows open.

Using Remote Mail with Other Mail Services

The Microsoft Mail service's Remote Mail capabilities are very robust and configurable. Other Windows Messaging services such as CompuServe require no special configuration at all. To use Remote Mail to access your CompuServe Mail, select Tools, Remote Mail, CompuServe Mail from the Windows Messaging menu. Similar dialog boxes appear as in Remote Mail for Microsoft Mail explained in the previous section, and they all work the same way.

Viewing Received Mail

To view and work with your received mail, you must have the Microsoft Windows Messaging program running. This section explains how you can see your received mail and how to keep the Windows Messaging window organized at the same time.

How Things Are Organized in Windows Messaging

Windows Messaging contains, by default, four Personal folders, each of which holds a different kind of message. The folder names show the function of the folders:

- **Inbox.** Where messages that come in to you are initially stored.
- **Deleted Items.** Stores messages that you have deleted from other folders.
- **Outbox.** Stores messages you are sending until you actually send them.
- **Sent Items.** Stores messages you have sent after they are successfully sent.

TIP It is very useful to see all four Windows Messaging folders on your screen. If you display all four folders, you can tell what kind of message you are seeing.

To display all four folders described earlier, choose View, Folders on the Windows Messaging menu bar. You also can click the Show/Hide Folder List icon on the toolbar.

When you choose to display the folder list, your Windows Messaging window divides into two parts. On the left side of the window, you see the list of the four folders. When you highlight a folder on the left side of the window, the contents of that folder appear on the right side of the window.

For example, if you highlight the Inbox folder, you see the contents of your Inbox folder on the right side of the window. The contents of the Inbox folder are your received messages and faxes. If a message in the inbox appears in **boldface**, the message is new and has not yet been read.

The types of messages that you can see in your inbox depend on the Windows Messaging services that you installed. If you installed Microsoft Fax, for example, you can see faxes. If you installed The Microsoft Network, you can see mail from MSN members and from the Internet. If you have Microsoft Mail installed for your workgroup network, you can see workgroup Mail messages. With Internet Mail installed, you can see mail from your own Internet mailbox.

Figure 27.18 shows an inbox that contains several types of messages. You can manipulate these messages in several ways. You examine how to manipulate and work with those received messages in the next sections.

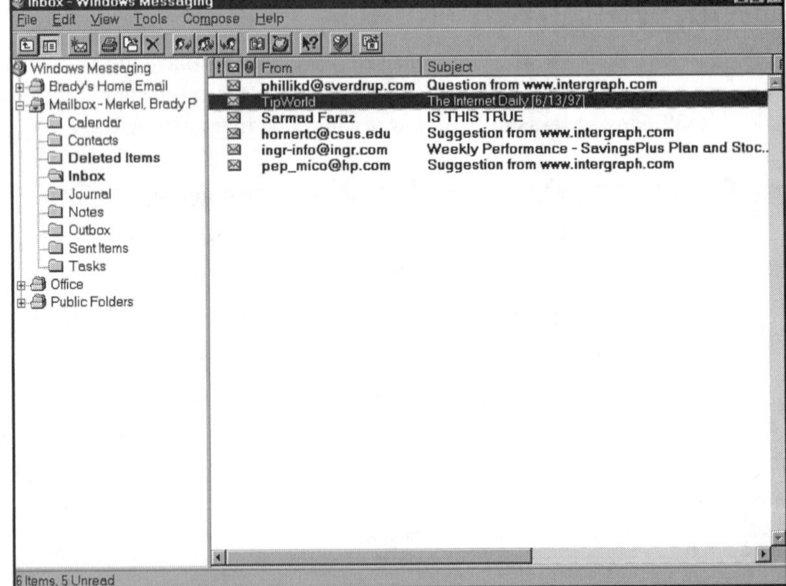

FIG. 27.18
The Windows Messaging inbox is where all your new messages are placed.

Reading Mail Messages

To read a mail message, double-click the message in your inbox. The standard message form opens, displaying the message. The Subject appears in the message form title bar. Figure 27.19 shows a received mail message.

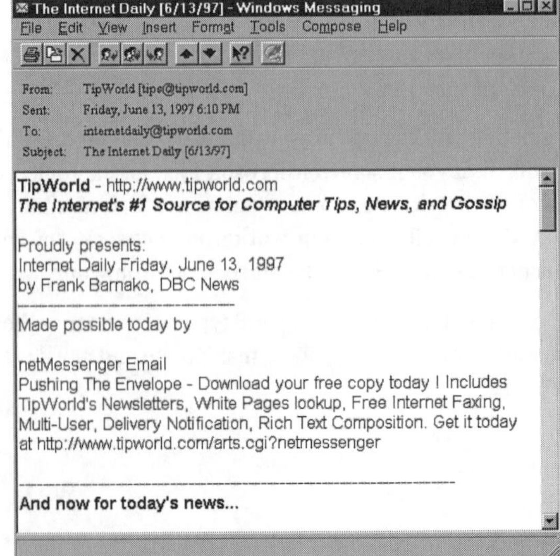

FIG. 27.19
Opening a mail message in your inbox displays the message.

Editing, Replying to, and Forwarding Messages

The standard message form (refer to Figure 27.8) is an important place where a great deal of messaging action takes place. Notice that the form looks very much like a Windows word processor, complete with Formatting toolbar. All the Rich Text tools are available, just as they are when you compose a message. In fact, the standard message form for composing a message is identical to the form for viewing, editing, replying to, and forwarding mail messages.

> **TIP** As a shortcut to send, reply to, forward, or edit a message without displaying it first, select the message in your inbox and then right-click.

While you are working with a received mail message, you can edit it if you want. Add text, files, or OLE objects; then use the tools in the Compose menu to whisk your reply on its way (see Figure 27.20).

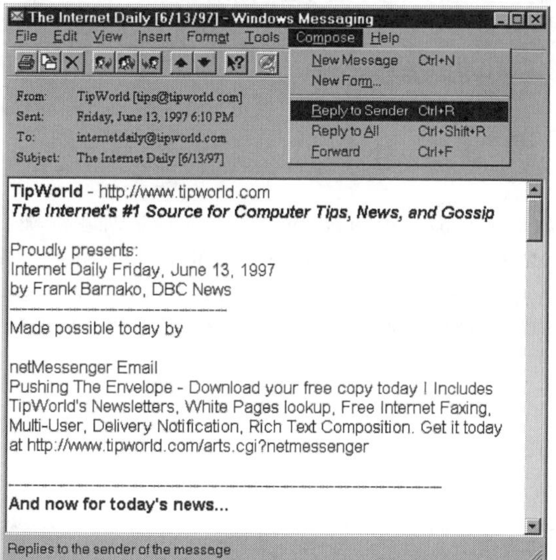

FIG. 27.20
The Compose menu has Reply and Forward options.

Sorting Messages

Above the messages in any of the Windows Messaging folders are column headings. These headings indicate the following:

- The importance of the message (according to the sender)
- The item type
- Whether files are attached to the message
- The sender's name

- The subject
- The date and time the message was received
- The size of the message (in kilobytes)

You can sort the messages in any of the Windows Messaging folders in the following ways:

- Click the column heading to sort the messages in the folder by the value in that column, in ascending order.
- Right-click the column heading to change the sort from ascending to descending order.
- Choose View, Sort in the main Windows Messaging window to access more elaborate sorting functions. Figure 27.21 shows these functions.

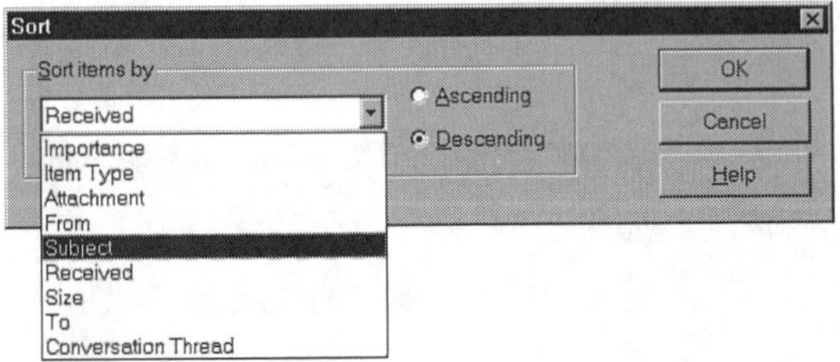

FIG. 27.21
You can use these advanced options to sort your messages.

NOTE The default From, Subject, Received, and Size columns in Windows Messaging are only the tip of the iceberg. You can display many more columns if the column headings are relevant to your work. You will find loads of column options, many of which are rather obscure. The options available depend on the message services you have installed. What works for one service may not work for another.

Deleting Messages

When you finish working with a message in your inbox and you want to delete it, highlight it and press the Delete key. The message is removed from the inbox, but it is not really deleted. Rather, it is moved to the Deleted Items folder.

CAUTION

Deleting a message from the Deleted Items folder completely removes it from your system. It is not placed in the Recycle Bin.

Using the Message Finder

You can use Windows Messaging to search through all of your folders, looking for messages that match certain criteria. You can choose among many options, shown in the following list. You can find items matching the following:

- The name of a sender you specify with the From option
- A message you sent to a certain recipient with the Sent To option
- A message sent Directly to you, or Copied (Cc) to you
- A message with a particular subject, by choosing the Subject option
- Certain text in the message with the Message Body option

To use Message Finder, choose Tools, Find in the main Windows Messaging window, and then choose the search option you want to use. For example, if you are looking for messages sent to John Jones, enter **John Jones** in the Sent To text box. Windows Messaging displays a list of messages matching the criteria you have chosen.

Working with User Profiles in Windows Messaging

When you installed Windows Messaging, you worked with the Inbox Setup Wizard. You gave the wizard information about yourself, and you installed one or more communications services. You also gave the wizard information about the services you chose, such as User ID and Mailbox Name.

When you finished installing Windows Messaging, the wizard saved all the information you gave it. The wizard saved your information in something called a *user profile.*

The user profile in Windows Messaging is where all your personal information and the information on all your communications services are stored. The name of the user profile created by the wizard for you is Default Settings. Default Settings becomes the default user profile for your computer.

You can add as many user profiles as you need by following the steps in the following section.

This default profile is fine for one user. If your computer has more than one user, however, you may want to create a special user profile for everyone who uses your machine.

Suppose that you share a computer with coworkers who work the second shift. If you do not use The Microsoft Network, but your coworkers do, they may want to set up their own user profiles. Then they can configure and personalize Windows Messaging to suit their needs without disturbing the settings that you use during your shift.

Adding Multiple User Profiles in Windows Messaging

To create an additional user profile, follow these steps:

1. Open the Start menu and choose Settings, Control Panel.
2. In Control Panel, double-click the Mail and Fax icon.
3. Choose Show Profiles. You see the list of existing Windows Messaging profiles.
4. Choose Add to create a new user profile. The Inbox Setup Wizard starts to run.

5. Select the communications services that you want to use with the new user profile you are creating (see Figure 27.22). Then choose Next.

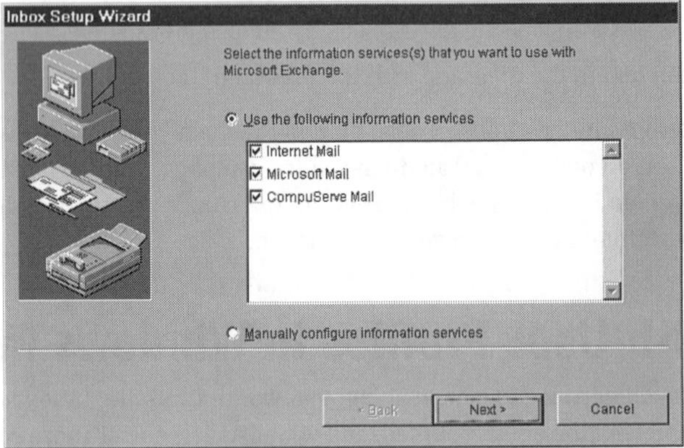

FIG. 27.22 Choose the services to use with your new user profile.

6. Type the name for your new user profile in the Profile Name text box (see Figure 27.23). Then choose Next.

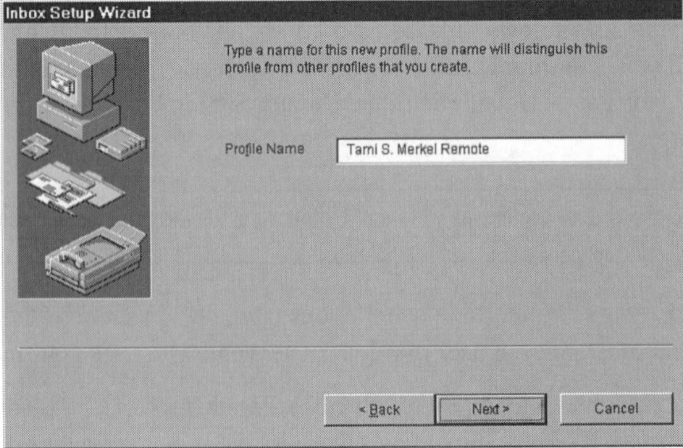

FIG. 27.23 Choose an appropriate name for a new user profile.

7. You now work with the wizard to set up the communications services you chose in step 5. This works the same way it did when you first installed Windows Messaging.

▶ **See** "Installing and Configuring Windows Messaging," **p. 670**

When you finish the Inbox Setup Wizard, your new user profile is ready to use. Your screen returns to the Mail dialog box you saw in step 3. Your new user profile is added to the list of profiles (see Figure 27.24.)

FIG. 27.24
Your new user profile has been added to Windows Messaging.

When you have more than one user profile installed, you will want Windows Messaging to ask you which profile to use each time Windows Messaging starts. Follow these steps to set up Windows Messaging so that it asks which user profile to use:

1. Start Windows Messaging by double-clicking the Inbox icon on your desktop.
2. Choose Tools, Options. The Options dialog box appears.
3. In the When Starting Windows Messaging area of the General page, check the Prompt for a Profile to Be Used box (see Figure 27.25).
4. Choose OK.

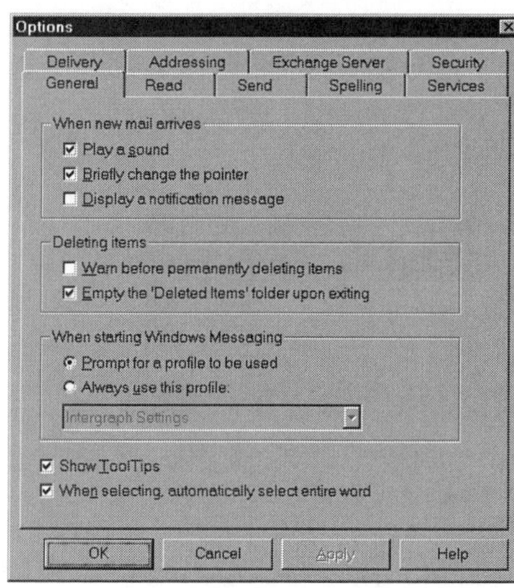

FIG. 27.25
When you tell Windows Messaging to prompt you for a user profile, you ensure that each user of your computer has the opportunity to pick their own Windows Messaging user profile.

TROUBLESHOOTING

I want to use Microsoft Fax, The Microsoft Network, and Microsoft Mail, but I do not see any references to those services in my Windows Messaging menus. Install the desired services in Microsoft Windows Messaging. In the Windows Messaging main window, choose Tools, Services, Add, and select the desired service from the list. A wizard guides you in setting up the service, if necessary.

NOTE If you have set up your computer with a different session profile for each user—so the user has to log on when Windows starts—you can ensure that each person's profile starts automatically. Each user should log on to Windows; open Windows Messaging; choose Tools, Options; and then click the Always Use This Profile option button and select the appropriate profile. ■

Enabling Mail and Message Security

Normally, when you run Windows Messaging, your mail folders display immediately in the Windows Messaging window. You can see and work with Inbox, Deleted Items, Outbox, and Sent Items as soon as Windows Messaging is running. This means that anyone who starts Windows Messaging on your computer can access all your mail in these four folders.

To make your mail secure, you must set a password for access to your mailbox so that nobody else can open your mailbox and read or work with your messages without your permission. Follow these steps to set up password security for your mail folders:

1. With Windows Messaging running, choose Tools, Options. The Options dialog box appears.
2. Click the Services tab, highlight Personal Folders, and choose Properties.
3. When the Personal Folders Properties sheet appears, choose Change Password. The Microsoft Personal Folders dialog box opens (see Figure 27.26).

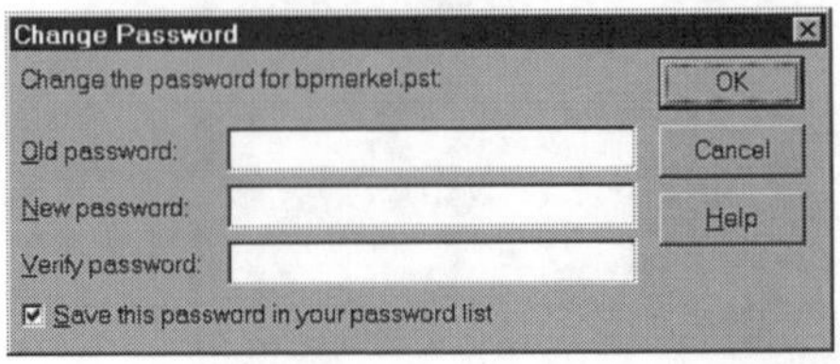

FIG. 27.26
Set a password for your mail folders for security.

Don't select the Save This Password in Your Password List option unless you've set up Windows for different users and each user has to log on using a password. If you select this option, you lose password security, because Windows enters the password for you whenever you start Windows Messaging.

4. Enter the password of your choice in the New Password text box. Then repeat the password in the Verify Password text box.
5. Choose OK.

The next time you run Windows Messaging, you have to enter your password to see the contents of your mail folders.

CAUTION

If you forget your mailbox password, you cannot access the contents of your mailbox again. You have to delete your personal folders and set up Windows Messaging again.

If you want to get rid of your mailbox password, follow steps 1 and 2. Then in step 3, type your current password in the Old Password text box. Leave the New Password and Verify Password text boxes blank. This means that you have changed back to having no password security for your mailbox folders. Then choose OK.

Working with the Workgroup Postoffice

Microsoft Mail requires that one of the computers on the workgroup network be set up as a Postoffice. This is usually a job for the network administrator or manager. If this is your function, this section is important for you.

The Postoffice machine is the place where all mail messages are stored for the workgroup. You can choose your machine for Postoffice duties or select a different machine.

The Postoffice must be installed somewhere on the network, in a shared folder that all members of the workgroup can access. Windows 95 comes with the Postoffice and a wizard that helps you install it.

You have to make the following decisions about your Postoffice:

- Which machine to install the Postoffice on (choose a machine that has a shared folder that everyone in the workgroup can access)
- Who will manage and maintain the Postoffice

If you're sure there is no Postoffice installed on your workgroup LAN, and if you're sure that you are the right person to set it up, the process is simple.

Installing the Workgroup Postoffice

When you are ready to install the Postoffice, follow these steps:

1. Open the Start menu and choose Settings, Control Panel.
2. Double-click the Microsoft Mail Postoffice icon.
3. Select Create a New Workgroup Postoffice, as shown in Figure 27.27. Then choose Next.

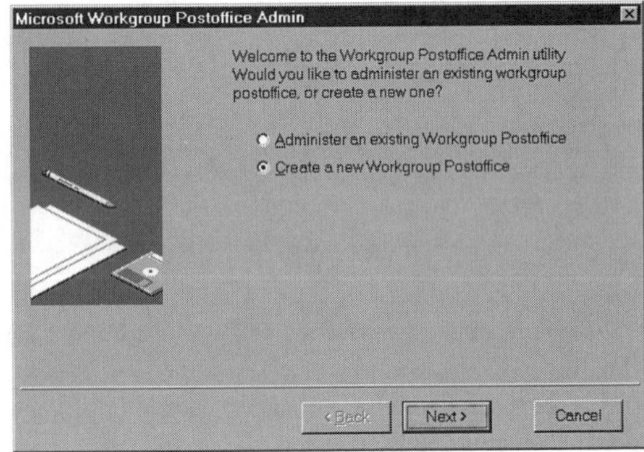

FIG. 27.27
Use the Microsoft Workgroup Postoffice Admin utility to create a new Workgroup Postoffice.

4. Type the full path to the folder you have chosen for the Postoffice in the Postoffice Location text box. Remember, this needs to be a shared folder that everyone on the Workgroup LAN can access. You can click the Browse button to find the folder.
5. Choose Next. The folder you have selected for the Postoffice displays for your approval. Choose Next again.
6. The next dialog box that appears requests administration details. Type your name in the Name text box, your mailbox name in the Mailbox text box, and your mail password in the Password text box (see Figure 27.28). Choose OK.
7. You'll see a message box reminding you to allow other users access to the Postoffice—which can be done from Windows Explorer. Choose OK. You have finished creating your Postoffice.

▶ **See** "Sharing Workstation Drives," **p. 863**

NOTE The other text boxes shown in Figure 27.28 may be filled in as you prefer, but are not required to set up the Postoffice. ■

Enter Your Administrator Account Details

Name: Brady P. Merkel
Mailbox: bpmerkel
Password: PASSWORD
Phone #1: (205) 555-2154
Phone #2: (205) 555-3161
Office: Building 24B Room 112L
Department: Corporate Web Management
Notes: Beeper: (205) 555-1234

OK Cancel

FIG. 27.28
Enter Postoffice Administrator information in this dialog box.

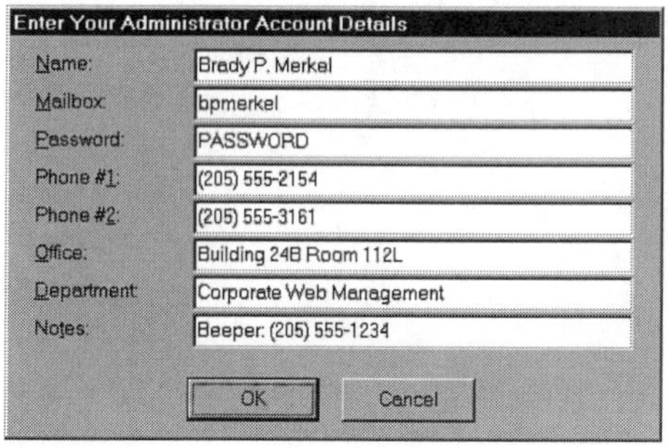

CAUTION

Create only one Postoffice on your workgroup network. If you create more than one, the mail system won't work properly.

CHAPTER 28

Using Fax, Address Book, and Phone Dialer

by Ken Poore and Brady P. Merkel

In this chapter

Overview of Microsoft Fax

Microsoft Fax works within Microsoft Exchange's Universal Inbox to provide a convenient place to compose, attach, or embed documents, and address a fax. Exchange gives you several ways to create faxes. You can use the Compose New Fax Wizard to send a simple typed message or an attached file. (Yes, you can transfer computer files using Fax, as you'll find out later.) You can use the same New Message window that you use to compose email, or you can create your fax in another application and send or print it to the fax system. Your faxes can include text, pictures, OLE objects, and files. This richness of function is one of the key benefits of using the fax capabilities within Microsoft Exchange.

Installing and Configuring Microsoft Fax

If you chose to install Microsoft Fax while using the Inbox Wizard, you see the Location Information dialog box shown in Figure 28.1. The wizard asks you to enter information about your telephone number: your area code, the number (if any) that you dial to get an outside line, and whether you are using pulse or tone dialing.

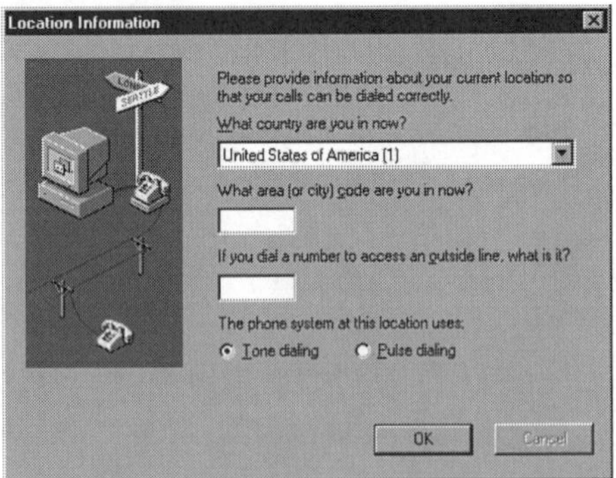

FIG. 28.1
The wizard's Location Information dialog box.

You are then asked whether you want to use a modem or a network-fax service (you can choose only the latter if you have installed network software; if you haven't, the wizard ignores your selection and assumes that you want to use a modem). Select the appropriate option button and choose Next.

The wizard now asks for information about the modem or network-fax service. If you have already installed a modem, you see something like the Microsoft Fax dialog box in Figure 28.2. (If you haven't yet installed a modem, the Install New Modem Wizard starts.)

▶ **See** "Installing and Configuring Your Modem," **p. 68**

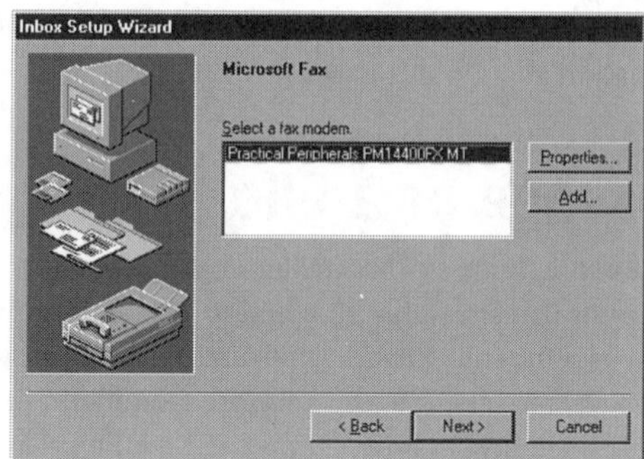

FIG. 28.2
The Inbox Setup Wizard's Microsoft Fax dialog box lets you specify the kind of device you want to use for sending and receiving faxes.

Select which modem you want to use for your fax messages—in the illustration, there is only one choice. You can add another fax modem—or a Network Fax Server—by clicking the Add button. Or modify the selected fax modem's properties by choosing Properties. When you've selected the fax modem (or added a Network Fax Server), choose Next.

If you want to be prompted to receive a fax when the phone rings, select Properties, Manual Answer mode. You can still pick up the phone and talk, too.

If you select a modem rather than a Network Fax Server, the wizard asks you whether you want Microsoft Fax to answer each incoming call on the phone line the modem is connected to. Choose Yes or No. (If you choose Yes, you may also want to change the Answer After *n* Rings value—you'll probably want the smallest value, two rings.) Then choose Next.

The Inbox Setup Wizard now asks for the information that will be used on any fax cover sheets you send along with your outgoing faxes, so people will know who sent them and how to fax back to you.

Enter your name and other information as requested in the dialog box shown in Figure 28.3. You must enter the fax number or you will be unable to continue. Then choose Next.

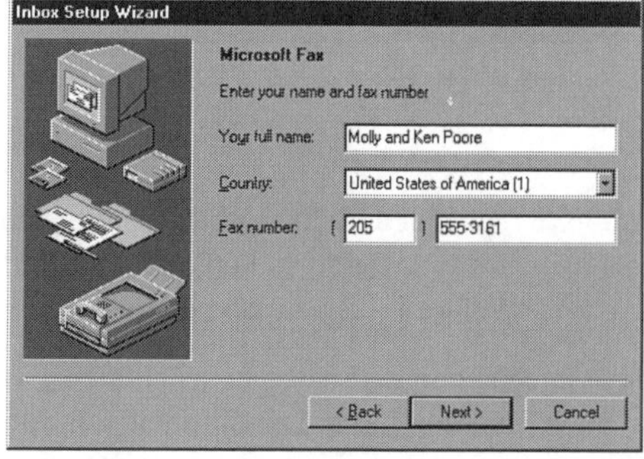

FIG. 28.3
Enter the personal information you want included on your faxes in this dialog box.

The Fax service is now installed. If you selected another service to install, the Inbox Setup Wizard now asks for information about that service.

Faxing a Quick Message or a File

You can also send a quick text message, or "fax" a file. This method lets you type a quick note (you cannot format the note) or transmit a file attached to the fax using the BFT fax technology. If you want to do more—such as send a nicely formatted fax message, put pictures inside it, or fax from your word processor—see "Sending a More Complete Message," later in this chapter. In the main Exchange window, choose Compose, New Fax. The Compose Fax Wizard appears.

A quick way to fax a file from within Explorer is to right-click the file and select Send To, Fax Recipient.

▶ **See** "Working with Phone Dialer," **p. 733**

The wizard first verifies the location from which you are sending the message, as shown in Figure 28.4. If you have created other dialing locations and moved your portable computer to one of them, choose I'm Dialing From and specify the new location. (Notice also that you can click the check box at the bottom of the dialog box to tell the wizard not to display this next time.) Then choose Next.

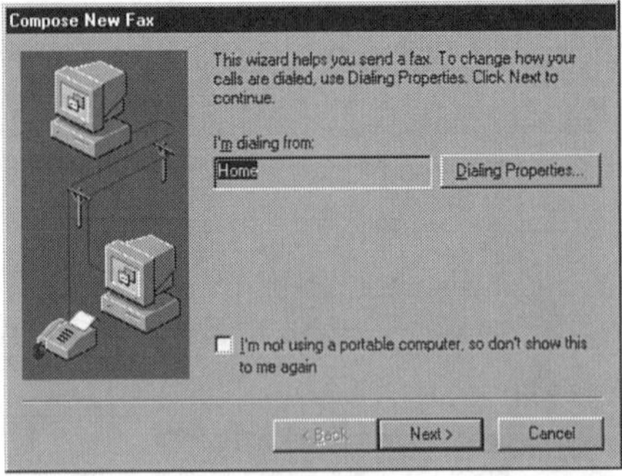

FIG. 28.4
The Compose New Fax Wizard confirms your dialing location.

Addressing a Fax

The wizard next prompts you for a recipient and offers to show you your Personal Address Book. If you want to choose a name from the address book, choose Address Book to display the address book (see Figure 28.5). Select a recipient and choose OK.

You also can type the recipient information in the text boxes named To and Fax #, without using the Personal Address Book. Use the Add to List button if you want to send the fax to several different numbers. Select the first and choose Add to List; select the second, and choose Add to List; and so on. Choose Next when you are ready to continue.

▶ **See** "Working with the Exchange Address Book," **p. 721**

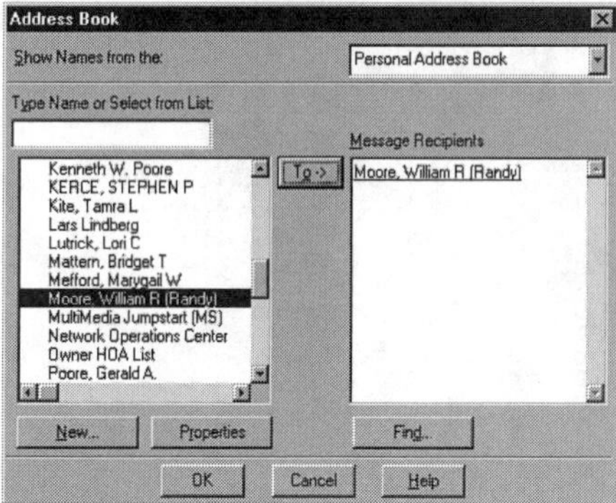

FIG. 28.5
Choose a fax recipient from your Personal Address Book.

Selecting a Cover Page

Next, the wizard asks whether you want to send a cover page with your fax. Windows has the following built-in cover pages:

- Confidential
- For your information
- Generic
- Urgent!

If you don't like any of the predesigned cover pages, use the Cover Page Editor to customize one of them or to create your own. See "Using the Fax Cover Page Editor," later in this chapter.

To use a cover page, select the page you want from the displayed list. Click the No button if you don't want to send a cover page.

Options for Fax Transmission

There are a variety of fax options that you can set before you move on. Choose Options to display the Compose New Fax Wizard's Send Options dialog box (see Figure 28.6). Use these options to control when your fax is sent, the format you use to send it, the paper size, and the security applied. In this dialog box, you also can choose the Dialing Location via the Dialing button, or you can choose a cover page to send with your fax as you did in the preceding section.

The following sections explain these options and how to use them.

Time to Send You can select a time to send your fax. Your choices are these:

- As Soon as Possible
- Discount Rates (night and weekends)
- Specific Time (which you can choose)

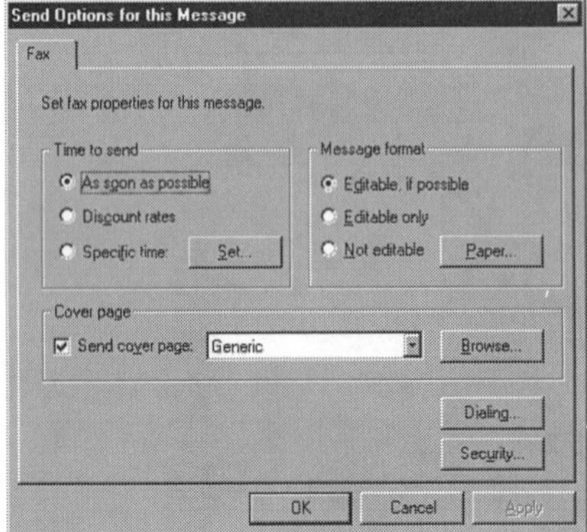

FIG. 28.6
This dialog box lets you specify various fax-sending options.

To set up the times for your discount phone rates, from the main Exchange menu, select Tools, Microsoft Fax Tools, Options, and choose the Set button next to the Discount Rates option.

Message Format The Message Format section deals with the *editable faxes* technology. A traditional fax is a single graphics image. Editable faxes are more like file transfers between computers, with the optional addition of a cover page. In fact, editable faxes are so much like file transfers that the technology behind them is called BFT, for *Binary File Transfer*.

An editable fax can be edited by the recipient in the application that created it or in any application that can open its file type. If you send a document created in Word for Windows (a DOC file), the recipient can open it in Word, WordPad, AmiPro, or WordPerfect, using import filters if necessary.

Sending editable faxes is very convenient, because the receiver's options are increased. The recipient can view or print the fax as you sent it, or edit the fax first.

You have three choices with the Message Format option:

- **Editable, If Possible.** Editable faxes can be exchanged only between computers using Microsoft Exchange and Microsoft Fax. This is the optimum way to send a fax.

  If the receiver is using a traditional fax machine, using editable format is not possible, so the fax is sent the old-fashioned way, as a graphic. If the recipient has a fax card in a computer but doesn't have Microsoft Exchange installed, the fax is delivered as a graphic. Exchange automatically determines which way to send the fax when it connects to the receiving machine.

NOTE In the near future, other systems may implement *Binary File Transfer* (BFT) in a way that is compatible with the Microsoft system. When that happens, you will be able to exchange editable faxes with those systems, too.

Editable faxes can be exchanged between Microsoft Exchange systems very quickly, because the format used is much more compressed than the format that regular fax machines use.

- **Editable Only.** This option works only for transfers between two Microsoft Exchange systems. If the receiving system is not a Microsoft Exchange system, the fax will not go through.
- **Not Editable.** You use this option when you want all your faxes to be sent as a single graphic image in traditional fax format.

Message Security Choose the Security button to see the Security options. Security works only with editable faxes. You have two basic choices: None and Password-Protected. If you choose None, your fax can be read immediately upon receipt. Choosing Password-Protected requires the recipient to type the password that you applied to that fax transmission in order to see it.

CAUTION

If you activate password security on a fax that is sent to a non-Microsoft Exchange recipient or fax machine, your fax will not go through.

Paper Size and Orientation, and Image Quality Choose Paper to access the Paper Size and Orientation options. These options are usable with noneditable faxes. You can choose letter or legal paper. You also can choose Portrait (vertical) or Landscape (horizontal) page orientation.

You also can change the Image Quality in this dialog box. This determines the resolution at which Exchange prepares the fax. As with a laser printer, the higher the resolution, the crisper and cleaner your fax will be when printed.

Pick one of the following three Image Quality options based on your need for a high-quality fax balanced against the additional time it takes to send the fax at a higher resolution:

- **Best Available.** This setting is recommended; it makes your fax look as good as possible on the receiving end.
- **Fine** (200 dots per inch, or dpi). Fine mode can result in incompatibilities if the receiving side doesn't support it. If it works with your recipient's hardware, it will look as good as possible.
- **Draft** (200×100 dpi). Draft mode looks coarser than Fine or Best Available, but transmits faster.

Cover Page To send a cover page with your fax, select the Send Cover Page option and choose which type of cover page to send.

When you finish selecting all the options you want to use, choose Next, and the Compose New Fax Wizard moves on to let you enter the Subject of the fax, and, if you want, a Note to put on the cover page.

▶ **See** "Using the Fax Cover Page Editor," **p. 713**

Fax Subject and Note When you finish working with all the options described in the preceding sections and you choose Next, the Compose New Fax Wizard displays a dialog box where you can enter the subject of the fax and add a note to accompany your fax.

Type the subject in the Subject text box. Optionally, you can type a note in the Note text box to go along with your fax. Click the Start Note on Cover Page check box to start your note on the cover page. If you leave the box unchecked, the note will start on a new page in your fax. Choose Next.

Adding Files to Your Fax

After the Compose New Fax Wizard finishes with the fax subject and note (covered in the preceding section), it offers you a dialog box where you can select files to include with the fax.

To include a file, choose Add File. You can use Explorer to browse and find the file you want to send with your fax.

After you choose the file, or files, to send with your fax, the wizard shows the files you selected in the Files to Send text box. When you finish selecting files to add to your fax, choose Next.

CAUTION

The files you choose can be sent only if the fax is sent in editable format. If you use any other format, Microsoft Fax will not send the fax or cover sheet.

For this reason, choose to add files to your fax only if you are certain that the recipient's system can support editable format, and that both your sending system and the recipient's receiving system are configured for editable faxing. (Configuring your fax in editable format was covered in "Options for Fax Transmission," earlier in this chapter.)

After you add any files you want to send with your fax, choose Finish, and Microsoft Fax sends your fax.

▶ **See** "Configuring Your Modem," **p. 77**

TROUBLESHOOTING

I'm trying to send a fax, but it won't go through. Do you hear the modem dial the fax? If not, make sure that you have a fax modem selected and that the settings are correct for your modem type. In Exchange, choose Tools, Services, Microsoft Fax, Properties; then click the Modem tab. You should see your fax modem displayed; if not, click Add to configure your modem.

If you can hear the modem dial the phone, but the modem disconnects just after dialing, repeat the preceding procedure. When you see your modem, select it and then click Properties. Make sure that the modem is set to allow enough time to connect after dialing (60 seconds is a good choice). This parameter often is set to 1 second by Windows for no apparent reason.

Sending a More Complete Message

There are a couple of other ways to send fax messages. First, you may want to use the same window you used to create an email message. The only difference between creating a fax message and an email message is in the way you address it. If you address the message to a fax "address," the message will be a fax message.

If you don't already have the fax address in your Address Book, you need to add it first. Then use the To button in the New Message window to add this address to the To line of your message.

Choose File, Send Options to modify fax options while working in the New Message window.

The advantage of sending a fax using this method is that you have all the New Message window's tools available. You can write a message, using all the text-editing capabilities. You can also attach files and insert pictures into your fax.

The other way to fax is directly from an application. For instance, you can fax from your word processor. Many applications have a Send option on the File menu. If an application you want to use *doesn't* have such an option, you can "print" to Microsoft Fax on the FAX print driver.

▶ **See** "Adding Names to Your Address Book," **p. 722**

Using the Fax Cover Page Editor

The Fax Cover Page Editor is a miniature word processor that allows you to work with graphics as well as rich text. Use the Fax Cover Page Editor to create custom-made cover pages or to modify one that is supplied with Exchange. You can do the following things with cover pages that you create or edit:

- Insert data from the Personal Address Book into your cover page.
- Paste items from the Clipboard into your cover page.
- Import text or graphics (such as a logo) into your cover page.

To use the Cover Page Editor, open the Start menu; choose Programs, Accessories, Fax; and then click Cover Page Editor. The Cover Page Editor program starts up.

When you first start the Cover Page Editor program, there is no cover page file loaded. From here, you can design a new cover page. If you start designing a new cover page and then decide you want to start over again, choose File, New, or click the New File icon on the toolbar.

Fax cover pages have a file name extension of CPE. The cover pages that come with Exchange are located in the C:\WINDOWS folder.

To edit and customize an existing cover page, choose File, Open. Then select the cover page you want to work with.

The most useful feature of the Cover Page Editor is the ability to insert information from your Personal Address Book into your cover sheets. You do this by choosing Insert from the menu bar and then choosing from the options on that menu and successive submenus (see Figure 28.7). Information you can insert includes:

- Recipient's or Sender's Name
- Recipient's or Sender's Fax Number
- Recipient's or Sender's Company

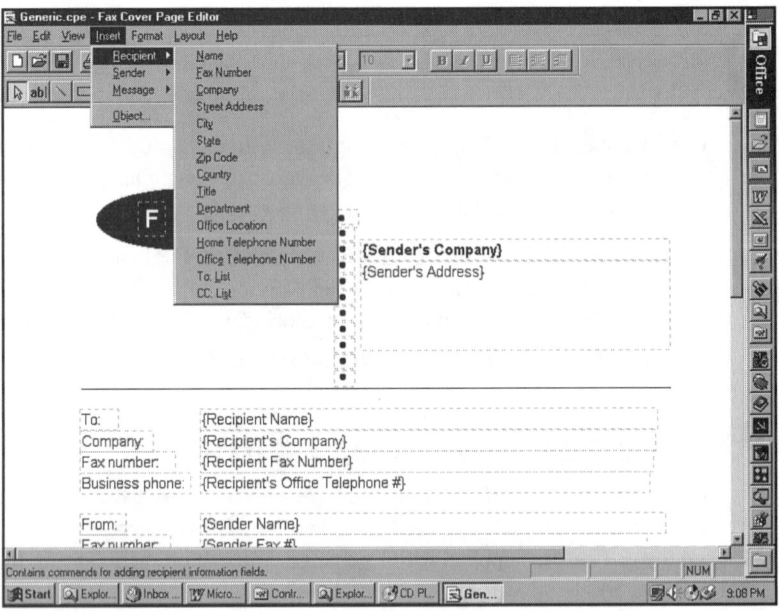

FIG. 28.7
Insert Address Book information into your fax cover sheet.

Viewing Received Faxes

The Exchange Inbox can display both email and faxes that you've received (see Figure 28.8). You can see the fax sender's phone number as well as the date and time the fax was received.

When you double-click a normal, noneditable fax, the Fax Viewer opens and displays the fax. When you double-click a received editable fax, though, or a fax that has attached files, the message window opens. Inside this window, what you see depends on what you received. If you received a fax that the author created in the New Message window, you see exactly what the author saw; the text looks the same, any icons representing attached files look the same, and so on. If, however, you are receiving a fax from another application (sent using the File, Send option), you see an icon representing the fax. Double-click this icon to open the application associated with that type of file. For instance, if you double-click a DOC file that you've received, the program associated with it opens: Word or WordPad.

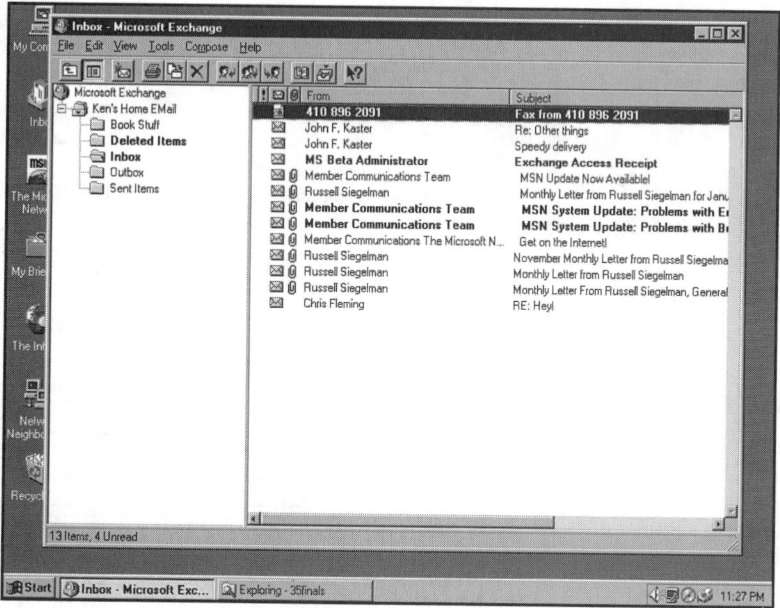

FIG. 28.8
The Exchange Inbox shows a received fax.

NOTE If you receive a fax that the author "printed" to Microsoft Fax on the fax driver, it comes through as if it were a normal fax from a fax machine. Double-clicking the fax in the Inbox opens the Fax Viewer, not the Message window.

For instance, Figure 28.9 shows a fax received from Notepad. Notice the Notepad icon in the message form to the left of the Notepad window. When the icon was double-clicked, Notepad opened and displayed the fax text. You can edit the text just as though you created the file on your own computer.

TROUBLESHOOTING

Someone is trying to send me a fax, but I'm not receiving it. Make sure that your fax modem is installed. From the Exchange window, choose Tools, Services. Select Microsoft Fax and choose Properties. Then click the Modem tab and make sure your modem is shown in the list of Available Fax Modems. If it is, click the Properties tab and check to see whether the modem is set to answer automatically. If not, select the Answer After check box, and set the number of rings to wait before your fax modem answers calls.

Using Other Fax Options

In addition to the options available when using the Compose New Fax Wizard, there are a few other very useful features that you can enable whenever a fax is sent.

▶ **See** "Options for Fax Transmission," **p. 709**

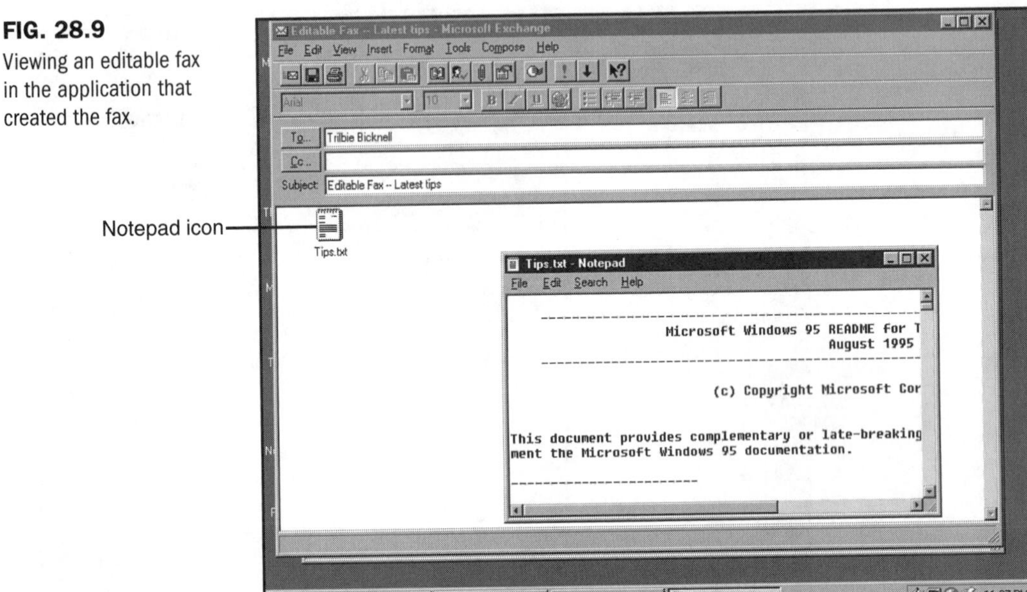

FIG. 28.9
Viewing an editable fax in the application that created the fax.

Using Advanced Fax Security

Security for ensuring that nobody else can view the contents of your faxes is built into Microsoft Fax; by default, however, it is not enabled. To enable the advanced security, select Tools, Microsoft Fax Tools, Advanced Security from the Exchange menu. This type of security is based on key encryption, which is different from the password-based security mentioned earlier. As you would guess, password-based security is based only on a single password; a recipient on the other end must know that password to unlock your fax.

Key encryption is more advanced and more secure, requiring more setup. It works by sending a "public" version of your key to all the people from whom you will eventually receive encrypted faxes. They keep this public key on their systems and use it when they only want you to decrypt whatever they send. Likewise, you must get their public keys and store them on your system so that you can send them encrypted material that only they can decrypt. Whenever you send them a secure fax, it is encrypted using the public key they already sent to you. When they receive the encrypted fax, their system uses their own private version of the key to decode the message.

Setting Up Your Encryption Keys The first steps in using Advanced Fax Security for Microsoft Fax are the creation of your key encryption set and establishing yourself in the encryption "system." For the encryption system to maintain its integrity, the system itself must be protected by your own password; otherwise, anyone else who logs on to your computer might access your encryption system. This is the first line of defense. All of your subsequent key encryption is based on this same password, so you must keep this to yourself or the entire scheme is compromised. Click the New Key Set button to establish your keys (see Figure 28.10).

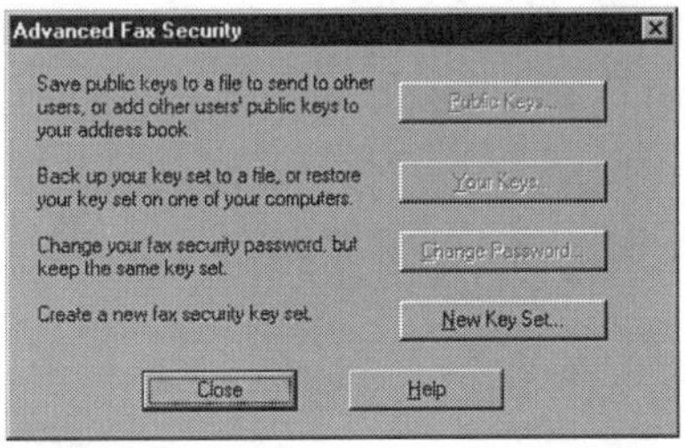

FIG. 28.10
Setting up Advanced Fax Security involves the creation of encryption keys.

Figure 28.11 displays the dialog box in which you enter your password to build your encryption keys. This same password is used to lock the encryption system. Type in your Password and Confirm it by typing it in again. Checking the Save the Password in Your Password List option saves you from typing in your password each time you receive an encrypted fax, but it also leaves your faxes wide open to anyone who can sit down at your computer and get into your email. If you need the maximum available security, do not select this option. If you keep your password secure, you probably won't have to regenerate your keys in the future. Click OK to return to the Advanced Fax Security dialog box.

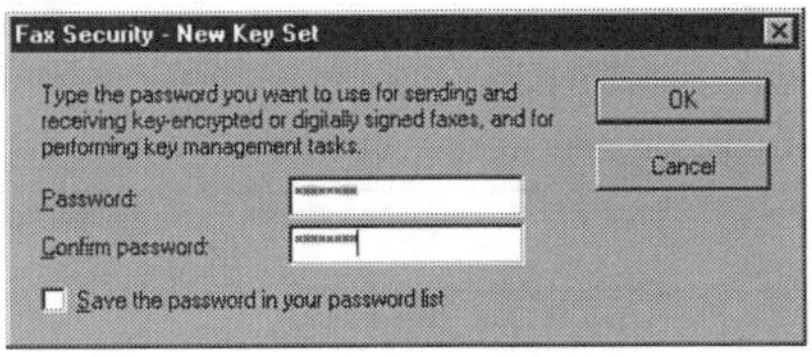

FIG. 28.11
You must first establish your password within the key encryption system.

NOTE Your encryption keys are *not* the same as your password; your keys are made up of an encrypted mixture of your password and your user information. The resulting keys themselves are totally unrecognizable (they're a mish-mash of bits) and virtually unbreakable.

Sharing Your Public Keys To send your public keys to the people who will be sending you encrypted faxes, you must first write your public key to a file so you can later send it via email. Click the Public Keys button on the Advanced Fax Security dialog box, and then click the Save button (see Figure 28.12).

The next dialog box appears, this time asking whose public keys you want to save to the public-key file (see Figure 28.13). If you had other public keys available in your Address Book, they would be listed on the left next to your public key. During the first run through this, only your public key is likely to be available, so click your name and add it to the To: list, then click OK.

FIG. 28.12 There are several options to help you manage your public keys.

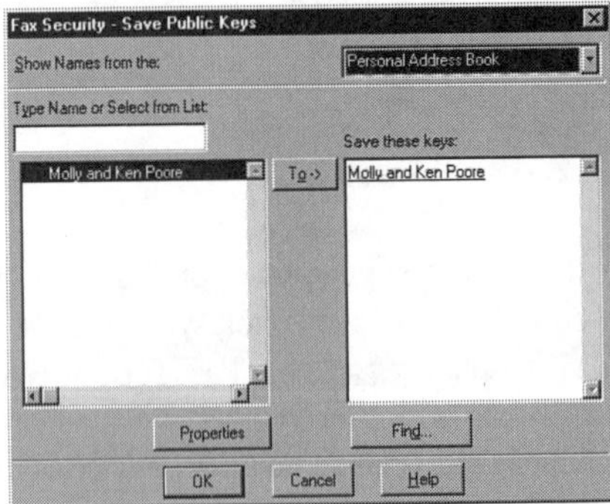

FIG. 28.13 Selecting your public key.

A Save Public Keys dialog box appears (see Figure 28.14), prompting you to write your public key to a file. Choose a folder and click Save.

All public key files end with an .AWP extension. It's a good idea to put these files in a folder other than your main Windows directory so you can easily keep track of them.

FIG. 28.14 Writing your public key to a file.

Now you should send this file in a mail message to those whom you will receive encrypted faxes from (you can send it to them on a floppy, too). Go back to the main Exchange Window and select Compose, New Message. Select those who will be sending you encrypted faxes, attach the file containing your public keys, and then send it. Be sure to ask them to send you their public keys as well.

When you receive a message from someone containing a public key as a file attachment to an email message, save the attached file. Then, from the Exchange menu, choose Tools, Microsoft

Fax Tools, Advanced Security; then select Public Keys from the Managing Public Keys dialog box (refer to Figure 28.12). Click Add and choose the file you just extracted from the email attachment. You will then see the dialog box shown in Figure 28.15.

Choose the names of the users you want to add to your Address Book's public key list by selecting them from the list and clicking OK.

FIG. 28.15 Adding public keys to your system.

Sending a Secure Fax Now that all your public keys are set up, you can send a key-encrypted secure Fax. Choose Compose, New Message. When the New Message dialog box appears, choose File, Send Options, and click the Fax tab. Click the Security button and you can now choose Key-Encrypted Security. If you didn't save your password by using the Save the Password in Your Password List option when you first created your keys, you will have to type in your password next. Close the options dialog boxes and return to composing your fax. Select the recipients, being careful to only choose those recipients for whom you've received a public key. Complete your fax and send it.

Changing Fax Dialing Options Most fax machines have the capability to continually redial the destination fax if the line is busy—Microsoft Fax does, too. Other options such as making toll calls within your area code and various dialing settings are also available. All these options are available by choosing Tools, Microsoft Fax Tools, Options (see Figure 28.16). The following list describes the options in the Microsoft Fax Properties dialog box.

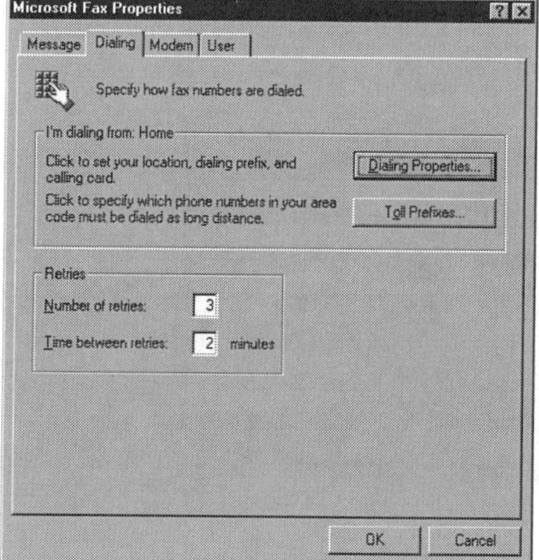

FIG. 28.16 Fax dialing options.

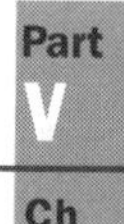

- On the Dialing page, the Toll Prefixes option allows you to select which exchanges in your area code are toll calls requiring the fax to dial 1 and the area code before dialing the number (see Figure 28.17).

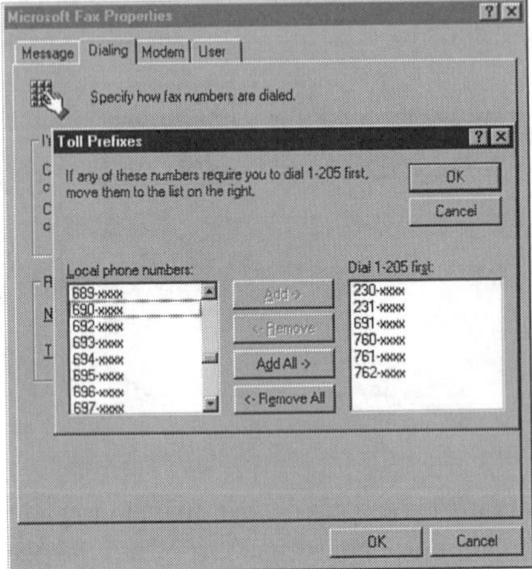

FIG. 28.17
Choosing phone exchanges that are toll calls.

- Choose Dialing Properties to configure your location and to enter the codes needed to block call waiting and other dialing options.

  ▶ **See** "Configuring Your Modem," **p. 77**

- You can change how your modem redials after getting a busy signal by setting the Number of Retries and the Time Between Retries.
- Your user information is inserted into cover pages. If you would like to change your user information, click the User tab and modify it (see Figure 28.18).

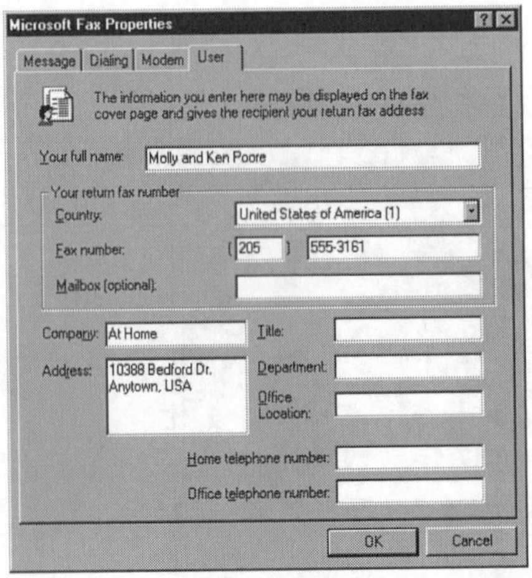

FIG. 28.18
Setting up user information for your fax cover pages.

Working with the Exchange Address Book

The Exchange Address Book can help you keep track of how to contact your correspondents. You enter names into the Address Book and specify the type of communications to use (fax, Internet mail, Microsoft LAN Mail, CompuServe Mail, and so on). The Exchange Address Book makes sure that your messages are addressed properly.

The entire Exchange Address Book is built from several different modular, building-block address books. The number of these building-block address books is determined by the communications services you installed when you set up Exchange.

Some of the services you installed come with their own building-block address book modules. For example, if you installed The Microsoft Network online service, a building-block address book for MSN was installed in your address book. The MSN Address Book is configured by Microsoft to contain the names and email addresses of all the members of The Microsoft Network.

Microsoft Mail for your workgroup LAN has a building-block address book—built by the network administrator—that is part of your Exchange Address Book. In Exchange, the Microsoft Mail Address Book is called Postoffice Address List.

The final module making up your address book is called the Personal Address Book. Here, you can store the names and addresses you use most often. You can transfer names into your Personal Address Book from the other address books.

The Exchange Address Book also has options you can use to control how it displays the names you store.

Now, to display and work with the address book from the Microsoft Exchange window, choose Tools, Address Book; or press Ctrl+Shift+B.

Setting Display Preferences

By default, names appear with the first name followed by the last name (John Jones). If, however, you have a rather long list or know several men called John, you may find viewing the list sorted by last names to be faster.

You can use the Personal Address Book Properties settings to change the order in which first and last names display. To change the order, follow these steps:

1. From the Exchange main window, choose Tools, Address Book. The Address Book opens.
2. Select Personal Address Book from the Show Names From The: drop-down list. The names in your Personal Address Book appear.
3. Choose Tools, Options. The Addressing dialog box appears.
4. In the When Sending Mail list, select Personal Address Book.

5. Click Properties. The Personal Address Book properties sheet appears.
6. Now you can choose to show names by first name or last name. Click First Name or Last Name on the Personal Address Book page, as shown in Figure 28.19.

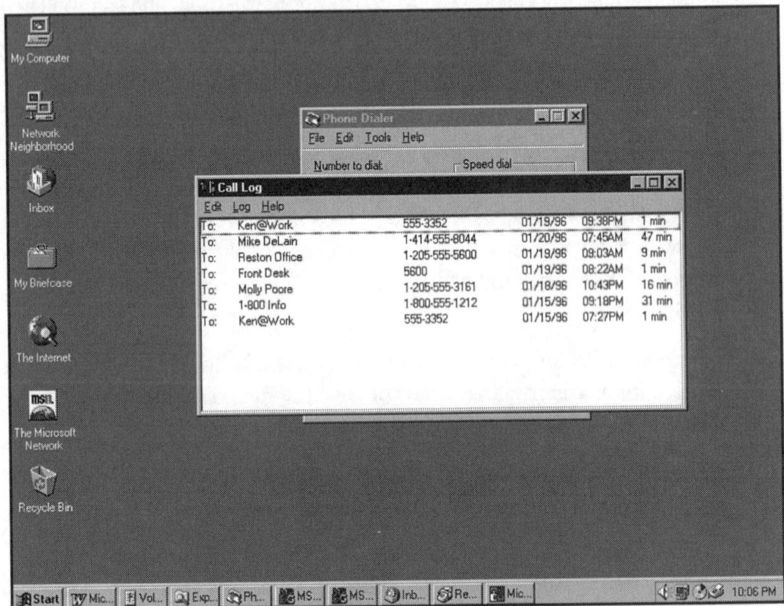

FIG. 28.19 Use this properties sheet to select how to display names in the Personal Address Book.

7. You also can give the Personal Address Book a more descriptive name. You might want to call it Business Contacts, for example. Type the name you want to use for the Personal Address Book in the Name text box.
8. Click the Notes tab, and type any information you want to record about your Personal Address Book in the text box.

Adding Names to Your Address Book

You want to use Exchange as the powerful communications tool it can be. Part of harnessing the power of Exchange is as simple as keeping a well-organized address book so that you have all the mail addresses and fax numbers you need conveniently at hand.

1. Open the Exchange Address Book by choosing Tools, Address Book. You also can click the Address Book button on the toolbar.
2. In the Show Names From The: drop-down list, select Personal Address Book.
3. Choose File, New Entry. You can also choose the New Entry button on the toolbar. The New Entry dialog box appears (see Figure 28.20).

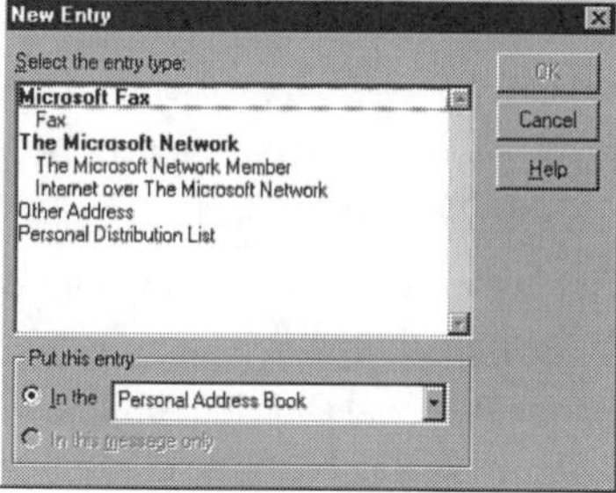

FIG. 28.20
The power of Exchange is evident in the range of address types to which you can send messages.

4. Select the type of address you want to add to your Personal Address Book. In this example, you're adding a Microsoft Fax entry to the book. Then choose OK. The New Fax properties sheet appears.
5. The properties sheet that you see in Figure 28.21 has text boxes for all the names and numbers required to reach your recipient. Type the pertinent information in each page. Then choose OK. The properties sheet closes, and the new entry appears in your address book.

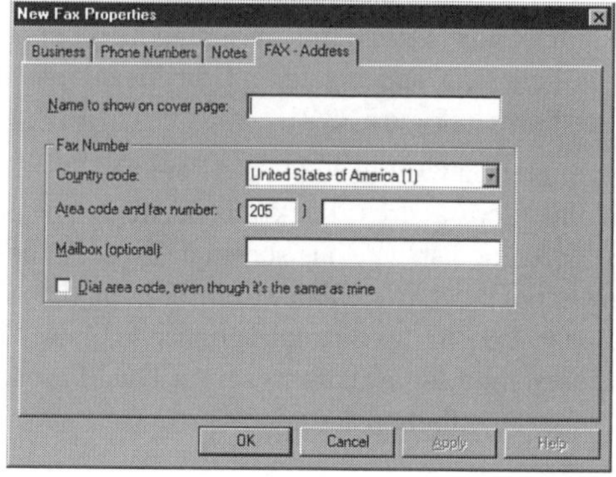

FIG. 28.21
The New Fax properties sheet is typical of the properties sheets you fill out when adding entries to your address book.

You follow the same steps as those for a Microsoft Fax entry to add different types of addresses such as Microsoft Network addresses or Internet Mail addresses.

The difference between adding the fax address you illustrated and the other possible address types is that after you select the entry type from the New Entry dialog box (step 4 in the previous list), the New Properties sheet that appears is different.

Adding Groups to Your Address Book

To send a message to a group of recipients, create a Personal Distribution List. Once you have a Personal Distribution List, you only have to create a message once, and you can send it to all the members of the list with one click.

Follow these steps to create your Personal Distribution List:

1. Open the Address Book by choosing Tools, Address Book.
2. Choose File, New Entry. The New Entry dialog box appears (refer to Figure 28.20). The New Entry dialog box contains a scrolling list of address types.
3. The last entry in the scrolling list is the Personal Distribution List entry type. Select Personal Distribution List at the bottom of the list.
4. In this example, you're putting your Personal Distribution List in your Personal Address Book. At the bottom of the New Entry dialog box is a setting that says Put This Entry In The. Make sure Personal Address Book shows in the text box. If it doesn't, click the drop-down arrow and scroll to select Personal Address Book.
5. Choose OK. The New Personal Distribution List Properties sheet appears.
6. Name your list. Type the name for your list in the Name text box. In this example, you name your Personal Distribution List **Staff Members on Project X**.
7. If you want to make some notes about the list, click the Notes tab and type your comments in the text box. You might use this space to document how the group members were chosen. You can enter anything that's useful in this text box.
8. Click the Distribution List tab.
9. Build the Distribution List now. You do this by adding members to the list. Choose Add/Remove Members. A dialog box appears, titled **Edit Members of** (name of your Distribution List), as shown in Figure 28.22.
10. Perhaps one of the people you want to add to the Personal Distribution List is already in another of your building-block address books. If so, choose the proper address book by selecting it from the scrolling list, which is shown in Show Names from The: list. When you choose an address book in Show Names from The:, all the address entries in that address book become visible. In this example, choose to Show Names from The Microsoft Network. Next, add some addresses from The Microsoft Network online service to your Personal Distribution List.

NOTE You can only use the Microsoft Network address book while online. If you select this address book while offline, the Connect dialog box appears so you can log on.

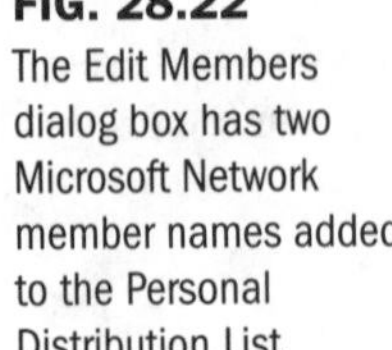

FIG. 28.22
The Edit Members dialog box has two Microsoft Network member names added to the Personal Distribution List.

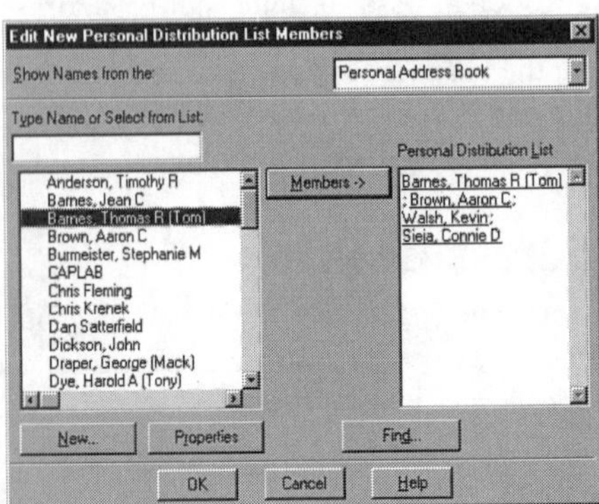

To add other names from existing address books, select Show Names From The:, and select the next address book from the scrolling list. Then repeat the preceding steps from step 10.

You also can put people on your Personal Distribution List who are not already in any of your address books. However, you have to put that person into your Personal Address Book first.

▶ **See** "Adding Names to Your Address Book," **p. 722**

Choose New. Then follow the steps discussed earlier for adding a name to your Personal Address Book. Once you make the addition to the book, that name is added to the Personal Distribution List automatically. When you finish adding members to your Personal Distribution List, choose OK.

Your Personal Distribution List appears in your Personal Address Book, along with any individual addresses you have stored there. By choosing the list as a recipient in a message you create, the message is sent to all members of the Personal Distribution List.

Using the Windows Address Book

When you install Outlook Express, you also install a new and improved Windows Address Book. The new address book is fully integrated with Outlook Express but can also run as a stand-alone contact management application. In Windows Address Book, you can store home and business addresses, email addresses, telephone numbers, fax numbers, security certificates, and other contact information. Some of the features of the Windows Address Book enable you to do the following tasks:

- Manage your personal contacts
- Create distribution lists for your email messages
- Search for people on the Internet
- Manage security certificates
- Print your address book to keep with you
- Import or export contact information for other address books
- Import or export vCards

To start Address Book, choose Start, Programs, Windows Address Book. You can also start Address Book from within Outlook Express: choose Tools, Address Book, or click the To, Cc, or Bcc buttons in a new message window. Outlook Express also uses the Address Book to resolve names to an email address.

Use the Start, Find, People to search for people in your address book or on the Internet using Directory Services.

Adding and Editing Contacts in Your Address Book

The Windows Address Book allows you to quickly and easily manage your personal contacts. To add a contact to your address book, follow these steps:

1. In the Address Book, click the New Contact toolbar button, or choose File, New Contact. The new contact properties sheet displays, as seen in Figure 28.23.

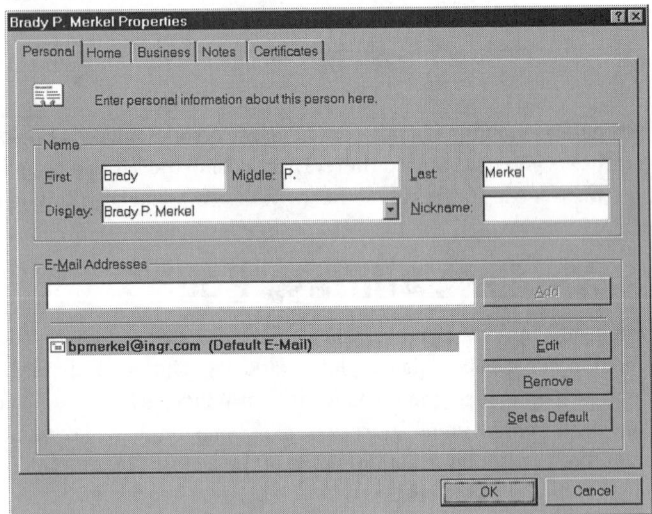

FIG. 28.23 Enter your contact information in the new contact properties sheet.

2. On the Personal tab, type the contact name, display name, and email addresses.

Each contact requires a display name. If you do not enter one, Address Book will create one for you using the first, middle, or last name, nickname, or company name.

3. On the Home and Business tabs, type the addresses of the contact, in addition to the phone, fax, and cellular numbers. If your contact has an Internet Web site, type the URL.
4. On the Notes tab, type other important information about your contact that might come in handy, such as their spouse's and children's names, birthdays, and so on.
5. Use the Certificates tab to import and manage security certificates for your new contact. You use security certificates when you send encrypted messages to a contact, or you want to verify a contact's digital signature.

   Once you import a certificate, select it and click Properties. In the Certificate Properties dialog box, you can review the validity, expiration dates, and issuing institution, and determine whether you trust the certificate. If you do not trust a certificate, indicate so in the Trusted option list.
6. Click OK to add the new contact.

In Outlook Express, you can quickly add names to your Address Book. Simply right-click a recipient's name and choose Add to Address Book.

Once you add a contact to your Address Book, you can use it in other applications such as Outlook Express.

If you ever need to go back to an Address Book entry to update the contact information, simply double-click the entry in the address book and modify the information as needed. Alternatively, you can select the contact in the list and click the Properties toolbar button, or choose File, Properties.

To delete a contact from your address book, select the contact in the list, and click the Delete toolbar button; or choose File, Delete. If the contact is a member of any of your groups, it is removed from each of the groups as well.

Creating a Group

Suppose you frequently invite several of your contacts to a weekly meeting, and you want an easy way to address the whole group in each invitation message. The way you do that is by using a *group*, or distribution list. You create a group and add the invited contacts to it. Then, when you send a message to the group, you address it to the group name, rather than each contact. Address Book allows you to create as many groups as you need, and each contact can be in more than one group, if desired. To create a group, follow these steps:

1. In Address Book, click the New Group toolbar button, or choose File, New Group.
2. In the Group Properties dialog box, give the group a meaningful name such as **Staff**.
3. Click Select Members to add your contacts to the group distribution list.
4. In the Select Group Members dialog box, select each contact you want in the group (you can even select other groups you have defined) and click Select.
5. Click OK when you have identified the members of the group.
6. Click OK again to save your new group. It should appear in your Address Book with a group icon next to the name.

If you no longer need a group, you can delete it. Deleting a group removes only the group collection and does not remove the contact members from the Address Book. To delete a group, select it in the Address Book list, and click the Delete toolbar button, or choose File, Delete.

Adding and Removing Contacts in a Group

If you want to add new members to a group, you can open the group and choose additional members. In addition, you can remove contacts you no longer want included in the group.

To add new contacts to a group, follow these steps:

1. Double-click the group you want to modify in the address book list. Or select the group name and click the Properties toolbar button, or choose File, Properties.
2. Click Select Members, and then select each additional contact from the Select Group Members dialog box.
3. Click OK to add the new members to the group.
4. Click OK again to save your new group membership.

To delete contacts from a group, follow these steps:

1. Double-click the group you want to modify in the address book list. Or select the group name and click the Properties toolbar button, or choose File, Properties.
2. For each contact in the Members list that you want to remove, select the contact and click Remove. Note: Removing a contact from a group does not remove it from your Address Book.
3. Click OK to save your changes.

Sorting Names in the Address Book List

As your address book begins to grow, you may find it difficult to locate contacts in the Address Book list. To make it easier to locate a contact, you can sort the Address Book list by any of the column headings. Simply click the appropriate column heading that interests you. To sort in the reverse direction, click the column heading again.

If you want to sort by first name or last name, use the View menu. Choose View, Sort By and select First Name or Last Name.

Searching for Names in Your Address Book or a Directory Service

If you are trying to locate someone, the Windows Address Book provides an easy way to find them in your Personal Address Book, or on the Internet.

To search for names in your address book or through a Directory Service, follow these steps:

1. In the Address Book, click the Find toolbar button, or choose Edit, Find. The Find People dialog box displays.
2. In the Search list, select the location to search: your personal Windows Address Book, or an Internet Directory Service.
3. Type the name you want to search for in the Name text box. If you know additional information such as the E-mail address, enter it as well to reduce the number of potential responses (especially when searching an Internet Directory Service).
4. Click Find Now.
5. The search results display at the bottom of the Find People dialog box, as shown in Figure 28.24. When searching a Directory Service, you can configure the number of responses and the time allowed for the search.

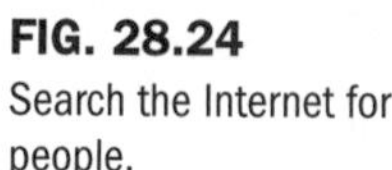

FIG. 28.24
Search the Internet for people.

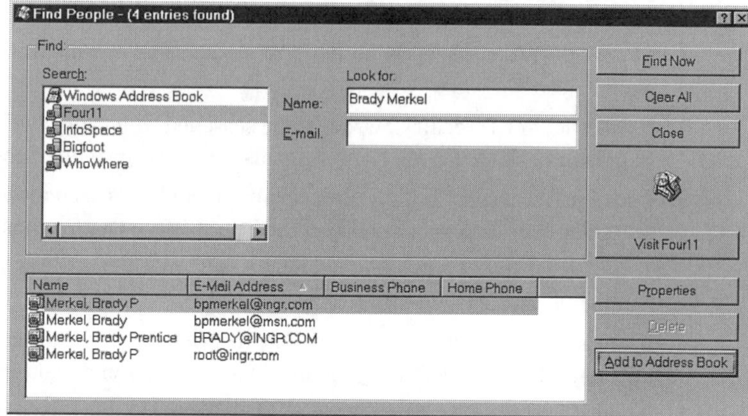

6. If you get multiple responses to your search, select each entry that looks promising, and click Properties to see additional information about the person. Click a column heading to sort the list.

   If you found a person from a Directory Service that is not in your Windows Address Book, and you want to add it, select the entry and click Add to Address Book. If you want to visit a Directory Service's Web site, select the Directory Service in the Search list and click the Visit Directory Service button. Some Directory Services allow you to add or update your own entries.

You can also use Tools, Check Names within Outlook Express to resolve names to your Windows Address Book and Internet Directory Services. See the next section for details on choosing which services should be searched.

Understanding Directory Services

The Windows Address Book uses a new and exciting capability to search Internet sites for people: *Directory Services.* Windows Address Book uses a technology known as the Lightweight Directory Access Protocol (LDAP) to search for the information.

When you install the Windows Address Book, it comes configured with four Internet Directory Service providers. If you prefer, you can add others, edit their properties, or delete the ones you no longer need.

NOTE Unlike the Address Book, you cannot view the entire contents of a Directory Service. In addition, Directory Service searches limit the number of responses, so you may need to provide additional information to reduce the search results.

Part V
Ch 28

To add a Directory Service entry, follow these steps:

1. In the Windows Address Book, choose File, Directory Services.
2. Click Add to add a Directory Service. Type the name of the Directory Service in the Friendly Name text box.

3. Type the Internet address of the Directory Service in the Directory Server text box.
4. Choose the required server authentication type, and provide the user name and password if needed.
5. If you want this Directory Service to be searched when you check names in Outlook Express, check the Check Names Against This Server When Sending Mail check box.
6. Click the Advanced tab. Type the maximum number of seconds you want to wait when searching this Directory Service in the Search Time-Out text box.

   Type the maximum number of responses you are willing to wait for in the Maximum Number of Entries to Return text box.

   If you are not getting any search results from a Directory Service, try increasing the time-out value and decreasing the maximum number of responses value.
7. If your Directory Service requires an LDAP base identifier, type it into the Search Base for this Directory Service text box. Contact the Directory Service administrators for this value.
8. Click OK. Your new Directory Service is added to the list.

To review or edit a Directory Service entry, follow these steps:

1. In the Windows Address Book, choose File, Directory Services.
2. Select a Directory Service in the list and click Properties. The Directory Service's properties sheet appears, as shown in Figure 28.25.

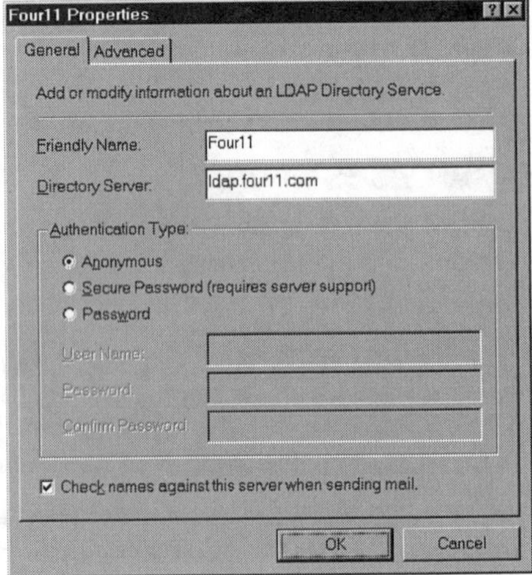

FIG. 28.25
You can review or edit the Directory Service's properties.

3. On the General tab, review the Directory Service connection settings and edit the values if you need to. If you want this Directory Service to be searched when you check names in Outlook Express, check the Check Names Against This Server When Sending Mail check box.
4. On the Advanced tab, as shown in Figure 28.26, you can tune the amount of time and number of responses you will wait for when searching the Directory Service.

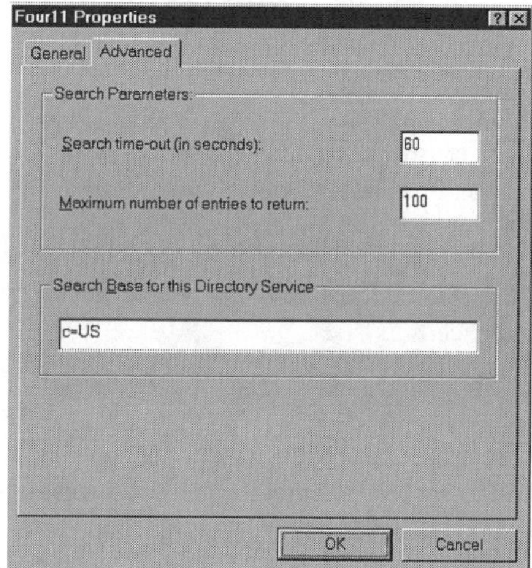

FIG. 28.26 Adjust the time-out and maximum response values to tune the amount of time it takes to perform a Directory Service search.

5. Click OK to save your settings and dismiss the dialog box.

When you check names while composing a new message in Outlook Express, first, your Personal Address Book is checked and then the Directory Services you have enabled. To define the order of Directory Services to search when checking names, follow these steps:

1. In the Windows Address Book, choose File, Directory Services.
2. Click the Options tab. If you see no Directory Services in the list, you need to enable one or more to be searched when you check names. See the previous text on editing a Directory Service entry.
3. Select a Directory Service and click Up or Down to change the order. Directory Services are searched in a top-down manner.
4. Click OK to save your settings and dismiss the dialog box.

To delete a Directory Service, follow these steps:

1. In the Windows Address Book, choose File, Directory Services.
2. Select a Directory Service in the list, and click Remove.
3. Click OK to save your settings and dismiss the dialog box.

Printing Your Contacts

If you are traveling, you can print your Address Book for easy reference. Choose File, Print, and select from the choice of printing in three different formats:

- **Memo.** For all address book information.
- **Business Card.** For only business-related information.
- **Phone List.** For only contact names and telephone numbers.

Importing Other Address Books

The Windows Address Book supports importing contact and group information from other address books, such as from Microsoft Exchange, Netscape Navigator, or Qualcomm Eudora. To import contacts from other address books, follow these steps:

1. Within Windows Address Book, choose Tools, Import, Address Book.
2. In the Windows Address Book Import Tool dialog box, select the type of address book you want to import and click Import.
3. The Import tool will attempt to locate the address book to import. Follow the prompts to facilitate locating the desired address book. For example, if you are importing a Microsoft Exchange Personal Address Book, you may need to log in to the specific Exchange profile. If the Import tool cannot locate the address book file, it will offer you the opportunity to locate the file manually.
4. As the Import tool reads each new contact and group, it compares it with the contacts you already have in your Windows Address Book. The Import tool will ask you to replace any contacts where the names are the same.
5. You should see a confirmation box that informs you that the import was successful. Click OK and click Close to dismiss the address book Import tool.

Exporting to Other Address Books

You can export your Address Book if you need to upgrade to a mail system that uses its own Address Book (such as Microsoft Exchange or Outlook 97). Alternatively, you can export your Address Book into a comma-separated format so you can import it into a database or spreadsheet. To export your Address Book, follow these steps:

1. In Windows Address Book, choose Tools, Export, Address Book.
2. In the Windows Address Book Export Tool dialog box, select the type of address book you want to export and click Export.

   If you selected Comma Separated Values, locate the folder where you want to create the .csv file, and type the name of file.

   If you are exporting to a Microsoft Exchange Personal Address Book, you may need to log in to the specific Exchange profile.

3. As the Import tool writes each contact and group, it compares it with the contacts you already have in your address book. The Export tool will ask you to replace any contacts where the names are the same.
4. You should see a confirmation box that informs you that the export was successful. Click OK and click Close to dismiss the address book Export tool.

Exporting your contacts and groups does not remove them from your Address Book.

Exporting vCards

A *vCard* is an electronic business card. vCards use an industry-standard format for exchanging business card information between different types of programs such as email and address books. vCards are exchanged as files with the .VCF file name extension. To export a contact to a vCard, follow these steps:

1. Select a contact in your Address Book and choose Tools, Export, vCard..
2. Navigate to the folder where you want to create the vCard and type the file name.
3. Click Save.

Once you save a vCard to a file, you can attach it to email messages or transfer them to your personal data assistant. Exporting a contact to a vCard does not remove it from your Address Book.

Importing vCards

If someone sends you a vCard, you can import it directly into your Windows Address Book. To import a vCard, follow these steps:

1. In Address Book, choose Tools, Import, vCard.
2. Locate the vCard on your local system or network drive.
3. Click Open.
4. In the Properties dialog box, review and modify any of the contact attributes.
5. Click OK to save the new contact in your address book. If the vCard contact name matches one that already exists in your address book, you will be prompted to replace it.

Working with Phone Dialer

The Phone Dialer is a handy accessory built into Windows 95 that acts as a speed dialer, remembering up to eight phone numbers. This may seem a bit redundant if you already have a speed dialer built into your existing phone, but this one is very easy to program and change, plus it can do the more intricate dialing needed to navigate voice-mail systems and make credit-card calls. Phone Dialer can even keep a log of your outgoing and incoming calls. You can access the Phone Dialer from the Start menu by choosing Programs, Accessories (see Figure 28.27).

FIG. 28.27
Use Phone Dialer to make calls with your modem.

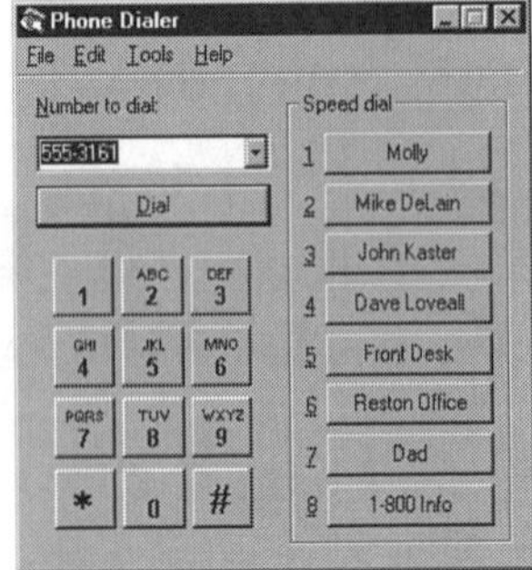

NOTE If you don't see the Phone Dialer on the Accessories menu, open the Start menu and choose Settings, Control Panel. Then double-click the Add/Remove Programs icon, click the Windows Setup tab, and select the Communications component. Select Details and be sure the Phone Dialer is selected. Click OK twice to save your changes.

Adding Phone Dialer Entries

When it's first started, your Phone Dialer has no speed-dial entries set. Your first task is to add names and phone numbers to the eight blank dial memories. Click any blank entry and type in the Name and Number you want to save (see Figure 28.28).

FIG. 28.28
You can enter a short name for each Phone Dialer entry.

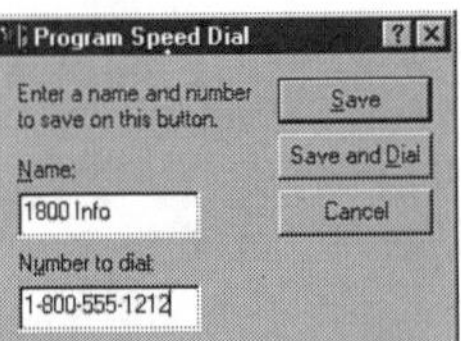

Both the Save and the Save and Dial buttons are now available. You can immediately use your new entry to dial the phone by clicking the Save and Dial button or use the Save button to program your speed-dial entry and exit the dialog box.

If you have a phone number that contains letters (555-FOOD or 1-800-555-SNOW), just put quotes ("") around the letters, for example, 1-800-555-"SNOW."

Once your number is entered and saved, clicking the speed-dial entry immediately starts the phone dialing and opens the Dialing dialog box shown in Figure 28.29. While waiting for your call to be answered, you can type in a description of the call as you want it to appear in the phone log.

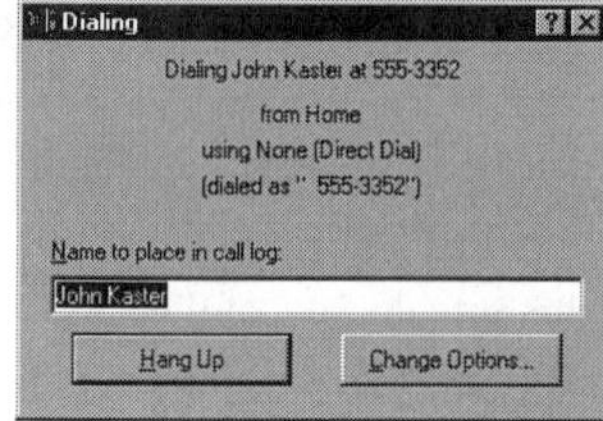

FIG. 28.29
Enter a log entry while the phone is dialing.

Click the Hang Up button if you want to abort the call immediately. The Change Options button gives you a chance to stop the call and redial with a number you type into the Number to Redial field (see Figure 28.30). This allows you to specify exactly what you want the modem to dial, ignoring any properties (such as your calling card number) set in the Dialing properties sheet. After typing in your number, click the Redial Number button to dial your new entry. If you click the Dialing Properties button, any changes you made in the Number to Redial text box are discarded, and your original speed-dial number appears with your current Dialing properties applied to it.

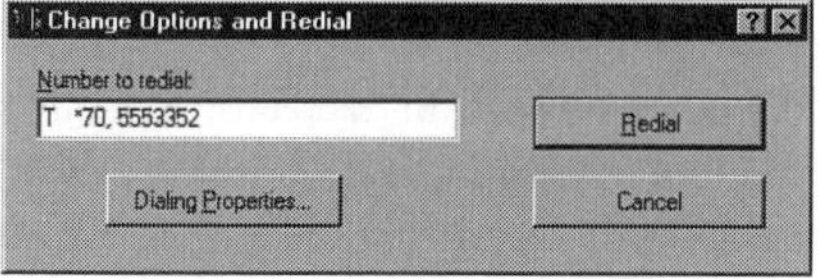

FIG. 28.30
You can make a temporary change to a Phone Dialer number when dialing.

Using Complex Phone Number Sequences

The convenience of voice-mail has an annoying side effect: All those voice menus prompting you to "Press one to leave a message, Press two to talk with an operator" can drive you crazy and waste a lot of your time. Likewise, credit cards and various long-distance carriers have required us to use dozens of numbers and procedures to make connections. A few built-in extras in your modem can handle things such as credit-card dialing, long-distance service connections, and navigation through many voice-mail hierarchies.

- To wait for the prompts within a voice-mail system, you can use the comma (,) to insert a two-second pause within your dialing sequence. Use more than one comma for a longer pause.
- If you need to wait for a secondary dial tone, use the letter **W**.
- If you need to wait for silence on the line, you can insert an @ sign.
- If you are making a credit-card call and need to wait for the tone from your long-distance carrier, insert a dollar sign ($) followed by your card number.
- You can also use * and # characters within the phone number to make those voice-mail menu selections.

For example, let's say you want to make a personal long-distance call from your office and charge it to your AT&T calling card. You know that your company's long-distance carrier is MCI, so you'll have to access the AT&T network to get the cheapest rates. Here's how to build your Phone Dialer sequence:

1. Type a **9** followed by a **W** to access the outside line, and wait for the dial tone.
2. Type the AT&T network access code: **10"ATT"** followed by a zero (**0**) to start the credit-card call.
3. Type the phone number you're trying to reach, such as **(205)-555-3161**.
4. To wait for AT&T to give their signal for you to enter your calling card number, type **$**.
5. Type in your credit-card number, such as **314-555-222-4321**.

Putting all these pieces of your dialing sequence together, it would read:

9W10"ATT"0(205)-555-3161$314-555-222-4321

That would be a definite candidate for saving in the Phone Dialer!

Using the Phone Dialer Log

The Phone Dialer comes with a log in which it will keep a record of your outgoing and incoming calls (see Figure 28.31). Each time you connect a phone call, an entry is placed in this text file. You can cut, copy, and delete from this log using the Edit menu commands, and you can redial an entry in your Log by double-clicking it or by selecting Log, Dial.

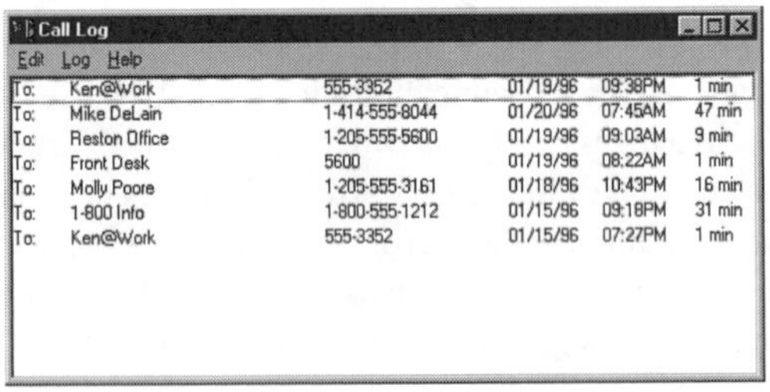

FIG. 28.31
Log entries can be used to redial or copy and paste into other documents.

Call Log

Edit Log Help

To:	Ken@Work	555-3352	01/19/96	09:38PM	1 min
To:	Mike DeLain	1-414-555-8044	01/20/96	07:45AM	47 min
To:	Reston Office	1-205-555-5600	01/19/96	09:03AM	9 min
To:	Front Desk	5600	01/19/96	08:22AM	1 min
To:	Molly Poore	1-205-555-3161	01/18/96	10:43PM	16 min
To:	1-800 Info	1-800-555-1212	01/15/96	09:18PM	31 min
To:	Ken@Work	555-3352	01/15/96	07:27PM	1 min

CHAPTER 29

Using WordPad and Paint

by Ron Person

In this chapter

Using WordPad

WordPad is a simple but powerful word processor that comes with Windows 95. WordPad offers many of the editing and formatting capabilities—such as cut, copy, and paste— commonly found in more advanced applications, along with the ability to share information with other applications and files using OLE.

WordPad is easy to use. The techniques and features you've learned to use in other word processors—such as how to select commands and how to enter, format, and print text—also work here. Because the margins, a font, and tabs are already set, you can actually begin a new WordPad document as soon as you start the application. WordPad's Help command can assist you if you run up against something new.

Starting WordPad

To start WordPad from the desktop, follow these steps:

1. Open the Start menu and choose Programs and then choose Accessories.
2. Choose WordPad. WordPad starts up and displays the WordPad window (see Figure 29.1).

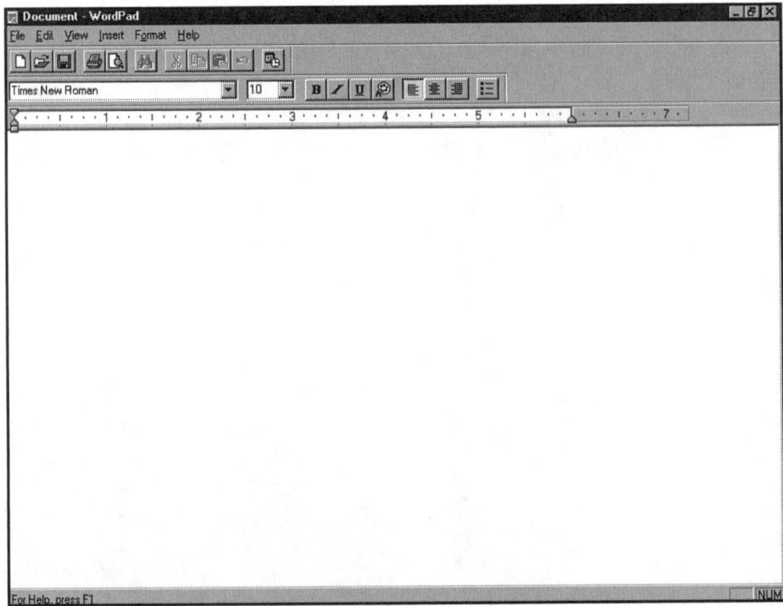

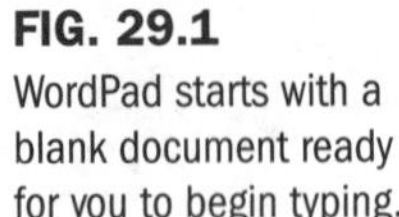

FIG. 29.1
WordPad starts with a blank document ready for you to begin typing.

Unlike more robust Windows applications, WordPad does not support MDI (Multiple Document Interface) and therefore can contain only one document at a time. When you open a new blank document, you will be asked if you want to save the current document.

Because WordPad is not as resource-hungry as "more robust Windows applications," you can open multiple instances of WordPad to edit multiple WordPad documents of different formats, including Word, ASCII, RTF, and Windows Write.

You can create new documents in any one of three formats in WordPad. When you choose the File, New command, the dialog box shown in Figure 29.2 appears. Select one of the following document types:

- **Word 6 Document.** This format can be opened and edited in Microsoft Word 6.0 or Microsoft Word 97. This is handy if you use WordPad on your laptop and Word 6 or Word 97 on your desktop. If you save a Word document from WordPad, you will lose advanced features such as columns that were created in Word.

CAUTION

If you're working in Word 97, and you open a document created in WordPad and then save it as a Word 97 document, you will not be able to reopen it in WordPad. If you want to be able to work with the document in WordPad, save the document as an .RTF file in Word 97.

- **Rich Text Document.** This format (RTF) is compatible with several word processing programs and includes fonts, tabs, and character formatting. RTF files are also used to create Windows Help files using the Microsoft Help compiler.
- **Text Document.** This format includes no text formatting and can be used in any word processing program. Use this format for creating DOS batch files.

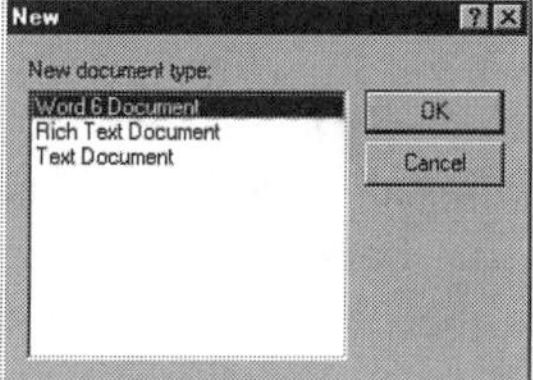

FIG. 29.2
You can create new documents in any one of three formats.

WordPad is an OLE 2-compliant application, so you can insert objects from other OLE applications into a WordPad document or insert all or part of a WordPad document into an OLE application. You can, for example, insert a graphic created in Windows Paint as an object into a WordPad document and then double-click the Paint object and edit the graphic in place. The WordPad menus and toolbars are replaced with the Paint menus and toolbars while you edit the object. Use the Insert, Object command or the drag-and-drop method for exchanging information with other OLE applications.

WordPad also is MAPI-enabled, which means you can use it with Microsoft Exchange to send mail and faxes. To mail or fax a document from WordPad, choose the File, Send command.

You can drag and drop files and folders from any common File Open dialog box (including WordPad's) into Explorer, onto the desktop, or into any OLE-compliant application such as Word 97. You can, for example, insert a WordPad document into a Word document by dragging it from the File Open dialog box in WordPad and dropping it into the Word document where you want it to be inserted.

TROUBLESHOOTING

When I try to save a file in WordPad with a non-default extension, WordPad appends the file name with the DOC extension. When you save a file with an extension that is not associated with an application in the Registry, WordPad appends the default DOC extension to the filename. In Notepad, the default extension TXT is appended to the filename. To avoid this, enclose the file name in quotation marks.

I am unable to print multiple or collated copies from WordPad. These features are unavailable in the File Print dialog box. WordPad does not support multiple or collated printing. Unless these features are supported with the printer driver for your printer, you cannot print multiple or collated copies from WordPad.

I selected a block of text in a WordPad document and tried to print just the selection, but the Selection option is unavailable in the File Print dialog box. Although this option is shown in the File Print dialog box, the capability to print selected text is not supported in WordPad. To work around this limitation, copy the text to a new WordPad document and print that document.

Using WordPad to Create and Edit System, Batch, and Text Files

WordPad is very useful for creating and editing TXT and system files (that is files with the extension BAT, SYS, INI, and so on), especially when the file in question is too large for Notepad. When you open a SYS, INI, BAT, or TXT file in WordPad, edit or view it, and then save it again, it is saved with its original file extension. This feature eliminates any worry about inadvertently saving a system file with the wrong extension, as can happen in a regular word processing program. And, WordPad provides more features (such as the replace command) for editing your files than does Notepad.

To create a new text file in WordPad, choose File, New and select Text Document in the New dialog box. When you save the document, it is given the TXT extension automatically. If necessary, change the extension, for example, to BAT for a DOS batch file.

Create a shortcut for WordPad in the SendTo folder so you can quickly open any file with WordPad from Explorer or a folder window.

▶ **See** "Adding Items to the Send To Menu," **p. 770**

You can change the association for TXT files so that they open in WordPad instead of Notepad when you double-click them or choose Open in the context menu in Explorer or My Computer. To change the association, follow these steps:

1. Choose View, Options in Explorer or My Computer and select the File Types tab.
2. Select Text Document from the Registered File Types list.
3. Choose Edit, select open in the Actions list of the Edit File Type dialog box and choose Edit.
4. Choose the Browse button and locate and select WORDPAD.EXE, which is located in the Program Files\Accessories folder.
5. Choose OK and make sure that .txt is selected in the Default Extension for Content list.
6. Choose Close twice.

Creating Post-It Notes on Your Desktop

Because WordPad is an OLE 2-compliant application, you can drag and drop selected portions of a WordPad document into other OLE applications or onto the desktop. When you drag a selection onto the desktop, you create a scrap; double-click the icon for the scrap, and WordPad opens up and displays the information in the scrap. You can use these scraps as electronic Post-it notes; bits of information you might otherwise lose track of, secured to your desktop.

If you create desktop notes frequently, for example, while on the phone, you can add WordPad to your StartUp folder so that it is immediately available or simply create a shortcut on the desktop to WordPad.

To create a note on your desktop, follow these steps:

1. Open WordPad and create the note.
2. Select the note and drag and drop it on the desktop. The scrap appears as a desktop icon, labeled with the first few words of the note. The data is saved as a file in the desktop folder.

You can rename the scrap. Note that you don't have to save the note in WordPad. Whenever you double-click the scrap icon, the note is opened in WordPad. If you make changes, however, you do need to save the changes because the scrap file isn't saved automatically.

If a Word for Windows file will not open, try opening it in WordPad. If it opens, you may see symbols and characters you do not recognize. Start a new instance of Word for Windows and open a blank document. Base this new document on the same template as the document that would not open. Now return to WordPad and copy the entire document. Switch to the blank document in Word for Windows and paste. Reapply paragraph styles as necessary. WordPad seems to be able to open documents that contain file errors that make Word balk.

Using Windows Paint

Paint is simple and easy to use, but it also may be as powerful a graphics application as you will ever need. You can use your creations in other Windows applications, such as WordPad or Word for Windows.

Here are some of the graphic effects you can create with Paint:

- Lines in many widths, shades, and colors
- Brush strokes in a variety of styles, widths, shades, and colors
- Unfilled or filled shapes with shades or colors
- Text in many sizes, styles, and colors
- Special effects such as rotating, tilting, and inverting

Because Paint is a bitmap graphics application, the shapes you create are painted on screen in one layer. Although you can't layer objects, you can move, flip, and tilt them. You also can change the color of your painting, or erase it completely and paint something new.

Starting Windows Paint

To start Paint, Click Start, Programs, Accessories, Paint. Paint starts up and opens a new, empty Paint file (see Figure 29.3).

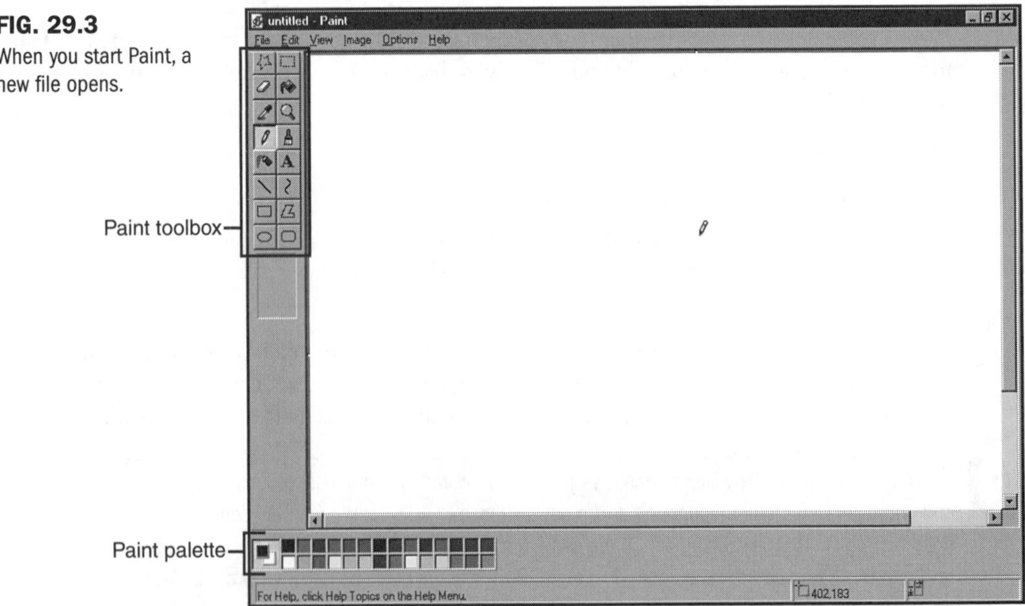

FIG. 29.3
When you start Paint, a new file opens.

To open a previously saved Paint file, choose File, Open. Select the file from the Open dialog box.

Selecting Tools and Colors

To paint, draw, fill, color or shade, write, and edit in Paint, you first must select the appropriate tool and shade or color. Figure 29.4 shows the individual tools in the toolbox located on the left side of the screen.

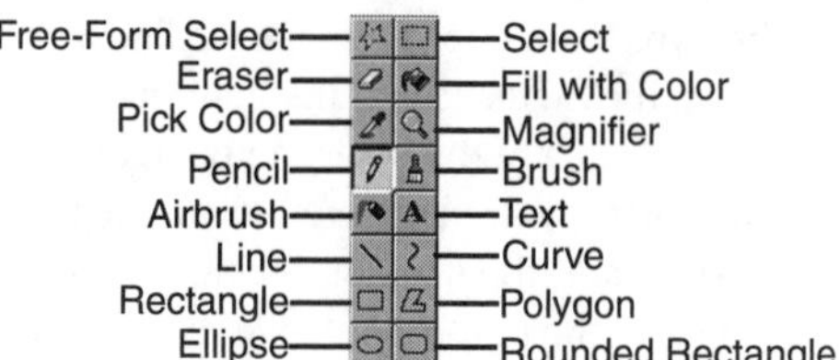

FIG. 29.4 The Paint toolbox provides the tools you need to create and modify a picture.

The palette offers two choices: foreground and background shade or color. At the left end of the palette (see Figure 29.5) is a box overlaying a box. The *top* box is the *foreground* color; the *bottom* box is the *background* color. The color you use depends on which mouse button you use to draw lines, brush strokes, and shapes. The left mouse button draws with the foreground color; the right mouse button draws with the background color. For example, when you draw a shaded box with the left mouse button, the foreground color borders the box and the background color fills the box. If you draw with the right mouse button, the foreground and background colors are reversed. (Drawing is discussed in the next section, "Using the Paint Toolbox.")

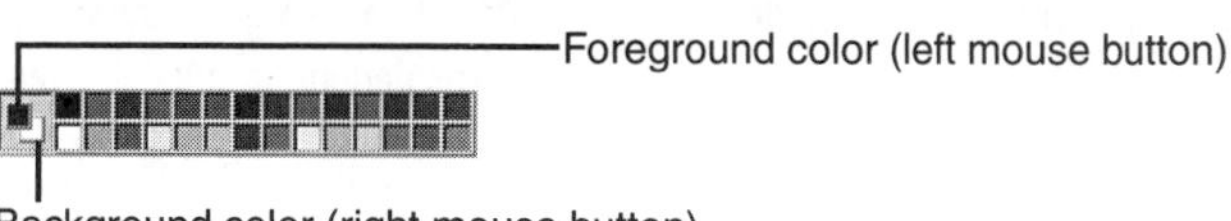

FIG. 29.5 Choose foreground and background colors from the Paint palette.

To select a tool or color, position the pointer on the tool or foreground color that you want and click the left mouse button. To select a background color, point to the color you want and click the right mouse button. You must use the left button when selecting a tool—the right mouse button can't be used to select a tool.

Using the Paint Toolbox

The Paint toolbox includes tools for selecting areas, airbrushing, typing text, erasing, filling, brushing, drawing curves or straight lines, and drawing filled or unfilled shapes. Most of the tools operate using a similar process, as described in the following steps.

To draw with the tools in the Paint toolbox, follow these steps:

1. Click to select the tool you want to use.
2. Position the pointer where you want to begin drawing, then press and hold down the mouse button as you draw with the mouse.
3. Release the mouse button to stop drawing.

Three exceptions to this process are:

- The Text tool, that you first click to select the text location, then type the text.
- The Paint Fill tool, which works by pointing and clicking.
- The Curve tool, which works by clicking, dragging, and clicking.

Aligning Drawn Objects When you want lines or shapes to line up accurately on screen, refer to the cursor position indicators in the Status Bar at the bottom of Paint's window. The two numbers that display tell you the position of the insertion point or drawing tool on screen. The position is given in X, Y coordinates, measured in pixels, from the top left corner of the painting. The left number is the X-coordinate (the position relative to the left edge of the painting); the right number is the Y-coordinate (the position relative to the top of the painting). If the numbers in the Cursor Position window read *42, 100*, for example, the cursor is 42 pixels from the left edge of the painting and 100 pixels down from the top of the painting.

Whichever tool you use, Edit, Undo is a useful ally. Use it to undo your most recent action. Undo undoes up to the last three actions. Just continue to select Undo to undo the number of actions you desire.

TROUBLESHOOTING

When I select the Undo command to undo a procedure I am in the middle of completing, the current procedure as well as the previous action are reversed. This is a bug in Paint. If you don't complete an action and you try to undo it, the previous action, as well as the current, incomplete action will be undone. You can reverse the action that was undone by choosing the Edit, Repeat command.

Several tools, including the Selection and Shape tools, use the right mouse button to undo. To cancel the shape you're currently drawing, click the right mouse button *before* you release the left mouse button.

The following sections describe how to use each of the toolbox tools.

Selecting a Free-Form Area The Free-Form Select tool enables you to select an area by drawing a free-form boundary. Click the Free-Form Select tool, then select either the Transparent (doesn't include the background) or Opaque (does include the background) tool at the bottom of the toolbox. Draw any shape to enclose an area of the drawing. If you make a mistake while using the Free-Form Select tool, click the left mouse button outside the cutout area to cancel the cutout and try again. Once enclosed, an area can be moved, cut, or copied (and then pasted), resized, tilted, flipped, or inverted with the Edit menu commands. If you cut an area, the selected background color shows the color the cleared area will be. With an area selected, press Delete to delete it from the picture.

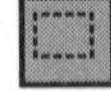

Selecting a Rectangular Area The Select tool enables you to select an area by dragging a rectangular box. Follow the instructions for the Free-Form Select tool in the previous section to use this tool.

Erasing Parts of Your Picture The Eraser tool erases as you drag it over your picture, just like an eraser on a chalkboard. Click the Eraser tool and then select the eraser size from the bottom of the toolbox. Drag across the picture with the left mouse button pressed to erase.

The selected background color shows the color the erased area will be. Choose Edit, Undo if you want to restore what you have erased.

Filling an Area with Color The Fill With Color tool fills in a shape. Click the Fill With Color tool and select foreground and background colors from the palette. Position the pointed tip of the Fill With Color tool inside the shape that you want to fill. Click the left mouse button to fill with the foreground color, or the right mouse button to fill with the background color.

You can use the Options, Edit Colors command to create a custom color palette from Paint's 48 colors or from colors you define by choosing the Define Custom Colors button in the Edit Colors dialog box.

TROUBLESHOOTING

I created a custom color palette, but when I try to use the colors in this palette to edit a 256-color bitmap, different colors than those I selected from the palette appear in the picture. This is a known bug in Paint with no current workaround. You have to use the standard color palette to edit 256-color bitmaps.

Picking Up a Color from the Drawing The Pick Color tool picks up the color on which you click for use in the current tool. To pick up the color of the spot where you click, click the Pick Color tool and then click anywhere in the painting. You can resume using the previous tool or select another tool and paint with the new color.

Magnifying the View of the Drawing The Magnifier tool magnifies the view of the drawing. Click the Magnifier tool and then select a magnification value at the bottom of the toolbox (1x, 2x, 6x, or 8x). Position the rectangle over the area you want to enlarge and click the left mouse button. You can work with the individual pixels that make up the painting. You can use any of the tools in the magnified view.

Drawing a Free-Form Line The Pencil tool draws a one pixel-wide, free-form line in the currently selected color. Draw with the left mouse button pressed to use the foreground color; draw with the right mouse button pressed to draw with the background color.

Painting with a Brush The Brush tool provides a selection of brush shapes with which you can paint lines of various widths and shapes. Click the Brush tool button and select from the brush shapes that display at the bottom of the toolbox. Paint with the left mouse button pressed to use the foreground color; paint with the right mouse button pressed to use the background color.

Painting with an Airbrush The Airbrush tool paints with a mist of color; the more densely you spray, the heavier your coverage. Click the Airbrush tool and select from the sprayer sizes that display at the bottom of the toolbox. Select a color from the Color palette: the left mouse button sprays with the foreground color; the right mouse button sprays with the background color. Hold the tool in one position longer to spray more densely.

Adding Text to a Picture Use the Text tool to add text to your painting. Click the Text tool and, in the area below the toolbox, select Opaque (the background color fills the text box behind the text) or Transparent (the picture appears behind the text). Next, in the picture area, drag to determine the size of the text box. Choose View, Text Toolbar to turn on display of the Font toolbar (only required the first time you use the Text tool). Select a font, point size, and bold, italic, or underline options. Click in the text box and type. Use the limited set of editing tools, including word-wrap and Backspace. Text appears in the foreground color.

If your painting includes a lot of text, type the text in Word or WordPad, select and copy it, and then paste it into Paint.

TROUBLESHOOTING

The Text Toolbar is not available from the View menu. You must click the Text tool and drag a text area before the Text Toolbar is available from the View menu.

An error message appears saying that I need to resize the text box. The text box isn't large enough to hold the text you are pasting into it. Enlarge the box and try again.

I was in the middle of typing text into a Paint picture and I opened Help. The text disappeared and did not reappear when I closed Help. There are a few problems that occur when you open Help in Paint:

- If you open Help when you are using the Text tool, the text disappears.
- If you have selected a portion of a picture with the Select or Free-Form Select tools, the selection is lost when you open Help.
- If you are using the Curve or Polygon tools to edit a picture, you will lose what you have created with the tools when you open Help.

One workaround for these problems is to save the picture before you open Help and reopen the saved image after you've closed Help. You also can click elsewhere in the picture or select another tool to set the element you were working on before you open Help. Selections made with the selection tools cannot be preserved when you open Help.

Drawing a Straight Line The Line tool draws a straight line. Click the Line tool and select a line width from the display at the bottom of the toolbox. To draw a straight line, click the mouse where you want to start the line and then drag the mouse. To cancel the line that you're drawing, click the right mouse button before you release the left mouse button. If you're drawing with the right mouse button, click the left button to cancel the line. To draw a line that is perfectly vertical, horizontal, or at a 45-degree angle, press and hold down the Shift key as you draw.

Drawing Curves The Curve tool draws a curve. To draw a curve, follow these steps:

1. Click the Curve tool.
2. Select a line width from the display at the bottom of the toolbox.

3. Draw a straight line and release the mouse button.
4. Click the left mouse button and drag away from the line to pull the line into a curve.
5. When you've achieved the shape you want, release the mouse button to complete the line. Repeat the process on the other side of the line to create an *s*-shaped curve.

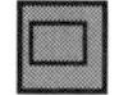

Drawing Rectangles and Squares The Rectangle tool draws a rectangle or square with different borders or fill color. Click the Rectangle tool and select Border Only, Border and Fill, or Fill Only from the bottom of the toolbox. To create the size box you want, press and hold down the mouse button and drag to that size. Release the mouse button when you have the size you want. Use the left mouse button to border with the foreground color and fill with the background color; use the right mouse button to border with the background color and fill with the foreground color. The size of the border is determined by the last line size you selected.

To draw a square, select the Rectangle tool, then press and hold down the Shift key as you draw.

Drawing Objects with Many Sides (Polygons) The Polygon tool draws a multi-sided shape. Each side on the shape is a straight line. To draw a polygon, follow these steps:

1. Click the Polygon tool and select Border Only, Border and Fill, or Fill Only from the bottom of the toolbox.
2. Click and drag to draw the first side of the polygon. As with the Line tool, you can use the Shift key to draw a straight line segment for the polygon.
3. Release the mouse button and click to draw other sides of the polygon.
4. Double-click at the next-to-last vertex point to finish and close the polygon to its first point.

Drawing Ellipses and Circles The Ellipse tool draws an *ellipse* (an oval) or circle. Click the Ellipse tool and select Border Only, Border and Fill, or Fill Only from the bottom of the toolbox. To draw a circle, press and hold down the Shift key as you draw.

Drawing Rectangles with Rounded Corners Use the Rounded Rectangle tool to draw a rectangle with rounded edges. Click the Rounded Rectangle tool and select Border Only, Border and Fill, or Fill Only from the bottom of the toolbox. Press and hold down the mouse button and drag to create the size rectangle you want. Release the mouse button when you have the size you want.

Editing a Painting

As you edit, be aware that completed objects cannot be edited, only erased or painted over and replaced. You can edit any object while creating it, but not after you complete the object. The method that you use to complete an object depends on the object. To complete a straight line, for example, you *release* the mouse button; to complete text, you *click* the mouse button or select another tool. You can cancel a line or curve before you complete it, for example, by clicking the opposite mouse button; you can change the appearance of text *before* you complete it by making a selection from the Text Toolbar.

TROUBLESHOOTING

I tried to clear my screen of the current contents, but the Image, Clear Image command is unavailable. The Clear Image command is unavailable if the Text tool is selected. Select any other tool and the command is available.

Moving a Selection

You can move an object or area on screen after you select it. (The object is still selected if you just pasted it.) Paint has several tricks for moving selections.

To move a selection, follow these steps:

1. Use one of the Select tools to select an object or area of the drawing. Select either Transparent (to leave the background showing) or Opaque (to hide the background). A dashed line encloses the selection.
2. Move the crosshair over the selection. The crosshair becomes an arrow.
3. Press and hold down the left mouse button to drag the selection to its new location. To copy the selection to a new location rather than moving it, hold down the Ctrl key as you drag the object to its new location.
4. Release the mouse button to place the selection, then click outside the selection to fix it in its new location.

Getting Different Views of the Painting You can zoom in to get a closer look at your painting or zoom out to see the whole page. Use either the View, Zoom command or the Magnifier tool.

The larger magnifications of the picture display the *pixels*, or tiny squares of color, which make up your painting. You can paint pixels in the selected foreground color by clicking the dots with the left mouse button and in the background color by clicking the right mouse button.

To zoom in for a close-up view of your painting, follow these steps:

1. Choose View, Zoom. Select Normal Size (Ctrl+Page Up), Large Size (Ctrl+Page Down), or Custom. If you select Custom, the View Zoom dialog box appears. Select 100%, 200%, 400%, 600%, or 800%.
2. Use the scroll bars to display the part of the painting you want to see.

To zoom back out to regular editing view, choose View, Zoom and select Normal Size or click the Magnifier tool and then click in the picture.

Select the area you want to flip, rotate, stretch, or skew. Place the pointer over it, and click the right mouse button to display a shortcut menu.

To use your painting or part of your painting as wallpaper, follow these steps:

1. Display the painting you want to use as wallpaper.
2. If you want to use only part of the painting on the desktop, select that part.
3. Choose File, Set as Wallpaper (Tiled) to repeat the painting as a pattern over the desktop, or Set as Wallpaper (Centered) to display the painting in the center of the desktop.

Saving Paint Files

When you save a Paint file, Paint assigns the extension .BMP to the file name and saves the file in Windows bitmap format.

To save a Paint file, click File, Save As. Type the name in the File Name text box. Click the Save As Type box to select one of the following file formats:

Format	**File Extension Assigned**
Monochrome Bitmap	BMP
16 Color Bitmap	BMP
256 Color Bitmap	BMP
24-bit Bitmap	BMP

Then click Save.

TROUBLESHOOTING

Many graphics files seem to use PCX format, but Paint won't save this format. Paint saves only with the BMP format. You can open PCX files with Paint, but if you want to make any changes and save the file again, you will have to save it as a BMP file. One way you can work around this is to use Microsoft Paintbrush from Windows 3.1 within Windows 95. You can copy the files PBRUSH.EXE, PBRUSH.DLL, PBRUSH.HLP, and PBRUSHX.CDX from the WINDOWS directory in Windows 3.1 into a Windows 95 folder. You can create a new folder within the PROGRAMS folder called Paintbrush. With Paintbrush, you can open and save PCX files.

You may want to convert your PCX files to BMP format. Microsoft has a graphics converter available and there are many free converters available through bulletin board services.

CHAPTER 30

Using Calculator, Calendar, and Other Accessories

by Ron Person

In this chapter

Calculating with Calculator

Like a calculator you keep in a desk drawer, the Windows Calculator is small but saves you time (and mistakes) by performing all the calculations common to a standard calculator. The Windows Calculator, however, has added advantages: You can keep this calculator on screen alongside other applications, and you can copy numbers between the Calculator and other applications.

The Standard Windows Calculator, shown in Figure 30.1, works so much like a pocket calculator that you need little help getting started. The Calculator's ***keypad***, the on-screen representation, contains familiar number ***keys***, along with memory and simple math keys. A display window just above the keypad shows the numbers you enter and the results of calculations. If your computational needs are more advanced, you can choose a different view of the Calculator, the Scientific view (see Figure 30.2).

FIG. 30.1
The Standard Calculator.

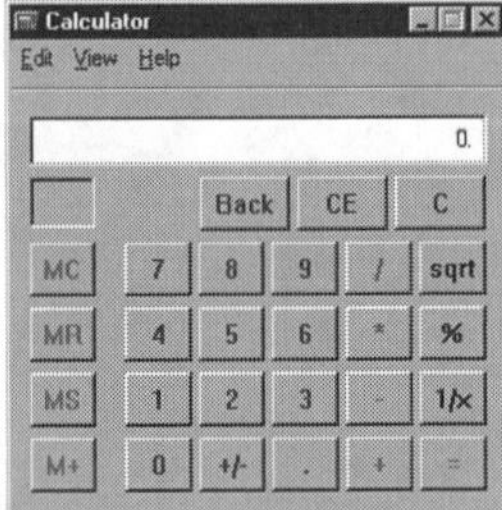

FIG. 30.2
The Scientific Calculator.

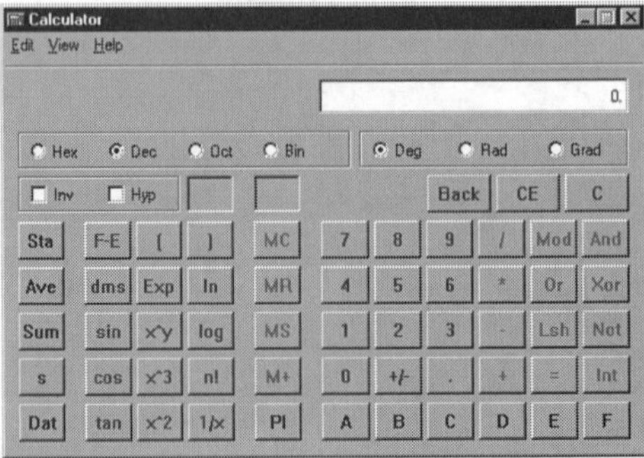

To display the Calculator, open the Start menu and click Programs and then click Accessories. Finally, click Calculator. The Calculator opens in the same view (Standard or Scientific) that was displayed the last time the Calculator was used.

To close the Calculator, click the Close button in the title bar. If you use the Calculator frequently, however, don't close it; click the Minimize button to minimize the Calculator to a button on the taskbar.

The Calculator has only three menus: Edit, View, and Help. The Edit menu contains two simple commands for copying and pasting; the View menu switches between the Standard and Scientific views; and the Help menu is the same as in all Windows accessories.

Operating the Calculator

To use the Calculator with the mouse, just click the appropriate numbers and sign keys like you would press buttons on a desk calculator. Numbers appear in the display window as you select them, and the results appear after the calculations are performed.

To enter numbers from the keyboard, use either the numbers across the top of the keyboard, or those on the numeric keypad (you first must press the NumLock key if the NumLock feature is not enabled). To calculate, press the keys on the keyboard that match the Calculator keys. Table 30.1 shows the Calculator keys for the keyboard.

Table 30.1 Keyboard Keys for Using the Calculator

Calculator Key	Function	Keyboard Key
MC	Clear memory	Ctrl+L
MR	Display memory	Ctrl+R
M+	Add to memory	Ctrl+P
MS	Store value in memory	Ctrl+M
CE	Delete displayed value	Del
Back	Delete last digit in displayed value	Backspace
+/–	Change sign	F9
/	Divide	/
*	Multiply	*
–	Subtract	–
+	Add	+
sqrt	Square root	@
%	Percent	%
1/x	Calculate reciprocal	R
C	Clear	Esc
=	Equals	= or Enter

NOTE To calculate a percentage, treat the % key like an equal sign. For example, to calculate 15 percent of 80, type **80*15%**. After you press the % key, the Calculator displays the result of "12."

You can use the Calculator's memory to total the results of several calculations. The memory holds a single number, which starts as zero; you can add to, display, or clear this number, or you can store another number in memory.

Copying Numbers Between the Calculator and Other Applications

When working with many numbers or complex numbers, you make fewer mistakes if you copy the Calculator results into other applications rather than retyping the result. To copy a number from the Calculator into another application, follow these steps:

1. In the Calculator display window, perform the math calculations required to display the number.
2. Choose Edit, Copy.
3. Activate the application you want to receive the calculated number.
4. Position the insertion point in the newly opened application where you want the number copied.
5. From the newly opened application, choose Edit, Paste.

You can also copy and paste a number from another application into the Calculator, perform calculations with the number, and then copy the result back into the application. A number pasted in the Calculator erases the number currently shown in the display window.

To copy a number from another application into the Calculator, select the number in the application and choose Edit, Copy. Next, activate the Calculator and choose Edit, Paste.

If you paste a formula in the Calculator, you can click the equal (=) button to see the result. If you copy *5+5* from WordPad, for example, paste the calculation in the Calculator, and click the = key, the resulting number 10 appears. If you paste a function, such as @ for square root, the Calculator performs the function on the number displayed. If, for example, you copy @ from a letter in WordPad and paste it into Calculator while it is displaying the number 25, the result 5 appears.

Numbers and most operators (such as + and –) work fine when pasted in the Calculator display, but the Calculator interprets some characters as commands. Table 30.2 lists the characters that the Calculator interprets as commands.

Table 30.2 Calculator Command Characters

Character	Interpreted As
:c	Clears memory.
:e	Lets you enter scientific notation in decimal mode; also the number E in hexadecimal mode.
:m	Stores the current value in memory.
:p	Adds the displayed value to the number in memory.

Character	Interpreted As
:q	Clears the current calculation.
:r	Displays the value in memory.
\	Works like the Dat button (in the Scientific Calculator).

Using the Scientific Calculator

If you have ever written an equation wider than a sheet of paper, you're a good candidate for using the Scientific Calculator. The Scientific Calculator is a special view of the Calculator.

To display the Scientific Calculator, activate the Calculator and choose View, Scientific.

The Scientific Calculator works the same as the Standard Calculator, but adds many advanced functions. You can work in one of four number systems: hexadecimal, decimal, octal, or binary. You can perform statistical calculations, such as averages and statistical deviations. You can calculate sines, cosines, tangents, powers, logarithms, squares, and cubes. These specialized functions aren't described here but are well documented in the Calculator's Help command.

Using the Taskbar Clock

It's convenient to have a clock always on the screen, and Windows includes one in the taskbar. If yours isn't displayed, you can turn on the clock, adjust the time, and even select a time zone. You'll be surprised at how much control you have over that little clock (see Figure 30.3).

FIG. 30.3
The taskbar clock.

The following table describes the taskbar clock options:

Action	Result
Point to time	Displays the date.
Double-click the time	Displays the Date/Time Properties, where you can set the date and time or select a time zone.
Right-click the time, and then click Properties	Displays Taskbar Properties, where you can turn Show Clock on or off.

Using Notepad

Notepad is a miniature text editor. Just as you use a notepad on your desk, you can use Notepad to take notes on screen while working in other Windows applications. Notepad uses little memory and is useful for editing text that you want to copy into a Windows or DOS application that lacks editing capability.

Notepad retrieves and saves files in text format. This feature makes Notepad a convenient editor for creating and altering text-based files. Because Notepad stores files in text format, almost all word processing applications can retrieve Notepad's files.

Starting Notepad

To start Notepad, click Start, Programs, Accessories, and choose Notepad. Notepad starts up and displays a blank document in the Notepad window (see Figure 30.4). You can begin typing.

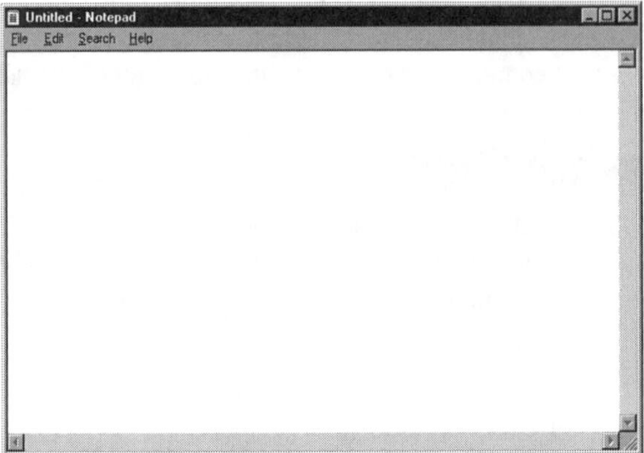

FIG. 30.4
The initial blank Notepad file is ready for text.

Working with Documents in Notepad

Unlike most word processing applications, Notepad doesn't, by default, wrap text to the following line. You must choose Edit, Word Wrap to activate this feature.

You can move the insertion point by using either the mouse or the keyboard. You select and edit text in Notepad the same way you select and edit text in WordPad.

Limited formatting is available from the File, Page Setup command. You can change margins and add a header or footer. You cannot format characters or paragraphs in any way, although you can use Tab, the Space Bar, and Backspace to align text. Tab stops are preset at every eight characters.

With Notepad's Edit commands, you can cut, copy, and move text from one place in a file to another. Text that you cut or copy is stored in the Clipboard. When you paste text, this text is copied from the Clipboard to the document at the insertion point.

▶ **See** "Using Simple Editing Techniques," **p. 618**

▶ **See** "Copying and Moving," **p. 619**

Creating a Time-Log File with Notepad

By typing a simple entry at the top of a Notepad document, **.LOG**, you can have Notepad enter the current time and date at the end of a document each time you open the file. This feature is convenient for taking phone messages or for calculating the time spent on a project. The text ".LOG" must be entered on the first line of the document and must be uppercase. As an alternative, you can choose Edit, Time/Date or press F5 to insert the current time and date at the insertion point.

Notepad can open binary files, which WordPad cannot. Although most of what you see when you open binary files is unreadable, you can sometimes find helpful information in the header of the binary file. This is a good reason to keep Notepad on your computer, even if WordPad is more suitable for most tasks.

Inserting Symbols with Character Map

The Character Map accessory gives you access to symbol fonts and ANSI characters. *ANSI characters* are the regular character set that you see on the keyboard and more than a hundred other characters, including a copyright symbol, a registered trademark symbol, and many foreign-language characters. One symbol font, Symbol, is included with most Windows applications. Other symbol fonts may be built into the printer. When you set up and indicate the model of the printer, font cartridges, and so on, the printer tells Windows what symbol fonts are available. (Printer fonts appear in Character Map only when they include a matching screen font.)

▶ **See** "Installing and Deleting Fonts," **p. 158**

To start Character Map, open the Start menu and click Programs, then click Accessories. Finally, click Character Map. You are presented with the Character Map window shown in Figure 30.5.

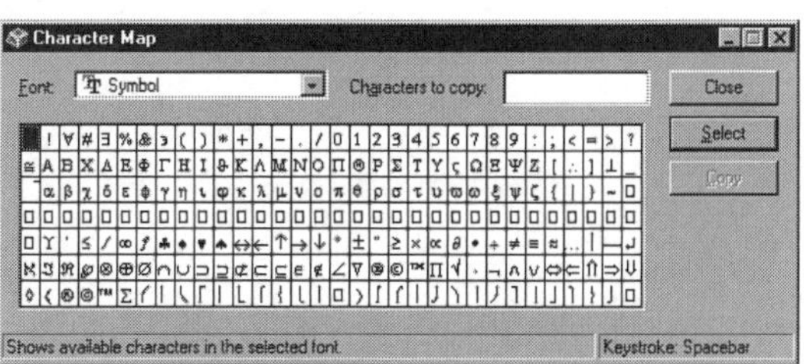

FIG. 30.5
Use Character Map to insert any of hundreds of special characters and symbols into a document.

The Character Map window includes a drop-down Font list box from which you can select any of the available fonts on the system. After you select a font, the characters and symbols for this font appear in the Character Map table. Each set of fonts may have different symbols. Some fonts, such as Symbol and Zapf Dingbats, contain nothing but symbols and special characters.

To insert a character in a Windows application from the Character Map, follow these steps:

1. Start the Character Map accessory.
2. Select the font you want to use from the Font list.
3. View an enlarged character by clicking and holding down the mouse button on a character or by pressing the arrow keys to move the selection box over a character.
4. Double-click the character you want to insert or click the Select button to place the current character in the Characters to Copy text box.
5. Repeat steps 2 through 4 to select as many characters as you want.
6. Click the Copy button to copy to the Clipboard the characters you've selected.
7. Open or switch to the application to which you want to copy the characters.
8. Place the insertion point where you want to insert the characters and open the Edit menu and choose Paste (Ctrl+V).

If the characters don't appear as they did in Character Map, you may need to reselect the characters and change the font to the same font in which the character originally appeared in the Character Map.

If you plan to use Character Map frequently, you may want to create a shortcut for this application so that you can start Character Map directly from the desktop.

PART VI

Customizing Windows 95 and Sharing Data Effectively

CHAPTER 31

Customizing the Taskbar and Start Menu

by Paul Sanna and Ron Person

In this chapter

Customizing the Taskbar

The more you use Windows, the more you appreciate its customization options. You can save time by setting features so that they normally appear or act in the way you prefer. You can change the look and feel of almost every component of Windows, from the taskbar, Start menu, and desktop to the date and time formats, language used, keyboards, mouse settings, and more. After you use Windows 95 for a while, you probably will want to modify at least some Windows 95 features to suit your personal taste and needs.

Two features of Windows 95 that you might want to customize right away are the taskbar and Start menu. These are features that you use constantly in Windows, so it makes sense that they should look and work the way you want. For example, you can customize your taskbar to appear only when you want it to, giving your applications more room onscreen. You can also position the taskbar in locations other than at the bottom of the screen. If you frequently use the same applications, you can add them to the Start menu so they are easy to find.

In this chapter, you will learn how to do all these things and more. In the following two chapters, you will learn more about customizing the desktop, screen colors, sounds, and many other aspects of Windows.

In Chapter 14, "Managing Files Using Web View," you learned how to use the taskbar to navigate between your open applications. The taskbar is one of the most useful new features in Windows 95; it's a tool you will use constantly throughout the day. When you first start Windows 95, the taskbar is located at the bottom of the screen and remains visible all the time—even when you maximize an application. In this section, you learn how you can customize the taskbar to give it the look and feel that best suits your needs and preferences.

Resizing the Taskbar

You can change the size of the taskbar to accommodate a large number of buttons or to make it easier to read the full description written on a button. To resize the taskbar, follow these steps:

1. Point to the edge of the taskbar. The pointer becomes a double-pointing arrow.
2. Hold down the left mouse button and drag to the size you want.

The taskbar resizes in full button widths. If the taskbar is horizontal against the top or bottom of the screen, you can change its height. If the taskbar is positioned vertically against a side, you can change its width.

Moving the Taskbar

You can position the taskbar horizontally along the top or bottom (default) of the desktop or vertically along the side of the desktop (see Figure 31.1). To reposition the taskbar, point to a position on the taskbar where no button appears, hold down the left mouse button, and drag to the edge of the screen where you want to position the taskbar. A shaded line indicates the new position of the taskbar. Release the mouse button to place the taskbar.

When the taskbar is positioned at the side of the desktop, it can be so wide that you don't have enough space to work. If so, you can drag the edge of the taskbar to give it a new width. When the taskbar is against a side, you can change its width in pixel increments, not just in full button widths.

FIG. 31.1
Reposition the taskbar for your convenience.

Using the Taskbar Menu

As in other Windows screen areas, you can click the right mouse button in a gray area of the taskbar to display a shortcut menu (see Figure 31.2). Use the taskbar menu to rearrange windows on the desktop, to reduce applications to buttons, and to change the properties of the taskbar.

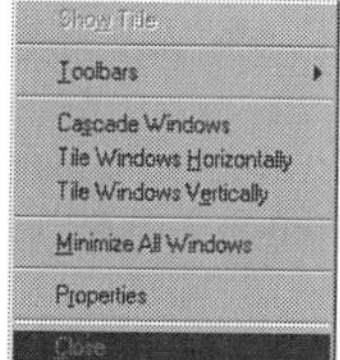

FIG. 31.2
Right-click the gray area of the taskbar to display the shortcut menu.

The following table describes each of the commands on the taskbar menu.

Command	Description
Cascade	Displays windows one over the other from left to right, top to bottom
Tile Horizontally	Displays windows top to bottom without overlapping
Tile Vertically	Displays windows left to right without overlapping
Minimize All Windows	Reduces all open windows to buttons on the taskbar
Properties	Displays the Taskbar Properties sheet, where you can change the Start menu or taskbar options

Changing the Taskbar Options

You can hide or display the taskbar by using the Taskbar Properties sheet. Figure 31.3 shows the commands available from the Taskbar Options tab. You also can turn the clock area of the taskbar on and off.

To change taskbar properties, follow these steps:

1. Point to a position on the taskbar where no button appears, either below or between buttons, and right-click. Choose Properties.

   Or, open the Start menu and choose Settings, Taskbar.
2. Click the Taskbar Options tab.
3. Select or deselect a check box to turn an item on or off. The options are explained in Table 31.1.
4. Click OK.

Table 31.1 Options on the Taskbar Options Tab

Option	Description
Always on Top	Displays the taskbar over all open windows.
Auto Hide	Hides the taskbar to make more space available on your desktop and in application windows. To see the taskbar, move your mouse pointer to the bottom of the screen (or where the taskbar is if you moved it) and the taskbar reappears. When you move the pointer away, the taskbar disappears again.
Show Small Icons in Start Menu	Displays the Start menu with small icons and without the Windows banner. This enables you to see more of what's onscreen while in the Start menu.
Show Clock	Hides or displays the clock in one corner of the taskbar.

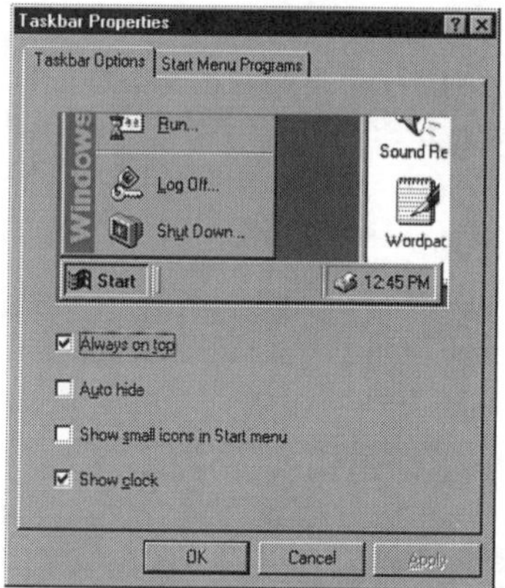

FIG. 31.3
Use the Taskbar Properties sheet to customize the taskbar.

When you select the Auto Hide option, the taskbar is reduced to a gray line at the edge of the screen. When you move the mouse pointer over this line, the taskbar reappears. You can modify the width of this line by right-clicking the desktop and choosing Properties. Select the Appearance tab, and select Active Windows Border from the Item list. Modify the value in the Size text box to the desired width and choose OK. Note that this affects the border width of your application windows as well.

Working with Taskbar Toolbars

When you use Internet Explorer 4 with Windows 95, functionality of the taskbar is extended somewhat. To provide quick access to related applications, you can add sets of shortcuts to the taskbar. These sets of shortcuts are labeled as toolbars. The shortcuts appear as small buttons on the taskbar, grouped with the other buttons in the toolbar. You can display any of the four toolbars that are provided with Internet Explorer 4 at the same time if you want, or you can build and use your own. Figure 31.4 shows the Quick Launch toolbar provided with Internet Explorer 4. In this section, you learn how to select toolbars to display on the taskbar, as well as how to build your own.

Displaying a Taskbar Toolbar

Displaying a taskbar toolbar is no more difficult than any of the taskbar tasks explained in this chapter so far. You display a taskbar toolbar by right-clicking a blank spot on the taskbar and choosing Toolbars and then the toolbar you want from the menu that appears. If you create a new taskbar toolbar, that toolbar appears on the list with those provided by Microsoft. Here is a description of the four toolbars shipped with Internet Explorer 4:

Toolbars	Description
Quick Launch	Shows links to Internet Explorer 4 and Outlook Express; toggles clean display of the desktop by minimizing all applications to the taskbar; and toggles display of the Active Channels page.
Desktop	Shows all of the shortcuts on the Windows 95 desktop.
Links	Shows contents of the Links menu displayed in Internet Explorer.
Address	Toggles display of the URL address drop-down list.

FIG. 31.4
Internet Explorer 4 provides a toolbar that gives quick access to the most useful Internet applications.

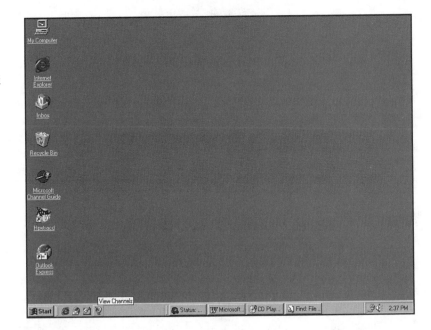

Creating a Taskbar Toolbar

It's easy to create a new toolbar to display on the taskbar. Part of understanding how to do so, however, requires knowing the secret behind toolbars. Each toolbar is nothing more than the display of all the contents of any folder on your computer. For example, the Quick Launch toolbar simply displays the contents of the \WIN95\Application Data\Microsoft\Internet Explorer\Quick Launch folder.

When you create a toolbar for display on the taskbar, you specify a folder on your system. This simplicity comes with a caveat, however; you must use care in selecting a folder, keeping in mind that if you select a folder with many items, such as the Windows 95 folder, every item in that folder will appear on the toolbar.

To create a new taskbar toolbar, follow these steps:

1. Right-click a blank spot on the taskbar and choose Toolbars, New Toolbar. The New Toolbar dialog box appears (see Figure 31.5.)

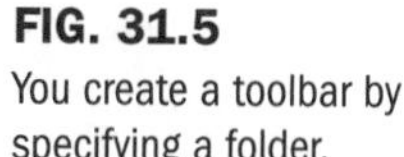

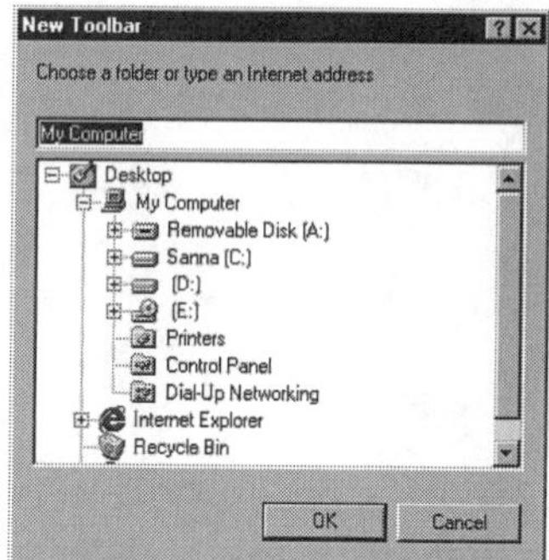

FIG. 31.5
You create a toolbar by specifying a folder.

2. Choose the folder that contains the items you want to display on the toolbar and choose OK. The toolbar appears on the taskbar.

Sometimes folders created by applications when they are installed include files that you do not want displayed on a taskbar toolbar. To display just the items you want on a taskbar toolbar, create a new folder and then copy shortcuts to the items you want to appear on the toolbar to that folder. This way, when you create a toolbar based on that folder, only shortcuts you copied appear on the toolbar.

Customizing the Start Menu

You can customize the contents of the Start menu. You can add a list of applications you use frequently and then launch those applications directly from the Start menu. By adding programs to the Start menu, you avoid having to display additional menus.

To quickly add a program to the highest level of the Start menu, drag the program's file from the Explorer or My Computer window and drop it on the Start button.

Adding and Removing Programs in the Start Menu

To add a program to the Start menu, follow these steps.

1. Right-click a gray area between buttons on the taskbar. Choose Properties.

   Or open the Start menu and choose Settings, Taskbar.
2. Click the Start Menu Programs tab (see Figure 31.6).
3. Click the Add button to display the Create Shortcut dialog box shown in Figure 31.7.
4. Click the Browse button to display the Browse dialog box. This dialog box looks very similar to an Open File dialog box.

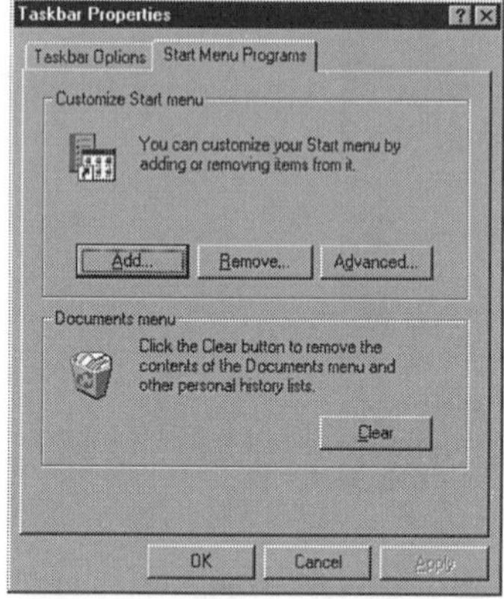

FIG. 31.6
The Start Menu Programs tab enables you to add programs to the Start menu.

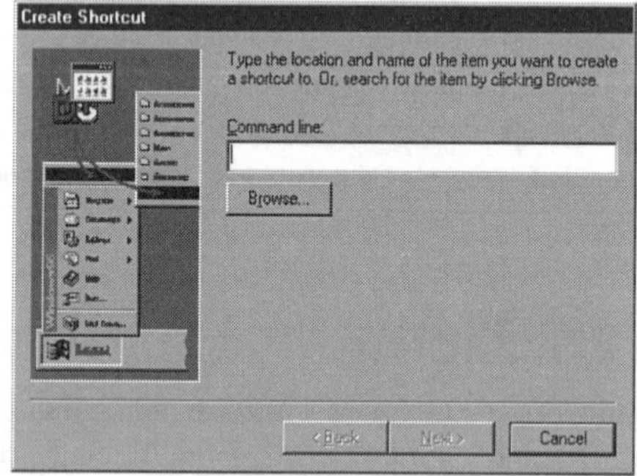

FIG. 31.7
In the Create Shortcut dialog box, type or select the file of the program you want to add to the Start menu.

5. Find and click the file for the program or document you want to add to the Start menu. Choose the Open button after you select the file.

   You can limit the displayed files to program files by selecting Programs from the Files of Type list at the bottom of the dialog box. For example, if you want to start Excel, open the Program Files folder, open the Microsoft Office folder, and finally, open the Office folder. Find and click EXCEL.EXE in the Office folder. Most program files use an EXE extension.

Adding a document's file to the Start menu enables you to open the document in its related application, assuming the document type is registered. See "Customizing the Shortcut (Right-Click) Menu," later in this chapter.

6. Click the Next button to display the Select Program Folder dialog box (see Figure 31.8).
7. Select the folder that corresponds to the location on the Start menu where you want the program to appear. Choose Next.

   For example, if you want the program you selected to appear at the top of the Start menu, select the Start Menu folder. If you want the program to appear as an item on the Programs menu, select the Programs folder.

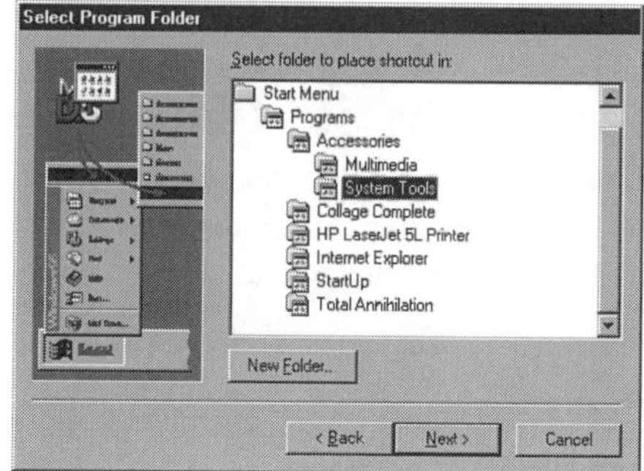

FIG. 31.8
You can position your document or application anywhere on the Start menu.

8. Type the name or words you want to appear on the Start menu in the Select a Name for the Shortcut text box. Choose Finish.

You can make it easy to launch the applications you added to the top of the Start menu by using the keyboard. Right-click the Start button and choose Open. Rename each application item, adding a number to the beginning of the name. To launch an application from the Start menu, press Ctrl+Esc to open the Start menu, and then type the number for the application you want to start.

To remove a program from the Start menu, you follow a similar process:

1. Display the Taskbar Properties sheet, as described earlier in this chapter.
2. Click the Start Menu Programs tab.
3. Click the Remove button to display the Remove Shortcuts/Folders dialog box shown in Figure 31.9.

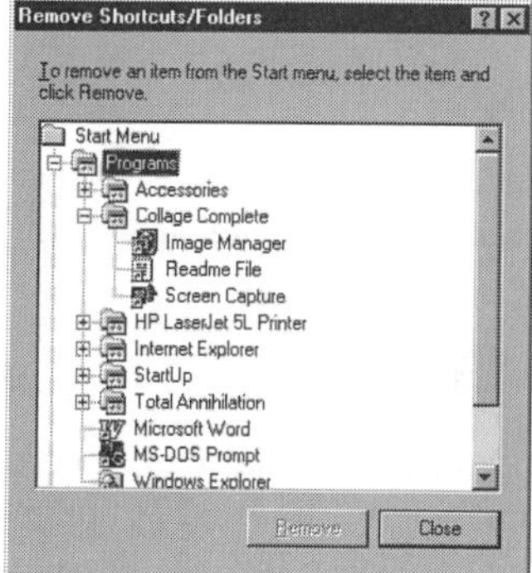

FIG. 31.9
You can easily remove any item from the Start menu by using the Remove Shortcuts/ Folders dialog box.

4. Select the shortcut or folder you want to remove from the Start menu.
5. Click the Remove button to remove the file or folder.
6. Remove additional items or choose Close. Choose OK when you return to the Taskbar Properties sheet.

▶ **See** "Starting from Shortcuts," **p. 230**

Clearing the Documents List in the Start Menu

The Start menu contains a Documents item that shows a list of recently used documents. At times, this list can become too long, or you might want to clear the list so documents are easier to find. To clear documents from the Documents menu, follow these steps:

1. Display the Taskbar Properties sheet.
2. Click the Start Menu Programs tab.
3. Click Clear in the Documents Menu area.
4. Choose OK.

Adding the Control Panel, Dial Up Network, and Printers Menus to the Start Menu

You can directly access all the items in the Control Panel by adding a special Control Panel folder to the Start Menu folder. To create this folder, follow these steps:

1. Right-click the Start button and choose Open. The Start Menu window appears.
2. Right-click in a blank area of the Start Menu window and choose New, Folder.
3. Name the folder Control Panel.

Now, when you click the Start button, you see Control Panel at the top of the Start menu. When you select Control Panel, a cascading menu of all the Control Panel items opens.

NOTE It might seem simpler to create a folder named Control Panel in the Start Menu folder, select all the items in the Control Panel window, and then drag and drop them into the new folder to create shortcuts. This works just fine, but the words `Shortcut to` will appear in front of each item. The previous method results in a cleaner looking menu. ■

You can create menus on the Start Menu for one other item using this method. For the Printers folder, create a folder in the Start Menu folder with the name "Printers."

Customizing the Send To Menu

The Send To menu is a very useful tool for using the mouse to move, open, print, fax, and perform many other actions with files and folders. The Send To command is instantly available by right-clicking a file or folder in the Explorer, in a folder window, or on the desktop.

Adding Items to the Send To Menu

When you first start Windows 95, there are a few standard items that appear in the Send To menu, such as your floppy disk drive and My Briefcase (if you installed the Briefcase).

However, you can add many other items to the Send To folder, including folders, printers, zip drives, applications, and so on.

To add items to the Send To menu, follow these steps:

1. Open the Send To folder, which is in the Windows folder.
2. Open the folder containing the item you want to add to the Send To menu.
3. Drag and drop the item into the Send To folder by using the right mouse button.

   You can also drag items from the desktop into the Send To folder.
4. Click Create Shortcut(s) Here.
5. Edit the filename to remove the words "Shortcut to."
6. Repeat steps 2–5 for any other items you want to add to the Send To menu.

Some suggestions for items you can add to the Send To menu include:

- Folders, for moving files to commonly used folders
- External drives, such as a Zip drive
- Printers
- Applications for opening a file (WordPad, for example)

If you have more than one printer, add each one to the Send To menu. That way, you can choose what printer to use to print a file. Or if you set up different configurations for the same printer (such as high and low resolution modes), include both of them in the Send To menu.

Figure 31.10 shows a Send To menu with several items that have been added.

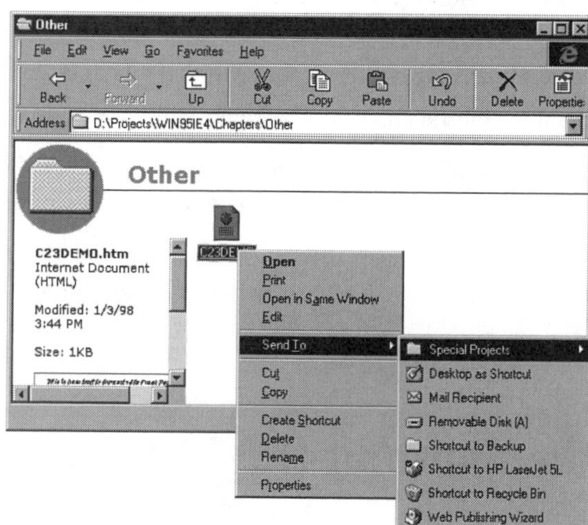

FIG. 31.10
You can add many items to the Send To menu to speed up processing your files.

NOTE When you send a file to a folder on the same disk, the file is moved. If you send the file to a different disk, it is copied. Be careful not to move EXE files by using the Send To menu.

Add the Recycle Bin to the Send To menu to quickly delete a file or selection of files. One benefit of using the Send To menu to send files to the Recycle Bin is that you don't have to see the Confirm File Delete message box.

You can even add Send To to the Send To menu. Create a shortcut to the SendTo folder in the SendTo folder. Now, when you want to add an item to the Send To menu, right-click the item and choose Send To, SendTo.

Creating Submenus in the Send To Menu

If you routinely use the Send To menu to move files from folder to folder, you might want to create submenus of folders on the Send To menu. This keeps the main Send To menu from becoming cluttered with a long list of folders. By using this technique, you can categorize your folders, making it easier to find the folder to which you want to send a file. For example, you might create a folder named Book Chapters in the Send To folder that contains shortcuts to the folders you create for each chapter.

To create submenus on the Send To menu, follow these steps:

1. Create a new folder in the Send To folder and assign a name indicating what category of folders it will contain.

   Using the previous example, name the folder Book Chapters.

2. Open the new folder and create shortcuts to the destination folders that you want to appear in the submenu.

   In this example, you create shortcuts for each of the chapter folders.

   You might want to edit the names of the folders to remove the words `Shortcut to`.

Now, when you open the Send To menu and select the parent folder (Book Chapters), a submenu appears with a list of folders from which you can select to move your files (refer to Figure 31.10).

You can use this same procedure to create submenus for other items. If you have several printers, for example, you can create a Printers folder in the Send To folder and create shortcuts to each of the printers inside this folder.

Customizing the Shortcut (Right-Click) Menu

You can add or modify the commands on the shortcut menu that opens when you right-click a file in the Explorer, in a folder window, or on the desktop. You can do this by specifying the application(s) that will act on this type of file. For each application, you can specify different actions the application will take on, such as opening, printing, or running a macro with the file. Applications that have macro languages or startup switches can use those macros or startup switches to control what happens when you start the application by using the shortcut menu command.

There are many actions that can occur with a file type. When you double-click a file, the action that has been designated as the default action is executed. Usually, the default action is opening the file, but you can change the default to another action. In this section, you learn how to register a new file type (when the file type is not already registered) and how to customize the actions associated with a file type.

Registering a New File Type

Registering a file type is analogous to associating a file in Windows 3.1, although you now do a lot more than simply tell Windows with what application to open a file. You can associate multiple applications with one file type and specify several actions that can occur with a file type; for example, you can tell Windows to print the document or open a new document of the same type.

To register a new file type, follow these steps:

1. In the Explorer, choose View, Options.
2. Click the File Types tab of the Options dialog box (see Figure 31.11).

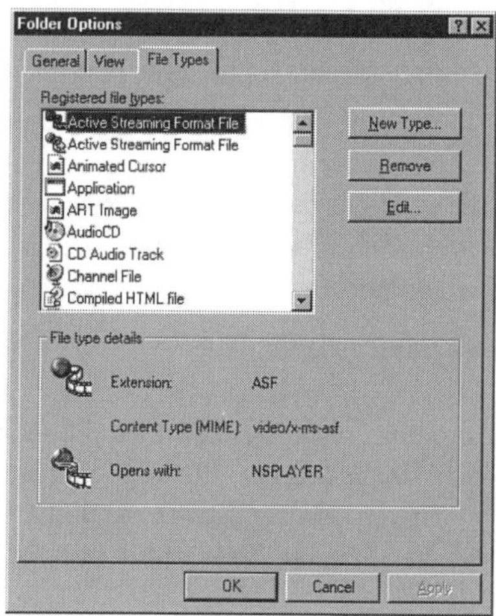

FIG. 31.11
Register and modify file types on the File Types page of the Options dialog box.

3. Choose the New Type button. The Add New File Type dialog box appears (see Figure 31.12).

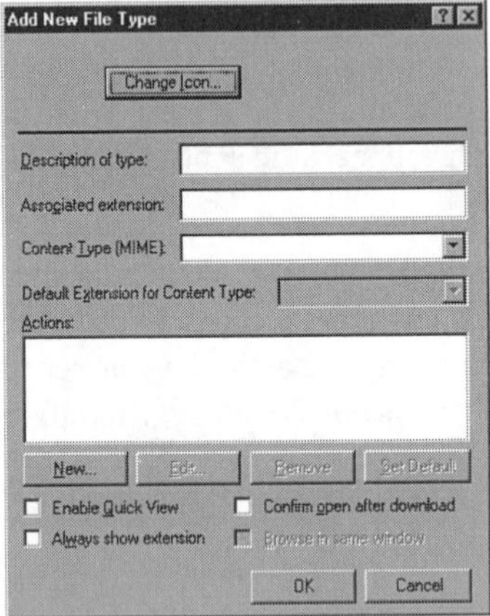

FIG. 31.12
Enter the information for a new file type in the Add New File Type dialog box.

4. Enter a description of the file type in the Description of Type text box.

   This description appears in the Registered File Types list on the File Types page of the Options dialog box. For example, if you want to double-click mainframe text files that use commas to separate data and have that file load into Excel, you might use a description similar to Comma Separated Values (CSV).

5. Enter a the file extension to be associated with this file type in the Associated Extension text box. This is the three-letter file extension associated with DOS-based files. For example, a comma-separated values file uses the extension CSV.

6. Choose New to add a new action to the file type in the New Action dialog box. The action is actually a custom command that appears on the shortcut menu when you right-click the file.

7. Type an action, for example, **Open CSV in Excel**, in the Actions text box. What you type appears as an item on the shortcut menu for this file type. You can type anything, but commands usually start with a verb. If you want the command to have an accelerator key, precede that letter with an ampersand (&).

8. Select the application to be used to perform the action in the Application Used to Perform Action text box.

   You can enter the path and directory to the EXCEL.EXE file—for example, "**C:\Program Files\Microsoft Office\Office\EXCEL.EXE**." Include the quotation marks if the filename has spaces in it. You can also choose Browse to find and select the application to use. Designate a shortcut menu action and the program used to perform that action in the New Action dialog box.

9. While the New Action dialog box is still displayed, select the Use DDE check box if the program uses DDE (dynamic data exchange).

   If you select the Use DDE check box, the dialog box expands, displaying the DDE statements used to communicate with the DDE application. If you know how to write DDE statements, you can customize the action performed with the associated application.

10. Click OK.
11. If you have more than one action listed in the Actions box, select the one you want to be the default action, and then choose the Set Default button.

    The default action is the one that is performed when you double-click a file of this type in the Explorer or My Computer.
12. Select the Enable Quick View check box if the file type supports Quick View. Quick View enables you to view a file without opening it.
13. Select Always Show Extension if you want the MS-DOS file extension for this file type to always be displayed in the Explorer and My Computer, even when you have selected the Hide MS-DOS File Extensions option on the View page of the Options dialog box.
14. Choose Close twice.

▶ **See** "Previewing a Document with Quick View," **p. 302**

Editing an Existing File Type

At times, you might want to change existing file type options. For example, say you want to change the action that opens BMP files in Paint so they will open in a different image editor. You must edit the BMP open action to include the path and filename for that image editor instead of Paint.

You can also add new commands to the shortcut menu for a registered file type. For example, you might want the option of opening BMP files with either Paint or another image editor. Instead of editing the open action already in place, you must add a new open command associated with the other image editor. You also can change the description, icon, and other aspects.

To edit an existing file type, follow these steps:

1. In the Explorer, choose View, Options.
2. Click the File Types tab to display the File Types page of the Options dialog box (refer to Figure 31.11).
3. Select the file type you want to edit in the Registered File Types list.
4. Click the Edit button.
5. Edit the characteristics for the file type by using the same procedures outlined earlier for creating a new file type in the section "Registering a New File Type."

   To edit an action, select that action from the list. Actions for a file type depend on parameters or arguments understood by that file type. Some applications can accept macro names as actions, whereas others accept "switches," and still others accept arguments left over from DOS commands. To learn more about the actions, check the technical reference manual for the application you are starting.

   To add a new action for a file type already registered, click New in the Edit File Type dialog box and follow the procedures outlined earlier for creating a new file type. This is how you customize the shortcut menu for a file type to include new commands for acting on that file type. For example, `Open with CorelDRAW!`.

6. Click OK.
7. Repeat steps 3–6 for any other file types you want to edit.
8. Click Close.

You are not limited to one occurrence for a particular action in a shortcut menu. For example, you can have two Open commands in the shortcut menu for a registered file type, each of which uses a different application to open files of that type. The example for opening BMP files with either Paint or CorelDRAW! is such a case. When you name the action in the New Action dialog box, give the command a name that enables you to distinguish it from the other commands in the menu.

Removing a File Type

If you no longer want a document to start a specific application, you can remove its file type description:

1. In the Explorer, choose View, Options.
2. Click the File Types tab to display the File Types page of the Options dialog box (refer to Figure 31.11).
3. Select the file type you want to remove in the Registered File Types list.
4. Click Remove.
5. Click OK.

Changing the Icon for a File Type or Other Object

You can change the icon used to designate a file type, drive, folder, and other objects on your computer. To change the icon used for a particular file type or object, follow these steps:

1. In the Explorer, choose View, Options.
2. Click the File Types tab to display the File Types page of the Options dialog box (refer to Figure 31.11).
3. Select the file type or other object whose icon you want to change in the Registered File Types list.
4. Choose the Edit button.
5. Click the Change Icon button to display the Change Icon dialog box shown in Figure 31.13.
6. Select a new icon from the Current Icon scrolling list.

   The name of the file containing the icons currently shown is listed in the File Name text box. You can use the Browse button to search for a new file containing different icons. All Windows programs come with their own icons, and you can obtain collections of icons from bulletin boards, the Internet, and other sources. Programs are even available that enable you to create your own icons.
7. Click OK three times.

FIG. 31.13
Use the Change Icon dialog box to select a new icon for a file type or other type of object.

CHAPTER 32

Customizing the Desktop Settings

In this chapter

Customizing the Desktop Colors and Background

Changing colors is just one way you can customize the windows you see on-screen. You also can change the pattern used in the desktop background, add a graphical wallpaper as a background, change the border width of windows, and more.

Wallpaper options you select for the desktop background can include graphics that come with Windows—including some wild and colorful ones—and designs you create or modify with Windows Paint. The graphic images you use as wallpaper are nothing more than computer drawings saved in a bitmap (BMP) format. You also can use the Windows Paint program to create your own bitmap drawings to use as screen backgrounds.

You can put wallpaper over just the center portion of the desktop, or you can tile the desktop with wallpaper. When tiling, the wallpaper reproduces itself to fill the screen.

▶ **See** "Saving Paint Files," **p. 749**

Changing Windows Colors

After working in the drab and dreary DOS or mainframe computer world, one of the first changes many people want to make is to add color to their Windows screens. You can pick colors for window titles, backgrounds, bars—in fact, all parts of the window. Predesigned color schemes range from the brilliant to the cool and dark. You also can design and save your own color schemes and blend your own colors.

Using Existing Color Schemes Windows comes with a list of predefined color schemes. Each color scheme maps a different color and text to a different part of the screen.

You can select from existing schemes, or you can devise your own (described in the next section). To select one of the predefined schemes, follow these steps:

1. Right-click the desktop, choose Properties, and then select the Appearance tab.

   or

   Open the Start menu and choose Settings, Control Panel; then click the Display icon and select the Appearance tab.

   The Appearance tab of the Display Properties dialog box appears, as shown in Figure 32.1.
2. Select the Scheme list; then select a predefined color and text scheme from the list. The sample screen at the top of the dialog box illustrates what this color scheme looks like.
3. Choose OK to use the displayed color scheme, or return to step 2 for other predefined schemes.

Creating Custom Color and Text Schemes You can change all or some of the colors in a scheme, change the color of the text, and even change the color and width of borders. To create new color schemes while the Appearance tab is open, follow these steps:

1. If you want to use an existing scheme as a base (as opposed to using Windows Standard as a base), select the scheme from the Scheme list.

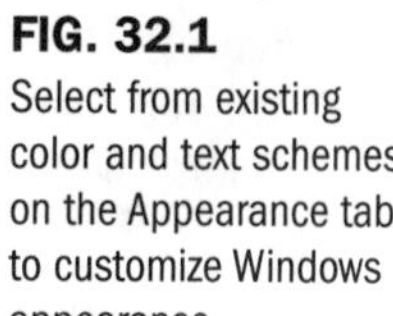

FIG. 32.1
Select from existing color and text schemes on the Appearance tab to customize Windows appearance.

2. Select from the Item list the screen element you want to modify. Or click a screen element in the sample window at the top of the dialog box. You can select elements such as the Menu Bar, Button, Active Border, and so on.
3. Select from the Size, Font, and Color lists how you want to change the selected element. Some options are available only for certain elements.
4. Choose one of these alternatives for the colors you have selected:
   - If you want to color another window element, return to step 2.
   - If you want to use these colors now but not save them for the next time you run Windows, choose OK or press Enter.
   - If you want to save these colors so you can use them now or return to them at any time, choose the Save As button. Then type a name in the Save Scheme text box and choose OK.
   - If you want to cancel these colors and return to the original scheme, select that scheme from the Scheme list if it was saved, or choose Cancel.

To remove a scheme from the list, select the scheme you want to remove from the Scheme list and click Delete.

Wallpapering Your Desktop with a Graphic

Using a graphic or picture as the Windows desktop is a nice personal touch. For special business situations or custom applications, you might want to use a color company logo or pictorial theme as the wallpaper.

Windows comes with a collection of graphics for the desktop. You can modify these images or draw new images for the desktop with the Windows Paint program. For high-quality pictorials, use a scanner to create a digitized black-and-white or color image.

Figure 32.2 shows one of the many wallpaper patterns that come with Windows. Figure 32.3 shows a logo used as a backdrop. Many companies scan and then enhance their corporate logo as a BMP file, and then they use it as the desktop background. Most of the patterns must be tiled to fill the entire screen, which you learn how to do in the following steps.

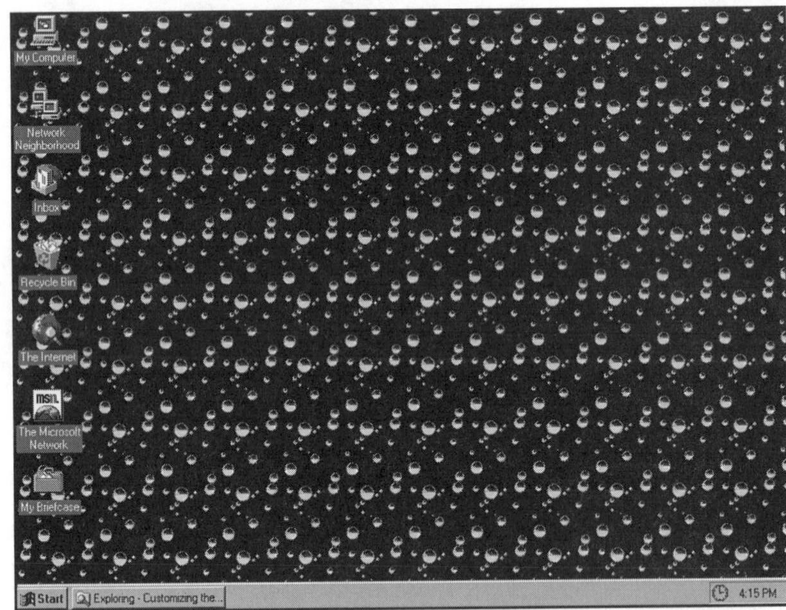

FIG. 32.2
This is Bubbles, one of the many Windows images you can use to wallpaper your desktop.

FIG. 32.3
Edit existing wallpaper files or create your own with Paint.

To select wallpaper, follow these steps:

1. Right-click the desktop, choose Properties, and then select the Background tab.

   or

   Open the Start menu and choose Settings, Control Panel; then click the Display icon and select the Background tab.

   The Background tab of the Display Properties dialog box appears (see Figure 32.4).

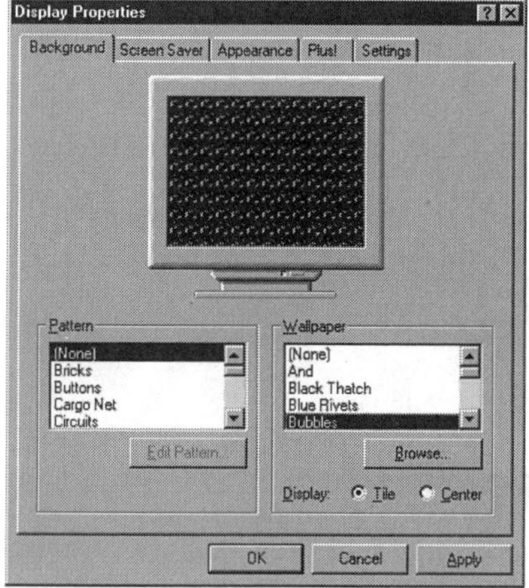

FIG. 32.4
Use the Background tab in Display Properties to select new wallpapers and patterns.

2. Choose a wallpaper from the Wallpaper list box. If the graphic file (with a BMP extension) is located in a folder other than Windows, choose the Browse button to find and select the graphic file.
3. If the graphic is large enough to fill the screen, select Display Center to center the wallpaper in the desktop. If the graphic is small and must be repeated to fill the screen, select Display Tile.
4. Choose OK if you are finished or make other display property changes.

When you choose a wallpaper from the Wallpaper list box, you see a miniature rendition of it in the display shown in the upper part of the Display Properties dialog box. This allows you to preview wallpapers before selecting the one to use. Remember, however, bitmap images displayed as desktop wallpaper use more memory than a colored or patterned desktop.

Wallpaper is created from files stored in a bitmap format. These files end with the BMP extension and must be stored in the Windows folder. You can edit BMP formats with the Windows Paint program. You also can read and edit files with PCX format in Paint and save them in BMP format to use as a desktop wallpaper.

You can create your own desktop wallpapers in one of three ways:

- Buy clip art from a software vendor. If the clip art is not in PCX or BMP format, use a graphics-conversion application to convert the image to one of these formats. Use

Windows Paint to read PCX format and resave the figure in BMP format. Computer bulletin boards, online services, and the Internet have thousands of BMP graphics files.

ON THE WEB

Check out **Anonymous FTP: bongo.cc.utexas.edu** through the path: /gifstuff/ftpsites.

You might also look at **Anonymous FTP: ftp.cica.indiana.edu** through the path: /pub/pc/win3/* for bitmaps for Windows.

- Scan a black-and-white or color picture using a digital scanner. Save the scanned file in BMP format or convert it to BMP format.
- Modify an existing desktop wallpaper, or create a new one with Windows Paint or a higher-end graphics program. Save the files with the BMP format.

Store your new BMP (bitmap) graphics files in the Windows folder so they will appear in the Wallpaper Files list box in the Display Properties dialog box.

To remove a wallpaper file from the Wallpaper Files drop-down list, delete or remove its BMP file from the Windows folder. To remove the wallpaper from the desktop, repeat the preceding steps but select (None) as the type of wallpaper.

Changing the Background Pattern

Wallpapers, while pretty and often amusing, can consume a lot of memory. If you want a simpler background or want to conserve memory, you can use a background pattern. The pattern is a small grid of dots that repeats to fill the screen. In Figure 32.5, the example area shows how one background pattern appears. Windows comes with predefined patterns you can select; you also can create your own. The color of the pattern is the same as the color selected for Window Text in the Color dialog box.

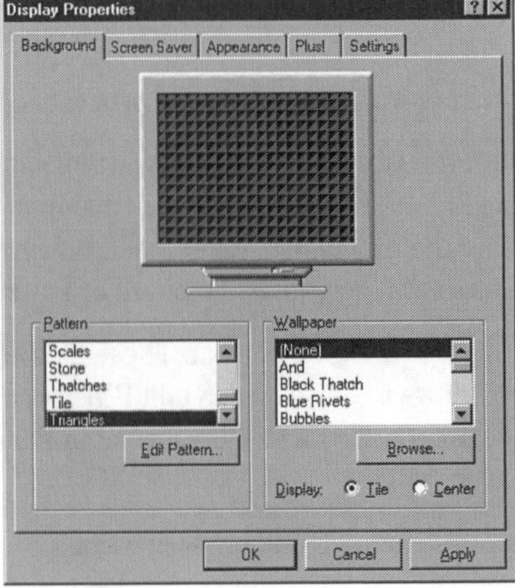

FIG. 32.5
Background patterns are simpler and conserve memory.

To select a pattern, follow these steps:

1. Right-click the desktop, choose Properties, and then select the Background tab.

   or

   Open the Start menu and choose Settings, Control Panel; then click the Display icon and select the Background tab. The Background tab of the Display Properties dialog box appears.
2. Select a pattern from the Pattern list. Some of the built-in repetitive patterns you can select are 50% Gray, Boxes, Diamonds, Weave, and Scottie.
3. Choose OK to add the pattern to the desktop. Alternatively, use the following procedure to edit the pattern just selected.

You can edit or create new patterns only if you have a mouse. To edit an existing pattern or create a new pattern while the Background tab is displayed, follow these steps:

1. Select a pattern from the Pattern list.
2. Click the Edit Pattern button to display the Pattern Editor dialog box, shown in Figure 32.6.

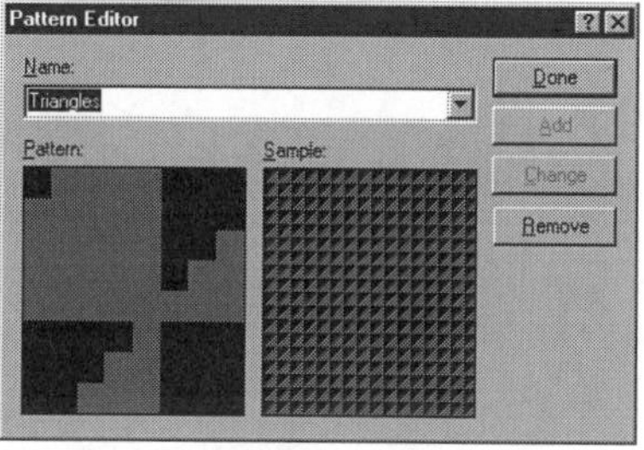

FIG. 32.6 Editing your pattern by using an existing pattern as a base can be easier than working from the (None) pattern.

3. Click in the editing grid in the location where you want to reverse a dot in the pattern. Watch the Sample area to see the overall effect.
4. Continue to click in the grid until the pattern is what you want.
5. When you finish creating or editing, continue with one of the following options:
   - If you want to change an existing pattern, click Change.
   - If you want to add a new pattern, type a new name in the Name list box and choose the Add button.
6. When you finish editing, click Done. Choose OK in the Display Properties dialog box.

To remove an unwanted pattern from the list, select the pattern and click Remove. Confirm the deletion by choosing Yes. The Remove button is available only after you select a new pattern name.

Working with Desktop Themes

The Microsoft Plus! Desktop Themes provide you with appealing graphics and sounds to decorate your desktop and highlight system events (see Figure 32.7). Each Desktop Theme offers a coordinated set of elements, so you can set the appropriate mood for your computing experience. Plus! provides Desktop Theme combinations for computers displaying 256 colors and for computers displaying 16-bit or higher color. If you did not install the high-color Desktop Themes, you can rerun the Plus! Setup at any time to do so. The following are the Desktop Themes provided with Plus!:

256 Color:

Dangerous Creatures

Leonardo da Vinci

Science

The 60's USA

Sports

Windows 95

High Color:

Inside Your Computer

Nature

The Golden Era

Mystery

Travel

When you choose a Desktop Theme, you can specify whether to replace Windows screen elements you specify using the Control Panel. Desktop Themes provides these desktop elements; you can choose which of these you want to use for your system:

- *Screen Saver.* Displays the Theme screen saver when you leave your computer idle.
- *Sound Events.* Assigns the Theme sounds to system events such as Windows startup and exit.
- *Mouse Pointer.* Applies the Theme pointer styles for different types of pointers, such as the pointer used to select text or the one that appears while Windows is busy performing an operation.

NOTE If you need a high degree of accuracy when pointing with the mouse, the Mouse Pointer option for several Themes might make your pointing more difficult because of the pointer shapes assigned by the Theme. If you have trouble with this, clear the Mouse Pointer option for the current Theme. ■

- *Desktop Wallpaper.* Covers the desktop with the decorative background provided by the Theme.

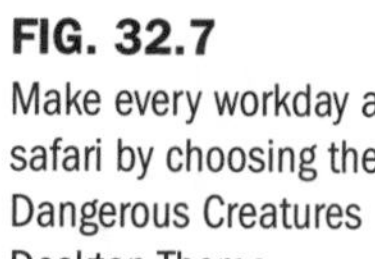

FIG. 32.7
Make every workday a safari by choosing the Dangerous Creatures Desktop Theme.

- *Icons.* Assigns custom Theme icons to desktop objects such as the My Computer object and Recycle Bin.
- *Icon Size and Spacing.* Makes desktop icons use the icon size and spacing specified by the Theme; remember that larger icons use more computer memory, so if your system is low on memory, don't use this option.
- *Colors.* Applies the Theme colors to windows and other screen elements.
- *Font Names and Styles.* Uses the Theme fonts for screen elements such as window titles.
- *Font and Window Sizes.* Uses the Theme font sizes and default window sizes.

As mentioned earlier, the Theme replaces the desktop elements you specify using the Control Panel. You should note, however, that the most recent element you select using either method (Desktop Themes or the Control Panel) becomes active. For example, if you apply a Desktop Theme but aren't quite satisfied with the screen saver, you can use the Control Panel to choose another screen saver to use.

Selecting and Setting Up a Theme

Plus! Setup! creates an object icon for the Desktop Themes in the Windows 95 Control Panel, which contains other objects for controlling Windows' appearance and operation. Use the following steps to use the Desktop Themes object to select a Theme:

1. Open the Start menu and choose Settings, Control Panel.
2. In the Control Panel window, double-click the Desktop Themes icon (see Figure 32.8). The Desktop Themes dialog box appears, as shown in Figure 32.9. Use this dialog box to select and set up a Theme.

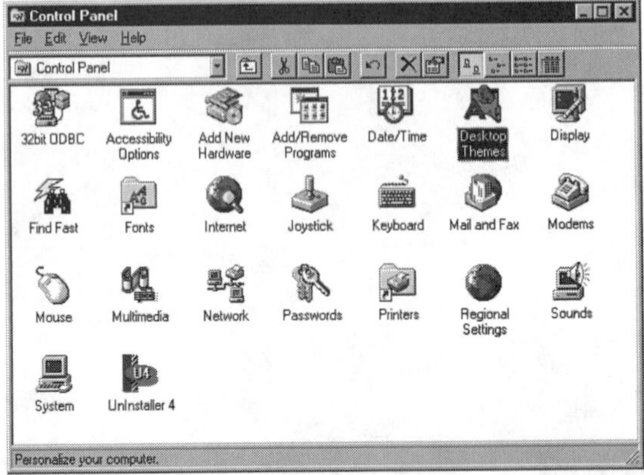

FIG. 32.8
Select a Desktop Theme using the Control Panel.

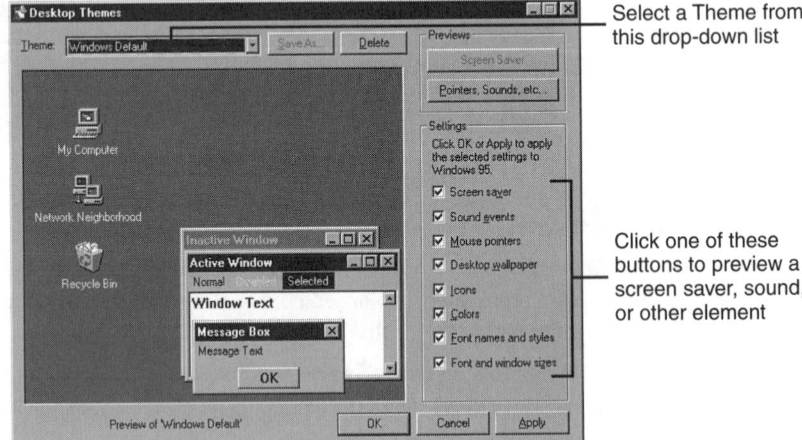

FIG. 32.9
Plus! provides numerous options for setting up the Desktop Theme of your choice.

3. Click the down arrow beside the Theme drop-down list to display the available Desktop Themes. Click the name of the Theme you want to use. A dialog box tells you that the Theme files are being imported. When that dialog box closes, the preview area of the Desktop Themes changes to display the appearance of the Theme you selected, as shown in Figure 32.10.
4. On the right side of the dialog box, choose the Settings to use for the Theme you selected.
5. (Optional) To preview the selected Theme's screen saver, click Screen Saver in the Previews area. The screen saver appears on-screen. Move the mouse or press a key to conclude the preview.

FIG. 32.10
After you select a Desktop Theme, you see a preview of your Windows desktop.

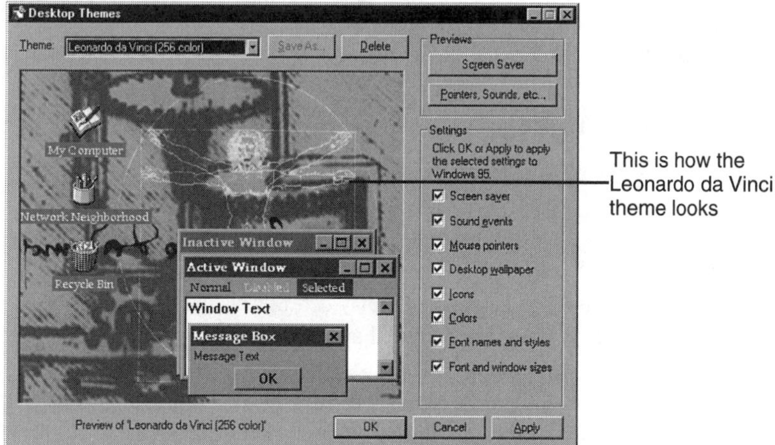
This is how the Leonardo da Vinci theme looks

6. (Optional) To preview several of the selected Theme's other elements, click Pointers, Sounds, etc... in the Previews area. A Preview dialog box for the Theme appears; the dialog box has three tabs for Pointers, Sounds, and Visuals. Click the tab you want to view. Each tab offers a list box with the elements for the Theme. For the Pointers and Visuals tabs, simply click an element in the list to see a preview in the Preview or Picture area. For the Sounds tab, click an element in the list; then click the right arrow icon near the bottom of the dialog box to hear the sound. Click Close to conclude your preview.
7. After you select a Theme, choose settings, and preview elements to your satisfaction, choose OK to close the Desktop Themes window. The selected Desktop Theme appears on your system.

Saving a Custom Theme

Any Control Panel changes you make after selecting a Theme take precedence over the Theme settings. In fact, you can make desktop setting changes in Control Panel and save those settings as a custom Theme. To do so, follow these steps:

1. Use Control Panel to change any settings you want, including the wallpaper, screen colors, sounds, and so on.
2. If the Control Panel window isn't open, open the Start menu and choose Settings, Control Panel.
3. In the Control Panel window, double-click the Desktop Themes icon.

TIP To permanently delete a Desktop Theme, select it in the Theme drop-down list; then click Delete. Click Yes in the dialog box that appears to confirm the deletion.

4. Open the Themes drop-down list and choose Current Window settings. The Save As button becomes active.
5. Click the Save As button. The Save Theme dialog box appears.

6. (Optional) Choose another folder in which to save the Theme.
7. Enter a unique name for the Theme in the File Name text box.
8. Click Save to save the Theme and return to the Desktop Themes dialog box. The newly saved Theme appears as the Theme selection.
9. Click OK to accept your new Theme and apply it to Windows 95.

Adjusting Plus! Visual Settings

Plus! adds new features to the display settings available in the Windows 95 Control Panel. These visual settings are designed primarily to make your desktop more attractive. Plus! enables you to specify new icons for My Computer, the Network Neighborhood, and the Recycle Bin desktop icons. You can choose to show the contents of a window (rather than just an outline when you drag the window). Choose whether you want to smooth the appearance of large fonts on-screen. You also can choose to show icons with all possible colors or expand the wallpaper (when centered using the Background tab of the Display Properties dialog box from Control Panel) so it stretches to fill the entire screen.

NOTE Most of the Plus! visual settings require more system resources than the normal display settings. In particular, showing window contents while dragging and using all colors in icons consumes more RAM. Consider all your computing requirements before you use up RAM by selecting any of these features. ■

To work with the Plus! visual settings, open the Start menu and choose Settings, Control Panel. In the Control Panel window, double-click the Display icon. The Display Properties sheet appears. Click the Plus! tab to display its options, as shown in Figure 32.11. To assign a new Desktop icon, click the icon you want to change in the Desktop Icons area. Click Change Icon. In the Change Icon dialog box that appears, scroll to display the icon you want; then click OK to accept the change.

To enable any of the other Plus! display features, select the feature in the Visual settings area of the Plus! page. If you want more information about a particular feature, right-click the feature, and then click What's This?. A brief description of the feature appears. Click or press Esc to clear the description. To accept your visual settings and close the Display properties sheet, click OK. Close the Control Panel window, if you want.

Changing Icon Size and Spacing

You can change the size of the icons and the spacing around icons on the desktop by using the Appearance tab of the Display properties sheet. Click the Item drop-down list. Choose Icon Spacing (Horizontal) to change the text area available for the text below the icons on your desktop. You can enter a number in the Size box from 0 to 150. Using 0 creates a narrow space for the text, so **Recycle Bin** changes to **Re** on one line and **Bin** on one line. Using 150 enables you to use longer names for your icons; 43 is the default. Choose Icon Spacing (Vertical) to adjust the space above and below an icon from 0 to 150, with 43 being the default.

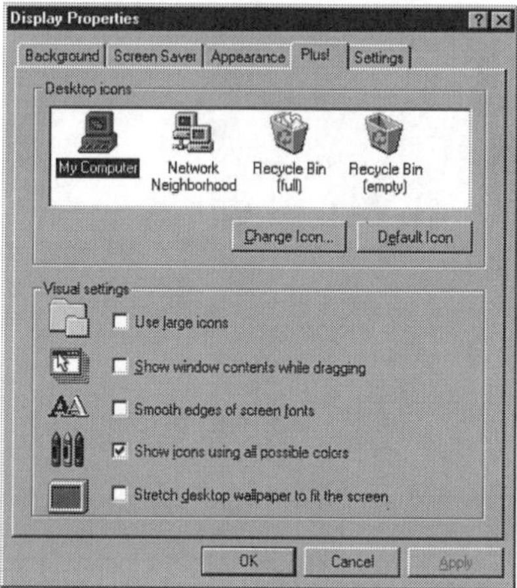

FIG. 32.11
Plus! enables you to make additional adjustments to the Windows Display Properties.

Changing the Name of Desktop Icons

You can change the name of any Desktop icon by clicking the name to select it and then clicking the name again to reveal the Rename text box. Enter the new name and press Enter. Name changes remain in effect until you change them again.

Having Fun with the Screen Saver

Screen savers display a changing pattern on-screen when you haven't typed or moved the mouse for a predetermined amount of time. You can specify the delay before the screen saver activates, and you can set up various attributes—including a password—for most of the screen savers.

To select and set up a screen saver, follow these steps:

1. Right-click the desktop and choose Properties; then select the Screen Saver tab.

   or

   Open the Start menu and choose Settings, Control Panel; then click the Display icon and select the Screen Saver tab.

   The Screen Saver tab of the Display Properties dialog box appears (see Figure 32.12).
2. Select a screen saver from the Screen Saver list.
3. The miniature display shows you a preview of the screen saver. To see a full screen view, click Preview. Click anywhere on-screen to return to the dialog box from the preview.
4. To customize the appearance and properties of your screen saver, click Settings. The options and settings for each screen saver are different. Figure 32.13 shows the options for customizing the Flying Windows screen saver.

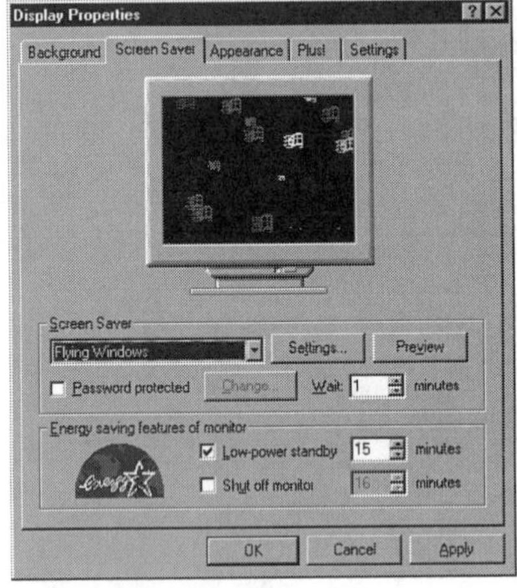

FIG. 32.12
Customizing your screen saver can display information, attract attention, or warn people away from your computer.

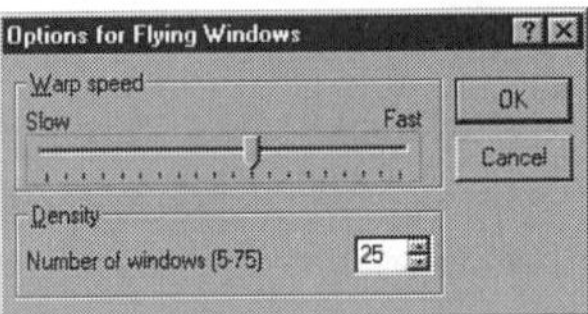

FIG. 32.13
You can customize screen savers so they act differently.

5. In the Wait text box, type or select the number of minutes you want the screen to be idle before the screen saver appears. A range from 5 to 15 minutes is usually a good time.
6. Choose Apply to apply the Display Property changes you have selected so far. You will see the changes take effect, but the Display Properties dialog box stays open. Choose OK to accept the changes and close the dialog box.

Protecting Your Computer with a Screen Saver Password

Although each screen saver has unique settings, all except Blank Screen have an area where you can specify password protection. If you don't want uninvited users to use your computer, you can specify a password that is associated with a screen saver, so only those who know the password can clear the screen saver and use your computer.

To protect your computer by using a password, follow these steps:

1. Right-click anywhere on the desktop; then choose Properties to open the Display properties sheet.
2. Click the Screen Saver tab.
3. Select a screen saver from the Screen Saver drop-down list and set its options.
4. Select the Password Protected check box and choose Change.
5. Type your password in the New Password text box, and confirm your password by typing it again in the Confirm New Password text box.

Asterisks will appear in the text boxes as you type your password to prevent others from seeing it (see Figure 32.14).

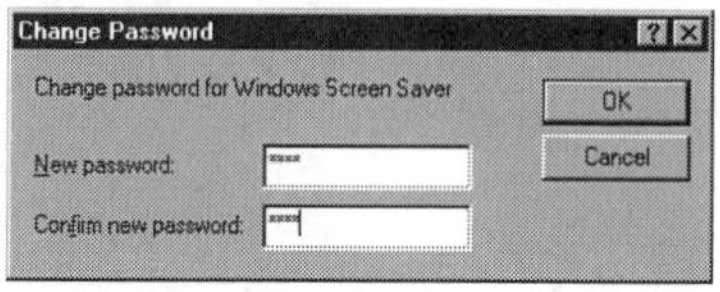

FIG. 32.14
Enter a password for the screen saver in the Change Password dialog box.

6. Choose OK. When the confirmation message appears, choose OK again.

Now, when the screen saver appears and you press a key on the keyboard or move the mouse, a dialog box appears in which you have to type your password to clear the screen saver.

Using Your Display's Energy-Saving Feature

If you leave your computer on continuously, or if you leave your desk for long periods of time while your computer continues to run, you will want to conserve energy by using the energy-saving features that are built in to many newer monitors. Although the energy used by one monitor might seem small when multiplied by the millions of computers in use across the nation, it is easy to see that selecting this option one time can save a lot of energy and reduce pollution. When you consider the cost of running the tens of thousands of monitors in a single large corporation, the dollar savings can be significant.

Monitors that satisfy EPA requirements usually display an "Energy Star" sticker on the monitor or in the manual. Older monitors do not have the energy-saving feature.

If you have a monitor that is an Energy Star but the Energy Saving Features of Monitor options are not available in the Screen Saver tab, you should install the correct display drivers for your monitor. To check which display driver is installed, open the Display Properties sheet, choose the Settings tab, and then choose the Change Display Type button. From the dialog box that appears, you can install the display driver for your manufacturer and model. After you have the correct driver, select the Monitor Is Energy Star Compliant check box. (Selecting this check box does no good if the monitor is not compliant.)

To set Windows so it takes advantage of the energy-saving features of Energy Star-compliant monitors, follow these steps:

1. Right-click the desktop and choose Properties.
2. Choose the Screen Saver tab (refer to Figure 32.12).
3. Select the Low-Power Standby check box, and select the number of minutes the computer should be idle before the monitor goes into low-power standby. This mode reduces power requirements but keeps the monitor ready to be instantly used.
4. Select the Shut Off Monitor check box, and select the number of minutes the computer should be idle before the monitor shuts down. This mode completely turns off your monitor.
5. Choose OK.

When you return to your workstation, you can press any key or move the mouse to return to normal monitor use from low-power standby. The Shut Off Monitor mode shuts off the monitor rather than putting it in Standby mode. This saves the most energy. The manual for your monitor will describe the best way to turn the monitor on again.

▶ **See** "Understanding the Device Manager," **p. 183**

▶ **See** "Using Power Management," **p. 197**

Changing the Screen Resolution, Font Size, and Color Palette

With Windows, you have the ability to change how your application displays, even while you work. This can help if you run applications that operate with different screen resolutions, or if you use programs that look better in different font sizes. Some applications, such as graphics programs or multimedia, work better when they use 256 colors and higher resolution.

The resolution is the number of dots shown on-screen. The more dots on-screen, the more detail you can work with. However, with a high-resolution screen, icons or fonts that appear an adequate size on a VGA screen can now appear small.

Changing the resolution while Windows is running enables you to switch between VGA mode (640 × 480 pixels on-screen) and the more detailed and wider view of SVGA mode (800 × 600 pixels). This can come in handy when you work on different types of tasks. You might, for example, have a laptop computer that displays on its LCD screen in VGA mode. When you work at your desk and have a high-resolution monitor connected to the laptop, you want to work in SVGA mode.

Changing the Screen Resolution

You can change the screen resolution, the number of dots on the screen, if your display is capable of running Super VGA 800 × 600 resolution or better and Super VGA or better is currently set as the monitor type.

You can change the resolution by following these steps:

1. Open the Display properties sheet and click the Settings tab.
2. In the Desktop Area box, drag the slider to the desired resolution.
3. Click OK.
4. When the dialog box appears, informing you that Windows will adjust the resolution, click OK.
5. Click Yes when the message box appears, asking if you want to keep the settings.

If you don't have the correct monitor type selected, you may not be able to change your screen resolution. To find out what monitor type you have selected or to change the monitor type, follow these steps:

1. Open the Display properties sheet and click the Settings tab.

2. Choose the Change Display Type button to display the Change Display Type dialog box.
3. Choose the Change button next to the Monitor Type area.
4. Select the manufacturer for your monitor in the Manufacturers list box and the model for your monitor in the Models list box.

   If you are unsure, choose Standard Monitor Types from the Manufacturers list box and choose a monitor from the Models list box.
5. Choose OK; then choose Close.
6. When you return to the Display properties sheet, you can change other display properties. Choose OK.

When you exit the Display Properties sheet, you might need to restart Windows to implement the new monitor type. You will be asked whether you want to restart at that time.

If you have the OSR2 version of Windows 95 installed, the steps for changing the monitor type are slightly different:

1. Open the Display properties sheet and click the Settings tab.
2. Click Advanced Properties.
3. Click Change.
4. Select Show All Devices in the Select Device dialog box.
5. Select the manufacturer and model for your monitor in the Manufacturers and Models lists.
6. Choose OK and then Close.
7. When you return to the Display Properties sheet, you can change other display properties. Choose OK.

NOTE Depending on the video card that you have installed in your system, you may find additional tabs in the Display Properties sheet or additional features on the Settings tab. See the documentation that comes with your video card to find out more about the custom features that come with your card. ■

CAUTION

Changing to an incorrect monitor type that cannot be implemented might cause your screen to be unreadable. If that happens, shut off your computer. Restart your computer and watch the screen carefully. When the phrase "Starting Windows 95" appears, press F8. This displays a text menu that enables you to start Windows in *safe mode*. Safe mode displays Windows on any screen, but many resources will not be available, such as networking and CD-ROM. While in safe mode, repeat the steps described in this section and select either a monitor type you are sure of or a resolution that will work from the Standard Monitor Types list.

After your monitor is in Super VGA mode or better, you can change between screen resolutions by dragging the slider in the Desktop Area section of the Settings tab.

Changing the Number of Colors Available to Your Monitor

Depending on your display adapter and the monitor, you can have the same resolution screen, but with a different palette of colors available. For example, you might have some business applications that use only 16 colors, while most games and multimedia use 256 or more colors.

To change the size of your color palette, click the Color Palette down arrow in the Settings tab. Then click the number of colors you need.

Changing Font Sizes

Need glasses to read the screen? You can enlarge (or reduce) the size of the font Windows uses on-screen. All text on-screen will change size. You have to restart Windows, however, to see the change.

You can select from any of the following font size options:

- Small Fonts scales fonts to 100 percent of normal size.
- Large Fonts scales fonts to 125 percent of normal size.
- Custom displays the Custom Font Size dialog box where you can specify your own size.

To change the size of screen fonts, follow these steps:

1. Right-click the desktop and choose Properties. The Display properties sheet appears.
2. Click the Settings tab. Figure 32.15 shows the Properties sheet.

   The Settings tab has changed in the OSR2 version of Windows 95, as shown in Figure 32.16.

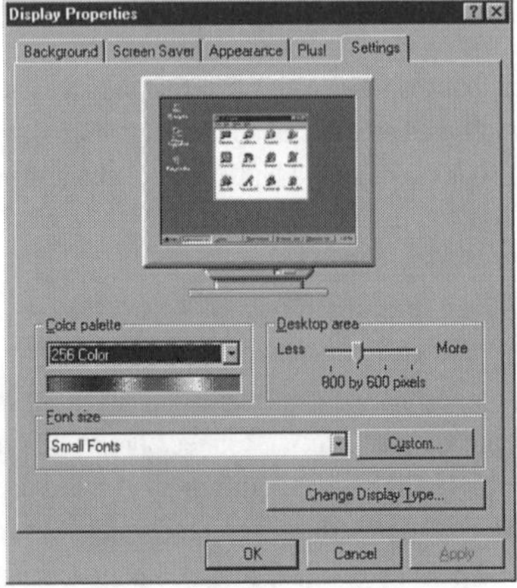

FIG. 32.15
Change your display's appearance in the Settings tab.

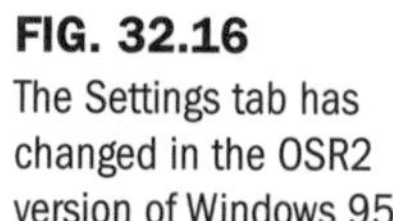

FIG. 32.16
The Settings tab has changed in the OSR2 version of Windows 95.

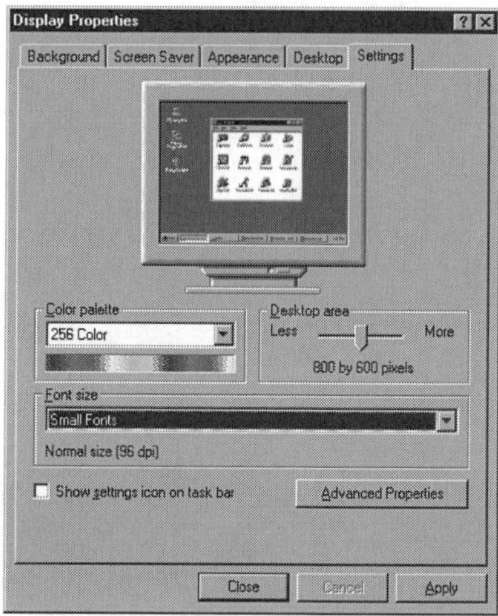

3. Choose Large Fonts or Small Fonts from the Font Size list box.

   or

   Click Custom to display the Custom Font Size dialog box (see Figure 32.17). Type or select a percentage of normal size in the Scale text box, or drag across the ruler and then release the mouse button to resize. Notice the sample font and its size below the ruler. Choose OK.

   In the OSR2 version of Windows 95, there is no longer a Custom button (refer to Figure 32.16). Select Other from the Font size list to open the Custom Font Size dialog box.
4. Click OK to accept the change and close the Display properties sheet.

FIG. 32.17
You can create your own custom font size.

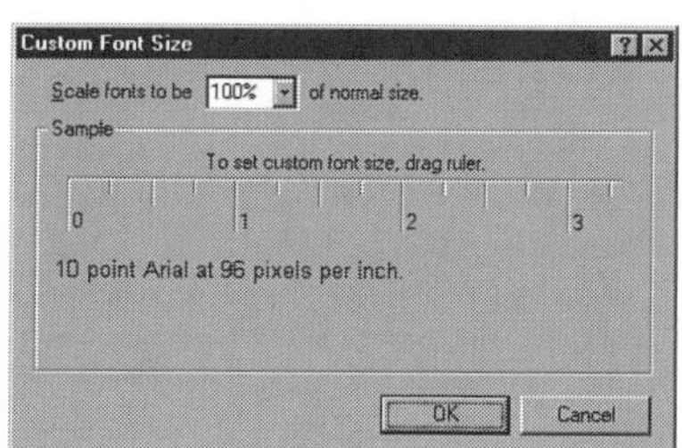

CHAPTER 33

Customizing Your System Settings

by Ron Person, Robert Voss, and Paul Sanna

In this chapter

Changing the Sounds Associated with Windows Events

In the previous two chapters, you learned how to customize many elements of the Windows 95 screen to change how Windows looks and operates. In this chapter, you will learn how to customize additional settings that affect the way Windows works for you. These settings include customizing the mouse and keyboard settings, enhancing the accessibility of Windows for hearing-, sight- and movement-impaired individuals, changing the date, time, and language settings, and several other system-related settings.

Windows plays sounds when different events occur, such as errors, closing programs, shutting down Windows, emptying the Recycle Bin, and so on. You can change the sounds used for each of these events; you can even use your own sound files.

To change the sounds associated with an event, follow these steps:

1. Open the Start menu, and choose Settings, Control Panel.
2. Choose Sounds to display the Sounds properties sheet shown in Figure 33.1.

FIG. 33.1
You can assign your own sound files to different Windows events.

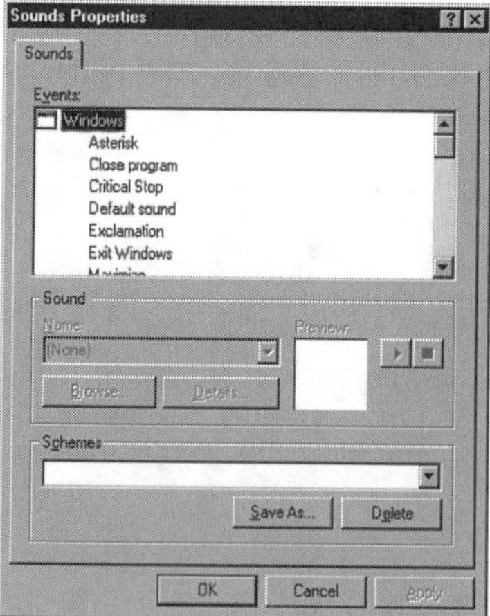

3. Scroll through the Events list until you see the event sound you want to change; click that event.
4. Select the WAV file that contains the sound for that event by clicking the Browse button and selecting a WAV file. Click OK. The Browse dialog box opens in the WINDOWS\MEDIA folder, but you can change to any folder.
5. Preview the sound by clicking the Go button to the right of the Preview icon.
6. Click OK.

NOTE You can create your own collection of WAV files by following the procedures described in Chapter 4, "Configuring Multimedia Windows 95." You can also check public bulletin boards, online services, and the Internet to find thousands of free WAV files.

Entire collections of sounds have been grouped for you as sound schemes. To change all the sounds involved in a sound scheme, select the scheme you want by choosing it from the Schemes drop-down list.

If you create your own scheme of sounds/events, you can save it with a name so that you can return to it by clicking the Save As button, entering a name, and clicking OK.

Customizing the Mouse

If you are left-handed, or if you like a fast or slow mouse, you need to learn how to modify your mouse's behavior. You can change mouse options in the Mouse properties sheet, as shown in Figure 33.2.

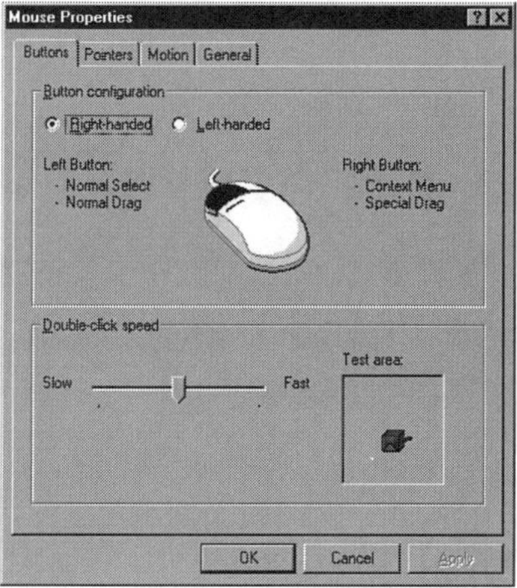

FIG. 33.2
You can change the speed of your mouse and more in the Mouse properties sheet.

To change how your mouse behaves and appears, follow these steps:

1. Open the Start menu and choose Settings, Control Panel; then choose the Mouse icon. The Mouse properties sheet appears.
2. Click a tab and make the changes you want.
3. Click Apply to accept the change and to continue making changes, or click OK to accept the change and close the Mouse properties sheet.

Mouse options are grouped on four tabs: Buttons, Pointer, Motion, and General. Table 33.1 describes each tab.

Table 33.1 Tabs of the Mouse Properties Sheet

Tab	Description
Button	Select either a Right-Handed mouse or Left-Handed mouse. Set the Double-Click Speed, and then double-click the Test box to determine if you set a speed you're comfortable with. When you double-click at the right speed in the Test area, you will be surprised by what appears.
Pointers	Change the size and shape of the pointer. You can select schemes of pointer shapes so all pointer shapes for different activities take on a new appearance.
Motion	You can set the Pointer Speed to make the mouse move more slowly or quickly across the screen. You can add a Pointer Trail to the mouse to leave a trail of mouse pointers onscreen. This feature is especially useful if you have an LCD screen where the mouse pointer can sometimes get lost. This option cannot be shown for video display drivers that don't support it.
General	To add a new mouse to your system, click Change, and the Select Device dialog box displays. Make your selection from there. You also can add a new mouse with the Add New Hardware Wizard, available from the Control Panel.

Double-click a pointer shape while in the Pointers tab to replace one shape in a scheme.

▶ **See** "LCD Screen Mouse Trails," **p. 220**

NOTE Many mouse manufacturers include other options for customizing the mouse. Check the Mouse Properties dialog box for additional options that you can use to customize your mouse. ■

Customizing the Keyboard

Although changing the keyboard speed doesn't result in a miracle that makes you type faster, it does speed up the rate at which characters are repeated. You also can change the delay before the character repeats.

To change keyboard properties, follow these steps.

1. Open the Start menu and choose Settings, Control Panel; then choose Keyboard. The Keyboard properties sheet appears (see Figure 33.3).
2. Click a tab and make the changes you want.
3. Click Apply to accept the change and to continue making changes, or click OK to accept the change and close the Keyboard properties sheet.

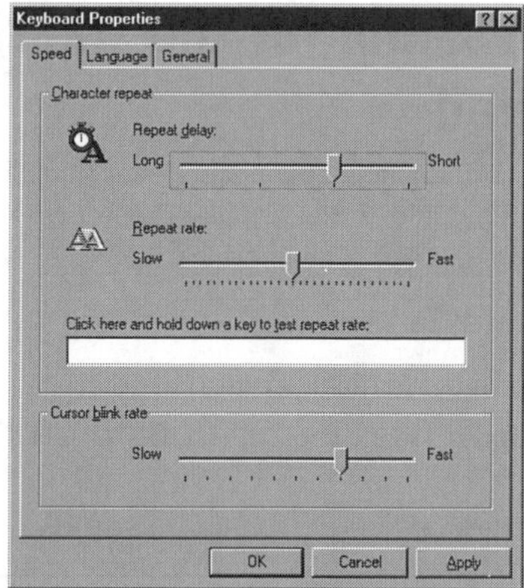

FIG. 33.3
You can change features such as the keyboard repeat and more in the Keyboard properties sheet.

Keyboard options are grouped on three tabs: Speed, Language, and General. Table 33.2 describes these tabs.

Table 33.2 Tabs of the Keyboard Properties Sheet

Tab	Description
Speed	Change the keyboard repeat speed. Drag the Slow/Fast pointer to change the Repeat Delay Speed (how long before the first repeat) or the Repeat Rate. Click the Click Here box to test the results. Drag the Slow/Fast Pointer for Cursor Blink Speed to change the speed at which the cursor blinks.
Language	Use the Language tab to select the language you use. Click Add to display the Add Language dialog box and select a language from the drop-down list. Click Properties to select an appropriate keyboard layout. Click Remove to remove a language from the list. Click the up and down arrows to change the order of the languages you have selected. Changing this option enables your applications to accurately sort words that might contain non-English characters, such as accent marks. However, changing the language setting does not change the language used by Windows. You need to purchase a different language version of Windows to accomplish this.
General	To change keyboards, click the Change button, and the Select Device dialog box appears. Make your selection from there. You can also add a new keyboard with the Add New Hardware Wizard, available from the Control Panel.

Making Windows Accessible for the Hearing, Sight, and Movement Impaired

In an effort to make computers more available to the more than 30 million people who have some form of disability, Microsoft has added Accessibility Properties. You can use these properties to adjust the computer's sound, display, and physical interface.

To make accessibility adjustments, follow these steps:

1. Click the Start button and choose Settings, Control Panel.
2. Choose the Accessibility Options icon. The Accessibility properties sheet appears (see Figure 33.4).
3. Make your selections and click OK.

TROUBLESHOOTING

Accessibility Options does not appear in my Control Panel. From the Control Panel, choose Add/Remove Programs, and then choose the Windows Setup tab. Choose the Accessibility Options choice, and then choose OK. You will be prompted for the Windows 95 installation media to complete the install.

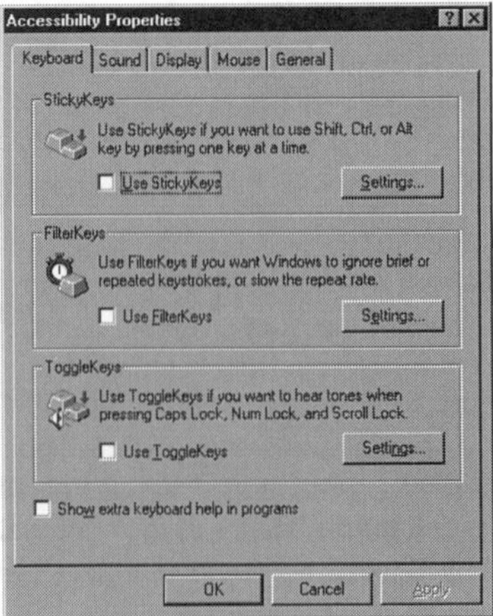

FIG. 33.4
Use the Accessibility properties sheet to make Windows easier to use for a person with a disability.

The Accessibility properties sheet includes the tabs outlined in Table 33.3.

Table 33.3 Tabs of the Accessibility Properties Sheet

Tab	Description
Keyboard	Makes the keyboard more tolerant and patient. Select Use StickyKeys if you need to press multiple keys simultaneously but can press keys only one at a time. Select Use FilterKeys to ignore short or repeated keystrokes. Select Use ToggleKeys to make a sound when you press Caps Lock, Num Lock, and Scroll Lock.
Sound	Provides visual warnings and captions for speech and sounds. Select Use SoundSentry to make Windows use a visual warning when a sound alert occurs. Select Use ShowSounds to display captions instead of speech or sounds.
Display	Selects colors and fonts for easy reading. Select Use High Contrast to use color and font combinations that produce greater screen contrast.
Mouse	Controls the pointer with the numeric keypad. Select Use MouseKeys to use the numeric keypad and other keys in place of the mouse. The relationship of keys to mouse controls appears in the following table.
General	Turns off accessibility features, gives notification, and adds an alternative input device. Use Automatic Reset to set Windows so accessibility features remain on at all times, are turned off when Windows restarts, or are turned off after a period of inactivity. Notification tells users when a feature is turned on or off. The SerialKey device enables Windows to receive keyboard or mouse input from alternative input devices through a serial port.

Some of these accessibility features might be difficult for a disabled person to turn on or off through normal Windows procedures. To alleviate this problem, Windows includes special *hotkeys*. Pressing the keys or key combinations for the designated hotkey turns an accessibility feature on or off or changes its settings. Table 33.4 provides the hotkeys for different features.

Table 33.4 Hotkeys for Accessibility Features

Feature	Hotkey	Result
High-Contrast Mode	Press left Alt+left Shift+Print Screen simultaneously	Alternates the screen through different text/background combinations.
StickyKeys	Press the Shift key	Turned on or off five consecutive times.
FilterKeys	Hold down right Shift	Turned on or off key for eight seconds.
ToggleKeys	Hold down Num Lock key	Turned on or off for five seconds.
MouseKeys	Press left Alt+ left Shift+Num Lock	Turned on or off simultaneously.

MouseKeys can be very useful for portable or laptop computer users and graphic artists, as well as for people unable to use a mouse. Graphic artists will find MouseKeys useful because it enables them to produce finer movements than those done with a mouse. After MouseKeys is turned on, you can produce the same effects as a mouse by using these keys:

Action	Press this key(s)
Movement	Any number key except 5
Large moves	Hold down Ctrl as you press number keys
Single pixel moves	Hold down Shift as you press number keys
Single-click	5
Double-click	+
Begin drag	Insert
Drop after drag	Delete
Select left mouse button	/
Select right mouse button	-
Select both mouse buttons	*

CAUTION

Use the numeric keypad with MouseKeys, not the numbered keys across the top of the keypad. Make sure the Num Lock key is set so the keypad is in numeric mode rather than cursor mode.

Setting the Date and Time

Use the Date/Time properties sheet to change the date or time in your system (see Figure 33.5). You also can change the format of the date and time to match another country's standard.

FIG. 33.5 You can change the system date and time in the Date/Time properties sheet.

TIP To display the current date, point to the clock on the taskbar, and the date will pop up.

To change date and time properties, follow these steps.

1. Double-click the clock on the taskbar, or open the Start menu and choose Settings, Control Panel; then choose Date/Time.

   The Date/Time properties sheet appears.

2. Click a tab and make the changes you want. See the following table for a description of things you can change.

3. Click Apply to accept the change and to continue making changes, or click OK to accept the change and close the Date/Time properties sheet.

Date and time options are grouped on two tabs: Date & Time and Time Zone. Table 33.5 describes these tabs.

Table 33.5 Tabs of the Date/Time Properties Sheet

Tab	Description
Date & Time	To change the Date, click the down arrow and select a month, or click the up and down arrows to select a year. Click the day of the month in the calendar. To change the time, click the element you want to change in the digital time display. For example, to change hours, click the first two numbers. Click the up and down arrows next to the time display.
Time Zone	Click the down arrow to select a new time zone (see Figure 33.6). Select the Adjust for Daylight Savings Time check box to have the time automatically adjust for daylight savings time.

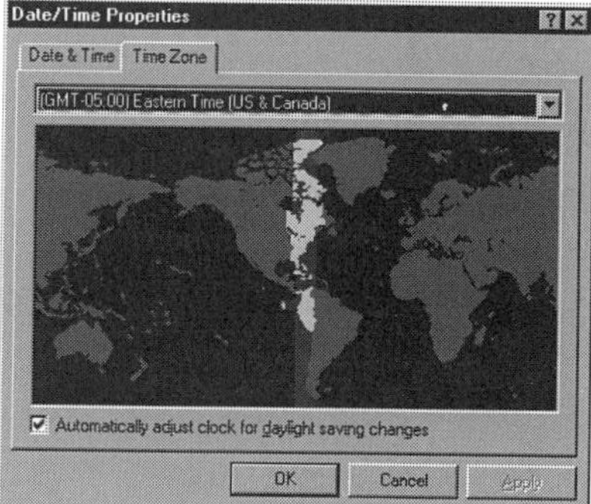

FIG. 33.6 You can change the time zone to reflect the time in any area of the world.

Customizing for Your Country and Language

Windows has the capacity to switch between international character sets, time and date displays, and numeric formats. The international settings you choose in Control Panel affect applications, such as Microsoft Excel, that take advantage of these Windows features.

NOTE Although you can change the language and country formats, doing so does not change the language used in menus or Help information. To obtain versions of Windows and Microsoft applications for countries other than the United States, check with your local Microsoft representative. Check with the corporate offices of other software vendors for international versions of their applications.

The Regional Settings properties sheet provides five tabs (see Figure 33.7). The region you select on the Regional Settings tab will automatically affect the settings in the other tabs.

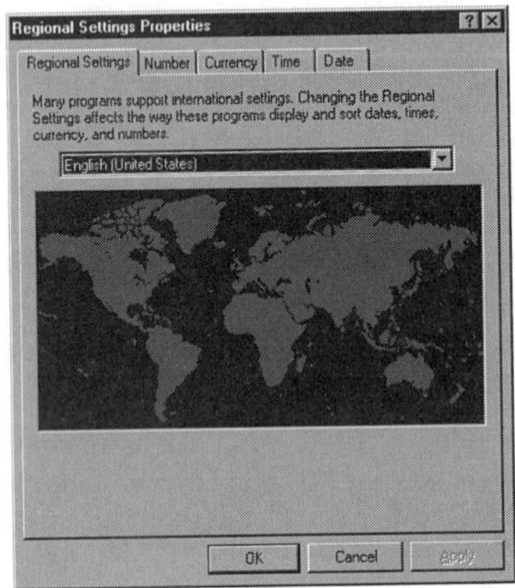

FIG. 33.7 You can change settings, including the formats used for numbers, dates, times, and currencies by selecting a region in the Regional Settings tab.

To change Regional Settings properties, follow these steps:

1. Open the Start menu and choose Settings, Control Panel; then choose Regional Settings. The Regional Settings properties sheet appears.
2. Click a tab and make the changes you want.
3. Click Apply to accept the changes and to continue making changes, or click OK to accept the change and close the Regional Settings Properties screen.

Table 33.6 describes each tab in the Regional Setting properties sheet.

Table 33.6 Tabs of the Regional Settings Properties Sheet

Tab	Description
Regional Settings	Click the down arrow and select your geographic region, or click your region on the global map. This selection automatically changes other settings in the dialog box.
Number	To make a change to the format, click the down arrow next to the box you want to change and choose what you want, or click in the box and type what you want.
Currency	To make a change to the format, click the down arrow next to the box you want to change and choose what you want, or click in the box and type what you want. To select some currency symbols, you might have to select a different keyboard first. The No. of Digits After Decimal setting can be overridden by some applications, such as spreadsheet programs.
Time	Change the symbols, separator, and style of the time display. To make a change to the format, click the down arrow next to the box you want to change and choose what you want, or click in the box and type what you want.
Date	To make a change to the format, click the down arrow next to the box you want to change and choose what you want, or click in the box and type what you want.

Changing Custom Settings for Each User

Windows accommodates situations in which people share a computer or move between computers. Windows enables you to store your custom settings for colors, accessibility features, desktop icons, and so on with your logon name. When you log on to the computer, Windows resets the computer with your settings.

User profiles are stored with your user logon ID. But you must tell Windows that you want to store user profiles for each different logon ID.

To create or remove a custom user profile for each logon ID, follow these steps:

1. Open the Start menu and choose Settings, Control Panel; then choose Passwords. Figure 33.8 shows the User Profiles tab.
2. Select one of the following:
   - Select All Users of This PC if you want all users to use the same settings. Go to step 4.
   - Select Users Can Customize Their Preferences if you want Windows to use the customization setup during the last use of that logon ID. Go to step 3.

3. If you make the second selection in step 2, you can choose from the following:
    - Select Include Desktop Icons and Network Neighborhood Contents in User Settings if the user profile should remember changes to these items.
    - Select Include Start Menu and Program Groups in User Settings if the user profile should remember changes to these items.
4. Click OK.

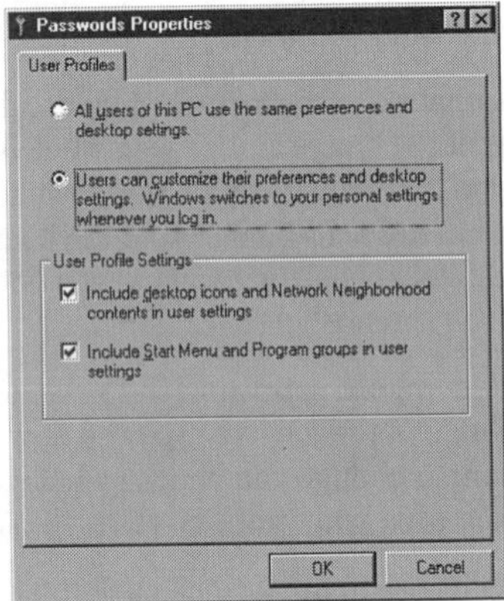

FIG. 33.8. You can create user profiles so people sharing the same computer can save their custom settings.

When you are done with a Windows computer shared by multiple users, log off the computer so others can log on and use their custom user profiles. To log off, click the Start button, and choose Shut Down, Close All Programs and Log On as a Different User. Choose OK.

If you selected Users Can Customize Their Preferences, then whenever a person logs on to Windows and customizes settings, those settings are saved with that logon ID. The next time someone logs on with that logon ID, Windows changes to the settings for that ID.

Running the User Settings Wizard

To further customize Windows 95 for individual users, you may run the User Settings Wizard. The Wizard helps specify what types of information should be stored for each user. This wizard should be run for each user sharing the Windows 95 computer. The first time the Wizard is run, the user is prompted for a username and password. After the inital run, the Wizard performs according to these steps.

To specify options for a new user, follow these steps:

1. Open the Start menu and choose Settings, Control Panel; then choose Passwords. Figure 33.9 shows the User Settings tab.
2. Choose New User. The User Settings Wizard is launched. Choose Next.
3. Enter a username and then choose Next.
4. Enter a password and then choose Next

5. Choose the items that will be personalized on a user-by-user basis. Also specify whether these copies of the current settings should be created, such as background images, or whether new default settings should be used to save space.
6. Choose Next and then choose Finish. Windows 95 will prompt you to restart your computer.

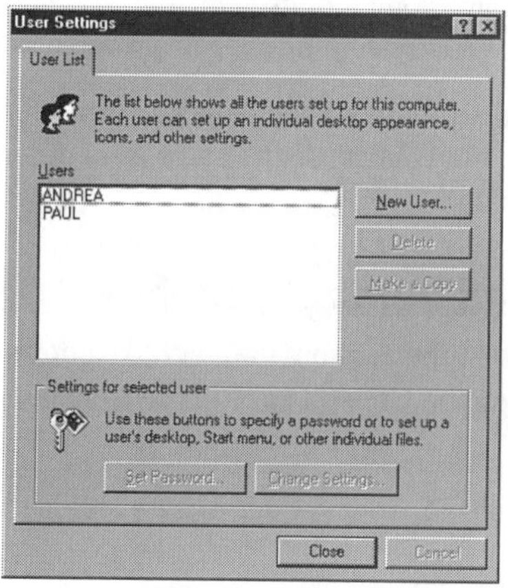

FIG. 33.9.
You can create new users and customize which system settings are saved for each.

Preventing Others from Using Windows

You might work in an area where you need to keep your computer secure. For example, your work might involve financial, market, or personnel data that is confidential. One way you can help to protect this information is to require a password before Windows will start.

To create or change your Windows password, follow these steps:

1. Open the Passwords properties sheet as described in the previous section.
2. Click the Change Passwords tab. Then click the Change Windows Password button to display the Change Windows Password dialog box. If you have network passwords, they will be listed so you can change them to match your Windows password.
3. Type your old password in the Old Password text box.
4. Type your new password in the New Password and Confirm Password text boxes.
5. Choose OK, and then choose OK again.

Windows provides security for the network environment from the other tabs on the Password properties sheet.

▶ **See** "Maintaining Workgroup Security," **p. 861**

Reviewing Your Computer's System Information

One of the more gruesome aspects of using DOS or earlier versions of Windows was working with configuration files when you wanted to customize or optimize your computer. People who wanted to install sound cards or network adapters, change memory usage, or specify I/O (Input/Output) or IRQ (interrupt request) settings faced immersion in the arcane world of configuration files. Configuration files gave you no help; yet if you made an error, part of your hardware might not be recognized, your system might run slower, or it might not run at all.

Windows 95 makes specifying configurations easier. Now you can select only allowable options from straightforward dialog boxes, and you can see settings from other hardware devices that might cause conflicts.

Reading Your Registration and Version Number

You can see your registration number, the version number of Windows, and the type of processor on which Windows is running on the General page of the System properties sheet. To see this page, follow these steps:

1. Open the Start menu and choose Settings, Control Panel to display the Control Panel window.
2. Choose the System icon.
3. Click the General tab of the System properties sheet (see Figure 33.10).

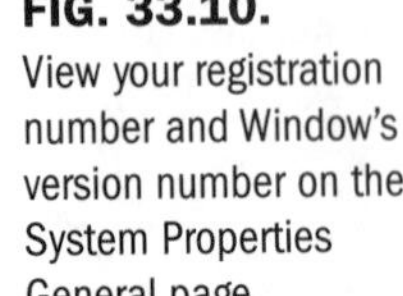

FIG. 33.10.
View your registration number and Window's version number on the System Properties General page.

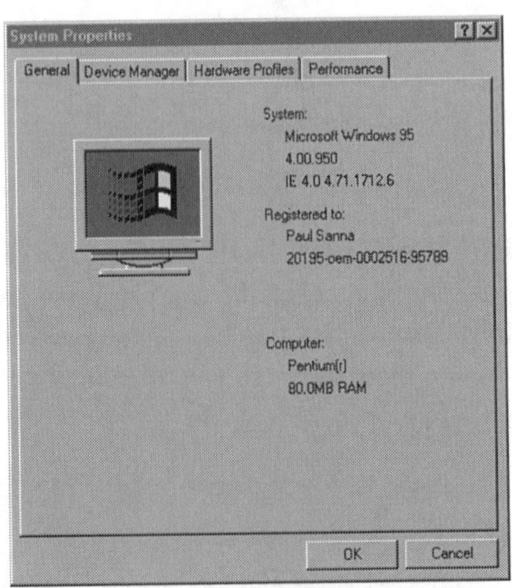

NOTE If you have the OSR2 version of Windows 95 installed, you will see a "B" after the 4.00.950 designation. This is a handy way to determine whether or not OSR2 is installed on a system.

Examining the Hardware on Your Computer

You might need to examine the configuration settings and drivers for hardware connected to your computer. You can use the System properties sheet to help you troubleshoot hardware. If you need to see a list of IRQ and I/O settings, you need to use the Device Manager.

To display the Device Manager page, follow these steps:

1. Open the Start menu and choose Settings, Control Panel to display the Control Panel window.
2. Choose the System icon.
3. Click the Device Manager tab of the System properties sheet (see Figure 33.11).

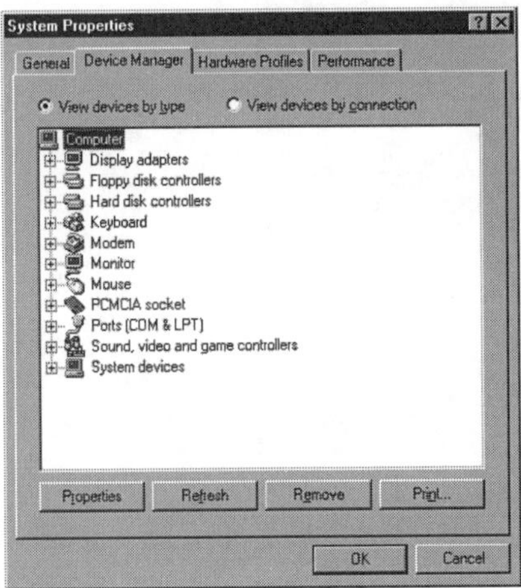

FIG. 33.11. View the hardware devices and their drivers on the System Properties Device Manager page.

4. To see the drivers installed for a device, click the + sign to the left of the device. To see information about a device or to remove the device, select one of the following buttons:

Button	Action
Properties	Displays a listing of properties appropriate to the device. Select the Computer item to see IRQ and I/O settings.
Refresh	Windows reexamines the installed hardware and attempts to update the list.
Remove	Removes the selected device or driver.
Print	Prints a report of configuration settings.

5. Choose OK.

▶ **See** "Installing Plug and Play Hardware," **p. 168**

▶ **See** "Installing Plug and Play CD-ROM Drives," **p. 125**

Checking IRQ, I/O, DMA, and Memory Settings Hardware devices each require a unique section of memory (I/O address). Some hardware devices also require an interrupt request (IRQ) or direct memory access (DMA) to operate. If any of these settings conflict with the settings for another device, either or both of the devices might not work.

You can see a list of these settings in your computer by selecting the Computer icon on the Device Manager page of the System properties sheet and then clicking Properties. Select from the option buttons to display the list of settings you want to see. Figure 33.12 shows the list of IRQ settings.

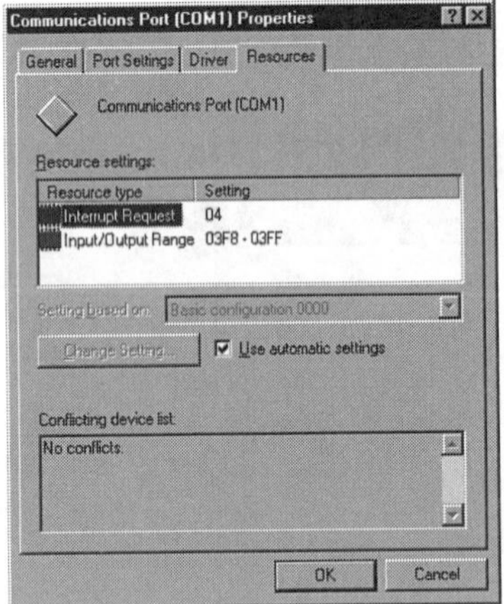

FIG. 33.12.
Use the View Resources page to track down conflicts in IRQ and I/O settings.

In MS-DOS and in prior versions of Windows, it was difficult to tell the cause of conflicts between hardware devices. In Windows 95, the Device Manager shows you lists of IRQ and I/O settings. You can scan through the lists and see where you accidentally installed two device drivers for the same device or you set two different devices to the same or overlapping IRQ or I/O settings.

If you find you installed two drivers for the same device, you can delete one of them. If you find a conflict because two hardware devices are using the same memory or IRQ settings, you can resolve the conflict easily through the Device Manager. The approach you might take to resolve a conflict is to look through the lists in the Device Manager to find an open IRQ or I/O setting, check the two manuals for the particular devices to determine what other IRQ or I/O settings they will work with, and change the settings for one of the devices so it doesn't conflict.

TROUBLESHOOTING

One of the hardware devices on a computer is not working. Click the Device Manager tab on the System properties sheet and check for an **X** through a device. This means the hardware has been disabled. Double-click that device to check its settings. If a device icon has a circled exclamation point, the hardware has a problem. Double-click the icon to inspect the type of problem.

It took a couple attempts with different driver selections before some of the hardware would work. Now some of the devices on the system work slowly, intermittently, or incorrectly. Check the Device Manager page of the System properties sheet to see if you have multiple drivers installed for the same hardware device. Delete all the drivers except the driver for your specific manufacturer and model. If there are multiple drivers, but not one specific to your hardware device, keep the generic driver.

The computer works with either a sound card or a network adapter card, but not both. The usual cause of this problem is a conflict between IRQ ports and I/O addresses. Each hardware device must have its own IRQ port and its own I/O address. Sound cards and network adapters are notorious for conflicting with each other over these. To see the IRQ port and I/O address used by each device, display the Device Manager page, select the Computer icon, and choose Properties. On the View Resources page that appears, you can select the Interrupt Request (IRQ) or Input/Output (I/O) option to view a list of settings for each device on your computer. Write down the current settings and watch for conflicts. Then change the settings for devices that conflict with others.

▶ **See** "Installing a Plug and Play Modem," **p. 69**

▶ **See** "Installing and Configuring Your Modem," **p. 68**

Creating, Naming, and Copying Hardware Profiles

Hardware profiles are collections of hardware settings; they're useful if you use different collections of hardware on your computer. For example, you might have a laptop computer that uses a VGA LCD monitor on the road but uses an SVGA large-screen monitor on the desktop.

By saving a collection of hardware settings as a profile, you only need to choose the profile you want rather than manually change hardware settings when you want to run a different combination of hardware.

When you start a Windows 95 computer that has multiple hardware configurations, you have the option of choosing the named hardware profile you want to use. From a text screen in Startup, you see something similar to this:

```
Windows cannot determine what configuration your computer is in.
Select one of the following:

1. Original Configuration
2. Multimedia
3. Desktop
4. None of the above

Enter your choice:
```

Type the number of the profile you want to use and press Enter. Windows 95 then starts with that configuration of hardware, only loading the hardware drivers required.

To make use of the distinct hardware profiles, you must first copy the existing default profile. The default profile is named Original Configuration. After you copy a profile, you can edit the devices included in it and rename it to help you recognize it. To copy or rename a hardware profile, follow these steps:

1. Open the Start menu and choose Settings, Control Panel to display the Control Panel window.
2. Choose the System icon.
3. Click the Hardware Profile tab of the System properties sheet (see Figure 33.13).

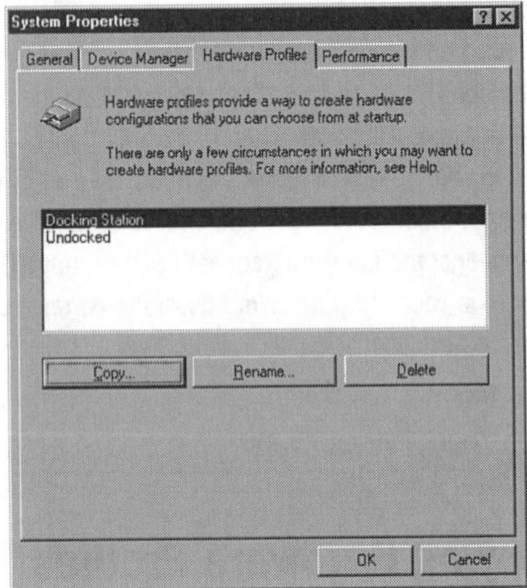

FIG. 33.13. Keep different combinations of hardware devices stored as a named hardware profile.

4. Select the hardware profile you want to work with and then click one of the following buttons:

Button	**Action**
Copy	Displays a Copy Profile dialog box in which you can enter a new name. Copies the hardware configuration from the selected profile to this new profile.
Rename	Changes the name of a profile.
Delete	Deletes a profile.

5. Choose OK.

To create a new profile or change an existing profile, follow these steps:

1. If you want to create a new profile, copy an existing profile as described in the preceding steps. Use a unique, descriptive name for the profile.
2. Click the Device Manager tab on the System properties sheet.
3. Click the plus sign next to the hardware type you want to change for the configuration; then double-click the specific hardware you want to change. This displays the device's properties sheet.
4. In the Device Usage area of the properties sheet, deselect any hardware profile you don't want to use this device with. By default, all of your devices will be used with all of your profiles until you make changes.

5. Choose OK.
6. Repeat steps 3 through 5 until you have configured all the hardware for this profile.
7. Choose OK.

Depending on the changes you made, you might be prompted to restart your computer.

▶ **See** "Using Your Laptop with a Docking System," **p. 190**

Checking Performance Settings

You can check the performance parameters of your computer on the Performance page of the System properties sheet. To see this page, follow these steps:

1. Open the Start menu and choose Settings, Control Panel to display the Control Panel window.
2. Choose the System icon.
3. Click the Performance tab of the System properties sheet (see Figure 33.14).

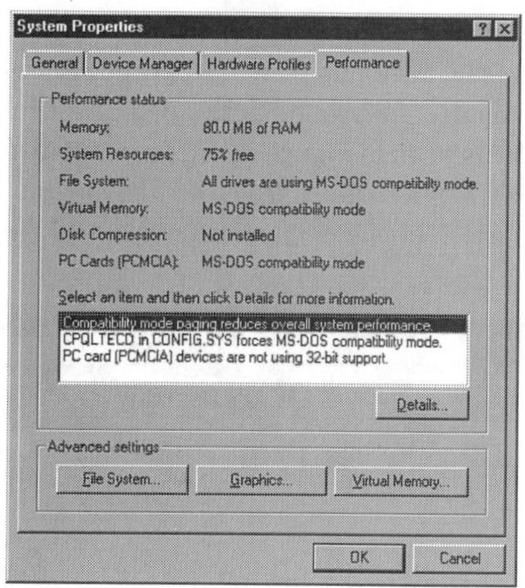

FIG. 33.14. The System Properties Performance page provides information on your computer's performance parameters.

4. View the performance status parameters on the Performance page, or choose File System, Graphics, or Virtual Memory for advanced performance tuning options.
5. Choose OK.

CAUTION

In general, do not change the settings available on the Performance page. Windows 95 usually sets these parameters optimally.

▶ **See** "Improving Performance with Disk Defragmenter," **p. 352**

Using the Task Scheduler

Task Scheduler is a new application that comes with Internet Explorer 4.0 that can be used to schedule tasks to run at regular intervals. You might, for example, schedule Disk Defragmenter and ScanDisk to run every evening at 8 pm as part of your routine disk maintenance. Task Scheduler starts every time you start up Windows and runs in the background, so you don't even have to think about a task once it is scheduled. You can easily change the schedule for a task, or temporarily suspend all scheduled tasks, if you are busy on your computer during times when tasks are scheduled to be completed.

The Task Scheduler consists of a folder, called Scheduled Tasks, which you can view in My Computer. Each scheduled task is an object in the Scheduled Tasks folder and as with any object in Windows 95, a task has a property sheet. You use the property sheet to set up and schedule a task and to set other parameters for the task. The folder/property sheet paradigm, which is so familiar in Windows 95, makes it easy to create and define a task in Task Scheduler.

Starting Task Scheduler

You can open Task Scheduler from either from the Start Menu or from My Computer. To open Task Scheduler from the Start menu, click Start, then Programs, Accessories, System Tools, Scheduled Tasks. From My Computer, choose the Scheduled Tasks folder. Either method opens the Scheduler Tasks folder, shown in Figure 33.15. As with any folder window, you can select different views to show more or less detail from the View menu. In Figure 33.15, the Details view has been selected, which presents more information about your scheduled tasks.

FIG. 33.15.
Tasks scheduled in Task Scheduler are found in the Scheduled Tasks folder.

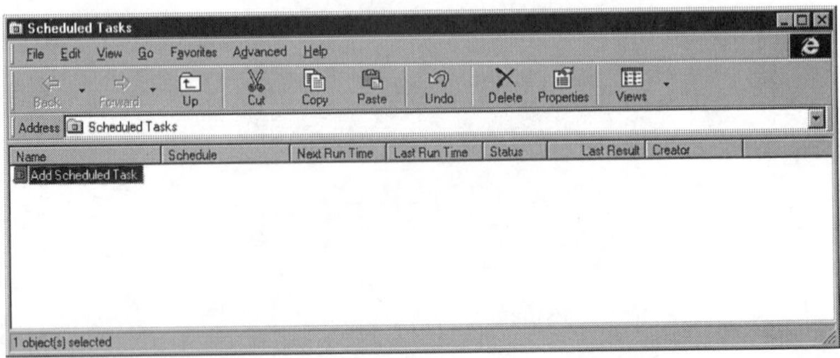

Once you have opened the Scheduled Tasks folder, you should check to make sure Task Scheduler is actually running. To do this, choose Advanced, Start Using Task Scheduler. If the command Stop Using Task Scheduler appears in the Advanced menu, then Task Scheduler is already running. When Task Scheduler is running, the Task Scheduler icon will appear in the lower-right corner of the taskbar.

Scheduling a New Task

Adding a new task to the Scheduled Tasks folder consists of adding a task object to the Scheduled Tasks folder, just as you would add a new folder to a folder window, and then defining the task using the property sheet for the task. A wizard walks you through the steps of creating a new scheduled task.

To schedule a new task, follow these steps:

1. Open the Scheduled Tasks folder in My Computer or by clicking Start, then Programs, Accessories, System Tools, Scheduled Tasks.
2. Choose Add Scheduled Task from the list. The Wizard is launched. Choose Next.
3. Choose the application you want to launch from the list of applications registered with Windows 95. If you do not see the application you want to launch, use the Browse button to track it down.
4. Enter the name of the task as it will appear in the list, and then select the interval at which you want the task to run. Then choose Next.
5. Depending on the interval, a specific dialog appears allowing you to customize the time at which the task runs. For example, if you choose a Daily frequency, the dialog box shown in Figure 33.16 appears. Specify the interval options for launching the task, then press Enter.

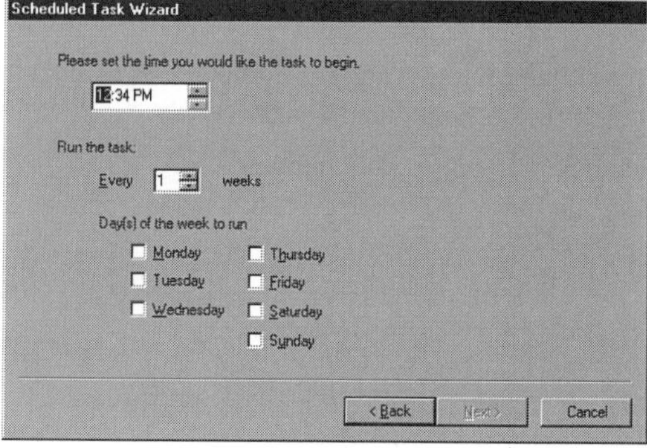

FIG. 33.16. You can customize the Task Schedule to launch an event at a specifc time.

6. Enter the username and password that Task Scheduler should use to launch the task. Choose OK.
7. Choose Finish to complete the new scheduled task, or to specify an advanced option, select the check box and then press Finish. Advanced options allow you to specify the Start In folder for a task, for how long Task Scheduler should repeatedly launch a task, as well as edit most of the options you specified with the Wizard.

Suspending Task Scheduler

Suppose you need to put in extra hours to catch up on your work and you don't want to be interrupted by tasks scheduled to run at night. You can temporarily suspend Task Scheduler so that all scheduled tasks are put on hold.

To pause Task Scheduler, follow these steps:

1. Open the Scheduled Tasks folder, using My Computer or the Start menu.
2. Choose Advanced, Pause Task Scheduler.

   The Task Scheduler icon will appear with an "X" through it in the taskbar when it is paused.

   If a task misses its scheduled time while the Task Scheduler is paused, it won't run until the next scheduled time.
3. To resume the Task Scheduler, choose Advanced, Continue Task Scheduler.

To suspend a specific task without suspending other scheduled tasks, open the property sheet for the task and clear the Enabled check box on the Task sheet.

Turning Off Task Scheduler

When you turn off Task Scheduler, scheduled tasks will not run and Task Scheduler will not start up when you start Windows. To turn off Task Scheduler, follow these steps:

1. Open the Task Scheduler folder from My Computer or by clicking Start, then Programs, Accessories, System Tools, Scheduled Tasks.
2. Choose Advanced, Stop Using Task Scheduler.

CHAPTER 34

Simple Ways of Sharing Data Between Applications

by Rob Tidrow with Bob Voss

In this chapter

Understanding the Data-Sharing Capabilities of Windows 95

Windows 95 supports data exchange using Clipboard object linking and embedding (OLE). All Windows applications provide some means of sharing data with another application. All applications, for example, have access to the Windows Clipboard, to which you can copy or cut data. Not all Windows applications, however, have OLE-capability.

Sharing data among applications can help you automate redundant tasks. Data-sharing capabilities also enable users to create more powerful, more informative, and more advanced documents that tap into the abilities of multiple applications. Many applications that adhere to Windows 95 standards let you copy an element from one type of application and use it in another application. You can, for example, create a picture from Paint and use it in a WordPad document, as shown in Figure 34.1.

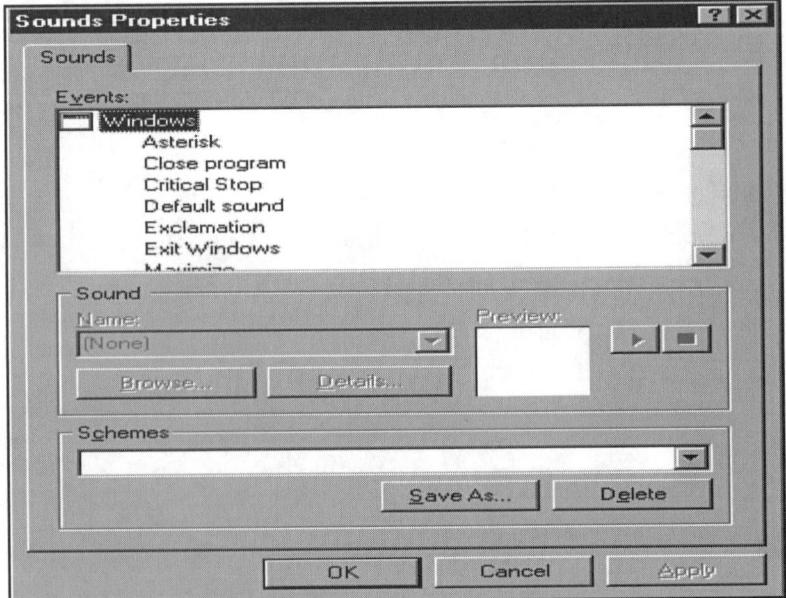

FIG. 34.1
This picture was copied from Paint into WordPad.

Using the Windows Clipboard

The most basic way to exchange data from one source to another is to use the Windows 95 Clipboard, an area in memory that applications can access to share data. When you use the Clipboard, you *cut* or *copy* data to the Clipboard and then *paste* that data in your document.

Copying places a replica of the material that you selected in the Clipboard. Cutting removes the data from your document and places it in the Clipboard. Pasting places the data from the Clipboard into your document.

NOTE When you paste data from the Clipboard, you don't remove it from the Clipboard. You can paste the data from the Clipboard into your document as many times as you like. The Clipboard retains your cut or copied data until you clear the contents manually, or until you cut or copy something else to the Clipboard.

Cutting, Copying, and Pasting Data

Applications that let you access the Clipboard generally use standard menu commands or keyboard shortcuts. In many Windows 95 applications, you can transfer data to and from the Clipboard by choosing commands from the Edit menu.

To cut or copy something from a WordPad document, follow these steps:

1. Select the text in the document that you want to cut or copy, as shown in Figure 34.2.

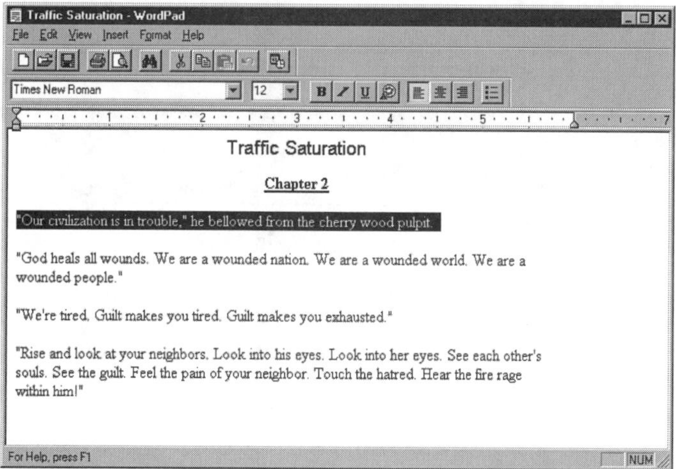

FIG. 34.2 Select the text you want to cut in the source document.

2. Choose Edit, Cut to cut the text to the Clipboard, or choose Edit, Copy to copy the text to the Clipboard.

   In many cases, you also can right-click the selection to display a shortcut menu and choose Cut or Copy from the menu.

Now that you have something in the Clipboard, you can paste it somewhere in the document, or into another document. To paste, follow these steps:

1. Position your cursor at the place in the document where you want to paste the element (if you're copying to a document in another application, open that application and document, then position the cursor).
2. Choose Edit, Paste to paste the contents of the Clipboard into its new location, Figure 34.3 shows WordPad text pasted into a Paint drawing.

Another standard way to use the Clipboard is to use the buttons in an application's toolbar. Figure 34.4 shows the Cut, Copy, and Paste buttons on the WordPad toolbar.

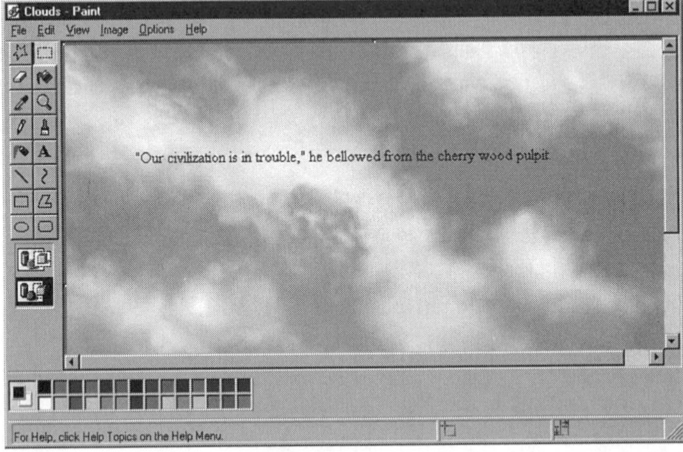

FIG. 34.3
Pasting text from a WordPad document into a Paint drawing.

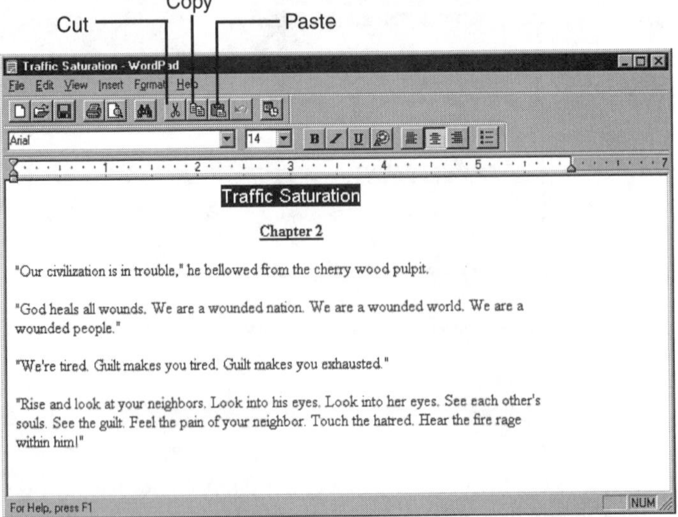

FIG. 34.4
Cut, Copy, and Paste buttons provided in the WordPad toolbar.

Quick View Plus is an add-on product for Windows 95 created by Inso Corporation. Quick View Plus enhances the Quick View feature that comes with Windows 95 in several ways. These include the capabilities to preview many more types of files, and to copy and paste information from a file that you are viewing. This feature allows you to view a file created by an application you don't have on your computer and then to copy and paste information from that file into another document.

For more information on Quick View Plus, contact Inso Corporation at (312) 329-0700. You can download a trialware version of the program from the Internet at the following address:

http://www.inso.com

Using Keyboard Shortcuts

Windows 95 supports a common set of keyboard shortcuts that, unless the shortcut has been reassigned, you can use in any application that supports data sharing. Table 34.1 shows these shortcuts.

Table 34.1 Cut, Copy, and Paste Keyboard Shortcuts

Action	Windows 95 Shortcut Keys
Cut	Ctrl+X or Shift+Delete
Copy	Ctrl+C or Ctrl+Insert
Paste	Ctrl+V or Shift+Insert

Copying Information to a Dialog Box

You can use a keyboard shortcut to help you fill in a dialog box. The Letter Wizard dialog box in Microsoft Word, which is used to create letters (see Figure 34.5), is requesting the recipient's name and address. You can type the information or copy it from somewhere else. For this example, assume that you have the recipient's name and address stored in a Notepad document and that you want to copy and paste that information into the dialog box.

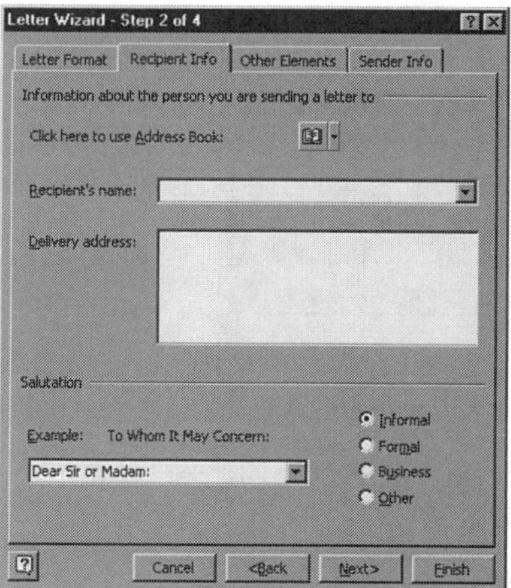

FIG. 34.5
You can cut or copy information to Windows 95 dialog boxes and wizards.

To copy information from the Notepad document to the Word Letter Wizard dialog box, follow these steps:

1. Select the information that you'll replace.
2. Switch to the open Notepad document by clicking the button in the taskbar at the bottom of the screen.

3. In the Notepad window, select the information that you want to copy, as shown in Figure 34.6.

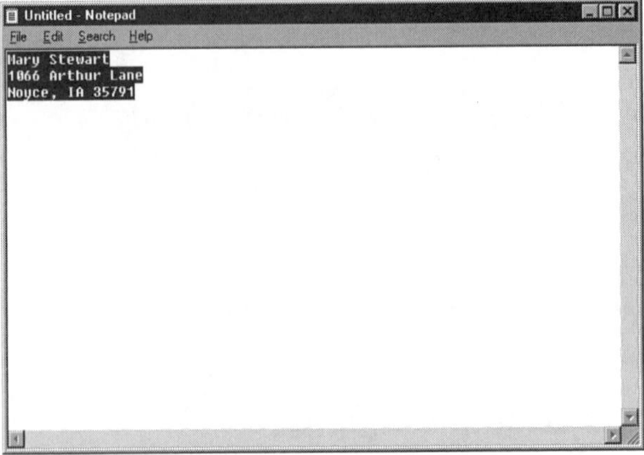

FIG. 34.6
Highlight text in the Notepad document to copy to the Clipboard.

4. To copy the highlighted text, choose Edit, Copy, or press Ctrl+C.
5. Click the Word button on the taskbar to return to the Letter Wizard dialog box in Word. The old entry in the recipient's text box should still be highlighted.
6. Press Ctrl+V to paste the information from the Clipboard to the text box. Figure 34.7 shows the completed text box.

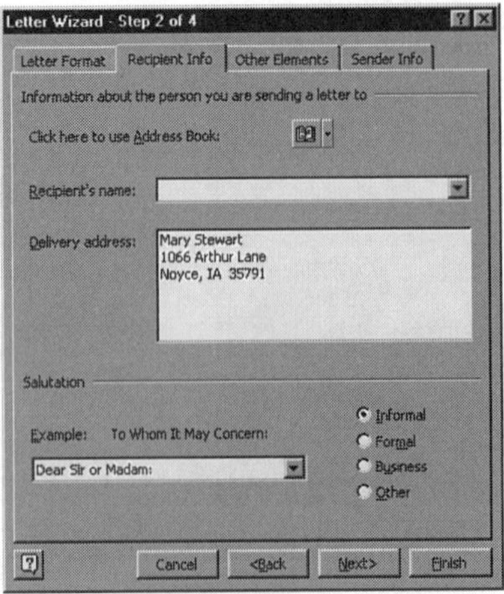

FIG. 34.7
The information from the Clipboard is pasted into the text box.

NOTE You can't use the Edit menu or any button on a toolbar while you're in this dialog box. The only way to copy from the Clipboard is to press Ctrl+V or Shift+Insert. The same holds true when you're trying to cut or copy from a dialog box. Press Ctrl+X to cut or Ctrl+C to copy highlighted text in a text box.

Capturing Screens with the Clipboard

Many Windows screen-capturing programs are available, but you also can use the Clipboard to capture the contents of the screen. When the screen image is captured, it's held in the Clipboard in bitmap format.

To capture the entire screen and paste it into a WordPad document, follow these steps:

TIP You also can capture the contents of the active window onscreen by pressing Alt+Print Screen or Shift+Print Screen, depending on your keyboard.

1. Press the Print Screen key to capture the entire screen and place it in the Clipboard.
2. Open or switch to WordPad.
3. In a new or existing document, choose Edit, Paste. The screen image, in bitmap format, is pasted into the WordPad document.

▶ **See** "Using Windows Paint," **p. 741**

Using Drag and Drop to Move or Copy Information Within an Application's Documents

A second method for moving information is to use the mouse to drag and drop selected pieces of information, which can be text, graphics, or data, from one location to another. When you drag and drop information, you are moving or copying it directly from one location to another, without using the Clipboard as a go-between. In this section, you learn how to drag and drop information within an application.

NOTE To use drag and drop, you must be working in an application that supports it. Most applications in the Microsoft Office suite, for example, support drag and drop, including Word, Excel, PowerPoint, and Access. Check the manual that comes with your application for information on using drag and drop. ■

To copy information with drag and drop in WordPad, follow these steps:

1. Open WordPad, and then open a document or create a new document that contains some text.
2. Select the text that you want to move or copy.
3. To move the text, position the mouse pointer over the selected area and drag the text.

   To copy the text, hold down the Ctrl key as you drag the text. A plus sign (+) appears next to the mouse pointer.

Up to the point that you release the mouse button to drop the text, you can press or release the Ctrl button to either copy or move the selection.

The mouse pointer changes as you drag, as shown in Figure 34.8.

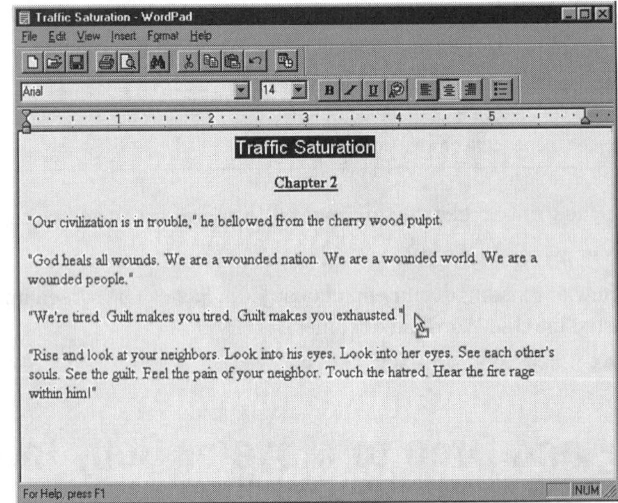

FIG. 34.8
The gray dashed line indicates where the text will be placed.

4. Drag the text to the position in the document where you want to place it. The gray vertical bar indicates the position of the new text.
5. Release the mouse button to complete the move or copy procedure.

Some applications, such as Word for Windows, allow you to move or copy text between two documents using drag and drop. To do so, make sure you can see both documents on screen at the same time, and then drag the item from one document to another following the steps just described.

TROUBLESHOOTING

When I copy information with drag and drop, the original document loses its information. You used the move feature instead. Make sure that you hold down the Ctrl key throughout the process. Release the mouse button first and then release the Ctrl key. The plus sign (+) next to the box in the mouse pointer indicates that you are copying the selection.

My copied text appears in the middle of existing text. Don't forget to watch the gray dashed line that's part of the mouse pointer. This line shows exactly where the copied text will be inserted.

I get a black circle with a slash through it when I try to copy. The black circle with the slash indicates that you can't drop the item in the area where the mouse is, such as the title bar or status bar. Make sure that you go all the way into the other document before you release the mouse button.

Although most Windows 95 users use Windows-based applications, millions of copies of DOS applications are used on Windows systems. Applications such as Lotus 1-2-3 for DOS, WordPerfect 5.1 for DOS, and the MS-DOS prompt remain very popular. Windows 95 lets you copy information from a DOS application or from a DOS command prompt to a Windows application.

Windows 95 supports the following ways to transfer information from DOS applications to Windows documents:

- You can transfer text from DOS to Windows, from Windows to DOS, and between DOS applications by means of the Clipboard.
- You can transfer graphics from DOS to Windows applications by means of the Clipboard.
- You can copy text from the MS-DOS command prompt to the Clipboard.

Using the Clipboard to Exchange Data

Some DOS applications use their own Clipboard equivalent, but none provide an area that lets you transfer text and graphics between applications. When you want to transfer text between applications, you usually have to use text converters or file-conversion utilities that transform the text into a format that the application can read. In many cases, you have to convert the text to an ASCII text file, which strips out your formatting and special character enhancements.

When you want to share data from a DOS application to a Windows application, you use a process known as *mark, copy, and paste*. The Mark, Copy, and Paste commands are located in the control menu of a DOS window. You also can find the Mark button on the MS-DOS Prompt toolbar.

To copy a list of your files at the DOS command prompt to a WordPad document, follow these steps:

1. Open the MS-DOS Prompt into a window (see Figure 34.9). You can change the way your DOS window looks by going into its properties and then changing the font or screen options.
2. Click the Mark toolbar button, or choose Edit, Mark from the Control menu. A blinking cursor appears at the top of the DOS window, indicating that you're in marking mode.
3. You now need to mark the area that you want to copy by drawing a box around it with your mouse pointer. To do so, place your mouse pointer where you want to start marking, hold down the left mouse button, and then drag the box around the text that you want to copy. Your screen should look something like the one shown in Figure 34.10.

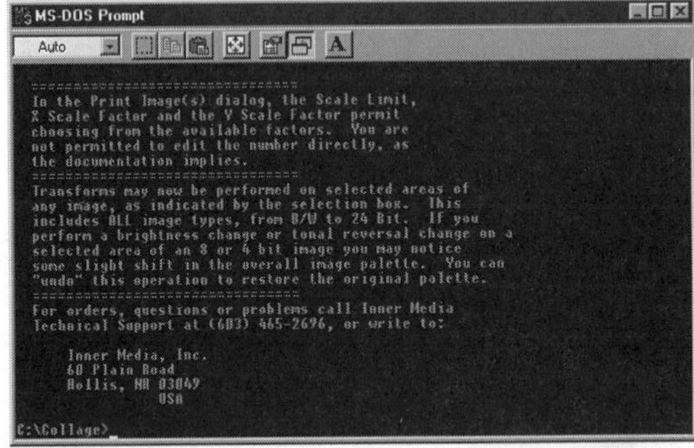

FIG. 34.9
You can copy text from the DOS window to a Windows document.

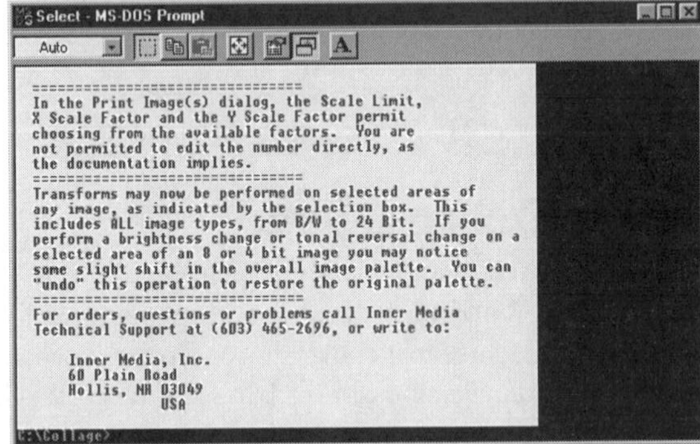

FIG. 34.10
Mark the text that you want to copy.

4. When you're satisfied with the selection, release the mouse button.
5. Click the Copy button in the toolbar; choose Edit, Copy from the Control menu or press Enter to copy the selection to the Clipboard.
6. Switch to WordPad, and place the cursor where you want the text to be placed.
7. Click the Paste toolbar button, or choose Edit, Paste. The text from the DOS window is placed in your WordPad document (see Figure 34.11).

▶ **See** "Understanding and Configuring MS-DOS Application Properties," **p. 657**

Copying Data from Windows to DOS

You also can copy data from a Windows application to a DOS application by cutting or copying the data to the Clipboard and then pasting the data into the DOS application. When you do this, all the formatting that you placed in the Windows document is lost.

To copy data from Windows to DOS, follow these steps:

1. In your Windows application, such as WordPad, select the text that you want to copy.
2. Choose Edit, Copy, or Edit, Cut.

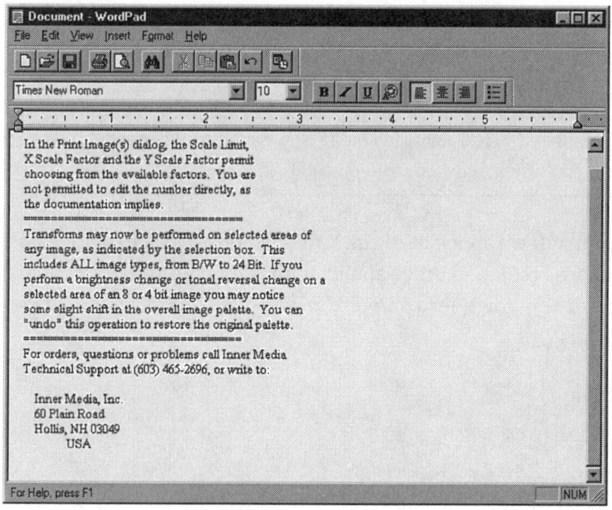

FIG. 34.11 You can insert text you copied from a DOS window into a WordPad document by pasting it from the Clipboard.

3. Switch to the DOS application, such as WordPerfect 5.2 for DOS. (Make sure the application is in a window and not full screen.)
4. Place the text or mouse cursor where you want to paste the text.
5. Choose Edit, Paste from the Control menu of the DOS application. The text now appears in the document.

Transferring Data by Using File Converters

Rather than cut and paste parts of a document into another document, you sometimes need to import an entire file into a different application. You may, for example, want to import a Windows Write file into WordPad. (Write was distributed with Windows 3.x.) Many software companies distribute Write files with their software to announce updates or changes in the software.

To open files that were created in other programs, many Windows applications include built-in file converters. *File converters* take the file format and transform it to a format that the application can read. During a file conversion, text enhancements, font selections, and other elements usually are preserved. Sometimes, however, these elements are converted to ASCII format.

To convert a Write file to WordPad format, follow these steps:

1. Start WordPad and choose File, Open.

TIP Click the Files of Type drop-down list to view the types of files you can open in WordPad.

2. Locate a file with the extension WRI and open it. WordPad starts to convert the file.

You now can edit the file as a WordPad file.

The type of converters you have installed for an application may depend on the installation options you chose at setup. See the application's documentation for specific converters.

Many other Windows applications include file converters to allow you to read and edit file formats that are created in other applications. Depending on the type of installation you perform, Word for Windows, for example, includes the following set of converters:

- Rich Text Format
- Text File
- Unicode Text Files
- Schedule+ Contact List
- Personal Address Book
- Outlook Address Book
- MS-DOS Text with Layout
- Text with Layout
- All Word Documents
- Word (Asian Version) 6.0/95
- Word for Macintosh 4.0-5.1
- Lotus 1-2-3
- WordPerfect 5.x
- WordPerfect 6.x
- Microsoft Excel Worksheet
- HTML Document

Rich Text Format (RTF) files have become the common language for exchanging files between word processors. You can preserve much of the formatting you apply to a document when you save it as an RTF file. If you don't have the correct converter for exchanging a file from one application to another, try creating an RTF file from the document and importing the document into the receiving application.

Another way to convert files is to save the file in a different format during the Save As process. When you need to import a Word for Windows file into WordPerfect or Word for Macintosh, for example, you can select those formats from the Save As Type drop-down list in the Save As dialog box. This list contains the types of formats in which you can save a Word for Windows document (see Figure 34.12).

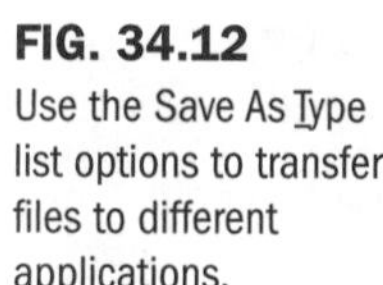

FIG. 34.12
Use the Save As Type list options to transfer files to different applications.

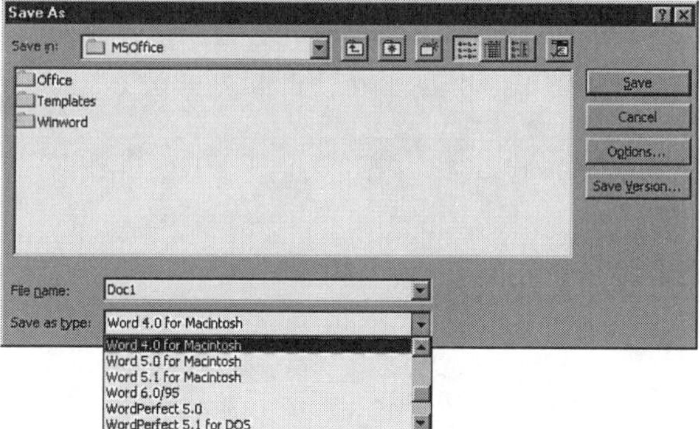

Understanding Data Linking

A more sophisticated way to exchange data in Windows 95 is through the use of linking. Before the arrival of the OLE standard, DDE (dynamic data exchange) was the technology used to link data. Now OLE offers both linking and embedding. OLE allows you to create links from one document or file to another document or file. These links can be between documents that are created in the same application (such as Word) or documents that are created in different applications (such as Word and Excel).

After you establish a link, you can update the information automatically by editing the original source of the information. This procedure lets you use data in various places but updates it in only one place. You must set up a *link* between two applications (or two documents) that support OLE. The application that requests data is called the *client* application. The other application, called the *server* application, responds to the client application's request by supplying the requested data.

With linked documents, you can work in the client application and make changes in data that's linked to the server application. When you change the data in the client application, Windows 95 automatically changes the data in the server application. The advantage to exchanging data by links is that data is kept up-to-date in the client and server applications.

One possible use of linking is taking data from an Excel worksheet and placing it in a Word document. If you need to change the Excel data, you need to change it only in Excel; the data is updated in Word automatically. In Figure 34.13, for example, data for the regional sales of TechTron is shown in an Excel worksheet. Figure 34.14 shows the same numbers in a Word document that can be distributed to the staff in the form of a memorandum.

Suppose that you want to put together a new memo each month to detail sales for the entire year, but you want to create the memo document one time and update the sales data in the Word document automatically. You can do this by using an OLE link. In this example, to change the worksheet data in the Word document, you need to change the data while you're working in Excel.

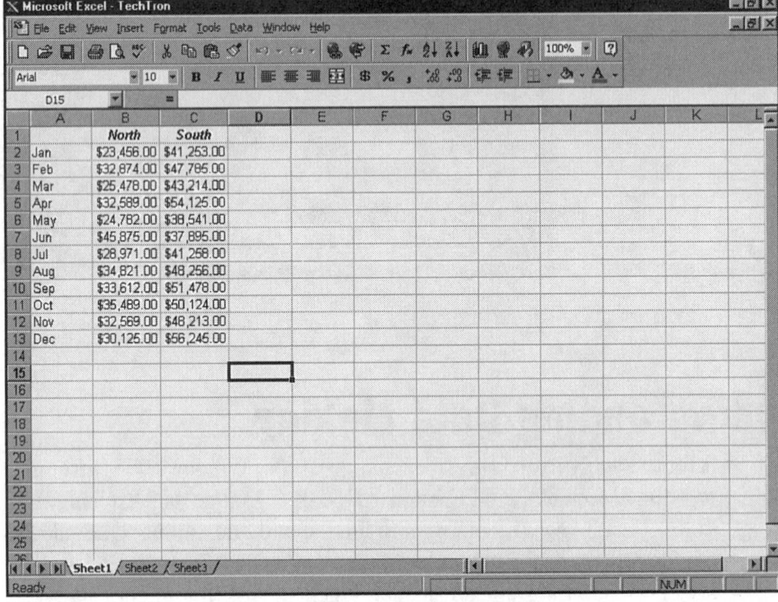

	North	South
Jan	$23,456.00	$41,253.00
Feb	$32,874.00	$47,785.00
Mar	$25,478.00	$43,214.00
Apr	$32,589.00	$54,125.00
May	$24,782.00	$38,541.00
Jun	$45,875.00	$37,895.00
Jul	$28,971.00	$41,258.00
Aug	$34,821.00	$48,256.00
Sep	$33,612.00	$51,478.00
Oct	$35,489.00	$50,124.00
Nov	$32,569.00	$48,213.00
Dec	$30,125.00	$56,245.00

FIG. 34.13
Data from an Excel spreadsheet can be linked to a Word document.

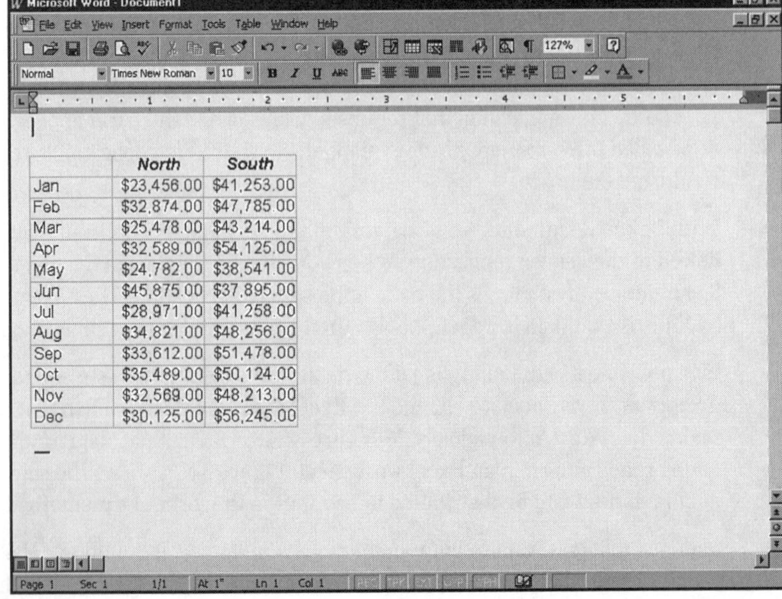

	North	South
Jan	$23,456.00	$41,253.00
Feb	$32,874.00	$47,785.00
Mar	$25,478.00	$43,214.00
Apr	$32,589.00	$54,125.00
May	$24,782.00	$38,541.00
Jun	$45,875.00	$37,895.00
Jul	$28,971.00	$41,258.00
Aug	$34,821.00	$48,256.00
Sep	$33,612.00	$51,478.00
Oct	$35,489.00	$50,124.00
Nov	$32,569.00	$48,213.00
Dec	$30,125.00	$56,245.00

FIG. 34.14
The Word document reflects any changes that you make in the Excel document.

Windows 95 provides two ways to use linking: interactively and through a macro language. The easiest way to use linking is the interactive method, which is based on the Clipboard copy-and-paste method you used earlier in this chapter but has some important differences. The macro method, which involves creating a macro in the application's macro language, isn't discussed in this book. See *Special Edition Using Excel Visual Basic for Applications, Second Edition*, published by Que, for more information on creating links using a macro language.

When you establish a link between applications, you use the Edit menu's Copy and Paste Link or Paste Special commands. If you have an Excel worksheet that you want to link to a Word document, follow these steps:

1. Open an Excel worksheet. You also can create a new worksheet from which you will link data.
2. Select some data in the worksheet, as shown in Figure 34.15.

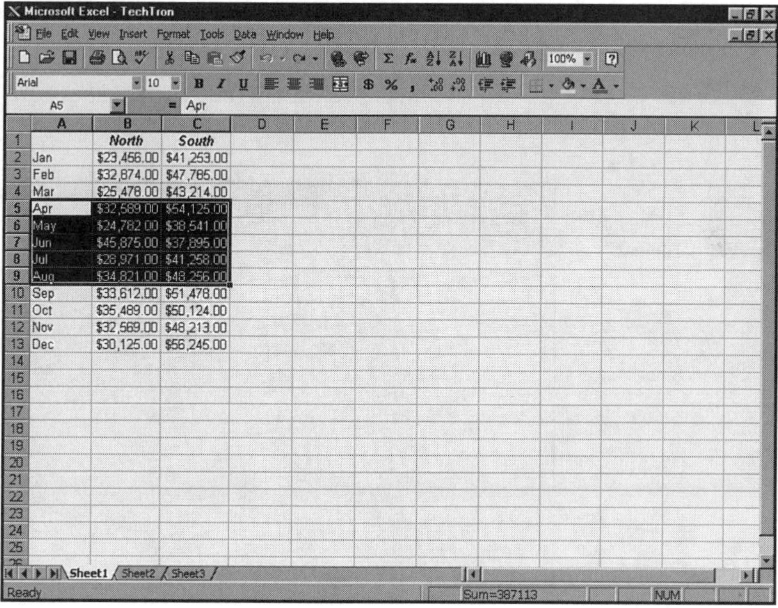

FIG. 34.15
Select data in Excel to link to Word.

3. Choose Edit, Copy to copy the selected data to the Clipboard.
4. Open Word and then open an existing document or start a new document.
5. Choose Edit, Paste Special and the Paste Special dialog box appears.
6. In the Paste Special dialog box, click the Paste Link option (see Figure 34.16). If you don't click this button, Word inserts the data from Excel as a table without linking.
7. Select Formatted Text (RTF) in the As list box.

   If you select Microsoft Excel Worksheet Object, the selected cells are inserted as an object (using OLE) into the Word document, instead of as a linked table.

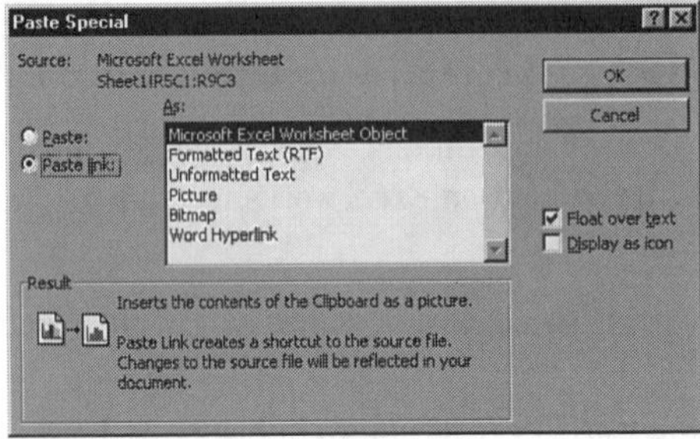

FIG. 34.16
Make sure you click the Paste Link button to establish a link.

8. Choose OK. The Excel data is inserted into the Word document as a table (see Figure 34.17).

When changes are made in the data in Excel, those changes are reflected in the Word document.

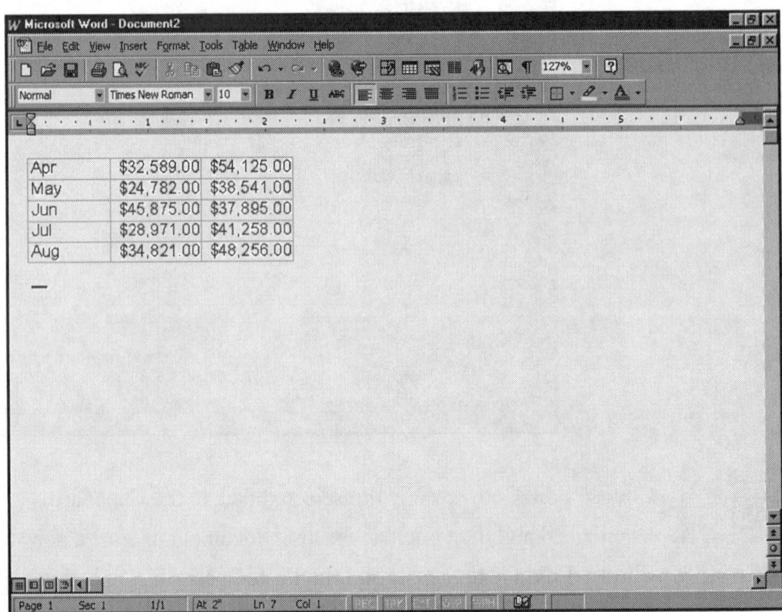

FIG. 34.17
Excel data is now linked to the Word document.

To see changes take place, switch back to the Excel worksheet and then follow these steps:

1. Change some of the data or formatting in the area that you linked to the Word document (see Figure 34.18).
2. Press Enter or click outside the cells that you edited. The data changes in the Word document to reflect your changes.
3. Switch to the Word document to see the updated data (see Figure 34.19).

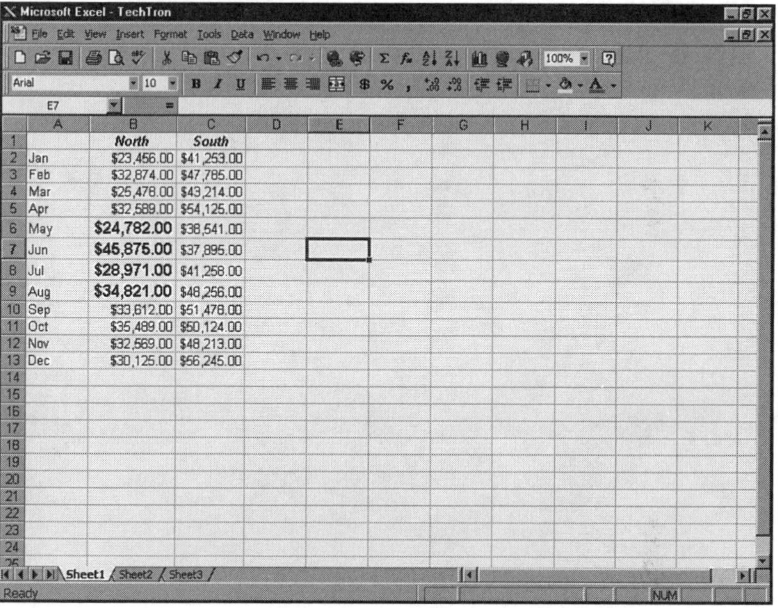

FIG. 34.18
Change some data in the Excel worksheet.

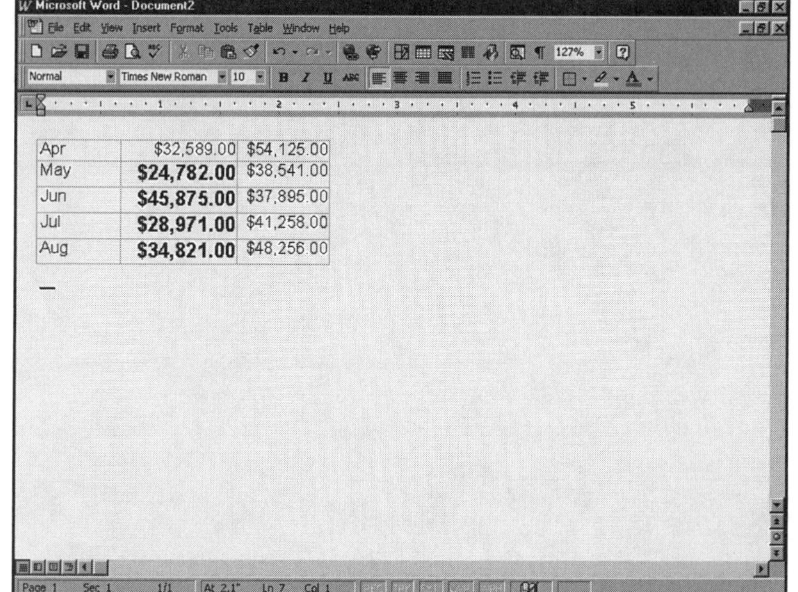

FIG. 34.19
The Word document is updated to reflect your changes.

NOTE If you change the name or path of your client or server documents, you must re-establish your links. You should make a habit of changing or creating file names and directories for your documents before you create a link. Otherwise, your data won't update properly, causing you to work with old data.

PART VII

Networking with Windows 95

CHAPTER 35

Setting Up a Windows 95 Peer-to-Peer Network

by Craig Zacker with Robert L. Bogue

In this chapter

Using the Peer Advantage

A Windows 95 peer-to-peer network can operate as part of a client/server network, or it can function on its own, without the presence of a server. A high-powered client/server NOS like NetWare or NT Server greatly increases the efficiency of the file and print services for which the local area network was originally designed. It also provides the potential for the evolution to higher level network services such as shared databases and communication applications. However, despite the added power, there is a basic functional drawback to the client/server model.

With the client/server arrangement, when one user needs access to a file on another user's local hard drive, the only solution is to copy the file to a server drive, so that both users can access it from there. There is no direct communication between workstations, as shown in Figure 35.1. On a peer-to-peer network, the file can be accessed directly, without bothering its owner. When one user needs to briefly use an application installed on another's machine, the user can simply access the application from the other's drive.

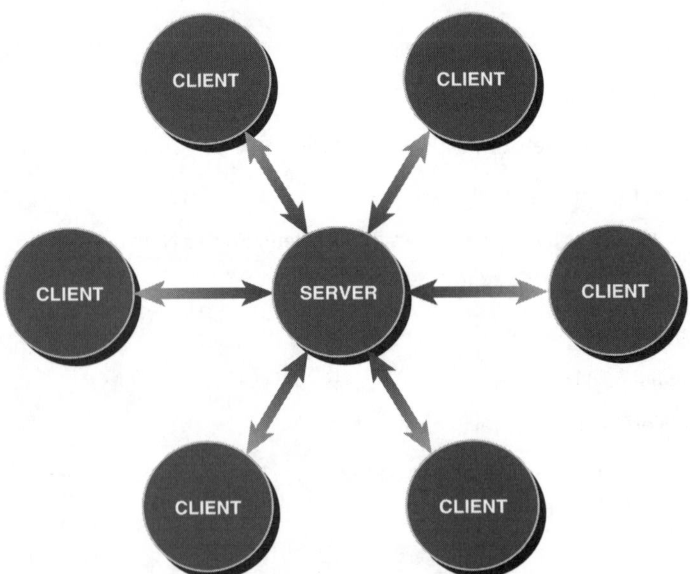

FIG. 35.1
The client/server model allows a workstation to communicate only with host servers.

Thus, it is clear that the peer-to-peer networking model does offer something that the client/server model lacks. Instead of every workstation communicating only with a central point, the server, every machine is theoretically capable of communicating with every other machine, as shown in Figure 35.2.

Peer-to-peer networking also allows users to share their workstations' hardware resources more efficiently. With Windows 95, you can allow other network users to access your CD-ROM drive, printer, or fax modem with little effort beyond the normal installation procedure for the device. On a client/server network, configuring any of these devices for network access is a more complicated undertaking, sometimes requiring additional server hardware or software.

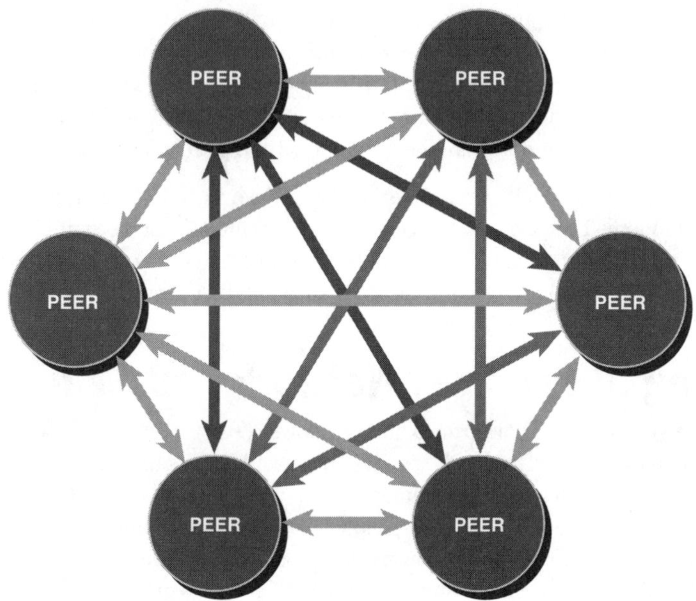

FIG. 35.2
Peer-to-peer networking can allow any workstation to access the resources of any other workstation.

Combining client/server with peer-to-peer networking is easy with Windows 95. You can construct a peer-to-peer network for a small business and add servers later, or add peer functionality to your existing client/server network. In either case, Windows 95 simplifies the conversion because all of the necessary client software is integrated into the operating system. You can therefore have a network that grows with the needs of the organization and offers the best features of both the client/server and peer-to-peer networking models.

Integrating Peer Networking into the Windows Environment

Like Windows for Workgroups and pre-version 4.0 Windows NT before it, Windows 95 incorporates both peer-to-peer and client/server networking functionality into the base operating system package. Windows 95 surpasses its predecessors, however, by automating more of the network configuration process and by providing a user interface in which peer network objects are presented side by side with server resources and those of the local machine.

Whichever organizational model you use in your network—client/server, peer-to-peer, or a combination of the two—your users will be working with the same interface. All other computers on the network appear as icons, with their shared resources displayed hierarchically beneath them.

Interestingly, Windows for Workgroups possesses much of the same basic networking capability that Windows 95 now does; that is, the ability to integrate client/server and peer-to-peer functionality into one operating system. The primary and crucial difference between the two is the ease and efficiency with which this is done.

With Windows 95, the process of adding peer-to-peer networking functionality almost never conflicts with the operation of an existing client/server configuration, as it often does in Windows for Workgroups. This allows you to create a business network that takes the fullest advantage of both network types. When every computer is capable of communicating with every other computer, the working environment is completely flexible.

You can create small teams of workers, called workgroups, that function with a greater amount of autonomy because of the access they are granted to each other's computing resources. You can therefore organize the network to accommodate the needs of the business, rather than organize the business around the constraints of the network.

Creating a New Peer Network with Windows 95

Like Windows for Workgroups and Windows NT before it, you can outfit a group of computers with network interface cards, connect them with cables and, using no software other than Windows 95, have them communicate with each other to great effect. Peer users can share their files, printers, fax modems, and CD-ROM drives without the intervention of a network administrator. You also can provide users with higher-level services, such as e-mail, group scheduling, and remote system administration, just as on a client/server network. Further, the addition of Plug and Play technology eliminates one of the largest stumbling blocks to the do-it-yourself network: selecting, installing, and configuring the hardware.

For a small business or home network of 10 workstations or less, purchase identical thin Ethernet Plug and Play network interface cards, insert one in each machine, connect them with prepackaged 50-ohm coaxial cables, and you have a network. Windows 95 identifies the cards and installs the correct drivers for you, and the basic installation is finished. Configuration and administration of your new network will take a little more effort, but that will be covered in this chapter and those immediately following.

Wiring a Small Network

Whereas Thin Ethernet is not the most recent technology in general use today, it's one of the most inexpensive and the simplest to install (which is why it's also known as *Cheapnet*). The professional standard in office networks is another Ethernet variety, 10BaseT, which uses twisted-pair, or telephone-type cabling. The complicating factor in a 10BaseT network is the need for a concentrator (or wiring hub), to which every workstation must be connected. This incurs additional expense. Thin Ethernet cables can simply be strung from one machine to the next, using the T-connectors supplied with the interface cards, and with a terminator plug installed on both ends. This wiring layout is called a *bus* topology. You must have at least six feet of cable between each pair of machines, and the total bus length cannot exceed 186 yards. The biggest problems with this kind of arrangement are:

- **Grounding problems.** Sometimes buildings will not have good grounds. The result is that the machines each have a different potential voltage (don't worry about what potential voltage actually is) and this can cause problems with machines communicating with one another. The solution is to have an electrician verify all of the outlets that the computers are plugged into.

- **Bad Ts or Terminators.** Just like everything else, there are a few bad Ts and Terminators. If either of these two types of devices fails, you may have some network communication, or no network communication. Review each T and terminator for visible damage, and keep a spare of each on hand to test, one by one, if a problem is discovered.
- **Cabling.** 10Base2 cabling is notoriously sensitive to tight bends. Try to allow 10Base2 cabling to make gentle arcs rather than tight corners. Tight corners can cause the cable to become unreliable.

Installing Peer-to-Peer Services

Manually installing Windows 95's peer networking capabilities is merely an extension to the network client installation procedure. Windows 95's Client for Microsoft Networks allows a workstation to see and access resources on both client and server machines running the Windows NT, Windows for Workgroups, or Windows 95 operating systems.

➤ **See** "Installing the Client for Microsoft Networks for Windows NT 4.0," **p. 929**

All machines with a functioning Windows client are visible to all users on the network, even those that are not configured to share any resources. The only step that remains for a Windows 95 machine with the Client for Microsoft Networks already installed is to add a service into the networking configuration that will allow the computer to share its own resources with other users on the network. To install the service, follow these steps:

1. Double-click the Network icon from the Windows 95 Control Panel and click Add.
2. Select Service, click Add again, highlight Microsoft and then File and Printer Sharing for Microsoft Networks. Click OK.
3. Click File and Print Sharing on the Network's Configuration page (see Figure 35.3), and select whether you want to share your drive(s), printer(s), or both. Click OK twice to complete the installation and restart Windows when you are asked to do so.

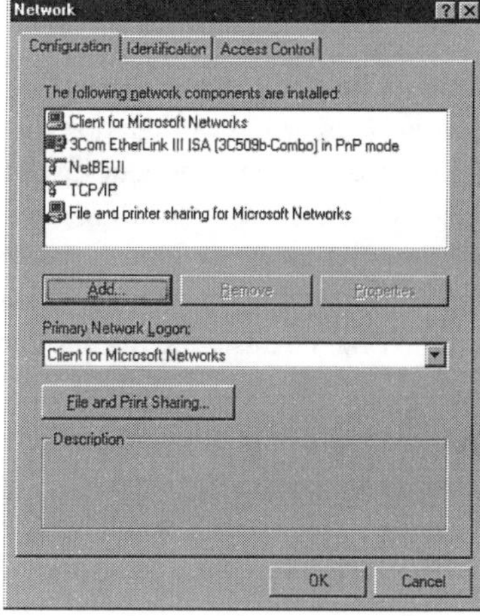

FIG. 35.3 The File and Print Sharing service enables the workstation to share its resources with others.

CAUTION

When installing the service, be sure not to choose the File and Print Sharing for NetWare Networks service by mistake. This is a completely different module that performs roughly the same workstation-sharing tasks, but in a NetWare environment. It uses NCP, the NetWare Core Protocol, instead of SMBs, Server Message Blocks, and makes a workstation appear to the network just as though it were a NetWare 3.12 server. It cannot run at the same time as the File and Print Sharing for Microsoft Networks service. One must be removed before the other is installed.

Windows Networking and Server Message Blocks

The SMB protocol was developed by Microsoft, Intel, and IBM to provide core networking functions between computers running the Windows network operating systems (Workgroups, NT and 95), as well as LAN Manager, LAN Manager for UNIX, AT&T StarLAN, IBM LAN Server, 3Com® 3+Open®, 3+Share®, and DEC PATHWORKS operating systems. Similar in functionality to Novell's NetWare Core Protocol (NCP), SMB provides commands that control four of the most fundamental networking operations: session control, file and print services, and messaging.

Session control is used to establish and break down connections to other machines on the network. File and Print commands initiate communications of the appropriate type for the transmission of data files and print jobs, and messaging commands are used whenever an application sends or receives messages from another workstation.

Whereas the basic Windows 95 Client for Microsoft Networks provides the client-side SMB functionality, the addition of the File and Printer Sharing service adds the capability for the Windows 95 machine to act as a server, by installing the VSERVER.VXD virtual device driver. Windows 95 machines with both of these components installed are peers in that they possess both client and server functionality in the same machine. This is why you may hear a workstation referred to as a "server," when the discussion involves the sharing of its resources.

Configuration Options

The File and Printer Sharing Service has only two configuration options:

- **Browse Master.** Used to designate whether this workstation should be the Browse Master for the workgroup. A Browse Master is a workstation that maintains a list of the other machines in the local workgroup. This arrangement saves time and network traffic by not forcing each machine to search the entire network segment for other machines each time it is browsed. The Windows 95 operating system cooperatively assigns a default Browse Master for each workgroup, but you can use this option to override the assignment. The current workstation can be designated a permanent Browse Master or prevented from ever being assigned Browse Master status.
- **LM Announce.** Used to control whether or not the workstation's presence should be advertised to LAN Manager 2.x workstations on the network. The default value of this parameter is No, and it needs to be set to Yes only if you have clients running LAN Manager 2.x that will be accessing the resources of your workstation.

These options are accessible from the service's properties sheet in the Network.

Integrating Windows 95 Peer Services into a Client/Server Network

In a client/server network environment running Windows NT or NetWare servers, Windows 95 can add the peer-to-peer functionality described at the beginning of this chapter to the existing infrastructure, and it can do it far more easily than Windows for Workgroups ever could. What this means is that, in addition to connecting to servers, workstations also can communicate directly with each other.

Thus, Windows 95 users can easily create their own local peer networking groups within the overall structure of the existing client/server network. Nearby users can share hardware conveniently, and users can perform the bulk of the configuration and administration tasks without the constant intervention of the network administrator.

CAUTION

Always consult with your network administrator before adding peer-to-peer networking to a working environment on any substantial level. You may weaken the performance of the network for other users, and the network administrator may waste a great deal of time trying to track down the cause of the performance degradation.

Users can easily access both client/server and peer networking functions because of Windows 95's improved ability to present and manipulate network entities within a logical, usable interface that fully integrates servers and other workstations into the desktop metaphor. In Chapter 35, you learned how users can access client/server resources, and how the Windows 95 interface can empower network users to achieve a greater level of network understanding than before.

In the rest of this chapter, you see how Windows 95 integrates peer networking entities into the desktop metaphor, how you can organize them into logical groupings, and how to use login and security procedures to grant appropriate access rights to all network users.

Peer Networking and Routability

A large business network is actually more accurately described as an *internetwork*—a network of networks. Individual LANs, or network segments, each containing a limited number of machines, form natural divisions between departments, divisions, or geographical locations within a company. The default transport protocol used in most of the Microsoft networking products is called NetBEUI, and unlike NetWare's IPX and TCP/IP, NetBEUI is a nonroutable protocol. This means that communication between Windows network machines is limited to those within the local segment, as shown in Figure 35.4, unless you take explicit steps to provide routing between networks. This situation is quickly changing, however; NT Server and Workstation 4.0 were the first Microsoft network operating systems to use TCP/IP as their default protocol.

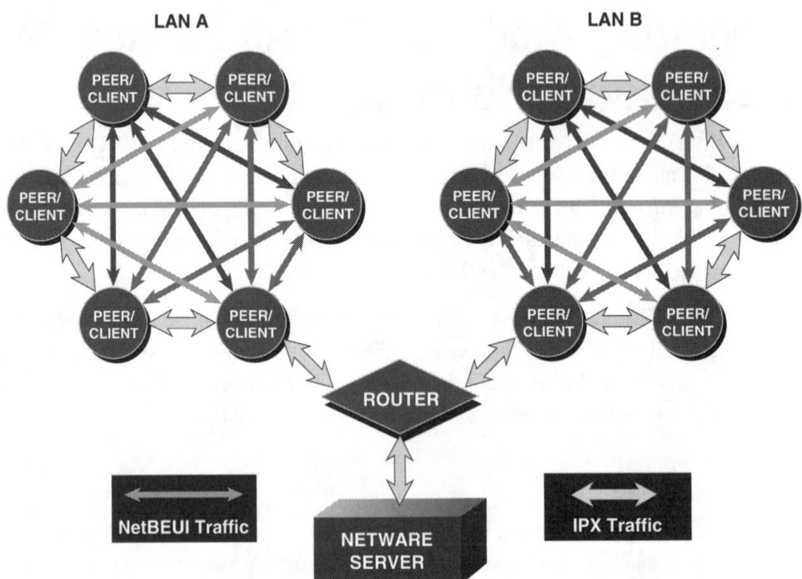

FIG. 35.4
All of the workstations on both LAN A and LAN B can function as clients to the NetWare server, because IPX (the default NetWare protocol) can be routed between network segments.

A workstation on LAN A, however, can enter into a peer networking relationship only with the other workstations on the same segment, because the NetBEUI protocol cannot be routed.

In order to route NetBEUI traffic between network segments, you must configure the Client for Microsoft Networks to utilize a second protocol, in addition to NetBEUI. When you add the Microsoft IPX/SPX-compatible or TCP/IP protocol to the network configuration and bind it to the Client for Microsoft Networks, the new protocol provides the routability that allows users to communicate with workstations on other network segments.

Although perceived by some as a shortcoming, the nonroutable nature of NetBEUI can actually be an advantage on large networks where peer and client/server networking are combined. The NetBEUI protocol operates at peak performance on relatively small network segments. Further, using NetBEUI limits the amount of additional network traffic generated when you add peer-to-peer functionality to an existing network.

Peer Networking and Controlling Traffic Levels

The signal traffic on a local area network consists of a great deal more than just the files, print jobs, and other data being sent from one place to another. Networked computers communicate on a great many levels, and countless transactions are being conducted between machines, even when the computers all seem to be idle. Just the practice of a computer making its presence known to the other machines on the network adds traffic.

On a purely client/server NetWare network, for example, each server periodically sends out communications packets to inform all the other servers of its presence. If a large network has 50 servers and 1,000 workstations, the increase in this type of traffic incurred by having all of the workstations advertise their presence would be enormous. This is why it's usually best to keep peer networking traffic limited to the local segment whenever possible. That way, each LAN is subject only to the additional burden generated by its own machines.

In the networking scenario being presented here, it would not be the responsibility of the average Windows 95 user to monitor traffic levels on the network, even if he or she were to function as a peer network administrator. This is a very complex undertaking, requiring special tools and expertise. It's important, however, to be aware of the consequences of your actions. The object here is to remove some of the burden from the professional network administrator, not add to it.

A network that is already approaching high traffic levels on a regular basis is likely to be pushed into the danger zone by the addition of peer traffic. Users, of course, are not likely to have any knowledge of this, and many other factors affecting network performance throughout the enterprise. It's important to always consult your network administrator before implementing any new services that could negatively impact other users.

Creating Workgroups

A single network segment can contain dozens of machines—far more than a normal user would need to access on a regular basis. Microsoft peer networks are therefore broken up into still smaller collections of machines called workgroups, as shown in Figure 35.5. A *workgroup* is a number of users whose relationship can be defined by any criteria that is convenient to the organization of the company or the network. Workgroup members may be users performing the same task, members of the same department or project team, or simply a group of people that sit near each other. For whatever reason, these users form a logical grouping based on their need to share the resources of each other's machines.

When browsing through the Entire Network display of the Network Neighborhood, workgroups are listed at the top level. Expanding a workgroup icon will display the workstations contained within it. Belonging to a workgroup does not limit the user's access to resources outside of the group.

The workgroup to which a Windows 95 workstation belongs is defined in the Identification page of the Control Panel's Network dialog box, as shown in Figure 35.6. Every Windows machine on a network must have a unique name, and must belong to a logical grouping, either a workgroup or a domain (see the next section for more information on domains). When it's time to create and access shares, these will later be used as part of a UNC name to identify the resources on this machine to the rest of the network (see Chapter 36, "Sharing Windows 95 Peer-to-Peer Resources").

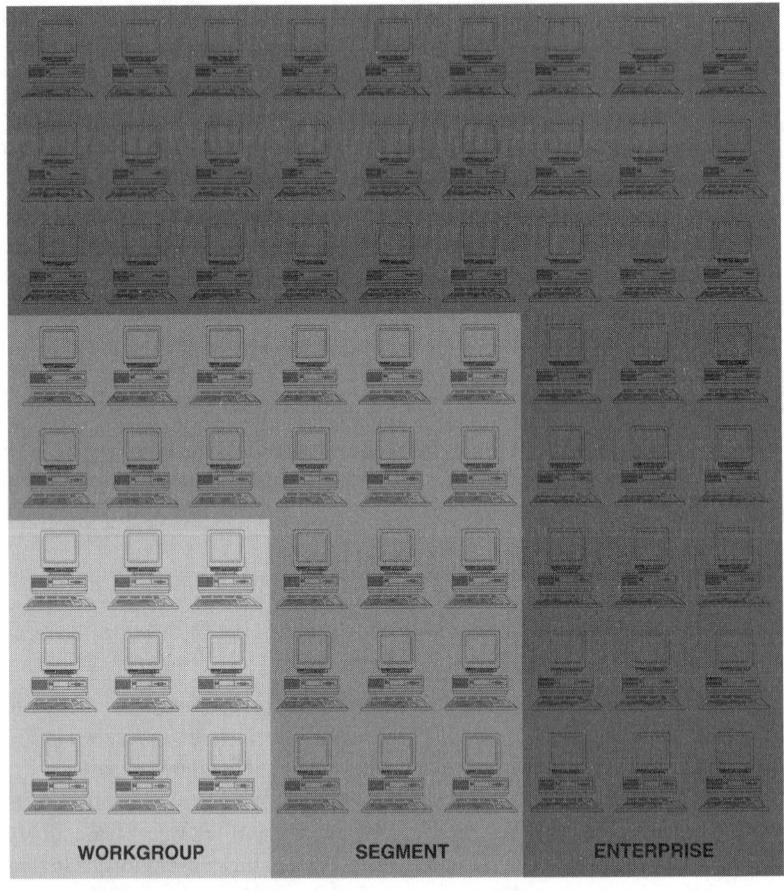

FIG. 35.5
A workgroup is a small collection of users within an existing network that have a regular need for access to each other's machines.

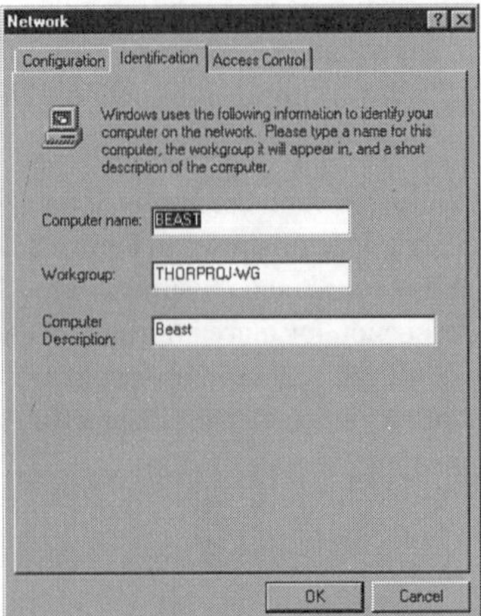

FIG. 35.6
Every networked computer must be identified by name and by a logical grouping.

A workgroup need not already exist for it to be named in the Identification page. Every machine on the network could create its own workgroup simply by entering a unique name in this text box. The Computer Description text box has no function other than to further identify this computer to the rest of the network. It could contain the full name of the user, the machine's purpose, or nothing at all.

CAUTION

Care should be taken not to assign names to workgroups that duplicate existing server names. This may prevent other users from accessing the server.

When a Windows 95 machine is a part of a workgroup, it is solely responsible for maintaining security over its own resources. As described in the next chapter, shares are created to allow other users access to a machine's drives and printers. These shares are, in a workgroup, individually password-protected by each machine. This is one reason workgroup computing should be limited to relatively small groups where security is not a major issue.

Using Domains

On a network that uses Windows NT as its network operating system, users are probably already using a domain login to gain access to client/server network resources. A *domain* is a logical grouping of computers that is entirely controlled and administered from a Windows NT server. Whereas share passwords in a workgroup are stored on the individual machines where the shares are located, passwords and all security information for domain users are stored on a server that has been designated a *domain controller*. In order for one workstation to access a drive on another workstation, both users must have valid accounts on the domain controlling server.

Network Browsing and Using a Domain

When utilizing Windows 95 in a network environment, you can normally only browse peer resources that are on your local network, even though you have access to machines on other networks. This is because the Windows 95 browser is designed to keep information only for local machines.

However, if you set the workgroup name of the Windows 95 machines to be the same as a Windows NT domain name, you will be able to browse all of the resources in this NT domain–including the Windows 95 machines.

This is a result of the additional architecture involved in a domain and is quite useful if you need to browse and share peer-to-peer resources over multiple networks.

Two screens in the Windows 95 Network dialog box are essential to the use of a domain logon. The properties sheet for the Client for Microsoft Networks contains a Login Validation section, as shown in Figure 35.7. To log on, the user must enable this section and specify a domain name. The Access Control page of the main Network dialog box allows the selection of

Share-level or *User-level* access control to the devices on that workstation. You must specify the domain name here if you intend to use the domain's security information to control access to shared devices.

NOTE User-level access control is not limited to Windows NT domains. A NetWare server also can be specified if the File and Printer Sharing service for NetWare networks has been installed.

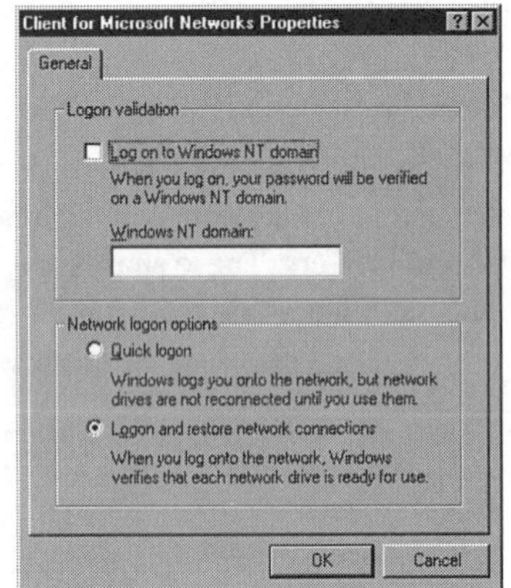

FIG. 35.7 Logon Validation must be enabled and a domain name supplied in order to perform a Windows NT domain logon.

User-Level versus Share-Level Security

When deciding which type of security validation to use, keep in mind the nature of the resources being protected. Traditional network security policies dictate that sensitive data should always be stored on server drives for protection against both intrusion and accidental loss.

Adding peer networking as an adjunct to a client/server arrangement is supposed to be a tool of convenience, and user-based security can sometimes defeat that purpose. If you regularly have a network administrator create user accounts on the Windows NT server in order to grant access to workstation devices, you then defeat the purpose of implementing a peer system, in part. You must, therefore, also consider your network's existing security policies before selecting an access control method.

Share-level security has its drawbacks as well. It is relatively limited in its access rights, allowing only a choice between read-only and full access to a shared drive, whereas user-level access rights can be more specifically customized. Share-level security also is subject to the whims of each workstation's user. If a member changes passwords, for example, without informing the other workgroup members, problems may result.

Situations like this are not insurmountable. Workgroup members can agree on a set of security policies that may involve, for example, the use of the same passwords for all group resources, or agreements on the sharing of particular resources. Remember, peer-to-peer is not just a technology, it's also a philosophy.

Building a Workgroup Administrator

Very often the best run departmental networks are those that have a knowledgeable networker among the regular members of the group. Some corporations are moving heavily toward decentralizing a portion of their MIS personnel. Instead of having specialized people concerned with only one aspect of the enterprise network, such as dedicated wide-area technicians and others who deal only with telephony, they are hiring (or cross-training) people for more general use and assigning them to specific departments.

This practice has two natural results. The corporation develops more well-rounded and generally capable MIS personnel; and, the administrator becomes a member of the department that he or she is dedicated to servicing. A sense of team spirit develops that leads the administrator to fight for the rights of coworkers when it comes to allocation of resources and equipment.

Implementing Windows 95 peer networking within a client/server environment will require at least one person who is familiar with the networking capabilities of the operating system and the administrative tools that are included within it. This workgroup administrator should be responsible for designing and implementing the resource-sharing policies observed by the users in the group. The job description is flexible, based on the needs of the users and the services already provided at the corporate level.

The Role of the Workgroup Administrator

The primary function of the workgroup administrator is to make the computing tasks of the less knowledgeable workgroup members easier. This is most often done by limiting their network environment to the resources they actually need to access regularly. One of the ironic qualities of Windows 95 is that it is easily capable of providing the user with an embarrassment of riches. Unlimited access to the contents of 100 different workstations is not going to make an employee's job easier.

A well-functioning workgroup has policies that limit user access to necessary resources. Such policies include the sensible creation of shares on each machine and a well-designed policy for the storage of files as well.

It is a good idea to create similar directory structures on all of the workgroup's computers. This practice gives users a basic familiarity with the layout all of the machines in the workgroup. Synchronizing directories also makes it easier for users to share applications that have been installed on other machines.

The administrator should also designate specific directories for the location of shared data files. The files may be grouped according to application, by project, or using any system convenient to the operation of the department. By collecting them all on the same place on each machine (such as a directory called \SHARED FILES), the administrator can create a documented standard for his workgroup's organization. With such a standard in place, new users will be able to come up to speed quickly and occasional users of the workgroup's equipment will find themselves in familiar surroundings.

The administrator also works behind the scenes to see that no one computer is carrying too much of the workgroup's weight. One of the primary drawbacks of peer networking is when a computer's background activities as a server detract from its efficiency as a client. If a dozen users are all constantly accessing files on a single computer, the performance level of the machine functioning as the server will suffer. The workgroup administrator must distribute shared hardware and software resources evenly throughout the group, and maintain an even level of traffic for each user so that all of the group members can remain productive.

Windows 95 provides the administrator with the tools that he or she needs to perform these organizational tasks. ●

CHAPTER 36

Sharing Windows 95 Peer-to-Peer Resources

by Craig Zacker with Robert L. Bogue

In this chapter

Creating Shares

Resources on a Microsoft Windows network are called *shares*. A share can be a hardware device, such as a modem or a printer; it can be a storage device, such as a CD-ROM or optical drive; or a share can be a logical entity on a hard disk drive, such as a volume, a folder, a directory, or a file. The owner of the server or workstation must explicitly designate a particular resource in that machine as shared in order for other users to access it over the network.

NOTE Whenever a computer on a Microsoft Windows network shares any device or resource, that computer is considered to be a server. **Peer-to-peer** means that computers can function as both clients and servers at the same time. ■

Sharing a Drive

To create a shared drive, make sure that the File and Print Sharing dialog box in the Network dialog box has I Want to be Able to Give Others Access to My Files enabled and that you have selected the desired access control method in the Access Control sheet (see Chapter 42, "Network Management and Security," if you're uncertain how to do this). Then do the following:

1. Open the My Computer window or launch the Windows Explorer. Select the local drive or folder you want to share.

NOTE Any storage device attached to the workstation and mounted as a drive letter can be shared with other network users. ■

2. Choose File, Properties and click the Sharing tab, or click the right mouse button and choose Sharing from the context menu.
3. Click the Shared As button to activate the option fields.
4. Enter a Share Name to identify the device to the network. Any text you enter in the optional Comment field also appears on all share listings.

When assigning share names, remember these things:

- A share name need not describe the exact location of the share on the server—you can use any descriptive name.
- Appending a dollar sign ($) to the end of the share name prevents the share from being advertised to other machines browsing the network. Remote users gain access by specifying the correct UNC name.

The appearance of the rest of the Sharing page depends upon whether you have chosen to use share-level or user-level access control in the Network dialog box. To complete the drive-sharing process, follow the procedure outlined in the following section that is appropriate for the type of access control you have selected.

▶ **See** "User-Level versus Share-Level Security," **p. 852**

Using Share-Level Access Control

When you configure a workstation to use share-level access control, the Sharing page of the properties sheet takes on the appearance shown in Figure 36.1.

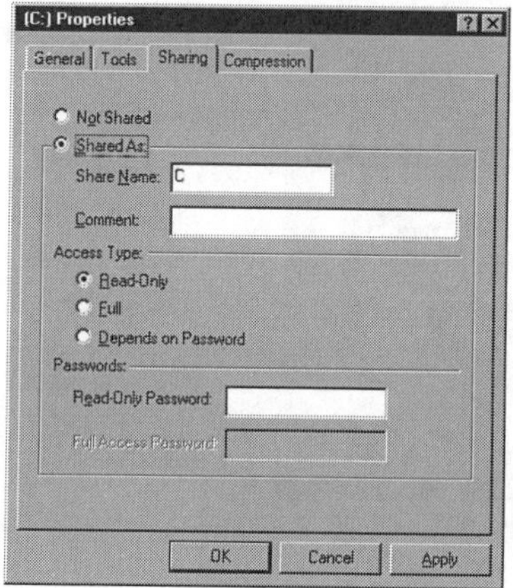

FIG. 36.1
Share-level access enables any user with the correct password to access a shared drive.

Use the following procedure to grant share-level access:

1. Select an Access Type to denote whether users are granted Read-Only or Full access. The Depends on Password option enables users of both levels to access the share, based on the password entered.
2. Enter password(s) for Read-Only and/or Full Access, depending on your Access Type selection.
3. Click the OK button. Confirm your password(s). Click OK again to create the share.

To prevent unauthorized access, always assign a password for all shares.

Using User-Level Access Control

When you configure a workstation for user-level access, a slightly different Sharing page appears in the properties sheet (see Figure 36.2).

To grant access to shares on workstations configured for user-level access control, use this procedure:

1. Choose the Add button and select a user or group from the list presented by the Windows NT validation server (see Figure 36.3). You could also use a NetWare server, but NT will be used throughout this example.

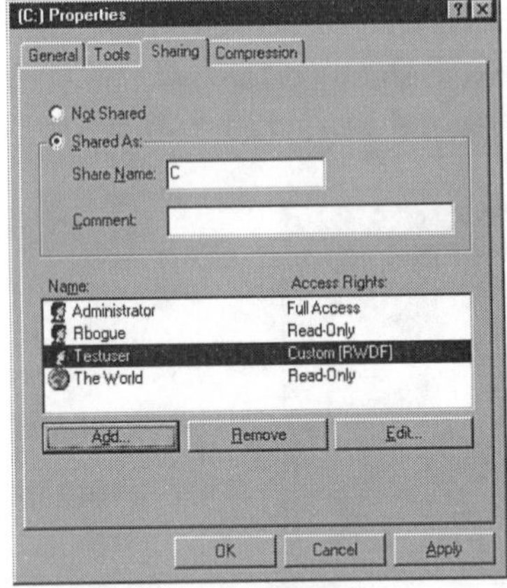

FIG. 36.2
User-level access requires a Windows NT server for user validation.

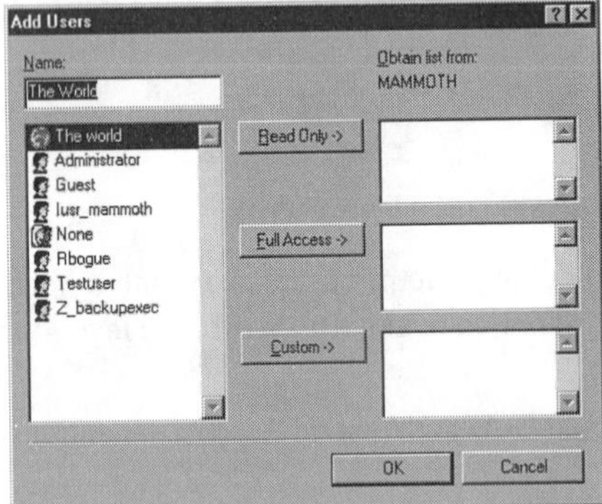

FIG. 36.3
The list of users and groups presented comes from the Windows NT server specified in the Access Control dialog box.

2. Select the level of access for that user: Read Only, Full Access, or Custom. Selecting Custom produces the Change Access Rights dialog box, from which you can select for that user any or all of the rights shown in Figure 36.4.

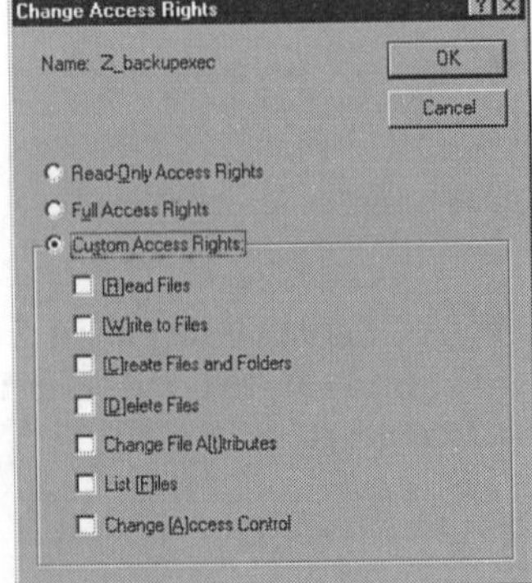

FIG. 36.4
You can grant a custom user any combination of these rights.

3. Click OK to add the user. Repeat the process for additional users or groups, if necessary. Then click the OK button to create the share.

After you have shared a drive or a folder, the icon that displays in the local drive of the My Computer and Explorer windows changes to include an outstretched hand, as shown in Figure 36.5.

FIG. 36.5
An extended hand is added to the icon for a shared local resource.

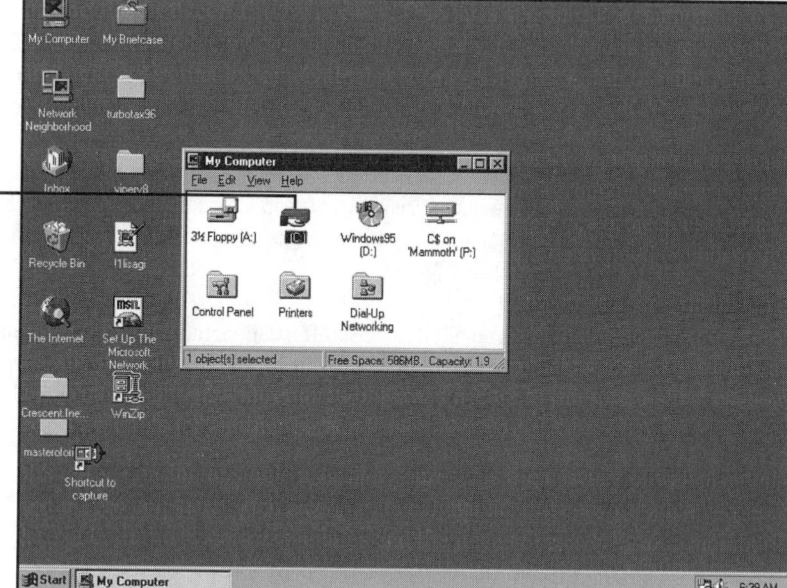

Shared drive

NOTE When user-level access control is enabled, each user sharing the drive must be added to the access list, either individually or as part of a group. Individual user and group accounts are maintained on a Windows NT or NetWare machine. If NT is used, this NT machine must be either the primary domain control server for the domain specified in the properties sheet of the Client for Microsoft Networks or a Windows NT machine specified by name in the Access Control screen of the Network dialog box.

Share-level access control enables any network user who furnishes the correct password to access the share.

CAUTION

If you switch your workstation's access control method from share-level to user-level (or vice versa), all of your shares are lost. You must reshare all folders, printers, and fax modems, and assign rights under the new method before users can access them.

Configuring Access Rights

As with most file systems, the permissions for shared drives in Windows 95 travel downward through the directory structure. When you grant a user full access to the root of your C: drive, you also grant that user rights to every folder and file on that drive. In Microsoft networking parlance, these rights are called ***implied rights***. NetWare calls them ***inherited rights***. When you use share-level access control, these rights, once granted, cannot be rescinded by any processes, other than disconnecting the user or ceasing to share the drive. You cannot grant or deny rights to individual files in Windows 95, as you can in Windows NT and NetWare. If you share a subdirectory of a previously created share and assign it more limited rights, the network user then has access to two different shares, each with its own permissions. The rights of the original share are unaffected by the creation of the new share.

NOTE As a security precaution, you can share only local drives on a Windows 95 workstation. You cannot "reshare" a network drive to provide access to another user who has insufficient rights to the source of the share.

You can effectively overlap shares with different permissions. If you grant read-only access to the root of a drive, and full access to a folder located farther down the tree, you provide the user with both forms of access to that subdirectory, depending on which share the user chooses to access.

TIP You can tell if a folder is already included as part of another share by looking at the very top of the Sharing page of the folder's properties sheet, where the name of any enclosing share is listed.

Filtering Access Rights

When user-level access control is in effect, you can grant users or groups lesser rights to a subdirectory than they have to the parent. This capability adds an important measure of flexibility to the effective creation of shares on Windows 95 machines.

NOTE Windows 95 uses the term **folders** to refer to what the rest of the PC world calls **directories**. The two terms are, in most instances, interchangeable.

For example, suppose that you are sharing a folder called \DATA\IRS and that read-only access has been granted to all users (The World, in Windows NT parlance). If you then create a share of the folder \DATA, granting full access to The World, the Change Security dialog box appears and notifies you that folders within the new share have already been granted different security rights (see Figure 36.6).

You are then given several choices:

- *Apply These Changes to Inside Folders*, causing full access to be granted to the \DATA\IRS folder, in this case.

- *Do Not Change Any Inside Folders*, retaining the read-only access to \DATA\IRS and granting full access to the rest of \DATA.
- *Display Each Folder Name Individually*, causing another dialog box to appear and asking if security changes should be applied to the \IRS folder within the \DATA share. If you select Yes, the \IRS folder in both shares will have read-only access. You answer the same question for any other folders within the \DATA folder that have been shared.

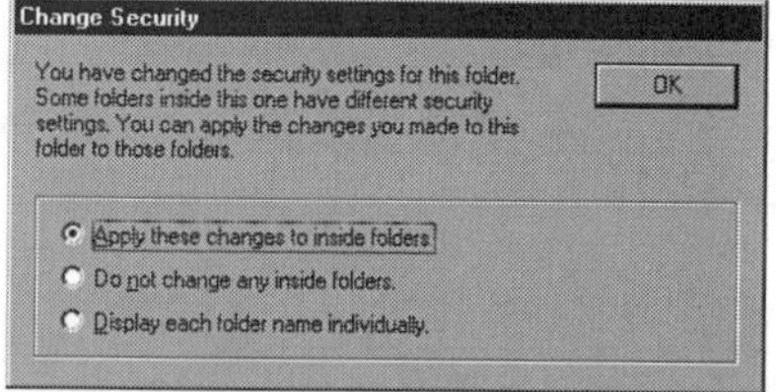

FIG. 36.6 User-level access control enables you to assign individual access rights to folders within a share.

The second or third option is preferable in most situations. You can allow users and groups to have full access to \DATA and yet limit them to read-only access for \DATA\IRS. This arrangement is similar to the Inherited Rights Mask in the NetWare file system.

Accessing the Sharing page of any shared folder's properties sheet displays the **effective rights**, that is, the rights currently in force for that folder.

TROUBLESHOOTING

I've created a user-level share and assigned access rights to a particular user, but he is being denied access. What is wrong? Check the status of the user's account on the Windows NT validation server. The user's access will be subject to any restrictions specified on that server.

Maintaining Workgroup Security

The shortcomings of share-level security and the complexities involved in maintaining user-level access are reason enough for many network administrators to reject peer networking as a viable option on a corporate network. Network operating systems like Windows NT and NetWare are more flexible in enabling rights-allocation; you can grant users access to individual files and restrict access to a particular directory branch at any point. On a peer network contained within a client/server network, however, workstation security is less of a concern because users still have access to server drives where they can store their most highly sensitive files in complete safety.

Even though most workgroups are made up of users who share a certain degree of trust, you must have sufficient network protection to guard against the inadvertent intrusion, as well as the malicious one. If you organize a workstation's directory structure properly from the outset, you best enable effective sharing.

Connecting to Shared Drives

After you have successfully created a share out of a drive or folder, it immediately appears on the network as a subordinate object to its host machine. The Entire Network display in the Network Neighborhood or the Windows Explorer displays the names of all the workstations contained in the workgroup and the names of all the shares on each workstation, as shown in Figure 36.7.

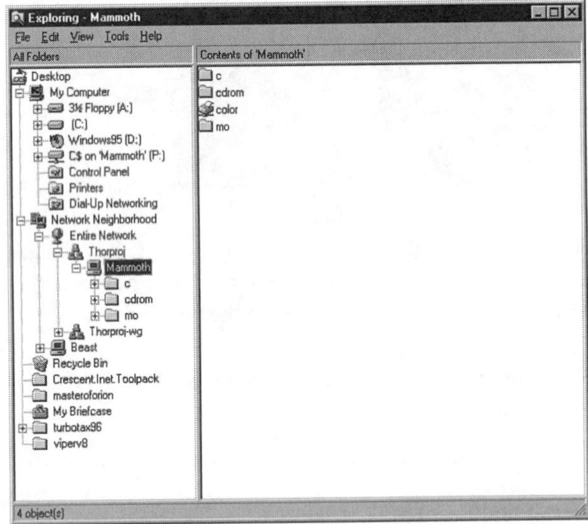

FIG. 36.7
The Windows Explorer shows all the shares available on the workgroup.

Clicking a share for the first time brings up a password validation screen that contains the usual option to save the password to the cache for future access. After access is granted, the folders and files of the share appear on a remote machine like those of a local or a client-server network drive.

You also can map a drive letter to a share on a peer workstation. The procedure is exactly the same as the process for mapping to drives on a client/server network. The UNC name specified in the Map Network Drives dialog box, or the NET USE command line, should appear as follows:

\\WORKSTATION\SHARE_NAME

NOTE The NetBEUI protocol, by default, limits a Windows 95 workstation to 10 simultaneous connections to other Windows network machines, including servers. If you work in what is primarily a Microsoft shop, this number may not be sufficient. To increase the limit, open the Network dialog box in the Control Panel. In the Advanced page of the properties sheet for the NetBEUI protocol, raise the number in the Maximum Sessions setting. You can set this value as high as 117, but set it only as high as you need for normal use. ■

Locating Computers

Despite the emphasis of this chapter on peer networking within the workgroup, Windows 95 is in no way limited to accessing the shared resources of nearby machines. You can access any peer workstation on the local network segment, and depending on the protocols being used, possibly any machine on the entire enterprise network.

▶ **See** "Peer Networking and Routability," **p. 847**

In a large-enterprise network environment, the sheer number of available machines may make it difficult to locate a particular server or workstation that you don't access frequently. For this reason, Windows 95 includes in its Find feature the capability to search for networked computers, files, or folders.

To locate a computer on the network, follow these steps:

1. Choose Find from the Start menu, or choose Tools, Find in the Explorer or Network Neighborhood window and then choose Computer.
2. Begin entering the UNC name of the machine in the space provided in the Find: Computer dialog box (see Figure 36.8). Entering even a partial name displays all the machines matching your selection.
3. Click the Find Now button to begin the search. The Find utility locates machines of all types: Windows NT servers; Windows NT, Windows 95, or Workgroups workstations; and NetWare servers.
4. Use the File, Explore command or double-click a found machine name to view its contents.

FIG. 36.8
The Windows 95 Find utility can locate any machine visible on the network.

Sharing Workstation Drives

In Chapter 34, "Simple Ways of Sharing Data Between Applications," you learned about enabling users to access files stored on network server drives. Setting up a workstation drive share is a bit different. Whereas a network is a public space, an individual's workstation may seem more like his or her "home."

To make this arrangement work successfully, peer-to-peer networking participants need to follow certain rules of etiquette. Remote users must leave things more or less the way they found them, and the host must keep anything not fit for public display behind closed doors. Establishing specific policies for the workgroup is the best way to ensure that standards are maintained.

Another safeguard is to limit the shared areas of each workstation drive. Allowing a remote user free access to one's entire drive (or *house*) is asking for trouble, no matter how friendly the relationship between coworkers. Unlimited access also makes finding specific items or files harder for the remote user.

You can choose specific directories or files for shared access on NetWare or Windows NT server drives. On a Windows 95 machine, however, you may need to modify the directory structure to accommodate the need for security. In many cases, if you grant access to a folder, you cannot prohibit access to anything contained within that folder.

Sharing Applications

To create an effective file-sharing arrangement, you must first decide exactly what material on each user's drive needs to be shared. This decision isn't as easy as it used to be. At one time, if you just copied the contents of the \WP51 directory from one computer to another, you had a fully functional copy of WordPerfect. You cannot simply copy a directory with today's Windows applications, which often require INI settings and library files located in several different directories. Even users who have become rather adept at modifying Windows 3.1 INI files may be daunted by the prospect of the Windows 95 registry.

To effectively share a Windows 95 application, you usually need to perform a network installation to the machine doing the sharing. This way, remote users can install the program themselves from the share, and add the appropriate settings to their own configuration files but leave the actual executables on the shared drive.

This technique can be an effective means of conserving hard disk space, especially when several people use an application only occasionally. Licensing issues may interfere with this practice, however. Many applications today protect themselves against users installing multiple copies of a single-user product on a network. In other cases, the terms of the license may deem this practice to be perfectly acceptable, as long as only one person is using the application at a time.

You can also effectively share smaller binaries over the network. DOS command-line utilities should cause no problems, and many small Windows utilities will function properly from a remote workstation.

NOTE Even the simpler Windows programs, like small utilities used for managing compressed files or viewing graphics, are comprised of several files in addition to the actual executable. Typically, some of the other files are dynamic link libraries (.DLLs) that are called while the program is running. Many installation programs copy .DLLs to the \WINDOWS\SYSTEM directory, so they are always available for use. (When a program searches for one of its files, it always checks the \WINDOWS\SYSTEM directory before running the PATH.)

Storing a copy of any required DLLs in the actual program directory will, in some cases, allow the program to run from another workstation on the network without installing it, as long as the Working Directory in the remote icon's properties sheet specifies the program directory on the host machine. Other applications cannot be run this way because they may require that their OLE objects be entered into the local machine's registry.

Sharing Data Files

Aside from sharing applications, the other major reason for sharing drives is to access data files. Administrators must take particular care regarding the granting of simultaneous read-write access to such files by multiple users.

Depending on the file type, more than one user may or may not be able to access the file at the same time. Applications usually deal with a second user attempting to open a file in one of three ways:

- **By denying the user any access at all.** The file locks open and any attempt to address it by another process generates an error message.
- **By allowing the user read-only access.** Some applications open a copy of the file, denying write access to the original but enabling the user to save it to another file name, if desired.
- **By sharing the file between the two users.** Only files specifically designed for sharing should be accessible by multiple users. Usually, this method is possible only with some database file types that lock individual records (divisions within the file) rather than the entire file.

When sharing data files, the administrator needs to be conscious of the way that the associated applications deal with simultaneous accesses. If, for example, a workgroup uses a particular Microsoft Excel spreadsheet file to document and track the progress of a project, users may then need only to refer to the file sometimes, and at other times they may need to update it.

Most likely, only one user will have read-write access to the file. Any other users will be in read-only mode, as imposed by the application. However, Microsoft Excel enables a user to explicitly open a file in read-only mode by marking a check box in the Open dialog box. In this case, a conscientious workgroup member who requires only read access to the spreadsheet can leave the read-write access available for another person's use.

Successfully enabling the sharing of single-user files represents the essence of well planned workgroup computing. To construct such a cooperative dynamic, the network administrator must be fully aware of both the system capabilities and the needs of all workgroup members.

Sharing CD-ROMs and Other Removable Drives

Although almost every home computer now sold includes a CD-ROM, this component is not usually standard equipment on the average business machine. One of the outstanding advantages to peer networking is the capability to share a CD-ROM drive among several users without the need to install it on a file server (a complicated process in a NetWare environment).

NetWare and CD-ROM Drives

Loading a CD-ROM onto a NetWare file server requires the use of NLMs devoted to that task. You must allocate memory to support the additional disk space of the CD-ROM, and you must remount

continues

continued

the volume every time the disk is changed. These tasks result in increased expense and aggravation for the network administrator.

On the user side of the equation, a NetWare-mounted CD-ROM appears as a new volume on the server. The name of the volume is taken from the volume label of the CD itself, so each disk creates a different volume. Although this technique provides a good way of knowing what disk is currently in the drive, it also forces users to map a new drive letter whenever they access a different CD-ROM.

When a CD-ROM drive is installed on a Windows 95 workstation, sharing the drive is an easy matter. The procedure is the same as that for sharing a local hard drive.

▶ **See** "Creating Shares," **p. 856**

Except in rare cases, you should create a CD-ROM share at the root of the drive. Although you can create a share from a specific directory on a CD-ROM, creating a share at the root enables you to use that same share for any disk loaded in the drive. You need only provide read-only access to a CD-ROM.

NOTE Even though a CD-ROM is a read-only device, limiting the CD-ROM share to read-only access provides benefits to the user. When a user with full access attempts to save changes to a write-protected drive, an error message is generated, forcing the user to Cancel or Retry the operation. When a user is granted read-only access to the share, issuing a Save command bypasses the error and automatically produces the Save As dialog box. The user can write the changes to another drive if necessary. ■

Using Networked CD-ROMs

CD-ROMs are rapidly becoming the preferred method of software distribution for users and manufacturers alike. When installing software from a CD-ROM drive accessed over the network, take note of whether the product is being completely installed to the local hard drive, or if it requires later access to the CD-ROM.

Many informational resource CDs, as well as games, install a viewer or other executable to the local drive and access the bulk of their application files from the CD-ROM itself. In these cases, the application sets up pointers to the original location of the drive so it can easily find the drive later. These pointers are nearly always in the form of drive letters.

Therefore, take the following steps to ensure that applications on CD-ROM are installed properly:

- Map a drive to the CD-ROM when installing software that requires access to the disk to run properly. Do not use the Network Neighborhood to browse the drive, unless the software is expressly designed for use with Windows 95.
- Make the drive mapping a permanent one if you want to access the data on the CD repeatedly.

This latter step is necessary because changing the drive letter of the CD-ROM drive may prevent the application from locating its data files. Some applications (like the Windows 95 Setup program) are well-behaved when this obstacle occurs and prompt you to specify the location of the CD when the application cannot find it. Other applications are more belligerent and refuse to run unless you reinstall the application from the new drive letter.

Using Networked Optical, JAZ, and ZIP Drives

When sharing other types of drives with removable media, follow the same procedure as for a CD-ROM, with the exception of the rights assignment. When you are creating a drive-sharing plan, you must consider the access rights to removable drives with read-write capability (such as magneto-optical drives) just like those of any hard disk. Again, though, create the share at the root of the drive so you can change the media without resharing.

You can share CD-ROM drives mounted on Windows for Workgroups workstations over a Microsoft peer network. To do so, be sure to include the /S switch on the line in the AUTOEXEC.BAT file that loads the Microsoft Windows CD extensions (MSCDEX.EXE).

Networking Tape Drives

Tape drives fall into still another category because you typically don't mount these devices as drive letters on the local machine. Instead, the devices are directly addressed through software specifically designed for that purpose.

Traditionally, network backup software runs on a server and addresses tape devices directly attached to that server. For a tape drive attached to a workstation, you must instead use a stand-alone backup software package. However, many workstation backup products can also back up network drives.

Cheyenne Software and Arcada Software (now owned by Seagate), which also include agent services for their network backup products in Windows 95, have both released workstation backup packages for Windows 95. These products can preserve long file names and back up any device (local or network) that is mapped to a drive letter, including Windows NT and NetWare drives. Thus, you can back up an entire workgroup's data to a single tape, not by sharing the tape drive's functionality with the workstations, but by bringing the workstations' data over the network to the tape.

Sharing Workstation Printers

To allow peer network users to access a printer installed on a Windows 95 workstation, you must first install the printer in the normal manner and enable the I Want to be Able to Allow Others to Print to My Printer(s) feature in the File and Print Sharing page in the Network dialog box. As with drive sharing, be sure to select the desired access control method in the Access Control page of the Network dialog box.

To create a printer share, use the following procedure:

1. Open the Printers window from the Settings option on the Start menu or through the Control Panel.
2. Highlight the printer you want to share and choose Sharing from the File menu or from the printer's context menu (see Figure 36.9).

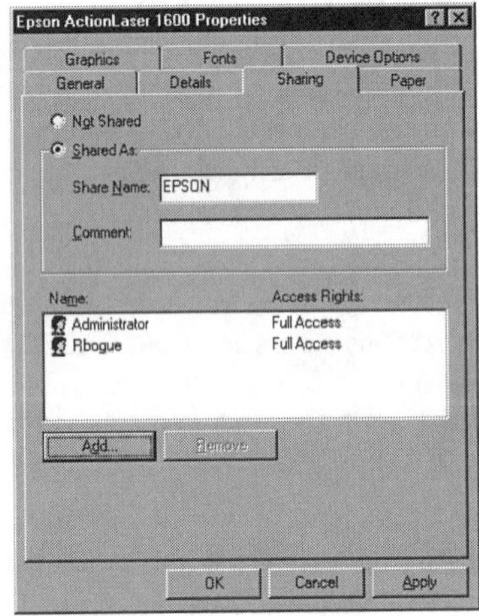

FIG. 36.9
Use the Sharing page to assign the printer a networking name and to provide access control.

Notice that the Sharing dialog box is actually one page of the printer's properties sheet, where you can access it via the Sharing tab.

3. Select the Shared As option button and enter a Share Name. The printer appears with this name to the rest of the network. You also may (optionally) enter further descriptive information for the printer in the Comment field.
4. If you are using share-level access, enter a password to protect access to the printer. For user-level access, select the users or groups who are permitted to use the printer. Click OK to create the share.

Whether your workstation is configured for user-level or share-level access control, a shared printer has only two security options: full access or no access. After you have created the share, an outstretched hand is added to the printer's icon to indicate its status.

Accessing Shared Printers

Configuring Windows 95 to access a shared workstation printer is no different than if the printer were installed on a server. You can launch the Add New Printer Wizard by any of the following methods:

- Open the Printers window and double-click the Add Printer icon.

- Locate the printer share in the Network Neighborhood or Explorer window and choose File, Install.
- Drag the Shared Printer icon from the Network Neighborhood or Explorer window to the Printers window.

- Launch the Add New Hardware icon from the Control Panel and select Printer from the list of devices.

Administering Workstation Print Queues

Windows 95's all-or-nothing printer security limitation affects the administration of print queues on workstations. As with a server-based printer, users can double-click a shared workstation printer's icon and open a window displaying all the pending print jobs in the queue. In Windows 95, all users have equal access to the queue. Any user with permission to access the printer can reorder the pending jobs, as well as pause or cancel any job in the queue.

However, the queue for a server-based printer is located on that network server, and the rights to manipulate the queue are also controlled by the server. NetWare and Windows NT both have a more extensive array of permissions in regard to accessing print queues. You can limit users' access to only the rights that they require, giving them a distinct advantage in the area of printer management. This should not be a significant problem in a cooperative workgroup, but if the resources of a client/server network coexist with the peer network, you may choose one of several alternatives to workstation-based print queues.

The first alternative is to avoid workstation-based printers entirely and run all printers from the client/server network. A unit equipped with a network adapter such as the HP JetDirect can be located anywhere a network connection exists. HP JetDirect also utilizes a server's print queue, providing additional administrative security and lessening the burden on the workstation that would otherwise be servicing the printer. The additional expense of the network card for the printer is negligible when you consider the average company networking budget.

NOTE You must install the additional RPC (Remote Procedure Call) Print Provider service with the Client for Microsoft Networks to provide Windows 95 with the capability to administer print queues on Windows NT servers. The service is installed through the Network protocol by adding a new service, clicking the Have Disk button, and browsing to the ADMIN\NETTOOLS\RPCPP directory of the Windows 95 CD-ROM.

The other alternative to standard Windows 95 printer sharing is to leave the printer attached to the workstation but utilize a NetWare print queue.

Sharing a Workstation's Fax Modem

Windows 95 incorporates fax services into the operating system using its Microsoft Exchange front end. Users can fax documents directly using the File, Print command of any application or the File, Send command of any application that uses the messaging application programming interface (MAPI). When both sender and recipient are using the Microsoft At Work binary file transfer protocol, you can even edit the faxed documents.

Windows 95 also can share the use of a workstation's fax modem, just as easily as it can share a drive or a printer. The workstation essentially becomes a fax server, enabling multiple network users to submit documents to its queue for sequential servicing by the modem.

NOTE Incoming faxes are held at the workstation where the modem is installed. Windows 95 alone does not have the capability to automatically route the faxes to their intended recipients, although this can be accomplished with the inclusion of Exchange Server on the network. In the absence of Exchange Server, the person designated as the fax server administrator must perform this task manually.

Before configuring a workstation for modem sharing, you must install the modem on the fax server workstation. You also must install Microsoft Exchange and Microsoft Fax on both the fax server and the client workstations.

To configure a workstation modem for network sharing, use the following procedure:

1. Double-click the Mail and Fax icon in the Control Panel. Select Microsoft Fax and click the Properties button.

TIP You can access the same sheet from the Microsoft Exchange Inbox window by choosing Tools, Microsoft Fax Tools, Options.

2. Select the Modem tab in the Microsoft Fax properties sheet and enable the option to Let Other People on the Network Use My Modem To Send Faxes (see Figure 36.10).
3. Click the Properties button, and a sharing sheet appears, similar to the sheet box for sharing a drive or a printer.

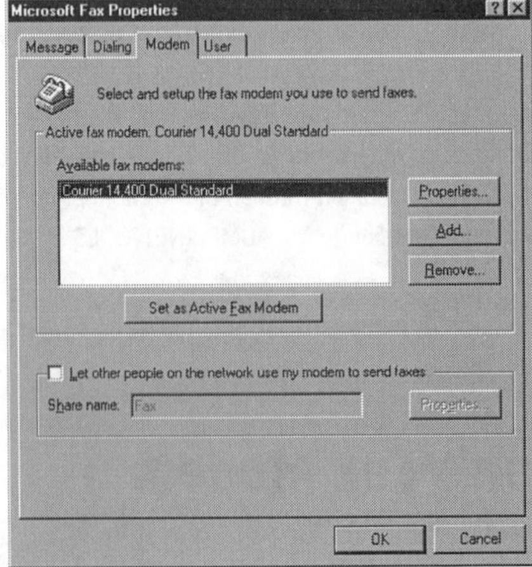

FIG. 36.10 You can install and configure modems through the Microsoft Fax properties sheet.

NOTE When you share a fax modem, a new shared directory is created on the workstation's C: drive. The path to that directory (C:\NETFAX, by default) appears in the title box of the properties sheet. This directory is where queued faxes are stored pending transmission. The seemingly incongruous options for read-only and full access that are provided when you create the modem share are actually referring to the access rights for this directory. You also can control access to network fax services from the directory's own Sharing dialog box. Always assign network users full access rights to the shared directory if they will be using the fax server. ■

4. Click the Shared As option button and enter a Share Name for the modem. If you are using share-level security, select Full for the access type and enter a password if you want. For user-level security, select users or groups who will have access to the share.
5. Click OK. Verify your passwords, if necessary, and then click OK again to create the share.

Accessing a Shared Fax Modem

After you have completed the preceding steps, any Windows 95 workstation on the network can make use of the shared fax modem. To configure the workstation to utilize the shared modem, use the following procedure:

1. Open the Microsoft Fax properties sheet as you did in step 1 of the preceding section.
2. Select the Modem tab and click the Add button next to available fax modems.
3. Select Network Fax Modem and click OK.
4. Enter the UNC name for the shared modem in the Connect to Network Fax Server dialog box. Click OK to close each dialog box.

NOTE The Connect to Network Fax Server dialog box does not contain a browse feature to facilitate the location of the fax modem. Notice the UNC name of the modem before you begin the procedure. ■

All of the functionality provided by Microsoft Fax is now available to the remote workstation. In fact, performance will be better than using a local modem, because the remote workstation does not have to process the fax transmission in the background. Windows 95 returns all system resources to the user as soon as the printing operation is complete.

Using Remote Network Access

Windows 95 defines the term *networking* more generally than most other operating systems. The connection of two computers via modems and a telephone line is considered a network interface just like a LAN connection. Windows 95 integrates these functions into the Network protocol along with the other networking components.

The Windows 95 Dial-Up Adapter is a driver like any other adapter driver, except the operating system uses the adapter to direct network traffic to a modem rather than a network interface card. A workstation can use this adapter to connect to an Internet service provider, to another Windows 95 workstation, Netware Communications Server, or to a Windows NT remote access server.

This section teaches you how to configure a Windows 95 workstation to be a dial-up server or a client. With this arrangement, a remote machine can dial into a Windows 95 workstation that is connected to the office LAN, and access not only the workstation's resources, but the LAN's resources as well. The remote machine can attach to the network like any workstation with a direct connection and perform any of the normal network functions, albeit more slowly.

NOTE Do not confuse **remote access** with **remote control**. Some communications products enable an offsite computer to dial into a host workstation and commandeer its interface by redirecting screen, keyboard, and mouse signals to the modem. When the remote user runs a program, all the microprocessing tasks are performed by the host computer. This process is remote control.

With Windows 95, the remote machine literally connects to the host as a peer. The host, despite functioning as a remote access server, continues to operate as a normal network workstation. Both the host and remote users can run different programs, with each machine doing its own microprocessing. This procedure is remote access. ■

Before configuring Windows 95 to function as a remote access server (or client), you must install a modem and the Dial-Up Networking module from the Windows 95 CD-ROM, as well as the File and Print Sharing for Microsoft Networks service.

▶ **See** "Configuring Your Modem," **p. 77**

Using the Dial-Up Server

The Windows 95 dial-up server enables a single computer running any one of the following clients to access its internal resources using a modem connection:

- Windows 95
- Windows NT
- Windows for Workgroups
- The Windows 3.1 Remote Access Server (RAS) client
- Any other Point-to-Point Protocol (PPP) client

The server also functions as an IPX/SPX or NetBEUI gateway, enabling these clients to access other network resources that are available to the dial-up server through these protocols.

NOTE Although the Windows 95 dial-up server included in Microsoft Plus! can route NetBEUI and IPX/SPX traffic to the remote client, it cannot perform this function for TCP/IP. As a result, a remote user cannot access a corporate Internet connection by dialing into a Windows 95 workstation. Such access would require a Windows NT server, which functions as an IP router to its remote access clients. ■

Configuring the Dial-Up Server

The dial-up server module is available only on the Microsoft Plus! for Windows 95 CD-ROM. You must install the dial-up server during the standard Setup procedure for the package.

After installing the dial-up server, use the following procedure to configure the workstation to be a dial-up server:

1. Open the Dial-Up Networking window from the Start, Programs, Accessories menu.
2. Choose Connection, Dial-Up Server (see Figure 36.11).

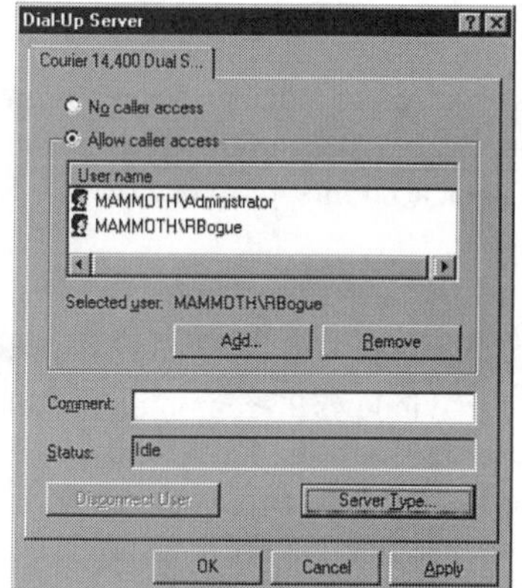

FIG. 36.11 Use the Dial-Up Server dialog box to configure a modem for remote access.

3. Choose the Allow Caller Access option button.
4. Click the Change Password or Add button, depending on your access control method.
   - For workstations configured for share-level security, click the Change Password button. Enter and verify a password for entry to the server, and click OK twice to close the dialog box.
   - For workstations configured for user-level security, click the Add button to select users or groups who are allowed access to the dial-up server. Click OK to close the dialog box.

When you close the dialog box, the dial-up server is ready to receive calls.

NOTE The Server Type button in the Dial-Up Server dialog box contains settings you should not need to alter for a Windows 95-to-Windows 95 connection. The Type of Dial-Up Server, when left at its default setting, causes the server to attempt first to initiate a PPP connection, and then drop to a Remote Access Server (RAS) connection, if necessary. The PPP server defaults to the use of software, not hardware, compression. For a RAS connection, the opposite is true.

The Point-to-Point Protocol (PPP) is a medium-speed Data-link layer protocol used for direct serial communications between two nodes, two routers, or a node and a router. It is most commonly used for Internet communications.

Ensuring Dial-Up Security

Securing a dial-up connection is much more important than the workgroup security considerations covered in "Configuring Access Rights," earlier in this chapter. An unprotected phone line is a gateway not only to your workstation, but possibly to your network. Always require a password for any form of dial-up access to any computer.

Windows 95's access control mechanisms, both user-level and share-level, only provide the means to allow or disallow a remote computer's access to the server. Beyond that, the server's resources are protected by the security measures implemented during the creation of the shares. In short, dial-up users are subject to the same share restrictions as any other network users.

When you implement user-level access control for a dial-up server, requiring a correct user name protects the machine against the risk of intrusion by someone outside the company. For this reason, avoid granting access to Guest accounts, or to groups like Everyone or The World when dial-up access is used.

Installing and Configuring a Remote Network Access Client

For the purpose of connecting to another Windows 95 computer, the following instructions assume that the client computer is not already attached to a local area network. Before you configure a Windows 95 machine to be a Remote Network Access (RNA) client, the following components must be installed on the workstation (all the software is available on the Windows 95 CD-ROM):

- A modem
- The Client for Microsoft Networks
- The Dial-Up Adapter
- The NetBEUI protocol (and the IPX/SPX protocol, if your network uses it)
- The Dial-Up Networking module

With the Windows 95 machine, you must create a new client (and an associated icon) in the Dial-Up Networking window for each different computer or service provider you connect to. Each client maintains its own settings and scripts, if needed, for logging into the host computer. Use the following procedure to create a dial-up client:

1. Open the Dial-Up Networking window from the Start, Programs, Accessories menu.
2. Double-click the Make New Connection icon to activate the Make New Connection Wizard, as shown in Figure 36.12.
3. Enter an identifying name for the new client you are creating, and be sure that the modem you want to use on the client machine is specified. You may click the Configure button to alter the settings for the modem, if needed. Click the Next button to proceed to the next screen.
4. Enter the area code, telephone number, and the country code for the computer you will be calling. Click the Next button to go to the next screen.

5. Click Finish to complete the process and create a new icon in the Dial-Up Networking window.

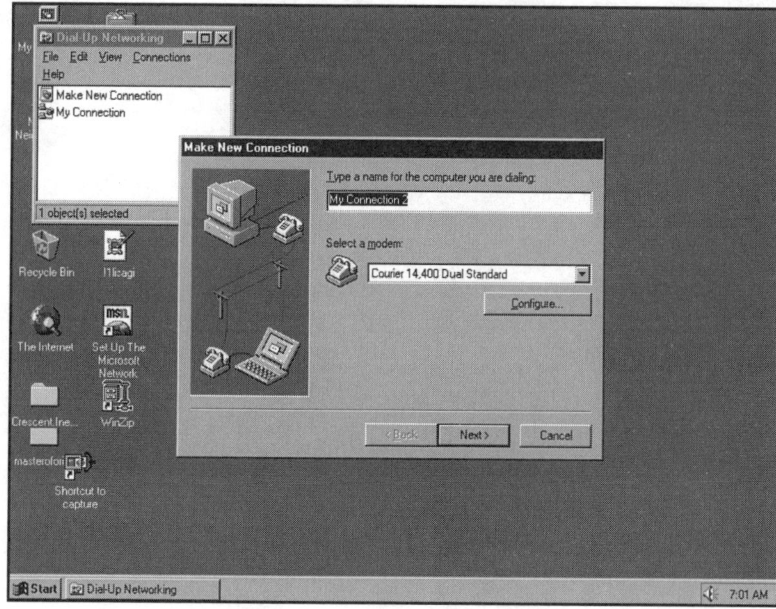

FIG. 36.12 Use the Make New Connection Wizard to configure Windows 95 to dial into a particular host server.

After you have configured the client, double-click the new icon and enter the required password to initiate the call to the host computer. The status of the call attempt appears as you progress through the connection and password-checking sequences. After the computers have successfully established a connection, access to the host computer's resources is available to the remote machine through the normal Windows 95 interface.

The newly created icon in the Dial-Up Networking window has a properties sheet through which you can alter the same modem settings as in Step 7 of the preceding steps as well as additional settings provided through an Options page. One setting you may find useful is on the Connection page of this sheet (see Figure 36.13). After you connect to a host, the remote resources are so completely integrated into Windows 95 that you may find yourself forgetting that a dial-up connection is active. Enabling the call disconnect feature under Call Preferences is a good idea so your connection terminates after the specified period of inactivity.

Clicking the Server Types button in the properties sheet of your new connection icon presents a dialog box that enables you to modify the client for use with a variety of hosts (see Figure 36.14). When you are connecting to a Windows 95 dial-up server, the default settings usually suffice. The sole exception may be the Require Encrypted Password check box under Advanced Options. You must set both the client and the server to either use (or not use) password encryption.

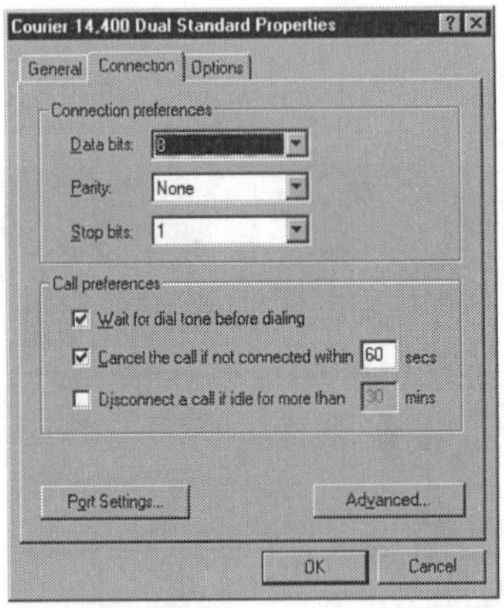

FIG. 36.13
The client's properties sheet contains a number of settings you may alter to suit that particular client.

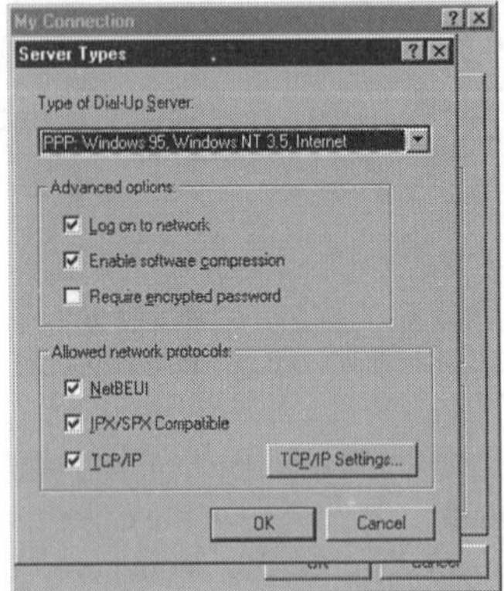

FIG. 36.14
The Server Types dialog box enables you to modify the client for use with various host computers.

Sharing Drives over the Internet

On a client/server network with Windows NT servers, TCP/IP has become a very popular protocol, and is the default on Windows NT 4.0. Windows NT has features that overcome the protocol's primary administrative drawback: the need to assign unique IP addresses to every machine on the network. NT's *dynamic host configuration protocol* (DHCP) dynamically assigns addresses to network workstations. The *Windows Internet naming service* (WINS) maintains host tables for the rapidly changing network more efficiently than a traditional *domain naming service* (DNS).

WINS also performs routing functions for TCP/IP, and one of the WINS's byproducts is its capability to allow Windows NT drives to be shared over the Internet. When you configure a Windows NT server on your network to use the WINS module and give it an external IP address (that is, an address visible from outside the company's firewall), then you can set up any Windows 95 machine with an Internet connection to contact that server through the WINS.

For more information on WINS server, try

http://www.winserve.com

Open the TCP/IP Properties sheet in the Network protocol of a remote Windows 95 machine and enable WINS Resolution in the WINS Configuration tab, specifying the correct IP address for your company's WINS server. Once you have done this, you can connect to any Internet service provider using either a dial-up or a direct connection and access shares on the WINS machine.

Unlike a local area network connection to the Windows NT machine, the shared resources are not browsable. In other words, you cannot open the Network Neighborhood window and see your Windows NT machine there. You must know the address of the server and the UNC names of the shares and have appropriate rights to access them. With this information, you can then map a drive or use the Run command on the Start menu to specify the share name and gain access.

This feature could be an enormous convenience for companies that must provide remote network access to distant users. Instead of maintaining a modem pool on the Windows NT machine and having users incur long distance phone charges to dial into the home office, the company can set up the NT server with WINS and have users call a local Internet provider (wherever they happen to be) and gain virtually the same access to that server. Instead of using a high-priced telephone network to establish a remote connection, telecommuters can use the Internet. The possibilities for increasing the flexibility and economy of remote data communications using this technology are unlimited.

Of course, some users may perceive this capability as a gigantic security hole. Some servers may already be accessible from outside the company, without their administrators even knowing it. When administrators are aware of its capabilities, however, WINS can offer users remote network access, with no additional investment in modems and telephone lines.

NOTE Microsoft has included a protocol in Windows NT called the Point-To-Point Tunneling Protocol (PPTP). This protocol allows communications to be encrypted over the Internet to minimize the security concerns.

Unfortunately, Microsoft has not released a PPTP protocol driver for Windows 95. This effectively limits the usefulness of this technology to connecting two NT networks together, or allowing Windows NT workstations to dial in.

Look for Microsoft to support PPTP in Windows 95 soon. ■

Balancing the Load

The overall performance of a workstation may degrade significantly if a large number of other users continually access its resources. On a peer network, therefore, the best arrangement is to spread the shared resources of the workgroup evenly among the workstations.

To achieve this balance, you may need to store a shared application on a different computer than its data files, or you may need to distribute files of a similar type among several machines. You also should spread hardware around the workgroup.

Creating a Dedicated Peer Server

There is an alternative approach to the problem of balancing resources within a workgroup. If multiple users rely heavily on Windows 95 to provide fax and print services, you may want to dedicate a computer to duty as a fax or print server.

Windows 95 provides a number of controls that enable the user to adjust the priority allotted to various system activities. You can optimize a machine that is not used as a production workstation to provide peak performance for tasks like printing and faxing, which are usually background processes.

The use of a dedicated machine may seem contradictory on a peer network, and the concept of a peer server is something of an oxymoron, but many different factors contribute to the way in which a network is designed. Modest needs call for modest solutions, and Windows 95 has emerged as the much needed filler of a significant gap between single-user systems and fully realized network systems.

For example, if a limited group of users requires fax services, only two ready solutions were available at one time. You could equip each user's workstation with its own modem and its own dedicated telephone line, each of which would remain idle most of the time. You could also invest a significantly greater amount of time, money, and administrative effort on a network server-based faxing system. Now, for the price of a single modem and phone line, users who need fax services can access them using the operating system software they already possess.

Using Workgroup Applications and Utilities

The Windows 95 operating system's peer networking capabilities are by no means limited to hardware sharing. Workgroup members can use Windows 95 to communicate among themselves at many different levels. If you do not already have a corporate e-mail system in place, Microsoft Exchange provides that capability. The \OTHER directory on the Windows 95 CD-ROM also contains several groupware utilities that have been part of Windows since Windows for Workgroups was first released, but which still may be useful to Windows 95 users.

Chat

Chat enables a Windows 95 user to select another Windows network user from a list and page them for a text-only chat. This feature can be a useful form of intermediate communication, falling somewhere between email and the telephone. Chat is particularly valuable for contacting someone while they are talking on the phone.

Clipbook Viewer

The Clipbook viewer extends the capabilities of the Windows Clipboard, enabling network users to share captured information. Users working with the same data can easily share quotes, excerpts, or boilerplate text between their open applications on different machines. ●

CHAPTER 37

Connecting Windows 95 to a Novell Network

by Craig Zacker

In this chapter

Introducing the Windows 95 Client for NetWare Networks

The arrival of Windows 95 supplied NetWare users with a new client that was immediately heralded as state-of-the-art. With its full 32-bit protected-mode architecture, the Microsoft Client for NetWare Networks uses no conventional memory. Gone are the memory management considerations that have for years plagued the use of DOS terminate-and-stay-resident (TSR) drivers for networking, and in their place are increased performance, simplified configuration, and easy installation.

In addition to the key features discussed in following sections, the Windows 95 Client also provides support for login scripts, global drive mappings, and command-line processing. Service releases of Windows 95 have also added support for NDS support.

NOTE Login script processing, while a major advantage to this client, is not yet completely effective. Although there are no problems with the basic commands such as drive mappings, difficulties have been reported with more complicated scripts, particularly those using IF...THEN loops. It is recommended that you fully test login scripts for successful completion before putting them into regular use. ■

Key Features of the Windows 95 Client

Microsoft's Client for NetWare Networks provides users with several new features not found in any other NetWare client, as well as enhancements of some existing ones. The following sections describe these key features.

Speed File transfers to and from NetWare drives are noticeably faster under Windows 95. Microsoft claims that its new client is twice as fast on large block transfers as a real-mode client running with Windows 3.1. The client also offers full support for the NetWare Core Protocol Packet Burst protocol as well as Large Internet Packets.

Integrated RAM Caching Windows 95's protected-mode networking is integrated with its file system. The clients are actually file system drivers, allowing network data to be serviced by Windows 95's 32-bit VCACHE, right along with local files. Files cached in memory do not have to be read and reread from the network drive during repeated use.

Plug and Play Networking All of the components of the Client for NetWare Networks are Plug and Play-capable, meaning that they can be dynamically unloaded without disturbing running processes or restarting the machine. You can remove a PC Card network adapter from its slot, and all of the networking components associated with it will be unloaded. Replace the card, and all of the components are reloaded again, without interruption of other processes.

Network Reconnection The NetWare client possesses excellent reconnection capabilities. A temporary detachment from the network doesn't disturb other system processes, either. Connections, drive mappings, and printer support are resumed when the machine is reattached.

Long File Names The protected-mode clients allow Windows 95 long file names to be transmitted over the network and stored on NetWare volumes (if they have been appropriately equipped with OS/2 name space).

Installing the Windows 95 Client for NetWare Networks

The last chapter covered the installation of a new network adapter, the Client for Microsoft Networks, and the NetBEUI protocol. The following procedure adds NetWare connectivity to this equation. Of the components already installed, only the adapter driver is required to attach to a NetWare network. You will be adding an additional client and a second protocol to the configuration. Both clients and protocols will be accessing the same adapter driver, as shown in Figure 37.1.

▶ **See** "Installing a Network Adapter," **p. 924**

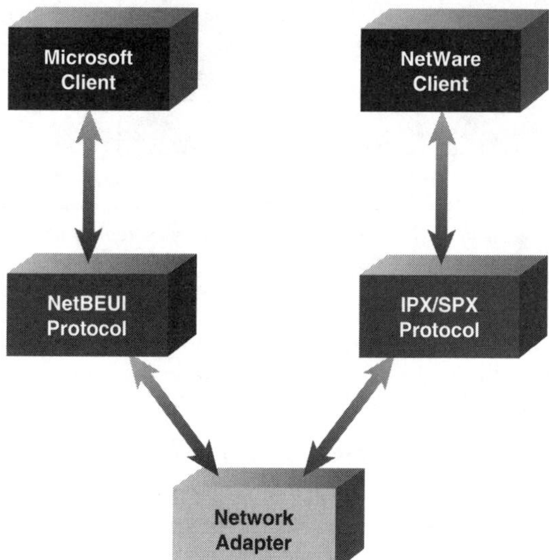

FIG. 37.1
Multiple protocols can be bound to a single adapter, each servicing a different client.

To add NetWare connectivity using the Windows 95 Client for NetWare Networks, use the following procedure:

1. Double-click the Network icon in the Windows 95 Control Panel and choose Add.
2. In the component list of the Select Network Component Type dialog box, double-click Client.
3. Select Microsoft under the Manufacturers listing and Client for NetWare Networks under the Network Clients listing. Click OK.

4. Select the Client for NetWare Networks, which should now appear in the Configuration page of the Network dialog box (see Figure 37.2), and click Properties.

FIG. 37.2
Protected-mode clients for Microsoft and NetWare networks can be installed on the same Windows 95 machine.

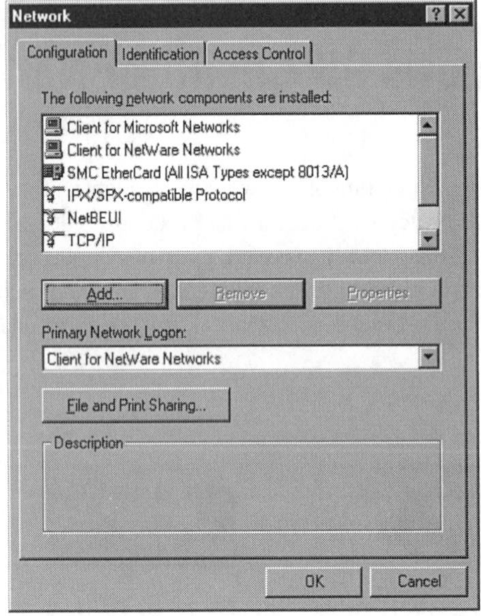

The network component listing in the Network dialog box is always sorted by component, in the following order: Clients, Adapters, Protocols, Services.

5. In the properties sheet, click the General tab and supply the name of your preferred NetWare server; this is the server that you always log into first. Your login scripts, if you elect to use them, reside on this server.
6. Click the check box to Enable Login Script Processing, if you want. Click OK.
7. Set the Primary Network Logon selector on the Configuration page to Client for NetWare Networks, if you want the NetWare login screen to appear first, each time you start Windows 95.

NetWare uses the term "login," whereas Microsoft prefers "logon." The terms are interchangeable.

8. Click OK to close the Network applet and complete the installation. You will be prompted to reboot your system. After you reboot, your computer should be capable of connecting to a NetWare server.

Examining the Installation Process

The preceding installation procedure was a very simple one, but it is worth examining more closely to see what actually occurred.

Step 3 of the process was the selection of the client to be installed. After clicking Add, you may have noticed that not only did the Client for NetWare Networks appear in the Network Configuration screen, but the IPX/SPX-compatible protocol appeared as well. The IPX/SPX protocol is essential for NetWare communications, and Microsoft's client automatically installs the 32-bit version that is supplied with Windows 95. If you remove the IPX/SPX-compatible protocol, the Client for NetWare Networks are also removed.

NOTE Novell's own IPX ODI version of the same protocol also ships with the operating system. It is primarily included for use with Novell's real-mode clients, but it will also function with the Microsoft Client for NetWare Networks in cases where the IPX/SPX-compatible protocol cannot be used. Likewise, the IPX/SPX-compatible protocol can be used with Novell's real-mode clients. ■

Furthermore, if you select the IPX/SPX-compatible protocol, click the Properties button and examine its Bindings. You will see that the protocol has also been bound to the Client for Microsoft Networks. So, what you have at this moment is a network configuration that looks like Figure 37.3. Both the NetBEUI and IPX/SPX-compatible protocols are being used by the Client for Microsoft Networks.

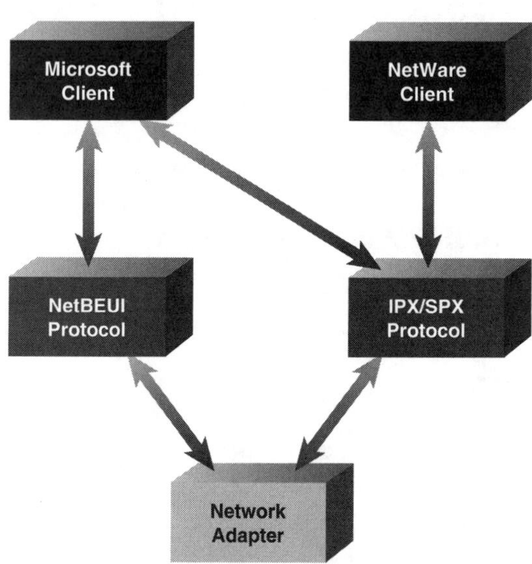

FIG. 37.3 Newly installed protocols are automatically bound to all available clients and adapters that can make use of them.

For many networks, the binding of the IPX/SPX-compatible protocol to both installed clients is a desirable situation because the IPX/SPX-compatible protocol can provide internetwork routing services to the Client for Microsoft Networks that NetBEUI cannot. Notice, however, that NetBEUI has not been bound to the Client for NetWare Networks because NetWare can make no profitable use of the protocol, and Windows 95 knows not to bind it.

If you had multiple adapters installed in the Windows 95 system, both protocols would have been automatically bound to both adapters, resulting in an interwoven network configuration in which all adapters are bound to all possible protocols, which in turn are bound to all possible clients.

Modifying the Default Installation

In some cases, this cross binding of clients, protocols, and adapters may be called for, but some of the automatic bindings may be unnecessary. You should remove unnecessary bindings because they consume system resources and slow down network performance.

In the case of your installation, if you are working on a single segment network, or all of the Windows NT machines that you need to access are located on the local network segment, the binding of the Client for Microsoft Networks to the IPX/SPX-compatible protocol can safely and profitably be removed.

Performing this task is a simple process:

1. Double-click the Network icon in the Control Panel.
2. Select the IPX/SPX-compatible protocol and choose Properties.
3. Click the Bindings tab and remove the check mark next to Client for Microsoft Networks (see Figure 37.4).
4. Click OK twice and the binding is removed as soon as the system restarts.

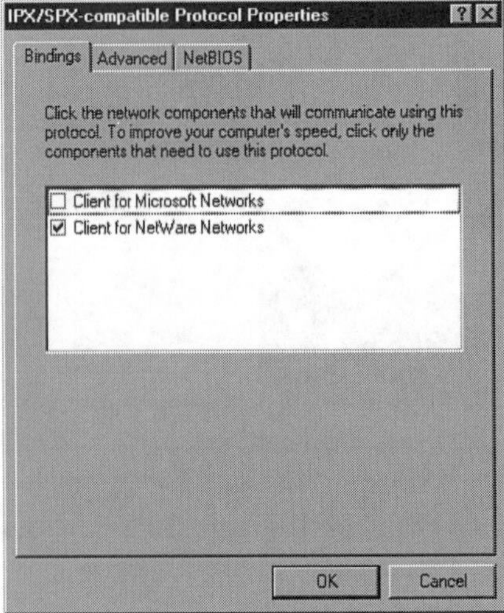

FIG. 37.4
Unbinding a protocol from a client is as easy as clearing a check box.

Another situation in which you should remove extraneous bindings is if a Windows 95 machine is using NetBEUI or the IPX/SPX-compatible protocol to connect to a LAN, but is also using a dial-up connection to an Internet service provider. A second adapter, called the Dial-Up Adapter, would have to be installed, along with the TCP/IP protocol. In this case, it would be beneficial to remove the bindings of the two LAN protocols from the Dial-Up Adapter, as well as that of the LAN adapter to the TCP/IP protocol. You would then have a system in which each adapter was using only the protocols that it needed, conserving system memory and optimizing performance.

Installing Windows 95 on an Existing NetWare Client

The simplest way to gain network connectivity with Windows 95 is to have a functioning network client present when the operating system is installed.

The Windows 95 setup program scans the machine's configuration files and the DOS memory control blocks (MCBs) for the presence of a Microsoft client, as well as a NetWare shell (NETX.EXE or NETX). The program also looks for other network-related TSRs that are running, all in an attempt to ensure that once Windows 95 has been installed, the workstation retains the same level of network connectivity that it had before the process began.

Always keep in mind that while Windows 95 examines the contents of startup files like AUTOEXEC.BAT, CONFIG.SYS, and WINSTART.BAT, it bases its installation decisions primarily on the network drivers that it finds in memory at the time of the installation. If, for example, your system is set up to use the NetWare NETX redirector, but you boot the machine from a floppy using NETX.EXE, the installation routine considers this a NETX machine, and behaves accordingly.

In most cases, the recommended method for installing Windows 95 to a network workstation is to start with the machine in its normal working state, before running **SETUP.EXE**.

In order to maintain the workstation's networking capabilities, Windows 95 modifies its installation routine in accordance with the results of its memory and disk scans. A file called NETDET.INI, located in the Windows directory, contains instructions for the installation program to follow under specific circumstances.

NOTE In networking situations in which you want to upgrade a large number of workstations to Windows 95, you can modify the NETDET.INI file to accommodate the specific needs of the environment.

In its default configuration, Windows 95 attempts to install the Microsoft Client for NetWare Networks, using the IPX/SPX-compatible protocol and a 32-bit protected-mode adapter driver. This is the optimum arrangement for Windows 95 running on NetWare. The installation program specifies other components only when they are required to maintain the same level of network connectivity as before the installation began.

This installation process remarks out entries in the AUTOEXEC.BAT and SYSTEM.INI files that are not needed in the new network environment and migrates settings found in configuration files like NET.CFG and PROTOCOL.INI to the Windows 95 Registry. The installation may also move the commands to launch required networking TSRs from the AUTOEXEC.BAT file to WINSTART.BAT. Any configuration settings that conflict with the capabilities of the default client installation may cause other actions to be substituted.

Supporting NetWare Directory Services

In the most common exception to this default installation, an existing real-mode NetWare client is retained because SETUP.EXE detects a workstation running VLMs to connect to a NetWare 4.x NDS tree. At the time of the initial Windows 95 release, no protected-mode client with NDS support was available, and retaining the VLMs was the only alternative.

NOTE The most recent release of Windows 95 (OSR2) includes the protected-mode client for NDS, but it is available only on preinstalled computers and cannot be used to upgrade existing Windows installations. The installation procedure has therefore remained the same: If SETUP detects a VLM installation connecting to an NDS tree, real-mode networking is preserved. ■

As you learn later in this chapter, a choice is now available for clients supporting NetWare Directory Services. The installation routine favors Microsoft's implementation, but after comparing the two, you may prefer to use the Novell client.

NOTE Windows 95 is capable of detecting whether a VLM-equipped workstation is logging in to a NetWare Directory Services database. If you are running VLMs to connect to a NetWare 3.x server, or a NetWare 4.x server in bindery emulation mode, the Microsoft protected-mode client is installed. ■

Supporting Other Networking TSRs

Aside from an NDS connection, Windows 95's SETUP also attempts to detect any other TSRs that involve network communications. These may include requesters for server-based database engines, network application protocol drivers, or modules providing connectivity to mini- or mainframe computers. When SETUP detects such modules, the installation program may take several different action stops to preserve their functionality:

- TSR load lines may be migrated from AUTOEXEC.BAT to WINSTART.BAT.
- The Client for NetWare Networks may be configured to utilize Novell's IPX ODI protocol, instead of Microsoft's IPX/SPX-compatible protocol.
- A real-mode client may be retained, but the IPX/SPX-compatible protocol substituted for Novell's IPX ODI protocol.
- A real-mode client may be retained in its entirety.

WINSTART.BAT and Windows 95

WINSTART.BAT is a Windows convention that dates back to version 3.1 and before, but has acquired new significance for Windows 95 users. WINSTART.BAT is simply a batch file that, when located in the Windows directory, automatically executes any commands within it as Windows is loaded. Any TSR programs executed are unloaded from memory when exiting Windows.

When Windows 95 is configured to use any of the Microsoft protected-mode clients, no network connectivity is established until after the processing of the AUTOEXEC.BAT file is completed. Any network-dependent TSRs in that file will, therefore, fail to load. The WINSTART.BAT file, however, is executed after a network connection is established. Migrating these TSR load lines there allows them to initialize properly.

As a result of these measures, a Windows 95 upgrade usually leaves a workstation with the same networking capabilities that it had before the process started.

Using NetWare Client Alternatives

Windows 95's backward compatibility and open architecture provides NetWare users with several alternatives to Microsoft's Client for NetWare Networks. Two of these alternative clients take the form of looking backward: Both of Novell's 16-bit real-mode DOS/Windows clients can be used with Windows 95; others look forward, providing even more features than are available with the Windows 95 client. The following sections consider all of these alternatives, outline their capabilities and their drawbacks, and cover their installation processes.

Gateway Services for NetWare

The first alternative method for gaining NetWare connectivity is actually not a client at all, it's a service. And what's more, it doesn't even run on a Windows 95 machine—it's for Windows NT Server.

Gateway Services for NetWare is an optional service available for versions 3.5 and later of Microsoft Windows NT. It allows a Windows NT machine to log into a NetWare server as a single user. As a result, a gateway is created so that all of the Windows network users that are logged into the NT server can access the volumes on the NetWare server, just as though they were normal Windows NT shares.

In this way, a workstation running Windows for Workgroups, Windows NT Workstation, or Windows 95 need not have a NetWare client installed at all. With only a Windows client, they can still gain access to NetWare-based file and print services.

Of course, Gateway Services for NetWare is not a practical alternative for prolonged use by a large number of workstations, as it pipes all of the NetWare requests through a single connection. But, for the user who needs only occasional access to NetWare files, or as a temporary measure to facilitate the transition between network operating systems, this can be a very useful tool.

File and Printer Sharing for NetWare Networks

Windows 95 has another unusual method for granting native NetWare users access to Windows 95 files, called File and Printer Sharing for NetWare Networks. Just as File and Printer Sharing for Microsoft Networks allows the Windows network client to share his workstation resources with other users, so File and Printer Sharing for NetWare Networks allows users of Microsoft's Client for NetWare Networks to do the same. To all NetWare users on the network, a Windows 95 machine running this setup appears to be a NetWare 3.12 file and print server.

Installation of the service creates a subdirectory called NWSYSVOL in the machine's Windows directory, which becomes the "server's" SYS: volume. When you share other Windows 95 drives or directories in the normal manner, they become additional volumes on the server.

Only user-level access to this server is allowed, and an actual NetWare server must be used as a "validator." You must select users that are to be allowed access to the shared drives from the actual NetWare server's user list, as shown in Figure 37.5. You then grant each user access rights to the shares, according to the standard NetWare model.

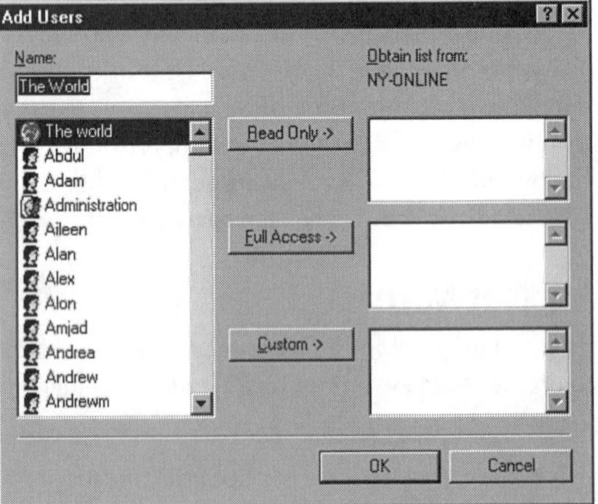

FIG. 37.5 Users for the new "server" are selected from a true NetWare server's user list.

Two options are available, in the service's Properties dialog box, for the way in which the new server is to be advertised on the network. *Workgroup advertising* means that the computer is seen as part of the regular Windows workgroup listing. *SAP Advertising* means that the machine appears to be a legitimate NetWare server to any other NetWare client workstation, through the SLIST command or any other utility that lists the NetWare servers on the network. You must use SAP (Service Advertising Protocol) advertising if you want users of the Novell NETX and VLM clients to be able to access the machine.

CAUTION

Use of the SAP Advertising feature in the File and Printer Sharing for NetWare service has been known to cause enormous increases in the overall SAP traffic on a network. Be sure to check with your network administrator before enabling this feature.

This service could be useful, for example, by granting Windows 3.1 NetWare users remote access to a CD-ROM drive without having to mount it as a volume on a real server, or access to a printer without having to attach it to a NetWare print server and a queue. However, use of a desktop computer as a file server is not recommended because these machines are not designed for the increased network traffic associated with the role of file server.

Using Novell Real-Mode Clients

Microsoft's NDS service for the Windows 95 Client for NetWare Networks and Novell's Client32 for Windows 95 both provide NDS access while retaining the advantages of a 32-bit protected-mode client. Both of these alternatives are considered later in this chapter.

Although there are other reasons to continue using the Novell real-mode clients, none of them have anything to do with performance. The real-mode clients are slower in every way than their protected-mode counterparts. They are also subject to the same conventional memory utilization problems as they were with Windows 3.1. It may be necessary, even with Windows 95, to implement a full memory management regimen, using the standard tools—EMM386.EXE, or a third-party package such as QEMM—to load some of the modules into upper memory.

However, situations such as those mentioned earlier in this chapter (when special TSRs are needed to gain access to critical network services) are still valid cases in which the real-mode clients might be needed—at least until the services in question can be upgraded. These cases are becoming less and less common, though, as many such TSRs are being rewritten as Windows 95 clients and services.

Using the NETX Client

When a workstation equipped with the NETX client is upgraded to Windows 95, it is automatically upgraded to the Client for NetWare Networks, unless TSRs are present that are incompatible with the 32-bit protected-mode client. If you want to continue using NETX with Windows 95 for any other reason, you need to remove the newly installed client first, in most cases, in order to restore NETX's functionality.

NOTE Even though Windows 95 may disable a workstation's existing networking configuration to install a new one, it will never delete the original files. Reinstalling the original client from the Control Panel locates and reactivates the original files. ■

Installing the NETX Client

When you install the NETX client in Windows 95, you should have a functional NETX client already installed on the machine, even if it isn't operating. Otherwise, you will be prompted to supply the necessary files during the installation.

CAUTION

The NETX and VLM client files do not ship as part of the Windows 95 package. You are responsible for supplying appropriate versions of all the necessary files. It's strongly recommended that the latest versions be installed on the system before the real-mode client is installed in Windows 95.

To install the NETX client in Windows 95, follow these steps:

1. Double-click the Network icon in the Windows 95 Control Panel.
2. If the Client for NetWare Networks, or any other NetWare client, is currently installed, select it and click the Remove button.

The NETX client can safely coexist with the protected-mode Client for Microsoft Networks on the same machine. Both can use the same IPX protocol, or two different ones can be installed. However, NETX cannot be used with the real-mode version of the Client for Microsoft Networks. Only one real-mode network client can run on a single machine.

3. In the component list of the Select Network Component Type dialog box, double-click Client.
4. In the Manufacturers list on the left side of the Select Network Client dialog box, select Novell. On the right side, choose Novell NetWare (Workstation Shell 3.X [NETX]). Click OK.
5. Notice that the NETX client, an adapter labeled Existing ODI Driver, and the Novell IPX ODI protocol have been added to the Network screen (see Figure 37.6). Click OK again to complete the installation. You will be prompted to restart your system.

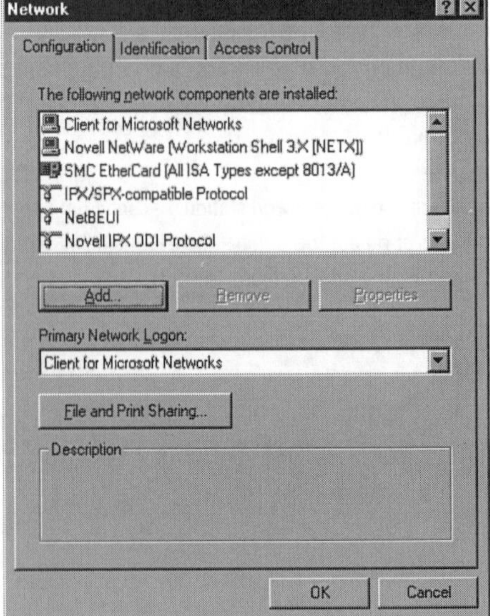

FIG. 37.6
Installing the NETX client automatically causes the Existing ODI Driver and the Novell IPX ODI Protocol to be installed.

NOTE Whereas the installation of the NETX client automatically includes the Novell IPX ODI Protocol and a 16-bit real-mode ODI adapter driver, either the Microsoft IPX/SPX-compatible protocol or its protected-mode NDIS 3.1 adapter drivers, or both, can be used instead.

Other NETX Client Issues

You need to consider several other issues when running the NETX client on a Windows 95 machine:

- Windows 95, by default, sets the LASTDRIVE= entry to the letter Z. To use NETX, you must include a line in the CONFIG.SYS file that indicates what the first NetWare drive letter will be. For example, adding LASTDRIVE=E will cause F: to be the first NetWare drive.
- If you will be running a login script that utilizes the %OS_VERSION variable, you must modify the Windows SETVER table by issuing the following command at a DOS prompt:

  SETVER NETX.EXE 7.00

SETVER, the MS-DOS version compatibility table, is no longer a separate TSR utility. It is now integrated into Windows 95 and automatically loaded with the operating system.

- Be sure that the NETX version of the NETWARE.DRV file is present in the Windows directory (see the "Windows 95 Clients and NETWARE.DRV" sidebar).
- You will not be able to store Windows 95 long file names on NetWare servers using NETX, or any real-mode client.

Windows 95 Clients and NETWARE.DRV

Whenever you elect to use a NetWare real-mode client with Windows 95, it's crucial that the correct version of the NETWARE.DRV file be installed in the Windows directory. There are different versions of this file for the NETX and VLM clients, and for Windows 95's own clients. Their approximate sizes are:

NETWARE.DRV	Windows 95	approx. 1.6K
NETWARE.DRV	VLM	approx. 160K
NETWARE.DRV	NETX	approx. 134K

Windows 95 replaces the current NETWARE.DRV with its own version when it updates a real-mode to the protected-mode NetWare client. The old version is renamed, however, as NETWARE.DR~ , so that it can be restored if necessary.

Using the VLM Client

The VLM client, if you are using it to log into a NetWare Directory Services tree, isn't replaced with the protected-mode client by the default Windows 95 installation routine. Like the NETX client, its settings are assimilated into the Windows 95 Registry and is loaded into conventional memory—unless you take steps to prevent this occurrence.

In addition, you must be aware of other concerns when using the VLM client with Windows 95, as well as issues that you must address when installing the client on an existing Windows 95 machine.

The VLM client offers considerably more functionality than NETX, but some of its features are not compatible with Windows 95. Its primary attribute is its ability to run NetWare NDS utilities like NWADMIN, NETADMIN, and CX, and to log into an NDS tree. To ensure this compatibility, you should use the DOS-based installation routine included with the VLM package to perform a complete client installation (with full Windows support). You should also make sure that you are installing the latest available version of the client software.

Obtaining the Latest Novell Client Software

The latest releases of the Novell NETX and VLM clients are required when you are running them with Windows 95. The most reliable source for Novell upgrade files is the Novell Support Connection Web site, located at **http://support.novell.com**.

All of the downloadable files can be found on the Novell Product Support page. This can be accessed by either clicking the Product Support icon or going directly to **http://support.novell.com/home**.

All of the Novell release files are self-extracting archives that you should execute in an empty directory. All contain extensive README files that you should read carefully before applying any updates.

Installing the VLM Client

When installing the VLM client onto a Windows 95 machine, use the Novell client installation program for the initial process rather than the Control Panel. When doing so, you must be sure to retain access to the VLM installation files throughout the process. You should therefore run the installation program either from floppy disks or a CD-ROM, or copy it to a local hard drive, rather than run it from a server drive.

To install the VLM client on a Windows 95 machine, use the following procedure:

1. Double-click the Network icon in the Windows 95 Control Panel and remove all existing network support components. Click OK to close the dialog box.
2. When asked whether to restart the computer, choose No. Open the Start menu, select Shut Down, choose Restart the Computer in MS-DOS Mode and click Yes.

The computer can also be started in MS-DOS mode by holding down the F8 key during the boot process and making the appropriate selection from the boot menu.

3. Run the VLM installation program from the DOS prompt in the normal manner. Be sure to include Windows support. If you are asked whether to overwrite the NETWARE.DRV file, select Yes.

4. Restart the computer and again open the Network dialog box. Windows 95 should detect that the VLM client has been installed and add the appropriate settings.
5. Click OK, and restart the computer once again.

Other VLM Client Issues

You must take note of the following issues when you use the VLM client with Windows 95:

- Due to a problem in the way that it makes calls to NETWARE.DRV, Windows 95, during its load sequence, attempts to restore any Windows-permanent network connections that you have specified before the NetWare login dialog box appears. This situation causes Windows 95 to generate error messages. One workaround is to ignore the errors and use the NWUSER program's Restore Now feature. Alternatively, you can log into the network before loading Windows to allow the permanent connections to be restored normally.

Placing a LOGIN command in the AUTOEXEC.BAT or STARTNET.BAT file causes the system's boot sequence to pause for user input and allows you to log into the network before the Windows 95 GUI loads.

- The VLM client's NWUSER program has an option to allow private drive mappings. These are drive mappings made in a DOS session that exist only in that session. This feature does not function under Windows 95. Be sure to leave the Global Drives and Paths box in the NWUSER program checked at all times. All drive mappings in Windows 95 are global. Changes made to drive mappings within a DOS session are always propagated throughout the whole system.
- As with Windows 3.1, all search drives must be mapped from a DOS prompt or a login script before starting Windows 95. Search drives cannot be mapped from a DOS session within Windows 95.
- As with NETX, Windows 95 long file names cannot be stored on NetWare servers with the VLM client. Instead, they are truncated to their DOS 8.3 equivalents. However, support is provided for the storage of user profiles on NetWare servers.

Using the Microsoft Service for NetWare Directory Services

Microsoft was well aware of the problems created by the lack of NetWare Directory Services (NDS) support in the Client for NetWare Networks at the time of the Windows 95 release. Within two months of that release, Microsoft resolved the problem by providing a Service for NetWare Directory Services (MSNDS).

This add-on service originally required the user to download the installation files from Microsoft's Web site, but the latest OEM Service Release (OSR2) includes the service in the base product. OSR2 is available in one form: preinstalled on new computers. If you have an older copy of Windows 95, or you have purchased Windows 95 as an upgrade, you must download MSNDS manually.

The addition of the service provides NDS users with full container, object, and user login script support, the ability to browse for NetWare resources through the NDS hierarchy, and access to all of the NDS-related NetWare utilities.

ON THE WEB

The Service for NetWare Directory Services is available for download from Microsoft's World Wide Web site at **http://www.microsoft.com/windows/software/msnds.htm**.

Installing the Service for NDS

NOTE Users of OSR2 do not need to download MSNDS. These users can simply install MSNDS from the Network Control Panel by clicking Add, Service, and Microsoft. The Service for NetWare Directory Services will be listed.

If you don't know if you are running the OSR2 version of Windows 95, open the System applet in the Control Panel. OSR2 is identified as version 4.00.950B. ■

To install NDS support into the Client for NetWare Networks, follow these steps:

1. Download MSNDS.EXE from one of the Microsoft online services.
2. Put the file in a directory by itself and execute MSNDS.EXE to extract the contents of the archive.

3. Double-click the Network icon in the Windows 95 Control Panel.
4. Click Add, double-click Service in the Select Network Component Type dialog box, and click the Have Disk button in the Select Network Service dialog box.
5. Enter the location of the directory containing the MSNDS files into the Install from Disk dialog box, and click OK twice.
6. Select the Service for NetWare Directory Services entry in the Network applet's Configuration page and click the Properties button.
7. Enter the name of your preferred NDS tree, and the full context of your workstation. Click OK twice to complete the installation.

CAUTION

When using the NDS Service to connect to a NetWare 4.01 NDS tree, only full-context names can be used. For example, a context of **.USER.ORGANIZATION** will not be acceptable. Enter instead: **.CN=USER.OU=ORGANIZATION**.

NOTE The installation of the Service for NetWare Directory Services adds a line to the system's AUTOEXEC.BAT file that runs a batch file called _NWNDS.BAT during the next system reboot. The batch file need only be run once, but this line will remain in the AUTOEXEC.BAT file. You can safely remove it after the installation is complete. ■

Other Service for NDS Issues

Although the Service for NDS provides users with the ability to access the NetWare Directory, you must address a number of compatibility issues before the service can be a suitable alternative to the VLM client. Some of these issues are easily addressed, some can be avoided by altering usage practices, and others are yet to be corrected. The following sections discuss these issues in detail.

NetWare Library Files Running the NWADMIN directory maintenance utility, as well as many other Windows network utilities, requires the support provided by the following NetWare library files:

- NWCALLS.DLL
- NWLOCALE.DLL
- NWIPXSPX.DLL
- NWNET.DLL
- NWGDI.DLL
- NWPSRV.DLL

These files are part of the NetWare VLM installation kit and are also available in the NWDLL2.EXE archive, both of which can be downloaded from Novell's NetWire service. If the VLM client has previously been installed on the workstation, these files should already be available. They must be located in the \Windows\System directory, or in another directory on the computer's PATH.

Windows 95 does not load these files into memory by default. It is possible that some networking applications may expect these libraries to be available in memory and will not function properly as a result. To work around this issue, Windows 95's System Policies feature can be used to preload these files.

NOTE The NW*.DLL files listed previously are not shipped with Windows 95. They are Novell release files and their use is subject to Novell's licensing restrictions. ■

Other applications may require access to the Unicode tables that are located in the \PUBLIC\NLS directory on a NetWare 4.x server. Adding this directory to the search path prevents any "Failed to Find Unicode Tables" errors from occurring.

Adding NDS Printers When using the Add New Printer Wizard with the Service for NDS to browse for printers, NDS printers are not visible. Bindery-based printers appear as they normally do. This discrepancy is due to a problem with the SHELL32.DLL file, which has been remedied by the release of Windows 95 Service Pack 1, available via Microsoft's Web site at **http://www.microsoft.com/windows95**.

▶ **See** "Working with Network Printers," **p. 951**

Service for NDS and NWUSER The Microsoft Service for NDS does not support the use of the NWUSER program that is included as part of the VLM client package. Most of the functions performed by NWUSER can be duplicated by other means in Windows 95.

Multiple Login Scripts When the Client for NetWare Networks and the Service for NDS are used alongside the Client for Microsoft Networks, Windows NT logon scripts always runs before NetWare login scripts, no matter which client is selected in the Primary Network Login dialog box.

Using the NetWare Client32 for Windows 95

Since the release of Windows 95, Novell has created its own protected-mode NetWare client, the NetWare Client32 for Windows 95. This client, as well as MSNDS, provides Windows 95 users with the basic NDS access that they requested. Novell's client, however, has proven to be a significantly more ambitious project than Microsoft's, and with good reason.

Client32 provides Windows 95 with NDS support, but it goes a great deal further by—for the first time—positioning NetWare Directory Services as a truly beneficial enterprise management platform. Client32's ability to deliver network applications to multiple users in the form of icons on the Windows 95 desktop is the first step toward making the Directory as useful for mid-sized and small networks as it is for giant enterprises.

Installing NetWare Client32 for Windows 95

Client32 provides a number of options with respect to its installation. Designed for the corporate environment, in which network administrators may be faced with the task of installing the client on hundreds of machines, it offers both automated and customized installation features.

For a network-based installation, Client32 can be added to the Windows 95 source files, and the installation script modified to make Client32 the default instead of Microsoft's NetWare client.

Client32 can also be configured to install itself automatically during a normal NDS login. A user's login script can be used to detect whether the client has already been installed on the workstation. If it hasn't, it performs the installation immediately.

Client32 can also be installed on demand by running a standard Windows 95 SETUP.EXE file from the source directory. All three of these processes can be customized to the administrator's exact preferences for multiple network installs. By default, they remove all existing NetWare client support from the Windows 95 machine and install the new client in its place.

For most single-user installations, running the SETUP program (see Figure 37.7) is the recommended installation procedure.

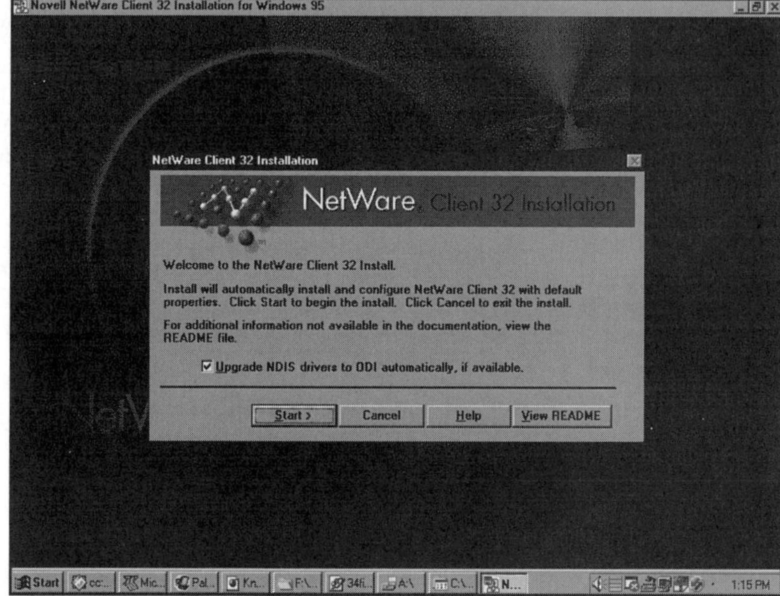

FIG. 37.7
The Novell NetWare Client32 for Windows 95 SETUP.EXE program completely automates the installation process.

The package also ships with its own 32-bit ODI drivers that, when compatible with the installed hardware, are recommended for use by Novell. Otherwise, you can use one of the NDIS 3.1 adapter drivers that ship with Windows 95.

Finally, Client32 can be installed using the normal Control Panel procedure, as follows:

1. Download NetWare Client32 for Windows 95 from Novell's World Wide Web site, place it in a directory by itself, and execute the file to expand it.

NOTE The Novell NetWare Client32 for Windows 95 can be downloaded from Novell's Web site at **http://support.novell.com** and then navigated to the appropriate page. To access the Client32 download page directly, point your browser at **http://support.novell.com/home/client/c3295/updates.htm**.

2. Double-click the Network icon in the Windows 95 Control Panel. Remove any existing NetWare support that has been installed.

NOTE Client32 is designed to automatically remove any existing NetWare client from Windows 95 before installing itself. However, in some instances, it can fail to do so, particularly when the Microsoft Service for NDS is present on the workstation. For large-scale client-upgrade projects, testing should be conducted on the existing environment to see if the installation method you choose behaves properly.

3. Click Add and double-click Client in the Select Network Component Type dialog box.
4. Click Have Disk and set the selector to the drive and directory containing the Client32 installation files.
5. When Client32 for NetWare Networks appears in the Select Network Type dialog box, select it and click OK.
6. After files are copied, the display returns to the Network's Configuration page, where the Novell NetWare Client32 is visible, as well as the IPX 32-bit Protocol for Novell NetWare Client32 (see Figure 37.8). If you want, and if your hardware is supported, you can manually install one of the 32-bit ODI adapter drivers included with Client32 at this time.

FIG. 37.8
Client32 is integrated into the Windows 95 networking environment, just as a Microsoft client would be.

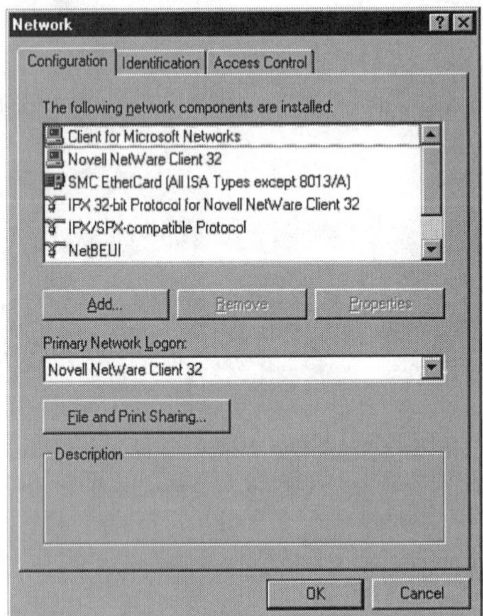

7. Before closing the dialog box, if you will be logging into an NDS tree for the first time, select the client and click the Properties button. Then select the Client32 tab and fill in the names of your preferred server and NDS tree, the context of your user object, and select a letter to be your first NetWare drive letter.
8. Click OK twice to close the dialog box and complete the installation. Restart the computer when you are prompted to do so.

Other Client32 Issues

Once installed, Client32 makes itself your primary login client, and as soon as the machine restarts, you'll see how this client differs from Microsoft's. Additional features abound from the very first login screen.

Client32 provides support for browsing to a different preferred server or tree, executes a specific login script or user profile, specifies values for login script variables, or just performs a simple bindery login.

The client modifies the My Computer, Network Neighborhood, and Windows Explorer displays to include icons representing NDS trees, as well as other NetWare features not provided by any other client (see Figure 37.9). The network can also be browsed either through the NDS hierarchy or through a server list. Support is even provided for logging into multiple NDS trees simultaneously.

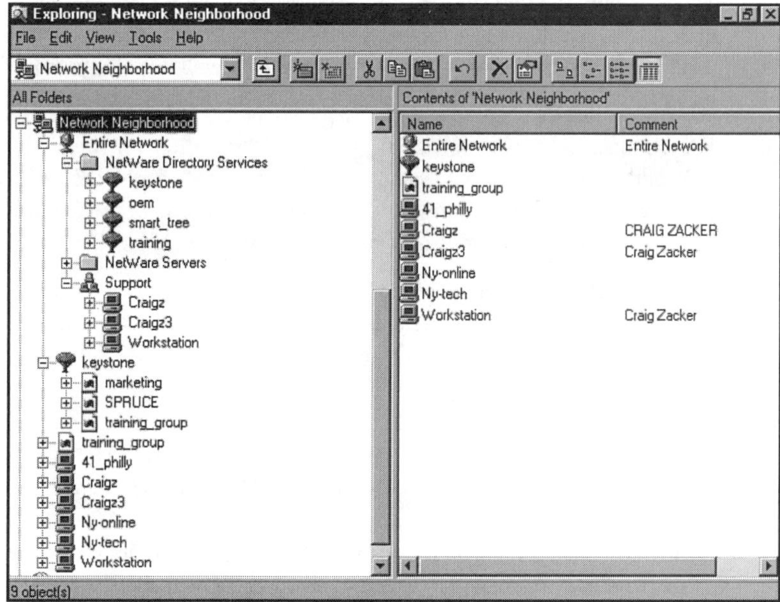

FIG. 37.9
Client32 integrates the NDS tree structure into the Windows Explorer.

Of course, you can run NWADMIN and all of the other NDS-related NetWare utilities using Client32. All of the necessary library files are included in the package, so even if you have never run a NetWare client on the workstation before, no other downloads are needed.

NOTE Novell has recently released an updated version of the Netware Administrator for Windows 95, called NWADMN95. This release addresses some issues found when using the Windows 3.x version of NWADMIN under Windows 95, and can be downloaded from Novell's Web site.

Most impressively, the package includes a module called APPSNAP.DLL that adds additional schema to the NDS database, that can be used by the NWADMIN utility. Once the module is installed, you can create application objects in the NDS database, just as you would create user, group, or any other NDS objects.

When you assign a user rights to an object representing a network-based application, the icon for the application appears in a window on his desktop when he runs the NetWare Application Launcher, a utility that is also included with the client. By placing this launcher in the Windows Startup group on all users' computers, a network administrator can deliver an entire customized suite of applications to as many workstations as needed, simply by assigning rights to users, groups, or containers in NWADMIN.

Choosing an NDS Client

The possibilities suggested by the NetWare Application Launcher are numerous, and most enticing. Although it started slowly, NetWare 4 sales are increasing tremendously, and NDS finally seems to be garnering the attention that Novell has always hoped it would, from both users and developers.

For the majority of users, especially those who are better off shielded from the intricacies of NDS and networking in general, the Microsoft Service for NetWare Directory Services is the preferred alternative. It offers excellent performance, all of the features that the average user needs, and it merges seamlessly with the existing Windows 95 client installation.

At a price, Client32 offers power users a host of very attractive features, including advanced configuration options. Navigating through a network server or tree display is markedly slower than with the Microsoft client. Delays of several seconds are commonplace while scanning network directories.

Client32 ships with files that allow it to be managed by the Windows 95 system Policy Editor. Access to selected features can be restricted in order to customize the interface to suit the users' skill level.

It should be noted that network file transfer performance does not seem to be affected as much as simple directory scanning. Client32 provides its own client-side caching, while the Microsoft clients are able to share the unified Windows 95 system cache (VCACHE). ●

CHAPTER 38

Using Novell Network Resources in Windows 95

by Glenn Fincher with Sue Plumley

In this chapter

Using Windows 95 and Novell Utilities

Windows support for Novell's NetWare makes performing general maintenance tasks, as well as requesting information from the server, quick and easy. You can perform many NetWare functions through Windows, such as mapping drives, listing your server connection, managing network print jobs, and so on, without ever using a command line.

Windows enables you to use many of NetWare's commands and utilities directly within Windows. You can check the status of network volumes, change your password, and use several administrative utilities from the MS-DOS prompt or the Run dialog box.

Mapping Drives

Windows provides an easy method of mapping drives from within the Network Neighborhood so you can avoid using Netware's MAP command. When you map a drive, you assign a drive letter to a network resource, such as a drive or folder. Mapping drives makes access to network resources faster and easier than opening several layers of windows to find the resource on the server or network.

You can make mapping permanent so you don't have to set the mapping each time you log in to the server.

Additionally, if you're running a login script, mapping drives provides the search and drive maps created by the system administrator. If you choose not to run the login script, you can map the drives yourself within Windows.

You also can choose to connect the map as a root of the drive, which not only helps keep path statements from getting too long but makes your maps a bit more permanent. For example, you can map to a document directory using the path: F:\CARLOS\NOTEBOOK\WPDOCS.

Now suppose you go into the F:\CARLOS\NOTEBOOK directory and access the REPORTS directory. The next time you want to use the original mapping to the WPDOCS directory, the map has changed to the F:\CARLOS\NOTEBOOK\REPORTS directory.

Connect the map as a root of the drive to alleviate this problem. In this example, connect F:\CARLOS\NOTEBOOK\WPDOCS as "J." Whenever you want to access the WPDOCS folder, you simply type **J**. Not only is the path shorter and easier to enter, the path remains the same even if you access different folders within the NOTEBOOK directory.

NOTE If you have used Windows for Workgroups, mapping a drive in Network Neighborhood should seem familiar because it is similar to mapping a drive from File Manager.

The basic procedure for mapping a network drive is as follows:

1. Open the Network Neighborhood and select the shared folder you want to map to.

2. Choose File, Map Network Drive. The Map Network Drive dialog box appears, as shown in Figure 38.1. Alternatively, you can right-click the share and choose Map Network Drive.

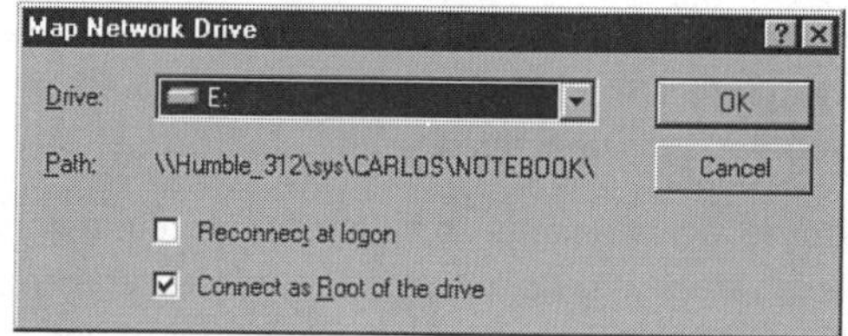

FIG. 38.1
Windows displays the path you've mapped out by selecting each folder.

3. By default, Windows assigns the next available drive letter on your computer to the folder that you select to map. To assign a different letter, select it from the Drive drop-down list.
4. To reconnect to this drive or directory automatically, select the Reconnect at Logon check box. Choosing this option makes the mapping permanent.
5. If you want, choose Connect as Root of the Drive.
6. Choose OK to close the dialog box. View drive mappings in the My Computer window (see Figure 38.2).

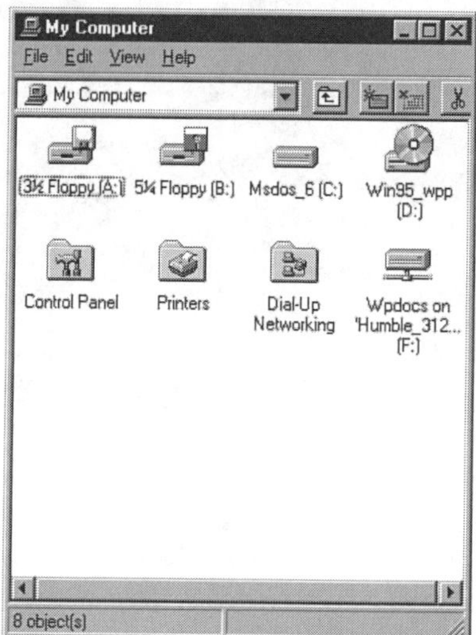

FIG. 38.2
Click the mapped drive icon to open the folder you want without wading through several other folders.

TIP If the toolbar is not showing in the Network Neighborhood window, choose View, Toolbar.

NOTE Windows supplies the Map Network Drive icon on the toolbar of the Network Neighborhood. However, mapping in this dialog box does not work with NetWare, but it does work with Microsoft peer-to-peer networking.

To disconnect a mapped drive, open My Computer and select the mapped drive. Right-click the mouse while pointing to the selected drive and choose Disconnect. The drive icon disappears from the window and the drive is disconnected.

If you want a list of the drives and mappings on your system, you might find the NetWare MAP command the best way to do so even though you can view mapped drives in the My Computer window. Enter **MAP** at the DOS prompt or in the Run dialog box, and you should see a screen similar to Figure 38.3.

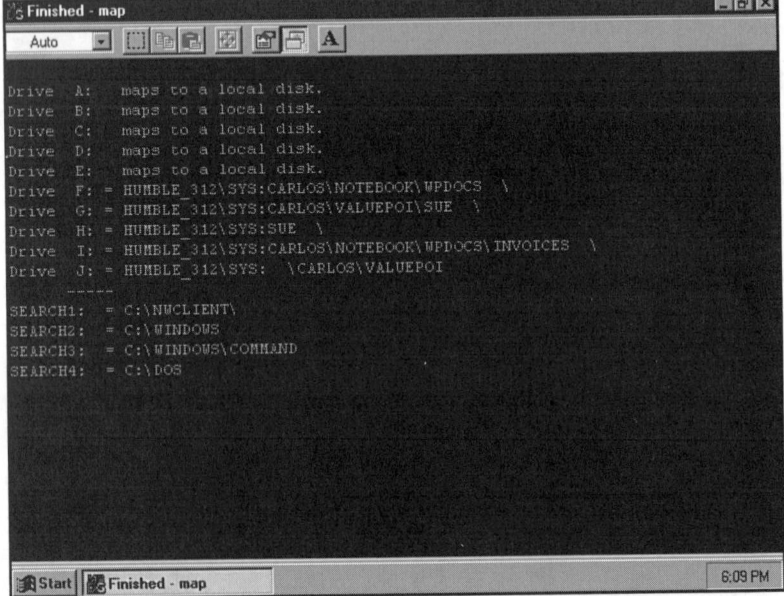

FIG. 38.3
The MAP command lists all the drive letters and the actual resources to which they are connected.

The drive mapping displayed in Figure 38.3 shows drives F through J as mapped drives that you've created in Windows. These drives make it easier for you to access your work on the server. The search section of the drive mapping shows the search paths that the server follows when you try to access a file or folder. The search drives were added by the login script that ran when Windows first logged in to the server.

TROUBLESHOOTING

I connected a path as a root of the drive but now I cannot move up one level in the path. What am I doing wrong? You're not doing anything wrong; the problem is with connecting as a root of the drive. You cannot move up a level within the path. If, for example, you want to move up one level from

F:\CARLOS\NOTEBOOK\WPDOCS to F:\CARLOS\NOTEBOOK, you have to create a new mapping or enter the entire path. When connecting as a root of the drive, your only choice is the entire path.

I typed MAP in the Run dialog box, but I got a message that said "Cannot find the file 'run'." What do I do now? If you ran the login scripts and the search paths are established, then you can just type **MAP** in the Run dialog box; otherwise, type the path to the MAP command, beginning with the server, public folder, and then the command. A sample path might be \\HUMBLE_312\SYS\PUBLIC\MAP. HUMBLE_312 is the server, and SYS is usually the name given to the first drive volume on the server. PUBLIC is the directory normally used to store NetWare commands.

Changing Your NetWare Password

The only way you can change your NetWare password, short of asking the system administrator, is to use the SETPASS command. SETPASS enables you to create or change a password on one or more file servers. You must be attached to the server before you can set the password on it.

If you're attached to more than one server with the *same* password, SETPASS enables you to synchronize passwords (setting all passwords at one time to the same word).

To use SETPASS, follow these steps:

1. Open the Start menu and choose Run. The Run dialog box appears.

If you're unsure of the path, choose the Browse button and look for the PUBLIC folder (in SYS: volume). Then find the command.

2. In the Open text box, enter the path and the SETPASS command. An example of the path might be: \\HUMBLE_312\SYS\PUBLIC\SETPASS.
3. Choose OK. Windows opens the MS-DOS prompt with the prompt asking for a new password, as shown in Figure 38.4.
4. Enter the new password and press Enter.
5. Re-enter the new password to confirm and press Enter. SETPASS notifies you the password has been changed.
6. Click the Close button to close the MS-DOS prompt.

Checking the NetWare Version

You can check the version of the NetWare server from within Windows. You'll need to know the NetWare version if a specific application you use is version-specific or version-sensitive.

TIP

You can also find the NetWare server version information by running NVER.EXE in a DOS window.

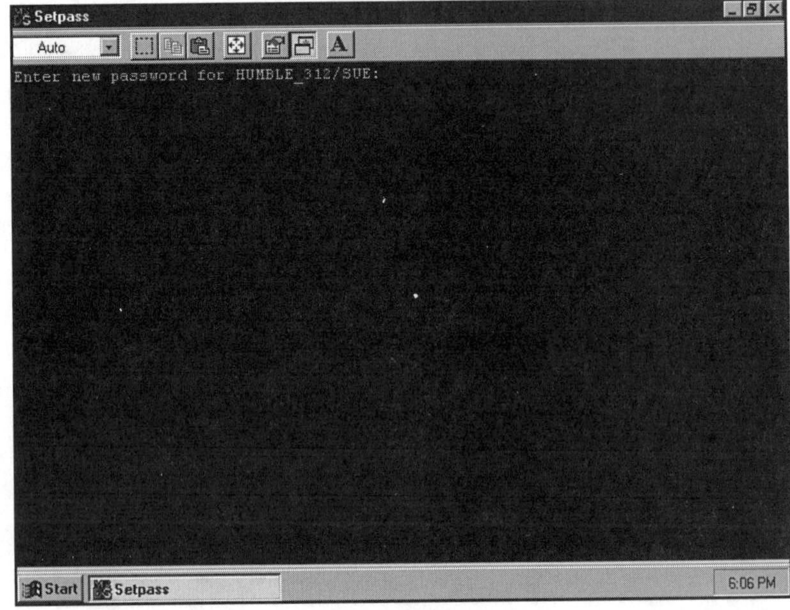

FIG. 38.4
Set a new password using the SETPASS command.

To find the version of the NetWare used on the server, follow these steps:

1. Open Network Neighborhood and select the server.

You also can display the properties sheet by right-clicking the server icon and choosing Properties.

2. Choose File, Properties. The properties sheet appears, as shown in Figure 38.5.
3. Once you have the version information, choose OK to close the properties sheet.

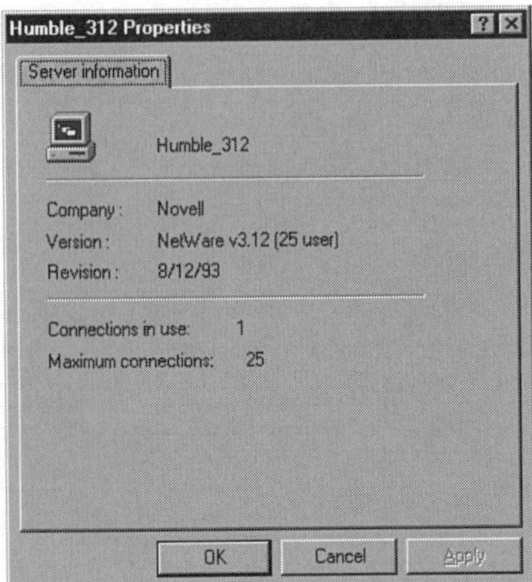

FIG. 38.5
The properties sheet lists NetWare server version information.

Checking the Status of Network Volumes

A *volume* is a physical portion of the hard disk that stores information on the file server. You can check the space on a volume as well as find out other information about different volumes on the server by using two NetWare utilities: CHKVOL and VOLINFO.

NOTE Usually the SYS is the first volume on a server and VOL1 is the second, VOL2 the third, and so on. Although these are the names Novell suggests, they are not always the names used. ■

To check on the status of the current volume, follow these steps:

1. Open the Start menu; then choose Programs, MS-DOS Prompt.
2. At the MS-DOS prompt, change the directory to the primary server drive (usually F:).
3. Type **CHKVOL**, and then press Enter. The results appear, as shown in Figure 38.6.

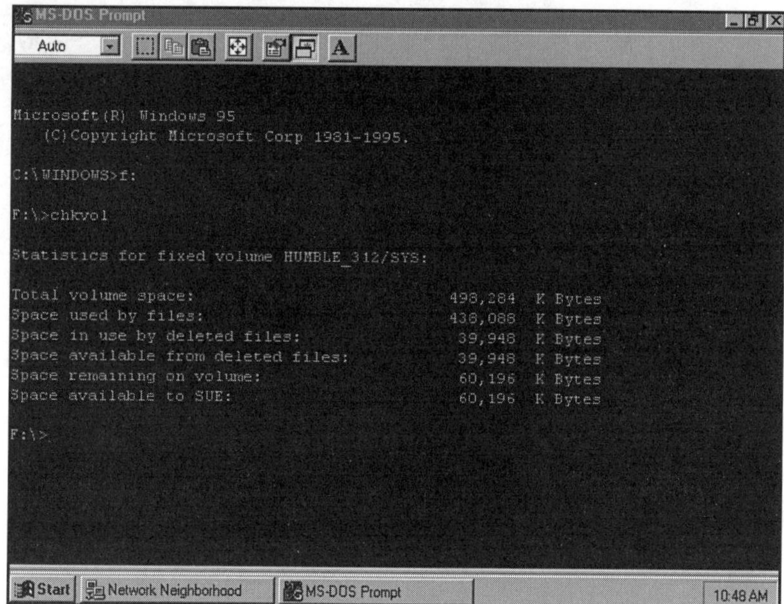
MS-DOS Prompt
Auto
Microsoft(R) Windows 95
(C)Copyright Microsoft Corp 1981-1995.
C:\WINDOWS>f:
F:\>chkvol
Statistics for fixed volume HUMBLE_312/SYS:
Total volume space: 498,284 K Bytes
Space used by files: 438,088 K Bytes
Space in use by deleted files: 39,948 K Bytes
Space available from deleted files: 39,948 K Bytes
Space remaining on volume: 60,196 K Bytes
Space available to SUE: 60,196 K Bytes
F:\>
Start
Network Neighborhood
MS-DOS Prompt
10:48 AM

FIG. 38.6 Run CHKVOL at the MS-DOS Prompt or from the Run dialog box.

NOTE You may need to enter a path to the CHKVOL.EXE command; an example path might be \\HUMBLE_312\SYS\PUBLIC\CHKVOL.EXE. ■

4. Close the DOS window when you finish looking at the CHKVOL statistics.

The CHKVOL statistics list the total amount of space on the volume, the space used by files, the space in use by deleted files as well as the space available from deleted files, space remaining on the volume, and the space available to you.

Another NetWare information tool that you can use is VOLINFO.EXE, which quickly checks the status of drive usage. To use VOLINFO, follow these steps:

1. Open the MS-DOS Prompt and change to the primary server drive.
2. At the prompt, type **VOLINFO** and press Enter. The Volume Information utility appears (see Figure 38.7).

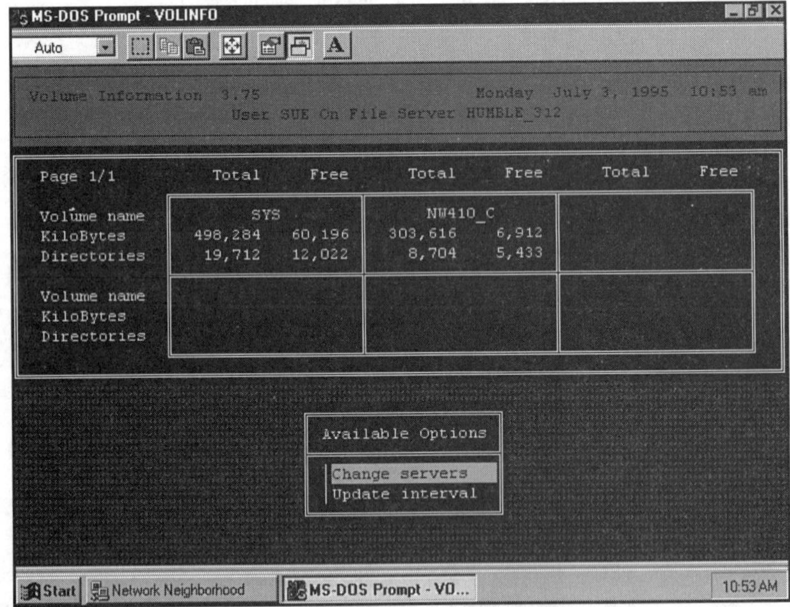

FIG. 38.7
Use Volume Information to view various volumes and their resources.

3. After viewing the volume information, press the Esc key. The Exit VolInfo dialog box appears.
4. Choose Yes, and then press Enter.
5. At the MS-DOS prompt, type **exit** and press Enter, or click the Close button in the title bar, to return to the Windows desktop.

VOLINFO reports the name of the volume you are viewing and refers to the storage capacity of that volume in kilobytes. It will report space in megabytes if the server has more than one gigabyte of storage space.

Listing Your Server Connections

Windows 95 provides a WhoAmI feature that is a graphical user interface (GUI) approach to NetWare's WHOAMI utility. This simplified version of the command shows only the most basic results: your user name and connection number. To see this information, right-click a server in the Network Neighborhood and choose Who Am I. The results are similar to Figure 38.8.

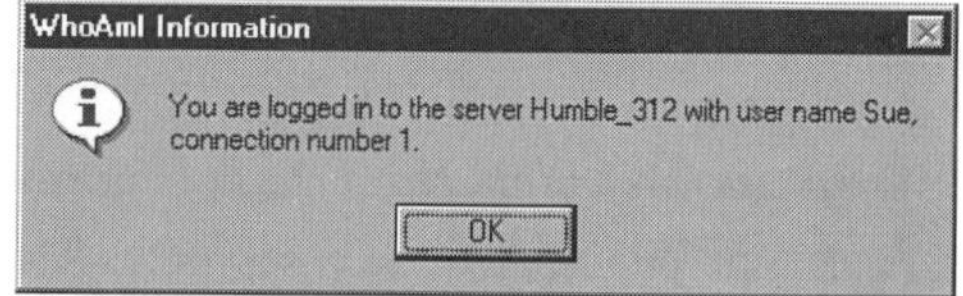

FIG. 38.8
The WhoAmI feature shows your user name, the server to which you're connected, and the connection number.

The NetWare command-line version is much more useful. For instance, if you enter **WHOAMI** at the DOS prompt, you get the same user, server, and connection information. Additionally, WHOAMI lists the NetWare version and allotted user number, date, and time of login, as shown in Figure 38.9.

If you're connected to more than one server, the WHOAMI command also lists those servers and your name on each, the software version on each, your login date and time for each server, and your rights and security equivalencies on each server.

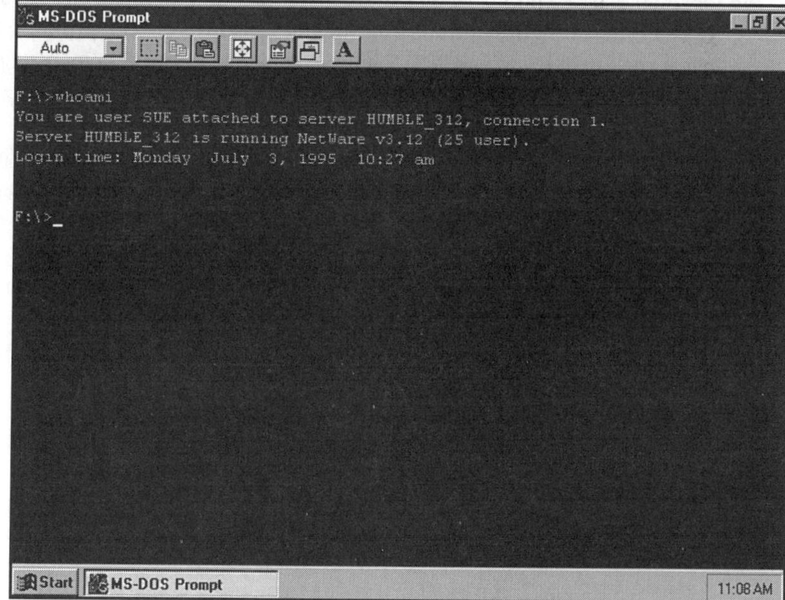

FIG. 38.9
Typical output from NetWare's WHOAMI utility.

You can enhance the command-line version's output with several parameters. Enter the command as **WHOAMI [servername] [option]**. The most useful parameters are those outlined here:

Parameter	Description
/s	*Security* lists the security equivalencies on each server you specify.
/g	*Groups* lists your membership in groups on each server specified.

continues

continued

Parameter	Description
/w	*Workgroup* lists workgroup manager information.
/r	*Rights* lists your rights on each server to which you're attached.
/a	*All* lists all the available information, including your group memberships, your security equivalencies, your rights, object supervisor, workgroup manager, and general system information.

Managing NetWare Printers

▶ **See** "Understanding Network Printing," **p. 952**

▶ **See** "Solving Common Network Printing Problems," **p. 964**

If you are comfortable with using NetWare and have done much work printing to a NetWare printer, you have probably seen or used NetWare's PCONSOLE utility for controlling print jobs. Windows 95 improves on PCONSOLE by adding to the printer's control applet in Windows 95 almost all these printer control functions for NetWare printers. Every common task for which you are likely to use PCONSOLE can be done from Windows. For example, checking the status of a print job and rearranging jobs in the queue (if you have sufficient user rights).

NOTE Even though Windows shows nine printer ports you can capture, Novell limits you to capturing on three: LPT1, LPT2, and LPT3. With Novell NetWare, Windows also tells you that LPT4 and higher are out of range. ■

PCONSOLE runs just as before, so if you are already familiar with it and want to continue using it, or if you want to access some advanced feature not available in Windows, you can still do so. However, if you only want to see how many print jobs are in front of you in the queue or to delete a print job that you sent accidentally, you can perform all these basic tasks in Windows, as described in Chapter 41, "Working with Network Printers."

Using Administrative Utilities

Most other NetWare utilities that you previously ran from a DOS prompt should now work in Windows 95 as well as from the DOS prompt. You might even find that some network utilities that were difficult to run in DOS 6.x, due to memory constraints, are easier to run in Windows 95 because more conventional memory is now available.

Table 38.1 lists some common Novell utilities that run in Windows 95. Many other unlisted utilities run as well.

Table 38.1 Some Novell DOS Utilities that You Can Run Under Windows 95 Command Prompts

Novell DOS Utility	Function
FCONSOLE	Monitors the file server and lets you perform such functions as broadcast console messages, down the file server, check file server status, and so on
RCONSOLE	Gives you access to the file server console from a workstation (NetWare versions 3.11, 3.12, 4.02, and 4.1)
FILER	Determines file creation date, last access date, size, owner, and so on
SALVAGE	Undeletes files from a NetWare volume
SESSION	Maps network drives with a menu
CAPTURE	Assigns network printers to local LPT ports
SLIST	Displays all NetWare servers on the network (through version 3.x)
SYSCON	Controls accounting, file servers, group, and user information (through version 3.x)

CAUTION

Deleted files and folders from a network drive are deleted permanently and do not go to the Windows Recycle Bin. There is no Undo, so be careful. If you do mistakenly delete an item you want, try the SALVAGE command as quickly after deleting the item as possible. When you delete files, the space it occupied remains on the server until the server needs space and is recoverable until that time.

Some utilities cannot run under Windows 95 when you use the Windows Client for NetWare Networks rather than the Novell VLM network drivers. You use these commands in NetWare 4.x networks that employ the NetWare Directory Services (NDS) to manage a multiserver domain. Table 38.2 lists these utilities, which operate under Windows 95, only when the Novell VLM network drivers are used.

Table 38.2 Novell Utilities that Work Only with Novell VLM Network Drivers

Novell Utility	Function
NWADMIN	Administers the NDS directory tree under Windows
CX	Changes contexts within the NDS directory tree
NETADMIN	Administers the NDS directory tree under DOS

NOTE NWADMIN, CX, and NETADMIN are all supported with NetWare's Client32 for Windows 95, which can be downloaded from the Novell Web site. In addition, if you are running OSR2 of Windows 95, you get MSNDS (Microsoft NetWare Directory Services), which allows a Windows 95 workstation access to NDS-based server resources. MSNDS also supports these Novell utilities.

In addition to the utilities listed in Table 38.2 that do not work with the Windows Client for NetWare Networks, the NWUSER Windows 3.x utility is not supported under any configuration in Windows 95. This should not pose a problem because the Explorer application provides all the functionality of the NWUSER utility.

NWPOPUP, a utility administrators use to broadcast messages across the network, does not work in Windows 95; however, you can install WinPopup to work in its place. WinPopup is a Windows utility in which you can send and receive messages on the NetWare network. Find the WinPopup utility on the migration Planning Kit CD that ships with Windows 95 and look in the Admin95 folder, Apptools.

TIP In WinPopup, choose the Messages menu, Options button and select Pop Up Dialog on Message Receipt to be notified immediately of messages from the network.

You can add WinPopup to your Startup group (Start menu, Settings, Taskbar, Start Menu Programs tab) so WinPopup automatically starts when you start Windows, so you'll always know when a network message is broadcast.

TROUBLESHOOTING

I tried to enter a NetWare command in the Run dialog box but I got the message "Cannot find the file...." What did I do wrong? You may need to specify a path to the server and the folder in which the command or utility resides. If that still doesn't work, close the Run dialog box and use the MS-DOS prompt instead. In the DOS window, change the drives to the primary network drive (usually F:) and then enter the command and the path. Some NetWare commands just do not work from the Run dialog box.

I've forgotten where I placed a file on the server. Is there a NetWare command I can use to find the file? The easiest way to find a file or a folder in Windows is to use the Windows Find feature. You can use it for network drives as well as for your own drive. Choose Start, Find, and then Files or Folders. In the Find Files dialog box, choose the Browse button. In the Browse for Folder dialog box, double-click the Network Neighborhood. Double-click the server and then choose OK. Enter the file or folder name in the Named text box and choose Find Now. Windows searches the server drive for your file or folder.

Connecting to Other Servers

Connecting to and using the resources on servers within the local network is easy, but how do you connect to servers other than your usual "preferred server"? You accomplish this connection just as you would expect: by using all the standard tools previously discussed.

To connect to other servers, follow these steps:

1. Open the Network Neighborhood; all attached servers appear in the list.
2. Select the server name and then choose File, Attach As, or right-click the server name and choose Attach As. The Enter Network Password dialog box appears.
3. Enter your user name and password. Additionally, you can choose from the following options:
   - Save this password in your password list. Choose this option to save your password in a list so the next time you make this connection, you do not have to retype the password.
   - Connect as Guest. Log on as a guest if you do not have access to that server. Logging on as a guest gives you only limited access to the server.
4. Click OK to establish the connection. Note that your user name and password may vary from server to server.

If you have logins on multiple servers, this method is probably the easiest. Of course, if you frequently need to connect your computer to the same server, you might create a shortcut on the desktop for this connection.

Using Network Tape Drives

Windows includes a Backup program you can use to back up your files to a network tape drive. Windows 95 works only with 1992 or later versions of certain tape drives (find the list in Backup Help). You might also call the tape drive manufacturer for information about backup software you can use with Windows 95.

Several drives are not compatible with Windows 95, including Archive drives, Irwin AccuTrak tapes and Irwin drives, Mountain drives, QIC Wide tapes, QIC 3020 drives, SCSI tape drives, Summit drives, and Travan drives.

▶ **See** "Backing Up Your Files," **p. 378**

In addition, Windows 95 includes an automatic backup feature, a backup agent that efficiently and regularly backs up your system, using industry-standard technology from Arcada (Backup Exec) and Cheyenne (ARCserve). These agents require network connections to a server.

NOTE These backup agents require the appropriate software running on the NetWare server. Windows 95 does not include the Arcada or Cheyenne backup software. Additionally, Arcada and Cheyenne are not Novell's native TSA backup agents.

Microsoft considers these agents a service. To install the service to Windows 95, follow these steps:

1. Open the Network dialog box from the Control Panel.
2. On the Configuration page, choose Add. The Select Network Component Type dialog box appears.
3. Select Service and choose Add. The Select Network Service dialog box appears (see Figure 38.10).

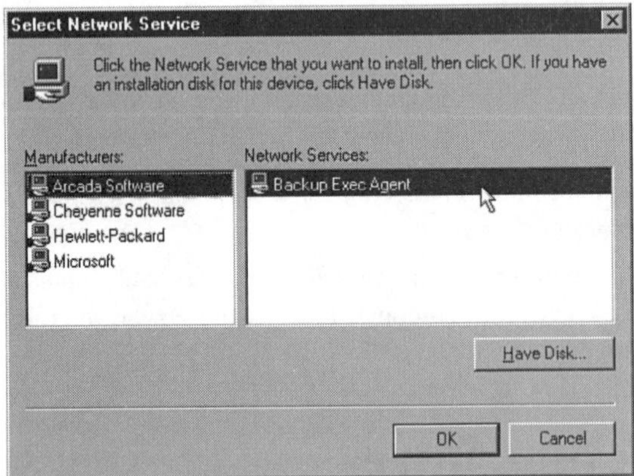

FIG. 38.10
Choose the service from the Select Network Service dialog box.

4. In Manufacturers, choose Arcada Software, and in Network Services, Backup Exec Agent becomes selected.

   Alternatively, choose Cheyenne Software in the Manufacturers list and choose ARCserve Agent.
5. Choose OK to select the service. Windows may prompt you to insert the Windows 95 CD. Follow directions on screen.
6. Windows returns to the Network dialog box. Choose OK to close the dialog box. Windows may copy more files from the Windows 95 CD.
7. Windows prompts you to restart your computer. Choose Yes.

The following sections take you step by step through a typical setup of both of these services. Remember, without one of these backup servers, you cannot use the backup agents.

NOTE If your NetWare server uses different backup software, you probably can still use it if you can run it from a DOS command line. Although Windows 95 might not support the software directly, you should still be able to run the software from DOS just as you could with previous releases of Windows.

Backing Up with Arcada

The Arcada Backup Exec agent as delivered with Windows 95 requires Arcada Backup Exec for NetWare, Enterprise Edition, or Single Server Edition, version 5.01. If your NetWare server is running either of these Arcada products, you can use the Arcada backup agent to archive important data regularly from your workstation.

Setting Properties After installing the Arcada service from the Select Network Service dialog box, follow these steps to set up the service:

1. In the Network dialog box, click the Configuration tab.
2. In the components list, double-click Backup Exec Agent. The Backup Exec Agent properties sheet appears, as shown in Figure 38.11.

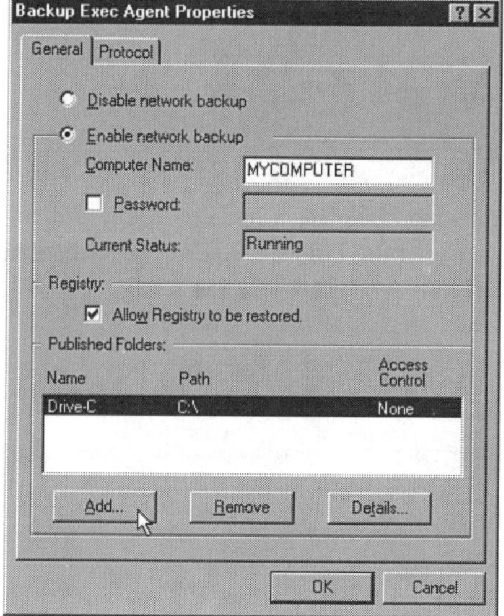

FIG. 38.11
Configure the Backup Exec Agent in the Backup Exec Agent properties sheet.

3. Click the General tab and choose to Enable Network Backup. The NetWare server software now considers the Windows 95 computer to be a backup source.
4. Enter the name of your computer (as the network knows it) and your password.

NOTE Select the Allow Registry to Be Restored check box if you want to enable the software to restore the Registry. If you select the Allow Registry to Be Restored check box, the software overwrites any changes that you made since your last backup.

TIP You can also choose to back up floppy and CD-ROM drives in the Select Folder to Publish dialog box.

5. In the Published Folders area, Drive C indicates your entire drive. If you do not want to back up the entire drive, choose Remove.

   To add specific folders, choose Add and the Select Folder to Publish dialog box appears (see Figure 38.12). Choose the folders you want to add to the backup and choose OK. The selected folders are added to the Published Folders list on the Backup Exec Agent properties sheet.

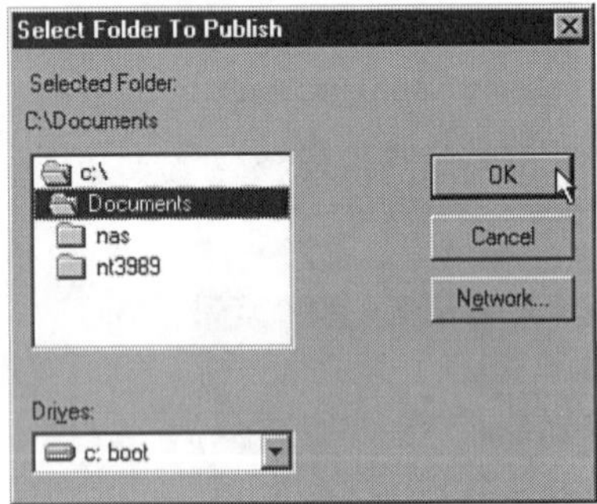

FIG. 38.12
Add drives and/or folders to the Published Folders list (backup list).

6. In the Published Folders area of the Backup Exec Agent properties sheet, select a folder or drive and choose Details. In the Folder Details dialog box, you can browse the folder's contents and set access limits (see Figure 38.13).

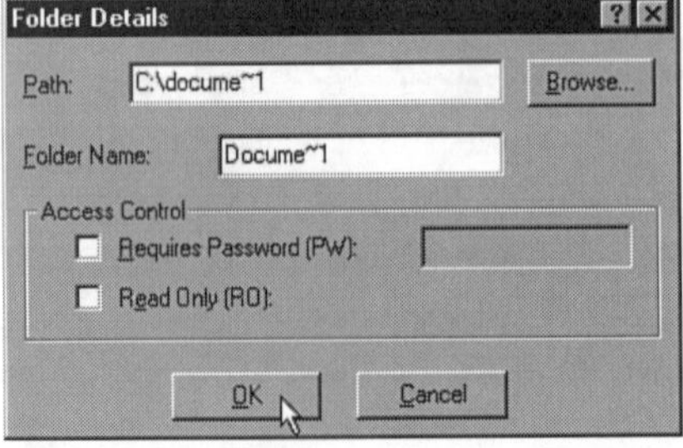

FIG. 38.13
In the Folder Details dialog box, you can assign the required access control.

7. Choose OK to close the Folder Details dialog box. The dialog box closes and the access control limits appear in the Published Folders area of the Backup Exec Agent properties sheet (see Figure 38.14).

8. Click OK to close the Backup Exec Agent properties sheet.

NOTE When you first install your software, the properties sheet's Current Status indicates "Not Running." After you install and configure the agent, this status changes to "Running."

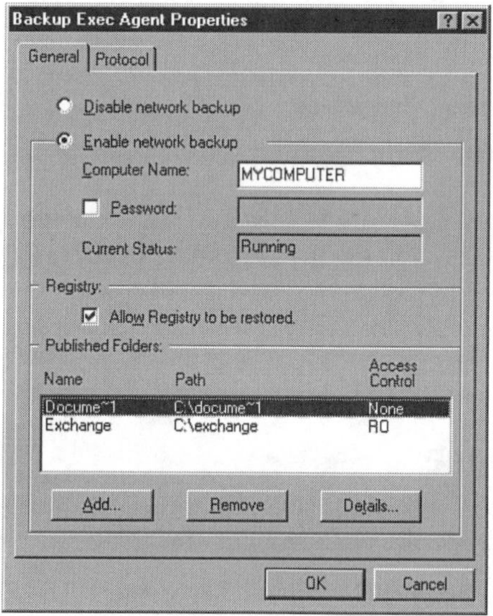

FIG. 38.14
The Published Folders area of the Backup Exec Agent properties sheet indicates the access control that you have set.

Setting Protocol You must set the protocol of the agent to match that of the server. To set the protocol for the Backup Exec Agent, follow these steps:

1. On the Backup Exec Agent properties sheet, click the Protocol tab (see Figure 38.15).

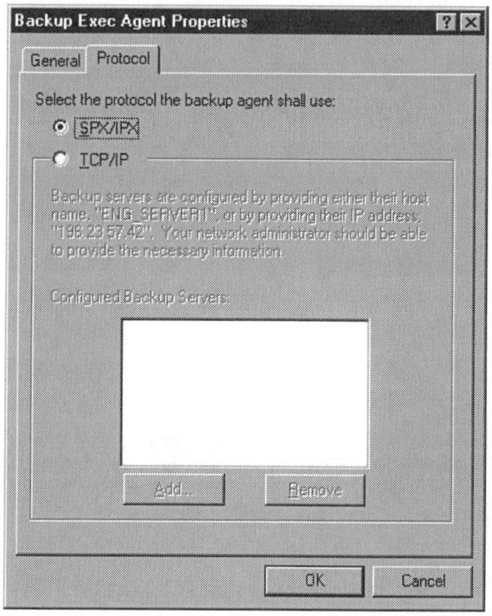

FIG. 38.15
The Protocol page of the Backup Exec Agent properties sheet.

2. Choose the SPX/IPX protocol for the backup agent.
3. Choose OK to close the dialog box.
4. Choose OK in the Network dialog box.
5. When Windows prompts you to restart the computer, choose Yes.

NOTE To use the Arcada Backup Agent, you might have to check whether the system administrator has the latest versions of the Arcada network loadable modules (NLMs) that have been updated for Windows 95. The necessary updated files are NRLTLI.NLM, TNRLAPT3.NLM, TNRLAPT4.NLM, TNRLTCP.NLM, and TNRLSPX.NLM. To get these files, you can contact Arcada directly or call Arcada's BBS at (407) 262-8138.

Backing Up with Cheyenne

If your server is running the Cheyenne backup software, and you've installed the ARCserve backup agent, you can set properties for the agent by following these steps:

1. In the Network dialog box, double-click ARCserve Agent. The ARCserve Agent properties sheet appears.
2. Click the General tab and choose Enable Network Backup. The Enable Network Backup area becomes available, as shown in Figure 38.16.

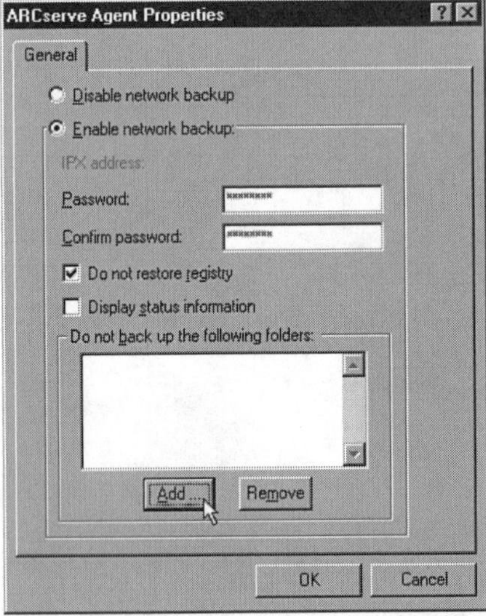

FIG. 38.16 Enable network backup on the ARCserve Agent properties sheet.

3. Specify the settings to configure the Cheyenne software:
   - **Password**. Enter your password.
   - **Confirm Password**. Enter your password again.

- **Do Not Restore Registry**. Select this option if you do not want your system's registry settings restored when your system is restored.
- **Display Status Information**. Displays information during the backup.

4. The Do Not Back Up the Following Folders list should contain only those folders you *do not* want to back up. By default, all folders will be backed up.

   To enter folders in the Do Not Back Up the Following Folders list, choose Add. The Add dialog box appears (see Figure 38.17).

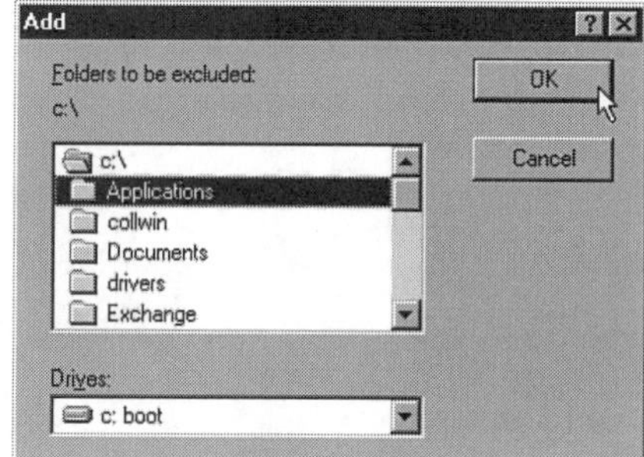

FIG. 38.17
Select the folder you *do not* want to back up in the Add dialog box for Cheyenne ARCserve agent.

NOTE If you mistakenly added a folder you do want to back up, select the folder and choose Remove.

5. Choose OK in the Add dialog box to return to the ARCserve Agent properties sheet. The folders you do not want to back up appear in the Do Not Back Up the Following Folders list box, as shown in Figure 38.18.

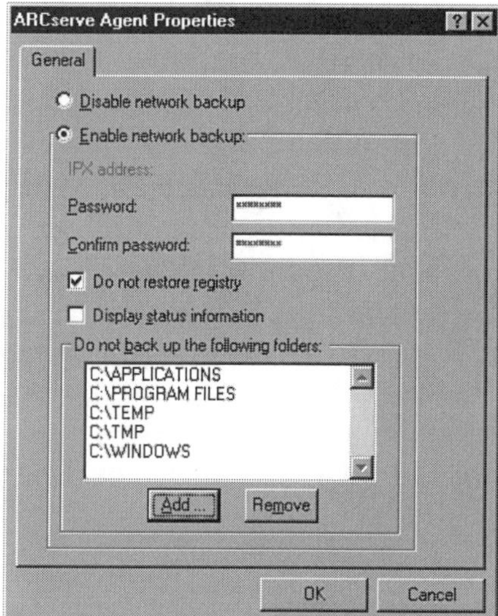

FIG. 38.18
The folders listed in the dialog box are those the agent will *not* back up.

6. Click OK to close the properties sheet.
7. Choose OK in the Network dialog box.
8. When Windows prompts you to restart the computer, choose Yes.

NOTE Cheyenne has updated the network loadable modules (NLMs) specifically for Windows 95. These updated files are APROCESS.NLM, ARCOPY.NLM, and WSTAPE.NLM. To obtain these files, contact Cheyenne directly at (800) 243-9832.

As you have seen in this chapter, Windows 95 and NetWare servers can coexist, and in fact, Windows 95 makes it easier to use NetWare server resources than previous releases of Windows. Microsoft has made Windows 95 truly a "well-connected client."

CHAPTER 39

Connecting Windows 95 to Windows NT Server 4.0

by Jerry Honeycutt and Craig Zacker

In this chapter

Installing a Network Adapter

A personal computer's network interface consists of two parts: the network adapter device itself, which usually takes the form of an expansion card or NIC (network interface card), and the adapter driver, which allows communication between the hardware and the network client software. Both the hardware and software components must be properly configured for network communication to occur.

When you install hardware conforming to the Windows 95 Plug and Play (PnP) standard, the operating system performs these configuration tasks for you automatically. However, many companies still purchase and use network interface cards that do not conform to the standard. When you install a non-PnP network adapter, you must configure the hardware and software yourself. Fortunately, even without Plug and Play, Windows 95 makes this configuration process easier than it has ever been before for a PC.

NOTE If you are using a PC Card network adapter, Windows 95 requires that you install a PC Card driver before the driver for the adapter. In many cases, the PC Card driver will provide Plug and Play recognition of the network adapter and its properties, even in computers without a Plug and Play BIOS. ■

Configuring Network Adapter Hardware

Every network interface card requires access to certain hardware and memory resources of your computer, such as an IRQ, a memory address, an I/O port, or any combination of these. The types of resources required differ for various adapters, but in nearly all cases, you must assign specific resource settings for the exclusive use of the card. The main obstacle to successfully installing a network adapter is locating settings acceptable to the card that are not already being used by the computer's other hardware.

You adjust your network adapter's hardware settings either by physically manipulating jumper blocks or DIP switches on the card itself, or by running a configuration program supplied the hardware. The program directly addresses the permanent memory on the card and stores your selected settings there.

Unless you are familiar with the IRQ, memory address and I/O port settings of all the components in your computer, the installation of a network card will be primarily a trial-and-error process. You insert the card into the computer, load the operating system, and see if there are any conflicts with the other hardware in the computer. If there are, you adjust the settings of the card and try again.

Windows 95 provides tools that can simplify this process, but before you can use them, you must first install driver support for the network adapter. You can do this from the Network properties in the Control Panel, but the easier method is to use the Add New Hardware Wizard.

Using the Add New Hardware Wizard

The Add New Hardware Wizard takes you through the process of identifying your network interface card to the operating system and installing the appropriate adapter drivers. You may elect to install the adapter hardware before running the wizard (although it is not essential), but it is recommended that you leave the task of resolving any hardware conflicts until afterward. Once you have installed the adapter driver, you can use the Windows 95 Device Manager to determine what devices are in conflict.

Before beginning the actual installation process of a new network adapter, it is a good idea to make a note of the adapter's default settings, either by examining the card itself, consulting the card's documentation, or by running the configuration software supplied with it. You may then physically insert the card into the computer (although this also may be done after the driver installation) and start the machine.

To install support for a network adapter, follow these steps:

1. Select the Add New Hardware icon in the Windows 95 Control Panel.
2. When asked if you want to let Windows 95 attempt to automatically detect your new hardware, select No.
3. From the list of Hardware Types, choose Network adapters and click the Next button. The Select Device dialog box, shown in Figure 39.1, appears.

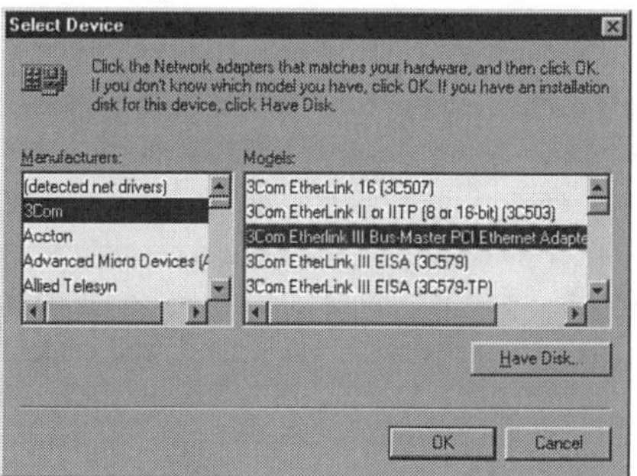

FIG. 39.1
The Select Device dialog box lists all of the network adapter drivers that ship with Windows 95.

4. Select the manufacturer of your network adapter from the scroll box on the left, and select the model on the right. If your adapter does not appear on the list, or if you have an updated driver that you want to install, click the Have Disk button and specify the location of the files.

NOTE The drivers supplied with the shipping version of the Windows 95 operating system support a large percentage of the network adapter cards in current use and available on the market today. However, new hardware is continually being released, as are updated drivers. Microsoft has posted a large number of updated hardware drivers on their online services. Updated drivers can also be obtained directly from the hardware manufacturer. While you may encounter cases in which newer

continues

continued

drivers are needed to enable certain networking features, you will rarely see the default Windows 95 installation package fail to achieve a network connection using the drivers provided.

Microsoft's updated adapter drivers can be found as part of the Windows 95 Driver Library, available on their World. Wide Web site at **http://www.microsoft.com/windows/software/drivers/network.html**.

5. Once you have made a hardware selection, click OK and Windows 95 displays a screen listing the hardware settings that must be specified for the operation of the adapter, as well as the default settings supplied by the driver software. These settings are not necessarily those to which the hardware has been configured. In a non-Plug and Play installation, the operating system is unable to detect the actual settings of the hardware. The values shown are proposed software settings for the driver to be installed.
6. Compare the driver settings displayed by the wizard with the adapter's hardware settings you have previously noted before the installation process began. If these values differ, then you must reconfigure either the hardware or software settings, or both. But first, the driver installation must be completed; click Next.
7. Windows 95 will now access its installation files and copy the appropriate driver files to the hard drive. You may be prompted to locate your Windows 95 installation source files. Click Yes when you are asked if you want to restart your computer.

TROUBLESHOOTING

After installing a new network interface card, my computer fails to boot properly. It either boots into Safe Mode or fails to boot at all. What's wrong? The network interface card is currently conflicting with the other hardware in your computer. Remove the card, boot the computer, and install support for the card using the Add New Hardware Wizard. (You can do this whether the card is physically installed or not.) Use the Windows 95 Device Manager to find new hardware settings that don't conflict with the rest of the system. Shut down the computer, reinstall the card with the new settings, and reboot.

Using the Windows 95 Device Manager

Unlike older operating systems, Windows 95 can monitor the hardware resources being used by every device in the computer (provided, of course, that you've also loaded the corresponding device driver). Windows 95 also includes a Device Manager that displays an inventory of the computer's contents. If you have determined during the adapter driver installation that adjustments to the hardware settings are necessary, you can use the Device Manager to see which hardware devices conflict and which settings must be altered.

You can access this inventory from the Windows 95 Control Panel by opening the System properties and selecting the Device Manager tab. This tab displays a tree, such as that shown in Figure 39.2. When you select a device on the tree, click the Properties button; then click the Resources tab. The hardware resource settings of the device's driver appear.

At the bottom of the Resources tab, there is a Conflicting Device List. If any of the current settings of your network adapter conflict with another device in the computer, then the setting and the device name appear in the Conflicting Device List.

If you attempt to modify a device's configuration to use a resource that has already been allocated, a message box warns you that you must make configuration changes.

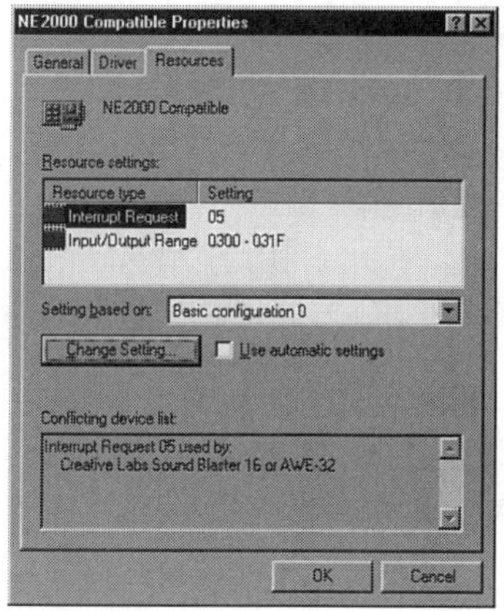

FIG. 39.2 The Device Manager screen displays an inventory of the computer's currently installed hardware.

Modifying the Network Adapter Configuration

At this point in the installation of the network adapter, you use the Device Manager to perform two distinct tasks:

- Determine whether the current hardware settings of the adapter are in conflict with other devices.
- Modify the resource settings of the network adapter's software device driver.

It is important that you distinguish between these two tasks. While you can use the Device Manager to examine the current hardware settings, it cannot modify them. You must do this by using the adapter's configuration program or by adjusting the hardware itself. Use the following procedure to locate proper hardware resource settings and configure the adapter driver to use them.

1. Double-click the System icon in the Control Panel, and click the Device Manager tab.
2. In the Device Manager tab, select your network adapter by name, and click the Properties button.
3. Click the Resources tab. A display of Resource Settings appears.
4. Click the first Resource Type in the Resource Settings selector; then click the Change Setting button. You'll see a dialog box similar to the one shown in Figure 39.3.
5. Modify the Value in the Edit dialog box to match your adapter's current hardware setting (which you noted before the installation process began). If another installed device appears in the Conflict Information window, that value cannot be used.

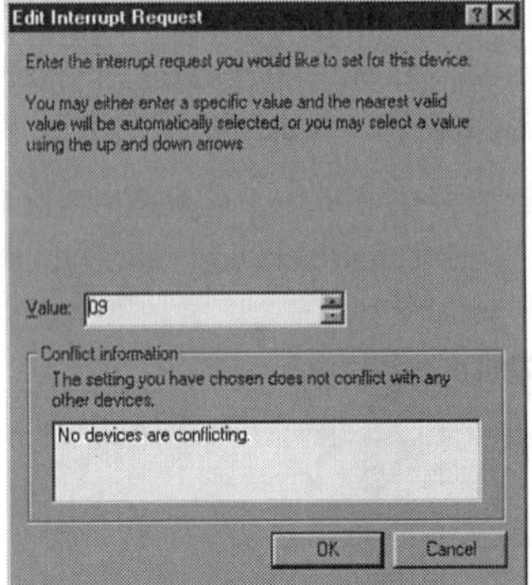

FIG. 39.3
You use essentially the same dialog box for editing IRQ's, DMA channels, and I/O addresses.

6. If necessary, modify the setting again to a Value that displays a No Devices Are Conflicting message in the Conflict Information window. Notice the new Value that you have selected for later use, and click OK.
7. Repeat steps 4–6 for each hardware setting displayed on the Resources tab. When you are finished, the Conflict Information window on the Resources tab should indicate that No Conflicts exist.
8. Click OK to close the dialog box.

Windows 95 displays a message stating that you should now shut down and power off your computer, and then modify your adapter's hardware settings. You need do this only if you encountered conflicts during the preceding steps. To change the settings, follow the instructions included with your network adapter. You may not have to power down the machine if a software-based setup program is available for the adapter. You do need to reboot the system, however, after any hardware settings are changed.

TROUBLESHOOTING

What do I do if I have tried all of the values for a particular resource setting, and they all result in a conflict? Today's network adapters usually provide a large selection of possible values for their resource settings. Other devices in your computer, however, may offer a different selection. If you cannot locate an nonconflicting value for a particular network adapter setting, you will have to modify the configuration of another device in your system to free up a resource for your network adapter.

The best way to handle this problem is to remove the network adapter from the computer and concentrate on reconfiguring another device, using either the Device Manager, a Control Panel application, or a dedicated configuration program to make the changes. Once you are certain that the other device is functioning properly, reinsert the network adapter and modify its resource setting to the newly available value.

I have modified the settings in the Device Manager so that there are no hardware conflicts, but my network adapter still does not function. What's wrong? If you made changes to the adapter driver settings, then you must also configure the hardware itself to use those settings. This can only be done by physically manipulating the hardware, using jumpers or DIP switches, or by using a software-based configuration program.

Installing the Client for Microsoft Networks for Windows NT 4.0

The adapter and its driver are the components that communicate directly with the network. For Windows 95 to access the resources on an NT server, you must next install the Client for Microsoft Networks, which communicates with the rest of the operating system, and a protocol, which links the client and the adapter.

The following procedure describes the installation of the Client for Microsoft Networks, and all of the other components necessary to gain access to a Microsoft network and attach to a Windows NT server.

1. Double-click the Network icon in the Control Panel and click Add.
2. In the Select Network Component Type dialog box (see Figure 39.4), double-click Client.

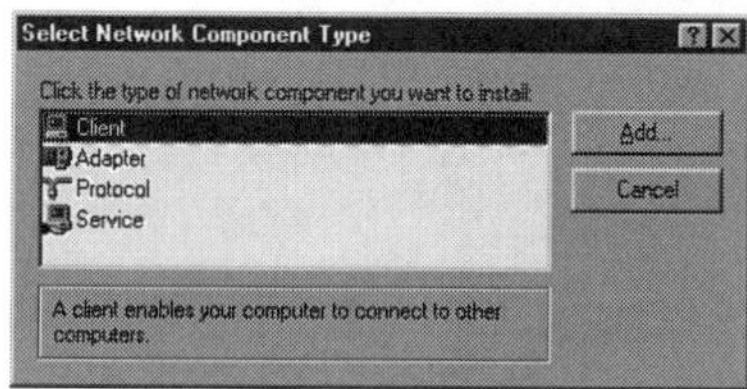

FIG. 39.4 Select the component to be installed from the list.

3. Choose Microsoft from the left side of the Select Network Client dialog box (see Figure 39.5) and choose Client for Microsoft Networks from the right side. Click OK. Back at the Network applet's Configuration tab, the client appears in the component list.

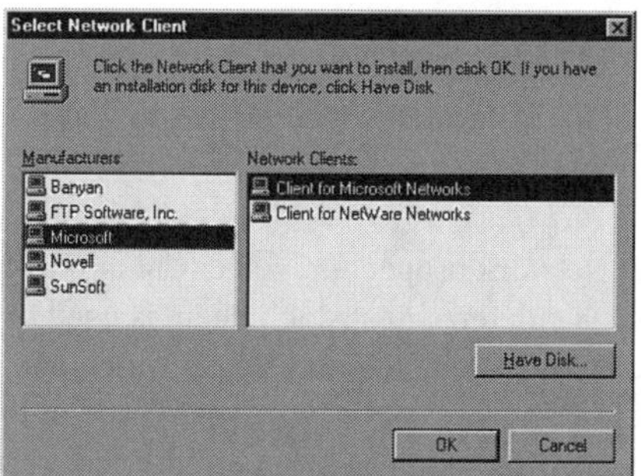

FIG. 39.5 Select the Client for Microsoft Networks to connect to a Windows NT server or a Windows peer-to-peer network.

NOTE If you had not already installed an adapter, you would be asked at this time to specify one, or allow Windows 95 to attempt to auto-detect one. You can install an adapter directly from the Network applet, or see "Using the Add New Hardware Wizard," earlier in this chapter.

4. Click the Add button again, and double-click Protocol in the Select Network Component Type dialog box.
5. Choose Microsoft from the left side of the Select Network Protocol dialog box and NetBEUI from the right. This is the default protocol for Windows NT and LAN Manager client/server networks, as well as for Windows peer-to-peer networks. Click OK. The Configuration screen of the Network applet should list the installed protocol, as shown in Figure 39.6.

NOTE With the introduction of Windows NT 4.0, Microsoft installs TCP/IP as the networking protocol of choice. Many networks still use NetBEUI, however. If your network is using TCP/IP, see "Installing TCP/IP for Windows NT 4.0 Networks," later in this chapter.

6. Review the following sections entitled "Primary Network Logon," "The Identification Tab," and "Domain Logons" and change any settings so that you can connect to the network after you restart your computer. After changing the settings described in those sections, click OK to complete the component installation process, and click Yes when you are asked if you want to restart the computer.

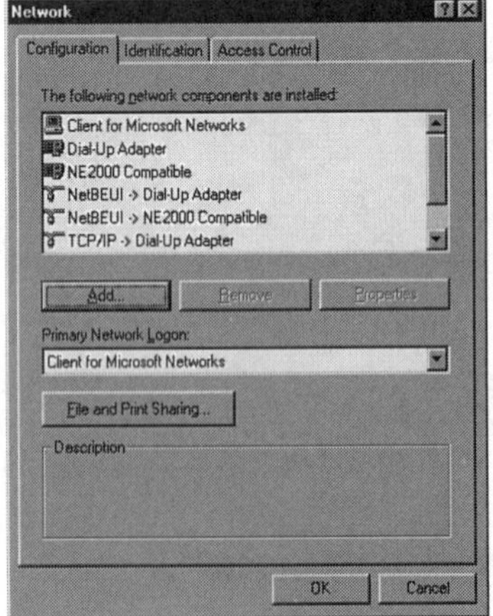

FIG. 39.6 A Windows 95 Network screen showing all of the basic components necessary to attach to a Microsoft Network running Windows NT Server 4.0.

Primary Network Logon

On the Configuration tab of the Network properties, select Client for Microsoft Networks in Primary Network Logon. This value determines which client is used to validate your logon. When multiple network clients are installed, you may select which one is to be the default login using this selector. If you choose Windows Logon, you'll see the Windows logon when you start your computer, and the passwords required to access the resources on Windows NT Server are retrieved from the password list.

The Identification Tab

On the Identification tab of the Network properties, enter a Computer Name and (optionally) a Computer Description. Windows 95 will use the names entered here to identify your computer to the network. Do not confuse the Computer Name with the user name that you use to log onto a network. A single Windows 95 computer can support many users, but it has only one single computer name. Also, for Workgroup, enter the name of the network workgroup or NT domain in which your workstation will belong.

Domains versus Workgroups

Microsoft Windows networking recognizes two types of logical machine groupings: domains and workgroups. A domain is a group of machines whose security is administered from a central location, that is, a Windows NT server. All users, groups, and passwords are stored on the server and administered by the server administrator. If you are logging onto an existing Windows NT network, there is probably a domain to which you will have to be granted access. Domain security information can only be stored on a Windows NT server; you cannot create a domain on a Windows 95 peer-to-peer network.

A *workgroup* is also a collection of Windows machines, any of which may be running Windows 95, Windows NT, or Windows for Workgroups. In a workgroup, each workstation is responsible for maintaining its own security information. The selection of which resources are to be shared and their access passwords are all controlled and stored on each individual workstation itself.

Every Windows computer running a Microsoft network client must declare itself to be a member of a domain or a workgroup, even if the workgroup consists of only one machine. Membership in a workgroup or a domain in no way prevents access to resources in other workgroups or domains.

Domain Logons

Since you'll be logging into an existing domain on the network, double-click the Client for Microsoft Networks in the Configuration tab of the network properties, and select the General tab in the Properties dialog box. Select Log on to Windows NT Domain, and enter the domain name in the Windows NT Domain field. You'll need to ask the network administrator for the domain name. Your username and password will be validated by the named domain controller.

Installing TCP/IP for Windows NT 4.0 Networks

TCP/IP (transmission control protocol/Internet protocol) is now the *de facto* standard protocol suite for all UNIX operating systems, as well as for the Internet. As well, most network installations of Windows NT Server 4.0 use TCP/IP instead of NetBEUI because NetBEUI packets can't be easily routed across subnets.

Windows 95 is the first popular desktop operating system to ship with fully integrated TCP/IP protocol support that is simple to use. It is also compatible with virtually every desktop Internet application available today. Microsoft's TCP/IP is installed like any other protocol and can be used as a general purpose LAN protocol. It can also be used to connect to the Internet, either through a LAN connection, or a dial-up connection. The Dial-Up adapter driver included with Windows 95 is explicitly made for this purpose.

Configuring TCP/IP for use on a Microsoft Network is more complicated than configuring NetBEUI. There are no default Plug and Play settings. You cannot expect to use the protocol without configuring certain options correctly, because they require unique values for every workstation on the network. In several cases, it will be necessary to ask your network administrator or Internet service provider for the correct settings. Before you read the following sections, which show you how to correctly configure TCP/IP, install the protocol on your computer:

1. Double-click the Network icon in the Control Panel, click Add, and double-click Protocol in the Select Network Component Type dialog box.
2. Choose Microsoft from the left side of the Select Network Protocol dialog box and TCP/IP from the right.
3. Click OK to add the protocol to your configuration. Review each of the remaining sections, and then change any settings described in them to make sure you've correctly configured TCP/IP. Then click OK to complete the component installation process. Click Yes when you are asked if you want to restart the computer. When your Windows 95 restarts, it'll prompt you for your NT user name and password.

The TCP/IP properties contains the standard Bindings, Advanced, and NetBIOS tabs that you can largely ignore. There are four other tabs that you must consider, however, which are described in the following sections.

DNS Configuration

A Domain Name Server is a server whose basic function is name resolution. That is, the DNS associates numeric IP addresses, such as 123.45.67.89, with named addresses, such as **www.microsoft.com**. The DNS does this by maintaining static tables of equivalent addresses, and by querying network entities for information to update the table.

The correct DNS address (or addresses) to use should be furnished by your network administrator or service provider Figure 39.7. You may enter multiple addresses in the DNS tab, so that if an entry is not found on one, the subsequent entries will be checked. You must also enter a host name for your machine, and the domain name for your organization (for example, **microsoft.com**). Use of a DNS is optional, because a DHCP server can be used for the same purpose.

Gateway

A gateway routes traffic from one network (subnet) to another. You'll usually have to configure a gateway when you participate in a network that's connected to another network and you need to access a resource on the remote network. For instance, if the network in accounting is attached to another network on which you participate via an IP router, you'd have to configure the IP router as a gateway if you wanted to access resources (such as the payroll) on the accounting network.

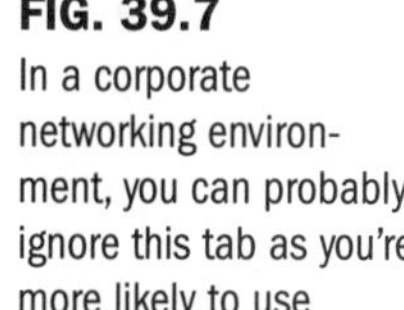

FIG. 39.7
In a corporate networking environment, you can probably ignore this tab as you're more likely to use DHCP in combination with WINS.

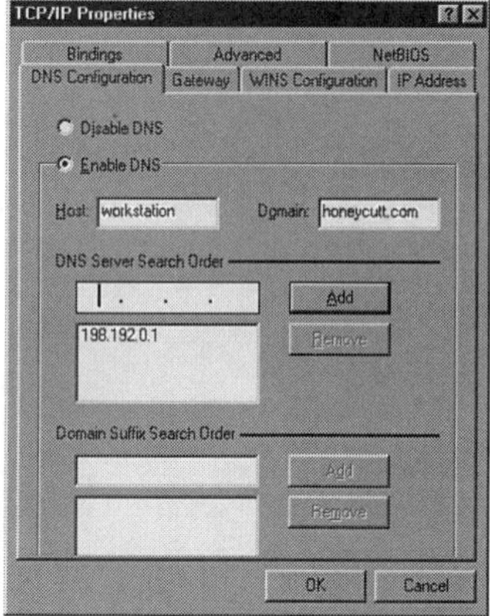

You use the Gateway tab to specify a gateway as shown in Figure 39.8. In fact, you can specify several gateway addresses. The protocol will proceed to the alternates when the first address is unreachable. This address should be supplied by your network administrator or service provider.

FIG. 39.8
If you've configured multiple gateways, TCP/IP will only use the second gateway in the list if, and only if, the first gateway is not working properly.

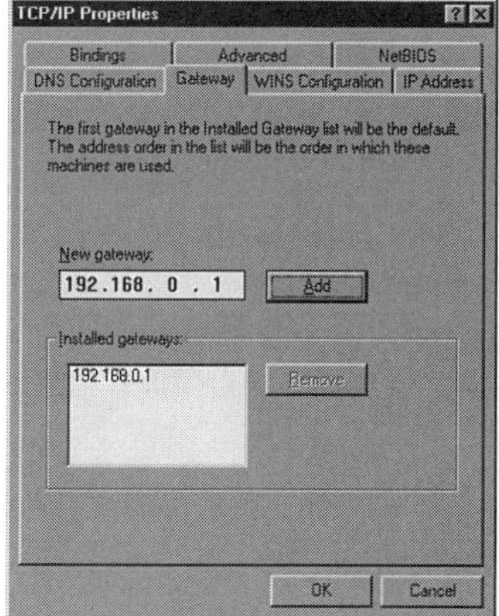

WINS Configuration

WINS, or *Windows Internet Naming Service*, is a realization of an existing published standard, implemented by Microsoft as a service for Windows NT Server. A WINS server performs essentially the same function as DNS, except that the WINS server does not require static addresses to maintain its data tables. They can be adjusted dynamically. When using a DHCP server to assign IP addresses, use of a WINS server is almost required, as a DNS server could not keep up with the continual IP address changes.

Configuring the TCP/IP protocol for the use of the WINS server in most cases simply involves entering the addresses of a Primary and Secondary WINS server in the spaces provided in the

WINS Configuration tab shown in Figure 39.9. Alternately, you can select the option that allows a DHCP server to provide the necessary addresses automatically.

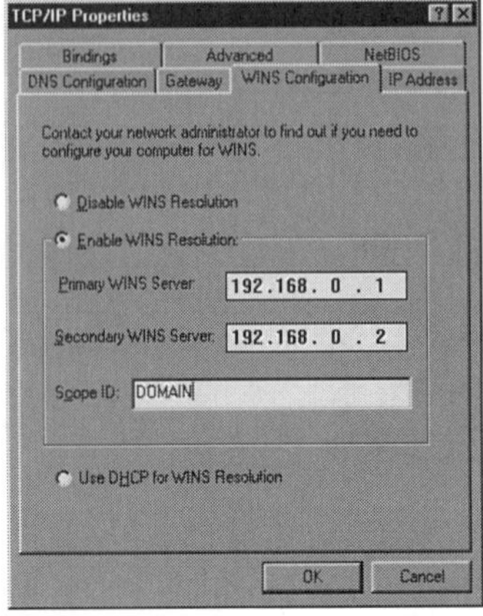

FIG. 39.9
If your network administrator configured DHCP to automatically provide WINS address, select Use DHCP for WINS Resolution.

IP Address

The IP address is the unique identifying address of your computer. It is composed of four octets of up to three digits each, separated by periods. In some cases, your computer may be assigned a specific IP address by your administrator or service provider. In that case, Select Specify an IP Address, and fill in the address and subnet mask supplied to you, as shown in Figure 39.10.

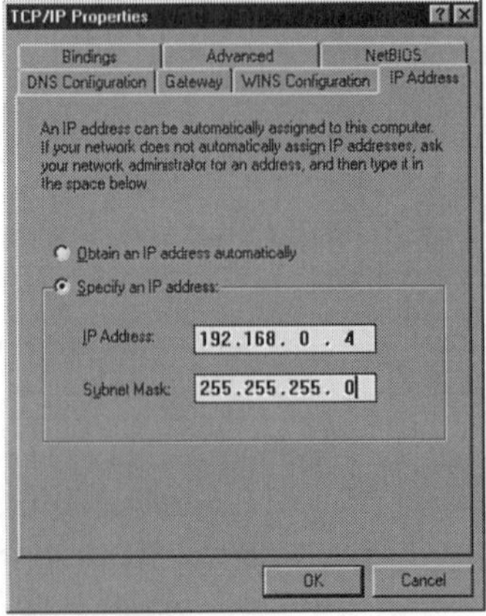

FIG. 39.10
It's more common to use DHCP than statically assigned IP addresses on a corporate network using Windows NT Server 4.0.

At other sites, a Windows NT server may be configured to act as a DHCP (*dynamic host configuration protocol*) server. This is a service that runs on Windows NT Server 4.0 that allocates IP addresses to network workstations requesting them, ensuring that no conflicts occur from two workstations using the same address. Such a server can also deliver a subnet mask, DNS and WINS information to the workstation. If your network uses DHCP, select Obtain an IP address automatically.

NOTE If you use dial-up connections to more than one Internet service provider, then individual IP address and DNS settings can be specified for each connection.

After completing the steps in this chapter, you should be able to connect to your Windows NT network. There's not much to look at yet, however, because you haven't learned how to use the resources on it. The next chapter, Chapter 40, "Using Windows NT Server Resources in Windows 95," shows you how to use such NT Server resources as shared drives and printers.

CHAPTER 40

Using Windows NT Server Resources in Windows 95

by Jerry Honeycutt and Craig Zacker

In this chapter

Logging onto an NT Network

When you configure Windows 95 to log onto an NT server, it displays a login screen each time you boot your computer. The choice of the primary client determines the type of network login screen. When Client for Microsoft Networks is installed, Primary Network Logon on the Configuration tab of the Control Panel's Network application offers two possible choices:

- **Client for Microsoft Networks.** Your username and password are validated by domain controller (Windows NT Server 4.0).
- **Windows Logon.** Your username and password aren't validated; but, Windows 95 uses both to open a password list (see "Working with the Password List," later in this chapter).

Additional entries will also appear in this list if you've installed additional network clients. When you select one of the network clients as the primary logon, that client's login screen appears first whenever the machine is booted, requiring the entry of a user name and password. The computer name that you have entered in the Identification tab of the Network properties is supplied as the username, by default, but you can change this to any valid network username, and the setting will be retained for future logins.

Logon onto an NT Server

When logging onto a Microsoft Network using the dialog box shown in Figure 40.1, Windows 95 uses the Logon Validation option specified in the General tab of the Client for Microsoft Networks' properties dialog box to determine whether a domain logon should be performed (see Chapter 39, "Connecting Windows 95 to Windows NT Server 4.0"). You must also specify a domain name on this tab. The General tab also contains an option to choose between a logon sequence that immediately verifies that each network drive is available for use, or one that waits until each individual drive is accessed before verification occurs. The tradeoff is between a brief delay when each drive is accessed, and a cumulative delay during the logon sequence, rarely more than a few seconds.

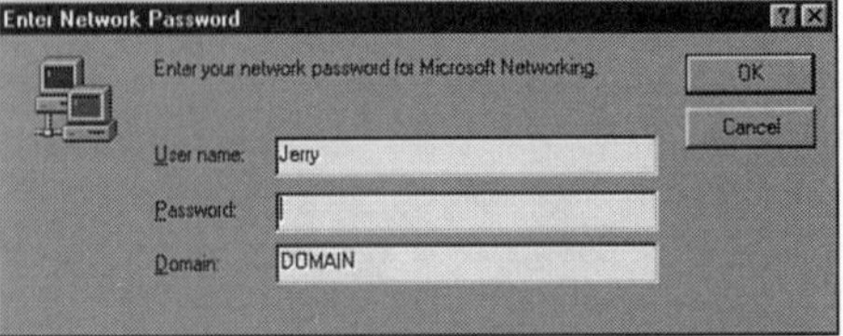

FIG. 40.1
The Microsoft Network logon screen allows access to Windows NT domains as well as peer workgroups.

After you log onto an NT server, the server executes a logon script. The logon script is a batch file that runs on the server. It does things like set environment variables or run programs. You can set an environment variable using the DOS command **set** as in **set PATH=C:\WINDOWS**. Then batch files or other programs can look up the variable called PATH and use the value you've assigned to it.

NOTE Windows 95 is incapable of setting environment variables that have been specified in Windows NT Server logon scripts in the normal manner. As a workaround, a utility called WINSET.EXE is provided in the \ADMIN\APPTOOLS\ENVVARS directory of the Windows 95 CD-ROM. You can use this program to set environment variables from a DOS session command line, a batch file, or a logon script. The syntax of WINSET.EXE is the same as that of the DOS SET command, except that entering the command without any parameters does not display the contents of the environment, as SET does.

TROUBLESHOOTING

Why doesn't a network login dialog box appear when I start Windows 95, no matter what the setting of the Primary Network Logon selector? If you select Shut Down from the Start Menu and then choose Close all Programs and log on as a different user, the correct login dialog box appears, after which everything functions normally. To eliminate this problem, open the Windows 95 Registry Editor (REGEDIT.EXE, located in the \WINDOWS directory), and proceed to the following key:

```
HKEY_LOCAL_MACHINE\SOFTWARE\Microsoft\Windows\CurrentVersion\Network\RealModeNet
```

Delete the value *AutoLogon=x*. A value of zero for the AutoLogon parameter causes the failure of the login dialog box to appear, and 1 is the default, but deleting the entire parameter is preferable to just changing the value. Save your changes and restart the computer. The primary login screen should now appear.

Working with the Password List

When logging into more than one network at the start of a Windows 95 session (Netware and NT Server, for example), you do not have to supply a duplicate password for each network, as long as both logins utilize identical usernames. Windows 95 automatically stores the secondary password in an encrypted password file called *username*.PWL, where *username* is your logon name, located in the workstation's \WINDOWS directory. You can use the Password application in the Windows 95 Control Panel to synchronize differing passwords used by the network logins.

The primary network login password unlocks the password file for use during that Windows 95 session. As work progresses, the operating system automatically caches passwords for NT Server networks, and secures Internet resources and workgroup resources in this same file. Password-protected applications written to the Master Password API also can store passwords in this file. All passwords are stored in the file in encrypted form. No unencrypted password is ever sent over the network.

NOTE On December 13, 1995, Microsoft released a patch file that significantly enhances the security of Windows 95 .PWL files. This was in response to an algorithm posted on the Internet that could be used to crack the existing password files. The fix upgrades the encryption key to 128 bits (from 32), increasing the difficulty of cracking the file by 79228162514264337593543950336 (2^{96}) times. The patch file is called MSPWLUPD.EXE and is

continues

continued

now available as part of the Windows 95 Service Pack 1, on Microsoft's World Wide Web site at **http://www.microsoft.com/windows/software/servpak1/sphome.htm.** You don't need this patch if you're using OSR2. ■

Most logins to network devices include an option for password caching, such as a check box labeled "Save This Password in Your Password List." A network administrator also can use the System Policy Editor to globally disable password caching for specific users or user groups. This action forces users to log into network resources individually, each time they access them.

CAUTION

Password caching is a useful convenience, but it also can be a dangerous security hole if not used carefully. When system administrators work at a user's machine, for example, they must be careful not to insert their passwords into the user's cache and leave the user with a greater level of access to the system. If this does occur, one method of repairing the damage is to delete the user's .PWL file from the \WINDOWS directory, causing all of his cached passwords to be lost. The user now has to log into each network resource individually until Windows 95 assembles a new cache file.

There is an alternative to this solution, however. On the Windows 95 CD-ROM is a password file editing utility called PWLEDIT.EXE. You can install it by using the Add/Remove Programs applet in the Windows 95 Control Panel. Select the Windows Setup tab and use the Have Disk button to get to the \ADMIN\APPTOOLS\PWLEDIT directory on the CD-ROM.

Changing Your NT Server Password

You can change your NT server password at any time. Follow these steps:

1. Double-click the Password icon in the Control Panel, and the Password Properties dialog box appears.
2. Click Change Other Passwords, and you'll see the Select Password dialog box.
3. Select Microsoft Network from the list and click Change.
4. Fill in the Old Password, New Password, and Confirm New Password text boxes. Then, click OK. Windows 95 displays a dialog box telling you that it successfully changed your password.
5. Click OK to close the confirmation dialog box.

Understanding the UNC (Universal Naming Convention)

Windows 95 and most other network operating systems use a syntax called the *Universal Naming Convention*, or UNC, for addressing network resources. The syntax for the UNC is as follows:

```
\\SERVER\SHARE\DIRECTORY\FILE
```

Because most Microsoft operating systems offer both client/server and peer-to-peer networking capabilities, you must use naming conventions that are capable of addressing workstation as well as NT server resources. In actuality, the SERVER name listed in the syntax refers to any machine that is sharing its internal resources over the network, and not just Windows NT servers. A workstation that is configured to share its CD-ROM drive with a neighboring workstation is functioning as a server in that respect, and its machine name is used in place of the SERVER name shown in the preceding example.

SHARE refers to a logical name assigned by a user or administrator to a particular network resource that he is sharing with the rest of the network. All drives, printers, fax modems, and other devices that you can access over a Microsoft network are called *shares*, whether they're located on an NT server or a workstation. As a result, a share can be an entire drive on a particular machine, a single directory on a drive, a printer, or a fax modem attached to the NT server.

The name for a share is selected by the person electing to share it. It need not reflect the share's actual location on the NT server. In other words, in terms of file sharing, you need not give a user any way of knowing on which server drive a share resides, or whether or not that share represents the entire contents of the drive. Access rights flow downhill on a Microsoft network. When you assign a user rights to a share, you include all of the directories and subdirectories contained beneath it. The directory names are the same as they appear on the NT server itself, however. You cannot assign them share names unless you configure them separately as additional shares.

Finding Computers on an NT Network

You can search for a network computer using the UNC by typing ***SERVER***, where ***SERVER*** is the name of the computer you're looking for. This is particularly useful if the machine doesn't show up in the Network Neighborhood, but you're absolutely sure that it's on the network. Choose Find, Computer from the Start button; type the name of the computer for which you're looking in Named; and click Find Now. If Windows 95 finds the computer, you'll see it in the Find window as shown in Figure 40.2.

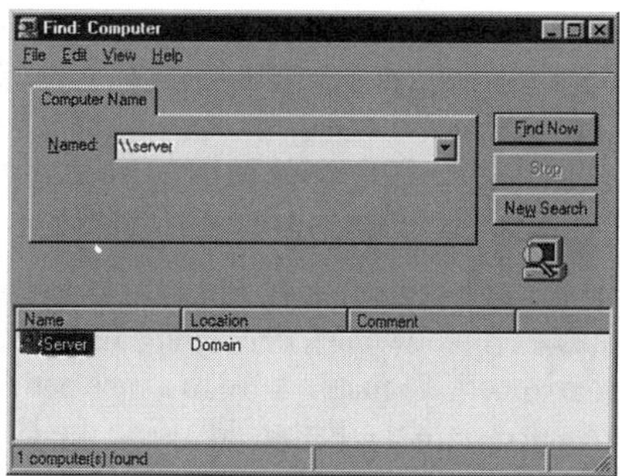

FIG. 40.2
Double-click the computer's name to see what shares it makes available to you.

You can also open a folder that contains a computer's share by launching that computer's UNC name. Choose Run from the Start button, type the UNC name of the computer (**TheServer**, for example), click OK, and Windows 95 will open all of that computer's shared resources in a folder.

TROUBLESHOOTING

Why do I see some peer computers in Network Neighborhood, but not all of them? In order for you to see a peer computer in the Network Neighborhood, the peer has to be configured to participate in the same workgroup you do. See Chapter 39, "Connecting Windows 95 to Windows NT Server 4.0," to learn how to configure the workgroup in which you participate.

Sharing NT Network Drives

Unquestionably, the first and primary purpose of networking is to enable simultaneous multiple-user access to application and data files stored on hard disk drives. Although networking capabilities continue to expand, disk sharing is still the primary function of most local area networks.

Microsoft Networks provide two different ways you can access a shared network drive. You can use the traditional drive mapping method or you can use the Windows 95 Network Neighborhood. You learn about each in the following two sections.

Using the Map Network Drive Dialog Box

Drive mapping, the original network file sharing paradigm, which persists to this day, attempts to package network resources as though they are local devices by mapping NT server disk locations to workstation drive letters. The DOS conception of the drive letter is thus extended to include not only internal workstation devices, but network drives as well. In this case, the network client functions as a redirector, channeling requests generated by an operating system designed for stand-alone machines to devices at other locations on the network.

Within the Windows 95 graphical user interface, the Map Network Drive dialog box (see Figure 40.3) provides a simplified means to map Windows NT Server or workgroup shares. The dialog box, which you can access from the Tools menu in the Windows Explorer or from the toolbar, contains two fields. The Drive field has a drop-down list with which you select the drive letter that you want to map. If a drive shown in the list is already mapped, you'll see the UNC path to which it is mapped just to the right of the drive letter. If you don't see a UNC path next to the driver letter, it hasn't been mapped and is available for you to use.

In the Path field, you specify the network share that you want to associate with the selected drive letter. The Path field also has a drop-down list, containing all of the network shares that you've recently accessed or have mapped. To map a drive to a new path, you must manually enter the name of the network resource into the Path field, using the UNC. If you are not currently attached to the resource you have specified, and if there is no password information in the cache for that resource, then you will be prompted to log in before the drive mapping is completed. Select Reconnect at logon to have Windows 95 to remap the drive letter each time the machine is started. In other words, make the drive mapping persistent.

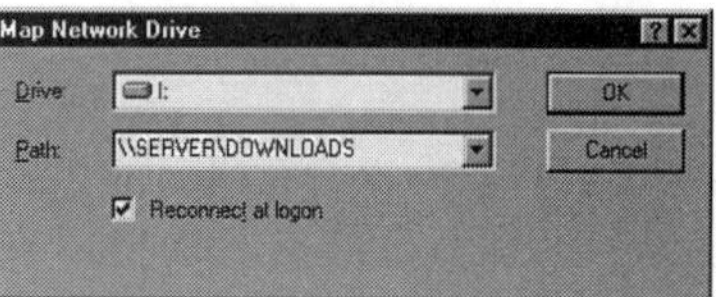

FIG. 40.3 The Map Network Drive dialog box allows network shares and volumes to be permanently associated with particular drive letters.

You also can access the Disconnect Network Drive dialog box from the Tools menu or toolbar of the Explorer or Network Neighborhood window. This dialog box displays a listing of the currently mapped drive letters and performs the opposite function of the Map Network Drive dialog box, allowing you to remove the selected mapping and free up its drive letter. Select a drive mapping and click OK to disconnect it. Click Cancel if you don't want to disconnect any drive mappings.

Using the Network Neighborhood

Besides supporting traditional drive-mapping methods, Windows 95 also provides another way of accessing network drives. The Network Neighborhood window displays all of the NT servers to which the user is currently attached as icons (see Figure 40.4). Double-clicking a server icon reveals the available Windows NT shares as folders.

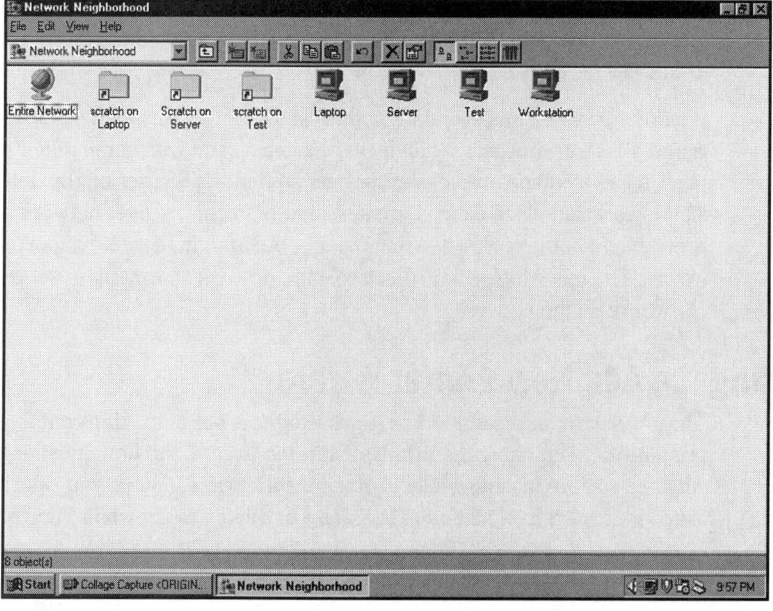

FIG. 40.4 The Network Neighborhood window displays all of the servers and workstations currently attached to the host machine.

When a user double-clicks the Entire Network icon, all of the NT servers on the network are displayed, expanding his view even further. A user (with the appropriate permission) can access any shared drive or folder on the network from this interface, simply by double-clicking its icon. If the user is not currently attached to the NT server containing the share, he is automatically logged in, if a cached password is available, or presented with a login dialog box.

The Windows Explorer integrates My Computer with the Network Neighborhood to provide a single navigable interface for the more advanced user. Mapped drives coexist with NT server objects, even when both are referencing the same network machine, and users can manipulate files on both interchangeably by dragging and dropping, as well as with context menus. Many of the same tools are available in the Explorer and My Computer.

You can map network shares in Network Neighborhood, too. Right-click a share, and choose Map Network Drive. You see the dialog box shown in Figure 40.3.

For example, if the CD-ROM on an NT server is shared by the network administrator, you can access it through Network Neighborhood. Double-click the Network Neighborhood icon on the desktop, and then double-click the icon representing the NT server. You'll see a folder that represents the CD-ROM. Double-click that folder icon to view the contents of the disc that's currently loaded into the player.

Using NT Network Printers

Aside from drive-sharing and storage capabilities, the other fundamental reason for the widespread adoption of local area networking in the business world is the sharing of printers. As with hard drives, the original method for printer sharing was to redirect the local DOS output to the network, where it was stored in a queue on a print server, until it could be serviced by a printer. The introduction of Windows helped overcome this deception by adding the capability to address network printers directly.

Windows 95 takes this evolution several steps further. Installing support for a network printer is now a far easier process than it ever has been, and with some minor print server configurations, it can be made even easier for every Windows 95 user on the network. Windows 95 also allows workstations to exert a greater amount of control over network printing than they have been able to in the past, while maintaining the margin of safety important to network administrators. The following section discusses the process of printing to server-based devices located elsewhere on the network.

Using the Add New Printer Wizard

The procedure for installing a network printer is not much different from installing a local printer. After launching the Add New Printer Wizard, the first question that you are asked is whether you are installing a local or a network printer. When you select Network, you are then asked to furnish the location of the share or queue, as shown in Figure 40.5.

FIG. 40.5
The Add New Printer Wizard simplifies the installation of a network printer.

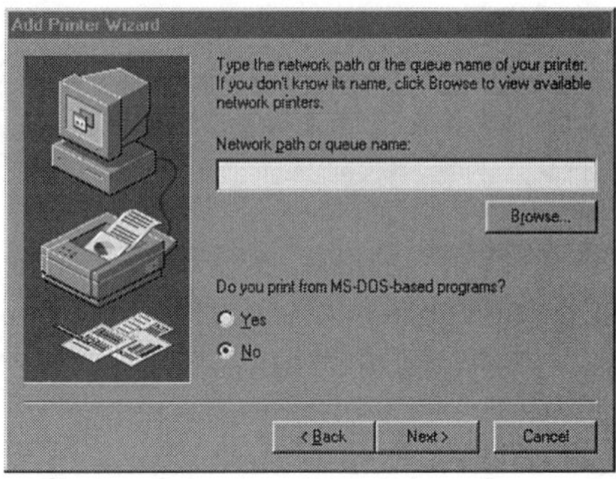

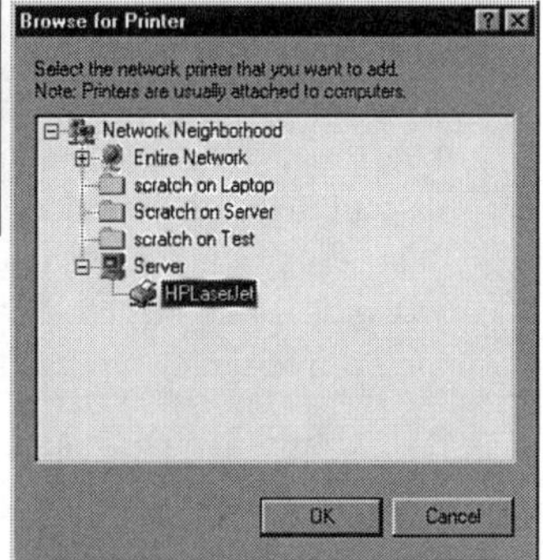

It is assumed that the printer you are installing has already been properly configured for network use. This involves the creation of a share on a Windows NT server. When you click the Browse button for the Network path or queue name field in the wizard, a Network Neighborhood display appears, in which you can expand servers until you have located the appropriate print queue. The correct path to the share or queue also can be entered directly into the dialog box, but it must be specified using a correct UNC path name; see the section "Understanding the UNC (Universal Naming Convention)," earlier in this chapter.

If the printer cannot be located at the path given, you receive a message to that effect, but you can still proceed with the installation. A network printer may be temporarily invisible to the network for any number of reasons.

The Invisible Printer

One of the basic tenets of network printing is to keep the user working whenever possible. That is why network printing systems are usually designed to function normally, even when the actual printer is not working. Unlike printing to a locally attached device, all network print jobs are *spooled*. Spooling is the process by which an NT server accepts print jobs from applications and stores them on a disk until the printer can service them. Network users can continue to send jobs to print queues, even when the printer has run out of paper, jammed, or been stolen during the night.

The spooling process has two major effects:

- The actual time that the user's application spends printing is greatly reduced, because a hard drive can accept data at a much greater rate than any printer.
- The user cannot be sure that his job has been successfully printed until he actually walks over to the printer and checks.

continues

continued

The administrative capabilities of Windows 95 can help to make the latter point less of a problem. Printers become more interactive each year, and it is now possible to perform a number of maintenance tasks from a remote network workstation. This eliminates trips to the printer and avoids a backlog of jobs in the queue.

The second question asked in the Add Printer dialog box is whether you print from DOS-based programs. While most of the remaining major DOS applications, such as WordPerfect and Lotus 1-2-3, are capable of network printing, some Windows users may drop to the DOS prompt to use the small utilities that they have grown accustomed to over the years. These small programs are often not network-aware and print by default to the LPT1 port. What the wizard is asking with this question is whether it should configure the printer driver to capture local printer port output to the network queue.

The wizard then presents a standard Select Hardware dialog box to identify the printer model. Next, the wizard asks you to furnish a name for the printer. You may think it silly to name a locally attached device, but if you're printing on a network, printer naming can be essential.

Part of the advantage of network printing is the ability to access printers all over the network. This has obvious benefits when the printers are of different types. You may need access to a wide-bed dot-matrix printer for spreadsheets, a laser printer for correspondence, and a color printer for presentations. However, even in a company that has 50 identical laserjets on its network, the ability to send a document to someone in another department simply by printing it to his printer can be a real time-saver. For this reason, it is a good idea to name your various printers descriptively, identifying the printer type and its location.

After its interrogation is complete, the wizard then copies the appropriate printer drivers from the Windows 95 source files (possibly prompting you to insert a floppy or CD-ROM) and creates an additional icon in the Printers window. You may now use this printer just as if it were a local device, dragging and dropping files onto the icon or selecting it directly from your application.

Using Point and Print

One problem that is often faced by network users is how to know exactly which printer model to select during the installation process, when the printer itself may be some distance away from both their workstation and the file server.

A network printer may have to be associated logically with an NT server, but it does not have to be physically attached to it, except through the network medium itself. One of the most popular solutions for network printing today is to install a special network interface card, that also functions as a print server, into a laser printer. Print jobs can be spooled to a print queue on a server and then systematically fed to a printer located anywhere on the network.

NOTE The Hewlett-Packard JetDirect card is one of the most popular network interface cards, and Windows 95 includes a service with the operating system that provides an interface to the print server on the card. ■

So how do users know which printer to use and what printer driver to install? Point and Print is a Windows 95 mechanism that solves both these problems by associating the appropriate printer model with a print queue, and storing the correct printer drivers on the network, where all users can access them. If you remove from the Add New Printer Wizard the procedures by which the printer is identified and the drivers located, you are left with a ridiculously easy installation process that can be performed by anyone.

In fact, when you have set up a network printer for Point and Print, users need only browse the Network Neighborhood for the printer that they want to use and drag it into the Installed Printers window. Users are still asked if they print from DOS applications and whether the selected printer should be the Windows default. After those questions, however, the necessary drivers are automatically downloaded from the NT server and installed, and the printer is ready for use.

Monitoring NT Network Printers

Aside from simplifying the printer installation process, Windows 95 has also improved the administrative features devoted to network printing. When you double-click a network printer icon in the Printers window, a screen showing the current contents of the network print queue appears, as shown in Figure 40.6. The source application of each pending job is listed, as well as the network user who generated it, its size, and the time that it was submitted. A user can, therefore, tell when his job has been completed or estimate the delay until it is serviced.

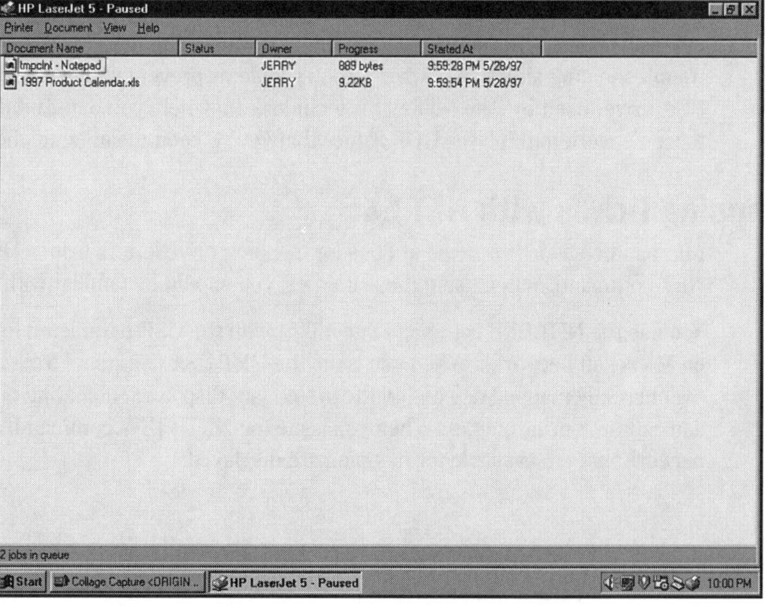

FIG. 40.6
The print queue window allows network print jobs to be manipulated directly from within Windows 95.

Accessing NT Network Resources from DOS

For users who first became acquainted with personal computing through DOS applications, perhaps you remember your first exposure to Windows and how long it took for you to gather up Windows versions of all of the DOS utilities you had collected. During those times when you just couldn't bring yourself to abandon your favorite DOS word processor or spreadsheet, it was a pleasure to exit from Windows and run that application in native DOS, rather than a DOS session.

Windows 95 is still capable of this, even when network support is required. Bring up the boot menu by pressing F8 as you start your computer, and you can easily boot to a DOS prompt. What you cannot do is boot directly to DOS mode with network support. You can, however, enable Windows 95's real-mode network clients with the NET START command, and map your drives with the NET USE command. Or you can create a batch file to perform all of these steps for you.

CAUTION

NET START can only be issued from the real-mode DOS prompt. It will not function in a Windows 95 virtual machine session. However, NET USE and many other commands can be used in a DOS window in place of their GUI counterparts.

Issue the NET START BASIC command from the DOS prompt to load the real-mode Client for Microsoft Networks. You then can map drives to any of the Windows shares available on the network, using the following syntax:

```
NET USE D: \\server\share
```

If you still use WordPerfect for DOS and need access to your network data files, using the real-mode client from the DOS prompt is the best way to run it under Windows 95. Also, in a troubleshooting situation in which video problems prevent you even from loading the standard VGA driver used by Safe Mode, this technique may help you out. And then, of course, there are those network multiplayer DOS games that you've been meaning to check out.

Mapping Drives with NET.EXE

Microsoft Networks provide utilities for mapping drive letters from a DOS prompt. You use the NET command. When using these utilities, you should be familiar with UNC.

You use the NET.EXE command line utility, with the USE parameter, for mapping drive letters on Microsoft networks. When you issue the NET USE command from any DOS prompt, all of the currently mapped devices on the system are displayed, including peer-to-peer mappings and captured print queues. When you issue the NET VIEW command, all of the shares on the network that are available for mapping are displayed.

The syntax for mapping a drive with NET is as follows:

```
NET USE X: \\SERVER\SHARE
```

NET USE also is capable of mapping LPT ports to shared network printers and contains many other options to control how drive mappings are created. This includes whether passwords are cached and whether the drive-mapping process should be interactive.

Performing Other Tasks with NET.EXE

NET is an extremely powerful command that you can use to perform nearly all of the network-related tasks that are possible from the Windows 95 GUI. It also has a number of real mode functions that can be used only when you boot Windows 95 to the command prompt; these functions will not operate from a DOS session within the Windows interface. Following is a summary of NET command functions. More detailed information about each one is available by typing the command followed by a **/?** at a Windows 95 DOS prompt (for example, **NET USE /?**).

NET CONFIG	Displays your current workgroup settings.
NET DIAG	Runs the Microsoft Network Diagnostics program to display diagnostic information about your network.
NET HELP	Provides information about commands and error messages.
NET INIT	Loads protocol and network-adapter drivers without binding them to Protocol Manager.
NET LOGOFF	Breaks the connection between your computer and the shared resources to which it is connected.
NET LOGON	Identifies you as a member of a workgroup.
NET PASSWORD	Changes your logon password.
NET PRINT	Displays information about print queues and controls print jobs.
NET START	Starts services.
NET STOP	Stops services.
NET TIME	Displays the time on or synchronizes your computer's clock with the clock on a Microsoft Windows for Workgroups, Windows NT, Windows 95, or NetWare time server.
NET USE	Connects to or disconnects from a shared resource or displays information about connections.
NET VER	Displays the type and version number of the workgroup redirector you are using.
NET VIEW	Displays a list of computers that share resources or a list of shared resources on a specific computer.

TROUBLESHOOTING

When using the NET USE command to map drives, why does the utility refuse to read passwords from the cache file and force me to enter them every time? The patch for the Windows 95 password cache file mentioned earlier in this chapter alters the NET.EXE utility. After the service pack containing the patch is applied, passwords are no longer extracted from the cache when you use NET commands. All passwords must be explicitly specified at all times.

CHAPTER 41

Working with Network Printers

by William S. Holderby

In this chapter

Examining Windows 95's New Network Printing Features

Windows 95 incorporates several new features and enhancements that markedly improve network printing. These new features include the following:

- *Network Point and Print* enables users to copy printer drivers automatically from network print servers to their local PC. This reduces the time it takes to set up a new printer and eliminates the need to find and copy vendor-driver software. This feature also eliminates the chance of configuring the wrong printer. You can access Network Point and Print from network servers running Windows 95, Windows NT Advanced Server, Windows NT Workstation, Windows for Workgroups 3.11, or Novell NetWare.
- *Windows 95's Network Neighborhood* provides tools to configure print resources quickly on Windows 95, Windows NT, and Novell servers. You can use this feature to find, use, and manage print jobs on printers interfacing any of these devices. Formerly, the user had to memorize locations and complex network commands. Network Neighborhood virtually eliminates this need through its new network user interface.
- *Compatibility with NetWare's PSERVER* enables you to access print jobs from NetWare's print spooler.
- *Deferred printing* provides you with the ability to save printouts until you reattach your printer. Deferred printing automatically stores print jobs after you detach your PC from the network, and automatically restarts them after you reestablish the connection.
- *Printer driver* provides command resources to remotely stop, hold, cancel, or restart print jobs located on shared printers.

Understanding Network Printing

Before delving too deeply into the nuts and bolts of network printing, you first must become familiar with the terminology you will see frequently in this discussion:

- *LAN Administrators* provide a management function to the local area network by assisting users and directing what resources are available on the network.
- *Systems policies* are software controls that are created by LAN Administrators to define what users can and cannot do on their desktops and the network. For example, you might use a system policy to restrict access to certain network programs.
- A *client* is a workstation that uses the services of any network server that can include server-based software systems, printers, and mass storage devices.
- *Print queues* contain print jobs that are not immediately printed. A queue holds the job until the printer is ready to print.
- *Windows Redirector* is the software module contained in the Windows network architecture that identifies software references to network devices and connects those devices to the workstation through the network.

- *Network resources* are software and hardware features that are available from servers and other workstations on the LAN. Resources such as shared drivers and server-based programs are available for network users.
- *Printing resources* are LAN resources that are dedicated to serving network users for the purpose of printing. These include shared printers, network printers, and print queues.
- *Print servers* service the printing needs of network clients.

Three network printer types are found on most networks:

- Printers attached to the network through a Microsoft Network-compatible server.
- Printers connected to a server running a compatible network operating system other than Windows, such as Novell NetWare and Banyan VINES.
- Printers directly attached to a network through a special printer network interface card (NIC).

Printing from Applications

Printing to network printers from within applications requires the same commands and menu items that you use to print locally. Windows handles the network communications and creates a printer driver for each attached network printer. As with local printers, you can access network printer configuration information in the Printer Properties sheet. In this sheet, you can change the network printer's properties for default or specific printing tasks.

CAUTION

Remember that other users can change a network printer configuration. Before printing, check all important parameters, including paper orientation and resolution. Don't assume that they are already set the way that you want them. Printing mistakes on network printers take extra time to recover.

When applications create a print file, they send a print stream to the network server through the Windows 95 Network Redirector. A print file contains spooled printer data and commands that are being temporarily stored prior to printing. The Network Redirector, which is part of Windows 95 network architecture, determines whether the print stream destination is a local printer. A print stream is the data that is being sent to a printer containing both printable and unprintable characters. Unprintable characters are used to control the printer. It also uses Windows network drivers to locate the designated printer.

Drag-and-Drop Printing

To perform drag-and-drop printing, you use the same procedure as you do for local printing. Remember, however, that drag-and-drop printing sends the print job to the system's default printer. If the selected printer is not the default printer, Windows asks you to make it the default printer prior to printing the file. When initially connecting your PC to a network, this printer might not be available. Be sure to log in to the network and verify the printer's network connection before setting it as the default printer.

▶ **See** "Drag-and-Drop Printing from the Desktop," **p. 142**

Installing a Network Printer

Network printers are usually installed in one of two ways:

- The *Add Printer Wizard* from the Printers folder can be used for any printer connected to the network. The installation of a network printer doesn't change the printer, it simply loads an appropriate printer driver on your PC. Windows 95 uses that driver during printing.

NOTE If other users share a network printer, changes to the printer can affect every user. If you change a cartridge or make printer menu changes, you can affect everyone using your printer from the network. ■

- *Point and Print installation* from the desktop can be used for printers attached to servers that are Microsoft Client-compatible.

▶ **See** "Setting Up a Windows 95 Peer-to-Peer Network," **p. 841**

▶ **See** "Connecting Windows 95 to a Novell Network," **p. 881**

Using the Add Printer Wizard Installing a network printer involves the same Add Printer Wizard as the local printer installation described in Chapter 5, "Controlling Printers." However, there are some differences.

When you configure a local printer, the location of your cable to a specific printer port determines the port's selection. The network printer, on the other hand, requires an address. In the example shown in Figure 41.1, an HP 1200 CPS print queue is located on the AlphaNT server.

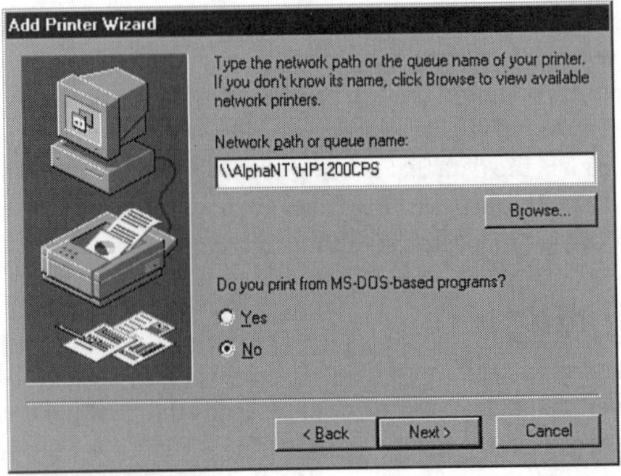

FIG. 41.1
The Add Printer Wizard requires a network address for printer installation.

If you're not sure of the correct address for the network printer, you can choose to browse the network. Browsing enables you to check which network printers are currently available. Some servers require passwords to view what network resources they have available. If you desire access to a server, but do not know the password, contact your LAN administrator.

To configure a network printer, you need to know its make and model. You can get this information from your network administrator. Microsoft network servers enable you to install printer drivers quickly.

To set up a network printer with the Add Printer Wizard, follow these steps:

1. Choose Start, Settings, Printers, and then double-click the Add Printer folder.
2. From the first Add Printer Wizard screen, click the Next button. Windows 95 displays the next Wizard screen which asks you to decide if you are adding a Network or a Local Printer.
3. Choose the Network Printer option to connect your PC to a network printer. Click the Next button located at the bottom of the window.
4. You must then identify the network path to the printer (refer to Figure 41.1). Click the Browse button to view the Network Neighborhood.
5. The Network Neighborhood displays a list of all servers and workstations connected to your network. Find the appropriate printer, select it, and click the Next button. The Wizard accesses the selected printer and determines whether its server can download an appropriate printer driver. If a driver is available, the Wizard automatically loads the driver and sets a default configuration for the printer. If a driver is not available, the Wizard asks you to specify the printer's make and model.

Use the Add Printer Wizard again if you have difficulty connecting to a printer using the Point and Print procedure.

6. Select the manufacturer and printer model by scrolling the Wizard screen lists; then click Next. The screen now offers a default name for your printer. The name should adequately describe the printer for later identification.
7. The Wizard asks whether you want this printer to be your default printer; select Yes or No. Follow this decision by clicking the Next button.
8. The final wizard screen provides the controls to print a test page on the printer you just installed. Choose Yes to print the test page, or choose No to not print the test page. As a general rule, you should always print a test page to verify the successful completion of the Add a Printer Wizard.
9. Click Finish.

Using Point and Print Point and Print enables a workstation user to quickly connect to and use a printer shared on another Windows 95 workstation, a Windows NT Advanced Server, or a Novell NetWare server. When first connecting to the shared printer, Windows 95 automatically copies and installs the correct driver for the shared printer from the server.

1. Choose the Network Neighborhood icon on the Windows desktop.
2. Choose the Entire Network icon. Windows displays all the servers attached to your network.
3. Choose the Server that supports the printer you want to attach to your workstation. If you don't know which Server that is, ask the LAN administrator or select each server in sequence until you find the name of the appropriate printer or print queue. Windows displays the server's screen showing its shared resources.
4. Drag a network printer icon from a server's window and drop it on the desktop. You receive a diagnostic message that says "You cannot move or copy this item to this location. Do you want to create a shortcut to the item instead?" Answer Yes. Windows creates a shortcut icon and drops it on the desktop.
5. Drag a document from a local folder and drop it on the New Printer folder icon. Windows displays an information screen such as that shown in Figure 41.2. If you select Yes, Windows automatically connects to the printer and downloads the appropriate printer driver from the network printer's server. After loading and configuring the driver, Windows 95 begins printing to the network printer.

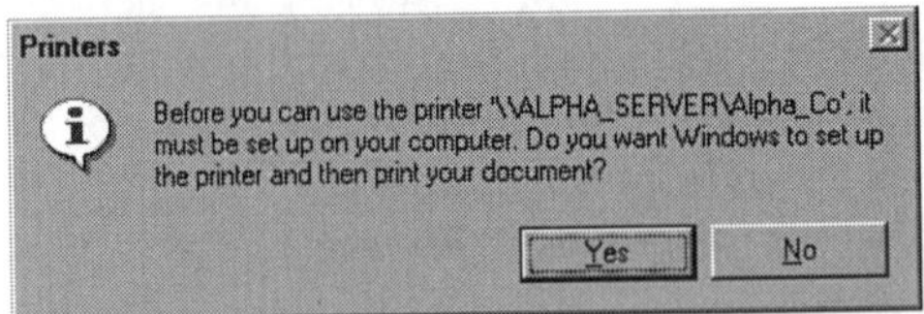
Printers
Before you can use the printer '\\ALPHA_SERVER\Alpha_Co', it must be set up on your computer. Do you want Windows to set up the printer and then print your document?
Yes
No

FIG. 41.2
If the printer driver is not loaded when you use Point and Print, Windows lets you install the driver on-the-fly.

Printing on a NetWare Network

To use a NetWare print queue, you must be logged onto a NetWare server. Windows 95 utilizes a PSERVER that can redirect print jobs from NetWare print queues to printers connected to Windows 95 workstations. In addition to the PSERVER capability, your PC must also use the Microsoft Client for NetWare Networks. Windows 95 automatically adapts to NetWare's security for printer and print queue access.

NOTE The network administrator can control how NetWare shares printers. If the administrator uses a *policy file* to disable print sharing, the network cannot access the printers. A policy file contains a set of commands that are used by your network administrator to set rules for the operation and configuration of Windows on a network. When entering a new network, check with your network administrator for a sharing policy before attempting to configure shared printing. ■

NetWare Print Servers Windows 95 provides printer services for NetWare networks, including a 32-bit PSERVER capability. PSERVER connects NetWare queues to printers shared by Windows 95 PCs. A NetWare print queue contains all the jobs waiting (queued) for a specific printer.

To connect your workstation to a Novell NetWare print server, follow these steps:

1. Choose the Network Neighborhood icon on the desktop. Notice that all servers (Microsoft and NetWare) appear in the Network Neighborhood screen. This screen displays an icon for each network drive currently attached to your system.
2. If you want to attach your workstation to a NetWare printer, choose the appropriate server by double-clicking its icon. The server dialog box opens and displays the shared directories, files, and print queues that are attached to the selected server.
3. Select the appropriate print queue. Choose File, Print and then select the Capture Printer Port control button.
4. The capture printer port dialog box contains the name of currently unattached LPT ports. Select the Reconnect at Logon check box if you want to maintain this connection and have it attached when you restart Windows. Then click OK to attach this print queue to your PC.

   Capturing the printer port attaches the NetWare print queue to the specified port. It does not, however, attach the associated printer to the desktop.
5. To attach the printer associated with that print queue, choose File, Create Shortcut. Windows displays a message warning that you cannot configure a shortcut printer icon in the Create Shortcut dialog box, but that you can create the icon on the desktop. Click Yes to create the icon.
6. Double-click the printer icon. Windows asks whether you want to set up a printer. Choose Yes.
7. Windows then displays the Add Printer Wizard. Follow the Wizard to finish installing an appropriate printer for the desktop.

NOTE You must know the type of printer attached to this print queue. This procedure is different than installing a printer attached to a Microsoft print server. ■

After configuring the printer, you can print by using the Point and Print procedure on the desktop.

Microsoft Client for NetWare Windows 95 Microsoft Client for NetWare Networks enables you to connect to new or existing NetWare servers to send files and interact with server-based software. With Microsoft Client for NetWare Networks, you can browse and queue your print jobs using either the Windows 95 network user interface or existing Novell NetWare utilities. The Microsoft Client for NetWare interfaces work equally well with both NetWare 3.x and 4.x servers running bindery emulation.

NOTE The Microsoft Client for NetWare does not support NDS-based NetWare 4.x networks. OSR2 comes with an option called MSNDS (Microsoft Netware Directory Services) that allows Windows 95 access to NDS-based server resources. Alternatively, you can use the 32-bit NetWare client available from the Novell site. ■

To use Microsoft Client for NetWare Networks, follow these steps:

1. Choose File, Print.
2. Your application might ask you to choose a destination printer. Most applications display a list of attached printers from which you can choose. If so, choose an appropriate network printer and choose OK.

   The Windows Redirector accepts the print stream and sends it to the selected printer over the network. Information concerning the status of the printing process automatically returns to you.
3. To monitor the status of your print job on a network printer, open the printer's folder and double-click the appropriate icon. The printer's local Printer Driver opens a status dialog box listing all print jobs in the printer's queue.

Point and Print for NetWare Print Queues

You can enable a Point and Print procedure to use a NetWare-compatible client as a destination. To do so, use the Point and Print procedure discussed earlier.

To print from the desktop to a network printer, follow these steps:

1. Open the folder that contains the document you want to print.
2. Select a document. Hold down the left mouse button and drag the selected document to the network printer's icon on your desktop. The document now appears as an outline.
3. Release the outlined document icon over the printer's icon. Windows 95 interprets the file type, starts the application associated with the file, commands the application to print the document, redirects the print job to the selected printer, and shuts down the application when the print job finishes.

NOTE Before Windows can perform the desktop printing operation, you must associate the document with an installed application. If the document is not associated with such an application, Windows displays a message box informing you that it cannot perform the printing task. ■

Printing on a Microsoft Network

To share files and printers on Microsoft networks, you also can set user rights remotely through the User Manager in a Windows NT Advanced Server.

To connect to a Microsoft print server, follow these steps:

1. Click the Network Neighborhood icon on the desktop. Notice that all servers (Microsoft and NetWare) appear on the Network Neighborhood window. This screen displays an icon for each network drive currently attached to your system.
2. To attach a printer through a Microsoft server, choose the appropriate Microsoft server by double-clicking that server's icon. The server dialog box, named after the appropriate

server, appears and displays the shared directories, files, and printers attached to the Microsoft server.

3. Select the appropriate printer queue. Choose File, Print and then select the capture printer port. The Capture Printer Port dialog box is displayed containing the name of a currently unattached LPT port.
4. In the Capture Printer Port dialog box, select the Reconnect at Logon check box if you want to maintain this connection and have it attached when you restart Windows. Click the OK button to attach this print queue to your PC.

NOTE Capturing the printer port attaches the printer to a specified port, but does not attach the associated printer to the desktop. ■

5. To attach the printer associated with the selected print queue, you must choose File, Create Shortcut. Windows displays a diagnostics message warning that you cannot configure a shortcut printer icon in the Create Shortcut dialog box, although Windows creates the shortcut on the desktop. Click Yes to create the icon.
6. Double-click the printer's shortcut icon. Windows asks whether you want to set up a printer. Choose Yes. Windows then displays the Add Printer Wizard.
7. Follow the Wizard to finish installing an appropriate printer for the desktop. The Add Printer Wizard identifies which printer make and model you are installing and completes the printer connection quickly.

After configuring the printer, you can print by using the Point and Print procedure on the desktop.

TROUBLESHOOTING

I can see a network printer using Network Neighborhood, but I can't print to it. Try the following:

- Check with your network administrator about your access rights to the printer.
- Verify that the printer is properly configured on your PC.
- Check with other users to determine whether they can access the printer.
- Try to print to another printer on the network to check your network connectivity.

I can't stop, cancel, or delete a print job in a network queue. Try the following:

- Check whether you have proper authorization from the network administrator to change the print settings. You might be authorized to change only your own print jobs, not others.
- If the print queue is on a shared printer, reload the printer driver or reset the printer properties. The system might not recognize that this printer is attached to your PC.

continues

continued

The network printer doesn't tell me that it is out of paper or toner. Have the network administrator configure WinPopup to broadcast printer-problem announcements. WinPopup is a utility that comes with Windows. This utility allows the network and network users to send "popup" messages that identify events and get the attention of other network users.

Optimizing Print Resources

Network printing involves many of the same facilities as local printing. Applications create print files that the Network Redirector streams to the destination network printer. When working with network resources, however, you must consider several other issues to ensure that you're getting the most from your system.

Network Printer Configuration and Management

The Printer Properties sheet contains information on each local and network printer attached to your PC. Each printer's properties are specific to its make, model, and hardware configuration.

▶ **See** "Applications with Special Print Options," **p. 136**

You can make several changes to the properties to enhance your printing. The print quality can be enhanced by specific printers, setting device options, graphics, and the procedures for handling TrueType fonts. The following general procedure explores some of these changes:

1. After attaching a network printer, open its Printer Properties sheet by right-clicking the appropriate printer. From the drop-down menu that appears, choose Properties and then click the General tab. The pages in the Properties sheet are specific to your printer and display the options and selections that match the printer's current hardware and printer driver configuration.
2. Click the Device Options tab. Notice the options that the network printer offers.
3. Change the Device Options settings to match your printer's specifications. These options include such pertinent information as printer memory size and page protection. (If you don't see these options, check with your LAN administrator.)
4. Click the Details tab. Check the spool settings to determine whether the printer is set to print after the first or last page spools. Usually, waiting until after the last page spools yields better results. Experiment with this setting to gain a better understanding of your configuration.
5. Click the Graphics tab. Change the dithering settings to identify which setting yields the best results for both speed and printout quality.

TROUBLESHOOTING

When I print to a printer on the network, my printout quality and settings are not consistent. Try the following:

- Before printing, check the printer's Properties sheet. Change the settings, if required.
- Check with the system administrator for the printer settings, features, and hardware configuration. The printer might not be capable of handling your print job.
- Relate printout quality to changes in the property settings. Change your printer's properties and make test printouts to see how these changes affect the printouts.

Network Printer Drivers

Windows uses printer drivers to deliver your print files through the network to your printer. How well Windows performs this printing depends on how well the drivers perform. If you use drivers that are several revisions old, you might experience a slowdown. It is a good policy to check your printer drivers and update as revisions become available.

1. In the Control Panel, choose the System icon. Then click the Device Manager tab.
2. Verify that the network interface card driver is a virtual mode driver with a V×D extension. The driver will be listed including its extension. If a real-mode driver with a DRV extension is installed, contact your LAN administrator or printer manufacturer for an updated revision.
3. Verify that the configured printer driver is also a virtual mode driver. The driver should also have a V×D extension. If a real-mode driver with a DRV extension is installed, contact your LAN administrator or printer manufacturer for an updated revision.
4. Ask your LAN administrator whether your system is configured with the latest driver version for your network printers. If the drivers are not the most current revision, request the latest update from either your LAN manager or the printer's manufacturer.

Managing Print Files and Sharing

After creating print files and sending them to a network printer, you must verify that the print jobs are finished, on hold, or need to be purged. You can check the print job status on both local and remote printers by using the Windows Printer Driver. Print job control is a complex task that involves user security rights on remote printers.

Viewing a Network Print Queue

Although you can view queue information, you cannot change any print job characteristics unless the LAN administrator has authorized you to do so. For some systems, the network administrator is the only user who can control all print jobs, while another user can control only his or her local shared-printing resources. LAN administrator policies determine which users can delete, pause, or purge documents from the queue. Usually, users can change the status of their individual print jobs, but not those of other users.

To view the queue, simply double-click the printer's icon in the Printers folder or on the desktop. Windows displays the Printer Driver and print queue.

Shared Printing

Shared printing or *peer-to-peer sharing* provides other network workstations access to your local printer. Shared printing access is useful for transferring documents between workstations and for sharing expensive resources with other users. It is also an excellent way to maximize the use of often expensive printing hardware.

To share a printer, follow these steps:

1. Choose Start, Settings, Control Panel. In the Control Panel folder, double-click the Network icon. The Network tabs will appear. These tabs include Configuration, Identification, and Access Control.
2. On the Configuration page, select the Add button. The Select Network Component Type dialog box appears.
3. Choose Service and then click the Add button.
4. Choose Microsoft from the Manufacturers list box.
5. If your primary network logon client is Microsoft Networks, choose File and Printer Sharing for Microsoft Networks. If your primary network logon client is NetWare, choose File and Printer Sharing for NetWare Networks.
6. Choose OK to close the Select Network Service dialog box. For these changes to take effect, you must restart the computer.

TROUBLESHOOTING

My shared printer is unavailable to other workstations on my network. Try the following:

- In the Control Panel, double-click the Network icon. Choose the File and Print Sharing button. In the File and Print Sharing dialog box, verify that the I Want to Be Able to Allow Others to Print to My Printer(s) check box is selected.
- Verify that all users are running a compatible protocol.
- Verify that your PC shows up in the network browser on other connected PCs.
- Verify that you can print successfully to your attached printer.
- Use the Extended Printer Troubleshooting (EPTS) application available in your Help file.

Enabling Shared Printing After configuring the network setup by following the preceding steps, you must enable the sharing feature as follows:

1. From the taskbar, choose Start, Settings, Control Panel. In the Control Panel folder, double-click the Network icon.
2. In the Network dialog box choose the File and Print Sharing button.
3. In the File and Print Sharing dialog box, select the I Want to Be Able to Allow Others to Print to My Printer(s) check box (see Figure 41.3).

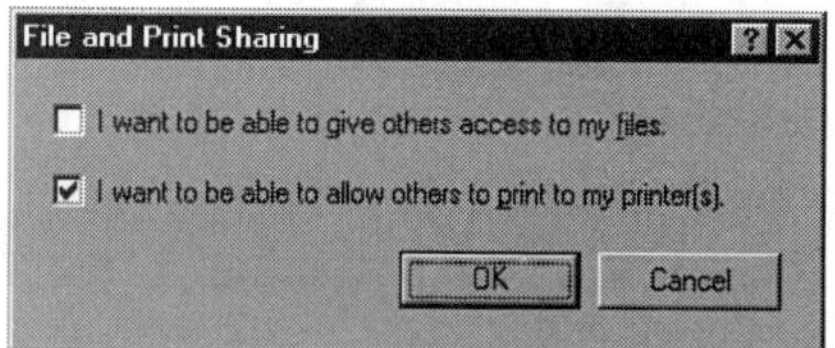

FIG. 41.3 The File and Print Sharing dialog box contains check boxes that enable you to share files and printers with other network users.

4. Choose OK to close the dialog box, and click it again to close the Network Control Panel. You must restart the computer for these changes to take effect.

NOTE If the I Want to Be Able to Allow Others to Print to My Printer(s) check box is grayed (disabled), your system does not support print sharing.

Disabling Shared Printing After your workstation printer is shared, you might find that too many users are creating an overload. To disable the share, follow this procedure.

1. From the taskbar, choose Start, Settings, Control Panel. In the Control Panel folder, double-click the Network icon.
2. In the Network dialog box, choose the File and Print Sharing button.
3. Deselect the I Want to Be Able to Allow Others to Print to My Printer(s) check box.
4. Choose OK to close the dialog box, and choose it again to close the Network Control Panel.

Creating Shared-Printer Security In Windows 95, creating shared-resource security is a multistep procedure. In order to effectively share a resource, you must be able to control who accesses that resource and, to some extent, what they do with it. If you share your printer, you can impose some level of security. Securing your printer requires several steps.

1. Choose the Passwords icon in the Control Panel folder. The Password Properties sheet appears. This Properties sheet has three tabs: Passwords, Remote Administration, and User Profiles.
2. Choose the Enable Remote Administration check box on the Remote Administration page.

3. Type a user-access password in the Passwords text box.
4. In the Confirm Passwords text box, retype the password. Record the password in your system workbook or manual.
5. Select OK.

Network users can now gain access to your system by using the password that you have just created. To access your shared printer, however, users must have the appropriate password information.

Deleting Connections to a Shared Printer When you delete a shared connection between your workstation and a workstation sharing its local printer, disabling sharing keeps your local printer from being shared by the network.

1. From the taskbar, choose Start, Settings, Printer's Folder. Windows displays a list of all printers, local or network, attached to your workstation.
2. Select the shared printer you want to delete.
3. Choose File, Delete.
4. Windows displays a dialog box warning that it will delete the selected printer. Click Yes.
5. Windows next displays a dialog box asking whether you want to delete this printer's drivers. Click Yes to delete the drivers.

CAUTION

Before you click Yes (and thus delete the printer's drivers), verify that you do not have any other printers attached of the same make and model. If you delete this printer's drivers, you might also disconnect other printers.

Solving Common Network Printing Problems

Windows 95 adds some basic Help tools to aid you in solving network printing problems. These basic tools include the following:

- Windows quickly displays descriptive information in diagnostic messages that appear when Windows encounters printing problems.
- The Help facility includes an interactive Printing Problem Help tool that takes you step by step through the most common solutions to problems.
- An enhanced Help tool incorporates even more detailed steps that can solve quite difficult network printing problems.
- The System Monitor is useful in diagnosing local PC problems caused by network connections.

Diagnostics

The facilities of the Windows Help system can help you diagnose printing problems as follows:

1. Choose Help, Troubleshooting, and Print Troubleshooting from your application or Windows. Windows displays a Windows Help screen with the Print Troubleshooter dialog box.
2. Answer each question by clicking the button next to the appropriate answer. The Help screens provide suggestions for many common troubleshooting problems.

If the troubleshooting Help information is inadequate for solving your problems, Windows provides the Enhanced Print Troubleshooter (EPTS):

1. Go to the Windows Explorer.
2. Choose the EPTS.EXE executable file. EPTS displays a Help screen that contains hypertext buttons. Next to each button is a brief statement describing a printer problem. Start by selecting the statement that best describes your problem.
3. Answer each EPTS question with the choice that best matches your problem. The EPTS helps you identify the most probable cause of your network printing problems.

Diagnosing network printing problems is more complex because the printers are not local and perhaps not readily accessible. After using EPTS, if you are still having difficulty printing to a network printer, call the local Help desk or your LAN network administrator.

Server Overload

A PC that shares a local printer with the network is a *print server*. If your PC is a print server, a percentage of your PC's resources are dedicated to the network. That percentage varies with the number of network connections to your PC. If your system slows down significantly, it might be suffering from *server overload*. This occurs when too many network users are either attached to or overusing your printer.

To test network loading, use the System Monitor to record your PC's server activities. Your Monitor charts might show large changes in network connection activity.

1. Choose Start, Programs, Accessories, System Tools, System Monitor.
2. Choose Edit, Remove to clear all Monitor chart variables.
3. Choose Edit, Add. Windows displays the Add dialog box.
4. Choose the Server Threads option from the Network Server category.
5. Choose the Bytes/sec option from the Network Server category.
6. Choose the NBs (network buffers) option from the Network Server category and then choose the OK button to complete the additions.
7. Choose Options, Chart. Set the update interval to one minute using the slide control in the Chart dialog box.
8. Choose View, Line Charts.

You have now configured the Monitor to show the level of resource loading associated with network clients. If the System Monitor displays large variations in the number of threads or bytes-per-second variables, discontinue printer sharing for a test period. This test period should help you determine whether you can eliminate overload as a cause for system sluggishness.

Using Custom Print Managers and Utilities

Windows 95 provides a standard platform that other vendors use to create software drivers and applications. These custom software packages integrate a specific product with Windows. As a result, many printer vendors work with Microsoft to create new drivers. Some vendors have created printing applications that can substitute for or replace the Windows Printer Driver. Many printer vendors provide custom property configuration utilities for accessing their printers' custom features. Two of these vendors are Hewlett-Packard (HP) and Digital Equipment Corporation (DEC).

- The HP JetAdmin Utility is a substitute for the Windows Printer Driver.
- The DEC utility provides additional property screens that the Windows Printer Driver can call.

Using the HP JetAdmin Utility

You can use the HP JetAdmin Utility to install and configure networked Hewlett-Packard printers that use the HP JetDirect network interface. The HP JetAdmin Utility substitutes for the Windows standard Printer Driver. You also can use JetAdmin to interface printers connected to a NetWare LAN.

Figure 41.4 shows the JetAdmin Utility's main screen. The dialog box is displaying a list of printers connected to a Novell NetWare network. The network printers are of diverse makes and models. The utility can identify most of these printers. However, if incapable of identifying a printer's make, model, or network adapter card, JetAdmin displays a large, yellow question mark to designate the unknown printer.

To obtain information about the printer, double-click one of the printers shown listed in the dialog box. The Printer screen shown in Figure 41.5 appears. The screen identifies the printer's make and model as well as its location, capabilities, and status.

Notice the traffic light indicator at the screen's lower-left corner. This indicator is useful for quickly isolating network printing problems. The following are traffic light patterns for diagnosing problem printers:

- A red light indicates that the printer has a critical error that you must correct before printing. Such critical errors include a lack of paper or an open door interlock.
- A yellow light signifies a noncritical error that will soon require service. For example, if the printer's toner is low, the yellow light comes on.
- A green light indicates that the printer is online and functioning normally.

FIG. 41.4
The HP JetAdmin Utility is a vendor-supplied Printer Driver that monitors and controls HP network printers.

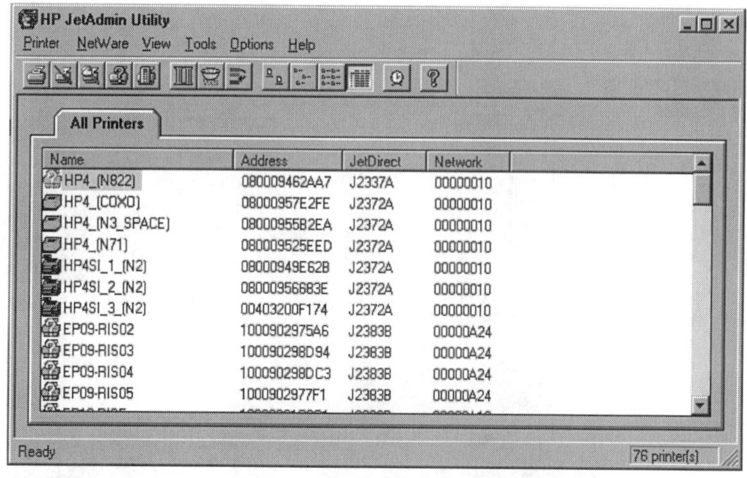

FIG. 41.5
The HP JetAdmin Utility's Printer screen displays current information about the selected printer.

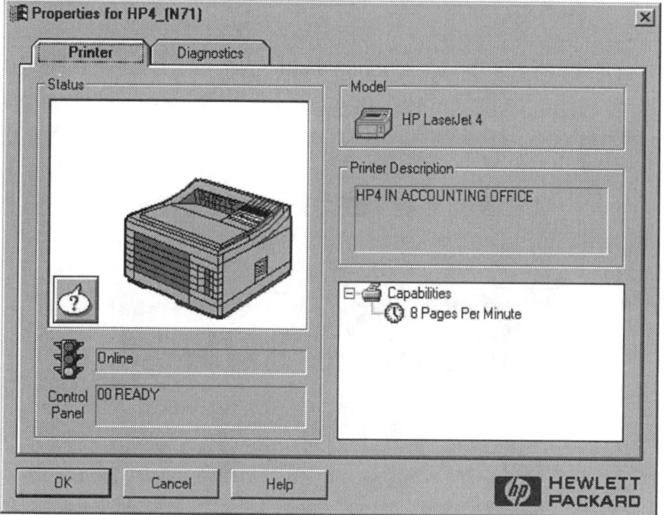

Figure 41.6 shows the Printer screen for a problem printer. JetAdmin has identified that the printer has a problem, as the question mark in the Status section denotes. Notice the traffic light patterns on this printer's display compared to that shown in Figure 41.5. The traffic light is now red, indicating a critical error has occurred.

Using the DEC Printer Utility

The DEC printer utility adds features to the standard Windows 95 Printer Driver and updates printer drivers. The utility includes a detailed Help file for configuring both local and network printers. In addition, the utility creates an enhanced set of property menus and screens for configuring DEC printers.

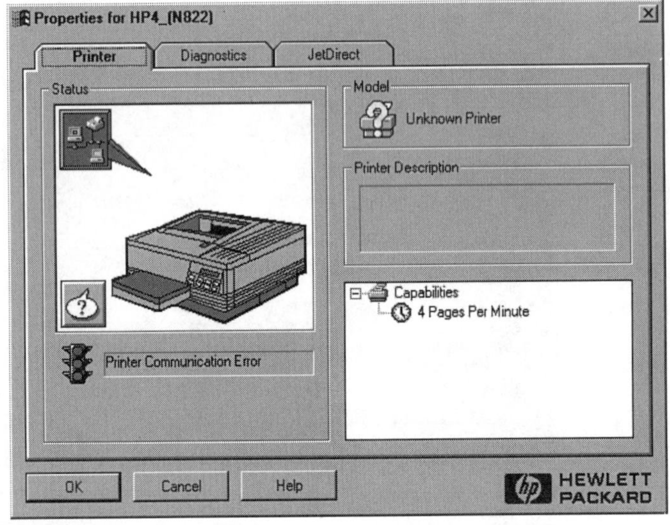

FIG. 41.6 The HP JetAdmin Utility's Printer screen shows the status of a printer whose current configuration is unknown.

Figure 41.7 shows the Device Options dialog box, which presents in detail the current conditions associated with the network printer. This dialog box also enables the user to install and quickly set special device options.

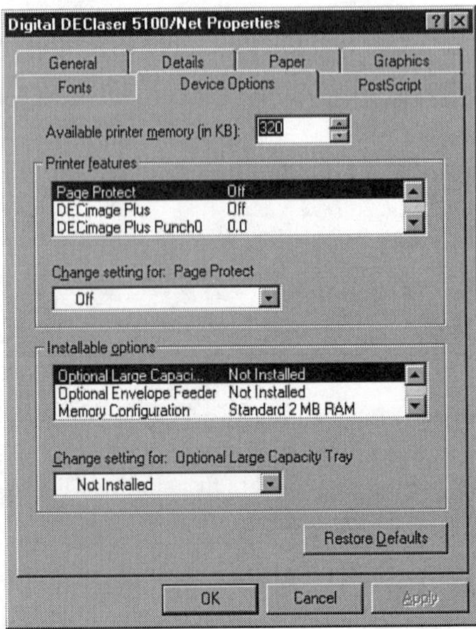

FIG. 41.7 The DEC printer utility's Device Options dialog box adds unique features to the standard Windows 95 Printer Driver.

As other printer vendors change their products and software drivers, other highly customized Printer Drivers will be available for use with Windows 95. ●

CHAPTER 42

Network Management and Security

by Gordon Meltzer

In this chapter

Creating Network Resources

The basic philosophy of peer-to-peer networks is that every file on every disk on the network is available for sharing by all members of the network. By extension, anyone can print to any printer on the network—and also delete any file, wipe out any directory, and erase any disk anywhere on the network.

That kind of peer-to-peer network, where everybody on the LAN is connected to everybody else's disks and printers, is an unmanageable network. If you draw a diagram of the connections in such a network, you'll see a crazy quilt of connections. With more than a few machines on the LAN, you'll be unable to follow all the connections. The worst parts of thoughtlessly connecting everybody to everybody are:

- **Confusion**. Time is always lost searching for data all over the LAN.
- **Data Loss**. Needed files get erased from one disk because somebody thought somebody else had a copy on another disk.

Don't be tempted to set up your Windows 95 peer network the crazy quilt way. The problem is that after you set up your network and declare your computer's hard drive to be shared, if you take no steps to manage the network, you've opened the door to network data-loss danger and file-finding confusion. You need to bring safety and sanity to your network environment, and you need to work with the other members of your workgroup to accomplish those tasks.

Data Storage Tips

Networks are designed to make office life easier. Peer-to-peer networks are supposed to eliminate something called the sneakernet, which is used when all computers in an office are standalone. Following are the steps involved in making a sneakernet connection:

1. You decide that you want to edit a document on which several people have been collaborating.
2. You visit each collaborator's computer, find the file in question, and record the date and time when the file was last modified. You're looking for the most recent version.
3. When you find the computer that has the most up-to-date version of the document, find a formatted floppy disk, copy the file to the disk, and take the disk back to your computer.
4. Copy the file from the floppy disk to your hard drive.

You think that you won't have to go through all that when you set up a network. All the computers will be connected, and you can copy the file to your hard disk over the wire. In fact, however, the default setup for peer-to-peer networks such as Windows 95 leaves each person's version of a collaborative file on his or her own hard disk, where other workgroup members cannot easily find it.

The solution to this problem is setting up your peer-to-peer Windows 95 network in a client/server model. The following sections show how this model enables all members of the network to get their work done but retains the flexibility that is the best feature of peer nets.

Choosing a Storage Area for Your Work

You really don't want to set up each computer on the peer network as a server; you want to make one computer on your network the server, the central storage area for data files. Data files are *work products*—the files created by the programs that you use. If you're not sure about which files are data files, remember that Microsoft Word creates files that have the DOC extension and that Excel creates worksheet files that have the XLS extension. The files with DOC and XLS extensions are the work product (data files) created by Word and Excel.

Files of this nature should be stored on only one computer in your workgroup so that everyone will know where to find them. If you don't do this, you have to search all the computers on your network for a file—and that makes the process very time-consuming and not superior to sneakernet at all.

Using a Dedicated Server

You don't have to have a dedicated server in your Windows 95 network, but if you can afford to dedicate one computer on your network to storing everybody's work product, do so. Following are the benefits of storing all the workgroup's data files on one machine:

- The individual workstations can use smaller, slower, less expensive hard drives.
- You don't have to search for the computer that holds the files that you want.
- Complex drive mappings are eliminated.
- In a LAN where all work product is stored on one central file server, File and Printer Sharing will not need to be turned on in Control Panel, Networks, on most of the computers in the LAN. Memory is used more efficiently on all the machines that do not use file and printer sharing.
- Backing up everyone's work is as simple as backing up one disk, because all the work is on that disk.

Setting Up a Data File Storage Server

Once you've decided that good network management involves setting up a central server, where you and your network neighbors will store their data files, follow these steps:

1. Choose the network machine that you want to use as the data server. This machine will always be turned on.
2. Enable File and Printer Sharing on the data server. Do this by going to the machine that will be your storage server. Use Control Panel and double-click the Network icon. Then choose File and Print Sharing and put a check in the box that says I Want to Be Able to Give Others Access to My Files.

NOTE If the server you're working on also has a printer attached, and if you and your workgroup members want to print on that printer, also put a check in the box that says I Want to Be Able to Allow Others to Print to My Printer(s).

3. Set up a directory structure that will make storing and finding documents easy.

NOTE You may create one folder for each user and then create subfolders for the users' projects. You may create a folder for each client and allow the workgroup members to store their work for that client in the client's folder. Setting up folders by project is okay, too, if the projects are long-term. Ideally, the directory structure on the data server should be long-lasting and timeless so that everyone in the workgroup can get used to it. ■

4. Map the server's network drive to each workstation using the same drive letter (for example, Z:).
5. Set up the applications on each workstation so that the default data directory for each application is the same.
6. Have workgroup members start saving their work to the appropriate subfolder on the network drive (not to their local C drives).

Getting the Best of Peer-to-Peer and Client/Server LAN Features

Although using a central server makes our workgroup look like a big client/server network, the flexibility of a peer-to-peer network still is available. You can call on this flexibility when you want to use a resource on the network that's attached to another computer—a color printer, for example. You can designate the printer as a shared resource, no matter whose computer the printer is attached to. You can't do that in a traditional client/server network.

Drive Mappings

Following a plan like the one shown in the section "Setting Up a Data File Storage Server" is important. If you don't, your workgroup ends up with a drive-mapping scheme that looks like a bowl of spaghetti. You don't want everybody in the network to be connected to everybody else's machines and drives. Point everybody in the workgroup to one machine for storage of working data files, and you'll always be able to find what you're looking for.

Suppose that you have a 10-user workgroup. If you set up the network in full peer-to-peer fashion, so that everyone is looking for files stored on other people's computers, your drive mappings look like Figure 42.1.

You can see why this kind of drive mapping is called spaghetti-code mapping. On each workstation, you have at least nine drive mappings to deal with. You'll have to look for files on all nine of the local hard drives if data files are stored on the local drive of each workstation.

Of course, you may be confused by having so many drive mappings and connections in place all the time. You may be dismayed by the drain on your system's performance caused by connecting to so many other workstations and having those workstations connect to yours. You are likely to disconnect from the other members' drives for normal work. Later, when you want to send a file to or retrieve a file from another computer, you must connect to the other computer, map that computer's drive to yours, and do your file transfer work.

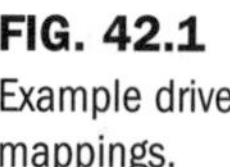

FIG. 42.1
Example drive mappings.

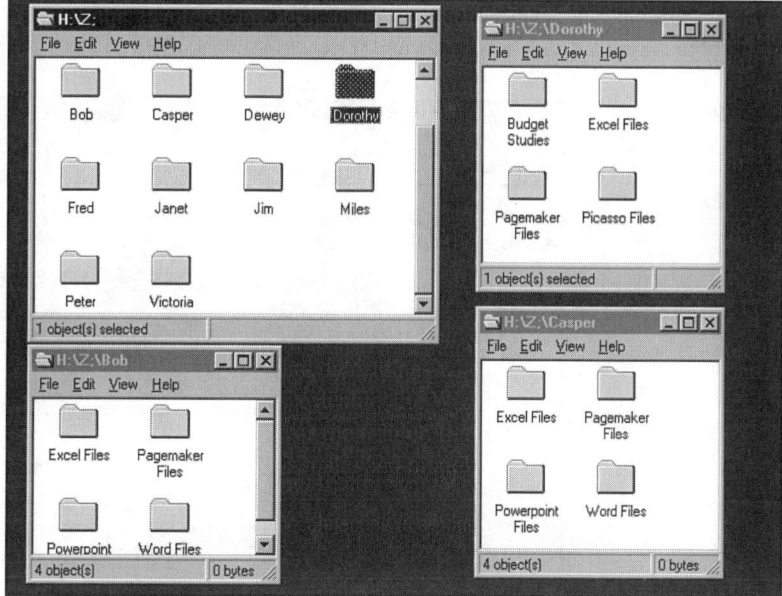

One more reason why all the computers in the workgroup should connect to one central data storage computer is that you can keep your computer connected to that computer at all times. This persistent connection can be configured to occur automatically when you start your computer or only when you actually try to access the drive. Because you don't have to worry about drive mappings or about connecting and disconnecting network drives, you can consider the network drive to be a permanent part of your computer—the place where you store your work.

Figure 42.2 shows three windows. The parent window shows a mapped network drive called Z. The first child window shows 10 folders on drive Z—one for each member of the workgroup. The smallest child window shows the folders in user Bob's main folder. The other users have similar folders. The number of folders that may appear in other users' main folders depends on the type of work each user does and the program he or she uses.

NOTE A parent window is the first window displayed by a program. Child windows appear as subsequent windows. ■

You don't have to structure the folder hierarchy on the data-server drive in any particular way. You should, however, have one data-server drive for your workgroup. All the members of the workgroup should connect to that drive permanently and store their work on that drive.

Keeping Applications and Data Separate

The preceding sections discussed only data files—the files that you generate by using your applications. But where should you store application files—your programs? The best method is to store applications locally on each user's C drive (if you have the space on your hard drive), because applications load and run noticeably faster if they run from the local hard drive.

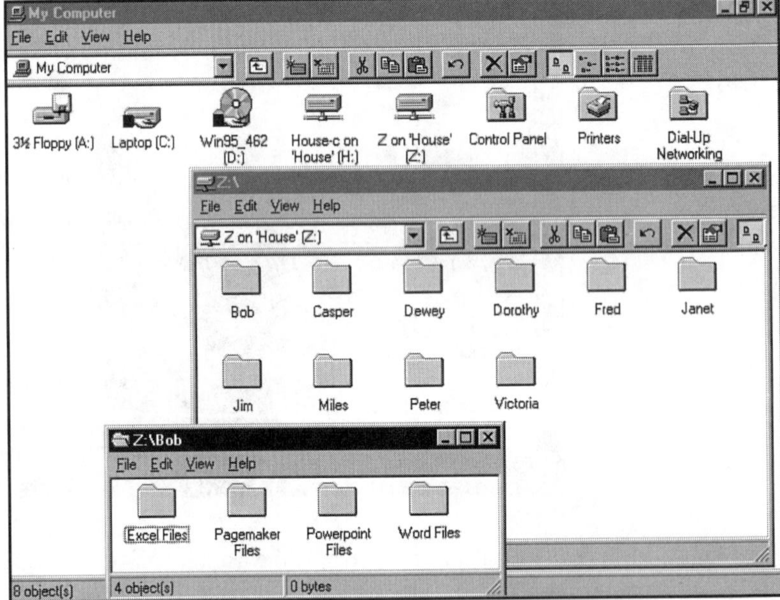

FIG. 42.2 This shows user Bob's folder structure on mapped network drive Z:.

Networks, and application-program vendors, certainly provide the capability for everyone in your workgroup to run programs from a single shared copy, located somewhere on a network file server. This method seems, at first, to be a very interesting way to operate, because that huge 15M installation of your favorite word processing program won't have to go on every computer—just on a file server. But the additional network traffic generated by the continual loading of program files over the network wastes bandwidth. Because Windows programs only load part of themselves from the disk into memory at one time, additional network traffic will be created as various parts of the program are called into memory as needed. If the application were stored on the local hard drive, all this unnecessary network traffic could be eliminated.

The users may complain that the program, coming to them from a server over the network, loads and runs too slowly. Finally, if the integrity of the network is interrupted, even momentarily, while a shared copy of an application is running, chances are good that every system running that application at that time will freeze while the application is being loaded. This could make some users think they need to reboot their machines. This procedure, of course, means that any unsaved data is lost in all applications.

The point here, of course, is that your workgroup will run much more smoothly if each user stores executable program files on his/her own computer's hard drive.

Being a Good Network Neighbor

If your workgroup is to function effectively, all the members of the workgroup must be good network neighbors. You can implement this simple concept by considering what resources are available on your computer and designating those resources as shared if other members of your workgroup need access to them.

▶ **See** "Sharing CD-ROMs and Other Removable Drives," **p. 865**

If yours is the only CD-ROM drive in the workgroup, for example, make it available for other members to use.

You also need to consider the continuity of shared resources. If you have the only CD-ROM drive or the only color printer and other users are connected to those resources, consider the effect on the rest of your workgroup if you turn off your computer without warning. In such a case, your resources disappear from the network and are no longer available to the other workgroup members. Don't discontinue sharing your resources without informing the rest of the workgroup. Use the WinPopup accessory program to send a message to your workgroup saying you are going to take your shared disk or printer offline. In your message, say how long it will be until you shut down. Communicating about a change in status of a shared resource you control is part of being a good network neighbor.

CAUTION

If a disk resource on your peer-to-peer network is disconnected from the network unexpectedly—if a computer that hosts a shared folder is turned off or if the folder-sharing properties are turned off—network users can lose data.

Network Management Tools

Windows 95 includes several useful tools that help you learn about and manage your peer-to-peer network. Although *network management* is a very broad term, management tools simply allow you to see how your network is functioning and to change almost everything about the entire network from your own computer. You can use these network management tools to enable or disable sharing of resources, add or delete passwords, disconnect users, and so on.

When you look at network management as being a series of toggle switches, with one switch for each possible setting on each possible resource, management tools become less mysterious. The trick is knowing how to set each parameter for optimum network efficiency.

NOTE Don't feel that you have to make every connection and map every drive just because you can. Simple is better.

Net Watcher

Net Watcher is installed in the Accessories, System Tools group, which you can find by opening the Start menu and choosing Programs. This utility is useful for examining which resources on which computer are shared. Net Watcher tells you about these resources, as well as who is using the shared resources and which files are open on the shared resources.

Net Watcher is a "per-server" utility. In order to display meaningful information, Net Watcher shows information about only one server computer at a time. Net Watcher shows information about computers that are sharing their disks or printers. These computers have File and Print Sharing for Microsoft Networks enabled.

Net Watcher provides three main views of the workgroup for each server:

- A view showing the users connected to the server called View by Connections. To see this view, start Net Watcher and choose View, Connections.
- A view showing the shared folders on the server called View by Shared Folders. To see this view from the main Net Watcher window, choose View, Shared Folders.
- A view showing the files that are open on the server called View by Open Files. To see this view, choose View, Open Files.

In the View by Connections, a list of users who are connected to the server appears on the left side of the screen. The right side of the screen displays the folders and printers to which the users are connected, as well as the files that the users have open. If multiple users are connected, you select one user at a time on the left side of the screen. You can then manage how that user interacts with the network, as you'll see next.

Figure 42.3 represents the View by Connections. In this example, you are looking at a server called HOUSE (as defined in the caption bar), to which one user, called LAPTOP, is connected.

View by Shared Folders shows detailed information about the disk folders and printers that have been declared sharable on the server. On the left side of the screen is a list of shared folders on the server, the names under which the folders are shared, the type of access available to the folder (full access or read-only), and any comment about the shared resource that was typed in the Comment box when the folder or printer was designated as sharable.

Figure 42.4 shows the Show Shared Folders view. In the figure, LAPTOP is connected to several shared folders and to one printer on the computer known as HOUSE.

View by Open Files is a full screen display. In Figure 42.5, Net Watcher shows the name of two open files on the server, the share name of the server on which the file is located, which computer is accessing the file, and whether the file is open for reading only or for reading and writing.

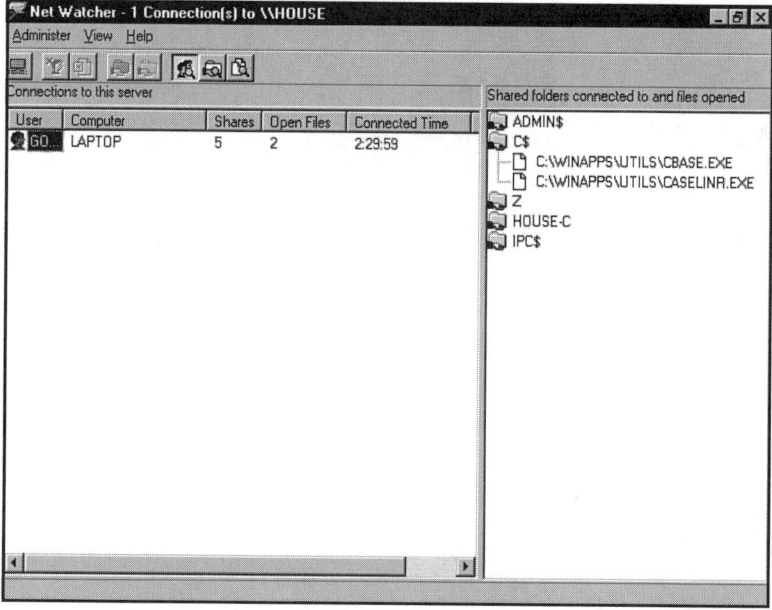

FIG. 42.3
The Net Watcher management program in View by Connections mode, showing user Laptop connected to server House.

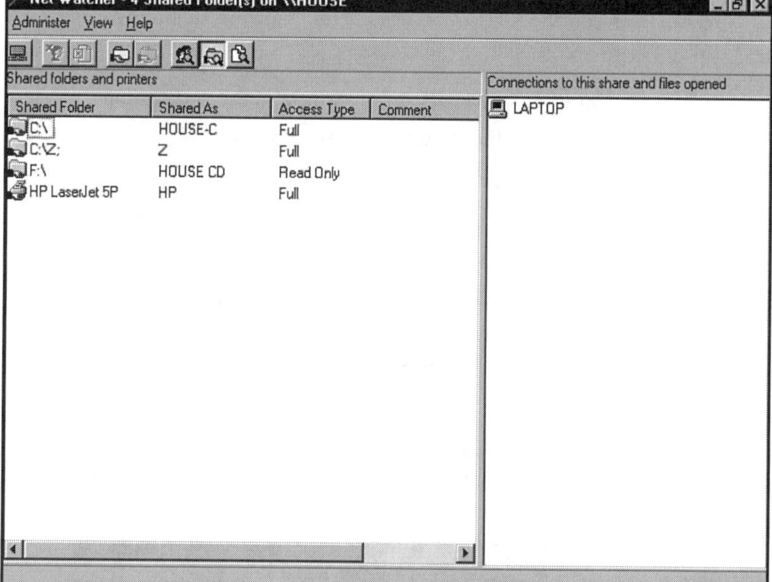

FIG. 42.4
The Net Watcher management program in View by Shared Folders mode, showing four shared folders on the server named House.

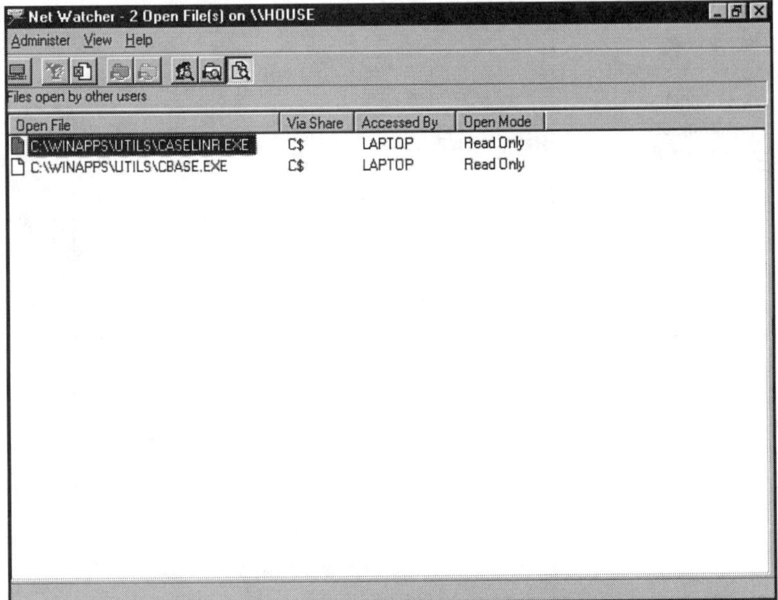

FIG. 42.5
The Net Watcher management program in View by Open Files mode, showing two open files on the server named House.

Net Watcher can do far more than simply report on network status, however; as a management tool, it can restructure the network. The following sections explain how you can use Net Watcher to accomplish these tasks:

- Disconnect a network user anywhere in the workgroup
- Close an open file anywhere in the workgroup
- Add a shared folder to any server in the workgroup
- Stop sharing folders on any server in the workgroup
- Change the properties of shared folders in the workgroup

Disconnecting a User from a Peer Server If you want to stop a user from connecting to your computer's shared folders and printers, use Net Watcher's Show Users view. Select the user whom you want to disconnect and then choose Administer, Disconnect User.

Disconnecting a user can have serious consequences for that user because data can be lost if there is any unsaved data at the time the disconnection occurs. In fact, Net Watcher issues a warning when you issue the Disconnect User command, as shown in Figure 42.6.

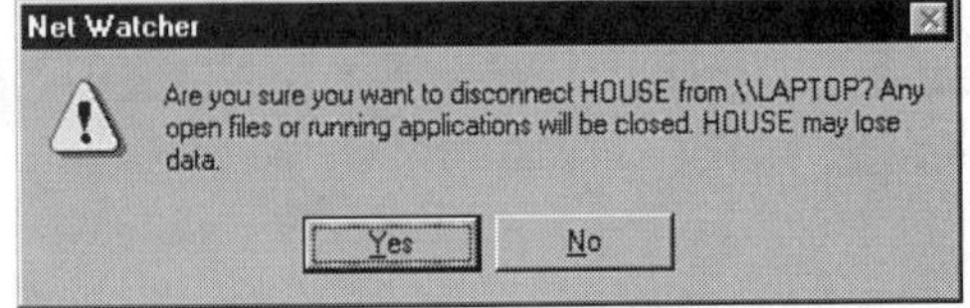

FIG. 42.6
The Net Watcher management program issues a warning when you use it to disconnect a server from a connected user.

Adding a Shared Resource on a Peer Server Adding a shared resource can be useful when you need access to a resource on another computer in your workgroup. Net Watcher can make the folder that you need sharable. Figure 42.7 shows the shared resources on the peer server called HOUSE—three shared folders and one shared printer. Anyone on a Windows 95 peer network can declare a share on any folder in which they have permission on the workgroup if the computer they are targeting is a server (has enabled File & Printer Sharing Services).

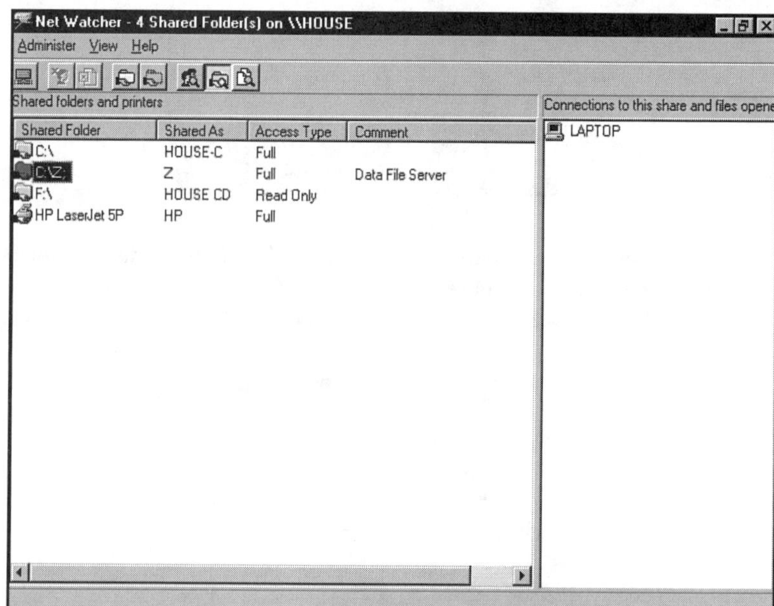

FIG. 42.7
Net Watcher in View by Shared Folders mode, showing three shared folders.

Suppose you want to access programs in the folder named SECURE on the computer named HOUSE. SECURE is not a shared folder, however, so you need to declare it to be sharable. You can do this, from any machine on the workgroup LAN, using Net Watcher. The three requirements are:

- Remote Administration is enabled on the server you are targeting (on which you want to set a resource shared).
- The folder, drive, or printer you want to share is on a server computer. A server computer has File and/or Printer Sharing enabled.
- No password has been established, controlling access to the folder or resource you want to share.

Starting from View by Shared Folders view on peer server HOUSE, choose Administer, Add Shared Folder, or use the Add Share button on the Net Watcher toolbar. Next, you'll see a dialog box asking for the path you wish to share. Then browse for the folder name, or type it in the Path box. Figure 42.8 shows the dialog box where you enter the path to the folder you want to share.

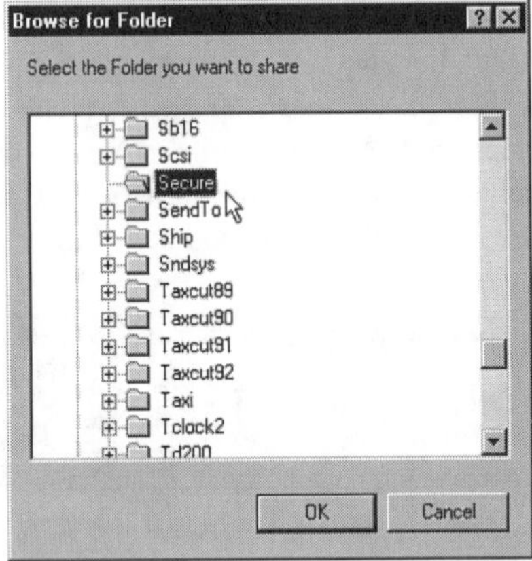

FIG. 42.8 To share a folder on your workgroup LAN using Net Watcher, browse for the folder you want to share and double-click to enter it in the Enter path dialog box.

When you select the folder you want to add, Net Watcher displays the Shared Folder properties sheet, shown in Figure 42.9. In this sheet, you declare the folder to be shared and set its shared properties: Shared As, Share Name, Comment, Access Type, and Passwords.

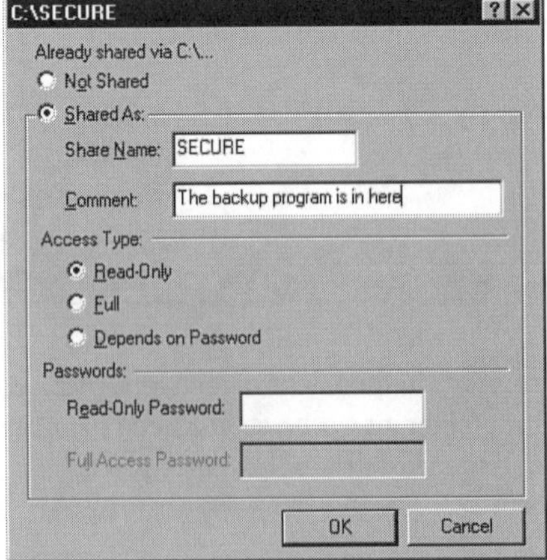

FIG. 42.9 In Net Watcher, you can edit the properties of your newly shared folder.

When you choose OK on the Shared Folder properties sheet, the folder becomes a shared resource on the workgroup and is added to Net Watcher's list of shared folders (see Figure 42.10).

CAUTION

The process of adding a shared folder just described has deep implications. Any member of the Peer-to-Peer workgroup LAN can add a shared drive or folder on any server computer in the network. The owner of the computer targeted to have a drive or folder shared doesn't need to agree. In fact, the owner of the targeted computer may not even know that a drive or folder has been set as shared, until she happens to examine the drive properties with My Computer or Windows Explorer, and notices the Shared Resource icon attached to one of her drives or folders.

Notice too, that any member of the workgroup, using Net Watcher to add shared drives or folders on server computers on the LAN, can also set passwords for access to the folders he declares as shared, effectively preventing anyone but himself from accessing those drives or folders over the LAN. Again, the owner of the computer containing these shared drives or folders will not know a password has been set without examining the properties for the shared drive or folder.

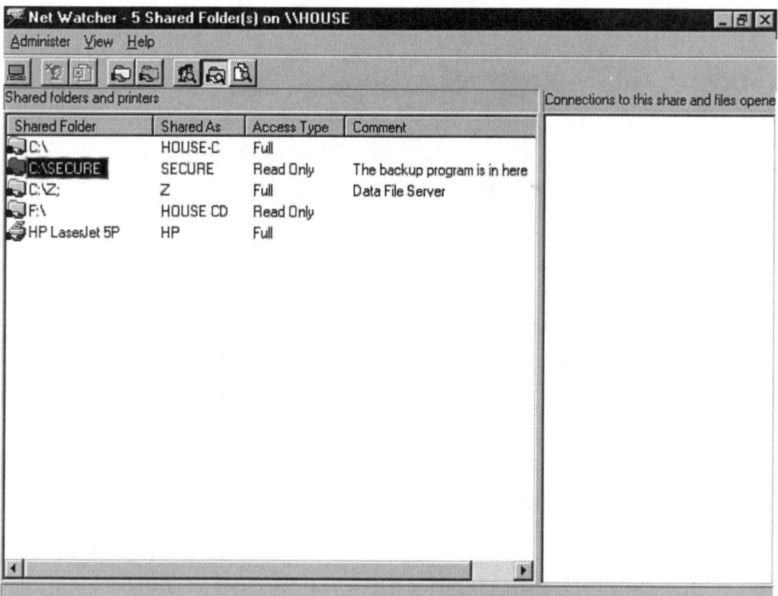

FIG. 42.10
The Net Watcher program has added your newly shared folder, C:\SECURE, to its list of shared folders on the peer server HOUSE.

TROUBLESHOOTING

Files on my hard disk drive are changing. Some are being deleted, some are just being modified. I haven't done anything to them. Why is this happening? The answer may be that another member of your workgroup LAN is causing these changes on your computer. If you have enabled File and Print Sharing in your network setup, another member of your LAN may have declared your hard drive and its folders to be shared. That person can then work with your files, modify them, delete them, or add new files to your disk.

Two ways to prevent having your drives and folders shared by others without your knowledge are:

- Turn off File Sharing in Control Panel, Network. Then, your computer is not a server and nobody can access your drives or folders over the LAN.

continues

continued

- Turn off Enable Remote Administration. You do this by using Control Panel, Passwords, and then clicking the page called Remote Administration. Only one setting is on this page. In the sole check box, deselect Enable Remote Administration of This Server.

Stop Sharing a Folder To stop sharing a folder, start in the View by Shared Folders view of Net Watcher. Select the Shared Folder that you want to stop sharing on the network and then choose Administer, Stop Sharing Folder. You also can choose the Stop Sharing icon on the Net Watcher toolbar. The warning message shown in Figure 42.11 appears. Click Yes to stop sharing the specified folder.

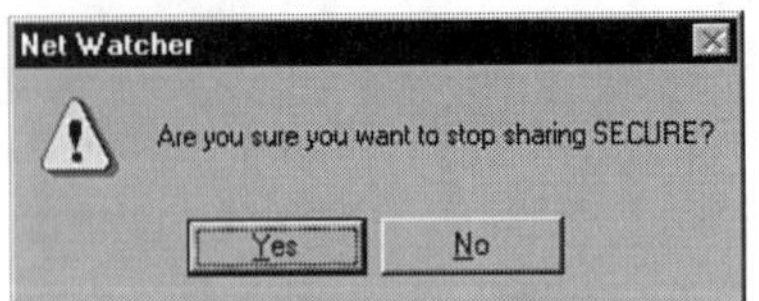

FIG. 42.11
When you use Net Watcher to stop sharing a folder, this confirmation dialog box appears.

Change a Shared Folder's Properties This option allows you to stop sharing a shared folder, but it also allows you to change the name of the shared resource on the network, change the access type, and set a password for access. In Net Watcher's Show Shared Folders view, select the folder that you want to stop sharing on the network and then choose Administer, Shared Folder Properties.

Now you can perform these kinds of changes on the folder you selected:

- You can set the folder as Not Shared.
- You can set the folder as Shared. If you do this, you must also enter a Share Name. By default, Windows selects the folder name as the Share Name, but you also can change it.
- If you've set the folder to be Shared, you can set the access type to Read-Only, or Full, or Depends on Password. You also may enter a password for access to the folder.

Figure 42.9 shows the dialog box to change a shared folder's properties.

Stop Sharing a Printer If you need to stop sharing a printer on the workgroup, start in View by Shared Folder view of Net Watcher. Select the printer in the list of shared resources and choose Administer, Shared Folder Properties. The printer properties dialog box appears (see Figure 42.12) showing the name of the printer you're working with in its title bar. To stop sharing the printer, choose Not Shared in the dialog box.

Then, choose OK. No warning message appears before the printer is made unavailable to the workgroup.

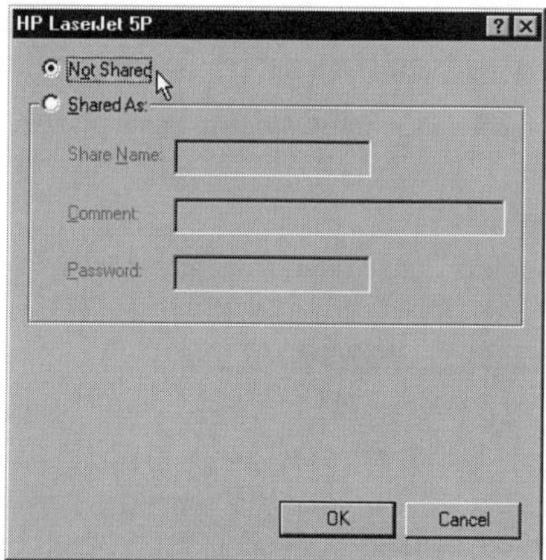

FIG. 42.12
Net Watcher uses this dialog box to allow you to stop sharing a network printer.

User Profiles as a System Management Tool

Many workgroups have users who may use more than one computer. Because Windows 95 is very customizable, a user who is sitting at what is not his or her main computer may be unable to work. Network connections may not be the same. Connections to the shared folders that the user needs may not be available. Printer connections may not be what the user expects. Menus may be different. In general, the workstation may be so customized for the primary user that another user may be lost.

▶ **See** "Changing Custom Settings for Each User," **p. 809**

Some computers on your workgroup may have no primary user but a group of users, all of whom may have different needs or expectations. You also may have users who are true floaters who have no primary machine but need to be able to be productive on any computer.

To deal with all these cases, Microsoft introduced User Profiles to Windows 95. With User Profiles, the following settings on any computer can be customized for any user:

- Shortcut lists and their contents
- Items in the Start menu
- Items that can be configured by Control Panel
- Menu configurations (for Windows 95 programs and the applications bundled with Windows 95), toolbar configurations, status bar configurations, and font and display settings
- Appearance of the desktop, including shortcuts and icons
- Fonts in use
- Screen saver, screen background, screen colors, color depth, and screen resolution
- Network settings (such as persistent connections and printer connections)
- Network Neighborhood configuration

Enabling User Profiles on the Workgroup To use User Profiles, you must be sure the proper options are selected on the Passwords properties sheet. Follow these steps:

1. Open the Start menu and choose Settings, Control Panel, Passwords. The Passwords properties sheet appears.
2. Click the User Profiles tab.
3. Choose Users Can Customize Their Preferences, as shown in Figure 42.13.

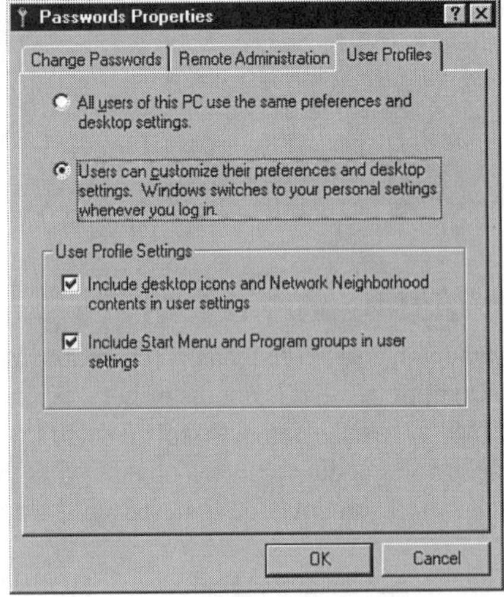

FIG. 42.13
Use the Passwords properties sheet to enable multiple User Profiles.

4. To make your User Profiles more powerful, choose Include Desktop Icons and Include Start Menu.
5. Click the Change Passwords tab.
6. Make sure that a logon password appears in this tab. You must have a password when you begin to work with User Profiles.

Working with User Profiles When a user logs on to a Windows 95 computer that has User Profiles enabled, the machine asks for a user name and password. The computer then creates a User Profile using default settings.

When you finish working at a profile-enabled computer, shut down with the Close All Programs and Log On as Different User option. This option prevents anyone from changing your profiled settings and preferences.

As the user sets up network connections, desktop preferences, and all the other customizable features of the workstation, Windows 95 waits for the user to log off and shut down the machine. Windows then saves all the settings that User Profiles can track (the settings listed in the preceding sections). Windows writes the User Profile information into the Registry, in the USER.DAT file, and saves the desktop and Start menu in the C:\WINDOWS\PROFILES folder, as shown in Figure 42.14. This figure shows profiles for five users on this computer; the hierarchy of subfolders is expanded for one of the users listed on the left side of the screen.

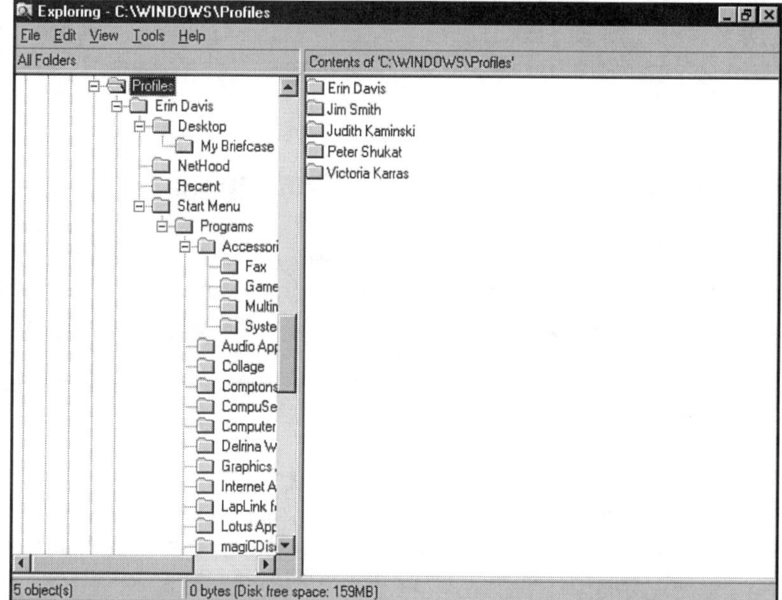

FIG. 42.14 Windows Explorer shows five User Profiles in the right half of the screen when five users have created Profiles.

User Profiles on the Network The preceding sections show how one machine can be customized for any number of users. This process is a local use of User Profiles. An even more powerful type of User Profiles allows anyone to log in on any machine in the workgroup and have his or her settings restored, even if that user has never set up his or her profile at that machine before. This option requires the use of an NT or NetWare server. On an NT or NetWare network, you can log in from any computer on the LAN and use your customized User Profile. You can do this because your User Profile is stored on the NT or NetWare file server, not on the workstation.

Because the profile is stored on the NT or NetWare server, it can be accessed by any workstation on the LAN.

On an NT server, use the User Manager tool to create a home directory for each member of the workgroup. When a user logs off the Windows 95 workstation—if User Profiles are enabled— Windows copies the profile information to the NT server. When that user logs on to any other computer on the workgroup, the profile on the NT server is accessed and used to set up the current workstation. (This may not work in cases where you have a shortcut to an application such as Word, and the machine you log in from does not have Word installed.)

The same system works in a NetWare environment.

NOTE If the User Profile on the current workstation is newer than the copy on the server, the workstation copy is used, and the server is updated. The procedure also works in reverse, so that the user always has the most recent configuration available.

NOTE If you use Microsoft Exchange on a computer that has User Profiles enabled, set Exchange to query for an Exchange profile to use at startup, because User Profiles do not control Exchange profiles. (For more on Exchange, see Chapter 27, "Using Microsoft Exchange and Windows Messaging.")

System Policies and Network Management

System Policies do many of the same things as User Profiles. System Policies are not used along with User Profiles but they are used instead of User Profiles. The members of a workgroup do not set System Policies, as they do for their own User Profiles. In this section, you'll see how the System Policy Editor can change the look and feel of your Windows 95 computer. Some features documented in this book may not be available to you if your network administrator has disabled some features using System Policy Editor. Let's see what can happen using System Policies which are created by the System Policy Editor program.

NOTE The System Policy Editor program, POLEDIT.EXE, is included on the CD-ROM version of Windows 95. It is not included on the floppy disk version of the operating system. If you do not have the CD-ROM version, you can download it from Microsoft's Web site (**http://www.microsoft.com**). The file is called POLICY.EXE and is included in the CD-ROM Extras.

The simplest way to understand System Policies is to know that these policies, which are created by a system administrator, are used to enforce predetermined User Profiles on a workgroup. The purpose of System Policies is to create a controlled workplace in which access to certain features of Windows can be restricted or eliminated. System Policies may restrict a user from accessing Control Panel or from getting to a DOS prompt, for example. These policies also may prevent a user from connecting to or disconnecting from shared resources on the network.

Used wisely, System Policies can increase the stability of a Windows workgroup by preventing users who like to experiment from disrupting needed network connections and thereby crashing the system. Used unwisely, System Policies can prevent the natural growth of understanding that is essential if members of a workgroup are to learn how to use their computers to maximum benefit.

System Policies are set through a tool called System Policy Editor, which is the most powerful of the network management tools included with Windows 95. This tool, which is designed to be used only by the network administrator, is inaccessible to users on the workgroup. The System Policy Editor should be kept in a nonshared folder on the administrator's computer.

With System Policy Editor, the administrator can set two types of policies. The first type of policies applies to individual-named computers on the network. The policies created for the named computer determine the default settings that are used when a user logs on to that computer.

The second type of policies applies to individual users, determined by user name at the time of logon. If policies exist for an individual user, they are combined with the System Policies that are in effect for the computer that is being used.

System Policies for Individual Computers The System Policy Editor can control the following settings on a per-computer basis:

Controlling the Network Group of Settings

- Access Control can be set to User Level. This requires the use of authentication on an NT or NetWare server to access the shared resources on the network.
- Logon features can display a warning at startup, saying that only authorized users should try to log on. Logon also can require validation by an NT server to access Windows 95.
- Settings for Microsoft Client for NetWare can be controlled.
- Settings for Microsoft Client for Windows Networks can be controlled.
- Password settings can be modified. Use of mixed alphabetical and numeric passwords, for example, can be required, and password caching can be forced off.
- Sharing can be disabled for the computer. In this case, no resources can be declared shared, and all shared information tabs disappear from properties sheets.
- Remote updating can be enabled.

Controlling the System Group of Settings

- The administrator can enable User Profiles.
- The network path to a shared copy of Windows Setup and Windows Tour can be specified.
- Items to be run at startup can be specified.

System Policies for Individual Users This area is where System Policy Editor can really show its power. Many options for individual users exist. For users, System Policy Editor works on five groups of settings.

Controlling the Control Panel Group of Settings

- The administrator can restrict the appearance of the Networks, Display, Password, Printer, and System icons in the Control Panel.

Controlling the Desktop Group of Settings

- The wallpaper and color scheme can be controlled.

Network Settings

- File and print sharing can be turned off for the user.

Controlling the Shell Group of Settings

- Custom Folder Functions can be disabled.
- Custom Programs Folders can be disallowed.
- Custom Desktop Icons can be disallowed.
- Start menu subfolders can be hidden.
- Custom Startup Folders can be disallowed.
- Custom Network Neighborhood can be disallowed.
- Custom Start Menu can be disallowed.
- The Run command can be removed from the Start menu.
- Folders and settings can be hidden so they won't show in the taskbar.
- The Find command can be disabled from the Start menu.
- The display of drives in My Computer can be hidden.
- Network Neighborhood can be hidden.
- Hide All items on the desktop can be hidden.
- The Shutdown command can be disallowed.
- Windows automatic saving of settings at shutdown can be disallowed.

Controlling the System Group of Settings

- Registry editing can be disallowed.
- The administrator can set up a list of allowed Windows applications and only the allowed applications can be run.
- The MS-DOS prompt can be disabled.
- MS-DOS mode can be disabled.

Figure 42.15 shows what the user would see if the administrator chose to restrict part of the System icon in Control Panel. The File System and Virtual Memory buttons in the System properties sheet are missing and the Device Manager and Hardware Profiles tabs are missing.

Figure 42.16 shows the System properties sheet before restrictions were applied by System Policy Editor.

CAUTION

System Policy Editor can be unpredictable. If the administrator selects a function and then deselects it, the function may not return to the state that it was in before editing. As a result, user settings can be destroyed without warning. The workaround is to tell your administrator to leave the setting neither selected nor deselected, but dimmed. Dimmed is an option when you edit a policy file.

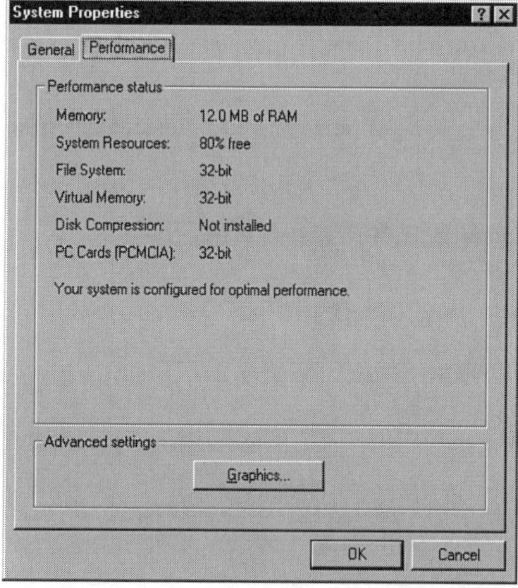

FIG. 42.15
System Policy Editor has removed features from System Properties in Control Panel.

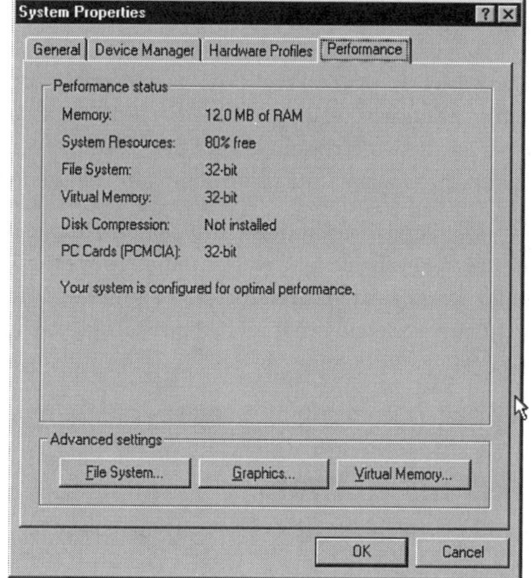

FIG. 42.16
System Properties in Control Panel looks like this before System Policy Editor removed features.

WinPopup

WinPopup is an applet that is included in the Accessories group when you install the network component of Windows 95. This tool normally is used to send short messages from one computer on the workgroup to another. WinPopup is designed so that when a message is received, the message pops up over anything else that is on-screen.

The real usefulness of the WinPopup program is that it automatically sends messages from a network printer when a print job finishes. WinPopup sends the message only to the computer that sent the print job for processing.

Figure 42.17 shows the simple network management function of a "print job is finished" notification.

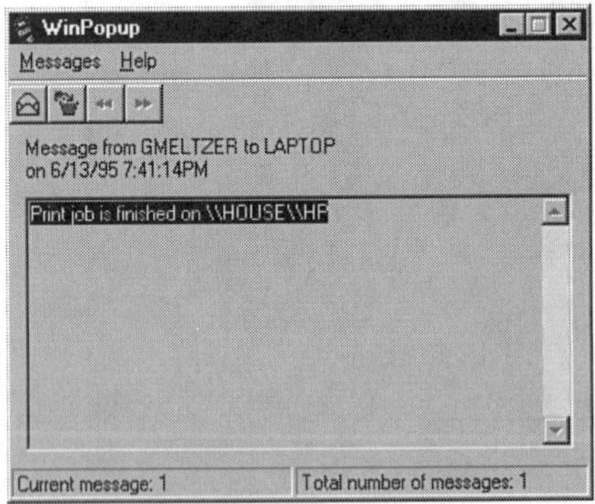

FIG. 42.17
WinPopup has sent a message to a user that the network print job is finished.

Network Security

Security on computer networks is designed to prevent unauthorized or accidental access to the information located on the disk drives on the network. Security can extend to preventing unauthorized users from using any network resource, such as a printer. Security systems also are intended to prevent unauthorized users from using computers on the network.

Windows 95 provides a wide range of network security options. Some of the most powerful security tools, however, are not available for a workgroup network that consists of computers that run only Windows 95. These functions require that a Windows NT or Novell NetWare server be connected to the network and programmed in a special way to enable Windows 95's advanced security functions.

The following sections examine the security tools that you can use in both environments.

All-Windows 95 Workgroup Network

In an all-Windows 95 workgroup, three types of security are available:

- Logon security
- Share-level password security
- System Policies security

Next, you will learn to use each of these security methods on your workgroup LAN. Whether you use one, two, or all of these techniques, the bottom line is that using security will prevent data loss.

Logon Security Although Windows 95 requires a logon password, you need to understand that the only things protected by this password are network resources, such as shared folders and shared printers. Windows 95 provides absolutely no password protection at the workstation level; anyone can sit down at your computer and access your local disks and attached resources.

If you need to control access to individual computers so that only a user with the right password can start the operating system, you should consider using Windows NT, not Windows 95, on individual workstation computers. NT requires a password before any user can work with the computer at all.

When Windows 95 starts, you see a screen that asks for your user ID and password. No matter what you do at this point, including clicking Cancel, Windows continues to load and to give you access to all the drives and printers on your computer.

Now that you understand that no logon security exists for the workstation in Windows 95, consider logon security for the network.

Windows Logon Password When Windows 95 starts for the first time, a logon dialog box asks for your user ID and password. Depending on your settings in Control Panel, Networks, you are prompted to log on to Windows 95 or the network. If your Network setting sets your Primary Network Logon as Client for Microsoft Networks, your logon screen looks like the one shown in Figure 42.18.

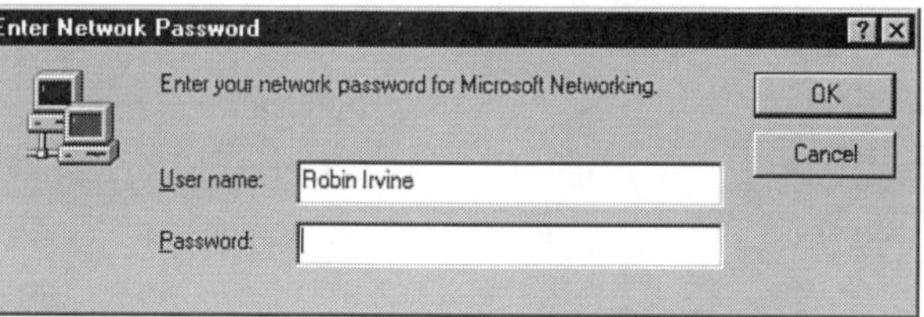

FIG. 42.18 This will be your logon screen if your Primary Network Logon is set to be Client for Microsoft Networks.

If you set your Primary Network Logon to be Windows Logon, you see a logon prompt like the one shown in Figure 42.19.

▶ **See** "Removing Cached Passwords," **p. 994**

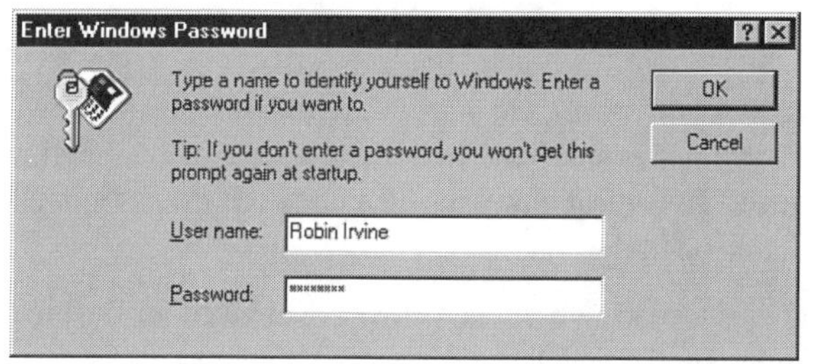

FIG. 42.19 The first time you run Windows 95 on your computer, you'll see this dialog box.

When you type the correct password for network access, you have access to all the shared resources on the network, as long as you know the password required to access them. In fact, you won't have to enter the passwords for network resources more than once; Windows stores the passwords that you enter in a cache so that they are entered for you automatically the next time you log on. Although the cache can be disabled by System Policies and by the Password List Editor program, in a normal installation, the password cache is active.

This chapter has mentioned passwords in connection with shared resources. The following sections examine the way that passwords work.

Access Control in Workgroups: Share-Level Access Control Earlier, you learned how to enable peer-to-peer resource sharing on a Windows 95 workgroup. In this section, you set some passwords for those resources so that only authorized users can find them over the network.

Figure 42.20 shows two types of shared resources.

FIG. 42.20
There are two resources shared in this view of My Computer.

Notice that the icon for the local hard drive—Drive C—is shared. The icon includes the outstretched hand that signifies sharing. The hand does not mean that the disk is completely open to any user, however. To control how you will share your drive, right-click the icon and choose Sharing from the pop-up menu.

Figure 42.21 shows the sharing properties that are enabled for the local hard drive. Two passwords are set. You want to give full read-and-write access to users who know the full access password. Other users will be able only to read the disk, not to modify it in any way.

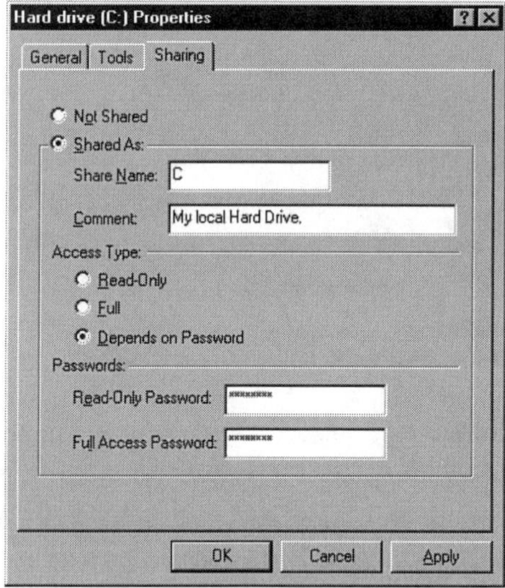

FIG. 42.21
The Hard Drive properties sheet controls password access to the drive.

This type of security is called *share-level access*, and it is the only kind of access protection available to workgroups in which Windows 95 (or Windows for Workgroups 3.1x) peer server is the only type of server on the network. To see how this access control is enabled, open the Start menu and choose Settings, Control Panel, Network; click the Access Control tab; and select the Share Level access-control option. The other option is not available for Peer-to-Peer networks.

Share-Level Access and Network Neighborhood If you enable sharing on a disk, folder, or printer on your computer, the shared resource appears in Network Neighborhood, from which users may try to connect to your resource or map a drive letter to it.

At times, you want to share a resource but not broadcast that fact to the workgroup. A mechanism for hiding shared resources exists. To do this, add a dollar sign character to the end of the share name. The resource still behaves in accordance with its password restrictions, but it does not appear in Network Neighborhood. Another member of the workgroup must know the exact name of the resource to connect to it.

Mapped Drives and Their Security Figure 42.20 earlier in this chapter, showed two types of shared resources in the My Computer window. This section examines the properties of the resources whose icons look like disks attached to cables. These resources are shared drives and folders on other computers. The owners of those resources may have enabled share-level security passwords for those resources. That security determines what you can do with the folders—whether you can write to them as well as read from them.

If the owner of a shared folder changes the password required to access that resource, your cached password no longer gives you access to the resource. You see a network drive icon with an *X* through the connection, like the one shown for the Z on House connection in Figure 42.22.

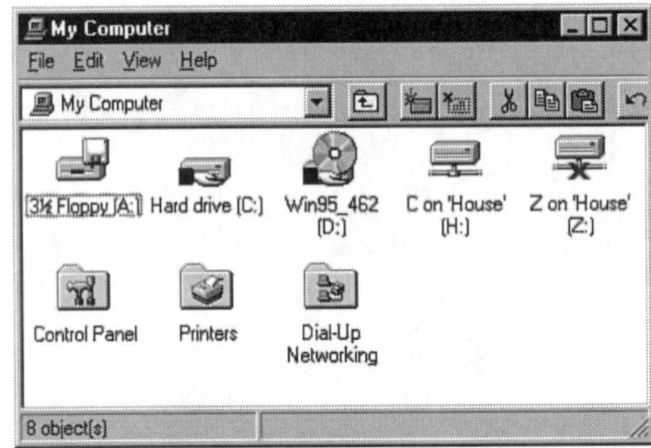

FIG. 42.22 An inaccessible network drive is shown with an X through its icon.

To access the resource again, learn the new access password. Then, when you want to access the shared drive again, you will have to restart Windows.

Removing Cached Passwords Because password caching is enabled in Windows 95 automatically, the system creates an encrypted file, in which it stores the password entries for all resources used by the computer. By default, the file name is SHARE.PWL. If User Profiles are enabled on the computer, the PWL files are not called SHARE but are created from the user names. When User Profiles are active, each user has a different PWL password list file, such as TOM.PWL.

If you are having trouble with a cached password, use the Password List Editor program, PWLEDIT.EXE. This program does not show you the actual passwords—it shows you that a password exists and gives you the opportunity to remove the password. This procedure forces you to log in with the correct password the next time you want to connect to the resource that you edited.

NOTE The Password List Editor program, PWLEDIT.EXE, is included on the CD-ROM version of Windows 95. It is not included on the floppy disk version of the operating system.

Figure 42.23 shows a Password List Editor screen. Password List Editor shows every password in effect on the computer on which it's running. In Figure 42.23, only one password is in effect. Although the display is not very informative, the text "Rna" shown in the Resource column is a hint that the password is for Dial-Up Networking. Rna, in Windows jargon, means Remote node access.

The only option is to remove the password.

Using Windows 95 with a Microsoft NT or Novell NetWare Server

If your network includes an NT or NetWare server, your options for workgroup security are greatly enhanced. You can use the features of those servers to provide and enforce user-level security on the workgroup. In this case, the NT or NetWare server is acting as a security provider and validator. This function works because those two network systems maintain lists of authorized users and those users' network rights and access privileges. This function does not exist in Windows 95 Peer-to-Peer networks.

FIG. 42.23 The Password List Editor program can remove passwords from any type of password protected resource on your computer.

Table 42.1 compares the features available in user- and share-level access control.

Table 42.1 Access-Control Comparison

Feature	User-Level	Share-Level
Read Files	X	X
Write to Files	X	X
Create Files and Folders	X	
List Files	X	
Delete Files	X	
Change File Attributes	X	
Change Access Control	X	

You can see that user-level security gives you much finer control of shared resources because you can enable any, all, or none of the preceding sets of rights. If you enable only List Files, for example, users who connect to the folder can execute programs from the folder, but they cannot delete or change anything.

User Lists in User-Level Security

In a Windows NT environment, the administrator uses the User Manager program to set up the security permissions for each user name. Windows 95 uses these permissions to set access rights for the listed resources. An NT administrator also can create groups and simplify workgroup administration by granting the same rights to several users or perhaps an entire workgroup.

The only thing to remember is that in the case of multiple NT domains, the Windows 95 computer must select one domain server to be the security and list provider.

In NetWare, the same list principles apply. Instead of using User Manager, however, NetWare relies on the Bindery feature. As a result, NetWare 4.x servers must be running Bindery emulation to act as security hosts for Windows 95 computers.

General Network Security Guidelines

As you've seen by now, network security in a Windows 95 workgroup LAN must be configured, cooperatively, by the network neighbors who are connected to the LAN. To avoid loss of your workgroup's valuable data, accidentally or otherwise, consider the following four guiding principles:

- Although setting up a completely open, password-free network is easy, resist the temptation. Even though you may not have to enter passwords with password caching enabled, require them because they will increase your options later.
- If you can make access to a shared resource read-only, do so. Use full read/write access only when it is necessary. This practice can prevent accidental deletion of important files and directories.
- Make sure that you and your network neighbors keep their passwords guarded and not written in plain sight on or near the computer.
- Don't use an obvious item, such as your name, as your Windows password.

Troubleshooting and Network Management Tools

If you're having problems accessing resources that you can see in Network Neighborhood, check to see whether you have the rights that you need to do your work. Windows provides an easy way to use Net Watcher for this purpose. In Network Neighborhood, right-click the computer that holds the resources that you need; choose Properties; and then click the Tools tab. Figure 42.24 shows the list of management tools that are available.

From this point, you can select Net Watcher and use it to see whether the folder that you want to use is shared. If not, you can designate the folder as shared. If the problem is that the folder is read-only and you need full access, use Net Watcher to adjust that situation, too.

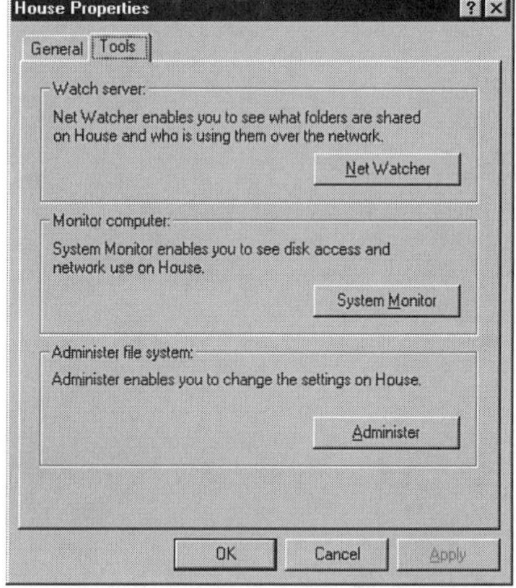

FIG. 42.24 Windows 95 provides Net Watcher, System Monitor, and Administer tools for network management.

Using Dial-Up Networking

Just as you can connect to shared resources on a network using a network interface card and network wiring, you can connect to the same kind of resources using a modem and telephone wires. This type of networking is called Dial-Up Networking. Dial-Up Networking is discussed in Chapter 8, "Special Features for Notebook Users," as this feature will be of most interest to laptop and notebook PC users. However, if you want to configure Dial-Up Networking to work on your desktop computer, all of the procedures are the same. ●

APPENDIX

Appendix

Additional Help and Resources

by Ron Person

In this chapter

Getting Telephone and FAX Support for Windows 95 and Microsoft Products

Microsoft has a wide array of telephone support systems for Windows 95. Numerous third-party companies are also dedicated to supporting individuals and corporations who use Windows 95.

If Windows 95 or other applications came preinstalled on your computer, your technical support for the preinstalled software will probably be through the hardware vendor who supplied your equipment.

Microsoft Telephone and FAX Support

For customer service and product upgrade information, call (800) 426-9400.

At the time this book was published, Microsoft used three methods of supporting Windows 95 with live support personnel. These numbers and support levels are outlined here:

Description	Type	Telephone
Support for 90 days from your first support call.	Free. Initial 90-day support.	(206) 635-7000
$35 charge to a credit card until the specific problem is resolved. Make sure you keep the charge code ID and incident ID assigned by Microsoft.	$35 per incident charged to a credit card.	(800) 936-5700
$35 charge to a telephone number until the specific problem is resolved. Incident ID is assigned by Microsoft.	$35 per incident charged to telephone.	(900) 555-2000

This support is available Monday through Friday, 6:00 A.M. to 6:00 P.M. Pacific Time, excluding holidays.

You also can receive help on Windows 95 via a fax that lists the most frequently asked questions and their answers. To get answers from FastTips, call (800) 936-4200.

Telephone Support from Non-Microsoft Vendors

Microsoft encourages the use of a stable of service providers who can give you or your company help on Windows 95. See the following list of service providers:

Name	Description	Support Options	Telephone
Sitel	Technical services	Wide range of services available	800-363-5448
Stream International	Backup for in-house support or staff	Windows 95 education and training	(800) 274-4707
Unisys Corporation	Support for home users and businesses	$35 per incident $2.95 per minute Prepaid callbacks	(800) 863-0436 (900) 555-5454 (800) 757-8324

Online Technical Support

You can also find support online through the Microsoft Download Service, the World Wide Web, and other computer bulletin board forums.

Microsoft Download Service

Microsoft maintains a software library containing sample programs, device drivers, patches, software updates, and programming aids. You have free access to the software in this library. Use HyperTerminal, which comes with Windows 95 and other PC communication software, to connect, search, and download files. You can connect to Microsoft Download Service at:

(206) 936-6735

World Wide Web

The World Wide Web is a huge, constantly changing collection of data. Because of this, you can waste considerable time searching for specific information on the Web. Your most productive searches for information will be through sites sponsored by Microsoft, PC Magazine, and vendors. Some valuable URLs are listed in Table A.1.

Table A.1 Helpful Web Sites

Name	Description	URL
Microsoft	Main Microsoft Web page	**http://www.microsoft.com/**
Microsoft	Table of contents for Windows	**http://www.microsoft.com/windows/**
Microsoft	Windows page and Windows 95 topics and software	**http://www.microsoft.com/windows/**

continues

Table A.1 Continued

Name	Description	URL
Microsoft Knowledge Base	Searchable database of white papers, technical notes, troubleshooting, tips, bugs, and workarounds.	**http://www.microsoft.com/kb/**
Microsoft	Home page for product support services	**http://www.microsoft.comsupport**
Microsoft	Free product upgrades, templates, and add-ons	**http://www.microsoft.com/windows/support**, select a product, and then click **Go**
Microsoft TechNet	Troubleshooting database, drivers, upgrades; all the information from the TechNet CD-ROM	**http://www.microsoft.com/technet**

▶ **See** "Connecting to the Internet," **p. 422**

Computer Bulletin Board Forums

Computer bulletin boards are computer services that enable you to retrieve information over the telephone line. Some bulletin boards contain a wealth of information about Windows and Windows applications. One of the largest public bulletin boards is CompuServe.

CompuServe contains *forums* in which Windows and Windows applications are discussed. You can submit questions electronically to Microsoft operators, who will answer questions usually within a day. CompuServe also contains libraries of sample files and new printer and device drivers. The Knowledge Base available in Microsoft's region of CompuServe has much of the same troubleshooting information that Microsoft's telephone support representatives use. You can search through the Knowledge Base by using key words. The Microsoft region of CompuServe is divided into many areas, such as Windows users, Windows software developers, Microsoft, Excel, and Microsoft languages, as well as sections for each of the major Microsoft and non-Microsoft applications that run under Windows.

After you become a CompuServe member, you can access the Microsoft user forums, library files, and Knowledge Base. (You must join CompuServe and get a passcode before you can use the bulletin board.) When you join CompuServe, make sure you get a copy of WinCIM, the Windows CompuServe Information Manager. It enables you to avoid typing many commands, and thus makes using CompuServe significantly easier.

Some of the Windows 95 services available on CompuServe are listed in Table A.2.

Table A.2 Windows 95 Services on CompuServe

Name	Description	Access With:
Windows Support	CompuServe's table of contents for Windows support, shareware, and so on	**GO WIN95**
Microsoft Connection	Entry service for Microsoft services	**GO MICROSOFT**
Microsoft Knowledge Base	Searchable database of troubleshooting tips, technical papers, and so on	**GO MSKB**
Microsoft Software Libraries	Free libraries of tools, software, patches, and drivers	**GO MSL**
Microsoft Windows Service Pack 1 upgrade	Free upgrades to Windows 95	**GO WINNEWS**
Windows 95 Setup	Specific setup questions for Windows 95 supported by WUGNET	**GO SETUP95**
Windows Users Group Network	Collections of useful software and information gathered by WUGNET	**GO WINUSER**

For information on joining CompuServe, contact a retail software store for a CompuServe starter kit or contact CompuServe at the following address:

CompuServe
5000 Arlington Centre Blvd.
P.O. Box 20212
Columbus, OH 43220
(800) 848-8990

Technical Support on Microsoft CD-ROM

One of the most valuable resources of technical knowledge on Windows and Windows applications is TechNet. TechNet is a compilation of troubleshooting procedures, technical papers, product descriptions, product announcements, drivers, and so on. It is available on a monthly CD-ROM for a fee or available over the World Wide Web for free. If you are a company with many Windows users or a consultant using Microsoft products, you must learn how to use TechNet.

If you support only a few people or do not have to frequently download files, the free Knowledge Base on the Web might work well for you. The Knowledge Base contains much of the same information as the TechNet CD-ROM, but it is free.

ON THE WEB

www.microsoft.com/kb

Although Knowledge Base is available for free on the Web, there are many times when you might want it on CD-ROM. If you frequently need files or need large files from TechNet, the CD-ROM is much more convenient than slogging through the Web. TechNet on CD-ROM has a much more flexible and faster search engine so you can quickly browse for related topics; for example, you can quickly find an answer while a client is on the phone. With the advent of CD-ROM drives built into portables, the TechNet CD is an indispensable tool for the traveling Windows consultant.

To subscribe to TechNet, contact them at this address:

Microsoft TechNet
One Microsoft Way
Redmond, WA 98052-6399
Fax: (206) 936-7329, Attn: TechNet
Voice: (800) 344-2121
Internet: **technet@microsoft.com**
Web: **www.microsoft.com/technet**

The Microsoft Windows 95 Resource Kit

Microsoft split the user documentation for Windows 95 in two parts. The first part contains the User's Guide, help files, tutorial, and so on. This part is aimed at the average Windows 95 user and covers the Windows 95 user interface and features.

The Windows 95 Resource Kit comprises the *rest* of the Windows 95 user documentation. This kit provides more depth and detail about topics that (in Microsoft's estimation) the average user isn't likely to need. You can find information about customized setup and installation, network configuration, and so on. The Windows 95 Resource Kit includes a manual, help files, and supplementary software utilities aimed at network administrators and others who must support other Windows 95 users.

It's important to understand that the Windows 95 Resource Kit is *not* a programmer's reference or software development kit—that's another area entirely. The Windows 95 Resource Kit is still part of the user-level documentation; it's just aimed at a higher-level user than the rest of the Windows 95 documentation.

The Microsoft Windows 95 Resource Kit is a book-software combination. The book and software come on the Windows 95 CD-ROM from which you might have installed Windows 95.

You can also download the book and software from online services or purchase it as a bound book from larger bookstores.

If you have the full CD-ROM version of Windows 95, you already have a copy of the Windows 95 Resource Kit. The Resource Kit chapters appear in the Windows 95 Resource Kit Help file, WIN95RK.HLP, which is located in the /ADMIN/RESKIT/HELPFILE directory. Double-click this file to open its help window. You can search and print in the file as you would any help file.

You can also find a number of useful user and network utilities on the Windows 95 CD-ROM. Look in the /ADMIN/APPTOOLS and /ADMIN/NETTOOLS directories to find these utilities. You also can find software tools on online bulletin boards. Many of these were listed earlier in this appendix, in the section "Online Technical Support."

NOTE Microsoft does not include the Windows 95 Resource Kit files when distributing Windows 95 on floppy disks. Also, other suppliers who are licensed to sell Windows 95 with their computer systems might not include the Windows 95 Resource Kit files. ■

Books from Macmillan Computer Publishing

Macmillan Computer Publishing (MCP) is the largest publisher of computer books in the world. Que Corporation is MCP's most successful book imprint. Que is the publisher of *Platinum Edition Using Windows 95* and the *Special Edition Using* series of books. Some of the best-selling books in this series are:

- *Special Edition Using Windows 95*
- *Special Edition Using Excel for Windows 95*
- *Special Edition Using Word for Windows 95*

For catalogs or individual or corporate purchases, contact Que and Macmillan Computer Publishing at:

201 West 103rd Street
Indianapolis, IN 46290
(317) 581-3500
(800) 428-5331

ON THE WEB

You can also search and browse book descriptions and download software at the Macmillan SuperLibrary site on the World Wide Web. To go there, use the URL:

http://www.mcp.com

Online WinNews Newsletter

Microsoft publishes WinNews, an online newsletter, that is available to anyone who can receive e-mail from the Internet (this includes CompuServe and America Online). WinNews includes information about new and free Windows 95 software, operating tips, releases of new hardware drivers, and references to additional information. It is published on the first and third Mondays of every month.

If you want to subscribe to WinNews, follow these steps:

1. Create an Internet e-mail message using the same account in which you want to receive WinNews.
2. Use a blank Subject line.
3. Type only the following as the message body:

   SUBSCRIBE WINNEWS

4. Send this Internet e-mail to:

   enews99@microsoft.nwnet.com

To stop receiving a copy of WinNews, follow the same instructions but use the following text as the only text in the message body:

UNSUBSCRIBE WINNEWS

Referrals to Consultants and Training

Microsoft Solution Providers develop and support applications written for the Windows environment with Microsoft products. They are independent consultants who have met the strict qualifying requirements imposed by Microsoft.

Microsoft also certifies training centers. A certified training center has instructors who have passed a competency exam and who use Microsoft-produced training material.

You can find the Microsoft Solution Providers and training centers in your area by calling (800) SOL-PROV. ●

Index

Symbols

A

B

C

D

E

F

G

H

I

J-K

L

N

P

Q

R

S

T

U

V

X-Z

Complete and Return This Card for a *FREE* Computer Book Catalog

Thank you for purchasing this book! You have purchased a superior computer book written expressly for your needs. To continue to provide the kind of up-to-date, pertinent coverage you've come to expect from us, we need to hear from you. Please take a minute to complete and return this self-addressed, postage-paid form. In return, we'll send you a free catalog of all our computer books on topics ranging from word processing to programming and the Internet.

Mr. ☐ Mrs. ☐ Ms. ☐ Dr. ☐

Name (first) ☐☐☐☐☐☐☐☐☐☐☐ (M.I.) ☐ (last) ☐☐☐☐☐☐☐☐☐☐☐☐☐☐☐

Address ☐☐☐☐☐☐☐☐☐☐☐☐☐☐☐☐☐☐☐☐☐☐☐☐☐☐☐☐☐☐☐☐☐☐☐

☐☐☐☐☐☐☐☐☐☐☐☐☐☐☐☐☐☐☐☐☐☐☐☐☐☐☐☐☐☐☐☐☐☐☐

City ☐☐☐☐☐☐☐☐☐☐☐☐☐☐☐ State ☐☐ Zip ☐☐☐☐☐ ☐☐☐☐

Phone ☐☐☐ ☐☐☐ ☐☐☐☐ Fax ☐☐☐ ☐☐☐ ☐☐☐☐

Company Name ☐☐☐☐☐☐☐☐☐☐☐☐☐☐☐☐☐☐☐☐☐☐☐☐☐☐☐☐☐☐☐☐☐

E-mail address ☐☐☐☐☐☐☐☐☐☐☐☐☐☐☐☐☐☐☐☐☐☐☐☐☐☐☐☐☐☐☐☐☐

1. Please check at least three (3) influencing factors for purchasing this book.

- Front or back cover information on book ☐
- Special approach to the content ☐
- Completeness of content ☐
- Author's reputation ☐
- Publisher's reputation ☐
- Book cover design or layout ☐
- Index or table of contents of book ☐
- Price of book ☐
- Special effects, graphics, illustrations ☐
- Other (Please specify): ____________ ☐

2. How did you first learn about this book?

- Saw in Macmillan Computer Publishing catalog ☐
- Recommended by store personnel ☐
- Saw the book on bookshelf at store ☐
- Recommended by a friend ☐
- Received advertisement in the mail ☐
- Saw an advertisement in: ____________ ☐
- Read book review in: ____________ ☐
- Other (Please specify): ____________ ☐

3. How many computer books have you purchased in the last six months?

- This book only ☐
- 2 books ☐
- 3 to 5 books ☐
- More than 5 ☐

4. Where did you purchase this book?

- Bookstore ☐
- Computer Store ☐
- Consumer Electronics Store ☐
- Department Store ☐
- Office Club ☐
- Warehouse Club ☐
- Mail Order ☐
- Direct from Publisher ☐
- Internet site ☐
- Other (Please specify): ____________ ☐

5. How long have you been using a computer?

- ☐ Less than 6 months
- ☐ 6 months to a year
- ☐ 1 to 3 years
- ☐ More than 3 years

6. What is your level of experience with personal computers and with the subject of this book?

	With PCs	With subject of book
New	☐	☐
Casual	☐	☐
Accomplished	☐	☐
Expert	☐	☐

Source Code ISBN: 0-7897-1553-8

7. Which of the following best describes your job title?

Administrative Assistant ☐
Coordinator ☐
Manager/Supervisor ☐
Director ☐
Vice President ☐
President/CEO/COO ☐
Lawyer/Doctor/Medical Professional ☐
Teacher/Educator/Trainer ☐
Engineer/Technician ☐
Consultant ☐
Not employed/Student/Retired ☐
Other (Please specify): ________________ ☐

8. Which of the following best describes the area of the company your job title falls under?

Accounting ☐
Engineering ☐
Manufacturing ☐
Operations ☐
Marketing ☐
Sales ☐
Other (Please specify): ________________ ☐

9. What is your age?

Under 20 ☐
21-29 ☐
30-39 ☐
40-49 ☐
50-59 ☐
60-over ☐

10. Are you:

Male ☐
Female ☐

11. Which computer publications do you read regularly? (Please list)

____

***Comments*:** ____

Fold here and scotch-tape to mail.

NO POSTAGE
NECESSARY
IF MAILED
IN THE
UNITED STATES

BUSINESS REPLY MAIL

FIRST-CLASS MAIL PERMIT NO. 9918 INDIANAPOLIS IN

POSTAGE WILL BE PAID BY THE ADDRESSEE

ATTN MARKETING
MACMILLAN COMPUTER PUBLISHING
MACMILLAN PUBLISHING USA
201 W 103RD ST
INDIANAPOLIS IN 46290-9042

Technical Support

If you need assistance with the information provided by Macmillan Computer Publishing, please access the information available on our web site at **http://www.mcp.com/feedback**. Our most Frequently Asked Questions are answered there. If you do not find the answers to your questions on our web site, you may contact Macmillan User Services at **(317) 581-3833** or email us at **support@mcp.com**.

Read This Before Opening Software

By opening this package, you are agreeing to be bound by the following:

This software is copyrighted and all rights are reserved by the publisher and its licensers. You are licensed to use this software on a single computer. You may copy the software for backup or archival purposes only. Making copies of the software for any other purpose is a violation of United States copyright laws. THIS SOFTWARE IS SOLD AS IS, WITHOUT WARRANTY OF ANY KIND, EITHER EXPRESSED OR IMPLIED, INCLUDING BUT NOT LIMITED TO THE IMPLIED WARRANTIES OF MERCHANTABILITY AND FITNESS FOR A PARTICULAR PURPOSE. Neither the publisher nor its dealers and distributors nor its licensers assume any liability for any alleged or actual damages arising from the use of this software. (Some states do not allow exclusion of implied warranties, so the exclusion may not apply to you.)

The entire contents of this disc and the compilation of the software are copyrighted and protected by United States copyright laws. The individual programs on the disc are copyrighted by the authors or owners of each program. Each program has its own use, permissions, and limitations. To use each program, you must follow the individual requirements and restrictions detailed for each. Do not use a program if you do not agree to follow its licensing agreement.